The Family and Local History Handbook

incorporating
The Genealogical Services Directory

7th Edition

In collaboration with

BRITISH
ASSOCIATION
FOR LOCAL
HISTORY
www.balh.co.uk

D1339119

Edited & Compiled

by

Robert Blatchford

Contents

6 Feature Articles

Editorial

Welcome to the 7th Edition of the Handbook. I hope you find the articles interesting and helpful with their advice and guidance. In commissioning articles I have been mindful of suggestions made in reviews and by individual readers. The layout has been changed so that our major listings are now in the yellow section with Local History articles and listings in the blue section. In addition, I have included a general Index as well as the usual Index to Advertisers

The designation of Counties and other Local Government always presents a conundrum for the listings. For example, should Hull be listed under Yorkshire - East or under Hull? There has been much change to administration boundaries since 1974 and each Local Authority jealously guards its independence from its neighbour. I have taken account of readers comments and hope the present listings layout is more consistent.

This 7th Edition has over 110 new articles and well over five and a half thousand contacts for anyone researching family or local history. The *Handbook* has certainly grown over the years. The first edition was smaller in size and consisted of eighty five pages. Now the 7th Edition of the Handbook has grown to 448 pages. I am constantly surprised by the critical acclaim we receive for each edition. Again we have been able to commission leading family and local historians to provide articles on many interesting subjects.

All design, layout and preparation is done in house on Apple Macintosh computers, a G4 Desktop and a G3 Power Book,using Quark Xpress 4, Adobe Photoshop 6 and Adobe Acrobat 4. The *Handbook* is produced electronically and is transferred to paper only when it is printed.

Please support our advertisers as their contribution to the production of the *Handbook* is essential. If you do contact any of the advertisers please tell them that you saw their advertisement in *The Family and Local History Handbook.*

It may seem repetitive but I must acknowledge all the many people, too numerous to name individually who have helped me in so many ways. I am especially grateful to my wife, Elizabeth, and the family for their patience and forbearance. The technical help and advice from my printers Alan and Sandra Williamson has been invaluable, as is the support from the BALH and Michael Cowan. Last but not least I am grateful once again to Nancy Redpath and Daphne Hambrook for the sterling work in the final stages of preparation before the book goes to the printer.

Suggestions from our readers are always welcome and where possible they are implemented in the next edition.We hope that you, our readers, enjoy this 7th edition as much as the previous ones.

Robert Blatchford

Starting Out
A Beginners Guide to Family History
Doreen Hopwood
guides you through the early stages

Every family has its own, unique history, and our ancestors have helped to make us what we are today. For those of you about to embark on the ancestral trail, here are some basic guidelines to help you to proceed effectively and efficiently.

Until recently, it was the families of the rich and famous (or infamous!) whose histories were researched, but the same investigative techniques must be applied whatever the status of the family in order to produce a family tree. Patience and perseverance are two 'musts' for the prospective family historian, along with a 'sense of the past'. As research takes you back in time, be prepared for surprises – and maybe the odd shock! We need to step back into the contemporary world of our forebears to understand their daily lives and you'll soon find yourselves delving into local and social history to find out more. What did a puddler do for a living? Court Heneage in Aston Manor may sound like a very grand address, but was a set of back- to-back houses in Victorian Birmingham!

Success with research may also depend on the survival of records, whether your family moved frequently, their status and even the popularity of the surname being studied. Perhaps you have an unusual surname and want to find out more - but be aware that in the nineteenth century many of our ancestors were illiterate and you may well encounter changes in spelling as they were written down as they sounded. On the plus side, however, names like Jones aren't prone to this problem!

Whilst this directory contains information about all of the major repositories in the United Kingdom – the Public Record Office, the Family Records Centre, county record offices and libraries – these are NOT the places to start your research. Your first steps should be to talk to members of your family and gather together as much information as you can. In addition to 'official' documents such as birth, death and marriage certificates, wills etc, the following may provide valuable information to aid research:

A family bible – a great find, as it usually records dates of events as they happened.

Memorial cards, obituaries and grave papers.

School reports, apprenticeship papers, graduation certificates, occupational pensions.

Military service records, medals or other awards.

Society/club membership cards or trade union subscription cards.

Diaries, scrapbooks, letters, newspaper cuttings, old address or birthday books.

Photograph albums are particularly helpful as 'memory joggers' when talking to older members of the family, and if possible, make a recording of any interviews. Whilst there are certain questions you need to ask, take care not to be too demanding - several short interviews may be more productive than one long one. This is also a good time to ensure that you have recorded on your own photos 'who, when and where'. Future generations will thank you for it!

Don't discount the family myth or legend – every family has at least one. They are usually firmly based on the truth, but like Chinese whispers, they tend to become embellished or distorted as they are passed on from generation to generation. Set out to verify the information with documentary evidence and share your findings with other family members. You may find out that someone is already researching your family's history, or is interested in joining in with you. This is an excellent way of sharing the workload – and the costs. There are numerous books about genealogical research available – and you may be able to borrow some of these from your library. Monthly family history magazines usually contain a 'Readers Interests' section in which people submit details of the surname, period, and area of their research, and you may find a possible entry for your family. If you do respond to any of these, please remember to enclose a stamped address envelope or international reply coupon.

Joining your local family history society will bring you into contact with individuals with the same interest – the addresses of members of the Federation of Family History Societies can be found on the Internet at www.ffhs.org.uk As well as regular meetings, you'll receive newsletters containing details of their publications and a 'members interest' section. As you progress with your research, you may also want to join the society covering the area where your ancestors lived.

Attend a family history class. There is a whole range available, ranging from one-off workshops to academic courses leading to formal qualifications. Your local Education Authority will be able to advise you of locally run courses and look out for information at libraries and in family history journals.

In this electronic age, more and more information is becoming available through the Internet. This is a great way of finding out about resources held in the area you are interested in and there are some excellent genealogical websites. However, don't expect to be able to compile your family tree solely from the World Wide Web. Whilst there are many indexes and resources accessible in this way, you will need to carry out research in numerous repositories – and this is part of the fun of family history. Nothing is more rewarding than seeing a 150-year old signature of one of your ancestors in a parish register, or visiting the church where family events were celebrated!

YOU are the most important person in your family tree, because you must always work from the known back to the unknown, generation by generation - yourself, parents, grandparents, great grandparents and so on. Never try to come forwards with your research – you may end up with an impressive family tree, but not necessarily your own. For most of us the first major national source we encounter is the General Register Office (GRO) Index, which includes every birth, death and marriage registered in England and Wales since the introduction of civil registration on 1 July 1837. Scotland and Ireland have their own registration systems, which commenced in 1855 and 1864 respectively. The index has separate volumes for birth, death and marriage and until 1984, when it became an annual cumulative index, it is split into four quarters:

March:
 events registered in January, February and March
June:
 events registered in April, May and June
September:
events registered in July, August and September
December:
events registered in October, November and December
Each index is arranged alphabetically by surname, then by forename(s) and shows the district where the event was registered, the volume and page number. As a period of up to 42 days is allowed between the birth and its registration, check the quarter following the birth.

Your birth certificate shows your parents names and mothers maiden name   THEN
Your parents marriage certificate shows the names of both grandfathers THEN
Your parents birth certificates show your grandparents names and grandmothers maiden name   THEN
Your grandparents marriage certificates show the names of both greatgrandfathers.......and so on.......

The General Register Office Index is now available in many libraries and other repositories. The Office of National Statistics (ONS) at Smedley Hydro, Trafalgar Road, Birkdale, Southport, Merseyside, PR8 2HH can provide details of local holdings. Once you have traced the entry you require, the full copy certificate can be purchased by post from the above address, from the register office at which the event was registered or by personal visit to the Family Records Centre at Myddleton Place, Myddleton

Street, London EC1R 1UW. In the latter case, the certificate can either be collected a few days later or posted to you.

Before the establishment of civil registration, it was the responsibility of the Church to record baptisms, marriages and burials, and in order to utilise the church registers, you will need to know the parish where the events took place. A census – a count of the population – has been taken every 10 years since 1801 with the exception of 1941. The census of 1841 is the earliest to contain information about individuals and as there is a 100-year closure on public access to the census enumerator's books, the latest that is currently available (for England and Wales) is the 1901 census. For the first time this has now become available online and has a full name index, so you do not need to have an address in order to trace individuals. There are also facilities to search by area.

Census returns contain lists of all inhabited buildings, showing the names, ages, occupations, marital status, birth places and relationship to the head of household of everyone resident on the night the census was taken – but with less detail on the 1841 return. It is usually necessary to know an address – or at least a street to 'find' a household as the returns are arranged by enumeration district, but there is a surname index to the 1881 census of the whole of England and Wales. Many local family history societies have produced indices for their own locality in respect of other returns. The census enumerators books for the whole of England and Wales are available at the Family Records Centre, whilst county record offices and main libraries usually hold copies covering their locality.

The Church of Jesus Christ of Latter Day Saints (the Mormon Church) has produced the International Genealogical Index (IGI), which is a worldwide resource and regularly expanded in its on-line form as FamilySearch on the Internet. Much of the information has been taken from original parish registers and complemented by family histories submitted by Church members. In its microfiche format, it is arranged by country then region/county and within these, alphabetically by surname, then forename and chronologically by event. For England and Wales, the majority of entries cover baptisms and marriages in the Established Church and may go back to the introduction of parish registers in the mid sixteenth century. The IGI can be found at major libraries, county record offices and at Church of Jesus

published books of monumental inscriptions transcribed from (legible) gravestones in church burial grounds. You can "browse" the catalogue of the Public Record Office (PRO) on-line prior to paying a visit and so organise your time effectively. The series of information leaflets is also available on the Internet at www.pro.gov.uk, and these cover a wide range of topics for family history. Servicemen who died during the First and Second World Wars can be traced on the Commonwealth War Graves Commission website at www.cwgc.org.uk

Since 1858 it has been the responsibility of the Government to administer wills and grant probates. The national, annual indexes (Index of Wills and Letters of Administration) can be found in major libraries and other record offices and the extracts include sufficient information to enable a full copy will to be purchased. They are arranged in alphabetical order by surname, then forename, and appear in the index covering the year in which the probate was granted - which may be several years after the date of death. Don't assume that only the rich or gentry left wills – a glance at the above indexes shows how many 'ordinary' people made wills – and whilst the monetary value may be negligible, the amount of genealogical information can be enormous.

Christ of Latter Day Saints Family History Centres. Their addresses can be found in telephone directories. Once an entry has been found on the IGI/FamilySearch always obtain a copy of the entry from the relevant repository as this will, in most cases, provide additional information, including the signatures of the bride groom and witnesses at marriages. Whilst some churches still hold their parish registers, the majority will be found in the Diocesan Record Office – which is often based at the County Record Office. As well as registers of baptism, marriage and burial, the 'Parish Chest' contains numerous other records relating to the Church, its officers and its parishioners. You may find that one of your ancestors was a prominent member of the church and appears as a Churchwarden or other parish official. Alternatively, an ancestor may have hit hard times and appear in the Overseers of the Poor's accounts as being in receipt of parish relief.

More and more 'finding aids' and indexes are being produced for family history. Such as the National Burials Index available on CD, and complements the

Do keep an open mind as you carry out research – whilst official documents provide evidence of names, dates, occupations and addresses, there are many other sources that will help to put your ancestors in their contemporary setting. Maps and photographs of the area in which the family lived will show how much (or how little) it has changed over time, whilst local newspapers give an account of what was going on in the area. National and global events – such as the world wars of the twentieth century – affected our families and the demise of a local industry/employer might have instigated migration or a complete change of occupation for family members.

You may have thought that your family was 'Brummie born and bred' but as you progress back in time, you will probably find that your ancestors came from all over the British Isles – and maybe beyond. The search will take you far afield in geographical terms as well as in time, adding to the fascination that is family history.

Maps for Family History : A Guide to their Use and Location
Doreen Hopwood

Have you ever walked along a street and wondered what it was like a hundred years ago – or if it was in existence then? Dramatic changes have occurred as the urban landscape has taken over the surrounding countryside and in some places the only recognition of former land use may be in the name given to the street or suburb built on it. Since earliest times maps have been produced for a variety of purposes – to show land ownership, for taxation, to chart defences, communication routes and even the distribution of public houses. Maps range in size and scale according to the purpose for which they were produced and by looking at a range of maps over a period of time we can get an overall picture of the places where our ancestors lived.

Maps can help the family historian to locate buildings from details given on civil registration certificates and census returns and to pinpoint likely places of work, worship and education. Used in conjunction with gazetteers, historical atlases, directories and Victoria County Histories they can enhance our knowledge of how our ancestors lived and worked. Large scale ordnance survey maps can tell us if the houses in which they lived had electricity and water. Ecclesiastical and civil parish maps indicate the likely church they attended and to whom they paid rates, whilst political maps show the electoral registration district covering their address.

From the 1570s political factors encouraged the production of county maps and the drawing up of estate plans from the end of the century. From about 1612, when Speed included town plans with his set of county maps, they started to be produced in greater numbers. The earliest known surviving town plan is a manuscript sketch of Bristol dating back to about 1479. Many of the early county maps have been commercially reproduced either as single maps or in county atlases and should be found in main reference libraries and county record offices

As can be expected, maps of London were produced in the greatest numbers. One which was published between 1792and 1799 at a scale of 26 inches to the mile, professed to show every court, alley and vacant plot. Between 1800 and 1805 over 200 maps of the capital were published but very few towns have any prior to 1800 – Leeds has 29 prior to this date with a further 90 produced in

the first half of the 19th century. Some towns were owned by a single family/landowner - such as Whitehaven in Cumbria – and maps may still be in the family archive or deposited in the relevant county record office.

The rapid growth of the urban population placed huge demands on the authorities and by the late 17th century "improvement schemes" encompassing the paving and lighting of streets became the responsibility of the Street Commissioners through the passing of local acts. Large-scale maps were drawn and these often included the names of landowners not only of affected areas but also of those adjacent to it. From 1794 all improvement scheme proposals required a private Act of Parliament and these had to be accompanied by large-scale plans which may be found in the local county record office or reference library. Copies were also deposited in the House of Lords Record Office. Whenever new sewers were to be dug or gas lighting (later electricity) installed, a new Act was brought into force and new plans drawn. Similarly, from the mid 16th to 19th centuries, Commissioners of Sewers could be appointed wherever it was necessary to protect land from flooding, to drain marshland or to supervise the flow of water into millstreams. Drainage maps show the "level" under the control of the Commissioners and there are plenty of surviving maps for the The Fens, which are held at the local county record office. Poker's map of Romney Marsh, dated 1617 includes "Highwayes, Lanes, Parish Churches, Dwelling Houses and Cottages within the said

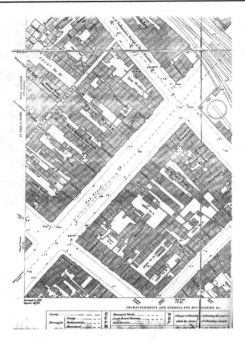

several levels".

From the 19th century, town improvement generally meant the creation of new streets or housing estates and the first step was for the municipal authority to purchase the land and existing buildings. When Joseph Chamberlain "parked, paved, assized, marketed, gas and watered" Birmingham in the 1870s, the plans consisted of several large hand-coloured maps showing the owners/tenants of buildings to be demolished as well as the proposed development. In some areas, individual lots are depicted, along with the name of the first purchaser. When a residential estate was completed in Hatton Gardens in 1694, a site map was drawn on which the names of each tenant was included.

Tithe Maps are a further useful resource for the family historian, and surviving copies (these were produced in triplicate) can be found at the Public Record Office, County/Diocesan Record Offices or in main reference libraries. These were generally produced in the 1840s following the Tithe Commutation Act of 1836 and completed for about two-thirds of the parishes in England and Wales. An apportionment register was produced for each tithe, showing the names of the landowner, the occupier and land use (arable, pasture or meadow), and sometimes its valuation. Each number on the tithe map corresponds to the number in the apportionment register, and it is not unusual to find several tithes owned or occupied by the same person spread around the parish.

Maps and plans were increasingly required for taxation purposes and to show ownership of land

or to settle boundary disputes. Many of the early estate maps were "one-offs" and as such in manuscript form. Survival rates vary and many such plans and maps remain uncatalogued amongst family papers or in solicitors archives. The detail on the maps also varies, according to the purpose for which it was drawn. Some include all buildings on an estate – including the estate workers cottages, but the omission of a building does not mean that it did not exist at the time the map was drawn – its inclusion may have been deemed to be unnecessary. From the 19th century estates were being broken up as parcels of land were sold and often include precise details of the affected area and those adjoining it.

The Church, municipal corporations and City Guilds are/were substantial landowners and as the price of land in urban areas escalated, it was in their own interest to have maps which clearly defined the boundaries of their properties. Some of these even give the names of tenement tenants, as in a plan drawn in the early 17th century by the Clothworkers Company to cover its property in London. Like the Public Record Office, many county record offices do not have specific map collections. Plans and maps which accompanied leases, mortgages or conveyances of land are likely to be found attached to these documents – and possibly not catalogued as being with them. Most of the maps deposited at the PRO are from material generated by government departments, courts of law and other such bodies and remain with the original documents.

Property plans from the 16th century often show the Church of England as the landowner, and records may be found amongst the parish chest papers of individual parishes in Diocesan Record Offices. Glebe Terriers contain descriptions of properties owned by the church – often at some distance from the parish itself – and provide information about sources of income. Parish maps were prepared to enable the officers of the parish to levy and collect rates and to distribute poor relief, but these may have been single copies and may still be hanging on the vestry wall of the church!

The Parochial Assessments Act of 1836 authorised Poor Law Commissioners to "..order a survey with or without a map or plan, on such a scale as they may think fit, to be made of the Messuages, Lands and other Hereditaments liable to Poor Rates". Again, the quality varies from place to place, but the surviving Parochial Assessment Maps (completed by 1845) are probably the most reliable local early Victorian maps. Phillimore's *Atlas and Index of Parish Registers* includes county maps showing the location of parishes up to the 1830s and is extremely useful in ascertaining neighbouring parishes and those on county boundaries.

Ordnance Survey maps are the best known (and used) maps of Great Britain, but when it was founded in 1791 – out of the Board of Ordnance – maps were produced specifically for military use. Its original concern was to map Great Britain at a scale of one inch to the mile and the first county map of Kent was published in 1803. By 1873 all of England and Wales (except the Scilly Isles) was covered in a series (The Old Series) of 110 sheets at this scale. The Ordnance Survey website at http://www.ordsvy.gov.uk provides a brief history and details of the scales used at different periods. The maps show the changing British landscape in a wide range of scales from the early 19th century to the present day. Generally speaking, the smaller the scale of the map, the less detail it contains, but you have a greater chance of locating these for the area in which you are interested. As the century progressed, maps became more sophisticated and eventually all cultivated areas were covered at 25 inches to the mile and uncultivated/wasteland and mountainous regions covered at 6 inches to the mile. The first annual report of the Ordnance Survey in 1855 stated "All large maps are greatly improved by colours, to clearly distinguish the houses from the courts or gardens attached to them ......and for clearly defining the direction of the roads." Coloured copies sold at 6d more than their uncoloured counterparts.

The revisions of the Old Series of maps were not made simultaneously, but as the need arose, so areas of rapid urban growth or industrialisation have more coverage than rural areas. Only the date of publication, not the date of the survey appears on Old Series maps, and there may have been as much as 20 years between these dates. The New Series, consisting of 360 sheets was started in the 1840s and all towns with a population of more than 4000 were mapped at a scale of 1:1056. There was a fullscale national revision during the 1890s with all sheets published by 1899.

The 1:500 scale was introduced in 1855 and by 1895 covered all large towns with a 4000+ population. Unless local authorities were prepared to pay for it, no mapping at this scale has been undertaken since 1910. These very detailed maps enable us to get a clear view of the areas in which our ancestors lived and worked as buildings are named and entries between courts/tenements are shown. This can be particularly useful if an address on a civil registration certificate cannot be traced in a census enumerators book. In some cases, the enumerator gained entry to a court from one street and listed it as such, even though the "official" address was off a different street. As our urban ancestors tended to "move house" on a fairly regular basis, and often go only a short distance, contemporary maps provide the location of similar properties in the vicinity. The mapping tended to extend to the edge of the built up area, irrespective of a municipal boundary and there is a near complete set in the British Library with local maps held in reference libraries and county record offices.

By 1896 the County Series at 1:2500 (25.344 inches to the mile) covered the whole of what was considered to be the cultivated area of Great Britain. Between 1891 and 1945 all English and Welsh counties were revised at least once.

The National Grid Series on a scale of 1:2500 began in 1948 and was completed in the 1980s, with those produced after 1970 showing metric values. Shortly before the Second World War a special emergency edition – for air raid precaution purposes – was produced for all places with a population of over 2000.

Along with improvement schemes, all transport schemes required private Acts of Parliament and from 1792, the accompanying plans had to show "The exact delineation of the land traversed" and all ownership of land en route had to be specified in a book of reference. From 1807 a duplicate set of plans had to be deposited with the Clerk of the Peace, and these should be found in county record offices with the court records. Occasionally, each of the affected landowners were supplied with a complete plan, but more often than not, just the part of his estate was provided. These may be in family/solicitors archives, with the full plans at the House of Lords Record Office. Routes of migration of ancestors sometimes follow the transport networks, particularly if your ancestor worked on the railways or canals or was a carter/haulier. National transport maps are particularly helpful in locating routes between towns and directories detail the coach routes.

Over a thousand Turnpike Trusts, administering some 23000 miles of road were established by Acts of Parliament by the end of the 18th century and as well as the legally required plans, commercial maps were frequently published. Records relating to these can be found locally and amongst the Quarter Session records as Justices of the Peace had the power to order a map for any diversion or closure of a highway. The increasing use of roads for commerce - and later for leisure – meant that reliable maps were needed and the spread of the postal and coaching services resulted in more maps being published. Town and county directories often included maps and these used in conjunction with present day street atlases and A-Z guides can help to build up a picture of the changes that have occurred in an area over time.

Ordnance Survey Scales & Dates of Publication

1843 – 1893 First edition – First county series survey
1891 – 1912 Second edition – First county series revision
1904 – 1939 * Third edition – Second county series revision
1919 – 1943 * Fourth edition – Third county series revision
1945 → First National Grid Edition – First National Grid Survey
* Generally only available for urban areas in these editions

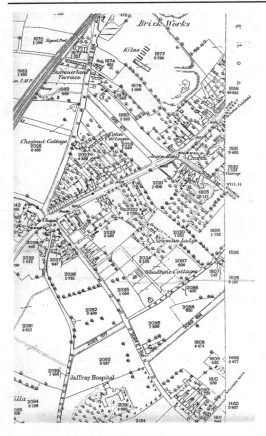

ceased work, miners moved –sometimes long distances – to another mining area. Associated trades can be identified and the adaptation of skills as changes in demand occurred. The large scale migration of Yorkshire worsted workers to the more lucrative cotton trade in Lancashire is an example of this. The large scale Ordnance Survey maps show individual factories and workshops in urban settings making it possible to identify likely places of employment for the skilled and unskilled urban workers.

A large range of miscellaneous maps has been produced. Maps charting the location of outbreaks of disease often appear in Medical Officer of health reports, and many local school boards produced maps showing the locations and types of school under its authority. Some Victoria County Histories include lists and locations of schools which can be used in conjunction with maps. Cemeteries/burial grounds can also be located by examining a local map together with the relevant contemporary town guides and directory.

Social commentators such as Booth and Mayhew showed areas of poverty. These depict how poverty was often trapped by physical boundaries such as railway lines, canals and new streets. In the St Bartholomew District of Birmingham a particular blind alley was know as "Catchems' Corner" until the area was redeveloped in the 1930s. Temperance Societies aimed to link the large numbers of public houses with poverty by drawing up maps showing the locations of pubs. In 1858 the Reverend Hume depicted the "Pauper Streets, Semi-Pauper Streets, Streets of Crime and Immorality" on his ecclesiastical and social map of Liverpool.

Historical educational maps and atlases are useful in identifying the former names of countries and member countries of the British Empire were usually coloured in red on these.

Religious maps can be used to identify areas in which certain denominations were concentrated, but it was often an opposing denomination who commissioned the map! In 1871 The Royal Standard published a map showing all of the "Romish establishments" in London. Dioceses often produced their own maps and these include the numbers of seats in each church as well as parish boundaries.

"Canalmania" swept the country at the end of the 18th century and by 1830 there were over 2000 miles of canals. As with road and improvement schemes, plans were legally required and as well as the repositories mentioned above, maps/plans may be found amongst the British Transport Historical Records at the PRO or with the archives of individual canal companies. There were two waves of "Railwaymania" in the 1830s and 1840s, resulting in some 46000 miles of railway by 1850. Each new line, extension or alteration to a line required a parliamentary act and where these were to pass through a built up area, or where a terminus was to be constructed, larger scale maps and plans had to be provided. As well as in the repositories already mentioned, the archives of individual railway companies may hold copies of the plans. As all urban transport schemes had to be accompanied by three sets of plans – ranging from the turnpike roads to modern motorways – it should be possible to locate these, either the CRO (Clerk of the Peace copy), the PRO (British Transport Commission) or House of Lords Record Office (Parliamentary copy).

Industrial maps showing the distribution of specific industries across regions can be helpful in tracing ancestors who moved from place to place. Mining is an example of this, as a particular mine

Although fire insurance maps can be traced back the 18th century these grew in number from about 1885 and were designed to provide insurance companies with information concerning the degree of risk. These continued until well into the 20th century with the principal publisher being Charles E Goad. They show great detail and were revised as necessary every 5 to 6 years. Whilst they only cover the main commercial districts of each town

Some Dates Relating to Ordnance Survey Maps	
1791	21 June: Founding Act of Ordnance Survey
1795	Survey for 1 inch map of Kent commenced
1801	1 January. Publication of 1inch map of Kent
1810	'Ordnance Survey' first recorded on maps
1825	Survey of Ireland at 6 inch scale commenced (Completed in 1846)
1840	Approval of 6 inch scale for surveys of Northern England and Scotland
1851	'Battle of the Scales' commenced as it was recommended that there should be a return to the 1 inch scale map
1854	First use of Photography in map production
1858	End of 'Battle of the Scales' on recommendation that national mapping should be at 1:2500, 6 inch and 1 inch scales
1870	Completion of mapping of England and Wales at 1 inch scale
1888	Inclusion of the statement ' All rights of reproduction reserved' appears on maps
1897	Full colour publication of 1 inch
1911	The statement 'Crown Copyright Reserved' added to all maps
1914 – 1918	All resources or Ordnance Survey put into production of maps for World Wars
1939 – 1945	All resources or Ordnance Survey put into production of maps for World Wars
1920	Publication of the first tourist map
1938	Introduction of a new scale – 1:250
1947	First 1:250 scale maps produced
1969	Agreement on metrication of maps of 1:2500 scale and larger
1974	Replacement of 1 inch series by 1:50000 scale (Completed 1976)
1991	Digitisation of all 1:250 maps complete

they include the names and numbers of properties which are not on contemporary OS maps.

The Valuation Office Survey of 1910-15, (known as the Lloyd George Domesday) was implemented under the Finance Act of 1910. This provided for a tax to be levied on any profit made on the sale of a property which arose from "public amenities" such as road and drainage systems. Land and properties were valued as at 30 April 1909, and even though many properties were exempt from the tax, an assessment was carried out. The valuation records include a description and valuation of each property, the names of owners and tenants and most are deposited in Class IR 58 at the PRO. Details of the National Farm Survey (1940-43), which involved some 300000 farms and smallholdings during the Second World War, can also be found in the PRO leaflet DR 106.

Whilst maps are designed to prevent us from losing our way, its easy to "lose yourself" in a map and find yourself tracing the routes your ancestors took to work, school, church – or even the local pub!

STEPPING STONES DATA CD'S LTD
Census Areas Available

Census Area	Release date	Pre-release price	Normal Price	P/P
West Riding of Yorkshire	Out Now		£29.95	£2.00
N & E Riding of Yorkshire	Out Now		£24.95	£2.00
Lancashire	Out Now		£34.95	£3.00
Durham	Out Now		£24.95	£2.00
Northumberland	Out Now		£24.95	£2.00
Middlesex incl. part **London**	TBA	£29.95	£39.95	£2.00
Staffordshire	Out Now	£19.95	£29.95	£2.00
Kent	Out Now	£19.95	£24.95	£2.00
Norfolk	Out Now	£19.95	£29.95	£2.00
Surrey incl. part **London**	TBA	£19.95	£29.95	£2.50
Essex	TBA	£19.95	£24.95	£2.50
Derbyshire	TBA	£19.95	£24.95	£2.00
Lincolnshire	TBA	£19.95	£24.95	£2.00
Devonshire	TBA	£19.95	£29.95	£2.50
Cheshire	TBA	£19.95	£24.95	£2.00
Cumberland	TBA	£19.95	£24.95	£2.00
Oxfordshire	TBA	£19.95	£24.95	£2.00
Cambridgeshire	TBA	£19.95	£24.95	£2.00
Dorsetshire	TBA	£19.95	£24.95	£2.50

Check our Web Page for
further releases & **New Products** in 2003
STEPPING STONES DATA CD'S LTD   PO Box 295 York YO32 9WQ
Tel: - 01904 400503   Email: - judd@mjudson.freeserve.co.uk
Fax: - 01904 400602   Secure Web Shop: - www.stepping-stones.co.uk

County & Country Codes (Pre 1974 counties)

England	ENG	Cardiganshire	CGN	Cavan	CAV	Manitoba	MAN
All Counties	ALL	Carmarthenshire	CMN	Clare	CLA	New Brunswick	NB
Bedfordshire	BDF	Denbighshire	DEN	Cork	COR	Newfoundland	NFD
Berkshire	BRK	Flintshire	FLN	Donegal	DON	North West Terr	NWT
Buckinghamshire	BKM	Glamorgan	GLA	Down	DOW	Nova Scotia	NS
Cambridgeshire	CAM	Merionethshire	MER	Dublin	DUB	Ontario	ONT
Cheshire	CHS	Monmouthshire	MON	Fermanagh	FER	Prince Edward Is	PEI
Cornwall	CON	Montgomershire	MGY	Galway	GAL	Quebec	QUE
Cumberland	CUL	Pembrokeshire	PEM	Kerry	KER	Saskatchewan	SAS
Derbyshire	DBY	Radnorshire	RAD	Kildare	KID	Yukon Territory	YUK
Devonshire	DEV			Kilkenny	KIK		
Dorsetshire	DOR	**Scotland**	**SCT**	Leitrim	LEI	**Europe**	
Durham	DUR	Aberdeenshire	ABD	Leix(Queens)	LEX	Austria	OES
Essex	ESS	Angus	ANS	Limerick	LIM	Belarus	BRS
Gloucestershire	GLS	Argyllshire	ARL	Londonderry	LDY	Belgium	BEL
Hampshire	HAM	Ayrshire	AYR	Longford	LOG	Croatia	CRO
Herefordshire	HEF	Banffshire	BAN	Louth	LOU	Czechoslovakia	CS
Hertfordshire	HRT	Berwickshire	BEW	Mayo	MAY	Czech Republic	CZR
Huntingdonshire	HUN	Bute	BUT	Meath	MEA	Denmark	DEN
Isle of Wight	IOW	Caithness-shire	CAI	Monaghan	MOG	Estonia	EST
Kent	KEN	Clackmannanshire	CLK	Offaly(Kings)	OFF	Finland	FIN
Lancashire	LAN	Dumfriesshire	DFS	Roscommon	ROS	France	FRA
Leicestershire	LEI	Dunbartonshire	DNB	Sligo	SLI	Germany (1991)	BRD
Lincolnshire	LIN	East Lothian	ELN	Tipperary	TIP	German Old Emp	GER
London (city)	LND	Fifeshire	FIF	Tyrone	TYR	Greece	GR
Middlesex	MDX	Forfarshire	ANS	Waterford	WAT	Hungary	HU
Norfolk	NFK	Invernessshire	INV	Westmeath WES		Italy	ITL
Northamptonshire	NTH	Kincardineshire	KCD	Wexford	WEX	Latvia	LAT
Northumberland	NBL	Kinrossshire	KRS	Wicklow	WIC	Liechtenstein	LIE
Nottinghamshire	NTT	Kirkcudbrightshire	KKD			Lithguania	LIT
Oxfordshire	OXF	Lanarkshire	LKS	**Channel Islands**	**CHI**	Luxembourg	LUX
Rutland	RUT	Midlothian	MLN	Alderney	ALD	Netherlands	NL
Shropshire	SAL	Moray	MOR	Guernsey	GSY	New Zealand	NZ
Somerset	SOM	Nairnshire	NAI	Jersey	JSY	Norway	NOR
Staffordshire	STS	Orkney Isles	OKI	Sark	SRK	Poland	POL
Suffolk	SFK	Peebleshire	PEE			Romania	RO
Surrey	SRY	Perthshire	PER	**Isle of Man**	**IOM**	Russia	RUS
Sussex	SSX	Reffrewshire	RFW			Slovakia	SLK
Warwickshire	WAR	Ross & cromarty	ROC	**Australia**	**AUS**	Slovinia	SLO
Westmorland	WES	Roxburghshire	ROX	Capital Territory	ACT	Spain (Espagne)	ESP
Wiltshire	WIL	Selkirkshire	SEL	New South Wales	NSW	Sweden	SWE
Worcestershire	WOR	Shetland Isles	SHI	Northern Territory	NT	Switzerland	CH
Yorkshire	YKS	Stirlingshire	STI	Queensland	QLD	Ukraine	UKR
YKS E Riding	ERY	Sutherland SUT		South Australia	SA	United Kingdom	UK
YKS N Riding	NRY	West Lothian	WLN	Tasmania	TAS	United States	USA
YKS W Riding	WRY	Wigtownshire	WIG	Victoria	VIC	USSR	SU
				Western Australia	WA	Yugoslavia YU	
Wales	**WLS**	**Ireland (Eire)**	**IRL**				
Anglesey	AGY	Antrim	ANT	**Canada**	**CAN**	Papua New Guinea	PNG
Brecknockshire	BRE	Armagh	ARM	Alberta	ALB	Rep South Africa	RSA
Caernarvonshire	CAE	Carlow	CAR	British Columbia	BC		

These codes are used to avoid confusion in the use of abbreviations for countries and counties. Created by Dr Colin Chapman they are universally recognised and should always be used.

Lochin Publishing 6 Holywell Road, Dursley GL11 5RS England

Census Returns

A Census has been taken every 10 years since 1801 except in 1941 during the Second World War.
The census returns for 1801, 1811, 1821, 1831 were not preserved.
However there are some areas where returns for these years have been found.
The first census that is useful to researchers is the one taken in 1841.
The Census returns were taken on:

1841	7th June 1841	1851	30th March 1851	1861	7th April 1861
1871	2nd April 1871	1881	3rd April 1881	1891	5th April 1891
		1901	31st March 1901		

These census returns can be consulted. They were subject to public closure for 100 years because of the sensitive personal information they contained.

The Institute of Heraldic and Genealogical Studies

The Institute of Heraldic and Genealogical Studies is a charitable educational trust that was established in Canterbury, Kent in 1961 to promote the study of the history and structure of the family. To fulfil this aim a series of day, residential, evening and correspondence courses are run throughout the year for the benefit of family historians and genealogists. The courses range from those suitable for complete beginners to the subject, to those aimed at individuals wishing to pursue genealogical research as an income earning profession.

The day and residential courses offered in 2003 are —

The Professional Approach	Day School	**1 February**
Heraldry for Family Historians	Day School	**12 April**
Introduction to Family History	Day School	**17 May**
Palaeography	Day School	**21 June**
Tracing Your Family History	Residential Course	**21-25 July**
Introduction to Family History	Day School	**27 September**
Advanced Genealogy	Residential Course	**15-17 November**

Accommodation for the residential courses is provided at one of the historic hotels or guesthouses in the delightful medieval city of Canterbury, close to the Institute's comprehensive library.

The Institute also runs an evening course that encompasses the whole of its syllabus required for qualification in genealogical research. This course, *Family History*, is held each year in central London at the London School of Economics. The course leads to graded assessments and examinations for certificates and diploma.

Family History	35 week evening course at the LSE	**3 September**

A six week evening course aimed at beginners to the subject of genealogy will also be held at the Institute's premises in Canterbury

Introduction to Family History	6 week evening course at the IHGS	**27 September**

For those students not able to study in Canterbury or London, the Institute runs a very popular correspondence course that is accredited by the Open and Distance Learning Quality Council. This is composed of a series of 24 in-depth assignments, each requiring written answers to questions on the particular topic. Individual tutorial guidance is given. The course is also open to students from abroad with an interest in British genealogical research and takes two or three years to complete, studying on a part-time basis.

Full details of the courses can be obtained from the Registrar on receipt of a large SAE.
Please send your enquiry to IHGS, 79-82 Northgate, Canterbury, Kent, CT 1 1BA
Tel 01227 768664   Fax 01227 765617   registrar@ihgs.ac.uk   http://www.ihgs.ac.uk

Catch 'em Young

Jean Cole on encouraging the younger generation's interest in history

Knowing that my twelve year old great nephew, Christopher, was interested in history and after giving him a book on the subject for Christmas, he came in to say thank you and tell me how fascinated he was by everything to do with history. I then suggested to him that, if I was able to arrange it, perhaps I could take him to the Wiltshire and Swindon Record Office at Trowbridge to look at some original documents. This Christopher greeted with enthusiasm.

Steve Hobbs, an archivist at Trowbridge, was amenable and we made a date for Christopher's day. Steve then came up with some suggestions that on our way to Trowbridge we should look at the Avebury Stone Circle and he would have ready an 18th century map showing where cottages were situated before they were demolished before World War 2, to make way for the raised stones. Through Devizes where we would be able to see windows that had been bricked in after the imposition of the Window Tax and cunningly painted to look like proper sash windows. Out of Devizes across the bridge where the prisoners which included, as late as the 1860's, children as young as 11 years of age who had contravened the law, and had been conveyed to the House of Correction or the gaol (now long demolished) to serve out their harsh sentences often with hard labour. Down the steep Caen Hill (the hill of canal locks) known as Cane Hill in the early 17th century, through the picturesque village of Seend towards the Semington roundabout where I would point out to Christopher the old Poor Law Union workhouse (now converted into prestigious flats). Shortly after, armed with a new A4 lined book, file, pencils, "A Secretary Hand ABC Book" by Alf Ison (Berkshire FHS Research Centre 2000) all in a brief case donated by my husband, we would arrive at the Record Office to look at various documents which would also include plans of Christopher's grandparents' house when it was first built.

After that, Steve said, Christopher could help me! I compiled a brief family history with some of its relevant documents which we could look at and obtain photocopies. I also decided to show Chris just one of the projects on which I am working at the moment - vagrants' passes.

The Visit
The visit on 6 June 2002 (the 58th Anniversary of WW2 D Day Landings in 1944)

The journey to Trowbridge takes around an hour and passes through beautiful countryside and some of the most ancient archaeological sites in Wiltshire. I felt much like a coach guide on a grand tour of the historic Wiltshire countryside pointing out all the places of interest - on your left is Silbury Hill; if you look towards your right you will see the Beckhampton Racing Stables and its string of horses coming home from their morning exercise, together with other notable places en route.

On arrival Steve was there to greet Chris and take him around the archives showing him various records including the oldest archives in the Wiltshire collection dating from early 12th and 13th centuries, with the seals of Maud and Richard the Lionheart. At this point, I frantically searched my memory so that I would be able to explain who these people were and to try and place Maud (in reality, Matilda) in the historic scheme of things. Eventually, I remembered that Maud had been the daughter of Henry 1 and that after his death she had been obliged to rule with Henry's nephew, Stephen - both of whom were 'wheelers and dealers' in trying to obtain the upper hand! Richard of course, was the King who spent much of his reign off adventuring in the Holy Land with the Crusades and who was locked up for a couple of years until rescued by his faithful minstrel, Blondin.

Next came an old parish register showing baptisms, marriages and burials and I informed Chris that parish registers began in 1538 and were always records of christenings, marriages and burials, not births and deaths. He was shown one or two early 17th century wills including a will made by a woman together with some inventories of goods and chattels. There were maps of all types and sizes - small maps, medium sized maps and some looking for all the world like large rugs enclosed in linen bags. Chris was suitably impressed with all he had been shown and I was more than pleased to hear him make some observant remarks.

Then it was into the search and map room to look at the large coloured map of Avebury which Steve explained in detail. There were some 1703 window tax documents for New Sarum (Salisbury) as none had survived for Devizes. As we pored over these documents I explained that the Window Tax had been imposed in 1696/7 and, as always with a new tax, it was a highly unpopular one and open to various devious ways and means by the people to evade paying, as we had witnessed by the blocking up of various windows in Devizes. The tax was eventually abolished in 1851.

Then came the plan of his grandparents' house which had to be copied into his book as the book was far too large to photocopy. One of the large boxes of vagrants' passes that I have been working on came next and we selected two of the more interesting ones to photocopy whilst I spelt out the implications in the past of being a vagrant - that they were beggars

Wiltshire Record Office
Research Room

roaming the countryside and according to the 'powers that be' were a scourge upon the country and parish finances and therefore vagrants were to be apprehended by parish officers and various upright citizens, punished by a whipping, and sent on their way back to their own parishes, all at great cost to the authorities, hence these records of 'passes'. That it had been decided to transcribe this massive collection which referred to men, women and children from all corners of the British Isles, in the hope that family historians who had managed to 'lose' some of their forebears would be able to discover their whereabouts.

Christopher was intensely interested in the letter concerning his three times great grandmother, Mary Collier, written by her uncle, David Cowley of Wroughton, to the Miss Elizabeth Benet Charity, requesting a new frock, worth ten shillings, for her as 'she have no mother... she have been a very good girl and deserving of the Money...' We also looked at Removal Orders for some of his ancestors who had been sent back to their parishes of settlement; marriage licence bonds and various other family documents, all of which were photocopied for his collection.

I was presented with the bill and was happy to pay up. After some more research we decided that it was time to go home - Chris was tired out and come to think of it, so was I by this time! We fell into the car and not much was said until we arrived home and Chris's Mother came to collect him and take him home, happy but exhausted.

The Result of the Exercise
At this point I have to say that I, for one, have long felt there is a great need for our younger generations to become interested in history as it was, about real people, and not the dry, dull stuff that I, for one, was taught when I was at school all those years ago, and I won't say how long! Without the youngsters of today, such as Christopher, perhaps, coming along to take our place, not only as family historians, but in all

aspects of social and local history, much of our work could be lost or forgotten in the future.

So, has the object of this exercise to encourage a love of all things historic in this particular youngster been achieved? Only time will tell. Will Chris, in the years to come, say that his dotty old great aunt encouraged in him an everlasting love of history? I sincerely hope so.

I leave almost the last word here with Christopher about his day amongst the archives and with being allowed to go 'behind the scenes' where other researchers are not allowed!   'Brilliant, I absolutely loved it and will always love history, thank you.'

And, Chris' father had the absolute final word when he 'phoned me that night to say, 'what on earth have you done with my son, its only seven o'clock and already he's in bed fast asleep, exhausted but happy!' And that was just how it should have been, shouldn't it?

Jean Cole is Vice President of Wiltshire Family History Society and Honorary Member of Wroughton History Group. She is a freelance writer and her 'Questions and Answers ' column is a regular feature in Family Tree Magazine. She is also the Co-author with John Titford of 'Tracing Your Family History' (Countryside Books 3rd edition) as well as being Co-author with Rosemary Church of 'In and Around Record offices in Great Britain' published by Family Tree Magazine.

Founded   1968
Incorporated   1998
Renamed   2001

The Association of
Genealogists & Researchers in Archives

(formerly The Association of Genealogists & Record Agents)

was founded in 1968 to promote high standards and professional conduct amongst family historians providing a research service to the public. Membership is open to those with recognised qualifications or inspection of case work by AGRA's Board of Assessors. Successful applicants must agree to abide by a Code of Practice.

An annual publication is produced listing members, their addresses and areas of expertise. This can be purchased from **The Society of Genealogists**, **Guildhall Library** or **The Secretaries, AGRA, 29 Badgers Close, Horsham, West Sussex RH12 5RU.** Please send £2.50 or 6 IRCs.

Web site: www.agra.org

---

www.genfair.com
Online Family History Fair
and Genealogy Bookstore

Over 60 UK societies and 30 other suppliers. Over 12,500 items for sale. Secure credit card payment facility

Books, fiches, CDs, software, indexes, transcriptions: parish registers, census indexes, monumental inscriptions, burial records, Poor Law records, marriage indexes, criminal and military records, poll books, old maps, trade directories, memoirs, local and county histories, genealogy guides, Family and Local History Society membership subscriptions, search services, birth marriage and death search and certificate ordering service, magazine subscriptions, &c., &c.

incorporating
GEN*fair*Direct
for superfast dellivery

Cornish Roots CDs
Fife Deaths Index CD
Gazetteer of Scotland CD
The Master Genealogist
National Burial Index CD
Trade Directories on CD
Victorian OS Maps

Enquiries from Societies & other suppliers welcome:

GEN*fair*
**36 Brocks Hill Drive,
Oadby
Leicester LE2 5RD UK**

E-mail: info@genfair.com

GENEALOGICAL.

The Rector. "A VERY NICE-LOOKING YOUNG WOMAN, GILSON. DID I HEAR RIGHTLY THAT SHE WAS YOUR DAUGHTER?"   *Rustic.* "YES, SIR, SHE WAR—SUSY WAR!"

The Rector. "HOW DO YOU MEAN—WAS?"

Rustic. "WELL, YOU SEE, SIR, FAITHER, HE MARRIED AGAIN, AND IN COURSE I CALLED HIS MISSUS 'MOTHER,' AND WHEN HE DIED SHE MARRIED BILL TOMKINS, SON O' JACK TOMKINS, AND I'M BLESSED IF MY SUSY DIDN'T SET UP AND MARRY JACK, WHO WAR A FRESHISH OLD CHAP. NOW, WHAT I WANT TO KNOW IS, AIN'T SUSY MY GRANDMOTHER?"

Friends' Organisations
Simon Fowler

Many county archives, and a few national one ones as well, have established organisations of Friends to help index the records and raise money to buy documents and equipment which otherwise the archive might not be able to afford. One of the largest is the Hampshire Archives Trust. Funded by Hampshire County Council, with subscriptions from several District Councils and a growing number of individuals, societies, and other corporate bodies, the Archives Trust has set out to safeguard archives within the county and encourage new initiatives in the field. Its work has included:

- surveying records in private hands and advice on their storage;
- liaison with military, naval, and other specialist museums with archive collections, with grants for conservation and improved packaging where appropriate;
- providing a continuing survey of business records in conjunction with supporters from the business field;
- organising exhibitions and conferences on themes of archive interest
- working with Hampshire County Council to establish and run the Wessex Film and Sound Archive.

Membership, for individuals, is £5 per annum. Members receive two newsletters a year and the opportunity to go on visits to archives and museums in Hampshire as well as outside the county.

More typical are the Friends of Gloucestershire Archives, which was formed to provide help and support to the Gloucestershire Record Office and to educate the public in the importance of preserving the county's archives. Membership is £5, and members receive a regular newsletter which covers matters of interest at the Record Office as well as what the Friends are doing. There are opportunities to join in a wide range of activities, such as:

- Transcribing and indexing projects.
- Staffing exhibitions and Open Days.
- Training at the Record Office.
- Special lectures and social events.
- Visits behind-the-scenes at the Record Office.
- Visits to local historic buildings and other Record Offices in the county and elsewhere.

In Northern England, the Friends of Lancashire Archives was formed in June 1986, with the aim of promoting, supporting, assisting and improving the Lancashire Record Office in its crucial work of protecting and conserving the archival heritage of the county, and making it available to the public. They provide a forum through which the Record Office can explain, publicise and promote its work and policies while users can put forward ideas and suggestions for improvement and can comment upon proposals. The FLA also makes a positive contribution to the work of the Record Office and has funded several projects.

The Friends meet socially and enjoy visits to other Record Offices and to places of historical and archival interest, including those not normally accessible to the general public. Membership is open to all who are concerned for Lancashire's archives and want to play a part in ensuring that their future is secure. The majority of the 350 Friends live or work in "historic" Lancashire, but many come from elsewhere.

The Friends have a stimulating and varied programme of events and activities, including:
- Trips to places of archival interest in the North West of England.
- Open days and similar events at the Lancashire Record Office.
- Social evenings and entertainment - an opportunity to meet and talk with other Friends.
- Discussion meetings to consider topics of concern to users of the Record Office.
- One-day workshops, with guest speakers on a wide range of subjects.
- Supervised groups of Friends doing voluntary work in the Record Office. Will flatteners, for instance, meet on Monday and Wednesday mornings.
- A quarterly Newsletter, which gives news about the Record Office, details of forthcoming events, catalogue updates, and an opportunity to air views and experiences.

In turn the Friends of Lancashire Archives have helped the Record Office by:
- Purchasing a set of the 1851 census to mark the 50 Anniversary of the Record Office.
- Providing assistance towards the purchase of the Towneley Papers.
- Buying a £600 computer for public use in the Searchroom to help family historians.
- Providing £1000 towards employing a student to sort Land Tax documents into township order.
- Creating an index to the Amounderness wills.
- Purchasing some 1793 records of the Lancaster Canal Company.

Britain's national archive, the Public Record Office, also has a Friends organisation. The objectives of the Friends of the Public Record Office is to educate the public in the knowledge of the public records and to support and assist the work of the PRO. Established in 1988, the Friends form a registered charity and are managed by an elected Council. Membership, which currently stands at just over 500, brings many benefits including *PROphile* the Friends magazine, and discounts on PRO conference and event fees and on purchases in the PRO bookshop. The Friends carry out many activities, but they are probably best known for their voluntary indexing projects. The result of the first of which (the indexing of some 300,000 wills and administrations in the Prerogative Court of Canterbury) is now available. The Friends are also completing work on an index to soldiers' documents between 1760 and 1854. Membership is £10 per annum, as well as *PROphile* members can go on several trips a year, attend an annual lecture with a top historian, and receive 10% discount in the Office's bookshop and 20% off events, such as lectures and conferences, organised by the PRO.

A rather different creature is the London Archive Users Forum (LAUF), which exists to represent the interests of all users of archives within the Greater London area. It is a little known fact that the capital has more archives than museums: from national and metropolitan institutions, such as the PRO and the London Metropolitan Archives (LMA), to small borough local studies libraries and special repositories. Over the years LAUF has campaigned for improving in services, such as opening hours, and against cuts in archival services and regularly meets the LMA to talk about the service they offer the public. Over the years its campaigns have directly improved facilities and opportunities to use record repositories for thousands of family and local historians. The Forum also publishes a well-regarded newsletter, sent free to members, that offers one way to keep up to date with the rapidly changing world of the London archives. We also organise an annual conference on some aspect of the records. Recent conferences have been on subjects as diverse as electronic records, charities and transport. One of the most popular features are the six trips each year LAUF members make to many of the capitals' archives and libraries. Recent trips have included the College of Arms, the Foundling Hospital, and the National Art Library. Membership is £5.

If you use a particular record office a lot, have time on your hands and fancy something a little different, or just want to give something back to help future generations of local and family historians then joining a Friends' organization is an excellent idea. The local archive will be able to tell you whether such a body exists and how to join it. An incomplete list is also given below.

List of friends organizations
Here are details of most Friends organisations, although there may be other bodies which I have been unable to find information about.
Friends of Devon's Archives, Membership Secretary, Mrs G.D. Adams, Stacombe Farm, Doccombe, Moretonhampstead, Devon TQ13 8SS
www.devon.gov.uk/dro/friends.html
Friends of Dorset Archives Service c/o, the Dorset Record Office, Bridport Road, Dorchester, Dorset DT1 1RP,
www.dorset- cc.gov.uk/CorporateHome/ CorporateServices/ArchivesService/
Friends of Dundee City Archives Hon. Treasurer, c/o Archive & Record Centre, 21 City Square, Dundee DD1 3BY   www.fdca.org.uk/
Friends of Gloucestershire Archives, Membership Secretary, Jill Barlow, 39 Tivoli Road, Cheltenham GL50 2TD
http://beehive.thisisgloucestershire.co .uk/ default.asp?WCI=SiteHome&ID=2947&PageID=13686
Friends of Hackney Archives, 43 De Beauvoir Road London N1 5SQ
www.hackney.gov.uk/history/data/h_fha.htm

Hampshire Archives Trust, Membership Secretary, Hampshire Record Office, Sussex Street, Winchester SO23 8TH.
www.hants.gov.uk/record-office/trust.html.
Friends of Lancashire Archives Membership Secretary, Mr. C. Spencer, 17 Black Bull Lane, Fulwood, Preston, PR2 3PT,
www.lancashire.gov.uk/education/lifelong/ro/fla/fla.htm
London Archive Users Forum, Membership Secretary, Paul Hadley, 28 Poole Rd, London E9 7AE, www.londonarchiveusers.org.uk
Friends of the PRO, Membership Secretary, Cedric Jeffery, 48 Elm Road, London SW14 7JQ
www.pro.gov.uk/yourpro/friends.htm
The Friends of the National Libraries, The Secretary, c/o Department of Manuscripts The British Library 96 Euston Road London NW1 2DB
www.bl.uk/about/cooperation/friends2.html
Friends of the Suffolk Record Office, secretary, Bill Wexler, Lowestoft Record Office, Central Library, Clapham Road, Lowestoft, NR32 1DR,
www.suffolkcc.gov.uk/sro/friends_of_sro.html
Friends of East Sussex Record Office, c/o East Sussex Record Office, The Maltings, Castle Precincts, Lewes BN17 1YT,
www.eastsussexcc.gov.uk/archives/search_page.htm
Friends of Westminster City Archives, 10 St Ann's Street, London SW1P 5DE,
www.westminster.gov.uk/libraries/archives/friends.cfm

Married ~ by Banns or by Licence

Pauline M Litton BA FSG (Assoc)
Vice President Federation of Family History Societies

Banns, Certificate or Licence
If your ancestor married before 1837 within the British Isles, the event should have been preceded by the calling of Banns or the granting of a Marriage Licence (marriage by licence was very rare in Scotland). If you find a record of a marriage, it is always worth trying to track down either the banns or the documentation accompanying the issuing of a marriage licence as, from these, you may be able to glean additional information to that given in the marriage entry. A Certificate was issued if the couple came from different parishes; the banns had to be called in both and a certificate handed to the clergyman performing the marriage confirming that the banns had been published in the other parish and no objection made.

Hardwicke's Marriage Act, which tightened controls on where marriages could take place, came into effect in 1754. Before this date (but not afterwards) a certificate might also be issued when a couple called the banns in their home parish but married elsewhere as when, in 1717, Joshua Stizaker and Anne Shepherd both of Lancaster were married at Thornton Lonsdale in Yorkshire *by certificate from Mr Christopher Gibson Curate of Lancaster*.

Since the introduction of civil marriages in 1837, a Superintendent Registrar's Certificate can be issued twenty one days after notice of a marriage has been given and this currently permits the marriage to take place in church (with the incumbent's consent) or *in a register office, registered building or approved premises*.

Validity of Banns, Certificates and Licences
All are valid for three months. If the marriage does not take place within this period, they become invalid and, in theory, the process has to begin again. To cater for the current trend to book wedding venues well in advance it has, since 1998, been possible to obtain a Certificate for Marriage up to twelve months in advance but formal notice must still be given three months before the ceremony.

Location of records
Written records of **Banns** (where they survive: see below) will usually be found in the same county record or archive office, or diocesan registry, as the Parish Registers. Few certificates survive; occasional ones may be found slipped into the relevant page of the PR and others may be located with parish chest material. Where marriage registers are viewed on microfilm or microfiche check whether any separate Banns Books have been filmed. Also be aware that some printed parish registers do not include details from such books and a few omit details of banns called if the couple did not marry in the parish. County volumes of the *National Index of Parish Registers*, and record repository guides, normally list separate Registers of Banns where these exist.

Documentation relating to **Marriage Licences** will generally be located in the same repository as Bishops' Transcripts, often a diocesan registry. Bear in mind that (as can be the case with PRs and BTs) Banns Registers/Books and Marriage Licence documentation may be held in different repositories. Also be aware that a diocese rarely coincided neatly with a county so that a diocesan registry may contain records from part of a county or from several counties. Many counties included areas known as Peculiars (areas not subject to the ecclesiastical jurisdiction of the diocese in which they are situate), a number of which were empowered to grant licences whose documentation may be filed separately from the main diocesan series. *Bishop's Transcripts and Marriage Licences, Bonds and Allegations: a Guide to their Location and Indexes* (5th edition 2001), compiled by Jeremy Gibson and published by the Federation of Family History Societies (Publications) Ltd. is a most useful publication.

Marriage by Banns
The word Banns originally meant 'proclamation' and, in the Christian Church, it was decreed that an intended marriage should be proclaimed or published (made generally known; it did not mean written down or printed) in a church for three Sundays preceding the marriage so that anyone wishing to object to the marriage had time to do so. In England, Ireland and

Wales, if the information is given at all, you will generally find the words *by Banns* or *by Publication* following the marriage entry; in Scotland *by Proclamation* is more commonly used. Until 1837 *by Banns and Certificate* or merely *by Certificate* indicates that more than one parish is involved, even if this is not stated in the marriage entry. In such cases the banns entry should be sought as it may well name the other parish, often many miles away.

Before 1754 there was no requirement to record Banns and their survival rate is almost nil. The exception to this, in some areas, is the period from 1653-1660, when marriage was a civil, not a religious, ceremony, with banns being called either in the market place or in church and with the couple being married by a Justice of the Peace (on production of a certificate confirming the calling of the banns). For many parishes neither banns nor marriages survive for these years but it is always worth checking in the area where you think a couple might have married because some incumbents did continue to enter events, particularly banns, in their registers. An Act in 1653 specified that, 21 days before an intended marriage, the couple should *deliver in writing unto the Register for the respective parish, where each party to be married lives, the names, surnames, additions, and places of abode of the parties so to be married, and of their parents, guardians or overseers.* Banns for *Thomas Browne taylor of this parish [Cheadle, Cheshire], son of James Browne of Cheadle deceased, and Ellen Berch of Didsbury parish of Manchester, daughter of John Berch of Didsbury deceased,* recorded in 1655 in registers at Cheadle, Didsbury and Manchester and who supposedly married at Stockport (where no record survives), demonstrate just how useful banns for this period can be.

From 25 March 1754 banns in England and Wales had to be recorded in writing but nothing was said about the format in which this should be done. As with marriage registers, individual printers interpreted Hardwicke's Act differently. Some combined the banns and marriage entry into one unit; others bound the marriage register at one end of the book and the banns book at the other; yet others produced two separate books, a Banns Book (sometimes referred to as a Publications or a Notices Book) and a Marriage Register. It is the separate Banns Books which are usually listed in guides. Great care should be exercised when searching for banns within a parish register; particularly if looking through microfilm or microfiche they can be very easy to overlook. Also be aware that the survival rate of Banns Books is patchy. They were not regarded as being of the same importance as registers and many have been lost.

Banns versus Licence

Marriage by banns has always been more common than marriage by licence, although in a few churches the latter was the norm (according to J.S.Burn's *The History of Parish Registers in England etc.* both St Paul's Cathedral and Westminster Abbey were precluded from performing marriages in 1754 because Hardwicke's Act specified that marriages must take place in a church or chapel *where Banns of Matrimony have been usually published* and no publication of Banns had ever taken place in them). It

is recorded in the marriage register for Leeds parish church, covering March 1754 to May 1760: *Number of Marriages in this Volume 1495; in all 1299 by Banns and 196 by Licence* but the ratio would vary from area to area, and time to time.

Marriage by licence was not restricted to the middle and upper classes, as is sometimes believed. Members of the aristocracy did marry by banns; some labourers married by licence. There were many reasons for opting for marriage by licence. These ranged from a desire for privacy (calling the banns in church meant that the entire neighbourhood would know what was being planned) to the convenience of being able to marry immediately the licence had been obtained. Licences were often preferred if the bride-to-be was heavily pregnant; the man was in the armed forces and about to march away; or the couple thought that there was likely to be opposition to their marriage. It was easier for minors to obtain a licence by lying about their ages than it was for them to avoid detection by parents or relatives as the banns were called three times. Roman Catholics and Nonconformists, bound by law between 1754 and 1837 to marry in the parish church, could often stomach the necessity for marrying in an Anglican church but did not want their banns called there. If the couple came from different parishes, and especially if these were a long way apart, it was often easier, if not cheaper, to obtain a licence. This removed the need to have the banns called in both parishes and to obtain a certificate from one of them, possibly several days' journey away.

Marriage by Licence

Licences could be issued by Archbishops (Canterbury, York and Armagh), Bishops and some Archdeacons or their surrogates (deputies), incumbents of some Peculiars and, after 1837, also by Superintendent Registrars. Almost all licences were of the type known as 'common' or 'ordinary' licences. 'Special licences', granted by the Archbishops of Canterbury and Armagh and, occasionally, by the Bishop of Sodor and Man, permitting couples to marry in any place (consecrated or not) and at any time, accounted for less than 1% of pre-20th century licences. According to the latest edition of *Whitaker's Almanack* (which contains a useful section on current marriage practices) there is a tendency for (common) licences issued by Superintendent Registrars to be referred to as 'special licences'.

Despite the use of the phrase 'married by licence' very few family historians will have seen an actual marriage licence. This was handed to the groom (very occasionally to the bride if she had applied for the licence), to hand to the minister at the church, and a few only survive among parish records. The documentation which may still be found in record repositories includes Marriage Allegations and Bonds and, for some dioceses, registers of marriage licences (which often do not include as much information as the allegation and bond). An allegation (sometimes known as an affidavit) states the couple's intention to marry, alleges that there is no reason why they should not marry, and names a church where the marriage should take place. The (approximate) ages of the couple, their places of residence and the groom's occupation may also be given. A bond serves as surety for the truth of the allegation and is usually entered into by the groom and one other, often a relative of bride or groom, an employer or a neighbour. Bonds ceased to be obligatory by law in 1823 but the practice of requiring them continued in some areas.

The survival rate of this documentation varies widely. Many dioceses have good coverage from the late 16th century; others have nothing before the mid-18th century. Consult the **Gibson Guide** mentioned earlier for details and bear in mind that, as the guide shows, much licence documentation has been either transcribed, calendared or indexed, and sometimes printed; it pays to check before beginning a long search of original documents or microform. Marriage licences are very rare from the mid-1640s and were not issued between 1653 and 1660 except in a few Peculiars. They were reinstated in 1660.

Many series of allegations and bonds begin around this date and a number of dioceses begin to use printed forms, particularly for bonds. Look out for those dioceses which handwrote the allegation onto the printed bond, sometimes on the back. Until 1732 the documents were often in Latin but names, ages and occupations can usually be picked out. Useful words in this context are: *aet[atis]* (age), *cael[ebs]* (single); *vid[uus* or *ua]* (widower/widow); *opp[idum]* (of this town) and *ille/illa* or *suus/sua* meaning his or her(s). From 1733 separate printed forms are commonly used for bonds and allegations so look for both.

Before 1714 incumbents were not bound to state in their registers whether a marriage had taken place following banns or the issuing of a licence. Individual bishops had been attempting to introduce this practice much earlier (Chester in the 1670s, York by 1710) but many clergy continued to ignore the requests; it is always worth checking to see if any licence documentation survives.

Prior to Hardwicke's Marriage Act, allegations often specified several churches where a marriage could take place and some did not name a church; after 1754 the allegation had to specify a church in the parish in which one of the parties had been resident for at least four weeks. Thus, before 1754, you may find marriage allegations/bonds (and the marriage) in unexpected places. Licences normally had to be obtained from the bishop or his surrogate and this could involve a long journey, often to the cathedral of the diocese or to the church occupied by a surrogate. Possession of the licence concerned many couples (who might, in any case, not be able to read it) and clerics far more than what it said. Particularly in cathedrals, there were usually clergymen only too willing to marry a couple as they emerged clutching their 'piece of paper' so, if the allegation specifies a church but the marriage does not take place there, try the cathedral. The Diocese of Lichfield covered the counties of Derbyshire and Staffordshire, and parts of Shropshire and Warwickshire (and marriage licence documentation for all these counties is held at Lichfield). Couples from all these counties can be found in the Lichfield Cathedral marriage register,

even though the cathedral was rarely named as a church where the marriage could take place.

When bride or groom was under the age of 21, allegations will often (before 1754) and should (after 1754) include their exact ages, together with the written consent of a parent or guardian of the minor. The ages of adults given in allegations are less reliable. The wording on the form, *he/she is of the age of ... and upwards*, was open to interpretation. In general, if a precise age is given, it is likely to be accurate to within five years (remembering that many people before the late 19th century did not know their precise ages) but *of the age of 21 and upwards* should be treated with extreme caution. The person might be telling the truth, be younger than 21 but marrying without parental consent, or be much older.

Between September 1822 and mid-1823, when a short-lived law required those applying for a licence to provide details of their baptisms, it is evident just how misleading ages on allegations can be. When widower Lawrence Peel of Ardwick in Lancashire and widow Elizabeth Radcliffe of Ecclesall Bierlow in Yorkshire applied for a licence it was stated that they were both aged over 21. Their baptism certificates showed that he was 65 and she was 47.

One final warning: Banns might be called, or a Licence might be issued, but neither is any guarantee that the marriage took place. Never assume that a couple married until you have seen the entry in the marriage register.

Transported to Bermuda
Jill Chambers

Far away in the Atlantic, the Islands of Bermuda lie like a number of tiny specks of coral, limestone, and rich vegetation in an ocean of deep blue. Their climate is, in general, warm and moist; beauty and fertility are their birthright.'
(The English Prison Hulks by W. Branch Johnson)

'Set in crystal waters, warmed by the sun, cooled by the gentle Gulf Stream breezes, adorned with sparkling beaches and lush vegetation, Bermuda is a shimmering paradise when experienced from the perspective of the privileged classes ashore, or the many thousands of tourists who have visited the colony during the 20th century.
(The Intolerable Hulks by Charles Campbell)

It is unlikely that the three hundred convicts who dropped anchor at Ireland Island, in Bermuda on board the *Antelope* in February 1824, or the thousands that followed them, would recognise these descriptions of Bermuda.

Under the provisions of the Act of 1776, convicts had been housed on board ships, or hulks, and had been kept to hard labour in some of H.M. Dockyards and other Public Works. By an Act, dated 4th July, 1823, offenders convicted in Great Britain and sentenced to

breakwater and the clearance of a wood on the hillsides around the cove. The names of these first 300 convicts who arrived on the *Antelope* can been found among the Home Office papers at the Public Record Office, in HO7/3, and in the Quarterly Returns in HO8/1. There returns give each man's name, age, crime, date and place of conviction, and sentence. Many of them were teenagers or in their early twenties. .

Early in 1826 the *Antelope* was joined by the *Dromedary*, with another 300 convicts. Three hundred more arrived on the *Coromandel* in 1828, with an additional 300 arriving in the *Weymouth* on 28th February 1829. By the end of December 1846, the number of convicts in Bermuda totaled 1,759, distributed among the hulks as follows: *Dromedary* 418, *Coromandel* 470, *Tenedos* 407, *Thames* 284. (CO37/119) In 1848 five hulks were listed in operation at the Dockyard at Ireland Island, *Dromedary, Coromandel, Weymouth, Tenedos,* and *Medway*, with the *Antelope* and *Thames* was stationed in St George's. It was in 1848 that the *Tenedos* was fitted out as a hospital ship and moved to moorings off Boaz Island.

Our idea of what conditions on board the hulks were like depends on who was describing them. In 1859,

HARVEY, Daniel	16	Stealing a sugar basin	MDX Sept 1823	14 years
MORLEY, John C	16	Felony	MDX Dec 1821	Life
MORTON, John	16	Felony	LAN Jan 1823, Salford	7 years
SHEARLEY, George	16	Felony	MDX 10 Sept 1823	7 years
MEMORY, Edward	16	Felony	MDX 10 Sept 1823	7 years
JAY, Benjamin	16	Burglary	WAR 5 April 1823	Life
NEWMAN, Martin	16	Stealing a jacket	SRY 3 March 1823	7 years
NASH, Thomas	16	Stealing wearing apparel	LIN 22 July 1823, Sleaford	7 years
LAKE, Thomas	16	Stealing 11yds black silk	Old Bailey Sept 1823	7 years
CAMPBELL, James	17	Stealing wearing apparel	NTT March 1823	7 years
FINCH, Timothy	17	Stealing Bombazine	NFK April 1823	7 years
TROUP, Alexander	17	House breaking	Aberdeen April 1823	7 years
HEATHCOTE Wm	17	Stealing a shirt	HRT July 1823	7 years
BALL, Henry	17	Stealing in a dwelling house	GLS July 1823	7 years
HUNTER, Henry	17	House breaking	BRK July 1823	7 years
FARRIER, John	17	Stealing a top coat	MDX Sept 1823	14 years

transportation, could now be removed to other parts of His Majesty's dominions outside England. They could be confined either on land or on board any ship, and kept to labour on H.M. Dockyards and Public Works overseas. The *Antelope*, a deactivated frigate, was acquired by the Home Office from the Royal Navy and after repairs and modification, she was provisioned for a voyage to Bermuda. Under the command of Lieutenant Henry HIRE, R.N., she sailed from Spithead on 5th January 1824, and arrived in Bermuda on 8th February, with a cargo of 300 convicts. Also on board were 200 Royal Marines, they were to perform the duty of the Dockyard guard. On 25th February, 1824, the *Antelope*, lying off the Dockyard at Ireland Island, was paid off and handed over to Commissioner BRIGGS, who now held legal authority over the convicts in Bermuda. The first convicts were to be employed with construction of a

Chaplain to the hulks, Reverend J.M. GUILDING, wrote, *'in the close and stifling nights of summer the heat between decks is so oppressive as to make the stench intolerable, and to cause the miserable inmates frequently to strip off every vestige of clothing and gasp at the portholes for a breath of air.'*

Captain Ferdinand WHITTINGHAM, an army officer, published an account of life in Bermuda based on his observations made during an 18 month posting to the garrison in Bermuda. According to him the convicts had an easy life, and enjoyed more privileges and comforts than British soldiers or honest labourers back home in England. William JONES, alias William SYDES, was supposedly released from the Bermuda convict station in May 1845 and wrote a scathing report of life on the

Bermuda hulks, saying that they were ten times worse than those in England. In the Original Correspondence for 1851 I found a copy of a letter from the Home Office enclosing an extract from the Journal of the Chaplain of the Gaol at Lewes, in Sussex including statements made by a returned convict named John MORGAN, respecting the treatment of convicts at Bermuda. MORGAN is reported to have said, 'that he was a great deal better off abroad than any Tradesman at home - he had more money to spend and was never without 3 or 4 dollars in his pocket, that on Xmas day he spent 15/- of his own money extra on Eating and Drinking - that he worked 8 hours a day for Government, & over that for himself - that's how he used to get his money - that he would not have come back only he was brought back, & that sooner than he would know distress he would go a thieving & be transported again. *What time you are in England is the worst of it, you are kept more closer - when you get abroad you Don't care a d - - -'*. Later in the statement we learn that MORGAN's dinner on Xmas day cost him 3 dollars, and he had *'roast pork, baked taters, roast Duck, plum pudding and a bottle of rum.'* (CO37/138 folios 98-100)

Periodic outbreaks of dysentery were responsible for many deaths among the convicts on board the hulks in Bermuda. They also suffered from ophthalmia, due to the glare of the sun on sea and limestone rocks, this would cause men to stumble and fall as they walked even along a straight and smooth path. The worst scourge of all, however, was Yellow Fever. There were outbreaks in 1829, 1837, 1843, 1844 and 1856, but the worst epidemic of all occurred in 1853. It was believed to have arrived on a ship from Cuba, in July of 1853, and swept over the islands until December that same year, claiming a total of more than 650 victims from the civilian, military, and convict population. 160 convicts lost their lives. Colonial Office Dispatches (CO37/150) is entirely given over to reports on the 1853 outbreak of Yellow Fever. There are the answers given by various people to set questions relating to conditions on board the hulks, giving such information as, weekly diet - 'Fresh meat, 4 lbs; salt pork, 1lbs; soft bread, 7 lbs; biscuit, 1 lb; potatoes, 2lbs; rice, 12oz; cocoa, 1 lb 5oz; tea, 1oz; sugar, 10oz; grog, 1 gill daily; cocoa mornings, and tea evenings.' We are told the space allotted to each prisoner 'is from 190 to 200 cubic feet.' We are also told the number of men on each hulk 'attacked' by the disease, and the number who died. There is a list of all the patients who died of Yellow Fever in the *Tenedos* Convict Hospital Ship between the 9th July and the 9th December 1853. So we learn that the first prisoner to die, William FOREMAN, age 21, was admitted from Boaz Island Prison on the 5th July 1853, having been 'attacked' by the disease on the 1st July. The last death from fever on board the *Tenedos* was that of 25 year old Alfred HUMPHRIES, from the *Medway* hulk. He had arrived on board the *Tenedos*, as a Bedmaker, in September, succumbing to the fever on the 2nd December and died on the 9th December. I now

have a list of all the convicts who died of Yellow Fever during this outbreak, and I am in the process of matching their names with those in the Quarterly Returns to find out where and when they were tried and what their offences were.

So far I have only looked at a selection of Colonial Office Dispatches from Bermuda, but enough to see that they contain a wealth of information about the prisoners held on the hulks.

It is sometimes possible to find letters from friends and relations of the convicts among the Dispatches. For example I found the following letter in CO37/138 folio 319)

> Workhouse, Londonderry June 1851
> Gentlemen,
> I beg to acquaint you that my husband James Deeham was sentenced at Londonderry in 1847 to 21 years transportation. He was in Bermuda in the Summer of 1849 when I applied to your Honors that I might be sent out with my two children to him, and was then informed that if he was in Australia on a Ticket of Leave that my request might be complied with, since that time I have learned that many of the convicts then in Bermuda have been removed elsewhere and humbly beg leave to request you will have the kindness to inform me whether he has been removed or whether I could now be permitted to join him with my two children
> I have the honor to be Gentlemen
> Your obedient Humble Servant
> Rose Deeham

The following is a copy of the reply sent to Rose Deeham. (CO37/138 folio 321)

> 3 July 1851
> Rose Deeham,
> In reply to your letter of the 17 ulto. I am directed by Earl Grey to express to you his Lordship's regret that from enquiries he has caused to be made it appears that James Deeham died at Bermuda on the 11 February 1848. Lord Grey apprehends that this information had not yet been brought under the notice of the Secretary of State for the Home Dept. on the date of your former Memorial asking to join your husband in the Colonies.

Among the Colonial Office records are numerous discharge certificate relating to released convicts. As well as the date and place of trial they give the prisoners age, height, hair and eye colour and complexion. They also show the amount of money paid to the man after deducting his passage home. Attempts were made to escape from the hulks in Bermuda, but to date I have not looked into any of

these attempts. In *The English Prison Hulks*, Branch Johnson gives the following account of the attempted escape of John SMITH, alias Sydney Jack.

'He had been concerned with four other men (one of them his brother) in the murder of a Berkshire clergyman about 1850, but, by turning King's Evidence, had managed to save his own skin and was transported to Sydney. Thence he escaped and reached England; soon afterwards he was re-captured and sent to Bermuda. At Bermuda he made two attempts; both were unsuccessful, and, in addition to being flogged, he was compelled to serve his full time instead of (as was usual) being sent home with some months of his sentence remitted. On the first occasion he seized a boat, provisioned it by robbing a house, crossed the reef, and was well on the way to the American coast when a change of wind blew him back. He was captured by a whaler, whose captain was deaf alike to his threats and his entreaties. Brought again to the hulks, he was loaded with irons, partly as punishment, partly to prevent a second attempt; but it was just while he was at this apparent disadvantage that the second attempt was made. He and several other prisoners similarly ironed were being marched to church by a warder when they secured their guard and ran into the forest. Sydney Jack determined at first to fend for himself. Knocking off his fetters, he spied a boat drawn up on the beach, and attempted to make away in her; but her ballast had been removed, and she capsized when he jumped in. He had no option, therefore, but to follow the rest; though they succeeded for some time in eluding pursuit, all four were eventually re-taken.'

The 1840s saw a large influx of Irish prisoners to Bermuda, due mostly to hard times brought about by the famine following the failure of the potato harvest. Captain ELLIOT, who served as Governor of the Bermudian Island Group during 1848 and 1849 showed particular concern for these Irish prisoners

In June 1848 he sent the following dispatch to Earl Grey, the Home Secretary.

'It will be remarked with anxiety, on examining the list of 704 prisoners, sent from Ireland, in the *Medway* and *Bangalore*, that many of them were convicted of stealing food, and agrarian offences; the first, no doubt, chiefly attributed to the dreadful calamity which befell the poorer classes of people during the last two years, and the last in a high degree to the inflammatory practices of others, in the time of desperate need. Perhaps Her Majesty's Government may be pleased (taking all these circumstances into consideration, on the return of a state of comparative tranquility in Ireland), to permit me to appoint a Commission in this colony, for selecting individuals from the Irish prisoners, whom it may be permissible to recommend for removal to Australia, on the ticket of leave or conditional pardon. These prisoners are for the most part friendless men in humble stations of life, and your Lordship will feel that they are entitled to any extenuating considerations which I can advance in their behalf, whilst they are conducting themselves steadily and submissively at this depot.'(CO37/121 folio 52

I have not yet followed up what happened to these Irish prisoners.

Governor ELLIOT also showed particular concern over the large number of juvenile prisoners who were among those to arrive on the *Medway* and *Bangalore*.

'Poor and scanty food and the hard things of their infancy have for the most part left these lads with a lower stature and more childish appearance than their age alone would suggest, though it will shock H.M. Government to learn that twelve of them are under sixteen years of age, and that of the thirteen-year-olds one has been sentenced to fifteen years transportation for sheep-stealing!' (CO37/121 folio 93)

He ordered them to be kept separate from the rest of the prisoners, and not be allowed to work in gangs with the men. Instead they were to be taught trades such as shoemaking, tailoring and carpentry.

The problem of keeping the aging hulks in a habitable condition presented an enormous expense each year and it was eventually decided that the convict workers would be better housed in a shore prison, and by 1847 plans were being brought forward for the development of a site on Boaz Island. The first of the convicts were moved to Boaz Island Prison in August 1852, and although the Dockyard authorities proudly announced that by May 1854, the whole of the prisoners had been transferred from the hulks to Boaz Island Prison, returns for the *Medway* show that this hulk continued to accommodate around 600 prisoners until it finally closed in 1861. Records for the *Tenedos* show that about 200 prisoners were housed on board between 1857 and 1860. In 1861 the number of convict workers held in Bermuda had been reduced to such an extent that they could all be housed ashore.

By 1863 the 130 convicts remaining in the Convict Establishment sailed for England on board the *Sir George Seymour,* and the building turned over to the military authority. They embarked on the 25th March 1863. It was found necessary to punish, 'corporally and otherwise', seven of the prisoners on the eve of their departure, 'in consequence of insubordinate conduct.' The dispatch continues, 'as there is some reason to anticipate that they may shew a similar spirit during the voyage where there are few or no means of repression, I have specially warned that a repetition of such behaviour will be followed by the loss of the remainder of their mitigated time. I have instructed Assistant Overseer DOUGLAS, who is in charge of the Prisoners, to report specially on these men on their arrival and I request your Grace to be good enough to cause the requisite communication to be made to the Prison Authorities at home should it be found necessary to enforce further punishment against them.'

The names of the seven men are listed as follows:-
No.1812 B CARNEY
No.1875 J BUSHELL
No.1917 W NORBURY
No.2073 J BAMBER
No.2103 C MAHONEY
No.2029 A SHORT
No.2012 W TAYLOR.
(CO37/186 folio 323-325)

References:
The English Prison Hulks - W. Branch Johnson
The Intorerable Hulks - Charles Campbell
Forty Years of Convict Labour, Bermuda 1823-1863 - C.F.E. Hollis Hallett
Original Correspondence, Bermuda - CO37/119; CO37/121; CO37/138; CO37/150; CO37/186
Quarterly Prison Hulk Returns - HO8/1
Hulks in Bermuda - HO7/3

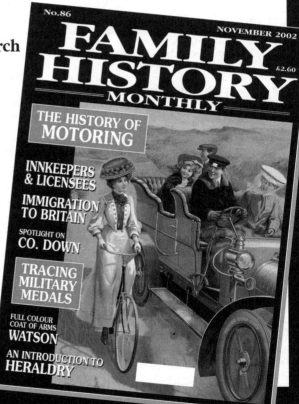

We've got a murderer in our family tree

Paul Williams discusses Murder Files

MURDER *files*

Information available
on UK murders
Research undertaken

There is nothing more attention grabbing when pouring over a family tree with friends and relatives than having a murderer pointed out amongst all the names and bits of information. What was till then perhaps a bit like watching other people's holiday slides, unless you are a budding genealogist, your mind suddenly goes into overdrive with thoughts of the jeering crowd around the scaffold, the sudden gasp as the body dangles for a few seconds on the end of the rope life now extinct. Similar thoughts also occur when the family member is the victim. How did he or she die? Did the victim suffer? Who did the evil deed? All of a sudden the fact that a few minutes earlier you had been told there was an Admiral or a Lord who committed a bit of hanky-panky back in the late 1800s pales into insignificance.

Most people have an inborn fascination with man's inhumanity towards man. When reading the newspapers the article referring to the discovery of a body in a neighbouring village or town is automatically one of the lead articles to be read. We may not like what we read but we automatically read it. The fact is that in the case of family trees we, through this unfortunate victim or perpetrator for some reason want to be associated with this dastardly crime. We may not have done it ourselves but we are linked. He or she was a relative.

When I was responsible for the famous Black (or Crime) Museum , amongst others, at New Scotland Yard in London, we received many enquiries from people all over the world requesting information on a particular murder. Generally the enquirer may perhaps have heard a rumour in the family that a relative had committed a murder earlier in the Century and was he or she the same 'Joe Bloggs' who was hanged at Wormwood Scrubs Prison by public hangman Albert Pierrepoint. Commonly they would add that unfortunately no living family member will talk about it. It was a taboo subject and best forgotten.

Unfortunately time and more pressing police duties meant we could give just scant information back if it was readily to hand. Cases occurring outside London were referred to the relevant Force. Hands were also tied in that Police records were strictly confidential and obviously details could not be released.

When I left in 1986 fate took a strange turn. I had been friends for some years with a publisher who had arguable the largest private murder library in the country. On one of my visits to his house when the subject was naturally about murder, he took me

to a large cupboard under the stairs and pointed to several extremely large packing cases and plastic bags. "Are those any use to you?" he asked. "I shan't need them anymore". Inside were literally thousands and thousands of press cuttings relating to murders during the last century! As I picked up the top handful I read of cases which, just months earlier, I had told enquirers we couldn't help them. From that moment Murder Files was born and after 18 months of sorting the cuttings became the initial collection, details of which could be available to enquirers.

Since then the collection has been greatly expanded. Murder Files now receive enquiries from all over the world from family historians gleaning information about that family rumour, TV researchers seeking information for a forthcoming documentary, the writer looking for missing details of a particular murder or whatever. It would be nice to say Murder Files had information on every murder that had occurred in the UK over the last 200 years but unfortunately I can't. But it does have records on literally thousands and is increasing rapidly especially with snippets of information being received from so many different avenues.

Although many of the murders researched may perhaps not be headline grabbers several cases come to mind where the enquirer has been surprised by what Murder Files had been able to find. A lady from Middlesex wrote to say that she had heard through her family that her great aunt, Maria Marten, had been murdered in the early 1800s and she wished to know more. Research discovered that a William Corder had been hanged for her murder in 1828. Maria was an attractive 25 year old who lived in the village of Polstead. She had met a rich

Murder of Maria Marten

Maria Marten's ghost shows where she is buried

21 year old farmer, Corder, in 1826, and when Maria became pregnant he promised to marry her. Although the child died, Maria's parents still urged Corder to marry.

On 19 May 1827 he stated he was taking her to Ipswich to marry her but said that the matter must be kept secret or she would, he told her, be arrested for having bastard children. He told her to go to her parents' home and change into male clothing. In the meantime he took some of her clothing to the Red Barn, a red roofed building on his land. He later called for her and they both walked to his home where, he told her, was waiting a horse and carriage to take them both to Ipswich.

Two days later he returned, saying Maria was still in Ipswich as there were problems in getting a marriage licence. On 29th September Corder declared he was going to London to meet and marry Maria. Three weeks later he wrote saying they were now married and living on the Isle of Wight. Her mother, however, had a dream that night that Maria had been murdered and buried in the Red Barn. So adamant was she that on the 19 April 1828 the barn was searched and Maria's body found.

Corder signs his confession in presence of the Prison Governor

Corder had by now married another girl in London. He was arrested and charged with Maria's murder. At his trial at Bury St Edmunds Assizes in August 1828 he pleaded Not Guilty and said that Maria had shot herself with one of his pistols that she had taken from his home. He did admit it was rather foolhardy in trying to conceal her body. The Jury were not convinced by this and listened to Corder's brother who said he had seen Corder leaving the barn with a pickaxe the day Maria disappeared. The Jury accordingly found Corder guilty of murder and he was hanged outside of Bury St Edmunds jail on Monday 11 August 1828 in front of a massive crowd. Strangely enough the murder was to be become the subject of several musicals for some years to follow.

Corder's Execution

Another interesting case Murder Files researched was one from a gentleman in Hampshire who wrote asking for any information on a man called Kent Reeks who was murdered in 1914. Reeks was his mother's cousin. He knew that no-one had been caught for the murder but wanted to know more about the actual case. Reeks had indeed been murdered. His body was found near a disused pit shaft at Ettingshall on 20 January 1914. He had been shot three times in the head. Bullets had gone through his brain and left eye and another through the centre of his skull. Three live cartridges and four spent ones were found lying near the body. The body was covered over by a coat but there were no bullet holes in it.

Reeks had landed at Liverpool from Halifax, Nova Scotia, on 17 January and visited his uncle in Manchester the same day. That night the uncle had put him on a train to join another train at Liverpool. Prior to departure Reeks had shown him a wallet full of dollar bills. However, only American and British coins were found in Reeks' pockets. Police never discovered the murderer nor was any trace found of the murder weapon. Even more mystifying was why the body was not thrown down the 400 foot water-filled shaft just yards away from where the body was found.

A lady from Natal, South Africa, wrote to enquire about a relative, Florence Nightingale Shore, who was murdered in 1920 on a train at or near Hastings Railway Station. Murder Files uncovered that a woman travelling alone in a 3rd class compartment was found with unexplained injuries

PILLBOX MURDER CHARGE

By KEN ROGERS

A MAN was charged last night with murdering a boy found dying with severe head injuries in a seashore pillbox last Thursday.

The man is Malcolm Keith Williams 30, a power station fitter, of Mountain View, Llwynypia, Rhondda Valley.

'The boy was Andrew Bonnick, 14, who lived with his parents and three sisters at The Old, Gileston, Glamorgan.

Despite a brain operation, he died soon after he was found in the pillbox, near his home.

Five Hours

Yesterday Williams spent more than five hours at Bridgend, Glamorgan, police headquarters before being taken six miles by police car to Cowbridge police station and charged.

Later Detective Superintendent John du Rose, of Scotland Yard, who heads investigations into Andrew's death, said: Williams would appear in court at Cowbridge today.

MAN ACCUSED OF PILLBOX MURDER

DAILY TELEGRAPH REPORTER

A MAN will appear in court at Cowbridge, Glam, to-day charged with the murder of Andrew Bonnick, 14, found dying in a pillbox on the beach at Gileston, near Barry, last Thursday. He is Malcolm Keith Williams, 20, fitter's mate, of Mountain View, Pontypridd.

Williams travelled from his home to Bridgend County Police Headquarters yesterday. He waited there for the return of Det. Supt. John de Rose, of Scotland Yard's murder squad, and Det. Insp. Norman Davies, of Glamorgan CID, from the forensic laboratory in Cardiff.

After spending two hours there they went with Chief Det. Supt. Tom Williams, head of Glamorgan CID, to the power station being built at Leys, near where the boy was found. After inquiries at Gileston, where the boy lived, they returned to Bridgend to question Williams.

AFTER FIVE HOURS

After about five hours he was taken to Cowbridge police station, where he was charged and detained in custody for his court appearance.

Supt. du Rose and Det. Insp. John Fyall, of Scotland Yard, were called in on Saturday to help local police in the investigations. The boy died in hospital after an emergency operation four hours after he had been found with severe head injuries in the pillbox.

---

on arrival at Bexhill Station on Monday afternoon 12 January 1920. She had a severe wound to the head and was hardly able to give an account of what had happened to her. As a result she was taken to the East Sussex Hospital in Hastings where she told nurses her name was Florence Nightingale Shore. She said she was attacked by a man who had left the train before it reached Bexhill. She described him as being slight, clean-shaven and about 28 years of age. He was wearing a light brown suit and looked like a clerk or shop assistant.

Extensive police enquiries were immediately made along the London to Hastings route, but despite Miss Shore's description of her attacker, no one was ever arrested for her murder – she having died on 16 January. The victim was Florence Nightingale's goddaughter and followed her into nursing where she was decorated for her work during the second Boer War.

An enquiry earlier this year involved a murder that occurred on 29 December 1960. A man (he later gave his name as Malcolm Keith Williams) had been collecting driftwood on the Lays Beach near the little village of Gileston in Glamorgan. Williams told police later that he had gone to place the wood in one of the wartime pillboxes on the beach to dry and had found a young boy, later named as Andrew Bonnick aged 14, lying in the box unconscious and with injuries to his face and head. The man had then run to the boy's mother and told her. The mother in turn had then raced to find her husband who had been out shopping and who was about to go down to the beach himself similarly to look for driftwood and to meet up with his son. Running to the scene the father and Williams carried Andrew out of the pillbox and applied some warm clothing to him to keep him warm. At this stage Mr Bonnick noticed that the boy still had his belt about his waist but his jeans were down to his legs.

Andrew was conveyed to the RAF Hospital at St Athan and seen by the medical officers and taken into the theatre. It was apparent to the medical officer that the injuries had been caused by violence. Later that night the boy passed away having had his heart twice restarted during an emergency operation.

At the scene of the crime police took away blood covered pebbles, large pieces of wood and an iron bar for examination at the Forensic Science Laboratory at Cardiff. Williams was also interviewed by Superintendent John du Rose, one of the famous 'big four' at Scotland Yard. Blood stains were found on Williams's clothing and fibres from his jacket found under the boy's fingernails. Hairs from the boy's head were also found adhering to a stick 19inches long and over 2 inches thick. Williams was later charged with murder. In Court he pleaded Not Guilty but at Glamorgan Assizes was found guilty and sentenced to Life Imprisonment. The enquirer incidentally turned out to be Andrew's sister. She had always wanted to know the full story of what actually happened.

Years ago the majority of murders would have been reported in the newspapers. Murder was regarded as a heinous crime. During the War years however more important issues took their place and finding details of murders during those periods is indeed difficult. In latter years only the more prominent cases seem to reach the headlines unless of course some other world event on the day overrules its inclusion. Similarly the archiving and destruction of police records has meant that the paperwork of many of the old 'famous' murders has long since gone and many were lost during the blitz.

Another aspect of Murderfiles is that it has details of over 200 British Police Officers murdered on duty from 1700 to 2000. Two CD-Roms are available, Part 1 being those murdered between 1700 to 1899, Part 2 being 1900 to 2000. The cost of each is £15 sterling or £26 sterling for the two. Cost includes postage. If you wish to purchase them please send a cheque or postal order made payable to '**Murderfiles**' to the address below.

Information is also available on the British hangmen and those they 'switched off'. Readers will no doubt be aware of the hundreds of hangings that took place at the Tyburn in London until 1798 after which they were moved to Newgate Prison. Murderfiles has hundreds of files relating to these and other hangings around the Country.

Murderfiles is a private collection of information on murders that have occurred in the UK over the last 300 years. Information from this collection is available to serious enquirers and details of cost involved are available on request. Should you wish to know whether any information is stored on a particular case please do not hesitate to write or email giving as much information as possible. Please forward a stamped addressed envelope (if you are located in the UK) for your reply or an International Reply Coupon if enquiring from outside the UK.

If you need to know more about any 'skeletons in your cupboard' I can be emailed on enquiry@murderfiles.com or written to at Dommett Hill Farm, Hare Lane, Buckland St Mary, Somerset TA20 3JS

Albert Pierrepoint The last British Hangman

Paul Williams worked for the Metropolitan Police in London for 26 years during which time he not only spent several years in their Criminal Record Office but was for over 8 years responsible for their Force Museums. One of these Museums was the world famous Black Museum which holds crime exhibits from notorious criminal cases. Whilst there he lectured, with the Curator, to police officers, members of the Judiciary and eminent people including members of the British and foreign Royal families. Amongst the many interesting visitors he met were Albert Pierrepoint, the last British Hangman and Professor Sir Bernard Spilsby, the pathologist.

As well as running Murder Files, Paul Williams, who is also a Winston Churchill Fellow, writes articles for books, magazines and CD-Roms as well as providing storylines for TV dramas. His first CD-Rom *The Ultimate Price – The unlawful Killing of British Police Officers 1700 – 2000* is available by writing to the above address.

Don't Believe All You Read In Print:
Two Cautionary Tales
John Titford advises us to verify facts

As family historians we are well advised to be suitably sceptical about what we read in print. Here are two cautionary tales which reinforce the point.

The Bloodworth Family

The origin of the surname Bloodworth is not difficult to determine. Occurring variously as Bloodworth, Bludworth, Blodworth, Bloudworth, Bleudworth, Bludsworth, Blardsworth, Bloodwork, Bloodwick, Bludwick, or simply Bludder, it is derived from the village of Blidworth in the Sherwood Forest area of Nottinghamshire, five miles south-east of Mansfield.

Not so very far from Blidworth, across the border into Derbyshire, is the former mining town of Heanor; a Heanor family bearing the surname Bloodworth were friends of mine, and I used to amuse myself by sending them references to their distinctive surname whenever I came across them. For some members of the extended family the genealogical hunt was very much in earnest, as it turned out, since various Bloodworths had always hoped to share in what was known as the "Bloodworth Millions", part of the unclaimed Angell estate which was worth 240 million pounds in the 1930s. All this was of no great concern to me - I just enjoyed unearthing Bloodworths for the fun of it.

The most famous Bloodworth, alias Bludder, was Sir Thomas Bloodworth, Lord Mayor of London at the time of the Great Fire of London in September 1666. History has not been kind to Sir Thomas. Woken from his drunken slumbers in his house in Maiden Lane at three o'clock in the morning on 2nd September, and not best pleased at being disturbed, he was shown burning houses in Pudding Lane and streets nearby. As he watched, St.Margaret's Church opposite the Star Inn in Fish Street Hill burst into flames. Sir Thomas was not impressed. "Pish!" he exclaimed, "a woman might piss it out!" They say that a sped arrow and words spoken can never be fetched back, though maybe Sir Thomas in later years may have wished he could have eaten such words before they reached the ears of those around?

Events soon overtook the hapless Sir Thomas, as Pepys reported in his diary:
At last met my Lord Mayor in Canning-Street, like a man spent, with a handkerchief about his neck. To the King's message, he cried, like a fainting woman, "Lord! What can I do? I am spent: people will not obey me. I have been pulling down houses: but the fire overtakes us faster that we can do it..."
Five days later, Pepys is reporting that:
People do all the world over cry out of the simplicity of the Lord Mayor in generall; and more particularly in this business of the fire, laying it all upon him.

Poor Sir Thomas - he was obviously not a man with the mental or physical resources to respond to a catastrophe of such proportions.

A Bloodworth researcher would no doubt be keen to establish the identity of Sir Thomas's parents, and to find out where he came from; in common with most Lord Mayors of London over the years, he was not a Londoner by birth. One obvious printed source would be *Le Neve's Pedigrees of Knights*, published by the Harleian Society from an original eighteenth century manuscript in 1873. Pages 48 and 49 of this work helpfully provide a fairly extensive pedigree, founded upon the assertion that "Sir Thomas Bludder", Lord Mayor, was the son of Sir Thomas Bludder of Flanchford in Reigate, Surrey by his wife Elizabeth, daughter of Robert Brett, Esq. This particular pedigree is continued back in time, for those who wish to pursue it, in the Harleian Society's *Visitation of Surrey 1530, 1572 and 1623* (1899).

Goodness only knows where Le Neve got his information from, since he was alive at the time of Sir Thomas and worked at the College of Arms. Not only that, but George W.Marshall's introduction to the Harleian Society volume is not slow to praise Le Neve's assiduous accuracy and attention to detail:

He appears to have been a man of no mean ability, though perhaps somewhat eccentric, and was a zealous and indefatigable antiquary - and one who, if we may judge from the following pages, never made an assertion when beyond his mere personal knowledge without quoting his authority, or shrank from stating the truth from the now, alas! too prevalent fear among persons addicted to genealogical pursuits, of giving offence to, or incurring the displeasure of, those whose vices or follies when recorded become no unimportant part of a genealogical tree...

Alas, Marshall's confidence in his subject is not borne out in the case of the Bloodworth pedigree with its Flanchford line of descent. This was a fairy story which would be repeated, as these things tend to be: the I'Anson manuscripts in Guildhall Library perpetuate the same myth, as does that most respected of genealogical works, Percival Boyd's *Citizens of London*. It was John Strype in his edition of *Stow's Survey of London* (1720) who was to sound the first warning bell by stating that Sir Thomas was "son of a Derbyshireman". So it would turn out to be.

Oddly enough, considering the fact that Sir Thomas Bloodworth/Bludder was Master of the Vintners'

Company in 1665, no-one seems to have thought of examining the apprenticeship register of that company for more information. J.R.Woodhead may have been the first to do so; in any event, he relates the true state of affairs in *The Rulers of London 1660-1689*, published in 1965. Sir Thomas Bloodworth, apprenticed in 1635 to Martin Linton, was not the son of Sir Thomas of Flanchford, but of "Edward Bludworth of Hennar, Derbyshire, yeoman." "Hennar", of course, being "Heanor", we are back where we started! My friends could well be distantly related to Sir Thomas Bloodworth, after all.

In cases such as this, if you mistrust the accuracy of one source, you might also have cause to mistrust later books or manuscripts. Only scholars with time and determination will check every primary source; an error, once made, is likely to be perpetuated and repeated *ad nauseam*.

The Hassard Family
I once had great fun working for an American client on the English origins of a family named Hassard or Hazard who arrived in Massachusetts in the mid-seventeenth century. The starting point was to look at a number of late nineteenth century books printed in America on the family; these, predictably enough for their period, proved to be an intriguing mixture of accurate genealogy and wild guesswork. A book of 1879 boldly asserts that:
The Hazard family take their name, we think, from the two words 'has', high, and 'ard', nature, meaning 'of high disposition, proud, independent'.

Where *do* they get this stuff from? A later work proudly informs us that:
At the time of the Conquest they were living on the borders of Switzerland...

This might be useful information - if only it were true, verifiable and based upon any evidence whatever - but it's not. Authors of family histories such as these do themselves a great disservice by the use of such fantastic claims, since they so often undermine the credibility of a lot of carefully researched pedigree work which follows.

We never did finally establish the English origins of the Hassards beyond doubt, though they were enough attractive possibilities before we'd finished. "Robert" was a favourite Christian name for this family, and a man of that name was a Member of Parliament for Lyme Regis in Dorset in the late sixteenth century. Normally in such instances one would be happy enough to turn to the series of printed works - now also available on CD-ROM - known as *The History of Parliament* for more information, since it is famed for its punctilious scholarship, both in terms of biography and genealogy.
Robert Hassard is featured in the appropriate volume in the series (*The House of Commons 1558-1603, Members D-L*, by P W Hasler, 1981). The trouble is, that as "Robert Hassard (1553-1627) of Lyme Regis, Dorset" he is featured in the book not once, but twice. A fundamental editing error has taken place. Two separate biographies are provided, but the heading of the first entry should read: "John Hassard (1531-1612) of Lyme Regis, Dorset", this John being a cousin of Robert. There is carelessness in evidence here; even a great and worthy compilation can make mistakes, so do be careful! Or maybe it's only the entries that interest me that have errors in them?

The editor of *The House of Commons 1558-1603* is not alone in having failed to make a likely identification between Robert Hassard of Lyme Regis and of Colyton in Devon and a man of the same name whose children were being baptised in the London parish of St.Catherine Coleman, London, in the 1580s, having apparently moved there from Devon during the period 1582-1587. This Robert had a son, another Robert, who became Clerk of the Jewels to King James I, and married Anne Moyse of Banstead in Surrey. Robert and Anne named their first child 'Edmund' in honour of his godfather, Edmund Tilney, who was a cousin of Robert Hassard, senior. No ordinary man, Edmund Tilney; he had been Master of the Revels from 1579 until his death in 1610, the man to whom it fell to authorise many of Shakespeare's plays and who, as

Lond. Sr Thomas Blodworth or Bludder Citizen of London K^ted at the Hague
Surr. May 1660 he was after Sheriff . . . . Alderman . . . . Lord Major 1666.
When the great fire broke out 1666 he haveing been drinking overnight and loath to rise said when called between sleep and wakeing he could piss it out. he dyed . . . . and was buried at Lederede in Surrey where he had a pretty seat. See my coppy of the Visitation of Surrey made 1623 folio 19.

Dame Elizabeth Bludder made her will dated 6 of October 17 Car. 2^d A.D. 1665. George farington her husband living to whom she gave lands in Surrey. John Dunn her son Henry fleetwood her nephew Roger James of Rygate & Thom. Turges executors. buried at Rygate. had farms called Iwood and batts com. Surr. farm called Knights in South Mimms given to her husband George farington.

Sr Thomas Bludder of Flanchford═Eliz. d^r of Robt Brett of
in Rygate K^t 22^d Apr. 1618.   Rotherby Leic. esq^r.

1st wife Mary d^r of═Sr Thomas Bludder of Lederede═2^d w. Mary d^r of . . . .
Walter Rogers of │Surr. and of London Sheriffe │relict of . . . . Ber. of Lon-
Lederede Gent.   │Alderm^n Ld Major.   │don Slopseller.

Eliz.
Walter. } all dyed s. p.
John.   A

Charming but inaccurate.
Part of a Bloodworth family pedigree from *Le Neve's Pedigrees of Knights*, published by the Harleian Society in 1873 from an original eighteenth century manuscript. Le Neve is in error here: the father of Sir Thomas Bloodworth or Bludder, Lord Mayor of London in 1666, was not Sir Thomas Bludder of Flanchford, Surrey, but Edward Bloodworth of Heanor in Derbyshire. Notice the phonetic spelling of 'Leatherhead' in Surrey as 'Lederede'.

"Master Tilney", is portrayed as rather a buffoon in the film *Shakespeare in Love*.

It is still my fond hope that Thomas Hassard, born about the year 1610, the original emigrant to Boston, Massachesetts, may turn out to be the brother of Edmund, but so far any baptismal or other relevant record eludes us. It is SO tempting, isn't it, to wish to lay claim to a pedigree peopled by grand or fascinating characters? Not that these people are more worthy than most of our humble and modest "ag lab" ancestors, but there is normally so much more than be discovered about them. Men and women of high social status appear more fully in written records of the past for obvious reasons, not the least of which being that they had property to

which they wished to prove their title, and they would have recourse to the law courts in order to claim or protect it at all costs. Just the occasional high-status ancestor or two would be nice to have sometimes, wouldn't it, to help balance those about whom we know so little? We can but hope.

John Titford is a professional genealogist and writer, author of The Titford family 1547-1947 *(1989),* Writing and publishing your family history *(1996) and* Succeeding in family history *(2001) and co-author, with Jean Cole, of* Tracing your family tree *(3rd.edition, 2000). He has recently finished writing a practical guide to help readers identify the origin and meaning of surnames, which is due to be published by Countryside Books in the Autumn of 2002.*

The 19th & 20th century British 'Merchant Navy' and its Links to State and Empire

Len Barnett

The British, through media such as television and the press, are regarded as a nation who has had salt water running through their veins for hundreds of years. Britannia, we continue to be emphatically told, ruled the waves. Personally, as a maritime historian and one time mariner, I would dispute this on many levels. However, the importance of the sea to Britain's economic and political long-term place in the world cannot be underestimated. If anything, I would opine it was mercantile endeavour that was the greatest governing factor in Britain's wealth over the centuries.

Wrapped up with Britain's past glory is the 'Merchant Navy'. This is a title widely used and misunderstood. It can be argued that the 'Merchant Navy' as such did not exist in reality until 1941, when the Reserve Pool of merchant seamen was introduced. Of course the term had previously been used, certainly back to the Great War 1914-19. One of this war's official histories was specifically named *The Merchant Navy*. But, whilst from 1916 to 1921 and the 1930s to 1950s there had been much State input into the operation of merchant shipping, the mercantile industry remained in the ownership of commercial entities and occasionally even individuals.

It is also a term which is difficult to delineate. It could be said that it constituted civilian sea activity, as opposed to armed service. At best this could only accurately relate to a period in the 19th century of less than ten years though. Anyway, important categories of civilian sea activity have not been mercantile: fishing and whaling for instance. But, both categories have been included within 'mercantile' records. Whilst passenger transport can be regarded as 'mercantile' because even the great 'liners' also carried a very substantial percentage of total cargo shifted, should vessels devoted entirely to cruising be included in the 'Merchant Navy'? It seems so, if only because of the difficulties of definition.

Instead of the 'Merchant Navy', there are other descriptions which prior to 1941 are perhaps more apt though and ones which I tend to use. There is 'merchant service', or 'mercantile service'. Alternatively, the 'Merchant' or 'Mercantile Marine' can be used. The latter are often regarded as modern American terms, but are not.

Merchant Navy Insignia

Prior to the 1850s British State interest in mercantile activities fell into a few distinct categories. Unsurprisingly, the oldest concern undoubtedly dealt with raising tax revenue and can be traced back as far as the 13th century. Primarily this was the concern of officials in what can be loosely called 'Customs and Excise', the 'Colonial Office' and the 'Board of Trade'. Partially linked to the above (as taxes were overwhelmingly spent by monarchs in conducting operations of war) what has become known as the Royal Navy was also highly active in recruiting men from mercantile service for naval vessels. This was especially so in times of war. Various schemes of registering men were tried, as well as more practical means: including the press. The Admiralty, as overseeing the bureaucracy of the monarch's navy was also involved in maintaining order through legal processes: in Courts of Instance and Prize. For a number of reasons from about the 1840s onwards more concern of mercantile activity was taken. It is the result of these that the modern State records on merchant mariners have grown.

Britain's links with its Empire are also widely misunderstood. Far from being strong and controlled from London, it was essentially weak and relied on confidence. When studying events in detail, all too often it is seen that British might was lacking in the extreme: the Royal Navy did not rule the waves as it was too stretched and the army was small and only fit for limited action. Overwhelmingly British Parliaments and Cabinets spent little time on colonial matters and the vast expanses of map coloured 'red' were ruled, or ruled themselves, in various ways: often without recourse to London.

But, by the decades following the Revolutionary & Napoleonic Wars British interests abroad were enormous and essentially were mercantilist. For complex political, economic and social reasons the British had a short-term industrial advantage. Later, when steam power at sea became commercially viable and by beneficial fortuity the most suitable coal lay under southern Wales, British mercantile power could be regarded as ubiquitous. Notwithstanding the imperial tariff protection arguments of some Victorians and Edwardians, the 'free trade' which had replaced the highly restrictive Navigation Acts of old had not meant an economic free-for-all by any means. Although there was increasing foreign competition in many areas of trade, often this was subsumed in shipping conferences (cartels). And, until trade patterns changed drastically; with the emergence of more industrialised countries with their own tonnage; the increased use of oil fuel products; and new routes opening up (especially due to the Panama Canal in 1914) strong trading links between the 'old country' and her colonies remained. The 'imperial preference' introduced post 1918 was economic 'tilting at windmills' however. In many respects the damage had already been done during the war years, when trade patterns had been deliberately shifted away from the Antipodes toward North America: in a government effort to use shipping most effectively.

Another World War not only finished Britain economically; it also accelerated the loss of Empire. With trading massively disrupted, new patterns emerged but not necessarily to the past colonial masters' benefit. With Marshall Plan money European competitors re-tooled and within twenty years completely overtook the British in many areas. The United States of America, looking outwards by this time and following up its military success with economic investment eclipsed the worn-out British. Air and road transport techniques, developed for war, were used increasingly effectively in peace: affecting sea trade adversely. Changing business patterns, such as 're-flagging' tonnage in Third World ports of convenience, have ultimately lead to the demise of the British 'Merchant Navy'.

The rest of this article deals briefly, by organisation, with the reasons why the State went to the effort and expense of compiling records on merchant mariners. This can be of use to genealogists in understanding what information is recorded and its limitations. Detailed information on the discussed documentation can be found on my website, at http://www.barnettresearch.freeserve.co.uk.

The Admiralty
For those seeking information on merchant mariners in British service the first bodies of records that are of *real* use are those generally referred to as the 'Ticketing System'. Although there had been earlier experiments, this was a related series of paper-exercises between 1835 and 1857 with the express aim of locating suitable mariners for forcing onto warships in time of war. Although pressing had always been a thorny issue, with reams of emotive words for and against, due to the social unrest post 1815 at least some of the gentlemen at the Admiralty realised that continuing the press could be very problematical. Over time with the limited introduction of iron hulls, armour-plate, steam power plants (driving paddles then screws) and new weaponry utilising shells, it must have become increasingly obvious that seamen straight from merchant service, without further training, would no longer be of much use on warships. As of 1853, instead of seamen signing on per voyage (on warships as in mercantile service) engagements of continuous service were introduced for those on the lower deck. This was an important factor in forming the modern Royal Navy as is now understood.
In 1850 the Admiralty's office of the Registry of Seamen had already been transferred to the 'Lords of Her Majesty's Privy Council appointed for the Consideration of Matters relating to Trade and Foreign Plantations' - more conveniently shortened to the Board of Trade. Whilst the maintenance of the registers was discontinued, much of the paperwork was retained for this board's own increasing role in mercantile affairs.

This was not the end of naval input in the lives of merchant mariners though. Even though seaborne

skills were diverging, the Royal Navy still required reserves of manpower: even if it was reticent to admit this. As of 1859 the first tentative elements of the Royal Naval Reserve were formed and it is important to emphasize that the R.N.R. was drawn exclusively from professional merchant mariners.

In the first forty-five years or so, overwhelmingly this consisted of gunnery reserves: of sorts. Through time other branches were formed, such as engineering. And, a few of the 'great' liner companies extracted building subsidies in order to provide vessels to the Crown as armed merchant cruisers in war.

After 1905, which incidentally could have seen it's disbandment, the R.N.R.'s future became more secure. During the First World War there were massive expansions, with a great many roles given to these reservists. Similarly, the R.N.R. was called on during the Second World War. In the 1950s, although retaining the title of R.N.R., this reserve of professional mariners was amalgamated with the reserve of volunteer amateurs: the R.N.V.R.

That has not been the end of naval use of the 'Merchant Navy' and has been used in various operations. During the Falklands War of 1982 H.M. Government requisitioned merchantmen. They were officially known as S.T.U.F.T. - Ships Taken up From Trade. But, it was not only post 1945 that the Royal Navy has used merchantmen for the transportation of men and matériel. However, as surviving records (of the Admiralty Transport Department) are not particularly useful in genealogical research, I have not covered these in this article.

The Marine Department of the Board of Trade
The reasons for the formation of this department are complex. Essentially it would seem that this became expedient through the results of abandoning tariff controls and taking on 'free trade' practices. Even before this, with the blockade of France, especially after the battle of Trafalgar (1805), Britain's mercantile presence had already been expanding rapidly. Post 1815 even though this was seen as the way to economic prosperity there were downsides. Small ventures rose dramatically in number and importance, in contrast to the great monopolistic companies that had been underpinned by the Navigation Acts. The Admiralty was known to be concerned about lowering standards of seamanship, seen to be a direct result of these new forms of business. In 1823 legislation on apprenticeships was enacted, in order to remedy this, but can hardly be regarded as having been effective. From the voluminous reports of House of Commons Select

Royal Naval Reserve Insignia

ROYAL ALFRED AGED MERCHANT SEAMEN'S INSTITUTION (opened in 1867).—30th Election.—The following CANDIDATES were duly ELECTED this day, June 21, 1882, at the Cannon Street Hotel, Captain Hon. Francis Maude, R.N., in the Chair, for admission into the House at Belvedere on 1st July.

Names.	Age	Years at Sea	Rank.	Port	No. of Votes
Williams, Richard	77	40	Seaman	Southampton	462
Davies, Joseph	60	40	Mate	Stepney	415
Bowen, William	65	45	Seaman	Poplar	397
Harkess, L. W.	69	50	Seaman	London	291
Taylor, John	74	60	Master	London	141
Nominated by Committee according to Rule 2.					
Pearson, Thomas	70	57	Master	Plymouth	—
For Out-pensions at various ports.					
Netting, R. P.	65	47	Boatswain	Poplar	504
Worwood, William	73	43	Mate	London	428
Adams, William	70	60	Master	Dundee	400
Tindle, J. S.	74	44	Master	North Shields	350
Betts, John (Blind)	66	35	Master	Sunderland	341
Jenkins, Samuel	64	35	Seaman	Cardigan	341
Fitchet, John	80	50	Master	Montrose	396
Scobey, John	67	40	Master	Penzance	274
Bucksey, Thomas	71	21	Seaman	London	250
Burrows, Robert	72	45	Seaman	London	247
Farrier, Richard	69	55	Mate	Bermondsey	239
Robinson, Thomas	78	60	Master	Sunderland	238
Nominated by Committee according to Rule 2.					
Huntingdon, Joseph	70	50	Seaman	N. Shields	—
Evans, Henry	67	40	Seaman	Aberforth	—

"They that go down to the Sea in ships."

The Committee beg to inform the public that, by this Half-yearly Election, they are enabled to admit to the much cherished benefits of this Charity, either as inmates to the Institution at Belvedere or as out-pensioners, only 20 out of 20 candidates, all aged and distressed merchant seamen. The remaining 75 applicants, eligible from age as well as distress, and most earnestly craving for these benefits, which the Committee are painfully compelled to limit from the want of necessary funds, are thus sent back to canvass again and to compete with fresh candidates. The Committee, earnestly hope that the public will generously help them in their anxious desire to alleviate the wants, and to contribute to the comfort of the sailor in his old age.

Donations and subscriptions will be gratefully received by the Bankers, Messrs. Williams, Deacon, and Co.; by the Chairman, Capt. Hon. Francis Maude, R.N.; and by the Secretary, at the Office, 58, Fenchurch Street, E.C.
W. E. DENNY, Secretary.

Committees on shipwrecks in the 1830s and into the conduct of steamships in the 1840s, their anxiety was justified. Within the 'Board of Trade' there had also been attention and submissions to supervise a regulated mercantile industry under a specialist department of this board. The perception of the prime lobbyist was that market forces left unchecked were producing inferior ships' officers, which was causing damage to the 'national character' and the monetary bottom line for British interests. The Foreign Office was also known to have addressed the issue of excessively drunken and violent behaviour of British merchant mariners ashore abroad: apparently this offended their genteel sensibilities.

By the 1840s there had also been some attempts within legislation to alleviate some of the worst aspects of seamen's lives. One of these dealt with the compulsory issue of 'Lime or Lemon Juice and Sugar daily' to stave off scurvy. Another tried to put crimps out of business.

With the formation of the Marine Department of the Board of Trade in 1850 which came into being to oversee 'matters relating to the British Mercantile Marine', the first compulsory schemes of certification of seamen officers were instituted. (Twelve years later a limited percentage of engineers also required certification.) The department's earliest work was concerned with codifying large tracts of marine law on subjects outstanding from various earlier Select Committees. The result was the 1854 Merchant Shipping Act.

This brought many more responsibilities, but the department was still working to the budgetary and manning requirements of the 1850 Act. Short-term solutions were found, in shuffling staff around from other departments and bringing in temporary staff (at lesser rates). Supposedly overworked and underpaid, if possible elements of paperwork were abandoned. This was already happening under the Admiralty regime and is why there was no sea service entered in the *Register of Seamen's Tickets* for 1849-1850 & 1852-54.

Though suffering chronic under-financing through the decades more responsibilities were acquired: wanted

or otherwise. With wartime reorganisation in 1916 the Marine Department was moved to another Ministry, but was returned in 1921. Again in 1939 the Board of Trade was shorn of its Mercantile Marine Department.

The Board of Trade could be seen as a supervisory body, with the office of the Registrar General of Seamen (as of 1872 also including shipping in its title) dealing with the records coming into their hands: including information on the certification of officers. Mercantile Marine Offices around the British Isles and within Empire conducted affairs locally: including examination of officers for certification. Elsewhere in the world, diplomatic and consular officials were responsible for the necessary routine contact with British merchantmen.

The nature of some of the retention of some classes of records is not entirely known or understood. As in days of the 'Ticketing System' crew-lists and articles were to be surrendered to pertinent port officials, either on completion of voyages or six monthly: later to be forwarded to London. However, as stated in the original legislation this only covered ports within the British Isles. It appears that the Mercantile Marine Offices in the great ports of Empire operated their own 'local' systems though. It is thought that some of these records were definitely destroyed through enemy action in the Second World War and others may not have survived independence. At the time of writing the author is making enquiries into modern locations of such possible documentation.

Ships' official logs often cause confusion. There were numerous types of information required to be kept by masters in these documents, which included diseases, births, deaths, marriages, offences committed by crew-members and subsequent punishments. This is a complex subject and will be dealt with in my other article in this publication.

It is important to emphasize that surviving records tend only to be *those stipulated in law as essential to maintaining the system*. So, whilst there were lots of other types of working documentation, such as discharge certificates, there was no requirement for further recording, copying or retention.

Wartime Ministries
To manage merchant tonnage to best advantage and with the scale of war increasing evermore, the Marine Department became the centre of a new Ministry of Shipping: founded in late 1916. The following year the successor ministry took over Admiralty chartering and other concerns: such as shipbuilding.

During the Second World War initially a Ministry of Shipping was set up once more. In 1941 to co-ordinate land and sea transport, this organisation was amalgamated with the Ministry of Transport: to become the Ministry of War Transport. In April 1946 the Ministry of Transport took on this work.
© Len Barnett 2002

Punishment and Crime

Fred Feather - Chairman of Essex Society for Family History and former Curator of the Essex Police Museum

Proud indeed is the family able with certainty to successfully boast that its members have never transgressed the commandments and endured the rigours of the British judicial system. Although I am occasionally contacted by enquirers who report their ancestor hanged, or even that they were descended from a hangman, there are certain categories of involvement in crime that I seldom hear mentioned. This article will offer an unscientific comment on the times when it was necessary to control our islands after the armies returned from the Napoleonic Wars. Whilst we had our transatlantic dominions the system seemed to hold a balance between supplying the colonists with cheap labour and frightening the population into tranquillity with executions and public humiliations. There were dungeons, but prison was an expensive option and at that time not so often a dumping place for felons. Then in 1783 we lost America and the situation changed. Within a few years transportation was transferred to Australia and our ancestors were sent to the Antipodes. Many stayed there. Records of those sent to both destinations are available. What is not so widely known is that the British government was intriguing with the faction of the Russian Imperial Court that had a scheme afoot. It was to populate with British prisoners and their families the areas of Southern Russia that Count Grigori **Potemkin** was then capturing from the Tartars. Potemkin died in 1791. Anyone doubting this prognostication might choose to locate and visit the grave of the best known prison reformer John **Howard** (now commemorated by the name of the *Howard League for Penal Reform*) who is buried in Kherson in the Ukraine under a stone marked "Ask not who lays here – he was your friend." I have been to Kherson. But for the vagaries of Czarist politics many Australians could have found themselves Crimean.

The Condemned cell, York Prison ©Robert Blatchford Collection

To the Treadmill

Have you ever considered that your ancestor was the victim of a cruel and unusual punishment? If they were daring men or women of the 18th and 19th century, and unruly, but not so unruly that they were executed or transported; then they might be imprisoned. Prisons were gradually being built, supplementing and replacing dungeons. Reformers like John Howard and Elizabeth **Fry** devoted their lives to seeking relief from the suffering imprisonment resulted. To subdue an unruly prisoner, and to give them painful work was an aim of some of those who developed prisons, and the treadmill provided one means. Several systems were developed, in some prisoners walked inside the wheel like hamsters, later they ground corn and stone by their efforts and the wheels became ever more sophisticated. Other systems had the person endlessly walking on the outside, with a drop below them if they faltered. But, there was still a humane streak in society as can be illustrated by the story of a newspaper campaign.

The issue of the weekly newspaper *"John Bull"* for the 18th January 1824 drew attention to the Magistrates for the County of Surrey, it was complaining about the treadmill having been employed and abused in their Brixton and Guildford Prisons. The paper then began a campaign concentrating on the use of the treadmill in general, but particularly when used for women and those who were not yet convicted of crime. I repeat: it was used to punish prisoners on remand who should have been "innocent until proven guilty."

Inmates at Guildford also complained about injuries. Many prisoners were young and serving sentences between 12 and 24 months:
Edward **Broughton**,(20), Robert **Willey**, (17), John **Dowley**, (19),), Edmund **Carroll** (35), William **Redman**, (28), Edward **Messer**, (25), Thomas **Hart**, (21), William **Milford**, (28), Ebeneezer **Oakley**, (22), Robert **Warner**, (20), George **Whitmore**, (22), Christopher **Lamborn**, (21), Joseph **Cohen**, (18) Joseph **Lay**, (26), Thomas **Farrage**, (18), Joshua **Gaushy**, (21) and William **Nash**, (27). But the problem was more serious when you note the age of the following felons; Thomas **Webbe**, (51), Richard **Bell**, (52), Thomas **Smea**, (55) Charles **Etherington**, (68). In the Brixton prison the following prisoners complained; William **Perkins** (19), John **Fitzgerald** (18), Wm. **Lock**, (18), Henry **Oakley** (18), Robert **Bignall** (21), Thomas, (19), James **Reid**(18) Thomas **Boniface** (23), James **Norton** (28) and John J. **Haynes**, (36) had received injury or been sent to the hospital.

A letter of the 7th February 1824 described the wheel in use at Leicester as 24 feet in height and of the type where the punished had to walk on the inside. Other reports identified Joseph **Sumner** as having died on a

York Castle and Prison 1920s © Robert Blatchford Collection

treadmill in 1821, and Thomas **Saunders** who had been killed in July 1823. Swaffham Magistrates in Norfolk also reported a convict fatality and there were stories of serious accidents at Aylesbury in Buckinghamshire and Shepton Mallet in Somerset. In Yorkshire's Northallerton House of Correction John **Hopper** had become entangled in the mechanism and his arm had to be amputated. And, this was before he had been put on trial. Apparently, at the whim of the magistrates and turnkeys you could be so punished, then be tried and found to be innocent.

An unfeminine punishment.
The prison reformer Mrs Elizabeth Fry was concerned to assuage the current use of this punishment, maintaining that it was unsuitable for women. One woman had been recorded with a pulse of 156. On 1st February 1824 the Middlesex Magistrates had investigated the system in use at their gaol at Coldbath Fields and listened carefully to the complaints of Superintendent Mrs **Heam** (appointed at Elizabeth Fry's instance). They then sacked Mrs Heam with a week's pay in lieu of notice, without giving a reason and she thereby lost her annual salary of 52 shillings. A suggestion had been made that Miss **Steele**, another disciple of Mrs Fry, had been permitted to teach the prisoners to read and had been giving presents of tea to sick inmates.

At Chelmsford in Essex, on 1st February 1824, the bench met and the Magistrates voted by 25 to 7, to rescind permission for two of Mrs Fry's colleagues to visit the prisoners. This despite that 3 of 5 visiting magistrates had given their permission. However, "*John Bull*" then went over the top, reporting that "Not only at Coldbath but at Chelmsford the secret system is carried on. At Chelmsford there is a treadmill." It told of horrid cruelties, two women seriously injured and that one woman had miscarried on the wheel. Also that Mrs Fry's colleagues "two benevolent females" had been excluded. In the following week's issue (8th February) Thos. **Cawkwell**, the chief gaoler at Chelmsford wrote a letter to the editor and shot the paper clear out of the

water, by denying the horrid cruelties and irrefutably pointing out that the Chelmsford House of Correction did not have a treadmill."

This did little to stop the editor's crusade although a Berkshire Magistrate then reported that the treadmill in that county was no longer to be used to punish women. Next, statistics were brought into the argument. Comparing Guildford and Coldbath it was found that the former punished women inmates by making them climb to the top of the wheel up to 50 times in winter and up to 76 times in Summer. At Coldbath the relevant figures were 44 to 61 respectively. How could women endure this, fed on a half pound of bread for breakfast, the same for dinner with a pint of soup and half a pound of boiled potatoes for their supper. This was the sustenance for the destitute poor, who may have been committed for begging or being homeless.

The pressure continued. At Coldbath Fields it was reported that on 17th October 1823 Sarah **Evans** had dropped off the wheel. Anne **Wilson**, Caroline **Davis**, Sarah **Brown**, Caroline **Dyer** and Mary **Kelly** (aged 48) had accidents thereon. At Brixton on 24th December 1823 there had been incidents, then on 17thJanuary 1824 Catherine **Macauley** fell from the wheel and was unable to walk weeks later. Jane **George** and Maria **Lake** were also injured then a week later a woman of 50 fell off twice. Again at Coldbath Fields it was established that Mary **England** and Mary Ann **Coram** had each fallen off 4 times, whilst Mary **Waghorn**, Mary **Coffin** and Mary **Head** had each fallen off twice.

There were allegations of injustices. On 11th April 1824 Daniel **Keefe** (40) and James **McCormack** committed by Bloomsbury magistrates were in St. George's Hospital as a result of such injuries, as was Rebecca **Shepherd**. Her complaint was that she had been put on the treadmill because she had been mistaken for Mary **Shepherd** a constant troublemaker. James **Naggett** and Thomas **Wilson**, both soldiers, were reported to the Surrey Quarter Sessions as having been handcuffed to the wheel on 22nd December 1823. Brixton Prison staff reported that the men were the most recalcitrant prisoners they had and that only after this extreme measure had been taken did they gain control of them.

A survey was made of prisons and a conclusion was reported that those who did not employ the treadmill were in areas where there was decreasing crime. It reported that these prisons included Horsemonger Lane in London (1300 prisoners annually), Tothill Fields Bridewell (2500 annually), Shrewsbury Gaol (800 annually) and Giltspur Street House of Correction (4500 annually). Those who had a treadmill included Coldbath Fields (4000 annually), Ipswich Gaol (300 annually), Durham Gaol (350 annually) and Hertford Prison (225 annually). This may have been a biased report as those with wheels were county gaols and many without were places of detention for shorter periods.

The prison system in the shires was sometimes on a much smaller scale. An unusual use for the treadmill was in the tiny Norfolk town of Walsingham, better known for religious fervour than criminal activity. The Bridewell had been built in 1787 on plans made by the aforementioned John Howard, who also designed the nearby Wymondham Bridewell. He was also the first person to campaign for separate prison accommodation for men, women and children. Until 1822, known as the "spital," it became the County House of Correction, co-inciding with the removal of the Quarter Sessions to the town from Aylsham. It was enlarged to 53 cells in 1843. In this rural setting the inmates were set to work on four treadmills at a nearby corn mill. It seems that prisoners were fed as payment for their work. No work and they went hungry. In 1854 the town was allocated a police station and some of the cells were in future to be used for police prisoners. In 1861 when the governor was

Mr Money **Curtis** the prison was finally closed.

Back in 1824 penal reform was in the air, as Parliament produced new measures to control the soldiers and sailors, unemployed after Waterloo, who had brought down Napoleon. It enacted the Vagrancy Act of 1824, still on the statute book, and identified new categories of criminals such as the "Idle and Disorderly Person," the "Rogue and Vagabond" and the "Incorrigible Rogue." But, that is another story.

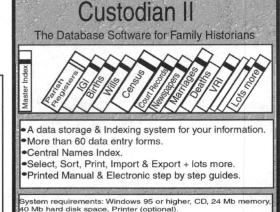

Personal Labels
Gabriel Alington

Tom, Dick and Harry; Mary, Catherine, Anne. What's in a name? The simple answer is who you are. A name gives recognition; it is, you might say, your personal label. A more complex answer, as suggested by the question, is how your name reflects your character. Which, of course, it does, like it or not. From an early age; your character and name become synonymous. But that is leading into deeper waters. Here we are concerned more with nomenclature, the system of naming, how it has changed through the centuries.

Today we take it for granted that everyone has a surname preceded by a Christian name, or first name in this multi-faith age; the Americans use the term given name. These two names provide your identity, they are used in introductions. Meet my friend, Sue Jones. I'm Roger Brown.

But once upon a time there were no surnames; each person was known by a single name. According to the Elizabethan historian, William Camden, 'Every person had in the beginning one only proper name'. Camden was right. Certainly in England that was the custom. It was not until the Middle Ages that surnames came into general use; in Wales it was the 17th century; the Highland clans of Scotland took a century longer.

Camden goes on to say that the exceptions to this rule were 'the savages of Mount Atlas in Barbary, which were reported to be both nameless and dreamless.' This delightfully random statement probably reveals more about Camden's conversational and often fanciful style, than the ways of the native Barbarians. Camden was a distinguished scholar; his topographical study *Brittania* was hailed as a landmark when published in 1586, and the Camden Society, established in the 19th century to promote the publication of historical works, was named after him. In his book *Remaines* he includes lists of names with their etymologies, their explanation and meaning - all invented by Camden according to later historians. The fact is there was then scant information available on the etymology of names. so perhaps Camden judged that imaginary accounts were better than nothing. At least his own interpretations are entertaining. It was not until the 19th century that a detailed study of nomenclature was published. The author of *A History of*

Christian Names was the novelist, Charlotte M.Yonge. Since then numerous books have been written on every aspect of names world-wide.

Little is known of English nomenclature before the 6th century BC when Celtic tribes, who had spread throughout Europe, settled in Britain. Celtic names, which are Indo-European in origin, are 'compound' names, that is, they are formed by two short words put together. The meaning of these words, often apparent nonsense, was unimportant. Their significance lay in their association with the family. Compound names were sometimes shortened; *Caturix* became *Catoc*, *Caractacos* became *Certic*.

It was about 45 AD that the Roman legions invaded Britain, occupied the land, built garrison towns linked by straight, paved roads, and remained there as masters for four centuries. Early Britons, taken as slaves, would have learned and, to some extent, benefited from the highly civilized life-style of the Romans. There was, up to a point a mingling of the Roman and Celtic peoples, some inter-married; their children would have had Roman names.

The Roman system of nomenclature, developed through time, was highly complicated. In an exception to Camden's single name rule, the Roman form, as applied to men - there was a different form for women - consisted of three names, the praenomen, the proper name, the cognomen, a personal nickname, and the name of the family or tribe. The praenomen, a name such as *Appius,*

Lucius, Marmericus, Cornelius, was taken from a recognised list !, which, according to the earliest known records, contained 32 names. By 27 BC, however, the list of praenomen in current use had shrunk to 18, and, as several of these were reserved for certain patrician families, the choice was, in fact, smaller still. As brothers were often given the same praenomen, the addition of a cognomen was virtually essential. Even then, with a limited number of available names, there must have been problems of identity.

The form for women seems to have varied from the time of the Republic to the period of the Empire but, for the most part, before marriage, women were known by the nomen of their father plus a praenomen, which was the feminine form of a masculine name; *Lucia*, for instance, from *Lucius, Valeria* from *Valerius*. Married women added their husband's name to their own, but in the genitive form; *Cornelia Secunda Caesaris* was *Cornelia Secunda* the wife of *Caesar*. Which somehow suggests she was his property, she belonged to him. And in a sense she did, feminism not being an issue then. Likewise a slave belonged to his owner, whose praenomen, again in the genitive form, was the slave's one name. Slaves who were released from servitude added the nomen of whoever set them free to their single name, as well as a praenomen which they chose themselves. To be a freeman meant expanding to the status of three name form.

Perhaps, in time, Roman names caught on, perhaps the idea spread beyond the Roman towns so that Britons chose to call their sons by names such as *Cassius, Quintus, Numerius*.

It is possible. But whether it happened we shall never know. For following the departure of the Romans came tribes from northern Europe, Angles, Saxons, Danes, who swept away the culture of the previous occupation, including the Roman nomenclature; these new invaders had a system of their own.

Names belonging to the Anglo-Saxon period are known as Old English. Like the Celts each person had a single name, a two-part compound name made up from a 'bank' of name-making words. Some of these were used for the first part of the name, *Ead*, for example, *Aethel* or *Gis*, others such as *beorht, frid, ric*, were specifically for the second part, which generally also indicated the gender. The little that is known about Old English names comes from lists attatched to documents and charters. These lists are the names of witnesses, inevitably men of prominence, landowners, the ruling class. Their impressive sounding names, *Wigfrith, Eadweard, Cuthwulf*, for example, were not universal. The peasants or serfs of the lower class are believed to have been known by single syllable names, short, hard words such as *Ragge, Hilde, Bugge*. Once again, however, evidence is scant for, following the Norman Conquest of 1066, Old English names all but disappeared. A few survived and, modified into their current form, *Alfred*, for example, *Edith* and

Geoffrey, are familiar today.

In Norman England records were kept, numerous records, which indicate clearly the most popular names. Apart from a scattering of less usual names such as, *Sampson, Ives, Aldwin* and *Odo*, there were hundreds who answered to *William, Richard, Walter* and *Hugh*, names we know well and meet frequently. What's more these Norman names kept their places at the top of the charts despite the growing influence of the Church.

Though Christianity had been filtering into Britain since the time of the Roman occupation, it was not until the late 12th century that scriptural names were widely used. The 11th century Domesday Book contains no more than a handful; there is a single entry of *Peter, Matthew, Andrew* and *John*. But a hundred years later the growing influence of the Church had had its effect. This meant a far greater choice for, as well as the remaining Old English names and the more recent Norman ones, there were those of the apostles and other saints. Women's names taken from the Bible are found in records dating from the early 13th century. The first *Mary* was recorded in 1203, *Elizabeth* in 1205; *Anne*, the legendary saint appears 1218. The names of other female saints particularly *Margaret, Agnes* and *Catherine*, are also found in records around that time.

Besides this wide variety of names, records from the late 12th and early 13th centuries contain other names which may sound odd to us, but which also go to show that the present fondness for inventing names is nothing new. Parents searching for novelty christened their children *Extrania, Melodia, Oriolda*, which may, for them, have been trendy and amusing; for their daughters, rather less so, possibly most of these odd names are feminine, though a few, *Splendor* and *Pharamus*, for instance, were given to sons. Unsurprisingly such names soon disappeared - as generally happens with the more outrageous personal labels.. Names go in cycles, like fashion they are changing constantly. The name of someone in the public eye, a film star, a singer, a sportsman perhaps, will suddenly become popular. Having heard it once or twice, you meet it frequently, before long it is everywhere. Then, when another star appears, their name takes over as favourite.

Names come and go. There are some, however, a dozen or so, that never lose their popularity. Records from the 16th century show that *John, William*, and *Thomas* were then the most usual names for men; for women it was *Mary, Elizabeth* and *Anne*. They are classic names, quintessentially English. Of course there are others in that category, *Richard, Philip, James, Sarah, Margaret, Jane*, and the annual listing published in The Times, show how they jostle to take top place. Never mind that in our day they are more likely to be used as second names, they are still perennial favourites. They can stand the test of time. One answer, perhaps, to what's in a name.

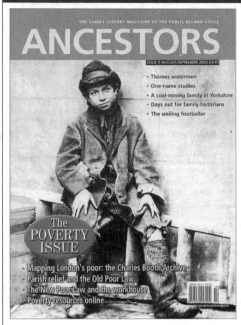

Directories
Angela Petyt

Yellow Pages. Thomson Local. The Phone Book. Useful publications, giving us details of businesses, people and their addresses in our communities. They are the descendants of a source which is unrivalled in its capacity to educate and enthral family and local historians - trade and street directories.

Background
The origins of directories stem from two main developments. Firstly, lists of traders kept by what were called registry offices. These were in existence even in the middle ages. Secondly, the growth of trade amongst London merchants. What was common to both was the driving force of commerce.

England's first directory was published in 1677. It comprised a list of City of London merchants. However, nothing similar was published until the mid-eighteenth century - the Industrial Revolution bringing unprecedented economic growth, and with it, the profession of the commercial traveller. Where London led, others followed, and in the provinces the burgeoning towns began to produce their own directories, with alphabetical lists of traders. By the late 1700s, directories appeared which covered far wider geographical areas, perhaps several counties. One of the most ambitious publications was the *Universal British Directory*, issued in five volumes between 1790-1799. This encompassed most of the important towns in the country. However, by the Victorian period the trend was to more localised and detailed directories. This type of publication continued until well into the twentieth century.

Many of the producers of directories were local printers and publishers, but bigger firms also began to appear. James Pigot, a Manchester engraver, brought out a successful national series and went into partnership with Isaac Slater. William White, William Parson, Edward Baines and many, many others put their name to directories. As with all forms of enterprise, publishers regularly came and went. But one name has come to be synonymous with trade and street directories - Kelly's. Founded by Frederick Kelly in 1845, his firm produced London and county 'Post Office Directory' volumes and became by far the most successful.

Contents of directories
As directory publishing developed, there came to be a standard format for compilation. Professional agents were employed to enquire at each house or business premises, either calling personally or leaving a circular to be filled in and collected. There was no charge to be included, unless you wished to have additional information added to your entry. For historical and topographical detail, publishers engaged the services of gentry, clergy, legal and poor law officials to supply information about their local area. The frequency of publication varied between publishing firms - perhaps a new edition would be produced every couple of years, on the other hand, several years might pass before the next book came out.

As directories might cover one large city, one county, or several counties, it is difficult to generalise as to their contents. However, it is safe to say that some, if not all, of the following categories will be included, and I have extracted some examples from various directories to give an indication of content and style.

Firstly, the essential sections-
At the beginning of the directory should be a comprehensive index of place names.
Historical, Topographical and General Services Description - at the head of the entry for each city, town, village and hamlet.

> **Ackworth** is a township, parish and large village, on rising ground near the source of the river Went. 3 miles from Hemsworth station on a branch of the London and North Eastern railway from Doncaster to Wakefield...Ackworth consists of the hamlets of High and Low Ackworth, Moor Top and Brackenhill...it is in the Hemsworth division of the Riding, upper division of Osgoldcross wapentake, petty sessional division of Upper Osgoldcross, Pontefract county court district, Hemsworth union, rural deanery and archdeaconry of Pontefract and diocese of Wakefield.
> The church of St. Cuthbert is a building of stone in the Early Decorated style, consisting of chancel with aisle, nave, aisles and an embattled western tower, with pinnacles, containing a clock and 6 bells, two of which are of pre-Reformation date...The register dates from the year 1558 and is in excellent condition.
> The church of All Saints, Moor Top, erected in 1889-91, at a cost of £2,400, as a chapel of ease to St. Cuthbert's...There are also a Wesleyan chapel, a

HISTORY,
GAZETTEER AND DIRECTORY
OF THE COUNTIES OF
LEICESTER AND RUTLAND,
CONTAINING
General Surveys of each County
AND SEPARATE
HISTORICAL, STATISTICAL AND TOPOGRAPHICAL DESCRIPTIONS
OF ALL THE
HUNDREDS, TOWNS, PARISHES, TOWNSHIPS, CHAPELRIES, VILLAGES, HAMLETS, MANORS & UNIONS
THE SEATS OF THE NOBILITY AND GENTRY;
MAGISTRATES AND PUBLIC OFFICERS;
AND A GREAT VARIETY OF OTHER
ARCHÆOLOGICAL, ARCHITECTURAL, AGRICULTURAL, BIOGRAPHICAL, BOTANICAL AND GEOLOGICAL INFORMATION.

THIRD EDITION.

BY WILLIAM WHITE,
AUTHOR OF SIMILAR WORKS FOR
LINCOLNSHIRE, NORFOLK, SUFFOLK, ESSEX, HAMPSHIRE, YORKSHIRE, AND MANY OTHER COUNTIES.

PRICE—CLOTH, 30s.; HALF-BOUND, 35s.

SHEFFIELD:
WILLIAM WHITE, 18 & 20 BANK STREET.
LONDON: SIMPKIN, MARSHALL, & CO.
1877.

ENTERED AT STATIONERS' HALL.

meeting house for the Society of Friends at Low Ackworth, and a Primitive Methodist chapel at Moor Top.

The charities amount to about £150 yearly.

The Society of Friends' school here, built in 1758 for the Foundling Hospital, was purchased in 1777 by Dr. John Fothergill, a member of that society, and refounded for its present purpose...

The Ackworth Adult School Social Club, built in 1907 at a cost of about £500, has 120 members...At Moor Top and Brackenhill are several large quarries, from which great quantities of stone are sent to all parts of England and abroad.

The soil is clay and gravel; subsoil, various. The area is 2,641 acres of land and 4 of water; rateable value £19,743; the population in 1921 was 4,831 in the civil and 4,746 in the ecclesiastical parish, including 345 in the Society of Friends' School...The kennels of the celebrated Badsworth hounds are in this parish, 1 mile from the village; Pontefract, Doncaster and Wakefield are convenient places for hunting visitors.

Brackenhill is a hamlet of this parish about 1½ miles south-west from the village, in the midst and inhabited chiefly by the men employed in the stone quarries and the Hemsworth colliery. The Ackworth Moor Top Working Men's Club and Institute was built in 1907 at a cost of £1,750.

Parish Clerk, Fred Lindsay.

Post, M.O., T. & T.E.D. Office, Ackworth – Mrs. Emma Alice Asquith, sub-postmistress. Letters from Pontefract

Post, M.O. & Telephone Call Office, Ackworth Moor Top – Henry Hawley, sub-postmaster. Ackworth, 1 mile distant, is the nearest telegraph office

Post Office, Brackenhill – Mrs. Rose Hannah Penn, sub-postmistress. Ackworth Moor Top is the nearest money order office & Ackworth the nearest telegraph office

Schools

Society of Friends', Ackworth, has about 340 scholars; Gerald Kenway Hibbert M.A., B.D., J.P. supt

Public Elementary, High Ackworth (infants), enlarged in 1880, for 137 children; Miss Catherine Paley, infants' mistress

Miss Rachel Howard's (endowed) (girls & infants), Low Ackworth, erected in 1830, for 98 children; Miss Alice Paley, mistress

Public Elementary, Moor Top (mixed & infants), erected in 1896, for 420 children; T.J. Bedford, head master; Miss Towler, infants' mistress

Public Elementary, Brackenhill (mixed & infants), erected in 1908, for 420 children; J. Swinbank, head master

Police Stations, Sergeant Harold Barker, High Ackworth; George Henry Smith, constable, Low Ackworth; Joseph Edward Rance, constable, Moor Top

Conveyance – motor omnibuses run constantly to Pontefract, Wakefield, Leeds & Barnsley

Ackworth Station (telegrams are received &

despatched from here, but not delivered); William Scarth, station master

[Source - edited extract from the Ackworth entry in *Kelly's Directory of the West Riding of Yorkshire 1927*]

Trades - in the early directories, or for a village, this will be a simple A-Z list. In towns and cities, they will be classified. County directories will often also include a classified master A-Z county index of all tradespeople.

Accock, William, *Stuff Manufacturer*
Atkinson, Samuel, *Currier*, between Skipton and Launceston
Bailey, John, *Woolstapler*
Baynes, George, *Tanner*
Baynes, Mrs. *Tea-dealer and Linen-draper*
Birtwhistle, John, and Sons, *Drovers*
Braishaw, Daniel, *Innkeeper*, Hole in the Wall
Brown, Bartholomew, *Wood Merchant*
Campbel, Charles, *Tea-dealer and Linen-draper*
Carr, Robert, *Innkeeper*, Black Horse
Chamberlain, Abraham, *Ironmonger*
Chamberlain, Thomas, *Grazier*
Chamberlain, Richard, *ditto*
Chippendale, Thomas, *ditto*
Chippendale, William, *Mercer and Woollen-draper*
Chippendale, Ann, *Tea-dealer and Distributor of Stamps*
Clerk, Thomas Carr, *Master of the Free Grammar School*

[Source - edited extract from the Skipton entry in *The British Directory 1784*]

Carvers and Gilders
Roach Charles, Kirkgate
Whittaker Ann, Kirkgate
Chair Makers
Olivant Edward, Northgate
Reading Thomas, Kirkgate
Cheese Factors and Mongers
Birkinshaw George, Cross Square
Leadley John, Silver Street
Sutton T. (& butter & salt) Westgate
Woodson Richard (& bacon) Ratten Row
Clock and Watch Makers
Allison Thomas, Westgate
Button Thomas, Kirkgate

An extract from Leicester street directory, included in White's Directory of Leicestershire and Rutland 1877

Coates B.E. (and watch glass manufacturer) Silver Street
Crosland William, Market Place
Hitchen Robert, East Moor
Jaques John, Wrengate
[Source - edited extract from the Wakefield entry in *Baines' Directory of the West Riding of Yorkshire 1822*]

Streets - included from the mid-nineteenth century onwards and only for the larger towns and cities. The streets will be listed by name from A-Z, and numbered. Intersections of other streets, yards and courts will be indicated.

PEMBERTON STREET
(107 Dewsbury Road)
9 Walker Charles, cloth dresser (J)
19 Appleyard Thomas, tailor
51 Oger John, clerk
53 Marsden Richard, grocer
4 Bachoffner Edwin, picture restorer
6 Hewitson Richard, commercial traveller
24 Sayner John, bookkeeper
42 Oldfield James, pottery salesman
56 Greenwood Joseph, bootmaker
74 Blagg John, detective
86 New Fleece Inn (beerhouse) Madeley W
96 Taylor William, storekeeper
[Source - extracted from *White's Directory of Leeds 1872*]

HALL STREET 320 City Rd. (E.C.) (FINSBURY) MAP M7
Pillar Letter Box
5 Leach Mrs. Charlotte, dressmaker
9 Murton David, livery stables
...here is Parrs Place...
16 Jones Frederick Jn. Wheel brush maker
20 Reliance Engraving Co. Limited
...here are Goswell Road & New Charles St...
22 *Oakley Arms*, Charles Baxter
34 Gold George, tailor
37 Dilger Emil, watchmaker

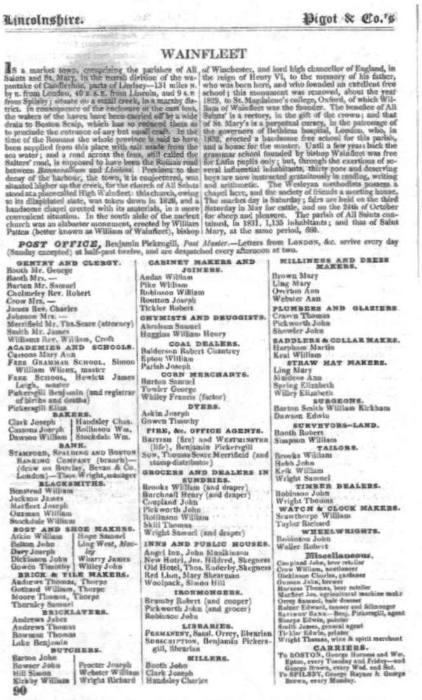
Lincolnshire. Pigot & Co.'s

WAINFLEET

Is a market town, comprising the parishes of All Saints and St. Mary, in the marsh division of the wapentake of Candleshoe, parts of Lindsey—131 miles N. by E. from London, 40 E.S.E. from Lincoln, and 9 S.E. from Spilsby; situate on a small creek, in a marshy district. In consequence of the enclosure of the east fens, the waters of the haven have been carried off by a wide drain to Boston Scalp, which has so reduced them as to preclude the entrance of any but small craft. In the time of the Romans the whole province is said to have been supplied from this place with salt made from the sea water; and a road across the fens, still called the Salters' road, is supposed to have been the Roman road between *Bannovallum* and *Lindum*. Previous to the decay of the harbour, the town, it is conjectured, was situated higher up the creek, for the church of All Saints stood at a place called High Wainfleet: this church, owing to its dilapidated state, was taken down in 1820, and a handsome chapel erected with its materials, in a more convenient situation. In the south aisle of the ancient church was an alabaster monument, erected by William Patten (better known as William of Wainfleet), bishop of Winchester, and lord high chancellor of England, in the reign of Henry VI, to the memory of his father, who was born here, and who founded an excellent free school; this monument was removed, about the year 1829, to St. Magdalene's college, Oxford, of which William of Wainfleet was the founder. The benefice of All Saints' is a rectory, in the gift of the crown; and that of St. Mary's is a perpetual curacy, in the patronage of the governors of Bethlem hospital, London, who, in 1832, erected a handsome free school for this parish, and a house for the master. Until a few years back the grammar school founded by bishop Wainfleet was free for Latin pupils only; but, through the exertions of several influential inhabitants, thirty poor and deserving boys are now instructed gratuitously in reading, writing and arithmetic. The Wesleyan methodists possess a chapel here, and the society of friends a meeting house. The market day is Saturday; fairs are held on the third Saturday in May for cattle, and on the 24th of October for sheep and pleasure. The parish of All Saints contained, in 1831, 1,135 inhabitants; and that of Saint Mary, at the same period, 660.

POST OFFICE, Benjamin Pickersgill, *Post Master*.—Letters from LONDON, &c. arrive every day (Sunday excepted) at half-past twelve, and are despatched every afternoon at two.

GENTRY AND CLERGY.
Booth Mr. George
Booth Mrs. —
Burton Mr. Samuel
Cholmeley Rev. Robert
Crow Mrs. —
James Rev. Charles
Johnson Mrs. —
Merrifield Mr. Tho. Seare (attorney)
Smith Mr. James
Williams Rev. William, Croft

ACADEMIES AND SCHOOLS.
Cassons Mary Ann
FREE GRAMMAR SCHOOL, Simon William Wilcox, master
FREE SCHOOL, Hewlett James Leigh, master
Pickersgill Benjamin (and registrar of births and deaths)
Pickersgill Eliza

BAKERS.
Clark Joseph
Cassons Joseph
Dawson William
Handsley Chas.
Rollinson Wm.
Stockdale Wm.

BANK.
STAMFORD, SPALDING AND BOSTON BANKING COMPANY (branch)—(draw on Barclay, Bevan & Co. London)—Thos. Wright, manager

BLACKSMITHS.
Benstead William
Jackson James
Marfleet Joseph
Ouzman William
Stockdale William

BOOT AND SHOE MAKERS.
Atkin William
Belton John
Davy Joseph
Dickinson John
Gowen Timothy
Hope Samuel
Ling West, *Mosley*
Wharry James
Willey John

BRICK & TILE MAKERS.
Andrews Thomas, Thorpe
Gothard William, Thorpe
Moore Thomas, Thorpe
Thornley Samuel

BRICKLAYERS.
Andrews Jabez
Andrews Thomas
Bowman Thomas
Lake Benjamin

BUTCHERS.
Barton John
Bowser John
Hill Simon
Kirkby William
Procter Joseph
Webster William
Wright Richard

CABINET MAKERS AND JOINERS.
Andas William
Pike William
Robinson William
Routton Joseph
Tickler Robert

CHYMISTS AND DRUGGISTS.
Abraham Samuel
Huggins William Henry

COAL DEALERS.
Balderson Robert Chantrey
Epton William
Parish Joseph

CORN MERCHANTS.
Burton Samuel
Towler George
Whiley Francis (factor)

DYERS.
Askin Joseph
Gowen Timothy

FIRE, &c. OFFICE AGENTS.
BRITISH (fire) and WESTMINSTER (life), Benjamin Pickersgill
SUN, Thomas Seare Merrifield (and stamp distributor)

GROCERS AND DEALERS IN SUNDRIES.
Brooks William (and draper)
Burchnall Henry (and draper)
Coupland John
Pickworth John
Rollinson William
Skill Thomas
Wright Samuel (and draper)

INNS AND PUBLIC HOUSES.
Angel Inn, John Maulkinson
New Hotel, Jos. Hildred, Skegness
Old Hotel, Thos. Enderby, Skegness
Red Lion, Mary Shearman
Woolpack, Simon Hill

IRONMONGERS.
Brumby Robert (and cooper)
Pickworth John (and grocer)
Robinson John

LIBRARIES.
PERMANENT, Saml. Orrey, librarian
SUBSCRIPTION, Benjamin Pickersgill, librarian

MILLERS.
Booth John
Clark Joseph
Handsley Charles

MILLINERS AND DRESS MAKERS.
Brown Mary
Ling Mary
Overton Ann
Webster Ann

PLUMBERS AND GLAZIERS.
Crawn Thomas
Pickworth John
Showler John

SADDLERS & COLLAR MAKERS.
Harpham Martin
Keal William

STRAW HAT MAKERS.
Ling Mary
Maidens Ann
Spring Elizabeth
Willey Elizabeth

SURGEONS.
Barton Smith William Kirkham
Dawson Edwin

SURVEYORS—LAND.
Booth Robert
Simpson William

TAILORS.
Brooks William
Hebb John
Kirk William
Wright Samuel

TIMBER DEALERS.
Robinson John
Wright Thomas

WATCH & CLOCK MAKERS.
Scawthorpe William
Taylor Richard

WHEELWRIGHTS.
Robinson John
Waller Robert

Miscellaneous.
Coupland John, beer retailer
Crow William, auctioneer
Dickinson Charles, gardener
Gunson John, brewer
Harness Thomas, beer retailer
Marfleet Jos. agricultural machine makr
Orrey Samuel, hair dresser
Rainer Edward, tanner and fellmonger
SAVINGS' BANK—Benj. Pickersgill, agent
Sharpe Edwin, painter
Smith James, general agent
Tickler Edwin, printer
Wright Thomas, wine & spirit merchant

CARRIERS.
To BOSTON, George Harness and Wm. Epton, every Tuesday and Friday—and George Brown, every Wed. and Sat.
To SPILSBY, George Rayner & George Brown, every Monday.

90

Example of a town listing in a trade directory taken from Pigot's Directory of Lincolnshire, 1841

42 Brooks Thomas, watch jeweller
44 Holloway John, gold blocker
45 Locke Mrs. Elizabeth, midwife
[Source - extracted from *Kelly's Post Office Directory of London 1902*]

Miscellaneous sections-
Court section - a consolidated A-Z list of 'private residents' (middle and upper-class) in the district or county. These people will also be listed before tradesmen in the separate town and village entries.
Postal section - variety of information on national postal rates and services.
Clerical and Parochial section - lists of churches, addresses, service times and ministers.
Conveyance section - depending on the date of the directory, this could include county or district lists of stage coaches and their routes, railway companies, carriers by road, canal transport etc.

And Finally-
Advertisements - elaborate display adverts for national and local businesses.
Maps - large fold-out maps included at the front or back of the directory. These are either county maps or street plans, and can be extremely detailed.

Use and Limitations
Naturally, directories are a veritable feast of surnames. A thorough search through every trade category and street in your locality of interest can pay enormous dividends, as members of the wider ancestral family may well be found. Try neighbouring towns and villages as well, perhaps using the map provided in the directory. If there is a consolidated county list of principal residents or tradespeople, take a look for names there too. By using a series of directories over the years, see how the family business grew and prospered - or maybe did not. The street section is a vitally useful tool to be used in conjunction with census returns, and if occupations are included, this can give an indication as to the social status of the neighbourhood.

It must be emphasised that there is much more to a directory than a list of names. The history and topography section in particular, which precedes the entries for each town and village, is a mine of information about the community in which your ancestors lived and worked, and can lead you on to research in other sources. To discover the history of the parish church, the lord of the manor, the local schools, the post offices, the railway station, the type of soil and crops grown, as well as the butcher where your ancestor bought their bacon, and the pub where they drank their beer, can paint such a vivid picture of a moment in time.

Don't forget the advertisements at the back of the directory as these are fascinating in their own right. Many local firms, some of which may still be in existence today. Strange machinery and even stranger patent medicines - a wealth of colourful description.

Nevertheless, directories have their drawbacks. The

main one is the gap between the agents collecting the information, and it being published. This could be anything from a few months up to a year, so the business or household might have moved by the time the directory was in print. Some publishers repeated old information year after year. Others blatantly copied details from rival publishers, not stopping to check their accuracy. This was the subject of several bitter lawsuits between the owners of directory firms. Moreover, not all traders would be included. Particularly in the early days, some refused to allow their names in print in case their tax liabilities increased or through fear of being unwittingly recruited into the county militia! Similarly in the street listings, not all residents of the street are included, just heads of household, and not all streets are included by any means. It is known that agents would refuse to canvass residents of streets that had the reputation of 'no-go areas', particularly slums in the industrial cities.

Where to find directories
Although thousands of copies of directories were published, survival rates may be patchy. They were not really designed to be kept and treasured - as soon as a new edition was published, the old one was thrown away. Original directories are now highly collectible and these rare gems may be discovered in second-hand bookshops. The biggest and best national collections are held at the Guildhall Library, the Society of Genealogists and the Family Records Centre, all in London. The National Libraries of Scotland, Wales and Ireland hold directories for their respective countries. Local studies departments of reference libraries will usually have good collections relating to their area. See Further Reading below for invaluable guides to the location of directories.

New developments
However, it is now possible to view a directory in the comfort of your own home. Imagine being able to spend time just browsing, soaking up the wealth of information. Or the convenience of having a directory from a far-flung part of the country at your fingertips, without the long journey to a distant library. This prime source for historical research is available in several formats -

Facsimilies - some directories have been re-published in paperback as complete reproductions of the original.

Microfiche - a useful way of condensing a large book into a small space. Each fiche will contain many pages, in either positive or negative form. These can then be viewed on your own microfiche reader, or the local library's machine.

Transcripts on the internet - the GENUKI website has lots of transcriptions of directory entries, as do a multitude of personal sites constructed by historians. These are often for selected towns or villages rather than whole-

scale transcripts of the complete directory. Investigation through one of the web search engines can come up with productive results.

Family History Society publications - these booklets may be in the form of transcripts, or consolidated alphabetical lists of traders extracted from the various classified categories, to make searching for names easier.

CD-ROM - by far the most significant development in making directories available to a wider audience is that of digitally scanning each page and producing it in computer-readable format. This can make viewing the directory on the monitor as easy and pleasurable as reading it in book form, but with added advantages - for example, to 'zoom in' and make the print larger, to view every minute detail of the map and to easily print extracts to include in your research files.

Family history magazines and searches on the internet will give details of the various organisations who produce directories in book, fiche, web and CD versions.

Further Reading
Guide to the national and provincial directories of England and Wales, excluding London, published before 1856, J.E. Norton (Royal Historical Society, 1950)
British Directories: a bibliography and guide to directories published in England and Wales (1850-1950) & Scotland (1773-1950), G. Shaw and A. Tipper (Leicester University Press, 1989)
The directories of London 1677-1977, P.J. Atkins (Mansell, 1990)

Angela Petyt lives in Wakefield, Yorkshire. She has a BA (Hons) in History and Language Studies from the University College of Ripon and York St. John, and (DA301) Studying Family and Community History from the Open University. Angela works as a lecturer in family and local history.

Tradesmans' advertisements - included in
Kelly's Directory of Lincolnshire and Hull, 1892

Photographs & Memorabilia - just how do you store them?
Colin and Sue Parkinson

"I really must start to sort out my family photos and bits of memorabilia." Could that be you talking?

We are asked on a regular basis at Family History Fairs and particularly those new to the joys of genealogy how best to store and organise photographs and items of memorabilia.

Many family historians have inherited albums of old photos and bundles of ephemera. As the families historian you may become the custodian of related family items. This can be a wonderful gift for you but also a terrible responsibility. Just what do you do with those boxes of irreplaceable photo's? The mass of certificates, postcards, letters, memorial cards etc. unique to your family can be daunting. Just how do you make any sense in organising it all?

Some existing photo albums can be unsuitable for the genealogists needs. Written notes on the reverse side of a photograph cannot be seen, old glue or mounts can damage the photograph, wrap over transparent vinyl sheets can stick to the photo and any attempt to remove will probably lift off the surface of the photograph. Not to display and store cherished items is a wasted opportunity to the genealogists as this can richly embellish family histories.

Some years ago one of our customers suggested it may be useful if we supplied binders or albums specifically for storing those odd and varied sized items that genealogists collect, accumulate and acquire. As a supplier of specialised certificate binders it seemed a natural progression for us to supply and offer photograph and memorabilia albums. Our certificate binders and clear polypropylene and polyester certificate pockets worked well for storing, protecting and displaying birth, marriage and death certificates. (See our article in The Family and Local History Handbook 5th Edition, *"Plastic, that will do nicely"*, on the types and use of safe polymer pockets.) But this size format of certificate pockets was too large for small items.

The affordable solution we found was a range of A4 polypropylene pages. These pockets are safe, clear and ideal for long term storage of treasured items. The pockets are available in a range of A4 formats, from a single pocket (293 x 215mm) to 20 pockets (48 x 53mm) on an A4 page. The most popular are the 1, 2 and 4 pocket formats, however the flexibility in having a range of pages is essential to store the variety of sizes of items to be saved. Single A4 pockets can be found in many stationery outlets and can be very inexpensive. Other

sizes are available from specialist archival and conservation retailers. The pages should be multipunched to enable you to store pages in a ring binder of your choice. A standard A4 binder will take about 40 pages whilst the deeper lever-arch binder will take approximately 120 pages.

The beauty of transparent pockets is that it allows you to store and title or describe items in any manner that suits you. For example writing on the back of photos can be seen through the reverse side of the transparent pocket. Alternatively, a description can be placed in the adjoining pocket so it faces the item it refers to. Or, if you use acid free card or paper with archival mounts or safe low tack glue then it can be mounted in the pocket with a title or description.

A word or two on writing on photographs would be appropriate here. Any photo's you have should be marked on the reverse saying who the photo is of, giving full names and dates where known. You might know it is your Aunt Bessie's wedding photo but the next generation of genealogists may have no idea. It is advisable never to write on the front of a photo. Any original writing on the reverse should be retained. For example this could be your grandparents writing which will always be fascinating to see. A problem if you write on the reverse of a photograph is if you make a mistake or want to add further details in the future then it can become messy. Safe, peelable labels seem to be difficult to find but you can make your own with safe peelable glue or use peelable 'post-it' labels, either would be easy to replace if you need to correct or update details. If you have to write on the back of a photograph then use a soft pencil and press lightly or an impression of your writing will appear on the front of you photograph.

The beauty of using clear pockets is that they can be mixed and matched. Different sizes can be interfiled to suit your individual needs. Furthermore, typed or written text, family trees, etc. can either be placed in a clear pocket or holes punched for direct insertion into a ring binder. Ring binders allow you to alter the sequence of pages that you use and allow you to add pages as you progress through organising your collection of ephemera. The mass of items you have can be daunting. The process of organising and sorting it all into clear, safe pockets and ring binders can be carried out as slow or fast as your time and pocket permits. Many of our customers order from us at intervals as they proceed through their collection of photographs and memorabilia.

We receive feedback from customers indicating that some sort their data in a "This is your Life" style. Binders and pockets allow photographs, text, certificates (reduced to A4 size), family trees and miscellaneous documents and items to be sorted in a detailed, colourful and informative manner. This can be done for individuals or families and is far more interesting than the bare bones of certificates and family trees.

Arranging your photographs and memorabilia into some organised sense is achievable. Even though it can appear overwhelming a methodical approach at your pace can be immense fun and rewarding. Generations to follow will gain great interest from it. Is it worth undertaking? Well it is your family history.

Researching My Family History ~ In the Beginning
Glenys Shepherd

When I was about eleven years old and living in Hindley near Wigan in Lancashire, I used to cycle to my Granny Dixons home in Spring View, (a misnomer if ever I heard one) near Wigan

As she was my only living grandparent, I loved to hear the stories she told me of the life she had had with Grandad George. He had been a little drummer boy in the grenadier guards at a very early age, progressing to be a musician. After they were married he became an orchestra leader in some of the very large theatres which abounded in the industrial areas. Whilst grandad was doing this, granny raised a large family and also, "took in theatricals"

Over the years, I scribbled down stories which I had been told by granny and other family members, with the intention of one day "writing a book'
One thing I did not have was actual dates and places,but more of that later.
In October 2001 I was just a year away from retirement so I decided that for the next year I would concentrate on collecting as much evidence as I could for my history. I copied a letter christmas card and put it in to family members telling them what I hoped to do. To my delight,over the next few months I received telephone calls of reminiscences, photographs, documents and letters. At this time I was working in Croydon and I was told that I had a distant relative living nearby in Suffolk.It only took a phone call to establish contact and before long we were off to Great Cornard for the week end. My newly found relative had had a grandfather called William and he had been one of my granny's six brothers. We were told stories in abundance ; shown photographs and taken to see the cottage where the Cant family had been born, as well as the school they had all attended. With the help of a map from a web site we established the size of the village they had grown up in. A visit

to a local second hand book shop found a Postal Street Directory from 1954. All the little villages were listed. Each village had every house named or numbered and each main residents name was listed. From consulting this we found that almost all of the family were still very near to their original birth place.Granny had come from a very rural village and her father was a farm labourer. Granny had gone to London to be "in service'; at a grand house, 153, Sloane Street, Chelsea. It was from Chelsea that she met and married grandad, who by then was a musician in the second battalion of the Grenadier Guards based at the barracks in Chelsea. A few dates were now beginning to emerge via their wedding certificate.

I have been very fortunate in having a great deal of information sent to me by my twin cousins Mavis and Kathleen. They are a little older than me and live in Blackrod near Bolton. Initially they included copies of photographs, but when I asked if they would send me the originals for a short time, they did so with the comment that it was my family as much as theirs. When the originals arrived, I was delighted to discover that the information on the reverse sides contained a great deal of information. I felt that I had struck gold! I took the photographs of vintage vehicles to the Bexhill-on Sea Centenary of British Motoring in 2002 and one of the organisers, Mr Paul Ffoulkes Habard was able to tell me the makes and date and place of registration (Edinburgh), This fitted in with a photograph of "Four of grandads brothers in their shop in Edinburgh. Waiting for George to visit". As a previous photograph was of great grandad George, a Professor of Music in York in the mid 1800's and a birth certificate of one of their sisters was registered as Scarborough. I did not know the connection. When did the move from Yorkshire to Edinburgh occur? Where were the sons born? I still have to investigate that part of the story.

After my grandparents were married, the children arrived approximately every two years. Nellie, Edie (or Edith), Florence (my mum), Beatrice (Beattie), George (a boy at last), Mary and Herbert. By the time the youngest ones were born, it was time for the oldest girls to follow in their mothers footsteps and go into service. Life must have been very busy for the Dixon family.The first children were born in Scunthorpe where grandad was at the Palace Theatre.Then came a very brief stay in Stockport. Then to Bolton (the Grand Theatre) then Wigan and the Wigan Hippodrome card I have a few dates but still have gaps.The children and all the theatres seem to have happened in a 20 year period from about the late

Four of grandad's brothers in their shop in Edinburgh.
Waiting for George to visit

Grandfather's Funeral procession, Lower Ince, Wigan

1890's to about 1919.

As the story unfolds, I am fascinated by coincidences in the generations. My great grandfather the professor; my grandfather the orchestra leader ; my musical cousins; my son who is a church musician and my daughter who is a flautist. The photographs too are uncanny. The one of Uncle Herbert could be the twin of one of granny's brothers; one of Auntie Beattie as a little girl is identical to one of my cousins. Roll on gene therapy history.

Some time in the future I intend to spend some time at the Guards Museum in Chelsea to find out what his battalion were doing at the time grandad was in it. I also need to find out when he died. I have a copy of a grand funeral which shows two of his brothers walking behind grandads funeral carriage and they seem fairly young.

I do know that later on granny re-married. It was a double wedding. Mother and daughter (granny and auntie Beattie) married father and son (Mr.Howerd and Alexander) A sad story as Alex became ill and died very shortly after the marriage.This wedding added a step sister and a brother to the family.Granny's last home was the one where I had visited her, in Taylors Lane.

When I sedously began to collect definite resources, I had no idea that both granny and grandad came from such large families.I have learned a lot in a comparitively short space of time but the more I know the more I would like to know.I was delighted with the initial response from some family members and a bit surprised at the lack of information from others. I just have to think that perhaps there are the usual family skeletons in our family as the there are in others. I still would like to know whether there is a family link with Reginald Dixon of Blackpool Tower fame.Some say yes and and some say no, Time will tell.I would like to know more about "Lilly". She was an older sister of grandad.Her real name was Amelia Ellen and she went to live with granny in Wigan after a broken romance.How intriginaly I do not suppose I will ever know whether Auntie Nellies first husband really did

write some popular songs of the 20's which were allegedly claimed by the famous singer to whom he sent them. But whether I find out or not, I am having fun trying.

I was sent information not only about my own family, the Boardman, but also about my husbands family history too, (Edwards and Shepherds After a while, I began to realise that I would have to have all this information in a manageible order. Each new photograph I photocopied, scribbling any information on to the photocopy and then placing in protective sleeves. All the cerificates and letters I also copied so I don't handle the originals more than necessary. I obtained a computer which I am still getting used to. I very soon realised the need for accurate dates. I put a search on a genealogical web site for "George Dixon" and it came up with 1,200 between 1800 and 2000 in England and America.

I also now am discovering that some of my friends are as hooked as I am and are prepared to share resources (when we have the time)

The Industrial Revolution has played a large part in my history My father Thomas was a fireman in the Lancashire coal mines (setting explosives, not putting fires out) until 1948,The Music Halls flourished in the heavily populated industrial areas. After leaving the coal mines, dad had a pet and animal foodstuffs shop before becoming one of the first Travel Agents in the Wigan Area.He then invested in a double decker bus and a coach.My brother Frank worked with Dad from this time. It was a time not only of King Coal but also of King Cotton.The bus and coach were used some of the time to take the mill girls to and from the huge cotton mills in and around Westhoughton and Bolton in Lancashire. At the week end the mill girls underwent a dramatic change.From the turbans and pinny's they changed like butterflies and then the coaches would take them to the large dance halls in the big towns (including Blackpool)and they would enjoy themselves to the

My Mother and Granny Dixon at Blackpool c1930

Gustave 'Gus' Dixon one of Granbdad's brothers
1899 Dedion Bouton 3$^1/_2$ HP - Registered Edinburgh 1903

Big Bands of the era such as Johnny Dankworth. During the 1950's my parents went on a continental familiarisation tour with other travel agents.I have a photograph taken then in Heidelberg at the castle and surprise surprise, fifty years later Rick and I had our photograph taken at exactly the same spot.

A few years later, Frank and Dad bought a piece of land (part of a colliery spoil tip). They cleared it and built their own National Benzole Petrol Filling station and car repair bay.Frank continued to run it until he retired. I don't know much about my parents life when they were young. I do know that they were founder members of the Wigan Cycling and Touring Club in the early 30's.They had a tandem bicycle with a sidecar on it for baby Frank. But within a very few years they changed it for a motor cycle combination.ie a motor cycle with an attached sidecar for little Frank.They spent many week ends and holidays camping (some times even in the snow) in North Wales(I think this must have influenced their choice of names for me and my other brother,Trevor) They also went as far as Edinburgh.The Lakes and Dales were also explored. As well as taking the mill girls, Frank also took groups from St.Peters Church in Hindley to Cropthorne in Worcesteshire and mens groups on fishing trips at £2.10 for a whole day!
When I was in my teens I had a Lambretta scooter , so all in all, our family know their countryside pretty well. The cycling theme has gone right through the family with the great uncles in Edinburgh my parents and also my brother Trevor who runs a very succesful Cycling goup in Hindley, catering for all ages and abilities.

As well as the usual photographs, certificates and stories, small items of family memorabilia have contributed to the history too. Three pretty china cups and saucers were given to two of my cousins and myself in 1952.At that time they were 120 years old and had been part of my granny's grandmothers wedding service.This link takes me back to 1832 approximately and made me wonder

why, if great great grandmother was a village country girl, she had such a lovely set? A letter from Jack Judge who sang "Its a long way to Tipperary' confirms the stories about music halls, theatricals and paying artists.

A postcard from 1914 posted in Denton, Manchester, draws together the story of Ellen Amelia or Lilly as she was known. She was the one of grandad's sisters who had a mental breakdown after a broken romance. Also, the Edith who sent the postcard to granny was another of his sisters.There is a lovely photograph of her with her son Lees. I think she must have married an affluent Denton business man judging by the clothes they were wearing.

Well, I really do have a good start to write about my family history but what of my husbands? So far I have been given copies of certificates, photographs and told verbal stories. The leads are taking us to Llanelly and a family of nine Payne sisters at the end of the 1800's; Scottish ancestry; war stories etc. so a good excuse to visit Llanelly. That will be another story.

Glenys Shepherd was born in Hindley Green near Wigan in Lancashire She has been married to Rick for almost 40 years and they have two children. She has a Certificate in Education from Lancaster University; a B.A. degree: Adv Diploma in Special Education from the Open University. She was warden of of a Tudor Almshouse in Croydon for eleven years until she retired to Bexhill in East Sussex in October 2002 © Glenys Shepherd

The Coaches of Regency Yorkshire

Prudence Bebb

My great-great-grandmother, Harriet Cooke, was nine years old in 1815. She lived in one of those typical Georgian houses which bordered the streets. One night, after she had gone to bed, she heard a commotion in the road. Inquisitive, she got up, ran downstairs and opened the front door. The London coach was rattling and rumbling down 'road; the driver was waving his whip and shouting: "We've beaten Boney We've beaten Boney!" So the news of Waterloo reached Stratford-upon-Avon.

Harriet recounted this memory to her niece, who eventually lived to be a hundred, and told it to her daughter who, in turn, told it to me.

Many people in Yorkshire would receive the news of Wellington's victory in much the same way because coachmen were the harbingers of news. They could bring newspapers recounting disasters as well as success. In May 1812 they carried accounts of the assassination of Britain's Prime Minister, Spencer Percival: "It is under feelings of horror, grief and dismay, that we record an event unparelleled in the history of our country...Mrs Percival and her children, 12 in number, are plunged into inexpressible grief..."

Even the names of the stage coaches popularised people and events. In 1815 a new coach started to travel from York to London and was named Prince Blücher, after the Prussian general who came to Wellington's aid at Waterloo. Advertisements for the new vehicle showed

drawings of Blücher's profile emphasizing his acquiline nose and Germanic moustache.

If you wanted to travel from London to York, you did not go through Selby like the modern trains; the road between there and York was too full of muddy ruts for a coach. At Doncaster the coachman branched north-westwards for Tadcaster, a town where as many as 32 coaches might change horses each day. No wonder there were three coaching inns - the Angel, the Rose and Crown, the White Horse - all supplied teams for the heavy vehicles which arrived with steaming horses to be changed. One coach came to Tadcaster with a black flag flying but this didn't announce a death; it told Yorkshiremen that Mr Bowes had won the Derby and his colours were black.

The road from Tadcaster to York was just one stage and a smooth one, too, unlike some roads where passengers were jolted sickeningly.

Not that people always had a smooth ride even on town roads. When the coach for Hull was driven over the Foss Bridge in York, two people were crushed between the coach and the wall. William Storrey was the coachman and he had to admit that he had squashed them with his coach "for want of proper attention by which means they were much injured." One wonders if he was the same man as the "William Storry" who, considerably worse for drink, trundled the mail coach late into Scarborough and was fined £5.

Most stage coaches were jointly owned by two inns, one at each end of the route. They provided the horses for the stages nearest to them and the middle stages were horsed by other inns or by 'horse-keepers', (the father of John Keats the poet was one).

The London to York coaches arrived at the Black Swan or the George and these two inns faced each other across Coney Street. Unfortunately neither the George nor the Black Swan has survived.

An inn yard was a very

The Edinburgh Mail in front of The Mansion House, York

THE RAM AND THE REINDEER INNS DONCASTER

noisy place with wheels on cobbles, heavy booted footsteps, stamping hooves, whinneys and agitated shouts. Small boys, dwarfed by the high—piled coaches, watched eagerly and decided to be coachmen themselves when they grew up.

If travellers from London wanted to go on to Scarborough, they changed coaches in York, leaving the Wellington and boarding the Lord Nelson to take them to the Bell at Bland's Cliff. The Bell's building , which still dominates Prospect Place, was run by the Harrison family. After poor John Harrison was kicked to death by a horse, William Harrison became mine host.

Passengers for Whitby had to traverse the heather clad moors via Saltersgate until they arrived at the Angel inn, much altered now but still there. William Yeoman was the innkeeper and he knew the difficult roads his guests had rumbled and swayed across. He took the authorities to law in a successful effort to get the surfaces of the roads improved. The York gentlemen, who often had to go that way, rewarded him with a silver-gilt goblet.

People wanting to go from York to Manchester used one of the cross country coaches which left from the Black Swan. Those making the shorter journey to Leeds boarded the Old True Blue at two in the afternoon. If you wanted to visit Harrogate, you had to go to the White Horse in Coppergate; from there the Eclipse coach took arthritic or hypochondriac persons in the Season to drink the sulphur waters at the Spa Well.

Those wishing to travel (or nervously about to do so) went to the appropriate inn's Booking Office, which was so named because the passenger's name was written in a book with details of amount paid, luggage and eventual destination.

It cannot have comforted the timid to read in the York Herald a notice inserted by several coach owners: "In consequence of the many Fatal Accidents that have lately occurred by the overturning of coaches, the proprietors of the under mentioned coaches are determined not to allow any of their servants to race with the other coachmen."

As the employers were not able to see their drivers at work on a stretch of country road, it was still perfectly possible for a rival coach to try and overtake another. As the two heavy vehicles raced, literally neck and neck, along a road far too narrow for passing, the passengers could only cling to their hanging straps and pray to survive.

It was much wiser to travel on the mail coach - not as colourful, of course, because each stage coach had its own gaudy paintwork to attract custom. The mail coach, on the other hand, had a distinctive livery which proclaimed it to be the property of His Majesty's Post Office.

The mail's wheels and undercarriage were scarlet except when they were covered in mud. The lower door panels were maroon whilst either side of the windows was a black panel painted with one of the stars of knighthood. The royal cipher was on the box underneath the coachman and on the black boot was the number of the individual coach, the only way in which it differed from the rest of the fleet. Since they were all alike, spare parts could be carried and the guard was trained to effect repairs by the roadside. Nothing was supposed to delay the mail coach and that is why it travelled at night.

When other equipages were in their coach houses, His Majesty's mails hurtled through shadowy valleys and across bleak moors. It was possible to

YORK MAIL.

ONE MONTH'S SETTLEMENT, ENDING SEPTEMBER 21ST, 1816.

Proprietors' Names.	Money Received.	Miles.	Shares and Payments.
	£ s. d.		£ s. d.
John Willan, London	567 16 6	14	51 5 19
James Dyson	—	9½	34 16 1
William Chuck	7 0 0	10½	38 9 4
Jane Meyer	—	13	47 12 6
Ernest Hubner	11 1 10	15	54 19 1
H. L. and M. Sibley, Stilton ...	0 6 0	12	43 19 4
John Lawson	41 10 0	14	51 5 10
Richard Newcombe...	—	8	29 6 2
William Dunhill	13 13 10	13	47 12 6
John Makings	—	14	51 5 10
William Thompson	40 4 11	14	51 5 10
Richard Pease	—	10	36 12 8
George Clarke, Barnby Moor ...	—	14	51 5 10
Robert Day, Doncaster	47 12 8	7½	27 9 6
George Alderson, Ferrybridge ...	—	7½	27 9 6
John Hall, Ferrybridge	7 13 6	11	40 6 0
John Hartley, Tadcaster	1 8 10	10½	38 9 4
John Wilson...	363 17 6	197½	
	1,102 5 7		
Deduct for Newcastle Company ...	158 16 6		
	943 9 1		

DISBURSEMENTS.

J. Willan	Bookkeeping, £5 5s.; Coachman, £2 8s.; Coach Hire, at 3d. per mile, daily, £68 18s. 6d.; Stamp Duty, £114 6s. 8d.	190 18 2
James Dyson	Share of Inspector's Salary at Waltham Cross	1 5 3
W. Chuck	Two Coachmen	4 16 0
E. Hubner	Paid out on Parcels	0 0 6
John Lawson	Paid out on Parcels	0 7 0
William Dunhill	Coachmen, £8 ; paid out on Parcels, 2s. 6d.	8 2 6
William Thompson	Paid out on Parcels	1 4 6
R. Day	Paid out on Parcels	1 19 8
John Hall	Paid out on Parcels	0 19 4
John Hartley	Bookkeeping, £2 ; Coachmen, £4 ; Oil for Lamps, £2 ; Packing Paper and Card, 4s. ; New Coach Book, £1 1s. ; Inspector, £1 1s.	10 5 0
	£723 11s. 2d., divided at £3 13s. 3¾d. per mile.	943 9 1

THE GEORGE INN, YORK.

go at an exceptional sixteen miles an hour at night although one couldn't keep up an average of more than twelve.

There wasn' t room for many passengers; four inside and three on the roof were all that were permitted. More than that would slow the vehicle. Those on the roof were forbidden to talk to the guard who was responsible for keeping to schedule. He carried a blunderbuss and two pistols which is why you felt safe. It was death to rob the mail.

It could be dangerous for the guards as well. William Redford lost his left hand when his blunderbuss burst and two years later fell to his death from his perch on the hind boot where the mail sacks were kept padlocked. York people collected donations for his widow and children. However, some mail guards found their job very lucrative. A wage of ten shillings and sixpence a week was far more than doubled by the gratuities paid by passengers who asked the guard to care for their gold watches, jewellery and any other valuables during the journey. Even this does not entirely explain how Matthew Creaser, guard of the Whitby-York mail coach, was able to buy an impressive house in Whitby. Local rumour said that he had been taking lobsters on the mail and selling them in York.

The guard on the mail's dicky seat made a cheerful splash of colour. Each guard wore a uniform of red coat trimmed with gold braid, and black hat with a cockade. He carried a horn with which he blew a warning to the next gatekeeper. Then the tollgate

would be opened ready for the mail which swept through it without stopping for the mails did not have to pay tolls.

Some of the coachmen were great characters, too. Thomas Pye was the innkeeper of the New Angel at Doncaster. The mail coaches left there for London at eleven each morning and Mr Pye was often on the box seat . He'd been a coachman before he took over the New Angel and he regularly drove the London mail from Doncaster to Stamford where he left it in the hands of another driver.

Like York, Doncaster was a place where many coaches started and others changed horses. It had several important inns and many people, coming up from London, changed coaches there so they could go to places not on the London—York route. From Doncaster you could get a coach to Sheffield or Wakefield in the West Riding or you could enter a coach for Thorne if you were making for the Humber area. You might even be driven by an artist for Herring, the famous painter of horses, was working in Doncaster then. He hadn't yet achieved the status of painter of royal equines, so he made a living for himself and his young wife as a coachman.

Mail guards and drivers had some hair-raising adventures particularly in the severe winter weather of 1814. The Post Office expected strict observation of the time; no mail guard was allowed to be late. "Keep the duty regular," was the instruction. If the coach stuck in a snowdrift, the guard was to free one of the horses and set off with the mail sacks. The unfortunate passengers must fend for themselves.

Moses James Nobbs
Coachman

Barnsdale Bar
Great North Road

It was not only snow which endangered vehicles. Some roads had large potholes Thomas Hasker wrote to the Postmaster-General: "The York coachman and guard were both chucked from their seats going down to Huntingdon last journey and, coming up, the guard is lost this morning, supposed from the same cause, as the passengers say he was blowing his horn just before they missed him."

In the notorious winter of 1814 even the mails were late. So deep was the snow that men were employed to walk in front of the coach digging a way for it. On January 29th the York Herald recorded: "In our last we mentioned that the heavy fall of snow had prevented the arrival of the south mails…so completely blocked were the roads they did not arrive before Monday evening, when four mails were due - they came together to the number of thirtysix bags. A similar circumstance never occurred in the memory of man."

If your ancestor was a mail guard, he was an intrepid man.

Bibliography
The York Herald 1811-1820
Old Coaching Days of Yorkshire - Tom Bradley 1889
Gary's New Itinerary - John Gary 1809
The Mail Coach Men of the Late 18th Century
Edmund Vale 1960

The Poppleton Tithe Barn

Prudence Bebb

'Rupert's Barn' - The Tithe Barn, Nether Poppleton, York

It had a crumbly look about it. The walls, of narrow bricks, bulged and the pantiled roof gaped in places where winter gales had torn its tiles away. Pigeons roosted in its rafters and coated the mud floor with their droppings. Yet the old barn fitted into its surroundings - the pond, the Norman church, the old farmhouse and the Tudor dovecot It seemed to belong to the ancient lane which petered out by the field gate. Besides, there was probably more to it than that.

Local tradition maintained that Prince Rupert and his men had used it for shelter before they marched to Marston Moor. Could he have done so? Surely the bricks were eighteenth century and Rupert fought his battle a hundred years before that. It was worth a look inside the barn.

Worth it but dangerous; the floor was so uneven, the wind whistled through the air-holes and tugged at the loose tiles. But it didn't shake the sturdy oak pillars.

Then came the shattering news. The Council proposed to sell it so that it could be converted into two executive dwellings. A feasibility study was started and plans made to restore it; dendrochronologists dated its timbers. They were made from a tree felled in 1542.

That made sense. The barn stood on land which once belonged to St Mary's Abbey, York; at the Dissolution the land was let complete with the right to the tithes in Poppleton, to the Lawton family. They needed a barn for the tithes of harvested corn to be stored. It would be like a Dutch barn with a thatched roof and sturdy wooden pillars and it would be erected in the 1540s.

So those oak pillars and rafters were there when Rupert and his men, having raised the siege of York, crossed the river at Nether Poppleton. Thomas Stockdale, a Roundhead officer, wrote to Parliament a letter which still exists, telling the members that 'the enemy' crossed the river at Nether Poppleton on a bridge made of boats and spent the night in the village.

This was in July 1644 when the wheat and barley still stood in the fields because the harvest had not yet been cut. So the barn would be empty. How convenient! There were only a few cottages in Poppleton and fewer hedges than there are today. A large empty barn would be a perfect shelter; they could hardly be so silly as to lie on the open ground beside their restless horses when cover was to be found nearby.

What about the brick walls? They came later. Of course they did. The village was enclosed by Act of Parliament in 1769, the tithes were commuted to a money payment and a tithe barn was no longer required.

But a threshing barn was needed. No wonder the owner of Manor Farm built walls to enclose the barn. Those walls have a very large doorway on one side and directly opposite to these double doors is a single smaller door. That is typical of a Georgian threshing barn; the big doors allow a high—piled wagon to enter. With the large and small doors open there is a cross—draught between them and the men worked for hours there, beating the corn with flails on the mud floor whilst the draught blew the lighter chaff away.

How could we let Rupert's barn be turned into an executive dwelling? We didn't. Led by Janet Hopton, there was an enthusiastic village response and after several years of fund—raising, studying architects' plans and seeking archaeological advice, the deed was done with the help of lottery money.

There it stands beside a wildlife area, near the lych-gate; its air-holes have been unobtrusively glazed, its mellow walls have been strengthened, new pantiles cover the old rafters and inside a floor of rustic slabs has been laid.

People come now to the tithe barn for Christening parties, weddings, village meetings and concerts. It can be hired (Contact Number 01904 794433) and on a dark evening light shines from its air-holes and the old barn comes to life once more.

The Federation of Family History Societies

Carol McLee and Maggie Loughran provide an update

The Federation of Family History Societies (FFHS), a registered charity, was formed in 1974 to meet a growing interest in the study of family history. Membership consists of over 200 societies including overseas, national, regional, and one-name study groups. The FFHS Council is comprised of member societies representatives which defines policies to be implemented by an elected executive committee, holds debates, and exchanges views.

FFHS principal aims are:
• to co -ordinate and assist the work of societies and bodies interested in Family History, Genealogy and Heraldry
• to initiate and foster co-operation with projects in these subjects locally and nationally
• to assist in preservation and encourage wider access to local and national records
• to represent the views of its members and liaise closely with national bodies
• to promote better standards of family history education
• to raise awareness through regular meetings, discussions and social events conducted by member societies at courses, seminars and conferences.
• to publish a bi - annual journal, *Family History News & Digest* and many educational leaflets on general interest topics
• to market, via its trading company, publications covering aspects of research and archival records for everyone interested in family and local history.

FFHS (Publications) Ltd stocks a comprehensive range of titles of interest to family, local and social historians, including many works from other publishers. Most of the regional and specialist societies produce their own publications details of which can be found in *Current Publications by Member Societies*. More details are available from FFHS (Publications) Ltd, Units 15 –16 Chesham Industrial Centre, Oram St, Bury Lancs BL9 6EN. Tel 0161 797 3843 Fax 0161 797 3846 e-mail sales@ffhs.org.uk or at www.familyhistorybooks.co.uk

Many national projects are co-ordinated by the Federation so that the work of societies can be integrated to the benefit of all concerned. At the present time the transcribing and indexing of the 1851 Census Returns for England & Wales is almost complete on a county - by - county basis, whilst the immense 1881 Census Returns Index, in partnership with the Genealogical Society of Utah ,was completed in 1996.

Other project work such as the recording of war memorials for the Imperial War Museum Project and monumental inscriptions throughout the UK, is co-ordinated at a local level by each society, the Federation giving each encouragement, advise or using its liaising capabilities with local and national bodies when needed.

The National Burial Index (NBI) contains records from parish, non-conformist, Roman Catholic and cemetery registers throughout England and Wales dating from the 16th C to modern times, although it is stressed that not all locations and dates are yet covered. Wherever possible, transcriptions are made from original source records but others, such as microfiche transcriptions or printed registers, are used. The first edition, with more than 5.3 million names, was produced on CDROM in 2001 with plans to publish a *cumulative* NBI every three years. Each entry presents the following information (if available in the original source):
Forename(s), surname, date, age, location with county where event was recorded. Also included is the name of the society or group which provided the record. To date, over 50 Family History Societies and Associated Groups have provided over 7 million records.
Could You Help This Project? The success of the first edition should encourage more volunteers to continue this worthwhile work. To contribute in some way, please contact direct the following:
General information:
Carol McLee 3 The Green, Kirklevington, N. Yks TS15 9NW Email nbi.project@ffhs.org.uk
To be a Group Co-ordinator:
Peter Underwood 174a Wendover Rd, Weston Turville, Bucks HP22 5TG
Email: nbi.data@ffhs.org.uk

Individual volunteers:
Sandra Turner 2 St Annes Close, Winchester, Hants SO22 4Ql Email nbi.individuals@ffhs.org.uk
A group or individual with existing computerized data to donate:
John Hanson 16 Audley Mead, Bradwell Village, Milton Keynes, Bucks MK13 9BD Email nbi.bulk@ffhs.org.uk

Co-operation between groups and individuals, archivists, and many others is essential as more and more people become involved in the study of the family structure, their roots and heritage. We hope that you will assist this project to further this aim.

NBI 1st Edition is available from most Family History Societies and FFHS (Publications) Co: email sales@ffhs.org.uk or write to FFHS (Publications) Co., Units 15-16, Chesham Industrial Centre, Oram Street, Bury, Lancs BL9 6EN; or on-line www.familyhistorybooks.co.uk for details and costs. For a listing of Family History Societies (with web page links) and other FFHS information see www.ffhs.org.uk or contact the FFHS Administrator, PO Box 2425, Coventry, CV5 6 YX Email info@ffhs.org.uk

Ron's Story ~ Part 2

Richard Ratcliffe FSG

Ron in Clacton

Since writing up Ron's story for the 6th edition of the Family and Local History Handbook, his research has progressed by leaps and bounds. Ron Silberbach is a member of my Clacton on Sea Family History Class who suffers from MS. Having obtained every Silberbach/Silverback Birth, Marriage and Death Certificate located via the indexes at the Family Records Centre with the help of his "gofer"[his tutor], Ron's main aim in 2001 was to locate the burial sites of as many of his Silberbach ancestors as possible. As many of them settled in the East End of London, Ron purchased the latest edition of the booklet *"Greater London Cemeteries and Crematoria"*[6th edition,SOG,1999] Almost without exception, the Cemetery Superintendents, officials and Local Studies Library staff have been extremely helpful and provided him with a wealth of information. With the help of Abney Park Cemetery and Hackney Archives, Ron has found the burial sites of more than 40 relatives in Abney Park Cemetery of his Silberbach and Wines families. But his biggest break came via the Abney Park website on which researchers can list surnames that they have located in the cemetery records.

In May 2002, Murray Silver of Wagga Wagga, Australia logged on to this website, saw Ron's interest in the surname Silberbach and contacted him on the Internet. Within a month, Ron had received information about 527 descendants of his Great/great grandfather Carl Frederick Alexander Silberbach.

Carl Frederick Alexander Silberbach had 6 children by his wife Charlotte [nee Glockler] of which 5 survived infancy. The eldest child, Alexander George Silberbach married Eliza Emma Evans at St Thomas's Parish Church, Stepney in

1874. Alexander and Eliza had 6 children who were born between 1875 and 1888 - George [1875], Alfred [1878], Frederick [1880], Charles and William [twins born in 1886] and Minnie [1888]. Alexander died in 1889 aged 38. A thorough recheck of the Marriage and Death Indexes at the Family Records Centre failed to locate any further references relating to Eliza and her 5 children. Their whereabouts were unknown until Murray made contact. Murray referred Ron to Rachel Silver in Palmerston North, New Zealand, giving Ron both her E-mail address and her telephone number. Ron immediately rang Rachel, even though it was in the "wee small hours of the morning" and got more than he bargained for.

It turned out that Rachel was not only the family archivist but she had organised a Silver/Silberbach Reunion in 1992 to honour Eliza who had emigrated to New Zealand with 5 of her 6 children in 1891- the eldest George having already left home to become a ship's engineer. On their arrival in New Zealand the family name was changed from Silberbach to Silver. After Eliza's death in 1900, her children settled in New Zealand , married and raised families - their biographies were included in the Reunion Booklet "Eliza - a Woman of Courage" which Rachel compiled for the big get together. Rachel Silver [nee Bak]is the wife of Desmond Silver who is elder of 2 children of William one of the twins. Rachel has supplied Ron with detailed information about 527 relations in New Zealand and Australia as well as dozens of family photographs and a copy of the Reunion Booklet.

Alice Maud Silberbach nee Parkes Ron's greatgrandmother with his grandfather Stephen and great aunt Florence

Walthamstow, London

As a result of making contact with Murray and Rachel, Ron has made contact with several other descendants of Eliza, including Christina Crossman, great/grand daughter of Charles Silberbach, the other twin. She made contact with him in July 2002 by seeing his surname listed in "Ancestry.com" Christina of Whyalla Norrie, South Australia, had only been able to trace the Silberbach/Silver family back to Eliza. Ron was able to provide her with information going back to 1670 in East Prussia as well as telling her that she was living less than 4 hours drive from some of her Australian cousins! Now they E-mail each other on a daily basis.

A small advertisement in the Anglo-German FHS Magazine Mitteilungsblatt 59 in March 2002 offering issues 1-28 and a book on Sugar Bakers to anyone interested led to more amazing discoveries. Ron obtained the lot and in issue 26 [December1993]found a list of surnames of families who were recipients of St George's Lutheran Church Society of Ladies Charity between 1821-1846, 1868-1883. In the list were the surnames Silberbach and Glockler. The list had been compiled by Len Metzner a member of the Anglo-German FHS. Ron contacted him and got back transcriptions of 4 entries.

3rd December, 1835 Glockler, John, 2 Philipp Street, Commercial Road. Has at this moment got employment at a sugarhouse at 26/- a week but is uncertain how long it will continue & having been a long time out of work is much reduced. There are only 2 children a girl of 5 [Ron's Great/ great grandmother Charlotte] and a boy of 1[John William]
Full suits and 2 pairs of shoes were ordered.

4th May, 1837 Glockler J and Mrs, 2 Philipp Street, Commercial Road. Clothed in December 1835. Having been out of regular work since the beginning of December is in great distress. In addition to the two children last clothed the eldest of whom goes to our school, they have had a baby since.
Full suits for a girl of 7, two boys of 3 yrs and 8 months & 2 prs of shoes were ordered.

10th December, 1868 Silberbach, Alexander and Charlotte, 54 Richard Street.[Last relieved 6th December,1866] - Still residing at 54 [formerly9] Richard St, circumstances quite unaltered; husband still in Colney Hatch Asylum. 2 boys of 9 and7, [Alexander and Charles], both in Infants School, 1 girl of 14 [Margaret] free of our school.
Full suit, 2 prs of shoes, 1 shawl & 2 tailors suits.

8th December,1870 Silberbach, Alexander and Charlotte + 3k, 54 Richard Street. [Last relieved 10th December, 1868] - Husband still at Colney Hatch Asylum. The eldest girl sickly at home. 2 boys, of 12 years free of school & of 9 years.
2 tailors suits & 1 pr of shoes.
[Alexander is of course Carl Frederick Alexander Silberbach referred to earlier].

Richard Pether Silberbach
Ron's great grandfather
who is the son of
Carl Silberbach
and
Charlotte Glocker

In the same issue of Mitteilungsblatt, Ron found a list of German Churches in London and details of their deposited records. St George's Lutheran Church Records which include baptisms, marriages, burials, school admission and leaving records and school attendance registers have been deposited with Hackney Archives. Ron contacted the Archivist who found baptisms of the Silberbach boys - not Margaret who was born in East Prussia in 1855 - and entries in the school attendance registers showing that the Silberbachs, Margaret in particular, were frequently late, lazy and irregular in their attendance.

This is not surprising since their father, Alexander had been committed to Colney Hatch Asylum in 1864 and was to remain their until his death in 1907. Efforts to examine the Colney Hatch records relating to Alexander have so far been unsuccessful. London Metropolitan Archives have confirmed that they have them on deposit but records relating to individuals are subject to a100 year closure rule. Thanks to the help of the Cemetery Superintendent at Manor Park Cemetery, Ron has discovered that both Alexander and Charlotte are buried there only a stones throw from Ron's own father who died in1999.

Oxfordshire County Record Office has also turned up trumps this year by supplying Ron with Wills relating to his Gondoux and Carpenter families. The Record Office has also supplied cuttings from Oxfordshire newspapers reporting the mysterious death of his 5x great grandfather John Gondoux at Charlbury in 1811 and also putting him in touch with Mrs Lois Hey, the village historian at Charlbury. Lois was in the final stages of writing her history of Charlbury and was delighted to hear from Ron as the Gondoux story is one of the most intriguing events in the history of the village. Sadly just a few months after her book "A History of Charlbury" [Wychwood Press 2001] was published Lois died but Ron treasures his signed copy which refers to his connection with this North Oxfordshire village.

As well as continuing to prove relationships by obtaining more certificates of birth, marriage and death [via the Family Records Centre] and confirming places of residence with the help of the 1901 Census [mostly due to his "gofer" using the microfiche at the Public Record Office at Kew], Ron has made extensive use of the Internet in 2001/2. He has gained most success via Ancestry.com, familysearch, surnames.com, Abney Park, whitepages[telephone directories] and Family History Society sites. He also subscribes to Family Tree Magazine, Practical Family History, Family History Monthly and Ancestors and is a member of Essex SFH, Suffolk FHS, Oxfordshire FHS, East of London FHS, and the Anglo-German FHS.

As he says when you get hooked on Family History you should never leave any stone unturned.

Photographic Pioneers - the photographers and processes
David Tippey

Since the industrial revolution, science has played an ever increasing role in our lives and although the Victorians didn't have the plethora of technological gadgetry we have today, they still had plenty of new innovations to excite them. One which appeared and matured during Victoria's long reign was to gain instant popularity and make a lasting impact on our lives: photography. The Victorian era heralded the creation of the photographic arts and with it, a new breed of entrepreneur. As the processes improved, the few portrait painters who had catered for rich clients at the beginning of the 19th century were replaced in the second half of the century by hundreds of portrait photographers who catered for all classes.

As early as 1725 there had been experiments with light sensitive materials, but the first successful permanent photograph was produced by Niépce in 1826 using a rather unwieldy bitumen process which required several hours exposure. Henry Fox Talbot 's experiments in 1835 with the *Photogenic Drawing Process*, using a system of paper negatives and prints, led to the Calotype and was the start of photography as we know it.
By 1840 the first commercial Daguerrotype process had been developed and introduced, bringing much better quality images.

Ambrotype Photograph

Although many different variations were tried, nineteenth century photography centred on four major processes the earliest being the calotype, daguerrotype and wet collodian processes. These were eventually superseded by the dry plate and it's bromide gelatine emulsion which in turn led to the development of roll film and the photographic materials and equipment which is still in use today.

Fox Talbot's **Calotype** system commercially introduced in 1841, used a paper negative allowing several copies of a photograph to be made and was the first process used to provide photographic book illustrations. Although relatively cheap, the picture quality was fairly poor due to the texture of the paper and it's exposure time was too slow for portraiture.
Prints were made on paper painted with a sensitising solution and exposed with the aid of sunlight. These salt prints were also used later to print negatives from the wet collodian process and remained in use well into the 1850s when the albumen print took over. You are unlikely to find a salt print from a calotype negative in the family album, it's main uses were in landscape and architectural photography, but you may be have a distinctive, **Daguerrotype** photograph, which was the first commercial process suitable for portraiture.

This process was invented by Louis Daguerre and photographers had to pay a license fee to use the process. The process produced only a single copy, using a polished copper plate coated with silver and the polished silver surface with it's delicate image can only be viewed when held at certain angles. The photographs are usually presented in a small, velvet lined, hinged, protective case, surrounded by ornate gilded mounts.
Early portrait photographs were often taken in studios that resembled greenhouses, to capture the maximum available daylight, and the darkroom would be situated next door, as this was a wet process which required the exposure to be made as soon as the plate was prepared. The exposure times were slow to begin with, between 10 & 15 minutes in bright sunlight, so not suitable for portraits. Subsequent improvements in sensitising and processing the plates and particularly in lens design, succeeded in reducing the exposure times to around a minute or so, but to prevent any movement blurring the image, subjects were seated in special chairs with neck braces to help them keep still. Sitting still in a greenhouse to have your portrait taken, wearing heavy Victorian clothes must have been rather an ordeal, no wonder none of them seem to be smiling.

Daguerrotypes were expensive, costing about a guinea each, so only the better off could afford them, but the market was still far greater than it's predecessor, the portrait miniature. When the original patent ran out in 1853, many new studios sprang up, but its popularity was soon to be usurped by the Collodian process and it's use had much declined by the end of the 1850s, although in some studios it remained in use through the 1860s and beyond.

Cabinet Card

Variations on these two early processes were tried, including Gustave le Gray's waxed paper process, an improvement on the calotype, but the next major step forward was Frederick Scot Archer's wet **Collodion** process. This allowed a light sensitive coating to be applied to glass plates, creating a glass negative which produced high quality images and it could be used to reproduce a great many prints or used to create the "one off" Ambrotype. This rapidly grew in popularity, despite being a difficult process to master. Although the process never displaced the other photographic processes entirely, it was to revolutionise photography, with its relatively short exposure times and excellent detail, plus the freedom from patent and licensing costs made it more affordable.

The introduction of the new process meant that photography blossomed and like mobile phone shops today, studios sprang up everywhere, taking advantage of the Victorians particular desire for portraits and new "must have" technology.

These early photographic processes all required the plates to be wet when exposed, because they lost their sensitivity when dry. This meant photographers always had to work within reach of a darkroom both to coat the plates and then to develop them after exposure. Because of this limitation photography was mainly carried out in the studio, although the particularly intrepid photographer could carry a portable darkroom with him on location, and several variations of the portable dark-tent were available during the 1850s. Roger Fenton was one such pioneering photographer and he can probably lay claim to being the father of photo journalism too. In 1855 he converted a horse drawn wine merchant's van and headed for the Crimea to create a remarkable early record of the soldiers life in a war zone, albeit carefully posed.

Although most of the early photographers didn't encounter the dangers of war, their chosen art wasn't short of discomfort and hazard. The greenhouse studios would be uncomfortable to work in, but the main hazards lay in the darkroom, as the processes used a wide variety of dangerous chemicals. These included chlorine to sensitise plates, a bath of heated mercury to develop the Daguerrotypes and the mixture of guncotton and ether, which formed the basis of the emulsion in the wet collodian process. None of these substances would be very pleasant to work with, or particularly good for your health in the close confines of the darkroom.

The early negatives produced by the wet collodian process were used to produce salt prints which had a soft image due to the fact that the light sensitive salts were distributed all through the paper. The invention in 1850 of an albumen based emulsion, which was used to coat the surface of the paper rather than soak it, led to a great increase in sharpness and detail, as well as to the first factory farming of hens to produce enough eggs for the albumen!

The albumen coated print papers produced excellent prints but were very thin and easily damaged, so the results were then mounted on cards creating the familiar carte-de-visite and it's larger cousin the, cabinet print. Although the enlarger was invented in the 1840s, materials fast enough to exploit it's potential were not available until the late 1850s, but contact printing was much more common and most prints you will see were produced by contact printing, creating images the same size as the negative.

Unlike the one-off family portraiture market, catered for by the daguerrotype, the carte-de-visite led to a brisk trade in the sale of photographs of famous people and places. These were eagerly collected, so if you find a picture of the pyramids or a member of the royal family in the family album, don't jump to hasty conclusions. Paris also became the centre for a much more risque trade, creating soft porn images for gentlemen to pass around with the port and cigars after dinner, so that scantily clad beauty probably wasn't your Great Aunt either.

As well as being used to provide negatives for multiple prints the wet collodian process was also used to create a cheaper version of the one-off daguerrotype portrait. These are sometimes referred to as collodian positives, but more often as Ambrotypes. These are not really positives at all, but a rather thin negative image produced on a glass plate. When backed by black paper or varnish, the image appears to be a positive. The images were often hand tinted before being fitted into velvet lined cases with chased brass mattes similar to those used for the more expensive Daguerrotypes. Cheaper versions with less elaborate framing, brought them within the reach of working class people with a shilling or so to spend and they were often taken to commemorate special occasions such as weddings. Photographs were frequently hand tinted, adding a little colour to cheeks and flowers and often gold to bring attention to the jewellery. The images on tinted Ambrotype are usually laterally reversed because it was easier to carry out tinting on the emulsion side of the plate, the emulsion was then protected by a cover glass and brass matte. Ambrotypes are the more common cased Victorian photograph and are often mistakenly referred to as Daguerrotypes by dealers who don't know the difference. Daguerrotypes are easily recognisable by the fact that when held at the wrong angle only the silver plate and a very thin negative image can be seen.

An even cheaper version of the Ambrotype process used a black enamelled tin plate with an emulsion coating. This **Tintype** or **Ferrotype** process was often used to take very small "Gem" portraits, with cheap card mounts. This enabled them to be sold for only 6d (2.5p) or 1s (5p) and they were popular at fairs or other places of leisure such as the seaside. They were less prone to damage than the glass plates used in the Ambrotype and were very popular in America, but although used in Britain you are probably less likely to find them here than an Ambrotype.

Although there had been various dry processes tried, they all suffered from a lack of speed, so the faster wet Collodion process remained in use alongside the other well established wet processes until the development by Dr Richard Maddox of a gelatin coated dry plate in 1871. This innovation finally freed the photographer from the proximity of the darkroom. The silver bromide gelatin emulsion was then applied to photographic print paper too and the foundations of modern Black & White photography were established, a system which has changed little and is only now starting to

be challenged by the digital camera and computer.

Coating machines to apply the photographic emulsion to glass plates and papers were introduced in the 1880s and it then became possible to buy mass produced photographic materials over the counter and photography started to become a popular hobby with the better off, as well as being a profession.

In 1888 George Eastman created the forerunner of today's disposable cameras, although neither roll film or a pre-loaded camera were a totally new idea even then! He produced the Kodak No.1, a very simple pre-loaded camera which took 100 exposures on a special paper based film with a strippable emulsion. The complete camera had to be sent back for processing and it cost 5 guineas. This combination was a new idea, and now you could take photographs without worrying about how to set the camera controls and never have to go into a darkroom yourself.
It only took another year for the Eastman Company to produce a roll film with the emulsion coated onto the transparent base and in 1892 he bought the Boston Camera Company who had the bright idea of backing the film with black paper which was printed with numbers to align the film in the camera. He now had a roll film which could be loaded into the camera in daylight, the like of which is still available today.

The turn of the century heralded a new age in photography, with the public starting to take their own "snaps". Cameras and film became cheaper and easier to handle. With the appearance of roll films and the 5 shilling "Box Brownie", it was no longer a hobby just available to the rich, most people could now start to record their lives and surroundings. Now the real innovation was able to switch to the cameras, with the bulky box designs soon being joined by "vest pocket" folding cameras making them much more portable and convenient. However these changes didn't put the studio portrait

Photographic Time Line

1845	1850	1855	1860	1865	1870	1875	1880	1885	1890....1910.......1930

Daguerrotype 1841-1855

Albumen Print 1850-1880---

Ambrotype 1852 -1890--

Tintypes 1856-1930--

Carte-de-Visite 1860 -1910--

Gelatine Prints 1880- To present ----------

photographer out of business, families still had their formal studio portraits taken, although they were busy using the new technology to record themselves at their leisure. The dry plate still continued in use well into the 20th century for portraiture and high quality work for publication and it was finally replace by flexible based sheet films.

Although the 20th century brought the development of colour film and big improvements in cameras and optics, the process would still be recognisable to the photographer who was plying his trade over 100 years ago. However we have now entered a new chemistry and darkroom free phase, where digital cameras capture images without film, to be viewed and printed instantly via our computers. It seems we have almost turned full circle, although we can instantly preview our photos, we still have to be near our "digital darkroom" to print them, so are we much better off than those photographic pioneers?

If you want to learn more about the history of photography, try to visit to National Museum of Photography Film & Television in Bradford or alternatively take a look at some of the excellent websites listed below which are full of interesting information and examples.

Bibliography
Victorian Photographers at Work by John Hannavy and *Victorian Cartes-de-Visite* by Robin and Carol White are low cost and extremely informative books by Shire Publications.

Internet Bibliography
• Examples of cartes-de-visite from different decades to aid dating, can be found at:
http://homepages.tesco.net/~roger.vaughan
• Robert Leggatt's informative, narrative site on the history of photography from it's early beginnings.
www.rleggat.com/photohistory
• 19th Century Photography (a US site including clues to dating old photographs)
www.ajmorris.com/roots/photo/photo.htm
• The Daguerreian Society, a visually interesting site with lots of data on this early photographic process which still has followers.
www.daguerre.org/home.html
• National Museum of Photography Film & Television *www.nmsi.ac.uk/nmpft*
• Royal Photographic Society
www.rps.org
• The George Eastman Museum of Photography has possibly the best timeline of photography amongst it's

other interesting pages.
www.eastman.org
• Victorian Photograpers in the British Isles
www.mywebpage.netscape.com/hibchris/instant/about me.html
• Old Photo Guide useful information and forms for dating.
www.city-gallery.com/guide
• An index to listings of photographers working in various towns can be found at.
www.users.waitrose.com/~rodliffe/index.html

Also worth looking at are:
www.victorian.fortunecity.com/carroll/642/pixs/carte. htm
www.cwreenactors.com/Collodion
www.gclark.com/phototree/index.htm
www.bbc.co.uk/history/community/family/victorian_ph oto1.shtml

The Fragility of Life ~ Infant Mortality in England and Wales
Doreen Hopwood

In Britain today a long and healthy life is considered to be the birthright of a baby, but even up to the mid twentieth century, mothers - particularly those living in poverty - were conscious of the fragility of their offspring. They were painfully aware of the many forces outside of their control, which could thwart their child's development. Prior to the discovery of modern medical therapies, the onset of illness in a baby was a cause of dread. An innocent seeming cold may be the beginning of a lethal case of pneumonia or bronchitis and all of the infantile developmental stages - such as teething - were fraught with danger. The first English childcare manual "The Boke of Chyldren" was published in 1544 and lists some of the "grevous and perilous diseases of chyldhode" as "apostume of the brayne ..... neasing out of measure .....bredying of teeth .... colyke and rumblying in the guttes." Without doubt, some of the remedies included in the manual were the means of the demise of the tiny patient rather than the cure, such as that recommended for teething:

"......annoint the gummes with braynes of a hare, myxt with as much capos grease and honney...."

In Tudor times, whilst the birth of a child may have been celebrated with the lighting of a bonfire and feasting, the infants' first months of life were rarely recorded other than by an entry in the parish baptism register. At a time when the average life span was about 30 years, parents were well aware of the fragility of new human life, and babies were christened very soon after birth. An entry of private baptism in the register may well signify that the infant was sickly and not expected to live,

so there may be a corresponding entry of burial in the register. Until the mid-17th century an entry may be found in the registers for a Chrisom Child. The chrisom was the white linen cloth placed on a child at the time of baptism. The priest anointed the child with holy oil (chrism) in the form of a cross and the cloth was the means of preserving the chrisom marks. It was worn by the child for seven days but if the baby died before then, the cloth became its shroud, and it was termed a Chrisom Child.

Statistics relating to infant mortality become more reliable after 1875, when they are included in detail in the reports of the Medical Officers of Health, with aggregate figures for England and Wales shown in the Registrar General's reports. The charts printed here show the extent of the problem in the latter part of the 19th century and beginning of the 20th century, but rates of infant mortality had always caused concern.

In 1624 an act was passed in an attempt to eradicate what became known as "baby-dropping" - the dumping of an infants' corpse. The Act presumed that the mother of an illegitimate baby was guilty of murder if she tried to conceal the birth by secreting its corpse, and carried a penalty of two years imprisonment. The onus was on the mother to prove that the infant had been stillborn or had died naturally - and applied only to illegitimate births. Concealment continued to be an offence, and carrying a lesser penalty than that of murder or manslaughter, it was often the verdict of a jury when cases were brought to trial.

The Foundling Hospital took in many of the infants who may otherwise have become dumped corpses, but the infant mortality rates in institutions such as this were very high. In 1765, Jonah Hanway, a Poor Law official and hospital governor, asserted that " ..... poorhouses or workhouses are, in general, slaughterhouses to infants" when presented with the fact that out of 133 babies born in the St Giles Workhouse, only 26 could be confirmed as still being alive.

The boarding out of infants to rural homes or to wet nurses became the standard practice of the Foundling Hospital and Poor Law Guardians, and this may account for the discovery of the burial of a family member some

distance from where the family lived. The Overseers of the Poor records in the parish of origin may indicate if they had a regular village to which infants were sent. Where Parish Officers paid a lump sum to a wet nurse, rather than making regular payments, this was an incentive for the unscrupulous to "do away" with the infant - in whom the parish no longer had any interest and whose continued existence ate away at her profits.

Bills of Mortality for London show that out of a total of 1,178,346 recorded deaths between 1730 and 1779, some 526,973 were of children under the age of five, and it was estimated that 75% of children died before reaching this age. John Wesley was one of 19 children, 6 of who reached adulthood and the following appeared in the Gentleman's Magazine in 1740:

"It is a wonderful Part of the Providence of God that so many little Creatures seem to be born only to die".

Under the Registration Act of 1836 - which established the system of civil registration in England and Wales - burials could take place without a death certificate so long as the person conducting the funeral notified the registrar within seven days of the burial. Medical certificates were not required for the issue of a death certificate - the person present at the death or who attended the deceased during the illness simply stated what was thought to be the cause of death. "Midwives" who had attended the delivery could attest that the child had been born dead and no birth or death certificate was necessary. This was amended in 1858, so that a medical certificate had to be produced prior to burial. The registration of stillbirths did not come into effect until 1926, but from 1874, in an effort to stop the fraudulent passing off of livebirths as stillbirths, a written statement by a doctor had to accompany the body to the burial place.

Parish burial registers occasionally include entries for stillborn babies, such as the following at Wickham in County Durham:

"1626. Anna Gaskell, wife to Anthony Gaskell bore at one birth fower [sic] p'fect children, whereof one had life and stirred after it was borne, the rest all three still borne and were all buried in one grave. 25th of March".

Proof of "separate existence" - that the infant had drawn breath - was sufficient to indicate that the child had lived and so necessitate the registration of both the birth and death after 1837. The absence of a forename in the General Register Office Index of Births may be an indication that the child did not survive. Such registrations usually appear in the alphabetical index under the parental surname and the "forename" column reads "female" or "male". A search should then be made for a corresponding entry in the General Register Office Index of Deaths. After 1865, these indexes include the age at death, so the figure "O" will appear against any child who had not reached its first birthday. Prior to this, the entry in the index could relate to a day old infant or an octogenarian! If you find a possible entry, application should be made to the register office at which the registration took place, stating that the certificate is required only if it is that of a child aged ....., the son or daughter of ...... together with any other information known about the family, such as the home address, fathers' occupation etc. Infant mortality rates were particularly high amongst immigrant communities in large cities, and in the Italian Quarter of Birmingham at the beginning of the 20th century the "little white boxes" containing tiny bodies were all too familiar a sight. Vincenzo Volante mourned the death of three of his young children within two years, and the birth and death of Fiore Grecco in 1902 was recorded by the Registrar as "Flower Grecco" (*fiore* = flower). He was just one of the many little flowers who did not bloom in the overcrowded and insanitary districts of Britain's large towns and cities.

Monumental inscriptions, such as the following at Aston Parish Church, often record the short lives of those buried in family graves:

"Thy will be done. Charles Frederick the beloved son of Charles and Mary Ann Summerfield who was killed at the Charity Sports Aston Lower Grounds July 6 1895 aged 10 years.
Also Nellie Elizabeth sister of the above who died April 8 1897 aged 8 months.
If love and care could death prevent
Thy days would not so soon be spent
Life was desired but God did see
Eternal life was not for thee"

Many family history societies have published books of such inscriptions - usually with an alphabetical surname index - and a search of these may provide information about the burial of an infant. It was not unusual for a child to be interred with grandparents, so a search under their names may be successful. The distribution of "death" or remembrance cards was customary amongst the better off and these may have survived with family papers. Where there is a family bible, the dates of birth, death and burial are likely to be meticulously recorded on its flyleaf.

Another source of concern was the practice of buying burial insurance for young children - the government deemed it to be the cause of the deaths of large numbers of working class children whose parents "cashed-in" on the policies. The

first "Men from the Pru" were recruited in the 1850s, and it was estimated that by 1890 about 4/5ths of all working class childen were insured. Local burial clubs also proliferated, such as the "Philanthropic" in Stockport, which for a weekly payment of a penny in the 1840s would pay out £3.8s 6d plus 2/- worth of drink on the death of an enrolled child. However, such clubs were open to abuse as children could be insured by more than one and some sensational cases did arise. When three of the four insured children of Robert Sandys died in quick succession he was tried for murder. Most working class parents paid the weekly penny or two to avoid the humiliation of a pauper or parish burial and the death benefits received barely covered the funeral costs as shown by the following account of that of a two month old Lambeth baby in 1911:

Funeral	£1.12s.0d
Death certificate	1s.3d
Grave Diggers	2s.0d
Hearse Attendants	2s.0d
Women to lay out body	1s.0d
Flowers	6d
Mourning clothes	1s.0d
	£2.19s.0d

The burial insurance paid out only £2.

The sudden death of an infant would result in an inquest by the coroner and the family would be subjected to close examination of their living habits, especially where the death of the infant was due to "overlaying" - suffocation in bed with parents and/or other siblings. Middle class observers saw this as a way of limiting the size of a family by the working classes, rather than what it really was - the result of chronic overcrowding and lack of money for proper sleeping accommodation. Surviving coroners reports (which are closed to public inspection for 75 years after the date of the inquest) can generally be found in county record offices, the Public Record Office or major libraries, and give an insight into the circumstances surrounding the infants' death. Even if the coroners papers have not survived, the local press usually included a report of the proceedings and where a prosecution took place, court records may provide more information.

Infanticide was responsible for only a small proportion of infant deaths, but received widespread coverage in the national press from the mid-9th century. The finding of a baby's corpse in the river or street in London was still accepted as sad inevitability, but the numbers rose and attracted attention from the public, press and police.

After 276 infants bodies had been found in the streets of London in 1870, investigations into the activities of local midwives were instigated. These unqualified women (registration was not introduced until the Midwives Act of 1902), were suspected of performing illegal abortions, delivering large numbers of stillbirths and getting rid of new-born babies by boarding them out to what came to be called "baby farms". These institutions were rarely out of the news in the 1860s and 70s as the source of spectacular mass murders of infants in their "care", even though some of the deaths occurred with the tacit approval of the parents. As a result of such cases, the Infant Life Protection Society was formed in 1870 and was instrumental in gaining protective legislation for all children as the century wore on. Whilst so much energy was spent in tightening up the laws concerning infanticide, little was being done to counteract the root cause of high rates of infant mortality - poverty. In his paper "The Waste of Infant Life" in 1867, Dr John Brendon Curgenven highlighted the huge differences between death rates across the social classes:

Well-to-do	11%
Urban working class	35 - 55%
Illegitimates	60 - 90%

Whilst the death rates amongst all age groups other

WHAT EVERY BABY NEEDS.

1. **FRESH AIR.** (1) Outside by day. (2) Open window by night.
2. **WATER** to drink (from a teaspoon).
3. **FOOD.** (1) Best Food—Mother's Milk. (2) Best substitute—Cow's Milk.
4. **A DAILY BATH.**
5. **REGULARITY OF ALL HABITS.**
    (a) Regular feeding hours.
    (b) No food between meals.
    (c) Bowels must be opened every day.
6. **CLEANLINESS.** (1) Clean food. (2) Clean feeding utensils. (3) Clean clothes.

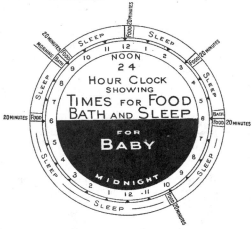

DONT'S.

1. **DON'T** give anything but milk until baby has cut some teeth.
2. **DON'T** keep baby's milk warmed ready for use.
3. **DON'T** use a "long tube" feeding bottle.
4. **DON'T** use a comforter or dummy.
5. **DON'T** use Patent foods, soothing syrups, or teething powders, except by Doctor's orders.
6. **DON'T** give a baby Castor Oil or any other purgative, without Doctor's advice.
7. **DON'T** omit to have baby weighed regularly.

If you are uncertain about anything, come to the Centre.

Adapted from "Feeding and Care of Baby" by Dr. Truby King.

than those under one year fell steadily throughout the 19th century, infant mortality rates remained stubbornly static, sticking at around 150 per 1000 births until the first decade of the 20th century. Many different arguments have been put forward as to why the rates finally declined both by contemporary observers and modern historians and all point to economic roots. As the Medical Officer of Health of Birmingham stated in 1910 "The heavier the purse, the lighter the mortality"

In general, infant mortality rates were about 25% lower in rural areas than in towns, but in the latter rates could vary as much as 300% between babies born in wealthy suburbs and those born to tenement dwellers. When infant mortality rates began to fall, this was also related to class - the higher the social class, the more rapid the decline. The introduction of compulsory vaccination against smallpox was a contributory factor in the fight to reduce this "waste of infant life" and surviving returns of the Vaccination Officers can be found amongst the Poor Law Union papers from 1853. The causes of infant deaths fell into four main categories - wasting diseases, gastric/diarrhoeal infections, respiratory conditions and developmental problems (such as teething). Many were due to natural deficiencies - maternal

exhaustion and malnutrition produced weak babies, exacerbated by damp, overcrowded and insanitary housing and low incomes. These causes were all identified by Medical Officers of Health in the last quarter of the 19th century, but apart from some eccentric schemes, little or nothing was done to alleviate the root cause - poverty. At the turn of the century, the Lord Mayor of Huddersfield, Benjamin Broadbent, issued promissory notes to new mothers, promising to pay a pound when the infant reached his/her first birthday. No records survive to show how successful the scheme was, but is assumed that the notes would have been carefully preserved for presentation at a time when £1 represented a working class family's weekly income.

A survey taken just before the outbreak of the First World War received responses from 348 women, who between them had
1396 live births
83 still births
218 miscarriages
- an average of over 5 pregnancies per woman. By this time, the care of the expectant mother was recognised as being important for the health of future generations, and infant welfare centres flourished in towns and cities. The Birmingham Infants Health Society was founded in 1907, and its aims were typical of all such welfare organisations:

• To lower the incidence of infant mortality in Saint Bartholomews Ward.
• To raise the standard of motherhood.
• To study, and as far as possible, elucidate some of the problems associated with infant mortality.

Until the establishment of the National Health Service in 1948, the visit of a doctor was a luxury which could not be afforded by a large proportion of the population and when he was called, it was often too late - after a variety of home remedies had been tried. Before 1858, when the Medical Register came into being, there was no standard medical qualification, and the wooliness of causes of death recorded on civil registration certificates is testimony to this.

As the professionalisation of health care has increased and medical techniques improved, the rate of infant mortality has continued to decline throughout the century and the ailments which killed so many of our forebears, such as diptheria, whooping cough and measles are no longer life-threatening.

Such vague terms as "wasting, debility, lack of vitality" and even "utterly unknown" appear all too often in the death registers, interspered with "Visitation of God" where the death was sudden or unaccounted for.

The First Jewish Master of The Rolls and the First Jewish Queen's Counsel
Doreen Berger *looks at the life of Sir George Jessell*

George Jessel, the first Jewish Master of the Rolls. The unfortunate disgruntled litigant was later found to be insane and confined to Broadmoor.

Sir George Jessel was born in 1824, youngest son of Zadock Aaron Jessel, pearl and diamond merchant, of Saville Row, Burlington Gardens and Putney. It is believed the original family name was Aarons. Zadock's father had emigrated to England from Frankfurt. Although the family were of humble origin, Zadock became a well-to-do merchant, and married in 1819 at the Great Synagogue, London Miss Mary Harris. In the entry for this marriage, Zadock's father is described as "learned". Zadock himself had a great interest in minerals and fossils, leaving at his death, in 1864, an important collection of these objects to charity.

The future Master of the Rolls was educated privately and then attended University College, where he distinguished himself. He was called to the Bar in 1847 and took large chambers on the ground floor in Stone Buildings. In after years he presented the unusual spectacle of a Solicitor-General finding the first chambers he took sufficient for him.

It was the last Friday in February of the year 1878. As the Master of the Rolls was alighting from a cab in Rolls Yard, a pistol shot was heard. The weapon was discharged so close to his lordship that the report stunned for the moment the Master and his Court-keeper, on whose shoulder he was leaning while stepping out of the cab. The culprit was immediately seized. The weapon was found to be a several-barrelled pistol, but it was believed it was not loaded with an actual bullet. The pistol was fired by Rev. Henry Dodwell, late of Brighton, who had made repeated applications to the Court, which had been refused on the grounds of irregularity.

On taking his seat in the Royal Court, shortly after the occurrence, Mr. Roxburgh, the senior member of the Bar present, addressed his lordship, and said that he desired, on behalf of the Bar, to express the grief with which they had heard of the attempt made on his lordship, and to express their gratitude to God for preserving a life so valuable.

The gentleman who had been shot at was Sir

It was not long before he obtained a large and remunerative practice; his ability for comprehending a complicated case and reducing it to a few plain issues ensured him many successes, and obtained him favour at the equity bar and among solicitors. It was in 1865 he was made a Queen's Counsel and at the same time a Bencher at the Inn. His practice now increased in a manner which was almost without precedent in the memory of the "oldest inhabitant" of the Law Courts of that time.

In November, 1868 George Jessel entered Parliament as a representative of Dover and "a strong supporter of Mr. Gladstone". He was not a success in Parliament, being considered too dry and dogmatic, lacking grace of delivery and boring the Members. However, in 1871 Mr. Gladstone had an opportunity of testifying his appreciation and George was called upon to accept the position of Solicitor-General - an appointment which, as a daily newspaper pointed out at the time, was rendered inevitable by the "force of intellect" which the comparatively young Queen's Counsel had shown. When, in 1873, Lord Romilly retired from the presidency of the Rolls Court, Sir George Jessel was acknowledged to have peculiar claims to the succession. He was the first Jew who, through a distinguished legal career, was enabled to reach the Judicial Bench. In August, 1873 he was sworn in as a Privy Councillor, and in November, 1875 became a Judge of the Supreme Court. In 1880, he became the first graduate to be elected by the Senate of the University of London as Vice-Chancellor.

He did have problems with the letter H and the story goes that when one day a patent case came before him concerning an air machine, he interrupted: "Wait a minute; do you mean the 'air of the 'ead or the hair of the hatmosphere?'"
At the Bar he never tried to make himself popular. On one occasion he was briefed to argue a case in the House of Lords from a decision of Lord Cairns and found his Lordship presiding over the appeal. Tactlessly he opened his case by saying it was an appeal from a judgement which, if it might not be thought disrespectful, he should call absurd. He had a reputation for being curt and for having unpolished manners and when Solicitor-General in the Court of Queen's Bench clashed immediately with Mr. Justice Blackburn, who interrupted him while reading an Act of Parliament. After this clash, no-one dared to interrupt him again.
Sir George Jessel's forte was in detail. Under the Judicature Act of 1873 a long series of rules of Court were drafted, which re-established a new code of practice for the Courts. He was chairman of the Committee of Judges, which supplied the draft, and took an active part in all modifications, and a member of the Royal Commission to inquire into the working of the Medical Acts. Before Sir George achieved the position of Master of the Rolls, it was not unusual for an undefended case to last many years. Sometimes whole families were ruined and estates remained undistributed for decades. The judgements of the new Master of the Rolls were quickly given, clear and short and hardly ever reversed on appeal. Business was despatched with a speed never before seen and Sir George Jessel became the organiser of the Court of Chancery in its present form.

Sir George died on 21st March, 1883, four days after taking to his bed, and five days after his last appearance at Court. At his death he was widely mourned. When the news came through to the Court of Appeal at the Royal Courts of Justice, Lord Justice Cotton, under feelings of strong emotion, referred to the great judicial knowledge and brilliant intellect which the Master of the Rolls displayed. The scene in Mr. Justice Chitty's court was affecting. On taking his seat the Bar rose, and their example was followed by every one in court.

Mr. Justice Chitty was unable to speak for some time, during which silence was observed, and he felt constrained to adjourn the court.
The funeral was attended by the Solicitor-General, a deputation from the Incorporated Law Society, several of the Benchers of the Honourable Society of Lincoln's Inn and the Prime Minister sent a kind message to condolence to Lady Jessel.
Many were the anecdotes told of Sir George Jessel after his death. The Times referred to Sir George's trial of the Epping Forest suit. This case lasted twenty two days, a length of time unparalleled in the history of his court. The lords of nearly a score of manors were defendants, and about an equal number of counsel appeared. The documents to be considered reached back to the reign of King John; nearly one hundred and fifty witnesses were examined. But judgement was delivered immediately on conclusion of the argument, without a moment's hesitation or preparation and it put an end to all litigation.

The Solicitor's Journal, in its obituary notice, related one anecdote to show the deceased Judge's kindness to members of the junior Bar. A nervous junior once appeared at the Rolls with his first briefing. His leader was absent and he rose to suggest to the Court the case should be postponed. The Master of the Rolls asked the junior to state his case. When he had done so, he restated the case, putting it in the best light for parties represented by the junior. Having done this, he turned to the leader on the opposite side and said "That is the case you have to meet; now what have you got to say?"

The Right Hon. Sir R.J. Phillimore, Justice of the Probate, Divorce and Admiralty Division, took his leave of the Bar on the same day that the Master of the Rolls passed away. The following poem referring to this was published in Punch on the 30th March, 1883.

A light of Law, none stronger or more keen,
Quenched in death's stone shadow, to be seen,
A steadfast beacon of clear Right no more;
Lost matchless judgement, lost unrivalled lore,
The sharp, swift insight, the unerring skill,
The strong unbending and unshaken will,
That lived to high fame and pride of place
The virile scion of a virile race.
And even as men mourn their cold eclipse,
Another light extinguished not, yet slips
From the full gaze of countryman and friend,
They won great life yet brightens to the end,
Sad seem the lines that, on one morning, tell
Of Jessel's death and Phillimore's farewell.

Sir George had married in 1856 Amelia, eldest daughter of Joseph Moses of Montagu Square and Leadenhall Street. Eight weeks after his death, in recognition of his father's great services, a baronetcy was conferred on his eldest son, Charles James. His second son, Herbert Merton, Mayor of Westminster 1902-3, was named for political

The Opening of The Royal Courts of Justice 1882

services as Lord Jessel of Westminster, also took his seat in Parliament, and was mentioned in despatches. One of his grandsons and namesake, was severely wounded in the Great War, mentioned in despatches and received the M.C. Another grandson, the Hon. Edward Herbert Jessel, married in 1923 Helen Vane-Tempest Stewart, daughter of the 7th Marquess of Londonderry and filled the office of Deputy Speaker of the House of Lords 1963-77. Other members of the family who entered Parliament are Toby Jessel and Peter Jessel. The baronetcy, motto Perseverance, has been extinct since 1990.

Portraits of Sir George Jessel were published in the October, 1873 issue of the journal Queen and the May, 1880 issue of Men of Mark. In addition, a bust by W.R. Ingram can be seen in the Royal Courts of Justice.

It was the day after his seventieth birthday and Sir Francis Henry Goldsmid, Bart., M.P. for Reading, arrived at Waterloo Station at 7.45 p.m. and behind time. The carriage door opened before the train had stopped and the Baronet stepped from the carriage. The result may be imagined.

The funeral cortege of this eminent man consisted of a hearse drawn by four horses, forty mourning coaches and about fifty private carriages. In Reading every shop was either partially or completely closed on the morning of the funeral, and almost every window had their blinds drawn,

while the church bells were tolled. In the afternoon, the Mayor and Corporation assembled, the mace and insignia being draped in crepe, and a note of condolence to the widow was unanimously sent.

The Daily Telegraph, in a leader, commented that the deceased gentleman held a prominent place in society and was universally respected and, by those who knew him intimately, beloved. Following the death of Sir Frances, the President of the Board of Trade was asked in the House of Commons if he was prepared to obtain from Parliament powers to compel railway companies to so construct footboards of passenger carriages as to prevent a recurrence of such an accident.

At the inquest on the Baronet, the Superintendent Inspector at Waterloo Railway Station said he did not consider six inches was too wide a space between the carriage and the platform. The rules of the Company stated "No carriage door should be opened before the train stops or after the train starts". Mr. W. Napier, surgeon, said he was the medical attendant of the deceased. Since the accident he had been at Waterloo Station and had measured the distance between the floor off the platform and carriages. He found it was 31 inches in a direct line. There were two steps. The lower one was useless, being on a level with the platform or below it, and the higher one was a short iron step. The deceased was a short-sighted man, and he believed was under the impression the platform was of the usual depth. It was rarely he travelled on the South-Western line. The foreman of the jury said they were of the opinion the practice of opening carriage doors by porters was calculated to contribute to accidents and recommended some portion of the train should not be higher than the other, and the space of six inches between footboard and platform was greater than it should be. Such was the sad death of a very great man.

Sir Francis, the first ever Jewish Queen's Counsel, was second son of Sir Isaac Lyon Goldsmid, founder of University College, merchant banker and philanthropist, who had married his cousin, Isabel, daughter of Abraham Goldsmid, another well known philanthropist. He was born in Spital Square, London in 1808 and in 1833 was the first Jew to be called to the Bar, being allowed to take the oath on a copy of the Old Testament. Practising for a short time in the Chancery Court, he obtained silk in 1858 and a seat in Parliament in 1860 on behalf of the Liberals, relinquishing his connection with legal matters. He had advocated political emancipation for his co-religionists at a time when the battle for their being allowed to take up a seat in Parliament was being fought. In Parliament, he was greatly esteemed as the spokesman for Jewish affairs

Sir Francis had married in 1839 his cousin, Louisa Sophia, the only daughter of Moses Asher Goldsmid of London. After his death the baronetcy devolved upon his nephew, Julian Goldsmid, MP.

A drinking fountain to his memory was erected at the lower end of Leman Street, Whitechapel in 1879 bearing the following inscription: "This fountain was erected by Emma, wife of Nathaniel Montefiore, in memory of her brother, Sir Francis Henry Goldsmid, Bart., M.P. for Reading. Born May 1, 1808. Died May 2, 1878. Write me as one who loved his fellow men. - Leigh Hunt."
These two eminent Victorians played leading parts in the legal history of this country.

The new volume in The Jewish Victorian series, by Doreen Berger, containing genealogical information from the Jewish newspapers, including thousands of birth, marriage and death entries, is available from Robert Boyd Publications, 260 Colwell Drive, Witney, Oxfordshire OX8 7LW (BOYDPUBS@aol.com). The newest volume covers 1861 to 1870 and is on the same lines as the 1871-80 volume.

THE YORKSHIRE COAST

SUNDAY 14 SEPTEMBER

2003

FAMILY HISTORY

FAIR

SPA COMPLEX
SCARBOROUGH

10am to 5pm

Admission £2 Adults
accompanied children free

Greenfairs
PROMOTIONS

The Spa

Following the Paper Trail

Dave Obee

On a sunny afternoon in October, 1894, Charles H. Marble climbed into a hot-air balloon at the annual exhibition in New Westminster, British Columbia. The balloon rose high above the fair grounds, and over the nearby Fraser River. Marble's plan was to cross to the south side of the river, then descend to the ground by parachute.

But something went wrong, and he landed instead in the river itself. By the time rescuers could reach Marble, the young aeronaut in the pink tights was dead, although doctors tried for almost an hour to bring him back to life. Marble left behind a grieving mother and an angry stepfather. He also set in motion a paper trail that crossed into the United States from Canada, and serves a fine example of the potential of using newspapers for genealogical research. It's possible, using newspapers, to learn much about the life of a young man who died more than a century ago.

In family history research, official records are generally more accurate than newspaper accounts. The Marble case is a reminder that sometimes, the newspapers should be trusted, and the official accounts should be ignored.

It takes a bit of time to learn about Marble, following the paper trail in an attempt to discover the truth. Marble's name appears in a rather enticing entry in an index at the B.C. Archives in Victoria, an entry that demands further investigation. He died, according to the listing of coroner's inquests and inquiries, by "drowning in the Fraser River after descending by parachute from a balloon."

The balloon performance at New Westminster was typical of those at fairs throughout Europe and North America in the decades before the Wright Brothers got off the ground. Adventurers had been rising into the air in balloons, then descending using parachutes, since the late 18th century. The ascents had become among the most popular shows at exhibitions, with performers using a balloon inflated by burning wood and coal to rise high above the crowd, where they would perform trapeze stunts before descending by parachute. Marble did several stunts on the trapeze bar after setting off in the

balloon at about 4 p.m. on Wednesday, Oct. 10, 1894. Within a few minutes, however, he was dead.

The first reports in newspapers in both British Columbia and Washington were wrong. They reported that the victim of the drowning had been Prof. Soper, a man they said was a professional aeronaut from Saginaw, Michigan.

The Victoria Daily Colonist reported that the balloon had risen several thousand feet above the river, then slowly descended. The aeronaut should have dropped from the balloon, the newspaper said, but stayed with it all the way down. *"It was discovered afterwards that the parachute became entangled, and balloon, parachute and man fell into the river. A boat was quickly rowed to the spot and Soper was taken out of the water alive, but died within a few minutes,"* the Colonist said.

The mistake about the victim's name was understandable; the man who was supposed to be in the balloon was, in fact, named Soper. He had hired Marble to do the ascent in his place.

The coroner in New Westminster in 1894 was Capt. George Pittendrigh, a 63-year-old who had been heavily decorated during the Crimean War. In B.C., he tried farming, but didn't like it, so he took on virtually every public service position available in New Westminster. Along the way, he was married twice, and sired a grand total of 20 children.

Pittendrigh wasted no time in calling an inquisition into the death of Marble. He immediately appointed a jury of five local men, including foreman James Wise and jurors Patrick Fourney, John Ridley, William Crispin Loye and Henry Symcock. The inquisition started the day after Marble died, and the jury delivered its verdict 24 hours later. The star witness was the "professor" himself, Alfred Henry Soper, although he dropped any claim to the title for the duration of the legal proceedings. Soper's testimony — found in court documents — was, to be kind, self-serving.

"I have known the deceased Charles H. Marble for five or six weeks," he said. *"He came and asked me if I wanted an aeronaut. I said I had several jobs to carry out and if he was a first-class one I would employ him. He agreed to work for me."*

Soper said Marble told him he had made balloon ascents throughout California, and was well experienced in the stunt work required. At the New Westminster fair, Soper said, he watched Marble perform several stunts before his balloon ascent. Marble's performance on the trapeze bar

convinced Soper that Marble was a "first-class man".

The balloon, Soper said, was one of the best available, made from cotton the previous year in Seattle. It was 88 feet in diameter, and made to carry two people. He said it was in good repair, with only a few small holes near the mouth that had been caused by sparks from the burning wood that was used to propel the balloon into the sky. Soper said he cautioned Marble several times not to go into the water, but to cut loose from the balloon before he reached it. "He came to me before starting and said that he would cross to the other side of the river, but I told him not to do so as the wind was blowing strong and shifting. *I told him not to mind the balloon, but to cut away. He said it would be too short a distance and would spoil the exhibition, but I did not consent.*"

Marble tied himself to the bar on the balloon with a rope, then set off. It rose into the air, then went east and south from the fair grounds, on the north side of the Fraser.

Soper said he saw the balloon start to come down, and the parachute opened partially. But Marble did not, he said, cut away from the balloon on time, so the parachute could not open properly. Soper also said Marble could have descended safely by holding on to the bar of the balloon as it came down. "*I think the deceased was sensible when he struck the water,*" he said.

Soper said it was *"usual, in some cases"* to have a boat on the water in case a balloon came down there, but he had not arranged for one because he had cautioned Marble not to go to the river. He also said he had employed two people to follow Marble on horseback, and help the young aeronaut if he struck a tree or any other object. *"I wanted to provide him with a life preserver and was going to town to purchase one when he said, "You need not go for if you get one I will not put it on as I am a first-class aeronaut."*

What was Marble paid? Soper didn't really answer. *"The wages of an aeronaut varies from 10 to 25 dollars a day. I boarded the deceased from the time he first asked me to employ him."*

William Huston, New Westminster's chief of police, also testified. He said he had been present at the filling of the balloon, and spoke with Marble. *"I warned him of the danger of going onto the river and asked him if he could swim. He said that he could, but there would be no necessity for it as he would land across the river,"* Huston told the jury.

"I said as soon as he would strike the centre of the river that he would find the wind changed and that it would be blowing up the river. He said, in that case, he would be able to swing her over so as to reach the other side. "I saw his performance on the bar and I thought he was doing all right," Huston said.

William Charles Bournes, who was fishing on the Fraser when Marble went in, told the jury he saw the balloon coming toward the river from the park at New Westminster. *"The man who was attached to the parachute appeared to be struggling and seemed to me to attempt to climb a rope up towards the top of the parachute. After this I noticed that the whole affair was descending towards the river,"* Bournes said. *"As soon as I knew of the danger of it coming into the river I rowed towards it as fast as I could."*

Bournes said Marble appeared to be sitting on the bar of the parachute. As he went into the water, the parachute fell on top of him. *"I saw him struggling in the water from the time of seeing the balloon, if he had cut away from it then he would have fell into the river."* Bournes said there was another boat about five chains (about 100 yards) from where the balloon came into the river. *"When I got there the men in the other boat had got hold of the parachute and had it partly in their boat. I saw them fiddling with the lines and made them pull in another line."*

Pulling that line brought Marble's body to the surface. Bournes said the aeronaut appeared to be dead when he was taken from the water. He said a rope about 20 feet long and three-eighths of an inch thick connected the parachute to a belt around Marble's body. "I cut the rope about six or eight feet from the body. It appeared to be attached to a ring in the belt", Bournes said. He also removed Marble's belt.
"I took the body into my boat and took him ashore and sent for a doctor", Bournes said.

The physician was Dr. Hugh M. Cooper, a Toronto native who had served in the field during the Civil War in the United States. Ironically, he had also worked for a time in Saginaw, Michigan, the city Soper had claimed as his home. *"A man rode to my office and told me I was wanted on the river bank opposite the asylum,"* Cooper told the jury. The doctor said he was told that *"the man who went up*

in the balloon has fallen in the river and was nearly drowned."

"I hastened to the place, and on Front Street met some men bringing a body in an express wagon. I made a slight examination of the body and considered it dead but ordered it to be taken to the first place they could find to heat it and I would . meet them there."

The men took Marble to the Guichon Hotel, where Cooper and the new doctor in town, Dr. George E. Drew, *"used all effort at restoration",* as Cooper described it, for nearly an hour. *"My opinion is that the man died by drowning,"* he said.

The jury agreed with Cooper, and further declared that Marble had died "accidentally, casually and by misfortune" by drowning and suffocating in the waters of the Fraser. The jury declined to attach blame to anyone. It did recommend, however, that the boatmen who recovered Marble's body from the water should get $5 each.

The inquisition left many questions unanswered. Was Marble really an experienced aeronaut? What was he really paid? Why were the two men who reached him first not called to testify? And, most important of all, who was he?

The official records in B.C. have little information on Marble. He was, the death registration said, 26 years old, and had been born in Los Angeles, California. There is nothing on his family or his background, beyond what little Soper told the jury.

There's a story to be told, however, using the newspapers of the day.

For a start, the Columbian, New Westminster's daily newspaper, offered eyewitness accounts of Marble's death. It said Marble, who went by the name Dr. Ray when performing, performed several daring feats on the trapeze bar when he was a few hundred feet in the air. The strap on his belt secured him, so he would not fall more than a few feet if he lost hold.

Marble continued his performance until the balloon had reached 1,500 feet or more, when the balloon

slowly started to return to the ground. Witnesses said it appeared Marble was trying to reach the opposite side of the river, but the balloon started dropping faster and faster. As a result, it was only 50 or 60 feet above the water when Marble was still just halfway across the river.

Marble then cut loose the parachute, and was seen to be hanging with his head down when he struck the water. *"If this is the case, it would indicate that he was in a state of collapse from fear or some other cause,"* the Columbian said. The aeronaut was enveloped by the parachute when he hit the water, making it impossible for him to swim.

The newspaper account offers the only clue as to why the first two people on the scene had not been called to testify to the jury. It had to do with race. *"Two Indians, in a fishing boat, went to the drowning man's assistance,"* it said. Marble *"had ceased struggling when rescued, although his heart was still beating and his body warm,"* the newspaper said.

The reporter who attended the inquisition noted that Marble's face *"bore a calm and natural expression."* No bruises were visible. The Columbian said Marble had friends in Edison, Wash., and his remains were to be sent there.

In Victoria, the Daily Colonist also had a further report on Marble's death, as well as on his activities prior to the ascent. *"The hero of the afternoon strutted about in his pink tights among the moving mass of humanity,"* said the Colonist, which also reported some of the comments made by spectators: *"There's the fool that's going to risk his neck in a balloon", "Such things shouldn't be allowed", "He gets $300 for three ascensions",* and *"He'll drop in the river, for sure."*

Marble was apparently oblivious to the comments as he continued his preparations. *"The immense canvas monster of the air was put in position, a few holes sewn up, and a wood and coal fire built underneath, so that smoke, gas and all entered the balloon, and slowly, very slowly, the great bulk swelled, Marble inspecting minutely every detail,"* the Colonist said.

By 4 p.m., the balloon was full, and a crowd of about 8,000 people had gathered. *"The guys were loosened and the balloon ascended swift as a rocket,"* the newspaper said. *"First the large bulk, then yards of rope, then the folded parachute, then more yards of rope, then a trapeze, and dangling in the air at the end of all was the figure of Marble."*

Within seconds, Marble was performing trapeze stunts for the crowd, who *"silent as death kept their fascinated yet unwilling eyes on the daring aeronaut."* The crowd expected Marble would open the parachute and leave the balloon, which would then collapse and fall to the ground. But he stayed with it all the way down, until trees blocked the view of the crowd. One of the spectators protested, saying Marble should not be paid a cent since he hadn't done the parachute drop that had been advertised.

"Then the crowd of thoughtless humanity forgot about the man and his balloon and lined about the fence to watch the match in progress between the seniors from Vancouver and New Westminster," the Colonist reported. The newspaper was critical of the efforts made to revive Marble. It was a mistake to take him to a warm room, it said, because when death by drowning is possible the patient *"should always be attended in the open air."*

The Colonist added a bit more information about Marble and Soper. Marble was from Seattle, and was employed by Soper, who was originally from Saginaw, Mich., but now lived in the Puget Sound area of Washington. Marble was about 21 years old, the newspaper said, and had a mother and stepfather. The stepfather was identified as George Cook, an insurance agent in Auburn, Wash.

The Colonist said Marble had been hired for the paltry sum of $10, with Soper planning to pocket the $300 for himself. *"There is no doubt that Marble has never made a balloon ascension before,"* the newspaper said. *"Soper admits that he did everything wrong, got rattled, and waited too long before he dropped, and the doctors finish matters by saying that Marble was not drowned, his heart having stopped, or nearly so, before he touched the water " that he died from the shock, probably being frightened to death."*

The day after Marble's death, Soper hired another daredevil to go up in the balloon. They had already started inflating it when customs officers seized it, with a demand for the payment of $24.

The following day, another aeronaut went up without incident. He was identified in the press only as a quiet-mannered German named Markeberg. The ascent had been, he said, his 138th. Another ascent the next day was scrubbed with the balloon only about 100 feet in the air, because "a blundering onlooker" became entangled in the ropes. Markeberg offered a bit more information about Marble, saying the dead aeronaut had worked as his assistant for a long time.

On Saturday, three days after Marble died, the Victoria Times reported that Marble's body was to be shipped to Tacoma for burial. It had been held in New Westminster for two days, the Times said, because Soper had been unable to pay the undertaker's expenses.

The next step in researching Marble is to check the newspapers from Tacoma, Wash. One newspaper account had said Marble's body was being shipped to Tacoma for burial; another had said Marble's stepfather worked in an insurance business in

Auburn, which is a few miles east of Tacoma. A third had said Marble had friends in Edison, which is in South Tacoma.

The Tacoma Ledger reported soon after the accident that Marble was from Auburn, and Soper had a restaurant in Seattle. The following day, it said Marble was actually "a Tacoma boy", who had been working at a restaurant in Seattle. The Ledger identified his stepfather as A.A. Cook, of Edison. It was the Tacoma Morning Union, however, that turned Marble's death into a major news story. It said Marble was about 20 years old, with no experience in ballooning. He had fired for Soper during ascensions at Edison, and Soper had hired him to work in a restaurant in Seattle with the understanding that Marble would go up in the balloon when needed.

"Friends of the family of A.A. Cook are indignant, and seemingly justly so," the paper said, because they believed Soper was *"directly responsible for the death of Charles Marble."*

The Morning Union said Soper was to have received $200 for the ascent in New Westminster. Marble had told a doctor in Edison that he was to receive $75 for his work. But Soper was now saying that Marble was to have received only $10, and Soper refused to pay it in any event. Soper had notified Marble's family of his death by sending a telegram collect. Cook, Marble's stepfather, asked for the body to be sent to Tacoma, but Soper refused to do so until he received $65 to cover the costs.

The Morning Union said Marble knew nothing about ballooning, "and more than any other boy who had never had anything to do with such a vehicle save make a fire under it."

Cook *"is very much exercised over the death of his stepson and the manner in which it occurred. It is said he will prosecute Soper if he returns to this side of the line,"* the newspaper said.

(After Marble's body was finally brought to Tacoma, the Morning Union wrote that his face bore "the flush of youth", and he seemed to be merely asleep. Twice, the report referred to Marble as being Soper's "victim")

The newspaper trail then leads to Seattle, where the Press-Times reported that Marble had been in the city for about two weeks, working as a dishwasher at the Michigan Restaurant at 216 Washington Street. Marble was 21, and had previously worked as a driver for C.P. Lacey of Auburn. He had planned to leave for California soon. The following day, the Press-Times was critical of Soper, in a roundabout way. "The telegraphic report of the death of young Marble at Vancouver, falling from a balloon, states that the aeronaut, Soper, testified that Marble was an experienced aeronaut," it said. "That must be a mistake of the reporter, for Marble was a dishwasher in Mr. Soper's 10-cent restaurant, the Michigan, on Washington Street, and he was a total stranger to the professor when he went to work there, the proprietor being ignorant of his name, even, for several days after employing him."

When Soper returned to Seattle, the newspaper interviewed him. The account appeared in the Press-Times five days after Marble died. *"He applied to me for work and said that he was without a cent to buy a meal; he wanted work in my restaurant and said nothing about having any profession or trade,"* Soper said. *"I did not require any additional help, but I told him to eat at the Michigan and to help about the place whenever he could be useful, and during the rush at meal time if he happened to be around."*

Soper said that when Marble learned that Soper had a job in British Columbia, he told both Soper and Soper's wife that he was an experienced aeronaut and trapeze performer who had done more than 20 ascensions under the name Charles Ray, and that he billed himself as Professor Ray.

"He wanted to go in with me on the job I had and I agreed to give him a certain amount of the profits of the exhibition. I had a contract for three

ascensions at so much for each. I paid his way there and all the expenses and gave him some cash on account, but one ascension was made and I sustained an actual loss, so that there would not have been anything whatever due him."

Soper claimed to have been in the business for 30 years, and said Marble was *"the finest trapeze performer I ever saw in the air."* He said that in New Westminster, he had used his hat and his cane in a vain attempt to signal Marble to drop from the balloon. *"I never had a greater grief. I sent his body home, but I had to beg the money of strangers, as I was broke from my losses there. His stepfather wired me at my expense to send the body home in a rough box, but I would not do that. I am well regarded in Seattle and I do not wish to be regarded as careless or heartless."*

"I was as blameless in the matter as you were," Soper said. Cook didn't see it quite the same way. The Tacoma Daily News reported that Cook had written to New Westminster's mayor, Henry Hoy, alleging that Soper was guilty of murder in the death of Marble. *"Cook says that his son was not of age, and had had no experience with balloons. He was working in a restaurant in Seattle for Soper, and was persuaded by him to make the ascent for $75."*

Cook said Soper was a fraud, with no practical knowledge, who always hired someone else to make ascents. His efforts to have Soper charged with murder would prove to be in vain, given that the coroner's jury in New Westminster had already determined the death was an accident, and that the chief of police was one of the witnesses for the jury.

Marble was buried in Tacoma.

The newspapers don't tell everything about him, of course, but the 1880 census can be used to fill in a few details. A.A. Cook and his wife, known simply as E.J. Cook, were enumerated in Georgiana, Sacramento County, California. They were listed with three of E.J.'s sons: George W. Marble, J.H. Marble, and Charles A. (not H.) Marble, as well as their one-year-old daughter, Mattie E. Cook. Charles Marble was six years old at the time of the census, so the newspaper accounts listing his age as 20 or 21 were accurate. His birthplace was Massachusetts, although his family was originally from Maine.

The official records in British Columbia contain only two details about Marble — *his age and birthplace* — and both are wrong. A researcher relying on official documents would have hit a dead end; newspaper accounts, however, provided valuable clues about Marble's origins.

When several newspapers are used together, it's possible to learn a lot about people such as Charles

Marble. There were errors, large and small, in several of the newspaper accounts (the errors don't end there; it's likely Marble's middle initial is not correct in the census). But used in conjunction with one another, a solid collection of facts can be assembled. It pays, of course, to compare the various accounts, and determine which ones are using original reporting, and which ones are simply repeating information contained in other newspapers.

An error doesn't become a fact just because it's carried in more than one publication. The last word on Marble's death belongs to The Province, a magazine published in Victoria:

"These balloon ascents with parachute attachment are dangerous and useless. They serve no better purpose than the one-man power cockle shells which periodically cross the Atlantic, and they should not be allowed. The public will go for miles to see an exhibition provided there is a fair probability of being in at the death of a fellow creature who risks his life at their amusement; but the spectacle is not an elevating one, quite the reverse."

Dave Obee is a genealogical lecturer and one of the owners of Interlink Bookshop and Genealogical Services of Victoria, British Columbia, Canada

HERALDRY · CALLIGRAPHY & ILLUMINATION

Family Trees · Coats of Arms · Poems · Charts · Maps

written and painted using fine quality materials.

For further details, prices and samples please contact:

MARIE LYNSKEY

109 Nutcroft Grove, Fetcham, Surrey. KT22 9LD Tel. 01372 372334

Website: http://www.ml.clara.net

Cornwall Family History Society

Cornwall has many advantages for the family historian – it's unique! Unique in history because the people have always been aware of being separate from England, unique in emigration patterns mostly because of the worldwide mining community, and even unique in its shape as Cornwall is only linked with one other county.

During the second half of the nineteenth century, almost twenty five per cent of the population of Cornwall emigrated. As well as those who crossed the River Tamar to England, the Cornish left in large numbers for the United States of America, Australia, Canada, New Zealand, Central and South America and later to South Africa. It has been estimated that there are some six million folk around the world with Cornish ancestors, and as the Cornish have very strong traditions of family and worship, the overseas communities have maintained strong identities. There are many overseas Cornish associations who hold regular gatherings, and are thriving and expanding their interests.

At the same time, the Cornish are fierce individualists – just ask for the proper pasty recipe, you'll get several, all different, all the genuine original, and if you want to hear a truly fierce academic argument, ask about the old Cornish language! When speaking to a true Cornish man or woman, you must always be aware of the difference between Cornwall and England – the phrase 'going up England' is still heard occasionally. It follows that if you have a Cornish ancestor, there's a welcome awaiting.

So it is perhaps not surprising that Cornwall was one of the first counties to set up a Family History Society, founded in 1976, a Society which has become one of the largest with over 5000 members, and certainly one of the most wide-spread with a very high proportion of the membership outside UK. We are very fortunate in having our own premises in the centre of Truro, housing our Library which is open to the public. We have one full time employee, our hard-working Secretary, so there will always be someone to take your phone call or answer your email or letter.

Cornwall FHS has always had a very enthusiastic group of volunteers, some staffing our library, some working at providing information for our members by post and email, and many beavering away at transcription of original records. We have built up a good working relationship with our County Record Office, and are working hard at extending links with all groups interested in family and local history in Cornwall. We were one of the first Societies to invest in computer equipment, and have built up an extensive database of some three million items which is growing continuously.

We have recently invested in a broadband internet connection to speed up communications.

Like many family history societies, our library is packed with information. We have on fiche the full set of census returns for Cornwall, the full set of General Record Office (GRO) indexes, the complete International Genealogical Index (IGI) as well as many other sources. As work progresses on transcription, an increasing amount of this information has been indexed and is available on our database. We also have a large number of publications on local history and many individual family pedigrees deposited by our members.

With such an extended membership 'family', Cornwall FHS is noticing the effects of modern communications very quickly. We have a high proportion of our membership with internet access, and partly because of this and partly because of the head start we have with our large genealogical database, Cornwall FHS is one of the first family history societies to join the Federation of Family History Societies' new online service. This is perhaps the most exciting event in recent years for family history, and Cornwall is proud to be up with the best.

At the same time, we shall never forget our members who prefer not to join the electronic revolution, so our large range of paper publications will continue to extend. We are proud of our quarterly Journal, some forty pages of interest and information, with a good mix of the academic and the homely, and a selection of appropriate advertising. The 'Helping Hands' section is always popular and an entry there always seems to bring a response. The Journal is packed for posting by another group of enthusiastic volunteers in a village hall once a quarter before being despatched to (almost) all corners of the world.

We have established a presence on the internet with our website. This site will probably change in response to the new online information service, but at the moment provides information to members regarding their research interests and many contact links. Do have a look at http://www.cornwallfhs.com

For those of our members living in Cornwall, we have monthly meetings to listen to an interesting range of speakers. A new innovation is a short course on using computers for family history. We ran our first half day recently at Truro College, and this was greeted with such enthusiasm by those attending that the next one will be a full day.

The Society holds its annual general meeting in

November each year, when we take over a hotel for the weekend, so that this becomes a family history fair as well. The meetings can be lively, and the 'chat' goes on well into each evening.

Cornwall FHS has links with other societies in the area as a member of the South West Area Group. This group is busy organising its next conference to be held in Exeter in April 2003. In cooperation with other groups, our Society contributes to several gatherings in England and Wales through the year, and had a prominent part to play in the Dehwelans Cornish Homecoming held at Falmouth in May 2002.

One aspect of a family history society that is often overlooked is its social side. Members, especially our volunteers living locally, form good friendships. All visitors to the Library are warmly welcomed, and correspondence with members overseas, especially in these days of rapid email communications, has extended this to our wider membership.

However far away you live, you are sure to visit Cornwall one day – do make sure that we are on your list of 'must see' places. So, when you visit the cathedral city of Truro, pop in to our Library, it's next to Malletts – ask any shopper. The Library is open every weekday except Tuesdays, (our work day), from 10.a.m. to 4 p.m.on Monday, 11 a.m. to 3 p.m.Wednesday to Saturday. You'll be greeted with a smile and an offer of help.

Successful Writing
for Family and Local History Publications
Simon Fowler

If you've fascinated by history, then you might be able to exploit this interest by writing about an ancestor or an aspect of local history that interests you. Why keep all this to yourself when there are people out there who want to read about the people and places you have researched. In this article I give some tips about how to start, to write interesting articles, and to get editors to accept your pieces.

If you think you've got an idea for an article you can either write it up and submit it on spec or contact the editor to see whether they might be interested in commissioning the piece. Personally, I'm always happy to discuss ideas with potential writers. However, if you are uncertain of yourself you might want to submit something cold – although here you risk seeing hours of hard work wasted if it is rejected.

You can increase your chance of acceptance by doing your research before hand, so that you have a good idea of the sort of articles that the magazine already publishes and the style in which they are written. It's no good, for example, sending a local family history society an article about an ancestor who didn't have a link with the area. However good the piece might be the editor is unlikely to be interested. So spend a few minutes reading your target journal to see whether what you propose fits in with what they cover and the approach that they use.

First impressions are important, particularly when sending stuff to commercial magazines (see below). Simple rules to follow when submitting manuscripts are:
• Always submit a typed copy, clearly laid out, wide margins, double space, with the title of piece and author's name at the beginning.
• Check for spelling and basic proof reading errors. It is particularly important to get historical dates and spelling of names correct, otherwise you spread doubts in the editor's mind about the accuracy of the rest of the article.
• Keep the piece short – few magazines or journals publish articles longer than 2000-3000 words. Most family and local history society journal articles are 1000 words or less.
It's often a good idea to include a short bibliography about the subject. It should contain no more than half-a-dozen books or record sources you have consulted, a couple of relevant web sites, and perhaps a useful address or two. And a short biographical note about yourself should reinforce the point that you are knowledgeable about the

subject you've written about. If the magazine is illustrated you can suggest possible pictures or offer to supply illustrations for inclusion.

Writing interesting articles is difficult. There's no real short cut: good writing is a skill, every bit as difficult as conducting historical research. And like historical research, however, everybody thinks it's easy, but you've got to practice. It's a good idea to try to emulate a journalist or writer whose pieces you enjoy reading. My old history teacher recommended George Orwell for the clarity of expression and simple style. You might want to read a couple of his collected essays to see why. However do not be tempted to copy the style of the tabloid press or thriller writers. It is both almost impossible to imitate them successfully and is, in any case, it is an inappropriate style to adopt for a respectable journal or magazine.

The most interesting articles are:
• Simply and clearly written. The old adage applies here as so often in life: KISS (Keep It Simple Stupid). Use short sentences with one idea in each and fairly short paragraphs (containing 4 or 5 sentences). Don't forget to use short words rather than their long Latinate equivalents, as they are easier to understand.

• Do not engage in flights of fancy or speculation, although this should not stop you being analytical where appropriate (that is interpreting and explaining what and why something has happened). You should be able to justify and provide evidence for any assertion. Remember Occam's Razor: the simplest explanation is normally the correct one.
• Enjoyable to read, and the reader finishes it having learnt something new or had to reassess their previous knowledge of the subject.
• Offers a clear narrative structure, with a beginning, a middle and end. The beginning indicates what you are going to write about and why you are doing it, the middle tells the story, and the end summarises what went before and underlines your conclusion. It's all too easy to write something that is meaningless without realising it.
• Is to the point, that is does not introduce irrelevant points, or become repetitious.
• Takes a fresh approach avoiding the obvious, particularly on well-covered subjects.
• It uses plenty of good and fresh examples to illustrate and support the story you are telling.
• Avoids cliché, current slang, abbreviations and jargon. Both cliché and slang date easily, while jargon mystifies the reader- exactly what you are trying to avoid. Sometimes, particularly with articles on computers and the internet, it is unavoidable, however you should endeavour to explain abbreviations and jargon if you think your readers are unlikely to understand them.

There are very few history magazines, so it is very unlikely that you are going to make a fortune from writing solely on historical subjects. That said history and heritage magazines, of whatever kind, are always looking for interesting items.. The market-leaders (contact details below) are:

• *History Today* - which was founded as long ago as 1951. It is the most academic and the most prestigious. Most of their authors are established academics and historians, but they will take serious articles from lay writers.
• *BBC History Magazine* – is the new boy on the block and has by far and away the largest sales of any history magazine. They prefer shorter more approachable pieces on mainstream history.
• *Family Tree Magazine* – is the oldest British genealogical monthly and is also the best selling. Articles are generally short often with a personal theme, many of which are supplied by its readers.
Practical Family History – sister publication of Family Tree Magazine, designed for people new to the hobby. The articles it contains are not dissimilar to its sister but with more of a practical bias.
• *Family History Monthly* – probably the best genealogical magazine, although as it's editor I'm biased! Most articles look at subjects rather than take a personal approach.
• *Ancestors* – published by Britain's national archives, the Public Record Office, is attractively presented genealogical magazine. Articles are usually about the Office's immense collections of historical material and tend to be written by PRO staff. However they do commission articles and from ordinary users of the archive.

• *Local History Magazine* – is a bi-monthly magazine for local historians. It is an essential read for all local historians. However, from the writer's point of view it rarely pays for articles.

In addition, there are many magazines for enthusiasts, particular for people interested in railways, military history and aircraft. To write for them you need to be familiar with the subject matter. And of course there are a number of heritage magazines (national, regional and local) which commission articles from freelancers about the history of their areas they cover. Here again you will have to demonstrate familiarity both with the area and the subject. And of course every family and local history society produces a journal for members or sometimes with a wider circulation. You'll not get paid but it is both a good way to practise your writing skills and to tell people about what you are researching and why it fascinates you.

Contact details:
History Today 20 Old Crompton St, London W1D 4TW (020) 7534 8000
BBC History Magazine (52,000) 80 Wood Lane, London W12 077 (020) 8433 2433
Family Tree Magazine (40,000) 61 Great Whyte, Ramsey, Huntingdon PE26 1HJ (01487) 814050.
Practical Family History (10,000) As above
Family History Monthly (20,000) 45 St Mary's Rd, London W5 5RQ Tel: (020) 8579 1082
*The Family and Local History Handboo*k (10,000) 33 Nursery Road, Nether Poppleton, York YO26 6NN
Ancestors (4,000) PO Box 38, Richmond TW9 4AJ
Local History Magazine (2,000) 3 Devonshire Parade, Lenton, Nottingham NG7 2DS (0115) 970 6473.

Simon Fowler is editor of Family History Monthly and has written many books and articles on local and family history.

Electronic Self Publishing for pleasure or profit?

David Tippey

When a printed book was the only option, publishing your own family or local history was a very costly affair, the computer has now changed all that and we can all now indulge ourselves by publishing the results of our hard work to share with others. We have all learnt that our research is never really complete, you can always find something to add, but the beauty of self publishing your work is that it can be easily and cheaply updated when you make any significant new discoveries. Some people like to create a website, which can then be regularly added to, but these all too easily cease to be available, as anyone who uses the web regularly will know. Once printed, your work could easily be available in 100 or more years time if you use good quality materials, and there is yet another option, the CD or DVD. These may not be accessible in 100 years, but they are more durable than a website and offer lots of interesting possibilities not available to conventional publishers.

Whether your ambition is just to share your work with family and friends or to dabble in small scale commercial publishing, you can easily write, edit and print a short booklet on your own computer. It's fairly simple to put together an A5 booklet of 30 pages or so. This size of publication can be printed on a standard A4 printer, folded and stapled with a printed card cover added. The results can look very professional, indeed some small scale publishers do just this, as it's easily possible to make 50 -100 copies per run on a laser printer.
The most difficult part, apart from deciding what to include, is in putting together the pages correctly so they are in the correct sequence when folded. Professional publishing programs can make this job easier, but you could use a simpler program such as ClickBook which works with your wordprocessor files and does the arranging for you.
Larger volumes are a little more difficult, although not impossible to make this way. You would have to print the book as a series of booklets and then get them professionally bound, still a much cheaper option than traditional small scale publishing.
Most people own an A4 printer and you can realistically only make A5 format books unless you use a commercial binder to perfect bind the result. This is where the pages are held together by glue along the spine. I'm not too keen on the system as the books often fall to pieces when used regularly. However an A3

printer offers the scope to print larger books up to A4 and if you get a print shop to guillotine the paper to size for you, the square, 2/3 A4 format can look very attractive, offering the extra space needed for more interesting page design.

The cost of the individual books can still be quite high when you take into account all the materials, especially colour ink jet cartridges, but you only pay for as many copies as you need and can always run off a couple of extra ones when required. However you don't have to publish in the traditional manner, now that CD burners are cheap you can publish your book on a CD and the material cost will only be £1 or so per copy. Using a CD also allows you to include material such as sound recordings and film clips, even add web links, none of which can be included in a conventional book. However it doesn't really matter which method of publishing you choose, the bulk of the writing and page design functions are more or less the same.

You will need a selection of programs to create a book, some of which you should already have; a good word processor which allows complete control over layouts, text and graphics or a publishing program such as PageMaker or MS Publisher are essential. So too is a graphics program such as PhotoShop or PaintshopPro, to edit the photographs and other graphics you want to include. A family history program can provide the reports to base a family history on, plus provide a variety of charts, but a specialist charting program such as Tree Draw will probably make a better job of pedigrees for publishing and they will be in the standard English format too.
It's one thing to create your book with the programs on your machine, but when you distribute it has to be in a format which everyone else can use. It is possible to create a CD book like a website, using HTML documents. The problem with this is that HTML is just a set of instructions to create a page and what looked wonderful on your browser could look completely different on a another machine. The most versatile and widely used publishing file system is the Adobe Acrobat PDF file, which enables your pages to be viewed exactly as you created them, no matter what platform or machine they are viewed on. This is a secure, cross platform system with free reader software available for a wide variety of computers. There are several shareware packages that will

convert documents to the Acrobat. PDF format, but having the full Adobe program allows you to do a lot of further work on PDF files once converted, offering many advantages to the home publisher over simple file conversion utilities.

If you want to add multimedia files to your CD then Quicktime Pro is a cheap and easy to use program which can make slide shows, movies and sound files which are compatible with Acrobat and can be imported into a PDF file or linked with it.

All your writing could be done on a good wordprocessing package such as Word, although publishing programs are usually easier to work with when it comes to page layout. It helps if you can establish a standard layout and type style at the outset, which you then just fill with the text and graphics. Before you can layout your pages, you first need to think about what exactly you are going to publish and formulate some ideas on how you are going to group the information. A family genealogy based purely on one of the reports from a family history program probably wouldn't make very interesting reading for others whose enthusiasm for the subject may not be as strong as yours. However the book style or narrative reports can be used as the basis of a more lively text, helping you to keep events in sequence as you write. You need to break all the information

down into chapters which could be organised by location, generation or family group for example. Local histories could be grouped around families, buildings, events or arranged along a timeline.

You now need to bring together the material you are going to use and start to write the basic text for each chapter. A good way to organise yourself is to make a list of all the chapter headings and then a list of contents for each one, both points to be covered in the text and illustrations. This gives you a framework to write on and will help stop you losing the direction and focus of your writing. Family historians will probably want to consult local and social history material to find interesting details to flesh out the bare facts about the family. A little about where they lived, their occupations and how it fitted in the local economy and the major events that happened in their lifetime, can all be used to add interest to the bare facts about earlier ancestors who are beyond family oral or written records. As you get nearer to the present you will probably have much more anecdotal material to work on, but consider carefully what you use, you don't want to upset anyone unnecessarily.

You will need sufficient charts, maps, photographs, documents and possibly multimedia clips to clarify the text and make the whole project more interesting and readable. Nothing looks more forbidding than page after page of solid black text, no matter how good the content is, so make sure you have enough supporting material, although for many it will be a case of deciding what should be left out, which can be more difficult. This isn't the same problem in CD publishing, as you can easily accommodate it all, but be selective and only include the best and most relevant, or you may put off your readers. By incorporating Quicktime files into your PDF document you can add music or oral history from tape recordings. You can also create slide shows from old photos, so rather than have just a single illustration on a page, that could become a link to a slide show about that person or family. Old cine film can be converted too, several firms offer a service, they can then be incorporated on the CD and linked to the relevant part of the document.

Having gathered everything together and written at least the first draft of your book, so you have some idea of it's length, you can turn your attention to it's presentation. A book published on a CD is very similar to the printed version and the design and layout of the pages is just as important. Rather too many booklets from family and local historians alike, look like average parish magazine, hastily duplicated and stapled together in coloured card covers. The cramped A5 format usually adopted for these is the main culprit for this, as it is very difficult to create interesting pages in such a small space. Spend some time in a good book shop or the library and find some examples of eye catching good book design, then borrow their layout ideas. Pages do not have to be full to capacity with text and graphics, incorporate some blank, white space in your design, it's easier on the eye. A typical A5 print area placed on a 2/3 A4 page with a wide margin, looks far better than a cramped standard A5 page. It also leaves a space for notes and for photos or graphics to expand into when necessary. Keep the typography simple, don't use too many fonts, I would suggest trying to stick with two; a display typeface for all your headings and titles and one for the text which also gives you the option using bold or italic lettering. It's generally accepted that text with serifs, for example Times and Garamond, makes the main text easier to read. Again follow the lead of the book designs which caught your eye.

With your basic page design decided and the text written you can now import all the text and position the graphics, trying to achieve a balanced look throughout the whole book, whilst keeping the supporting illustrations somewhere near the relevant area of text. Having got the first version assembled you can

carry on polishing both the text and the layout until you are happy with the final result. Don't forget to create a content page and index, these will be later linked using the features in Acrobat to give faster access to your electronic book. If you are going to include multimedia Quicktime files you need to decide how they are to be used and if necessary to incorporate buttons in the design, which will be used to trigger and play the files in the final PDF. For instance you could use one frame of the movie in your page layout and then make that the link to trigger the movie.

When you are happy that the text and graphics are done, the file can be converted into a PDF using Acrobat Distiller or the PDF writer depending on what program you used to create your original file. If you made each chapter a separate document, convert them all into PDF versions then Open the first with Acrobat and Insert each chapter, so that you end up with one complete file, which is easier to handle. You can now create Acrobat bookmarks to help you navigate the book, but it's neater just to have one or two to take you to the content and index pages or the beginning of chapters. All the items on your contents page can be made into links which will take you direct to that section and if you wished you could also do that with the index, but that may be a rather longer job. The multi media links are also created at this point, sound files are embedded in the PDF but movies aren't and you need to create a link to the associated movie file. With everything complete, give it a thorough testing, preferably asking a few other people to try it for problems. If you are creating your CD on a Windows machine and want to make sure it can be read on others such as a Mac, keep the file names as short as possible. If your CD has more than one file on it, long filenames are the main reason that links don't work on other machines, change them to the old DOS style or shorter, and your PDF external file links should work correctly. Don't forget that making your CD Autorun will only work on the same operating system, so make sure it's obvious where the starting point is for users of other machines.

It only remains to set the security settings before you are ready to actually burn your book onto CD. These are optional but they can be set to prevent anyone altering the text or selecting parts to copy and you can also prevent unauthorised printing if you wish.

Your final task is to design an attractive CD label and the jewel case inserts. Put the same effort into this as the rest of the design, they want to reflect the style of the book and make people want to read it. All that remains then is to get the finished book to your target audience, be it Christmas wrapped for the family or on sale in the local book shops. The latter will entail lots of legwork and promotion, you are unlikely to make your fortune, but hopefully you will make an important contribution to local or family knowledge.

Bibliography

TOMBO MEDIA have an excellent website and tutorial CD about electronic family history publishing.
www.tombomedia.com

The Sunshine Press publish a very nicely designed CD book on using Photoshop for genealogy and the author's website has some sample pages to give you ideas. A new book on presentation of research is due out soon.
www.sunshinepress.com
www.photosforgenealogy.com

Roy Stockdill has written a brief but useful guide to writing one-name journals and newsletters called "From the Desktop". It has some very good tips on design and layout and is published by the Guild of One-Name Studies.
www.one-name.org
© David Tippey 2001
The right of David Tippey to be identified as the author of this work has been asserted in accordance with the Copyright Designs and Patents Act 1988

Expect the Unexpected

Kate Thompson

One of the joys of family history is finding information in unusual and unlooked for sources – serendipity at its best! This article provides a good example of valuable information hidden in an unlikely place.

The Saffron Walden Town Archive is currently stored in the town hall but as soon as it has been fully catalogued it will be transferred to the Essex Record Office (and a digitised version made available in the town). Inevitably it contains material relating to other activities in the town as well as the records of the Town Council, and includes records of the Essex Regiment prisoners of war fund from the first world war [ref D/B2/BRL8/26/1-85]. Over 1,000 men of the

Essex Regiment were prisoners of war and the fund was established to send food and clothing to them. Apparently the food provided by the Germans and Turks was barely sufficient to keep them alive and they were 'entirely dependent' on the parcels. The honorary secretary of the fund was Mrs Stephenson, the wife of Major-General Stephenson, and in one letter she asked for 'adopters' for each man, saying that the personal interest taken by those back at home and the letters they received were a great additional comfort.

There are three detailed letters from soldiers who were helped by the fund, written once they had been repatriated; they are in fact contemporary transcripts, helpfully typed, rather than the original letters. The first is from Ernest George Staddon, number 35093, 10th Essex Regiment, written on 13 February 1918 from King George's hospital, Waterloo (sub-number 27):

Being a returned prisoner from Germany with a broken leg I feel that I must write and thank you for all that you and your fund did for me while in Germany. I can assure you that if it had not been for your parcels, which we received regularly, three a fortnight we should have absolutely starved, as the small portions of food which the Germans gave us was more often than not impossible to eat, you have my heartfelt gratitude, and I sincerely hope that the good work which you are doing may continue, to make some of our poor fellows lives out there a little brighter, only those who have been there and suffered can really understand the true state of affairs.

The most detailed is from Private A J Wilkinson, number 32099, 13th Essex Regiment, written on 14 February 1918 from Chelmsford (sub-number 28):

I write in answer to your kind letter. I do hope you will not think me a long time in answering [it] I cannot write much at a time you see it makes my eye ache, I have only one and I must not strain it too much so I have to write a little bit at a time but am only too pleased to do as you ask in return for the great kindness you have done for me. I will tell you right from where I was captured till I left Germany. We went over the top took our position stayed there about three hours when the Germans counter-attacked us: we had the order to retire but the Germans were all round us nobody knew where they came from we fought our way back as far as we could when I was hit by a bomb by one of the Germans which knocked me out for five or ten minutes I picked my rifle up and saw the German which hit me in a shell hole I fired at him hitting him through the fore-head then I tried to get back to our own lines killing about half a dozen on my

way then to my surprise I was surrounded by quite three dozen of them, I was so weak with loss of blood I had to give in else be killed they pulled my equipment off took my rifle jack knife and several other things left me with just what I stood up in the cruel beasts made me march over five killermeteros [sic]. I was so weak and exhausted I dropped like a log then they carried me on a stretcher I rode a long way in a motor ambulance when they took me out they tipped me off the stretcher on to the hard road then stood and laughed at me I was put in a red cross train one made up on purpose [with] wooden beds old straw mattresses and one blanket I laid in there five days without having my wounds dressed living on raw coffee and thin soup two little thin slices of bread a day. When we arrived at hospital we had a bath in water with just the chill off they scrubbed us with a short haired scrubbing brush no soap dressed our wounds and put us to bed and how thankful I was. The food they give us to eat was shocking black bread about 2? inches square and a inch thick soup made of cabbage leaves and potato peelings sometimes we had macaronie [sic] I lived for three months on this food. I was so weak I could not stand up in a room without holding on to the bed they gave us big old wooden clogs to wear with no socks it was terrible. When I got my first parcel I nearly went mad with joy if only the people knew what the parcels mean to the boys out there I am sure they would give the last penny they have. Yes every packet is worth a thousand pounds to the boys out there, we call them the staff of life because if it was not for those parcels we could not have stuck it the only way to help my poor comrades out there in my idea is that everybody should help a little by putting a few coppers in the prisoners of war fund box and I feel as if I should like to do a little so I kindly ask you if you could

send me 2 prisoners of war fund boxes. When I get them full I will send them straight to you then you can let me know how much I have collected sending me an empty one in return. I will now tell you about my wounds. I was hit in the left eye chest left shoulder arm and neck my chest is cracked I can lift very little without it hurting me the back of my eye was cut all to pieces leaving just the front I kept telling them about it paining me at times nearly sending me off my head all they done was bandin [sic] it up with paper bandages very seldom they use linen. I was full of pain till August 1917 it affected my right eye till I was blind with both eyes I heard that there was a Russian doctor in the hospital a good eye specilist [sic] he could speak broken English so I told him about it asked him if he would take my left eye out thinking my right eye would come allright he said he would and try his best to get the sight of my right eye back that same afternoon he had me moved into his barrack took my eye out the next morning he worked hard for me doing his best looked after me in every way I was blind folded for a month then one morning to my great surprise the Doctor took off my bandages I could see his dear old face he said there you are mister if you keep your spirits up your eye will soon be allright I did in two or three days I could see to walk about wearing a dark pair of specticals [sic] now I can see to get about without them only I cannot see in the dark for it is still weak but its much better with one weak eye than none at all. I cannot thank the Doctor enough for what he has done if it was not for him the Germans would never have troubled and I should have been stone blind this day and if I had never had the parcels you were so good to send me I could not have lived so you see its your dear madam I owe so much to as well as the Russian

Doctor if there is any thing I can help you in I am only to [sic] pleased to be at your service. When we left hospital well such as they are wooden barracks straw mattresses two blankets the water comes through the roof when it rains wake up in the morning the blankets wet through its awful not even a German sister in the hospital we had to look after each other we travelled by rail went to Langensalza stopped there about three days in the search barrack they took all my photos [sic] old letters about 2 dozen tins of conserved and other things we went from there to Manuem stayed three weeks living on German food because my parcels never came through there we went from there to Achen stayed there three days then we went right through to Holland you ought to have seen the fine red cross train we travelled in spring mattresses feather-beds and nice white sheets just to make Holland think we have been treated allright but it would take a lot of that sort of thing to make me forget the past days, we had a fine reception at Holland plenty to eat and drink it was fine trip across the water. I am very sorry to hear about my redgiment [sic] isint [sic] awful for the poor men to be cut up so how I wish this beastly war would end for the sake of my poor comrades. You said in your letter you would like me to go to Hylands: well I am ready to go any day you like if you will make arrangements for me when to go anytime it is convenient for the gentleman if you will kindly let me know I will be at your service. I am now home on two months leave which is up on the 15th March then I shall go to cliff Hospital Felixstowe thanking you many times for your kindness which I shall never forget not only for myself but for my comrades if you will kindly send me the prisoners of war fund boxes I may be able to help you a little which I am only to [sic] pleased to do. I think this is all so I draw my letter to a close.

The final letter was from Sergeant Evan Binnie, number 8594, 2nd Essex Regt, written on 26 March 1918 from Scheveningen, Holland (sub-number 33):

At last I am able to sit and write a letter in comfort, on the 11th of this month I left Germany and arrived here under the arrangement for the exchange of Non-Commissioned Officers. I wonder Madam, if it is possible for you to realize what this means to me, just fancy after 3 years of what can only be described as a time beyond imagination, to find yourself suddenly free, living in lovely quarters, with permission to go where you like, and mix with who you like, without any barb-wire and German sentries to stop you. My only wonder now is how I ever managed to get through the last 3 years, but still the old saying is All's well that ends well. It is impossible for me to describe my feelings as the train steamed slowly across the frontier, all I can say is that I sat in a sort of a trance until the train stopped at a station a little way into Holland, here our German sentries disappeared and we were met by several ladies and a British Officer. On being invited to leave the train just as we liked and sit down to a feed of nice white bread, ham and coffee, it slowly began to dawn on me, that life had once more changed, and that at last we were free. After this we went by express train on the rest of our journey, all the way down the line we received a hearty welcome arriving at Scheveningen about ten at night, and marched to the Hotel de Galeries between two lines of cheering comrades at the Hotel we were met by the Queen of Holland's representative the General in Command and several other noted people after several speeches by them we were sat down to a nice supper in fact to cut a long story short Madam, we received altogether a splendid reception. After 3 days stay in the Galeries we were shifted to our new quarters and I am now living in a large private house with about 40 other men, this house is situated in a main street in a very nice part of a large seaside resort and is only about 5 minutes walk from the sea front so you can tell that everything is just lovely.

I would try and describe what my life in Germany was like but find it impossible to put it to paper, and even if I could Madam, it would be just as impossible for anyone who has not been through it to understand; it was terrible. I should like to take this opportunity of expressing my heartfelt thanks for all the great kindness you have shown me during my captivity. If it had not been for the help and kindness shown us by our friends and relations at home, I am absolutely certain that three parts of us would not be here to-day. I am more than grateful Madam, and am sure you will understand as I do not know how to put my thoughts on paper. I will close now sincerely hoping that General Stephenson and yourself are enjoying the very best of good health.

These letters have been quoted in their entirety to demonstrate the wealth of information which can be gleaned from them. If any of their descendents are reading this article they will undoubtedly be thrilled at the detail they have discovered.

With thanks to Malcolm White, Town Clerk of Saffron Walden, for permission to quote from the letters.
© Kate Thompson

I Remember, I Remember

Anne Batchelor

provides more tips on recording your story for the delight and amazement of future generations

The boys and girls of Beechwood Infants (Top Class) looked at me in wonder. This white—haired dinosaur of a woman had actually been alive during THE WAR! They found my description of sweet— rationing hard to take in, raising their voices in a chorus of disbelief. Then came the questions - "Did children wear shoes in those days?" asked a concerned little girl. "And was it FUN in the War?" asked a boy.

I pointed out that when I was teaching, even in recent years, there was a space on each child's absence form for "No shoes" as an explanation for absence in the winter. As for "fun", I asked the lad how he would feel if he was lifted from his nice, warm bed in the middle of a cold winter's night, wrapped in a blanket and carried down the garden in pouring rain,to a brick and concrete shelter with no light or heating, there to sit for perhaps an hour until the "All Clear" brought the family back up the garden path. Not exactly my idea of "fun"!

Added to that was my childhood fear that Father Christmas would not be able to fly through the sky with his reindeer if it were full of enemy planes! Bless him, he always managed to get through, even the year my mother wrote him the following note, which I found recently when clearing her flat:
"Dear Father Christmas, Don't come to Anne this year. She has been a naughty girl. Signed - Anne's Mammy"
I wonder what I had done to make her so exasperated?

I do think it is very important for times past to be recorded either verbally or in writing. As I have often said, think how wonderful it would be to discover letters or a diary written by your 4xGreat grandparent. So one of my missions in life is to encourage people, especially family historians, to record their memories of times past and tell the story of their own life.

It matters not that the life is "ordinary", for every life is unique and special. In the future it will give a vivid picture of life as it was. The account of an ordinary life will become a valuable social document. I recently acquired, via a rubbish tip, the diary of Sarah Abigail Brown, a very ordinary housewife living in Hull in 1901. It describes the minute detail of her life - how many buns she baked for the Chapel Sisterhood, who preached the sermon on Sunday (and what she thought of it!), how her husband, Arthur, taught bookkeeping to a

young neighbour to supplement his modest income, the day Arthur mended the kitchen table and where she took Baby and Eddie for a walk. She tells how Joe, a relative, visited them and brought Eddie a walking stick " - made from a Boer shell." Remember, this is everyday life over a hundred years ago. I'm sure Sarah Abigail would be amazed to think that anyone today would be interested in her life. Incidentally, I had a letter just last week from a lady who had read my cries for help in Family Tree magazine and offered me two photographs of Sarah Abigail (known in the family as "Aunt Abbie"). You can imagine my delight. Now that I have her face as well as her words, she has become a real person.

So how to begin your story? Perhaps you don't have time to keep a daily diary. There are other ways. My sweet mother, Frances, some years before her death, was in the habit of saying, "I remember when I was a girl -". I would always interrupt with the demand, "Write it down!" I gave her an A4 notebook with hard cover and told her to write down her memories as they came to her, in any order. I could always rearrange them in sequence later.

I gave her a list to jog her memory –
Childhood and schooldays,
Our wedding day,
Life in service (tweenie, housemaid, cook & nannie)
Becoming a mother,
Life during the war (rationing, air raids & rabbits!)
Flat dwelling,
Growing older, health problems and bereavement.
My favourite things (books, poems, music, places,paintings)
My hobbies (dressmaking, painting, gardening, crochet)
Over the space of a few months she produced an amazing fifteen pages of close written, tiny handwriting before declaring, "I'm too tired now. I'll tell you and you write it down." This account, along with a tape recording of her childhood memories I had made in 1987, when she was seventy four, formed the basis for my book about her, "My Name is Frances."

Her memories were very vivid and often very touching. She wrote of her years in a Waifs and Strays Home at York
"First thing in the morning Sister would ring a bell for us to get up, so it was all bustle at first. Then we washed and dressed and went down to breakfast, which was usually porridge (lumpy!) and dripping and bread and a cup of tea. Then off to school we

Godfrey Walker Waifs and Strays Home
Annual Holiday at Filey - c1921
Frances is on the front row, second left in the white dress

will be a hundred years in the future, and how strange and quaint your life will appear to people in the twenty—second century. *"Imagine!"* they will say, *"They used to go to the shops in person and carry their shopping home! And their children used to go to a school building and meet their teacher in person, instead of learning over the Internet. They used to read from books and they wrote with a pen - on paper! How curious! How primitive!"*

When you relate events in your life to historical world events, your account will be twice as fascinating. So, for instance, anything you can remember about wartime will be "history". Remember food rationing? I remember my family receiving a food parcel from Australia containing amazing things I had never seen before, such as tinned peaches and Christmas cake full of fruit!

I remember all the fuss there was about bananas, and how my very first banana at the age of eight or nine was such a disappointment. It was black and squidgy, and had to be spread on bread because it was semi liquid.

I remember going to the cinema and, during the newsreel, having my mother's hands suddenly put over my eyes, for the newsreel showed the liberation of the concentration camps. Squinting through her fingers I saw, to my horror, skeletal figures on bunkbeds staring blankly at the camera.

I remember the Coronation of Queen Elizabeth II. About twenty neighbours squeezed into Nell and Dave's little house to watch it on television. No one else in the street had a set! We watched the frail figure of the newly crowned queen as she rose from the Coronation Chair, to be greeted by cries

went. I remember the mill on Holgate Road was working and we often met the miller on his cart with bags of corn. In winter we put our long black stockings over our boots to stop us slipping, and when we got to school we had to leave our boots and stockings by the fire. We had a big roaring fire with a fireguard round it, so the classroom was nice and warm. On the way home we often saw men breaking in horses in the fields, and each night we saw the lamplighter with his ladder, lighting the gas lamps in the street."

Of her wedding day she wrote
"Zillah (her sister in law) said I would make a beautiful bride because she said I had a lovely complexion, nice teeth and beautiful chestnut hair. When I was sitting in the wedding car after the ceremony, women came crowding round and peering in, saying, "Isn't she beautiful!" Those were the days! I'm not so beautiful now. "

The entry dated February 17th 1991 says, touchingly
"Today Bill passed away just before seven o'clock. We went to the hospital chapel to see him. He didn't look as if he was dead, but only sleeping. He looked so peaceful, so I couldn't wish him back, as he had suffered a lot, poor love"

Your life's story would be just as fascinating as hers to future generations. Consider how life has changed over the past one hundred years. My mother remembered life B.C. (Before Computers) when she got a great thrill out of hearing music from a wind—up gramaphone with a horn, and voices out of the air via the cat's whisker! She spent the first night of her honeymoon at Grandma Batchelor's little house in Rougier Street, York. The old lady was so suspicious of new fangled electricity that she wouldn't have it in her home in case it leaked out of the sockets, so the newly weds had to go upstairs by candlelight. How romantic!

Just imagine, if you can, how very different life

Frances in later life

A Beautiful Bride 27 June 1936

of "God save the Queen!" History indeed.

Your story will also reflect the changes in society and the attitudes of the times. I remember the first black family to live in Seacroft - a Jamaican bus—driver, his wife and two small children. They were lovely people. They came to our church every Sunday morning impeccably dressed - the tiny boy in a proper suit (the miniature of his father's) with a crisp white shirt, and his sister in a straw hat, pretty dress, white socks and white gloves. They made a terrific impression on us. However the people in their street got up a petition to have them removed from their council house because " - they are different and don't belong here!" How such attitudes shock us now.

Holidays have become more adventurous than in my teenage years. Our primitive week under canvas in the Dales was so thrilling to us - and so daring! Boys and girls camping together! What was the world coming to? Now the youngsters in the travel agent's casually book a visit to Nepal or go back—packing in Australia. A hundred years from now space travel will probably be quite common. Think what people will say to our memories of straw - filled matresses and hard wooden bunk beds in a converted barn at Pateley Bridge in the 1960s!

Of course, photographs are an important part of your personal archive. These can be stored, with your information, on a computer disc, but please also keep real photographs and real paper archives. Don t forget that technology moves on at a terrific pace. It would be awful if future generations tried to study your material on a disc which was not compatible with their equipment. I can't be the only person who has miles of recording tape from my old "reel—to— reel" original tape recorder (circa 1958) which I can no longer play.

Remember, too, that unidentified photographs are frustrating and quite useless. Every picture in your family archive must bear a note of who, where and when. If you can't identify them yourself then take them with you to all family weddings and funerals! If it is a group photograph, remember that most people in the picture will have a copy, so send copies to the local newspaper or to a family history magazine. Someone might just have a copy with names on the back - if you are lucky.

I once attended the funeral of a lady whose family had wanted to make her Order of Service very personal by adding a photograph and a full page description of her - her personality, likes and dislikes and so on. Why not write something similar about yourself?

I love the description Mary de la Rivièr Manley gave of herself in 1714 -
"Her eyes are the best feature in her face. Nothing can be more tender, ingenious and brilliant with a mixture so languishing and sweet. Her lips admirably colour'd; her teeth small and even, a breath always sweet; Her hands and arms have been publicly celebrated; Her neck and breasts have an established reputation for beauty and colour; From her youth she was inclined to fat."

You should describe your jobs, too. My late father was always so proud of his forty - two years working for Schweppes but it was only after his death that I discovered his collection of references from the eleven jobs he had in his young days. How lovely to read that -
"He was always energetic, willing, obliging, perfectly sober and trustworthy - honest, hardworking and a good timekeeper, very civil and conscientious in every degree."
If you have similar references of your own, don't be modest. Include them in your story for the delight of future generations.

Mary de la Rivièr Manley

A Child in Wartime 1942 - Anne Batchelor

People who know me as a family historian may not be aware that for thirty years I was a teacher. My first headmaster presented me with a blank timetable saying, "Fill that in with the things you would like to teach." Such freedom! How times have changed in schools. A hundred years from now teachers and schools may have disappeared, to be replaced by educational data bases. Gone, too, will be the special relationship between pupil and teacher, so remember to write about your special teachers.

Before that I was a librarian, lending out books made of paper! Will they exist in the distant future, I wonder? Whatever your job, it will be fascinating to researchers in the year 2050 or 3000. Think how much it enriches your research when you read about your straw—plaiting ancestors or the life of the good old " ag. lab." Even if, like my mother, you were - just a housewife!" your story is important.

Remember to include a list of your likes and dislikes. Your favourite book, music, flowers, colour, food, and holiday spot makes you a more real person to anyone reading your story in years to come. List your pet hates, too. Mine are noise, swimming baths and tripe! Wouldn't it be wonderful if your sixteenth—century ancestor had

left such a list. It would help put flesh on their dry old bones, which is what gives us family historians such delight.

My lovely mother died only recently, and I had the job of clearing her flat. It was not all sad, for in her sideboard I found hundreds of letters and cards full of love from family and friends going back over most of her 89 years. Inside the covers of her bibles and hymn books, and in her notebooks, she had carefully copied poems and prayers which revealed her deep and intense faith in God which carried her through life's difficult and worrying experiences. You too could include such things when you write your life's story.

I also discovered an amazing thirteen years of diaries, from 1968, in which she recorded the minute details of her very ordinary life. Reading them was a lovely experience for me, for my last memory of her, in her final days in hospital, was of a frail, tired old lady, but the diaries of thirty years ago show me the bright, vigorous, busy woman I had almost forgotten.

So you see, the written word has the great power to convey the essence of a person. That is why I feel so passionately that it is the duty of every family historian to leave an account of their life for the delight and wonderment of generations as yet unborn.

Please don't wait until you acquire one of those wonderful things called " a round tuit ". That could be too late. A dear friend of mine lost her sight in the space of a year. She can no longer do any research or any writing. Another much younger lady had a brain haemorrhage and can't find the words she needs for everyday conversation, let alone writing her life story.

So in the words of militant crowds of future family historians, "What do we want? Your story! When do we want it? Now!"

The Padcroft Experience –

Church of England Temperance Society London Police Court Mission Padcroft Boys' Home

Shani Cassady - Researcher & Lecturer - The Nottingham Trent University

You should see them!
You should really see them

THERE THEY ARE, forty-four boys, from fourteen
to eighteen years old, of all sorts, shapes and sizes,
living at Padcroft…
Whatever a lad's bent may be, they will sort it out at
Padcroft…
…Padcroft will analyse the boy's mind, and put him
to that for which he is best adapted.
[Mr Green] ..late of the Suffolk Yeomanry…with a
better understanding of human nature it would be
difficult to find.. ..will tell you stories…of boys who
have been through his hands and have turned out
absolute out-and-out thorough white men and
Englishmen.
Nearly all the boys call Mr Green "Father". He is
the only decent father most of them have ever
known.
It hardy seems possible that in a short space of three
months a boy can be transformed from leading a life
of crime into that of a good law abiding citizen, but
by the grace of God this miracle is performed about
a hundred and seventy times a year.
G. Burnside-Sprateley
Padcroft booklet circa 1928

Introduction

Padcroft was a Church of England Temperance
Society (CETS) London Police Court Mission
(LPCM) probation home for approximately 45
boys whose ages ranged from 14 to 18. It started
in 1902 under the care of Mr and Mrs Clements,
and followed 2 attempts at creating and
maintaining a boys' home (one of which was in
Gunnersbury and closed in 1899). Mr. Frank
Green (the manager for the majority of Padcroft's
existence) relates in later minutes (1948) that he
had been associated with Padcroft for 46 years, 32
of which were as a Probation Officer at Uxbridge
court. Most boys were sent to Padcroft for
larceny, embezzlement, being suspected persons,
wandering, or as they came under the Probation of
Offenders Act of 1907. Some of the boys went

Padcroft boys in the gym
Copyright RPS-Rainer

home for holidays, however the average length of
stay rose during the period of Padcroft's life, from
3 to 6 months. Following some complaints a
punishment book was created, however this does
not appear to have be used very frequently and
almost all cases of corporal punishment result
from incidents of absconding, theft or wilful
damage. Corporal punishment was only carried
out by Mr. Green, and assistant masters defying
this regulation faced instant dismissal. The boys
were used around the home for a variety of
household jobs, including painting and decorating,
maintenance, gardening, carpentry etc. Many were
found employment on leaving; in farming and
mining, and for some years there was a close
association with Pilkington's Glass in St. Helens.
After-care was also a priority and Mr Green wrote
to or visited ex-boys on a regular basis going to
Birmingham, South Wales, Leicester, Norfolk,
Suffolk, St. Helens, Yorkshire, Litchfield,
Worcestershire and Lincolnshire. Padcroft
eventually closed in 1949 and Mr and Mrs Green
(manager and matron for 47 years) took their
retirement.

Funding and finances[1]

There were several methods by which Padcroft
was financed. This appears to have been done
chiefly through subscriptions, donations, and
fundraising activities, however the Police Court
Mission (PCM) regularly contributed over 40% of
the total amount needed for its continuance.
Efforts were constantly made to reduce overheads,
and the minutes relate the cost of various items
including clothing, and also of food per head
(approximately 7/- per boy per week in early
minutes). The London Secretary pointed out to the
committee that any deficit of funds had to be met
by the LPCM and that this should be avoided at all
costs, however the jurisdiction of the mission
changed on the 1st January 1923, and this
effectively stopped any subsidization, although this
was rescinded at a later date when Padcroft was
facing financial crisis.

The annual anniversary (catering for
approximately 400 people) was also used to solicit
contributions to Padcroft and it was noted that on
one occasion £15 had been received from the 'Old
Boys at St. Helens' (via Mr. E. F. Davies manager
of Pilkington's home)[2.] The committee received
pecuniary gifts, donations and legacies from
individuals, sales of work and meetings in addition
to gifts of a material kind. Regular donators
included Miss Lovering who not only sent cheques
but also paid for the boys' annual trip to the Royal
Tournament at Olympia.

Directors of the HMV Gramophone Company donated a gramophone plus 24 records at Christmas, and others gave encyclopaedias, rose trees, day shirts, football shirts and shorts, books, groceries, fruit, shoes, a piano, and tins of Ovaltine.

Staff

The staff originally consisted of Mr and Mrs Green (manager and matron), a cook, two assistant masters and a chaplain (although labour or technical masters were employed once the workshop had been built. The number of assistant masters also increased during the 1930s). The first minute book recalls that Rev. R. Hartley curate of St. Margaret's, Uxbridge was appointed chaplain of the home at a remuneration of £30 per annum, however upon his resignation, the Vicar of Yiewsley was employed in his stead. Mr and Mrs Green managed Padcroft for much of its 'life' and other members of their family also assisted, particularly Frank junior who, like his father, worked in the local courts. In the early 1920s Mr and Mrs Green were paid a combined salary of £225 per annum, and assistant masters were given a salary of approximately £60 per annum. This may have been one of the reasons why the home appears to have had a reasonably high turnover of staff, although it should be noted that this is not unusual in institutions. Additionally apart from the manager and his wife, the staff were not permitted to remain at Padcroft once they were married, although this was relaxed during the 1940s as the home suffered staff shortages.

By the 1940s the working conditions were as follows:
Assistant masters had 3 evenings off a week and 1 weekend off in 3 on a rota basis.
They earned £3.6.6 + 13/6 per week, although after 6 months they earned £180 per annum + £12 yearly increments to a maximum of £252 + war bonus of £35.2.0. Their board and lodgings were free, and they also received 2 weeks leave.

Daily life, including recreation, facilities, and accommodation

Padcroft was a large house in its own grounds in Yiewlsey, Middlesex. It accommodated around 45 boys at any given time and the home was divided into 'houses' administered by assistant masters. In the 1930s the property next door to Padcroft, known as the Willows, was purchased to increase the amenities of the home. At first Padcroft's facilities were primitive and included outside toilets, basic bathrooms, dormitories, and the masters' accommodation. However in 1930 the Home Office inspector criticized sanitary arrangements at the home and as a result of this a new 'observation bathroom' was installed with a large communal bath. The minutes also relate how discussions took place on the provision of a chapel, where it was argued that whilst not a necessity in homes for children, was at the very least, desirable

The Criminal Justice Act of 1925 provided welcome respite from financial difficulties as the secretary drew attention to the clause in which local authorities were required to make financial contributions for those placed on probation within the area when an order of residence was given in the order. It was expected that this would impact positively on Padcroft as all the boys admitted there of late were placed on probation, and that the place of residence was fixed in the order as Padcroft.

At one point financial assistance came directly as a result of a failure by the PCM. Captain Shaw, collector for the mission had a sum of money to distribute that he had collected for a boys' hostel. It was decided that the hostel was not required and this allowed the money to be divided between the CETS Camberwell Road home for Lads, the Boys' Garden Colony at Basingstoke, and Padcroft. Indeed Padcroft received the lion's share that amounted to £942. However in 1942 Padcroft was effectively 'sold' to the LPCM as part of their separation from the CETS, although there is no evidence to suggest this had any financial impact on the home, merely one of management.

Additionally booklets were produced to solicit donations from members of the committee and the community at large, and on one occasion a new booklet was produced via a generous donation from two men in 'a large advertising company'. Furthermore in 1932 Mr Seymour Hicks made an appeal on BBC radio (29th May) for the Padcroft rebuilding fund which raised £949. Donations to the home were also gratefully received: The

as 'the Centre of the Religious influence of the Home.' The necessary money was eventually raised and St. George's Chapel (from the 1924 Wembley Exhibition) was purchased for their use, subsequently becoming a daily feature of life at Padcroft.

Between 1929 and 1933 a workshop (photographs of which were said to have appeared in the PCM annual report of 1929) was provided, however only 15 boys could be trained there at any given time and the rest were occupied in painting and decorating, gardening and household chores. Boys engaged in the workshop made (amongst other objects) benches, sheds, garages, slipper boxes, and doll's houses. It is recorded that one boy, described as an orphan, having previously travelled with the circus, became a carpenter's improver on large housing estate in Surrey, and this was cited as evidence of the value of training received at Padcroft. In 1932 the workshop was extended and a greenhouse provided, although in the 1940s engineering was added to the training programme and Messrs Vickers Armstrong donated a lathe for their use.

Eventually a sports pavilion was also provided, and extensive rebuilding created a new recreation room with billiard table, which was named as a memorial hall in respect of Louis and Winifred Rickards (by virtue of Misses Picard). A wireless set sent from the Boys' Garden Colony in Basingstoke (which closed in 1931), and a table tennis table in 1939 completed facilities within the recreation room, until a piano was obtained in the 1940s.

During the war boys undertook first aid courses, fire drills and extra gardening duties, and Sgt. C. R. Hart from the RAF officers' school Uxbridge attended Padcroft to teach physical training on two evenings a week. However despite the necessity to be accepted by the community in which they lived, Mr Green would not allow the boys to attend army training corps nor the home guard, and instead the boys were kept busy producing wooden boxes and 'digging for victory'. Additionally some boys were employed on nearby farms and went there on a daily basis accompanied by a master. The wages from any endeavours were apparently divided thus: 2/3 to Padcroft and 1/3 shared between the boys. Furthermore the home began to keep rabbits, and the Ministry for Agriculture and Fisheries issued information films about animal husbandry which the boys are said to have enjoyed at the local cinema.

The annual anniversary was always a cause for celebration amongst the residents of Padcroft, and the committee arranged for eminent officials to preach on the day and give out prizes to the boys. Amongst those invited to officiate were the Rev. Austin Thompson of St. Peter's Ealing, Sir Charles Biron chief metropolitan Magistrate, the Bishop of Kensington, the Bishop of London, Mr Cairns

Magistrate at Thames Court, Mr Short the ex-Home Secretary, Dr Alington headmaster of Eton, and Sir John Dickinson. For the most part the day was successful however in 1921 the anniversary was cancelled due to scarlet fever, and in 1926 it was cancelled due to railway difficulties. The war curtailed festivities and these were never resumed after hostilities had ceased.

As previously mentioned, the association between Padcroft and Pilkington Glass was a long one, no doubt initiated by Mr Davies of the Pilkington Boys' Hostel (operational from 1912 to 1926), who had in fact been an assistant master at Padcroft. The minutes state that he visited Padcroft and asked permission for the St. Helens Boy Scouts (of which he was district Scout Master) to camp on their meadow for a week commencing 31st July 1920, as they were attending the Great Scout Rally at the Olympia. This was agreed to and subsequently the minutes report:

On 31st July the London Jamboree contingent of the St. Helens association Boy Scout, Lancashire visited Padcroft, and were camped on the meadow, in tents etc., kindly lent by a gentlemen greatly interested in the Scout movement, among the number were several of our old boys who are at present working at Messrs. Pilkington's Crown Glass Works, St. Helens. In charge of the party was District Scout Master Davies who used to be on the Padcroft Home staff. On Sunday Morning 1st August they attended the Great Jamboree Service at Olympia, and in the evening a Special Scout Service was arranged by Rev. F. D. Sturgess at the Parish Church, which was greatly appreciated by everyone. The rest of the week was spent attending the Jamboree and seeing the sights of London etc. They left for St. Helens on 7th August 1920. Major Guy Pilkington DSO who is the Chairman of this association stayed at Padcroft during the week and was much interested in our Home and Work.

This was not the only visit made by the scout troupe as in 1924 Harry Pearson reported that a group of scouts from St. Helens had again visited Padcroft for 10 days in August, and that they had attended church parade at St. Matthews, returning to St. Helens on the 10th August.

Each year the boys celebrated November 5th with fireworks, frequently donated by Mr Jackson and the Uxbridge Combined Football Club, although their annual recreation was not confined to this one night. Mr B. Cooke from the Boys' Garden Colony visited Padcroft with their football team, the boys attended concerts at the St. Matthew's Church Rooms in Yiewsley, they also went to see the final for the Daily Telegraph Junior Football Cup and listened in to the opening of Wembley by His Majesty. Miss Lovering ensured that the boys attended the Royal Tournament at Olympia each year, the local cinema asked boys to screenings of films, and the Yiewsley community invited Padcroft to take part in the local athletics day in August. However although these events were reported in the minutes it should be noted that they were not frequent, and it appears that little was done to keep the boys occupied during their leisure time. From 1920 to 1928 no mention was made of any clubs, associations or otherwise that the boys attended in the evenings or at weekends.

From 1930 the boys received weekly conduct money in the following manner:
2 captains received 1/- each
2 vice captains received 9d each
20 boys received 6d each
Remainder received 3d each
This altered to 1/- per week per boy in the 1940s.

In 1930 the boys were invited to a holiday camp at Hayling Island where Mr Snell, Magistrate at Old Street Court had begun a permanent holiday camp for probationers. Padcroft was therefore closed for 2 weeks from August 30th 1930, and Mr Green later reported on the camp.

I shall never forget how excited our boys were the night before we started for the Rotary Camp, Fishery Lane, Eastoke, Hayling Island. The majority never had any sleep and at 3 a.m. they were looking out of

the dormitory windows longing for the sun to rise. So anxious were they to be ready in time that they decided to awake the master and ask if he had not over-slept. At 5 a.m. they were all astir, and every boy was ready for the great exodus by 8 a.m. "Just fancy" I overheard one lad say, "two whole weeks by the sea; I have never been out of London before". The two motor coaches which were to convey us to our destination arrived at 10 a.m. and after everyone was comfortably seated we left "Padcroft".

We had a very pleasant journey down. All the way the boys were singing and cheering to the accompaniment of a tin whistle and a mouth-organ. At last the camp was reached and the boys at once prepared to fill their paillasses and generally put the camp in order whilst Mrs. Brogan and her staff attended to the culinary department.

When everything was completed, the boys were allowed to go to the bathing pool and have a swim. This was thoroughly enjoyed and after a strenuous time they were assembled for tea to which they did full justice.

The camp is ideally situated. It overlooks Chichester Bay and on a fine day one can see the spire of the Cathedral. I should describe it as a natural camp which provides entertainment for boys of all temperaments.

On Sunday, 31st August, the service was conducted by the Reverend Barnett, which everyone attended. The following Sunday Mr T. H. Mills conducted the Service whilst Mr S. Holder gave the address on "The Importance of Small Things", and on Tuesday, the 12th instant, the Reverend Harrison conducted a Thanksgiving Service.

Through the kindness of Mrs Snell Senior, the boys were taken on a trip to Portsmouth Dock Yard. They were very interested in everything, especially the Royal Yacht and HMS Victory.

Thursday 11th instant, was devoted to Sports, etc. In addition to the usual races held on these occasions, a water polo match was arranged, which caused great excitement. Three events were contested for the House Cup, viz., a relay race, boat race and tug-of-war, resulting in a win for the Red House by two points to one.

Everyday there was always a full program of events, which included bathing in the sea, cricket, baseball and ball games on the sands, football, cricket, club swinging and vaulting horse in the meadow, and fishing and boating on the pool.

On the evening of the 12th instant – the last night at Camp, a huge fire was made and lighted at 8 p.m. From then until midnight the boys entertained us with a most excellent concert.

At first (and this was only to be expected) the boys were terribly excited, but soon settled down, and everyone without exception thoroughly enjoyed their holiday. Throughout the two weeks the boys behaved in a most exemplary way.

We had one accident. A. C. strained a muscle of his knee whilst playing football. This necessitated him spending the rest of his holiday in bed but he was never neglected by his chums, who sacrificed their pleasure to cheer him up. One very touching incident happened which goes to prove what a fine tone there is amongst our boys, which I will now briefly relate:-

On the day we had our races, A. C., the injured boy, was carried on his bed into the meadow to witness these events, and after Mrs Snell had presented the prizes, one boy who was there went direct to the sick boy and gave him one, a fountain pen.

Captain Ivan Snell visited the Camp each day and took a keen interest in every one. One Thursday the 11th instant, Mrs Snell kindly presented the prizes. Afterwards Captain Snell addressed the boys and congratulated them on their excellent behaviour. I suitably replied on behalf of the boys and staff.

Mrs Brogan and Mr King, her assistant Cook, were presented with a clock and a cigarette case respectively by the boys, as a mark of appreciation for the excellent way they catered for them whilst at Camp.

The camp was visited during our stay by Mr Clarke-Hall, Dr Bosworth-Wright, Mr F. W. Waites, Mr A. E. Cox, Mr T. H. Mills, Mr S. Holder, Mr F. J. Simpson and Mr F. J. Simpson Junior, Dr J. Adams, Mrs Snell and family and several other ladies and gentlemen.

We returned to Padcroft on the 13th instant, after having a most glorious time.

The boys are to be congratulated on the way they settled down to work on their return, which goes to prove how very much they appreciated every effort made for them.

Minutes also record the boys' diet:

	Breakfast 8 a.m.	Dinner 1 p.m.	Tea 5 p.m	Supper
Monday	Bread margarine cocoa apples	Meat potatoes 1 vegetable	Bread margarine jam, toast tea	Bread margarine cheese beetroot lettuce radishes
Tuesday	As above	As above	As above	As above
Wednesday	As above	As above	As above + bread pudding	As above
Thursday	As above	As above	As above	As above
Friday	As above	Fish	As above + bread pudding	As above
Saturday	As above	As for Monday	As above	As above
Sunday	Eggs ham, fish	As Above + Dessert	As Above + cake	As Above

Seasonal fare was provided at Christmas when the committee donated £5 for special purchases.

Their daily routine was as follows:
7 a.m. rise (winter)   **6.30 a.m.** (summer)
8.15 a.m. breakfast
9 a.m. chapel (taken by Mr Green)
Then on to working parties: carpentry, gardening or housework.
12 till 2 p.m. lunch and midday break
2 till 5 p.m. return to work
5 p.m. tea
After this was free time and the boys could go to the playing field or the gym.
Church every Sunday and religious instruction classes one day per week.
Bed at 10 p.m.

The war brought many changes to the lives of all those at Padcroft, and in September of 1940 it was recorded that they had received 50 air raid warnings since mid August, and that every one of these nights were spent in the shelter[3]. Additionally three incendiary bombs had dropped in Yiewsley during that time causing alarm amongst all who lived there. However on VE day the boys went to the zoological gardens and had two visits to the cinema. In the autumn of 1945 a programme of lectures and instruction were designed which included classes in horticulture, singing, handicrafts, model making and physical culture, and on VJ day the boys made trips to the local swimming baths and the cinema.

The Boys: Their health, their length of stay, their offences, behaviour and discipline.
Up until the end of 1927 it was reported that the total number of boys that had passed through Padcroft at that point amounted to 5511. Boys would sometimes be allowed home leave at Easter, Whitsun and Christmas, however the average length of their stay at Padcroft was 3 months (rising to 6 months when carpentry training became available).

It appears that the general health of the boys was good (serious illnesses were few), although it was noted on several occasions that their time spent at Padcroft increased the standard of health in almost every boy.

Offences tended to be in the categories defined under the Probation of Offenders Act of 1907 (see

allow myself to be confined as I like my freedom too much do not trouble to try and find me as it is impossible. Signed EDC[4]

Mr Green reported that he had had to pay 3d postage on the letter.

Additionally further offences were occasionally committed which necessitated the boy's removal to court, and boys could be discharged from the home due to illness or incorrigibility. Some boys were more notable than others. For example, BE (admitted on a charge of housebreaking) had tried 'to poison matron' (by putting carbolic into her tea), and had also caused wilful damage and so was returned to the Middlesex sessions.[5] The Committee placed on record that "In view of the badly behaved boys received lately into the Home, the Committee desired to place it on record that in the event of any unfortunate circumstances resulting from the admission of boys undesirable for the Home, the Committee will not hold themselves responsible".[6] Another boy, FR, was said to have been a member of the 'Self determination league' and as such, would not settle into life at Padcroft.[7]

appendix), however the majority of boys were sent to Padcroft for embezzlement, larceny, felony, sleeping out and begging. Some were suspected persons and many more were not charged but were merely beyond parental control. Most cases were sent through the courts, however there were examples of private cases brought by parents who were unable to cope with their child. The reasons for admittance changed over time, and eventually the notes show that although some were admitted under the Probation of Offenders Act 1907 others came under the Children and Young Person's Act of 1933. The first recorded transfer to an approved school occurred in 1936, and by the end of the 1930s, further changes to the reasons for admission to Padcroft can be detected when in the main boys came to Padcroft for the following reasons:

In need of care and protection
Aiding and abetting
Assault and battery
Common assault
Breaking and entering
Driving without owner's consent
Receiving stolen property
Breach of recognizance
Shop breaking

Despite being placed under a probation order, it appears that the majority of boys behaved in a reasonable manner whilst in Padcroft, and the role played by conduct money (that is, pocket money given in lieu of good conduct) was not underestimated by the manager. Certainly there were absconders, although these tended to be few in number. However one letter was appended to the minutes from one such absconder.

Dear Sir, I feel that this missive is necessary to explain my irrevocable conduct in absconding from your illustrious home. It grieves me greatly to think what trouble I must have put you to, but I could not

Some boys were said to negatively influence others. One high school boy was said to be the chief instigator of trouble at the home. His school report said that he was "Thoroughly unsteady. He is an extravagant type, always anxious to draw attention to himself and be popular, though never succeeding in the latter, as normal boys despised his childish and dishonourable behaviour." Mr Green continued, 'his conduct at school was so unsatisfactory that it was suggested to the boy's Father that he should not send him back…It is quite evident that (C's) romantic tales influenced the other boy (R) to abscond with him. The latter boy is a waif and so far as we are aware is still at large.'[8]

During the war however the numbers of boys being admitted increased and this brought with it further problems of control. The first instance of robbery with violence was recorded and taking a vehicle without the owner's consent increased, although the more common offences during this period were housebreaking and larceny. Additionally boys were placed at Padcroft on remand and Mr Green remarked that 'the war has had a very disturbing effect on the boys between 14 and 18'.[9] Nevertheless the boys were sometimes discharged before their probationary period had expired due to special circumstances, for example if their homes had been bombed or if they were needed for munitions work. By 1947 no boys under the age of 15 nor 18 and over could be admitted, and the length of stay for those under the Probation Act was a maximum of 6 months, whereas those admitted under some other means could serve a term of no longer than 12 months.

Punishment, or rather, corporal punishment (defined once in the minutes as four strokes of the cane) was administered by Mr Green, and any master defying this rule rendered himself liable to instant dismissal. A punishment book was presented to the committee and the punishments agreed to retrospectively, however its use lapsed around 1922, and it was not until 1929 that it was returned by order of the Home Office. Only 73 specific entries were ever recorded (for absconding, theft, smoking and wilful damage), although it was frequently stated that 1) punishments were agreed to although no number was given, or 2) there were no entries in the punishment book. It was not unusual for the latter entry, and it seems that six months was the longest consecutive period in which no punishments were administered. On one occasion Mr Green opined that a 'thrashing would in some cases be utterly useless, but in other cases a boy felt it to be a real disgrace, and it had a satisfactory remedial effect', however in September 1945 a new clause was added to the conditions of service for house staff (excluding the manager) formally forbidding the use of corporal punishment.[10]

Training, apprenticeships, duties and tasks of the boys:

Whilst resident at Padcroft the boys were engaged in domestic chores, painting, decorating and maintaining the home. Alternatively they chopped wood or worked in the workshop, however on leaving the home, it was usual for positions to be found for the boys who were not being returned to their parents. A variety of occupations were secured for the boys, although they tended to centre on farms, mining and manufacturing.

Mr Green occasionally details methods of disposal and in 1942 he stated that there had been 108 situations found for boys. 35 of these had gone into the forces, 43 into machine and munitions work, 4 railway engineers, 5 motor and general engineers, 11 carpenters, joiners, builders and decorators, 5

gardeners, 2 were retuned to parents and 3 had absconded. Furthermore many hundreds enlisted or were conscripted during the Second World War, although there is no account of where they served or if they survived.

After-care
After-care, or what would be termed, visits and correspondence with old boys, appears to have been fundamental to the operations of Padcroft, and Mr Green's travels to different parts of the country are well documented.[11]

Mr Green had visited Wales and the south of England to see boys employed on farms and in every case found the boys contented. However one boy CC who was sent to Llanybyther on the 14th of July had stolen a bicycle on the 16th. Subsequently he was arrested and sentenced to one month's hard labour at Carmarthen prison, although following his release he was re-employed by Mr B. Jones via the intervention of Mr. E. Lloyd CC of Cefremaes, Mydroilin Felinfach Cards, who not only interviewed farmers willing to take boys, but also concerned himself with their interests after their placement. Rev. J. Caleb Hughes MA PhD Diocesan secretary of the CETS Carmarthen had also promised to help in the area.

Mr Green – 'I have about 30 boys at present working on Farms in various parts of Wales, and I should like to pay a visit to them, and inspect their Homes etc., it is 5 years ago since such a visit was paid. I have a number of the Cardiganshire County Council who looks after their interests, but at the same time, I think a visit would be welcomed by both the boys and farmers.'

Mr Green visited Litchfield where he met old boys and made arrangements with farmers to take more boys. He stated that the reason why so few boys remained in contact with their probation officers was that they had made new friends and new lives, and therefore wanted to leave their past behind them.

Mr Green reported that he had visited Rugeley, Litchfield and district regarding situations for the boys, and had found several suitable openings with farmers.

Mr Green reported on his visit to farms in Wales: Mydroilyn, Llandyssul, Pencader, Llanybyther, Newcastle Emlyn. Only one boy FF seemed unsettled but this was soon rectified by Rev. E. M. Davies, vicar of Llandyssul. In four cases Mr Green secured an increase in wages for the boys concerned. He also relates how his chats with the farmers allowed for misunderstandings to be 'adjusted to the mutual satisfaction of all.'. He further states that the success of the boys in that district was due to the interest taken in them by Rev. D. Thomas Jones, vicar of Mydroilyn, who interviewed all the boys and advised Mr Green of vacancies. Mr J. Bisgood presented Mr Green with a set of goal nets and a punch ball for the boys at Padcroft.

Visits were made by Mr Green to Leicester, Worcester, Lancashire, Staffordshire, Lincolnshire. He noted that wages of boys on farms were controlled by the Agricultural Wages (Regulation) Act.

Mr Green visited Pilkington's where 'everything was shown to me from A to Z'. He was impressed with the safety of the industry there.

'The Secretary described the Hostel as a well constructed and very up-to-date building with elaborate arrangements for the well-fare of 200 boys for whom accommodation was provided. There were 120 in residence last month. The Secretary saw the Glass Works where the boys were employed. He formed a very favourable opinion of the treatment of boys in the Hostel[12] and the arrangements made for safe guarding them at the Works. He had made plans with the Superintendent, Mr Roache, to insure a regular report being sent to our Missionaries of the boys sent to St. Helens. The Committee approved the report and agreed that under the organised arrangements described by the Secretary, boys might again be sent to St. Helens.'
Mr Green visited 8 old boys on farms in Leicestershire.
Mr Green visited 16 boys on farms in Worcestershire, Leicestershire and Lincolnshire.
Mr Green visited 10 boys on farms in Staffordshire.
Boys visited on farms in Great Malvern, Litchfield, Leicester and Lincoln.

Additionally boys were contacted by letter, and in 1926 alone, 300 letters were sent out to old boys and at least 100 replies were received. Some old boys seemed anxious to relate how their lives had progressed beyond Padcroft.[13]

'On the 26th of June and old boy HC visited and presented the boys with 3 cricket balls. This is not an isolated case of our old boys appreciation.'

A letter was received from an old boy offering his thanks to everyone for turning him from someone who had been dealt with twice under the Probation of Offenders Act before coming to Padcroft, into a respectable member of society.

Green reported that a boy who had left Padcroft 21

years previously had returned to give his thanks for everything done for him. He was employed by Purley Insurance Company.

However from 1934 entries relating to contact with the boys on a personal level ceased, and the minute book contained an example of an after-care report sheet which was routinely sent to all probation officers in the six months following a boy's release. The curtailment of this duty of the manager probably resulted from the re-organisation of the probation service, which by that time was beginning to come under the auspices of the Home Office and was no longer the remit of the LPCM, however Mr Green continued to record after care statistics. In 1941 he noted that of the 230 boys admitted in the previous year, 190 after-care reports stated their progress as quite satisfactory, 20 not satisfactory, 10 had gone to borstal and 10 to an approved school. The total to date through the home at that point was 6,963.

The Last Word
Between 1902 and 1949 7,583 boys passed through the doors of Padcroft, and the home boasted an impressive 83% success rate. Perhaps then it should be left to Mr Green to sum up the operations and successes of Padcroft. This extract was taken from his last annual report.

Gentlemen,
I have much pleasure in presenting my report for the year ending 31st March 1948. I thought it would be interesting for you to know that I have completed 46 years service at "Padcroft", 43 years as Manager and 32 years as Probation Officer at Uxbridge Court.

In addition to the above, I, on behalf of the Mission, opened the Boys' Garden Colony at Basingstoke in 1918 which was, up to the time I was relieved of the responsibility, a great success. I have dealt with over 9,000 difficult boys during this period. I think I can now say, without being conceited that I consider myself an authority on this work.

However, in spite of my vast experience, I have never been invited to give evidence, or take part in any Government Departmental Enquiry, where my experience would be an advantage.

Of recent years, "Padcroft" has been used for the reception of problem boys, the difficult mal-adjusted type, who have caused all who were interested in them – Magistrates, Probation Officers, Social Workers and parents – grave anxiety…During their residence all these boys receive psychiatric treatment at the various clinics. These boys, in the past, looked with suspicion on all efforts to assist them, and would rather sink in the mire of despair, than grasp the hand of fellowship. Then again, there is the defiant aggressive boy, who refuses to recognize law and order, defies authority, and is a law unto himself. Every admission is studied and treated as a separate unit; each has his own peculiar weakness and requires individual treatment.

The class of boys admitted since 1939 is, in some respects, more difficult than before hostilities. This is due, in my opinion, to the apathy of the parents, and their lack of moral obligation and example. At the present time I realize that the number of offences that a person can commit is greater than before, but that is principally owing to restrictions and controls which, in turn, create "Black Markets".

During the year, the health of the boys has been generally good…We believe the physical efficiency brings moral tone, and the youth gains in alertness and self-respect. This is our motto, and Mr. Nicholls, our Physical Training Instructor, must be congratulated on his energy and example…The improvement in the boys' physical condition whilst in residence is remarkable. Regular meals, a balanced diet, and a well ordered life, make this improvement possible. The average weight gained per boy over a period of 6 months is 14 lbs.

…Mr. H. Carn, our Horticultural Instructor, is trying out a system of plots, so many boys to each plot. The idea is to create healthy competition and enthusiasm, and I am looking forward to the result of this venture.

…During the winter evenings, our boys have been fully occupied with their several hobbies – model making in metal and wood, artificial flower designing, etc., and quite recently they have founded an "Artists Club" with some very good results.
…We are constantly receiving letters from old boys and their parents…I know and realize how very keen the authorities are in 'After Care' but my experience over a long period proves to me that, unless done diplomatically and with caution, it is not appreciated by the person concerned. Their argument is this:- "I quite realize you are anxious for my future, and so am I, but I do not want to be constantly reminded that I have been in trouble. I want to forget it. Wouldn't you?"

…Our principle throughout our work here at "Padcroft" has been to 'Be just before being generous'. We have always tried to instill into those placed under our care that 'Whatever is worth doing at all is worth doing well'…

'The story of "Padcroft" is largely the life stories of two people, Mr. and Mrs. Frank Green. Forty-seven years ago, a young man who had already been a gold miner in Wales and had seen active service in the South African War, was appointed "Manager" of this Home for boys. Mr. Green's qualifications for this work were perhaps by modern standards, slender, but he had character in abundance, a simple faith in God and in the essential decency of ordinary folk, a wealth of common sense allied to a sense of humour, a ready sympathy,

and a belief in orderliness and discipline…

"Padcroft" closed its doors, but its work will live on for many years to come. It will live in the restored lives of thousands of men who in their youth had their first chance in life at "Padcroft".'
G. Morley-Jacob, General Secretary of The London Police Court Mission, Annual Report 1949 pp14-1

Examples of cases

13th annual report of the London Diocesan Branch of the Church of England Temperance Society, 1905
'E. C. H. was received from Enfield, a serious charge having been preferred against him. He had become associated with bad characters, but on his admission to the Home, resolved to lead a better life. His conduct is now beyond approach.'
'F. H., charged with sleeping out. He was entirely destitute, without father or mother, and had gradually sunk into the lowest depths. A few weeks in the Home worked wonders in every way, and he is now doing well in a situation.'

19th annual report of the London Diocesan Branch of the Church of England Temperance Society, 1911
'F. A., aged 16, was charged with stealing linen, etc., when employed at the Army and Navy Stores. He had been brought up in an atmosphere where the home influence was good, but he was to be seen night after night in the crowds which throng the picture-palaces and cheap music halls. Like many a lad he loved excitement, and it took this form with him. The effect upon him was bad, and he started to drift with the current and was soon upon the rocks. The Missionary at Westminster went to his rescue, and he was placed in the home at Yiewsley. In the situation found for him he has remained for sixteen

A REHEARSAL!

"NOW, DON'T YOU 'URRY THE HANDANTY (*ANDANTE*) THIS TIME, YOUNG FELLER!"

months and has done well. The Home is an Emergency Home of this kind and ready to receive such lads at the moment of danger.'

23rd annual report of the London Diocesan Branch of the Church of England Temperance Society, 1915

'J. S. was charged at the Chiswick Police Court with a petty theft. The Missionary asked that the boy might be taken to "Padcroft," and the Magistrate consented. Here he behaved well, and on leaving the Home he enlisted. He went to India with his Regiment, and on the outbreak of war he had attained Sergeant's rank. Attached to the Indian Contingent, Sergeant S. went through many engagements and won the D.C.M. at Festubert for attending and rescuing two wounded comrades under heavy fire.'

29th annual report of the London Diocesan Branch of the Church of England Temperance Society, 1921

'J. P., age 16, was charged at Acton Court with "wandering." Both his parents were dead, and the lad, with no home, had tramped the country, being knocked about "from pillar to post." He had worked on different farms, but was half starved, and had no friends to help him. The Magistrates showed their sympathy for this unfortunate boy, and he

found a home in Padcroft. By the kind assistance of a local farmer his knowledge of farm work was considerably extended, and eventually a situation was found for him with a lady in Carnarvonshire. His duties were to look after four cows, a pony and a horse, and he loved his work. This lady is very pleased with "Jimmy," and the lad is thoroughly happy, and the proud possessor of a bicycle, given him by his mistress.'

32nd annual report of the London Diocesan Branch of the Church of England Temperance Society, 1924

'A lad was charged at the court with stealing a coat and vest. On hearing that the boy had no home and that his parents were dead he was taken to Padcroft. While there he wrote to the Missionary who had brought him saying. "I am sending these few lines to let you know that I am very sorry to have caused all this trouble, but this has taught me a lesson. I hope you will go over it. I was led away by other boys, but I have made up my mind to go straight.'

43rd annual report of the London Diocesan Branch of the Church of England Temperance Society, 1935

'Henry was a foundling and brought up at a Children's Cottage Home in the country. His only friends in the world were the officials connected with the Home. He was like Oliver Twist in one respect – he "asked for more;" not more food, but trouble! And he got it. Henry was too much for the quiet and peaceful atmosphere of the Children's Home, and it was decided to send him where there would be more discipline. He was admitted to Padcroft, and the "young scamp" soon showed that he had plenty of spirit, but his conduct was excellent. One day the headmaster of a well-known school called to ask for "a good boy" to assist the butler. Henry was chosen, and has given satisfaction to the butler, and the headmaster and to himself.'

44th annual report of the London Diocesan Branch of the Church of England Temperance Society, 1936

'Harold was charged at Brentford with larceny, but his home was near the London Docks, and he had left it on account of the drunken habits of his mother and step-father. Harold's mother had taken to herself a third husband whose only qualification appeared to be that he was a good drinker. This poor boy when admitted was a miserable underfed child but to-day, thanks to regular habits, healthy environment and good food, he is a blue-eyed box of happiness, very good-tempered, and the life of Padcroft. He has been with us for six months and wants to stay six months more. Poor child, what a home was his! Padcroft seems to him a Paradise.'

A Mission of Mercy, The London Police Court Mission Report for 1938

'George lived in Bedfordshire with a step-father, and after leaving school he obtained a situation near his home. His earnings however were not sufficient for his guardian, and another job had to be obtained but with similar results. Again a change was made, and yet again but the step-father was never satisfied, and the dreadful truth gradually sank into George's consciousness – he was not wanted. Life under such circumstances must be terrible always to a sensitive nature, but still more so when the parent's feelings are expressed with brutal frankness. So at last George left his home for London, little knowing the pit-falls and troubles that might await a stranger in the great City. Hungry and footsore, he was tempted to take a bottle of milk from a doorstep. It was thus that George found himself in a Juvenile Court. He was placed on probation and sent to Padcroft – which was probably the most fortunate incident in his life. He quickly responded to all that was done to help him. He worked well and showed himself honest and good-tempered. When George left Padcroft it was to work at the house of a gentleman who took an interest in his progress. He was encouraged to be thrifty and industrious, and arrangements were made for him to attend evening classes. George is doing well, and hopes to become a draughtsman and thus further improve his position.'

Letters from old boys

13th annual report of the London Diocesan Branch of the Church of England Temperance Society, 1905
'D. A., 18, was charged with embezzlement, and finally bound over and taken to a Home. Two and a half years later, he wrote to the Magistrate as follows: "Dear Sir, I am D. A., who was bound over by you. I was sent by the Missionary to Padcroft, and I am very thankful I was sent there, as there is everything a young fellow can wish for. When I left the Home, the Master got a berth for me at the …………, in the Electrical Engineering Department, as an assistant circuit hand for nine months. My next situation was at …………..Road, Holborn, for 9 months. The cause of leaving is that Mr………..sold his motor-car. The reason I write this is that I know you would like to know how I have been getting on since I came from the Home.'

29th annual report of the London Diocesan Branch of the Church of England Temperance Society, 1921
'Dear Mr Green,
Just a line from one of your old boys, to let you know that I am still alive. I am now on one of the best ships in the Navy. We start on a two-years' cruise to the West Indies and North America on Monday, so I shall not see you for another two years…I shall be extremely pleased to hear from you again, as, although I was supposed to be rather a "dashing" boy, you took almost a fatherly interest in me, and I shall never forget your kindness. I suppose I am rather sentimental, but I have never been able to remember much of my own father, and since I met you I have looked upon you as my father…I hope you will find time to write to me as soon as you can. I remain, etc.'

32nd annual report of the London Diocesan Branch of the Church of England Temperance Society, 1924
'After 9 years, grown to manhood, he called on the Missionary at Court. He said he was in business for himself, had started as a fruiterer and greengrocer with the money he received on his discharge from the Army, and was doing well. He said he had honestly tried to carry out the advice which the Missionary gave him on his way to Padcroft and he always thanked God when he read in the Press of a lad being sent to the Home because he knew he would be given a good chance there.'

36th annual report of the London Diocesan Branch of the Church of England Temperance Society, 1929
'Dear Mr Green,
It gives me great pleasure in writing to one who had helped me through part of my life. Well Sir, I hope you will forgive me for keeping you so long without an answer. When I received your letter I was very pleased to hear you had not forgotten one of your old boys. Well, Sir, I have been to sea twice since I left you. The first day I sailed from England my mother died, I was on a Norwegian vessel. The second time I went was August, 1927, on an English vessel. I have been on land for 12 months now, I live with a friend of my mother's in the same house. I wish I were at sea. I have managed to save a £1.0s.0d. I get 22s. a week, when one has to buy clothes, cigarettes and pay for keep, one can imagine it does not go far. Well, Sir, I have not forgot the good times I had a Padcroft. It is a place where no lad can regret having been there. Well, Sir, I haven't anything else to write about at present, and I hope yourself, Matron, and Mrs Brogan are enjoying good health. I will close now as my tea is ready, thanking you for your pleasing letter.
Yours sincerely, C. D.'

44th annual report of the London Diocesan Branch of the Church of England Temperance Society, 1936
'We have often submitted that the chief cause of juvenile delinquency is to be found in unsatisfactory or broken homes. David was handicapped from the start, for his mother was never married and he could not remember anything of a father. Later he was brought up by an uncle and aunt who certainly did their best for him, but the start had been all wrong. So David stood in the dock charged with embezzlement. A kindly missionary suggested Padcroft, a proposal agreed to by the Court. Although David had fallen under the influence of persons of the wrong character, he showed signs which Padcroft recognised that there were latent possibilities of good in him. He was trusted by the Master and never failed. He obtained a good post on leaving, and his own appreciation of the efforts made on his behalf may be judged from the following letter (addressed to Mr. Green):-

Dear Sir,
This is to thank you for the great kindness with which you have helped me during my stay at Padcroft. I can assure you that I really do appreciate both you and Mrs. Green's help which you have already given me. I have now settled down to work hard and prove a success so that you will see I have appreciated your kindness. I find it hard to express my gratitude in words, but I am sure that you will understand. Thank you also for the

who remember me tell them I am in the "pink" and only wish they could be in the Army with me learning to make retribution for all the things they may have done. Well, Sir, so much for my "few lines." I think I have said enough, so will close with best wishes from myself and my parents.
Yours sincerely J. F.
P.S. – Please accept my small donation to the funds of the Home, and if Bob is still with you please ask him to write to me.

References and Resources:

1 It should be noted that throughout the report money is referred to in pounds, shillings and pence and not in decimal currency.
2 Padcroft minutes 1920
3 The shelter appears to have been of the Anderson type and built in the grounds. The boys slept on mattresses on the floor as opposed to using bunk beds. Additionally sanitation and ventilation gave some cause for concern.
4 Ibid 1928
5 Ibid 1922
6 Ibid
7 Ibid 1926
8 Ibid 1945
9 Ibid 1942
10 Ibid 1930
11 Ibid 1920 to 1932
12 Undoubtedly there would have been difficulties accommodating and containing nearly 200 boys aged 14 to 18, not only as many of them lacked the necessary 'discipline' expected of them, but also as they were apparently sent under duress as part of their probation period.
13 Ibid 1920 and 1926.

The resources used in compiling this report were from The Rainer Archive housed at the Galleries of Justice, High Pavement, Nottingham Telephone 0115 9520555.

This is an extract from a report commissioned by The Galleries of Justice and Mr David Pilkington CBE in March 2002.
A website offering information to ex-residents of London Police Court Mission Padcroft Boys' Home, Yiewsley, Middlesex. is at http://www.geocities.com/lpcmpadcroft

The home ran from 1902 to 1949 and some 8,000 boys aged between 14 and 18 passed through its doors during that time. Until now Padcroft's history has lain undiscovered and therefore the 'boys' have been unable to relocate their pasts. In exchange for their or their families memories they can gain an insight into the home.

way in which you provided for me to start work, clothes, etc. I think that it was very decent of you to fix me up as regards clothes. Please accept the gratitude and respects of my people, also myself. Please give my regards to Master Frank for the kindness which he has also shown to me. In fact, I want to thank everybody and let them see that whatever happens I shall always be indebted to them for helping me at a time when help was needed. Hoping that you will accept my humblest thanks. I close, etc.'

A Mission of Mercy, The London Police Court Mission report for 1939
"Dear Sir,
Just a few lines to let you know how I am getting on in life since I left Padcroft. I reported to H.Q.'s on the Saturday night after leaving you and was sent to Brixton War Station. Two weeks ago I was sent with the rest of the 1st Battalion to the above address. I am in the best of health thanks to Mr Buckie's training, and am living in the middle of the Forest in what was once the estate of Mr Hayley Morris. I have to thank Mr Stronnell for his training, too, as I should never have been able to fix up shelves and chairs and tables in what was once an empty Warden's cottage. It looks quite homelike except that there is no carpet on the floor, I've painted a notice on the door naming it the "Royal Albert Hall," we only want an organ now and we could give Concerts. Tell Mr Buckie for me that we all do 15 minutes P.T. in the morning after Reveille and we take turns in taking the class. I have introduced all the exercises that I was taught at Padcroft, excluding, of course, the Horsework. I wonder what Mr Hicklin is doing about his gardens now. I suppose the rain we have had lately has not done them any good. Well, Sir, I have received a letter from Mr Smith telling me that the Magistrate has kindly consented to my being allowed to be struck off the Probation list. I am now a free man, and I must thank Matron and you and all at Padcroft for the good report which Mr Smith mentioned in his letter. If there are any boys at Padcroft, please,

Ship, Steamboat Owners and Master Mariners

Neil Richardson discovers his maritime ancestry

It all stared while looking through a Local Directory. I found one of my family had been a Steam Boat Owner in the nineteenth century, Jacob Tweedy. Once I had this information I found the need to find out more about him and his boats. Unfortunately no one could tell me where to go to next. I tried Tyne and Wear Archive and found there were some Minute and Account Books for the Tyne Steam Tug Association, North Shields. Unfortunately these only dealt with the names of the boats and not their owners, so this is where I came to a halt for some years.

My fortune changed when I met a local historian, Bob Balmour. He told me of the research he had done in the Customhouse Records of the River Tyne. Then started what has become a bit of an obsession. I found their records I required were deposited in the Tyne and Wear Archive. There are three sets of records for the Tyne; Newcastle 1786 onwards, North Shields 1848 onwards and South Shields 1859 onwards.

My first search began with the North Shields records. I decided to start from the first record and work my way through. After a week of doing this Bob asked me if I would mind transcribing the names, numbers, rigs, where they had come from and their fates in a book he had begun many years before. Also, could I record any ship with a Blyth connection on a pro-former? This I agreed to do.

The first thing that caught my attention was the people who had shares in ships. There were all classes of society from the very rich to the likes of miners and shipwrights. To me this seemed like an excellent source of untapped information for the Family Historian.

The first stoke of luck was not for me but a lady in Australia for whom I do research. In the early records for North Shields, the Masters of the vessels were named and I found two references to Winspeare's, the name she is researching. Next again I found some information for a lady in Essex. Ships are sold in sixty four shares and a lot of the ships were part owned by the master. She is researching a Captain Joseph Dixon. I found him as a part owner of a ship with four other people. Joseph was born in Blyth but was living in North Shields; all the other owners were from Blyth. A little research and two of the four at least are relations. I went on to find more than ten vessels that Joseph was owner of and possibly Master as well. He was recorded as being a Master Mariner in all but one record and in that one he is down as a Ship Owner.

At last I found what I had been looking for. In 1853 I found Jacob Tweedy had 32/64 shares in the Steam Boat "Honer". What was surprising was the other owner was his brother Robert Tweedy of Blyth of whom I knew nothing and so started research into another member of the family. This vessel was brand new and to this day I still don't know where the money came from to buy this boat, Jacob had been a rope maker and Robert an agricultural labourer. They kept this boat for a year and then sold it.

About six months later in 1854 they bought their second boat, "Fury" again brand new, they kept this boat for three years and again sold it. A few months later 1n 1857 they bought their third and last Steam Boat, another called "Fury" [the other "Fury" had left the Tyne]. The next lot of transactions gave Jacob and Robert mortgaging the vessel twice. The first was to a Mary Swinney who later bought 12/64 shares when Robert sold out, Jacob taking the remaining shares, giving him 52/64 shares. Mary Swinney was a widow and when she died she left all of her estate to Jacob [the date of probate being granted and the names of the executors are recorded, for anyone owning a vessel, in the Custom House Records]. I again have yet to find out what the relationship was between Jacob and Mary. One other transaction took place William Tweedy, Jacob's son, bought one share. Jacob eventually lost the boat in 1880 when the mortgage was called in. Jacob died in 1885 in the Work House, possibly with Dementia perhaps this was the cause of him losing his boat, I have yet to find out.

© Robert Blatchford Collection

I now had the names of Jacob's boats so I could once again try and find out more about the vessels in the two books of the Tyne Steam Tug Association. The first book I looked at was the minute book. The main interests in this book were the disputes between the tugs for Foy money paid by vessels entering or leaving the Tyne. Although this book did not start until 1875 the "Fury" featured in three disputes. The first she lost, the second neither party turned up and in the third "Fury" won by default of the other tug making the claim to late.

In the Account Book again the "Fury" is mentioned on four occasions. In the first the boat is damaged, in the second she has a broken crank pin, in the third she has a broken shaft and has to be towed and lastly she is again damaged. The amounts paid vary from £2 0s 0d [£2.00p] to £16 8s 4d [£16.42p].

If I require any more information about the Steamboats that the Tweedy's Owned I will have to go to the PRO in London, the National Maritime Museum in Greenwich or perhaps the Maritime History Group in Newfoundland. Depending on your commitment there are lots of places to search; if you have the time and the money.

As for my obsession, along with Bob Balmour we have transcribed the names, tonnage, rig, the vessels last recorded location, present location and fate, for both the North and South Shields Custom Houses. These are well on he way to being indexed. Work has started on the Newcastle registers and they will be indexed in the near future. I have started on the Master Mariners on the North Shields registers. These only run from 1848 to 1854 when they can be found by other means [Lloyds Captains Register]. This index should be finished shortly.

I have also started to extract all of the owners on the North Shields Register. This will be followed by the South Shields Owners, then the Newcastle Owners and Master Mariners. This is a massive job and will

take a while. We hope that I will be able to publish on fiche in parts consisting of a suitable number of years, The Vessels, The Owners and the Masters of all of the Vessels registered on the River Tyne. This includes Seaton Sluice, Blyth and Warkworth Harbour [Amble].

If you think you may have a connection with the Sea, the Customhouse records are well worth looking at. This is a long and often-slow task but can be very rewarding.

Then again you could wait until I finish indexing and do it the easy way.

The other problem you may face is the need to know more about the terms used when describing vessels. The rigging donates the type of vessel you are looking at. There are Brig, Snow Barque, Schooner, Sloop rigged vessels, Standing Bowsprit's and much more but that is another lot of research.

The only thing to be careful of is shipping can be as addictive as Family History

Bibliography
Watts Christopher T and Watts Michael J.
My Ancestor was a Merchant Seaman.
Published by The Society of Genealogists.

Manchester Ship Canal
© Robert Blatchford Collection

Family History and the Militia from 1793 ~ 1815

Barbara Chambers

Many people are familiar with the fact that during the 2nd World War, military bases were established all over Britain. This led to people from other parts of Britain living in places many miles away from their homes and becoming involved with the local community.

Another War over a hundred years prior to this resulted in much the same situation occurring but for considerably longer. From 1793 to 1815 Britain was at war with France and during this time in addition to many men and indeed some women and children spending time overseas. Britain and Ireland had many military establishments throughout the length and breadth of the country. The places involved varied depending on the situation at the time but generally speaking stretched from Inverness in the north to the Channel Island in the south and all points east and west, including many in Ireland. These establishments ranged from barracks, and coastal defences to prison for prisoners of war, both in the form of hulks and land based prisons. Often more particularly as the war progressed the soldiers manning these establishments were men from a County Militia, invariably from another county. At

the start of the war the Counties were required to embody their Militia and raise varying numbers of men during the entire period to maintain their county militia. The Militia were not required to serve outside Britain and Ireland during this war.

Britain and Ireland were divided into military districts and sub district and although many of the places within these districts that had a military presence were found on the coast not all were. Although not stationed everywhere the Militia were being used to assist the regular Army in home defence, but also they were used to deal with civil unrest, guarding the ever increasing number of prisoners of war and carrying out duties in and around London normally carried out by the Foot Guards in their roll as members of the Household Brigade, these involved duties at such places as Windsor and the Tower of London. Prison hulks were based at Chatham, Portsmouth and Plymouth, and among the land prisons the furthest north was Perth and purpose built prisons included Dartmoor in Devon and Norman Cross just outside Peterborough.

As to who the men in the County Militia were, contrary to reports I have read, in general the Militia Regiments were made up of men from their own county or sometimes an adjoining one or men from elsewhere who had moved to that county. Certainly my experience gained from research during this period shows this to be the case. It may be that some confusion has arisen between the Militia and Volunteers in the Fencible Cavalry and Infantry. Individuals raised these units during the early period of the war; most were disbanded by the year 1802. They initially raised men from an area, but also appeared to collect recruits where ever in the country they were stationed.

Although there were variations in the rules concerning the requirements and service of the Militia during this period; as new legislation was passed to deal with the situation at a particular time. Generally men were balloted from a list of men from the parish between the ages of 18 and 45 years and they served for a term varying between 3yrs and 5yrs. They were then discharged and were then excluded from the ballot until their name came round again in rotation, some men chose to sign on at the end of their term. Some of those balloted were able to find substitutes to go in their place. It has been suggested that the parish disposed of their unwanted men by balloting and or substituting them into the Militia and that the Militia were generally 'riff raff'. This seems very unlikely, firstly from a practical point of view, because of the numbers involved over the period of 22yrs no one could have those many undesirables, secondly the Army including many of the best Regiments increasingly recruited from the Militia and were happy to take on these men, many of whom gave good service. There were men who were exempted from service like those already in the armed forces or other vital jobs in the war effort such as dockyards, also a man with a child under ten years was exempted. Those serving as volunteers and substitutes were also subject to exemption. these men however were exempted from being drawn for further service.

Each county had at least one Militia Regiment, however larger counties had more than one. Cornwall had the Cornish Miners as well as the Militia; Devon had an East, North and South; Essex East and West, Gloucestershire North and South, Hampshire North, South and Isle of Wight; Kent East & West; Lancashire 1st, 2nd and 3rd; Lincolnshire North, South and East; London East and West; Middlesex East West and Westminster; Norfolk East and West; Somerset 1st and 2nd; Suffolk East and West; Surrey East and West; Tower Hamlets 1st and 2nd; Yorkshire 1st, 2nd and 3rd West Riding, North Riding and East Riding. The counties of Monmouth and Brecon were combined and some of the smaller Scottish counties did not have separate regiments. The numbers to be raised and continually maintained by each county varied but at one time it ranged from eighty three for Rutland to Middlesex, excluding Tower Hamlets needing to raising over three thousand,

There are some exceptions to the Militia going far from home. It would appear that the Isle of Wight Militia remained on the island and the Tower Hamlet and East London Militia ventured no further than across the River Thames to Deptford and the surrounding area.

Just to give a few examples of locations in August 1799 you would have found Militia from Anglesey, Carmarthen, Dorset, Flintshire, Glamorgan and North Yorkshire on the Isle of Wight.

In August 1806 in Yarmouth in Norfolk, Militia from Anglesey and Rossshire were serving, the East Suffolk were in Aberdeen, the Aberdeenshire at Haddington and the Fifeshire at Dover Castle. While in August 1812 Guarding prisoners of war on prison ships stationed in Portsmouth, Gosport and Hilsea were regiments of militia from North Devonshire, East Essex, Hereford, Worcestershire, North Cork Militia and County Limerick. Meanwhile the Cambridgeshire Militia were in Peebles the Durham in Kinross the Inverness at Porchester Barracks, while over in Ireland in addition to twenty three Irish Militia Regiments, there were twenty eight Militia Regiments from England, Scotland and Wales.

How does this affect family history? In most parish registers where Regiments were stationed you will find marriages taking place between local women and soldiers, it is also quite probably that there will be baptisms and even deaths. The families frequently travelled with the Regiment. Perhaps that lost marriage is to be found among these records. Possibly the family you thought was from Kent or Ireland is connected to your family.

Finally a word of advice for those who research only exact spellings, the Army have no rules as far as spellings are concerned they can vary from one documents to another and often are spelt phonetically, so unless you are flexible with the spelling you may miss some interesting ancestors.

http://member.aol.com/BJCham2909/homepage.html

Where can you

- *Access over 100,000 items on local & family history?*
- *Use the largest collection of parish register & census index copies in Britain?*
- *Get immediate, valuable advice from experienced genealogists?*
- *Attend informative lectures presented by experts?*
- *Browse the best-stocked genealogical bookshop in the country?*
- *Surf a growing range of online records?*

You get all these and more from

The Society of Genealogists

The One-Stop resource for everyone in Family & Local History

Take advantage of our unique, newly refurbished **Library** with over 9000 Parish Register copies and wide-ranging material on Civil Registration, Censuses, County Records, Poll Books, Heraldry & Family Histories - on microfilm, fiche & PC.

Visit our **Bookshop** for an impressive range of books, microfiche, CDs, disks & IT genealogy programs at very competitive prices. Surf over 7000 items online at www.sog.org.uk via our secure server. Contact us at sales@sog.org.uk.

Join the Society - **Membership** gives you:

- Free access to the library & borrowing rights
- a 20% discount on all Society publications, lectures and courses
- free copies of the highly respected *Genealogists' Magazine*
- free access to an increasing range of online records

and all for **just £40 a year** *

For an information pack, simply email the Membership Secretary on

membership@sog.org.uk,
tel: 020-7553 3291

Make the most of your research with:

The Society of Genealogists
14 Charterhouse Buildings, Goswell Road
London EC1M 7BA

Tel: 020-7251 8799; Fax: 020-7250 1800

* special Direct Debit offer plus Initial Joining Fee £10.00

The Society of Genealogists
Else Churchill *Genealogy Officer*

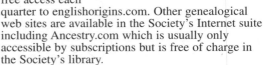

Founded in 1911 the Society of Genealogists (SoG) is Britain's premier family history organization. It arranges courses, lectures and visits and promotes two annual family history fairs.

Its extensive collections are particularly valuable for research before the start of civil registration in 1837 but there is plenty for the beginner too.

Its library contains Britain's largest collection of parish register copies and many nonconformist registers. Most cover the period from the sixteenth century to 1837. Register transcripts are arranged by county along with local histories, copies of monumental inscriptions, poll books, trade directories and census indexes.

Indexes of births, marriages and deaths for Scotland (1855-1920) for England and Wales and for many Britons overseas (1837-1925) are also available as are indexes of wills and marriage licences, and of apprentices and masters (1710-1774). The Society has a wide collection of miscellaneous manuscript research notes, printed and unpublished family histories and birth briefs submitted by researchers.

There are also sections of works relating to the professions, army and navy lists, clerical and medical directories, public and other schools, universities, religious denominations, biography, peerage and heraldry and standard genealogical periodicals. These include the Society's own journals Genealogists' Magazine and Computers in Genealogy and the journals of family history societies in the British Isles and many from societies worldwide.

Unique to the Society's library is its substantial Document Collection of miscellaneous manuscripts and an extensive collection of printed and typescript family histories. Additionally, there is a general card index of over three million references and references to about four and a half million chancery and other court proceedings in the Bernau Index.

Most of the books are on open access shelves and an increasing amount of material is now on film or microfiche and also on CD ROM. Thanks to the support of the Heritage Lottery Fund, the entire library catalogue is now on computer terminals around the building. If you expect to be carrying out extensive research in the British Isles then membership is very worthwhile and the overseas collections are useful too. Non-members can use the library for a small fee.

Membership is £40 per years (if paying by direct debit in the EU VAT area) plus a one-off joining fee of £10. This entitles a member to free access to the Library, certain borrowing rights, free copies of the quarterly Genealogists Magazine and various discounts of publications, courses, postal searches and free access each quarter to englishorigins.com. Other genealogical web sites are available in the Society's Internet suite including Ancestry.com which is usually only accessible by subscriptions but is free of charge in the Society's library.

The Society publishes many useful guides and these are available along with an enormous range of other books, maps and computer software from the bookshop as well as on line. Additionally, the Society publishes over one hundred books of interest to family historians including the vital National Index of Parish Registers and My ancestors series. All these publications are available together with a vast range of other books, maps, microfiche and computer software at the Society's shop - all available on-line at www.sog.org.uk. Catalogues are available on request. More details about the Society can be found on its extensive website at www.sog.org.uk

The Society has an important role in providing education and training. It runs a comprehensive programme of skills courses to help family historians get the most out of the library and other repositories and also to conduct and present their research in a methodical and accurate fashion. There is also a wide range of lectures and visits of interest to genealogists and the Society promotes the Family History Fair in London in May and an out reach event away from London in September.

The Society also has an important national voice in pressing for preservation of and better access to records of interest to genealogists.

Visitors are welcome to the Society. There are free tours of the Library on alternate Saturday mornings with free advice sessions available on the same afternoons. In addition there are two open Sundays each year with tours and demonstrations.

For a free Membership Pack contact the Society at 14 Charterhouse Buildings, Goswell Road, London EC1M 7BA Telephone 020- 7553 3291 Fax 020 7250 1800 Email: membership@sog.org.uk

Library & Shop:
Tuesday, Wednesday, Friday & Saturday:10am to 6pm: Thursday, 10am to 8pm
Administration: Monday to Friday, 9am to 5pm

Contacts:

Library Enquiries - Tim Lawrence
Tel: 020 7702 5485 Email: library@sog.org.uk
Membership - Jayshree Neghandi
Email: membership@sog.org.uk
Genealogy Enquiries - Else Churchill
Tel: 020 7702 5488 Email: genealogy@sog.org.uk
Shop - Ken Divall
Tel: 020 7702 5483 Email: sales@sog.org.uk
Lectures & Courses - Julia English
Tel: 020 7553 3290 Email: events@sog.org.uk
General Enquiries Sheila Marshall Tel: 020 7702 5480
Acting Director (Finance & Admin) June Perrin
Tel: 020 7553 3296 Email: asstdir@sog.org.uk
Library & Shop Fax: 020 7250 1800
Membership & Events Fax: 020 7251 6773

Library Searches
The Society is aware that not everyone is able to
visit the library; hence the library does offer a
limited search and copy service on some of the
indexes and finding aids within the collections. The
Society's resources are such that we cannot make
long searches in un-indexed materials. Nor can we
make searches outside the library. For example we
would not be able to extract all entries of a
particular name from a filmed parish register but if
the exact date is known copies can be made. Please
note we cannot search for a named individual
within the collections.

Payments
Indexes and collections can be searched on receipt
of the library search/copy fee of £11(members
£8.80) for each half hour or part thereof spent in
making the search. Most searches will not exceed
half an hour. The fee includes VAT and postage.
Requests must include payment in advance. Copies
of entries (If found) will be supplied (maximum c20
pages). Payment can be made by sterling cheque or
VISA/MASTERCARD.

Indexes and Special Collections
Bernau Index to miscellaneous chancery,
exchequer and other 17th & 18th century sources
Boyd's Marriage Index for England 1538-1837
(state either particular county or a 25 year time
period)
Boyd's Inhabitants of London (60, 000 London
families mainly 16th & 17th centuries)
Boyd's London Burials (250,000 abstracts of adult
male burials pre 1853)
Apprentices of Great Britain
(taxed apprenticeships) 1710-1774
London Apprenticeships 1568-1850
Teachers' Registration
Council Registers 1902-48
Trinity House Petitions 1787-1854
(also some Apprentice Indentures 1788 & 1818-45
and miscellaneous Pensions and Petitions 1790-
1889)
Great Card Index of miscellaneous sources (3
million entries)
Fawcett Index of Anglican Clergy and North
Country families
County Family Collections
Campling Collection – Norfolk families

Roger's Collection – Cornish families
Professions Trades and Occupations
Law Lists 1813-1973
Medical Directories from 1845 and Medical
Register from 1854
18th Century Medics
Schools Universities
Alumni Oxonienses 1500-1714, 1715-1886
Alumni Cantabrigienses to 1751,1752-1900
Other printed schools and university registers
Religions
Huguenot Society Proceedings & Quarto Series
Quaker Digests of pre 1837 registers
Crockford's Clerical Directories and Clergy Lists
(1828, then roughly every 10 years1840-1999)
Hyamson's Notes on Jewish families
Colyer Fergusson's notes on Jewish families
Wagner Collection of Huguenot Pedigrees

Armed Service
Navy Lists 1800-1946 Army Lists 1756-1946 (gaps
- later years held but not searched)
Soldiers Who Died in the Great War 1914-19
National Roll of Great War
Commissioned Sea Officers of the Royal Navy
1600-1819
Will Indexes
PCC wills (BRS and other indexes 1383-1800)
Other printed indexes (mostly BRS Index Library
volumes and some others. Please note we cannot
search calendars on microfilm)
Peerage Royalty
Complete Peerage
Burkes Peerages and Landed Gentries
Overseas Collections
Australia:
Civil Registration Indexes on CD ROM & fiche
New South Wales Convicts Indents (Index only)
1828 Census New South Wales
India:
Percy-Smith's India Index (notes on British families
in India – many marriages)
Anglo India Research Correspondence
West Indies
Smith Manuscripts – notes on British families in the
Caribbean
CD Roms
Included inter alia:
Palmer's Index to the Times Newspaper 1790-1905
Services of Heirs for Scotland 1700-1859
Griffith's Primary Valuation for Ireland 1848-1864
1880 US Census
Other CDS may be searched and a quote will be
given.
Indexes and Original Documents
The following indexes and databases can be
searched on www.englishorigins.com. The indexes
are available to view online for non members at £6
for 48 hours/150 records. Members have free access
four times a year. *Copies of the some documents
to which index entries refer are available at £10
(members £8)
Vicar General Marriage Licence Allegations
1694-1850*
Faculty Office Marriage Licence Allegations 1701-
1850*

Bank of England Wills 1717-1845*
PCC Wills 1750-1800
City of London Apprentices
Consistory Court of London Depositions
Archdeaconry Court of London wills
Special Manuscript Collections
The Society of Genealogists holds many special
manuscript research collections of research notes
and roll pedigrees. A search can be made in the
indexes to see if a surname is represented (free of
charge). A quotation can then be made for the costs
of copying the relevant materials if possible.
What's been done before?
The Society of Genealogists holds thousands of
printed family histories along with a huge document
collection of miscellaneous manuscript notes on
families. The Society will happily search its various
catalogues and bibliographies (free of charge) to see
if anything is held on a particular name. A quotation
can then be made for the costs of copying the
relevant materials if possible
Lengthy searches
Lengthy or complicated Searches are undertaken
only at the discretion of the Genealogy Officer, and
an estimate of fees will be provided. The work will
be undertaken only on receipt of the appropriate fee.

Enquiries should be made by:
Fax: (020) 7250 1800 Email: library@sog.org.uk
Post: SoG, 14 Charterhouse Buildings, Goswell
Road, London EC1M 7BA
Telephone 020 7702 5488 or 5489
For postal enquiries, please include a stamped self-

addressed envelope or, if
outside the UK, an addressed envelope and THREE
International Reply Coupons.

Notes
Requests for catalogue enquiries and searches are
dealt with in order of receipt. They are not
acknowledged but the Society endeavours to answer
within one month if possible. The Society does not
undertake professional genealogical research. Those
unable to conduct their own research may wish to
consider appointing a record agent or professional
genealogist. The Society will not recommend any
individual but several advertise in our own
Genealogists' Magazine and other journals such as
Family Tree Magazine. The Association of
Genealogists and Researchers in Archives (AGRA)
publishes a list of its members and this is available
from the Society's Shop at £2.50 (including UK
postage) or £3.84/$6.00 for airmail overseas. The
lists can also be found on-line at www.agra.org.uk

Personal searches can of course be made. Non-
members are also welcome to use the Library as day
searchers on payment of the appropriate fee
(currently £3.30 per hour, £8.80 four hours or
£13.20 a day). Photocopies or printouts can be made
personally at a cost of 20p (A4) or 40p (A3) or by
staff (in the case of fragile and or manuscript items
in the lower library) at 30p (A4) or 50p (A3) per
copy.

Probate Inventories
Angela Petyt

Anyone who is fortunate enough to locate a will of an ancestor knows how useful they are. However, if this will is accompanied by a probate inventory, the researcher will discover a most fascinating and evocative document - for to view an inventory is to peer into a looking glass of ages past...

"Their goods and chattels..."
From the 1530s onwards, it became the custom of the church courts (who had the jurisdiction to prove wills and letters of administration) to ask that the executors appoint two, three or four local men. These would often be friends or neighbours of the deceased. They were known as appraisers or valuers. Their task was to make a "true and perfect" inventory, which would detail the personal estate i.e. "goods, chattels, rights, credits" of the deceased and file it with the probate court. This practice lasted until the mid-18th century (and in some counties even later).

An inventory had three objectives - firstly, to work out the value of the estate, secondly, to decide the court fee to be paid for granting probate, and thirdly, to protect against fraud those who would benefit from gifts etc. under a will. The kinds of items listed in an inventory include - money, clothing, jewellery, furniture, linens, kitchenware,

books, farming equipment, livestock, crops, tools of the trade, leases and debts - both what was owed to the deceased and what was owing. Few stones were left unturned. Buildings and land were not to be included in an inventory, although leasehold land was permitted.

These documents, which may be long or short, minutely detailed or frustratingly brief, can often throw up more questions than answers. There are mysterious items and even more mysterious spellings. Was there a standard system for valuing goods? Why do the figures often not add up? Did the appraisers show bias? And the most poignant question of all - where are all these wonderful artefacts now?

Examples of inventories
What an inventory will reveal is the lifestyle of an ancestor - their home, their farming or business interests, their wealth and social status, perhaps even their hobbies. Here follow some extracts from various inventories, which will give an impression of the scope and contents of this particular historical source -

Christopher Pettyt of Ortontown in Westmorland.
This inventory dated 1702 is a typical example of a gentleman farmer, including -

Extract from the inventory of Christopher Pettyt
of Ortontown in Westmorland, 1702
[Carlisle Diocesan Probate records
held at the Cumbria Record Office (Carlisle)]

Item Bedsteads and Bedding	£9-9s-6d
Item Chists and Trunks	£2-0s-0d
Item Table linning	£4-7s-6d
Item " plate vessell	£10-5s-0d
Item " pewther	£1-12s-6d
Item Brasse and brewing vessell	£2-0s-0d
Item Barke spitt berkonrook and Tongs	£0-13s-4d
Item a frying pann	£0-1s-4d
Item wood vessell earthen vessell	
Glasse vasses and glasses	£1-14s-0d
Item Cardes and Spinning wheell	£0-1s-0d
Item poake Sacks and winowcloath	£0-3s-0d
Item a fowling peine	£0-10s-0d
Item Carts and wheels ploughs harrows	
Cartgeare and ploughgeare	£0-15s-0d
Item Horses and Mares	£8-0s-0d
Item Three Kine	£4-10s-0d
Item Two young Heiffers	£1-10s-0d
Item five Sheep	£0-15s-0d
Item five Hoggs	£1-0s-0d
Item Hay in the Lathes and in the stack	£6-0s-0d
Item Bigg and oats	£6-0s-0d
Item Books	£1-6s-8d
Item Mealle Mault and Beife	£0-14s-0d
Item poultery	£0-2s-6d

[Source: Carlisle Diocesan Probate records held at the Cumbria Record Office (Carlisle)]

Robert Petty of the Intack in Ravenstonedale, Westmorland.
A yeoman's inventory of 1722 lists

amongst its items -

Purse and apparel	£2-4s-0d
Fleece - wool	£0-48s-0d
Cheeses & c.	£0-11s-10d
Wood-vessel, Bottles &c.	£1-03s-0d
Pewter & China-Ware	£0-18s-6d
Sheep 34	£5-6s-0d
A Girdle, Frying pan, & other Iron &c.	£0-15s-1d
A Table Form, Dresser, Long settle &c.	£1-10s-0d
Books and Stockings	£0-8s-0d
Owing to ye Deceased on a Bond	£10-0s-0d

[Source: Carlisle Diocesan Probate records held at the Cumbria Record Office (Carlisle)]

Joseph Petty of Deerstones near Skipton, Yorkshire.
This linen weaver's inventory of 1717 illustrates how the appraisers have gone around the house, room by room, then into the workshop and barn, and includes -

In ye bodystead of the house	
1 old cupboard	£0-10s-0d
1 old table & 2 little meat boards	£0-05s-0d
One old longsettle & 4 old chairs & some cushions	£0-04s-0d
7 little pewter dishes, 1 salt and 1 mustard box a little glass case 1 smoothing iron 1 lantern 1 hourglass	£0-09s-0d
In ye parlour	
2 old bedstead with some bedding thereon	£1-0s-0d
In ye milkhouse	
1 churn 3 cheesefatts 1 butterbowl 6 pot bowls 2 creampotts some other small hustlements	£0-5s-0d
In the Chamber	
one old ark 2 pr of old bedstocks 2 straw skeps some yarn and some line and some small hustlements there	£1-0s-0d
In ye shops	
4 pr. of looms with geers of sev'll sorts & other materials and utencills belonging ye trade	£2-10s-0d
4 cowes without calf	£12-0s-0d
2 stirks 2 Sumer calves & 2 drinking calves	£5-10s-0d
1 old lame horse	£1-5s-0d

[Source: Borthwick Institute, York - Exchequer Court Inventory, Craven Deanery]

Edward Guy of Long Clawson, Leicestershire.
A Midland farmer's inventory of 1676 includes -

Item in the stair head chamber bacon	£0-15s-0d
Item A coverlid four pillows & two blanketts	£0-18s-0d
Item Two beds with the cloathes and two coffers	£1-0s-0d
Item A tester bed with bedding and curtains &c.	£2-0s-0d
Item in the Buttery two panns two tables and other smal things	£1-0s-0d
Item in the barn hay	£1-10s-0d
Item In the Cow house three cows	

and a calf	£7-0s-0d
Item Coales & manure a pig and pig trough	£0-11s-0d
Item in the house a cubberd & able & forms & stools	£1-10s-0d
Item Peuter in the house	£0-5s-0d

[Source: Archdeaconry Court of Leicester Probate records held at the Leicestershire Record Office]

Richard Guy of Knipton, Leicestershire.
Another farmer's inventory of 1723. This one, instead of detailing each item in the room, gives a sum total, including -

Goods in the Hall praised at	£5-0s-0d
Goods in the parlour praised at	£5-0s-0d
Goods in the Kitchen praised at	£3-0s-0d
Goods in other lower rooms praised at	£5-0s-0d
Goods in the chambers praised at	£19-0s-0d
In the yard horses & mares foles Colts and filleys Apraised at	£85-0s-0d
Waggons Carts Plougs Harrows & other Materials of husbandry	£34-0s-0d
Corn and Hay in the yard and Barns Appraised at	£240-0s-0d
Three Hundred Sheep apraised at	£91-0s-0d
Cows heifers and followers apraised at	£69-0s-0d
Swine praised at	£6-0s-0d
Things unseen and forgotten praised at	£0-10s-0d

The inventory of Joseph Petty of Deerstones, near Skipton in Yorkshire, 1717
(Exchequer Court Inventory, Craven Deanery. Reproduced from an original in the Borthwick Institute, University of York)

[Source: Archdeaconry Court of Leicester Probate records held at the Leicestershire Record Office]

Ann Petty of Storiths, near Skipton, Yorkshire.

A very short and simple 1701 inventory of a widow, which is reproduced in full below -

Imp. Her purse and apparel	£1-10s-0d
It. One Cupboard and two chests	£1-6s-8d
It. One bedstead and bedding	£1-6s-0d
It. Some pieces of brass and pewter	£1-5s-0d
It. Owing to the Testatrix though found to be desperate	£5-6s-6d
Total	£10-14s-2d

Apprzed by
James Phillips   Samson Lupton   Jos. Waite

[Source: Borthwick Institute, York - Exchequer Court Inventory, Craven Deanery]

Sylvester Petyt of London.

This inventory dated 1719 is in complete contrast to that of Ann Petty. It runs to twenty-six pages and accompanies an epic will of about the same length. Sylvester was a lawyer and money-lender, and consequently lived the luxurious life of an extremely wealthy City gentleman, as these extracts show -

One hundred King Edwards shillings	£5-0s-0d
one diamond Ring with seaven stones	£12-0s-0d
a fashionable Silver watch and Chaine	£3-0s-0d
one flat Silver watch and Chaine	£1-16s-0d
one Do. with a studded Case and Chaine	£1-10s-0d
one Smal Ovall Silver Watch	£0-15s-0d
remaineing in Mr. Lambs hands of money deposited with him by the Testator in his Life Time	£1264-17s-4d
Severall old Copper pieces of no value	£0-0s-0d
Copper Swedish money	£0-8s-9d
Eighty two old pictures of different sizes	£3-0s-0d
Mr. Petits and Mr. Catersons pictures in Ovall Gilt Frames	£1-1s-0d
one hundred and ninety four large & small prints Maps and Coats of Arms	£1-10s-0d
An Indian Card table lined with Crimson plush One Walnutt Tree inlaid Table A Smal Table & Tea board A writing Stand one Walnutt Tree ffiligree Table & eight Stands	£0-15s-0d
an Indian Beauroe	£1-5s-0d
A Walnut Tree Sriptore & a Chest	£1-10s-0d
a Black Chest on a frame	£0-10s-0d
Two playing Tables Box Dice	£0-8s-0d
one Looking Glass in an inlaid Frame & one Weather Glass	£1-5s-0d
nine Cane Chairs and a Cane Couch Squab and Bolster and two Worsted Damaske Stools Seven Turkey workt & two Stuffed Chairs a ship & Step Ladder	£1-0s-0d
an Old Iron Grate one Warming pan Some old Iron one Iron Lock and Key belonging to the Chambers	£0-14s-0d
One Worsted Damask Bed Compleat	

a Feather Bed and Bolster one pillow and two Ruggs	£4-10s-0d
a Fiddle and Case a Glass Case & some odd things	£0-2s-6d
A Walnut Tree Beauroe	£1-15s-0d
A large Clock with a Walnut Tree Case playing Sevll tunes	£5-0s-0d
A Fine Table Clock with Brass work & a case	£5-0s-0d
A plaine Table Clock with a Black Ebony Frame	£3-0s-0d
An Eight day Clock	£4-0s-0d
Twenty one images & Toyes over the Chimney & seven peices of Glass ware	£0-12s-0d
Two pictures of Mr. Wm. Petyt & one other of Mr. Silvester Petyt in Gilt Frames	£3-3s-0d
The pictures of King Wm. & Queen Mary in Oval Gilt Frames and of King Charles & ye. Duke of Brandon in Gilt Frames	£2-0s-0d
Two Crucifixes two Candlesticks one other Crucifix in an Ovall fframe Two Smal heads in round frames a Coat of Armes three wooden Cups one Tea Canister two Straw boxes & some odd Toyes	£0-6s-0d
two Doz. Of Earthen plates & two fruit dishes of the Same & two Cupps	£0-6s-0d
A muskett Baganett Sword and powder Box	£0-15s-0d
five Swords and a hanger	£1-15s-0d
A large Iron Chest with two padlocks	£2-10s-0d
A Smal Iron Chest broken	£1-10s-0d
The deceaseds Two Clokes and all his wearing apparell both Linnen and Woollen and two Lawyers Gowns	£5-5s-0d
about 100 Miscelaneous Books and pamphlets most Octa. & Quartos	£40-0s-0d

The inventory goes on to list in great detail all the debts owed to the deceased in his capacity as a money-lender. These include aristocracy and tradespeople from London and many counties of England. Every single signed bond had been carefully noted by the appraisers.

[Source: Public Record Office, Kew - PROB 5 / 2768]

Some explanations

As can be seen with this small sample, there is no such thing as a 'typical' probate inventory. Although it is quite common to begin with "his purse and apparel" and to end with "things unseen or forgotten" (which always seem to be given a value!) a multitude of variations in format can appear. Each county or locality will have its own traditions and customs as to how to record the deceased's personal effects.

The main problems encountered, as in many old documents, are handwriting and spelling. Handwriting styles can be deciphered with practice, and by consulting the many handbooks on the subject, such as *Reading Tudor and Stuart Handwriting* by Lionel Munby (British Association

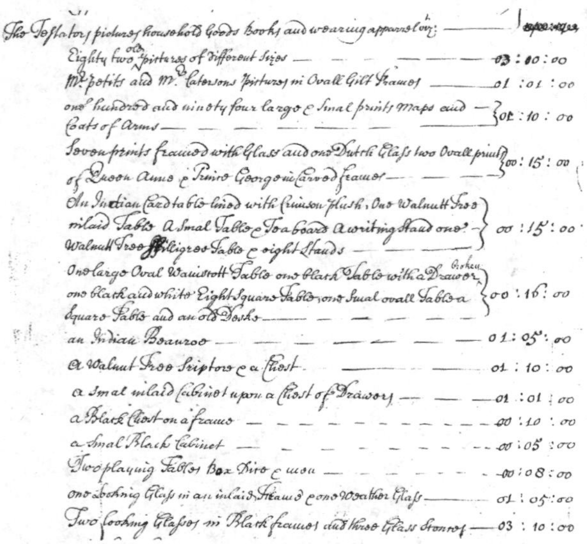

[handwritten inventory manuscript extract with columns of values]

Extract from the inventory of Sylvester Petyt of London, 1719
(Public Record Office, Kew, ref. PROB 5 / 2768)

for Local History, 1988). Spelling can be a different matter. The appraisers wrote down words how they thought they sounded phonetically. To make things more complicated, inventories often include descriptions of items in local colloquial terms, and dialect forms. This might be overcome by consulting the invaluable guide *A Glossary of Household, Farming and Trade Terms from*

Probate Inventories by Rosemary Milward (Derbyshire Record Society, third edition 1986). Dialect Societies exist for most English counties and they may also be able to assist.

Once the inventory has been deciphered and transcribed, it is worth thinking about the workings of the document. Great care must be taken when looking at values given to goods. It is thought that clothing, most household furniture, utensils and farm or workshop equipment are given a 'second-hand' value, which could be lower than their resale value. On the other hand, crops, livestock and foodstuffs to be sold at market, would be listed as nearer the current market price. Also, we are relying on the appraisers' personal opinions as to what items were worth - this could vary widely from villages to towns and in different counties. Look at some of the differing values given to goods in the above sample of inventories, which come from Westmorland, Yorkshire, Leicestershire and London.

Where to find inventories
It is vital to study the essential guide to the location of probate documents *Probate Jurisdictions: Where to Look for Wills* by Jeremy Gibson and Else Churchill (Federation of Family History Societies, 5th edition, 2002). The location of pre-1858 wills can be a minefield, but this book details all repositories, from the Public Record Office to County Archives. It is estimated that tens of thousands of inventories exist, although by no means do all 16th-18th century wills or admons include an inventory. Many have not survived. Please be aware that the inventory may have been filed with the original will, or it could be separate from the will and located in a different document class altogether. The archivist will be able to advise you.

The true value of inventories
As can be seen, probate inventories are one of the most intimately personal documents about an ancestor that a family historian is likely to encounter. It is a moving experience to read one. For the local, social and economic historian, inventories have for many years been the subject of intense scrutiny, and many published works are available covering most counties.

Much of what we know about 16th, 17th and early 18th century homes, work and lifestyle comes from analysing the unique data that inventories provide.

Angela Petyt lives in Wakefield, Yorkshire. She has a BA (Hons) in History and Language Studies from the University College of Ripon and York St. John, and (DA301) Studying Family and Community History from the Open University. Angela works as a lecturer in family and local history.

Vaccination Records for Family History
Doreen Hopwood

Smallpox has now been eradicated in the western world, but until the 18th century it was the worlds major killer disease, leaving survivors grossly disfigured, or blind, as a result of its ravages. It was recognised as an inocuable disease as early as the 16th century when inoculation – involving the use of live smallpox virus – was practised in the Near East. Working in Berkeley, Gloucestershire the physician, Edward Jenner, was intrigued by country folklore, which decreed that individuals who succumbed to cowpox were thereafter immune to the deadly smallpox virus. Jenner set out to test the hypothesis, and his first vaccination (taken from the Latin for cow), was performed on eight-year old James Phipps, using matter from a cowpox pustule on the hand of a dairymaid, Sarah Nelmes, in 1796. Two years later he published *An Inquiry into the causes and effects of Variole Vaccinae, a Disease discovered in some parts of the Western Counties of England, particularly of Gloucestershire, and known by the Name of Cow*

Pox. By the turn of the 19th century it was available in all major European languages and over 100,000 individuals had been vaccinated in England.

However, the introduction of compulsory infant vaccination some fifty years later, in 1853, became an issue of controversy on which municipal elections were fought, and against which Anti-Vaccination Leagues were formed. Ironically Gloucestershire, Jenner's native county, was one of the strongholds of Anti-Vaccination Law action.

The first Vaccination Act was passed in 1840, following a major national smallpox epidemic between 1838 and 1840, in which almost 42,000 people died. The highest proportion of deaths occurred in large towns and cities, accounting for 10% of all deaths in 1839, but in children aged under five years, it was responsible for some 80% of registered deaths. Since civil registration had been established on 1 July 1837, this was the first time that mortality statistics were available to reveal the full extent of an epidemic throughout England and Wales. The Poor Law Union was recognised as an effective administrative unit under which vaccination could be carried out, and Ellenborough's Bill of 1840, providing for universal, voluntary vaccination (paid out of the Poor Rate) was quickly passed. The Government anticipated that it would receive the full support of the medical profession, but, because the Poor Law Guardians were given the task of employing vaccinating doctors, they saw it as an insult to their profession and professionalism and the following extract appeared in the Lancet of 18 June 1840:

> "The popular prejudices are not likely to be subdued by men with the ogre – like countenances and abhorred voices of the Poor Law Commissioners. The invitation to 'come and be vaccinated' will terrify, not persuade".

Initially, vaccination stations were often set up in workhouses, so making them even less inviting to the general populace. The Public Vaccinator for Southwark performed vaccinations at his home until 1845, and in 1844 carried out over 1000 such operations. However, in 1846, when the station was moved to the workhouse, the number dwindled to less than fifty. This problem was recognised by the Government and amended in 1868 as " ... *the independent poor are unwilling to resort for vaccination to an institution connected with pauper relief*". Similarly, public houses could

PUNCH, OR THE LONDON CHARIVARI. [JULY 30, 18

TRIUMPH OF DE-JENNER-ATION.
[The Bill for the encouragement of Small Pox was passed.]

(Form D)

THE VACCINATION ACT OF 1867.

(30 and 31 Victoria, cap. 84.)

Medical Certificate of Successful Vaccination.

[To be delivered (pursuant to Section XXI.) to the Father or Mother of every Child successfully Vaccinated, or to the Person having the Custody of such Child.]

I, the undersigned, hereby certify, that¹ _Lucy Bird_ the Child of² _Elijah Bird_, aged³ _3 mths_ [stated to have been born at ⁴No. in _Level_ Street] in the Parish or Township of _Burley Hills_ in the County or Borough of _Stafford_ has been successfully vaccinated by me.

Dated this⁵ _1st_ day of _October_ 18 68.

(Signature of the Person certifying) _Edwd Smithite Mann_

Add " Public Vaccinator of the Union or Parish of," or " Medical Practitioner of," and add professional titles (i.e. M.D., L.A.C., or F.R.C.S., or otherwise, as the case may be.)

[☞ See Note on the other side.]

---

not be used as vaccination stations because *".... some think it necessary to pay for drink by way of acknowledgement to the landlord for the use of his premises"*.

The Government blamed indifference and apathy on the part of parents for the low numbers of vaccinations being carried out in the 1840s, but, instead of taking the responsibility away from the Poor Law Guardians, the Government chose to make infant vaccination compulsory in England and Wales. Bavaria had introduced this as early as 1807, and members of the newly established Epidemiological Society (of England) scrutinised the Bavarian and other European schemes. They reported that there was a powerful inverse relationship between deaths from smallpox and the strength of implementation of vaccination laws in a country. On the basis of the report a Bill was introduced in 1853 under which Vaccination Districts were to be formed under the control of Poor Law Authorities. As Registration Districts covered the same area as a Poor Law Union, each District Registrar was required to issue a notice to parents of an infant following the birth registration, to the effect that the child had to be vaccinated within three months. There was a dramatic increase in the numbers of infant vaccinations in the wake of the 1853 Act, but there was also a growing amount of opposition.

There was another major outbreak of smallpox in England in 1871/2, concentrated in London, Staffordshire, South Wales and Durham, and this put the legislation to the test. Despite the numbers of deaths, fewer vaccinated individuals died than those who had not been vaccinated.

Smallpox was the only one of the infectious killer diseases which had an effective, preventive measure to eradicate it, yet an increasing number of individuals joined together to form Anti-Vaccination Leagues, or refused to have their

infants vaccinated within 3 months of birth. This was the first occasion on which the Government had passed public health measures overriding the right of the individual's choice for the greater good of the wider community. At first, the Anti-Vaccination Movement was not so much against vaccination, as against the loss of the individuals right to choose. Opposition also stemmed from religious, social and cultural beliefs and, increasingly, fears that the practice of vaccination was itself unsafe. Members of the medical profession began to add their voices to the growing noises of dissent, often couched in emotive speech, such as that of Henry Port, FSA, in1882: "What! Are we to have healthy children, strong men and women, living to a good old age, and free from disease in a natural way, by allowing this rotten animal discharge to be inserted into their veins. What an absurdity!" They drew attention to the increasing number of cases of erysipelas (blood poisoning) and other diseases, which they attributed to the vaccination procedures. On the eighth day following the vaccination, the child had to be re-examined by the Vaccination Officer to establish whether or not it had been successful, and the parents were issued with a certificate as proof of vaccination.

Although vaccination had become compulsory in 1853, there was no requirement on the part of the Poor Law Authority to penalise non-compliance. As with other laws concerning individuals – such as the earlier Recusancy Acts – it was implemented forcefully in some authorities and virtually ignored by others. The Vaccination Acts were tightened in 1867 and 1871 when Vaccination Officers had to be appointed and action taken against parents whose children had not been vaccinated. Each registrar was required to make a half-yearly return of all birth registrations for whom no certificate of successful vaccination had been received, and the Poor Law Guardians were to contact the parents. If they chose to ignore a warning they were taken to court where a fine of 20 shillings (£1.00p) could be charged, and continue to be imposed for every child under 14 years of age until the parents complied. This law hit the poorest families hardest, for the wealthy could pay up, or have their children vaccinated privately.

The first Anti-Compulsory Vaccination League was formed in 1867, and by 1870 all of the major industrial towns and cities had their own, made up of mostly artisans, but often funded and supported by middle-class intellectuals. During the 1870s, virtually all parents who refused to comply in the counties of Buckinghamshire, Gloucestershire and Leicestershire were penalised, yet in London, Yorkshire and Lancashire, prosecutions were few and far between. Minutes of these societies may be found in County Record Offices, and leaflets were often published which may have been deposited there as well. Prosecutions can be found amongst the Justices records as well as the Vaccination Committee Minutes (from 1871). Demonstrations were reported in the local newspapers. When the Board of Guardians in Keighley refuses to appoint Vaccination Officers, the individuals were imprisoned in York Castle. The most famous demonstration against the Vaccination Laws was held in Leicester on 23 March 1885 when over 80,000 people processed through the town culminating in the burning of a copy of the Vaccination Acts. An effigy of Dr Jenner was tossed into the crowd where constables "… having secured the 'Doctor' solemnly marched him off to the police station, minus his head, which had disappeared." A list of 'Leicester Martyrs' was published and circulated and reports of the march appeared in the Times as well as the Leicester press. The laws were relaxed in 1898 when a Conscientious Objectors Clause was incorporated, celebrated in a Punch cartoon entitled 'De-Jenneration' on 30 July 1899, but it was not until 1 July 1948 that compulsory vaccination was completely abolished. The Poor Law Unions ceased to exist in 1930, and after this date, material relating to vaccination can be found amongst local authority records, but some of these are still closed to public access.

The survival rates of vaccination records from 1871 vary from one Poor Law Union to another. Where they can be found, the information can be extremely informative as the registers give almost as much information as a full copy birth/death certificate, and the area covered corresponds with existing and disestablished registration districts. However, the vaccination registers do not show the maiden name of the mother, which is generally the reason for the purchase of a birth certificate to facilitate a search for the parent's marriage. The birth registers include the name, sex, date, and place of birth of the child, the father's name and occupation (mothers names, if illegitimate) and details of the outcome of the vaccination.

The monthly returns of death detail children who died under the age of one year without being vaccinated. Whilst the cause of death is not included, the name of the child, sex and place of death are shown, as well as the father's (or mother's) name and occupation. Where the child's birth was registered in the same sub-registration district, the entry number in the birth register is given. The Vaccination Officers were also responsible for ensuring that infants who came into their Union were vaccinated, and these registers are in the same format as the others, but the information may not be wholly accurate. The address at the time of vaccination is generally included. Surviving records are usually held with the Poor Law Union records in County Record Offices or main libraries, and the dates covered for some districts are detailed in the Gibson guide *Poor Law Union Records*. Coverage generally covers the 1870s to the early 20th century, and can be helpful in 'filling in' gaps concerning children of a marriage in the post, or inter-censal years.

Mary, Mary quite contrary: the writings of Mary Wroth (1586(7?) – 1651) niece to Philip Sidney (1554 – 1586)

Dr Jane Batchelor

Sonnet XVI – Mary Wroth

Deare cherish this and with it my soules will,
      Nor for it ran away doe it abuse:
      Alas it left (poore me) your brest to choose
As the best shrine, where it would harbour still.

Then favour shew, and not unkindly kill
      The heart which fled to you, but doe excuse
      That which for better did the worse refuse;
And pleas'd Ile be, though heartlesse my life spill.

      But if you would bee kinde and just indeed,
Send me your heart, which in mine's place shall feede
      On faithfull love to your devotion bound.

      There shall it see the sacrifices made
Of pure and spotlesse Love, which shall not fade
      While soule and body are together found.

Mary Wroth and the Sidney family

Mary Wroth was the youngest of ten children born to an English aristocratic family. Her mother was the wealthy Barbara Gamage (married 1573), her father Robert Sidney (1563-1625) educated at Oxford and brother to the famed courtier-poet Sir Philip Sidney (1554 – 1586), which made her the niece of the same, and of Mary Sidney, his sister.

The influence of the aristocratic Sidney family on sixteenth and seventeenth century England cannot be under estimated. Like his father Henry Sidney Philip Sidney, Mary Wroth's uncle, was involved in politics at the highest level, successfully using his spoken skills to defend his father's Irish policy (1597), and preventing what he considered to be a disadvantageous marriage between Queen Elizabeth I and the Duke of Anjou (1580).

As well as taking an interest in politics Philip Sidney was an accomplished poet, poetry being the preferred form of choice for the aristocratic privileged audience to which he belonged. Philip Sidney's most well known works included the *Arcadia* (begun 1578) and *Astrophil and Stella* (begun 1591). The Arcadia was a mixture of poetry and highly elevated prose, presenting an idealised rural landscape of love inhabited by shepherds declaring their love to shepherdesses. *Astrophil and Stella* was a sonnet sequence of love poems apparently based on the "real life" but platonic relationship between Sidney and Penelope Devereux, married to Lord Rich (1581). Neither of these works was published before his death; other aristocrats would not have approved of such public showmanship. This is not to say he was shy. In fact Philip's works were circulated widely amongst other courtiers, and Sidney's death in 1586 after a fight with the Spanish was probably because of

"his refusal to wear heavy thigh armour", following the fashion for lighter decorative armour instead.

Mary Wroth's aunt Mary Sidney (1562-1621) was a poet and patroness, but her work has been (partly through her own choice) been hidden by the promotion which she gave to her brother's writings. Throughout her life Mary Sidney read and offered advice on Philip's writings, editing the *Arcadia* and, when he died, taking on the task of finishing off his *Psalms* (1593 – 1600), and writing *To the Angel Spirit of the Most Excellent Sir Philip Sidney* (1599) a poem eulogising him. This is not to say that Mary did not understand the value of her own writing, rather that she recognised the value in a male orientated world of basking in reflected glory, of showing her own writings to be following in the lineage of her illustrious brother. As she put it in a poem introducing the *Psalms* which she addressed to Queen Elizabeth I:
But he did warp, I weaved this web to end.

There were some advantages to this approach as opposed to the more openly challenging approach taken by her niece, as shall be seen later.

Mary Wroth's parents felt it was important to educate all their children, and it appears that she received a good education. The Sidney daughters were described as making goods progress in their book. Mary Wroth especially was seen as "forward in her learning, writing and other exercises she is put to". She may have been influenced by her aunt, who was a frequent visitor to Penshurst, and whom Mary Wroth herself visited at her home, Wilton House, and at Baynards Castle. It is possible that Mary Wroth may have travelled abroad as a child. In 1597 Lady Huntington suggested that the Sidney children should travel to the Hague "where they shall learn the French tonge."

The "perfect" match: Mary Wroth and Robert Wroth

A girl's education remained, especially among the aristocracy, a preparation for marriage. A match for Mary was found in Sir Robert Wroth (1576-1614), a member of a large landowning family who's ancestors included a Lord Mayor of London. In the modern terms of emotional "bliss" the Wroths seem to have been unsuited; soon after the marriage Robert Sidney commented "It were very soon for any unkindness to begin". But Sir Robert Wroth's friendship with James I gave him a privileged status, and Mary Wroth made the most of her high status at court to secure a grant for the rebuilding of Loughton Hall, their home.

Mary Wroth the writer

Like her uncle and aunt before her Mary Wroth had a keen interest in writing. As early as 1605 her poems were being read in court circles, and her friends included Ben Jonson and Lucy Countess of Bedford, the patroness of John Donne. But court life was expensive. After Sir Robert's early death Mary was left with money problems and an expensive estate to manage. Following the death of her son a large portion of the estate passed to an uncle. Mary was in debt, and her position was not helped by her long-running affair with William Herbert, the Earl of Pembroke, by whom she had two children. It was against this background and following the death of her aunt and mother that she published the *Urania* (1621), a prose romance, together with a selection of sonnets. Although this was modelled upon her uncle's Arcadia it clearly contained criticism of court life. In 1623 Mary called upon James I to protect her from the criticism it generated, and he did; nevertheless she later withdrew her work, saying that she did not wish to offend.

Wroth's *Urania* as social satire

It seems likely that Mary Wroth was indeed satirising some aspects of court life in her Urania. In it she relates the story of Sirelius who married a "very young wife" with the consent of his father; that is, the girl herself had little say in the matter. Mary appears to have little sympathy with Sirelius and his father, whom she describes as "vaine as Courtiers, rash as mad-men and ignorant as women" – the latter phrase taking on an ironic tone, as she is outlining male insensitivity. Sirelius uses his wife "ill" and she dies, after bearing him two children. Similarly, Denny's daughter Honor was married with consent to Lord James Hay, a favourite of James's. Honor later died, having given birth to two children. Annoyed, Denny compared Mary Wroth unfavourably to her aunt Mary Sidney:
Redeem the time with writing as large a volume of heavenly lays and holy love as you have of the lascivious tales and amorous toys that at last you may follow the rare, and pious example of your aunt.
"Holy love"; objections to Mary Wroth's work

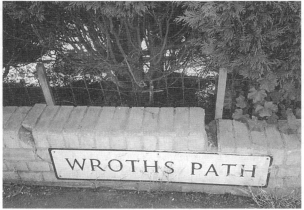

Wroths Path, near Baldwins Hill, Loughton, Essex
© Jane Batchelor 2002

generally may have been because she was writing a romance, that is venturing into male territory, instead of sticking to writing about religion, like her aunt. Women were meant to read romances, not to write them, as Thomas Powell declared in his Tom of all Trades:
In stead of Song and Musicke, let them learne Cookery and Laundrie. And in stead of reading Sir Philip Sydney's Arcadia, let them read the grounds of good huswifery. I like not a female Poetresse at any hand.

Note that in this example it is the *Arcadia*, in which Mary Sidney had a hand, which is held up as the "bad work" – Mary Sidney having carefully reinvented herself as a paragon of religious virtue, not a "female Poetresse". Mary Wroth however is not prepared to cloak the value she places on herself as a writer. In "traditional" pastoral discourse the shepherd declares his love to the shepherdess, but the *Urania* is characterised by long female soliloquies, as for example when the shepherdess laments her lowly birth, and when Pamphilia takes up her pen and "being excellent in writing" writes of her lover's inconstancy. The sonnet sequence *Pamphilia to Amphilanthus* continues the dialogue begun in the *Urania*. Its title is a parody of Sidney's *Astrophil and Stella*, but instead of the woman "Stella" being placed last. "Pamphilia" is placed at the front, that is in Wroth's sonnet sequence the woman comes first, questioning conventional values and thinking.

Marital bliss rejected? - the example of Wroth's Sonnet XVI

In Sonnet XVI of *Pamphilia to Amphilanthus* Mary Wroth, the subject of an arranged and possibly unhappy marriage, is exploring what the words of the Christian marriage service mean. She opens her sonnet:
> Deare cherish this and with it my soules will,
> Nor for it ran away doe it abuse
> Alas it left (poore me) your brest to choose
> As the best shrine, where it would
> harbour still.

"Doe it abuse" – from the first the speaker is challenging the authoritarian way in which love is often conducted. "Cherish this" is purposefully ambiguous, the woman protecting herself by keeping ambiguous how much love whether physical or spiritual she has given to the man. Essential to this ambiguity is the pun on the word "still". The speaker implies that either her soul would either stay be happy to stay "still" quietly in this relationship, or, more challengingly, her soul "would …still" that is conditionally wish to stay in the relationship, but only so long as it provides the "best shrine". She expects better, and in the second stanza she lays out her case:
> Then favour shew, and not unkindly kill
> The heart which fled to you, but doe excuse
> That which for better did the worse refuse
"For better did the worse refuse" is a parody of one of the best known lines in English religious tradition. In the Christian marriage ceremony,

marriage is made for better or for worse. Here is the religious high ground as personified by Mary's aunt taken one step further. "The worse" could refer to the physical violation of the virgin, but Mary is concerned with more than this; as "abuse" and "fled" make clear she seems to have in mind abuse which occurs in any relationship in which a long term relationship is made. If a relationship is bad, then it is not always right that love should be requited; in this sense the refusal of love instead of being the lover anguishing unloved is a positive step. But Mary does not stop here, as the archetypal pastoral lover would do. Instead, she takes her argument to her logical conclusion, and in doing so implicitly challenges the idea that it is wrong for women to be "amorous". She recognises that if there is commitment in a relationship then there is nothing wrong with requiting a relationship:

> But if you will be kinde and just indeed
> Send me your heart, which in mine's
>   place shall feede
> On faithfull love to your devotion bound.
>
> There shall it see the sacrifices made
> Of pure and spotlesse Love, which
>   shall not fade,
> While soule and body are together founde.

Mary may talk about love in this context in traditional terms of being "bound", "faithfull" and "making sacrifices", but the speaker stresses that she only offers this kind of love conditionally. The bond goes both ways; the lover must be "faithful" and his love "spotlesse", unsullied and given totally to her. She is happy to play the game of total devotion and unquestioning love – but these things work both ways. In this context it is important to notice the repetition of the idea of the soul. Love is about the soul as well as the body, it is about being pure spiritually, it is about bringing the same standards to love as you do to religion: that is for Mary as much as her aunt it is important to be seen to be virtuous, but here the virtue promoted is a woman's right to an equable loving relationship.

The uncompromising tone of the *Urania* and the criticism it generated may explain why in 1623 Mary called upon James I to protect her. He did so; nevertheless she later withdrew her work, saying that she did not wish to offend.

Finding out more Mary Wroth
Philip Sidney may have not had his work published in his lifetime, but his carefully groomed image and the attentions of his sister have ensured that since their first publication his writings have remained in print and relatively easy to obtain. For his niece however things have been rather different, and it has been a question of combing through information about the Sidney family in general to see what you can find. For a long time the easiest way to access Wroth's work was through the original edition of the *Urania* held in the British library, but more recently there have been several good modern editions of her work, for example Josephine Robert's *The Poems of Mary Wroth* (1983), which contains a good

biography and May Nelson Paulissen's *The Love Sonnets of Mary Wroth* (1982). Her work is also appearing more frequently in anthologies such as Germaine Greer's *Kissing the Rod* (1988) and Marion Wynne Davies's *Women Poets of the Renaissance* (1998), which also features Mary Sidney.

Mary Wroth and the Loughton connection
Mary Wroth an aristocrat came from a family of aristocratic writers, that is her family defined her. But if her family defined her, so did the lavish home which she and her husband established in Loughton, sign of their rising ambitions, and a continuance if you like of the Sidney dynasty. It is this local connection which again as so often is useful in revealing more about her. One of the most important people in establishing the value of Mary's work was William Chapman Waller (1850 – 1917), whose work *An Extinct Family: Wroth of Loughton Hall* represents a painstaking attempt to find more about the Wroths and specifically Mary Wroth, who she was and what she did, reflecting Chapman's detailed knowledge of local history. Loughton and District Historical Society have recently published a work by R S Morris on Chapman Waller and his work (2001), ordering details of which may be found on the internet at ourworld.compuserve.com/homepages/LOUGHTON_TC/4pubs.htm
A series of cuttings on Loughton Hall, the Wroth family home may be found under the heading "Loughton Hall: The Debden Community Centre" at Loughton Library.

Conclusion: Mary Wroth and understanding family and local history
In conclusion, in finding out about Mary Wroth it is important as always to see the person in her full family and history context. That means understanding that if Mary Wroth did come from a privileged family and was in some sense destined to be a writer then that was understandable, but equally interesting is to realise that just because she came from a certain background she did not accept it unquestioningly, subverting the Arcadia of her uncle and aunt to her own purposes, and refusing entirely to toe the family line. For this she paid a certain price, not least in the subsuming of her own work to her uncle's, whereas Mary Sidney benefited more obviously from the reflected glory which her brother's name afforded her. But if the history of Mary Wroth is the history of the Sidney family, it is also the history of the Wroths, of her own ambition to take her family connections and use them to promote herself as ferociously as possible – as her aunt and uncle had done. A family, a house, a marriage, a book of poems questioning contemporary morals: Mary Wroth may be from another age and another context than the modern reader but her connection with her locality, her family and her sense of self are still as vivid and understandable as ever.

Stonards Hill, off Epping High Street, Epping, Essex.
Probably named after the Stonards, a rich land-owning family from whom the Wroths were descended. There is also a Stonards Hill in Loughton,near Loughton Station,Essex

© Jane Batchelor 2002

Select Bibliography

Primary Sources

Mary Wroth, *Urania* and *Pamphilia to Amphilanthus* (London, John Marriot and John Grismand, 1621)

Marion Wynne-Davies, ed., *Women Poets of the Renaissance* (London, Weidenfeld and Nicolson, 1998) – includes works of Wroth and Mary Sidney.

Sidney, Sir Philip and Mary, *The Psalms of Philip Sidney and the Countess of Pembroke* (New York: New York University Press, 1963).

Sidney, Sir Philip, *Selected Poems*, ed. by Katherine Duncan-Jones, rev. edn (Oxford: Oxford University Press, 1973) – includes *Arcadia* and *Astrophil and Stella*, and gives biographical details.

Secondary Sources

A. A. Altwood, *Lady Mary Wroth* (Loughton, 1954) – one of a series of cuttings relating to Loughton Hall, kept under the heading *Loughton Hall: The Debden Community Centre* at Loughton Library in Essex.

Caroline Lucas, *Writing for Women: The Example of Woman as Reader in Elizabethan Romance* (Milton Keynes, Philadelphia: Open University Press, 1989) – for views of Thomas Powell and Thomas Salter see p. 16 and pp. 119 – 20.

Josephine A. Roberts ed., *The Poems of Lady Mary Wroth* (London, Louisiana State Press, 1983) – Wroth's biographical details from this source, pp. 1- 40.

Helen Hackett, "Yet Tell Me Some Such Fiction", in Women, Texts and Histories, ed. by Clare Brant and Diane Purkiss (London, Routledge, 1992), pp. 39 – 68 – details Wroth and Lord Denny scandal.

May Nelson Paulissen, *The Love Sonnets of Mary Wroth: A Critical Introduction*, Elizabethan and Renaissance Studies 104 (Salzburg: Institut fur Anglistik und Amerikanistik, 1982).

William Chapman Waller, *An Extinct Family: Wroth of Loughton Hall* (Essex, Transactions of the Essex Archaeological Society, undated) – describes Wroth ancestry pp. 156- 157, family tree on p. 181

Inside the Workhouse
Susanna Smith
- Property Manager
The Workhouse Southwell

The Workhouse, Southwell, Nottinghamshire © National Trust

The National Trust buying a workhouse? Whatever next?!
This was many people's reaction in 1997, when the National Trust stepped in to rescue the best-preserved workhouse in the country from redevelopment. In fact, this century-old national charity was pursuing its founding purpose of preserving places of historic interest permanently for the nation. Just as the stately homes and tracts of countryside and coastline, with which The National Trust is most associated, were once threatened with destruction, so the country's legacy of hundreds of former workhouses is dwindling and few survive complete. At least one example needed to be preserved as a reminder of the most ambitious national programme of construction, legislation and bureaucracy that the country had ever seen – the 1834 'New' Poor Law. The word 'workhouse' still has the power to strike fear in people, but how many know what it actually meant?

The Workhouse, Southwell, opened to the public in March 2002, with the help of the Heritage Lottery Fund, individual donations and legacies and the ongoing support of National Trust members. Many visitors come to find out what life was like in these institutions after discovering family connections with former workhouse inmates or staff. In this article I explain what workhouses were and who lived there, as well as how we researched The Workhouse, Southwell, ending with some hints on further research.

Workhouses and the New Poor Law
Our Workhouse is an imposing red brick building outside Southwell, in Nottinghamshire. Built in 1824, it was part of an experiment in management of the poor. Its founder, the Reverend Becher, sought a solution to the high cost of outdoor relief (or 'dole'). This solution was to care for the 'old and infirm', who could not work, and act as a deterrent to the 'idle and profligate', who, he suspected, would not work. After this prototype, the 1834 New Poor Law established similar workhouses and deterrent regimes across the country, with a national system of inspection and a head office at Somerset House.

Originally called Thurgarton Hundred Incorporated Workhouse, the building became Southwell Union Workhouse after the 1834 Act. The name Union refers to the union of parishes whose ratepayers supported the workhouse. The country was divided into hundreds of these unions so that there would be a workhouse for anyone who needed help. There were 60 parishes in Southwell Union and anyone settled in these parishes who applied for poor relief might be offered this workhouse.

Paupers were generally admitted after applying to a Relieving Officer for help, but could be seen in person by the Board of Guardians (the ratepayers' elected representatives) who considered each case. Applicants would hope to be given money or other assistance that would enable them to continue living at home. Often, however, they were told, 'No answer but the workhouse'.

On arrival, paupers' clothes were cleaned and stored while they put on workhouse uniforms. (Possessions were returned when a pauper left the workhouse). After medical inspection, they were segregated into 'classes', as the design of the building is based upon principles of classification and segregation. The Master's central, 'control' section of the building is flanked by wings. Men were confined to the east wing, women to the west and children placed in quarters at the rear. Paupers were further subdivided according to age and ability to work. The 'old and infirm' paupers were considered a 'blameless' class and given an easier regime than the 'able-bodied' or 'idle and profligate' paupers who had to work. Internally, double interlocking stairs ensured the categories could not meet except by permission of the staff.

Who was in The Workhouse?
These classes give an idea of the range of people inside a workhouse; from those who lost homes due to the infirmities of old age, to the working labourer, who might return to work within a week if harvest started. Such a man would bring his family with him, to be segregated in different parts of the house. (As well as being part of the deterrent regime, there were practical reasons for keeping such a wide mix of ages and sexes separate.) Family members were allowed 'interviews' with each other on application to the staff.

Master & Matron Willatt and dog - 1927 ©National Trust

More people were admitted alone: orphans, widows, widowers, and single mothers, many of whose children were born in workhouses. Increasingly the infirm sector outgrew the 'able'. Many were there due to mental or physical disabilities and censuses give 'occupations' of 'idiot' and 'lame'.

A deterrent regime
Work for able men involved breaking stones and old bones, unpicking old rope (oakum picking), weeding and gardening. Women carried out oakum picking, cooking, washing, milking, spinning and needlework. The diet consisted of milk or gruel and bread for breakfast and supper, with meat and potatoes or broth for dinner on set days of the week. Bad behaviour meant an even more boring diet (was it possible?) or confinement in a cell. While paupers could apply to leave officially, those who just absconded over the wall with their uniform might end up in the House of Correction.

The regime was intended to be harsher than life outside the workhouse so that only the truly needy would apply for help. It led to the fear and loathing of the very word 'workhouse' still remembered today, although workhouses are now a thing of the past. In practice, many alternative forms of relief continued alongside the new workhouses so that a vast majority of those receiving assistance never came into a workhouse.

Sticking to the truth
The Workhouse, Southwell, is not a museum, rather it offers the privilege of seeing a genuine site where so many lived and of searching for the clues it offers about life inside. We wanted to tell people about life in a workhouse in the midddle of the 19th century, when the system was fully established across most of the country. However, the building was completely empty in 1997. The 19th century beds and benches had long been gratefully discarded and replaced by more comfortable, modern ones as the institution moved into the 20th century. None survived to serve as models for replicas.

Television and film depictions show workhouses as dark, dingy corners of starvation. Research revealed that there was usually an institutional cleanliness, with paupers constantly whitewashing the walls and cleaning the floors as part of their work regime. Sharing rooms or even beds might seem hard to us but was something most had experienced in their own cottages, where they struggled to afford fuel and other necessaries. The diet, while plain, also tended to be better inside than most had experienced before arriving. It was the tedious, repetitive regime, the stigma and the lack of independence that were the real deterrent, not an intentional cruelty in the system.

How could we make a bare and tedious place an interesting visit for today's public? While many rooms looked authentically similar and repetitive (clean and bare), different people had inhabited each space. Perhaps former inmates could speak to the visitor in the parts of the building that belonged to them.

Welcome to The Workhouse
Visitors to The Workhouse today receive an audio guide, carefully based on archive sources, such as Guardians' Minutes, Punishment Books and Poor Law Inspectors' letters. Where clues were missing from our workhouse, we looked to other workhouse sources to fill in the gaps. Dickens' essays (not his more sensationalised fiction) were also useful.

Writer Robin Brooks was determined to use real 19th century language. For the Master's character, a master's diary from another workhouse revealed an overwrought and undermined man. We hear him conduct us around the workhouse. Pauper's accounts are rare and can be unreliable but reports investigating poverty, industry or agriculture at the time quote interviews, giving an idea of words used to describe conditions. So it is that in the able men's day room we meet a framework knitter, out

Reverend Becher
who visitors
meet in the
Introductory Film
© National Trust / Kate Fisher

of work in the 'hungry forties'. This contrasts with the mumbling of men in the old and infirm day room or the request for a bit more fresh air from the bedridden old man in his dormitory.

Visitors explore accommodation for each class of poor - the enclosed exercise yards at the front, work yards at the rear, day rooms on the ground floor and sleeping accommodation above. In the cellars and kitchen we meet Matron and her charges, the women. In the schoolroom, the hard-pressed Schoolmistress describes the children's workhouse education, better than many received outside.

Inventories and accounts helped us describe the sort of furniture that may have been in each room. We reinstated features (the paint colours, fireplaces and windows) where we are sure how they looked; where we cannot be certain, we provide visitors with accurate information on the audio guide to allow their imagination to furnish the rest.

Other features of the visit are a film where the Reverend Becher introduces the building and we see workhouse inhabitants at work. Census information contributed to a database of some of the inmates to give an idea of the range of people and occupations. One room has a conjectural recreation of a dormitory but as these are replica beds, visitors are free to touch or even sleep in them! A handling collection and oral history extracts add to the experience. Other displays and interactive computer exhibits look at the development of workhouses and welfare up to 1948 and then consider modern alternatives.

What happened to workhouses later?
Workhouses developed from deterrence to care, although the fearful reputation remained. By the 1870s, improvements in nursing care saw new workhouse infirmaries built. As well as the destitute, workhouses admitted those who were simply sick with no one to care for them. Casuals or tramps also continued to arrive for a night's board in return for work. By 1913, workhouses were being renamed 'institutions'. New names tried to put the stigma behind them. (Southwell became Greet House.) Searching among the archives you may find a simple address being used rather than a clearly institutional title. One such as Union Road can be a giveaway!

The introduction of health and unemployment insurance and pensions, along with improving nutrition and health care meant that many no longer needed these institutions. New, specialised homes were built for children and many were fostered out. 1929 legislation saw Guardians hand their duties to local authorities, who continued to run the 'public assistance' institutions until many became NHS hospitals, while others continued as residential homes until very recent times.

Researching workhouse residents
For inmates, I start with the census but it can be hard to trace people between each census. Masters and Clerks carefully kept admission and Discharge Registers but it is disappointing how rarely they survive. This may be due to sensitive staff shielding former inmates from the stigma of the workhouse but it is frustrating for researchers! Of Nottinghamshire Union records, all kept in Nottinghamshire Archives, only Nottingham Unions Register survives. Where such a register survives you can trace people being admitted and discharged, sometimes several times a year!

Other county record office sources are Union records such as Punishment Books, Daybooks, medical records *etc*. Guardians' Minute books discuss some individual cases so are certainly worth perusing if you know an approximate date. Apprenticeships and later school records can help – at Southwell, Guardians dismissed the schoolmistress in 1885 and sent children off to local schools with a sigh of relief.

Parish records may list their own paupers receiving 'in relief' in the workhouse. Paupers were usually buried back in their own parishes but there are some workhouses that had their own burial grounds. Many Workhouse Infirmaries provided local medical care several decades before the existence of the NHS, so finding a relation born or dying there may not signify that they came from a life of poverty but simply that they received specialist medical care.

Individual cases can be mentioned by School, Lunacy and Poor Law Inspectors, whose fascinating but time-consuming records and reports can be found at the Public Record Office (PRO), which publishes a helpful paper on Poor Law Records (www.pro.gov.uk).

Staff members are easier to trace. Hiring and firing is always mentioned in Minutes, with salary details and sometimes former or subsequent employment details. Even handier, in PRO MH9, are Registers of Paid Officers covering most of the workhouse period. Early Masters often came from the armed services and nurses were simply female inmates. Later, both became more professional. The Poor Law examinations made Masters professional administrators who ran hospitals and institutions alike and there was a professional association. Nursing qualifications ensured that paid nurses became Matrons with the right husband. The tradition of employing a married couple for Master and Matron continued well beyond 1948, although Superintendent had long replaced the title of Master.

Not sure where your local workhouse was, or where its archives are? Help is at hand! Gibson's Guides can be very useful on Poor Laws and Peter Higginbotham's amazing one-man Odyssey has resulted in an informative and well-researched website. Click on www.workhouses.org.uk and head for the Union maps as a really good starting point. This site is excellent for general background information, including regional variations, such as Scottish Poorhouses and the Irish Poor Law.

Were your family here?
We are keen to trace former inhabitants. Photographs of the people or the building are also rare finds. We do not have our own archives but have been fortunate in help from the public. If you have details of anyone from Southwell Union Workhouse, we are pleased to add details to the simple database we have started. Please give references for information and indicate if you are happy for the information to be made public.

How to visit
For more about The Workhouse, see www.nationaltrust.org.uk/workhouse and write to the Property Secretary, The Workhouse, Upton Road, Southwell, Nottinghamshire, NG25 0PT for

our book *The Workhouse, Southwell* currently at £2.95 plus £1 p&p. If you plan to visit, do remember that The Workhouse can be busy during holiday periods. To be sure of admittance at the time you want just book in advance on 01636817250. Opening times for 2003 are from April to October, every day **except** Tuesday and Wednesday from 12pm to 5pm, but from 11am during August. Do leave at least one and a half hours for your visit.

The National Trust is a registered charity independent of government. If you would like to become a member or make a donation, please telephone 0870 458 4000; write to: The National Trust, PO Box 39, Bromley, Kent BR1 3XL; or see our website at: www.nationaltrust.org.uk.

Further reading
M A Crowther *The Workhouse System 1834-1929* (Batsford, 1981)
S King *Poverty and Welfare in England 1700 – 1850: A Regional Perspective* (Manchester University Press, 2000)
M E Rose *The English Poor Law, 1780-1930* (David and Charles, 1971)
N Longmate *The Workhouse* (Maurice Temple Smith Ltd, 1974)
K Morrison *The Workhouse* (English Heritage, 1999)
Trevor May *The Victorian Workhouse* (Shire Publications, 1997)
©Susanna Smith for The National Trust

Black Sheep Search
(Machine Breakers, Rioters & Convict Research 1780 -1900)
**
Jill Chambers ~ 4 Quills ~ Letchworth Garden City ~ Herts ~ SG6 2RJ
e-mail: Jill_M_Chambers@compuserve.com
**
Publications include:
The Story of the 1830 Swing Riots Series
Berkshire Machine Breakers
Buckinghamshire Machine Breakers
Gloucestershire Machine Breakers
Hampshire Machine Breakers
Wiltshire Machine Breakers
**
Criminal Petitions Index 1819 - 1839
Part 1 - HO17/40-49
Part 2 - HO17/50-59
Part 3 - HO17/60-69
Part 4 - HO17/70-79
**
Machine Breakers' News
Newsletter, published three times a year. It contains articles on 18th and 19th century protest in England and Wales, and Convict Research
**
Convict Research 1780-1900
Convict research undertaken at the Public Record Office, Newspaper Library and from own indexes
**
Transportation Index 1780 - 1868
Coming Soon: This index will include all those sentenced to transportation between 1780 and 1868, whether or not they sailed for Australia, giving age, offence and in many cases native place, as well as date and place of trial and ship, hulk or prison details. It is to be published by county, starting with Yorkshire. Send for details.

A Family Secret –

Linda Wroe tells Robert Blatchford her story
of how she discovered she was adopted.

Several weeks ago I read an article in The Times newspaper where the article writer discussed the fact that she knew that one of her sisters was adopted. Apparently all the family, other relatives and some friends knew that the girl had been adopted. The girl, or young woman, had never been told about the adoption and the writer discussed the merits of whether or not she should tell her sister. She concluded that she was not going to be the member of the family who would tell the adoptee.

The article affected me considerably as some weeks previously I had talked to Linda and was well aware of the consequences of not telling some one who was adopted of the fact.

In our discussions Linda told me that she had been born on March 29th 1950 and with her family lived in the Dewsbury Road area of South Leeds until she was seven. She had a very caring and loving family, who, took her on holidays, gave her treats and everything a child could ever want. Moving to the Cottingley area with her Mum and Dad, this happy life continued through school and later college. Her first job was as a shorthand typist and through a work colleague she met Colin. By June 1968 they were engaged, marrying in May 1970 and moving to their first house in the Armley area which was near the local police station where Colin worked. In 1971 their first child Melanie was born and she was idolised by everyone. In 1974 Joanne came along followed in 1975 by Simon. Linda was overjoyed as she was an only child.

Moving to a bigger house in the Whinmoor area of Leeds Colin left the police and returned to being an engineer, travelling around the country wherever the work was. One day in 1979 Colin took Linda to work and when she returned home there was a note on the table saying he had left but he would return someday. The children were heartbroken and after a long period without contact they eventually divorced and Linda and the children started life again.

By May 1982 Linda was working in the Leeds Reference Library. She subsequently met Clive. Falling in love with him, and finding that her children readily accepted Clive, she could see that a great and happy family was emerging. Clive had never been married but taking Linda and the three children under his wing they married in 1989 and have been happy ever since.

Linda continued working at the library and was able to move around to different branches, large and small, meet many different characters and do many tasks all linked to the job. She now thought she should settle in a department and stop being a "library vagrant". In October 2000 she went into Local and Family History Department and that is where her life took on a lot of changes.

One morning in November 2000 the porters brought some boxes into the department and when Linda opened them they were the baptism records of St. Peters church in Dewsbury Road from 1950. She thought she would find an entry about herself in one of the registers because it was where she had attended Sunday School. She sifted through them and found her school friends' names but not her own.

Her curiousity roused, Linda telephoned her mother and asked why she was not in the Baptism Register. Linda's mother said that 'they couldn't decide where to have me christened so they chose Belle Vue chapel'. Linda had thought she had always been 'Church of England' but had now discovered she was a Non Conformist!

It was the Friday before

KIRKGATE & COMMERCIAL. ST, LEEDS.

Christmas and Linda thought that she would find herself in the St. Catherine's Index (now the GRO Index). She got index films for the four quarters of 1950 from the relevant filing cabinet and worked her way through them.

"Where was I, everybody born after 1837 should be registered. I telephoned my dad and asked him. 'Oh they will have missed you off like they have me", was his quick reply. 'Thanks', I said and put the receiver down".

That evening at home she discussed it with Clive and got out her birth certificate. It was only a short certificate which had been signed in November 1950 and all registrations should made within to six weeks after a birth. Linda had been born in March 1950.

At Christmas Linda, Clive and the children went to her parents' house for lunch. It was very enjoyable and nothing was discussed regarding Linda's work. With snow beginning to fall and feeling a bit uncomfortable Linda suggested that they all returned home.

On the Wednesday between Christmas and New year Clive and Linda went to the Register Office in Leeds. She took the short birth certificate, gave them her details and asked if they would issue her with a full certificate.

"I'm awfully sorry", said the counter assistant, "but you're neither on the computer records nor in the old journal. Try Southport and see what they have to say as all records are held there".

Linda hurried home in confusion and telephoned Certificate Services in Southport, gave them the numbers on the birth certificate, and the assistant said she would phone Linda back after she had spoken to another department, but it did sound as though the short certificate was an 'adoptive certificate'.

"Already on my knees the phone rang and she confirmed what she had said 10 minutes earlier.In sheer disbelief and tears flowing freely I asked her to forward all documentation that I was entitled to. I had no inkling about being adopted, I never had any reason to question it. So why?"

A few days later her full adoptive birth certificate arrived, so Clive and Linda went to her parents' house to ask them all about it.

"Feeling sick inside I asked them if they had anything to tell me about my childhood. At first they didn't want to say anything so I had to ask them. It was awful. Dad now 85 and Mum 82 just broke down and said they had been selfish and just didn't want to lose me. There was never a right time to tell me and they were frightened what my reaction might be".

Linda came away from the house absolutely devastated she knew she had to find who she was and realised all her attention would be focused on finding her birth mother. That same evening Linda visited her aunts, and asked them if they could enlighten her on her past. They too were stunned that Linda had found out - after all they had been loyal to her parents by not saying anything. The aunts told her that her mother was German and that she was adopted from a place called the 'Wyther' in Leeds and 'she kept me immaculate'.

Linda continually questioned herself about the reason for her adoption. What she needed was more information to discover why she had been adopted. Early in February 2001 Linda received a letter from Social Services telling her that her adoption papers had arrived and would she like to collect them.

"I couldn't get them quick enough, I went in my lunch hour and they told me the name of my mother, father and the reason why I was to be given a new home. My mother came over to England on a European Volunteers scheme as a domestic help and worked in the local hospitals. My father was an engineer and worked at a local factory. They started an affair and I came along but unfortunately my father wouldn't marry as he had another girl who he was in love with."

From this information Linda was able to get her real birth certificate, to find that her birth mother called her Pamela Beryl Rockel.

"My emotions were all over the place. I'm 51 years old, I have a different name, my religion is different, I'm half German, I'm adopted. Is there anything else?"

Linda's work colleagues were extremely supportive, intrigued and so very willing to help her. They looked in the electoral roll for past years to see where her father lived and found a local address, but there was no trace of her mother. Linda reasoned that her birth mother "was only young in a strange country, had just given birth and must have been lonely" so therefore returned to Germany to continue her life.

She wrote many letters to Germany, to the Land Registry and archives. The replies, translated by a friend and colleague, showed there was no trace of her, but Germany had been a divided country and their systems were completely different from the United Kingdom.

"Everyday I would wake wondering about her, why and would I ever find her as I knew time would be precious as she would now be 71 or 72. My emotions got the better of me and I started to have counselling sessions. Clive, my children and grandchildren were also starting to find coming to terms with the situation rather difficult.

BOAR LANE LEEDS.

very close to him in many ways. Aghast, they told me that my father had died in 1988 and his wife in 1982 but that he had had four boys and one girl. I've got brothers and a sister. Again I couldn't believe this, I was elated, on cloud nine."

After a few enquiries Linda discovered that her new found sister was living in south Leeds. Curiosity got the better of Melanie, Linda's eldest daughter, who went to see Linda's sister, Margaret. Melanie asked Margaret a few questions about her father and then as diplomatically as she could Melanie told Margaret that Linda, her mother, was Margaret's half sister. Taken aback Margaret asked where Linda was and asked to meet her straight away. After a telephone call from her daughter Linda drove to the pub.

"When I walked in rather apprehensive we embraced each other and started to talk and the feeling was that we had never been apart it was so emotional."

The following day Margaret phoned the four brothers and told them about Linda. There was a mixed reaction, which was only to be expected but they all wanted to meet her. Arrangements were made for them to meet the following Wednesday evening. Linda could not have wished for anything better, they had all accepted her, the thought of rejection wasn't even an issue, Linda felt wonderful.

At the meeting Linda met her four brothers, their wives and partners. All of them had two children some even had grandchildren. Suddenly Linda found herself part of a large and super family

The following Friday after Linda again looked at the GRO index to see if her mother had had any more children. In 1952 her mother had a boy and called him Kevin.

Linda felt that she was getting nearer to finding her mother. She discovered that there were only 30 people named Kevin with the same surname in England so she wrote to them all.

At 8.00 o'clock on the morning of 29th October a Kevin telephoned in response to her letter. In disbelief Linda told him what he wanted to know and confirmed there and then that they had the same mother. He had discovered a sister.

The only way I could describe the experience was that of the Indian earthquake where there was once a family and then they vanished very quickly. My father's family found this explanation very hard to comprehend and couldn't accept my feelings and views, it had been a secret for a long time. I didn't want to hurt anyone and that was so hard as I had so many different things to take on board and try to keep things as normal as possible."

October 4th 2001 will be a day Linda will always remember. A member of the public visiting the L:ibrary asked Linda how she was progressing in her search for her birth mother. Telling her that she was not making much progress Linda said her next step was to trawl through the Marriage and Death indexes of the GRO Index.

The lady volunteered to look through the indexes on Linda's behalf as she said she had the 1951 marriages and it seemed a good starting point.

"Within 10 minutes she came to me and said look I've found a marriage of your mum. What! I screeched. Here in Leeds. I couldn't believe it. I went to pieces, my glasses steamed up. Elation. I ran up to the register office and acquired the marriage certificate. My mum had married in Leeds in October 1951 and ironically it would have been their Golden wedding anniversary two days later October 6th. Another coincidence.

Back at work excitement was rife and the department buzzing as word got round, we looked in the old telephone directories as we had an address and on each page side by side were my father's and mother's names. The address of my father sent bells ringing in my head as I knew we had friends living on the same street.

I couldn't get home quick enough to tell Clive and contact our friends. They had lived next door to my father and knew all about him as they had been

Kevin told Linda where his mother lived in Leeds and gave her her telephone number and address. She had lived so close to Linda for all these years. In the excitement Linda called Kevin on the telephone instead of her mother. Kevin decided he would go and see his mother, tell her of the letter and ask why she had never mentioned Linda to him and would she see her. Linda thought it was a super plan and in an excited state she had to sit and wait for the call.

At 10.50 that same morning the telephone rang, it was Kevin. He was crying. When he had arrived at the house he had found his mother dead on the floor. Linda could not believe it, got in her car drove like she had never driven before.

"I ran into the house, it was true there was my mum on the floor. I hugged Kevin and we said what a way to meet. I went over to her, knelt down beside her, touched her and told her that everything would be OK now that I was here, it was Pamela. I'd never used that name in my life before but it just came out naturally. I was heartbroken. The police arrived with it being a sudden death, so we had to leave. It was traumatic."

Linda had known all along that she had to find her birth mother but fate decreed that she was too late by a few hours.

With emotions running high Linda wanted to see her mother in the Chapel of Rest but was advised not to as she had had a post mortem. Linda felt that was another blow and it was not meant to be.

As the funeral arrangements progressed Kevin automatically added Linda into the family obituary notice in the local newspaper and arranged for her to go with him to see the vicar.

Intrigued by their story the Vicar dedicated his sermon to Kevin and Linda and said it was her mother's gift to bring them together after all these years being apart.

Linda wrote a verse on the card with the flowers trying to reflect and understand what had happened and placed photographs of Linda and her family in her mother's coffin
> We were together at the beginning
> We were together at the end
> We were apart in the middle
> But you would have been my best friend
> RIP

Whilst at the funeral a neighbour of her mother told Linda that her mother had told her about her and that her mother was always wondering what Linda was doing, what she was like and what had happened to her. Linda knows now that her mother did not reject her but circumstances had necessitated her adoption. Linda did not blame anyone about the situation.

Linda has met Kevin and his family since 'that awful but happy day' and they are now regularly in touch exchanging photographs and memorabilia of her birth mother and father.

Linda tells me that the past twelve months have been absolutely wonderful and she is now coming to terms with everything putting it all into perspective. She knows with all the support she has from family, friends and work colleagues the future will be happy. She had no idea that she had been adopted. She was given all the love and care anyone could have wished for by her adopting parents and nothing will ever replace that.

Linda now has a new family enlarging the one she already had and she knows that whilst her parents were living she never came between them nor caused further heartache.

In her own words Linda says, "It is a feeling of elation, comfort and I will never be lonely again. I am so pleased I pursued all the issues although it was harrowing at times with many sleepless nights and no regrets".

Linda still works in the library in Leeds and says she is now better equipped to help others who were adopted in tracing their birth parents.

Ships' Official Logs for British Merchant Vessels

Len Barnett

Ships' logs for British merchantmen can often be a cause for confusion. Traditionally these have been associated with navigation: be they log-boards, or log-books (as well as other equipment such as log-bags, log-ships or patent logs).

The wording of the 1850 Mercantile Marine Act is not particularly helpful, but the 1854 Merchant Shipping Act is clearer. Both required *official* logs to be maintained, but the latter stated that this may 'either be kept distinct from the ordinary Ship's Log or united therewith'. From all examples I have so far seen, I would opine that masters of foreign-going vessels overwhelmingly kept their navigational logs completely apart from their official logs.

In compiling official logs the 1850 law required masters to make various notations on officers and crew. Primarily these were of illness onboard and treatment (if indeed there was any); deaths; desertions; poor behaviour and subsequent punishments; and assessments of conduct and ability. Master mariners were not required to report on themselves. The 1854 Act further ordered masters to note births, marriages and *all* deaths onboard.

Whilst the responsibilities of masters were adequately stated in this legislation, the retention of official logs was not. A relatively small percentage of these documents has survived and the traditional understanding as to why I find rather

wanting. I do not propose to explore this here. Instead I will attempt to show how the above information was recorded in practice and how it can add greatly to one's understanding of particular voyages and occasionally, individuals. Whilst most of the following text is drawn directly from official logs, in order to make a better narrative some reference is made to other records such as crew-lists and articles. Incidentally, complexities of the bureaucratic systems and the potential holdings of these logs are described on my website at http://www.barnettresearch.freeserve.co.uk

If taken in totality, ships' official logs would have overwhelmingly made boring reading. Even a relatively high percentage of those retained give little information. Sometimes, however, when voyages have gone disastrously wrong there is a wealth of commentary that can be absolutely fascinating.

I begin with a voyage of VERITAS, a year-old Liverpool registered schooner. She sailed from that same port on 3rd September 1859, under the command of Thomas Carrey then aged 26. Bound initially for Calcutta, a return cargo could be sought anywhere in the Far East for final discharge in the United Kingdom: taking a maximum of three years.

A few weeks later near the Canary Isles there were the first signs of potential problems. The Cook, Thomas Dent, requested to be taken off articles 'as

he was not qualified'. This was permitted. It should be explained that merchant mariners signed as qualified for particular duties and if found unfit their wages were 'reduced in proportion' to their 'incompetency'. Not uncommonly cooks also performed seamen's work when required, so he was probably rated as such.

The next sign of trouble came on 12th January 1860 in mid Indian Ocean. George Ohlmann, a German born Able Seaman refused to pump ship after six p.m. It was noted that the master had already had occasion to 'speak to him'. Reaching Calcutta around 30th January ten days later another A.B. was discharged by 'Mutual Consent'. Especially since his wages were paid, it may be that there had been negotiations with the local Shipping Master.

Interestingly, there had been an unusual entry in early January. The master and crew of another vessel, the full-rigged ship WINSCALES, had been picked up by VERITAS in the Bay of Bengal, it would seem they were helpless, since they were suffering from scurvy. Signed not only by the past master but also by the other distressed seamen, whilst they were apparently well cared for, it is clear Mr. Carrey intended claiming this expense back on return to England.

Obviously Thomas Dent had returned to his culinary duties. Still at Calcutta, on the morning of February 16th the Mate discovered a 'large Hole' had 'burned through the main deck'. The Cook had the night before allowed 'the Red Cinders to overrun his ash pan'. During the afternoon and exposing themselves to a charge of mutiny, the crew complained of 'the dirty, indifferent way that their food was cooked for them, often not Ready at the Proper time' - which was important at sea. Refusing to do any further duty Dent requested his discharge: which was refused. On board another two days without turning to, he then went ashore without leave. It seems the master regarded this initially as a case of 'rambling', but by the time of sailing around March 1st this was treated as desertion.

Whilst anchoring at Rangoon on March 21st George Ohlmann got himself into trouble, by being insolent to the Mate. The following day the German demanded his discharge and was refused. Withdrawing his labour, on the 23rd Ohlmann was taken before the local British Magistrate and was sent briefly to gaol. On release he would not return on board, was arrested once more and incarcerated ashore until brought back on May 17th. He still refused to work and was 'put in irons … to be kept on bread and water' until arriving back in England 'or to consenting to do duty'.

Meanwhile, on April 8th the following was logged:-

'The Chief Mate called my attention to the

misconduct of the Sailmaker Samuel Foulkes Refusing duty. On being called aft by me he said there was no more use of him doing any more duty on board. I put him under confinement in the Cabin previous to informing the Magistrates. At noon I asked him would he return to his duty and on reading the articles to him, he said he would, whereupon I released him from confinement. The Chief Mate informs me that he is in the habit of giving back answers when told by to do anything'.

A fortnight later two A.B.s, one who was French incidentally, went ashore on the Sunday without leave and were still missing the following day. They returned onboard at one p.m., but the police were called and one was 'confined for being drunk and disorderly'.

The Sailmaker and yet another A.B. also broke leave on the day that Ohlmann was brought back on board, but at six p.m. came back. Added to this, in May an A.B. who had been signed-on either at Calcutta or Rangoon (the records do not tally here) for the return voyage requested to be discharged, as the work was too severe. This was refused since hands were 'scarce'. The following day he disappeared 'having taken his clothes', though some days later he was discharged by mutual consent. (In all likelihood the cargo would have been of timber, Burma being heavily logged at this time for hardwoods. I believe that ships' crews were required to load this completely by themselves, which was not often normal practice in

last logged trouble was recorded. During a winter/spring afternoon in early August there was an altercation between the Mate and a passenger named Smith. The former having been ordered to his cabin, the latter then also set about the Master verbally. The following day the passenger apologised to the Master, who noted that he believed Smith had been 'under the influence of Liquor at the time'. This is interesting as it was stated in the articles that the crew was not allowed 'grog'.

VERITAS made a good, if not record-breaking passage home from there. The remaining crew finally paid off at Liverpool on 4th October 1860.

Another voyage where discipline disintegrated is worthy of mentioning, since there were other factors: usual and unusual. The Aberdeen registered (full-rigged) ship BALMORAL sailed from Liverpool on 13th November 1851. Under the command of William Budge, she was bound initially for Hong Kong.

At first there seems only a 'dirty', 'slovenly' and insolent character rated Cook and Steward for the command to contend with. Not seeing fit to carry out his duties as Steward, finding 'remonstrances' in vain Mr. Budge had the defaulter's wages reduced as a result.

However, by the end of January 1852 whilst in the southernmost reaches of the Indian Ocean a far more serious situation had begun to arise: the Mate and 2nd Mate were found quarrelling on deck. (Including the master there were only three officers onboard.)

Two days later the Carpenter and a Seaman had been caught fighting. (Apart from officers the crew consisted of the Carpenter, the Cook & Steward, six Seamen and one Ordinary Seaman.) The master noted that this was the 'first appearance of bad conduct amongst the crew' but added ruefully that he could not 'expect much else' after the incident with the Mate.

On February 8th there was another public argument between the two mates, over some Cape yams. Ten days later the Mate, William Davidson, had a violent disagreement with the Master over greasing rather than tarring rigging. Much of the crew witnessed this and it may be that they supported the Mate.

By the beginning of March they were within the myriad of Indonesian islands when the allowance

British merchantmen. Also, with the oppressive climate and primitive port facilities, this would have been *very* hard work.)

The return voyage was also eventful. George Ohlmann on his return had made threats and still refused duty. On 25th May, he escaped from the cabin and went forward. The Master, Mate and Boatswain found him on the 'Top Gallant Forecastle'. Armed with a capstan bar he threatened to 'nock' (sic) Carrey's 'Brains out'! Overpowered, he was returned to captivity in irons: whilst still 'giving insolence'. The Master's anger obviously shows in this entry, as he was ready to have the German locked up for the entire trip home. However, probably short-handed the following day he was set free 'on promising to behave himself in a proper and upright manner and to commence his duty again as AB'.

Entering the Indian Ocean between the Great Nicobar and Sumatra at six a.m. on 7th June the master arose to find VERITAS 'right on the opposite direction to what she should be going, with all sail set and making sail to send her more out of her course'. The officer on deck had been the Mate, Charles Fairbairn, who at 28 was slightly older than the master. Apparently the master's standing order was to be was to be awakened if she 'broke off' her intended track.

This was not his only order that was disregarded either. Later in June, the seventeen-year old 'Boy' (actually rated Ordinary Seaman) in charge of the livestock and fowls was 'chastised' by the Master with a rope's end for repeatedly not feeding them.

Having transitted the Indian Ocean and rounded the Cape of Good Hope into the South Atlantic, the of beef and pork was reduced slightly. This was a sure sign of a passage running longer than planned for and as the food allowance was not more than absolutely 'adequate', bode ill. The full meat allowance was restored later in the month and BALMORAL reached Hong Kong on 2nd April 1852.

There were all the classic signs of a seriously discontented crew whilst in port: arguments, fighting, drunkenness, leave-breaking and gaol ashore. The Mate was discharged on April 19th. (As the Master had declined to comment on his ability and conduct, Davidson may have had difficulty securing another berth.) Another Second Mate was procured. Shifting a considerable distance to Shanghai sometime in May probably for a cargo, BALMORAL began her voyage home mid June.

Although there had already been a case in Hong Kong which flared up again at sea, for nine days in July the Carpenter, Norman McLaren, was off duty suffering from venereal disease. 'Blue Pills and mercurial ointment' were administered by the master.

Another long passage (presumably around Cape Horn) by the time BALMORAL reached the North Atlantic in November beef was running short. Although by this time it would have been inedible by modern standards, the allowance was cut short for over a week.

Before reaching London docks on 28th November 1852 the Carpenter had another reason for being sent to the 'Seamen's Hospital'. Five days before whilst aloft furling the mainsail he fell from the Mainguard. Badly shocked, he was bled and given a 'purgative powder' onboard. These seem to have been the preferred treatments meted out by William Budge, the Carpenter had already received similar for being feverish and having a headache on the way out.

Logs occasionally show other character traits. Whilst at Foo Chow Foo in October 1858, an apprentice named Henry Heywood aboard the barque SPIRIT OF THE NORTH was assaulted by the Mate, William Affleck. Arising out of a petty matter, the Mate was obviously considerably drunk and the attacks were accompanied by derogatory language. Affleck after sleep, but still drunk, once again returned to insulting the apprentice.

Although the mate was logged onboard, Heywood, as per his rights took this further: initially stating his complaint before the Commanding Officer of H.M. Ship SAMSON. Advised to go the British Consul, this he did. Accordingly, a full hearing was due to be held a few days later and both mariners left the barque *together* to attend. When asked by the Consul if young Heywood 'wished to force the charge, he answered that he did not, so the case ended'.

Heywood's career at sea however did not: going on to be a deck officer with 'P & O'.

Accidents of various forms are also within these logs. One case concerns a collision between ZEBRA, a British coastal paddle-steamer and a Belgian mail-steamer off Dunkirk in February 1869. There is a wealth of detail in entries, including the fact that ZEBRA was at full speed, had all sail set, but was somewhat blind due to the amount of smoke she was making. Apparently there were no injuries, other than to the vessels.

However, reports on deaths can be noteworthy. Sometimes there was little to say, as in the example of 'Thomas Richardson Apprentice' of the barque INDIAN, in the Southern Ocean in September 1858. Whilst 'painting ship' he 'fell overboard and after every endeavour to save him, was drowned'. On other occasions much depth is entered on the loss of life. One such case covered the death of William Charles Pearson, Third Engineer on the steamship BAROTSE in November 1915. In the early stages of a voyage from London to South Africa and beyond, working on a badly leaking stay in the combustion chamber the poor man suffered horrific burns from an oil lamp. Although tenderly cared for, he died later in the day in the presence of the 1st Engineer and Chief Steward. In the Bay of Biscay, the following forenoon Mr. Pearson was 'committed to the Deep with Christian Burial'.

© Len Barnett 2002

Militia Attestation Records in the PRO

Jennifer A Edmonds

One of the most underused military document class at Kew is the Militia Attestation document. Although prior to about 1860 there are several different WO classes, I am going to concentrate on class WO96.

I am listing all 1522 boxes, but so far I have only done about a hundred. It will take me up to 30 years to complete. I find them both amusing and sad and in the next few paragraphs hope that I can bring the documents and men to life.

People say "No one in my family was in the military",. Perhaps their direct ancestor may not have been, but an uncle or great uncle may have been and he is still a valuable source of information for your direct father or grandfather. Whereas WO97 class is the regular army attestation and discharge papers, the militia form is filled in at joining and if the potential soldier was unfit then his document with descriptions, signatures etc. are still kept. For those who stayed in, their completed training days were listed as were any medals they collected along the way.

Normally the third and fourth battalions of a Regiment form the miltia, but another group was simply called the Royal Garrison Artillery (R.G.A. for short). In another class there is the Royal Field Artillery. For anyone looking for people born or serving in Cambridgeshire, look in the Suffolk Regiment under WO96/245 -252.

The years covered by this class are anything from 1860 to 1915, so while most soldiers who were away fighting were covered by Class WO 363 and Class WO 364, anyone serving at Home could be found in the Militia documents.The following Militia are listed until 1915... 16th Foot(Beds. and Herts.), 17th Foot (Leicester Regt.), 20th Foot(Lancashire Fusiliers), Royal Dublin Fusiliers, Dublin R.G.A., Edinburgh R.G.A., Forfar & Kincardine R.G.A.

The details shown on the main bulk of the documents are as follows....
Name; birthplace; whether British subject; where now resides (at time of attestation); where resided in last twelve months; age at attestation; Trade or Calling; whether apprenticed; Name and Residence of Master; whether single, married or widower; if married or widower how many children under 14 years of age; whether served, discharged in Army, Army reserve, Navy or Marines; whether sentenced to Penal Servitude; whether in receipt of a pension from any service; if rejected as unfit, was a notice served and by whom, and was it understood; Whether willing to serve for (normally) 6 years; county of registration; in which Militia; Signature

of Recruit; Date of joining and Signature of Witness and Magistrate or Commanding Officer.

Description on Enlistment; age; height in feet and inches; chest measurement (in some it also has expanded measurement); eyes; hair; complexion; Religous denomination; any distinctive marks; various certificates of fitness.

Statement of Services.... gives number and when and in which military group served. This can be a valuable tool because in some cases regular soldiers when they had finished their time in the Army either chose to be in the Militia or were drafted in to help in time of war. A lot of the men were over the fighting age. It will also detail things like absent without leave and character.

I was surprised to find that the Militia did not only fight locally but did go abroad, many to South Africa during the Boer War and in the case of the 72nd foot (Seaforth Highlanders) I really felt for them - the Government of the time took this island (Stornaway) people on 14 March 1900 and sent them out to Egypt.

Pages at times can give a wealth of information.. Just a short address or the parents and brothers and sisters with or without their full addresses and from as far afield as Canada, America or Australia. There is also a single sheet giving birthplace and place of signing-on and not much else for the Militia Reserve. These seem to appear in the Irish battalions more than in the English. Also with the Irish Battalions there is a declaration that their address is not a boarding house. One of the Scottish battalions has the original Service Certificate with the document. This does not come with every set of papers in these boxes.

On the lighter side I have found a Victor Hugo and an Arthur Negus (could this be the Arthur Negus?) I extracted a place name which made me smile - Ham (nr) Sandwich. Talking of place names - the men and the person making out the form did not have a very good knowledge of geography. To give you an example - 'Ipswich near Norwich' (about 50 miles apart and in different counties).

These documents are found at the Public Record Office, Ruskin Ave, Kew, and are the original documents. Can I please ask you to take care when handling them? Since I started listing and publishing the lists, I have found that when I have had to refer to them again, they are put in any old how.
© Jenifer A. Edmonds 2002

Reach over 120,000 North American Family Researchers through Family Chronicle

Family Chronicle is America's most popular genealogy magazine and is filled with articles from the world's best genealogy writers. America's top genealogy software, book and CD publishers, genealogy services companies and genealogists advertise regularly in Family Chronicle to reach this affluent market. If you want to reach the huge North American genealogy market you can do so very affordably with Family Chronicle.

Examples of Small Ads (Payable in US Dollars)

40 word Classified	$20
Marketplace (2$^{1}/_{4}$"x 3$^{1}/_{8}$")	$55
FC Library -Full Colour (2$^{1}/_{2}$"x 2$^{3}/_{8}$")	$100

Call Victoria Pratt at (416)491-3699 ext 114 for full details
on small space advertising programs or
Jeannette Cox at (416) 491-3699 ext 0 for details on large space (display)
advertisements or fax: (416)491-3996 E-mail: jeannette@moorshead.com
or write to
Family Chronicle, P.O.Box 1111, Niagara Falls, NY,14304-1111 USA
Visit us on the web at **www.familychronicle.com**

YorkshireAncestors.com
Brenda Green

Yorkshireancestors.com is believed to be the first purpose built Family History research library providing accommodation in the country. Anyone researching their ancestors, particularly in Yorkshire, or the history of a Yorkshire house will find a treasure trove.

I have been addicted to Family History for almost 30 years and like most family historians, have been frustrated that numerous record offices and libraries have rigid weekday opening hours & for many working people, research time has to be limited to holidays. Most of us have to plan our holidays around other family members. Many new researchers are unaware of the huge range of resources available & do not always feel confident asking. It can be quite daunting in the early stages of research to be confronted by an archivist who assumes we are familiar with churchwardens accounts, Dade registers & tithe maps, or the librarian who talks in abbreviations, the GRO, the IGI, the NBI & M.I.'s.

In a perfect world I could carry out my research during a blissful holiday where I could research day or evening,. Ask stupid questions without feeling foolish and relax in the knowledge that other family members were equally using their valuable leisure time profitably. And just for good measure, with a few good meals and pleasant countryside thrown in. We can all fantasize.

As my research progressed, so did my book collection. In particular I discovered the wealth of information contained in Trade Directories. An aunt of my husband's lent me Porter's Directory of Leeds 1872 (which I later inherited & is now available on CD) I was absolutely riveted to it and read every page and every name. Today's researchers miss such a lot with 'search & find' facilities.

In 1994 my husband, David and I became the proud owners of Upper Carr Caravan Park in Pickering, just south of the North York Moors national park. My collection of Yorkshire books, indexes, Parish Registers had grown and I made them available to visitors. Both the North & East Riding Record Offices & repositories at York were easily accessible. These brought the caravanners in, but most enquiries were from people wanting bed & breakfast or short breaks in self-catering accommodation & we did not have suitable space to expand. The arrival of the internet saw many new would-be family historians & the library housed in a tiny office was getting more & more popular and had outgrown it's limited accommodation.

Our first set of CDs were launched at the York Family History fair in June 2001 and we were amazed at the interest. We now have around 50 with many more in the pipeline, mostly relating to Yorkshire, taken from Trade Directories, Poll books, Parish Registers, Local Histories and other books similarly useful to Family or local historians.

In September 2001 we moved to a delightful old farmhouse, Studley House Farm in the picturesque village of Ebberston, 6 miles East of Pickering. We have attained a 4 diamond rating from the English Tourism Council for our Bed & Breakfast accommodation. We also have 2 self-catering cottages, one of them recently completed which is wheel chair accessible and a barn in the process of conversion. In addition, we can take 8 caravans, motorhomes or tents in a tranquil setting in the old apple orchard.

An extension to an old cart shed became our new library. The library is wheelchair accessible and parking is adjacent. There are also tea & coffee making facilities and for those who require a snack or meal, there is an excellent country pub in the village.

Opening Hours
The library is open to visitors who are staying with us, at times to suit the researcher. This could be before breakfast or up to 11pm in an evening or weekend.
We are also open to Day researchers. 10am – 7.30pm daily, strictly by appointment.

Firstly, I should stress, we are not a record office, and have very few primary sources, but what we do have compliments the official sources & covers the whole of Yorkshire. We have an excellent collection of family history source books, FH Society information, One-name studies collections, beginners books, specialist areas, religious records, SOG publications, Gibson & Mcloughlin guides, most Yorkshire CRO guides/holdings lists, Yorkshire Archaeological Society journal 1974 to date. There is an extensive accumulation of Family History & genealogical reading, the latest FH magazines & Yorkshire FH Society journals, books helpful to reading old, difficult & Latin handwriting, a collection of military books, hundreds of surname indexes, for census returns, marriages & marriages licences, burials, monumental inscriptions, Hearth Tax, criminal records, a large amassment of material relating to Leeds and we are continually sourcing books & indexes to increase the contents of the library.

Friendly help & advice is offered if required. We can also provide up to date information on internet mailing lists & websites or alternatively how to research if you do not have a computer.
We have 3 fiche readers, 2 computers linked to the internet, a photocopier, and a laminator. The full range of our CDs, a small selection of books & 1901 census vouchers are on sale in the library.

It is extremely rewarding, when on many occasions, a shriek of joy can be heard and someone else has found yet another elusive ancestor, waiting to be found, lurking in the contents of our library.

Wills and their Writers

Jill Groves

When looking at the wills of your ancestors, have you ever thought about the people who actually did the writing of their wills, who they were. These days wills are often drawn up by lawyers or will writing services run by people with some legal training. The basics of drawing up a will haven't changed much since the seventeenth century (and neither has the legal language). But who drew up the wills for people in the seventeenth and eighteenth centuries? What follows is what I have discovered from years of transcribing wills and inventories in North-east Cheshire (greater Altrincham area).

Literacy was a rare commodity in the seventeenth century, possessed by the educated gentry, and the clerics, but very few others. When a man or a woman needed to make a will at the beginning of the seventeenth century they turned to the local clergy. The reason for this was two-fold. Firstly, they could read and write. Secondly, the Church was very deeply concerned in everyone's will making, financially and spiritually. Originally a will was primarily for a person to bequeath their soul to God and some of their goods to the church for specific reasons (i.e. to endow a church, have priests say masses for their souls, etc.). Well into the eighteenth century the church courts, especially the consistory courts and the prerogative courts, were still very much concerned with wills and affairs attached to them. Not until the Inland Revenue got their claws into the estates of the deceased did the making and proving of Wills become a purely civil affair. But perhaps the will writers give clues about the secularising of probate documents.

How Wills were written

Anyone who studies wills and inventories for a particular area, as I do, begins to recognise the handwriting of the more popular will writers. By comparing the handwriting of the will with the signatures, it is possible to identify these people. A little delving into the history of an area, especially lists of local vicars, rectors, curates, schoolmasters and parish clerks, will usually tell you what these people were. I have identified twenty-five writers of wills in seven townships in North-east Cheshire. Those twenty-five include one vicar and one rector (Robert Janney, vicar of Bowdon, 1629; Thomas Mallory, rector of Northenden), one curate (Edward Berron, curate of Cheadle, 1613), four schoolmasters (Peter Hurdis of Bowdon, 1671; Francis Newton, 1688-1709; John Hollenpriest of Hale, 1674-1711; Thomas Renshaw of Sale, 1700-1720) and five lawyers (John Houghton of Bowdon, Baguley and later Macclesfield; George Clayton of Altrincham 1720-1730s; John Cook of Altrincham, 1727-34; John Stafford of Altrincham and later Northenden, 1720-1760; John Hobson of Sale and Altrincham 1742-1771; Isaac Worthington of Altrincham, 1743-54), and township and parish clerks (George Vawdrey of Bowdon, late sixteenth century to 1616; John Goulden of Hale, 1620s-1640s; Ralph Lowndes, then of Timperley, 1621, prior to becoming curate of Northenden after the death of the octogenarian rector, John Barrett, in 1627; three Renshaws of Sale, two called Thomas, and one called John from about the mid-seventeenth century to 1757). There are several others whose occupation I have been unable to identify. These include two sons of rectors of Northenden, James Barrett (1616) and John Mallory (1666). One of the Thomas Renshaws may have been a parish clerk in the 1680s, and the other may have been a schoolmaster (1679-1709).

Some of the parish clerks were local gentry, especially those of the parish of Bowdon. George Vawdrey of Bowdon was a gentleman from a prestigious local family. Although he was seventy-five in 1613, he rode out to Dunham Massey to write the controversial second will of Maud Tipping of Dunham Massey, widow. He was a member of a numerous and well-respected family, the status of whose members ranged from county elite to well-to-do yeomen, and he had some sort of lease or right to the vicarage and the tithes of Bowdon. His successors, Thomas Saunderson of Bowdon and his sons, were also members of the local gentry, although they didn't seem to write wills.

The normal way for a will to have been written seems to have been as follows. Someone falls ill, takes to his/her bed and if, they are not delirious with fever, calls for a member of the family to run and fetch the parish clerk/schoolmaster or, later on, a lawyer. The parish clerk

arrives with a quill pen, ink and a wad of paper. He (always he) sits at the bedside of the dying/very ill testator (not always he) and makes notes on how the testator wants to dispose of his/her personal (goods) and real (land) estates. In the main a testator did not have a lot of determination in how their estate was disposed of. Men with wives and children, specially unmarried children, had to leave one third to the widow and one third to the children. Which only left one third to be freely disposed of. Most of the land, freehold or rented, went to the eldest son, or to the widow until the eldest son was twenty-one. If no son survived the land would be divided between any daughters with the eldest getting the majority. Bachelors, childless widowers and widows, single women with no children could leave personal and real estate to whomsoever they choose, although most tended to keep it in the family. For example, William Davenport of Sale in 1729 left his real and personal estate spread around his Davenport and Sidall nieces and nephews. Benjamin Artinstall of Ashton-on-Mersey, a widower with no surviving children, left his estate divided between Artinstall nephews, although some were already handsomely provided for by their fathers.

The parish clerk/schoolmaster/lawyer would then listen patiently to the testator's wishes and grumbles about his family, including how his eldest son (and heir) had borrowed a lot of money from the testator, promised to repay it but never had. So the testator wanted his son, when he inherited the family farm, to pay to his mother and siblings equivalent to the money borrowed before he could even set foot in the courtyard. Also the testator didn't want that ne'er-do-well who had married his favourite daughter to get his hands on any money the testator might want to leave her and any present/future grandchildren. The parish clerk/schoolmaster/lawyer (and any interested persons present) would advise on trust-like ways of getting the money put out at interest (with interest paid by the executors to the daughter only).

Then the will writer would then retire to another room or even go home, write up the will in a fair/neat hand, and return to the testator, usually the same day, and read over the will to the testator in front of witnesses. The testator would approve the will, with or without amendments and the document would be signed/marked by the testator and witnesses (often including the will writer).

After the testator had died (often within a week after the will had been written or even the same day) the will writer was often called upon again to write the inventory of the testaor's goods, excluding those due to the eldest son and heir (if there was one) which could include fruit trees and crops such as carrots.[1]

Occasionally there were problems with a will, normally caused by second wills where the first will was written in haste when the testator first had a serious illness and he/she wished to revise the will later. Or, in the case of Maudie Tipping of Dunham Massey, Cheshire, in 1613, an old lady in her eighties, when her sons wished her to revise her will in favour of themselves and not her daughter Alice, thereby cutting out her son-in-law William Rowcroft. The

Tipping boys considered William had had far too much favour from the local landowner and their employer, Sir George Booth of Dunham Massey, as manager of his dairy in Wilmslow. Robert Tipping, eldest son of Maudie, was his steward, living at Carrington Hall, Carrington. In cases of disagreements over wills the services of the will writer could be called on as witness. To be caught in the middle of such a family quarrel was not pleasant, made less so by the fact that a lot of hitherto buried dirty linen, including that of the witnesses, got washed in public. In the case of Maudie Tipping the unbelievable shinanikins to persuade her to revise her will would take another article just to describe. It included the faking of the funeral of her daughter Alice (very much alive at the time) by her sons. The world and, more importantly, the ecclesiastical Chester Consistory Court meeting in Chester Cathedral also learnt that one of the witnesses to the fake funeral, a cousin called George Moores of Dunham Massey, had had a child by his young maidservant, Maud Artenstall. At the age of fifty-four and a widower, he was probably delighted to have fathered a son. The Consistory Court was less so. They demanded that he marry his maidservant, which he did two years later before another cousin, George Tipping, rector of Ashton-on-Mersey.

Another case from about the same period was when the relatives and friends of Ralph Chorlton of Altrincham, yeoman, who died in 1633, contested his will. Ralph was a reasonably well-to-do man, with £213 7s 7d owed to him on bond or mortgage and another £100 in personal estate. Yet he made bequests in his will as though he was only worth £50 or less, with a few pounds here, a pound or two there. So his family thought he was not of sound mind when he made the will. They thought he was suffering from mental illness, as well as a physical one, and depression, siting that he had offered to buy old horses and drive them to market at Tideswell in Derbyshire, that he was drinking too much and talking of his grief. Someone had gone to Hale to fetch John Goulden, the township clerk for Hale. From the Allegations before the Consistory Court, John Goulden may have had a little trouble in getting Ralph to focus his mind on what legacies he would leave to friends and family. The tone of the Allegations is that the Consistory Court would declare the will invalid, and attach some blame to John Goulden for having allowed Ralph to make it in the first place. It would not have helped that John wrote his customary long Puritan preamble to the Will. In 1635, that would have gone down like a ton of bricks. At the time the Consistory Court in Chester was punishing other Cheshire Puritans like John Bruen and William Prynne who were defying church and state. However, they only succeeded in making martyrs of the men.

'First and principallie I render and bequeath my soule unto my Lord God and Creator firmelie trusting that by the death and passion of his dearelie beloved sonne Christ Jesus my saviour and redeemer and by his onelie merritts and mediacon for mee I shall live and partake with his blessed Saints in his heavenlie kingdome of those Celestiall Joyes which of his Eternall goodness he hath prepared for his Elect of which number through his infinite mercie and compassion I doe confidentlie hope and beleeve That I am one'.[2]

However, all this was water off a duck's back to John Goulden who continued to write wills for Hale people with even longer Puritan preambles until the early 1640s. He would have been protected from the Consistory Court's censure by the powerful influence of the largest local landowner, Sir George Booth of Dunham Massey, and by the local clergy, all of whom shared John Goulden's Puritan convictions. It is possibly partly due to the influence of John Goulden, amongst others, that nearby Ringway Chapel (the chapel of ease for Hale people) was such a hot bed of Independent preachers early on in the English Civil Wars.

Will Writers Imposing their Religious Views on the Testators

Did will writers impose their religious views on testators? The answer is that in the seventeenth century they most certainly did, since most of the will writers were clergymen or parish/township clerks. Most just followed the normal local form, with puritan overtones in the early seventeenth century. However, as already noted, the Hale township clerk, John Goulden, made his views quite clear.

Enter the Lawyers

From the early seventeenth century to the 1670s most of those writing wills were clergymen or lay clerics such as schoolmasters and clergymen's sons. From the early eighteenth century onwards there is a little bit of overlap, but essentially the lawyers are beginning to take over.

Even with lawyers as rivals, schoolmasters and parish clerks continued to write a lot of wills. John Hollenpriest was by far and away the most popular writer of wills from the 1670s to 1711. He wrote wills in five neighbouring townships, Etchells, Northenden, Timperley, Baguley, and Hale. His nearest rival, in time period as well as numbers, was Francis Newton, a schoolmaster, another with a neat hand. It is possible that John was followed in the will writing business by a son, James, and then a grandson, Abraham, who wrote two wills in Baguley (1747-1759). Perhaps they became lawyers.

From the 1670s onwards lawyers/attorneys were increasingly used. In the beginning they were used by those who ordinarily used them as land/business agents. Attorneys like John Houghton who worked for John and Jane Eaton of Bowdon and Altrincham as their agent wrote their wills.[3] However, in the eighteenth century wills written by lawyers became the norm in most areas, although schoolmasters and parish clerks like the Renshaws were the more usual will writers in the parish of Ashton-on-Mersey until 1757.

Attorneys were often sons of clergymen like the Cookes and the Hobsons or schoolmasters like the Houghtons. George Clayton was not quite in this mould. He came from an old Altrincham family and was the son of George Clayton, yeoman, who died in 1713. George's main source of work seems to have been in providing wills to local people. To help him,

he had at least two apprentices/clerks living with him at any one time. In the 1720s they were John Stafford of Middlewich and John Carter.

The Depositions and Allegations to the Will of William Higginson of Altrincham (will no longer extant), 1726, shows how an attorney like George Clayton had his clerks draw up wills. William Higginson had had a will drawn up by George Clayton or one of his clerks, possibly a couple of days before or even some time before. William fell ill and sent to George Clayton for the will. John Stafford, then nineteen, was sent round to the Higginson house with the will as yet unsigned. John read it over to the client, who asked for changes to be made. John made notes of the changes William wanted made and duly trotted back to Clayton's. He gave the will to another apprentice attorney, possibly John Carter, to be written out again with the changes made. The following day, which was a market day in Altrincham, John went back to William Higginson with the amended will which the latter now signed in front of witnesses.

George Clayton probably offered the same service to others. He wrote the wills of Henry Worthington of Timperley in 1717, John Barlow of the Lowe House, Sale, yeoman, also in 1717 and John Higginson of the Brook, Timperley, yeoman, in 1727. He also wrote the will of another attorney, Ralph Houghton of Baguley, gentleman, in 1731.[4]

Clayton's apprentice, John Stafford, did not go into the will making side of the business after he left George's practice in the early 1730s. Instead, he took up the other way of making money for lawyers, he became the Steward for the Tatton family for the manors of Northenden and Etchells from the 1730s to 1760.[5] However, he had been writing wills for George Clayton's clients before that of William Higginson. In 1724, when he was only sixteen, John Stafford wrote the Will of Nicholas Waterhouse of Bowdon, the controversial Presbyterian minister of Ringway Chapel and later, after he and his congregation had been forcibly kicked out of Ringway by John Crewe of Crewe, the Chapel of Halebarns. He was called 'Mr Stafford', in deference to his profession, even though he was so young.

John Cooke, like George Clayton, could have been a member of an Altrincham family or he could have been the son of John Cooke, rector of Northenden from 1667 to 1675. He might also have been one of George Clayton's apprentice clerks, one of the first since he was old enough to be Mayor of Altrincham in 1712. Again like George Clayton, John Cooke mainly worked for yeoman farmers, writing their wills. He wrote the Will of George Ashley of Ollerbarrow Hall, Hale, yeoman, in 1729; the Inventory of George Trevis of Timperley, yeoman, 1728; the Will of James Ashton of Ashton-on-Mersey, yeoman, 1733; and the Will of Elizabeth Coppock of Timperley, spinster, 1734. He died in 1752.

Isaac Worthington probably started working for himself in the late 1730s. By 1742 he was established enough to be a 'sleeping partner' (providing capital and legal advice) in the malting business run by the wealthy gentleman and erstwhile Mayor of Altrincham, Ferdinard Langton of Altrincham. He also wrote out his friend's will in 1742, although the latter did not die until 1750. Isaac's will writing skills were used by a succession of well-to-do local people including Hannah Simpson of Dunham Massey in 1743, Thomas Davenport and William Royle of Bowdon, John Coppock the Timperley tanner in 1753 and James Walton of Bowdon in 1760. James Walton was the nephew of another lawyer, Thomas Walton of Dunham Massey, steward to the earl of Warrington. Isaac Worthington took over the stewardship when Thomas Walton died in 1756.

John Hobson may have been another of George Clayton's apprentices. He started working in Sale in 1742, possibly under the aegis of George Clayton. He wrote the Wills of John Byrom of Sale, husbandman, in 1742, of Hugh Holt of Bowdon, victualler, in 1757, the Will of John Duncalf of Ashton-on-Mersey, yeoman, in 1757 and the Will of John Renshaw of Sale, parish clerk of Ashton-on-Mersey, in 1757. He was also working for the Whitelegg family of Northenden and Stretford in 1771, who were the heirs of John Eccles of Altrincham, who died in 1727, in a complex matter over a piece of land known as the Mayor's Land, on which the current Mayor wanted the rents raised.[6] Before 1771 he had written the will of John Eccles's son William, shoemaker of Altrincham, in 1755. In 1753 he wrote the Will of Revd. Turner Vawdrey of Dunham Massey, chaplain to the Earl of Warrington.

He also wrote the following wills: James Neild of Dunham Massey, yeoman, in 1756; Thomas Walton of Dunham Massey, gentleman and steward to the Earl of Warrington in 1757.

In the seventeenth century lawyers and attorneys were rare creatures. They worked only for the large local landowners as stewards to their manor courts. Then from the early eighteenth century onwards there was a sort of explosion of attorneys in and around the greater Altrincham area. Why I am not sure, but perhaps the following is a reason. Altrincham, a market town, after a period of decline and depression following the English Civil Wars of the 1640s and the Interregnum of the 1650s, started to revive when the local landowner, the Earl of Warrington, had the Butter market built. The market became a centre for the buying and selling of cattle and dairy products. People became more well-to-do. They needed to borrow and lend more money with more security. So people needed attorneys to sort out their business affairs, to make sure they weren't cheated and represent them in court when debitors defaulted. Writing wills was all part of the service for clients for lawyers like George Clayton and John Hobson.

This is only what I have discovered about the will writers in my area after studying only 500 wills and inventories. What can you discover? Next time you transcribe a will, either of a relative or from an area you are studying, compare the signatures (if there are any) at the end of the will and see if you can discover who the writer was and then if you can discover anything else about him.

Notes
1. See Margaret Spufford's article, 'The limitations of the probate inventory' in *English rural society 1500-1800* edited by John Chartres and David Hey for details of what was and wasn't supposed to be listed in a probate inventory.
2. Preamble to the Will of Ralph Chorlton of Altrincham, yeoman, 1633.
3. Will of John Eaton of Altrincham, yeoman, 1675; Will of Jane Eaton of Bowdon, widow, 1693. John Houghton also wrote the Will of Robert Dean of Altrincham in 1673. He was also a moneylender to people like the well-to-do farmer, Richard Ward of Timperley.
4. Will of Henry Worthington of Timperley, 1717; Will of John Barlow of Lowe House, Sale, yeoman, 1717; Will of John Higginson of the Brook, Timperley, yeoman, 1727; Will of Ralph Houghton of Baguley, gentleman, 1731.
5. John Stafford married Lucy Tatton, daughter of his future employer, in North-east Cheshire in 1734.
6. Executors' papers attached to the Will of John Eccles of Altrincham, yeoman, 1727. John Eccles was Mayor of Altrincham in 1696 when a new long lease was drawn up for the Mayor's Lands.

First published in Open History, September 1994. Revised and Updated for The Family and Local History Handbook 7th Edition

The Public Record Office

John Wood - Public Services Development Team

The Public Record Office is the national archive of England, Wales and the United Kingdom. The government has announced that in April 2003 the functions of the Public Record Office and the Historical Manuscripts Commission are to come together to form a single new organisation, the National Archives, based at Kew. The PRO, as it is commonly known, near Richmond in Surrey houses one of the most definitive archive collections in the world representing the events and people of the past thousand years. Over 100 miles of records are stored here that defines nations history. Although the PRO is recognised as a major international research institution in fact around 75% of the online and onsite visitors are researching their family, community or local history.

Onsite facilities

The PRO truly has something for everyone. For the family or local historian there is an extensive range of information leaflets available onsite and online on the website at www.pro.gov.uk. The leaflets are the springboard for researchers setting out on the research trail, as they cover nearly 200 of the most popular searches at the PRO.

Over the past eighteen months the PRO has:
- *Introduced orientation tours for every new reader or visitor*
- *Enhanced the range and depth of services to callers via the Contact Centre*
- *Hosted over 180 family history coach parties from across the country*
- *Established the Education and Visitor Centre as a major attraction featuring icons from British History including the Domesday Book.*
- *Expanded the onsite bookshop.*
- *Consolidated the reputation and position of it's magazine for family historians, 'Ancestors' in the genealogical market.*
- *Automated the document ordering and delivery process.*
- *Introduced more microfilm readers and self service copying systems to meet demand*

First World War

In the summer of 2002 the PRO's prestigious First World War burnt documents project came to an end. This project brought the often heroic and frequently tragic lives of over 2 million soldiers who served in that war to a new audience. When viewed with the operational records and records of the medals awarded in the conflict, also available at the PRO, the microfilm records of these soldiers service records paint a vivid picture of the era. With the support of the Heritage Lottery Funding and the Genealogical Society of Utah, the PRO filmed

the soldiers' records that had survived enemy bombing in 1940. These records, known as the 'burnt documents' are of immense value to anyone with an interest in family, military and local history as well as to the soldier's descendants. They are amongst the most popular

First page of the service record of Arnold Loosemore VC

The microfilm reading room at Kew

records for visitors at the PRO for there is hardly a village town or family did not have a soldier serving in the 1st World War. When added to the records of the Royal Marines, Navy, Royal Naval Reserve, Royal Flying Corps that are also available at the PRO it ensures that the experiences of a generation and the impact on their communities are preserved for future generations.

PRO-Online

The gateway to the PRO is the website at www.pro.gov.uk where you will find
- The complete PRO catalogue online including a keyword search facility
- Hundreds of information leaflets on the PRO's holdings
- Established PRO-Online digital document service
- Introduced online name databases for early soldiers records
- Online bookshop and ordering facility
- Award winning interactive education and museum galleries.
- Details of all the PRO services and events.

In the past two years the PRO has taken vast steps to make available some of its most popular records online. PRO-Online (http://www.pro-online.pro.gov.uk/) is the Public Record Office's new digital document delivery service. By logging on to this website you can search and then download images of documents held by the PRO. Currently there are over 230,000 English Wills from the 19th Century (it costs £3 to download a copy of a will) and a range of other documents, for example papers relating to T.E.Lawrence (Lawrence of Arabia), Charlie Chaplin or Winston Churchill as well as newly released papers. Please check the website for details as material is being constantly added.

'A copy of the will of William Wordsworth'

Services and facilities for visitors

Admission is free and, other than for coach parties and large groups, **no** advance booking is required. Researchers need to obtain a readers ticket at Reception to gain admission to the reading rooms. The website has full details on the registration process or call the contact centre for individual information. All new readers are given an orientation tour to familiarise newcomers with PRO's range of research facilities.

The most popular records have made available in the self-service Microfilm Reading Room. There are always staff on hand to help you make the most of your research and to advise on the different avenues that you can follow.
The ground floor has public areas open to all and

contain:
- An extensive modern bookshop
- The Museum and visitor centre featuring important landmarks in world history
- Comprehensive restaurant facilities
- Cyber café.

Coach parties and groups
Coach parties are welcome to visit the PRO. As space is limited for coaches all parties *must* be pre-booked. Bookings are taken up to 18 months in advance. All coach parties receive a dedicated orientation tour for newcomers in their party and are provided with an advance reader ticket registration scheme. To enquire about available dates and reserve your coach group booking telephone the contact centre or use the email facility listed below. There is no access to the site for coaches that have not pre - booked.

Opening hours
The PRO is open 6 days a week throughout the year except bank and public holiday weekends and the annual stocktaking week - usually in December. Up to date details of opening times and closure dates are on the website or can be checked through the Contact Centre. It is always advisable to call the PRO contact centre before visiting for the latest information on opening times, records availability, travel conditions and events.

Transport and Access
The PRO is 200 yards level walk from Kew Gardens station, served by the District underground line and the Silverlink Metro rail service. Kew Bridge station is half a mile away. Local bus services run nearby. Road access to the motorway system is good. Free parking is available on site. Easy access facilities for those with disabilities, including a lift to all floors.

Essential contacts and information
The Public Record Office, Ruskin Avenue, Kew, Richmond, Surrey TW9 4DU United Kingdom
Website: www.pro.gov.uk
Contact centre: 020 8392 5200 Fax: 020 8392 5286
Email: enquiry@pro.gov.uk
Coach party bookings: 020 8392 5393
Or email: coaches@pro.gov.uk Events: 020 8392 5202
Publications or bookshop enquiries: 020 8392 5271

The Family Records Centre

Family Records Centre

1 Myddelton Street, London, EC1R 1UW
www.familyrecords.gov.uk
A service provided by The Public Record Office &
The Office for National Statistics (General Register Office)

The Family Records Centre provides access to the following:

Ground Floor
Indexes of births, marriages and deaths in England and Wales from 1837
Indexes of legal adoptions in England and Wales from 1927
Indexes of births, marriages and deaths of some British citizens abroad from the late 18th century, including deaths in the two World Wars
Certificates can be purchased of any entry in the above. If you need a certificate but cannot visit the Family Records Centre in person, you can place an order by post, fax or telephone. Please ring 0870 243 7788 for further information and details of fees.

First Floor
Census returns for England and Wales (1841-1901)
                (1901 Census : online service only)
Wills and administrations from the PCC up to 1858
Death Duty registers (1796-1858) and indexes (1796-1903)
Records of nonconformist births, baptisms and burials (mainly pre-1837) and marriages (mainly pre-1754)
Miscellaneous foreign returns of births, deaths and marriages (1627-1960)
These records are seen on microfilm

The Family Records Centre also offers the following services:
Bookshop and information point, selling publications on family history
Advice on family and local history research
Family history reference area, including books and maps
FamilySearch including the International Genealogical Index (IGI)
On-line indexes to Scottish registration and census records via Scot Link
Self-service or staffed photocopying service for census and wills
Regular users' consultations
Refreshment area with vending machines
Good facilities for customers with disabilities
Baby changing room

Contact Details
Births, Marriages, Deaths, Adoptions and Overseas enquiries:
Telephone: 0870 243 7788 Fax: 01704 550013
E-mail: certificate.services@ons.gov.uk
Census and general enquiries Telephone: 0208 392 5300 Fax: 0208392 5307 E-mail: enquiry@pro.gov.uk
Minicom: 020 8392 9198

Planning Your Visit
Opening Hours
Monday 9:00 am - 5:00 pm Tuesday 10:00 am - 7:00 pm
Wednesday 9:00 am - 5:00 pm Thursday * 9:00 am - 7:00 pm Friday 9:00 am - 5:00 pm Saturday 9:30 am - 5:00 pm
* On Thursday mornings the tills on the ground floor do not open until 10:00 am The Centre is closed on Sundays, Public and Bank Holidays Please check closure dates for Easter and Christmas (020 8392 5300 There is no need to book.

Group Visits
You are welcome to bring a group/coach party to the FRC at any time during our normal opening hours. However, we would advise you to plan your visits to avoid our busiest times - e.g. school holidays (particularly half-term weeks). We also tend to be busy on Tuesdays, Thursdays and Saturdays. On our busy days the lockers are often all in use so try to bring no more than you need for your research. Please let us know if you are planning to bring a large group to the FRC. We can then publicise this information for the benefit of other users.

How to get here
By rail
Angel – Northern Line (City Branch)
Farringdon – Hammersmith and City, Metropolitan, Circle Lines and Thameslink
King's Cross – Victoria, Northern, Piccadilly, Circle, Metropolitan, Hammersmith and City Lines and mainline services
By bus 19, 38 and 341 along Rosebery Avenue
63 along Farringdon Road
By Car There are NCP car parks in Bowling Green Lane (off Farringdon Road) and Skinner Street, both of which are within easy walking distance of the Centre. There is limited Pay & Display parking in the surrounding streets. **There is reserved parking for visitors with disabilities at the Centre, but spaces must be booked in advance. Please ring 020 7533 6436 before you visit.**

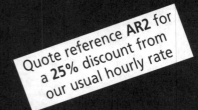

YORKSHIRE
FAMILY HISTORY FAIR
KNAVESMIRE EXHIBITION CENTRE
YORK RACECOURSE

SATURDAY 28TH JUNE 2003
10.00.a.m. to 4.30.p.m.

Many Stalls including:
Society of Genealogists, Federation Publications
The Family & Local History Handbook
(The Genealogical Services Directory)
Family Tree Magazine, Local Archives,
Family History Societies from all over Great Britain
Maps, Postcards, Printouts,
New & Second-hand Microfiche Readers
Genealogy Computer Programs
Advice Table

234 Tables in 2002

FREE CAR PARKING
ADMISSION £2.50

Further Details from:
Mr A Sampson
1 Oxgang Close, Redcar TS10 4ND
Tel: 01642 486615

NOTE FOR YOUR DIARY:

YEAR 2004 - YORKSHIRE FAMILY HISTORY FAIR
SATURDAY 26TH JUNE 2004
YEAR 2005 - YORKSHIRE FAMILY HISTORY FAIR
SATURDAY 25TH JUNE 2005
YEAR 2006 - YORKSHIRE FAMILY HISTORY FAIR
SATURDAY 24TH JUNE 2006

The House of Lords Record Office (The Parliamentary Archives)
David Prior

The Records of Parliament
The House of Lords Record Office holds the archives of both Houses of Parliament. The earliest documents that we have date from 1497. Records of Parliaments before that date were kept amongst the records of Chancery and are now to be found in the Public Record Office, but in that year the Chancery clerk assigned to Parliament retained at Westminster the Acts of the Parliament that had just met, so beginning a tradition of record keeping that has lasted over 500 years.

As the administration that supported Parliament developed so the accumulation of records grew, and came to include the journals of both the House of Lords and the House of Commons (these record the business of Parliament, but not debates), Bills, petitions, judicial records, committee books and plans deposited in connection with private Bills. Most of the records relating to the House of Commons were, however, lost in the fire of 16 October 1834 which destroyed the Houses of Parliament. Following the fire provision was made within the design of the new Palace of Westminster for a repository for the storage of records which eventually became known as the Victoria Tower. Following the tower's completion in 1855 the records of the House of Lords and then later those of the House of Commons were transferred to it's strong rooms. This situation was enhanced in 1946 by the establishment of the House of Lords Record Office.

The Record Office has a Search Room which is

open to the public from Monday to Friday, 9.30 am to 5.00 pm (certain public holidays and the last two weeks in November excepted). In order to guarantee a seat we recommend that you make an appointment. We are able to provide limited answers to questions about the nature and scope of the records in our care by post, telephone, fax or e-mail (see below). We also provide a copying service and a list of charges is available. For descriptions of the records see M. F. Bond, *Guide to the Records of Parliament* (London, 1971).

Sources for Family and Local History
The following are the main sources held by the Record Office for family and local historians:

Acts of Parliament
It is now much easier to identify Acts for research into family and local history since the titles of all Acts held by the Record Office can now be searched electronically; they are currently available at www.a2a.pro.gov.uk

Local Acts
Amongst the Acts of Parliament preserved in the Record Office are many which were promoted by individuals, local authorities or companies for specific projects. These often related to initiatives such as the construction of roads, railways, canals, harbours and bridges as well as to enclosures of common lands and provide details of the schemes and of the individuals involved. The Record Office is able to provide access to printed versions of these Acts as well as to the originals.

Personal Acts
Included in this category are Acts concerning divorce, changes of name, naturalisation and estates. Between 1670 and 1857 (when divorce by legal process without enactment became possible) approximately 300 divorces were effected by Act of Parliament. Details concerning individual cases can also be found in the journals of the House of Lords. Bills concerning Changes of name are fewer in number and the last was in 1907. Until 1844 naturalisations could only be obtained by Act of Parliament and from 1609 the individual concerned had to produce a certificate testifying that Holy Communion had been received. Estate Acts were concerned with a variety of issues connected to the holding of property including the sale of entailed estates and were most popular in the mid eighteenth century.

In addition to the Acts themselves relevant references can often be identified to the legislation in other sources such as committee books and amongst papers laid before the House of Lords. Lists of some of these records up to 1718 have been published by the Historical Manuscripts Commission and the Record Office. Personal Acts

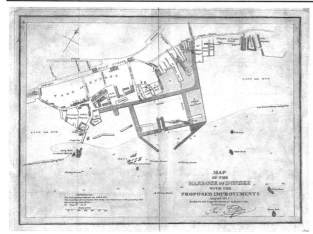

have not been printed and the Record Office can provide access either to the orginal or to a microfilm copy.

Deposited Plans

In 1793 the House of Lords required promoters of Bills concerning canals and other such navigations to deposit plans showing the route of the undertakings. This requirement was later extended to other catagories including railways, tunnels, bridges, harbours, town improvements and turnpikes. The House of Commons had a similar requirement.

The plans are usually accompanied by books of reference and other items such as subscription lists, lists of owners and occupiers of land that was to be compulsorily purchased with indications of their consent or otherwise to the Bill and lists of lessees. It is therefore possible to identify property owned or occupied by specific individuals and to obtain information not just about the work of construction itself but also about the nature and use of the surrounding area.

Private Bill evidence

Local Bills which were opposed were referred to a private Bill committee which took evidence. This evidence has been indexed in collaboration with the Transport History Research Trust and so it is possible to identify individuals who gave evidence and to discover what they said about a particular proposal, such as a plan to build a railway through a settlement. The significance of these records lies in the range of witnesses called – from the Duke of Cambridge to an unemployed agricultural labourer to a penny-ice salesman. For more details of this resource see *Witnesses before Parliament: A Guide to the Database of Witnesses in Committees on Opposed Private Bills 1771-1917* (House of Lords Record Office, 1997).

Protestation Returns

These returns contain the names of those who made the protestation 'to maintain the true reformed Protestant religion' in accordance with a

letter of instructions from the Speaker of the House of Commons dated 19 January 1642. Returns survive for almost one third of the parishes in England; details of the areas covered and of those returns which have been published are given in J. G. Gibson and A. Dell, *The Protestation Returns 1641-1642* (Federation of Family History Societies Publications Ltd, 1995).

Returns of Roman Catholics

These exist for 1680, 1706, 1767 and 1781 but not all of the returns give names. For details see the *National Index of Parish Registers,* vol. 3 (1974), *Historical Manuscripts Commission, Eleventh Report, Appendix, part 2* (1887), and E. S. Worrall, *Returns of Papists, 1767: dioceses of England and Wales except Chester* (Catholic Record Society, 1989).

Members of the House of Commons and the House of Lords

With the exception of the speeches recorded in the record of debates (Hansard), some photographs and material relating to peerage claims the Record Office holds little material relating specifically to members of either House. Searchers are advised to consult in the first instance the biographies of MPs produced by the History of Parliament Trust (see www.histparl.ac.uk for more information) or reference works such as *The Complete Peerage.*

How to contact us
By post: House of Lords Record Office, London SW1A 0PW
Tel: 0207 219 3075
Fax: 0207 219 2570
E-mail: hlro@parliament.uk
Information about the office can be found at www.parliament.uk

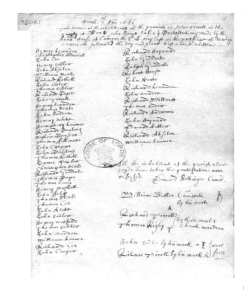

FEDERATION OF FAMILY HISTORY SOCIETIES (PUBLICATIONS) LIMITED

Publishers and Suppliers of a wide range of books on Family History (and related subjects) to Family History Societies, individual Family Historians, Libraries, Record Offices and Booksellers, etc.

- *Well over 100 titles commissioned by the Federation of Family Historians and produced at attractive prices, plus a fine selection of titles from other publishers.*

- *A wide range of 'Basic Series' and 'Introduction to' books with detailed guidance on most aspects of family history research.*

- *Gibson Guides giving explicit advice on the precise extent and whereabouts of major record sources*

- *Stuart Raymond's extensive listings of published family history reference material at national and local level*

Titles available from your local Family History Society and by post from:-

**FFHS (Publications) Limited,
Units 15 and 16 Chesham Industrial Centre,
Oram Street, Bury, Lancashire, BL9 6EN**

Visit our 'On-line bookshop' and Catalogue at

www.familyhistorybooks.co.uk

Tel: 0161 797 3843 Fax: 0161 797 3846

Email enquiries to: sales@ffhs.org.uk

Derbyshire Family History Society

The Society was formed in 1976 by a small number of individuals attending family history evening classes at Alfreton. The society called itself the Mid-Derbyshire Society and membership numbers grew. In 1980 the 'mid' was dropped from its name and the Society became the Derbyshire FHS. Derbyshire is a long and narrow but beautiful county, as you follow it down on a map you will see the famous Peak District National Park dominating the northern part, while the industrial Derwent valley, which is now a world heritage site leads to Derby and the lush rolling pastureland of the south of the county.

The Society quickly grew producing a lively and interesting quarterly magazine, monthly meetings at Alfreton Hall, a bookstall and the archive which started life in a shoe box was rapidly expanding. By the mid 1980's membership had exceeded 1000 and a second group had started at Chesterfield, where a small band of enthusiastic members were soon organising open days and monthly meetings. A decision was taken by the Executive Committee that there was enough support to open a third group in Derby, this happened in 1987 and this group also started monthly meetings, a bookstall and open days.

While all this was taking place the Committee and volunteers were busy recording Memorial Inscriptions (MIs), transcribing parish registers, census and almost any other documents they could lay their hands on. Some of this material was now being published by the Society and finding its way onto the bookstall. As computers played a more active role in family history a new computer was purchased which was put to various uses. At the end of the 1980's owing to various problems the Chesterfield branch ceased to operate.

The Derbyshire Society formed close links with the County Record Office at Matlock, the Local Studies Library in Derby and with the three family history societies of Leicestershire, Lincolnshire and Nottinghamshire. A 'Four Counties' Conference was held each year with each society taking turns to host the conference, many venue's have been used over the years and some very enjoyable conferences took place. Although the four societies now feel that these conferences have run their course we still meet with each other twice a year for a discussion on family history in general and our own societies in particular.

In 1989 the Society obtained its own 'room' at the Wycliffe Church in Alfreton where our library and archive could expand, members could visit, Committee meetings and projects meetings were also held here. Opening every Tuesday and Saturday the library proved be very popular, opening times were extended to include Thursday evenings and space soon became very short, it was realised within a few months of moving in that bigger premises would soon be required, but at this time the Committee felt we could not afford to move. A programme of open days around the county proved very successful, It was just about possible to move the archive in a large van to the venue and move it back again at the end of the day,

very tiring but well worth while as many of our members travelled long distances to be with us on the day.

In the 1990's the Society grew and grew the membership had exceeded 2000 members and was well on the way to 2500. The publications list had grown from two pages in the magazine to 12 pages, material produced on microfiche and floppy disc was proving to be as popular as books. The 1851 and the 1891 census were both indexed and published, these were extremely popular. Local history books were also proving to be good sellers. More MI's and parish registers were coming onto the library shelves; Federation publications are also very popular. The Committee was approached by a number of members from the north of the county and following discussions a third group was set up in Glossop, this group has worked very hard attracting many new members from north Derbyshire, Manchester and over the border into Cheshire. The Glossop group is now affiliated to the Tameside Local History Forum and has attended and organised a number of family history and workshop days.

In 1994 we accepted that we needed bigger premises to house the library and archive. After searching for some months we successfully negotiated with the Trustees and Derby Cathedral to take a lease on Bridge Chapel House in Derby. After weeks of planning the

THE
DERBYSHIRE
FAMILY HISTORY SOCIETY
www.dfhs.org.uk

For all your
Family History Research in Derbyshire
Visit our Website
or our
HEADQUARTERS AND RESEARCH CENTRE
at
THE HISTORIC BRIDGE CHAPEL HOUSE
ST MARY'S BRIDGE, DERBY

We are open every
Tuesday, Thursday and Saturday
From 10.00a.m. until 4.00.p.m.
Or contact our Secretary

Mr G Wells
76 Elms Avenue, Littleover, Derby DE23 6FD

We have Club Meetings every month at
Derby, Glossop and Shirland

Plus exhibitions and Open Days

Our Quarterly Magazine is packed with information

Come and Talk to us. We can Help

archive was moved from Alfreton into the newly decorated Research Centre and Library which was officially opened in April 1996. Bridge Chapel House is a ten roomed house on three floors, built in the 1750's it is attached to the Bridge Chapel, one of only six left in the Country and still used for regular worship. At the Research Centre and Library on the top floor members and non members can enjoy the facilities of the research rooms with a room dedicated to paper records, MI's, parish registers, census, local history and other societies publications. The microfiche and microfilm room has a number of viewers and printers where the IGI, various census and the Registrar General's indexes from 1837 to 1920 can be viewed. In the computer room visitors will find on a database a master index of our records, plus many other records on CD and disc. On the first floor are the kitchen and a comfortable coffee shop where visitors can enjoy a drink, a snack and chat to other members about family history. On the ground floor is the reception area, locker room, a well stocked bookshop and a quiet reading room. Outside is the garden which covers two sides of the building and the chapel. In August 2001 the Society was approached to produce a video showing how to trace your family tree. Filming took place at the Research Centre during one day and the result was very good, using the basic records and search aids that may be found in any county it shows a beginner where to go and what to look for. The video is on sale through our publications list.

The Committee and volunteers are justifiably proud of our headquarters which has now become part of the

newly created World Heritage Site Derwent Valley. Our HQ has seen many visitors and open days, it is open every Tuesday, Thursday and Saturday from 10am until 4pm and is staffed by a band of extremely hard working volunteers who are always on hand and use their knowledge and expertise to help point researchers in the right direction. The Society also offers a postal research service which is very well used and brings in revenue in order to purchase more material for the benefit of members. In January 2002 following an appeal to members for contributions the Society purchased the 1901 census for Derbyshire, this was quickly followed by Leicestershire, Nottinghamshire and Cheshire. Some of these counties were purchased after a successful bid for a lottery grant, also purchased from the grant was a new fiche / film- reader / printer.

We always welcome new members, our annual subscriptions are UK family - £11, European family - £12, other continents - £15. these subscriptions become payable on 1st January each year. Membership details can be obtained from the Membership Secretary, Mrs L Spare, 'The Brackens' Wards Lane, Stanton by Bridge, Derby, DE73 1HX. All other enquiries should be addressed to, Mr G Wells, Hon Secretary, Bridge Chapel House, St Mary's Bridge, Sowter Road, Derby DE1 3AT.
Alternatively you can visit the society's website at **www.dfhs.org.uk**

Hospital Records for Family Historians – *Victoria, Australia*

The project by The Genealogical Society of Victoria to index the Admissions Registers of the Goldfields Hospitals

The contents of Admission Registers of hospitals in Victoria Australia in the 1800s are probably typical of such registers elsewhere in the British Empire at the time. As well as given name and surname they contain admission date, discharge date, age, religion, a word or two about the medical problem for which they sought treatment, the result of that treatment, some information about where the patient resided and on whose authority the patient was admitted for treatment. In addition to this information the Victorian registers frequently contain a record of how long the patient had been in the colony and the place of birth – valuable information for genealogists.

It is well known that our ancestors who went to the "diggings" (as the goldfields were called) were sometimes lost to the usual records, there being no established government or church infrastructure in those earliest gold rush years.

As towns in the gold rush areas became established hospitals were built, and records of patients began. Some of those patients had left no paper trail except, perhaps, being recorded as a passenger on one of the many ships that carried gold seekers from the UK or Europe or elsewhere to Victoria, until they were admitted into hospital.

The Genealogical Society of Victoria has indexes to eight of the goldfields hospitals' admission records covering the period 1855 to 1900. One of special interest is not an admissions register but a record of the families of those admitted. It contains fields for the patient's parents (including the maiden name of the mother), the father's occupation, the year of the parents' marriage, and a list of children with their ages. While not every detail is present in every record the whole index contains 5,660 names and is obviously a very valuable one. It covers the period 1869 to 1884.

We plan to publish a CD of most, or all of these indexes for launching at the GSV hosted 10th Australasian Congress on Genealogical and Heraldry, in Melbourne, from 23 – 27 April 2003.

The Society is also indexing ward books of the Melbourne General Hospital from 1856 and admission registers of Fairfield Infectious Diseases Hospital from 1904 when this hospital was established. These indexes will progressively become available to researchers in the GSV library. The status of indexing projects and availability of indexes can be checked on the GSV web site www.gsv.org.au

Researching is Nicer in Somerset and Dorset

Those lucky enough to be researching family in Somerset and Dorset are doubly fortunate. Not only are they two attractive counties to be drawn to, but they also have an award winning family history journal in which to appeal for help from some 5,000 readers worldwide.

The Greenwood Tree, journal of the Somerset and Dorset FHS, won the best English-language family history journal worldwide, known as the Federation of Family History Societies' Elizabeth Simpson Award, in 2002.

The May 2002 edition was particularly innovative, for its 72 A4 pages were entirely devoted to Somerset and Dorset folk who migrated between the Channel Islands, more than 1,000 names being included.

Copies of this Channel Island Special are available £3.50 UK, £4.50 overseas, from Catherine Richards, 22 Pitchers, Salway Ash, Bridport DT6 5QS, (e-mail: catherine_richards@btinternet.com) cheques etc payable SDFHS.

The SDFHS, celebrating its 28th anniversary in 2003, has a host of indexes and other services. Details are available from

SDFHS, PO Box 4502, Sherborne DT9 6YL. Their website is www.sdfhs.org and e-mail society@sdfhs.org

---

Herefordshire Family History Society

Herefordshire is happy to once again be a County in it's own right, following the dissolution of it's ill-fated amalgamation with Worcestershire in the 1974 re-organisation of the Counties by the government. The "divorce" took place in 1998 and we are now governed by a "unitary authority". The area is mainly viewed as an 'agricultural county', which of course it is, but that is not to say there were not industrial workings in the county in the past. Many of the archaeological excavations of recent times have brought to the surface aspects of its unknown industrial heritage. Of course, it is on a small scale, as the geology of the county was (thankfully) not conducive to large scale mining. Perhaps the county is most recognisable as being the home of the 12th century *Mappa Mundi* world map, Herefordshire cider and the white faced Hereford cattle.

The Herefordshire Family History Society was formed in March 1980, at a meeting addressed by Mr Colin Chapman who spoke about the growing interest in family history research and the formation of new societies to cater for this interest. There were 14 people present, with the express intention of providing a family history society for the historic county of Herefordshire. In 1996 charitable status was granted. We are members of the Federation of Family History Societies and recently joined the South West Group of Family History Societies.

Membership. From the beginning there has been a steady increase in membership. Within two years, by the spring of 1982 the total stood at 120, and today where we have an annual membership of around 900. Anyone with an interest in Herefordshire is most welcome to join and an Application for Membership can be obtained by downloading one from our web site at www.rootsweb.com/~ukhfhs or by sending an SAE to the Membership Secretary, Mrs Heather Bufton, 3 Cagebrook Avenue, Hunderton, Hereford, HR2 7AS. The subscription fees are £9 for Single and £12 for Family within the UK and Europe. Australia, New Zealand and USA membership costs the equivalent of £12.

Projects. We have completed many indexing projects which are available for sale and are listed under our

Publications. We still have many on-going projects though. Herefordshire FHS took part in the national Burial Index project, and we decided to continue indexing burials from the parish records – working backwards from 1813. One of the longest on-going projects is that of recording all the surviving Monumental Inscriptions in the churchyards and cemeteries throughout the county. We've been at it for 20 years now, but it will be ongoing for quite a few more years to come. One of our latest projects involves working in the local Registrars Office to make indexes to the post-1837 Marriages. Another just beginning is to capture through digital photography those Parish Registers that have not yet been deposited at the County Record Office. Herefordshire being such a small & rural county, many parishes are still recording events in registers that began in the 19th century. Finally, having completed indexes to the 1851 & 1891 Census returns, we have started on the 1901 Census for Herefordshire.

Monthly Meetings are held in Hereford every 3rd Friday every month, except December. We always have a speaker at the meeting, together with our library, bookstall, Strays Index and exchange journals. We hold a bi-annual Open Day in Hereford - the next one is scheduled for Saturday April 3, 2004 at the Hereford Leisure Centre. All of the surrounding Family History Societies, and Local History Societies from within the county are invited to attend. The 2004 event will be our largest to date, and is being held at a larger venue than previously, so we are hoping to attract some organisations that require more space than we have previously been able to supply. We also attend many of the surrounding Family History Societies Open Days. Last year we attended 14 fairs and this year promises to be just as busy, and would like to invite anyone with an interest in Herefordshire to come and visit us at one of the many fairs in and around the West Midlands and Wales. Our web page has a full list of dates and venues.

Journal. As with most other Family History Societies we publish a quarterly journal called 'Herefordiensis' which is distributed to members as part of their membership. We encourage members and those with perhaps just a passing interest in Herefordshire to contribute articles, photographs, or research tips, to join our regular features of extracts from local newspapers '160 Years Ago', "Help Wanted" and "Members Interests".

Publications available include Monumental Inscriptions & Census Indexes on Microfiche. On CD-ROM we have an ever expanding list of titles, amongst them are the 1851 Census Index and the 1891 Census Index and Transcription for Herefordshire: the 1813-1839 Burial index: and an index on CD-ROM of all the names mentioned on the MI's recorded over the past 20 years of graveyard grovelling. All our publications are available either through www.genfair.com on the Internet, or by post from our publications officer, or in person at our monthly meetings.

Eardisland, Herefordshire

Local History Magazine no.89

2 free issues or a binder when you subscribe to *Local History Magazine*

During 2002 our **News section** covered a wide range of issues from the perils of copyright law to lottery funding for local history, and contained information about local history conferences, day schools, events and hundreds of courses.

'Local history at Westminster' by Paul Seaward is just one of **many articles** in recent issues. Other topics have included 'America's enduring legacy to London', 'Researching the history of a workhouse', 'The rise and rise of a village school', 'The Watlington Sewer Saga' and 'Images of England'.

News from societies features in every issue. As well as new societies, such as the Milestone Society, we also include progress reports from societies all over the country.

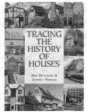

We carry more **book and periodical reviews** than any other magazine. We also sell the best in local history reference books at generous discounts.

In addition to all these features, *Local History Magazine* includes a unique **Noticeboard section** where every subscriber can place **50 words free** in every issue. Subscribers' notices are also included on our website (www.local-history.co.uk).

Our normal subscription price is £19.50 per year for six issues, posted direct to your home. Our **introductory offer** means that you can either pay £19.50 and receive 2 free additional issues or pay £35 and receive 12 issues plus a free binder, worth £7.50, which holds 12 copies.

To subscribe, send your cheque for £19.50 or £35, payable to Local History, to:
Local History
Freepost (NG7 2DS)
Nottingham
NG7 1BR
(no stamp needed). Please mention *The Family and Local History Handbook*.

Offer applies in the UK only. For details of overseas subscription rates, or of how to pay by credit card, e-mail us on editors@local-history.co.uk or telephone us on 0115 9706473.

Llyfrgell Genedlaethol Cymru The National Library of Wales
Eirionedd A. Baskerville - Editorial Officer Public Services

An interest in family history is part of the Welsh psyche. According to the Laws of Hywel Dda, it was necessary to know one's relatives to the ninth remove, and Giraldus Cambrensis on his crusading tour of Wales in 1188 noted that the humblest person was able to recite from memory his family tree, going back six or seven generations.

The National Library of Wales is the premier centre for family history research in Wales, holding as it does abundant records covering the whole of Wales. Its three main Departments all have something different to offer. The Department of Printed Books holds electoral lists, newspapers and directories, while the Department of Pictures and Maps has plans, sale catalogues, and tithe maps and schedules. However, the most important Department from the point of view of genealogical research is the Department of Manuscripts and Records, which holds a whole range of useful resources.

The Department has microform copies of the returns for the whole of Wales for each of the ten-yearly censuses 1841-91, and microfiche copies of the index to the 1881 census for the English counties as well as those for Wales. In addition, some of the returns have been transcribed and indexed by enthusiastic individuals and societies who have kindly made them available to the Library's users.

Civil registration of births, marriages and deaths was introduced in England and Wales on 1 July 1837, and microfiche copies of the General Register Office's indexes of the registration records from 1837 to 1992 are available for searching free of charge at the National Library. The Library does not issue certificates, but a search of the indexes can be undertaken for a fee.

Before the introduction of civil registration, the 'rites of passage' were noted in parish registers, following the order of 5 September 1538 that a register of every baptism, marriage and burial in every parish should be kept. However, the earliest surviving registers for most Welsh parishes do not commence until after 1660, although starting dates vary greatly. Parish registers held at the National Library are available on microfilm to readers. The Library also holds transcript copies of some parish registers, which have been kindly donated by the compilers. In addition, the 1988 edition of the International Genealogical Index, while far from complete, can prove a useful starting point for tracing the parish in which a baptism or marriage was registered.

Although the ravages of weather and rodents, inept vicars and disrespectful parishioners have resulted in the disappearance of many original parish registers, the bishops transcripts (annual returns submitted by Anglican parish clergy to the bishops containing copies of all the entries recorded in their parish registers during the preceding twelve months), often come to the rescue of the family historian. Transcripts were ordered to be sent annually from 1597 onwards, but there are no transcripts before 1661 in the records of the Church inhales deposited in the Library. Even after this date there are many gaps in the returns, only a few transcripts before 1723 being extant for parishes in the diocese of Llandaff, and hardly any for the eighteenth century for parishes in the archdeaconries of Cardigan and St David's.

The transcripts cease at dates varying from parish to parish

during the middle of the nineteenth century, although there are a few examples from the early twentieth century from some parishes. Transcripts of marriage entries normally cease with the introduction of civil registration in 1837. The transcripts held by the Library are listed in schedules available in the Department of Manuscripts and Records. At present the original transcripts are available to readers, but the task of preparing microfiche copies is underway.

Marriage bonds and allegations are the next most important class of Anglican Church record of use to the genealogist. These documents were executed in order to obtain a licence to marry without having banns called publicly in Church on three Sundays before the solemnisation of the marriage. Generally speaking, these records cover the eighteenth and nineteenth centuries and the first three decades of the twentieth century. The amount and nature of the information varies with the type of document, and are particularly valuable when the approximate date of a marriage is known but not its venue. The pre-1837 bonds and allegations in the Library have been indexed and may be searched on computer in the Department's Catalogue room. Also available for the diocese of St David's are registers of marriage licences, mainly for the nineteenth century.

Another class of records of paramount interest to the genealogist is wills and administrations, and those which before the introduction of Civil Probate on 11 January 1858 were proved in the Welsh ecclesiastical courts, have been deposited in the Library. Roughly speaking, the covering dates of the surviving probate records of each of the consistory courts are: Bangor, 1635-1858; Brecon, 1543-1858; Chester (Welsh Wills), 1557-1858; Hawarden, 1554-1858; Llandaff, 1568-1857; St Asaph, 1565-1857; St David's, 1556-1858. These wills have also been indexed and may be searched on computer.

For the period after 1858 the Library has custody of register copy wills from five registries, covering all but one (Montgomeryshire) of the Welsh counties, and a full microfiche set of the annual index of all wills and administrations granted in England and Wales (the Calendar of Grants), from 1858 to 1972.

Despite the fact that they are much less comprehensive than the records of the Anglican Church in Wales, Nonconformist records are an important source of information for genealogists. Many registers of dissenting congregations were deposited with the Registrar-General after the Civil Registration Act of 1836, and the Library has microfilm copies of these. A few registers of that period which never found their way to London and some other later registers are now deposited at the Library.

Other nonconformist records of genealogical value at the Library include manuscript lists of members and contribution books of individual chapels, printed annual reports, usually including lists of members and their contributions, which have been produced by many chapels since about 1880, and denominational periodicals, which often contain notices of births, marriages and deaths.

Records of the Court of Great Sessions of Wales, the most important legal and administrative body between the Act of Union and its abolition in 1830, may also prove useful for genealogical purposes. Occasionally challenge pedigrees were filed in connection with certain actions, and other documents of considerable value are depositions, which often state the age of the deponent, jury lists and coroners' inquests.

Whereas the official Quarter Sessions records for the county of Cardigan, held by the Library comprise little more than the order books from 1739, there are also some related materials among the archives of landed estates or solicitors' firms, for example a few sessional rolls and land tax records 1780-1839 from Cardiganshire, some land tax records (the most useful class of records for the genealogist) for Montgomeryshire and Breconshire, order books 1647-75 and rolls, 1643-99 for Denbighshire, and sessions records from Montgomeryshire.

Local government at a level between county and parish was practically non-existent before the formation of Poor Law Unions under the the Poor Law Amendment Act 1834 Most Poor Law Union records are now deposited at the appropriate county record office, but there are some records at the Library, mainly from Montgomeryshire. Civil parish records are also mainly held by the appropriate county record office, although the Library holds vestry books and other parochial records for many parishes for which parish registers have been deposited.

The manorial records held by the Library are mainly to be found with the estate records and listed with them They are most comprehensive for Montgomeryshire (mainly the Powis Castle and Wynnstay estate records), with substantial holdings for Glamorgan and Monmouthshire also (mainly the Badminton, Bute and Tredegar estate records). It should be noted that in many parts of Wales the manorial system never really took root.

The Library has recently prepared a manorial database for Wales in conjunction with HMC available to readers on the Internet
http://www2.hmc.gov.uk/Welsh_Manorial_Documents_Register.htm.
Most of the estate records and personal papers held by the Department of Manuscripts and Records are detailed in typescript schedules. The estate records contain title deeds, rentals, account books, correspondence, etc. Rentals may prove particularly useful in indicating a death or change of residence when a name disappears from a series of rentals.

The Department holds many manuscript pedigrees. These vary from descents of nobility, compiled in the later Middle Ages and copied time and again with additions by later genealogists, to charts which are the work of amateurs of modern times who have given copies of their compilations to the Library. For searchers particularly interested in the pedigrees of gentry families there are several important printed works available.

There is a general card index to most of the typescript schedules of the collections in the Department of Manuscripts and Records, and probably the most useful for the family historian are the sections devoted to wills, marriage settlements, inquisitions post mortem, and pedigrees. The index to the general collections of manuscripts (NLW MSS) may also be of use to genealogists. In addition, a basic inventory of the contents of the Library's Annual Report up to 1996 is available on-line in the Catalogue room.

For further information on sources for family history research at the National Library of Wales, it is worth consulting the Department of Manuscripts and Records' pages at the Library's web site at: http://www.llgc.org.uk/

Folk Medicines and their Practitioners

Eirionedd A. Baskerville - Editorial Officer Public Services

Homeopathic and complimentary medicine has seen a resurgence of interest in recent years, as an alternative to scientific medicine. However, for our forebears there was no choice – natural remedies was the only option and knowledge of medicinal herbs and potions was often handed down from generation to generation.

A great uncle of mine was well known in his locality as a herbalist and as a child I was subjected to some of his herbal concoctions. Strolling through country lanes he would show me the various herbs and try to get me interested in them, but I knew that at the end of my holiday I would be given a bundle of the herbs to take home, and the infusions would be dispensed for as long as the herbs lasted. My family were also great believers in the medicinal properties of honey, and when I had a whitlow the poultice which my mother wrapped around the suffering finger was a mixture of honey and Gypsy Lee ointment – bought at the local market and supposedly made from the flesh of the hedgehog. It had the required effect as, a day before the local GP was due to lance the top of my finger the wound opened on its own account. One old recipe which I refused to adopt, however, was my grandmother's cure for chilblains – to walk barefooted in the snow then beat the swollen toes with holly twigs until they bled!

Pondering on these 'cures' I decided to search the

National Library of Wales' collections for other medicinal remedies. The kinds of ailments mentioned in the manuscripts were those which affected all classes of people, but the poorest would not have had access to some of the ingredients involved; they would have had to rely on the produce of hedgerows and gardens.

There was, traditionally, a relationship between medicine and magic – the mother of the first recorded doctors in Wales, the Physicians of Myddfai in Carmarthenshire belonged to the world of magic. According to legend an elderly widow living at Blaensawdde in Carmarthenshire would send some of her cattle, in the care of her son, to graze on the Black Mountains, to a spot near Llyn y Fan Fach. One day, the son saw a lady come out of the lake and, as in all good fairy stories, he immediately fell in love with her. He offered her his lunch – cheese and barley bread- but she refused the bread saying that it was too hard. The next time he saw her he tried to woo her with unbaked dough, which was again refused, but the third time, when he offered lightly baked bread she accepted it, together with his offer of marriage. There was, however, one condition – she would return to her home in the lake if he should hit her without cause three times. She left the lake and called out of the water, by name, a vast quantity of cattle and livestock. The farmer's son and the lady of the lake were married and she bore him three sons.

However, the marriage was not to last for he did strike her three times – firstly, while preparing to attend a christening to which she was reluctant to go, he tapped her on the shoulder with a glove when he found that she had not fetched the horses; next at a wedding when she started to cry, and finally at a funeral when she burst out laughing. She then returned to the lake, taking with her all her cattle and other animals. However, some years later, when the three sons, Cadwgan, Gruffydd and Einion, were out walking, their mother appeared and gave them a bag full of medical prescriptions and instructions as to their use, and at a spot called Pant y Meddygon (the Physicians' hollow) she pointed out to them the various plants and herbs which they and their descendants would later use in their roles as the Physicians of Myddfai.

However, perhaps the real origin of the medical gifts of the Physicians of Myddfai, was more prosaic – they could simply have been the first to write down medical prescriptions which had been part of oral folk tradition for generations. Similar material is to be found in other collections of medieval recipes from all over Europe as is shown by Morfydd Owen in her article 'Meddygon Myddfai' in *Studia Celtica* 10/11, 1975-76. Such medicinal remedies were 'aimed at giving instruction for diagnosis, prognosis, treatment by surgery, by drugs, by letting blood and by cauterising'. The recipes of these Physicians were copied many times and can be found in various manuscripts. They were translated into English and published by John Pughe of Aberdyfi in 1861, and a facsimile of this was reprinted in 1993. The first part is based on two manuscript sources, the Red Book and 'Mr Rees of Tonn's manuscript', while the second, the larger of the two works, was transcribed in 1743 from a book of John Jones, the last of the lineal descendants of the Physicians of Myddfai, which is supposed to have been written by Howel, a descendant of Einion, one of the three sons of the Lady of Llyn y Fan Fach. There are remedies for curing dimness of sight, removing warts, a cure for the smallpox and other recipes for destroying fleas, producing golden hair and to cause the hair to grow. I was particularly interested to find that the book contained eight cures for a whitlow, one of them using bruised mugwort and 3 egg yolks and another involving taking a snail out of its shell and bruising it small, pounding to a paste and applying to finger. 'This will ripen and break it, then it should be dressed like any other wound'. Another, however, had one of the ingredients which my mother used on my whitlow, namely honey – 'take honey, yolk of eggs and wheaten flour, mix together and apply as a paste'.

National Library of Wales (NLW) Minor Deposit 1343B has a section called 'Herbanium Meddygon Myddfai' which contains numerous medicinal recipes and details of the healing properties of certain plants and flowers. They reflect the illnesses and 'agues' which affected people centuries ago and which continue to plague mankind today. The following are some of the 'cures' listed:

Blood pressure (high). Prepare a standard infusion of wallflower (yellow flowers), primrose and sorrel leaves. Dose 1 tablespoon daily
Blood pressure (low) Prepare a standard infusion of dandelion leaves or Lady's mantle. Dose 1 tablespoon daily
A standard infusion of eyebright, fennel, violet and nettle or parsley was prescribed as a kidney tonic, 2 tablespoons to be taken daily, and a nerve tonic was obtained by preparing a standard infusion of balm or lily of the valley, lavender or periwinkle, skullcap and valerian. Again the recommended dose was 2 tablespoons daily. I also liked the recipe 'To open the gateways of the mind. Water of magnanimity. Prepare a standard infusion of mugwort, chicory and loosestrife. Dose 1 glassful after fasting for 10 hours and before meditation'.

The leaves and stem of agrimony was recommended for dry coughs, the liver, and some forms of rheumatism, while alder leaves were useful for 'disorders of the renal system'. As a lotion it

was also good for sore, tired feet. The leaves and stem of angelica had several properties – it was a cure for flatulence, colic, heartburn, and as a gargle for sore tonsils and throat, while camomile leaves and flowers dissolved tumours, ulcers, and worms. Many of the recipes are for curing, or alleviating the pain of arthritis; the Herbarium lists candytuft in this respect together with cleavers (goose grass), the latter also having medicinal properties against fever, jaundice, and skin cancer, as a lotion for dandruff, and as a poultice for cysts, boils, and swellings. Marigold flowers were used in the cure of ulcers, open sores, catarrh, varicose veins, and circulation problems, but one which I would have greatly appreciated as a child was the use of an ointment made of crushed snowdrop bulbs for frostbite or chilblains – a much kinder alternative to my grandmother's remedy!

The descendants of the Physicians of Myddfai continued to practice their arts until well into the eighteenth century; in fact, Dr Rice Williams of Aberystwyth, who died on 16 May 1842 aged 85, was a great grandson of Rees Williams, who is recorded as one of the Physicians of Myddfai. The introduction to the English translation says of Dr Rice Williams, that he was 'the last, although not the least eminent, of the Physicians descended from the mysterious Lady of Llyn y Fan'.

There are many other collections besides the numerous copies of the remedies of the Physicians of Myddfai among the manuscripts held at the National Library of Wales, for example the small Commonplace Book of Abraham Howells of Montgomeryshire (NLW Minor Deposit 1031B). Whether the recipes were his own or had been passed down through the family, or whether he had copied them from another source is not known. As a cure for rheumatism, his remedy advised putting horseradish root, marsh trefoil (also called bog beans or marsh mallow) and mustard in a jug, covering with hot water and then drinking. There were many recipes which used beeswax and butter, for example, one cure for a burn was to boil beeswax, salad oil, unsalted

butter and unsalted lard together, and anoint the spot with the poultice and then wrap in flannel. For a sore throat – garlic, camomile, penny royal; boil together, place in a jug and cover and inhale the infusion for as long as you can, while the cure for heartburn was to knead a penny halfpenny worth of turmeric in half a pound of brown sugar and 'take at your pleasure'. Abraham Howell's recipe for curing colic lists some ingredients which are outside the scope of what would be available in hedgerows and gardens: '2 ounces of oak ferns, 1 ounce senna, 1 ounce juniper berries, pennyworth of hard ginger, 1 ounce of aniseed, 1 ounce of liquorice stick. Place in 3 quarts of liquid and stew until it makes 3 pints'. However, for shortage of breath his ingredients would have been available in every garden – it entailed collecting garden snails, boiling them in milk until it formed a cheese and then strain. This concoction was to be drunk hot. I doubt whether that remedy was ever used, but I'm sure that one for rheumatism, which I found in NLW MS 23472C, was very popular, as it meant putting 20 grains of grated rhubarb into a glass of white wine and letting it stand half an hour. The dose was to be drunk 14 mornings successively.

The basic ingredients for many of these cures would have been available to ordinary folk but sometimes the nature of the ailment meant that they had to resort to the 'unofficial' medical experts. 'The practice of folk medicine…is largely a matter of magic, sympathetic cures and charms…and the distinction between magic, domestic medicine and the practice of unlicensed practitioners is decidedly tenuous if not

non-existent' [MA thesis of Dr J G Penrhyn Jones, 'A History of Medicine in Wales in the Eighteenth Century', NLW MS 16125E]. One type of 'magician' to whom folk would turn was the *dyn hysbys*, literally 'wise man', basically someone who had, or claimed to have, access to secret or hidden knowledge. The *dyn hysbys* was also known by other names – *consuriwr* (conjuror) or *swynwr* (charmer) and *dewin* (magician), and was said to break spells by undoing the evil perpetrated by witches and others. Fevers and other illnesses were often attributed to the maledictions of witches, and a *dyn hysbys* would be called upon to remove spells and cast out evil spirits.

The tradition of the *dyn hysbys* has its origin in a period when people had very little knowledge of science or the forces of nature, and anyone who had more knowledge than the rest of the community (or claimed to have) was greatly respected. Often both the *dyn hysbys* and the physician possessed a book which contained knowledge of their craft. In an age when most people were illiterate, owning a book and being able to read it was a matter of wonder and raised the status of that individual. It was, therefore, to the dispensers of folk medicine with a touch of simple, crude magic in the bargain, in the person of the *dyn hysbys*, that many of the inhabitants of rural Wales turned to when illness or trouble befell them, as much as out of choice as of necessity. Although he took advantage of the ignorance and belief in the supernatural, the *dyn hysbys* fulfilled a special and sometimes valuable role in society. He did not confine his powers to giving advice on matters of medicine; in addition to healing the sick the *dyn hysbys* was also prepared to safeguard people and their animals from danger or a *rhaib* (bewitching) placed on them by a witch, another 'conjurer' or a jealous neighbour. To ensure good health or good luck he used charms, some based on local traditions, occasionally originating in ancient folk-lore, and usually consisting of a prayer or blessing written on a piece of paper in a hardly readable mixture of Latin and English together with the abracadabra in the shape of a triangle, the signs of the zodiac and sometimes secret symbols. If the charm was to keep a person from harm the individual would either keep it on his/her person, in a pocket or purse as a sort of pendant, or put it under a pillow. If the charm was to cure animals or ensure their well being, the charm would usually be put into a bottle and hidden in the building which contained the sick animals, and the owner instructed not to remove the cork from the bottle because the evil spirit troubling the animals was imprisoned inside.

They were also prepared to invoke the supernatural to help the farmer with his animals and crops, to forecast the weather and foretell the future, for example by reading a horoscope or reading hands. Quite responsible men were known to be *dynion hysbys* (wise men) - clerics, such as Edmwnd Prys and Walter Davies, men who had inherited their skill through being related to families such as the *dynion hysbys* of Llangurig, Montgomeryshire, and men who were familiar with medicine and magic who had learned their art from books, such as the Harries family of Pantcou, Cwrt-y-cadno, Carmarthenshire, the most notorious of the *dynion hysbys* at the turn of the 19th

century. John Harries (1785-1839) had received a certain amount of training in medicines or had taught himself, and had a substantial library consisting of both printed volumes of the chief medical books of the period and the works of classical authors and manuscripts in his own hand. Thus he combined the art of the physician with his abilities as a proper *dyn hysbys*. His son Henry (who died in 1862) spent a period in London where he studied sorcery before joining his father in the practice of the magic arts. John Harries died, according to local tradition, on the day which he had himself prophesied; he stayed in bed that morning to avoid his fate and was burned to death when his house caught fire.

John Harries's book of prescriptions in NLW Cwrtmawr 97A contain recipes for medicines, etc., to cure all kinds of illnesses – measles, tetanus, colic, pleurisy, whooping cough, diabetes and even puerperal fever. However, it also contains examples of the forms he used for sending bills to his clients.

Sir
Unless the above Amount is paid to me, on or before the day of next, adverse means will be resorted to, for the recovery

In his work as a healer of physical ailments there was nothing unusual, but as a doctor of mental problems he was more original and showed considerable understanding of the workings of the mind – an excellent sort of amateur psychologist. He also claimed to be able to find items that had been lost or stolen and to call forth spirits. When we remember that he lived at a time when Calvinistic Methodism had established strong roots in Carmarthenshire, it's no wonder that not everyone approved of John

Harries's work as a *dyn hysbys*, during his lifetime and even after his death attempts were made to blacken his name and say that he was a hoaxer or a quack. But the ordinary folk remained faithful to the *dyn hysbys*; the tradition was still strong at the end of the 20th century in north Cardiganshire.

The *dyn hysbys* and other practitioners of 'unconventional' medicine and cures of mind and body were thus an important feature of the Welsh rural community. To close I should like to share with you another recipe from the Commonplace Book of Abraham Howells, namely the recipe for Diod Anfarwoldeb (The Draught of Immortality):
Prepare a standard infusion from the following herbs: chervil, heather, honeysuckle, red clover and vervain. Dose one tablespoonful night and morning.

I wonder if it works!!

The Scottish Genealogy Society

Library & Family History Centre

Researching your ancestors in Scotland?

Make THE SCOTTISH GENEALOGY SOCIETY your first port of call. Situated in the heart of Edinburgh's Old Town, its Library and Family History Centre is a treasure trove of books, manuscripts, CDs, microfilm and microfiche to help you unlock the mysteries of your ancestors.

The Library has a large collection of graveyard inscriptions, family histories, maps, and many books on family and social history for sale. It's also within walking distance of New Register House, The National Archives of Scotland and The National and Central Lending Libraries.

The Library and Family History Centre is open during the following times:

		MONDAY	10.30AM - 5.30PM
TUESDAY	10.30AM - 5.30PM	WEDNESDAY	10.30AM - 8.30PM
THURSDAY	10.30AM - 5.30PM	SATURDAY	10.00AM - 5.00PM

THE SCOTTISH GENEALOGY SOCIETY

15 Victoria Terrace, Edinburgh, EH1 2JL. Tel & Fax: 0131 220 3677.
E-mail: info@scotsgenealogy.com Internet Web Page: http://www.scotsgenealogy.com

---

Ancestral Research Services

16 Forth Street
Edinburgh
EH1 3LH
Scotland

Tel: 0131 477 8214 Fax: 0131 550 3701
Email: stuart@scottish-roots.co.uk
Web: www.scottish-roots.co.uk

Professional Services established in 1984
Specialising in
Statutory Records
Old Parish Registers Census Returns, etc.

Send known details
for free estimate & brochure

Mastercard
&
Visa facilities

THE
LAIRG
HOTEL

11 Coates
Gardens
Edinburgh
EH12 5LG

A family run hotel in a charming Victorian Terrace, convenient for Princes Street and Register House.

All rooms en-suite and non-smoking.

Rooms from £28pp low season to £40pp high season.
Phone or email for Special Offers

Tel: (0131) 337 1050 Fax: (0131) 346 2167
www.thelairghotel.co.uk
Email: info@thelairghotel.co.uk

The Search for Scottish Sources ~ Planning a Genealogical Journey

Rosemary Bigwood MA MLitt

The enthusiasm for tracing Scottish family history continues to grow and there are a wealth of opportunities for carrying out a great deal of research at home with the aid of internet sites and contacts or the facilities of a Family History Centre near you. If circumstances allow, however, a journey to Scotland will prove enormously rewarding, allowing the discovery of rich resources not available to you locally or which can only be found intside Scotland, to widen your research and your knowledge both of your ancestors and their background.

Planning a visit to Scotland in the quest of the ancestral past is not always an easy matter, especially if time is of the essence. A question frequently asked is "Should I go first to Edinburgh to the National Archives of Scotland and the General Register House or search in local record offices?" As with all travelling, some pre-journey preparations will be valuable. In the past it has often proved difficult to find out what source material is kept where and also to determine what records might be most fruitful to consult. Fortunately, work is now in hand to put most of the catalogues of the National Archives of Scotland and those of local and specialised archives on-line. This will be of great assistance in carrying out the planning of your research programme in Scotland.

One of the great interests in carrying out genealogical research is that you never know with certainty where it will lead in the end but

in getting ready to embark on "on-site" work, it is important to make a list of your objectives – whether these are concerned with tracing back the family further, putting flesh on the bones by viewing the old family "stamping grounds" or trying to locate living relatives. Bring with you a summary of sources already searched so that you avoid duplication of work and a note of any index entries you have found relating to documents you may wish to view. Also, identify on a map the areas where the family are known to have lived in Scotland.

Where to start - Edinburgh

Many Scottish records which are concerned both with national and local administration are centralised in Edinburgh. Articles in the *Handbook* outline the rich resources of New Register House and the National Archives of Scotland. If you have work still to be done in extracting information from statutory registers of birth, death and marriage, in searching censuses or Old Parish Registers, then time spent in New Register House (also known as the General Register Office for Scotland) will be valuable. A day's ticket for access may seem expensive (currently £17) but, thanks to the self-service system which enables a visitor to consult not only indexes but all the actual records, including copies of the statutory register pages and census returns (1841-1901) a great deal can be achieved within this time.

Having exhausted the resources of New Register House, it is time to assess what is now known about the family in which you are interested. What did these ancestors do - were they lan llords or labourers? When did they live and where did they live? On this will depend the choice of records in which to carry out research "beyond" the parish registers.

Records are

made by the contact of one person with another, with a group of people (perhaps at work or in the community) or with an authority such as a legal court or the church, for example. Thus a merchant or proprietor may have owned land, have left a testamentary disposition, had business and family dealings which are recorded in registers of deeds. He may have been involved in trade and have had a place in society, perhaps as a burgess in a burgh, member of the town council or acting as a JP – all of which matters may have resulted in the making of records. A tenant farmer is less likely to have owned land but could have left a testament, have had dealings with a landlord or initiated some legal proceedings. The labourer may be mentioned in poor law records, have appeared before a court for some misdemeanour, be listed in the local kirk session minutes or have had to serve in the militia if he lived at the time of the Napoleonic Wars – all contacts offering possible scope for research in specific classes of records, many of which can only be consulted in Scotland.

The second evaluation must be of the records themselves. How likely are they to throw light on a particular person and their circumstances? Are there indexes or finding aids and how long will it take to search them? Will the records be in Scots or Latin and will they be readable? Many documents, particularly those concerning with the possession of land, were written in Latin till well on in the eighteenth century. Handwriting changed around the beginning of the 1700's and there may be difficulties in reading the earlier, Old Scots hand. And lastly, where will these records be held?

The National Archives of Scotland

The National Archives of Scotland hold a vast and sometimes bewildering collection of material – much of it of vital interest to family historians. Some of this will be found on microfilm in Family History Centres but a great deal of it will not. Testaments, registers of deeds (both in the Books of Council and Session and in the sheriff and burgh courts), sasines, charters, retours, court records and a vast collection of church material, especially regarding the Established Church, are held there. There are muniments of many Scottish families, as well as records relating to national government – taxes and trade records. These sources are likely to be of prime importance in genealogical research. The new on-line catalogue of the NAS will provide some guidance as to the content of each class of records and be of assistance in selecting what may be relevant to your search. A preliminary study of published guides to records such as Cecil Sinclair's two books - *Tracing Your Scottish Ancestors in the Scottish Record Office* and *Tracing Scottish Local History in the Scottish Record Office* will meantime be of assistance in helping to identify source material which may be of value. *Tracing Scottish Ancestors* (Rosemary Bigwood) offers help in evaluating and selecting various classes of records, as well as indicating what may be found in the NAS and what is kept in local archives or to be found in libraries.

In the West Search Room in Charlotte Square, Edinburgh, the NAS has a very large collection of plans, mostly extracted from collections of family papers. These can shed considerable light on family history – illustrating land use, the whereabouts of old townships now vanished, buildings, plans of towns, providing information or field names and sometimes showing where named individuals lived.

The National Library of Scotland

This library, situated on George IV Bridge, Edinburgh, is a copyright library and has a huge collection of printed items. Their catalogue is on-line – www.nls.uk. They also have an

CALLING OVER THE ROLL OF FAME.

Sergeant. "TUGAL M'TAVISH!"   Tugal (hurrying up, too late for parade). "HERE!"
Sergeant (indignant). "HERE! WHERE? YOU'LL ALWAYS CRY 'HERE!' WHEN YOU'RE ABSENT."

extensive manuscript collection – including papers on families, estates, legal and financial matters. At present their detailed catalogue of manuscript material is not on-line and it is necessary to go to the library to search it.

A visit to the Map Library, which is part of the National Library of Scotland, (Causewayside Building, 33 Salisbury Place, Edinburgh) will almost certainly be of value in offering opportunities to look at their extensive collection of old printed maps of Scotland. They also have some manuscript ones. The maps include Scotland, Scottish counties, town plans, battles, railway and canal plans - to name only a few. The two volume work *The Early Maps of Scotland* published by the Royal Scottish Geographical Society is a useful guide to what is available.

Local Council Archives
In the past, the main administrative units in Scotland were the parish, the burgh and the sheriffdom or county. In 1975, as the result of the reorganisation of local government, burghs and counties were abolished and Scotland was divided into nine Regional Councils with a number of District Councils in the tier below. In 1996 there was yet another change when the present system of thirty-two local councils took over in charge of Scotland's local administration. These are listed below, with the administrative headquarters given in brackets after each:

Aberdeen City (Aberdeen) Inverclyde (Greenock) Aberdeenshire (Aberdeen) Midlothian (Dalkeith) Angus (Forfar) Moray (Elgin) Argyll & Bute (Lochgilphead) North Ayrshire (Irvine) City of Edinburgh (Edinburgh) North Lanarkshire (Motherwell) Clackmannanshire (Alloa) Orkney Islands (Kirkwall) Dumfries & Galloway (Dumfries) Perth & Kinross (Perth) Dundee City (Dundee) Renfrewshire (Paisley) East Ayrshire (Kilmarnock) Scottish Borders (Melrose) East Dumbartonshire (Glasgow) Shetlands Islands (Lerwick) East Lothian (Haddington) South Ayrshire (Ayr) East Renfrewshire (Glasgow) South Lanarkshire (Hamilton) Falkirk (Falkirk) Stirling (Stirling) Fife (Glenrothes) West Dumbartonshire (Dumbarton) Glasgow City (Glasgow) Western Isles (Stornoway) Highland (Inverness) West Lothian (Livingstone)

It is envisaged that each council will have an archivist but lack of funding and premises has in some cases made this difficult to implement immediately. Those currently in place are listed in the *Handbook* section on Record Offices and Archives.

Records of the Local Council Archives
It is first necessary to identify the local council which covers the district in which you are

interested. Appendix 6 of *Tracing Scottish Ancestors* (Bigwood) gives a list of parishes and the local authority responsible for each.

The holdings of the various local council archives vary widely. In Fife, for example, an archivist has only recently been appointed but a valuable body of material is being collected in the local council archive, including school board minutes, Commissioners of Supply books, parochial board minutes and various burgh and town council minutes. The largest collection of records for the area, however, is still held in the St. Andrews University archives – including deposits of records of a number of the Fife burghs – but other primary material is scattered in various centres, such as in the local history department of Dunfermline Library or in the Kirkcaldy Museum and Art Gallery. In other parts of Scotland, records are more centralised and one local council archive may hold most of the records of the royal burghs within their areas, as well as other local material relating to local administration, such as deeds, town council minutes, court records, lists of burgesses and parochial board minutes. Records of some kirk sessions (of both the Established Church and dissenting congregations), trade records, papers of associations of various kinds, collections of family papers, individuals and businesses, maps and plans may also be found in these archives.

Exploring Scottish History (2nd edition) edited by Michael Cox, is a directory of resource centres for Scottish local and national history and is an invaluable guide to what is held where. It includes a broad description of the holdings of each local archive. The book also notes the web-sites which can be useful, though the information provided on individual sites ranges from bare particulars of times of opening to quite detailed listings of holdings.

The Scottish Archive Network - SCAN - is currently working on giving on-line access (by 2003) to the "top level finding aids" of participating Scottish archives, providing a single searchable access point to their catalogues. Their web-site is: www.scan.org.uk. These finding aids will summarise the nature and content of each collection and show whether more detailed catalogues are available and in what form they can be consulted. The archives contributing to the network include all Scottish university archives, most local council and health board archives, and many specialist repositories. Details concerning surveys on private archives carried out by the National Register of Archives (Scotland) will also be incorporated. The web-site is *www.hmc.gov.uk/nra/nra2.htn*

When planning to visit a local council or specialised archive, it is wise to contact the archivist in advance. Not all archives (Stirling, for example) are open every day and in some there is limited space for researchers. The scope of material held, amount of help given, ease of access to records and premises themselves will, however, vary from place to place. Some provide facilities for photocopying, a user friendly cataloguing system and a café in the building. In others, archivists are struggling with inadequate storage space, understaffing and old premises. A great many of the archivists compensate for any such problems with their compendious knowledge of the district and its records and their willingness to help researchers.

University Archives
Many of the Scottish Universities have extensive holdings of primary material which may include papers of local families, estates and firms and large photographic collections, as well as records relating to the university itself and its students. For an outline description of university archives, consult *Exploring Scottish History* (Cox). A number of Scottish Universities are participating in the SCAN project and their entries will be cross-referenced to the descriptions of holdings on their individual web-sites. Another web-site dealing with the holdings of British universities is Archives Hub at www.archiveshub.ac.uk. Some of the university holdings include specialised collections. The University of Glasgow Business Records Centre is especially valuable in having a large collection of records of businesses of various kinds.

Specialist Archives and Museums
A number of organisations and professional bodies have archives – such as the Royal College of Physicians, Regimental Museums or the Royal Highland and Agricultural Society of Scotland - to mention just a few. As well as documentary evidence, artefacts, old agricultural machinery, presentations showing how people lived in the past displayed in local or specialised museums often add an extra dimension to family history. A wide range of both specialised archives and museums are mentioned in *Exploring Scottish History*.

Libraries
Local libraries often have very useful collections of regional books, town directories and copies of old newspapers, some of which may have been indexed. Small collections of primary material and photographic material may also be held there. The local knowledge of a librarian can be invaluable in pointing a researcher in the right direction. The telephone directory for the area will list both the local council library

headquarters and also the branch libraries. For newspapers, *Directory of Scottish Newspapers* compiled by Joan P.S.Ferguson is invaluable in providing information about local newspapers, when they started publication and where runs of the paper are held in Scotland.

Family History Centres and Societies
Many family history centres and societies have premises which hold material of value to researchers – transcripts of monumental inscriptions, collections of published and unpublished genealogical works and reference books, as well as microfilm copies of parish registers, copies of the International Genealogical Index, and fiche indexes to census returns. Some of these centres make a small charge for non-members. Not all are open every day and it is well to check on this. Like the local libraries, these societies will provide opportunities for sharing local knowledge.

Rosemary Bigwood is a lecturer, researcher and genealogist, specialising in older Scottish records. Her handbook *Tracing Scottish Ancestors,* first published by Harper Collins in 1999, has been updated and republished in 2001. It provides detailed guidance on a wide range of sources, how to locate and use them. The book is available in the UK, America, Australia and New Zealand.

Where Is It?
A Short Introduction to Locating Place Names in Scotland
David W Webster FSA Scot

While this article is written for those searching their Scottish ancestry, the same basic principles will apply to other countries as well, but the relevant sources are not given here.

You might be fortunate when researching your Scottish family tree in the sense that all the families involved came from and never moved from a single, easily identifiable town, e.g. Ayr, or a city such as Glasgow (but see later…).

The much greater likelihood, however, is that the various families involved in your tree moved about at least a bit, and quite possibly a lot ! In which case, unless you already have a detailed knowledge of the geography of Scotland, you are going to have to develop such a knowledge.

First Steps
First you will need to develop an outline knowledge of the "shape" of Scotland, and, in particular, the pre-1974 county structure that stretched back centuries. For this, books such as Kathleen B Cory's "Tracing Your Scottish Ancestry" and Sherry Irvine's "Your Scottish Ancestry: A Guide for North Americans" are ideal.

Such books will also give you an understanding of the parish structure of Scotland, both as it relates to civil parishes (901 of them!) and church records. In gazetteers you may come across the terms "quoad sacra" and "quoad civilia" relating to Scottish parishes.

The term quoad sacra relates to a parish that derives from the ancient organisation of the church in Scotland, and which may no longer exist on its own for civil purposes, being incorporated into another civil parish. Sometimes the civil parish name will incorporate the names of two or more quoad sacra parishes, e.g. Tarland and Migvy in Aberdeenshire.

A quoad civilia parish is one that exists for civil purposes only, from 1855 onwards.

A quoad sacra parish can also be a quoad civilia parish, but a quoad civilia parish does not always have a quoad sacra equivalent.

I Know that My Scottish Ancestors Came from ………?
OK, you have a place of origin in Scotland, so what next? First, a massive word of warning !

It can be shown to be very common that a Scottish emigrant would not always give a census enumerator, or a registrar or other official the actual place of birth in Scotland, but, instead would give the name of the nearest town or city that the official was likely to know.

Let's face it, if your ancestor came from Auchenshuggle – don't laugh, it exists, and is not

far outside Glasgow, and known to very many Scots as it was a tram terminus, and therefore on the destination board of the tram, - what would that ancestor have been likely to tell the official,- Auchenshuggle or Glasgow? If he or she had been talking to a fellow emigrant, then that would be a different matter. Which leads me into the critical value of newspaper obituaries, intended not only for N American neighbours, but fellow Scots both in N America as well as back in Scotland, as it was common for Scottish newspapers to repeat such obituaries, but

that's a subject for a separate article. Suffice to say that obituaries can be well worth hunting down as they are very likely to give accurate information on the place of origin of the deceased.

From long hard experience I can assure you that the distance between the place quoted and the actual small town or village that turns out to be the true place of origin can be many miles, and lead to much confusion.

Your next step depends on your location, your preferences, and familiarity with computers and the world wide web.

Gazetteers
Personally I prefer to have a hard copy of a gazetteer in front of me so that I can flick back and forth between the pages with various entries. However much I'm highly computer literate that's just the way I am!

The gazetteer that I most often use is Groome's 1890s 6 volume Ordnance Survey Gazetteer of Scotland that has entries for Scottish places down to the smallest villages. I also have the 2 volume 1842 Fullarton's Gazetteer of Scotland. If you are fortunate to locate a copy of either of these in a condition approaching reasonable, you'll be lucky to pay less than US$200.

But the CD age is with us, and GENfair: http://www.genfair.com/shop/ system/index.html or http://www.genfair.com/gazetteer/ for a demo) has a CD version of "Groome's" for sale at only £25.50, ca. US$37 . If you will excuse the expression, this is pure peanuts for the absolute wealth of invaluable information that this CD provides.

If, like me, you prefer to have a hard copy in front of you, then you will need to be fortunate enough

to live near to a library that has, or can obtain a copy. That said, while I do have a copy of the CD of Groome's Gazetteer, it's always the hard copy that I use first !

General Register Office Scotland (GROS)
GROS also has an excellent place name index for Scotland, based inter alia on the place names that occur in the censuses. This can be accessed on the web at www.origins.net/GRO/places/places.html.
The Gazetteer Doesn't Show the Place Name that I Have – What Do I Do Now?
There are two possible explanations for this situation.

The first is that the spelling of the place name was or has been corrupted. If the person hearing the place name involved was unfamiliar with the accent of the person reporting the event involved and/or was unfamiliar with Scottish place names, then the spelling noted down may have differed from that generally accepted as the correct spelling.

Secondly, as with surnames, up to a 100 years or so ago, there weren't always consistent spellings, especially for smaller place names.

The solution to such a situation for me, as a native Scot and with an understanding of Scottish accents is relatively straightforward. This is to be able to look at a spelling of a place name and imagine how the actual name could be spelt. For someone who is not a native Scot, all I can advise is to make contact with someone who is, possibly via a genealogical newsgroup, and seek advice.

Alternatively, you can log on to the UK Ordnance Survey web site (http://www.ordsvy.gov.uk/) and consult the 250,000 place name index derived from the 1:50,000 (ca. 1 inch to the mile) maps of the UK that include Scotland. It is also possible to buy a hard copy, but this tome costs approaching £100, - ca US$150.

This place name index is superior to Groome's, Fulton's, and other gazetteers as it shows place names down to the levels of farms.

Although the Ordnance Survey 1:50,000 gazetteer is based on modern maps, place names are the longest surviving aspects of local history, so that place names on maps today are still likely to reflect accurately place names of two or three hundred years ago.

Local Geography
Once you have established the correct location(s) for your Scottish ancestors I would strongly recommend that you then invest some time and effort in developing a better understanding of the local geography both in the sense of how the location concerned fits into the larger Scottish picture, but also the more local situation.

While one generation may have come from one parish, other generations may have come from neighbouring parishes, never mind the fact that your family may have lived close to the border of a parish so that they appeared in that parish and the neighbouring parish with equal frequency.

In addition, precise parish boundaries varied over the decades and centuries so that, although a family may not have moved, they appear from time to time in different parishes due to such boundary changes.

Be aware as well that many parishes were historically not contiguous, with parts of the parish separated by some distance, and in the middle of other parishes. The reason for this goes back to the ownership of land being linked to the original structure of the church in Scotland, based on religious institutions such as abbeys and orders of monks etc. There is still one county in Scotland, Dunbartonshire, which, as a result, is not contiguous.

In fact, you will find that it's impossible to divorce the geography from history, both local and national.

Such a better knowledge of the geography will let you appreciate the lie of the country involved in terms of natural directions of local movement and travel. This, together with a knowledge of history will allow you to understand better the likely movements of ancestors, e.g. the development of roads, canals, and railways.

For example, especially after the opening of the Crinan Canal in the early 1800s it was much easier for someone living in the Inner Hebrides to travel to Glasgow than anywhere else in the Lowlands, never mind the attraction in terms of employment that Glasgow offered, but that's taking us into social history as well !

Especially valuable resources are the Statistical Surveys of Scotland. The Old Statistical Account is a compilation of entries describing a parish, often in considerable detail, obtained from the Church of Scotland ministers over the period between 1791 and 1799. The New Statistical Account followed in 1845. Both can be consulted in full at http://edina.ed.ac.uk/StatAcc/about.html.

If you are really into maps then there was also a series of 6 inches to the mile maps of Scotland (1:10,560) produced in the period 1846 to 1899 that show an incredible amount of detail, down to individual buildings. Unfortunately I'm not aware of which libraries outside Scotland, if any, hold copies of this 6 inches to the mile series. In Edinburgh, full sets of copies are available at New Register House and the National Library. They can also, however, be found on the web at www.old-maps.co.uk .

Conclusions
Be prepared to invest time and money in learning about the history and national and local geography of Scotland in order to ensure that you maximise your chances of tracing your Scottish family tree.

Bibliography
In addition to the books and www site mentioned above, there are also the following web sites of interest, -
Gazetteers
www.geo.ed.ac.uk/scotgaz
www.genuki.org.uk/big/Gazetteers.html
General Maps
www.genuki.org.uk/Regions/Scotland.html
www.rootsweb.com/~sctayr/counties.jpg
www.nls.uk/collections/maps
www.old-maps/co.uk
www.ukmultimap.com for present day street maps
County Maps
Ayrshire
home.clara.net/iainkerr/genuki/AYR/ayrparish.htm
home.clara.net/iainkerr/genuki/AYR/ayr_pmap.htm
www.rootsweb.com/~sctayr/ayr.jpg
Berwickshire
www.vivdunstan.clara.net/genuki/BEW/gazetteer/
Dumfriesshire
www.embra.force9.co.uk/genuki/DFS/Parishes/parish_map.html
Dunbartonshire
www.skyline.net/~lasmith/genuki/DNB/dnbpmap.html
East Lothian
Genealogy.rootsweb.com/~genmaps/genfiles/COU_Pages/SCO_pages/ein.htm
Fife
www.fifepost.freeserve.co.uk/map.htm
Kincardineshire
www.genuki.org.uk/big/sct/KCD/ParishMap.html
Lanarkshire
www.rootsweb.com/~sctayr/lanark.jpg
Peebleshire
www.genuki.org.uk/big/sct/PEE/map.html
Roxburghshire
www.vivdunstan.clara.net/genuki/ROX/gazetteer
www.genuki.org.uk/big/sct/ROX/mapList.htm;
Selkirkshire
www.genuki.org.uk/big/sct/SEL/map.html
www.genuki.org.uk/big/sct/SEL/mapList.html

General Register Office for Scotland

Registration of births, deaths and marriages in Scotland

Registration of baptisms and proclamations of marriage was first enacted in Scotland by a Council of the Scottish clergy in 1551. The earliest recorded event - a baptism of 27 December 1553 - can be found in the register of baptisms and banns for Errol in Perthshire. Following the Reformation registration of births, deaths and marriages became the responsibility of the ministers and session clerks of the Church of Scotland. Standards of record-keeping varied greatly from parish to parish, however, and even from year to year. This together with evidence of the deterioration and loss of register volumes through neglect led to calls for the introduction of a compulsory and comprehensive civil registration system for Scotland. This came into being on 1 January 1855 with the establishment of the General Register Office for Scotland headed by the Registrar General and the setting up of 1027 registration districts. In 2002 registration districts number 319.

Records in the custody of the Registrar General

The main series of vital events records of interest to genealogists are held by the Registrar General at New Register House in Edinburgh. They are as follows:

Old parish registers (1553-1854): the 3500 surviving register volumes (the OPRs) compiled by the Church of Scotland session clerks were transferred to the custody of the Registrar General after 1855. They record the births and baptisms; proclamations of banns and marriages; and deaths and burials in some 900 Scottish parishes. They are far from complete, however, and most entries contain relatively little information. Microfilm copies of these records are available world-wide and there are computerised and microfiche indexes to baptisms and marriages. A project to index the death and burial entries got under way in 1997 and is still ongoing.

Register of neglected entries (1801-1854): this register was compiled by the Registrar General and consists of births, deaths and marriages proved to have occurred in Scotland between 1801 and 1854 but which had not been recorded in the OPRs. These entries are included in the all-Scotland computerised indexes.

Statutory registers of births, deaths and marriages (from 1855): these registers are compiled by district registrars. They are despatched by the district examiners to New Register House at the end of each calendar year. Microfiche copies of the register pages are then made available in the New Register House search rooms. By the end of 2003 the microfiche copies will have been replaced by digital images.

Adopted children register (from 1930): persons adopted under orders made by the Scottish courts. The earliest entry is for a birth in October 1909.

Register of divorces (from 1984): records the names of the parties, the date and place of marriage, the date and place of divorce and details of any order made by the court regarding financial provision or custody of children. Prior to May 1984 a divorce would be recorded in the RCE (formerly the Register of Corrected Entries, now the Register of Corrections Etc), and a cross-reference would be added to the marriage entry.

Births, deaths and marriages occurring outside Scotland (The Minor Records): these relate to persons who are or were usually resident in Scotland.

> Marine Register of Births and Deaths (from 1855)
> Air Register (from 1848)
> Service Records (from 1881)
> War Registers for the Boer War (1899-1902) and the two World Wars
> Consular returns (from 1914)
> High Commissioners' returns (from 1964)
> Foreign Marriages (from 1947)
> Register of births, deaths and marriages in foreign countries (1860-1965)

Census records (from 1841): these are the enumerators' transcript books of the decennial census of the population of Scotland. They record the name, age, marital state, occupation and birthplace of every member of a household present on census night. Census records are closed for 100 years and only the schedules for the 1841 to 1901 censuses are open to the public.

To discover more details about the history of

these records please see GROS's publication "Jock Tamson's Bairns: a history of the records of the General Register Office for Scotland" by Cecil Sinclair, ISBN 1 874451 591, 52 pages, cost GBP5.00 (USD8.00). See http://www.gro-scotland.gov.uk for details of how to order.)

Searching at New Register House
New Register House was opened in 1861 as a purpose-built repository for Scotland's civil registration records. Today it provides 100 search places and is open to the public from 09:00 to 16:30, Monday to Friday. Access to the indexes requires payment of a statutory fee which allows self-service access to microform and digital copies of all the open records. The fee can be for a day, a week, four weeks, a quarter or a year. There are discount arrangements and a limited number of seats can be booked in advance. There is also provision for group evening visits.

Indexes to the statutory records (including overseas events), OPR baptism and marriage entries, and the 1881, 1891 and 1901 census records are available on computer. There is self-service access to the statutory register pages on microfiche and the OPR and Census records on roll microfilm. It is also possible to order official extracts of any entry.

Microfiche and microfilm copies of the records are being replaced by digital images which are linked to their respective index entries. This is part of the DIGROS (Digital Imaging of the Genealogical Records of Scotland's People) project which will be complete by the end of 2003.

Online Access to the New Register House Indexes
The all-Scotland computerised indexes can also be accessed from local registration offices which have links to the New Register House system. Some local registration offices provide search room facilities with access to microfiche copies of the statutory registers for their area. The Family Records Centre in London has also been provided with online access (the "Scotlink"); while the indexes to birth records over 100 years old, marriage records over 75 years old and death records over 50 years old have been made available for searching over the Internet on the pay-per-view website 'Scotland's People'.

To find out more see the GROS website at **http://www.gro-scotland.gov.uk**. Pay-per-view search website is **http://www.scotlandspeople.gov.uk**

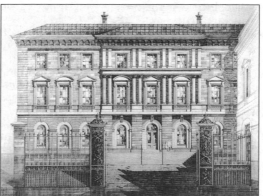

The Scotland's People Internet Service
Martin Tyson,
General Register Office for Scotland

Since September 2002, *Scotland's People* has been giving access to indexes and digitised images of GROS's historical records on the Internet. It is a fully searchable pay-per-view website provided in partnership with Scotland Online, a well-known Internet provider with a particular interest in Scottish heritage (and replaces the successful *Scots Origins* website).

Scotlandspeople.gov.uk gives access to a uniquely comprehensive range of Scottish genealogical data. This includes:
Indexed digital images of the statutory registers of births for Scotland, 1855-1902
Indexed digital images of the statutory registers of marriages for Scotland, 1855-1927
Indexed digital images of the statutory registers of deaths for Scotland, 1855-1952
Indexed digital images of the 1891 and 1901 census returns for Scotland
Browsable digital images of the 1841, 1851, 1861 and 1871 census returns for Scotland
Indexes to the 1881 census returns for Scotland
Indexes to the Old Parochial Registers of baptisms and proclamations/marriages for Scotland, 1553-1854

In addition, digital images of the Old Parochial Registers of baptisms, proclamations of banns/marriages and deaths, and of the 1881 census returns will become available on scotlandspeople.gov.uk during 2003.

The various cut-off dates detailed above have been applied to the statutory registers to avoid raising concerns about browsing on the Internet among records relating to living people. An additional year of index data and images will be added at the beginning of each year, so 1903 birth data, 1928 marriage data, and 1953 death data will be available from January 2004.

Features
The site includes a number of free features, including a free surname search where the user can see how many entries there are under their name on the indexes, a regularly updated feature on Famous Scots, giving access to data on the site regarding well-known figures in Scottish history, a place-name search, and news items. There will also be a demonstration of the search system.

Registration
Users need to register the first time they access the database. Once registered, users only need to use their username and password when they return to the site. It uses customer registration forms and order forms so that users can request particular products, but does not handle credit- or debit-card details. This information is entered once users have been directed to the Streamline secure payment gateway of the Royal Bank of Scotland Group, a major UK bank. Credit card or debit-card information, including account number, is not held by Scotland Online or GROS at any time.

It costs £6, payable by credit card, to access the index database. This gives 30 'page credits' and allows access for a period of 24 hours (starting from the time a credit card payment is authorised), however many times the user logs on and off in that time. Further credits can be purchased. Users can access any of the previous records they have downloaded from the past 100 days, outside the 24-hour registration period. Users can also order hard copies from any of the previously viewed records without having to pay the £6 again.

Searching
Searching is straightforward, with soundex and wild card search options available. The user can search across all the records on the database, or narrow their search by type of record, time period or geographical area. Each time a search is done, the number of records found is displayed; each record refers to a specific event, ie a particular birth/baptism, marriage or death. When the user decides to download these records to their PC, they are displayed in pages each containing a maximum of 15 records. Each page they choose to download costs 1 credit. The index page will indicate if a digital image of each record is available - if so, it can be accessed at the click of a mouse. To view a digital image costs 5 credits.

If a user wishes to order an extract of any register entry found in the index, they can do this on-line, again making a credit card payment. The system automatically transfers the request to the General Register Office for Scotland to fulfil the order and mail the extract. A fixed fee of £10 is payable per extract.

You can access the records of Scotland's people at http://www.scotlandspeople.gov.uk

The National Archives of Scotland

David J Brown - Head of Reader Services

The National Archives of Scotland (NAS) holds one of the most varied collections of records in Britain. Occupying some 60 kilometres of shelving, the records date from the 12th century to the present day. They include the formal records of pre- and post-Union government, the law courts, the public registers of deeds and sasines (land transfers), the records of the Church of Scotland as well as those of some other denominations, estate papers of landed families, a large collection of maps and plans, the Scottish railway archives, and the records of a variety of businesses, charitable institutions and public bodies.

Two books, both by Cecil Sinclair, give much fuller information about these and other records. They are: *Tracing Your Scottish Ancestors: A Guide to Ancestry Research in the Scottish Record Office* (Stationery Office, 1997, price £9.99) and *Tracing Scottish Local History* (Stationery Office, 1994, £9.99). Both will enable family historians to assess likely sources of information before they visit us, so as to make the best use of their time in our search rooms.

Before visiting the NAS, it is advisable to start investigating Scottish ancestry in the records held by the General Register Office for Scotland (GROS). Hopefully these should provide a skeleton tree, to be fleshed out from the records held by us. As most readers of this *Directory* will know, the GROS is located at New Register House, Edinburgh EH1 3YT. This is next door to our main building, HM General Register House. Both are at the east end of Princes Street. The GROS holds old parish registers of the Church of Scotland (up to 1854), statutory registers of births, marriages and deaths (from 1855) and census returns (from 1841- open up to 1901).

For family historians, the most popular NAS records are the **registers of wills and testaments**, dating from the 1513 to 1991. Since late 1999, NAS has been a partner in a major project, the Scottish Archive Network (SCAN). Financed principally by the Heritage Lottery Fund, partly by NAS itself and partly by the Genealogical Society of Utah, one object of the Network is to generate digital images of all the testaments for the years before 1876 and produce a union index for them. The index for the years 1513-1875 is now complete and may be seen at http://www.scottishdocuments.com. When the testaments are fully imaged, each image will be linked electronically to its index entry. It will then be possible to view the images in NAS, enabling readers to gain almost instant access to any testament. Website access, however, will be to the index only and SCAN will sell paper and electronic copies of images to enquirers. Copies of these images will become progressively available for purchase from the summer of 2002. You can register at the site to receive updates about progress.

This imaging process has taken some time, and the original testaments for the years 1514 to 1875 were progressively withdrawn from public access at NAS by the end of 2002. With a few exceptions, where copying is still in progress, consultation of these records in NAS is now generally by digital image.

NAS still provides copies of testaments after 1875. There is a good annual index to testaments from 1876 to 1991 but before we can search for particular entries we need clear details of the name, date and place of death of the deceased. While we are happy to search for one or two entries in this way, however, we will not search for lists of names and you will have to do this yourself, either personally, through a friend or perhaps by hiring a researcher.

Scottish testaments after 1992 are held by the Edinburgh Commissary Office, 27 Chambers Street, Edinburgh, EH2 1LB.

The **church records** held by NAS are often consulted by family historians who have been unsuccessful in tracing an ancestor in the Old Parish Registers held by the GROS. These records, although catalogued, are not indexed. In consequence the most profitable searches tend to be those where a family has an association with a particular denomination and parish. The largest bodies of these records are those for the kirk sessions of the established Church of Scotland (minute books, communion rolls, etc) and those for the other Presbyterian churches which broke away from the Church of Scotland in the years after 1733, and which gradually reunited with it in the years after 1843. The collection is large, but not complete. Another group of church records meriting special mention is that of the Roman Catholic Church. These consist of bound sets of photocopies of Scottish Catholic parish registers for the years before 1855, particularly of baptisms and marriages. The earliest of these dates from the 18th century, but in most parishes they do not start until the 19th century. They are generally not indexed.

Another popular class of records is the **Register of Sasines**, beginning in 1617 and recording the transfer of lands and houses, together with transactions in which land was used to secure loans. Sasines contain information or clues about the individuals and families involved in these transactions, although they do not mention tenants. There are good indexes for the years after 1781, but before that the indexes are less straightforward and searching may have to be done using contemporary minute books. The Royal burghs kept separate series of their own for urban property transactions and the NAS holds most of these.

The **Retours** (or **Services of Heirs**) concern the inheritance of land. Although they deal only with landowners, a small proportion of the population, they can be a valuable resource. They run from 1530 until modern times, although they are of declining importance after 1868. When a vassal of the Crown died, his heir had to prove his right to inherit his ancestor's lands by obtaining an inquest by jury which delivered a return ('retour') to Chancery. People who were not Crown vassals could also use the procedure in order to provide evidence of their right to inherit land. Until 1847 the record was kept in Latin and the published indexes for the years before 1700 (the *Inquisitionum ad Capellam Regis Retornatarum Abbreviatio*) are also in Latin. Retours are very stylised documents, however, and a researcher will need only a minimum of instruction to understand their contents. The indexes from 1700 are in English.

The NAS operates two search rooms in Edinburgh. The Historical Search Room at General Register House, Princes Street, EH1 3YY, is used mainly by family historians. The second search room at West Register House, Charlotte Square, may hold relevant material and is the principal store both for judicial records and for our plans collection. Please telephone well before any visit, to check which search room is most appropriate for your work and to ask about any arrangements for consulting out-housed records. You should also make sure that your visit does not coincide with public holidays. The NAS has its annual stocktaking in November and the Historical Search Room is closed for the first two full weeks in that month, the West Search Room for the third.

We respond to every written or e-mailed enquiry but the pressure of correspondence is considerable and we cannot undertake research for enquirers.

The records mentioned above are described, with others, in more detail on the NAS website at www.nas.gov.uk. The Scottish Archive Network's website also has much useful information about Scottish family history and this can be viewed at www.scan.org.uk.

Enquiries: Telephone: 0131-535-1334
E-mail:research@nas.gov.uk
enquiries@nas.gov.uk **Website**: www.nas.gov.uk

Church Records of Scotland

Rosemary Bigwood MA MLitt

The Church in Scotland 1560 -

In 1560 John Knox's Confession of Faith was accepted by Parliament and this marked the start of the Reformed Kirk in Scotland. The ensuing one hundred and thirty years, however, were ones of conflict, change and compromise between Presbyterians and Episcopalians. The seventeenth century in particular was marked by the struggle between these opposing factions. Episcopacy was brought back in 1662 on the ascendancy of Charles II to the throne but the same parish registers continued to be kept (albeit irregularly and variably) for baptisms and proclamations of marriages throughout the whole period. In 1690 Parliament restored Scottish presbyterianism and the Church of Scotland became the established church. Dissent, however, was not far away and throughout the eighteenth and nineteenth centuries many new churches were formed – including the First Secession in 1733, the Relief Church in 1761 and the Free Church in 1843. Some of these secession congregations fragmented again but having united in the first half of the nineteenth century to form the United Presbyterian Church, they later rejoined the main stream Scottish church. A diagram demonstrating the complicated history of the main religious denominations in Scotland from 1690 to 1929 was drawn up and published by J.H. S. Burleigh in his book *A Church History of Scotland* (1960) and is reproduced in many genealogical publications .

The Established Church of Scotland - the Kirk Session

Up till the middle of the nineteenth century, the church was the most important authority in people's lives and its records are a rich source of information about all classes of society, but particularly about the ordinary parishioners. The main responsibility taken by the church was in looking after the moral welfare of those who lived in the parish but the kirk was also involved in the provision of schooling and the care of the poor. Its records, therefore, include very

interesting details relating to people and their relationships with each other and also provide an insight into social conditions of the past, enabling flesh to be put on the bones of our ancestors.

Before 1855, when statutory registration was introduced, one of the most important duties of the minister, aided by his session clerk, was to keep records of baptisms, proclamations of marriage and burials (the least well-kept of the registers) in what have become known as the Old Parochial Registers or OPRs. By the Act of Parliament of 1854, creating the post of Registrar General for Scotland, it was laid down that he should gather in and preserve the old parochial registers in Edinburgh but the minutes of the kirk sessions were not covered by this ruling and they can be found in various other places.

In certain parishes, the session clerks made no distinct separation between the minutes of the kirk session and the records they kept of baptisms, marriages and burials. This has resulted in a considerable number of entries relating to these events (partieularly burials) appearing in the kirk session minutes or accounts, rather than in the Old Parochial Registers. A useful summary of where these additional entries - in short or long runs - can be found is given in *Parish Registers in the Kirk Session Records of the Church of Scotland* by Diane Baptie (published by the Scottish Association of Family History Societies, 2001). The OPR catalogues, which can be consulted in New Register House, also contain three appendices. The first gives a list of Church of Scotland records (i.e. kirk session records) containing additional pre-1855 birth, death and marriage registers. The second lists kirk session and other material found in the OPRs and the third refers to miscellaneous records with the OPRs, containing entries from non-conformist churches described as "relevant to the OPRs." This last section contains some surprising registers such as a record of births and marriages relating the Gordon Highlanders 75th Regiment between 1803 and 1834, as well as registers of various Free Church congregations.

Other entries of birth/baptism, marriage and burial (not listed in Diane Baptie's book) may occur sporadically in kirk session records in the form of money received for proclamations or hire of the mortcloth and ringing of the bell at a funeral. Marriages performed without due proclamation or by someone other than the parish minister were termed irregular and were a source of income to the minister. The fines charged for these irregular marriages were often noted in the kirk session accounts and the details given there or in the hearing before the session

Crathie Church 1882

Rodhill Church, Isle of Harris

may fill apparent omissions in the relevant parish register.

In addition to records of burials, the session often kept a record of the ownership of lairs. Rights to lairs might be handed down from generation to generation – not always without dispute - and details given sometimes provide mini-genealogies. Lists of lairs are not always kept with the kirk session records and copies are often held by the church concerned or by companies or other bodies who administer local cemeteries.

In pursuance of their work in the parish, the minister, his session clerk and elders kept many lists of both the inhabitants and parishioners which provide much valuable information for family historians. Many of these lists only concern adherents of the Established Church, such as lists of communicants, rolls of male heads of families and examination rolls: others are more inclusive, such as the list of inhabitants of Ecclesgreig – another name for St.Cyrus - taken in 1798 which clearly states the denomination to which each family belonged. The majority of these lists date to the nineteenth century but some are much earlier – such as the inhabitants in Coll in 1776, parishioners of St. Cuthberts, Edinburgh for the years 1632-1639 and a list of inhabitants there in 1790. Communion rolls are mainly post -1800 but they can be a useful source of information, often covering a series of years and sometimes giving names of members of a household, residence and details of death or removal to another place (including references to emigration). In some parishes there are more comprehensive lists which are, in fact, early nominal census returns for 1801, 1811, 1821, and 1831. Most schoolmasters (whose responsibility it was at that time to act as enumerators) unfortunately only made numerical returns.

Another of the national duties of the parish officers was to draw up lists of men liable for service in the militia at the time of the Napoleonic Wars in the late 1790's and early nineteenth century, covering all those between the ages of about 18-45 (the age-range varied from time to time) capable of carrying arms. These lists, of course, included all persons in this category, not just members of the Established Church. A guide to many of the parish listings of various kinds will be found in the second section of Diane Baptie's book *Parish Registers in the Kirk*

Session Records of the Church of Scotland.

Further named lists have survived in matters concerning the rent of pews. These lists rarely giving more than names, but do sometimes afford more detailed information about the people concerned. The poor in various places had their own pews. More informative are the testimonials brought by incomers to the parish or granted to those leaving it which sometimes reflect their reputations, not always favourably. These (also referred to as testificates) may appear as part of the minutes or be kept as a separate series of records and provide clues as to the movement of people.

A large proportion of the kirk session minutes are concerned with disciplinary cases – fornication and adultery, swearing, breaking of the Sabbath, disorderly behaviour and illegitimacy. The proceedings are a source of detailed information about our ancestors and their relatives (who were often summoned to appear to give evidence) and also about the conditions of life at the time, as each case is examined in considerable detail. The hearings concerning illegitimacy are of particular value as the elders of the session carried out minute investigation into the circumstances in their efforts to find the name of the child's father. Such enquiries were continued in some parishes until well on into the nineteenth century and post-1854 cases may supply details which do not appear on a statutory certificate concerning the paternity of an illegitimate child.

The Poor
Until the Poor Law Act of 1845, responsibility for the care of the poor rested mainly with the parish. Among the accounts of the kirk session in most places there are lists of the poor with the amounts paid out to them. Unfortunately, these lists are rarely informative, providing insufficient detail to make it possible to identify the persons mentioned. In some cases, however, a poor person had to submit an application for parish assistance. The subsequent certificates of poverty may provide a history of the circumstances of the applicant. As parish funds were limited, there were occasions when two parishes might be in conflict as to which was responsible for the support of a poor person and details of the case might appear in the minutes of the parish heritors or be heard before the sheriff court – the evidence and ruling producing details of the life of the person concerned. After 1845, most parish relief was handled by the Parochial Boards who kept their own records.

Locating Kirk Session Records
Kirk session records are not indexed but there are often side-heads for each case and it is always worth spending time reading the minutes for a period which is relevant for general background information. Some sessions were more vigilant than others in recording the falls from morality of the parishioners. A few ministers were more concerned in recording the texts for their weekly sermons but most kirk session minutes are very rewarding from the point of view of social history, if not from genealogy. Listings may be found as part of the

kirk session minutes but in many cases they are in separate volumes or bundles. Similarly, the kirk session accounts may be found with the minutes in the same volume or they may be separate.

The National Archives of Scotland in Edinburgh hold a very large collection of kirk session records. The catalogue of church records is titled *Records of the Church of Scotland and other Presbyterian Churches*. It is divided into various sections – Records of the General Assembly (Class reference CH1), Synods and Presbyteries of the Church of Scotland (CH2) Records of the Kirk Sessions (CH2). The records of the dissenting churches are categorised as CH3. Each deposit has a number and there is then a more detailed individual description of the holding. The catalogues of the NAS are in process of being put on-line which will make it very much easier to check what is available. If the records for a particular parish are not found there, they may be held in a local council or other archive – and a few are still with the parishes concerned. It is always worth checking the list of holdings surveyed by the National Register of Archives, available on their web-site – www.hmc.gov.uk

The Presbytery
The presbytery which was formed of ministers and representative elders of a group of parishes was the administrative court above the kirk session. Cases which were more serious or on which the kirk session felt it was not able to give judgement – dealing with habitual offenders, with accusations of incest or witchcraft, for example - were sent on to the presbytery and a note to this effect is entered in the session minutes. Other matters which came within their remit were the supervision and appointment of ministers, parish visitations and upkeep of church and manse. Like the kirk session records, their records are a valuable source of social history – though containing less genealogical material. They are in the keeping of the National Archives of Scotland. Some have been published by various record societies. Details will be found in *Scottish Texts and Calendars* edited by D. and W. Stevenson (Scottish History Society 1987).

Synod and General Assembly
The business of the synods, the next up in the hierarchy of church courts, is generally of less interest to family historians but the records of the General Assembly can be of value. The General Assembly, attended by representive ministers and elders, was often involved in settlement of disputes over the appointment of new ministers and particularly in the first half of the eighteenth century there were a great many such cases. With the evidence heard there are often long lists of parishioners who supported one or another candidate or cause – particularly valuable between 1700 and 1750, a period for which fewer parish registers have survived or were kept. These lists may give only the name of each signatory but sometimes an occupation or residence is included. Concern about the number of Roman Catholics in each parish has resulted in much useful information about their adherents in the early part of the eighteenth century (see below).

The General Assembly sometimes heard appeals from the decisions of kirk session and presbytery and they were involved in a wide range of matters concerning education, their records providing the names of many schoolmasters.

The General Assembly papers (kept in the NAS – Class reference CH1) are catalogued (but not indexed) on an annual basis from 1690 to 1777. This makes it possible to select anything that might be relevant within that period of time.

Records of the Dissenting Churches
The Old Parish Registers were, in the main, only concerned with members of the Established Church of Scotland – though it was not uncommon for members of dissenting congregations, Episcopalians or even Roman Catholics, to have a baptism or marriage recorded there. Most parish registers unfortunately have many deficiencies, due to loss of records, variable dates of commencement, carelessness of session clerks or ministers, and numbers of parishioners who omitted to record baptisms or marriages. By the first half of the nineteenth century the numbers of recorded births/baptisms and proclamations/marriages in the parish registers was falling quite dramatically, largely due to the great number of those who had joined churches other than the Established Church. The enormous out-flow of members at the time of the Disruption, with the formation of the Free Church in 1843, exacerbated the situation.

Failure to find a desired entry in the OPRs, therefore, leads the family historian to face the possibility that an ancestor might have been a dissenter and the problem of discovering to which church the family might have belonged. A post-1854 marriage certificate may provide a clue if the ceremony was

Ancient Tomb - Isle of Harris

performed by a minister of one of these "non-conformist" congregations. Otherwise, it will be necessary to do some research to find out what other churches there were in a particular parish. The *First (or Old) Statistical Accounts* (published 1791-8) and the *Second (or New) Statistical Accounts* (compiled by the parish ministers in the 1840's) which cover every parish in Scotland, comment on the religious composition of most parishes and estimate the number of adherents to each church. The *Ordnance Gazetteer of Scotland* by Francis H. Groome (1882-1885) gives details of the various churches in towns and cities and when they were built. Many dissenters, lacking a church in their own parish, had to travel to worship in a neighbouring parish. It is, therefore, important to examine the religious components of adjoining parishes to the one in which an ancestor may have lived.

The administrative structure of these churches was similar to that of the Established Church, with kirk sessions, presbyteries and synods which dealt with parish and other church matters. The NAS catalogue of church records held there has sections covering the United Presbyterian Church (including the churches which joined – Associate, Relief, Burgher and Anti-burgher), records of the Free Church, the United Original Secession and Reformed Presbyterian Church. The NAS has separate catalogues for other denominations – Quakers, Methodists, United Free Church, Congregational Church and Unitarian Church.

Registers of the Secession Churches in Scotland by Diane Baptie (published by the Scottish Association of Family History Societies 2000) is a useful guide to baptismal, marriage and burial registers and listings of members found as part of the records of the Reformed Presbyterian, United Presbyterian and Free Churches held both in the NAS and elsewhere. The book does not cover minutes of the sessions. Unlike the parish registers of the Established Church, there was no legal requirement for dissenting congregations to lodge any of their records with the Registrar General. A great many have been deposited in the National Archives of Scotland : others are in local authority or other archives and libraries and some are still kept locally - or have been lost.

Roman Catholic Records

Relatively few records of the Roman Catholic Church in Scotland have survived, mainly due to the fact that Catholic Emancipation was not passed till 1829. The most useful guide to known registers or baptism, marriage and death is given by Michael Gandy in his book *Catholic Missions and Registers 1700-1880: Volume 6: Scotland* (privately published 1993). Microfilm copies of a number of these registers can be consulted in the NAS (the repertory is RH21) – most registers only start in the nineteenth century.

Some interesting information concerning Catholic families in the early decades of the eighteenth century can be found in the records of the General Assembly. The church was concerned at the spread of Catholicism and ministers were asked to make a return of all the Catholics in their parish. In many cases, these lists give quite a lot of information, sometimes including details of nearest kin who were protestants. Some of these lists have been published – a list of Popish parents and their children in various districts of Scotland given into the commission of the General Assembly 1701-1705 can be found in *Miscellany of the Maitland Club* in 1843 and a further list of Catholics in Aberdeenshire in 1704 was published by the Spalding Club in 1844.

The Episcopalian Church

After the restoration of the presbyterian form of worship as the Established Church in Scotland in 1690, Episcopalianism remained strong in certain areas – often associated with the Jacobite cause - but suffered severe harassment. Surviving registers of these congregations are all too few. There is a small number in the NAS (repertoried as CH12): others may be found in local authority or other archives or are still with the parish concerned. A list of some of those which have been identified are given in Appendix 11 in *Sources for Scottish Genealogy and Family History* by D.J. Steel (Phillimore 1970).

Other Congregations

Source material for other denominations is scattered. The Scottish Jewish Archives, 127 Hill Street, Glasgow holds synagogue registers and other primary material. A search of web-sites will often be very productive and more and more catalogues are appearing on-line. The National Register of Archives surveys may also indicate the location of relevant collections.

Rosemary Bigwood is a lecturer, researcher and genealogist, specialising in older Scottish records. Her handbook *Tracing Scottish Ancestors,* first published by Harper Collins in 1999, has been updated and republished in 2001. It provides detailed guidance on a wide range of sources, how to locate and use them. The book is available in the UK, America, Australia and New Zealand.

Lothians Family History Society

The Society was founded in 1996 by a group of enthusiasts based in Bonnyrigg, Midlothian, Scotland. They were interested in researching their family histories, both in the Midlothian area and beyond. In 1998, the Society expanded to cover the counties of East Lothian and West Lothian.

The current membership stands at just over 300 with members all over the world; those overseas are mainly in Canada and Australia. Members are keen to promote the study of genealogy and family history, to start and extend research into family roots and to further interest in, and facilities for, genealogical research.

Members of the Society meet each Wednesday evening from 7 till 9 pm (during school terms only), in the library of Lasswade High School in Bonnyrigg, seven miles south of the city of Edinburgh and close to the City Bypass. The second Wednesday of each month is a speaker evening with experts on a wide range of subjects, including 'Scots at War', 'Shipping in the Forth' and 'Agricultural Labourers in the Lothians'. On the fourth Wednesday of each month, there is an evening visit to New Register House in Edinburgh to enable members to do research. Visitors are welcome at all meetings and those from overseas are especially welcome.

The Society has its own library within the school, which holds a considerable amount of research material. This includes a large range of Edinburgh & Leith Post Office Directories; MIs for many of the Scottish counties; exchange journals for other societies; general reference books. The 1992 IGI is held on microfiche and the 1881 Census is on CD-Rom. A recent purchase is a set of 1837 Trade Directories on CD-Rom for the whole of Scotland. Several members have deposited copies of their family tree with the Society.

A transcription service is available at a small charge for members. This can be done for birth, marriage and death certificates as well as census details from 1881, 1891 and 1901. Transcriptions can also be made from the 1841 and 1851 censuses for those parishes in the Lothians that the Society has indexed. Completed indices are available for 27 parishes – Borthwick, Carrington, Cockpen, Colinton, Corstorphine, Cramond, Cranston, Crichton, Currie, Dalkeith, Duddingston and Portobello, Fala and Soutra, Glencorse, Heriot, Humbie, Inveresk, Kirknewton and East Calder, Lasswade, Liberton, Mid Calder, Newbattle, Newton, Penicuik, Ratho, Stow, Temple and West Calder. While most of these parishes were originally within the County of Midlothian (formerly Edinburghshire), boundary changes over the years mean that many are now within the boundaries of the City of Edinburgh, the County of East Lothian (Haddingtonshire) and the County of West Lothian (Linlithgowshire).

These censuses are published in printed form and can be purchased from the Society. Many volunteers have assisted in this project and work is continuing with the 1861 census and with the parishes of East Lothian.

The Society attends the SAFHS conference each year and has also participated for the last two years in the York Family History Fair.

For the year 2002-2003, membership costs £9 for individuals, £13 for a family, with an additional £1.50 for overseas members. Fees are payable in £ sterling and the membership year runs from 1st September. Membership enquiries should be made to Mrs Margaret Mitchell, 3 Stevenson Road, Penicuik, Midlothian, Scotland, EH26 0LU.
General enquiries should be addressed to the Lothians Family History Society (Dept. MM), Lasswade High School Centre, Eskdale Drive, Bonnyrigg, Midlothian, Scotland, EH19 2LA.
Further information is available on the Society's website at www.lothiansfhs.org.uk.

Lothians Family History Society

Ancestors in Mid, East or West Lothian (around Edinburgh)?
Maybe we can help you.

Membership details from:
Mrs Margaret Mitchell,
3 Stevenson Road,
Penicuik,
Midlothian,
Scotland,
EH26 0LU

Website : **www.lothiansfhs.org.uk**

Scottish Surnames and Christian Names

David W Webster FSA(Scot)

Up to the late 1800s in Scotland few people were particularly concerned about how they spelt their name. During his lifetime my great-grandfather McLennan used McLennan, MacLennan, Mclennan, Maclennan and Maclenan.

People were also at the mercy of the ear of the recorder. Galbraith is a well known surname in Ayrshire. Now I know that it is spelt that way, as it was in letters one foot high above the eponymous baker's shop in Ayr. But in Yorkshire it has become Gilbraith, because that's the way that it is pronounced in an Ayrshire accent and heard by a Yorkshire ear !

McMillen is a well known Scottish surname, but involve a broad Ulster accent, and what results can be McMullan.

My favourite example relates to an entry in the 1851 census for Dalry in the north of Ayrshire.

A family appears with the surname Araphady, not a surname that I can fit to anything recognisable, unless I imagine a broad southern Irish pronunciation of O'Rafferty heard by an Ayrshire ear unaccustomed to such accents. I can't prove it, but I defy anyone else to come up with an alternative explanation!

Prior to the start of statutory recording in 1855, i.e. in the early 1800s and earlier centuries the situation can be very difficult, in general the further back one goes in time the more difficult the situation can become, e.g. the standard work on Scottish surnames, Black's *The Surnames of Scotland*" quotes the following variants for Cook:

Cuk	398	Cowk	1492
Cuke	1402	Cuch	1231
Cuik	1566	Cwke Cuick	1645
Cuyk	1540	Cwyk Ceuk	1674
Cuyke	1519	Cwyke Coowk	1686
Cwik	1554	Kewk	1504
Kuyk	1504	Kok	1479

Another major factor is the frequency of occurrence of a surname. In other words, even in comparatively recent times, a surname that is uncommon is open to spelling variations. I recently did some work for a client by the name of Scallon, and came across the following variants in the late 1800s and early 1900s !!

Scullion Scalleon Scallion Scallan Scallon Scolan Scollan Scollin Scullon Scullen Scullian Sculin
And those don't take account of variants starting "Sk..", or variants with a "y" in place of the first vowel !! In other words you need to think very, very carefully about this aspect. I believe that the great majority of failures to find an expected statutory record is due to spelling variations.

Types of surname variants

1. Simple variants
The substitution of a single letter, e.g Wabster instead of Webster.
The addition of a letter at the end, e.g. Yorkstone instead of Yorkston, or Roberts instead of Robert.
The use of a double letter instead of a single letter, or vice versa, e.g. Morison

REFRESHMENT.

Hospitable Good Templar (to Visitor—average Scotsman). "WELL, NOW, WHAT WILL YOU TAK', MAC, AFTER YOUR WALK—TEA, OR COFFEE, OR PEASE-BROSE ?"!!.

and Morrison.
Or any combination or permutation of these types.

2. Complex variants, ranging from -
The deceptively simple but far from obvious elision of a letter or letters, e.g. Wason instead of Watson, or Yorson instead of Yorkston.
To the much more difficult Lindsay for McLintock, thought to be an Anglification of Maclintock.
But note that apparently similar spelling variants do not always have the same derivation, e.g. Yorson can derive from either Yorkston **or** Yorson, a distinct Scottish surname in its own right.

Similarly with Scullion and variants and Scallon and variants.

The occurrence of a variant is always more likely to be due to the recorder, be that the registrar, census enumerator, session clerk, etc., thinking that they are hearing a name with which they are already familiar, or writing down a name with which they are unfamiliar as they hear it.

In the OPRs it's quite amazing the difference in spellings that can result from a change of the minister or session clerk changes. A similar comment applies to census enumerators who were quite often schoolmasters. In both cases it was very common for the minister or schoolmaster to be from outside the area.

3. Surnames derived from Gaelic
Then that leaves us with Scottish surnames derived from the Gaelic The etymology of such names is a subject in its own right. There is no significance in the difference between "Mc" and "Mac". The full range of variants is "Mc", "Mac", "M'", "Mhic", and "Vc", all of which mean "son of", sometimes "descendant of".

Up until the early 1700s it was common for a man to be known not just by his father's name but also those of his grandfather and great-grandfather, e.g. –

> Duncan MacGille Chriosd mhic Dhomhnuill mhic Thormoid.
> MacGille Chriosd we know better as MacGillechrist; Dhomnuill as Duncan; and Thormoid as Norman, so that this is –
> Duncan son of Gillechrist son of Duncan son of Norman.
> There is also a feminine equivalent of Mac. This can be "Nic", a shortened form of "nighean mhic".

In certain Highland areas, where a particular "Mac" name was very common, you may come across the use of "aliases". This comes from the situation in which a name, say MacLennan, was so common, that another surname based on say, occupation, or some other aspect, was used in daily life. The OPR entry could then refer to, say, Roderick MacLennan alias Watson.

In the second half of the 18th century many Gaelic people wanted to conceal their origin and used a number of methods to "anglicise" their names. An English or Lowland name was adopted which sounded similar, e.g. Brodie for Brolachan, Cochrane for Maceachran, Hatton for Macilhatton, Charles for Tearlach, Daniel for Donald. The name was translated from Gaelic to English, e.g. Johnston for MacIan, Walker for Macnocatet, Weaver for Macnider.

The other common method was to drop the "Mac".

In the OPR you will come across many instances of the use of Gaelic patronymic surnames, aliases and the "translation" of Gaelic surnames. This is mostly limited to

---

Frequency of Occurrence of Scottish Surnames

The following is an extract from the Sixth Detailed Annual Report of the Registrar General of Births, Deaths and Marriages in Scotland (1864) – "Most Common Surnames":

Surname	Est Number	Surname	Est Number
1. Smith	44,378	11. Mackenzie	23,272
2. Macdonald	37,572	12. Scott	22,342
3. Brown	33,820	13. Johnston	21,569
4. Robertson	32,600	14. Miller	21,318
5. Thomson	32,560	15. Reid	20,047
6. Stewart	31,836	16. Ross	18,254
7. Campbell	31,555	17. Paterson	18,048
8. Wilson	29,741	18. Fraser	18,013
9. Anderson	28,300	19. Murray	17,606
10. Mackay	23,840	20. Maclean	17,375

It would be reasonable to expect that this situation would remain quite stable over a long period of time.

Highland and Island parishes. In general the number spelling variants of "Mac" names is greater that other Scottish surnames. For example, Black lists 36 variants for Mackay!

4. T-Names
In the North East of Scotland there are a number of fishing villages in which there are very few surnames.
In the 1920s in Gamrie a compilation of a roll of male voters found:

17 Nicols	19 Wisemans
26 Wests	68 Watts

This led, understandably, to the use of nicknames, or "to-names", sometimes just referred to as "t-" or "tee-names". While some of these were based on physical characteristics, others used the name of the fisherman's boat. The t-name was regularly used on a statutory certificate.

The above situation can have interesting consequences. When carrying out some research in Gamrie I came across the re-marriage of a widow who was shown as Jane Watt, formerly Watt, maiden surname Watt !

5. Patronymics
If your search takes you to Orkney or Shetland (Zetland) you will need to develop an understanding of patronymics, e.g. the first generation could be John Donaldson, his father Donald Ericson, his father in turn Eric Peterson, and so on……..

The use of such patronymics in these northern island groups only died out completely in the first decade or so of the 20th century. Note that there is a little known OPR forenames index. Unfortunately this has not been computerised and is only on fiche.

The Solution !
• Buy a copy of Black's *"The Surnames of Scotland"*
• Invest in a copy of the LDS 1881 UK census, - the use of wildcards, - "?" and/or "*" in the Scottish area disks can provide a wealth of information on possible surname variants
• Use your imagination !!!
• Find someone with a knowledge of Scottish, Irish, English and other accents

General Etymology of Scottish Surnames
As in many other countries the derivation of surnames can be summarised as follows:

Patronymic or Familial based
Location/Origin based
Occupation based
Nickname based

Physical characteristic based

Scottish Christian/Given Names
There was a comparatively small number of Scottish given names in use in the 19th and earlier centuries. There were distinct naming patterns, -

First son after father's father
Second son mother's father
Third son after father
First daughter after mother's mother
Second daughter after father's mother
Third daughter after mother

Thereafter, it was common to use uncles' and aunts' names, but I have only ever come across a very few instances of strict adherence to, -

4th son after fathers' eldest brother
5th son after mother's eldest brother
4th daughter after mothers' eldest sister
5th daughter after father's eldest sister

You may also come across

4th son after father's father's father
5th son after mother's mother's father
4th daughter after mother's mother's mother
5th daughter after father's mother's mother
Similarly you may come across rules for naming 6th and subsequent sons and daughters
but I have never come across a case where I can show such rules to be strictly followed.

In about 10% of cases where the naming convention was used you will find a switch in the maternal/paternal pattern, i.e.

1st son after maternal grandfather
2nd son after paternal grandmother
3rd son after father
1st daughter after paternal grandmother
2nd daughter after maternal grandmother
3rd daughter after mother

In situations where the father and grandfather had the same name, the pattern may be altered to avoid duplication, but it is also not at all uncommon to find two sons with the same given name, i.e. altho' the repeat of a name will often mean that the eldest died in infancy, this cannot be assumed without checking the naming pattern possibilities. There are also rare occurrences of 3 sons with the same name as the father and both grandfathers had the same name.

In some families, if a child died in infancy that name was never used again, whereas in others the name would be re-used, several times if necessary.

Before you make any final judgment as to whether a family used a form of the naming pattern, double check that you know all the births. It's quite possible for children to be born and die in between censuses, so that they can't be picked up that way, and can only be found in the statutory indexes or the Old Parochial Registers.

As to the period during which the naming pattern tradition was used you will find it relatively uncommon to come across strict usage from the early 1900's onwards, especially once the size of families started to decrease. Before that it was used widely, but you will find at the one extreme families who stick strictly to the conventions for a number of generations right through to families where there is no apparent usage of the convention. The most frustrating for a genealogist can be families that only partly used the convention and/or sometimes did and sometimes didn't

In any case naming pattern evidence should only ever be used as a guide, never as the sole confirmation of a link.

Many Christian name variants are known and obvious, e.g. Betty, Eliza or Lizbeth for Elizabeth. But did you know that further variants of this name are Bessie, Beth, Elsbeth, Elsie, Elspeth, Lillibet, Lisa together with foreign forms and diminutives such as Isabel, Elisabeth, Lisbeth, Elise, Lise and Isabella ?

There are many similar situations. Jane is interchangeable with Jean and Janet. Marion is a diminutive of Mary. In the 1700s Marjorie and Marjory were interchangeable with Margaret.

The best book that I know of is Leslie Alan Dunkling's "Scottish Christian Names".

There is one further, outside chance that you should consider. This is that it was the practice, especially in the North of Scotland, to use occasionally a boy's name for a girl, e.g. Nicholas, Bruce , John and Scot, and very, very occasionally a girl's name for a boy.

Associated with that aspect was

the practice of adding "ina" to a boy's name when the hoped for son turned out to be a girl. There are familiar examples such as Alexandrina, Williamina, as well as less frequent examples such as Johnina and Jamesina.

On the day after I wrote this article I came across an Angusina, and a female Roderick!

Frequency of Occurrence of Scottish Christian Names.

The situation in Scotland is complicated by the relatively small pool of given names in common use. In the tables below you will see that the 5

Extract from the Sixth Detailed Annual Report of the Registrar General of Births, Deaths and Marriages in Scotland (1864) "Most Common Male Christian Names (total 3,690 entries)":

Name	Number	Name	Number
1. John	563	16. Donald	28
2. James	508	17. Walter	26
3. William	473	18. Joseph	24
4. Alexander	318	19. Colin	22
5. Robert	225	20. Samuel	19
6. George	159	21. Henry	18
7. David	153	22. Daniel	17
8. Thomas	139	23. Neil	17
9. Andrew	102	24. Malcolm	16
10. Charles	65	25. Francis	15
11. Peter	64	26. Matthew	11
12. Hugh	49	27. Roderick	11
13. Archibald	49	28. Richard	9
14. Angus	40	29. Allan	9
15. Duncan	28	30. Edward	9

Extract from the Sixth Detailed Annual Report of the Registrar General of Births, Deaths and Marriages in Scotland (1864) "Most Common Female Christian Names (total 3,689 entries)":

Name	Number	Name	Number
1. Margaret	470	16. Grace	27
2. Mary	462	17. Eliza	25
3. Elizabeth	303	18. Betsy	21
4. Anne	271	19. Euphemia	18
5. Jane	262	20. Martha	17
6. Janet	213	21. Flora	16
7. Isabella	212	22. Charlotte	16
8. Agnes	193	23. Georgina	14
9. Catherine	166	24. Jemima	14
10. Helen	138	25. Susan	14
11. Christina (Christian) 107		26. Wilhelmina	14
12. Jessie	102	27. Alice	12
13. Marion	58	28. Joan	12
14. Jean (Jeannie) 48		29. Marjory	10
15. Barbara	32	30. Amelia	8

most popular male given names represent 56% of the total number, while the top ten represent an amazing 88%. The same figures for the girls' names are 48% and 73% !

Since the selection of Christian names was increasingly liable to changes in fashion during the 19th century, and into the 20th century, the above tables should only be used as a snapshot of the situation in the 1860s. For anyone particularly interested in the situation, there were and are regular reports on the popularity of given names.

Middle Names
Another commonly used naming convention in Scotland is the use, widespread only from the early 1800's onwards, of using the mother's maiden name, or one of the grandmother's maiden names as a middle name,- this practice can even extend back to a maternal grandparent of the parents, i.e. g-grandmother of the child, especially if the person in question died a short time before the birth in question. As far as I am aware there was no set pattern or sequence in the use of such maiden names, although it was most common for the mother's maiden name to be used first, with those of the grandmothers following. In some cases the same middle name was repeated for quite a few children.

Prior to the early/mid 1800s the use of a middle name normally means:

The child belonged to an upper class family, possibly aristocratic.

The child was illegitimate, there being a widespread custom to give the child the alleged father's surname as a middle name

Beware of a widespread belief in N America that Miss Jane BROWN became Jane Brown SMITH when she married Mr SMITH. Not true! Yes, Scottish women have never lost their maiden name on marriage, but there has never been a widespread custom of combining the maiden and married surname. It is not uncommon, however, to find Scottish men who adopted a

family surname as a middle name in later life.

Another aspect to watch out for is that it was not compulsory for someone to use his or her full name later in life. For example someone might appear on his or her birth certificate as Jane Brown Smith, but just plain Jane Smith on her marriage certificate.

Remember as well that the accuracy of the information on a death certificate depends very much on the knowledge of the informant.

Conclusion
Unless you invest time in understanding how surnames can evolve, you may well miss vital links in your family tree. You may be very fortunate in having a group of Scottish surnames that are not subject to spelling variations. Otherwise I cannot recommend too strongly that you make the effort to understand how the spelling of Scottish surnames can vary, even in comparatively recent times.

"NO FEAR."

Fisherman. "Take care, Donald—You'll be Drowned !"
Donald. "Trooned !—in a Dub like this ! If i was, I'd be ashamed to show my Face in Oban again ! "

Researching Your Irish Ancestry
On the Holy Ground Once More
Joseph O'Neill

In Britain we have the world wide web, an extensive network of Family History Centres and the myriad collections of Kew's Public Record Office. Yet those of us in search of our Irish ancestors must eventually retrace their footsteps and cross the sea to Ireland. This is a happy hardship.

Those with forebears from the North must go to Belfast. Despite all its misfortunes it remains a fine Victorian city with an ambience that is as attractive as it is unique. Nowhere in Ireland are the people as friendly and charming. Those with ancestors from the Republic have the opportunity to visit Dublin, Europe's most vibrant capital and the finest Georgian city in the world.

You may also decide to visit one of Ireland's fine family history and heritage centres to research your ancestors's locality. You can find details of these through the Irish Family History Foundation.

Dublin is wonderful but not cheap. To make the most of your time there be well prepared and do the spadework before leaving home. Use the Internet to search the electronic indexes online so that you are absolutely clear what you want and where it is to be found. Use your local library if you do not have a PC. Staff are invariably helpful and the benefits of the web are a good incentive to master the basics of information technology.

Always take the time and trouble to record this information carefully. Any time expended at this stage will pay ample dividends later.

The more information you gather about Ireland, especially the part of Ireland you are most interested in, the more benefit you will get from your research. This is particularly the case if you have lost contact with your Irish roots.

Today, in contrast with thirty years ago, Ireland and things Irish are very much in vogue. In spirituality, literature and music the Irish connection is an asset. One advantage of this is that information on Ireland is readily available in an attractive and digestible form. Roddy Doyle's A Star Called Henry, and Peter de Rossa's vastly superior Rebels provide accounts of the 1916 Easter Rising, perhaps the single most important event in modern Irish history. For an overview of recent Irish history Robert Kee's The Green Flag is still hard to better. Among Irish writers who are currently writing all the best ones provide an insight into Irish life. Patrick McCabe, William Trevor, Jennifer Johnston, Hugh Leonard, Bernard MacLaverty and Dermot Bolger are all unique, yet they all provide insight into the Irish psyche.

Few things are more useful when it comes to getting a feel for the sort of life your ancestors lived than histories of parishes. Local history societies all over Ireland have produced these in recent years and the general standard is excellent. One of the very best is also one of the most useful as its account of a poor parish in the west of Ireland is typical life all over Ireland. Portrait of a Parish, Ballynakill, Connemara, shows how the great events of Irish history impinged on the lives of ordinary people.

Most important of all is the need to establish exactly where in Ireland your family originated. Much information is arranged according to county. Yet, paradoxically, Ireland has no equivalent to the County Records Offices. The central depositories are in Belfast and Dublin, which is a bonus for the visiting family historian.

You should also be aware that although nearly all records are in English, Irish was the first language of most of the population until well into the 19th century. Consequently, many names are Anglicized versions of the original Irish. Thus, Goff became Smith.

You will, of course, record everything you uncover. But, just as important, note when nothing is found. If you search a source and uncover nothing of use, note the source and the date. At the very least this will save you the trouble of needlessly covering the same ground again. Note the date and the format of the source — original, transcript, microfilm — as something more accurate may become available later.

THE UNVEILING OF THE O'CONNELL STATUE AT DUBLIN

marriage certificates.

The first census in Ireland was in 1821 but there are many gaps in the records. Complete sets of the original enumerators' lists survive for only 1901 and 1911, though there are some from 1821 to 1851. What makes these returns particularly interesting is that as well as all the information contained in returns for other parts of the British Isles, they also record the length of the marriage and whether respondents were literate or could speak Irish. These are housed in either the PRONI or the Dublin National Archives, where there is a detailed list of the existing returns.

Referring to the pension records may fill some gaps in the census records. When Britain introduced the state pension in 1909, many claimants had no birth certificate. Officials sought proof of age in the census records and recorded their findings.

The gaps in the census, mean parish registers are even more important than when researching in England. Unfortunately, few of the pre-1820 ones survive and those that do generally have records of deaths. Baptismal entries include the names of both sponsors - usually relatives - and witnesses, who were invariably neighbours. These entries also record the mother's maiden name and the parents' townland.

The good news is that the National Library of Ireland has microfilm of pre-1880 registers. PRONI has copies for the six counties and the adjacent border areas of the Republic. The relevant parishes hold most of the post 1880 registers.

When researching these registers it is well to beware of the Irish custom of naming the eldest son for the paternal grandfather and the second son for the maternal one. In the same way the first two daughters took the names of their respective great-grandmothers. Clearly, this leads to a great deal of repetition of names.

Most people in Ireland were and still are Catholics. Yet the Church of Ireland was, from the Reformation until Gladstone's Act of 1869, the established church, though never did it enjoy the adherence of more than an eighth of the population. Keeping a parish register only became obligatory in the Church of Ireland in 1634, though some do survive from an earlier period. Most of its registers began in the 18th century but were unfortunately destroyed during the civil war of 1922. Noel Reid's A Table of Church of Ireland Parochial Records and Copies is invaluable in placing surviving registers. The Representative Church Body Library has many originals.

Nonconformist registers are generally more recent, most dating from the 1840s and are usually held by the churches to which they relate. The PRONI has some.

And you may not have to wait too long for the opportunity. Duplicates of many major sources are available within the two cities, both of which are compact with good public access.

Once in Dublin your first port of call should be the National Archives of Ireland. Situated in Bishop's Street, Dublin 8, the Archives is the equivalent of Britain's Public Record Office and also hold the records for Northern Ireland prior to 1922. The National Library of Ireland is the Irish equivalent of the British Library and also houses the Genealogical Office. The General Register Office, holds all the records for births, marriages and deaths for Ireland from 1864 to 1921 and for the Republic from 1921 to the present. The Representative Church Body Library, Braemor Park, Rathgar, Dublin 14, has most of the Church of Ireland's records.

If Northern Ireland is the focus of your research, you must visit three archives. The Public Record Office of Northern Ireland is at 66, Balmoral Ave., Belfast BT9 6NY. Apart from its official records it holds an extensive collection of personal and business papers.

The General Register Office of Northern Ireland is at Oxford House, 49-55 Chichester St., Belfast BT14HL. It produces an excellent guide, Records and Search Services,which is available on its website.

Finally, there is the Ulster Historical Foundation, 12, College St. East, Belfast BT15DD. As well as producing an extensive range of guides on all aspects of Irish genealogy it also offers research services and organises conferences for family historians.

The civil registration of births, marriages and deaths began later in Ireland than elsewhere in the United Kingdom, only coming into effect at the beginning of 1864. Fortunately for the family historian, Catholic registered their marriages from April 1845. These records are with the relevant GRO but unfortunately the local registrars hold all

Many nonconformists played a prominent role in Irish industry and commerce. Their wills make fascinating reading and tell us a great deal about family relationships and their material culture. However, it was generally only the landowning class — largely Anglo-Irish — and the small merchant class based in the urban areas who concerned themselves with such matters. Most of Catholic Irishmen had no occasion to make a will, having nothing to bequeath.

Until 1858 the validation of wills was the responsibility of the Church of Ireland. There was a great deal of social cachet in having a family will proved by the highest court, the Prerogative Court of Armagh. The less socially elevated used the various diocesan consistory courts.

This changed in 1858 when responsibility for probate passed to the state. Unfortunately, most of these wills were lost in 1922. However, indexes exist for some of them and details of others. The National Archives and PRONI hold the surviving records.

Having trawled the major governmental sources, spend some time looking at newspapers. In the absence of personal family records nothing is better for fleshing out the lives of your ancestors. This applies especially to the Irish who have always been avid readers of newspapers with an insatiable appetite for information about current affairs. Irish newspapers date from the 18th century and the National Library, Dublin, has most of them. The Newspaper Library of the British Library also has a splendid collection which you can search via the web. A word of warning. Old newspapers are engrossing, so allow plenty of time for this phase of your research.

Directories are second only to newspapers in evoking the ambience of an era. They give an insight into the normal, humdrum concerns of our ancestors, what was their everyday reality. As well as containing items for sale and prices and giving us a good idea of the range of commodities available and the types of business enterprises that flourished they provide details of our ancestors' retail trade.

The first of these trade and street directories for Dublin was published in 1751. The most comprehensive of these, which also includes details of official appointments, is Thom's. Pigot's, Slater's and Wilson's came later. The National Archives and the National Library both hold large collections. Likewise, PRONI has an extensive range of directories relating to the North.

Both the National Archives and PRONI have the records, including registers, of many state schools going back to the 1830s. They also have records from Trinity College —until 1849, Ireland's only university — and the four other institutions of

AGE CANNOT WITHER.

Paddy (to Fellow-Passenger). "OI'M SIVENTY YEARS OF AGE, AND IVERY WAN O' MY TEETH AS PERFECT AS THE DAY I WAS BORN, SOR'!

higher education established in that year in Dublin, Belfast, Cork and Galway. The National Archives's materials are searchable through their website.

If you wish to build up a picture of your ancestors' environment, you will find everything you need in the National Archives and the National Library. The first detailed maps showing land ownership date from the 1830s. By 1842 six inches to the mile maps existed for the whole country. These provide a detailed picture of a society which the Famine was soon to destroy. Complementing these are detailed descriptions of every parish in nineteen of the thirty-two counties. The Royal Irish Academy is the impressive setting for these sources. The National Library also has an impressive array of maps, all listed on its website.

Griffith's Valuation or the Primary Valuation of Ireland, is a survey of land and property compiled between 1846 and 1865. It lists all landowners and their tenants, one and a quarter million people in all, and it details the extent and value of their property. Nearly complete sets are available in the National Library, the General Register Office and PRONI.

While Griffith's is clearly an invaluable source, it is important to remember that it does not include most of even the male population. Most of the population were landless labourers or tenant farmers whose holdings did not warrant mention. Copies are available at the National Archives and PRONI.

Griffith's is not the only source of information on property. The Valuation Office of Ireland also

"EXCLUSIVE DEALING."

Irish Landlord (boycotted). "PAT, MY MAN, I'M IN NO END OF A HURRY. PUT THE PONY TO, AND DRIVE ME TO THE STATION, AND I'LL GIVE YE HALF A SOVEREIGN!"
Pat (Nationalist, but needy). "OOH SHURE, IT'S MORE THAN ME LOIFE IS WORTH TO BE SEEN DROIVING YOU, YER HONOUR. BUT"—(slily)—"IF YER HONOUR WOULD JIST DROIVE ME, MAYBE IT'S MESELF THAT MOIGHT VENTURE IT!"

contains property records from 1846. These give the acreage, rateable value and the name of the owner for every property valued. The Valuation Office is conveniently situated in the city centre.

You may gather more details of land holdings in the period 1823-38 may from the Tithe Applotment Books. Devised to simplify the collection of the tithe - payments to the Church of Ireland - they not only identify all landowners liable to the tax but also give details their holdings, including the quality of the land and the crops they grew. Similar information is to be found in the 1873 Return of the Owners of Land and the 1873 - 6 survey of land ownership. The latter is arranged by county, lists landowners and provides details of holdings and their valuation. Copies of both are available at the National Archives and the PRONI.

Hearth Money Rolls and the poll tax records also contain valuable information. An Act of 1663 imposed the hearth tax, waging a standard tax of two shillings on every household in the country. It lists the name of every hearth-owner. The poll tax of 1660 affected every person over the age of twelve years and the returns list all those liable to pay.

The Irish Linen Board is not a quango established to revive a traditional industry. It existed in the 18th century to promote a vibrant trade by encouraging farmers to plant at least an acre of flax. Those who did were rewarded as encouragement to continue their contribution to an enterprise which already had an international reputation. Their names are recorded togther with 60,000 others in the Flax Growers' Bounty List, housed in the National Archives.

While in Ireland, take the opportunity to visit one of the splendid folk parks. They give a real feel for how your ancestors might have lived and worked over the centuries. Two of these are more than

twenty years old and are world famous. Bunratty Castle, near the Shannon Airport development, has a selection of characteristically Irish dwellings and a complete 19th century Irish town with shops, a Post Office, printing works and a flour mill operated by a water mill.

Just as impressive is the Ulster-American Folk Park, Camphill, Omagh, County Tyrone. Like Bunratty it has a range of dwellings from every era of Irish history and demonstrations of rural crafts. A fascinating section devoted to the experience of emigration to North America allows the visitor to relive the emigrant experience.

Useful Addresses
The National Archives of Ireland
http://www.nationalarchives.ie
The National Library of Ireland http://www.nli.ie
The General Register Office, 8-11, Lombard Street East, Dublin http://www.groireland.ie
The Representative Church Body Library, Braemor Park, Dublin. http://www.ireland.anglican.org/library
The Valuation Office of Ireland, Irish Life Centre, Abbey Street Lower, Dublin 1. http://www.valoff.ie
Royal Irish Academy, 19, Dawson Street, Dublin 2. http://www.ria.ie
The Public Record Office of Northern Ireland http://www. proni.nics.gov.uk
The General Register Office of Northern Ireland http://www. nisra.gov.uk
The Ulster Historical Foundation
http://www. uhf.org.uk and http://www.ancestryireland.com
The Newspaper Library of the British Library http://www. bl.uk/collections/newspapers
Portrait of a Parish, Ballynakill, Connemara, produced by the Tully Cross Guild of the Irish Countrywoman's Association.
The Irish Family History Foundation with links to local research centres in Ireland — http://www.mayo-ireland.ie/general
Irish Family History Society
http://homepage.eircom.net/(dash)ifhs
The Local Ireland genealogy pages —
http://www.local.ie/genealogy
http://www.cyndilist.com

QUITE ANOTHER THING.

Paddy (the loser). "ARRAH, G'ALONG! I SAID I'D LAY YOU FOIVE TO WAN, BUT I WASN'T GOIN' TO BET MY HA'F-CROWN AGIN YOUR TATH'RIN LITTLE SIX-PENCE!"

The Public Record Office of Northern Ireland
Valerie Adams

The Public Record Office of Northern Ireland (PRONI) receives records ranging from government departments, courts, local authorities and non-departmental public bodies to those of landed estates, businesses, churches, societies, private individuals and families. This unique combination of public and private records makes PRONI the most important resource for any one researching their family tree or their local area. PRONI's extensive website will help researchers find out how to make best use of the records. There you will find, for example, answers to the most frequently asked questions, introductions to the major private collections, news of new developments that are taking place such as the digitisation of the Ulster Covenant signatures, how to get to PRONI and copies of our policies on preservation and copying.

Having carried out introductory research using the printed sources and consulted family members and papers for details of births, marriages and deaths, your research will inevitably lead you to PRONI. To view the records a Readers ticket is required for which proof of identity is needed. Admission is free except for commercial users.

Public Records
Among the most popular of the public records for family and local history are: the valuation records from 1856 to the present and the tithe applotment books, 1823 - 37, for the six counties of Northern Ireland which give details of landholders and the size of their farms; microfilm copies of the 1901 census for Northern Ireland; copy wills from 1858 - c1900 and all original wills from 1900 to 1996; the registers and inspectors observation books of c1,600 national/public elementary/primary schools dating mainly from the 1870's; the grant-aid applications of the Commissioners of National Education which document the history and state of schools from the 1832 to 1889; the Ordnance Survey maps at various scales from 1831 to the present; and the minutes and indoor relief registers from 1839 - 1948 of the Boards of Guardians who administered the workhouses. Guides to the tithe applotment books, educational records and probate records are available for consultation in PRONI.

Private Records
Because so many of the public records for the island of Ireland prior to 1922 have not survived, private records assume a much greater importance for family and local history The records of the great landed estates, solicitor's records, railway records, the working notes of antiquarians and genealogists and church records are particularly valuable. The major estate collections are described on the PRONI website -among the more notable are: Downshire (Cos Down and Antrim); Antrim (Co Antrim); Abercorn (Co Tyrone); Belmore (Cos Fermanagh and Tyrone); Gosford (Co Armagh); and Drapers' Co (Co Londonderry). A comprehensive listing of all the estate records will be found in the 'Guide to Landed Estates', available in PRONI. Also on the PRONI website you will find an index of reference numbers to the many church records held on microfilm but fuller details can be found in the 'Guide to Church Records' also available in PRONI.

Printed sources
Street directories are an important source of information for local and family historians. PRONI holds a very comprehensive set of the Belfast and Ulster Street Directories from c.1840 to 1996 and of Thom's Directories from 1845. A set of printed will calendars summarising every will proved in the civil courts from 1858 to 1996 is also available in PRONI.

Improvements to Service
This year has been characterised by continuous improvement as PRONI has been actively preparing for Charter Mark accreditation. A number of improvements have already been implemented such as: improved signage in the Public Search Room; the introduction of a new complaints system, a revised comments and suggestions form and telephone voice mail for out- of - office hours enquiries; the provision of an information folder for user consultation in the Waiting Room area; the introduction of corporate wear (uniforms) for those in the public service areas as well as name badges; the prominent display within PRONI of progress made against our performance targets; the provision of free Internet access to selected websites ie those of the National Archives in Dublin, the National Library of Ireland, the Public Record Office in London and the National Archives of Scotland; and a new front entrance from Balmoral Avenue which provides for a separate pedestrian entrance and exit.

We have also been able to extend the range of microfilms that are available on a self- service basis by adding the microfilms of the civil birth indexes for 1864 - 1922 and the tithe applotment books to the church records, the 1901census and the copy wills from 1858 - c1900 already available on microfilm on a self-service basis.

To improve consultation with our users a PRONI Forum is to be established which will enable us to get regular feedback on actual or proposed changes/improvements. The Forum will be representative of all PRONI's stakeholders and will meet at least 3 times a year.

New PRONI Outreach Centre
PRONI's fourth outreach centre was opened in the autumn of 2001 in partnership with Armagh City and District Council. It is based in the premises of Armagh Ancestry in St Patrick's Trian in Armagh City. Armagh Ancestry is one of a large number of local community based genealogy centres throughout the island of Ireland and has an extensive range of resources relating to County Armagh for family history. As in the other outreach centres in Ballymena and Londonderry, the new Armagh centre will hold PRONI's computerised subject and place name indexes, its web pages, the touch-screen inter-active video (which is an introduction to PRONI and the records it holds) and also a set of guides to various types of records. Having in one location the very comprehensive indexes of church and other records compiled by Armagh Ancestry and the finding aids of PRONI has created one of the best resources of material in Northern Ireland for family and local history.

The outreach centre at Blacklion in Co Cavan, run in association with the Border Counties History Collective, is currently closed but the History Collective hopes to be up and running again soon.

New Acquisitions
PRONI continued to identify and acquire public and private records of major importance to the family and local historian.

Public Records
For the historian of Belfast a large volume of 10 drawings for the Albert Bridge in Belfast, 1888 will be of interest as well as an extensive addition to the records of Belfast City Council which will soon be available for public consultation.

Estate Papers
Estate papers received included: a major addition to the Farnham papers, c.1810 - 1920, which relate to the Maxwell and Maxwell Barry family, Lords Farnham of Farnham, Cavan, Co.Cavan; rentals and account books, 1813 - 1918, for the Annesley estate, Castlewellan, Co. Down; and an 1891 map of the estate of Lord Templemore in Ballyhackamore, Co. Down.

Business Records
Among the business records received were: correspondence files and photographs, c.1970 - 2000, of prominent Irish property agents, Lisney; financial records relating to Robert Hogg & Co. Ltd, specialists in chinaware and crystal, Belfast, 1907 - 1975, and to John Magee & Co. Ltd, art dealers, picture frame makers and leather goods, Belfast, 1961 - 1975; additional Belfast Co-Operative Society papers including a substantial number of title deeds relating to their properties, c.1909 - 1970; and records relating to A.Glendinning & Co. Ltd, linen merchants, Belfast, c.1913 - 1945.

Papers of Notable Individuals
Records relating to notable individuals included a patent from George III to Richard Robinson, Archbishop of Armagh, appointing him Lord Almoner for the whole of Ireland, 1763; and additional papers, c.1975 - 1985, from Professor Robert Denis Collison Black, the former Dean of the Faculty of Economics and Social Sciences and Pro Vice-Chancellor of Queen's University, Belfast.

Individual politicians continue to deposit papers in PRONI and these included additional constituency papers of Ken Maginnis c.1986 - 1997, the former MP for Fermanagh-South Tyrone, and also the papers of Thomas W. Boyd of the Northern Ireland Labour Party, 1924 - 1977.

Sports Records
In response to previous appeals for sports records, PRONI was delighted to receive three new significant archives: scorebooks, annual reports, accounts, fixture lists, visitor books and scrapbooks, 1862 - 2000, of the North of Ireland Cricket Club, later the North of Ireland Cricket and Football Club, Belfast; minutes and annual reports of the Northern Ireland Amateur Athletic Association and the Northern Ireland Women's Amateur Athletic Association, 1934 - 1996; and minute books of the Irish Ladies Golf Union, 1911 - 1988.

Miscellaneous
PRONI's collection of architectural plans was added to by the purchase of five unexecuted plans of Killyfaddy House, Clogher, Co.Tyrone, designed by Thomas Colbourne, 1823. Material that will be of particular interest to genealogists are four microfilmed notebooks of W.H. Welpy of Greenisland, Co Antrim, containing c.1,500 abstracts of wills, relating largely to Cork and Cloyne dioceses, early 17th - mid 19th century. A large deposit of personal correspondence, photographs and printed material relating to the McCready and Ewart families of Belfast, c.1890-1970, was also received by PRONI. Two other deposits deserve mention: a bundle of 12 letters of John Tulloch of the 74th Highland Regiment, relating to the Indian Mutiny, 1852-1859, and a microfilm copy of the memoirs of Humphrey Thomson, a Co. Sligo gentleman, 1734 - 1809.

Church Records
PRONI continues to be proactive in acquiring either in original or microfilm form, significant deposits of church records. Of special importance are the records of Down Cathedral, 1730 - 1870, comprising a chapter book, rentals, a Cathedral Committee Improvements account book, a 1786 lease of lands in Ballyclander, Co.Down, and a translation of the Charter establishing the Cathedral of Down, Connor and Dromore, Co. Down.
The following Church of Ireland churches deposited their original records in PRONI, some of which are public records under the 1923 Public Records (NI) Act: Holy Trinity, Belfast, incorporating records of Trinity Parish Church, Belfast, 1855 - 1983; St Silas' Belfast, 1899 - 1994, St Brides, Belfast, 1938 - 1977, and Holy Trinity, Lisnaskea, Co.Fermanagh, 1889-2001.

Presbyterian records microfilmed by PRONI included those of 1st Lisburn, Co. Antrim, 1846-1975, Whitehouse, Co.Antrim, 1867 - 1960, and 1st Kilraughts, Co. Antrim, 1831 - 2001. A more unusual set of records microfilmed were nine visitation notebooks of the Rev. John Knox Leslie of Molesworth (3rd) Presbyterian Church, Cookstown, Co.Tyrone, 1842 - 1881.

Cataloguing
Cataloguing was completed on two significant mill collections: minute books, accounts, share registers, etc, 1909 - 1996, of Albion Clothing Co, based at Wellwood Street in Belfast, (including a number of associated companies, such as Comber Clothing Co. Ltd and Belfast Clothing Co. Ltd); and the records of Moygashel Ltd, Dungannon, Co. Tyrone (incorporating the records of Stevenson & Son Ltd, Braidwater Spinning Co. Ltd, Smyth's Weaving Co. Ltd, and their subsidiary companies). The latter include minute books; annual reports and accounts; ledgers, cashbooks, letter books; maps and plans and fabric sample books, 1866 - 1990. This is a particularly important collection because of the sheer scale of the Moygashel operation. The mills, which were owned by the Stevenson family since 1875, were the major source of employment in Dungannon for almost a century. By the time of the Second

World War, the Stevenson family had purchased Dungannon Park, the former seat of the Knox family, Earls of Ranfurly. The purchase of the estate led to a diversification into farming activities with the result that Stevenson & Son Ltd achieved the rare feat of running a linen mill and owning a herd of Ayrshire cattle and a herd of Larke White York pigs. During the Second World War, Dungannon Park was also the site of a prisoner of war camp, where over 300 German soldiers were imprisoned.

Cataloguing was also completed on the records of the Pharmaceutical Society of Northern Ireland which comprise minute books of the Council and its various committees, correspondence, photographs and a scrapbook of newspaper cuttings, 1925 - 1992.

External Relations
PRONI staff give talks and lectures to outside organisations, including family and local history societies about PRONI and the primary sources held. Some of these are held in PRONI but they are largely delivered off-site.

Of the in-house monthly lecture series that we run on a regular basis the least well-attended one is the talk on 'Sources for Local History'. It was decided therefore to try running these in conjunction with our outreach centres which might at the same time help to publicise the facilities that PRONI offers at these centres. The first of these was held at the outreach centre at Armagh Ancestry using the lecture theatre in St Patrick's Trian as the venue. A second one was subsequently held at the Ballymena outreach centre at Ballymena Museum. We hope to repeat this event at the other outreach centres. PRONI's website will give details of forthcoming talks.

Special Events
An Open Day, held in May as part of Adult Learning Week, was very successful. The public had the opportunity to attend talks on PRONI sources, go on tours of the Public Search Room and Reading Room and visit Conservation and the storage areas. It is intended that this will become a yearly event.

The Brian Waddell film crew worked in PRONI for a few days in July and August in order to film part of the 'Blood Ties' programme for BBC television which featured PRONI as the custodian of vital series of records for anyone wanting to trace their family history. The programme was screened during March and April 2002.

Projects
Funding from the Sharing Museum Skills Millennium Awards to Belfast Central Library enabled one of their librarians to spend some time in PRONI researching and compiling a web–based template for studying the history of a national school using both printed and manuscript material as well as oral history (interviewing past pupils and teachers) Although primarily for use by schools it would also be of interest to anyone researching local history and can be viewed on the PRONI website.

Opening Times
Monday - Wednesday & Friday 9.00 - 16.45;
Thursday 10.00 - 20.45 Documents are not produced after 16.15 (except for Thursdays when last orders must be in by 20.15) Closure for stocktaking takes place annually during the last week in November and first week in December.
While there are extensive catalogues, finding aids and leaflets on sources for family and local history, staff are always available at the Help Desk in the Public Search Room to give advice and help to researchers. The leaflet series is also available on the PRONI website.

If your local or family history group or any other organisation would like to know more about PRONI and the records held or want advice or help with aspects of family or local history contact us by phone, fax or e-mail

Public Record Office of Northern Ireland
66 Balmoral Avenue, Belfast BT9 6NY
Tel: 028 9025 5905   Fax: 028 9025 5999
E-mail: proni@dcalni.gov.uk
Web: http://proni.nics.gov.uk

National Archives of Ireland

Aideen M Ireland National Archives of Ireland

The National Archives comprises the holdings of the former Public Record Office of Ireland and of the State Paper Office. The combined holdings date from medieval times to the present day.

The holdings comprise the records of the former Chief Secretary's Office in Dublin Castle, including papers relating to the Rebellion of 1798, the Fenian movement of the 1860s, and crimes and convictions throughout the nineteenth century. The Transportation Records are of particular importance to Australians whose ancestors were transported from Ireland to Australia as convicts in the period 1788 to 1868. Microfilms and a computerised index of the most important records relating to transportation have been deposited in the Australian National Library in Canberra and copies of the microfilms are available at state libraries throughout Australia. Record collections include those relating to the employment of Resident magistrates and other local government officials. There are also excellent prison records.

The national Archives collections also comprise the records of the former Public Record Office of Ireland. This office suffered in 1922 during the Civil War and many of the records were destroyed. However, in many cases there are copies, transcripts, précis and indexes of this material. Many other records of genealogical and historical interest have been acquired since 1922.

Among other records which are available in the National Archives are the census returns of 1901 and 1911 (and nineteenth century census returns for the decades 1821 - 1851, if extant), which list all persons living in Ireland on the nights on which the census were compiled. There are also some eighteenth century census collections.

For the nineteenth century Griffith's Primary Valuation of Ireland of 1846 - 1863 lists all immediate house and land occupiers except those living in tenements. This is a return of the head of the family only. The Tithe Applotment Books of 1823 - 1837 list all those holding over one acre of (agricultural) land who were obliged to pay a tithe for the maintenance of the local Church of Ireland clergyman. This also is a return of the head of the family only. The Tithe Applotment Books are least satisfactory for urban areas. The census returns and the records of the Primary Valuation and of the Tithe Applotment are available in microform and there are comprehensive finding aids.

Wills, grants of probate, grants of administration, and schedules of assets survive for the twentieth century and are available for consultation if older than twenty years. Many of the records also survive for the nineteenth century and earlier - either in copy or precis form. Much of the testamentary material has been abstracted by professional genealogists in the period before 1922 or by the Commissioners for Charitable Donations and Bequests and is available for research. Some Inland Revenue returns of wills, grants of probate and grants of administration survive for the first half of the nineteenth century. The testamentary collection is a particularly rich and important source for genealogists. There are comprehensive finding aids to all these testamentary collections.

Records for the Church of Ireland survive in original, copy or extract form. The records in local custody have, in many instances, been copied on microfilm and are also available for research. There is a comprehensive finding-aid to all known surviving records.

Many other collections will also be of interest to the genealogist. These include the records of the National School system up to modern times (especially regarding the employment of National School teachers), admission registers to workhouses (where they survive), estate collections (including leases and tenants' agreements), Voters' registers (where they survive) and the records of local administration in Ireland throughout the nineteenth century.

The National Archives is open to the public, Monday to Friday from 10.00 a.m. to 5.00 p.m. Documents are not produced after 4.30 p.m. However, the reading room does not close over lunchtime. The office is closed for periods at Christmas and Easter and on Public Holidays. Staff are always available in the reading room to give advice and help researchers. There are comprehensive finding aids in the Reading Room and printed leaflets, which are updated regularly, are available to assist the researcher.

Bishop Street is easily accessible on foot from both St Stephen's Green and St Patrick's Cathedral.
From O'Connell Street via Trinity College - O'Connell Street O'Connell Bridge, Westmorland Street College Green (passing the Front Gate of Trinity College on your left), Grafton Street, St Stephen's Green West, Cuffe Street Kevin Street Lower, Bride Street Bishop Street (West end).
From the Four Courts via St Patrick's Cathedral - Inns Quay, O'Donovan Rossa Bridge, Winetavern Street (passing under the arch of Christ Church),Nicholas Street, Patrick Street (passing St Patrick's Cathedral on your left) Kevin Street Upper, Bishop Street (West end).
From the National Library and Genealogical Office - Kildare Street, St Stephen's Green North, St Stephen's Green West, Cuffe Street, Kevin Street Lower, Bride Street, Bishop Street (West end).
From the General Register Office -
Either Lombard Street East, Pearse Street, College Street and get the number 83 or 155 bus. - Or, Lombard Street East, Westland Row, Lincoln Place, Leinster Street, Kildare Street and continue walking as from the National Library.

The best bus routes from the City Centre to Bishop Street are the number 83 to Kimmage and the number 155 to Greenhills Get of at the stop on Redmond's Hill cross the road at the next traffic lights, walk along Kevin Street Lower, turn right onto Bride Street and almost immediately again onto Bishop Street and cross the street . The National Archives is the building in front of you as you cross Bishop Street.

The Church Of Ireland ~
Genealogy and Family History

The archives of the Church of Ireland, and particularly parochial registers of baptisms, marriages, and burials, are a primary source for genealogists and family historians. Although many registers were destroyed in the past, especially in the fire in the Public Record Office of Ireland in 1922, many others have survived in a number of custodies and are available to researchers.

Survival of Parish Registers
Almost half of the surviving registers were destroyed in 1922 and others have been lost at earlier periods. However, much of the lost information survives in transcripts and abstracts. The most recent published listing of parish registers is Noel Reid (ed) A table of Church of Ireland parochial records and copies (Irish Family History Society, Naas, 1994). In addition useful genealogical information may be had from other parish records especially vestry minute books, churchwardens' account books and cess applotment books.

Location of Parish Records
The Representative Church Body Library is the Church of Ireland's principal repository for its archives and manuscripts, and holds records from some 600 parishes in the Republic of Ireland. Records from a small number of parishes in the Republic are in the National Archives, and the remainder are in the custody of local clergy.

In Northern Ireland most parish registers are available in copy form in the Public Record Office of Northern Ireland (PRONI), while original parish records are either in the custody of the local clergy or in PRONI.

Names and addresses of local clergy may be had from the Church of Ireland Directory, published annually, which is available from the Religious Education Resource Centre, Holy Trinity Church, Church Avenue, Rathmines, Dublin 6 and the APCK Bookcentres at 61 Donegal Street, Belfast, BT1 2QH and St Ann's Church, Dawson Street, Dublin 2.

Access to Parish Records
Access to records in the RCB Library, National Archives and PRONI is straightforward but it is mutually beneficial if potential researchers contact the repository in advance to check on opening hours and conditions of admittance. However, repositories will not usually undertake genealogical research on behalf of enquirers.

Records in the custody of local clergy may be more difficult to see and the following procedure is recommended:
1. Write to the clergyman detailing the information which you need and ask if he will perform a search. If the clergyman agrees to perform a search there will be a fee of £5 per hour and it would be prudent to offer some payment in advance.

2. Clergy are not required to conduct searches on behalf of researchers, but they are required to make the registers available to researchers or their agents: this is a statutory requirement under the terms of the Constitution of the Church of Ireland, and relevant national archives and public records legislation in the Republic of Ireland and Northern Ireland.

If you are making the search yourself you should write to the clergyman to make an appointment and confirm that appointment by telephone before travelling. However, many clergy work alone and occasionally pastoral emergencies may cause the last minute cancellation of your appointment.The clergy are required to supervise your search and there is a fee of £5 per hour for this activity.

Reprography
Certified copies of entries in parish registers can be issued by local clergy or by the certifying officers in the repositories. Certified copies of entries of all baptisms and burials and marriages before 1845 cost £5 each. The cost of copies from civil marriage registers from 1845 is set by the respective governments and varies from time to time. Photocopying of parish records is forbidden on all occasions. Photography from parish records may only be undertaken with the written permission of the owner of the copyright. Further information on copyright matters may be had from the RCB Library.

Christ Church, Kilbrogan, Bandon, Cork, Ireland
now Bandon Heritage Centre
© Robert Blatchford 1994

Preparing for Searches
Most Church of Ireland parish registers do not have indexes and there is no single comprehensive index to all their contents. In general, in order to prosecute a successful search in parish registers you need a name, a date and a place name. However, there are a number of ongoing projects to index genealogical material on a county basis and some of these projects have included Church of Ireland records: details may be had from the Irish Family History Society.

The following publications and agencies can help with your preparations:
* Donal Begley (ed) Irish genealogy. A record finder (Heraldic Artists, Dublin, 1981)
* John Grenham Tracing your Irish ancestors (Gill & Macmillan, Dublin, 1992)
* Maire Mac Conghail & Paul Gorry Tracing Irish ancestors (Harper Collins, Glasgow, 1997)
* Brian Mitchell A new genealogical atlas of Ireland (Genealogical Publishing Co, Baltimore, 1988)
* Raymond Refaussé Handlist of Church of Ireland parish registers in the Representative Church Body Library (copies of this list, which is updated regularly, are available from the RCB Library at IR£2.50 including postage)
* Association of Professional Genealogists, c/o Genealogical Office, 2 Kildare Street, Dublin 2
* Irish Family History Society, PO Box 36, Naas, Co Kildare
* Irish Genealogical Research Society, The Irish Club, 82 Eaton Square, London SW1W 9AL
* National Archives, Bishop Street, Dublin 8
* Public Record Office of Northern Ireland, 66 Balmoral Avenue, Belfast, BT9 6NY
* Ulster Historical Foundation, Balmoral Buildings, 12 College Square East, Belfast, BT1 6DD

It may be helpful to visit the Directory of Irish Websites at http://doras.eircom.net/ and search for sites using the keyword "genealogy".

Other Genealogical Sources in the RCB Library
Apart from Church of Ireland archives, the RCB Library holds a number of collections with obvious attraction to genealogists. Among the more important are the biographical succession lists of Church of Ireland clergy, compiled by J B Leslie; collections of copy wills; extracts from the destroyed 1766 religious census; and collections of pedigrees.

New Book on Church of Ireland Records

One of the more remarkable of phenomena in Irish historiography in recent years has been the upsurge in interest in local history. Often this is spontaneous and arises from the curiosity of people who have moved to a new locality, but increasingly it is structured either through local historical societies or in schools, colleges and universities.

Central to most local historical endeavours in Ireland is the Church, which is the only institution to have survived from the earliest times to the present day. Its longevity combined with its sustained presence in almost every corner of the country suggests that it is, or has been, the most profound influence on the development of Irish society.

The Church of Ireland as the lineal descendant, legally at least, of the Church in Ireland following the Reformation, and, subsequently as the established Church until the late nineteenth century, has inherited responsibility for many of the sources which are fundamental to Irish local history. Records of parishes, dioceses and cathedrals, church buildings and graveyards, memorials in stone, glass and silver contain much valuable information not only about local Church of Ireland people but also the wider communities in which they lived and worked.

In order to make such resources better known a new series of guides entitled "Maynooth Research Guides for Irish Local History" is being developed under the general editorship of Dr Mary Anne Lyons from the history department of St Patrick's College, Drumcondra. The first guide in this series Church of Ireland Records, which has been written by the Librarian and Archivist of the Church of Ireland, Dr Raymond Refaussé, has just appeared.

Church of Ireland Records offers an introduction to the archives and manuscripts of the Church of Ireland and to the administrative structures which produced these records. Access

The National Library of Ireland derives its origins from the Library of the Royal Dublin Society, founded in 1731. In 1877 a substantial portion of the Royal Dublin Society library was purchased by the State and the new National Library of Ireland was established.

Situated in Kildare Street, Dublin, the Library aims to collect, preserve and make accessible materials on or relating to Ireland, whether published in Ireland or abroad, together with a supporting reference collection. The Library's current collection of some six million items constitutes probably the most outstanding collection of Irish documentary material in the world, an invaluable representation of Irish history and heritage. Books, serial publications, newspapers, manuscripts, maps, photographs, official publications, prints, drawings and ephemera make up the bulk of the collections.

The National Library has long been one of the key centres for family history research in Ireland. In recognition of this the Library's Genealogy Service - an expert service staffed by a panel of professional genealogists, together with experienced Library staff - is designed with the specific needs of family history researchers in mind. The Service, which is freely available to all visitors to the Library, offers the opportunity to consult with expert researchers who will advise on specific records and research procedure. Visitors to the Genealogy Service are offered expert advice on their research together with access to reference material and finding aids. Information

to the records, both intellectually and physically, is discussed, as are problems of interpretation. Church of Ireland Records is published by Irish Academic Press at IR£9.95 and is available through bookshops.

The staff of the RCB Library will be glad to offer advice on all queries concerning Church of Ireland archives and manuscripts and related printed and reference works. It should be stressed, however, that they will not undertake genealogical research on behalf of readers.

St Peter's Church, Ballymodan, Bandon, Cork, Ireland
©Robert Blatchford 1994

If you have any queries, please contact the RCB Library library@ireland.anglican.org - in the first instance.

National Library of Ireland
Colette O'Flaherty

leaflets, including a series on family history research in the Library, are readily available.

While the Genealogy Service is of particular value to first-time researchers, the Library also encourages more experienced family history researchers to continue to use the facilities for next-step advice from the genealogists and Library staff there.

The records most used by family history researchers in the National Library fall under the following headings:

(a) Parish Records
For most family history researchers parish registers are the earliest direct source of family information, providing clear evidence of links between one generation and another (via baptismal registers) and one family and another (via marriage registers). They are particularly important for any information they provide for the period before the commencement of civil or State registration of all births, marriages and deaths in 1864.

The National Library holds microfilm copies of almost all Roman Catholic parish registers up to circa 1880. Most of the registers begin in the period 1810-1830 but some - particularly in counties along the western seaboard - begin somewhat later. In a number of counties in the province of Leinster registers begin in the 1780-1790s, while in the cities the start dates may be as early as 1760. In the case of three dioceses - Kerry, Limerick and Cashel and Emly - formal written permission to consult registers must be obtained in advance from the relevant diocese. Contact addresses and telephone numbers for these dioceses are listed in National Library Family History leaflet no. 2 (Parish registers), a copy of which may be obtained from the Library.

The Library's parish register microfilming programme is ongoing, with gaps in the collection being steadily reduced. A comprehensive listing, by diocese, of the Library's holdings may be consulted in the Genealogy Service and in the main

Reading Room.

(b) 19th Century Valuation Records
The Library holds copies of Griffith's Valuation (on microfiche) and of the Tithe Applotment Books (on microfilm). A CD-ROM index to Griffith's Valuation is also available for consultation.

The county by county Index of Surnames, a listing of the surnames recorded in Griffith's Valuation and the Tithe Books, continues to be a much-used source. The Index of Surnames acts as a valuable aid to pinpointing relevant parishes and parish records, and to understanding the distribution of particular surnames in parishes throughout the country.

(c) Trade and Social Directories
The National Library has extensive holdings of Dublin, provincial and countrywide trade and social directories. The first of the Dublin directories dates from 1751. Dublin directories, which steadily expanded in scope over the years, continue in publication up to the present time. While the earliest of the provincial directories - Ferrar's Directory of Limerick - dates from 1769, the nineteenth century saw the widespread publication of such directories. The nineteenth-century also saw the publication of countrywide directories such as Pigot's Commercial Directory of Ireland (1820 and 1824) and Slater's Directories (1846, 1856, 1870, 1881 and 1894), all of which may be consulted in the Library.

(d) Newspapers
The National Library has the largest newspaper collection in Ireland, with complete files of many local as well as national newspapers. In newspapers, the bulk of information relevant to genealogical research occurs in the form of advertisements and biographical notices (of birth, death or marriage). As there are few indexes available, relevant family information can be difficult to locate. As with the trade and social directories, newspaper information tends to be exclusive of the majority of the population: most births, marriages and deaths went unannounced and daily life continued without advertisement or report. Nonetheless, while direct family information may not be available, newspapers are rich in context and provide a sense of the community and times in which particular ancestors lived.

A comprehensive listing of Irish newspapers, including the National Library's holdings, may be found in the publication NEWSPLAN - Report of the NEWSPLAN Project in Ireland (Revised edition, 1998. Edited by Sara Smyth). The Report includes a town and county index of places of publication, subdivided chronologically. The updated NEWSPLAN database may be consulted on the National Library of Ireland website.

(e) Manuscripts Records
The main components of the Library's manuscripts collections are Gaelic manuscripts, landed estates archives, maps, political material and literary papers. Of these, it is the archives of the former landed estates that are of particular interest to family history researchers. Among the more notable of these archives held by the Library are Castletown (Co. Laois), Clements (Cos. Leitrim and Donegal), Clonbrock (Co. Galway), Coolattin (Co. Wicklow), De Vesci (Co. Laois), Doneraile (Co. Cork), Headford (Co. Meath), Inchiquin (Co. Clare), Lismore (Co. Waterford), Monteagle (Co. Limerick), O'Hara (Co. Sligo), Ormond (Cos. Tipperary and Kilkenny), Powerscourt (Co. Wicklow), Prior-Wandesforde (Co. Kilkenny), Sarsfield (Co. Cork) and Wicklow (Co. Wicklow). Estate archives contain the records of the administration of estates by landlords and their agents, and generally include leases, rentals, accounts, correspondence and maps, mostly dating from the eighteenth and nineteenth centuries.

Also of interest to family history researchers in the Department of Manuscripts are a number of collections of wills and will abstracts.

Information on Department of Manuscripts catalogues and guides is readily available from the National Library. For those intent on searching for relevant estate material, the expert advice from the Library's Genealogy Service will be of assistance in pinpointing who the relevant landowner might have been.

(f) Maps
The Library's map collections comprise some 150,000 maps and include cartographic materials ranging from a 12th century coloured sketch map of Europe to the most recent Ordnance Survey maps. Special collections include the Down Survey maps (18th century copies of 17th century originals), 18th century estate maps - including the collection of surveyors Brownrigg, Longfield and Murray, maps commissioned by the County Grand Juries (late 18th -19th century) and Ordnance Survey maps (1830s onwards).

Both printed and manuscript maps are listed in a card catalogue. Manuscripts maps are also listed in the various manuscripts catalogues.

(g) Other Sources
Other sources regularly consulted by family history researchers in the National Library include many printed family histories, often compiled and published for private circulation by individuals who have researched their own family history. It should also be noted that publications of local history societies from around the country often contain valuable transcripts of local sources, including gravestone inscriptions, freeholders lists, etc. Other relevant material in the Library's collections include the annual printed Army Lists, Navy Lists, Royal Irish Constabulary (RIC) publications including the annual RIC Directories, the 1796 Spinning Wheel Premium Entitlement List (microfiche) and various other records of trades and professions, as well as a comprehensive series of Registers of Electors. Also, as research progresses, the appendices to nineteenth-century Parliamentary reports may prove useful.

The Library's photographic collections - held at the National Photographic Archive in Meeting House Square, Dublin 2 - may also be of interest. Collections acquired from various commercial photographic studios such as Poole (Waterford and surrounding counties) and Wynne (Castlebar) include studio portraits and an unparalleled collection of topographical images of Ireland.

There are comprehensive finding aids to Library collections available in the Library Reading Rooms. Regularly updated information leaflets - with information on various Library collections and services - are readily available.

Exhibitions and publications: Exhibitions are held in both the main Library building and in the National Photographic Archive. The Library publishes a wide range of materials including books and guides, reports, booklets, document facsimile folders, CD-ROMS, calendars and postcards. These are available in the Library shop.

Admission to the National Library of Ireland: For Genealogy (microfilms) and Newspaper research, passes - which may be obtained in the main Library building - are required. Other readers must apply for a Readers Ticket (for which proof of identity and two passport photos are necessary). To view manuscripts, a separate Manuscripts Readers Ticket, issued by the Duty Librarian, is required.

The Readers Ticket Office is open during the following hours: Mon-Wed 1000-1230, 1400-1700; Thu-Fri 1000-1230, 1400-1630; Sat 1000-1230).
Library Opening Hours:
Main Reading Room/ Microform Reading Room Mon-Wed 1000-2100 Thu-Fri 1000-1700 Sat 1000-1300
Manuscripts Reading Room
Mon-Wed 1000-2030 Thu-Fri 1000-1630 Sat 1000-1230
National Photographic Archive Reading Room
Mon-Fri 1000-1700
Contact details:
National Library of Ireland, Kildare Street, Dublin 2
Tel: +353-1-6030 200 Fax: +353-1-6766 690
Email: info@nli.ie Internet: http://www.nli.ie/

Irish Militia and Yeomanry Records

Kyle J. Betit and Simon Fowler

Militia Records of the Seventeenth Century
In the early 1600s Ulster was "planted" with Protestant settlers from Scotland and England. The 'undertakers' granted land in the Plantation were required to muster their Protestant tenants for inspection by the Muster Master General who recorded the names and ages of the tenants and the types of arms they bore. All Protestant males between the ages of 16 and 60 were liable to service in the militia. Copies of the seventeenth century Ulster militia records survive at the Public Record Office of Northern Ireland (PRONI). They list the undertakers, and sometimes divide the lists of tenants by parish or by barony. For more information, visit the PRONI's web site http://proni.nics.gov.uk/records/militia.htm.

Militia lists of the Eighteenth Century
Lists of men who were serving in 1761 in Cos Cork, P Derry, Donegal, Down, Dublin, Kerry, Limerick, Louth, Monaghan, Roscommon, Tyrone, Wicklow are with the Genealogical Office in Dublin. For details visit http://scripts.ireland.com/ancestor/browse/records/occupation/army.htm.

Militia Records 1793-1925
The Irish militia was reestablished in 1793 with

thirty-seven county or city battalions or regiments. During the period 1793-1816 the Irish militia was quite active. Militia units moved around Ireland, to England and other localities. If it is found that an ancestor or an ancestor's relative was born in a different county or country from the rest of the family, membership in a militia unit is one possible explanation.

If there is a "legend" of military service in the family, it may be that the ancestor served in the Irish militia rather than in a regular British Army unit. An ancestor may also have served in both.

Various militia records of the county and city militia, 1759-1925 are found in the WO 68 series at the PRO. This series is available on microfilm at the Family History Library in Salt Lake City, which can be ordered via LDS Church family history centres around the world. For information about soldiers, the Enrollment and Description Books in WO 68 are useful. They usually provide the soldier's place of birth (such as a parish or town within the county), age, date and place of attestation, service record, and other data. Some of the books go back to 1793, but others begin later depending on the county. The "Enrollment and Description Books" are in chronological order. The "Record of Officers Services" volumes provide extensive information on each officer including date and place of birth and detailed data on marriage and children.

Muster books and pay lists of the Irish yeomanry units between 1823 and 1834, and the Irish militia units are in WO 13 at the PRO. The Militia Attestation Papers (1806-1915) (WO 96) were filed at recruitment but also in most cases give the date of discharge, as well as date and place of birth. They are arranged in the order of precedence of the regular army unit to which a militia regiment was attached after the Army's reorganization in 1881. An example of a typical document can be found on this web site; www.jenlibrary.u-net.com/irish.htm

Militia soldier's documents, 1760-1872 (WO 97/1091-1112) are for soldiers discharged to pension. They are arranged in surname alphabetical order regardless of unit and give birth place, age at enlistment, and service data. The militia soldier's documents are also available on microfilm from the Family History Library (FHL).

Yeomanry Corps Records 1796-1834
The Irish yeomanry corps originated in 1796 as a civilian volunteer defense force to augment the regular army and militia. The yeomen were

primarily Protestant, although there were Catholic members. The yeomanry were expected to drill two days a week and could be called out to suppress public disorders and assist the regular army in case of invasion or insurrection. The yeomanry was officially disbanded in 1834.

Some records survive of individual yeomanry corps. The PRO has quarterly muster returns of various yeomanry companies in Ireland, 1823-1834 in WO 13. Some collections of records for specific localities in Ireland survive in various repositories. For example, there are nominal rolls in the Roscrea Yeomanry Papers, 1798-1821, at the National Archives in Dublin.

Armagh County Museum has typescript copies of lists of the officers of the yeomanry in Ireland for 1797, 1804, 1820, and 1825. The first was compiled by Dublin Castle, while the others were compiled by the War Office in London. The officers' dates of commission are given. The 1797 list is indexed while the later three are not. The lists are also available at the FHL. The Museum also has a "Description Book" of the Seagoe Yeomanry Corps, 1831-1855, giving a roll of men in alphabetical order from 1831 to c1855 with observations regarding transfers and deaths. Again this is also available from the FHL.

Addresses
Armagh County Museum: The Mall East, Armagh BT61 9BE, Northern Ireland; Tel: (028) 3752 3070. www.ulstermuseum.org.uk/armagh/
Family History Library: 35 North West Temple, Salt Lake City, UT 84150 USA; British Reference Tel: (801) 240-2367
www.familysearch.org/Eng/Library/
Genealogical Office of Ireland, Office of the Chief Herald, National Library of Ireland, Kildare St, Dublin 2, tel (01) 6030311, www.nli.ie/fr_offi.htm.
Public Record Office: Ruskin Avenue, Kew, Surrey TW9 4DU, England; Tel: (020) 8392 5200 www.pro.gov.uk A usefulgeneral leaflet on Irish genealogy can be downloaded from
http://scripts.ireland.com/ancestor/browse/records/occupation/army.htm

Public Record Office of Northern Ireland: 66 Balmoral Avenue, Belfast BT9 6NY, Northern Ireland; Tel: (028) 9025 5905
http://proni.nics.gov.uk

Further Reading
Bartlett, Thomas and Keith Jeffery, eds. A Military History of Ireland. (Cambridge University Press, 1996)
Bevan, Amanda, Tracing Your Ancestors in the Public Record Office (6th edition, PRO, 2002)
Blackstock, Allan. "A Forgotten Army: The Irish Yeomanry," History Ireland 4 (4) (Winter 1996)
Blackstock, Allan. An Ascendancy Army: The Irish Yeomanry 1796-1834. (Four Courts Press, 1998).
Collins, Peter. "Militia, Yeomanry Lists and Muster Rolls," Pathways to Ulster's Past .(The Institute of Irish Studies, The Queen's University of Belfast, 1998).
Gibson, Jeremy and Mervyn Medlycott. Militia Lists and Musters 1757-1876: A Directory of Holdings in

the British Isles. (4th ed, Federation of Family History Societies, 2000).
Hamilton Edwards, Gerald. In Search of Army Ancestry (Phillimore & Co., Ltd., 1977)
Hayes-McCoy, G.A. Irish Battles: A Military History of Ireland. (2nd ed, The Appletree Press, Ltd., 1989)
Herber, Mark D. "Militia Records," Ancestral Trails: The Complete Guide to British Genealogy and Family History (Sutton Publishing Limited, 1997)
Spencer, William, Records of the Militia and Volunteer Forces 1757-1945 (PRO Publications, 1997)
Spencer, William. Army Records for Family Historians. (Public Record Office, 2000)
Watts, Michael J. and Christopher T. Watts. My Ancestor Was in the British Army How Can I Find Out More About Him? (Society of Genealogists, 1992)

Kyle J. Betit, BS is a professional genealogist, lecturer and author residing in Salt Lake City, Utah. He was a co-editor of the popular journal The Irish At Home and Abroad, and is co-author of the newly published resource, A Genealogist's Guide to Discovering Your Irish Ancestors. Simon Fowler is editor of Family History Monthly.

Bringing It All Back Home ~
Tracing Your Irish Ancestors Without Crossing the Water
Joseph O'Neill

If you are one of seventy million people with Irish ancestry, do not be surprised when the genealogical bug bites. Before you finish it will test your patience. You'll find yourself in some dead-ends. If your family names are common and your ancestors achieved little status your task may prove difficult. You will curse yourself for embarking on this task. But you cannot escape it - it is in your blood.

Brendan Behan claimed that the Irish obsession with their past almost amounts to a psychosis. Listen to any Irish family and before long you will hear them identifying people through a network of relationships. More than any other modern European people the Irish are instinctive genealogists.

This is excellent news for the novice, starting on the search for his forebears. For of all genealogical research begins not with dusty archives or computerized indexes but with living memories. Your first and most valuable resource is what your family remembers. All subsequent research rests on this foundation.

Begin by finding out everything you can about your family. But be wary. Even the loquacious grandmother who can describe in detail the dress she wore on the day of her First Holy Communion is fallible. We are all prey to family lore and no memory is unerring. So it is essential to record everything and always specify the source. Then you must check and double check and on each occasion note how this fits in with your original information.

What sort of information are you looking for? Start with yourself - on the well-established principle that

in genealogy you always work backwards from what is known to what you hope to discover. Begin by researching your own birth certificate. It will confirm your parents' names, including your mother's maiden name. This may prove useful in providing clues to nicknames or names used only within the family.

After that you should try to gather any documentation relating to your parents, grandparents and earlier generations. Generally, official documents - certificates of birth, marriage or death, grave papers, academic, technical or professional qualifications or material relating to pensions, state benefits, rationing or proof of identity - are the most reliable and are invaluable for fixing the dates of key events in a person's life.

Official documents are important but semi-official documents which can be as useful and more fascinating. Memorial cards, newspaper obituaries, club and trade union subscription records all help to place our ancestors in their social setting. To place them within the network of relationships which were central to their lives and personality, few things are more useful than personal documents. Reading through a person's military service record, family Bible, letters, scrapbooks and photograph albums bring to life the unique flesh and blood person only glimpsed through documents.

For each family member you should complete an entry in your records which includes the following information: name; date and place of birth, date and place of baptism; education and qualifications; details of marriage - date, spouse, minister and witnesses; children's names and those of their spouses; occupations, with dates; claims to fame and achievements; date, place and cause of death; date and place of burial and details of any will. For each piece of information, record the source.

Keep your information on loose pages that can be fitted into a file. This makes it easy to expand and rearrange the information without the need to rewrite. If you are familiar with IT, you will consider the value of the available resources. There is an extensive range of software, with programmes to suit the computer competence and requirements of every family historian. This edition of the Handbook contains many advertisements and the fifth edition has an excellent review of one of the most popular programmes, *The New Generation Version 8 UK* Software, by

M Portlock. Before that you should read, in the same edition, D Tippey's splendid piece, *Do I Really Need a Computer?* which deals with the whole area of IT and genealogy.

Keep an open mind and be prepared for alternative spellings of family names and nicknames. Do not assume that anything is absolutely certain and that anything that appears to contradict it must be wrong. Even official sources contain errors and serious omissions. Yesterday my wife noticed that her birth certificate - which she has used as proof of identity when applying for her passport, marriage certificate, grants and admission to college and profession bodies - is technically invalid as the registrar had neglected to sign it.

Now it is time to begin work on the archives. The good news is that because of developments over the last twenty years a great deal of research is possible without the need to travel to Ireland. The longer it is since your ancestors arrived in mainland Britain, the further you can go without leaving the country.

If your parents were married in this country, your first resource is the GRO (General Registry Office). It contains a complete index - organised alphabetically by surname, forenames and district - of all births, marriages and deaths. Your parents' marriage certificate should be relatively easy to find. It will provide the names of both your grandfathers. This information should help locate your parents' birth certificates. Besides providing a check on the names of your grandfathers, their birth certificates will also provide the names - including the maiden names - of your grandmothers. By proceeding next to each set of grandparents' marriage certificate, and then their birth certificates, you can work your way back through the generations, building up the outline of your family history.

Access to the GRO index is possible at many locations. The Office of National Statistics will tell you the most convenient location and once you've

traced the details they can provide a full copy certificate. Remember, however, that compulsory registration began in England only in 1837 - in 1855 in Scotland and 1864 in Ireland - and prior to that responsibility for record keeping fell to the parish.

For most people with Irish ancestry that means the Catholic parish. The problem here is that the Catholic church in England had no parish system before the Great War. They often held religious services in hired accommodation and they called chapels missions.

Successful missions generated records of births and marriages but frequently produced little on the deaths of members of their flocks. First Anglican and then municipal cemeteries provided the final resting place for most Catholics. Invaluable in helping to track down these records are two volumes by Michael Gandy. For placing these communities in their wider historical context see the books by Bernard Kelly and the many diocesan and mission histories.

It is possible that your ancestors may have left a will. Do not dismiss this as improbable simply because most Irish immigrants remained at the bottom of the social and economic ladder. It was not only the wealthy who took the precaution of leaving their affairs in order.

The administration of wills and the granting of probate has been the government's responsibility since 1858. Many large libraries contain an index and will be delighted to explain how you go about obtaining a copy.

Inevitably you will consult the census. Taken every ten years from 1801 - apart from 1941 - the 1841 records are the first to include information on individuals. The census covers every dwelling in the country and gives everyone's name, age, marital status, occupation, place of birth and relationship to the head of the household.

Remember, the hard work may have been done already. Many areas have indexes to the census, the work of industrious local family history societies. Contacting those functioning in your areas of interest and chatting with an active member may save you many hours of labourious searching. This Handbook contains a complete up-to-date listing.

At some stage you will hope to find the end of that thread that will lead you across the sea to your ancestors in Ireland. The more precise information you can get about their Irish origins the better.

Failing a documentary clue to their place of origin, you must rely entirely on family memory, or even family lore - that story about a granduncle in Killarney or the memory of a Christmas parcel from Ballinasloe containing a goose, innards replete with a bottle of colourless liquid. In the absence of this, you should make enquiries among the nearest Irish community.

Should all this fail, do not give up. Irish surnames are even today concentrated in certain provinces, counties and even towns. The frequency and distribution of names can be determined by consulting a number of indexes, the most accessible of which is that of the Church of Jesus Christ of Latter Day Saints - the Mormons.

It's worth, at this stage, finding out if a pedigree exists for the name you are researching. John O'Hara's book remains the best source for this information.

Hopefully, by now you will have established the part of Ireland from which your family hails. Working through contacts in the local family history society you may well contact someone researching the same name. Subscribing to at least one national magazine - Family History Monthly and Irish Roots are the best and the most relevant - may prove invaluable in making such contacts.

IRISH HOUSEKEEPING.

Bachelor. "MARY, I SHOULD LIKE THAT PIECE OF BACON I LEFT AT DINNER YESTERDAY."
Irish Servant. "IS IT THE BIT O' BHACON THIN? SHURE I TOOK IT TO LOIGHT THE FHOIRES!"

This should not be too difficult as Irish emigration to Britain has been common since the early nineteenth century. Over that period the steady flow of immigrants has occasionally swollen to a torrent - especially during the famine decade which began in 1845. Officially, all these people were technically British until 1921. Irish people in Britain immediately on arrival acquire the rights of British citizenship. In 1961 one-million people of Irish birth were living in Britain.

Given this it is hardly surprising that a great deal of relevant material can be found in Britain. Much of it is housed in the Public Record Office, the UK national archive, which stores the records of the government and law courts activities for nine centuries. Their electronic catalogue is available on the web togther with many excellent guides. Irish Genealogy (Overseas records Information 9) is perhaps the most helpful.

Kew has many military records. This is important because the British army has played a large part in Irish life. Irishmen were well represented in every colonial army and the Fenians boasted that most men in all the major garrisons in British were sworn to the cause of Irish freedom - when the Empire was at its height. A higher proportion of Irishmen - 35,000 - died in the Great War than any other nationality on the Allied side.

Though Irishmen joined every regiment there were many specifically Irish ones and before the Great War they recruited primarily from within their own locality. But before you begin your search you need to be clear about the differences between officers, NCOs and other ranks.

The vast majority of servicemen were 'other ranks' -

ordinary soldiers. They list only officers in the Army, Navy and Air Force Lists. The former started in 1740 and lists every officer in the army while from 1839 - 1915 Hart's Army List provides an outline biography of some officers. Correspondence about the purchase of commissions in Irish regiments for 1768-1877 is held in HO123.

For other ranks before 1880, knowing the relevant regiment is useful. File WO97 contains the records of men granted a pension between 1760 and 1913 and provides details of enlistment and service, disciplinary record and the circumstances of discharge. Often they include details of immediate family living with the soldier on his service.

Muster rolls - which were compiled monthly and list every man in the regiment - also provide detail of individuals for the period 1732 to 1898.

Militia muster rolls for 1793 - 1876 are available as are musters of Volunteers for 1797 - 1814 and 1873-8. These are conveniently filed by county and contain an alphabetical list of names and details of age and parish.

The RAF and the Royal Navy make no distinction between Irish recruits and others.

Details of those who have fallen in wars since 1914 are the responsibility of the Commonwealth War Graves Commission. You can access its electronic index at http://www.cwgc.org. For each man listed it gives the location of his grave, his unit and the date on which he died. Every Irishman who lost his life during the Great War is listed on 'Ireland's Memorial Records, 1914-18', available at the Society of Genealogists. The corresponding records for the Second World War are also available at the

PRO and the Society of Genealogists libraries.

If the armed services were not the means by which your ancestor left Ireland then you may find it difficult to trace their route. Unfortunately, the best records are likely to be found in the country of destination or the Public Record Office of Northern Ireland. The PRO's records are limited as there was little incentive for the British government to record details of emigrants. Emigrants to North America during the 1773-6 period and those transported to Australia between 1788 and 1867 are listed at Kew. The National Archives of Ireland website lists all those transported from Ireland.

Passenger lists for those emigrating beyond Europe between 1890 and 1960 give emigrants' personal details, including their previous address. The only problem is that they are arranged by year and port of departure.

Almost daily more passenger lists of ships arriving in the USA are being published. The American Immigrant Ship Transportation Guild (www.istg.rootsweb.com), the National Archives of Canada (www.archives.ca) the National Archives and Records Administration USA (www.nara.gov), the National Archives of New Zealand (www.archives.govt.nz) and the National Archives of Australia all have information on Irish emigrants arriving in their country.

Among the most interesting records held by the PRO are ones which include detailed descriptions of the physical appearance and even photographs of individuals. Though these are a family historian's dream, you will hope they do not refer to your ancestors. For these are the registers of habitual drunkards, 1903-1914 (MEPO6) and habitual criminals, 1867-1940 (PCOM2 and MEPO6).

Dealing with criminals and drunkards in Ireland was, from 1836 to 1922, the responsibility of the RIC - the Royal Irish Constabulary. The service records of the 85,000 men who served are in HO184. You may access and search this information on the net.

The Family Records Centre in London provides an invaluable resource for the family historian. It has a useful site. It has indexes to all the major sources including the censuses for England and Wales and a large collection of reference books, indexes and maps.

You will also find there the records of men who served in the armed forces and census material. The 1901 census is available online.

Apart from its collection of records the library of the Society of Genealogists also has a host of finding aids, many of which are to be found nowhere else. Their website describes the services they offer.

The Family History Centres are the work of the Mormons and provide the most convenient access to a range of useful indexes and records. The most convenient way to find your nearest Centre is to consult their website.

Another invaluable resource is the British Library. Among other things it holds some Irish electoral registers. But perhaps one of their most valuable sources is a copy of Griffiths or the Primary Valuation. This inventory was an early rates system. It dates from the 1830s and shows the names of occupiers of land and buildings, the person from whom the land was leased, the amount of property held and its estimated value. It has a parish index.

By now you should have a full outline of recent generations of your family. You can pursue your research through the genealogical websites listed

IN THE EMERALD ISLE.

Impatient Traveller. "NOW, THEN, IS THIS TRAP READY? WHERE'S THE OSTLER?"
Small Boy. "SHURE, OI'LL P-HUT 'M OP FOR YE, SOR. THE OTHER *MAN'S* GONE IV A ARRAND!!"

below. These provide the best preparation for the next major step - researching in Ireland.

Resources referred to:
Michael Gandy, Catholic Missions and Registers, 1700-1880
The Public Records Office, Kew, Richmond, Surrey TW9 4DU; website: http://www.pro.gov.uk
The Office of National Statistics , Smedley Hydro, Trafalgar Road, Birkdale, Southport, Merseyside, PR8 2HH.
John O'Hara, Irish Pedigree, 1892 edition reissued by the Genealogical Publishing Company
The RIC Service Records www.esatclear.ie/~ric/.
The British Library, St Pancras, 96, Euston Road, LondonNW12DB www.bl.uk/
The Family Records Centre www.pro.gov.uk/frc/

The Society of Genealogists www.sog.org.uk/
The Mormons (Society of Latter Day Saints of Jesus Christ) LDS.www.org.uk
National Archives of Ireland
http://www.nationalarchives.ie
Cindy's List - provides links to 60,000 genealogical sites - http://www.cyndilist.com'
The Irish Family History Foundation with links to local research centres in Ireland - http://www.mayo-ireland.ie/general
Irish Family History Society - http://homepage.eircom.net/-ifhs
The Local Ireland Genealogy pages - http://www.local.ie/genealogy
The Ulster Historical Foundation - http://www.ancestryireland.com

Wills and What to do with them

Stuart A Raymond

There are millions of wills and other probate records dating from the sixteenth to the eighteenth centuries in the record offices of England and Wales. This is an enormous resource for genealogists and local historians, and offers considerable scope for research on a wide variety of topics, for example, inheritance, wealth, furniture, charitable giving, literacy, credit, etc., etc. The information they contain is extensive, and provides invaluable evidence for everyone interested in studying what it was like to be alive several centuries ago.

Wills and other probate records originated at a major stage in the process of inheritance. They do not, however, represent the only stage. This can be clearly seen by considering who made wills, and why they were written. Mostly, testators had sons who still needed to be established on a farm or in some trade; or had daughters who were unmarried. They had wives or young children to provide for. The process of dividing an estate between children frequently began with their marriages, and only ended with the death of the widow. Hence, if we look at wills alone, they provide a misleading picture of what each son or daughter received. Indeed, testators frequently excused a bequest of a few pence to a child on the grounds that they had already established them on a farm, or provided a dowry.

Wills alone cannot be relied on to tell us how the process of inheritance worked. Usually, they do not even mention freehold property. They can, however, be relied on for genealogical information. Seventeenth-century wills normally do mention all surviving children, even if they only receive token bequests. Wives and minors occupy a prominent position in most wills: they had not previously been provided for. An examination of 61 seventeenth-century wills of married men from Week St. Mary,

Cornwall, reveals that no less than 34 named their widows as sole executrixes, whilst a further 9 widows shared the task with their sons. Eldest sons were not named as executors unless they were only sons. The law of primogeniture ensured that the eldest son was provided for: wills were for the benefit of widows and younger children, and it was consequently they who looked after the administration of estates.

Most testators made their wills when they knew death to be imminent. Very few were made in advance, unless the testator was about to undertake some hazardous task such as going on a long journey. If you were reasonably fit, you did not make a will. As soon as it became evident that death was close, neighbours and friends would be brought to the deathbed to witness the will. Sometimes, it would be written by the testator himself, if he were fit enough to do so. Otherwise a neighbour would undertake the task. In Week St. Mary there were a number of people who regularly wrote wills; some may have been paid to do so. One of the most prolific was Cornelius Clifton who wrote no less than 14 probate documents in the parish, and probably more in neighbouring parishes. Clifton came from a family of minor attornies; an uncle had resided at Lyon's Inn, one of the inns of Chancery, where lawyers were trained; a cousin was clerk to one of the Six Clerks of the Court of Chancery; a nephew was serving his clerkship as an attorney at the end of the seventeenth century. There were some four or five scribes like Clifton in the parish during the century. If you have an interest in the history of the legal profession at grass-roots level, then the evidence of wills is important.

Semi-professional scribes did not, however, write all the probate documents for Week St. Mary. An examination of the hand-writing of 238 documents reveals that they were written by no less than 145 different people. That is important evidence for wide-spread literacy in a parish which had a population of c.400. Another way in which these documents can be used to study literacy is by analysing the signatures of witnesses. Did they sign, or merely make their mark? Those who signed had at least a smattering of literacy; those who did not were illiterate. This method does not, it should be noted, work as well in studying testators signatures: even if they were literate, they were on their death beds, and would frequently have been too feeble to do more than make their mark.

Occasionally, there was not time for a scribe to write a will before death. Nevertheless, the testator could speak his will in the presence of witnesses,

who could testify to its accuracy when it was written down after death. Such wills are termed nuncupative,.

Wills normally begin with the invocation of the deity, and a statement of the testators state of health: he is usually weak of body but of good and perfect remembrance,, or similar wording. This is followed by the bequest of the soul, sometimes a request for burial in a particular place, then the legacies, and finally the naming of the executor and residual legatee - normally the same person.

The bequest of the soul is of great interest to ecclesiastical historians, especially in the sixteenth century. If references to the Virgin Mary are included, the testator may be presumed a Roman Catholic; if the elect and predestination are mentioned, Protestant tendencies may be assumed. A count of the wills using these terms during the reformation period will show how quickly Protestant doctrines spread - although it is necessary to add the caveat that the doctrines expressed in wills may have been those held by scribes or local clergy, rather than those of testators themselves.

The request for burial in a particular place does not usually tell us much; mostly burial in the local church or churchyard is specified. However, if a different place is mentioned, it may indicate a different place of origin; such information could be useful to the genealogist.

Legacies often begin with charitable donations. Wills are a prime source for the history of charitable giving, and have been used extensively for that purpose. Such legacies may also reveal information about religious commitment. The origin of the practice of making wills was religious in character; they were a means by which the church ensured that it received alms from its sons at death. That is why probate jurisdiction was exercised by the church. But in seventeenth-century Week St. Mary, bequests to the church slumped dramatically. There were twelve bequests to the church before 1641, but none after 1662. Giving to the poor also fell. In the first two decades of the century, 55% of testators left small sums to the poor; in the last two decades the figure was 12%, despite the fact that testators were much wealthier at the end of the century than they had been at its beginning.

Most legacies were made to kin - usually to wives and children - for the reasons already given. From the testators point of view, wills were simply a means of ensuring that, as far as possible, his children were provided for.

Once the will had been written, and the testator died, the executor took the will to the relevant probate court. If there was no will, the next of kin applied for letters of administration. The structure of probate jurisdiction was extremely complicated; however, Gibson & Churchill provide the details needed to begin the task of locating particular wills. There are, incidentally, innumerable published indexes to probate records. In order to prove the will, the executor needed two or more people who could praise, i.e. value the descendants goods and chattels, and compile a probate inventory. Vast collections of inventories are

available; sometimes these are filed with wills, sometimes not. Where they are not, it may prove difficult to locate both will and inventory. For example, the Public Record Office holds the probate records of the Prerogative Court of Canterbury. It holds far more wills than inventories; most of the latter have disappeared.

Probate inventories are invaluable sources of information on the material conditions of life of our ancestors. They enable us to answer many of the basic questions about ordinary life several hundred years ago. What were the conditions in which men worked, ate and slept? What were their houses like? How much money did they keep in the house? How wealthy were they? What occupations did they follow? What furniture did they own? All these questions can be answered, at least partially, from probate inventories.

Inventories are basically lists of goods and their market values. Their preamble give the name of the deceased, sometimes his status or occupation, and his residence. The status or occupation given in a will should be compared with that given in the inventory. The will tells us what a testator thought of himself; the inventory tells us what his neighbours thought. The two are not always the same, and any differences may be significant. A man who described himself as a gentleman, and was described by his neighbours as a yeoman, or even a husbandman, clearly had an inflated view of his status in his neighbours' opinions. Sometimes a will provides a man's status e.g. gent., esquire, etc., and the inventory provides the additional information that he was a butcher or baker. A collection of probate records for a particular parish enables us to construct a picture of that parish's social and occupational structure.

The main body of the inventory is a list of goods owned by the deceased, with their values. These values are usually totalled, but the totals need to be checked, since seventeenth-century arithmetic is often suspect, especially when Roman numerals were used. Not everything was included; the most significant exclusion was land. Freehold property was excluded, although leases were listed. Consequently inventories are not fully representative of total wealth. Nevertheless, probate inventories do enable the historian to study the social and geographical distribution of wealth, and to trace its growth and decline. Week St. Mary was one of the poorest parishes in a poverty stricken area - but the disparity between the poorest and the wealthiest inhabitant was very much less than it was in the much wealthier areas of the South East. None of the inventories reveal really wealthy inhabitants in Week St. Mary, Conversely, there were few local people who were paupers. The poverty of the soil, and the remoteness of the parish, meant that people shared more equally in such wealth as there was.

It is also noticeable that wealth increased dramatically in the last quarter of the seventeenth century. A much higher percentage of inventories record values in excess of £100 after 1675 than was the case earlier in the century. This growth of wealth was followed by an increasing interest in material comfort. The seventeenth century house was bare by modern standards. Most people had very little furniture. The only item almost everyone possessed was a bed, and it is probable that even that was a recent innovation. In the sixteenth century, people slept on the floor, perhaps on some straw, with a blanket if they were lucky. If the value placed on beds is any guide then they became much more comfortable after the 1670s. There were far less people owning tables, and even fewer with any type of seating: presumably the floor served as a seat. Again, the number of tables and chairs recorded in inventories increased dramatically from the 1670s. The inventories also provide much information about kitchen and fireside utensils, cupboards and chests, lighting and heating.

In most parts of England, probate inventories also provide much information on housing. Praisors often listed goods room by room, and divided up the inventory accordingly, thus identifying the kitchen, the parlour, the hall, the chamber, etc., with some indication of the use of each room. This evidence enables us to see that houses were designed for work, eating, and sleeping. They were emphatically not designed for relaxation or recreation.

Work in seventeenth century Week St. Mary primarily meant agriculture, although the parish also had its rector, its blacksmith, its attorney, and other occupations. And everyone spun wool, as can be seen from the number of wool turns, i.e. spinning wheels,

mentioned in inventories. The latter show that c.80% of agricultural investment was in livestock. Poor soils meant little arable farming. The major investment was in cattle, for both beef and milk. Most people also had a pig; sides of bacon hanging from the roof, are frequently mentioned. Many also had two or three sheep, providing the wool needed for spinning.

These small farmers depended on credit, and much information on borrowing and lending can be derived from probate inventories. Some 40% of Week St. Mary probate inventories record the lending of money. It is probably that most people were active in lending money, even though they had no money on loan at the time of their death. There were many reasons for lending money at interest. For example, most adolescents were placed in service, outside of the family home, and they would stay in service until they had saved enough to marry. Bed and board were provided, so their cash earnings could be saved and placed at interest in the credit market. Another example is provided by the testator who left money for an infant son, to be lent at interest during the minority.

There were no banks or other credit institutions in the seventeenth century. The creditor had to deal directly with those who wanted to borrow. They are named in probate inventories, and such evidence may lead the genealogist to relatives. The reasons for borrowing are not usually stated, although in Week St. Mary debtors were probably needing to borrow in order to maintain their agricultural activities.

In addition to wills and inventories, the process of probate generated a variety of other documents. The probate court could require executors or administrators to enter into a bond, with a financial penalty that he/she would faithfully administer the estate. Occasionally, more might be required, for example, the maintenance of a child, or their education. The bond names the executor or administrator, and usually also a guarantor who stood bound with him or her. An account of the administration could also be demanded, although, if surviving accounts are any guide, this requirement was usually not enforced. Those accounts which do survive list everyone who received payment from the estate. Other probate documents were created when wills were disputed, or when executors declined to accept the dubious honour and nominated someone else.

Most post-Reformation probate documents are written in English, although the Latin used by court officials may also be seen occasionally. With practise, seventeenth-century handwriting is easy to read, and the effort is likely to be well-rewarded. Probate records contain an enormous amount of information, and constitute a major challenge for anyone seriously interest in studying the way of life of our ancestors.

Stuart A Raymond is the author of numerous bibliographies for family historians. He has just published ' Using Libraries: Workshops for Family Historians', which aims to provide basic guidance in the use of libraries and books, and develops the theme of this article. It is available from S.A. & M.J.Raymond, P.O.Box 35, Exeter, EX1 3YZ, price £3.40 (inc p &p). Stuart will also be happy to supply a full listing of his other publications.

mca
Maritime and Coastguard Agency

Registry of Shipping & Seamen
Neil Staples - Records Officer

This is a guide to the library of seaman and ships records held at the Registry of Shipping and Seamen (RSS)

1. Merchant Navy Seamen's Sea Service Records
1994 - 2001 Sea Service Records
This information is **taken from the ships official logbooks and crew agreements** on which the seaman sailed. There is a charge of £11.00 per logbook to extract this information, the details of which are then included on a Certificate of Sea Service in respect of the seaman.

1973 to 1993 Sea Service Records This office is not able to supply information concerning the sea service details of individual Merchant Seamen from 1973 to 1993. After 1973 the Registrar General was not required by legislation to keep these records.

1941 to 1972 Fifth Register of Merchant Seaman's Service These records are held at the Public Record Office in classification **BT 382. The Fifth Register of Seaman's Service 1941 to 1972.**
Records of individual Merchant Seamen's sea service details are held in alphabetical surname order. These details include the following information: Name of seaman, Date and place of birth, Discharge (Seaman's) book number, Rank. Details of the ships on which he served. These include: Name of ship and official number, date of engagement (Joining ship), Date of discharge (Leaving ship), whether ship was a foreign going or home trade vessel, and records in some cases National Insurance contributions. Details shown in these records are similar to those contained in an individual seaman's discharge book.

1913 to 1940 Fourth Register of Merchant Seaman's service. Public Record Office Classification: **BT 364 Register of Seaman, Combined Numerical Index (CR1, CR2 and CR 10).** Microfiche of these three index series are held in the following classes: **BT 348: Register of Seamen, Central Index, Numerical Series (CR 2), BT 349: Register of Seamen, Central Index, Alphabetical Series (CR 1)** and **BT 350: Register of Seamen, Special Index, Alphabetical Series (CR 10).** The original records for the above named classifications are now held at the following address: **Southampton Archives, Southampton City Council, South Block Civic Centre, Southampton, S014 7LY.**

1913 to 1940 Merchant Seaman's Pouches
These records are held at the **Public Record Office** in their classification **BT 372. Central Register of Seaman's Records ("Pouches").** These are held in numerical order of the individual seaman's discharge book (Seaman's) number. These pouches were a central repository for a seaman's documents; these would comprise of the many documents that the sailor would have had to submit to the Registry of Shipping over the whole of his career and copies of those documents issued to him. These would comprise of Applications for Discharge Books (including photographs of the seaman), Sea Service records, records of certificates issued etc. The Pouches can sometimes include records cards extracted from the Forth Register of Seaman's Service.
1857 - 1918 for gaps between these records see certificates of competency and service
1854 - 1856 Third Register of Merchant Seaman's service
This register of Merchant Seamen service was opened in 1854. This was arranged in alphabetical order and contained the following details of seaman: age, place of birth, details of voyage, including name of ship and port of departure. In 1856 it was considered that the obligation to maintain a register of seaman was satisfied by the crew list and the register was closed. Public Record Office Classification: **BT 116: Register of Seamen: Series 111.**
1845 - 1854 Second Register of Merchant Seaman's Service The Merchant Shipping Act 1844 stipulated that

every British seaman should have a register ticket. The details given when applying for a ticket were: Name, Date and place of birth, Date and capacity of first going to sea, Capacity since: any Royal Navy ship served in, and capacity; Present employment at sea, home address. Public Record Office Classification: **BT 113: Registers of Seaman's Tickets.** (1845-1853). In Certificate number order. **BT 114: Alphabetical Index to registers of Seaman's Tickets. BT 115: Alphabetical Register of Masters tickets.**
1835 to 1844 First Register of Merchant Seaman's service The registration of seamen was introduced by the Merchant Shipping Act 1835. Public Record Office Classification: **BT 120: Register of Seamen Series 1.** (1835-1836). These records are arranged alphabetically. **BT 112: Register of Seamen: Series 11.** (1835-1844). **BT 119 Alphabetical Index to Seamen.** This index provides the registration number of the seaman.

2. Log Books and Crew Agreements
Logbooks are the records of a period of time in the life of a vessel; these usually are in existence for a one-year to eighteen-month period. The logbook is divided up into two sections, the **tabular** section and the **narrative** section. The **tabular** section contains the information concerning "Notice of Freeboard" this is a record of all the ports the vessel docked at, and other information. This form is used for **tax purposes**. Births and deaths are also recorded in the tabular section along with other more routine information. The **narrative** section of the logbook contains written entries concerning various events that occur on each voyage: disciplinary matters, illness amongst the crew and accidents. There is a charge of £11 to extract a logbook from our records and also additional photocopying charges.Blank pages with no information are not photocopied.

Crew Agreements This document is a legal agreement between the crew of a vessel and the owners. It lists all the crew by name, includes their signatures and the last ship on which they sailed. When requesting a copy of a logbook the attached crew agreement would also be photocopied.

Log Books and Crew Agreements 1996 - 2001 These records are held at the Registry of Shipping and Seamen in their entirety. A certificate of sea service for individual seaman who sailed on ships from this period may be obtained from these records

Log Books and Crew Agreements 1977 - 1995 A 10% sample of all log books for the above period 1977 to 1995 Public Record Office Classification: **BT 99: Agreements and Crew Lists, Series 11.**

Log Books and Crew Agreements 1951 to 1976 A 10% sample of all logbooks from the above period are held at the Public Record Office, in classification **BT 99 Agreements and Crew Lists, Series 11.** 80% of the records are now held at the **Maritime History Archive, Memorial University of Newfoundland, St. John's, Newfoundland, Canada, A1C 5S7.** The remaining 10% of these logbooks and crew agreements are kept at the **National Maritime Museum, Greenwich, London, SE10 9NF.**Keeps the years ending in "5", i.e. 1955, 1965, 1975.

Log Books and Crew Agreements 1947 to 1950 The Public Record Office holds all surviving logbooks and crew agreements for 1947 to 1950. These include both Merchant and Fishing vessels in their classification **BT 99 Agreements and Crew Lists, Series 11.**

Ships Logbooks and Crew Agreements 1939 to 1946
Public Record Office Classification: **BT 381. WW 2 Log books and Crew Agreements** These are held in order of the ship's official number. It is therefore advisable to find out the official number of the ship in that you are interested before contacting this office. We would also require the name of the ship. NB: Please note that these records have only recently been transferred to the Public Record Office and some of the later years may not be available to the public as yet.

Allied Crew List 1939 - 1945 The following documents concerning allied vessels are held at the Public Record Office, in alphabetical order of ship's name: Return of British members of the crew of a foreign Ship that has been requisitioned or chartered by, or on behalf of H M Government. and **Account of Changes** in the crew of a foreign-going ship. Agreement and list of the crew of a foreign-going ship. Some Official Logbooks of these vessels are also held. The records also include those records of the British crew of allied vessels who were lost at sea. Please note that only in rare cases were logbooks of any kind attached to these crew lists. An additional record was also kept of the British seamen who served on **Dutch** and **Norwegian** ships. These are held in alphabetical ship order. Public Record Office Classification: **BT 387. Allied Crew List from WW 2**. These records have recently been transferred to the PRO and may not as yet be available.

Ships log books and Crew Lists 1861 to 1938 10% of logbooks and crew agreements for the above period Public Record Office Classification: **BT 99. Agreements and Crew Lists, Series 11.** 80% of the records are held at the **Maritime History Archive, Canada.**The remaining logbooks are held at the National Maritime Museum, Greenwich. They hold the years where the last digit ends in "5", from 1861 onwards: i.e. 1865, 1875, 1885 etc Log books and crew agreements not included in the above for the years 1861 to 1913 have been retained by some local records office. If you wish to obtain a list of where these records are held please write in to the Registry of Shipping and this will be supplied. **Ships Log Books and Crew Lists 1835-1860**

From 1835 onwards the masters of foreign going British ships over 80 tons were required to carry on board a written agreement with every seaman employed. These agreements contained the following: wage rate, The capacity he served in, and the nature of the voyage. Public Record Office Classification: **BT 98. Agreement and Crew Lists: Series 1.** Records prior to 1854 are arranged by the port of registry numbers, later records are arranged in official number order. From 1852 onwards the official logbook of the vessel was kept with the agreement and crew list.

Ships Log Books and Crew Lists 1747 - 1851 From 1747 onwards masters or owners of merchant ships were obliged to keep muster rolls of each voyage. These contained: names of the seamen employed on the ship, their home address, when they joined ship and the last ship on which they sailed. This system continued to be compiled until 1851. Public Record Office Classification: **BT 98: Agreements and Crew Lists: Series 1**.

Special Ships 1861 onwards A selection was made of logbooks and crew agreements from famous ships, for example the SS Titanic and Great Britain. Public Record Office Classification: **BT 100. Agreements and Crew Lists Series 111**. A 10% sample of similar records for fishing vessels of less than 80 tons can be found at the Public Record Office in category **BT 144. Agreements and Crew Lists Series 1V** for the period 1884 - 1919. Later records of fishing vessel are included in BT 99 (as above).

World War 1 Log Books and Crew Agreements Log books and crew agreements for 1914-1918 are held at the Public Record Office in classification **BT 165. Agreements and Crew Lists.**

Log Books containing entries of Births and Deaths at Sea Log books containing information concerning births and deaths at sea were segregated. These log books for the years 1902 - 1938 Public Record Office Classification: **BT 165. Ship's Official Log Books**. If you are planning to include a reproduction of a logbook or crew agreement or any part of these documents in a publication, you must obtain written permission from the RSS and acknowledge the Registry of Shipping and Seamen and include our full address.

3. Deaths at sea: Merchant Seamen and Passengers The registers of deaths at sea are public documents and are open to inspection by the public. The various registers concerning deaths at sea contain the following information regarding Merchant Seamen and Passengers: Name of person, Rank/Occupation, age/date of birth, address, date of death, place of death (This is often given in Lat. and Long.), cause of death: name, official number and port of registry of the ship.

Registers of Births and Deaths at Sea 1965 to present day These records are held at the Registry of Shipping and Seamen. A search may be made in these registers for the fee of £11.

Registers of Births, Marriages and Deaths at Sea Death Registers: 1891 to 1964 Public Record Office Classification: **BT 334: Registers and indexes of Births, Deaths and Marriages at Sea**. These records contain the death registers of those passengers and crew who died on the SS Titanic and SS Lusitania.

Registers of Births, Marriages and Deaths at Sea 1851 to 1890 From 1854 registers were compiled from ships official logbooks of births, marriages and deaths of passengers at sea. All these are recorded from 1854-1883, births and deaths only from 1883 -1887 and deaths only from 1888 onwards. Public Record Office Classification: **BT 158. Registers of Births, Marriages and Deaths of Passenger at Sea**. Masters were also required from 1874 to report births and deaths of UK subjects and foreign subjects to the Registrar General of Shipping and Seamen. Public Record Office Classification: **BT 160: Registers of Births of British Nationals at Sea** and **BT 159: Registers of deaths at sea of British Nationals.** From 1851 onwards Masters of UK ships were required to surrender to the Board of Trade the wages and effects of any seaman who died during a voyage. These records included the following information concerning the seaman: name, date and place of joining the ship, date and cause of death, name, official number (after 1854) and port of ship: name of master, date and place of payment of wages, the amount of wages and date of receipt by Board of Trade. Public Record Office Classification: **BT 153: Registers of Wages and Effects of Deceased Seamen (1852 to 1881).** To access these records you have to consult the following categories **BT 154: Indexes to Seamen's Names and Indexes to Ship's Names (1853 – 1889)** These provide the relevant numbers of the pages in the register.

Monthly Lists of dead Seaman 1886 - 1889 Monthly lists of dead seamen were compiled giving name, age, rating, nationality and birthplace, home address and cause of death. Lists for 1886 - 1889 are at the Public Record office in category **BT 156: Monthly Lists of Deaths of Seamen.** There are also nine manuscript registers of half yearly lists of deaths 1882-1888 Public Record Office Classification: **BT 157 Registers of Seaman's Death Classified by Cause.**

Deaths at Sea - Returns of Death When a death at sea occurs on an UK vessel the master is required to complete a Return of Death. This return includes the following information: name, official number and port of registry of ship, date and place of death, name, age, rank/occupation, address and cause of death of deceased.The reverse of the form includes an extract of the ship's logbook that gives an account of the events that led to the death at sea. Please note however, that the log book extract is not always included. The return of death forms the basis of the death registration (See above). The earliest surviving returns of death, date from1914 to 1919 are now held at the National Maritime Museum, Greenwich. No returns exist between 1920-1938, Returns from 1939 to 1964 are also held at the National Maritime Museum. Returns from 1965 to the present day are held at the Registry of Shipping. Please note that there are also some gaps in these records.

Inquiries into Deaths at Sea, Papers and Reports Inquiry reports concerning deaths at sea, conducted under the provisions of the Merchant Shipping Acts Public Record Office Classification: **BT 341. Inquiries into Deaths at Sea, Papers and Reports.** These documents contain statements, log book entries, medical reports and other relevant information regarding the particular death at sea. These cover the years 1939 to 1946 and the year 1964. The Returns of Death, which originally accompanied these papers, are now held at the National Maritime Museum (See above). These records are organised in year order and in alphabetical order of ship name. They correspond to the Registers of death held in BT 334.

Casualties and Deaths Lists (C & D) When a vessel was lost at sea, the ship's official logbook would have been lost with the vessel. In these circumstances the owners of the vessel would submit a copy of the crew list to the Registrar General of Shipping and Seamen. These lists would be used for the registration of the deaths of the crewmembers. Casualties and deaths lists (C & D) for the years 1920-1938 are held at the National Maritime Museum, Greenwich. **Casualties and deaths on fishing vessel's (List D)** for the years 1920-1938 have also been transferred to that office. These records are organised by the official number of the ship. The official numbers of ships can be obtained from the extensive collection of Lloyds registers held at the National Maritime Museum. Many lists C & D are included in the 1939 - 1950 logbooks and crew agreements held at the Registry of Shipping.

Graves of Seamen/Memorials The Registry of Shipping and Seamen holds no records of the last resting-place of seamen. Those who were lost/buried at sea and have no known grave are commemorated on the Tower Hill Memorial, London, and are also included in the Tower Hill Memorial Registers for both World Wars.For information concerning the Tower Hill Memorial, you may wish to contact the following address: **The Commonwealth War Graves Commission, 2 Marlow Road, Maidenhead, Berkshire, SL6 7DX.**

Merchant seamen who are buried in various graves and war cemeteries around the world are included on index cards that have been transferred to the Commonwealth War Graves Commission. These cards also record those seamen included on the Halifax Memorial. There is also a small collection of cards held at the National Maritime Museum, that date approx. 1939 to 1950 these include details of the deceased seaman and gives information regarding where the seaman is buried.

Rolls of Honour, Wars of 1914 - 1918 and 1939 - 1945 Public Record Office Classification: BT 339. These include the Rolls of Honour of the Merchant Navy and Fishing Fleets, Ships list and Seaman list, The Albert Medal register, Nominal lists and Runnymede Memorial.

4. Daily Casualty Registers 1939 - 1945 These records comprise of 7 volumes of the daily casualties to Merchant Shipping between 8th June 1940 to 15th September 1945. Public Record Office Classification: **BT 347.**

5. Registers of Certificates of Competency & Service Masters and Mates From 1845 masters and mates of foreign going vessels took voluntary examinations of competency. These exams became compulsory in 1850, and from 1854 masters and mates of home trade vessels were also required to take these examinations. The certificates were entered into registers arranged in numerical order and provide: name of seaman: place and date of birth, register ticket, if any, rank examined for, or served in, and date of issue of certificate. Some additional information concerning the seamen may also be included in this record i.e. Deaths, injuries, previous ships etc. Seamen judged by the examiners to have sufficient experience as a master or mate, and also men retiring from the Royal Navy were eligible, without formal examination, for certificates of service. Those without sufficient service or wishing to progress in the ranks were granted certificates of competency on passing examinations. These registers are arranged in 7 classes, which are held at the Public Record Office, Kew.

A. Certificates of Competency: Masters and Mates Foreign Trade. BT 122. (1845 - 1906). Held in Numerical order of certificate number.
B. Certificates of Service: Masters and Mates: Foreign Trade. BT 124. (1850 - 1888). Held in Numerical Order of Certificate number.
C. Certificates of Competency: Masters and Mates: Home Trade:, BT 125. 1854 -1921. Held in Numerical order of Certificate number.
D. Registers of certificates of Competency: Masters and Mates of Steamships: Foreign Trade. BT 123. (1881 - 1921) Held in certificate number order.
E. Registers of Certificates of Service: Masters and Mates: Home Trade BT 126. (1855 - 1888). Held in certificate number order.
F. Alphabetical Register of Masters. BT 115. 1845 - 1854.
G. Certificates of Competency, Master and Mates. Colonial BT 128 1870 – 1921.

The means of reference to these series are the indexes to the registers **BT 127: Index to the Registers** that give the date and place of birth and the certificate number & **BT 352 Index to Certificate of Competency** dates from 1910 to 1930. These cards are held in alphabetical order of seaman's name and list the certificates issued to the individual seaman with relevant number of the Certificate.

Application Forms for Certificates All surviving Board of Trade Office copies of the above named certificates are held at the National Maritime Museum, these date from 1845 to 1927. These are arranged numerically by certificate number. The accompanying applications forms record the personal details of the candidate together with a list of vessels he served on with relevant dates of service.

Registers of Passes and Renewals of Master' and Mates' Certificates 1917 to 1968 Public Record Office Classification: **BT 317.** These registers include details of individual seamen passing certificate of competency examinations and also the replacement of lost certificates. These records are in numerical order of certificate number.

Registers of Changes of Masters 1893 to 1948 Public Record Office Classification: **BT 336.** The registers contain lists of those masters who were in command of vessels registered in the United Kingdom. The registers are arranged in numerical order by the official number of the individual ship. Each entry contains the name of the vessel: the port where the master joined the vessel with relevant date and also the name and seaman's number of the master.

Engineers Examinations of competence were extended to engineers in 1862. The registers of certificates are held at the Public Record Office Classification: **BT 139: Certificates of Competency: Engineers. (1863 – 1921)** and **BT 142: Certificates of Service: Engineers.** (1862 – 1921). The means of reference to these records are the indexes to registers in **BT 141: Certificates of Competency: Engineers.** This index is arranged alphabetically by surname, and gives date and place of birth and the certificate number **BT 143 Registers of Certificates of Competency and Service, Miscellaneous.** (1845 – 1849)

Fishing Boats The Merchant Shipping (Fishing Boats) Act 1883 extended the examination system to the skippers and mates of fishing vessels. TPublic Record Office Classification: **BT 129. Certificates of Competency: Skippers and Mates of Fishing Boats.** (1880 – 1921) and **BT 130: Certificates of Service: Skippers and Mates of Fishing Boats.** (1883 – 1907) Public Record Office Classification: **BT 138. Indexes to Registers of Competency and Service: Skippers and Mates of Fishing Boats.** These records are held in alphabetical order according to the seaman's surname.

6. Merchant Seamen Prisoner of War Records 1939 to 1952 Public Record Office Classification: **BT 373.** These are organised by the name of ship from which the seamen were captured. The information is held in pouches in alphabetical order. These records contain the names of those men captured from merchant ships and where they were held in captivity. These records also include additional information supplied by the Red Cross and also information regarding the deaths of POW's.

7. Precedent Books, Esatblishment Papers etc, This section can be regarded as a miscellaneous section contains a number of different types of records; these include policy files, precedent books and black books. Public Record Office Classification: **BT 167. Marine Safety Agency** (Now the Maritime and Coastguard Agency): **Business Plans.** These date from 1994 to 1998. Public Record Office Classification: **MT 173.**

8. Apprentices Public Record Office Classification: **Index of Apprentices BT 150 (1824 -1953), BT 151 Apprentices Indentures (1845 - 1962) and BT 152. Apprentices Indentures for Fishing (1895 to 1935)** In accordance with the Merchant Seamen's act 1823 Masters of British merchant ships were required to carry a given number of indentured apprentices. In London they were registered with the Registrar General of Seamen, in other ports customs officers were required to submit quarterly list to the Registrar General. These papers consist of indexes of all apprentices whose indentures were registered (BT 150), together with specimens taken at five-yearly intervals of the copy indentures (BT 151 and 152).

9. Royal Naval Reserve (RNR): Rating Records of Service 1908 - 1955 Public Record Office Classification: **BT 377.** This series contains microfiche copies of service record cards of Royal Naval Reserve rating, mainly covering men who served during the First World War. The filmed cards are arranged in service number order. Indexes to service numbers are included in the class. The Royal Naval **Volunteer** Reserve (RNVR). This was a force of officer and ratings undertaking naval training in their spare time, but not professionally employed at sea like the RNR. During both world wars the RNVR was the principal means by which officers entered the Royal Navy for the period of the war only. In 1958 the RNVR was amalgamated with the RNR. Details of records related to the RNVR can be found in Public Record Office Handbook No 22. Naval Records for Genealogists. Records of the **Merchant Navy Reserve Pool** WW2 are held at the National Maritime Museum.

9. Passenger Lists 1878 - 1960 Passenger lists for the period before 1890 have not survived in England, with the exception of a few relating to vessels in the United Kingdom between 1878 and 1888. These, and the surviving lists for the period between 1890 and 1960, are held at the Public Record Office Classification: **BT 26. Inwards Passenger Lists 1878 to 1960.** The information given in these lists include the age, occupation, address in the United Kingdom and the date of entering the country of passengers entering the United Kingdom by sea from ports outside Europe and

the Mediterranean. They are arranged under the names of the ports of arrival. Public Record Office Classification: **BT 32. Registers of Passenger Lists 1906 to 1951.** Prior to 1920 they are under the different ports, the names of ships and the month of arrival and departure: after 1920 the date of arrival or departure is recorded. Before 1908 the registers relate only to the ports of Southampton, Bristol and Weymouth. **BT 27. Outward Passenger Lists. 1890 to 1960** These give the names of all passengers leaving the UK where the ship's eventual destination was a port outside Europe and the Mediterranean Sea. Names of passengers who disembarked at European ports from these ships will be included in these lists. They are arranged monthly by port of departure. For registers see **BT 32 (as above).** There have been several resources published specifically aimed at helping family historians locate passenger lists outside the UK. Copies of these are now held at the following address: **The Guildhall Library, Aldermanbury, London, EC2P 2EJ.** These include Filby, P.W.: **Passengers and immigration lists index (and annual supplements),** that cover North America. It can be found in the Reference Collection at R 325/2 and lists individuals by surname and shows where the passenger list can be found; **The Morton Allan Directory of European Steamship arrivals 1890 - 1930 at the ports of New York, Philadelphia, Boston & Baltimore,** Closed Access LB 286, is also useful. **British Immigration to Victoria - assisted immigrants 1839 - 1891** (microfiches 3), **Index of New South Wales Convict Indents** (microfiches 29) **Immigration Index to assisted immigrants arriving Sydney 1844 - 96,** Closed Access 387/5, and Hughes, 1A: **9 assorted list to Port Phillip, c 1839 - 51,** Closed Access 387/5, cover Australia.

Guildhall Library holds a number of shipping indexes that were compiled for the popular immigration ports in Australia and New Zealand. These include: **Shipping arrivals and departures, Victorian ports, 1798 - 1855** (2 vols.), **Shipping arrivals and departures, Sydney, 1788 - 1844** (3 vols.), **Shipping arrivals and departures, Tasmania, 1803 - 1843,** (2 vols.) and **Shipping to New Zealand 1839 - 1889** (known as the Comber Index), all Closed Access 387/2. Some other books held by the Library also provided potentially useful information, such as **Dictionary of Western Australians. 1829 - 1914,** Closed Access 325/941 and British settlers in Natal 1824 - 1857. Closed access 325/684.

Recommended Reading:
Records of the Merchant Shipping and Seamen. Public Records Office Readers' Guide No 20. PRO Publications.
1. The Registry of Shipping and Seamen, P.O. Box 420, Cardiff, CF24 5XR, Tel: 029 20 44 88 00, Fax: 029 20 44 88 20 MCA Website :http://www.mcagency.org.uk
2. The Public Record Office,, The National Archives,, Kew, Richmond, Surrey, TW9 4DU, Tel: 020 8876 3444, Fax: 020 8878 8905 Website: http://www.pro.gov.uk
3. The National Maritime Museum,, Greenwich, London, SE10 9NF, Tel: 020 8858 4422, Fax: 020 8312 6632 Website: www.nmm.ac.uk.
4. The Archivist, **Maritime History Archive** Memorial University of Newfoundland, St. John's, Newfoundland, A1C 5S7, Tel: 709 737 8428, Fax: 709 737 3123 Website: http://www.mun.ca/mha/, E-Mail: mha@morgan.ucs.mun.ca
5. The Guildhall Library, Aldermanbury, London, EC2P 2EJ, Tel: 020 7 332 1868/1870, Fax: 020 7 600 3384
6. The Southampton Archives Services, Southampton City Council, South Block, Civic Centre, Southampton, S014 7LY, Tel: 023 8083 2251, Fax: 023 8083 2156 E-Mail city.archives@southampton.gov.uk

Registry of Shipping and Seamen (RSS), P.O Box 420, Cardiff, CF24 5JW. Tel: 029 20 44 88 00. E- mail RSS@mcga.gov.uk. It also identifies records transferred to other locations.

The Family and Local History Handbook
Local History Section
produced in collaboration with the

Family and Local History
~ You can't have one without the other
Alan Crosby

I often give talks in this subject to organisations involved in both areas of research and I find that almost without exception people are excited by the challenge and the opportunities which linking these two themes can offer. It is in some ways obvious that the two subjects do go together, and are inextricably entwined. We cannot understand local communities - their origins,

PICTISH WALL IN S. BERNERA.

development and character - without giving the fullest possible attention to the people who made up those communities. After all, the farms and the fields, the streets and the houses, the industries and the churches, are all the product of untold human endeavour over the centuries. If we ignore the people we ignore the reason why, and that it absurd. Yet, at the same time, we cannot really understand the lives of individuals and the stories of families unless we consider their world, the environment they lived in and the lifestyles they enjoyed (or, maybe, didn't enjoy but rather suffered!).

How often, in researching your family history, have you wondered about what it was like for the people whose names, dates and brief historical record you have uncovered? What sort of housing did they live in, what clothes did they wear, what were their working conditions, what was the landscape which they knew from day to day and how did they fit into local society? Have you asked yourself why they moved from one place to another, what they felt about their fellow-citizens, how greater and lesser events impinged upon them, and what rituals and customs they encountered in birth, marriage and death. What sort of education was available to them - if any - and how did they tackle the burdens and oppressions of poverty, early and sudden death, natural disaster, illness and ill-health. What lightened their lives and what did they look forward to?

Local history can answer many such questions. It can set the lives of your forebears firmly in their proper context, helping to explain why they did what they did and what they met along life's path. All over the British Isles local history is a 'growth industry'. There are many hundreds of societies which are devoted to furthering the cause of local history - undertaking research, using original sources; holding lecture meetings and field visits; publishing the fruits of research and writing; campaigning for the extraordinarily rich heritage which is the legacy of the past and seeking to ensure its conservation and enhancement for future generations.

Local history is endlessly diverse, full of rewards and unexpected surprises, and something which is available and accessible to everybody. The British Association for Local History helps to further the cause of this fascinating and valuable subject. BALH promotes the study of, and interest in, our local heritage and history. All those who are interested in the history of the family will find that the study of local history can provide a much clearer and deeper understanding of where we came from and how it was in the past.

In collaboration with the British Association for Local History

A five thousand year old tradition

Alan Crosby

On 15 July we went bilberrying high on the moors near Blackburn. We do it every summer. For the uninitiated, bilberries (vaccinium myrtillus) are small purple-blue berries which grow on stout knee-high shrubby bushes on the moorland fringes of the Pennines and other upland areas of the British Isles: in Lancashire they are usually called whinberries. Picking them is, to the novice, a less-than-appealing prospect.

We – the cognoscenti of the bilberry world - all know our own special patch. Like the Russian mushroom-gatherers long ago described in nostalgic terms by Vladimir Nabokov, we go back to places where in previous years the berries have been particularly large, or the bushes better-laden. We breathe out with pleasure at the sight of those small purple globes hanging amid the crisp green foliage: 'they're really large this year' … 'wow, look at these' … 'Oh, Jim, don't get them all over your T-shirt'. The last, to a six-year old, reveals one of the characteristics of bilberries. They have copious purple-red juice, so your hands soon look like the aftermath of a terrible accident with a carving knife. Children naturally manage to get the juice everywhere.

But that is the least of the worries of the bilberry-picker. The real problems begin as soon as you bend down and brush your way through the bushes. A million flies, which have been waiting eagerly since the previous July, bored for almost twelve months but knowing that a feast is now imminent, descend in clouds, biting and buzzing, in and on ears, noses, eyes, backs of necks and bare exposed wrists. Instinctively, you slap: purple-red patches appear in all sorts of places. The sun beats down. Rivers of sweat flow mingled down with the grime and the juice and the squashed insects.

The berries are small, the bushes low: the back hurts, calves ache, knees complain, red bites start to swell on hands and cheeks, children want to go home, and … well, what is there to show for all this effort and discomfort? Bilberries are small. They are not cultivated and they cannot be cultivated. The bushes are not designed for pick-your-own activities. The labour is intensive and the results seemingly pitiful.

The rewards are various. First, the fruit is free: nature's bounty. Bilberries are abundant and there is no charge – except a heavy payment in stained clothes and stained skin, blood [given to insects] and sweat and toil and tears [those of fed-up children]. Then, the views are wonderful, and there is the priceless pleasure of being on the hills, looking out – in our case – across Lancashire to the Lake District fells thirty miles away and enjoying fresh air and sunshine. But the real reward is the taste. Bilberries have an exquisite and incomparable flavour and an almost equally delectable smell.

They freeze perfectly: I always make a bilberry tart on Christmas Eve, and in the middle of winter the scent instantly evokes the heathery moorlands of midsummer.

And what has this to do with local history? Simple. It is one of my very personal links with the past. For two hundred generations people – among them my ancestors – have been walking up onto those moors, in the summer sun, for that short period in July and August when the bilberries are ripe. My ancestors, five thousand years ago, were surrounded by the ancestors of the flies which bit me last July (quite a few thousand more generations of them, of course). The distant ancestors of Anna and Jim told their parents that they were bored and wanted to go home. Making use of the waste; exploiting the resources of the marginal lands; communal activity on the upland fringes … that's just what we did that afternoon. Though we did drive there in a Golf Estate!

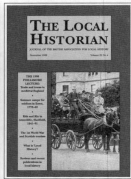

THE LOCAL HISTORIAN
Journal of the British Association for Local History

Volume 29, appeared in February, May, August and December 1999, containing some 16 articles. Once again, there was a considerable range in period, from the Anglo-Saxon (a study of sources for English beekeeping) to the almost contemporary (open-air schools in Birmingham, 1911-1970). Our contributors were representative of the wide variety of people who have an interest in local history, from the full-time teachers of the subject in further and higher education, to those who work as freelance researchers and writers; from retired professionals who have developed an interest in local history, to people who work in related fields, such as archivists and librarians. The geographical spread of contributions was restricted to the British Isles this year, although an article on the effects of the First World War on Scottish tourism did allow the author to mention the overseas destinations of Scottish travellers, and there was an Irish dimension in the discussion of the Irish in two London boroughs in 1851.

The nineteenth century still exercises a strong influence over the choice of research topics for local history, and this is reflected in two articles discussing aspects of enclosure (in Yorkshire and in Buckinghamshire), two making use of census material (the Irish in Hammersmith and Fulham, 1851; kinship ties in Sheffield, 1841–91), and another analysing retailing patterns (using Wolverhampton as a case study, and ranging in period from 1800 to 1950).

One very pleasing feature of the year was the use made of hitherto unrecognised forms of 'documentary' evidence. Scraps of clothing accompanying registration papers for foundlings led to a breakthrough in costume and textile history (infant fashion in the eighteenth century). An exploration and recording of those mysterious marks on the outside of letters, rather than the content of the letters themselves, gave an insight into postal routes and postal practice in Berkshire in the eighteenth century.

On a more traditional note, the potential of friendly society records for research was fully revealed, and we were challenged to think about the very nature and methodology of local history in an article which will probably continue to stir up debate well into the next year. The third Phillimore Lecture, published in November's issue, gave a masterly exposition of the current state of research and thinking into the patterns of trade and the role of towns in medieval England. We reviewed 27 books in some depth, and in his annual Round-up, the Reviews Editor surveyed some of the many publications issued to commemorate the 80th anniversary of the First World War.

www.thelocalhistorian.org
or details from BALH PO BOX 1576 SALISBURY SP2 8SY

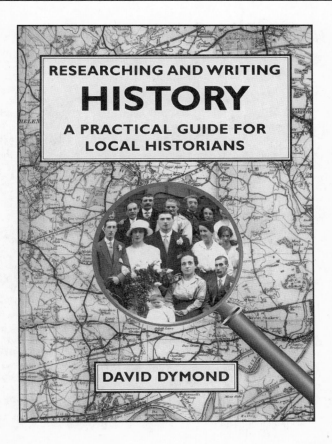

This book is essential reading for anybody who has written, is writing or might one day write local history. The earlier version of the book, Writing Local History, was first published in 1981 and became an instant classic. Now it has been totally rewritten, extended and updated so that local historians in the early 21st century, will have an even better reference book to help them produce work of the highest quality. David Dymond has spent most of a lifetime as a professional local historian, and he writes from that personal knowledge and experience. The contents of the book include an assessment of the present state of local history; the challenge of writing; choosing a subject; the search for sources; transcribing; analysing and assembling evidence; interpreting the evidence; writing techniques; the final draft; and numerous appendices which illustrate sample styles of local historians, show how to present information, and demonstrate good and bad practice in writing. It is, in short, an invaluable, stimulating and often entertaining exposition of how we should approach our subject.

180 pages   £12.00 (£10.00 for members)
from BALH (P) PO BOX 1576 SALISBURY SP2 8SY

Local Studies Collections

Alan Crosby

The continuing threats to the integrity and funding of county and borough local studies collections in libraries has recently been debated within the British Association for Local History, and nationally and locally there has been a series of campaigns to highlight this issue. Some have been prompted by specific crises, others by a more general concern for the future. Local studies collections face many problems. It would be wrong to suggest that in this

they are uniquely unfortunate within library services, for many other aspects of the work of libraries have also been suffering – the future of the superb music library in Manchester Central Library, for example, has been a major point of heated controversy during the last three years. Nevertheless, local studies collections are as vulnerable as any, though their usership is precisely that at which policies of inclusivity should be targeted, and their future is all too often uncertain.

One of the problems which has often been identified is the way in which specialist staff, who have proper expertise in local history and related subjects, and who know their collections intimately, have been replaced by staff who can be, and are, employed in any part of the library and who have no special knowledge or experience. Specialist staffing of particular departments does not fit in with the current fashion for the interchangeability of personnel – itself a direct result of cost-cutting and staffing

reductions. Probably quite a few readers will have experienced what I have not infrequently encountered – hearing a well-meaning but unknowledgeable member of library staff giving misleading or downright inaccurate information to an enquirer in a local studies section, simply because he or she does not 'know the ropes' and yet is heroically manning the desk alone.

The possibility of dispersal of special collections has often been raised as a threat. Local studies material is arguably less likely to suffer from this than some other categories (inevitably, perhaps, it is the valuable [i.e. 'we can raise some money by selling this junk'] or less frequently used [i.e. 'nobody will notice if we bin this lot'] resources which are likely to be affected). Local studies collections are not usually all that valuable in monetary terms, though beyond price in an intellectual and cultural sense, and they are reasonably well used, especially if the ever-popular family history resources are included as they certainly should be.

But their maintenance and upkeep, conservation and security, are all vital issues. I know of too many local studies libraries where books are badly housed, pamphlets are crammed into acidic brown paper envelopes, large quantities of material have gone missing, catalogues and indexes are hopelessly inadequate, and security is minimal. There are too many libraries where keeping the local studies collection up to date seems to be largely a matter of getting this year's *Yellow Pages*, putting the free newspapers in the racks, and buying the latest cheap and flimsy books: 'chilling' ghost stories, murders and true crime. The runs of periodicals and journals are stopped as an economy measure, and the undoubtedly expensive but relevant and essential proper books do not appear. This paints a depressing picture, yet it is far from the truth? How often does quickly outdated technological wizardry – 'see XYZ on line' – seem to receive all the money, while the old fashioned and unglamorous books, papers and pamphlets are neglected, and deteriorating.

Many readers will be able to point to shining examples to the contrary, and that is good. I do not (usually) blame the librarians who work ion local studies collections for this state of affairs, but rather the service chiefs who are seduced by technology and who forget their first principles that they learned, or should have learned, thity years ago when they were tidying the shelves in the small branch library. Today they are the ones persuaded by the glamour of screens and in-library cafes (or, in the case of the new Norwich library, pizza restaurants), potted plants and internet access. Yes, libraries should be attractive, welcoming places. Yes, they should be full of the new media. And yes, I say with feeling, they need to be places where a serious researcher can spend a day, a penny and a pound or two on food and drink. But all this should not be at the expense of books, paper, print, ink, bindings, pages to touch rather than pages on the screen, staff who know the subject rather than bored individuals who simply direct you to a terminal and say, more or less in these words, 'Dunno, you'll have to look there'. Printed books have been with us for half a millennium, paper and parchment and ink for centuries more. No civilised society should throw all that away for the sake of some computer equipment which will be out of date by three weeks next Tuesday, a plethora of unchecked and unvetted internet data, and library staff who have been downgraded to serve merely as receptionists. Support your local studies collection. Campaign for its proper funding. Make sure it is used and publicised. Fight for its continuation as one of the cornerstones of Britain's proud and honourable tradition of free accessible public library excellence.

Local History News Spring 2002

How lucky we are

Alan Crosby

Knowing that I am interested in the subject, an archivist friend recently lent me a small booklet, printed on cheap yellowed paper: The fate of Polish archives during World War II, published in Warsaw in 1964. The article recounts in heartbreaking detail the destruction of Poland's historical record, though it should be said immediately that to any honest reader the infinitely more heartbreaking knowledge is that of the fate of Poland's people. But the statistics of archival losses are awe-inspiring: during the 1944 Warsaw Rising the air raids and shelling of the Central Archives of Earlier Records resulted in the incineration of 400,000 bound volumes of manuscripts. Ten days later, 30,000 volumes of treasury records went up in flames. In late August 1944 the municipal archives were destroyed. Between September and November the Germans, having recaptured the city centre, deliberately burned all the remainder. In total, 92.8% of all the archives in Warsaw were destroyed, including most of the records of the Polish nation going back eight centuries and every single item from the records of the city of Warsaw itself. In addition, many trainloads of archives from all over Poland had already been seized and taken to Germany - many were subsequently destroyed, others lost, and only part of the total repatriated after 1945.

The proportion of such devastation is not unique, though its absolute magnitude probably is. Anybody researching Irish history or who is trying to trace Irish ancestors is virtually certain to have encountered the fateful date '1922'. On 30 June that year, at the outbreak of the brief and savage civil war between pro-Treaty and anti-Treaty forces, the munitions stored by the I.R.A. in the cellars of the Four Courts (which housed the Public Record Office of Ireland) exploded as the building was stormed by government forces. For three days the documentary history of Ireland rained down upon Dublin in a snowstorm of ash and burned fragments of paper. We on this side of the water have had our own losses - the probate records of the diocese of Exeter,

Bombardment of The Four Courts, Dublin 1922

destroyed during the Baedeker raid on the city in 1942, are an obvious example, and the near-miss (for the archives, anyway) of the Norwich Central Library fire in August 1994 is a reminder that these losses can occur in peace as well as war. And the destruction of archives is a continuing feature of wars and conflicts. The bitter struggles in 'former Yugoslavia', especially in Bosnia and Kosovo, led to wholesale loss of historical records - and often the deliberate destruction of archives - matching the devastation of historic towns and cities.

Thinking of these historical tragedies, and knowing how casually I use my own local record offices, I realise just how easily we accept that they are there for us and others and how little we think of the alternatives. When I grumble, as I often do, about the cost of photocopying, the lack of a catalogue for a vital (to me, at any rate) collection, the irritation of having documents counted out in penny packets, restrictions on the number of sheets of paper I can take into the searchroom, or the insistence that I must use a microform copy rather than the original, should I not be rather more conscious of my good fortune in being able to use a record office, look at an infinite variety of archival material momentous and trivial, work on a splendid richness of primary sources, and enjoy the opportunities which our modern access to archives brings? Being human, the answer I give to that rhetorical question is 'yes, I should, but no, all too often I'm not'. I, like most of us, take such things for granted. How lucky we are to have that luxury.

Local History News August 2002

Fresh Mersey Salmon, Sir?

Alan Crosby

One of my childhood nightmares was the river Irwell. My father once lifted me up to look over the bridge near Manchester cathedral, and I gazed down into a black and noisome canyon of buildings between which ran a sinister and malodorous inky black waterway, its texture seemingly viscous and treacly, its surface scattered with the ghastly detritus of a thousand polluting industries upriver. He told me that to drown in the Irwell was a fate worse than death. Nearly thirty years later, when the extinction of most of those Victorian industries meant that things were getting better, a pub with a riverside terrace was opened on the Salford bank, the rive droite of the Irwell. The pub is named the Mark Addy, after a 19th century local hero who, with awesome courage, regularly dived into those unspeakable waters to rescue unfortunates who had fallen in. I ate a ploughman's lunch there (though it is many centuries since a Salford ploughman tilled the soil by the Irwell). My tomato (what would the ploughman have made of that?) rolled off the plate and into the river, falling with a sticky 'plop' into the black sluggish waters, disappearing instantly from view, and suggesting that the density of suspended solids was still all too high. The powerful and distinctive miasma rising from the oily-glittering river reinforced the point.

Those waters flowed, not sweetly but stately, down to the docks, into the also-black Manchester Ship Canal, and on into the sullied and ruined Mersey. Two hundred and fifty years ago rural Widnes, on the north shore of the upper Mersey estuary, was a popular bathing-resort, its yellow sands frequented by holidaymakers who also relished the great pies which the landlady of the nearby tavern baked from locally-caught eels. A hundred years ago Widnes, transmogrified into one of the world's greatest chemical towns, was a byword for filth and pollution. The beach was still there, but the Mersey brought down all the dirt, sewage and effluent of south Lancashire, depositing it in an evil scum along the shore, and the air was laden with the smoke and acid fumes of industry. The eels had long gone. So had virtually every other living thing in those waters which rose high on the lonely Pennine moors and met their dark fate all too soon along their courses (though, at the risk of seeming to be partisan in these matters, it might have been even worse in Yorkshire: 22 years ago there was a headline in the local paper in Sheffield: 'ALGAE FOUND IN RIVER DON', this being acclaimed as a major improvement to the bright orange rusty-with-iron-waste waters).

Yesterday, though, I read some remarkable news. The first salmon for over a century had been caught in the Mersey. To those familiar with the foaming salmony Spey, or the glassy waters and rippling weeds of the trouty Test, that might seem less than newsworthy. Even those who know the now-freshish waters of the Thames will not find it remarkable (though isn't it said that a glass of London water has been drunk by seven people previously?). But, take my word for it, it is indeed extraordinary that the Mersey has salmon. Only thirty years ago, nobody could have imagined that salmon would venture into the Mersey, swim beneath the Runcorn-Widnes bridge, pass the Fiddler's Ferry power station, and head along their ancestral paths towards the soap powder works at Bank Quay in Warrington. This is truly an achievement of major historical significance. It symbolises a new chapter in the continuing environmental melodrama of north-west England, and holds out hope for the future. When we can see the bottom of the Irwell I'll believe that miracles have really happened, but one salmon does represent a genuine success – some change assuredly is for the better.

Local History News February 2002

Brobdingnagian Criticism
Alan Crosby

Last year I wrote a short piece about reviews and reviewers, lamenting the inadequacy of some reviews and the lack of charity of some reviewers. Recently, though, I realised that we are today but pygmies standing on the shoulders of giants, at least as far as devastating reviews are concerned. This revelation was occasioned by reading a volume of Lord Macauley's Critical and Historical Essays, published in 1898 but compiled from work of the 1830s. To me Macauley was one of those writers read about but never read, known by name but not by acquaintance. I'm not quite sure how the book itself (most of its leaves uncut) appeared on my shelf. I think it must have been inherited from my late grandfather-in-law, an enthusiastic picker-up of the sort of second hand books that others equally enthusiastically put down. I opened the book out of curiosity, and was immediately smitten by Macauley's wonderfully magisterial and cruelly crushing reviews of the work of his contemporaries. Here he is on Memoirs of the life and Administration of Lord Burghley, by the Reverend Edward Nares, Regius Professor of Modern History at Oxford (published in 3 volumes, 1828):

Coat of Arms - Lord Burghley

The Macauley pot called the Nares kettle black...

'The work of Dr. Nares has filled us with astonishment similar to that which Captain Lemuel Gulliver felt when he first landed in Brobdingnag, and saw corn as high as the oaks in the New Forest, thimbles as large as buckets, and wrens of the bulk of turkeys. The whole book, and every component part of it, is on a gigantic scale ... Compared with the labour of reading through these volumes, all other labour, the labour of thieves on the treadmill, of children in factories, of negroes in sugar plantations, is an agreeable recreation ... On every subject which the Professor discusses, he produces three time as many pages as another man; and one of his pages is as tedious as another man's three. His book is swelled to its vast dimensions by its endless repetitions, by episodes which have nothing to do with the main action, by quotations from books which are in every circulating library, ... Of the rules of historical perspective he has not the faintest notion ... Dr. Nares is a man of great industry and research; but he is so utterly incompetent to arrange the materials which he has collected that he might as well have left them in their original repositories'.

The Macauley pot called the Nares kettle black, for the review evolves into an extended essay on the life of Burleigh, full of marvellous phrasing and perceptive historical analysis. This is a Brobdingnagian review, carrying on for another 32 closely-printed pages, in which Macauley demolishes every argument and opinion of his victim, arguing cogently for a contrary view (he is not enamoured of Burleigh, seeing him as unprincipled and self-serving). It is, like his other essays, remarkably fresh and interesting to read, but also striking, for here - just as history was being invented as an academic discipline - is a professional historian who has looked at the sources, weighed up the evidence, sought a historian's understanding of what was going on in the reigns of Mary and Elizabeth. He saw no black and white but shades of grey: on the subject of religion, he notes, in a view revived in recent years, that the impact of the Reformation was patchy and uncertain, that many of the English were 'sometimes Protestants, sometimes Catholics; sometimes half Protestants half Catholics'. A fine phase, and a fine writer. Poor Edward Nares hardly stood a chance against this critical juggernaut.

Local History News May 2002

Enjoy!
Alan Crosby

Why do we choose a topic to investigate? Some of my work is commissioned by other people, so the initial choice is theirs rather than mine, but much of the rest is determined by what interests me at the time. I have a long list of 'articles that I'll write one day', and an equally long list of 'documents to work on when I have the time' and 'topics to research when I've done the five already in hand'. Other people have a more single-minded devotion to a specific subject, investigating and writing about it for many years, seemingly tapping an inexhaustible spring of information and showing an equally unfailing ability to deal with it. Some move from subject to subject, shifting abruptly from period to period and place to place. Perhaps something captures our interest and we switch from one theme to another, or we may have a long-term aim, a grand strategy which is a backdrop to our more immediate work, and over the years we accumulate material and shift the content round constantly in our minds, gradually formulating a structure, an argument, a sequence of ideas.

But we should avoid, if at all possible, anything which we don't find interesting. We should not regard local history as a penance. I think of Jim Dixon, the hero of Kingsley Amis's clever, sharply-observed and very funny Lucky Jim, as he struggles desperately to finish (well, actually to start) the article which might gain him tenure in the provincial university where he lectures in the history department: The economic influence of the development of shipbuilding techniques, 1450 to 1485 … 'it was a perfect title, in that it crystallised the article's niggling mindlessness, its funereal parade of yawn-enforcing facts, the pseudo-light it threw upon non-problems'. He can barely think of the words without yawning, and he fails completely to see the point of the subject, let alone of the article (except the obvious one of career advancement and even that is scarcely appealing). He finally writes it, sends it off to a journal editor, hears nothing for a very long time, and then finds that the editor has run away to an obscure Argentine

university and published the article under his own name. His reaction is almost one of relief.

Halfway through writing my doctoral thesis I became so wearied by it and – more seriously – so weary of its subject, that it was a real trial to finish. Newly-married, living at that time in two rooms in the top of a Victorian house in Norwich, I plodded through the last chapters and tried to stay awake while putting together the obligatory and pretentious 'review of the literature'. Only the severe strictures of my beloved compelled me to get it finished [written in longhand and posted chapter by chapter to my Mum to be typed – those were the days!]. I was awarded my doctorate and immediately and thankfully relegated, to the topmost shelf, the 100,000 words which had earned it.

That was a salutary lesson which I have always remembered: research something which you find interesting, and if you become bored with it think seriously about abandoning the whole thing. That may seem easier said than done, especially with a doctoral thesis, but sometimes we read books or articles where the author's lack of commitment, lack of enthusiasm, and lack of inspiration emerge from the page like a stupefying miasma. In very marked contrast is the preface to Peter Warner's excellent book Bloody Marsh: a seventeenth century village in crisis [Walberswick, Suffolk]* in which he discusses the background to the work and his feelings about the subject and what he has written. He explains the gestation of the project in a way rarely found in a local history book, noting how it didn't just happen, but instead gradually emerged, via a doctoral thesis, notes for teaching undergraduates, case material for use in history workshops, and a stimulating exercise in exploration for an author who normally focussed on other periods.

It is a most interesting preface, for our motives in writing about a particular subject, or beginning to investigate sources for a certain topic, are by no means irrelevant. Like Peter Warner, most of us find that the raw material from which we create our work, be it a lecture, an article, a book, or any other form, engages our interest, stimulates our imagination, spurs us to find out more, and – a very important element – may well encourage us to share our findings and thoughts with others. In reading the articles submitted to The Local Historian I am struck by the enthusiasm and the dedication which so many authors display, as well as by their high academic standards. That enthusiasm is a strength of our subject: there's no place for Jim Dixon here!

*Peter Warner, Bloody Marsh: a seventeenth century village in crisis
(Windgather Press, 2000)

Local History News May 2002

The inportants of corect speling

Alan Crosby

When I was a child in Surrey, notices in the omnibuses of the Aldershot & District Traction Company informed passengers (for such we were, as of course we had not yet become 'customers') that 'tickets must be shewn for inspection'. "What a funny word 'shewn' is", I used to think. Much more recently I was involved on the fringes of a debate as to whether, in a forthcoming book, the spelling 'inclosure' should be used rather than 'enclosure'. My view was that 'inclosure' was anachronistic, but the counter-argument was that it should be employed because that was how the word was spelled in the Inclosure (or Enclosure) Acts of the eighteenth-century. The vagaries of spelling in the past, and the way in which our own perceptions of correctness influence our views of what we are reading, are familiar problems for local and family historians. Once upon a time in a record office - this is an absolutely true story - I overheard a searcher ask the duty archivist whether she should correct the spelling of a surname in a seventeenth-century parish register: 'We've never spelled it like that, it's wrong'. The archivist, after a moment or two of stupefied astonishment, gently suggested that it would not be a good idea.

Spelling and its evolution is a fascinating and confusing subject. How many of us, embarking upon our early palaeography exercises, have been able to read the letters but then found that they've made an apparently impossible word? And how many of us, later on, are faced with that difficult choice: do we modernise the spelling and lose the 'flavour' of the original, or leave it as it was written and run several risks: i) that the reader won't understand; ii) that we will be accused of using original spelling just because it looks 'quaint'; iii) that readers will think that we can't spell; or iv) maybe the worst of the lot today, that we will make the computer spellchecker wish that it had never been born, and so perhaps we'll press the wrong button and leave some nonsense in the text (it's sometimes entertaining, at the end of a long day, to print out a piece of spellchecked historical writing in which we have opted for the first alternative choice each time ... a new form of creative writing, though I expect it's already been tried).

We are conditioned from the very beginning of our literate lives to the notion of a single correct spelling for every word, and therefore believe that if we don't conform to the official version we are simply, and unarguably, wrong. Such dogmatism admittedly goes back a long way now, to the rigidity of nineteenth-century educational regimes, and - though derided in the notorious and glorious 1960s - is now well back in favour. But of course the idea of a single universal spelling would have been laughable to our forebears 300 years ago. Those trendy lefties in the '60s were actually sticking pretty closely to the unspoken but well understood principles of ten generations earlier - spell it how you feel it should be spelled, don't worry too much about consistency, let the flow and sense of the text be your guide and not a [sterile?] insistence on the shape of the individual word. Let your poetic or literary or verbal instincts mould your words and their form. Let it all hang out, man! Radical stuff in 1967 - completely normal in 1667.

I certainly do not advocate that we should go back either to 1667 or 1967 - not least because the brightly-coloured velvet costumes and flowing locks of either period would hardly be suit me now - but I do relish the creative anarchy of spelling in the past. For me it is one of the incidental charms of the documentary sources, one of the delights of reading a manuscript for the first time. I like to see how a writer, perhaps unaccustomed to the art of writing itself, and certainly unfamiliar with the words (and with no comforting dictionary to hand) struggled to put down something which approximated to the sounds made when he or she said the word. And so we also gain a small understanding of how the word may have been pronounced. Here in Lancashire I note how our thus-converted seventeenth century dialects and speech patterns show close similarities with those of lowland Scots (qwich qhiet qwishon) and I hear in my mind the late fifteenth-century writer of a letter which begins, in formal style, rolling the words around the tongue in a way which is now definitely unEnglish, 'Deare honured faredr and modr'.

Sometimes in local history classes we read the texts aloud in this way and try to reproduce (how can we know if accurately or not) the sounds which our ancestors made - often harsher, usually more guttural, always more 'Germanic', more rhythmic and more ponderous than the fluid dexterities of modern English, with the vocal and verbal agilities which, traditionally, we owe to Shakespeare but which were really becoming general in the mid-sixteenth century as the language evolved into a new stage. The spelling may tell us how they spoke, and it is beautiful in its idiosyncrasy and individuality. How liberated they were, those relatively few who, four hundred years ago, could put pen to paper or quill to parchment. How good to be free of embarrassment if they could not spell embarasment. How lucky not to have to worry about the difference between 'practice' and 'practise'. But if Anna, aged 10, does not get 20 out of 20 for spelling in this week's test, there will be words of a different sort!

Local History News August 2001

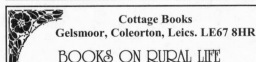

Dusty Archives and Viking Longships
Alan Crosby

Whenever a newspaper manages to find a story about archives, the Boy's Book of Cliches is pulled down from the shelf. Documents are always 'discovered' in archives by the researcher. The implication is that nobody, ever, at any time, was aware of the existence of that particular document before. Not even the archivist who catalogued it. Then, of course, they aren't just 'in the archives' – they are languishing, or hidden, or buried, or lost, or even mouldering. And the archives, naturally, are 'dusty'. The archivist is rarely described in newspaper articles, mainly I suppose because most archivists culpably fail to conform to the stereotype and so would conflict with the image in the mind of the reporter – to newspaper-people, all archivists are, by definition, thin elderly men, hunched and stooping, wisps of grey hair straggling from their bald heads.

They all wear ancient tweed jackets, frayed and tatty at the edges, and most have a pair of dirty gold-rimmed glasses perched precariously on the end of their (probably rather unclean) nose. They speak in cracked and high-pitched voices, a little uncertainly because they are quite unused to human company, and they lapse frequently into incomprehensible Latin. Most of these eccentric archivists live a troglodytic existence, rarely seeing daylight and working in subterranean burrows, deep down in basements which are piled with heaps of bundles of papers and rolls of parchment which spill from boxes and shelves.

Being married to an archivist who fails … in oh, just about every respect … to answer to this description, and who works in a 1970s concrete building on stilts, with huge plate-glass windows and vast airy spaces, I am wary of such cliched images. Even worse, none of her colleagues really fits the bill either. I suppose

that cliches are the lifeblood of reporters, but their uncertainties about the world of history are very great indeed. We have recently had a series of sensational stories in our local paper (a favourite source of alternative history) including the extraordinary revelation that Henry VIII dissolved the priory just outside the town on the grounds that the prior was immoral. That was a quite remarkable world exclusive, though unfortunately the original story had broken only a matter of 460 years earlier and so it should not really have merited stopping the presses. The headline (I forget the precise details, mercifully) was something like 'Naughty Prior Exposed in Tudor Sex Scandal'. But, sadly, no pictures were available.

The property pages are also good for new

interpretations on a familiar theme, as cliches are trotted out to embellish a dull little piece of text. Anxious to give a little novelty to a feature on a house, reporters add some spicy extras, helped by house-owners whose desire to get a good price transcends their truthfulness. Ships' timbers reused in houses are naturally a favourite, no matter how far from any possible navigable water a building might be – a public house near my own town, almost a thousand feet above sea level and eight miles from a waterway, is allegedly made of not just any old ships' timbers, but the timbers of Viking longships. Now that's what I call classy, especially as the building gives every appearance of dating from 1840. In the past few years I've read of a house which sheltered Oliver Cromwell's men after Bonnie Prince Charlie's rising [sic], a restaurant mentioned in the Domesday Book, a small 19th century terraced house which is 'where the monks at the local friary lived',and I've lost track of the number of priest holes and secret passages, those perpetual myths which are the bane of the lives of serious local historians.

Can we do anything about this? I fear that we are unable to influence the stereotypic view, to correct the cliches and to promote a more realistic view of history and those who engage in it. We can try, patiently, to explain how truth is exciting, how historical investigation can be fascinating without the need for name droping and linking with great events, and how documents may not always be dusty or languishing undiscovered. But even though almost everyone to whom I talk laments the approach to teaching history which focused on kings and queens, battles and inventions, it is that sort of headline-filling eye-catching name which is the last resort of the cub reporter who, shirtsleeves rolled up, green eyeshade pulled down, well-chewed biro clutched in hand, is

AND HOW CAN YOU BE SO SURE THE TIMBERS COME FROM A VIKING LONGSHIP?

frantically scribbling a story on a spiral-bound pad in time for final late-night edition …oh well, others have their stereotypes too.

For a view of the stereotype see The Local Historian Vol 31 No 4 page 252 – but it was 1880!

Local History News November 2001

Dead Language

Alan Crosby

Recent EU legislation requires medical products to be labelled in the language of Cicero so that everybody, from Turkü to Taranto, will understand what they contain. It's the irrepressible sense of quirky humour displayed by that lot in Brussels which is so endearing. English is now the *lingua franca* (I've always liked that joke, too) and another recent report (sociologist, Reading University, not 1 April) condemned, with awesome political incorrectness, the compulsory teaching of Welsh in the principality, arguing that it should be allowed to die because everybody west of Offa's Dyke speaks English anyway. Then, it was claimed, Welsh (once properly dead) could become the equivalent of Latin, a language used only for high-quality classical scholarship. Local historians, of course, don't see Latin as a classical language, and its deadness, like that of a monster in a horror film, is only partial. Instead, for most of us it is the last, and for many the insurmountable, vertical cliff-face on the uphill struggle towards the summit of total accomplishment.

Picture the hapless entrant into our world. He or she gets to grips with record office and library procedures, reads about county histories and pre-Conquest charters, Hooper's hedgerow dating and queenpost roofs, and then come the documents. Panic. Consternation. Funny writing, unintelligible script. Drunken spiders dipped in ink have crawled randomly across a page which starving mice have ravaged, chewing away corners and tattering the edges. What does document this say? How can I ever read this? Slowly, with much pain and humiliation, all becomes comparatively clear. The palaeography classes and the long evenings spent going over the same few words produce enlightenment. Seventeenth century wills hold fewer terrors, the delight of being able to read the original of something four centuries old replaces the longing for a nice clean bit of typescript circa 1930. But what's this at the top? I still can't read it.... or rather, I can read the letters but what do they say. Is it in 'Old English'. No, oh no, it's LATIN.

Why didn't I pay more attention at school. Why did I squander all those hours spent carving my name (in English) on the desk leg, or filling the ancient and dusty inkwell with even more bits of rubbish, or reading *Biggles* under the cover of an improving text. How on earth can I remember those endings, those agreements, those conjugations and declensions? Is being able to translate (badly) 'Having pitched camp near the enemy lines the troops were sent out to forage' going to help me in this exercise? The last is a fine example of a question which expects the answer 'no', for *amo amas amat* and *bellum bellum bellum* seem of questionable relevance when confronted by *Ad' Sess' pac' tent' apud Wigan in Com' lanc ' die lune vid' et vicesimo primo die Januar' Anno RR d'ni Caroli Ang '&c duod'mo*. Then come the subversive thoughts ... "I could just paraphrase", "Why not do only the date and leave the rest", "The endings don't really matter that much, it's the vocabulary which counts".

And those words, so familiar to so many and so much denounced by that happy band of local historians who have reached the summit and for whom 'doing the Latin bit at the top' no longer presents an obstacle: "Well, I can understand the gist of it". The only comfort in all this? Why did the clerk in 1637 abbreviate so many words. Could it really be true - did he not know the endings either!

(This piece first appeared in Local History News, No 52, Autumn 1999)

The Irish in Kilburn: Myth and Reality

Dick Weindling and Marianne Colloms

Famine', about a million Irish had already gone to America and perhaps 500,000 had made their way to Britain. But mass migration occurred during the ten-year period of the famine and its aftermath (1845-1855), when over two million people left.

The majority of Irish who settled in Britain were very poor, as the better-off tended to go to America. Emigration as a consequence of the famine increased the numbers from the poorer classes and it was estimated that up to 90 per cent of the emigrants between 1851 and 1855 were labourers. The majority were also Catholics. But MacRaild argues that there was more to the Irish communities than poverty, Catholicism and drink. These aspects were over-emphasised by the Victorians, and the Irish were used as scapegoats for a host of problems in the cities. Many writers of the period emphasised the negative aspects of the Irish in London, and rarely mentioned that most were well-behaved and worked hard to send money back home.

Before the famine, there were three groups of Irish who came to Britain on a temporary basis. Seasonal workers came during harvest time. The cowkeepers around London cultivated hay intensively and employed large numbers of Irish labourers for the harvest. Their presence could cause tension, and fights between the English and Irish workers were reported during the eighteenth century. For example, in 1774 there were pitched battles between English and Irish haymakers in Kingsbury, Edgware and Hendon. The increasing commercialisation of British farming at the beginning of the nineteenth century led to even greater temporary migration of the Irish. The women and children usually remained at home tending the smallholding, while the wandering reapers (known as spalpeen, an Irish term for rascal or scamp) spent up to half the year in Britain. In 1815 London's Irish population was said to have increased by 5,000 spalpeen in May and June as they waited for the harvest. A good summer meant the men could bring back £10-£12, but a poor harvest might yield little more than five shillings. In 1830 the crop failed and there were deaths from starvation

Kilburn, three miles from central London, developed on both sides of the old Roman road, Watling Street (now the Edgware Road and Kilburn High Road). This article explores the origins of the neighbourhood's large Irish population and tests our initial assumption that they first settled in Kilburn, as in other parts of London, during the large-scale exodus from Ireland during the Great Famine of 1845-1855. We examine the Irish-born people in Kilburn using the 1881 census, and also explore the Victorian myth of 'Irish equals Catholic plus poverty'. The study is carried forward to the present day, examining the new influences that stimulated Irish emigration in the twentieth century.

Ireland has a long history of migration: since the early eighteenth century about eight million people have emigrated, and by 1890 40 per cent of all Irish-born people were living outside Ireland. The Irish had been coming to England for temporary work since the Middle Ages and began to form permanent settlements in London by the Elizabethan period. However, the earliest significant migration from Ireland occurred in the eighteenth century - these were economic migrants and groups seeking religious freedom. During the Napoleonic Wars about 100,000 Irish departed for America and a larger number came to Britain. By 1845, the eve of the 'Great

among Irish labourers in Acton, Willesden and Hampstead, and a riot among the Irish in Barnet. By the 1880s the numbers of spalpeens had declined due to the increased use of machinery on farms. Reaping and threshing machines meant that the Irish labourers were now only needed to harvest potatoes, turnips and other root crops.

A second group of seasonal Irish workers were the navvies who worked on the construction of canals and railways. They moved their hastily-constructed shanty towns with them as they went. Renowned for their hard work and hard living, Irish navvies were set apart from the other workers, partly as they only spoke 'the Gaelic tongue'. They were generally better paid, with a diet rich in beef and beer, but their working life was short. It has been estimated that in 1851 about 10 per cent of navvies were Irish, but the proportion varied considerably from area to area. After 1798 a colony of Irish developed at Lisson Grove where the parishes of Marylebone and Paddington joined. Irish labourers were employed on the nearby Grand Union Canal, and they were attracted to the land as potatoes could be grown around the huts. In 1836 fights broke out in Hanwell between locals and Irish labourers working on the railway, and in 1846 a group of Irish navvies were charged with starting a riot during the building of the Round House (a large railway engine shed) in Camden Town). Hundreds of English were engaged in bricklaying on the site and similar numbers of Irish were working near Euston station.

The third itinerant group were Irish paupers, whose numbers increased during the post-war slump after 1815. Many London parishes expressed concern regarding the cost of supporting Irish paupers in their area. By the 1830s, after years of temporary migration, the permanently-settled Irish in London outnumbered the itinerants. The original Irish colony, dating from the early seventeenth century, was in the parish of St Giles (part of Holborn) but with time other settlements were made across the Metropolis, particularly in Whitechapel and Southwark. The overcrowded slums were called 'rookeries'. The Irish worked as labourers, porters, coalheavers, ballastmen, milksellers, costermongers, streethawkers, tailors and shoemakers, often catering for their own countrymen.

The Irish community in St Giles was much larger than that of other parishes: the area was called 'Little Dublin' in the eighteenth century. In 1796 the poor rate of £2,000 for the combined parishes of St Giles and St George's provided support for 1,200 Irish. But their numbers increased dramatically, so that by 1819 £20,000 of the total rate of £32,000 went to destitute Irish. The population was estimated at 6,000 Irish adults and 3,000-4,000 children, many living in common lodging houses. The tenants of a single room sometimes sublet to numerous other people, so that forty people might live in one cellar. Between 1844 and 1847 a new road was built joining Oxford Street to Holborn, involving the demolition of 259 houses in St Giles. But the Irish living in these properties just moved a few streets away and even continued to live in the condemned houses after the roofs had been removed. Mann found that the numbers of occupants in the houses in Church Lane (next to the new road) doubled between 1841 and 1847. For example, a house which had 29 occupants before the construction of the new road, later had 62 people. Further attempts to improve the area in the 1850s caused some of the Irish to move out to Somers Town and Lisson Grove. Others went to Agar Town, which Dickens called 'A Suburban Connemara' and in 1851 likened to one of the worst towns in Ireland. A modern analysis shows that, contrary to popular belief, the number of Irish in Agar Town was not that high and concluded that 'very few of its inhabitants had been born in Ireland, and very few seem to have relocated to Agar Town when the worst parts of St Giles were demolished'.

Census data

Lees made a detailed study of the Irish in five districts of London using the census data of 1851 and 1861. She selected three districts of London with the highest proportion of Irish-born (over 10 per cent): the old areas of Irish settlement in St Giles, Whitechapel, and the riverside area of Southwark. These were compared with two areas with lower percentages of Irish-born populations, Kensington (3.6 per cent) and Camberwell (2.9 per cent). The London Irish community was larger than the census indicated as the figures only included the Irish-born, not the second and third generations born in London. The sample showed that in 1851 English-born children of Irish parents made up 30 per cent of Irish households and this had risen to 40 per cent in the 1861 sample. Lees concluded that three types of Irish came to London. A small number of middle-class Irish, many of them Protestant and culturally similar to the English, chose the metropolis for its professional and educational opportunities. Craftsmen from Irish villages and small towns travelled to London for job opportunities. But the largest group were the rural labourers and small farmers who lacked skills and urban experience.

Our analysis of the early census data for Hampstead showed that in 1841 the Irish-born accounted for only 1.4 per cent of the population, rising by 1851 to 2 per cent, possibly due to the effect of the famine exodus. By 1861 it had fallen back to 1.4 per cent and in 1881 it was still only 1.6 per cent. We conducted a detailed analysis of the 1881 census, searching for all the Irish-born people resident in Kilburn. It is important to point out that while some entries show places of birth as, for example, 'Cork, Ireland', others may only show 'Cork'

century Kilburn was neither a notably Irish district nor was the Catholic population very large.

The main influx of Irish emigrants to the Kilburn area in fact took place much later than is generally believed, during the years immediately following the Second World War. Post-war Britain experienced a chronic labour shortage and many of the Irish who came to Kilburn were economic migrants, attracted by job opportunities in light industry and construction companies. Local people subsequently ascribed the large Irish population of Kilburn to the notion that it was as far as a

MALES				FEMALES		
Occupation	Number	%		Occupation	Number	%
Labourers	37	33.7		Laundress/Washerwomen	23	12.5
Clergymen/RC Priests	9	8.2		General/domestic servants	16	8.7
Painters	6	5.5		Scholars	13	7.1
Boot and Shoe makers	4	3.6		Dressmaker/tailoress	9	4.9
Scholars	4	3.6		Cook & Cook Domestic Servants	5	2.7
Tailors	4	3.6		Charwomen	4	2.2
Children under six (not scholars)	4	3.6		Nurses	4	2.2
Students	3	2.7		Children under six (not scholars)	4	2.2
Clerks	3	2.7		Housekeepers	3	1.6
Policemen	3	2.7		Annuitants	3	1.6
Costermonger and Hawker	2	1.8		Governess	3	1.6
House and light porter	2	1.8		Boot binder/closer	2	1.1
Iron merchant	2	1.8		Others	5	
Others	27			No information/occupation	90	48.9
Total	**110**			**Total**	**184**	

and many just have 'Ireland'. This means that a simple search for Ireland in the 'Country' column will not reveal all the Irish born people. A second search is therefore necessary in the 'Town' column. The results are summarised in the following table, showing the Irish-born in 1881:

One-third of the men were labourers. The nine priests and clergymen were associated with both Catholic and Protestant churches. There was a variety of tradesmen, professionals and skilled and semi-skilled workers. It is noticeable that the large majority of the men had jobs. In contrast, almost half the woman did not declare an occupation: they ran the home. There was a smaller range of occupations for the women with only 16 different types of job, and many were laundresses and servants. There were more Irish-born women than men (184 compared with 110). From the available evidence we concluded that despite the presence of a large Catholic church, towards the end of the nineteenth

man could comfortably walk from Euston Station, carrying a suitcase. In fact, during the 1950s the Legion of Mary would meet Irish people at Euston as they came off the boat train at 3.00 in the morning. They had a stall inside the station with jobs and accommodation advertised. The Legion had contacts with local landladies, contractors in the building industries, and foremen in factories. Paddy Fahey moved from Waterford to work in England during the Second World War. He remembers what life was like for the Irish in Kilburn, and also describes the role of the church of the Sacred Heart:

You had half a million people come over in the Fifties, but there was nothing organised, there was no community at all. But they had the dances, the Irish dance-halls were terrific! Now, I was always fond of dancing. I remember the tea-dances at the Banba Club in Kilburn - a half a crown to get in and you'd get a Spam sandwich and a cup of tea. On Sundays, that was 3.00 to 6.30, and some of them used to wait and hang on for the evening session, from 8 o'clock till 11. They used to do fox-trots, slow waltzes, and that: there was also Irish dancing: the Siege of Ennis and the Walls of Limerick. Rock 'n roll wasn't it, no way ... The Church was like a lamp to moths, the attraction... The Irish always settled around their churches.... It was also safety in numbers when it wasn't safe to be a Catholic. I remember the Oblate Fathers that were up in Kilburn: they did tremendous work. Apart from their spiritual duties, they organised hurling, Gaelic football, social events, outings. The Church was the main organiser of social functions. There were about seven or eight Oblate Fathers at the time, and most of their work was dealing with the affairs of Irish emigrants. An Irishman would return home annually and he would bring back the first cousin or a younger brother.

Father Quinn, the parish priest in Kilburn, recalled the 1960s as the decade of peak attendance at the Sacred Heart Church in Quex Road. Eighteen masses were held every Sunday, and over 10,000 people attended, 90 per cent of whom were Irish. It was at this time that locals often referred to the area as 'County Kilburn'. Gerry Conlon, one of the four people wrongly accused of the Guildford pub bombing of October 1974, was living in Hope House, a large Catholic hostel opposite the Sacred Heart Church, Kilburn, at the time of the bombing. In his autobiography he describes it as

a large place with a hundred beds, all occupied by single Irishmen. There are always thousands of guys like that floating around London, working on building sites and labouring jobs, staying a few days or months and then moving on, or out, or back. Father Carolan, I discovered later, was very reluctant to take us in, because he knew nothing about us. We could produce no letter from our parish priest back home, which was the normal passport you needed to a place like that, and we had no other kind of reference. But when he saw us looking like half-drowned rats from the rain he did the right Christian thing and said he would let us in.

While the impetus for the emigration to England in the 1950s and the 1980s remained largely unaltered from that of the famine years in the last century, namely a search for economic survival, other aspects had changed. Those coming to London in the 1980s were mostly from urban areas and more arrived from Northern Ireland than previously. By then the priests of the Sacred Heart were burying four or five a week of the early generation of immigrants and the Church no longer exerted as great an influence on newcomers. But the immigrants were still attracted to Kilburn because of its Irish population - it offered a sense of community and security. Many of the pubs in the Kilburn High Road had Irish landlords, and Irish papers were widely available. The large number of single Irish men in the neighbourhood were increasingly hard-pressed to find suitable accommodation, as property booms and gentrification took their toll on the supply of rented rooms and flats. By the end of the eighties, it was not unusual for ten men (either newcomers or London Irish) to arrive daily at the Quex Road hostel, looking for a room, where there was only space for two. A considerable number of those seeking accommodation were older men, who been displaced by the shrinking rental market. They could be found among the 100-200 people who gathered on the steps of the Sacred Heart Church every afternoon for a free meal provided by Mother Theresa's Missionaries of Charity. The 1991 census data showed 11,027 Irish-born people in Camden, representing 6.5 per cent of the population. The two wards on the Kilburn High Road had the highest proportion of Irish-born across the borough (11 per cent and 13 per cent). Of all of the London boroughs Brent had the highest number of Irish-born residents at 21,936 (9 per cent of residents). But, as in the nineteenth century, these figures were an underestimate, because they did not show the second and third generation children who were born in England, or those from Northern Ireland. The data shows that by 1991 Irish occupation was still concentrated along both sides of the Kilburn High Road but that it had had also spread further north-west, with larger numbers in the Cricklewood area of Brent.

As a result of the analysis we reject our initial hypothesis. The Irish did not settle in Kilburn in large numbers until after the Second World War. Many were Catholics, especially those arriving in the 1950s and 1960s, but it is a mistake to assume that all the Irish were Catholic, or that all the Catholics were Irish. Most of the available data does not specify ethnicity or religious belief, which makes it impossible to draw accurate conclusions about the precise numbers in either category. While much of the published information refers to single Irish men, it is important to realise that the majority of Irish in Kilburn during the nineteenth and twentieth centuries were married with children. Although the number of Irish in Kilburn has declined from its peak, there is still a strong Irish culture. In 2001 a new feature film called 'County Kilburn', portraying a week in the life of a group of Irish regulars at a local pub, was shown at the Tricycle Cinema in Kilburn; and at the Tricycle Theatre a play about a group of Irishmen was performed. It was called, 'The Kings of the Kilburn High Road.

This article is an abridged version of one which first appeared in The Local Historian volume 32 no.2 (May 2002).

Mushrooms, scandal and bankruptcy:
the short life of Mid Rhondda Football Club
Martin Johnes

parts of England where football was already well established, to work in the burgeoning coal industry. The semi-professional English Southern League was also actively encouraging the expansion of soccer in south Wales to help itself survive in the face of the growing power, popularity and prestige of the national Football League. The Southern League's promises of membership led to the formation of new clubs such as Swansea Town and Newport County. In 1912 an amateur club from Tonypandy in the Rhondda decided to seek elevation to the league.

In 1848, a visitor to the two valleys which make up the Rhondda wrote that that air was 'aromatic with wild flowers and mountain plants'. Fewer than 1,000 people lived there, but a great coal rush was about to descend and transform the Rhondda into a thriving series of interlocked communities, each dominated by the winding gear of its colliery. By 1911 the population was 152,000, and the rural beauty had become an urban sprawl of tightly packed terraced houses clinging to the mountainside under the shadow of looming tip heaps. Amid such environmental rape and the dangerous life of working underground, sport offered some relief to the people who inhabited a Rhondda that has become synonymous with south Wales.

The history of sport has come a long way since the 1970s, but local studies have tended to be confined to nostalgic studies of teams, grounds and sportsmen and women. Yet sports history has much to offer local history, for it sheds light on daily life in communities, the joys and tribulations of their inhabitants, and the local impact of wider events and agencies. This article explores the history of a small semi-professional soccer club which gave some vitality and colour to the cultural landscape of the Rhondda. Mid Rhondda FC only existed from 1912 to 1928, and has been largely forgotten by historians and people in the Rhondda itself, but its short and turbulent history sheds light on underexplored areas of the history of sport and also, perhaps, on the very nature of local history itself.

In Edwardian south Wales football, though overshadowed by rugby union, was growing rapidly. Professionalism was legalised in south Wales in 1900 and teams such as Aberdare and Treharris led the way in improving playing standards in the South Wales League (formed 1890). The increasing popularity of soccer was aided by the migration of people, from

Setting up a professional club was expensive and hazardous but the guarantee of entry to an established high-profile competition did much to offset potential risks and encourage promoters. Entry to the Southern League was secured with a simple promise of a plan for a senior club. Raising capital proved more problematic: two weeks before the first game of the season, the whole project was pronounced dead because not enough money had been collected. But, encouraged by the positive press coverage, the promoters decided to carry on. Just over a week before the season kicked off, the club found a manager and secured the local athletics and cycling arena as a ground, but still had very little money and no players. Yet it managed to scratch together a team of local amateurs and some imported professionals, and in its first game entertained Ton Pentre (another Rhondda town) before a thousand spectators.

The club's swift birth earned it the nickname of 'The Mushrooms', an image that symbolised the whole history of the Rhondda. The speed with which the club was set up helps to explain how the professional game was able to establish itself so quickly across Britain in this period. Setting up a club did not have to be a lengthy process and, once in existence, it could quickly attract support, even in a town with no experience of professional soccer. The name chosen for the new club was Mid Rhondda rather than Tonypandy, the name of the town where it was based. Because of their geography, towns in the valleys often lacked a focus and were instead collections of dispersed but adjoining settlements. Their populations identified more with the wider valley or the smaller village, than with the town or ward itself. To ensure as much support as possible, the name of the club had to appeal to such sentiments. The Rhondda was a world-famous coal-producing region and its inhabitants were proud of this. The club was keen to associate itself with such pride, rather than with Tonypandy, a name most famous for its 1910 riots.

Like most of its peers, the club registered as a limited liability company and thus its lists of shareholders and directors are held at the Public Record Office. Its first board of directors consisted of three licensed victuallers, a schoolmaster, an accountant, an ironfounder and a colliery weighman: a cross-section of the small tradesmen and workers' representatives that provided the civic leadership of the coalfield. All were from the Rhondda, and nearly half the club's shareholders were local miners.

Occupation	No. of shareholders	No. of shares held
Miner	41	162
Licensed Victualler	10	130
Not given	15	100
Valuer	2	42
Grocer	2	15
Clerk	2	12
Agent	2	12
Stationmaster	1	12
Councillor	1	10
Solicitor	1	10
Hairdresser	1	10
Fish merchant	1	10
Athletic Institution	1	10
Manager	1	10
Check weigher	1	10
Director	1	10
Porter	1	10
Boot merchant	1	5
Printer	1	5
Barman	1	2
Ironmonger	1	1
88		**588**

Although most of the miners only owned one or two shares each, the purchase still represented a significant financial outlay for working-class men. Dividends were very rarely paid by any club; shares were bought as declarations of support, rather than financial investments, and are a testimony to the importance that football held in many miners' lives.

The first years of the club were unremarkable. It was just one of a host of semi-professional teams across the south Wales valleys that struggled to make ends meet, employed players who also worked as colliers, and were supported by a small but enthusiastic band of fans. The first serious problem the club faced was the First World War. Like others, it struggled through the 1914-1915 season with reduced gates brought about by restrictions on travel and the timing of matches. After organised professional football was suspended in the summer of 1915, the club even ceased to play friendlies. In 1917 the secretary was forced to write to the registrar of Joint Stock Companies to explain the absence of annual returns: all the players and several directors had joined up, the remaining directors were engaged in important war work, he himself was too old to enlist but was working as a miner, and there was no ground to play on or money to pay an auditor.

Amid the general optimism of the immediate post-war years, the club was supremely ambitious. To attract quality players it was, like many Welsh teams in the Southern League, willing to match or even exceed the wages paid in the Football League. In 1920 Mid Rhondda won the second division of the Southern League, the Welsh League and the South Wales Cup. Jimmy Seed, who later found fame as an England international and manager, said 'it seemed like "non-stop football"'. He was taken with Mid Rhondda from the moment he had first got off the train and been cheered as if he were heavyweight champion of the world, rather than an unknown footballer unable to get an English club. The highlight of that season was a derby before 20,000 people against Ton Pentre in an FA Cup preliminary round. Seed remembered that

The rivalry was terrific and there was little else discussed in the miners' pubs and clubs a week before the match ... the mountainside overlooking the field was black with spectators who couldn't get inside ... there was more excitement from this crowd than any huge gathering I have since witnessed at Wembley, Hampden Park, Ninian Park or Windsor Park. Within a minute we were one up ... Our supporters just went crazy. They invaded the pitch singing, shouting, waving hats and rattles. Others hugged and embraced the home team ... it was five minutes before the game started once more.

Mid Rhondda's manager that year was Haydn Price, a colourful character and qualified schoolteacher from nearby Maerdy. In a ten-year playing career he had been a semi-professional at Aberdare, Aston Villa, Burton United, Wrexham, Leeds City, Shrewsbury Town and Walsall, but never really established himself at any of his larger clubs and won one of his five Welsh caps while in Villa's third team. He joined Mid Rhondda as secretary-manager in 1919 and set about dominating the club. At a time when the maximum wage for Football League players was £9, Haydn Price was paid £10 a week, although his wages were not always forthcoming because of financial difficulties. A well-attended public meeting in 1920 became heated when Price announced that he felt impeded by a hostile section of the directorate, angry because he had not consulted them in all the club's affairs. They were refusing to accept any responsibility or to help the club financially. The club already had monetary problems thanks to its wage bill and to improvements undertaken in stand accommodation. It was forced to borrow from a director, whom Price had not alienated, in order to make ends meet over the summer months when there was no income from gate receipts. Yet despite the financial instability, and buoyed by a successful season, ground improvements continued with a new press box, directors' room and gym. Small professional clubs were not havens of financial common sense.

In the summer of 1920, after just one season, Price joined Grimsby Town as manager, having previously sold four Mid Rhondda players to his new club. These dealings later came under the spotlight when he was accused of receiving larger fees for players than he had actually paid into Mid Rhondda's account. He quickly fell out with the Grimsby board, resigning very publicly after just four months, returning to Mid Rhondda, and promptly buying a player from Grimsby. He used his sporting connections, and Mid Rhondda notepaper, to act as a personal agent for an outfitter selling sports kit – that arrangement turned sour over an unpaid bill which landed Price in court. He was not the subservient employee or 'sacrificial clerk' that most inter-war managers have been portrayed as by historians, and he dominated his little corner of the football world.

Like the Rhondda itself, the history of Mid Rhondda FC was shaped by coal. In 1923, 87.2 per cent of the local insured population were employed in the coal industry and in 1926 an estimated 90 per cent of Mid Rhondda's supporters were miners. Thus, the 1921 national coal strike inevitably led to a collapse in the club's gates. It struggled financially and found itself in court in respect of £250 owed in wages to a former player. He settled for £150 plus costs but the club and its officials, including Price, were suspended by the Football Association of Wales (FAW) after complaints by other players, clubs, associations and officials. All football at Mid Rhondda's ground was banned. The club failed to produce the documentation demanded by the FAW and was only allowed to continue if a new board and guarantors were found and a deposit of £500 placed with the association. A packed public meeting, chaired over by the general manager of a local colliery company and with hundreds outside unable to gain admission, heard details of debts of over £4,000. In an atmosphere of civic duty, promises of nearly £650 were made, a new chairman found and a fund-raising performance at the local theatre organised.

Three months later the club went into voluntary liquidation, unable to meet the FAW's conditions to lift its suspension. Many other local teams had similar financial problems, as unemployment continued to rise after the end of the 1921 strike and the south Wales coal industry slipped slowly towards collapse. With it fell the majority of the semi-professional teams in south Wales because many fans were unable to afford the 6d admission. During the 1922-1923 season alone, Abertillery Town, Caerphilly Town, Maerdy, Porth Athletic and Ton Pentre all closed. Mid Rhondda was given permission to re-form for the 1923-1924 season and this time it successfully appealed to local miners to have 3d a week voluntarily deducted from their pay. Re-formation took place too late to enter the Southern League so the club was left with just the Welsh League and unpopular friendlies with local amateurs. The 'army of ignoble supporters' who watched matches free from a nearby railway embankment did not help, and the club resorted to asking the Great Western Railway to prosecute offenders for trespass. There was little it could do about local fans who shunned Mid Rhondda in favour of a short train journey and the more glamorous pull of Cardiff City and first division football. Professional sport could be as much about seeking quality entertainment as expressing civic pride through your local team.

By 1924-1925 the club was back in the Southern League, but it was playing too many games with too few players and no money for hotels. Yet, despite its financial problems and the surrounding unemployment, the club's management still harboured ambitions. It applied for membership of the Football League in 1925 - but failed to win a single vote. At the 1925 AGM, attended by a thousand people, controversy broke out again. There was to be a new FAW inquiry into the club, following allegations of illegal lotteries and betting competitions. Supporters expressed dissatisfaction with the way the club was being run and appointed a new management committee. Yet the old directors and management had not resigned and there were now two groups claiming the right to run a club which, no longer being a limited liability company, had no clear constitution.

Well tried!

The FAW inquiry revealed that the club had been profiting from an illegal sweepstake organised personally by a local grocer to help the club. One club director had already been suspended a few months earlier by the association after a similar scheme. More public meetings, fund raising and appeals for unity followed. But there must have been a wry smile in the club when Haydn Price found himself declared bankrupt less than a month later, when a building firm sued him for over £1,400 owed for the building of a new stand five years earlier. Price had been one of seven guarantors on the work but was sued for half the total cost of the stand. Evan Morris, another former director, went bankrupt in August 1925 (a week after Price), having been sued for the other half of the outstanding money. Morris told the judge: 'I thought as things were so bad locally, and owing to the unrest, it would be wise to have an antidote such as sport and music to keep the people quiet'. The judge asked him if he meant against Bolshevism to which Morris replied, 'Hardly that but I still think that if things got better people will support me'.

Meanwhile Mid Rhondda was dependent on loans from local tradesmen and in arrears with its playing staff yet again. The players were said to be loyal to the club and willing to compromise, but it is difficult to see what choice they had. It was either a lower wage or none at all. Directors found themselves harassed by court summons and in danger of losing their homes over the club's debts. The chairman bemoaned the closure of collieries, the loss of derbies because of the bankruptcy of local rivals, and the existence of an 'organised opposition to the club' which wanted to see it go to the wall and attended matches only to bring discontent amongst players by barracking. This club, like the surrounding community, felt under siege from the wider world and the 'economic blizzard' that had engulfed south Wales. Fifty thousand people moved away from the Rhondda in the inter-war years in search of a brighter future elsewhere. The majority of those who went were young men, the sector in society that watched soccer.

In May 1926 South Wales faced further turbulence, with a general strike and subsequent lock out in the coal industry. There was little spare money for entertainment. The club kicked off the 1926-1927 season having decided to employ no professionals until the miners were back at work. Its gates plummeted, and it had lost the weekly contribution given by 400 miners out of their wages. It needed crowds of 5,000 to survive financially, but when it rained gates could fall as low as fifty. The club could was reduced to asking for its share of away gates in advance to cover travel costs. In March 1928, the bank called in the overdraft and Mid Rhondda FC finally closed with debts of £1400. This brought to an end the story of a club that had given many individuals joy, pain and pride, and its financial backers more than their fair share of monetary grief.

Mid Rhondda was a club in which 'the people who made it' can shine through the historical record if we care to look, whether they be the supporters celebrating on the pitch a victory over a local rival or protesting against the sale of a star player; the part-time professional enjoying the adulation of the crowd or resigning himself to the hardship of yet more unpaid wages; or the director faced with an uncaring bureaucracy and the personal tragedy of bankruptcy resulting from trying to support his passion and his community. All these are human stories and deserve their place in history. As the historian Chris Williams has written,

Only by seeing history as full of individuals with their own stories is it possible to defy stereotypes and to bring a sense of proportion to studies of politics and trade unionism … It is the responsibility of the historian to arrive at histories that we think people could have reasonably lived … [Histories should not] patronise and demean their historical subjects … [but] restore to them the sense of agency and originality of thought they possessed.

Sport is about the agency and emotions of individuals: their joys and triumphs, their defeats and losses, the personal decisions they take and face. As historians we must strive to inject that personal touch and recover those stories as best we can.

Further reading:
Richard Holt, Sport and the British: A Modern History (Oxford University Press, 1989); Martin Johnes, Soccer and Society: South Wales, 1900-39 (University of Wales Press, 2002); Chris Williams, Democratic Rhondda: politics and society, 1885-1951 (University of Wales Press, 1996)

This article is an abridged version of one which first appeared in The Local Historian Volume 32 No.1 (February 2002).

Military Gravestones in south-east Essex:
classification and analysis of a neglected source

Stephen Murray

©Robert Blatchford

War memorials have attracted considerable interest among local and family historians, but the inscriptions on military gravestones do not seem to have been widely used as a source for local history studies despite a long tradition of gravestone-recording. One recent article on the use of churchyard gravestones for local history specifically omitted 'memorials from the Second World War'. There are inherent limitations in the use of gravestones for local history research but in conjunction with other sources such as nominal and statistical data on war casualties, death registers, and military service records, they and their inscriptions can illustrate aspects of local military history and how the dead are remembered.

The case study

In 1997 a survey was undertaken of gravestone inscriptions with military connections in part of south-east Essex, covering all accessible churchyards and cemeteries in the Rochford hundred, excluding Foulness, together with a few adjoining parishes in Barstable hundred. The area includes the borough of Southend-on-Sea, and the towns of Rochford, Rayleigh and Benfleet. The major military installations in the area were the Royal Artillery garrison at Shoeburyness (1849-1976) and the airfield at Rochford used by the Royal Flying Corps and Royal Air Force during the two World Wars. The survey included all gravestones of military personnel - soldiers, sailors and airmen - whether buried there or only mentioned on inscriptions, as well as of members of the merchant navy and auxiliary forces, and instances where the inscription states, for example, 'lost on active service 1943'. Military or ex-military personnel whose gravestones make no mention of a military connection, and those buried in unmarked graves, are by definition excluded from its scope. The analysis in this article does not include any names mentioned on war memorials but is restricted to gravestone inscriptions, copies of which have been deposited with the Society of Genealogists, the Essex Record Office, the Imperial War Museum, the Essex Family History Society and the Royal Artillery Historical Trust.

Type of gravestone	Number of gravestones	Number of military personnel buried	Number of military personnel commemorated
CWGC sole burial	317	317	2
CWGC plus non-military family member	44	44	-
CWGC plus military family member	6	12	3
CWGC plus other non-related military burials	9	18	-
CWGC multiple military burials	2	26	-
Private grave sole burial	60	60	-
Private grave plus family member	100	102	11
Private grave plus one other military burial	1	2	-
Gravestone of others commemorating military personnel	185	-	195
Total	**724**	**581**	**211**

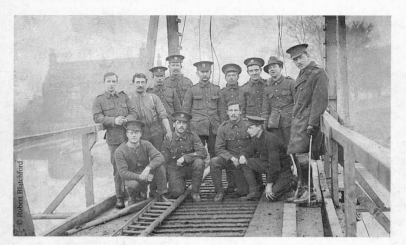

© Robert Blatchford

Types of gravestone

The survey identified 792 individuals, commemorated on 724 separate gravestones. Three types of gravestones commemorating military personnel can be distinguished:
i) Commonwealth War Graves Commission (CWGC) type gravestones
ii) private gravestones marking the graves of military personnel
iii) gravestones marking the graves of non-military personnel but commemorating military personnel within the inscription

In most churchyards and cemeteries within this survey, military graves are not located in separate areas but are placed alongside others of a similar date, although this does lead to some grouping of military graves associated with the two World Wars. There is a specific plot of 'service graves' in the municipal cemetery at Sutton Road, Southend, and the churchyard of St. Andrew at South Shoebury is notable for a large number of Royal Artillery officers' graves in a prominent position around the south porch.

Commonwealth War Graves Commission (CWGC) gravestones

The Commonwealth (formerly Imperial) War Graves Commission gravestones are of a standard design, with headstones 81cm high, 38cm wide and 75cm thick and made of Portland or Hopton Wood stone. The designs for the graves of foreign nationals are slightly different: those for Polish nationals have a pointed top, for Yugoslavs a flat top, and for Czechs tapered sides. The gravestones have a standard inscription, giving a service or regimental crest; the service number and rank of the individual; the name, usually initials and surname; the service unit or regiment; the date

of death and sometimes the age; and a religious emblem such as a cross or star of David. At the base of the stone there may be an inscription of up to 60 letters provided by the next of kin, usually a personal 'message' or a standard form of words such as 'always [or 'forever'] in our thoughts' (19 graves) 'til we meet again' (11), 'gone but not forgotten' (10), 'happy [or 'treasured' or 'beautiful'] thoughts' (9) or 'until the day break and the shadows flee away' (5 graves). Within the survey there are 378 CWGC gravestones marking the graves of 417 individuals. These people represent but a small fraction of the 172,044 Commonwealth service personnel buried in the United Kingdom and commemorated by the CWGC. Fifty gravestones also mark the burial place of another family member and of these 48 have additional headstones, footstones or kerbs indicating the burial of either one or both parents (15 graves), the widow (14), or siblings, children or another person of unspecified relationship. Two gravestones commemorate three service personnel sharing a common surname. There are also nine CWGC gravestones dated 1915 or 1916, each commemorating two people. Although the individuals commemorated in these joint graves were not necessarily from the same regiment or unit, the dates of death of each pair were within about a week of each other. There are two large gravestones marking the collective graves of 26 First World War servicemen, one commemorating eight individuals and the other eighteen.

Private gravestones of military personnel

Private gravestones of military personnel have a great variety of forms and styles following the fashion of the day: large Victorian arched headstones; marble-kerbed graves of the 1930s and 1940s; and simple square headstones from the 1960s to the present day. This category includes military graves prior to the First World War, and the more recent graves of personnel where the only indication of military service is mention of a rank, involvement in a conflict, or an award for bravery such as the Military Medal. There are 161 of these gravestones, marking the burials of 164 people. Two-thirds also mark the burial place of another family member, most commonly the widow (46 graves), or one or both parents (28). Eleven also commemorate a military family member who died, or is buried, elsewhere. Private gravestones often contain more information about military service or the circumstances of death than do the CWGC gravestones. The following is an example at St. Andrew's church, South Shoebury:

SACRED TO THE MEMORY
OF
GUNNERS WALTER EDWARD PEARSON
AND HARRY HUBBARD
ROYAL GARRISON ARTILLERY
WHO WERE KILLED IN A GUN ACCIDENT
AT THE NEW RANGES SHOEBURYNESS
9TH JANUARY 1913
FATHER INTO THY HAND I COMMEND MY SPIRIT
THIS STONE IS ERECTED BY THE OFFICERS
NON-COMMISSIONED OFFICERS AND MEN OF
THE EXPERIMENTAL DEPARTMENT

Commemorative gravestones: the absent dead

Gravestones in the third category mark the burials of non-military personnel but also commemorate military personnel in the inscription. In 1915, on the grounds of expense and equality, the government prohibited the repatriation of the bodies of service personnel killed abroad: 'so many men had no known grave that granting the privilege of bringing back only identified bodies would discriminate against about half the population'. This led to the establishment in 1915 of the Graves Registration Commission (later the Directorate of Graves Registration, then the Imperial War Graves Commission, and since 1960 the Commonwealth War Graves Commission) to trace and register the dead. For the relatives of the deceased a local focus for mourning the 'absent dead' was necessary. This led to the building of local war memorials in the early 1920s but also at a personal level to the commemoration of the deceased on gravestones of non-military relatives.

Within this survey there are 185 gravestones of non-military people commemorating 195 service personnel. Most commonly the graves are of parents (108 graves), although widows (15) and grandparents (8) also figure. Like private gravestones these often contain more information about the circumstances of death and burial place of the individual than do the CWGC gravestones. For example at St. John's church, Southend, is this inscription:

KILLED IN THE GREAT WAR
IN
LOVING MEMORY OF

WILLIAM CHIGNELL
AGED 22
WOUNDED SUVLA BAY AUG 21ST 1915
DIED 30TH AUG 1915
BURIED AT GIBRALTAR
GRAVE NO 3063
ALSO
IN LOVING MEMORY OF
[other family members]

Also included in this category are those gravestones which only make an indirect reference to military personnel. For example at St. Mary's church, South Benfleet:

REQUIESCAT IN PACE
MARY SUSANNA ALTHAM
BORN JULY IX 1809 DIED DEC XII 1883
DAUGHTER OF COLONEL COOK
28TH LIGHT DRAGOONS

Year of death

When military gravestones are analysed by the year of death, the large number of military personnel throughout the twentieth century compared with the nineteenth century reflects the much-increased size of the armed forces, particularly during the World Wars. Several gravestones from immediately after the First World War include inscriptions such as 'passed away ... from injuries received in France' and 'who was severely wounded in France'. Six of the graves for 1950-1959 are of men between the ages of 18 and 25, some of whom would have been national servicemen: indeed, one gravestone explicitly states 'died [1954] on his national service in Germany'.

Date	Number of gravestones
Before 1890	3
1890-1899	5
1900-1909	7
1910-1919	318
1920-1929	31
1930-1939	10
1940-1949	317
1950-1959	26
1960-1969	11
1970-1979	9
1980-1989	16
1990-1997	11

Service and Regiment

The proportions of military personnel can also be calculated. Comparison of these figures with overall numbers of service personnel is difficult as the numbers in each service varied over time. However, comparisons of the gravestone survey details of Second World War personnel with the overall numbers of UK service personnel mobilised and killed during that war confirms that military gravestones for that war in south-east Essex over-represent RAF casualties –

	Total mobilised		Total killed		Graves survey WW2	
	No	(%)	No	(%)	No	(%)
Royal Navy	923,000			(15.7)	50,758	
Army	3,778, 000	(64.2)	144,079	(19.2)	29	(11.6)
Royal Air Force	1,185,000	(20.1)	69,606	(54.5)	126	(50.6)
Total	5,886,000	(100)	264,443	(26.3)	94	(37.8)

Second World War casualty figures. For private gravestones, officers account for 64 per cent and other ranks 18 per cent. Therefore the other ranks are indeed seriously under-represented on private gravestones in comparison with CWGC graves. For commemorative gravestones, an intermediate position applies. This may be because when a gravestone was being carved and erected for a civilian, little additional cost was involved in adding an inscription to commemorate a military relative.

presumably because of the presence of Southend airfield - and under-represent those of the Royal Navy.

The army regiments most frequently mentioned on gravestones are the Royal Artillery (64), the Essex Regiment (38), the Royal Engineers (35) the Royal Army Service Corps (31), the Royal Garrison Artillery (27), the Royal Field Artillery (22) and the London Regiment (20). In total 112 army regiments and units are mentioned although 61 of these regiments are only represented by a single individual. The Royal Artillery and Royal Engineers have the largest number of military graves because of the long connection with the garrison at Shoeburyness. St. Andrew's churchyard at South Shoebury has 94 military gravestones of which 41 mention the Royal Artillery. The wide range of other regiments appears to be associated with the use of Southend-on-Sea as a receiving point for wounded personnel during both World Wars.

Military Rank

One of the limitations of this survey, as indeed of any gravestone survey, is that grave memorials give us a record of the middle class, and not of the whole community. In a military context it can therefore be hypothesised that officers will be better represented than other ranks. In the land forces during the Second World War, 13,245 officers died and 149,054 from other ranks, so officers represented 8.2 per cent of all casualties. In this survey there are 178 officers and 516 others, 25.6 per cent of gravestones being those of officers who are thus substantially over-represented. Although during the World Wars hospitals were provided in the area for all ranks, it is possible that more officers were treated and subsequently died and that may distort the local picture.

On CWGC gravestones that were provided for all ranks the officers represent about 12 per cent of all burials, NCOs and WOs 21 per cent and other ranks 67 per cent. Although these numbers relate to the entire period covered by the survey, the proportion of officers is close to the overall

Locals and strangers

To what extent did service personnel buried in south-east Essex have local connections? In order to answer the question it is necessary to

Connection with area	Churchyards		Municipal cemetery	
	No	(%)	No	(%)
Resident or next of kin living locally	72	(64.3)		
Not resident or next of kin not living locally 1	1	(9.8)	136	(46.6)
No information available	29	(25.9)	81	(27.7)
Total	112	(100)	75	(25.7)

address two issues: first, the differences between burials in local churchyards and those in municipal cemeteries; and second, discrepancies between location of death and location of burial. Of the 792 military personnel identified in this survey 35 per cent are buried or commemorated in churchyards and 65 per cent in cemeteries. It could be assumed that people buried in churchyards have a personal connection with the parish for, as James Stevens Curl says, 'there was an attachment to the parish burial-ground, to custom ... that was clearly very much alive and well at least until 1914, and, to a lesser extent, until 1939'. Several sources have been searched for residence or next of kin details for military personnel buried in a sample of 16 churchyards within this survey. This indicates that nearly two-thirds of burials in churchyards have a known local connection and only 10 per cent have no proven connection. Even an unproven connection simply means that no link can be discovered from the records, not necessarily that there was no connection with the area.

The burials at St. Andrew's, South Shoebury, are those of soldiers connected to the garrison, who do not necessarily have any other family association with the parish. The situation for the

254

large cemetery at Sutton Road, Southend, is more complex. Military personnel with both family and military connections are buried there. But the cemetery was also the burial place for people with no connection with the area who died locally, such as the wounded brought back from continental Europe. Less than half had a known local connection and over a quarter did not have next of kin living locally. Therefore there was a higher proportion of 'strangers' in this large municipal cemetery than was the case with churchyards, but it must also be acknowledged that are still many personnel for whom no information is available.

Place of death

Names and dates of death on the gravestones were checked against the General Register Office (GRO) death indexes at the Family Records Centre, to determine the registration district where the death was notified. Places of death may be unidentifiable because no date of death is given on the gravestone; or the details are not sufficiently specific to cross-reference with the registers (for example, 'Jack Smith died 1942'); or the death occurred elsewhere, such as in Scotland. Of the 519 military personnel in the survey who have an identified place of death in England and Wales, only 59 per cent died within the area (Rochford and Southend-on-Sea Registration Districts). When a serviceman died in his own country, the next of kin had the choice of having him buried in a civil cemetery or churchyard. Because the individuals who died elsewhere in England and Wales had been brought to south-east Essex for burial it is likely that most had families who wished them to be buried locally. There are many others buried in south-east Essex with no known local connection: their families may have been unable to bury them 'at home' or chose not to do so. Twenty-one of the 36 service personnel (59 per cent) who died in the eastern counties were RAF personnel. This is significantly higher than the overall proportion (17 per cent) of RAF personnel, and is related to the large number of airfields in East Anglia and the east Midlands during both World Wars. Other geographical connections, such as naval associations with deaths in Portsmouth, Chatham and Greenwich, can also be identified.

This brief study illustrates several points raised by the survey. Gravestone inscriptions can be cross-referenced to other local sources, and it is apparent that there was often a strong connection between military establishments, the local community and the churches. Some specific links can readily be identified, such as

the large number of Royal Artillery personnel buried in the area and associated with the garrison at Shoeburyness. The significance of the area during the World Wars, when training, launching military operations, and the hospitalisation of returning casualties were important, resulted in many burials of service personnel. Other areas may display similar patterns associated with their relationship to military establishments and geographical location.

Some general characteristics reflecting the situation in many graveyards and cemeteries can also be identified. The majority of military gravestones commemorate casualties from the World Wars but there are there are some interesting gravestones from earlier periods. However, military personnel may not be buried where they died, perhaps because of family considerations. It is also likely that officers will be better represented on private gravestones than other ranks. Gravestones are limited in value as a source when considered in isolation, because they may be unrepresentative of a population. However they can be used effectively in conjunction with other sources. Nominal and statistical data on war casualties can be used to suggest burial patterns for military personnel. Churchyards are likely to be the burial place for service personnel with local family or military connections, while larger municipal cemeteries will include the graves both of local military personnel and those without local connections. Military gravestone inscriptions could be used in other ways, such as the analysis of battle campaigns, investigations into cause of death, and work on the age profiles of military dead. Research on how the language of commemoration has changed over time, and on the status of women in terms of how they are identified in relation to men, are also subjects worthy of further investigation. Many local and family history societies have recorded the inscriptions in graveyards and cemeteries and this information is usually available in county record offices and local studies libraries, as well as the library of the Society of Genealogists which has an extensive collection. This paper shows that gravestone inscriptions are an underused source which can be used to support and illustrate local history, and it would be encouraging if similar projects could be undertaken elsewhere so that the results might be compared and the analyses extended.

This article is an abridged version of one which first appeared in The Local Historian
Volume 32 No.1 (February 2002)

History Societies & Organisations

British Isles National Organisations & Specialist Subject Societies

The Anglo-Zulu War Historical Society, Woodbury House, Woodchurch Road, Tenterden, TN30 7AE Tel: 01580-764189 Fax: 01580-766648 Email: WWW: www.web-marketing.co.uk/anglozuluwar, Records & Documentation of Zulu War

Association of Local History Tutors, 47 Ramsbury Drive, Earley, Reading, RG6 7RT Tel: 0118 926 4729

Association of Friends of Waterloo Committee, 2 Coburn Drive, Four Oaks, Sutton Coldfield, B75 5NT Tel: 0121-308-4103 Email: jwhite02@globalnet.co.uk
The Association promotes study and research into the Battle of Waterloo and the events of the Napoleonic Wars. Access to to database details of British combatants is possible.

Baptist Historical Society, 60 Strathmore Avenue, Hitchin, SG5 1ST Tel: 01462-431816 Tel: 01462-442548 Email: slcopson@dial.pipex.com WWW: www.baptisthistory.org.uk

The Battlefields Trust, 33 High Green, Brooke, Norwich, NR15 1HR Tel: 01508 558145 Fax: 01508 558145 Email: BattlefieldTrust@aol.com WWW: www.battlefieldstrust.com

Black and Asian Studies Association, 28 Russell Square, London, WC1B 5DS Tel: (020) 7862 8844 Email: marikas@sas.ac.uk BASA is collating information on the presence of people of African and Asian origin/descent in Britain and would appreciate family researchers help

Brewery History Society, Manor Side East, Mill Lane, Byfleet, West Byfleet, KT14 7RS Email: jsechiari@rmcbp.co.uk WWW: www.breweryhistory.com
Do not have information on publicans. Contact Pub History Society

British Association for Local History, PO Box 1576 Salisbury, SP2 8SY Tel: 01722-332158 Fax: 01722-413242 Email: WWW: www.balh.co.uk The BALH each year commissions a distinguished academic figure to deliver the Phillimore Lecture, in London, based on current research by the presentation of The Local History Awards.

British Association of Paper Historians, 47 Ellesmere Road, Chiswick, London, W4 3EA Email: baph@baph.freeserve.co.uk WWW: www.baph.freeserve.com
Interest in all aspects of the study of paper history including paper mills, paper making, watermarks, papermill equipment, types of paper and their conservation.

British Brick Society, 9 Bailey Close, High Wycombe, HP13 6QA Tel: 01494-520299 Email: michael@mhammett.freeserve.co.uk WWW: www.britishbricksoc.free-online.co.uk
Membership includes specialist in family history records associated with UK brickmaking others have some information on craft (bricklaying) and indenture/apprentice records.

British Deaf History Society, 288 Bedfont Lane, Feltham, TW14 9NU Email: bdhs@iconic.demon.co.uk Archive

British Records Association, 40 Northampton Road, London, EC1R 0HB Tel: (020) 7833 0428 Fax: (020) 7833 0416 Email: britrecassoc@hotmail.com WWW: www.hmc.gov.uk/bra The BRA brings together everyone interested in archives;owners, custodians, users. It publishes, informs, lobbies and plays an active part in the work of preserving records.

British Records Society, Stone Barn Farm, Sutherland Road, Longsdon, ST9 9QD Tel: 01782 385446 Tel: 01538 385024 Fax: Email: carolyn@cs.keele.ac.uk britishrecordsociety@hotmail.com WWW: www.britishrecordsociety.org.uk

British Society for Sports History, Dept of Sports & Science, John Moore's University, Byrom Street, Liverpool, L3 3AF

The Chapels Society, 25 Park Chase, Wembley, HA9 8EQ Tel: 020 8903 2198 Email: agworth296@hotmail.com
This society does not hold genealogical information. The society promotes the study of Chapel history

The Costume Society, St Paul's House, 8 Warwick Road, London, EC4P 4BN WWW: www.costumesociety.org.uk, Society for the study of dress, fashion and clothing history

Conference of Regional and Local Historians, The School of Humanities, Languages & Social Sciences, University of Wolverhampton, Dudley Campus, Castle View, Dudley, DY1 3HR Tel: 01902 321056 Email: M.D.Wanklyn@wlv.ac.uk, Promotes the study of regional and local history in Higher education

Congregational History Circle, 160 Green Lane, Morden, SM4 6SR

Current Archaeology, 9 Nassington Road, London, NW3 2TX Tel: (020) 7435-7517 Fax: (020) 7916-2405 Email: editor@archaeology.co.uk WWW: http://www.archaeology.co.uk
A leading British archaeological magazine, bridging the gap between the amateur and professional., CC accepted

The Ecclesiastical History Society, 6 Gallows Hill, Saffron Walden, CB11 4DA

The English Place Name Society, c/o School of English Studies, University of Nottingham, Nottingham, NG7 2RD Tel: 0115 951 5919 Fax: 0115 951 5924 Email: janet.rudkin@nottingham.ac.uk WWW: www.nottingham.ac.uk/english/

Family & Community Historical Society, 73 Derby Road, Cromford, Matlock, DE4 3RP WWW: www.fachrs.com

Friends Historical Society, c/o The Library, Friends House, 173-177 Euston Road, London, NW1 2BJ

Friends of Public Record Office, The Public Record Office, Ruskin Avenue, Kew, Richmond, TW9 4DU Tel: (020) 8876 3444 ext 2226 Email: friends-pro@pro.gov.uk WWW: www.pro.gov.uk/yourpro/friends.htm

Friends of War Memorials, 4 Lower Belgrave Street, London, SW1W 0LA Tel: (020) 7259-0403 Fax: (020) 7259-0296 Email: fowm@eidosnet.co.uk WWW: http://www.war-memorials.com

Garden History Society, 70 Cowcross Street, London, EC1M 6EJ Tel: (020) 7608 2409 Fax: (020) 7490 2974 Email: enquiries@gardenhistorysociety.org WWW: www.gardenhistorysociety.org

Glasgow Hebrew Burial Society, 222 Fenwick Road, Griffnock, Glasgow, G46 6UE Tel: 0141 577 8226

Heraldry Society, PO Box 32 Maidenhead, SL6 3FD Tel: 0118-932-0210 Fax: 0118 932 0210 Email: heraldry-society@cwcom.net

The Historical Association (Local History), 59A Kennington Park Road, London, SE11 4JH Tel: (020) 7735-3901 Fax: (020) 7582 4989 Email: enquiry@history.org.uk WWW: http://www..history.org.uk

Historical Medical Equipment Society, 8 Albion Mews, Apsley, HP3 9QZ Email: hmes@antiageing.freeserve.co.uk

The Hugenot Society of Great Britain & Ireland, Hugenot Library University College, Gower Street, London, WC1E 6BT Tel: 020 7679 5199 Email: s.massil@ucl.ac.uk WWW: (Library) www.ucl.ac.uk/ucl-info/divisions/library/huguenot.htm (Society) www.hugenotsociety.org.uk

Labour Heritage, 18 Ridge Road, Mitcham, CR4 2EY Tel: 020 8640 1814 Fax: 020 8640 1814

Lighthouse Society of Great Britain, Gravesend Cottage, Gravesend, Torpoint, PL11 2LX Email: k.trethewey@btinternet.com WWW: http://www.lsgb.co.uk
Holds databases of lighthouses and their keepers. SAE required for enquiries. Lighthouse Encyclopaedia 2003 edition published on CD Rom only

Local Studies Group of CILIP - Formerly the Library Association, 25 Bromford Gardens, Edgbaston, Birmingham, B15 3XD Tel: 0121 454 0935 Fax: 0121 454 7330 Email: prthomaspdt@aol.com

Local Population Studies Society, School of Biological Sciences (Dr SA Scott), University of Liverpool, Derby Building, Liverpool, L69 3GS Fax: 01423-560429 Email: sscott@liverpool.ac.uk WWW: home.att.net/~jkbfa

Mercia Cinema Society, 5 Arcadia Avenue, Chester le Street, DH3 3UH

Military Historical Society, Court Hill Farm, Potterne, Devizes, SN10 5PN Tel: 01980 615689 Daytime Tel: 01380 723371 Evenings Fax: 01980 618746

Museum of the Royal Pharmaceutical Society, Museum of the Royal Pharmaceutical Society, 1 Lambeth High Street, London, SE1 7JN Tel: (020) 7572 2210 Fax: (020) 7572 2499 Email: museum@rpsgb.org.uk WWW: http://www.rpsgb.org.uk CC accepted. Records of pharmacists from 1841 Research fee charged

Local Population Studies Society, School of Biological Sciences (Dr SA Scott), University of Liverpool, Derby Building, Liverpool, L69 3GS Fax: 01423-560429 Email: sscott@liverpool.ac.uk WWW: home.att.net/~jkbfa
Open University History Society, 111 Coleshill Drive, Chapel End, Nuneaton, CV10 0PG Tel: (024) 76397668 The Open University History Society is a natioanlly based Society with a widely scattered membership. To keep in touch with members a quarterly magazine Open History written mainly by members themselves
Oral History Society, British Library National Sound Archive, 96 Euston Road, London, NW1 2DB Tel: (020) 7412-7405 Tel: (020) 7412-7440 Fax: (020) 7412-7441 Email: rob.perks@bl.uk WWW: www.oralhistory.org.uk
Parish Register Transcription Society, 50 Silvester Road, Waterlooville, PO8 5TL Email: mail@prtsoc.org.uk WWW: www.prtsoc.org.uk
Police History Society, 37 Greenhill Road, Timperley, Altrincham, WA15 7BG Tel: 0161-980-2188 Email: alanhayhurst@greenhillroad.fsnet.co.uk WWW: www.policehistorysociety.co.uk Whilst the society is not primarily interested in family history and having no personal records of its own is unable to answer enquiries re individual officers. However members may contact each other
Postal History Society, 60 Tachbrook Street, London, SW1V 2NA Tel: (020) 7821-6399 Email: home@claireangier.co.uk
Pub History Society, 13 Grovewood, Sandycombe Road, Kew, Richmond, TW9 3NF Tel: (020) 8296-8794 Email: sfowler@sfowler.force9.co.uk WWW: www.uk-history.co.uk/phs.htm
Richard III Society - Norfolk Group, 20 Rowington Road, Norwich, NR1 3RR
Royal Geographical Society (with IBG), 1 Kensington Gore, London, SW7 2AR Tel: 020 7291 3001 Fax: 020 7591 3001 WWW: www.rgs.org
Royal Society of Chemistry Library & Information Centre, Burlington House, Piccadilly, London, W1J 0BA Tel: (020) 7437 8656 Fax: (020) 7287 9798 Email: library@rsc.org WWW: www.rsc.org
Royal Photographic Society Historical Group, 7A Cotswold Road, Belmont, Sutton, SM2 5NG Tel: (020) 8643 2743
Royal Society, 6 - 9 Carlton House Terrace, London, SW1Y 5AG Tel: 020 7451 2606 Fax: 020 7930 2170 Email: library@royalsoc.ac.uk WWW: www.royalsoc.ac.uk
Society of Antiquaries, Burlington House, Piccadilly, London, W1J 0BE Tel: (020) 7479 7080 Fax: (020) 7287 6967 Email: admin@sal.org.uk WWW: www.sal.org.uk
Society of Archivists, 40 Northampton Road, London, EC1R 0HB Tel: (020) 7278 8630 Fax: (020) 7278 2107 Email: societyofarchivists@archives.org.uk WWW: www.archives.org.uk CC accepted not American Express
Society of Brushmakers Descendants Family History Society, 13 Ashworth Place, Church Langley, CM17 9PU Tel: 01279-629392 Email: s.b.d@lineone.net WWW: http://www.brushmakers.com A society devoted to assisting research into the history and records of brush or broom maker ancestors.
Social History of Learning Disability Research Group, School of Health & Social Welfare, Open University, Milton Keynes, MK7 6AA
Society of Indexers, Globe Centre, Penistone Road, Sheffield, S6 3AE Tel: 0114-281-3060 Fax: 0114-281-3061 Email: admin@socind.demon.co.uk WWW: www.socind.demon.co.uk
Society of Jewellery Historians, Department of Scientific Research, The British Museum, Great Russell St, London, WC1B 3DG Tel: (020) 7323 8768Fax: (020) 7323 8118 Email: jwallace@thebritishmuseum.ac.uk WWW: www.thebritishmuseum.ac.uk
Society for Landscape Studies, School of Continuing Studies, Birmingham University, Edbaston, Birmingham, B15 2TT
Society for Nautical Research, Stowell House, New Pond Hill, Cross in Hand, Heathfield, TN21 0LX
Society for Name Studies in Britain & Ireland, 22 Peel Park Avenue, Clitheroe, BB7 1ET Tel: 01200-423771 Fax: 01200-423771

Strict Baptist Historical Society, 38 Frenchs Avenue, Dunstable, LU6 1BH Tel: 01582 602242 Email: kdix@sbhs.freeserve.co.uk WWW: www.strictbaptisthistory.org.uk
Tennyson Society, Central Library, Free School Lane, Lincoln, LN2 1EZ Tel: 01522-552862 Fax: 01522-552858 Email: linnet@lincolnshire.gov.uk WWW: www.tennysonsociety.org.uk
Thoresby Society, 23 Clarendon Road, Leeds, LS2 9NZ Tel: 0113 245 7910 WWW: www.thoresby.org.uk
United Kingdom Reminiscence Network, Age exchange Reminiscence Centre, 11 Blackheath Village, London, SE3 9LA Tel: 020 83189 9105 WWW: age-exchange@lewisham.gov.uk
University of London Extra -Mural Society For Genealogy And History of The Family, 136 Lennard Road, Beckenham, BR3 1QT
United Reformed Church History Society, Westminster College, Madingley Road, Cambridge, CB3 0AA Tel: 01223-741300 (NOT Wednesdays) Information on ministers of constituent churches not members
Unitarian Historical Society, 6 Ventnor Terrace, Edinburgh, EH9 2BL
Upholstery Old and New, 7 Selly Avenue, Selly Park, Birmingham, B29 7PE
Vernacular Architecture Group, Ashley, Willows Green, Chelmsford, CM3 1QD Tel: 01245 361408 WWW: www.vag.org.uk
The Veterinary History Society, 608 Warwick Road, Solihull, B91 1AA
Victorian Military Society, PO Box 5837 Newbury, RG14 7FJ Tel: 01635 48628 Email: beverley20@tesco.net WWW: www.vms.org.uk The leading Society covering military history of all nations and races from 1837 to 1914
The Victorian Society, 1 Priory Gardens, Bedford Park, London, W4 1TT Tel: (020) 8994 1019 Fax: (020) 8747 5899 Email: admin@victorian-society.org.uk WWW: http://www.victorian-society.org.uk, CC accepted
Victorian Revival, Sugar Hill Farm, Knayton, Thirsk, YO7 4BP
Voluntary Action History Society, National Centre for Volunteering, Regent's Wharf, 8 All Saints Street, London, N1 9RL Tel: (020) 7520 8900 Fax: (020) 7520 8910 Email: instvolres.aol.com WWW: www.ivr.org.uk/vahs.htm
War Research Society, 27 Courtway Avenue, Birmingham, B14 4PP Tel: 0121 430 5348 Fax: 0121 436 7401 Email: battletour@aol.com WWW: www.battlefieldtours.co.uk
The Waterways Trust, The National Waterways Museum, Llanthony Warehouse, Gloucester Docks, Gloucester, GL1 2EH Tel: 01452 318053 Fax: 01452 318066 Email: info@nwm.demon.co.uk WWW: www.nwm.org.uk
The West of England Costume Society, 4 Church Lane, Long Aston, Nr. Bristol, BS41 9LU Tel: 01275-543564 Fax: 01275-543564
Yorkshire Dialect Society, 51 Stepney Avenue, Scarborough, YO12 5BW

England

Avon
Avon Local History Association - See Somerset North
Avon, Bristol & Avon Archaeological Society - See Bristol

Bath & NE Somerset
Avon Local History Association See Somerset North

Bedfordshire
Ampthill & District Archaeological and Local History, 14 Glebe Avenue, Flitwick, Bedford, MK45 1HS Tel: 01525 712778 Email: petwood@waitrose.com WWW: www.museums.bedfordshire.gov.uk/localgroups/ampthill2/html
Ampthill & District Preservation Society, Seventh House, 43 Park Hill, Ampthill, MK45 2LP
Ampthill History Forum, 10 Mendham Way, Clophill, Bedford, MK45 4AL Email: forum@ampthillhistory.co.uk WWW: www.ampthillhistory.co.uk
Bedfordshire Archaeological and Local History Society, 7 Lely Close, Bedford, MK41 7LS Tel: 01234 365095 WWW: www.museums.bedfordshire.gov.uk/localgroups

Bedfordshire Historical Record Society, 48 St Augustine's Road, Bedford, MK40 2ND Tel: 01234 309548 Email: rsmart@ntlworld.com WWW: www.bedfordshirehrs.org.uk, CC accepted

Bedfordshire Local History Association, 29 George Street, Maulden, Bedford, MK45 2DF Tel: 01525 633029

Biggleswade History Society, 6 Pine Close, Biggleswade, SG18 QEF

Caddington Local History Group, 98 Mancroft Road, Caddington, Nr. Luton, LUL 4EN WWW: www.caddhist.moonfruit.com

Carlton & Chellington Historical Society, 3 High Street, Carlton, MK43 7JX

Dunstable & District Local History Society, 7 Castle Close, Totternhoe, Dunstable, LU6 1QJ Tel: 01525 221963

Dunstable Historic and Heritage Studies, 184 West Street, Dunstable, LU6 1 NX Tel: 01582 609018

Harlington Heritage Trust, 2 Shepherds Close, Harlington, Near Dunstable, LU5 6NR

Knoll History Project, 32 Ashburnham Road, Ampthill, MK45 2RH

Leighton-Linslade Heritage Display Society, 25 Rothschild Road, Linslade, Leighton Buzzard, LU7 7SY

Luton & District Historical Society, 22 Homerton Rd, Luton, LU3 2UL Tel: 01582 584367

Toddington Historical Society, 21 Elm Grove, Toddington, Dunstable, LU5 6BJ WWW: www.museums.bedfordshire.gov.uk/local/toddington.htm

Wrestlingworth History Society, Wrestlingworth Memorial Hall, Church Lane, Wrestlingworth, SG19 2EJ

Berkshire

Berkshire Industrial Archaeological Group, 20 Auclum Close, Burghfield Common, Reading, RG7 DY

Berkshire Local History Association, 18 Foster Road, Abingdson, OX14 1YN Email: secretary@blha.org.uk WWW: www.blha.org.uk

Berkshire Record Society, Berkshire Record Office, 9 Coley Avenue, Reading, RG1 6AF Tel: 0118-901-5130 Fax: 0118-901-5131 Email: peter.durrant@reading.gov.uk, Berkshire Record Society publishes editions of historic documents (including many with family history interest) relating to the ancient County of Berkshire

Blewbury Local History Group, Spring Cottage, Church Road, Blewbury, Didcot, OX11 9PY Tel: 01235 850427 Email: aud@spcott.fsnet.co.uk

Bracknell & District Historical Society, 16 Harcourt Road, Bracknell, RG12 7JD Tel: 01344 640341

Brimpton Parish Research association, Shortacre, Brimpton Common, Reading, RG7 4RY Tel: 0118 981 3649

Chiltern Heraldry Group, Magpie Cottage, Pondwood Lane, Shottesbrooke, SL6 3SS Tel: 0118 934 3698

Cox Green Local History Group, 29 Bissley Drive, Maidenhead, SL6 3UX Tel: 01628 823890

Datchet Village Society, 86 London Road, Datchet, SL3 9LQ Tel: 01753 542438 Email: janet@datchet.com WWW: www.datchet.com

Eton Wick History Group, 47 Colenorton Crescent, Eton Wick, Windsor, SL4 6WW Tel: 01753 861674

Finchampstead History & Heritage Group, 134 Kiln Ride, California, Wokingham, RG40 3PB Tel: 0118 973 3005

Friends of Reading Museums, 15 Benyon Court, Bath Road, Reading, RG1 6HR Tel: 0118 958 0642

Friends of Wantage Vale & Downland Museum, 19 Church Street, Wantage, OX12 8BL Tel: 01235 771447

Goring & Streatley Local History Society, 45 Springhill Road, Goring On Thames, Reading, RG8 OBY Tel: 01491 872625

Hare Hatch & Kiln Green Local History Group, Shinglebury, Tag Lane, Hare Hatch, Twyford, RG10 9ST Tel: 0118 940 2157 Email: richard.lloyd@wargrave.net

History of Reading Society, 5 Wilmington Close, Woodley, Reading, RG5 4LR Tel: 0118 961 8559 Email: peterrussell7@hotmail.com

Hungerford Historical Association, 23 Fairview Road, Hungerford, RG170PB Tel: 01488 682932 Email: mandm.martin@talk21.com WWW: www.hungerfordhistorical.org.uk

Maidenhead Archaeological & Historical Society, 70 Lambourne Drive, Maidenhead, SL6 3HG Tel: 01628 672196

Middle Thames Archaeological & Historical Society, 1 Saffron Close, Datchet, Slough, SL3 9DU Tel: 01753 543636

Mortimer Local History Group, 19 Victoria Road, Mortimer, RG7 3SH Tel: 0118 933 2819

Newbury & District Field Club, 4 Coombe Cottages, Coombe Road, Crompton, Newbury, RG20 6RG Tel: 01635 579076

Project Purley, 4 Allison Gardens, Purley on Thames, RG8 8DF Tel: 0118 942 2485

Sandhurst Historical Society, Beech Tree Cottage, Hancombe Road, Little Sandhurst, GU47 8NP Tel: 01344 777476 WWW: www.sandhurst-town.com/societies

Shinfield & District Local History Societies, Long Meadow, Part Lane, Swallowfield, RG7 1TB Tel:

Swallowfield Local History Society, Kimberley, Swallowfield, Reading, RG7 1QX Tel: 0118 988 3650

Thatcham Historical Society, 72 Northfield Road, Thatcham, RG18 3ES Tel: 01635 864820 WWW: www.thatchamhistoricalsociety.org.uk

Twyford & Ruscombe Local History Society, 26 Highfield Court, Waltham Road, Twyford, RG10 0AA Tel: 0118 934 0109

Wargrave Local History Society, 6 East View Close, Wargrave, RG10 8BJ Tel: 0118 940 3121 Email: peter.delaney@talk21.com history@wargrave.net WWW: www.wargrave.net/history

Windsor Local History Publications Group, 256 Dedworth Road, Windsor, SL4 4JR Tel: 01753 864835 Email: windlesora@hotmail.com

Wokingham History Group, 39 Howard Road, Wokingham, RG40 2BX Tel: 0118 978 8519

Birmingham

Alvechurch Historical Society, Bearhill House, Alvechurch, Birmingham, B48 7JX Tel: 0121 445 2222

Birmingham Canal Navigation's Society, 37 Chestnut Close, Handsacre, Rugeley, WS15 4TH

Birmingham & District Local History Association, 112 Brandwood Road, Kings Heath, Birmingham, B14 6BX Tel: 0121-444-7470

Small Heath Local History Society, 381 St Benedicts Road, Small Heath, Birmingham, B10 9ND Tel:

Birmingham War Research Society, 43 Norfolk Place, Kings Norton, Birmingham, B30 3LB Tel: 0121 459 9008 Fax: 0121 459 9008

Bristol

Alveston Local History Society, 6 Hazel Gardens, Alveston, BS35 3RD Tel: 01454 43881 Email: jc1932@alveston51.fsnet.co.uk

Avon Local History Association, 4 Dalkeith Avenue, Kingswood, Bristol, BS15 1HH Tel: 0117 967 1362

Bristol & Avon Archaeological Society, 3 Priory Avenue, Westbury on Trym, Bristol, BS9 4DA Tel: 0117 9620161 WWW: http://www.digitalbristol.org/members/baas/

Bristol and Gloucestershire Archaeological Society, 22 Beaumont Road, Gloucester, GL2 0EJ Tel: 01452 302610 Email: david_j._h.smith@virgin.net WWW: http://www.bgas.org.uk

Bristol Records Society, Regional History Centre, Faculty of Humanities, University of the West of England, St Maththias Campus, Oldbury Court Road, Fishponds, Bristol, BS16 2JP Tel: 0117 344 4395 WWW: http://humanities.uwe.ac.uk/brs/index.htm

Congresbury History Group, Venusmead, 36 Venus Street, Congresbury, Bristol, BS49 5EZ Tel: 01934 834780 Fax: 01934 834780 Email: rogerhards-venusmead@breathemail.net

Downend Local History Society, 141 Overndale Road, Downend, Bristol, B516 2RN

The West of England Costume Society, 4 Church Lane, Long Aston, Nr. Bristol, BS41 9LU Tel: 01275-543564 Fax: 01275-543564

Whitchurch Local History Society, 62 Nailsea Park, Nailsea, Bristol, B519 1BB

Yatton Local History Society, 27 Henley Park, Yatton, Bristol, BS49 4JH Tel: 01934 832575

Buckinghamshire

Buckinghamshire Archaeological Society, County Museum, Church Street, Aylesbury, HP20 2QP Tel 678114

Buckinghamshire Record Society, Centre for Buckinghamshire Studies, County Hall, Aylesbury, HP20 1UU Tel: 01296 383013 Fax: 01296-382771 Email: archives@buckscc.gov.uk

WWW: www.buckscc.gov.uk/archives/publications/brs.stm

Chesham Bois One-Place Study, 70 Chestnut Lane, Amersham, HP6 6EH Tel: 01494 726103 Email: cdjmills@hotmail.com

Chesham Society, 54 Church Street, Chesham, HP5 IHY

Chess Valley Archealogical & Historical Society, 16 Chapmans Crescent, Chesham, NP5 2QU Tel: 01494 772914

Pitstone and Ivinghoe Museum Society, Vicarage Road, Pitstone, Leighton Buzzard, LU7 9EY Tel: 01296 668123 WWW: http://website.lineone.net/~pitstonemus Also Pitstone Green Museum and Ford End Watermill

Princes Risborough Area Heritage Society, Martin's Close, 11 Wycombe Road, Princes Risborough, HP27 0EE Tel: 01844 343004 Fax: 01844 273142 Email: sandymac@risboro35.freeserve.co.uk

Cambridgeshire

Cambridge Antiquarian Society, P0 Box 376, 96 Mill Lane, Impington, Cambridge, CB4 9HS Tel: 01223 502974 Email: liz-allan@hotmail.com

Cambridge Group for History of Population and Social History, Sir William Hardy Building, Downing Place, Cambridge, CB2 3EN Tel: 01223 333181 Fax: 01223 333183 WWW: http://www-hpss.geog.cam.ac.uk

Cambridgeshire Archaeology, Castle Court, Shire Hall, Cambridge, CB3 0AP Tel: 01223 717312 Fax: 01223 362425 Email: quentin.carroll@cambridgeshire.gov.uk WWW: http://edweb.camcnty.gov.uk/archaeology www.archaeology.freewire.co.uk

Cambridgeshire Local History Society, 1A Archers Close, Swaffham Bulbeck, Cambridge, CB5 0NG

Cambridgeshire Record Society, County Record Office, Shire Hall, Cambridge, CB3 0AP WWW: www.cambridgeshirehistory.com/societies/crs/index.html

Hemingfords Local History Society, 8 Weir Close, Hemingford Grey, Huntingdon, PE28 9EJ Tel: 01480 464843 Email: hemlocks@hotmail.com

Houghton & Wyton Local History Society, Church View, Chapel Lane, Houghton, Huntingdon, PE28 2AY Tel: 01480 469376 Email: gerry.feake@one-name.org

Huntingdonshire Local History Society, 2 Croftfield Road, Godmanchester, PE29 2ED Tel: 01480 411202

Sawston Village History Society, 21 Westmoor Avenue, Sawston, Cambridge, CB2 4BU Tel: 01223 833475

Upwood & Raveley History Group, The Old Post Office, 71-73 High Street, Upwood, Huntingdon, PE17 1QE

Cheshire

Altrincham History Society, 10 Willoughby Close, Sale, M33 6PJ

Ashton & Sale History Society, Tralawney House, 78 School Road, Sale, M33 7XB Tel: 0161 9692795

Bowdon History Society, 5 Pinewood, Bowdon, Altrincham, WA14 3JQ Tel: 0161 928 8975

Cheshire Heraldry Society, 24 Malvern Close, Congleton, CW12 4PD

Cheshire Local History Association, Cheshire Record Office, Duke Street, Chester, CH1 1RL Tel: 01224 602559 Fax: 01244 603812 Email: chairman@cheshirehistory.org.uk WWW: www.cheshirehistory.org.uk

Chester Archaeological Society, Grosvenor Museum, 27 Grosvenor Street, Chester, CH1 2DD Tel: 01244 402028 Fax: 01244 347522 Email: p.carrington@chestercc.gov.uk WWW: http://www.chesterarchaeolsoc.org.uk

Christleton Local History Group, 25 Croft Close, Rowton, CH3 7QQ Tel: 01244 332410

Congleton History Society, 48 Harvey Road Road, Congleton, CWI2 2DH Tel: 01260 278757 Email: awill0909@aol.com

Department of History - University College Chester, Department of History, University College Chester, Cheveney Road, Chester, CH1 4BJ Tel: 01244 375444 Fax: 01244 314095 Email: history@chester.ac.uk WWW: www.chester.ac.uk/history

Disley Local History Society, 5 Hilton Road, Disley, SK12 2JU Tel: 01663 763346 Fax: 01663 764910 Email: chgris.makepeace@talk21.com

Historic Society of Lancashire & Cheshire, East Wing Flat, Arley Hall, Northwich, CW9 6NA Tel: 01565 777231

Fax: 01565 777465

Lancashire & Cheshire Antiquarian Society, 59 Malmesbury Road, Cheadle Hulme, SK8 7QL Tel: 0161 439 7202 Email: morris.garratt@lineone.net

Lawton Heritage Society, 9 Woodgate Avenue, Church Lawton, Stoke on Trent, ST7 3EF Tel: 01270-878386 Email: dmcall12280@aol.com

Macclesfield Historical Society, 42 Tytherington Drive, Macclesfield, SK10 2HJ Tel: 01625 420250 SAE for all enquiries

Northwich & District Heritage Society, 13 Woodlands Road, Hartford, Northwich, CW8 1NS

Poynton Local History Society, 6 Easby Close, Poynton, SK12 1YG

South Cheshire Family History Society inc S E Cheshire Local Studies Group, PO Box 1990 Crewe, CW2 6FF WWW: www.scfhs.org.uk

Stockport Historical Society, 59 Malmesbury Road, Cheadle Hulme, Stockport, SK8 7QL Tel: 0161 439 7202

Weaverham History Society, Ashdown, Sandy Lane, Weaverham, Northwich, CW8 3PX Tel: 01606 852252 Email: jg-davies@lineone.net

Wilmslow Historical Society, 4 Campden Way, Handforth, Wilmslow, SK9 3JA Tel: 01625 529381

Cleveland

Cleveland & Teesside Local History Society, 150 Oxford Road, Linthorpe, Middlesbrough, TS5 5EL, Membership Secretary: 43 Petrel Crescenet, Norton, Stockton on Tees TS20 1SN

North-East England History Institute (NEEHI), Department of History University of County Durham, 43 North Bailey, County Durham, DH1 3EX Tel: 0191-374-2004 Fax: 0191-374-4754 Email: m.a.mcallister@County Durham.ac.uk WWW: http://www.County Durham.ac.uk/neehi.history/homepage.htm

Cornwall

Bodmin Local History Group, 1 Lanhydrock View, Bodmin, PL31 1BG

Cornwall Association of Local Historians, St Clement's Cottage, Coldrinnick Bac, Duloe, Liskeard, PL14 4QF Tel: 01503 220947 Email: anne@coldrinnick.freeserve.co.uk

Cornwall Family History Society, 5 Victoria Square, Truro, TR1 2RS Tel: 01872-264044 Email: secretary@cornwallfhs.com WWW: http://www.cornwallfhs.com For anyone researching their family roots or local history the Cornwall Family History Society is in dispensible. Free help and advice, census returns, GRO index, IGI, marriage indexes, burial index

The Devon & Cornwall Record Society, 7 The Close, Exeter, EX1 1EZ Tel: 01392 274727 (Ansaphone) WWW: www.cs.ncl.ac.uk/genuki/DEV/DCRS

Fal Family History Group, 4 Downside Close, Treloggan, Newquay, TR7 2TD

Lighthouse Society of Great Britain, Gravesend Cottage, Gravesend, Torpoint, PL11 2LX Email: k.trethewey@btinternet.com WWW: http://www.lsgb.co.uk Holds databases of lighthouses and their keepers. SAE required for enquiries Lighthouse Encyclopaedia 2003 edition published on CD Rom only

Royal Institution of Cornwall, Courtney Library & Cornish History Research Centre, Royal Cornwall Museum, River Street, Truro, TR1 2SJ Tel: 01872 272205 Fax: 01872 240514 Email: RIC@royal-cornwall-museum.freeserve.co.uk WWW: www.cornwall-online.co.uk/ric

Cumberland

Cumberland and Westmorland Antiquarian and Archaeological Society, County Offices Kendal, LA9 4RQ Tel: 01539 773431 Fax: 01539 773539 Email: info@cwaas.org.uk WWW: www.cwaas.org.uk

Cumbria

Appleby Archaeology Group, Pear Tree Cottage, Kirkland Road, Skirwith, Penrith, CA10 1RL Tel: 01768 388318 Email: martin@fellside-eden.freeserve.co.uk

Appleby In Westmorland Record Society, Kingstone House, Battlebarrow, Appleby-In-Westmorland, CA16 6XT Tel: 017683 52282 Email: barry.mckay@brtishlibrary.net

Caldbeck & District Local History Society, Whelpo House, Caldbeck, Wigton, CA7 8HQ Tel: 01697 478270

Cartmel Peninsula Local History Society, 1 Barton House, Kents Bank Road, Grange-Over-Sands, LA11 7HD Tel: 01539 534814

Centre for North West Regional Studies, Fylde College, Lancaster University, Lancaster, LA1 4YF Tel: 01524 593770 Fax: 01524 594725 Email: christine.wilkinson@lancaster.ac.uk WWW: www.lancs.ac.uk/users/cnwrs Cc accepted Oral History Archives; Elizabeth Roberts Archive: Penny Summerfield Archive

Crosby Ravensworth Local History Society, Brookside, Crosby Ravensworth, Penrith, CA10 3JP Tel: 01931 715324 Email: david@riskd.freeserve.co.uk

Cumberland and Westmorland Antiquarian and Archaeological Society, County Offices Kendal, LA9 4RQ Tel: 01539 773431 Fax: 01539 773539 Email: info@cwaas.org.uk WWW: www.cwaas.org.uk

Cumbria Amenity trust Mining Socierty, The Rise Alston, CA9 3DB Tel: 01434 381903 WWW: www.catmhs.co.uk

Cumbria Industrial History Society, Coomara, Carleton, Carlisle, CA4 0BU Tel: 01228 537379 Fax: 01228 596986 Email: gbrooksvet@tiscali.co.uk WWW: www.cumbria-industries.org.uk

Cumbria Local History Federation, 10 Mill Cottages, Distington, Workington, CA14 5SR Tel: 01946 833060 Fax: 01946 833060 Email: gillyfoster@cumbrialocalhistory.org.uk WWW: www.cumbrialocalhistory.org.uk

Cumbrian Railways Association, Whin Rigg, 33 St Andrews Drive, Perton, Wolverhampton, WV6 7YL Tel: 01902 745472 WWW: www.cumbrian-rail.org

Dalton Local History Society, 15 Kirkstone Crescent, Barrow in Furness, LA14 4ND Tel: 01229 823558 Email: davidhsd@aol.co., WWW:

Distington Family & Local History Society, 10 Mill Cottages, Distington, Workington, CA14 5SR Tel: 01946 833060 Fax: 01946 833060 Email: gillyfoster@distington.idps.co.uk WWW: www.distington.idps.co.uk

Distington Oral Archive, 10 Mill Cottages, Distington, Workington, CA14 5SR Tel: 01946 833060 Fax: 01946 833060 Email: davidfoster@doarchiveidps.co.uk WWW: www.doarchiveidps.co.uk

Duddon Valley Local History Group, High Cross Bungalow Broughton in Furness, LA20 6ES Tel: 01229 716196

Friends of Cumbria Archives, The Barn, Parsonby, Aspatria, Wigton, CA7 2DE Tel: 01697 320053 Email: john@johnmary.freeserve.co.uk WWW: www.focasonline.org.uk

Friends of The Helena Thompson Museum, 24 Calva Brow, Workington, CA14 1DD Tel: 01900 603312

Holme & District Local History Society, The Croft, Tanpits Lane, Burton, Carnforth, LA6 1HZ Tel: 01524 782121

Keswick Historical Society, Windrush, Rogersfield, Keswick, CA12 4BN Tel: 01768 772771

Lorton and Derwent Fells Local History Society, Clouds Hill, Lorton, Cockermouth, CA13 9TX Tel: 01900 85259 Email: michael@lorton.freeserve.co.uk

Matterdale Historical and Archaeological Society, The Knotts, Matterdale, Penrith, CA11 0LD Tel: 01768 482358

North Pennines Heritage Trust, Nenthead Mines Heritage Centre, Nenthead, Alston, CA9 3PD Tel: 01434 382037 Fax: 01434 382294 Email: administration.office@virgin.net WWW: www.npht.com

Sedbergh & District History Society, c/o 72 Main Street, Sedbergh, LA10 5AD Tel: 015396 20504 Email: history@sedbergh.org.uk

Shap Local History Society, The Hermitage, Shap, Penrith, CA10 3LY Tel: 01931 716671 Email: liz@kbhshap.freeserve.co.uk

Solway History Society, 9 Longthwaite Crescent, Wigton, CA7 9JN Tel: 01697 344257 Email: s.l.thornhill@talk21.com

Staveley and District History Society, 1 Oakland, Staveley, Kendal, LA8 9JE Tel: 01539 821194 Email: Jpatdball@aol.com

Upper Eden History Society, Copthorne, Brough Sowerby, Kirkby Stephen, CA17 4EG Tel: 01768 341007 Email: gowling@kencomp.net

Whitehaven Local History Society, Cumbria Record office & Local Studies Library, Scotch Street, Whitehaven, CA28 7BJ Tel: 01946 852920 Fax: 01946 852919 Email: anne.dick@cumbriacc.gov.uk

Derbyshire
Allestree Local Studies Group, 30 Kingsley Road, Allestree, Derby, DE22 2JH

Arkwright Society, Cromford Mill, Mill Lane, Cromford, DE4 3RQ Tel: 01629 823256 Fax: 01629 823256 Email: info@cromfordmill.co.uk WWW: www.cromfordmill.co.uk CC accepted not American Express

Chesterfield & District Local History Society, Melbourne House, 130 Station Road, Bimington, Chesterfield, S43 1LU Tel: 01246 620266

Derbyshire Archaeological Society, 2 The Watermeadows, Swarkestone, Derby, DE73 1JA Tel: 01332 704148 Email: barbarafoster@talk21.com WWW: www.DerbyshireAS.org.uk

Derbyshire Local History Societies Network, Derbyshire Record Office, Libraries & Heritage Dept, County Hall, Matlock, DE4 3AG Tel: 01629-580000-ext-3520-1 Fax: 01629-57611 Email: recordoffice@derbyshire.gov.uk WWW: www.derbyshire.gov.uk

Derbyshire Record Society, 57 New Road, Wingerworth, Chesterfield, S42 6UJ Tel: 01246 231024 Email: neapen@aol.com WWW: www.merton.dircon.co.uk/drshome.htm

Holymoorside and District History Society, 12 Brook Close, Holymoorside, Chesterfield, S42 7HB Tel: 01246 566799 WWW: www.holymoorsidehistsoc.org.uk

Ilkeston & District Local History Sociey, c/o 28 Kensington, Ilkeston, DE7 5NZ

New Mills Local History Society, High Point, Cote Lane, Hayfield, High Peak, SK23 Tel: 01663-742814 Fax: 01663 742814

Old Dronfield Society, 2 Gosforth Close, Dronfield, S18 INT

Devon
Chagford Local History Society, Footaway, Westcott, Chagford, Newton Abbot, TQ13 8JF Tel: 01647 433698 Email: cjbaker@jetdash.freeserve.co.uk

Holbeton Yealmpton Brixton Society, 32 Cherry Tree Drive, Brixton, Plymouth, PL8 2DD, Tel: WWW: http://beehive.thisisplymouth.co.uk/hyb

Moretonhampstead History Society, School House, Moreton, Hampstead, TQ13 8NX

Newton Tracey & District Local History Society, Home Park, Lovacott, Newton Tracey, Barnstaple, EX31 3PY Tel: 01271 858451

Ogwell History Society East Ogwell, Newton Abbott, TQI2 6AR

Tavistock & District Local History Society, 18 Heather Close, Tavistock, PL19 9QS Tel: 01822 615211 Email: linagelliott@aol.com

The Devon & Cornwall Record Society, 7 The Close, Exeter, EX1 1EZ Tel: 01392 274727 (Ansaphone) WWW: www.cs.ncl.ac.uk/genuki/DEV/DCRS

The Devon History Society, c/o 82 Hawkins Avenue, Torquay, TQ2 6ES Tel: 01803 613336

The Old Plymouth Society, 625 Budshead Road, Whitleigh, Plymouth, PL5 4DW

Thorverton & District History Society, Ferndale, Thorverton, Exeter, EX5 5NG Tel: 01392 860932 Fax: 01392 860932

Wembury Amenity Society, 5 Cross Park Road, Wembury, Plymouth, PL9 OEU

Yelverton & District Local History Society, 4 The Coach House, Grenofen, Tavistock, PL19 9ES

Dorset
Bournemouth Local Studies Group, 6 Sunningdale, Fairway Drive, Christchurch, BH23 1JY Tel: 01202 485903 Email: mbhall@onetel.net.uk

Bridport History Society, c/o 22 Fox Close, Bradpole, Bridport, DT6 3JF Tel: 01308 456876 Email: celia@cgulls.fsnet.co.uk

Dorchester Association For Research into Local History, 7 Stokehouse Street, Poundbury, Dorchester, DT1 3GP

Dorset Natural History & Archaeological Society, Dorset County Museum, High West Street, Dorchester, DT1 1XA Tel: 01305 262735 Fax: 01305 257180

Dorset Record Society, Dorset County Museum, High West Street, Dorchester, DT1 1XA Tel: 01305-262735

Verwood Historical Society, 74 Lake Road, Verwood, BH31 6BX Tel: 01202 824175 Email: trevorgilbert@hotmail.com WWW: www.geocities.com/verwood_historical

William Barnes Society, Pippins, 58 Mellstock Avenue, Dorchester, DT1 2BQ Tel: 01305 265358 William Barnes is primarily (but not exclusively) a Dorset Dialect Poet

Durham

Architectural & Archaeological Society of County Durham & Northumberland, Broom Cottage, 29 Foundry Fielkds, Crook, DL15 9SY Tel: 01388 762620 Email: belindaburke@aol.com

Durham County Local History Society, 3 Briardene, Margery Lane, County Durham, DH1 4QU Tel: 0191 386 1500

Durham Victoria County History Trust, Redesdale, The Oval, North Crescent, County Durham, DH1 4NE Tel: 0191 384 8305 WWW: www.County Durhampast.net The Victoria History of the Counties of England c/o Institute of Historical Research, University of London

Elvet Local & Family History Groups, 37 Hallgarth Street, County Durham, DH1 3AT Tel: 0191-386-4098 Fax: 0191-386-4098 Email: Turnstone-Ventures@County Durham-city.freeserve.co.uk

Lanchester Local History Society, 11 St Margaret's Drive, Tanfield Village, Stanley, DH9 9QW Tel: 01207-236634 Email: jstl@supanet.com

Monkwearmouth Local History Group, 75 Escallond Drive, Dalton Heights, Seaham, SR7 8JZ

North East Labour History Society, Department of Historical & Critical Studies, University of Northumbria, Newcastle upon Tyne, NE1 8ST Tel: 0191-227-3193 Fax: 0191-227-4630 Email: joan.hugman@unn.ac.uk

North-East England History Institute (NEEHI), Department of History University of County Durham, 43 North Bailey, County Durham, DH1 3EX Tel: 0191-374-2004 Fax: 0191-374-4754 Email: m.a.mcallister@County Durham.ac.uk WWW: http://www.County Durham.ac.uk/neehi.history/homepage.htm

North Eastern Police History Society, Brinkburn Cottage, 28 Brinkburn Street, High Barnes, Sunderland, SR4 7RG Tel: 0191-565-7215 Email: harry.wynne@virgin.net WWW: http://nepolicehistory.homestead.com, North Eastern England police forces past and present from Teeside to Tweed. All history aspects.

Teesdale Heritage Group, Wesley Terrace, Middleton in Teesdale, Barnard Castle, DL12 0Q Tel: 01833 641104

The Derwentdale Local History Society, 36 Roger Street, Blackhill, Consett, DH8 5SX

Tow Law History Society, 27 Attleee Estate, Tow Law, DL13 4LG Tel: 01388-730056 Email: RonaldStorey@btinternet.co.uk WWW: www.historysociety.org.uk Extensive collection of photos, also some polling returns of Tow Law & District area

Wheatley Hill History Club, Broadmeadows, County Durham Road, Wheatley Hill, DH6 3LJ Tel: 01429 820813 Tel: Mobile 0781 112387 Email: wheathistory@onet.co.uk WWW: http://mypages.comcast.net/dcock104433/HISTORY/index.htm

The 68th (or County Durham) Regiment of Light Infantry Display Team, 40 The Rowans, Orgill, Egremont, CA22 2HW Tel: 01946 820110 Email: PhilMackie@aol.com WWW: www.68dli.com

Essex

Barking & District Historical Society, 449 Ripple Road, Barking, IG11 9RB Tel: 020 8594 7381 Email: barkinghistorical@hotmail.com Covers the London Borough of Barking and Dagenham

Barking Historical Society, 11 Coulson Close, Dagenham, RM8 1TY Tel: (020) 8590 9694 Email: pgibbs9@tesco.net

Billericay Archaeological and Historical Society, 24 Belgrave Road, Billericay, CM12 1TX Tel: 01277 658989 Group within Society recording MIs at Churches in Essex

Brentwood & District Historical Society, 51 Hartswood Road, Brentwood, CM14 5AG Tel: 01277 221637

Burnham & District Local History & Archealogical Society, The Museum, The Quay, Burnham On Crouch, CM0 8AS

Colchester Archaeological Group, 172 Lexden Road, Colchester, CO3 4BZ Tel: 01206 575081 WWW: www.camulos.com/cag/cag.htm

Dunmow & District Historical and Literary Society, 18 The Poplars, Great Dunmow, CM6 2JA Tel: 01371 872496

Essex Archaeological & Historical Congress, 56 Armond Road, Witham, CM8 2HA Tel: 01376 516315 Fax: 01376 516315 Email: essexahc@aol.com

Essex Historic Buildings Group, 12 Westfield Avenue, Chelmsford, CM1 1SF Tel: 01245 256102 Fax: 01371 830416 Email: cakemp@hotmail.com

Essex Society for Archeaology & History, 2 Landview Gardens, Ongar, CM5 9EQ Tel: 1277363106 Email: family@leachies.freeserve.co.uk WWW: www.leachies.freeserve.co.uk

Friends of Historic Essex, 11 Milligans Chase, Galleywood, Chelmsford, CM2 8QD Tel: 01245 436043 Fax: 01245 257365 Email: geraldine.willden2@essexcc.gov.uk The Friends of Historic Essex support the work of the Essex Record Office. Membership Secretary Ms M Scollan, 22 Abercorn Way, Witham, Essex CM8 2UF Tel: 01376 517863 Email: mjscollan@ouvip.com

Friends of The Hospital Chapel, 174 Aldborough Road South, Seven Kings, Ilford, IG3 8HF Tel: (020) 8590 9972 Fax: (020) 8590 0366

Friends of Thomas Plume's Library, The Old Vicarage, Great Totham, Maldon, CM9 8NP Tel: 01621 892261 No facilities for enquiries and no material relevant to Genealogists

Halstead & District Local History Society, Magnolia, 3 Monklands Court, Halstead, C09 1AB

(HEARS) Herts & Essex Architectural Research Society, 4 Nelmes Way, Hornchurch, RM11 2QZ Tel: 01708 473646 Email: kpolrm11@aol.com

High Country History Group, Repentance Cottage, Drapers Corner, Greensted, Ongar, CM5 9LS Tel: 01277 364305 Email: rob.brooks@virgin.net Covers the rural area of S W Ongar being the parishes of Greensted, Stanford Rivers, Stapleford Tawney and Theydon Mount

Ingatestone and Fryerning Historical and Archaeological Society, 36 Pine Close Ingatestone, CM4 9EG Tel: 01277 354001

Loughton & District Historical Society, 6 High Gables, Loughton, IG10 4EZ Tel: (020) 8508 4974 This Society keeps no records of Genealogical interest - any material given to the Society is passed to Essex Record Office

Maldon Society, 15 Regency Court, Heybridge, Maldon, CM9 4EJ

Nazeing History Workshop, 16 Shooters Drive, Nazeing, EN9 2QD Tel: 01992 893264 Email: d_pracy@hotmail.com WWW: www.eppingforectmuseum.co.uk/socvieties/php/NazeingHistoryWorkshop,

Newham History Society, 52 Eastbourne Road, East Ham, London, E6 6AT Tel: (020) 8471 1171 WWW: www.pewsey.net/newhamhistory.htm

Romford & District Historical Society, 67 Gelsthorpe Road, Collier Row, Romford, RM5 2LX Tel: 01708 728203 Email: caroline@wiggins67.freeserve.co.uk

The Colne Smack Preservation Society, 76 New Street, Brightlingsea, CO7 0DD Tel: 01206 304768 WWW: www.colne-smack-preservation.rest.org.uk

Thurrock Heritage Forum, c/o Thurrock Museum, Ossett Road, Grays, RM17 5DX

Thurrock Local History Society, 13 Rosedale Road, Little Thurrock, Grays, RM17 6AD Tel: 01375 377746 Email: tcvs.tc@gtnet.gov.uk

Waltham Abbey Historical Society, 28 Hanover Court, Quaker Lane, Waltham Abbey, EN9 1HR Tel: 01992 716830

Walthamstow Historical Society, 24 Nesta Road, Woodford Green, IG8 9RG Tel: (020) 8504 4156 Fax: (020) 8523 2399

Wanstead Historical Society, 28 Howard Road, Ilford, IG1 2EX

Witham History Group, 35 The Avenue, Witham, CM8 2DN Tel: 01376 512566

Woodford Historical Society, 2 Glen Rise, Woodford Green, IG8 0AN

Gateshead

National Inventory of War Memorials (North East England), Bilsdale, Ulgham, Morpeth, NE61 3AR Tel: 01670 790465

Gloucestershire

Alveston Local History Society, 6 Hazel Gardens, Alveston, BS35 3RD Tel: 01454 43881 Email: jc1932@alveston51.fsnet.co.uk WWW: www.bgas.org.uk

Bristol and Gloucestershire Archaeological Society, 22 Beaumont Road, Gloucester, GL2 0EJ Tel: 01452 302610 Email: david_j._h.smith@virgin.net WWW: http://www.bgas.org.uk

Campden and District Historical & Archaeological Society, 14 Pear Tree Close, Chipping Campden, GL55 6DB

Charlton Kings Local History Society, 28 Chase Avenue, Charlton Kings, Cheltenham, GL52 6YU Tel: 01242 520492

Cheltenham Local History Society, 1 Turkdean Road, Cheltenham, GL51 6AP

Cirencester Archaeological and Historical Society, 8 Tower Street, Cirencester, GL7 1EF Tel: 01285 651516 Fax: 01285 651516 Email: dviner@waitrose.com, WWW:

Forest of Dean Local History Society, Patch Cottage, Oldcroft Green, Lydney, GL15 4NL Tel: 01594 563165 Email: akearApatchcottage.freeserve.co.uk WWW: www.forestofdeanhistory.co.uk

Frenchay Tuckett Society and Local History Museum, 247 Frenchay Park Road, Frenchay, BS16 ILG Tel: 0117 956 9324 Email: raybulmer@compuserve.com WWW: www.frenchay.org/museum.html

Friends of Gloucestershire Archives, 17 Estcourt Road, Gloucester, GL13LU Tel: 01452 528930 Email: patricia.bath@talk21.com

Gloucestershire County Local History Committee, Gloucestershire RCC, Community House, 15 College Green, Gloucester, GL1 2LZ Tel: 01452 528491 Fax: 01452-528493 Email: glosrcc@grcc.org.uk

Leckhampton Local History Society, 15 Arden Road, Leckhampton, Cheltenham, GL53 OHG WWW: www.geocities.com/llhsgl53

Moreton-In-Marsh & District Local History Society, Chapel Place, Longborough, Moreton-In-Marsh, GL56 OQR Tel: 01451 830531

Newent Local History Society, Arron, Ross Road, Newent, GL18 1BE Tel: 01531 821398

Painswick Local History Society, Canton House, New Street, Painswick, GL6 6XH Tel: 01452 812419 Fax: 01452 812419

Stroud Civic Society, Blakeford House, Broad Street, Kings Stanley, Stonehouse, GL10 3PN Tel: 01453 822498

Stroud Local History Society, Stonehatch, Oakridge Lynch, Stroud, GL6 7NR Tel: 01285 760460 Email: john@loosleyj.freeserve.co.uk

Swindon Village Society, 3 Swindon Hall, Swindon Village, Cheltenham, GL51 9QR Tel: 01242 521723

Tewkesbury Historical Society, 20 Moulder Road, Tewkesbury, GL20 8ED Tel: 01684 297871

The Waterways Trust, The National Waterways Museum, Llanthony Warehouse, Gloucester Docks, Gloucester, GL1 2EH Tel: 01452 318053 Fax: 01452 318066 Email: info@nwm.demon.co.uk WWW: www.nwm.org.uk

Gloucestershire - South

Avon Local History Association, 4 Dalkeith Avenue, Kingswood, Bristol, BS15 1HH Tel: 0117 967 1362

Marshfield & District Local History Society, Weir Cottage, Weir Lane, Marshfield, Chippenham, SN14 8NB Tel: 01225 891 229 Email: weircott@luna.co.uk

Greater Manchester

Denton Local History Society, 94 Edward Street, Denton, Manchester, M34 3BR

Stretford Local History Society, 26 Sandy Lane, Stretford, Manchester, M32 9DA Tel: 0161 283 9434 Email: mjdawson@cwcom.net WWW: www.stretfordlhs.cwc.net

Urmston District Local History Society, 78 Mount Drive, Urmston, Manchester, M41 9QA

Hampshire

Aldershot Historical and Archaeological Society, 10 Brockenhurst Road, Aldershot, GU11 3HH Tel: 01252 26589

Andover History and Archaeology Society, 140 Weyhill Road, Andover, SP1O 3BG Tel: 01264 324926 Email: johnl.barrell@virgin.net

Basingstoke Archaeological and Historical Society, 57 Belvedere Gardens, Chineham, Basingstoke, RG21 Tel: 01256 356012

Bishops Waltham Museum Trust, 8 Folly Field, Bishop's Waltham, Southampton, S032 1EB Tel: 01489 894970

Bitterne Local History Society, Heritage Centre, 225 Peartree Avenue, Bitterne, Southampton, Tel: (023) 80444837 Fax: (023) 80444837 Email: sheaf@sheafrs.freeserve.co.uk WWW: www.bitterne.net

Botley & Curdridge Local History, 3 Mayfair Court, Botley, SO30 2GT

Fareham Local History Group, Wood End Lodge, Wood End, Wickham, Fareham, PO17 6JZ WWW:

www.cix.co.uk/~catisfield/farehist.htm

Farnham and District Museum Society, Tanyard House, 13a Bridge Square, Farnham, GU9 7QR

Fleet & Crookham Local History Group, 33 Knoll Road, Fleet, GU51 4PT WWW: www.hants.gov.uk/fclhg

Fordingbridge Historical Society, 26 Lyster Road,, Manor Park, Fordingbridge, SP6 IQY Tel: 01425 655417

Hampshire Field Club and Archaeological Society, 8 Lynch Hill Park Whitchurch, RG28 7NF Tel: 01256 893241 Email: jhamdeveson@compuserve.com WWW: www.fieldclub.hants.org.uk/

Hampshire Field Club & Archaelogical Society (Local History Section), c/o Hampshire Record Office, Sussex Street, Winchester, SO23 8TH

Havant Museum, Havant Museum, 56 East Street, Havant, P09 1BS Tel: 023 9245 1155 Fax: 023 9249 8707 Email: musmop@hants.gov.uk WWW: www.hants.gov.uk/museums Also Friends of Havant Museum - Local History Section Local Studies Collection open Tuesday to Saturday 10.00.a.m. to 5.00.p.m.

Lymington & District Historical Society, Larks Lee, Coxhill Boldre, Near Lymington, 5041 8PS

Lyndhurst Historical Society, 13 Northerwood Avenue, Lyndhurst, SO43 7DU

Milford-on-Sea Historical Record Society, New House, New Road, Keyhaven, Lymington, S041 OTN

North East Hampshire Historical and Archaeological Society, 36 High View Road, Farnborough, GU14 7PT Tel: 01252-543023 Email: nehhas@netscape.net WWW: www.hants.org.uk/nehhas

Somborne & District Society, Forge House, Winchester Road, Kings Somborne, Stockbridge, S020 6NY Tel: 01794 388742 Email: w.hartley@ntlworld.com WWW: www.communigate.co.uk/hants/somsoc

South of England Costume Society, Bramley Cottage, 9 Vicarage Hill, Hartley Witney, Hook, RG27 8EH Email: j.sanders@lineone.net WWW:

Southampton Local History Forum, Special Collections Library, Civic Centre, Southampton, England Tel: 023 8083 2462 Fax: 023 8022 6305 Email: local.ctudies@southampton.gov.uk

Southern Counties Costume Society, 173 Abbotstone, Alresford, SO24 9TE

Stubbington & Hillhead History Society, 34 Anker Lane, Stubbington, Fareham, PO14 3HE Tel: 01329 664554

West End Local History Society, 20 Orchards Way, West End, Southampton, S030 3FB Tel: 023 8057 5244 Email: westendlhs@aol.com WWW: www.telbin.demon.co.uk/westendlhs, Museum at Old Fire Station, High Street, West End

Hampshire (North)

Newbury & District Field Club, 4 Coombe Cottages, Coombe Road, Crompton, Newbury, RG20 6RG Tel: 01635 579076

Herefordshire

Council for British Archaeology - West Midlands, c/o Rowley's House Museum, Barker Street, Shrewsbury, SY1 1QH Tel: 01743 361196 Fax: 01743 358411 Email: mikestokes@shrewsbury-atcham.gov.uk WWW: www.shrewsburymuseums.com www.darwincountry.org

Ewyas Harold & District Wea, c/o Hillside, Ewyas Harold, Hereford, HR2 0HA Tel: 01981 240529

Kington History Society, Kington Library, 64 Bridge Street, Kington, HR5 3BD Tel: 01544 230427 Email: vee.harrison@virgin.net

Leominster Historical Society, Fircroft, Hereford Road, Leominster, HR6 8JU Tel: 01568 612874

Weobley & District Local History Society and Museum, Weobley Museum, Back Lane, Weobley, HR4 8SG Tel: 01544 340292

Hertfordshire

1st or Grenadier Foot Guards 1803 -1823, 39 Chatterton, Letchworth, SG6 2JY Tel: 01462-670918 Email: BJCham2809@aol.com WWW: http://members.aol.com/BJCham2809/homepage.html Military history, from a family history view point. Special interest in Napoleonic Wars.

Research and advice on this period are generally available.

Abbots Langley Local History Society, 80 Abbots Road, Abbots Langley, WD5 0BH WWW: http://www.allhs.btinternet.co.uk

Baptist Historical Society, 60 Strathmore Avenue, Hitchin, SG5 1ST Tel: 01462-431816 Tel: 01462-442548 Email: slcopson@dial.pipex.com WWW: www.baptisthistory.org.uk

Black Sheep Research (Machine Breakers, Rioters & Protesters), 4 Quills Letchworth Garden City, SG6 2RJ Tel: 01462-483706 Email: J_M_Chambers@compuserve.com

Braughing Local History Society, Pantiles, Braughing Friars, Ware, SG11 2NS

Codicote Local History Society, 34 Harkness Way, Hitchin, SG4 0QL Tel: 01462 622953

East Herts Archaeological Society, 1 Marsh Lane, Stanstead Abbots, Ware, SG12 8HH Tel: 01920 870664

Hertford Museum (Hertfordshire Regiment), 18 Bull Plain, Hertford, SG14 1DT Tel: 01992 582686 Fax: 01992 534797 Email: enquiries@hertfordmuseum.org WWW: www.hertfordmuseum.org

Hertford & Ware Local History Society, 10 Hawthorn Close, Hertford, SG14 2DT

Hertfordshire Archaeological Trust, The Seed Warehouse, Maidenhead Yard, The Wash, Hertford, SG14 1PX Tel: 01992 558 170 Fax: 01992 553359 Email: herts.archtrust@virgin.net WWW: www.hertfordshire-archaeological-trust.co.uk

Hertfordshire Association for Local History, c/o 64 Marshals Drive, St Albans, AL1 4RF Tel: 01727 856250 Email: ClareEllis@compuserve.com

Hertfordshire Record Society, 119 Winton Drive, Croxley Green, Rickmansworth, WD3 3QS Tel: 01923-248581 Email: info@hrsociety.org.uk WWW: www.hrsociety.org.uk

Hitchin Historical Society, c/o Hitchin Museum, Paynes Park, Hitchin, SG5 2EQ WWW:

Kings Langley Local History & Museum Society, Kings Langley Library, The Nap, Kings Langley, WD4 8ET Tel: 01923 263205 Tel: 01923 264109 Email: frankdavies4@hotmail.com alan@penwardens.freeserve.co.uk WWW: www.kingslangley.org.uk

London Colney Local History Society, 51A St Annes Road, London Colney, Nr. St. Albans, AL2 1 PD, Affiliated to BALH and Hertfordshire Heritage

North Mymms Local History Society, 89 Peplins Way, Brookmans Park, Hatfield, AL9 7UT Tel: 01707 655970 WWW: www.brookmans.com

Potters Bar and District Historical Society, 9 Hill Rise, Potters Bar, EN6 2RX Tel: 01707 657586 Email: johnscrivyer@aol.com

Rickmansworth Historical Society, 20 West Way, Rickmansworth, WD3 7EN Tel: 01923 774998 Email: geoff@gmsaul.freeserve.co.uk Search service for Rickmansworth (old Parish area) - militia lists, census, baptisms, marriage & burials, from 1700 app to 1st World War; Watford Observer quotes to 100 years ago

Royston & District Local History Society, 8 Chilcourt, Royston, SG8 9DD Tel: 01763 242677 Email: david.allard@ntlworld.com WWW: www.royston.clara.net/localhistory

South West Hertfordshire Archaeological and Historical Society, 29 Horseshoe Lane, Garston, Watford, WD25 0LN Tel: 01923 672482

St. Albans & Herts Architectural & Archaeological Society, 24 Rose Walk, St Albans, AL4 9AF Tel: 01727 853204

The Harpenden & District Local History Society, The History Centre, 19 Arden Grove, Harpenden, AL5 4SJ Tel: 01582 713539

Watford and District Industrial History Society, 79 Kingswood Road, Garston, Watford, WD25 0EF Tel: 01923 673253

Welwyn Archaeological Society, The Old Rectory, 23 Mill Lane, Welyn, AL6 9EU Tel: 01438 715300 Fax: 01438 715300

Welwyn & District Local History Society, 9 York Way, Welwyn, AL6 9LB Tel: 01438 716415 FH Coordinator: June Longmead, 9 York Way, Welwyn Hertfordshire AL 6 9LB

Isle of Wight

Isle of Wight Natural History & Archaeological Society, Salisbury Gardens, Dudley Road, Ventnor, PO38 1EJ Tel: 01983 855385

Newchurch Parish History Society, 1 Mount Pleasant, Newport Road, Sandown, PO36 OLS

Roots Family & Parish History, San Fernando, Burnt House Lane, Alverstone, Sandown, PO36 0HB Tel: 01983 403060 Email: peters.sanfernando@tesco.net

St Helens Historical Society, Gloddaeth, Westfield Road, St. Helens, Ryde, PO33 LUZ

St. Helens History Society, c/o The Castle, Duver Road, St Helens, Ryde, PO33 1XY Tel: 01983 872164

Kent

Appledore Local History Society, 72 The Street, Appledore, Ashford, TN26 2AE Tel: 01233 758500 Fax: 01233 758500 Email: trothfw@aol.com

Ashford Archaeological and Historical Society, Gablehook Farm, Bethersden, Ashford, TN26 3BQ Tel: 01233 820679

Aylesford Society, 30 The Avenue, Greenacres, Aylesford, Maidstone, ME20 7LE

Bearsted & District Local History Society, 17 Mount Lane, Bearsted, Maidstone, ME14 4DD

Bexley Civic Society, 58 Palmeira Road, Bexleyheath, DA7 4UX

Bexley Historical Society, 36 Cowper Close, Welling, DAI6 2JT

Biddenden Local History Society, Willow Cottage, Smarden Road, Biddenden, Ashford, TN27 8JT

Brenchley & Matfield Local History Society, Ashendene, Tong Road, Brenchley, Tonbridge, TN12 7HT Tel: 01892 723476

Bridge & District History Society, La Dacha, Patrixbourne Road, Bridge, Canterbury, CT4 5BL

Broadstairs Society, 30 King Edward Avenue, Broadstairs, CT10 lPH Tel: 01843 603928 Email: mike@termites.fsnet.co.uk

Bromley Borough Local History Society, 62 Harvest Bank Road, West Wickham, BR4 9DJ Tel: 020 8462 5002

Canterbury Archaeology Society, Dane Court, Adisham, Canterbury, CT3 3LA

Charing & District Local History Society, Old School House, Charing, Ashford, TN27 0LS

Chatham Historical Society, 69 Ballens Road, Walderslade, Chatham, ME5 8NX Tel: 01634 865176

Council for Kentish Archaeology, 3 Westholme, Orpington, BR6 0AN Email: information@the-cka.fsnet.co.uk WWW: www.the-cka.fsnet.co.uk

Cranbrook & District History Society, 61 Wheatfield Way, Cranbrook, TN17 3NE

Crayford Manor House Historical and Archaeological Society, 17 Swanton Road, Erith, DA8 1LP Tel: 01322 433480

Croydon Natural History & Scientific Society Ltd, 96a Brighton Road, South Croydon, CR2 6AD Tel: (020) 8688 4539 WWW: http://www.grieg51.freeserve.co.uk/cnhss

Dartford History & Antiquarian Society, 14 Devonshire Avenue, Dartford, DA1 3DW Fax: 01732 824741

Deal Library, Broad Street, Deal, CT14 6ER Tel: 01304 374726 1901 census

Deal & Walmer Local History Society, 7 Northcote Road, Deal

Detling Society., 19 Hockers Lane, Detling, Maidstone, ME14 3JL Tel: 01622 737940 Fax: 01622 737408 Email: johnowne@springfield19.freeserve.co.uk

Dover History Society, 2 Courtland Drive, Kearsney, Dover, CT16 3BX Tel: 01304 824764

East Peckham Historical Society, 13 Fell Mead, East Peckham, Tonbridge, TNI2 5EG

Edenbridge & District History Society, 17 Grange Close, Edenbridge, TN8

Erith & Belvedere Local History Society, 67 Merewood Road, Barnehurst, DA7 6PF

Farningham & Eynsford Local History Society, Lavender Hill, Beesfield Lane, Farningham, Dartford, DA4 ODA

Faversham Society, 10-13 Preston St, Faversham, ME13 8NS Tel: 01795 534542 Tel: 01795 533261 (Home) (Do not publish) Fax: 01795 533261 Email: faversham@btinternet.com WWW: http://www.faversham.org CC accepted. A detailed list of local Explosives Factory workers 1570-1934 to be published soon.

Fawkham & District Historical Society The Old Rectory, Valley Road, Fawkham, Longfield, DA3 8LX

Folkestone & District Local History Society, 7 Shorncliffe Crescent, Folkestone

Friends of Lydd, 106 Littlestone Road, New Romney, TN28 8NH

Frittenden History Society, Bobbyns, The Street, Frittenden, Cranbrook, TN17 2DG Tel: 01580 852459 Fax: 01580 852459

Gillingham & Rainham Local History Society, 23 Sunningdale Road, Rainham, Gillingham, ME8 9EQ

Goudhurst & Kilndown Local History Society, 2 Weavers Cottages, Church Road, Goudhurst, TN17 1BL

Gravesend Historical Society, 58 Vicarage Lane, Chalk, Gravesend, DA12 4TE Tel: 01474 363998

Great Chart Society, Swan Lodge, The Street, Great Chart, Ashford, TN23 3AH

Hadlow History Society, Spring House, Tonbridge Road, Hadlow, Tonbridge, TN11 0DZ Tel: 01732 850214 Email: billanne@hadlow12.freeserve.co.uk

Halling Local History Society, 58 Ladywood Road, Cuxton, Rochester, ME2 1EP Tel: 01634 716139

Hawkhurst Local History Society, 17 Oakfield, Hawkhurst, Cranbrook, TN18 4JR Tel: 01580 752376 Email: vcw@lessereagles.freeserve.co.uk

Headcorn History Society, Cecil Way, 2 Forge Lane, Headcorn, TN27 9QQ Tel: 01622 890253 WWW: www.headcorn.org.uk

Herne Bay Historical Records Society, c/o Herne Bay Museum, 12 William St, Herne Bay, CT6 5EJ

Higham Village History Group, Forge House, 84 Forge Lane, Higham, Rochester, ME3 7AH

Horton Kirby & South Darenth Local History Society, Appledore, Rays Hill, Horton Kirby, Dartford, DA4 9DB Tel: 01322 862056

Hythe Civic Society, 25 Napier Gardens, Hythe, CT2l 6DD

Isle of Thanet Historical Society, 58 Epple Bay Avenue, Birchington CT7 9HH

Kemsing Historical & Art Society, 26 Dippers Close, Kemsing, Sevenoaks, TN15 6QD Tel: 01732 761774

Kent Archaeological Rescue Unit, Roman Painted House, New Street, Dover, CT17 9AJ Tel: 01304 203279 Tel: 020 8462 4737 Fax: 020 8462 4737 WWW: www.the-cka.fsnet.co.uk

Kent History Federation, 48 Beverley Avenue, Sidcup, DA15 8HE

Kent Mills Group, Windmill Cottage, Mill Lane, Willesborough, TN27 0QG

Kent Postal History Group, 27 Denbeigh Drive, Tonbridge, TN10 3PW

Lamberhurst Local History Society, 1 Tanyard Cotts, The Broadway, Lamberhurst, Tunbridge Wells, TN3 8DD

Lamorbey & Sidcup Local History Society, 14 Valliers Wood Road, Sidcup, DA15 8BG

Leigh and District History Society, Elizabeths Cottage, The Green, Leigh, Tonbridge, TN11 8QW Tel: 01732 832459

Lewisham Local History Society, 2 Bennett Park, Blackheath Village, London, SE3 9RB Email: tom@trshepherd.fsnet.co.uk

Loose Area History Society, 16 Bedgebury Close, Maidstone, ME14 5QY

Lyminge Historical Society, Ash Grove, Canterbury Road, Etchinghill, Folkestone, CT18 8DF

Maidstone Area Archaeological Group, 14 The Quarter, Cranbrook Road, Staplehurst, TN12 0EP

Maidstone Historical Society, 37 Bower Mount Road, Maidstone, ME16 8AX Tel: 01622 676472

Margate Civic Society, 19 Lonsdale Avenue, Cliftonville, Margate, CT9 3BT

Meopham Historical Society Tamar, Wrotham Road, Meopham, DA13 0EX

Orpington History Society, 42 Crossway, Petts Wood, Orpington, BR5 1PE

Otford & District History Society, Thyme Bank, Coombe Road, Otford, Sevenoaks, TN14 5RJ

Otham Society, Tudor Cottage, Stoneacre Lawn, Otham, Maidstone, ME15 8RT

Paddock Wood History Society, 19 The Greenways, Paddock Wood, Tonbridge, TN12 6LS

Plaxtol Local History Group, Tebolds, High Street, Plaxtol, Sevenoaks, TN15 0QJ

Rainham Historical Society, 52 Northumberland Avenue, Rainham, Gillingham, ME8 7JY

Ramsgate Society, Mayfold, Park Road, Ramsgate, CT11 7QH

Ringwould History Society, Back Street, Ringwould, Deal, CT14 8HL Tel: 01304 361030 Tel: 01304 380083 Email: julie.m.rayner@talk21.com and jeanwinn@beeb.net WWW: www.ringwould-village.org.uk

Romney Marsh Research Trust, 11 Caledon Terrace, Canterbury, CT1 3JS Tel: 01227 472490 Email: s.m.sweetinburgh@ukc.ac.uk WWW: www.ukc.ac.uk/mts/rmrt/

Rye Local History Group, 107 Military Road, Rye, TN31 7NZ

Sandgate Society, The Old Fire Station, 51 High Street, Sandgate, CT20 3AH

Sandwich Local History Society, Clover Rise, 14 Stone Cross Lees, Sandwich, CT13 OBZ Tel: 01304 613476 Email: frankandrews@FreeNet.co.uk

Sevenoaks Historical Society, 122 Kippington Road, Sevenoaks, TN13 2LN Email: wilkospin@beeb.net

Sheppey Local History Society, 34 St Helens Road, Sheerness

Shoreham & District Historical Society, The Coach House, Darenth Hulme, Shoreham, TN14 7TU

Shorne Local History Group 2 Calderwood, Gravesend DA12 4Q11

Sittingbourne Society, 4 Stanhope Avenue, Sittingbourne, ME10 4TU Tel: 01795 473807 Fax: 01795 473807 Email: mandbmoore@tinyonline.co.uk

Smarden Local History Society, 7 Beult Meadow, Cage Lane, Smarden, TN27 8PZ Tel: 01233 770 856 Fax: 01233 770 856 Email: franlester@fish.co.uk

Snodland Historical Society, 214 Malling Road, Snodland, ME6 SEQ Email: aa0060962@blueyonder.co.uk WWW: www.snodlandhistory.org.uk

St Margaret's Bay History Society, Rock Mount, Salisbury Road, St Margarets Bay, Dover, CT15 6DL Tel: 01304 852236

Staplehurst Society, Willow Cottage, Chapel Lane, Staplehurst, TN12 0AN Tel: 01580 891059 Email: awcebd@mistral.co.uk

Tenterden & District Local History Society, Little Brooms, Ox Lane, St Michaels, Tenterden, TN30 6NQ

Teston History Society, Broad Halfpenny, Malling Road, Teston, Maidstone, ME18 SAN

Thanet Retired Teachers Association, 85 Percy Avenue, Kingsgate, Broadstairs, CT10 3LD

The Anglo-Zulu War Historical Society, Woodbury House, Woodchurch Road, Tenterden, TN30 7AE Tel: 01580-764189 Fax: 01580-766648 WWW: www.web-marketing.co.uk/anglozuluwar Records & Documentation of Zulu War

The Kent Archaeological Society, Three Elms, Woodlands Lane, Shorne, Gravesend, DA12 3HH Tel: 01474 822280 Email: secretary@kentarchaeology.org.uk WWW: www.kentarchaeology.org.uk

The Marden Society, 6 Bramley Court, Marden, Tonbridge, TN12 9QN Tel: 01622 831904 WWW: www.marden.org.uk

Three Suttons Society, Henikers, Henikers Lane, Sutton Valence, ME17 3EE

Tonbridge History Society, 8 Woodview Crescent, Hildenborough, Tonbridge, TN11 9HD Tel: 01732 838698 Email: s.broomfield@dial.pipex.com

Wateringbury Local History Society, Vine House, 234 Tonbridge Road, Wateringbury, ME18 5NY

Weald History Group, Brook Farm, Long Barn Road, Weald, Sevenoaks

Wealden Buildings Study Group, 64 Pilgrims Way, East Otford, Sevenoaks, TN14 5QW

Whitstable History Society, 83 Kingsdown Park, Tankerton, Whitstable

Wingham Local History Society, 67 High Street, Wingham, Canterbury, CT3 1AA

Woodchurch Local History Society, Woodesden, 24 Front Road, Woodclnurch, Ashford, TN26 3QE

Wrotham Historical Society, Hillside House Wrotham, TN15 7JH

Wye Historical Society, I Upper Bridge Street, Wye, Ashford, TN2 5 SAW

Lancashire

Aspull and Haigh Historical Society, 1 Tanpit Cottages, Winstanley, Wigan, WN3 6JY Tel: 01942 222769

Birkdale & Ainsdale Historical Research Society, 20 Blundell Drive, Birkdale, Southport, PR8 4RG WWW: www.harrop.co.uk/bandahrs

Blackburn Civic Society, 20 Tower Road, Blackburn, BB2 5LE Tel: 01254 201399

Burnley Historical Society, 66 Langdale Road, Blackburn, BB2 5DW Tel: 01254 201162

Chadderton Historical Society, 18 Moreton Street, Chadderton, OL9 OLP Tel: 0161 652 3930 Email: enid@chadderton-hs.freeuk.com WWW: http://www.chadderton-hs.freeuk.com

Ewecross History Society, Gruskholme, Bentham, Lancaster, LA2 7AX Tel: 015242 61420

Fleetwood & District Historical, 54 The Esplanade, Fleetwood, FY7 6QE

Friends of Smithills Hall Museum, 19 Leighton Avenue, Heaton, Bolton, BL1 4EH Tel: 01204 840506

Garstang Historical & Archealogical Society, 7 Rivermead Drive, Garstang, PR3 1JJ Tel: 01995 604913 Email: marian.fish@btinternet.com

Historic Society of Lancashire & Cheshire, East Wing Flat, Arley Hall, Northwich, CW9 6NA Tel: 01565 777231 Fax: 01565 777465

Hyndburn Local History Society, 20 Royds Avenue, Accrington, BB5 2LE Tel: 01254 235511

Lancashire Family History and Heraldry Society, 15 ChristChurch Street, Accrington, BB5 2LZ Email: jehuntingdon@08002go.com WWW: www.lancashire-fhhs.org.uk

Lancashire Local History Federation, 298 Blackpool Road, Poulton le Fylde, FY6 7QU Email: secretary@lancashirehistory.co.uk WWW: www.lancashirehistory.co.uk

Lancashire Parish Register Society, 135 Sandy Lane, Orford, Warrington, WA2 9JB Email: tom_obrien@bigfoot.com WWW: http://www.genuki.org.uk/big/eng/LAN/lprs

Leyland Historical Society, 172 Stanifield Lane, Farington; Leyland, Preston, PR5 2QT

Littleborough Historical and Archaeological Society, 8 Springfield Avenue, Littleborough, LA15 9JR Tel: 01706 377685

Maghull and Lydiate Local History Society, 15 Brendale Avenue, Maghull, Liverpool, L31 7AX

Mourholme Local History Society, 3 The Croft, Croftlands, Warton, Carnforth, LA5 9PY Tel: 01524 734110 Email: nt.stobbs@virgin.net

Nelson Local History Society, 5 Langholme Street, Nelson, BB9 ORW Tel: 01282 699475

North West Sound Archive, Old Steward's Office, Clitheroe Castle, Clitheroe, BB7 1AZ Tel: 01200-427897 Fax: 01200-427897 Email: nwsa@ed.lancscc.gov.uk WWW: www.lancashire.gov.uk/education/lifelong/recordindex

Centre for North West Regional Studies, Fylde College, Lancaster University, Lancaster, LA1 4YF Tel: 01524 593770 Fax: 01524 594725 Email: christine.wilkinson@lancaster.ac.uk WWW: www.lancs.ac.uk/users/cnwrs Cc accepted Oral History Archives; Elizabeth Roberts Archive: Penny Summerfield Archive

Saddleworth Historical Society, 7 Slackcote, Delph, Oldham, OL3 5TW Tel: 01457 874530

Society for Name Studies in Britain & Ireland, 22 Peel Park Avenue, Clitheroe, BB7 1ET Tel: 01200-423771 Fax: 01200-423771

Urmston District Local History Society, 78 Mount Drive, Urmston, Manchester, M41 9QA

Leicestershire

Desford & District Local History Group, Lindridge House, Lindridge Lane, Desford, LE9 9FD

East Leake & District Local History Society, 8 West Leake Road, East Leake, Loughborough, LE12 6LJ Tel: 01509 852390

Glenfield and Western Archaeological & Historical Group, 50 Chadwell Road, Leicester, LE3 6LF Tel: 1162873220

Leicestershire Archaeological and Historical Society, The Guildhall Leicester, LE1 5FQ Tel: 0116 2703031 WWW: http://www.le.ac.uk/archaeology/lahs/lahs.html

Leicestershire Archaeological & Historical Society, 37 Dovedale Road, Leicester, LE2 2DN Tel: 0116 270 3031 Email: alan@dovedale2.demon.co.uk WWW: www.le.ac.uk/archaeology/lahs/lahs.html

Sutton Bonington Local History Society, 6 Charnwood Fields, Sutton Bonington, Loughborough, LE12 5NP Tel: 01509 673107

Vaughan Archaeological and Historical Society, c/o Vaughan College, St Nicholas Circle, Leicester, LEl 4LB

Lincolnshire

Lincoln Record Society, Lincoln Cathedral Library, The Cathedral, Lincoln, LN2 1PZ Tel: 01522 544544 Email: librarian@lincolncathedral.com WWW: www.lincolncathedral.com

Long Bennington Local History Society, Kirton House, Kirton Lane, Long Bennington, Newark, NG23 5DX Tel: 01400 281726

Society for Lincolnshire History & Archaeology, Jews' Court, Steep Hill, Lincoln, LN2 1LS Tel: 01522-521337 Fax: 01522 521337 Email: slha@lincolnshirepast.org.uk WWW: www.lincolnshirepast.org.uk

Tennyson Society, Central Library, Free School Lane, Lincoln, LN2 1EZ Tel: 01522-552862 Fax: 01522-552858 Email: linnet@lincolnshire.gov.uk WWW: www.tennysonsociety.org.uk

Liverpool

Maghull and Lydiate Local History Society, 15 Brendale Avenue, Maghull, Liverpool, L31 7AX

Merseyside Archaeological Society, 20 Osborne Road, Formby, Liverpool, L37 6AR Tel: 01704 871802

London

Acton History Group, 30 Highlands Avenue, London, W3 6EU Tel: (020) 8992 8698

Barking & District Historical Society, 449 Ripple Road, Barking, IG11 9RB Tel: 020 8594 7381 Email: barkinghistorical@hotmail.com, Covers the London Borough of Barking and Dagenham

Birkbeck College, Birkbeck College, Malet Street, London, WC1E 7HU Tel: (020) 7631 6633 Fax: (020) 7631 6688 Email: info@bbk.ac.uk WWW: www.bbl.ac.uk

Brentford & Chiswick Local History Society, 25 Hartington Road, London, W4 3TL

British Records Association, 40 Northampton Road, London, EC1R 0HB Tel: (020) 7833 0428 Fax: (020) 7833 0416 Email: britrecassoc@hotmail.com WWW: www.hmc.gov.uk/bra The BRA brings together everypone interested in archives;owners, custodians, users. It publishes, informs, lobbies and plays an active part in the work of preserving records.

Brixton Society, 82 Mayall Road, London, SE24 0PJ Tel: (020) 7207 0347 Fax: (020) 7207 0347 Email: apiperbrix@aol.com WWW: www.brixtonsociety.org.uk

Bromley Borough Local History Society, 62 Harvest Bank Road, West Wickham, BR4 9DJ Tel: 020 8462 5002

Centre for Metropolitan History, Institute of Historical Research, Senate House, Malet Street, London, WC1E 7HU Tel: (020) 7862 8790 Fax: (020) 7862 8793 Email: olwen.myhill@sas.ac.uk WWW: www.history.ac.uk/cmh/cmh.main.html

The Costume Society, St Paul's House, 8 Warwick Road, London, EC4P 4BN WWW: www.costumesociety.org.uk, Society for the study of dress, fashion and clothing history

Croydon Local Studies Forum, c/o Local Studies Library, Catherine Street, Croydon, CR9 1ET

Croydon Natural History & Scientific Society Ltd, 96a Brighton Road, South Croydon, CR2 6AD Tel: (020) 8688 4539 WWW: http://www.grieg51.freeserve.co.uk/cnhss

East London History Society, 42 Campbell Road, Bow, London, E3 4DT Tel: 020 8980 5672 Email: elhs@mernicks.com WWW: www.eastlondon.org.uk

Edmonton Hundred Historical Society, Local History Unit, Southgate Town Hall, Green Lanes, London, N13 4XD Tel: (020) 8379 2724 Covers Tottenham, Wood Green, Palmers Green, Winchmore Hill, and Southgate (All London Postal Districts besides Enfield and Monken Hadley)

Fulham And Hammersmith Historical Soceity, Flat 12, 43 Peterborough Road, Fulham, London, SW6 3BT Tel: (020) 7731 0363 Email: mail@fhhs.org.uk WWW: www.fhhs.org.uk

Hornsey Historical Society, The Old Schoolhouse, 136 Tottenham Lane, London, N8 7EL Tel: (020) 8348 8429 WWW: www.hornseyhistorical.org.uk

London & Middlesex Archaeological Society, Placements Office, University of North London, 62-66 Highbury Grove, London, N5 2AD

London Record Society, c/o Institute of Historical Research, Senate House, Malet Street, London, WC1E 7HU Tel: (020) 7862-8798 Fax: (020) 7862 8793 Email: heathercreaton@sas.ac.uk WWW: http://www.ihrinfo.ac.uk/cmh

Mill Hill Historical Society, 41 Victoria Road, Mill Hill, London, NW7 4SA Tel: (020) 8959 7126

Museum of the Royal Pharmaceutical Society, Museum of the Royal Pharmaceutical Society, 1 Lambeth High Street, London, SE1 7JN Tel: (020) 7572 2210 Fax: (020) 7572 2499 Email: museum@rpsgb.org.uk WWW: http://www.rpsgb.org.uk CC accepted. Records of pharmacists from 1841 Research fee charged

Newham History Society, 52 Eastbourne Road, East Ham, London, E6 6AT Tel: (020) 8471 1171 WWW: www.pewsey.net/newhamhistory.htm

Paddington Waterways and Maida Vale Society (Local History), 19a Randolph Road, Maida Vale, London, W9 1AN Tel: 020 7289 0950

Royal Arsenal Woolwich Historical Society, Main Guard House, Royal Arsenal Woolwich, Woolwich, London, SE18 6ST Email: royalarsenal@talk21.com WWW: http://members.lycos.co.uk/RoyalArsenal

Richmond Local History Society, 9 Bridge Road, St Margarets, Twickenham, TWI IRE

The Peckham Society, 6 Everthorpe Road, Peckham, London, SE15 4DA Tel: (020) 8693 9412 Fax: (020) 8693 9412

The Vauxhall Society, 20 Albert Square, London, SW8 1BS

Walthamstow Historical Society, 24 Nesta Road, Woodford Green, IG8 9RG Tel: (020) 8504 4156 Fax: (020) 8523 2399

Wandsworth Historical Society, 31 Hill Court, Putney Hill, London, SW15 6BB Covers the areas of Balham, Southfields, Tooting, Wandsworth, Roehampton, Earlsfield, Putney, Battersea

West London Local History Conference, 25 Hartington Road, London, W4 3TL, This is a group of various Family and Local History Societies who organise a conference each Spring with a West London context. It is an organising body only and does not have a membership.

Willesden Local History Society (London Borough of Brent), 9 Benningfield Gardens, Berkhamstead, HP4 2GW Tel: 01442 878477 Covers the parishes of Cricklewood, Willesden, Kilburn, Park Royal, Harlesden, Neasden, Park Royal & Kensal Rise

Fulham & Hammersmith History Society, 85 Rannoch Road, Hammersmith, London, W6 9SX

Hendon &District Archaeological Society, 13 Reynolds Close, London, NW11 7EA Tel: (020) 8458 1352 Fax: (020) 8731 9882 Email: denis@netmatters.co.uk WWW: www.hadas.org.uk

Merseyside
Birkdale & Ainsdale Historical Research Society, 20 Blundell Drive, Birkdale, Southport, PR8 4RG WWW: www.harrop.co.uk/bandahrs

British Society for Sports History, Dept of Sports & Science, John Moore's University, Byrom Street, Liverpool, L3 3AF

Friends of Williamson's Tunnels, 15-17 Chatham Place, Edge Hill, Liverpool, L7 3HD Tel: 0151 475 9833 Fax: 0151 475 9833 Email: info@williamsontunnels.com WWW: www.williamsontunnels.com A registered charity with over a thousand members, Friends of Williamson's Tunnels works to ensure the preservation of the mysterious 19th century labyrinth under Liverpool

Historic Society of Lancashire & Cheshire, East Wing Flat, Arley Hall, Northwich, CW9 6NA Tel: 01565 777231 Fax: 01565 777465

Maghull and Lydiate Local History Society, 15 Brendale Avenue, Maghull, Liverpool, L31 7AX

Merseyside Archaeological Society, 20 Osborne Road, Formby, Liverpool, L37 6AR Tel: 01704 871802

Maghull and Lydiate Local History Society, 15 Brendale Avenue, Maghull, Liverpool, L31 7AX

Middlesex
British Deaf History Society, 288 Bedfont Lane, Feltham, TW14 9NU Email: bdhs@iconic.demon.co.uk Archive

Edmonton Hundred Historical Society, Local History Unit, Southgate Town Hall, Green Lanes, London, N13 4XD Tel: (020) 8379 2724 Covers Tottenham, Wood Green, Palmers Green, Winchmore Hill, and Southgate (All London Postal Districts besides Enfield and Monken Hadley)

Hounslow & District History Society, 16 Orchard Avenue, Heston, TW5 0DU Tel: (020) 8570 4264

London & Middlesex Archaeological Society, Placements Office, University of North London, 62-66 Highbury Grove, London, N5 2AD

Middlesex Heraldry Society, 4 Croftwell, Harpeden, AL5 1JG Tel: 01582 766372

Northwood & Eastcote Local History Society, 3 Elbridge Close, Ruislip, HA4 7XA Tel: 01895 637134 WWW: www.rnelhs.flyer.co.uk

Pinner Local History Society, 8 The Dell, Pinner, HA5 3EW Tel: (020) 8866 1918 Email: mwg@pinnerlhs.freeserve.co.uk WWW: www.pinnerlhs.freeserve.co.uk/index.html

Ruislip Northwood & Eastcote Local History Society, 3 Elmbridge Close, Ruislip, HA4 7XA Tel: 01895 637134 Email: www.rnelhs.flyer.co.uk

Sunbury And Shepperton Local, 30 Lindsay drive, Shepperton, TW17 88JU Tel: 01932 226776 Email: H.L.Brooking@eggconnect.net WWW: http://users.eggconnect.net/h.l.brooking/sslhs

Borough of Twickenham Local History Society, 258 Hanworth Road, Hounslow, TW3 3TY Email: pbarnfield@post.com

Norfolk
Blakeney Area Historical Society, 2 Wiveton Road, Blakeney, NR25 7NJ Tel: 01263 741063

Federation of Norfolk Historical and Archaeological Organisations, 14 Beck Lane, Horsham St Faith, Norwich, NR10 3LD

Feltwell (Historical and Archaeological) Society, 16 High Street, Feltwell, Thetford, IP26 4AF Tel: 01842 828448 Email: peterfeltwell@tinyworld.co.uk The Museum is at The Beck, Feltwell Open Tuesday & Saturday April to September 2.00.p.m. to 4.00.p.m.

Holt History Group, 6 Kelling Close, Holt, NR23 6RU

Narborough Local History Society, 101 Westfields, Narborough, Kings Lynn, PE32 ISY WWW: www.narboroughaerodrome.org.uk Narborough Aerodrome 1915-1919 ongoing research - Narborough Airfield Research group. Over 1000 names of Officers Men & Women who served at Narborough. 15 Military graves

Norfolk and Norwich Archaeological Society, 30 Brettingham Avenue, Cringleford, Norwich, NR4 6XG Tel: 01603 455913

Norfolk Archaeological and Historical Research Group, 50 Cotman Road, Norwich, NR1 4AH Tel: 01603 435470

Norfolk Heraldry Society, 26c Shotesham Road, Poringland, Norwich, NR14 7LG Tel: 01508 493832 Fax: 01508 493832 WWW: www.norfolkheraldry.co.uk

Richard III Society - Norfolk Group, 20 Rowington Road, Norwich, NR1 3RR

Northamptonshire
Bozeat Historical and Archaeological Society, 44 Mile Street, Bozeat, NN9 7NB Tel: 01933 663647

Brackley & District History Society, 32 Church Lane, Evenley, Brackley, NN13 5SG Tel: 01280 703508

Higham Chichele Society, 3 Bramley Close, Rushden, NN10 6RL

Historical Medical Equipment Society, 8 Albion Mews, Apsley, HP3 9QZ Email: hmes@antiageing.freeserve.co.uk

Houghtons & Brafield History, 5 Lodge Road, Little Houghton, NN7 IAE

Irchester Parish Historical Society, 80 Northampton Road, Wellingborough, NN8 3HT Tel: 01933 274880 Fax: 01933 274888 WWW: www.irchester.org www.iphs.org.uk

Northamptonshire Association for Local History, 143 Clophill Road, Maulden, MK45 2AF Email: enquiries@northants-history.org.uk WWW: www.northants-history.org.uk

Northamptonshire Record Society, Wootton Park Hall, Northampton, NN4 8BQ Tel: 01604 762297

Oundle Historical Society, 13 Lime Avenue, Oundle, Peterborough, PE8 4PT

Rushden & District History Society, 25 Byron Crescent, Rushden, NN10 6BL Email: rdhs.rushden@virgin.net WWW: www.rdhs.org.uk

Weedon Bec History Society, 35 Oak Street, Weedon, Northampton, NN7 4RR

West Haddon Local History Group, Bramley House, 12 Guilsborough Road, West Haddon, NN6 7AD

Northumberland see also Tyne and Wear
Architectural & Archaeological Society of County Durham & Northumberland, Broom Cottage, 29 Foundry Fielkds, Crook, DL15 9SY Tel: 01388 762620 Email: belindaburke@aol.com

Association of Northumberland Local History Societies, Centre for Lifelong Learning, King George VI Building, University of Newcastle upon Tyne, Newcastle upon Tyne, NE1 7RU Tel: 0191-222-7458 Tel: 0191-222-5680

Felton & Swarland Local History Society, 23 Benlaw Grove, Felton, Morpeth, NE65 9NG Tel: 01670 787476 Email: petercook@felton111.freeserve.co.uk

Hexham Local History Society, Dilstone, Burswell Villas, Hexham, NE46 3LD Tel: 01434 603216

Morpeth Antiquarian Society, 14 Southgate Wood, Morpeth, NE61 2EN

Morpeth Nothumbrian Gathering, Westgate House, Dogger Bank, Morpeth, NE61 1RF

National Inventory of War Memorials (North East England), Bilsdale, Ulgham, Morpeth, NE61 3AR Tel: 01670 790465 Email: gjb@bilsdale.freeserve.co.uk

North-East England History Institute (NEEHI), Department of History University of County Durham, 43 North Bailey, County Durham, DH1 3EX Tel: 0191-374-2004 Fax: 0191-374-4754 Email: m.a.mcallister@County Durham.ac.uk WWW: http://www.County Durham.ac.uk/neehi.history/homepage.htm

North East Labour History Society, Department of Historical & Critical Studies, University of Northumbria, Newcastle upon Tyne, NE1 8ST Tel: 0191-227-3193 Fax: 0191-227-4630 Email: joan.hugman@unn.ac.uk

North Eastern Police History Society, Brinkburn Cottage, 28 Brinkburn Street, High Barnes, Sunderland, SR4 7RG Tel: 0191-565-7215 Email: harry.wynne@virgin.net WWW: http://nepolicehistory.homestead.com North Eastern England police forces past and present from Teeside to Tweed. All history aspects.

The Ponteland Local History Society, Woodlands, Prestwick Village, Ponteland, NE20 9TX Tel: 01661 824017 Fax: 01661 824017 Email: jmichaeltaylor@talk21.com WWW: www.ponthistsoc.freeuk.com

Prudhoe & District Local History Society, Prudhoe Community Enterprise Office, 82 Front Street, Prudhoe, NE42 5PU

Stannington Local History Society, Glencar House, 1 Moor Lane, Stannnington, Morpeth, NE61 6EA

North Somerset - see Somerset - North

North & South Tyneside
National Inventory of War Memorials (North East England), Bilsdale, Ulgham, Morpeth, NE61 3AR Tel: 01670 790465

Nottinghamshire
Basford & District Local History Society, 16 Harcourt Crescent, Nuthall, Nottingham, NG16 1AT Tel: 0115 927 2370

Beeston & District Local History Society, 16 Cumberland Avenue, Beeston, NG9 4DH Tel: 0115 922 3008

Bingham & District Local History Society, 56 Nottingham Road, Bingham, NG13 8AT Tel: 01949 875866

Bleasby Local History Society, 5 Sycamore Lane, Bleasby, NG14 7GJ Tel: 01636 830094

Bulwell Historical Society, 21 Rowe Gardens, Bulwell, Nottingham, NG6 9ER

Burton Joyce and Bulcote Local History Society, 9 Carnarvon Drive, Burton Joyce, Nottingham, NG14 5ER Tel: 0115 931 3669

Caunton Local History Society, Beech House, Caunton, Newark, NG23 6AF Tel: 01636 636564

Chinemarelian Society, 3 Main Street, Kimberley, NG16 2NL Tel: 0115 945 9306 covers Kimberley

Cotgrave Local History Society, 81 Owthorpe Road, Cotgrave, NG Tel: 0115 989 2115

East Leake & District Local History Society, 8 West Leake Road, East Leake, Loughborough, LE12 6LJ Tel: 01509 852390

Eastwood Historical Society, 18 Park Crescent, Eastwood, NG16 3DU Tel: 01773 712080

Edwalton Local History Society, The Croft, Main Street, Edingley, Nottingham, NG22 8BE Tel: 01623 882507

Edwinstowe Historical Society, 12 Church Street, Edwinstowe, NG21 9QA Tel: 01623 824455

Epperstone Society, Sunny Mead, Main Street, Epperstone, NG14 6AG

Farndon & District Local History Society, Chinley Chine, 7a Wyke Lane, Farndon, Newark, NG24 3SP Tel: 01636 673900

Flintham Society, Flintham Museum, Inholms Road, Flintham, NG23 5LF Tel: 0163.6 525111 Email: flintham.museum@lineone.net WWW: www.flintham-museum.org.uk

Gotham & District Local History Society, 108A Leake Road, Gotham, NG11 0JN Tel: 0115 983 0494 Fax: 0115 983 0494

Hucknall Heritage Society, 68 Papplewick Lane, Hucknall, Nottingham, NG15 8EF Email: marion.williamson@ntlworld.com

Keyworth & District Local History Society, Innisfree, Thelda Avenue, Keyworth, Nottingham, NG12 5HU Tel: 0115 937908 Fax: 0115 9372908 Email: info@keyworth-history.org.uk WWW: www.keyworth-history.org.uk

Lambley Historical Society, 11 Steeles Way, Lambley, Nottingham, NG4 4QN Tel: 0115 931 2588

Lenton Local History Society, 53 Arnesby Road, Lenton, Nottingham, NG7 2EA Tel: 0115 970 3981

Newark Archaeological & Local History Society, 13 Main Street, Sutton on Trent, Newark, NG6 PF Tel: 01636 821781 (Evenings) Email: jill.campbell@ic24.net

North Muskham History Group, Roseacre, Village Lane, North Muskham, NG23 6ES Tel: 01636 705566,

Nottingham Civic Society, 57 Woodhedge Drive, Nottingham, NG3 6LW Tel: 0115 958 8247 Fax: 0115 958 8247 Email: membership@nottinghamcivicsoc.org.uk

Nottingham Historical and Archaeological Society, 9 Churchill Drive, Stapleford, Nottingham, NG9 8PE Tel: 0115 939 7140

Nottinghamshire Industrial Archaeology Society, 18 Queens Avenue, Ilkeston, DE7 4DL Tel: 0115 932 2228

Nottinghamshire Local History Association, 128 Sandhill Street, Worksop, S80 1SY Tel: 01909 488878 Tel: Mobile: 07773887803 Email: drossellis@aol.com

Numismatic Society of Nottinghamshire Tel: 0115 925 7674

Nuthall & District Local History society, 14 Temple Drive, Nuthall, Nottingham, NG16 1BE Tel: 0115 927 1118 Email: tony.horton@ntlworld.com

Old Mansfield Society, 7 Barn Close, Mansfield, NG18 3JX Tel: 01623 654815 Email: dcrut@yahoo.com WWW: www.old-mansfield.org.uk

Old Mansfield Woodhouse Society, Burrwells, Newboundmill Lane, Pleasley, Mansfield, NG19 7QA Tel: 01623 810396

Old Warsop Society, 1 Bracken Close, Market Warsop, NG20 0QQ

Pentagon Society, Dellary, Mill Road, Elston, Newark, NG23 5NR Tel: 01636 525278 covers Elston, Shelton, Sibthorpe, East Stoke & Syerston CC accepted

Pleasley History Group, 8 Cambria Road, Pleasley, Mansfield, NG19 7RL Tel: 01623 810201

Radford Memories Project, 25 Manston Mews, Alfreton Road, Radford, Nottingham, NG7 3QY Tel: 0115 970 1256

Retford & District Historical & Archaeological Society, Cambridge House, 36 Alma Road, Retford, DN22 6LW Tel: 7790212360 Email: joan@granto.demon.co.uk

Ruddington Local History Society, St Peter's Rooms, Church Street, Ruddington, Nottingham, NG11 6HA Tel: 0115 914 6645

Sherwood Archaeological Society, 32 Mapperley Hall Drive, Nottingham, NG3 5EY Tel: 0115 960 3032 Email: pjneale@aol.com

Sneinton Environmental Society, 248 Greenwood Road, Nottingham, NG3 7FY Tel: 0115 987 5035

Southwell & District Local History Society, Fern Cottage, 70 Kirklington Road, Southwell, NG25 0AX Tel: 01636 812220

Stapleford & District Local History Society, 25 Westerlands, Stapleford, Nottingham, NG9 7JE Tel: 0115 939 2573

Sutton Heritage Society, 8 Sheepbridge Lane, Mansfield, NG18 5EA Tel: 01623 451179 Email: lildawes@yahoo.co.uk

Sutton on Trent Local History Society, 14 Grassthorpe Road, Sutton on Trent, Newark, NG23 6QD Tel: 01636 821228

Thoroton Society of Nottinghamshire, 59 Briar Gate, Long Eaton, Nottingham, NG10 4BQ Tel: 0115-972-6590 Email: thoroton@keithgoodman.com WWW: www.thorotonsociety.org.uk

Tuxford Heritage Society, 140 lincoln Road, Tuxford, Newark, NG22 0HS

West Bridgford & District Local History Society, 30 Repton Road, West Bridgford, NG2 7EJ Tel: 0115 923 3901 Fax: 0115 923 3901

Whitwell Local History Group, 34 Shepherds Avenue, Worksop, S81 0JB
Wilford History Society, 10 St Austell Drive, Wilford, Nottingham, NG11 7BP Tel: 0115 981 7061
Woodborough Local History Group, The Woodpatch, 19 Sunningdale Drive, Woodborough, NG14 6EQ Tel: 0115 965 3103 WWW: www.woodborough-heritage.org.uk
Worksop Archaeological & Local History Society, 42 Dunstan Crescent, Worksop, S80 1AF Tel: 01909 477575

Oxfordshire
Abingdon Area Archaeological and Historical Society, 4 Sutton Close, Abingdon, OX14 1ER Tel: 01235 529720 Email: rainslie@hotmail.com WWW: www.aaahs.org.uk
Ashbury Local History Society, Claremont, Asbury, Swindon, SN6 8LN Email: marionlt@witrose.com
Banbury Historical Society, c/o Banbury Museum, Spiceball Park Road, Banbury, OX16 2PQ Tel: 01295 672626
Blewbury Local History Group, Spring Cottage, Church Road, Blewbury, Didcot, OX11 9PY Tel: 01235 850427 Email: aud@spcott.fsnet.co.uk
Chinnor Historical & Archealogical Society, 7 Cherry Tree Road, Chinnor, 0X9 4QY
Cumnor History Society, 4 Kenilworth Road, Cumnor, Nr Oxford, OX2 9QP Tel: 01865 862965 Fax: 01865 862965
Faringdon Archaeological & Historical Society, 1 Orchard Hill; Faringdon, SN7 7EH Tel: 01367 240885 Email: fdahs@bigfoot.com WWW: www.faringdon.org/hysoc
Goring & Streatley Local History Society, 45 Springhill Road, Goring On Thames, Reading, RG8 OBY Tel: 01491 872625
Lashbrook One-Place Study, 70 Chestnut Lane, Amersham, HP6 6EH Tel: 01494 726103 Email: cdjmills@hotmail.com Covers Bradford, Talaton, Thornbury in Devon and Shiplake, Oxfordshire see also Lashbrook One-Name Study (Under Family History Societies)
Longworth Local History Society, 7 Norwood Avenue, Southmoor, Abingdon, OX13 5AD Tel: 01865 820522 Fax: 01865 820522 Email: keene@thematictrails.u-net.com WWW: www.kbsonline.org.uk   http://freepages.history.rootsweb.com/~lhs1 Covers villages of Hinton Waldrist and Kingston Bagpuize with Southmoor
Oxfordshire Architectural and Historical Society, 53 Radley Road, Abingdon, Oxford, OX14 3PN Tel: 01235 525960 Email: tony@oahs.org.uk WWW: www.oahs.org.uk
Oxfordshire Local History Association, 12 Meadow View, Witney, OX28 6TY Tel: 01993 778345
Oxfordshire Record Society, Bodleian Library Oxford, OX1 3BG Tel: 01865 277164 Email: srt@bodley.ox.ac.uk
Volunteer Corps of Frontiersmen, Archangels' Rest, 26 Dark Lane, Witney, OX8 5LE
Wallingford Historical and Archaeological Society, Wallingford Museum, Flint House, 52a High Street, Wallingford, OX1O 0DB Tel: 01491 835065
Witney & District Historical & Archaeological Society, 16 Church Green, Witney, OX28 4AW Tel: 01993 703289 Fax: 01993 703281
Wychwood's Local History Society, Littlecott, Honeydale Farm, Shipton-Under-Wychwood, Chipping Norton, 0X7 6BJ, Enquiry letters should be accompanied by an SAE or 2 IRCs if from abroad
Yarnton with Begbroke History Society, 6 Quarry End, Begbroke, OX5 1SF
Oxfordshire (South), Berkshire Local History Association, 18 Foster Road, Abingdson, OX14 1YN Email: secretary@blha.org.uk WWW: www.blha.org.uk

Rutland
Rutland Local History & Record Society, c/o Rutland County Museum, Catmos Street, Oakham, LE15 6HW Tel: 01572 758440 Fax: 01572 757576 Email: rutlandhistory@rutnet.co.uk WWW: www.rutnet.co.uk/rlhrs

Shropshire
Cleobury Mortimer Historical Society, The Old Schoolhouse, Neen Savage, Cleobury Mortimer, Kidderminster, DY14 8JU Tel: 01299 270319 Email: paddy@treves.freeserve.co.uk

Council for British Archaeology - West Midlands, c/o Rowley's House Museum, Barker Street, Shrewsbury, SY1 1QH Tel: 01743 361196 Fax: 01743 358411 Email: mikestokes@shrewsbury-atcham.gov.uk WWW: www.shrewsburymuseums.com www.darwincountry.org
Field Studies Council, Head office, Preston Montford, Montford Bridge, Shrewsbury, SY4 1HW Tel: 01743 852100 Fax: 01743 852101 Email: fsc.headoffice@ukonline.co.uk WWW: www.field-studies-council.org
Shropshire Archaeological and Historical Society, Lower Wallop Farm, Westbury, Shrewsbury, SY5 9RT Tel: 01743 891215 Tel: 01743 891805 Fax: 01743 891805 Email: walloparch@farming.co.uk WWW: www.shropshirearchaeology.com
Whitchurch History and Archaeology Group, Smallhythe, 26 Rosemary Lane, Whitchurch, SY13 1EG Tel: 01948 662120

Somerset
Axbridge Archaeological & Local History Society, King John's Hunting Lodge, The Square, Axbridge, BS26 2AR Tel: 01934 732012
Bathford Society, 36 Bathford Hill, Bathford, BA1 7SL
Bristol Records Society, Regional History Centre, Faculty of Humanities, University of the West of England, St Maththias Campus, Oldbury Court Road, Fishponds, Bristol, BS16 2JP Tel: 0117 344 4395 WWW: http://humanities.uwe.ac.uk/brs/index.htm
Bruton Local History Society, The Dovecote Building, High Street, Bruton Email: bob.hatcher@bruton-town.org.uk
Castle Cary & District Museum & Preservation Society, 1 Fir Tree Cottages, Lower Ansford, Castle Cary, BA7 7JY,
Chard History Group, 17 Kinforde, Chard, TA20 1DT Tel: 01460 62722 Email: carterw@globalnet.co.uk WWW: www.users.globalnet.co.uk/~carterw
Freshford & District Local History Society, Quince Tree House, Pipehouse Lane, Freshford, Bath, BA2 7UH Tel: 01225 722339
Oakhill & Ashwick Local History Society, Bramley Farm, Bath Road, Oakhill, BA3 5AF Tel: 01749 840 241 Fax: 01749 841195
Somerset Archaeological & Natural History Society, Taunton Castle Taunton, TA1 4AD Tel: 01823 272429 Fax: 01823 272429 Email: secretary@sanhs.freeserve.co.uk
Somerset Record Society, Somerset Studies Library, Paul Street, Taunton, TA1 3XZ Tel: 01823-340300 Fax: 01823-340301
South East Somerset Archaeological and Historical Society, Silverlands, Combe Hill, Templecombe, BA8 OLL Tel: 01963 371307 Fax: 01963 371307
South Petherton L H Group, Cobbetts Droveway, South Petherton, TAI3 5DA Tel: 01460 240252
South Petherton Local History, Crossbow, Hele Lane, South Petherton, TA13 5DY

Somerset - North
Avon Local History Association, 4 Dalkeith Avenue, Kingswood, Bristol, BS15 1HH Tel: 0117 967 1362
Congresbury History Group, Venusmead, 36 Venus Street, Congresbury, Bristol, BS49 5EZ Tel: 01934 834780 Fax: 01934 834780 Email: rogerhards-venusmead@breathemail.net
Nailsea & District Local History Society, PO Box 1089, Nailsea, BS48 2YP

Staffordshire
Council for British Archaeology - West Midlands, c/o Rowley's House Museum, Barker Street, Shrewsbury, SY1 1QH Tel: 01743 361196 Fax: 01743 358411 Email: mikestokes@shrewsbury-atcham.gov.uk WWW: www.shrewsburymuseums.com and www.darwincountry.org
Berkswich L H Group, 1 Greenfield Road, Stafford, ST17 OPU
Birmingham Canal Navigation's Society, 37 Chestnut Close, Handsacre, Rugeley, WS15 4TH
Landor Local History Society, 38 Fortescue Lane, Rugeley, WS15 2AE Tel: 01889 582709,
Lawton Heritage Society, 9 Woodgate Avenue, Church Lawton, Stoke on Trent, ST7 3EF Tel: 01270-878386 Email: dmcall12280@aol.com
North Staffordshire Historians' Guild, 14 Berne Avenue, Newcastle under Lyme, ST5 2QJ
Ridware History Society, 8 Waters Edge, Handsacre, Nr. Rugeley, WS15 7HP Tel: 01543 307456 Email: davidandmonty@carefree.net

Stafford Historical & Civic Society, 86 Bodmin Avenue, Weeping Cross, Stafford, ST17 OEQ Tel: 01785 612194 Email: esj@supanet.com

Staffordshire Archaeological & Historical Society, 6 Lawson Close, Aldridge, Walsall, WS9 0RX Tel: 01922 452230 Email: sahs@britishlibrary.net WWW: www.sahs.uk.net

Suffolk

Brett Valley History Society, 17 Manor Road, Bildeston, Ipswich, IP7 7BG

Framlingham & District Local History & Preservation Society, 28 Pembroke Road, Framlingham, IP13 9HA Tel: 01728 723214

Lowestoft Archaeological and Local History Society, 1 Cranfield Close, Pakefield, Lowestoft, NR33 7EL Tel: 01502 586143

Suffolk Institute of Archaeology and History, Roots, Church Lane, Playford, Ipswich, IP6 9DS Tel: 01473-624556 Email: brianseward@btinternet.com WWW: www.suffolkarch.org.uk

Suffolk Local History Council, Suffolk Community Resource Centre, 2 Wharfedale Road, Ipswich, IP1 4JP Email: admin@suffolklocalhistorycouncil.org.uk WWW: www.suffolklocalhistorycouncil.org.uk

Surrey

Addlestone History Society, 53 Liberty Lane, Addlestone, Weybridge, KT15 1NQ

Beddington & Carshalton Historical Society, 57 Brambledown Road, Wallington, SM6 0TF

Beddington Carshalton & Wallington History Society, 57 Brambledown Road, Wallington, SM6 0TF Tel: (020) 8647 8540

Bourne Society, 54 Whyteleafe Road, Caterham, CR3 5EF Tel: 018833 492287 Tel: 01883 347143 Fax: 01883 341638 Email: robert@friday-house.freeserve.co.uk WWW: www.bournesociety.org.uk Covers the districts of Caterham, Chaldon, Chelsham, Chipstead, Coulsdon, Farleigh, Godstone, Kenley, Old Coulsdon, Parley, Sanderstead, Whyteleafe, Warlingham and Woldingham.

Carshalton Society, 43 Denmark Road, Carshalton, SM5 2JE

Centre for Local History Studies, Faculty of Human Sciences, Kingston University, Penrhyn Road, Kingston, KT1 2EE Tel: (020) 8547 7359 Email: localhistory@kingston.ac.uk WWW: http://localhistory.kingston.ac.uk

Croydon Natural History & Scientific Society Ltd, 96a Brighton Road, South Croydon, CR2 6AD Tel: (020) 8688 4539 WWW: http://www.grieg51.freeserve.co.uk/cnhss

Domestic Buildings Research Group (Surrey), The Ridings, Lynx Hill, East Horsley, KT24 5AX Tel: 01483 283917

Farnham and District Museum Society, Tanyard House, 13a Bridge Square, Farnham, GU9 7QR

Guildford Archaeology and Local History Group, 6 St Omer Road, Guildford, GU1 2DB Tel: 01483 532201 Email: H.E.Davies@surrey.ac.uk

History of Thursley Society, 50 Wyke Lane, Ash, Aldershot, GU12 6EA Email: norman.ratcliffe@ntlworld.com WWW: http://home.clara.net/old.norm/Thursley

Leatherhead and District Local History Society, Leatherhead Museum, 64 Church Street, Leatherhead, KT22 8DP Tel: 01372 386348 cc accepted

Nonsuch Antiquarian Society, 17 Seymour Avenue, Ewell, KT17 2RP Tel: (020) 8393 0531 WWW: www.nonsuchas.org.uk

Puttenham & Wanborough History Society, Brown Eaves, 116 The Street, Puttenham, Guildford, GU3 1AU

Richmond Local History Society, 9 Bridge Road, St Margarets, Twickenham, TWI IRE

Send and Ripley History Society, St Georges Farm House Ripley, GU23 6AF Tel: 01483 222107 Fax: 01483 211832 Email: slatford@johnone.freeserve.co.uk

Shere Gomshall & Peaslake Local History Society, Twiga Lodge, Wonham Way, Gomshall, Guildford, GU5 9NZ Tel: 01483 202112 Email: twiga@gomshall.freeserve.co.uk WWW: www.gomshall.freeserve.co.uk/sglshhp.htm

Surrey Archaeological Society, Castle Arch Guildford, GU1 3SX Tel: 01483 532454 Fax: 01483 532454 Email: surreyarch@compuserve.com WWW: www.ourworld.compuserve.com/homepages/surreyarch Covers the Historic County of Surrey

Surrey Local History Council, Guildford Institute, University of Surrey, Ward Street, Guildford, GU1 4LH

Surrey Record Society, c/o Surrey History Centre, 130 Goldsworth Road, Woking, GU21 1ND Tel: 01483 594603 This is a publishing society only. No research can be undertaken by the honorary officers.

The RH7 History Group, Bidbury House, Hollow Lane, East Grinstead, RH19 3PS

Walton On The Hill District Local History Society, 5 Russell Close, Walton On The Hill, Tadworth, KT2O 7QH Tel: 01737 812013

Walton & Weybridge Local History Society, 67 York Gardens, Walton on Thames, KT12 3EN Tel:

Westcott Local History Group, 6 Heath Rise, Westcott, Dorking, RH4 3NN Tel: 01306 882624 Email: info@westcotthistory.org.uk WWW: www.westcotthistory.org.uk

Sussex

Sussex Archaeological Society, Barbican House, 169 High Street, Lewes, BN7 1YE Tel: 01273 405738 Fax: Email: library@sussexpast.co.uk WWW: sussexpast.co.uk

Danehill Parish Historical Society, Butchers Barn, Freshfield Lane, Danehill, RH17 7HQ Tel: 01825 790292

Lewes Archaeological Group, Rosemary Cottage, High Street, Barcombe, near Lewes, BN8 5DM Tel: 01273 400878

Sussex Local History Forum, Anne of Cleves House, 52 Southover, High Street, Lewes, BN7 1JA

Sussex Past, Anne of Cleves House, 52 Southover High Street, Lewes, BN7 1JA Tel: 01273 405738 Fax: 01273 486990 Email: library@sussexpast.co.uk WWW: www.sussexpast.co.uk

Sussex - East

Blackboys & District Historical Society, 6 Palehouse Common, Framfield, Nr Uckfield, TN22 5QY

Brighton & Hove Archealogical Society, 115 Braeside Avenue, Patcham, Brighton, BN1 8SQ

Eastbourne Natural History and Archaeological Society, 11 Brown Jack Avenue, Polegate, BN26 5HN Tel: 01323 486014

Family & Community Historical Research Society, 56 South Way, Lewes, BN7 1LY Tel: 01273 471897

Friends of Sussex - East Record Office, The Maltings, Castle Precincts, Lewes, BN7 1YT Tel: 01273-482349 Fax: 01273-482341 WWW: www.esrole.fsnet.co.uk

Maresfield Historical Society, Hockridge House, London Road, Maresfield, TN22 2EH Tel: 01825 765386

Peacehaven & Telscombe Historical Society, 2 The Compts, Peacehaven, BN1O 75Q Tel: 01273 588874 Fax: 01273 589881 Email: paths@openlink.org WWW: www.history-peacehaven-telscombe.org.uk

Sussex Archaeological Society, Barbican House, 169 High Street, Lewes, BN7 1YE Tel: 01273 405738 Email: library@sussexpast.co.uk WWW: sussexpast.co.uk

Sussex History Forum, Barbican House, 169 High Street, Lewes, BN7 1YE Tel: 01273-405736 Fax: 01273-486990 Email: research@sussexpast.co.uk WWW: www.sussexpast.co.uk

Uckfield & District Preservation Society, 89 Lashbrooks Road, Uckfield, TN22 2AZ

Warbleton & District History Group, Hillside Cottage, North Road, Bodle Street Green, Hailsham, BN27 4RG Tel: 01323 832339 Email: junegeoff.hillside@tiscali.co.uk WWW: www.angmeringsociety.org.uk

Sussex - West

The Angmering Society, 45 Greenwood Drive, Angmering, BNI6 4JW Tel: 01903-775811 Email: editor@angmeringsociety.org.uk

Beeding & Bramber Local History Society, 19 Roman Road, Steyning, BN44 3FN Tel: 01903 814083

Billingshurst Local History Society, 2 Cleve Way, Billingshurst, RH14 9RW Tel: 01403 782472 Email: jane.lecluse@atkinsglobal.com

Bolney Local History Society, Leacroft, The Street, Bolney, Haywards, RH17 5PG Tel: 01444 881550 Email: constable@lespres.freeserve.co.uk

Chichester Local History Society, 38 Ferndale Road, Chichester, PO19 6QS

Horsham Museum Society, Horsham Museum, 9 The Causeway, Horsham, RH12 1HE Tel: 01403 254959 Email: museum@horsham.gov.uk

Mid Sussex Local History Group, Saddlers, Stud Farm Stables, Gainsborough Lane, Polegate, BN26 5HQ Tel: 01323 482215 WWW: www.derby.org/midland

Midland Railway Society, 4 Canal Road, Yapton, BN18 0HA Tel: 01243-553401 Email: BeeFitch@aol.com

Steyning Society, 30 St Cuthmans Road, Steyning, BN44 3RN

Sussex Record Society, West Sussex Record Office, County Hall, Chichester, PO19 1RN Tel: 01243 753600 Fax: 01243-533959 Email: peter.wilkinson@westsussex.gov.uk

Sussex History Forum, Barbican House, 169 High Street, Lewes, BN7 1YE Tel: 01273-405736 Fax: 01273-486990 Email: research@sussexpast.co.uk WWW: www.sussexpast.co.uk

West Sussex Archives Society, c/o West Sussex Record Office, West Sussex CountyCouncil County Hall, Chichester, PO19 IRN, 01243 753600 Fax: 01243 533959 Email: records.office@westsussex.gov.uk WWW: www.westsussex.gov.uk/cs/ro/rohome.htm

Wivelsfield Historical Society, Middlefield Cottage, Fox Hill, Haywards Heath, RH16 4QY

Tyne and Wear - see also Northumberland
Association of Northumberland Local History Societies, Centre for Lifelong Learning, King George VI Building, University of Newcastle upon Tyne, Newcastle upon Tyne, NE1 7RU Tel: 0191-222-7458 Tel: 0191-222-5680

Cullercoats Local History Society, 33 St Georges Road, Cullercoats, North Shields, NE30 3JZ Tel: 0191 252 7042

National Inventory of War Memorials (North East England), Bilsdale, Ulgham, Morpeth, NE61 3AR Tel: 01670 790465

North East Labour History Society, Department of Historical & Critical Studies, University of Northumbria, Newcastle upon Tyne, NE1 8ST Tel: 0191-227-3193 Fax: 0191-227-4630 Email: joan.hugman@unn.ac.uk

North Eastern Police History Society, Brinkburn Cottage, 28 Brinkburn Street, High Barnes, Sunderland, SR4 7RG Tel: 0191-565-7215 Email: harry.wynne@virgin.net WWW: http://nepolicehistory.homestead.com North Eastern England police forces past and present from Teeside to Tweed. All history aspects.

North-East England History Institute (NEEHI), Department of History University of County Durham, 43 North Bailey, County Durham, DH1 3EX Tel: 0191-374-2004 Fax: 0191-374-4754 Email: m.a.mcallister@County Durham.ac.uk WWW: http://www.County Durham.ac.uk/neehi.history/homepage.htm

North East England Local and Family History, University Of Newcastle, Newcastle Upon Tyne, NE1 7RL Tel: 0191 222 6546 Fax: 0191 222 7090 WWW: www.ncl.ac.uk/lifelong-learning/

Northumbria Historic Churches Trust, The Vicarage, South Hylton, Sunderland, England

Society of Antiquaries of Newcastle upon Tyne, The Black Gate, Castle Garth, Newcastle upon Tyne, NE1 1RQ Tel: 0191 261 5390 Email: admin@newcastle-antiquaries.org.uk WWW: www.newcastle-antiquaries.org.uk

South Hylton Local History Society, 6 North View, South Hylton, Sunderland, SR4 0LH Tel: 0191 552 6587 Tel: 0191 534 4251 Fax: Email: Douglas.Scrafton@aol.com WWW: www.shlhs.com

Warwickshire
Alcester & District Local History Society, Applecross, Worcester Road, Inkberrow, Worcester, WR7 4ET Fax: Email: cjjohnson@care4free.net

Council for British Archaeology - West Midlands, c/o Rowley's House Museum, Barker Street, Shrewsbury, SY1 1QH Tel: 01743 361196 Fax: 01743 358411 Email: mikestokes@shrewsbury-atcham.gov.uk WWW: www.shrewsburymuseums.com www.darwincountry.org

Kineton and District Local History Group, The Glebe House, Lighthorne Road, Kineton, CV35 0JL Tel: 01926 690298 Fax: 01926 690298 Email: p.holdsworth@virgin.net

Warwickshire Local History Society, 9 Willes Terrace, Leamington Spa, CV31 1DL Tel: 01926 429671

Watford
Watford and District Industrial History Society, 79 Kingswood Road, Garston, Watford, WD25 0EF Tel: 01923 673253

West Midlands
Aldridge Local History Society, 45 Erdington Road, Walsall, WS9 8UU

Barr & Aston Local History, 17 Booths Farm Road, Great Barr, Birmingham, 642 2NJ

Birmingham War Research Society, 43 Norfolk Place, Kings Norton, Birmingham, B30 3LB Tel: 0121 459 9008 Fax: 0121 459 9008

Black Country Local History Consortium, Canal St, Tipton Rd, Dudley, DY1 4SQ Tel: 0121 522 9643 Fax: 0121 557 4242 Email: info@bclm.co.uk WWW: ww.bclm.co.uk

Black Country Society, PO Box 71 Kingswinford, DY6 9YN

Council for British Archaeology - West Midlands, c/o Rowley's House Museum, Barker Street, Shrewsbury, SY1 1QH Tel: 01743 361196 Fax: 01743 358411 Email: mikestokes@shrewsbury-atcham.gov.uk WWW: www.shrewsburymuseums.com www.darwincountry.org

Local History Consortium, The Black Country Living Museum, Tipton Road, Dudley, DY1 4SQ Tel: 0121 557 9643

Quinton Local History Society, 15 Worlds End Avenue, Quinton, Birmingham, B32 1JF Tel: 0121-422-1792 Fax: 0121 422 1792 Email: qlhs@bjtaylor.fsnet.co.uk WWW: www.qlhs.org.uk

Romsley & Hunnington History Society, Port Erin, Green Lane, Chapmans Hill, Romsley, Halesowen, B62 0HB Tel: 01562 710295 Email: ejhumphreys@mail.com

Smethwick Local Hist Society, 47 Talbot Road, Smethwick, Warley, B66 4DX WWW: www.smethwicklocalhistory.co.uk

Wythall History Society, 64 Meadow Road, Wythall, Birmingham, B47 6EQ Email: val@wythallhistory.co.uk WWW: www.wythallhistory.co.uk

War Research Society, 27 Courtway Avenue, Birmingham, B14 4PP Tel: 0121 430 5348 Fax: 0121 436 7401 Email: battletour@aol.com WWW: www.battlefieldtours.co.uk

Wesley Historical Society, 34 Spiceland Road, Northfield, Birmingham, B31 1NJ Email: 106364.3456@compuserve.com edgraham@btconnect.com
Genealogical research is NOT undertaken. The Society holds no genealogical records. Methodist Records should be deposited in the Local Record Office or local recognised repository. Advice on Methodist given where possible. SAE required

Upholstery Old and New, 7 Selly Avenue, Selly Park, Birmingham, B29 7PE

Westmorland
Cumberland & Westmorland Antiquarian & Archaeological Society, County Offices Kendal, LA9 4RQ Tel: 01539 773431 Fax: 01539 773539 Email: info@cwaas.org.uk WWW: www.cwaas.org.uk

Wiltshire
Amesbury Society, 14 Stonehenge Road, Amesbury, SP4 7BA Tel: 01980 623123

Atworth History Group, 48D Post Office Lane, Atworth, Melksham, SN12 8JX Tel: 01225 702351 Email: joan.cocozza@btinternet.com

Chiseldon Local History Group, 24 Carisbrook Terrace, Chiseldon, SN4 0LW Tel: 01793 7400473 Records

Devizes Local History Group, 9 Hartfield, Devizes, SN10 5JH Tel: 01380 727369

Freshford & District Local History Society, Quince Tree House, Pipehouse Lane, Freshford, Bath, BA2 7UH Tel: 01225 722339

Highworth Historical Society, 6 Copper Beeches, Highworth, Swindon, SN6 7BJ Tel: 01793 763863

Marshfield & District Local History Society, Weir Cottage, Weir Lane, Marshfield, Chippenham, SN14 8NB Tel: 01225 891229

Melksham & District Historial Association, 13 Sandridge Lane, Melksham, Tel: 01225 703644

Mere Historical Society, Bristow House, Castle Street, Mere, BA12 6JF Tel: 01747 860643

Mid Thorngate Society, Yewcroft, Stoney Batter, West Tytherley, Salisbury, SP5 ILD

Pewsey Vale Local History Society, 10 Holly Tree Walk, Pewsey, SN9 5DE Tel: 01672 562417 Fax: 01972 563924 Email: westerberg@onetel.co.uk

Purton Historical Society, 1 Church Street, Purton, SN5 4DS Tel: 01793 770331

Redlynch & District Local History Society, Hawkstone, Church Hill, Redlynch, Salisbury, SP5 2PL Email: pat.mill@btinternet.com

Salisbury Civic Society, 4 Chestnut Close, Laverstock, Salisbury, SP1 1SL

Salisbury Local History Group, 67 St Edmunds Church Street, Salisbury, SP1 1EF Tel: 01722 338346

South Wiltshire Industrial Archaeology Society, 34 Countess Road, Amesbury, SP4 7AS Tel: 01980 622092 Email: goodhugh@btinternet.com, WWW:

Swindon Society, 4 Lakeside, Swindon, SN3 1QE Tel: 01793-521910

The Hatcher Society, 11 Turner Close, Harnham, Salisbury, SP2 8NX

The Historical Association (West Wiltshire Branch), 24 Meadowfield, Bradford on Avon, BA15 1PL Tel: 01225 862722

Tisbury Local History Society, Suzay House, Court Street, Tisbury, SP3 6NF

Trowbridge Civic Society, 43 Victoria Road, Trowbridge, BA14 7LD

Warminster History Society, 13 The Downlands, Warminster, BA12 0BD Tel: 01985 216022 Fax: 01985 846332

Wilton Historical Society, 3 Wiley Terrace, North Street, Wilton, SP2 0HN Tel: 01722 742856

Wiltshire Archaeological and Natural History Society, Wiltshire Heritage Library, 41 Long Street, Devizes, SN10 1NS Tel: 01380 727369 Fax: 01380 722150 Email: wanhs@wiltshireheritage.org.uk

Wiltshire Buildings Record, Libraries and Heritage HQ, Bythesea Road, Trowbridge, BA14 8BS Tel: 01225 713740 Email: dorothytreasure@wiltshire.gov.uk

Wiltshire Local History Forum, Tanglewood, Laverstock Park, Salisbury, SP1 1QJ Tel: 01722 328922 Fax: 01722 501907 Email: sarumjeh@aol.com

Wiltshire Record Society, County Record Office, County Libraries Hq, Trowbridge, BA14 8BS Tel: 01225 713136 Fax: 01225 713515

Wootton Bassett Historical Society, 20 The Broadway, Rodbourne Cheney, Swindon, SN25 3BT Small local history Society with no genealogical information.

Worcestershire

Alvechurch Historical Society, Bearhill House, Alvechurch, Birmingham, B48 7JX Tel: 0121 445 2222

Bewdley Historical Research, 8 Ironside Close, Bewdley, DY12 2HX Tel: 01299 403582 Email: angela.ironside@clara.co.uk Worcestershire (Bewdley Only)

Council for British Archaeology - West Midlands, c/o Rowley's House Museum, Barker Street, Shrewsbury, SY1 1QH Tel: 01743 361196 Fax: 01743 358411 Email: mikestokes@shrewsbury-atcham.gov.uk WWW: www.shrewsburymuseums.com www.darwincountry.org

Dodderhill Parish History Project - Discovering Wychbol's Past, 9 Laurelwood Close, Droitwich Spa, WR9 7SF

Droitwich History and Archaeology Society, 45 Moreland Road, Droitwich Spa, WR9 8RN Tel: 01905-773420

Feckenham Forest History Society, Lower Grinsty Farmhouse, Callow Hill, Redditch, B97 5PJ Tel: 01527-542063 Fax: 01527-542063

Feckenham Parish, Worcestershire One Place Study, 33c Castle Street, Astwood Park, Worcester, B96 6DP Email: benwright3@hotmail.com

Kidderminster District Archaeological and Historical Society, 178 Birmingham Road, Kidderminster, DY1O 2SJ Tel: 01562 823530 WWW: www.communigate.co.uk/worcs/kidderminsterhistorysoc/index.phtml

Kidderminster & District Local History Society, 39 Cardinal Drive, Kidderminster, DY10 4RZ Email: kidderhist.soc@virgin.net WWW: www.communigate.co.uk/worcs/kidderminsterhistorysoc/index.phtml

Kidderminster Field Club, 7 Holmwood Avenue, Kidderminster, DYL 1 6DA

Pershore Heritage & History Society, 6 Abbey Croft, Pershore, WR10 1JQ Tel: 01386 552482 Email: kenmar.abcroft@virgin.net

Wolverley & Cookley Historical, 18/20 Caunsall Road, Cookley, Kidderminster, DYL 1 5YB

Wolverley & Cookley History Society, The Elms, Drakelow Lane, Wolverley, Kidderminster, DY11 5RU Tel: 01562 850215 History of parishes of Wolverley & Cookley. Annual journal contact John Pearsall Tel: 01562 850915

Worcestershire Archaeological Service, Woodbury Hall, University College of Worcester, Henwick Grove, Worcester, WR2 6AJ Tel: 01905 855455 Fax: 01905 29054 Email: archaeology@worcestershire.gov.uk WWW: http://worcestershire.gov.uk/archaeology

Worcestershire Archaeological Society, The, 26 Albert Park Road, Malvern, WR14 1HN Tel: 01684 565190

Worcestershire Industrial Archealogy & Local History Society, 99 Feckenham Road, Headless Cross, Redditch, B97 5AM

Worcestershire Local History Forum, 45 Moreland Road, Droitwich, WR9 8RN Tel: 01905-773420 Subject to AGM September 2002

Yorkshire

York Archaeological Trust, 13 Ogleforth, York, YO1 7FG Tel: 01904 663000 Fax: 01904 663024 Email: enquiries@yorkarchaeology.co.uk WWW: www.yorkarchaeology.co.uk An educational Charity devoted to archaeological research and the education of the public in archaeology. Its archives and collections contain extensive records of archaeological material

Yorkshire Architectural & York Archaeological Society, c/o York Archaeological Trust, Cromwell House, 13 Ogleforth, York, YO1 7FG Email: www.homepages.tesco.net/~hugh.murray/yayas/

Yorkshire Dialect Society, 51 Stepney Avenue, Scarborough, YO12 5BW

The Yorkshire Heraldry Society, 35 Holmes Carr Road, West Bessacarr, Doncaster, DN4 7HJ Tel: 01302-539993

Yorkshire Philosophical Society, The Lodge, Museum Gardens, Museum Street, York, YO1 7DR Tel: 01904 656713 Fax: 01904 656713 Email: yps@yorkphil.fsnet.co.uk WWW: www.yorec.org.uk

Yorkshire Vernacular Buildings Study Group, 18 Sycamore Terrace, Bootham, York, YO30 7DN

Victorian Revival, Sugar Hill Farm, Knayton, Thirsk, YO7 4BP

Yorkshire - East

East Riding Archaeological Society, 455 Chanterland Avenue, Hull, HU5 4AY Tel: 01482 445232

Yorkshire - East Local History Society, 13 Oaktree Drive, Molescroft, Beverley, HU17 7BB

Yorkshire - North

Forest of Galtres Society, c/o Crawford House, Long Street, Easingwold, York, YO61 3JB Tel: 01347 821685

Northallerton and District Local History Society, 17 Thistle Close, Romanby Park, Northallerton, DL7 8FF Tel: 01609 771878

Poppleton History Society, Russett House, The Green, Upper Poppleton, York, YO26 6DR Tel: 01904 798868 Fax: 01904 613330 Email: susan.major@virgin.net WWW: www.poppleton.net/historysoc

Scarborough Archaeological and Historical Society, 10 Westbourne Park, Scarborough, YO12 4AT Tel: 01723 354237 Email: archaeology@scarborough.co.uk WWW: www.scarborough-heritage.org

Snape Local History Group, Lammas Cottage, Snape, Bedale, DL8 2TW Tel: 01677 470727 WWW: www.communigate.co.uk/ne/slhg/index.phtml

The Steel Bonnets - Re-enactment Society, 12 Marske Road, Saltburn by the Sea, TS12 1PZ Tel: 01287 625744

Stokesley & District Local History Study Group, 21 Cleveland Avenue, Stokesley, TS9 5EZ Tel: 01642 712559

Upper Wharfedale Field Society (Local History Section), Brookfield, Hebden Hall Park, Grassington, Skipton, BD23 5DX Tel: 01756-752012

Upper Wharfedale Museum Society & Folk Museum, The Square, Grassington, BD23 5AU

Wensleydale Railway Association PO Box 65, Northallerton, DL7 8YZ Tel: 01969 625182 (Railway Shop, Leyburn) WWW: www.wensleydalerailway.com

York Georgian Society, King's Manor York, YO1 7EW

Yorkshire - South

Barnscan - The Barnsdale Local History Group, 23 Rushymoor Lane, Askern, Doncaster, DN6 0NH Tel: 01302 700083 Email: barnscan@btinternet.com WWW: www.barnscan.btinternet.co.uk

Bentley with Arksey Heritage Society, 45 Finkle Street, Bentley, Doncaster, DN5 0RP

Chapeltown & High Green archives, The Grange, 4 Kirkstead Abbey Mews, Thorpe Hesley, Rotherham, S61 2UZ

Doncaster Archaeological Society - Group of the Yorkshire Archaeological Society, The Poplars, Long Plantation, Edenthorpe, Doncaster, DN3 2NL Tel: 01302 882840 Email: d.j.croft@talk21.com

Friends of Barnsley Archives and Local Studies, 30 Southgate, Barnsley, S752QL Email: hazel@snowie48.freeserve.co.uk

Grenoside & District Local History Group, 4 Stepping Lane, Grenoside, Sheffield, S35 8RA Tel: 0114 257 1929 Tel: 0114 245 6959 Email: info@grenosidelocalhistory.co.uk WWW: www.grenosidelocalhistory.co.uk

Wombwell Heritage Group, 9 Queens Gardens, Wombwell, Barnsley, S73 0EE Tel: 01226 210648

Yorkshire - West

Beeston Local History Society, 30 Sunnyview Avenue, Leeds, LS11 8QY Tel: 0113 271 7095 This is Beeston, Leeds and should not be confused with Beeston, Nottinghamshire

East Leeds Historical Society, 10 Thornfield Drive, Cross Gates, Leeds, LS15 7LS, Also East Leeds Heritage Centre

Halifax Antiquarian Society, 66 Grubb Lane, Gomersal, Cleckheaton, BD19 4BU Tel: 01274 865418

Kippax & District History Society, 8 Hall Park Croft, Kippax, Leeds, Yorkshire - West Tel: 0113 286 4785 Email: mdlbrumwell@tinyworld.co.uk WWW: www.kippaxhistoricalsoc.leedsnet.org

Lowertown Old Burial Ground Trust, 16 South Close, Guisley, Leeds, LS20 8TD, Reg Charity 1003823 Lowertown Old Burial Ground is at Oxenhope, Keighley. The Trust has transcribed the Memorial Inscriptrions and hold some family trees.

Northern Society of Costume and Textiles, 43 Gledhow Lane, Leeds, LS8 1RT

Olicana Historical Society, 54 Kings Road, Ilkley, LS29 9AT Tel: 01943 609206 The Olicana Historical Society organises a programme of lectures in the winter and excursions in summer. It has a lending library and has published several books of local historical interest

Ossett & District Historical Society, 29 Prospect Road, Ossett, Tel: 01924 279449

Thoresby Society, 23 Clarendon Road, Leeds, LS2 9NZ Tel: 0113 245 7910 WWW: www.thoresby.org.uk

Wetherby & District Historical Society, 73 Aire Road, Wetherby, LS22 7UE Tel: 01937 584875

Yorkshire Archaeological Society - Local History Study Section, Claremont, 23 Clarendon Road, Leeds, LS2 9NZ Tel: 0113-245-7910 Fax: 0113-244-1979

The Yorkshire Buildings Preservation Trust, c/o Elmhirst & Maxton Solicitors, 17-19 Regent Street, Barnsley, S70 2HP Tel:

Wales

The Chapels Heritage Society, 2 Sandy Way, Wood Lane, Hawarden, CH5 3JJ

South Wales Record Society, 13 St Cybi Drive, Llangybi, Usk, NP15 1TU Tel: 01633 450353

Anglesey

The Anglesey Antiquarian Society & Field Club, 1 Fronheulog, Sling, Tregarth, Bangor, LL57 4RD Tel: 01248 600083

Caernarvonshire

Federation of History Societies in Caernarvonshire, 19 Lon Dinas, Cricieth, LL52 0EH Tel: 01766 522238

Cardiff

Pentyrch & District Local History Society, 34 Castell Coch View, Tongwynlais, Cardiff, CF15 7LA

Carmarthenshire

Carmarthenshire Antiquarian Society, Ty Picton, Llansteffan, SA33 5JG Tel: 01267 241 727 Email: arfon.rees@btinternet.com

Gwendraeth Valley Hist Society, 19 Grugos Avenue, Pontyberem, Llanelli, SA14 5AF

Ceredigion

Ceredigion Antiquarian Society, Henllys, Lôn Tyllwyd, Llanfarian, Aberystwyth, SY23 4UH

Clwyd

Friends of The Clwyd Archives, Bryn Gwyn, 2 Rhodea Anwyl, Rhuddlan, LL18 2SQ Tel: 01745 591676 Fax: 01745 591676 Email: coppack@timyworld.co.uk

Conwy

Abergele Field Club and Historical Society, Rhyd y Felin, 47 Bryn Twr, Abergele, LL22 8DD Tel: 01745 832497

Denbighshire Historical Society, 1 Green Park, Erddig, Wrexham, LL13 7YE

Llandudno & District Historical Society, Springfield, 97 Queen's Road, Llandudno, LL30 1TY Tel: 01492 876337

Denbighshire

Denbighshire Historical Society, 1 Green Park, Erddig, Wrexham, LL13 7YE

Ruthin Local History Group, 27 Tan y Bryn, Llanbedr D.C., Ruthin, LL15 1AQ Tel: 01824 702632 Fax: 01824 702632 Email: gwynnemorris@btinternet.com

Flintshire

Flintshire Historical Society, 69 Pen y Maes Avenue, Rhyl, LL18 4ED Tel: 01745 332220

Ruthin Local History Group, 27 Tan y Bryn, Llanbedr D.C., Ruthin, LL15 1AQ Tel: 01824 702632 Fax: 01824 702632 Email: gwynnemorris@btinternet.com

Glamorgan

Glamorgan History Society, 7 Gifford Close, Two Locks, NP44 7NX Tel: 01633 489725 (Evenings Only) Email: rosemary_hewlett@yahoo.co.uk

Kenfig Society, 6 Locks Lane, Porthcawl, CF36 3HY Tel: 01656 782351 Email: terry.robbins@virgin.net WWW: www.kenfigsociety.supanet.com

Llantrisant & District Local History Society, Cerrig Llwyd, Lisvane Road, Lisvane, Cardiff, CF14 0SG Tel: 029 2075 6173 Email: BDavies203@aol.com

Glamorgan - Cardiff

Pentyrch & District Local History Society, 34 Castell Coch View, Tongwynlais, Cardiff, CF15 7LA

Glamorgan - Mid

Merthyr Tydfil Historical Society, Ronamar, Ashlea Drive, Twynyrodyn, Merthyr Tydfil, CF47 0NY Tel: 01685 385871

Gwent

Abertillery & District Museum, 5 Harcourt Terrace, Glandwr Street, Abertillery, NP3 ITS

Abertillery & District Museum Society, The Metropole, Market Street, Abertillery, NP13 1AH Tel: 01495 211140

Gwent Local History Council, 8 Pentonville, Newport, NP9 5XH Tel: 01633 213229 Fax: 01633 221812 Email: byron.grubb@gavowales.org.uk

Newport Local History Society, 72 Risca Road, Newport NP20 4JA

Pontypool Local History Society, 24 Longhouse Grove, Henllys, Cwmbran, NP44 6HQ Tel: 01633 865662

Gwynedd

Abergele Field Club and Historical Society, Rhyd y Felin, 47 Bryn Twr, Abergele, LL22 8DD Tel: 01745 832497

Caernarvonshire Historical Society, Gwynedd Archives, County offices, Caernarfon, LL555 1SH Tel: 01286 679088 Email: caernarvonshirehistoricalsociety@btinternet.com WWW: www.caernarvonshirehistoricalsociety.btinternet.co.uk Membership details from; The Membership Secretary, Hyfrydle, Caernarfon Road, Y Felinheli LL56 4NJ

Cymdeithas Hanes a Chofnodion Sir Feirionydd Meirioneth Historicial and Record Society, Archifdy Meirion Cae Penarlag Dolgellau, LL40 2YB Tel: 01341 424444 Fax: 01341 424505

Cymdeithas Hanes Beddgelert - Beddgelert History Society, Creua, Llanfrothen, Penrhyndeudraeth, LL48 6SH Tel: 01766 770534

Monmouthshire
Newport Local History Society, 72 Risca Road, Newport, NP20 4JA

Pembrokeshire
The Pembrokeshire Historical Society, The Castle Haeverford West, SA61 2EF Tel: 01348 873316

Powys
Radnorshire Society, Pool House, Discoed, Presteigne, LD8 2NW Email: sadie@cole.kc3ltd.co.uk

Wrexham County Borough
Denbighshire Historical Society, 1 Green Park, Erddig, Wrexham, LL13 7YE
Flintshire Historical Society, 69 Pen y Maes Avenue, Rhyl, LL18 4ED Tel: 01745 332220
Wrexham Maelor Hist Society, 37 Park Avenue, Wrexham, LL12 7AL

Scotland

Airdrie
Monklands Heritage Society, 141 Cromarty Road, Cairnhill, Airdrie, ML6 9RZ Tel: 01236 764192

Angus
Abertay Historical Society, 27 Pitcairn Road, Downfield, Dundee, DD3 9EE Tel: 01382 858701 Email: abertay@dmcsoft.com WWW: www.dcmsoft.com/abertay

Ayrshire
Ayrshire Federation of Historical Societies, 11 Chalmers Road, Ayr, KA7 2RQ

Ayrshire - East
Stewarton Library, Cunningham Institute Stewarton, KA3 5AB Tel: 01560 484385

Dundee,
Abertay Historical Society, 27 Pitcairn Road, Downfield, Dundee, DD3 9EE Tel: 01382 858701 Email: abertay@dmcsoft.com WWW: www.dcmsoft.com/abertay
Friends of Dundee City Archives, 21 City Square, Dundee, DD1 3BY Tel: 01382 434494 Fax: 01382 434666 Email: richard.cullen@dundeecity.gov.uk WWW: http://www.dundeecity.gov.uk/archives

Edinburgh
Scottish Records Association, National Archives of Scotland, H M General Register House, Edinburgh, EH1 3YY Tel: 0141 287 2914 Fax: 0141 226 8452 Publisher of journal, Scottish Archives and datasheets on holdings of Scottish Archives and libraries
Society of Antiquaries of Scotland, Royal Museum of Scotland, Chambers Street, Edinburgh, EH1 1JF Tel: 0131 247 4115 Tel: 0131 247 4133 and 0131 247 4145 Fax: 0131 247 4163 Email: r.lancaster@nms.ac.uk WWW: www.socantscot.org

Falkirk
Falkirk Local History Society, 11 Neilson Street, Falkirk, FK1 5AQ, Limited achive of material related to the Falkirk Council Area

Fife
Abertay Historical Society - see Dundee

Glasgow
Glasgow Hebrew Burial Society, 222 Fenwick Road, Griffnock, Glasgow, G46 6UE Tel: 0141 577 8226

Perthshire
Abertay Historical Society - see Dundee
Dunning Parish Historical Society, The Old Schoolhouse, Newtown-Of-Pitcairns, Dunning, Perth, PH2 0SL Tel: 01764 684448 WWW: www.dunning.uk.net

Renfrewshire
Bridge of Weir History Society, 41 Houston Road, Bridge Of Weir, PA11 3QR No archive material available
Paisley Philosophical Institution, 14 Newton Avenue, Elderslie, PA5 9BE
Renfrewshire Local History Forum, Museum & Art Galleries, High Street, Paisley, PA1 2BA Tel: 0141 889 3151 WWW: www.rlhfas.org.uk

Stirling
Drymen Library, The Square, Drymen, G63 0BL Tel: 01360 660751 Email: drymenlibrary@stirling.gov.uk Hold the IGI in disc form, the 1881 census on disc and have Internet access, as well as a selection of local history books relevant to their locale

West Lothian
Linlithgow Union Canal Society, Manse Road Basin, Linlithgow, EH49 6AJ Tel: 01506-671215 (Answering Machine) Fax: Email: info@lucs.org.uk WWW: www.lucs.org.uk, No genealogical information held
Scottish Local History Forum, 45 High Street, Linlithgow, EH54 6EW Tel: 01506 844649 Fax: 0131 260 6610 Email: chantal.hamill@dial.pipex.com

Isle of Man
Isle of Man Natural History & Antiquarian Society, Ballacrye Stream Cottage Ballaugh, IM7 5EB Tel: 01624-897306

Channel Islands
Jersey
Societe Jersiaise, 7 Pier Road, St Helier, JE2 4XW Tel: 01534 730538 Fax: 01534 888262 Email: societe@societe-jersiaise.org WWW: http://www.societe-jersiaise.org

Northern Ireland
Federation of Ulster Local Studies, 18 May Street, Belfast, BT1 4NL Tel: (028) 90235254
Presbyterian Historical Society of Ireland, Church House, Fisherwick Place, Belfast, BT1 6DW Tel: (028) 9032 2284 Opening hours: Mon to Fri 10am to 12.30pm. Wed afternoons 1.30pm to 3.30pm

County Tyrone
Centre for Migration Studies, Ulster American Folk Park, Mellon Road, Castletown, Omagh, BT78 5QY Tel: 028 82 256315 Fax: 028 82 242241 Email: uafp@iol.ie WWW: www.qub.ac.uk/cms/ www.folkpark.com

County Londonderry
Roe Valley Historical Society, 36 Drumachose Park, Limavady, BT49 0NZ

Ireland
Federation of Local History Societies - Ireland, Rothe House, Kilkenny, Ireland
Presbyterian Historical Society of Ireland, Church House, Fisherwick Place, Belfast, BT1 6DW Tel: (028) 9032 2284 Opening hours: Mon to Fri 10am to 12.30pm. Wed afternoons 1.30pm to 3.30pm

Dublin
Raheny Heritage Society, 4 Thorndale Drive, Artane, Dublin 5, Tel: 01 831 9028 Lists of individuals interests supplied on request to Hon Secretary with International Reply Coupon

County Mayo
Mayo North Family Heritage Centre, Enniscoe, Castlehill, Ballina, Tel: 00 44 096 31809 Fax: 00 44 096 31885 Email: normayo@iol.ie WWW: www.mayo-ireland.ie/motm.htm
South Mayo Family Research Centre, Main Street, Ballinrobe, Tel: 353 92 41214, Email: soumayo@iol.ie WWW: http://mayo.irish-roots.net/

The Commonwealth War Graves Commission
Peter Francis
Commonwealth War Graves Commission

The Commonwealth War Graves Commission, was established by Royal Charter of 21 May 1917, the provisions of which were amended and extended by a Supplemental Charter of 8 June 1964. Its duties are to mark and maintain the graves of the forces of the Commonwealth who died during two world wars, to build and maintain memorials to the dead whose graves are unknown, and to keep records and registers. The cost is shared by the partner governments - those of Australia, Canada, India, New Zealand, South Africa and the United Kingdom - in proportions based upon the numbers of their graves.

The Commission is responsible for 1.7 million commemorations, with war graves at over 23,000 locations and in some 150 countries. The work is founded upon the principles that each of the dead should be commemorated individually by name either on the headstone on the grave or by an inscription on a memorial; that each of the headstones and memorials should be permanent; that the headstones should be uniform; and that no distinction should be made on account of military or civil rank, race or creed.

Today, the Commission's major concern is the maintenance of those graves, cemeteries and memorials, to the highest standards, in the face of exposure to the elements and the passage of time - to ensure that "Their Name Liveth For Evermore". In addition to the day to day horticultural and structural maintenance of the cemeteries and memorials, an enquiry service is on offer to the public, whereby the commemorative details for any Commonwealth casualty who died during either of the two world wars can be provided. Commemorative information for Commonwealth civilians who died as a result of enemy action during the Second World War is also available on a Roll of Honour numbering over 66,400 names.

Originally, casualty data was stored on card indexes in over 3,000 drawers. After the First World War, details were compiled into some 1,500 cemetery registers. All enquiries were handled by a wholly manual process until 1995. The work was carried out, as it had been for decades, by dedicated, knowledgeable staff, using large ledgers. The ledgers are organised by country, name of cemetery and alphabetically by surname. To overcome the challenge of an enquirer only knowing a casualty's surname and not the place of burial, there are large volumes of alphabetical lists, cross-referenced by code numbers to the appropriate cemetery register. In late autumn 1995 the Commission's vast resource of information was computerised, allowing for a more efficient service to be offered to the public. The information for each entry was broken down into searchable 'fields' - For example, Surname, Age, Regiment, Cemetery Name, Date of Death e.t.c.

Not only do the computerised records allow for better access to the casualty details and place of commemoration, it also allows the operator to trace single casualties more quickly, from less information, and offer services like casualty-listing reports. This has become increasingly important as the value of the database for educational purposes is recognised and enquiries become more complex. Some of the most popular criteria for casualty listings include a same surname search, a regimental search and a home town search. It is even possible to trace, for example, how many Captains were killed on the first day of the Battle of the Somme.

In line with this public access policy, the Commission took the initiative to use the Internet to further promote access to the records. In November 1998, to coincide with the eightieth anniversary of the Armistice that brought to an end the First World War, the Debt of Honour Register was launched. The Register, a search by surname database, is available to the public via the Commission's web site at www.cwgc.org. The database provides known details of the casualty as well as the name of the cemetery or memorial, directions on how to find it and the exact plot, row, grave or memorial panel reference to enable the enquirer to locate the place of burial or commemoration should they make a pilgrimage to the cemetery or memorial. A second page on the web site prints the casualty details in the form of a commemorative certificate for the enquirer.

The launch of the Debt of Honour Register on the Internet has been an incredible success - the site averages 500,000 hits a week. The Register has widened public knowledge and interest in commemoration, reunited families with the records of their long-fallen loved ones, assisted the historian, researcher and the student and most importantly, proved a highly effective way of keeping the names of those the Commission commemorates alive in the hearts and minds of a new generation. Enhancements to the site since it was launched have reduced down time and increased the accessibility of the site still further. The Commission anticipates further enhancements to the site in the near future.

In 1926, the Commission's founder, Fabian Ware, said the cemeteries and memorials built and maintained by the Commonwealth War Graves Commission, 'will bear a message to future generations as long as the stone of which they are constructed endures.' With the launch of the Debt of Honour Register, names once kept alive only in stone are now readily available to be carried in the hearts and minds of a new generation. As we move further away from the two world wars the Commission will ensure the stone, the gardens, the records, the memory and the message endure - that 'Their Name Liveth for Evermore".

Further Information
The Commission welcomes enquiries from the public. We request that you supply the Commission's enquiries department with as much information as possible. This will enhance the chances of a positive trace.

A full list of the Commission's services and publications on offer to the public is available from:

The Records & Enquiries Section
The Commonwealth War Graves Commission
2 Marlow Road, Maidenhead, Berkshire, SL6 7DX
Tel: 01628 634221 Fax: 01628 771208
E-mail: casualty.enq@cwgc.org Web Site: www.cwgc.org

What's new at the Imperial War Museum

Sarah Paterson - *Department of Printed Books*

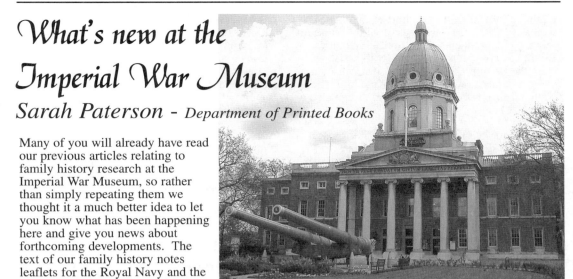

Many of you will already have read our previous articles relating to family history research at the Imperial War Museum, so rather than simply repeating them we thought it a much better idea to let you know what has been happening here and give you news about forthcoming developments. The text of our family history notes leaflets for the Royal Navy and the Royal Flying Corps/Royal Air Force is also included in this entry. The text of the leaflets for the Army, Merchant Navy and Prisoners of War can be found on the Museum's website, the address if which is www.iwm.org.uk We also have information sheets for tracing members of the Women's Royal Naval Service, Queen Mary's Army Auxiliary Corps and Voluntary Aid Detachments in the First World War.

The text of the Army leaflet was published in the 6th Edition of this Handbook, but an important change occurred on 1 July 2002, when the Army Records Centre at Hayes ceased to function. Anyone requiring Army service records dating from after1922 (officers) or 1920 (other ranks) should now apply to the **Army Personnel Centre, Historical Disclosures, Mailpoint 400, Kentigern House, 65 Brown Street, Glasgow G2 8EX**. Initial contact can also be made by telephone (0141 224 3030) and e-mail (apcsec@dial.pipex.com).

The Prisoner of War leaflet also featured in the 6th Edition, and a new publication was produced this year that will be of interest to anyone trying to research men of the Royal Air Force taken prisoner in the Far East during World War Two. The book by Les and Pam Stubbs is called **Unsung heroes of the Royal Air Force: the Far East Prisoners of War, 1941-1945** (Grantham, Lincolnshire: Barny Books, 2002). The ISBN is 1-903172-21-7. Anyone wishing to have a look at this or any other book in our collection is welcome to make an appointment to visit the Reading Room. This is open between 10.00am-5.00pm, Monday to Friday (and most Saturdays between the same hours although this is a limited service).

Appointments can be made on (020) 7416 5342.

If you have previously visited our Reading Room you will know that it is a delightful circular room (at the top of a winding staircase, although alternative facilities are available for those who would find it too difficult to reach). The Museum moved to its present site in 1936 – the building (dating from 1815) had previously been the home of the Bethlem Royal Hospital (more famously known as "Bedlam"). In 1967, the Reading Room of the library transferred to the Dome. This had formerly been the Chapel of the old Hospital, and its original use is remembered in the Ten Commandments still prominent on the walls. The Dome was designed by Sir Sydney Smirke (in the mid-1840s). A decade later he was to create the most famous reading room in the land – the circular reading room of the British Museum!

However, in 1968, a pacifist poet tossed a firebomb into the Reading Room and the Dome was destroyed. Colossal damage was done and enormous numbers of publications destroyed – mainly journals and newspapers (and, ironically, the poetry collection – this has since been rebuilt with the result that the Museum has an outstanding collection of twentieth century poetry). It re-opened in 1975, and 2002 marked the completion of the first redecoration since then. The catalogue room has had the banks of card catalogues removed and replaced with more computer terminals to enable the

public to look at the online library catalogues, as well as research the databases of all the Museum reference departments. The Special Facilities Room has also been renovated (with assistance from the Friends of the Imperial War Museum) and the database for the United Kingdom National Inventory of War Memorials can also be looked at here.

On the floor below, disabled visitors or those who find it difficult to use the stairs, can work in "D12". This has been refitted with a wide door, wheelchair friendly carpet, four new purpose-built workstations and a cord-pull emergency alarm system. A grant from the Friends of the Imperial War Museum also enabled us to purchase special closed circuit television and computerised equipment for blind and visually impaired readers. It is necessary to book an appointment, and if you are registered disabled you will be able to book a car parking space – it is best to book several days before you intend visiting.

Recent publications by the Department of Printed Books are listed below. All our publications can be purchased from **Mail Order, Duxford, Cambridge CB2 4QR**. (Tel: (01223) 499345; Fax: (01223) 839688; E-mail: mailorder@iwm.org.uk).

Wise eating in wartime prepared for the Ministry of Food by the Ministry of Information and originally published by HMSO in 1943. This useful little booklet covers food and nutrition in the Second World War costs £4.00.

Catalogue of the special collection of First World War German unit histories held in the Department of Printed Books costs £15.00. This lists the German Regimental histories the Museum received in the 1920s and 1930s. The German language and gothic script make the histories difficult to read, but these are a valuable resource, especially if one of your ancestors fought with the Germans, or you are interested in gaining the opposing viewpoint for British Army research.

Notes on trench routine and discipline by a Second in Command, originally published in 1916 by Forster, Groom and Co. Designed to fit in a small pocket and be a reference guide for a young officer, this is full of useful tips and advice for life in the trenches. A bargain at £1.50 (and features delightful contemporary adverts too!)

Notes on trench warfare for infantry officers issued by the General Staff in 1917 is an official publication full of illustrations showing plans for features such as dug-outs, barbed wire and latrines. The price is £2.50.

Four titles in our **Tracing your family history** series are currently available, covering the **Army**, **Royal Air Force**, **Royal Navy** and **Merchant Navy**. These sell for £5.50 each and are ideal introductions to the subject of tracing ancestors in each of these services from 1914 onwards, having been compiled in response to the many questions we get asked regularly. As well as providing information about where records can be found, they include information about the structure and organisation of the branch of service, medals, numbering, and suggestions for further research. Useful book titles, addresses and websites are also included.

If you wish to make an appointment to visit our Reading Room, or have a question you would like to ask (bearing in mind that we cannot embark on detailed research for you), please contact us in one of the following ways:
Telephone (enquiries): (020) 7416 5342
Fax: (020) 7416 5246
E-mail: books@iwm.org.uk
Website: www.iwm.org.uk

Tracing Royal Flying Corps and Royal Air Force Ancestry
Family History notes from the Imperial War Museum

The Imperial War Museum does not hold any personal service records or official documentation but can help the enquirer as long as some basic facts are known. The Department of Printed Books welcomes visitors by appointment and is able to provide useful reading material and advice for finding out more about those who served. Other reference departments in the Museum - Art, Documents, Exhibits and Firearms, Film and Video Archive, Photograph Archive, and Sound Archive - may also be able to assist.

The most important piece of information is the unit that an individual served with (it is a sad fact that those who died during the World Wars will be easier to trace than those who survived, and this information is readily obtainable from the **Commonwealth War Graves Commission**). The personal service record should be the starting point, but not all of these records for the First World War survived Second World War bombing. Records are located according to an individual's date of discharge.

The **Public Record Office, Ruskin Avenue, Kew, Richmond, Surrey TW9 4DU (Tel: 020 8392 5200; Website: www.pro.gov.uk)** holds all surviving First World War service records for officers who left the RAF before 1920. Surviving First World War service records for other ranks who ceased service before 1920 have recently been released to the PRO where they can be consulted on microfilm. The records of any First World War airman who saw service after 1920 or who rejoined the RAF will still be held by the **RAF Personnel Management Agency, PMA(Sec)1B, Building 248A, RAF Innsworth, Gloucester GL3 1EZ**. Further information concerning the RAF material now held by the PRO can be found in the publication *Air Force records for family historians* by William Spencer (Richmond, Surrey: PRO, 2000).

The **RAF Personnel Management Agency** holds the records for all those who served after 1920. The RAF PMA will release records to proven next of kin for a £25 fee but there may be a lengthy wait for this service.

The ranks and dates of promotion of RAF officers can be traced using the regular official publication the *Air Force List* and the Department of Printed Books holds an almost complete set of these from 1918 to date. (From 1914 RFC officers were included in the *Army List*. The Department of Printed Books also holds an almost complete set from 1914 onwards). It should be noted that, with the exception of some issues from the period between the two world wars, the *Air Force List* does not include any details of squadrons.

Casualty Records
The **Commonwealth War Graves Commission, 2 Marlow Road, Maidenhead, Berkshire SL6 7DX (Tel: 01628 507200)** has details of all service personnel who died between the dates 4 August 1914-31 August 1921 and 3 September 1939-31 December 1947. The CWGC may charge a fee for postal enquiries, but there is a website containing their computerised database, *Debt of honour* (which can be consulted at **www.cwgc.org**).

The **Department of Research and Information Services** at the **Royal Air Force Museum, Grahame Park Way, London NW9 5L Tel: 020 8205 2266 Website: http://www.rafmuseum.org.uk/** holds several series of official casualty records. Although detailed these records are not complete. The **Ministry of Defence, Air Historical Branch, Building 266, RAF Bentley Priory, Stanmore, Middlesex HA7 3HH** holds casualty records for RAF personnel killed, injured, reported missing or

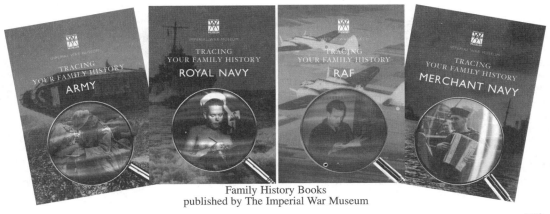

Family History Books
published by The Imperial War Museum

© Robert Blatchford

taken POW from 1919 onwards. The **RAF Personnel Management Agency** and the **Air Historical Branch** will release details of their records to proven next of kin only.

Sources held by the Department of Printed Books include a complete set of the CWGC's memorial and cemetery registers. Other useful sources are the books *Airmen died in the Great War 1914-1918: the roll of honour of the British and Commonwealth Air Services of the First World War* compiled by Chris Hobson (Suffolk: J B Hayward, 1995) and *The sky their battlefield: air fighting and the complete list of Allied air casualties from enemy action in the First War: British, Commonwealth, and United States Air Services 1914 to 1918* by Trevor Henshaw (London: Grub Street, 1995).

For the Second World War it should be noted that the register of the Runnymede Memorial (one of those published by the Commonwealth War Graves Commission) lists in alphabetical order the names of over 20,000 airmen who lost their lives in operations over north-west Europe and the Atlantic and have no known grave. The six volume *Royal Air Force Bomber Command losses of the Second World War* by W R Chorley (Leicester: Midland Counties Publications, 1992-1999) is a useful reference work.

Rolls of honour for other later conflicts are also held and in addition the DPB has a large collection of published rolls of honour for localities, schools, institutions etc. Squadron histories and journals sometimes contain rolls of honour.

The airman's own home area should not be forgotten when researching an individual's service - there may be local war memorial records, a local account of war service may have been published, and contemporary local newspapers can prove very helpful. It is also possible that school, church or workplace records may still exist.

Medal records
Campaign medals are those given to airmen who are eligible for them because they were in a

particular theatre of war within given dates. The PRO holds the First World War Medal Roll which provides a listing of all those who qualified for the 1914 Star, 1914/15 Star, British War Medal, Victory Medal, Territorial Force War Medal and/or the Silver War Badge. If an airman's record was destroyed some basic information about his service may be found in this.

Gallantry medals are those medals awarded for an especially heroic deed or action. Records for these are held at the **PRO**, but may not be very detailed. Notifications and citations (if these were published, which was not the case for awards such as Mentions in Despatches) were published in the official journal *London Gazette*. A complete set of this, and the all important indexes, is held at the PRO. The Department of Printed Books does have some published listings of medal awards for decorations such as the Victoria Cross, Distinguished Flying Cross and Distinguished Flying Medal. Usually you will need to go either to the official operations unit record book (held at the PRO) or to a published squadron/unit history to see whether you can find out more about the action for which the decoration was awarded.

Other sources
The Department of Printed Books has a good collection of books on the RFC/RAF including a number of squadron histories. (The reading room is open between 10am-5pm, Monday to Saturday, by appointment.) It should be noted however that the number of such histories is relatively small compared with the total number of squadrons that have existed in the RAF. Service and ex-service periodicals and newspapers should not be overlooked. *Flypast* (**Key Publishing Ltd., P.O.Box 100, Stamford, Lincolnshire PE9 1XQ; website: www.flypast.com/**) publishes appeals from enquirers on aviation history topics including the tracing of former RAF personnel.

The Royal Air Forces Association produce a quarterly journal called *Air Mail* (**RAFATRAD Ltd, Unit 17 Sovereign Park, Coronation Road, London NW10 7QP**). The website address is **www.RAFA.org.uk**

The Royal Air Force website at **www.raf.mod.uk/** is worth a visit as it has very comprehensive links.

Tracing Royal Naval Ancestry
Family History notes from the Imperial War Museum

The Imperial War Museum does not hold any personal service records or official documentation, but can help the enquirer as long as some basic facts are known. The Department of Printed Books welcomes visitors by appointment and is able to provide useful reading material and advice for finding out more about those who served. Other reference departments in the Museum – Art, Documents, Exhibits and Firearms, Film and Video Archive, Photograph Archive and Sound Archive – may also be able to assist.

Where to find Royal Navy Service Records
The Imperial War Museum only covers the period from the First World War onwards. Most of the relevant records relating to naval genealogical research are either still held by the **Ministry of Defence** (MOD) or the **Public Record Office** (PRO). Genealogical enquiries to the various departments of the MOD must be made in writing, but do not receive priority as the principal concern is to respond to official enquiries concerning welfare, pensions and other legal matters. The basic search fee, if levied, is currently £25.00.

Personnel records available to the public are now held by the **Public Record Office, Ruskin Avenue, Kew, Richmond, Surrey TW9 4DU (Tel. 020 8392 5200; Website: www.pro.gov.uk)**. Please note that the PRO does not undertake research on behalf of the public; it is necessary to either visit in person or employ a professional researcher, details of which are available direct from Readers' Services at the PRO. For anyone intending to do their own research the Public Record Office has produced

invaluable guides to their holdings; of particular importance are ***Tracing your ancestors in the Public Record Office*** 6th revised edition, edited by Armanda Bevan (Richmond, Surrey: PRO, 2002) and ***Naval records for genealogists*** by N A M Rodger (Richmond, Surrey: PRO, 1998). In principle, personnel records are transferred to the PRO when they are seventy-five years old.

Pre-First World War service records, and ratings' personnel files dating to 1923, are now held at the PRO. The transfer of officers' records has recently been completed. For service records dating from 1923 to 1939 please write to the **Ministry of Defence, DR(2)A Navy, Bourne Avenue, Hayes, Middlesex UB3 1RF**.

For records of officers and ratings who saw service from 1939 (including 'Hostilities Only' service in the Second World War and Korea), write to the **Directorate of Naval Pay and Pensions, NPP (Acs)1E Centurion Building, Grange Road, Gosport, Hampshire PO13 9XA**.

Service records for officers in the **Royal Naval Reserve** and **Royal Naval Volunteer Reserve** for the First World War have now been transferred to the PRO. Officers' records up to 1950, and ratings' records up to 1945 are held at MOD Hayes. RNR and RNVR records from after these dates are held at Centurion Building.

Records of those who served in the **Royal Naval Air Service** can be found at the PRO. **Fleet Air Arm** records are held at Centurion Building. **Royal Naval Division** records of service are now at the PRO. Records of **Royal Marines** officers and men in service up to 1924 are at the PRO.

Naval Review
at Spithead
1914

The Battle of Jutland 1916

© Robert Blatchford

Subsequent records are still held by the **Royal Marines Drafting and Record Office, Centurion Building, Grange Road, Gosport, Hampshire PO13 9XA**.

The careers of Naval officers can be traced through the *Navy List*, a regular, official publication. (No such listing exists for other ranks). These contain seniority lists of all officers, cross referred to individual ships. A full set is held by the PRO but the Department of Printed Books holds a near complete run from 1914 to date.

Casualty Records

Casualty records are available for consultation at the PRO. In addition, the **Commonwealth War Graves Commission, 2 Marlow Road, Maidenhead, Berkshire SL6 7DX (Tel. 01628 507200; Website: www.cwgc.org)** holds details of the burial place or commemoration site for all those who died in service during the period 1914-1921 and 1939-1947. A search fee may be levied. Access to the CWGC's *Debt of Honour* database is free on their website. Details of naval personnel who were buried at sea are contained in memorial registers produced by the Commission. The Department of Printed Books holds a complete set of memorial and cemetery registers, together with various operational and unit histories, some of which may make reference to casualties, and some published rolls of honour.

Details of service personnel buried in 'non-World War' graves are available from the **Ministry of Defence, NP-Sec2(b), Room 222 Victory Building, HM Naval Base, Portsmouth, Hampshire PO1 3LS**.

Medal Records

Records of campaign and gallantry awards and available citations, for the period up to 1921, are lodged with the PRO. For awards after that date write to the **Directorate of Naval Pay and Pensions, NPP (Acs)1F Centurion Building, Grange Road, Gosport, Hampshire PO13 9XA**. The PRO holds a full set of the *London Gazette*, another good source of reference for awards and citations, complete with indexes. However, please note that during the Second World War, publication of all citations for gallantry awards was suspended. For possible information on these 'unpublished' citations write to the **Ministry of Defence, Honours and Awards, Room 115 Victory Building, HM Naval Base, Portsmouth, Hampshire PO1 3LS**.

The Department of Printed Books holds published sources only, but recommends in particular the volumes *Seedie's roll of honour and awards* compiled by B C Dickson (Tisbury, Wiltshire: Ripley Registers, 1989).

Other Sources

The **Royal Naval Association, HMS Nelson, Portsmouth, Hampshire PO1 3HH** produces a monthly magazine *Navy News* (Tel: 02392 726040; Website: www.navynews.co.uk) which carries a column for contacting and tracing ex-servicemen. Details of other publications and associations, which offer a similar service, are available from the Department of Printed Books. Researchers will also find operational accounts, unit and ships' histories held by the Department, invaluable for background detail. Official documentation such as operational records, unit diaries and ships' logs are now with the PRO.

There are many magazines on the market which offer

advice and guidance on family history; one of which is *Family Tree Magazine* published monthly by **ABM Publishing, 61 Great Whyte, Ramsey, Huntingdon, Cambridgeshire PE26 1HJ**. Genealogical societies such as the **Federation of Family History Societies, c/o Mrs Maggie Loughran, FFHS Administrator, PO Box 2425, Coventry CV5 6YX** are also able to offer advice. The website can be accessed at www.ffhs.org.uk/

Once the recommended archives have been approached, researchers are welcome to forward their findings to the Department of Printed Books for advice on other relevant works and addresses. The Printed Books reading room is open to the public, by prior appointment, from Monday to Saturday between 10.00am and 5.00pm.

Other museums that might be able to help you further are:

Royal Naval Museum, HM Naval Base (PP66), Portsmouth, Hampshire PO1 3NH
Tel: 02392 727562

Website: www.royalnavalmuseum.org/
Fleet Air Arm Museum
Box D6, RNAS Yeovilton, near Ilchester, Somerset BA22 8HT
Tel: 01935 840565
Website: www.fleetairarm.com/

The Royal Marines Museum
Southsea, Hampshire PO4 9XP
Tel: 02392 819385
Website: www.royalmarinesmuseum.co.uk/

Royal Navy Submarine Museum
Haslar Jetty Road, Gosport,
Hampshire PO12 2AS
Tel: 02392 529217
Website: www.rnsubmus.co.uk/

National Maritime Museum
Greenwich, London SE10 9NF
Tel: 020 8858 4422
Website: www.nmm.ac.uk/

THE REGIMENTAL MUSEUM OF THE BORDER REGIMENT AND THE KINGS OWN ROYAL BORDER REGIMENT

at

Queen Mary's Tower, The Castle, Carlisle. CA3 8UR

The Museum relates the history of Cumbria's County Infantry Regiment, the Border Regiment and its successor The King's Own Royal Border Regiment and local Militia, Volunteer and Territorial Army units from 1702 to the present day.

The Castle. founded in 1092, is a superb Border fortress still owned by the Crown and maintained by English Heritage within its walls are the barrack and other military buildings dating from the nineteenth century, which formed the Regimental Depot.

The Museum has extensive Regimental Archives and family history and other enquiries are welcome. Researchers are welcome at the Museum but strictly by appointment.

School/Educational visits - all groups welcome; visits to schools by arrangement.

Location - north side of the City centre (within easy reach from M6 J.43 & 44), 10 minutes from railway station. Adjacent car-parking. Museum admission included in entry charge to the Castle.

For further details contact:
Curator: Stuart Eastwood, BA AMA.
Tel: 01228-532774   Fax: 01228-521275
E-mail: RHQ@kingsownborder.demon.co.uk

The Commonwealth War Graves Commission Civilian Roll of Honour

Peter Francis
Commonwealth War Graves Commission

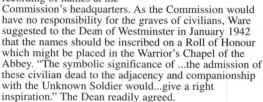

In 1938, the Imperial, now Commonwealth, War Graves Commission unveiled the Australian Memorial at Villers-Bretonneux. It was the last of the Great War memorials to be completed from the war that was to end all wars and yet within a year the Second World War had started and the Commission was called upon to prepare for a new harvest of death. This second catastrophe of the twentieth century was a very different conflict to the one that had taken place only twenty or so years previously. The war was one of quick movement - the German Blitzkrieg sweeping all before it and forcing the Commission to temporarily relinquish control of the cemeteries and memorials in occupied Europe.

With the conquest of mainland Europe complete, Hitler's forces concentrated their efforts on the invasion of the United Kingdom. In order to invade, Germany had first to achieve total air superiority and so began the Battle of Britain and the large-scale bombing of airfields, factories and later in an attempt to smash the morale of the British people, cities. Distinctions between soldiers and non-combatants were non-existent. The phrase Total War was coined to represent the fact that civilian populations as well as front line troops were now considered targets.

On 7 September 1940 the first major air raid on a British city was carried out by the Luftwaffe. The Commission's founder, Fabian Ware, witnessed first hand the deaths of women, children, firemen and air-raid wardens. This new and horrifying war was impacting on communities like never before. Surely, he reasoned, each casualty deserved a fitting commemoration? Soon London itself was a target of the Blitz. Ware decided to act and wrote to the Prime Minister, Winston Churchill, on 18 September, urging the commemoration of those civilians killed by enemy action. In his words, "The deliberate slaughter of civilians was creating a new category of normal war casualties. Theirs should be counted an equal sacrifice".

Churchill, who had so successfully argued for the Commission's principle of equality of treatment for the war dead while Chairman of the Commission during the parliamentary debates on commemoration of the early 1920s, had no objection. In fact, he believed that civilian deaths might well outnumber military casualties - fortunately, he was not proved correct.

In January 1941, the Commission began to keep records of all civilian deaths caused by enemy action and its Royal Charters were adjusted to give it the necessary powers to do so. The biggest single obstacle to this task was obtaining the names and addresses of those killed. The information provided by the authorities, like the Registrar General, was not always complete and often did not include the addresses of next of kin. In February 1941, to encourage a greater flow of information and further publicise the commemoration of civilians, Ware decided to make a tour of the hard-hit areas. During his tour he enlisted the help of mayors and local authorities and the information provided to the Commission greatly improved. In November 1941, he made a further appeal on national radio and in the press for help and the records began to take shape - the Commission already

had over 18,000 individuals recorded.

However, Ware was not satisfied with the mere recording of names at the Commission's headquarters. As the Commission would have no responsibility for the graves of civilians, Ware suggested to the Dean of Westminster in January 1942 that the names should be inscribed on a Roll of Honour which might be placed in the Warrior's Chapel of the Abbey. "The symbolic significance of ...the admission of these civilian dead to the adjacency and companionship with the Unknown Soldier would...give a right inspiration." The Dean readily agreed.

In December 1942 the first typed lists, leather bound in three volumes, were deposited for safekeeping at Westminster. The volumes were not put on display until after the war because it was believed that if the extent of civilian casualties were known, it might damage the morale of the nation. It was not until 1956 that the completed volumes of the Civilian Roll of Honour were handed to the Dean of Westminster by the Duke of Gloucester. Today, there are six volumes with over 66,000 names recorded. In a fitting tribute to those commemorated, the books are still on display to the public at the Abbey. A new page of the Civilian Roll of Honour is turned every day and so unfolds 66,000 tragic stories - the sudden death of a pensioner aged one hundred or of an infant a few hours old, of 163 people killed in an instant when a V2 rocket fell on Woolworth's at New Cross, and of the 1,500 dead of Malta.

What information does the Civilian Roll of Honour have? The casualty details available include the person's name, age, date of death, last known address and the particulars of the next of kin. The entries are structured along the lines of the old Borough system and then alphabetically by surname. Just one moving example reads: Betty Francis, Civilian War Dead. Died 9 April 1941, Aged 2. Daughter of Emily and the late Tom Francis of Clevedon Road, Balasall Heath. County Borough of Birmingham. The civilian records, like the military records, are still updated to this day. Amendments made on the computerised system are later added to the leather bound volumes at the Abbey twice a year by a member of the Commission's records department. In this way, that 'equal sacrifice' is preserved for future generations.

For the family historian, all of this information is available from the Commission's enquiries department in Maidenhead and the Debt of Honour Register at www.cwgc.org The Civilian Roll of Honour is a highly moving tribute not only to the many innocents who had their lives brutally cut short by war but to the bravery of services like the Fire Brigade and Ambulance crews who risked their lives to save others. The Commonwealth War Graves Commission keeps faith with them all, ensuring that

Their Name Liveth For Evermore.

Military Campaigns over the last 200 years

David Barnes

Perhaps the best place to start is by looking at the major campaigns or actions in the last 200 years that units of the British Army have been involved in, for which medals or honours were awarded. Some of the minor campaigns and those in which only a small number of British troops served in have been excluded from the list below

The first medal to be distributed to all ranks of the British Army was the Waterloo Medal and was authorised by the Prince Regent in March 1816. Some 39,000 medals were issued to all the survivors of actions at Ligny (16 June), Quatre Bras (17 June) and Waterloo (18 June 1815) and to the next of kin of men killed in action. This was also the first medal to carry the recipient's name rank and unit impressed by machine around the rim of the medal

The Military General Service Medal commemorates British Army actions in the French Revolutionary and Napoleonic Wars between 1801 and 1814, but this was not issued until 1848, and the veteran had to submit a personal application. There were some 29 battle or campaign clasps which were eligible to be issued with the medal and multiple clasps are fairly common. There were 21 campaign bars for actions in the Peninsular War 1808-1814, there were bars for Egypt, Madia, Martinique, Guadaloupe, Java and three were for actions in the War of America. The maximum number of clasps awarded to any one person was 15 and there were only two recorded recipients; James Talbot, 45th Foot and Daniel Loochstadt, 60th Foot and King's German Legion. Eleven men were awarded fourteen bars.

French Revolutionary & Napoleonic Wars 1801 -1814	Second China War 25 May 1857 -13 October 1860
Peninsular War 1 August 1808 - 10 April 1814	Abyssinian War 4 October 1867 - 19 April 1868
War of America 18 June 1812 - 1815	Ashantee War 9 June 1873 - 4 February 1874
Nepal War 1 November 1814 - 27 April 1915	Zulu War 25 September 1877 - 2 December 1879
Waterloo Campaign 16 - 18 June 1815	2nd Afghan War 21 November 1878 - 1 September1880
Kandian Rebellion, Ceylon 1818	First Boer War 1880 -1881
Burma April 1824 - February 1826	Egyptian Campaigns 1882 - 1891
Indian Campaigns 1799-1826	Sudan 1884 and 1896-1922
South African Campaigns 1834 -1853	Rebellions in South Africa 1890 - 1897
First Afghan War April 1839 - October 1842	Campaigns in India 1895 - 1939
First China War 5 July 1840 - 29 August 1842	Anglo-Boer War 11 October 1899 - 31 May 1902
Indian Campaigns 1843 -1849	Boxer Rebellion, China 10 June-31 December 1900
Second Burma War 1852	Campaigns in Africa 1900 - 1956
Crimean War 2 March 1854 - 30 March 1856	Tibet 13 December 1903 - 23 September 1904
Indian Mutiny 10 May 1857 - 20 December 1858	First World War 4 August 1914 - 11 November 1918

Bombardment o
Alexandria
by Ironclads
11 July 1882

Egyptian Campaign
1881 -1882

The Western Front - France and Flanders

Action	Date
Mons	23-24 August 1914
Audregnies	24 August 1914
Le Cateau	26 August 1914
Retreat from Mons	24 August - 5 September 1914
Nery Marne	7-10 September 1914
Aisne	12-15 September 1914
La Bassee	10 October - 2 November 1914
Messines	12 October - 2 November 1914
Armentieres	13 October - 2 November 1914
1st Battle of Ypres	19 October - 22 November 1914
Langemarck	21-24 October 1914
Hollebeke Chateau	25-30 October 1914
Gheluvelt	29-31 October 1914
Nonne Bosschen	11 November 1914
Festubert	23-24 November 1914
Wytschaete	14 December 1914
Givenchy	20-21 December 1914
Givenchy	25 January 1915
Neuve Chapelle	10-13 March 1915
Hill 60	17-22 April 1915
2nd Battle of Ypres	22 April - 25 May 1915
Gravenstafel	22-23 April 1915
St Julien	24 April - 4 May 1915
Hill 60 Counterattack	4 May 1915
Frezenberg	8-13 May 1915
Aubers	9 May 1915
Festubert	15-25 May 1915
Bellewarde	24-25 May 1915
Hooge	19 July, 30 July, 30 August 1915
Loos	25 September - 8 October 1915
Bois Grenier	25 September 1915
Pietre	25 September 1915
St Eloi Craters	27 March - 16 April 1916
Mount Sorrel	2-13 June 1916

Battles of the Somme

Albert	1-13 July 1916
Beaumont Hamel	1 July 1916
Schwaben Redoubt	1 July 1916
Bazentin	14-17 July 1916
Delville Wood	15 July - 3 September 1916
Fromelles	19 July 1916
Attacks on High Wood	20-25 July 1916
Pozières	23 July - 3 September 1916
Guillemont	3-6 September 1916
Ginchy	9 September 1916
Flere Courcelette	15-22 September 1916
Morval	25-28 September 1916
Thiépval	26-28 September 1916
Le Transloy	1-18 October 1916
Ancre Heights	1 October - 11 November 1916
Ancre	13-18 November 1916

Battle of Arras

Vimy	9-14 April 1917
1st Battle of the Scarpe	9-14 April 1917
2nd Battle of the Scarpe	23-24 April 1917
Arleux	28-29 April 1917
3rd Battle of the Scarpe	3-4 May 1917
Bullecourt	3-17 May 1917
Action at Roeux	13-14 May 1917
Action at Oppy Wood	28 June 1917
Hill 70	15-25 August 1917
Battle of Messines	7-14 June 1917
3rd Battle of Ypres	31 July - 10 November 1917
Pilckem	31 July - 2 August 1917
Westhoek	18 August 1917
Langemarck	16-18 August 1917
St Julien	22-27 August 1917
Menin Road	20-25 September 1917
Polygon Wood	26 Sept - 3 October 1917
Broodseinde	4 October 1917
Poelcappelle	9 Oct - 12 October 1917
2nd Battle of Passchendaele	26 Oct - 10 November 1917
Battle of Cambrai	20 Nov - 7 December 1917
Gouzeacourt	20-21 November 1917

German Offensive in Picardy

1st Battles of the Somme	21 March - 5 April 1918
St Quentin	21-23 March 1918
Fontaine-les-Clercs	21-22 March 1918
Cugny	23 March 1918
1st Battle of Bapaume	24-25 March 1918
Rosieres	26-27 March 1918
1st Battle of Arras	28 March 1918
Avre	4 April 1918
Ancre	5 April 1918

Offensive in Flanders

Lys	9 - 29 April 1918
Estaires	9-11 April 1918
Messines	10-11 April 1918
Hazebrouck	12-15 April 1918
Bailleul	13-15 April 1918
1st Battle of Kemmel	17-19 April 1918
Bethune	18 April 1918
Pacaut Wood	22 April 1918
Villers Brettoneaux	24-25 April 1918
2nd Battle of Kemmel	25-26 April 1918
Scherpenberg	29 April 1918

Offensive in Champagne

Aisne	27 May - 6 June 1918
Bligny	6 June 1918
Bois des Buttes	6 June 1918
Hamel	4 July 1918
Soissonais-Ourcq	23 Jul - 2 August 1918
Tardenois	20-31 July 1918
Battles of the Marne	30 July - 2 August 1918
Battle of Amiens	8-11 August 1918
Harbonnieres	8 August 1918
2nd Battles of the Somme	21 August - 3 September 1918
Albert	21-23 August 1918
Albert(Chuignes)	21-23 August 1918
Scarpe	26-30 August 1918
Mont Vidaigne	29 August 1918
Mont St Quentin	31 August - 3 September 1918
2nd Battles of Arras	26 August - 3 September 1918
2nd Battle of Bapaume	31 August - 3 September 1918
Drocourt-Queant	2-3 September 1918

The Somme Battlefield 1916

Battles of the Hindenburg Line

	12 Sept - 9 October 1918
Havrincourt	12 September 1918
Epehy	18 September 1918
Canal de Nord	27 September - 1 October 1918
St Quentin Canal	29 September - 2 October 1918
Battles of Ypres	1918 28 September - 2 October 1918
Beaurevoir	3-6 October 1918
Cambrai	8-9 October 1918
Courtrai	14-19 October 1918
Le Cateau	918 17-18 October 1918
Selle	17-25 October 1918
Tieghem	31 October 1918
Valenciennes	1-2 November 1918
Sambre	4 November 1918
Sambre (Le Quesnoy)	4 November 1918
Pursuit to Mons	4-11 November 1918

Other Theatres of Operation

Action	Date
WEST AFRICA	**6 August 1914 - 17 February 1916**
Cameroons	6 August 1914 - 17 February 1916
Kamina	8-26 August 1914
Duala	26-27 September 1914
Garua	31 May - 10 June 1915
Banyo	4-6 November 1915
EAST AFRICA	
	15 August 1914 - 25 November 1918
Kilimanjaro	5-21 March 1916
Beho Beho	3-4 January 1917
Narungombe	19 July 1917
Nyangao	16-19 October 1917
SOUTH WEST AFRICA	**20 August 1914 - 9 July 1915**
Gibeon	25-26 April 1915
CHINA and AUSTRALASIA	
Herbertshohe	12 September 1914
Tsingtao	23 September - 7 November 1914
MESOPOTAMIA	
	6 November 1914 - 5 November 1918
Basra	6 November 1914 - 14 April 1915
Shaiba	12-14 March 1915
Nasiriya	5-24 July 1915
Kut el Amara	28 September 1915
Ctesiphon	22-24 November 1915
Defence of Kut el Amara	7 December 1915 - 28 April 1916
Tigris 1916	14 January - 24 April 1916
Kut el Amara	16 December 1916 - 25 February 1917
Baghdad	25 February - 30 April 1917
Ramadi	28-29 September 1917
Tigris 1917	1 October - 6 December 1917
Khan Baghdadi	26-27 March 1918
Sharquat	28-30 October 1918
INDIA North West Frontier	
	28 November 1914 - 10 August 1917
Waziristan	2 March -10 August 1917
Baluchistan	18 February - 8 April 1918
EGYPT	**26 January 1915 - 8 February 1917**
Suez Canal	26 January 1915 - 12 August 1916
Defence of the Suez Canal	3-4 February 1915
Wadi Majid	25 December 1915
Halazin	23 January 1916
Agagiya	26 February 1916
Rumani	4-5 August 1916
Magdhaba-Rafah	23 December 1916 - 9 January 1917
Rafah	9 January 1917
DARDANELLES - Gallipoli	
	25 April 1915 - 7 January 1916
Landing at Helles	25-26 April 1915
Helles	25 April - 6 June 1915
Landing at Anzac	25-26 April 1915
Anzac	25 April - 30 June 1915
1st Battle of Krithia	28 April 1915

2nd Battle of Krithia	6-8 May 1915
Defence of Anzac	8 May - 30 June 1915
3rd Battle of Krithia	4 June 1915
Landing at Suvla	6-15 August 1915
Suvla	6-21 August 1915
Sari Bair	6-10 August 1915
Sari Bair - Lone Pine	6-10 August 1915
Scimitar Hill	21 August 1915
Hill 60 (ANZAC)	27 August 1915
SOUTHERN ARABIA	
Aden	3 July 1915 - 31 October 1918
MACEDONIA - Salonika	
5 October 1915 - 30 September 1918	
Kosturino	7-8 December 1915
Horseshoe Hill	17-18 August 1916
Struma	30 September - 31 October 1916
Doiran	24-25 April 1917 and 8-9 May 1917
Roche Noir	1-2 September 1918
P' Ridge	12 September 1918
Doiran	18-19 September 1918
PERSIA	**10 January 1915 - 8 August 1919**
Persian Gulf	10 January - 9 September 1915
Baku	26 August - 15 September 1918
Merv	1 November 1918
Persia	11 April 1916 - 8 August 1919
SUDAN	
Darfur	March - 23 May 1916
Fasher	1 September-23 November 1916
PALESTINE	**26 March 1917 - 31 October 1918**
1st Battle of Gaza	26-27 March 1917
2nd Battle of Gaza	17-19 April 1917
3rd Battle of Gaza	27 October - 7 November 1917
Gaza- Beersheba	27 October - 7 November 1917
Huj	8 November 1917
El Mughur	13 November 1917
Capture of Jerusalem	7-9 December 1917
Defence of Jerusalem	26-30 December 1917
Jaffa	21-22 December 1917
Jericho	19-21 February 1918
Tell Asur	8-12 March 1918
Jordan	21 March-11 April 1918
1st Battle of Jordan (Es Salt)	
	24-25 March 1918
Jordan (Amman)	27-30 March 1918
2nd Battle of Jordan (Es Salt)	
	30 April-4 May 1918
Megiddo	19-25 September 1918
Sharon	19-25 September 1918
Nablus	19-25 September 1918
Damascus	1 October 1918
Syria	1-26 October 1918
ITALY	**12 May 1918 - 4 November 1918**
Piave	15-24 June 1918
Vittorio Veneto	24 October - 4 November 1918
RUSSIA	**29 June 1918 - 12 October 1919**
Murman	29 June 1918 - 12 October 1919
Archangel	1 August 1918 - 27 September 1919
Dukhovskaya	23-24 August 1918
Siberia	8 August 1918 - June 1919
Troitsa	10 August 1919

Third Afghan War	1919
Mesopotamia	1919 - 1920
Ireland	21 January 1919 - 11 July 1921
North West Frontier, India	
	1930, 1936-1937, 1937 - 1940
Palestine	1936 - 1939

Second World War
3 September 1939 - 2 September 1945

Norway	21 April - 26 May 1940. 27 December 1941
North West Europe	1940-42 10 May 1940 - 19 August 1942
Abyssinia	1 July 1940 - 28 November 1941
British Somaliland	4-17 August 1940
Iraq	2 - 31 May 1941
Syria	7 June - 12 July 1941
Persia	25-28 July 1941, 25 : 26 August 1941
Malta	11 June 1940 - 20 November 1942
North Africa (Western Desert)	
	12 June 1940 - 9 May 1943
North Africa (1st Army Operations)	
	17 November 1942 - 30 April 1943
North Africa (1st and 8th Army Operations)	5-12 May 1943
Greece	10-29 April 1941
Crete	20 May - 1 June 1941
Middle East	20 May 1941 - 21 November 1944
Hong Kong	8-25 December 1941
Malaya	8 December 1941 - 15 February 1942
South East Asia	8 December 1941 - 9 March 1942
Burma	20 January 1942 - 15 August 1945
South West Pacific	20 February 1942 - 15 August 1945
South Pacific	7 August 1942 - 25 June 1944
Madagascar	5 May - 6 November 1942
South East Asia	1942, 1945-1946
Sicily	9 July - 17 August 1943
Italy	3 September 1943 - 22 April 1945
North West Europe	6 June 1944 - 5 May 1945
Greece 1944-45	16 September 1944 - 15 January 1945

The various regiments and units that took part in actions or campaigns are often awarded a 'Battle Honour', this appears on the Regiment or unit's Colour, and is a way by which the Sovereign acknowledges the part the unit played in the action, battle or campaign. Details of how Battle Honours are awarded, which have been awarded and the units receiving them are covered in; 'Battle Honours of the British and Commonwealth Armies' by Anthony Baker, Published by Ian Allen Ltd, Shepperton, Surrey 1986 ISBN 0 7110 1600 3

Information arranged by Regiment for Battle Honours awarded for the First and Second World Wars and on the earlier Battle Honours

Palestine	1945 - 1948
Malaya	1948 - 1960
Korean War	2 July 1950 - 27 July 1953
Kenya	1952 - 1956
Cyprus	1955 - 1959
Suez	1956
Arabian Peninsula	1957 -1960
Brunei and Borneo	1962 -1966
The Radfan	1964
South Arabia	1964 - 1967
Northern Ireland	1971 - Present
Falkland Islands	2 April - 14 June 1982
Gulf War	2 August 1990 - 3 March 1991

(arranged alphabetically) can be found in 'A Companion to the British Army 1660-1983' by David Ascoli, published by Harrap Ltd 1983. This book also lists the titles by which regiments have been known, lists regimental orders of precedence and illustrates a number of Regimental and Corps Headdress badges.

Information on the Medals awarded for the campaigns and actions mentioned earlier, along with medals awarded for gallantry, can be found in 'Medal Yearbook', which is published annually by Token Publishing Ltd, P.O. Box 14, Honiton, Devon EX14 9YP. In addition to descriptions of the Decorations and Medals, which are nicely illustrated, there is a coloured chart showing the medal ribbons for each medal.

General information on Medals can be found in the series of books written by Peter Duckers and published by Shire Publications Ltd;
British Gallantry Awards 1855 - 2000 Published 2001, ISBN 0 7478 0516 4
British Campaign Medals 1815 - 1914 Published 2000, ISBN 0 7478 0465 6
British Campaign Medals 1914 - 2000 Published 2001, ISBN 0 7478 0515 6

Of course the nature of warfare has changed in this period also. The tactics and scale of warfare

German Flamethowers, Hooge- July 1915

Chateau d'Hooge 2002

have altered dramatically, along with technological advances in the soldier's individual weapons, support weapons, transport, uniforms and equipment.

Some of these changes are highlighted in 'The Fighting Man - The Soldier at War from the Age of Napoleon to the Second World War' by Paul Lewis Isemonger and Christopher Scott, published by Sutton Publishing Ltd, Gloucestershire 1998. ISBN 0 7509 1413 0. This interesting book shows photographic re-enactment of the lifestyles of soldiers through the last 200 years.

Nº.55. A FIELD-AMBULANCE BEHIND THE FIRING LINE, DARDANELLES.

book titles are suggested in the bibliography for further reading on subjects touched upon in the various chapters.

For an excellent general history of the British Army, see 'The Oxford Illustrated History of the British Army' Edited by David Chandler and Ian Beckett, published by Oxford University Press 1995. Along with a chronology of important events in the British Army there are a number of other

If you are interested in a specific campaign or regimental histories, then there are many books available that can give you details on uniforms, tactics, the conditions of the period, as well as the campaigns themselves.

The Keep Military Museum, Dorchester
Lt.Col (Rtd.) Dick Leonard - Curator and *Helen Jones* M.A

Standing imposingly on the Bridport Road leading out of Dorchester, the Keep has a distinctly medieval appearance although it was built in 1879 as a gatehouse and armoury for the Dorsetshire Regiment Depot and training centre. Built by Messrs H Bull and Sons of Southampton it formed part of Marabout Barracks (built at a total cost of some £38,000) that was formally opened by Lieutenant General Prince Edward of Saxe-Weimar in September 1879.

The Depot carried out its training function from 1879 to 1958 with only one break during the Second World War when the barracks was used by the 701st Ordnance Light Maintenance Company and the 1st Quartermaster Company of the American Army. Following the amalgamation of the Devonshire and Dorsetshire Regiments in 1958 the decision was taken to have the Depot of the new Regiment in Exeter. 1960 saw the barracks sold off to the Dorset County Council and the Royal Mail. The Keep remained as the Museum of the Dorset Regiment and in 1994 the present title was adopted when the Keep became the Military Museum of the counties of Devon and Dorset.

The Keep (or gateway) is built in random rockwork Ridgeway stone with 2 massive towers that rise to a height of 20 metres (65 feet). At the base of the structure was the guardroom, prisoner's cells and exercise yard. Although one cell remains as a part of

the museum display the others have been converted to provide wash room amenities and the exercise yard is now a cafeteria. The entrance to the Keep today is through the old guardroom now converted to a modern shop. On moving through to the Gallery of the Regiments you pass over what was the main roadway from the town into the barracks. As you pass through the jungle display visitors should look up and note that the ceiling is convex in shape as this was the old powder room and the design was to help cushion any explosion.

Once through this room you face the old lift that was used to haul weapons and heavy stores to the upper floors. The lift, made by Burnett and Company of New Cross, is a grade 2 listed piece of industrial machinery and the Keep itself is a Grade 2 listed building. The spiral staircases lead to 3 successive floors above that were used to store 2,500 weapons and their accoutrements. The Keep now holds the artefacts of 'The Queen's Own Dorset Yeomanry', 'The Royal Devon Yeomanry', 'The Devonshire Regiment', 'The Dorsetshire Regiment' and 'The Devonshire & Dorset Regiment'. Campaign equipment, military decorations and medals, uniforms, weapons and paintings from the formation of these Regiments in the 17th Century to the present day are housed in the building.

Our public floors have a variety of displays, including

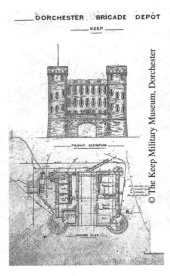

DORCHESTER BRIGADE DEPOT
KEEP

© The Keep Military Museum, Dorchester

medals, uniforms and weapons. Special attention is given to our five Victoria Cross winners, including Lieutenant Colonel H. Jones of Falklands War fame, who was once a member of the Devon and Dorsets. Our Museum tells the story of our Regiments and men, and the social history of the times in which they lived and fought. We also have Hitler's desk! We include topical displays, linking in with current affairs, which are changed on a regular basis. We offer three children's trails to keep the younger visitors amused, and our touch-screen computers and introductory video offer audio-visual interest as well.

Having viewed the exhibitions on each of the floors by ascending the West Tower (the one with the old lift) a visitor can gain access to the roof to be met with spectacular views of Dorchester and the surrounding countryside. Ask at reception for a map of the town to help you identify the landmarks you see around you. The East Tower does not provide a means of getting onto the roof, as the isolation room was located at the top of this tower. Soldiers suffering from *the itch* (the common term for Scabies) were isolated and

disinfected in this room which is now used to house the main water tank for the Museum.

The Keep is open to the public from 9.30am-5pm, Mondays to Saturdays with last admissions at 4pm. In July and August we are open on Sundays from 10am-4pm.
We are closed on Mondays from October until the end of February and during the Christmas holiday period. As a private charity, we need to make a small admission charge of £3 per adult, £2 for children, OAPs and students. Family tickets and group discounts are also available. We welcome tours and are happy to provide educational activities on the theme of World War 1 or World War 2 for pre-booked for school parties. The Museum is 'wheelchair friendly', with a modern lift – only the roof being inaccessible to wheelchairs. There is a shop selling military books, family history research books, regimental souvenirs and gifts on a military theme. We also offer a mail order service. "The Plassey Tea Room" is open from Easter until the end of September and sells a range of home made cakes, light snacks and drinks. We have our own small, free car park, for the use of Museum visitors only!

As a Regimental Museum, we are happy to help researchers with enquiries about the Devon & Dorset Regiments and the men who served with them. We do not, however, hold any personal service records, and are usually unable to answer queries about individual soldiers without this. We need the soldier's name, unit, rank and number if possible. Once you have the service record, we can help you with details of actions and locations, regimental history and perhaps photos or extracts from the many scrapbooks, diaries, journals and documents in our archives. No charge is made for this, but donations are very welcome to cover the cost of postage, photocopying, archive conservation and staff! If writing to us, please enclose as much relevant information as you can find and please allow 2-4 weeks for a reply. Our archives are not open to the public, but we will arrange for one of our research volunteers to search our records on your behalf. Staff and volunteers are currently undertaking a project to transcribe and publish some of the many war diaries in the Museum's collection, and these should be of interest to historians and researchers alike.

We also publish our own guide to researching military ancestors. Although the focus of this booklet is the county of Dorset and the Dorset Regiments, it does include plenty of general advice as well as addresses and URLs to help the new researcher locate the records needed for successful military research. A fully illustrated CD Rom telling the history of the regiments is also available. Contact us for more details. Those of you wishing to combine military with family history research may find it useful to know that we are located almost next door to the Dorset County Record Office, and just a few minutes walk from the Reference Library. The Dorset County Museum is also close by.

If you have not visited recently do call in and

© The Keep Military Museum, Dorchester

The Keep was built in 1879 as the Gateway to the Dorset Regimental Depot. This photograph, from an original taken in 1881, shows the first Quarter Guard. The avenue of trees on the left is now the A35 Trunk Road.
© The Keep Military Museum, Dorchester

discover the military and social history of the men and women who have given service to their county and country.

For more information, please contact us at:
The Keep Military Museum,
1 Bridport Road,
Dorchester,
Dorset,
DT1 1RN
Tel:01305 264066
Fax: 01305250373
Email: keep.museum@talk21.com
Visit our website http://keepmilitarymuseum.org

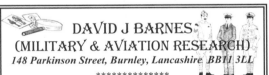

A Journey of Exploration Along The Western Front

Michael Kelly BA. (Hons) - Group Leader Bartletts Battlefield Journeys

Our vehicle bumped from side to side with the motion transmitted from the uneven Belgian road surface. It was the third time that I had ridden this stretch of road and now, after close examination of the 1917 trench map I felt that my three guests and I were at last making an achievement. One of my guests Ron was visibly strained. We were looking for the area of action where his father had been wounded. Clearly the direction of the road remained as it did in 1917 but the little farm where the Kings Royal Rifle Corps had passed by was harder to find. We turned onto a narrow uneven track; I had seen the corner of a farmhouse jutting Out from some trees. Was there a name to the farm that could assist us? Voila, there it was, the name of the farmhouse was the same named building on the trench map. Ron was ecstatic

As a tour leader working on the Western Front Battlefields, moments such as these are indescribably rich and rewarding. Many of our guests travel thousands of miles to find the ground/grave of their relatives. For many families it is the first opportunity to visit the battlefields and the feeling of well being that is abound having made this achievement is always a high point.

Of course many of the farms, trees and forests are no longer in existence, but to the trained eye there is evidence of the 'War to end all Wars'. French and Belgian farmers use in abundance the Great War picket fences that once supported the miles of barbed wire. Certain areas are still pock-marked by the fierce artillery barrages that once pounded the landscape, and preserved trenches can still be found The farmers staunchly guard their rights of privacy in the woods, but if permission can be gained to enter them, without application of too much imagination one can step back 80 years to these battles to gain yards not miles

I once took 11 guests to the Somme and Ypres. Each party member had a particular quest in mind; to find Grandfather's grave, to explore the

Thiepval Memorial

The Menin Gate, Ypres

battlefield where Uncle was killed; to simply look at the name of a relative killed and without a known grave and inscribed on the Thiepval Memorial or the Menin Gate. In addition to this, I had researched the particular units involved in order to ascertain the area of involvement just prior to the relative's demise. Armed with copies of trench maps and unit histories, war diaries and GPS, it was amazing how my guests, none of whom had met prior to the journey became involved in each other's objectives. There were moments of sadness as recognition of the truth finally dawned upon them; there were also moments of great hilarity as we realised the navigational errors we had made and finished up in some unholy place, a great distance from where we had intended to be. We were not ashamed, sadness and laughter were emotions that all of our soldiers witnessed in the Great War.

There is now great beauty to be found on these fields of what was once described by Sassoon as 'A sunlit picture of hell.' I know of no place I would rather be than in the grounds of the cemetery at Authuille close to Thiepval on the Somme. An Infantry Officer at the height of the Somme battles witnessed the same solitude in 1916. Charles Doui in his book The Weary Road' described this area during a burial and a lull in the fighting,

'One evening I stood there looking over the broad marshes of the Ancre and the great mass of Aveluy Wood beyond. There was a lull in the firing, and everything was still. The sun was setting, perhaps the majesty of Nature had stayed for one moment the hand of the Angel of Death. The river and marshes were a sea of gold, and the trees of the wood were tinged with fire, a cool evening breeze blew gently through the graves of our dead.'

The eloquence of Doui is untainted by his experiences. School children, students of history and those who believe visiting the Battlefields to be a glorification of war should read his book. The majesty Charles Doui witnessed here at Authuille should be experienced by all.

American Battle Monuments Commission - Cambridge American Cemetery

The American Battle Monuments Commission (ABMC), established by law in 1923, is an independent agency of the Executive Branch of the US Government. The Commission is responsible for commemorating the services and achievements of United States Armed Forces where they have served since April 6, 1917 (the date of US entry into World War I) through the erection of suitable memorial shrines; for designing, constructing, operating and maintaining permanent US military cemeteries and memorials in foreign countries; for controlling the design and construction of US military monuments and markers in foreign countries by other US citizens and organizations, both public and private; and encouraging the maintenance of such monuments and markers by their sponsors.

Cambridge American Cemetery, 30.5 acres in extent, was constructed on the site of a temporary cemetery established in 1944 on land donated by the University of Cambridge. After the war, it was selected as the only World War II American cemetery in the British Isles. A high portion of those buried here were temporarily interred in England and Northern Ireland and represent American servicemen and women who served as crew members of British based American aircraft. Most of the others died in the invasions of North Africa and France as well as the training areas of the United Kingdom and the waters of the Atlantic.

The cemetery is situated on the north slope of a hill from which Ely Cathedral, 14 miles distant, can be seen on clear days. It is framed by woodlands on the west and south. The road to Madingley runs along the cemetery's northern boundary.

The memorial chapel, is built from Portland stone, as is St. Paul's Cathedral and many other monumental buildings in London. On the north face of the Memorial are five pylons, each inscribed with one of the years from 1941 to 1945, during which the United States participated in World War II.

The entrance of the Memorial at the west end is framed by two pylons. On the pediment above them is the dedication: TO THE GLORY OF GOD AND IN MEMORY OF THOSE WHO DIED FOR THEIR COUNTRY 1941 - 1945. The main entrance doors are of teakwood. They bear bronze models of various military equipment and naval vessels. On the South exterior of the Memorial is a great map which depicts each location in the United Kingdom where an American unit or battalion or larger size was stationed during WWII. The places where units of brigade-size or larger were stationed are indicated by name. The map also shows the principal air and sea approach routes to Great Britain from the United States. It is embellished with the sculptured coat of arms of the United States and the United Kingdom. The significance of the colors and signs used is explained in the legend.

Inside the Memorial, the impressive map. "The Mastery of the Atlantic - The Great Air Assault," is the outstanding feature of the museum room. The wall bearing the map is of Portland stone. On the map, the lower land elevations are indicated in polished Portland stone. while the higher elevations are in polished Hauteville. Lunel Clair, and Lunel Fonce marble. Below the map are seven plaques, six of which contain key maps recording the development of the war against Germany and Japan. The seventh, a bronze plaque in the centre, bears a description of the operations portrayed by the

great map.

The seal of the War and Navy Departments as well as the principal decorations awarded our Armed Services are depicted in glass panels beside and above the main door to the Memorial. They include the Air Medal. Distinguished Flying Cross. Silver Star. Distinguished Service Cross, Medal of Honor - Army. Distinguished Service Medal - Army. Soldier's Medal, Purple Heart, Bronze Star, Legion of Merit, Navy Cross. Medal of Honor - Navy, Distinguished Service Medal - Navy, and Navy and Marine Corps Medal. The other windows of the Memorial contain stained-glass replicas of the seals of the States of the Union arranged from left to right, in the order in which they entered the Union. Above them are the seals of the United States (obverse and reverse), the District of Columbia, Alaska, Hawaii and Puerto Rico.

The chapel is reached through a teakwood doorway above which is the following inscription in bronze characters: INTO THY HANDS O LORD. The words FAITH and HOPE in bronze letters are set into the chancel rail. A cloth of mail is spread over the Portland stone altar on which is set a large bronze cross. At the altar base rests the Tablets of Moses. Flanking the altar are two large ornamental candelabra embellished with mosaic. A mosaic depicting the Archangel trumpeting the arrival of the Resurrection and the Last Judgment covers the wall above the altar and continues across the entire ceiling of the Memorial, with pictures of ghostly aircraft. accompanied by angels. making their final flight. The ship and aircraft depicted above the altar memorialize the members of the naval and air forces who are buried or commemorated at the cemetery.

The tablets of the missing are inscribed on a wall of Portland stone. which is 427 feet long. Recorded on the Tablets are the names and particulars of 5126 Missing in Action, lost or buried at sea, or those "Unknown" whose remains were either never found or positively identified prior to interment. An asterisk points out those subsequently identified. Along the wall are four statues carved by English craftsmen: a soldier, an airman, a sailor and a Coast Guardsman. The paving is of English York sandstone.

The graves area contains 3,812 headstones: Stars of David for those who professed the Jewish faith and Latin crosses for all others. They represent about 42 percent of those temporarily interred in England and Northern Ireland. The headstones in the fan-shaped graves are arranged in seven curved grave plots. A-G. The headstones within the plots are aligned in seven concentric arcs whose wide sweep across the green lawns may best be viewed from the mall near the Memorial. From the north edge of the flagpole platform another feature of the pattern is evident - the headstones are also aligned like the spokes of a wheel. Among the headstones are two which represent burials of two and three servicemen, respectively, whose names are known but could not be separately identified. Their remains were buried together and bronze tablets over the graves record their names.

The plantings which complement the woodland frame on the west and south include rows of Japanese pagoda trees, rose of Sharon, firethorn, forsythia, and cotoneaster. The reflecting pool is bordered by roses. Double-pink hawthorn trees line the north side of the graves area. Each grave plot is enclosed by a boxwood hedge. Tulip trees, catalpa, beech, oak, and liquidambar (sweetgum) are also present.

The architects for the cemetery and memorial were Perry, Shaw. Hepburn and Dean of Boston, Massachusetts. The landscape architects were the Olmsted Brothers, Brookline. Massachusetts. The mosaic is by Francis Scott Bradford, of Cornwall Bridge. Connecticut. The battle map was designed by the American artist Herbert Gute and the statues along the Tablets of the Missing were designed by Wheeler Williams, New York City. Construction of the cemetery was completed and the dedication ceremony held on 16 July 1956.

Cambridge American Cemetery
Coton., Cambridge, England
CB3 7PH
Tel: (44) 01954 210350
Fax: (44) 01954.211130
Email:
    Cambridge.Cemetery @ abmc-er org

Website: http://www.abmc.gov
Information and editorial provided by James A Schoenecker,
The Superintendent,
Cambridge American Cemetery

Eden Camp ~ The People's Museum

Nick Hill - Museum Archivist

Camp Origins

In early 1942, a small contingent of Army personnel, under the command of a Sergeant, arrived at Malton, midway between York and Scarborough in North Yorkshire. Their task was to construct a barbed wire enclosure and erect tents to house the steady flow of enemy prisoners of war captured in North Africa. The site was named Eden Camp and the first inmates were two hundred and fifty Italian prisoners. These prisoners were put to work constructing a larger permanent camp, consisting of forty five huts. The Italians were at the Camp from 1942 to 1944, then the Germans from 1944 to 1948. While at the Camp the prisoners worked on the local farms under the control of the War Agricultural Officer.

In 1986, local business man Stan Johnson discovered that POW Camp 83 was still generally intact and that thirty five of the original huts were in roughly the same condition as when the last of the 1,200 inmates left for the 'Fatherland" in 1948. Mr Johnson bought the site and initially invested £750,000 to create, within the original Camp, the world's only Modern History Theme Museum. In his own words, Stan wanted Eden Camp to act 'as a tribute to all the people who served during the Second World War. From the school children, to the people in the home, the factories and all branches of the services'.

It was this desire that makes Eden Camp such a unique place. Many visitors recognize that the museum serves as a tribute to the 'ordinary' men, women and children who experienced the events of World War Two at first hand. Many of them are keen to be part of the tribute and share their own or their families' experiences.

Approximately 85% of all the exhibits on display have been donated or given on loan by members of the public. They visit and then go home and search through their drawers, cupboards, attics, cellars and garages to re-discover their own items of wartime history. In order to build up our archives over the last 15 years that Eden Camp has been open as a museum, we have been pleased to accept everything that has been brought in or offered - from a brass button to an armoured car. This means that a large part of the archives contain 'personal' items - photographs, documentation and items of kit that belonged to specific individuals. All that you see on display around the museum accounts for approximately 50% of Eden Camp's full collection of wartime memorabilia.

Every item that is brought or sent into the museum is catalogued and recorded in both a conventional paper filing system and on a computer database. The database now contains in excess of 40,000 records and entries and, although not yet directly accessible to the general public, the methods which we use to record and store items does mean that any and every item can normally be located and retrieved within a couple of minutes.

As the veterans of the Second World War grow older, many of them have brought in their memorabilia to ensure that it is in a safe place and that it will be looked after once they have passed on. In the same way, many families see Eden Camp as the best location to keep family items together rather than spreading them around the family which could eventually lead to items being accidentally lost or misplaced.

One of the greatest compliments that the museum receives is from those veterans and families who wish to donate medals. There are over 90 sets of medals on display in the Garrison Cinema Bar corridor - Hut 19. Each set of medals are mounted in their own display cabinet with a photograph and a written history of the donator. The medal cabinets also contain other items of personal memorabilia - cap badges, insignia, berets,

Identity tags, Pay Books, trophies etc.

One of the most impressive things about the medal displays is that they represent an extremely wide and diverse cross section of men and women who answered their country's call to arms. Those represented include Harold Eardley and Stan Hollis, both holders of the Victoria Cross. Flight Sergeant James 'Ginger' Lacey DFM who shot down the German plane that bombed Buckingham Palace and went on to be Britain's highest scoring Battle of Britain Hurricane pilot. Elizabeth Ward, an English girl who went to America to work as a housemaid but who ended up working in the Ceramics plant of the Linde Air Products Company, Tonawanda, New York which contributed towards the Manhattan Project - the creation and construction of the Atom Bomb.

Marjorie Philpot's Imperial Service and British Empire medals are also displayed. With the outbreak of war, Marjorie went to work in a munitions factory in Luton inspecting ammunition and testing bombs. Later she worked on Barrage Balloons at RAF Cardington in Bedfordshire. She also dedicated 26 years of her life to collecting and promoting the National Savings Scheme.

Finding Old Friends, Family Members and Forces Reunion.

Many families donate items in memory of loved ones. One of the simplest donations is a photograph. Hut 22 - Forces Reunion was specifically created so that families, friends or veterans themselves could have their photograph displayed. Hut 22 now contains over 1000 photographs, and has proved to be the instigator and source of many happy reunions. A number of visitors have also identifyed family members in group shots. This has led to us putting them in contact with the person who originally donated the photograph which has subsequently led to the donator providing the person enquiring with details about where their father/mother served and other previously unknown (some good, some bad!)

information. Some visitors have also picked up on the surnames and 'family likenesses' of some of those featured in Hut 22 which has resulted in the reuniting of long lost cousins and Uncles/Aunts.

The Home Front

Many of the original PoW accommodation huts have been re-equipped to portray the social and civilian history of Britain from 1939 to 1945. So many Museums simply display exhibits in cabinets and on walls and are pretty dull affairs, but not Eden Camp. Realistic tableaux, with moving figures, authentic sounds and smells have been created to "transport you back in time". In one scene there is a living room of a typical wartime home in Britain. The family are seated in front of the fire, listening to the radio as Chamberlain announces "the declaration of war". You see the man move his arm to adjust the wireless set, the woman breathes, the tin bath sits in front of the flickering fire and the scene comes alive.

Each hut covers a different aspect of the story, starting with the rise of the Nazi Party, Hitler and The Outbreak of War. Other topics include: Rationing, the Utility Scheme, 'Save It' Campaigns, Evacuees, Propaganda, Home Guard, Home Front, The Blitz, Air Raid and Gas Precautions, Animals at War, The Street at War, Women at War, The Land Army and Timber Girls, The Munition Factories, The Observer Corps, The Auxiliary Fire Service, The WVS, The Red Cross, Civil Defence, The Rescue Services, The Bevin Boys, etc.

Military Conflicts

Other huts have been allocated military themes – War at Sea and U-boats, LDV & The Home Guard, Bomber Command, Path Finders, R.E. & R.A.F. Bomb Disposal, S.O.E., Escapers and Evaders, Resistance, Women at War, The life of a Prisoner of War etc.

From 1990 to 1995 a series of huts were opened, creating a "Museum within a Museum". In these huts the military and political events of the Second World War around the world are covered in detail. Scenes such as Dunkirk, The War in the Desert, War at Sea, The Dambusters, The Great Escape, D-Day, V.E. and V.J. Days etc can be found along with displays covering The Holocaust, The Middle East, The Far East, Italy, Europe etc. In 1995 the museum also reconstructed (in Hut 29), from archive photographs, the Chapel which the PoW's had built whilst held captive.

Rolls of Honour

The Eden Camp Chapel acts as a memorial to all those that have been killed as a result of military conflict throughout the 20th Century. Its walls are lined with dozens of plaques dedicated to Associations, Regiments and other military and civilian groups and bodies. Many Associations and regional branches of Associations combine a reunion with the dedicating of a memorial plaque or laying up of a Standard. Some of the plaques list individual names - Rolls of Honour. Other Rolls of Honour can be found incorporated into a number of displays around the site, whilst more are held within the museum's archives. The Chapel allows both young and old to spend a quite moment and reflect on everything that they have seen on site.

During 1992 a prefab was reconstructed on site which is an excellent example of the post war housing efforts. Additionally a Dig for Victory garden was created and a Garden of Remembrance.

Before and After World War Two
The year 2000 saw the refurbishment and redevelopment of Hut 13, Post-WWII Conflicts. This hut covers all those conflicts that British military forces have been involved in worldwide since the end of the Second World War. The hut covers events in Palestine, Cyprus, Egypt, Suez, Malaya, Korea, Kenya, Aden, The Falklands, The Gulf War, Bosnia, Kosovo and information is being added about the recent events in Afghanistan.

The new Millennium also heralded the refurbishment and expansion of Hut 18, The War News Reading Room. Newspaper pages from virtually every day of the war can be browsed through to see what was happening between 1939 and 1945, whilst the media theme was extended to include different forms of communication and media presentation with a large display of radio and telecommunications equipment covering most of the 20th Century.

September 2001 saw the opening of Hut 11, which takes you back to World War One. Visitors experience what life was like in the trenches, brought to life with realistic sights, sounds and smells. The second part of the exhibition is more of a traditional format with text boards and display cases containing documentation, photographs and artifacts that relate to all aspects of the Great War.

'For you the war is over'
2002 marked the beginning of a major refurbishment of Hut 10 - Life as a Prisoner of War. This display will incorporate the wealth of material and memorabilia that has been brought into the museum over the last 15 years by ex-PoW's, Guards and the civilians who befriended PoW's. It will cover the life of both Allied and Axis PoW's. The display will be on going and will contain totally unique material and personal experiences and stories.

Being housed within the grounds of an original PoW camp has led to Eden Camp becoming a focus for PoW related enquiries, not only from within Britain, but also around the world, mainly via the internet. In the past we have had visitors

call into our Office and enquire as to whether we have lists of names of the PoW's that were held at Eden Camp.

When we first opened, we did try and source such information, in fact we tried to locate any 'official' documentation relating to Eden Camp being established and used as a PoW Camp between 1942-1948. Following correspondence with the MoD, the IWM, the PRO and the British and International Red Cross, the nearest we came were addresses in Germany and Italy of the Governmental departments to which documentation relating to PoW's was returned to help with prisoner repatriation in the late 1940's. The only PoW names that we have are those which appear on 100 or so Identity Cards which were donated by an ex-guard who had taken them as a souvenir when the camp said farewell to the last of its prisoners towards the end of 1948. We also have a list of the names of the occupants of one hut which were written on a page from an exercise book and kept by a German PoW who handed the list to us when he revisited his 'old home' shortly after we had opened as a museum.

Legacy of the PoW's
The saddest situation that we have ever had to deal with has actually occurred on four separate occasions. On each occasion we have had a man/woman contact or visit us in the hope that we would be able to provide them with information about an ex-Eden Camp PoW.

As the Prisoners held at Eden Camp were deemed to be of a low security threat they did enjoy a relative amount of freedom and were able to mix with the local population once the war in Europe

answer specific questions relating to the displays and subjects covered on site.

In addition to the museum's many indoor displays, we are always adding to our collection of military vehicles displayed around the site, these include T34, Sherman and Churchill Tanks, Scammel Heavy Recovery Wagon, White M16 half-track, DUKW, a large collection of artillery pieces and full size replica Spitfire and Hurricane aircraft as well as a V1 Doodlebug Flying bomb. Our most recent addition is a gun from a British submarine.

On a number of special days throughout the year, Eden Camp becomes the temporary home of a number of re-enactment teams. This allows visitors to come face to face with 'German' PoWs, British soldiers, an American M.P. or even the great British bobby.

For some light relief, you can visit the Eden Camp Music Hall where you can sit down and watch a puppet show in which some of the great entertainers of the time are portrayed. The audience is invited to join in and sing "We'll meet again".

Eden Camp is a Museum with a difference, it is historical, exciting and appeals to all ages and sexes. There is something for everyone. It is open 10.00am-5.00pm 2nd Monday in January – 23rd December, every day. We are located on the outskirts of the Market town of Malton, on the side of the A64 which runs from Leeds to Scarborough Tel. 01653 697777 Website: www.edencamp.co.uk

had ended. This naturally led to friendships and relationships being formed, the consequences of which has resulted in the four people who learnt, 50 years on, from a dying relative that their father wasn't the man they had been brought up to call dad, but was really a PoW from Eden Camp. We have learnt of similar sad stories around the country. In 2001, a gentleman came over from Germany to Yorkshire. He was trying to trace his half sister. Seriously ill, his father had confided that he had fathered a baby girl whilst a prisoner in Yorkshire, had wanted to stop with the mother and 'do the right thing' but had been forced to return to Germany.

Support of the Veterans

As a nationally recognized military museum we are continually forming partnerships with many different military and civilian veteran groups, Associations and Old Comrade clubs. This in turn has led to many organizations depositing their own collections of memorabilia and archives with us. This has allowed us to establish and create a number of unique exhibitions, for example Escapers and Evaders, Human Torpedoes, The Civil Defence, R.A.F. Bomb Disposal and British Forces in Palestine 1945-48.

The forming of partnerships has also led to the museum hosting a growing number of reunion events which allow veterans to get together and reminisce about the good (or in some cases not so good) old days. These reunions are often quite emotional, with pals meeting up again and being reunited after, in some cases, 50 years. Our main all Services veterans' parade takes place in September. We also host annual reunions for Escapers and Evaders (usually April - May) and veterans of Palestine (October).

As Eden Camp is a privately run museum we do not have any access to official records. However, we do hold files of useful names and addresses that we can pass on to visitors who call in to our Reception or contact us -Veterans Associations, Regimental Museums, official sources of military records etc, and museum staff will endeavour to

British Army Divisions in The First World War
David Barnes

Each Division was composed of several units , the War Office 'Field Service Pocket Book' 1914 gives a typical breakdown of the components and personnel based on 'War Establishment'

When the original six Divisions of the British Expeditionary Force went to war in 1914, they conformed strictly to the numbers laid down in the 'War Establishment'. Divisions formed later could not always adhere to the numbers suggested, particularly as there was a shortage of artillery and these figures are provided as a guide

The following list sets out the type of each division, it's title, major components and the main theatres of war in which they served:

Regular British Divisions
1st Cavalry Division
1st, 2nd, 3rd, 4th and 9th Cavalry Brigades
Western Front - France and Belgium
2nd Cavalry Division
3rd, 4th and 5th Cavalry Brigades
Western Front - France and Belgium
3rd Cavalry Division
6th, 7th, 8th and Canadian Cavalry Brigades
Western Front - France and Belgium Guards Division
1st, 2nd and 3rd Guards Brigades
Western Front - France and Belgium
1st Division
1st Guards, 1st, 2nd and 3rd Infantry Brigades
Western Front - France and Belgium
2nd Division
4th Guards,5th, 6th, 19th and 99th Infantry Brigades
Western Front - France and Belgium
3rd Division
7th, 8th, 9th and 76th Infantry Brigades
Western Front - France and Belgium
4th Division
10th, 11th and 12th Infantry Brigades
Western Front - France and Belgium
5th Division
13th, 14th, 15th and 95th Infantry Brigades
Western Front - France and Belgium; Italian Front Nov 1917 - April 1918; Western Front - France and Belgium
6th Division
16th, 17th, 18th, 19th and 71st Infantry Brigades
Western Front - France and Belgium
7th Division
20th, 21st, 22nd and 91st Infantry Brigades
Western Front - France and Belgium; Italian Front Nov 1917 to end of War
8th Division
23rd, 24th and 25th Infantry Brigades
Western Front - France and Belgium
27th Division
80th, 81st and 82nd Infantry Brigades
Western Front - France and Belgium; Salonika Nov 1915-Feb 1916; Macedonia Front to 30 Sept 1918; Trans Caucasia to Aug 1919
28th Division
83rd, 84th, 85th, 228th and 242nd Infantry Brigades
Western Front - France and Belgium; Egypt Nov 1915;

'War Establishment'. Divisions

CAVALRY DIVISION	Officers	Other Ranks
1 Headquarters	15	81
4 Cavalry Brigades	340	6,532
1 Headquarters Cavalry Divisional Artillery		
	3	17
2 Horse Artillery Brigades	38	1,324
1 Royal Engineer Field Sqn	7	184
1 Signal Squadron	8	198
1 Headquarters Cavalry Division, A.S.C.		
	4	22
4 Cavalry Field Ambulances	24	472
Total in the Field	**439**	**8,830**

CAVALRY BRIGADE		
within a Cavalry Division		
Headquarters	6	41
3 Cavalry Regiments	78	1,569
1 Signal Troop	1	23
Total	**85**	**1,633**

CAVALRY BRIGADE		
not within a Cavalry Division		
Headquarters	7	47
3 Cavalry Regiments	78	1,569
1 Horse Artillery Battery	7	215
1 Ammunition Column	2	115
1 Field Troop	3	74
1 Signal Troop	1	42
1 Cavalry Field Ambulance	6	118
Total	**104**	**2,180**

INFANTRY DIVISION		
1 Headquarters	15	67
3 Infantry Brigades	372	11,793
1 Headquarters Divl Artillery	4	18
3 Field Artillery Brigades	69	2,316
1 Field Artillery (Howitzer) Brigade	22	733
1 Heavy Battery and Ammunition Column	6	192
1 Divisional Ammunition Column	15	553
1 Headquarters Divl Engineers	3	10
2 Royal Engineer Field Companies	12	422
1 Signal Company	5	157
1 Cavalry Squadron	6	153
1 Divisional Train	26	402
3 Field Ambulances	30	672
Total in the Field	**585**	**17,488**

INFANTRY BRIGADE		
Headquarters	4	23
4 Battalions	120	3,908
Total	**124**	**3,901**

Salonika early 1916; Macedonia Front to 30 Sept 1918;
Dardanelles Forts and Turkey to Oct 1923
29th Division
86th, 87th and 88th Infantry Brigades
Gallipoli 1915; Egypt - Suez January - March 1916;
Western Front - France and Belgium

**Territorial Force Mounted Divisions and First Line
Territorial Force Divisions**
1st Mounted Division
*1st, 2nd, 3rd and 4th Mounted Brigades, 1st, 2nd, 3rd
and 4th Cyclist Brigades*
Home Defence
2nd Mounted Division
1st, 2nd, 3rd and 4th Mounted Brigades
Egypt April - August 1915; Suvla; Egypt Nov 1915
2nd/2nd Mounted Division
*1st, 2nd and 3rd Mounted Brigades and 5th Cyclist
Brigade, 11th, 12th and 13th Cyclist Brigades*
Home Defence
3rd Mounted Division

4th Mounted Division
*13th, 14th, 15th, 16th Mounted Brigades, 5th, 6th, 7th
8th Cyclist Brigades*
Home Defence
Yeomanry Division
6th, 8th and 22nd Mounted Brigades
Palestine

42nd (East Lancashire) Division
125th, 126th and 127th Infantry Brigades
Egypt (Suez Canal Defence) Sept 1914 - May 1915;
Gallipoli May 1915 - Jan 1916; Egypt (Suez Canal
Defence) Jan 1916 - Feb 1917; Western Front - France
and Belgium March 1917 to end of War
43rd (Wessex) Division
*Hampshire, South-Western and Devon and Cornwall
Brigades*
India; Battalions to Mesopotamia, Palestine and Aden;
Detachment in Third Afghan War May-Aug 1919
44th (Home Counties) Division
Surrey, Middlesex and Kent Brigades
India; Battalions to Burma and Mesopotamia; 3
Battalions in Third Afghan War May-Aug 1919
45th (2nd Wessex) Division
*2nd/1st Hampshire, 2nd/1st South-Western and 2nd/1st
Devon and Cornwall Brigades*
India; Battalions to Mesopotamia and Palestine;
Detachment in Third Afghan War May-Aug 1919
46th (North Midland) Division
137th, 138th and 139th Infantry Brigades
Detachments to Egypt briefly 1916; Western Front -
France and Belgium
47th (London) Division
140th, 141st and 142nd Infantry Brigades
Western Front - France and Belgium

48th (South Midland) Division
143rd, 144th, 145th Infantry Brigades
Western Front - France and Belgium; Italian Front Nov
1917 to end of War
49th (West Riding) Division
146th, 147th and 148th Infantry Brigades
Western Front - France and Belgium
50th (Northumberland) Division
149th, 150th and 151st Infantry Brigades
Western Front - France and Belgium
51st (Highland) Division
152nd, 153rd and 154th Infantry Brigades
Western Front - France and Belgium
52nd (Lowland) Division
155th, 156th and 157th Infantry Brigades
Egypt June 1915; Gallipoli July 1915 - Jan 1916; Egypt,
Suez Defences March 1916; Palestine March 1917 -
March 1918; Western Front - France and Belgium May
1918 to end of War
53rd (Welsh) Division
158th, 159th and 160th Infantry Brigades
Eastern Mediterranean July - Dec 1916; Egypt (Suez
Canal Defence) Dec 1916; Palestine until Nov 1918;
Egypt Nov-Dec 1918
54th (East Anglian) Division
161st, 162nd and 163rd Infantry Brigades
Eastern Mediterranean July - Dec 1916; Egypt, one
Brigade to Western Desert for Senussi Uprising, (Suez
Canal Defence) April 1916; Palestine until Nov 1918;
Egypt Nov-Dec 1918
55th (West Lancashire) Division
164th, 165th and 166th Infantry Brigades
Western Front - France and Belgium
56th (London) Division
167th, 168th and 169th Infantry Brigades
Western Front - France and Belgium

**Second Line Territorial Force Divisions, Home
Service Divisions and 74th and 75th Divisions**
57th (2nd West Lancashire) Division
170th, 171st and 172nd Infantry Brigades
Western Front - France and Belgium
58th (2nd/1st London) Division
173rd, 174th and 175th Infantry Brigades
Western Front - France and Belgium
59th (2nd North Midland) Division
176th, 177th and 178th Infantry Brigades
Western Front - France and Belgium
60th (2nd/2nd London) Division
179th, 180th and 181st Infantry Brigades
Western Front - France and Belgium June - Nov 1916;
Salonica Dec 1916 - June 1917; Egypt (Suez Canal
Defence July 1916; Palestine
61st (2nd South Midland) Division
182nd, 183rd and 184th Infantry Brigades
Western Front - France and Belgium
62nd (2nd West Riding) Division
185th, 186th and 187th Infantry Brigades
Western Front - France and Belgium
63rd (2nd Northumbrian) Division
*188th, 189th and 190th Infantry Brigades [Became
Royal Naval Div 19 July 1916]*
Western Front - France and Belgium
64th (2nd Highland) Division
191st, 192nd and 193rd Infantry Brigades
Home Defence - Norwich 65th (2nd Lowland) Division
194th, 195th and 196th Infantry Brigades
Ireland
66th (2nd East Lancashire) Division
197th, 198th, 199th and South African Infantry Brigades
Western Front - France and Belgium
67th (2nd Home Counties) Division

Broodseinde

200th, 201st, 202nd and 214th Infantry Brigades
Home Defence - Brentwood / Colchester / Ipswich
68th (2nd Welsh) Division
203rd, 204th and 205th Infantry Brigades
Home Defence - Norfolk / Suffolk
69th (2nd East Anglian) Division
206th, 207th and 208th Infantry Brigades
Home Defence - Yorkshire
70th Division
NEVER FORMED
71st Division
212th, 213th and 214th Infantry Brigades
Home Defence - Essex Coast
72nd Division
215th, 216th and 217th Infantry Brigades
Home Defence - Ipswich
73rd Division
218th, 219th and 220th Infantry Brigades
Home Defence - Essex / Hertfordshire
74th (Yeomanry) Division
229th, 230th and 231st Infantry Brigades
Egypt (Suez Canal Defence) April 1917; Palestine until
April 1918; Western Front - France and Belgium May
1918 to end of War
75th Division
232nd, 233rd and 234th Infantry Brigades
Egypt June 1917; Palestine, Egypt until April 1920

New Army Divisions
9th (Scottish) Division
26th, 27th, 28th and South African Infantry Brigades
Western Front - France and Belgium
10th (Irish) Division
29th, 30th and 31st Infantry Brigades
Gallipoli; Salonika; Macedonia; Egypt;
Palestine
11th (Northern) Division
32nd, 33rd and 34th Infantry Brigades
Suvla; Egypt (Suez Canal Defence);
Western Front - France and Belgium July
1916 to end of the War
12th (Eastern) Division
35th, 36th and 37th Infantry Brigades
Western Front - France and Belgium
13th (Western) Division
38th, 39th and 40th Infantry Brigades
Eastern Mediterranean; Egypt (Suez Canal
Defence); Mesopotamia
14th (Light) Division
41st, 42nd and 43rd Infantry Brigades
Western Front - France and Belgium
15th (Scottish) Division
44th, 45th and 46th Infantry Brigades

Western Front - France and Belgium
16th (Irish) Division
47th, 48th and 49th Infantry Brigades
Western Front - France and Belgium
17th (Northern) Division
50th, 51st and 52nd Infantry Brigades
Western Front - France and Belgium
18th (Eastern) Division
53rd, 54th and 55th Infantry Brigades
Western Front - France and Belgium
19th (Western) Division
56th, 57th and 58th Infantry Brigades
Western Front - France and Belgium
20th (Light) Division
59th, 60th and 61st Infantry Brigades
Western Front - France and Belgium
21st Division
62nd, 63rd, 64th and 110th Infantry
Brigades
Western Front - France and Belgium
22nd Division
65th, 66th and 67th Infantry Brigades
Western Front - France and Belgium; Salonika Nov
1915; Macedonia Front to end of War
23rd Division
24th, 68th, 69th and 70th Infantry Brigades
Western Front - France and Belgium; Italian Front Nov
1917 to end of War
24th Division
17th, 71st, 72nd and 73rd Infantry Brigades
Western Front - France and Belgium
25th Division
7th, 74th, 75th and 76th Infantry Brigades
Western Front - France and Belgium
26th Division
77th, 78th and 79th Infantry Brigades
Western Front - France and Belgium; Salonika Dec 1915;
Macedonia Front to end of War
30th Division
21st, 89th, 90th and 91st Infantry Brigades
Western Front - France and Belgium
31st Division
4th Guards, 92nd, 93rd and 94th Infantry Brigades
Egypt (Suez Canal Defences) Jan - March 1916; Western
Front - France and Belgium 32nd Division
14th, 95th, 96th and 97th Infantry Brigades
Western Front - France and Belgium 33rd Division
19th, 98th, 99th and 100th Infantry Brigades
Western Front - France and Belgium 34th Division
101st, 102nd, 103rd, 111th and 112th Infantry Brigades
Western Front - France and Belgium
35th Division

Neuve Chapelle

New Cemetery

104th, 105th and 106th Infantry Brigades
Western Front - France and Belgium
36th (Ulster) Division
12th, 107th, 108th and 109th Infantry Brigades
Western Front - France and Belgium
37th Division
63rd, 102nd, 103rd, 110th, 111th and 112th Infantry Brigades
Western Front - France and Belgium
38th (Welsh) Division
113th, 114th and 115th Infantry Brigades
Western Front - France and Belgium
39th Division
116th, 117th, 118th, 119th Infantry Brigades
Western Front - France and Belgium
40th Division
119th, 120th and 121st Infantry Brigades
Western Front - France and Belgium
41st Division
122nd, 123rd and 124th Infantry Brigades
Western Front - France and Belgium
63rd (Royal Naval) Division
1st RN, 2nd RN and RM Brigades, and 11th, 189th and 190th Infantry Brigades
Western Front - France and Belgium

More detailed breakdowns on the formation of British Army Divisions can be found in;

Order of Battle of Divisions
Part 1 - The Regular Battalions - 1st, 2nd, 3rd Cavalry; Guards, 1st - 8th, 27th, 28th and 29th

Part 2a - The Territorial Force Mounted Divisions and the First Line Territorial Force Mounted Divisions - 42nd - 56th

Part 2b - The Second Line Territorial Force Divisions - 57th - 69th and Home Service Divisions - 71st - 73rd, 74th and 75th

Parts 3a/3b - New Army Divisions - 9th -26th, 30th - 41st and 63rd (Royal Naval) Division
Also of interest in this series are;

Order of Battle
Part 4 - Army Council, G.H.Q.'s, Armies and Corps
Order of Battle - Overseas Formations
Part 5a - Divisions of Australia, Canada and New Zealand

Part 5b - Indian Army Divisions

All the above can be obtained from Ray Westlake -

Military Books, 53 Claremont, Newport, South Wales NP20 6PLTele 01633 854135.

Some 39 units produced Divisional Histories after the end of the First World War, and these have been very collectable over the years, often commanding priced between £65 - £200 per volume. There are currently plans to reprint these volumes, and they will be available at considerably less cost than an original edition. It should be remembered that an individual soldier is not likely to be named in a Regimental History unless he was awarded a Decoration for Gallantry etc, but these books do give a valuable insight into what tasks units were engaged in and an insight into the conditions men were fighting in

The reprints currently available are;
Guards Division; 2nd Division 1914 -1918; 7th Division 1914 - 1918; 8th Division in the Great War; 9th (Scottish) Division; 19th Division 1914 - 1918; 25th Division; 34th Division 1915 - 1919; 47th (London) Division 1914 - 1919; 50th Division; 51st (Highland) Division; 56th 91st London Territorial Division); 63rd Royal Naval Division

Again all these items are available through Ray Westlake - Military Books (53 Claremont, Newport, South Wales NP20 6PLTele 01633 854135) who is a specialist dealer in Military Books about the First World War

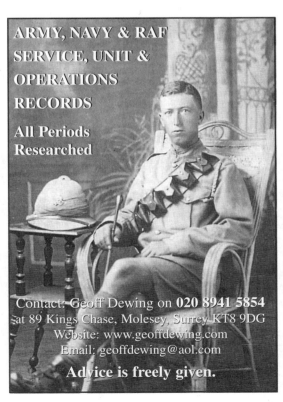

The Luftwaffe Aerial Reconnaissance over the United Kingdom

Nigel J Clarke

On the 1st of January 1938, the German Defence Ministry established the 5th Abteilung of the Luftwaffe General staff. The stated aim of this new unit was to establish an intelligence operation to monitor foreign air forces and prepare detailed target information to be used in time of war. Targets were to include both military and economic infrastructure of potential hostile countries. Major Josef 'Beppo' Schmidt was given command of the unit.

Most of the aerial reconnaissance photography of the United Kingdom was taken by the Luftwaffe between 1939 and 1943. The German High Command had realised early in the war the importance of up to date aerial intelligence, and the Blitzkrieg tactic necessitated the need for accurate reconnaissance of targets, so that subsequent bombing would disrupt the supply lines and industrial strata of the defending country. The Luftwaffe were well prepared for war with the United Kingdom. Their aircraft had been flying over the country, since the late 1930's, at high altitude, producing an aerial photographic mosaic of Britain.

In 1937, the German civilian airline, Lufthansa handed over two civilian versions of the newly developed Heinkel He III to the German military airforce, known as the Luftwaffe. The planes still bore the markings of the civilian airline, though they were secretly adapted for their new spying role. The engines were modified to make them both faster and able to fly at higher altitudes, and the planes were fitted with hidden cameras. These planes flew high altitude reconnaissance missions of over Great Britain, Poland, Russia and the Baltic coast.

The Dornier 17 was another plane used for these early missions. The reconnaissance section was initially based at Oranienburg on the outskirts of Berlin. By 1939, the Luftwaffe had established a very efficient photo reconnaissance capability; there were a total of 23 long-range reconnaissance units. Each unit had its own photo-laboratory, where film was developed, analysed and distributed to the relevant military organisations. Master prints were sent to the intelligence library at Zossen (12 miles south-east of Berlin).

Luftwaffe Reconnaissance over Britain

After the fall of France and the allied retreat from Dunkirk, the German High Command proposed the invasion of the United Kingdom. The whole of the southern coast of the United Kingdom was studied; aerial reconnaissance flights looked for possible invasion landing sites; areas for German bridgeheads were selected; models were made, maps produced, ports were put under intense aerial scrutiny, and the coastal defences of southern England were mapped out.

Generalfeldmarschall Hermann Goering, the commander-in-chief of the Luftwaffe, promised Adolf Hitler complete German domination of the air. The German High Command planned for the invasion of Britain after the fall of France. The initial stages of the operation were to be the elimination of the Royal Air Force as an effective fighting group, and the disruption of all marine and port activities. This first phase of the proposed German invasion was fought in the skies above England.

The Battle of Britain

At the outbreak of the Battle of Britain, the Luftwaffe allocated 2,600 aircraft for the operations against the UK. The reconnaissance section consisted of 140 aircraft, with a further 30 available from the Norwegian sector. The initial reconnaissance missions were undertaken by Dornier bombers to establish the potential strength of the defending British forces. These initial flights were solo missions, and the Luftwaffe reconnaissance planes also dropped flares and small incendiaries to try and goad the Royal Air Force into action.

By 1941, after suffering tremendous losses, and with the start of the war on the Russian front, all thoughts of a British invasion by the Germans had disintegrated. The Luftwaffe had suffered its first major defeat of the war, and the resources of men and aircraft were no longer available for the western sector of German operations. Many of the front line units were transferred to the invasion of Russia and eastern Europe. From 1942, photo-reconnaissance by the Luftwaffe

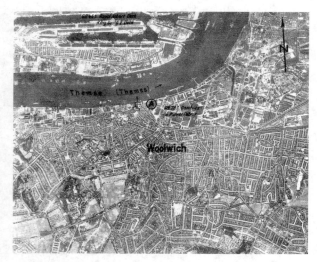

London

Newton Abbot

had become insignificant over the United Kingdom. The use of radar and new and faster fighter cover had made reconnaissance flights very hazardous. The Luftwaffe introduced night-flash photography to beat the fighter screen. A plane would drop a bomb containing an intense flash explosive that lit the target area, while at the same time taking photographs. One of these bombs was discovered, unexploded in Bristol.

The aerial reconnaissance flights continued throughout the war, though never with the same intensity of the 1938-1942 period. The Luftwaffe failed to modernise its fleet of reconnaissance aircraft, and restrictions in supply of new planes curtailed operations. The Germans routinely monitored the country for troop movements and for the selection of bombing targets. Towards the end of the war, the Germans searched for the embarkation points, prior to the D-day landings, but the aircraft available for reconnaissance missions were few, and the skies of Britain were well protected by fighters.

In the last stages of the war, the Luftwaffe introduced the new jet planes, the Arado Av 234 and the Messerschmitt Me 262, as long range reconnaissance aircraft, flying missions over the south east of England, reconnoitring the coastal ports looking for embarkation points for the invasion of France, and to make damage assessments of the German V-rocket attacks.

At the end of the war, vast quantities of material were captured by both the American, British and Russian forces. The British and Americans set up a joint allied operation to collate and sort the information. The material was transferred to R A F Medmenham and the subsequent project was named Operation Dick Tracy. The information obtained from this project was shared by the joint allied command.

The Russian Army captured much of the original Luftwaffe reconnaissance records which had been stored near Berlin, but as the fighting drew close, the library was transferred to river barges. While they were being transported away from the fighting, the barges were attacked and destroyed, and it is thought most of this collection was lost. Other reconnaissance archives did exist at military bases in Germany and the occupied countries, and it was from these sources that most of the present records come.

After the war, the Luftwaffe records were eagerly sought by both the West and the Eastern block countries. The Soviets were interested in intelligence about Western Europe, whilst the only photographic records of Russia and the former Eastern Block countries available to the Allies prior to the American spy flights were the Luftwaffe records. Much of the material remained the domain of the interested intelligence services. The American collection was not released for public access till the 1970's, and even some of this material appears to be censored.

Adolf Hitler's Aerial Survey of Great Britain and Ireland.

The aerial photographs in this collection wast the first ever aerial survey of the United Kingdom. There is a list at www.njcpublications.demon.co.uk The photographs are now over fifty years old, but they still have many modern uses: from environmental research on such topics as the loss of hedgerows; the calculation of coastal erosion; to soil contamination from heavy industries and research on family history.

My initial interest in these aerial reconnaissance photographs had little to do with any concern about the workings of the German War machine of the Second World War. I was fascinated by the changes of the landscape that had occurred over the last fifty years: the loss of coastline, hedges, farms and woodland. I wanted to know what my local town looked like from the air fifty years ago.

I had originally found some old and worn aerial photographs of Dorset, and with the aid of a local town map identified the towns in the pictures. The changes I noticed were immense. New roads had replaced village lanes, roads had become wider, housing and trading estates had all mushroomed on the outskirts of towns. In many cases it was hard to identify the towns photographed by the Luftwaffe fifty years ago. Bomb damage and planners had created change on an enormous scale.

Portishead

A local newspaper contacted me about the photographs, and printed a view of Weymouth, taken by the Luftwaffe in 1939, under the heading, "Adolf Hitler's Dorset Holiday Snaps".
The interest in the photographs was tremendous, and I received numerous requests for copies of the photos from individuals, museums and businesses. I also received many letters about the pictures, which helped me to fill in the background to the locations and subject of the photographs.

In the summer of 1994, I was contacted by a Mr Phillips, who had seen some photographs of Exeter taken by the Luftwaffe, which the local paper had published. During the Second World War, Mr Phillips' father had been a staff driver to General Horrocks, and had served throughout France and Germany. Towards the end of the war, while waiting for the General at a newly liberated Luftwaffe airfield in northern France, Mr Phillips decided to explore some of the subterranean command bunkers, abandoned by the German airforce. The airfield had been hurriedly evacuated and many of the rooms were littered with documents. In one of the bunkers was an operations briefing room, and scattered about were hundreds of photographs of Britain. Staff driver Phillips filled his tunic up with the most interesting and at the end of the war brought the photographs back to his home in Devon. The photographs were soon forgotten and left to gather dust, in an old box, on the top shelf, behind the counter at a small agricultural merchant's shop, in Exeter.

Mr Phillips died in 1993, and his son discovered the box containing the collection of photographs, and telephoned me after reading the article in his local newspaper about the aerial photographs. I was able to examine these unique prints, and have been allowed to include them in this book, for which I am grateful.

There is one photograph in the collection that amused me. During the war, Sir John Betjeman published a poem which said ,"Come Friendly Bombs Fall On Slough", a town which he though had little architectural merit and would have been improved by bombing.

Use of information by the Luftwaffe.
A target folder for the United Kingdom would contain up to six documents. The main part would have been the operation plan which would give the location, description and other topographical details about the target. The pack also included an extract from the British Ordnance Survey which was re-scaled by the Germans to either 1:100,000 or 1:50,000 depending upon the target.

Further documents would normally have included both oblique and vertical annotated aerial photographs, with the bombing area marked in red, and details about the target, such as size and description. Also included was a large scale extract of the ordnance survey showing all the nearby features. It is these photographs that form the main section of this book.

Nigel J Clarke has written and published two books on the Luftwaffe Archives:
Adolf Hitler's Holiday Snaps
(covers the South west of the England)
Adolf Hitler's Home Counties Holiday Snaps
(covers London and the home counties)
Nigel J Clarke Publications, Unit 2, Russell House, Lym Close, Lyme Regis, Dorset DT7 3DE
Tel:and Fax: 01297 442513
Email: mail@njcpublications.demon.co.uk
Website: www.njcpublications.demon.co.uk

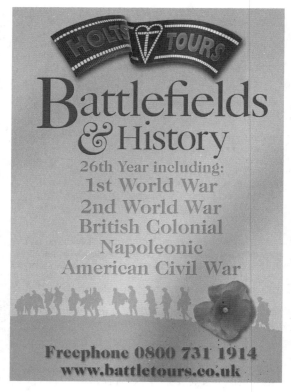

HMS Belfast ~ Imperial War Museum
Nick Hewitt - *Temporary Exhibitions Officer*

HMS *Belfast* is a modified *Southampton* class cruiser. She was launched in March 1938 and served throughout the Second World War. Badly damaged by a German magnetic mine in November 1939, she was repaired and went on to escort convoys to Russia **(Fig 1)**, and play a leading part in the destruction of the German battle cruiser *Scharnhorst* at the Battle of North Cape on Boxing Day, 1943. In June 1944 she provided fire support for the D-Day landings and in 1945 she sailed for the Far East but the Second World War ended before she saw action against the Japanese.

In 1949 HMS *Belfast* was flagship during the Yangtse River incident, when HMS *Amethyst,* a small British warship, was trapped in the Yangtse River by Chinese Communist gun batteries. Between 1950 and 1952 HMS *Belfast* served off the coast of Korea during the Korean War, the last time her guns fired in anger. She continued to serve with the Royal Navy until 1965, and in 1971 she became the first warship to be saved for the nation since Nelson's flagship HMS *Victory.* She is now moored near Tower Bridge as a branch of the Imperial War Museum. **(Fig 2)**

HMS *Belfast* is the only big-gun armoured warship from the Second World War remaining in Europe, and her permanent displays offer a unique opportunity for those researching the Royal Navy service of an ancestor to understand the nature of the life they lived. Much of the ship is open to the public, including all of her upper decks, her boiler and engine rooms, her six inch turrets, shell rooms and magazines, officer's cabins, galley and sick bay. Restored mess-decks recreate both the harsh conditions experienced by those who served aboard HMS *Belfast* in Arctic waters in 1943, and the relative comfort enjoyed by those who served aboard for her post-war cruises in the Far East.

On 31st October 2002 a new permanent exhibition , "Life at Sea" opened on board HMS *Belfast*. Designed to complement "HMS *Belfast* in War and Peace", the existing historical exhibition, which tells the story of the ship, the new exhibition will concentrate on the lives and experiences of the ship's companies during her various commissions and so as much use as possible will be made of eyewitness accounts and personal testimonies, particularly sound recordings.

The exhibition is to be particularly relevant and accessible to schools and a key feature is a range of interactive displays which can be used by the ship's Education Staff for class teaching. However, "Life at Sea" is intended to appeal to all of the ship's visitors, and it is hoped that the personal testimonies will be of particular interest to those with an ancestor who served in the Royal Navy during the Second World War.

For further details about HMS *Belfast* or the new exhibition, contact:
Nick Hewitt
Temporary Exhibitions Officer
HMS *Belfast*, Morgan's Lane, Tooley St
London SE1 2JH Tel: (020)7940 6343
Email: nhewitt@iwm.org.uk

Fig 2 Resplendent in her wartime dazzle paint, HMS *Belfast*
in the Pool of London
© Imperial War Museum

A Guide to Military Ephemera
David Barnes

If members of the family served in the armed forces, it is not unusual for odd items from their service to be kept in the family. Soldiers would often 'liberate' some item from the enemy or a place they passed through or retained an item of kit as a 'souvenir'.

During the First World War, for example, items made from brass shell cases were popular, these could be a complete, empty shell case, which was polished and placed by the hearth of the family home as a receptacle for the poker for the coal fire. The brass could be worked and by using other bits and pieces, such as empty bullet cases, brass buttons etc, the British 'Tommy' produced all kinds of 'trench art', such as letter openers, with the name of an town, such as Ypres, worked in the brass, cut down shell cases for tobacco or trinkets, representations of tanks, guns and aircraft.

There could be other items in the house that contains odd items. Check out that old tin that has buttons in it, you might be surprised at that you find. There can be brass buttons in there that could lead to clues to tracing a relative's service. However it should be pointed out that both brass and plastic buttons exist which depict the Royal Arms, unfortunately these were on general issue to a lot of units and are not helpful when searching for clues and you need to look a little further.

Uniform Cap Badge and Buttons

By far the easiest way to identify a unit is to find a cap badge, shoulder title or button. These can usually identify a regiment or unit and from there you can try to find regimental history etc

Again a word of caution, soldiers being souvenir collectors sometimes exchange cap badges with men in other regiments, so any material found may not necessarily lead to the correct identification of your relative's unit.

It should also be remembered that men transferred from unit to unit so it could also be possible that the person you are researching did have more than one unit's cap badge issued to him.

The following books listed cover Military, Fire,

Police, Transport as well as Civilian badges and buttons and are excellent for identification purposes. Collectors/Researchers may find these can be used on a regular basis for identifying items in their collection. A number of the books listed are out-of-print but you may be able to borrow copies from libraries or buy copies of them on the second-hand market or through specialist book dealers.

Akers, MA. 1985. *British Fire Service Cap Badges - Volume 1 - 1974-1985*. ISBN 0951093207: MA Akers
Akers, MA. 1989. *British Fire Service Cap Badges and Buttons - Volume 2 - 1947-1974*. ISBN 0951093215: MA Akers.
An excellent book with full colour photographs of every cap badge in the period covered (1947-1974). Buttons are described but not illustrated.
Audax, CE. 1992. *Badge Backings and Special Embellishments of the British Army*. ISBN 0951434209: UDR Benevolent Fund.
A superb unique reference work - the only book on this subject. Many pictures and information direct from the regiments concerned.
Baily's. 2000. *Baily's Hunting Directory*. ISBN 0953318109: Pearson Publishing.
Describes hunt uniforms and illustrates hunt buttons for the UK, Ireland, America, the Commonwealth and Europe. The most useful book dealing with hunt buttons
Bennett, RW. 1994. *Badges of the Worcestershire Regiment*. ISBN 0952423103: RW Bennett
Bloomer, WH & KD. 1973. *Scottish Regimental Badges 1793-1971 including Commonwealth Forces*. ISBN 0853684294: Arms and Armour Press.
Bouchery, J. *The British Soldier. Volume 1 From D-Day to VE-Day*. Histoire & Collections, Paris. The British Tommy in North West Europe 1944-1945, covers Uniforms, Insignia and Equipment. Excellent colour photographs throughout
Bouchery, J. *The British Soldier. Volume 2 From D-Day to VE-Day*. Histoire & Collections, Paris. The British Tommy in North West Europe 1944-1945, covers Organisation, Armament, Tanks and Vehicles. Excellent colour photographs throughout
Bragg, RJ & Turner, R.. 1979. *Parachute Badges and Insignia of the World*. ISBN 0713708824: Blandford Press Ltd.
Bragg, RJ & Turner, R. 1985. *Parachute Wings*. ISBN 0950642622: Peter A Heims Ltd.
This book is one of the major references in the field of military badge collecting. Each badge is numbered and many badge dealers refer to their stock using 'Bragg and Turner' numbers from this book and their earlier similar work.
Burns, KV. 1986. *Badges and Battle Honours of HM Ships*. ISBN 0907771262: Maritime Books
Carroll, W. 1997. *Eagles Recalled*. ISBN 0764302442: Schiffer Publishing.
Air Force Wings of Canada, Great Britain and the Commonwealth 1913-1945
Churchill, C & Westlake, R. 1986.

Reverse of Postcard posted Egypt 1916

British Army Collar Badges 1881 to the Present - An Illustrated Guide for Collectors. ISBN 0853688958: Arms and Armour Press.

Churchill, C. 2001. *History of the British Army Infantry Collar Badge.* Naval & Military Press, Contains 2000 illustrations and descriptions of badges

Cole, HN. 1993. *Formation Badges of World War 2 - Britain, Commonwealth and Empire.* ISBN 0853680787: Arms and Armour Press.

Congdon, P. 1985. *Behind the Hangar Doors.* ISBN 0951013904: Sonik Books.
Written by a serving RAF Regiment officer, this is an interesting and wide-ranging book covering history, heraldry and etiquette of the Royal Air Force. There are excellent sections on insignia.

Corbett, DA. 1980. *The Regimental Badges of New Zealand.* ISBN 0908596057: Ray Richards, New Zealand.
An excellent book suitable for both beginners and advanced collectors. Cap badges, collar badges, shoulder titles and buttons. 320 pages with photographs of over 1000 badges. An illustrated history of the badges, mottoes and battle honours of the Regular and Volunteer units of the New Zealand Army from the 1840's to the 1970's.

Cossum, JK. 1994. *Australian Army Badges - A Collectors Reference Guide - part 1 - 1930 - 1942.* ISBN 0949530115: JK Cossum.

Cossum, JK. 1994. *Australian Army Badges - A Collectors Reference Guide - part 2 - 1900 - 1930.* ISBN 0949530123: JK Cossum.

Cossum, JK. 1994. *Australian Army Badges - A Collectors Reference Guide - part 3 - 1948 - 1985.* ISBN 0949530131: JK Cossum.

Cossum, JK. 1986. *Australian Army Badges - The Rising Sun Badge.* JK Cossum.

Cox, RHW. 1982. *Military Badges of the British Empire 1914-18.* ISBN 0510000827: Ernest Benn Ltd.
An excellent book with photographs of over 3200 First World War badges. This is one of the few books to cover British Empire badges in depth. Out of print, but second-hand copies are well worth buying.

Cross, WK. *Charlton Standard Catalogue of First World War Canadian Infantry Badges* A record of Cap, collar and shoulder badges worn by the 1st - 260th Battalions, Canadian Expeditionary Force. Over 600 photographs

Davis, BL. 1985. *British Army Cloth Insignia 1940 to the Present.* ISBN 085368 7099: Arms and Armour Press, 600 black and white photographs of cloth badges

Davis, BL. 1993. *British Army Uniforms & Insignia of World War Two.* ISBN 0713717378: Blandford Press.

Davis, BL. 1988. *NATO Forces - An Illustrated Reference to their Organization and Insignia.* ISBN 185409159X: Arms and Armour Press.

Edwards, D & Langley, D. 1984. *British Army Proficiency Badges.* ISBN 0950942707: Wardley Publishing.

Forty, G. 1998. *British Army Handbook 1935 - 1945.* ISBN 0750914033: Sutton Publishing.
An impressive 369 pages covering mobilisation & training, command structures, weapons, equipment, vehicles, tactics, abbreviations, signals codes, badges and medals. The text is backed-up with over 300 photographs.

Froggatt, DJ. 1986. *Railway Buttons, Badges & Uniforms.* ISBN 0711016496: Ian Allan Ltd.

Gaylor, J. 1996. *Military Badge Collecting.* ISBN 0850525241: Leo Cooper.
6th revised edition of a photographic reference covering 800 military badges from the period 1881 to 1996, with an explanation of the evolution of military badges, and advice on the acquisition, mounting and storage of badges. Includes sections on tartan badge-backings and feather hackles.

Glyde, K. *Distinguishing Colour Patches of the Australian Military Forces 1915-1951* Over 1.500 colour patches are illustrated and described

Gordon, DB. 1998. *Tommy - Volume One.* ISBN 1575100428: Pictorial Histories Publishing.
A useful, well-researched hand-book covering WW2 British uniforms, equipment. weapons and vehicles-written by a re-enactor for re-enactors. Lots of illustrations.

Harfield, AG. 1982. *Head Dress, Badges and Embellishments of the Royal Corps of Signals.* ISBN 0902633813: Picton Publishing (Chippenham).

Hobart, MC. 2000. *Badges and Uniforms of the Royal Air Force.* ISBN 0850527392: Pen & Sword Books.
Recently published - excellent book on Royal Air Force insignia - includes Royal Observer Corps and Air Cadets. This is the only specialist RAF badge book still in print.

Kipling, AL & King, HL. 1995. *Head-Dress Badges of the British Army - Volume 1 - Up to the end of the Great War.* ISBN 0584109474: Muller, Blond & White Ltd.
An excellent book with black and white photographs of nearly 1900 cap badges. Each badge is numbered and the numbers are used by dealers and collectors to refer to cap badges. If you are going to buy any books on cap badges, then you need this book and Volume 2.

Kipling, AL & King, HL. 1994. *Head-Dress Badges of the British Army - Volume 2 - From the end of the Great War to the Present Day.* ISBN 0584109482: Muller, Blond & White Ltd.
An excellent book with black and white photographs of many cap badges. Each badge is numbered and the numbers are used by dealers and collectors to refer to cap badges. Essential reference book along with Volume 1

Linaker, D & Dine G. 1997. *Cavalry Warrant Officers' and Non-Commissioned Officers' Arm Badges.* ISBN 0951060333: Military Historical Society.

Litchfield, N. *Militial Artillery 1852-1909* Contains lineages of units along with details of badges and uniform . 225 photographs

Litchfield, N. *Territorial Artillery* Contains hundreds of badge and uniform photographs

Loughran, JL. 1995. *Brown's Flags and Funnels of Shipping Companies of the World.* ISBN 0851746349: Brown, Son & Ferguson.
Although this book does not specialise in uniform, it is useful for identifying Merchant Navy buttons and insignia - 1088 illustrations of shipping company liveries.

May, WE; Carman, WY & Tanner, J. 1974. *Badges and Insignia of the British Armed Services.* ISBN 0713613440: A & C Black Ltd
An excellent book with 6 colour plates, 39 black 7 white photographs and 765 line drawings. The book is in 3 sections to cover the Royal Navy, the Army and the Royal Air Force. The authors were senior directors of the national museums of the respective services. It is a particularly good reference for Royal Naval branch & trade insignia. Unfortunately no longer in print, it contains much information unavailable elsewhere.

McDonnell, J. *Buttons of the Irish Militia 1793-1881* 134 buttons are illustrated and described

Mills, J. 1993. *A People's Army - Civil Defence Insignia and Uniforms 1939 - 1945* Wardens Publishing
Includes many good quality photographs

Mills, J. 1997. *Doing Their Bit - Home Front Lapel Badges 1939-1945.* ISBN 0952811405: Wardens Publishing
A superb unique reference work covering lapel badges worn during the Second World War 1939-1945. The badges are illustrated in colour, together with dates and history of each badge. The badges were worn on civilian

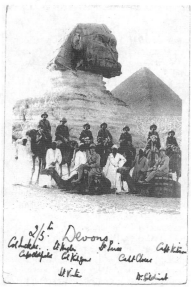

Front of Postcard posted Egypt 1916

clothes to denote that wearers were 'doing their bit' to contribute towards the war effort. This is the only book on the subject and is also a useful research reference regarding the many short-lived organisations that appeared during WW2.

Mills, J. & Carney, T. 2001 *In the Space of a Single Day- The Insignia and Uniforms of the LDV and Home Guard 1940 - 1944 and 1952-1956* ISBN 09 528 114 13: Wardens Publishing . Includes many good quality black and white as well as colour photographs. It is the most comprehensive record produced to date

Nevill, T. 1999. *The Scottish Regiments.* ISBN 1861262841: Crowood Press
A colour guide to the legendary Scottish regiments of today's British Army. The regular units covered are: The Scots Guards; The Royal Scots Dragoon Guards; The Royal Scots; The Royal Highland Fusiliers; The King's Own Scottish Borderers; The Black Watch; The Highlanders; and The Argyll and Sutherland Highlanders. The text details the units, their organization, equipment, weapons and vehicles and their uniforms and insignia. Illustrated with more than 100 colour photographs of Scottish soldiers in combat dress, training and working in the field, and on parade, this book is part of the "Europa Militaria" series

Owen, CR. 1990. *The Military Badges and Insignia of Southern Africa.* ISBN 0620154381: Chimperie Agencies. A unique work containing 3,991 black and white photographs of helmet plates, glengarry, cap and collar badges and shoulder titles, along with 2,300 cloth and metal items in colour

Parkyn, HG. 1956 (re-printed 1986). *(Military) Shoulder-Belt Plates and Buttons.* ISBN 0950853054: Ray Westlake

Poulsom, NW. A series of books all published in 1998, featuring black and white line drawings of pre-1947 buttons. Comprehensive research including dates and changes of unit titles.

Buttons of the Indian Army - Volume 1 - Cavalry. ISBN 0854200797: Military Press International.
Buttons of the Indian Army - Volume 2 - The Bengal Army Infantry. ISBN 0854201599: Military Press International.
Buttons of the Indian Army - Volume 3 - Punjab Frontier Force, Madras Army Infantry, Hyderabad Infantry. ISBN 0854201513:
Buttons of the Indian Army - Volume 4 - Bombay Army Infantry, Gurkha Infantry. ISBN 0854201610: Military Press International.
Buttons of the Indian Army - Volume 5 - Arms and Services pre-1947. ISBN 0854201718: Military Press

International.
Buttons of the Indian Army - Volume 6 - index covering sections 1-5, Summary of Battle Honours to 1914 Awarded to Each Regiment, and Summaries of the Post-1922 Amalgamations. ISBN 0854201815: Military Press International.

Ripley, H. 1983. *Buttons of the British Army 1855-1970.* ISBN 085368569X: Arms and Armour Press.
Ripley, H. 1983. *Police Forces of Great Britain and Ireland - their Amalgamations and their Buttons.* ISBN 0901718297: R Hazell & Co.
Ripley, H & Darmanin, D. 2000. *Police Buttons - Volume 2.* ISBN 0952793814: Police Insignia Collectors Society of Great Britain.
Ripley, H & Darmanin, D. 1996. *Rifle Volunteer Buttons 1859-1908.* ISBN 0951060341: Military Historical Society. 352 Buttons are illustrated
Ripley, H & Moodie, B. 1994. *Local Militia Buttons.* ISBN 0952446103: H Ripley.
Seaman, P. 1994. *Arm Badges of the British Cavalry Regiments.* ISBN 0952426102: P Seaman. Illustrated with some 300 photographs
Smylie, E. 1996. *Buttons of the Canadian Militia.* ISBN 1551250047: Vanwell Publishing, Canada.
Squire, Gwen 1972. *Buttons - A Guide For Collectors.* ISBN 0584100353: Frederick Muller Ltd.
This is the best book on uniform buttons, but unfortunately is no longer published. Second-hand copies are difficult to find - if you are serious about button collecting you can expect to pay up to £60.00 for a good copy.
The book illustrates and identifies buttons from the United Kingdom and many overseas countries. In addition to military and police buttons, it covers ambulance, fire service, prisons, hospital, blazer, clubs, livery, hunts, public and private companies, hotels, American state seals, town crests, schools, customs & excise, airlines, shipping,
Squire, Gwen 1976. *Livery Buttons - The Pitt Collection.* ISBN 0950474800: Leghorn Company.
Taylor, M. M & Wilkinson, V. L. 1995. *Badges of Office - An illustrated Guide to the Helmets and Badges of the British Police 1829 - 1989.* ISBN 0901718521: PICA GB. Some 2,000 clear photographs of badges from various forces throughout the British Isles
Taylor, P. 2000. *Allied Special Forces Insignia 1939 - 1948.* ISBN 0850525829: Leo Cooper.
Taylor, P. 1998. *Collecting Anodised Cap Badges.* ISBN 085052637X: Leo Cooper.
This book lists nearly every anodised cap badge which has ever been used by the British Forces. Over 400 black & white line drawings of badges.
Thomas, C & Endean Ivall, D. 1976. *Military Insignia of Cornwall.* ISBN 0903686147: Penwith Books.
Thomas, M & Lord C. 1995. *New Zealand Army Distinguishing Patches 1911-1991 - Part One.* ISBN 0473032880: Thomas & Lord, New Zealand.
Thomas, M & Lord C. 1995. *New Zealand Army Distinguishing Patches 1911-1991 - Part Two.* ISBN 0473032899: Thomas & Lord, New Zealand.
Thompson, L. 1999. *Badges and Insignia of the Elite Forces.* ISBN 0713713291: Blandford.
Thornton, WM. 1997. *Submarine Insignia of the World.* ISBN 0850525365: Leo Cooper.
Westlake, R. 1997. *Collecting Metal Shoulder Titles.* ISBN 0850525055: Leo Cooper.
This is an excellent book with black and white photographs of over 1800 British Army metal shoulder titles, and descriptions of many more. Each badge is numbered and the numbers are used by dealers and collectors as the 'industry-standard' to refer to shoulder titles. If you are going to buy a book on British Army

shoulder titles, then you need this book.
Whittaker, LB. 1990. *Stand Down - Orders of Battle for the units of the Home Guard of the United Kingdom.*
ISBN 1871167140: Ray Westlake Military Books.
An excellent book on the Home Guard, including locations, dates, insignia and unit commanders.
Windle, D. 2000. *Badges and Insignia of the Royal Air Force.* ISBN 1854095293: Cassell Military.

Personal Documents etc

In addition to the badges worn on the uniform, there are other items which the soldier carried on him that could also be useful and may be found in the family.

Soldiers Service and Pay book

This was to be carried with the soldier at all times and information contained in this book included;
Soldier's Regimental Number
Last Name and First Name(s)
Date and Place of Birth
Religion
Date and Place of Enlistment
Terms of Enlistment
Measurements
Distinctive Marks
Postings [Details of units not given]
Medical Information, listing inoculations, wounds etc
Address of Next of Kin or contact to be advised in the event of soldier being wounded or killed
Soldiers Will

Identity Discs

Identity Discs were made of compressed fibre, there was a red circular disc and a dark green octagonal disc and these were worn around the soldier's neck. The information recorded on them was Service Number, Religion, Initials and Surname

Initials were used for the religion :-

C E	Church of England
C I	Church of Ireland
PRES	Church of Scotland & Presbyterian
R.C.	Roman Catholic
METH	Methodist
CONG	Congregationalist
J	Jewish
SA	Salvation Army
CSCI	Christian Scientist
U	Unitarian
PB.	Plymouth Brethren
Q	Quaker

In case of death in action, the green octagonal disc was to be buried with the body, in order to allow identification at a later date by the graves registration service. The cap badge, regimental title or any item bearing the soldiers number, were, as far as possible, left with the body in a service issue cigarette tin. The red disc was to be used for recording purposes.

Some soldiers carried a privately purchased engraved discs and tags or sometimes the details were stamped on the smoothed off side of a foreign coin, which then had been drilled so that it could be worn by the soldier.

Although the soldier's unit is not identified on these tags, using the search facilities on the CD Rom 'Soldiers Died in the Great War', or the 'Army Roll of Honour - World War Two' it is now possible to

check if the soldier was killed simply by typing in the service number, which was unique to the individual soldier. This search technique can be employed on other items that may record the serviceman's name and number.

Chits

There were many official forms to be completed during a soldier's service and sometimes these can survive. Call up papers, Graduation Certificate, request for leave, furlough pass, attending courses, transfer to another unit, education certificates , Transfer to Reserve Certificate, Discharge certificate etc, etc.
Many will be dated, so a timeframe can be established for what the soldier was doing, or intending to do. Examination of any 'Official ' stamps or markings can also be interesting.

Letters and Postcards

Letters and postcards can sometimes reveal information, but not from the contents of what was written, which was censored, to ensure that no military information was included that could be of use to the enemy, before being sealed and posted.
The envelope to the letter or the address side of the postcard can carry a postmark, this is often a military postmark, from a Field Post Office or an Army Post Office. Sometimes there is an additional censors stamp and a signature or initial of the officer censoring the mail.

Whilst these units are only identified with a number, and units exchanged these numbers on a regular basis, research over the years by postal history collectors has enabled information to be published that enables you to find out who these units were, and where they were serving.

Further reading
"The Postal History of the British Army in World War One, Before and After 1903-1929" by Alistair Kennedy and George Crabb, published by George Crabb, Epson 1977
"The History of the British Army Postal Service, Vol I 1882-1902" by E B Proud. Published by Proud Bailey Co. Ltd, Dereham, Norfolk 1986
"The History of the British Army Postal Service, Vol II 1903-1927" by E B Proud. Published by Proud Bailey Co. Ltd, Dereham, Norfolk 1980
"The History of the British Army Postal Service, Vol III 1927-1963" by E B Proud. Published by Proud Bailey Co. Ltd, Dereham, Norfolk 1982
"The Postal History of the Naval and R.A.F. Postal Services" by E B Proud. Published by Proud Bailey Co. Ltd, Dereham, Norfolk
Specialised Group of Collectors; Forces Postal History Society. Contact Hon. Secretary; Mr M Dobbs, 52 Leamington Avenue, Bromley, Kent BR1 5BL

The subject matter on the front of a postcard can often provide clue for research, especially as a lot of those from the First World War and some of those from the Second World War were photographs of the individual in uniform.

A guide to the 'Identification and dating of British Military Uniforms' appeared on page 218-220 of the 6th Edition of The Family and Local History Handbook.

Royal Navy *Submarine* Museum Portsmouth
George Malcolmson Business Services Manager

The Royal Navy Submarine Museum in Gosport Hampshire is a unique attraction. Not only is it the countries only museum dedicated to the history of submarines, it boasts the only walk through guided submarine tour in the UK!

On arrival visitors are booked in for a tour of HMS Alliance that includes an audiovisual presentation about the Submarine Service in an atmospheric control room cinema. Visitors are then shown through the Museum's star exhibit, HMS Alliance, a post-war diesel-electric submarine. Approximately 290 feet in length she was built between 1945 and 1947 and saw active service with the Royal Navy until 1973.

Visitors can see first hand how her crew of 65 lived and worked - the cramped bunks and tiny galley where one chef prepared three meals a day for 65 men. One of the highlights of the tour is the control room, where visitors brace themselves for a depth-charge attack.

Visitors can also stroll around the Museum galleries where the stirring heritage of the Submarine Service is brought to life. The Submarine Weapons Gallery, featuring a real Polaris submarine launched missile, shows the development of underwater weapons from primitive 19th century torpedoes to the latest submarine launched cruise missile. The Historical Galleries lead visitors around chronological displays that recreate the story of the Service from its birth in 1901 up to the modern day. The thought-provoking exhibits range from Jolly Roger's, scoring a war-time submarine's successes, to poignant last letters home, also included are replicas of the 14 Victoria Crosses won by British submariners and an unclaimed raffle prize of a bottle of whisky

The Lower Historical Gallery illustrates the post-war nuclear submarine era and includes the actual working periscopes and Captain's Cabin of HMS Conqueror of Falkland war fame. Visitors can scan the whole of the Portsmouth harbour area.

The Royal Navy's first submarine, Holland I, has undergone a period of revolutionary conservation to treat her hull. Holland I foundered in 1913 as she was being towed to the breaker's yard, she was salvaged in 1981. The 100 year-old submarine boat known as HM Submarine Torpedo Boat No.1, is now back on display in an exciting new purpose built gallery and exhibition hall.

The Museum is host to a collection of Diving equipment on loan from the Museum of Diving and Underwater Exploration. Housed alongside examples of submarine escape equipment that also includes: LR3, the Royal Navy's decommissioned Deep Submergence Rescue Vessel, JIM 18 an articulated atmospheric diving suit and a Diving Probe, also decommissioned from service with the Royal Navy.

The Museum has been officially recognised by the National Historic Ships Register as holding two important national maritime treasures. HMS Alliance, which, laid down in 1945 and having seen service through three decades, is probably the youngest vessel on the Register. Holland I, as the Royal Navy's first submarine, is the mother of all submarines afloat around the world today. It is of great significance that the importance of preserving these two particular vessels has been nationally endorsed.

The museum is also home to the only surviving example of a World War II British midget submarine X24. These craft were used to attack enemy shipping in heavily defended harbours. X24 is split into two halves so that visitors can see the intricate workings of these amazing mini submarines. Many top gallantry awards were won by the crews of the X craft force.

Museum facilities and services include free onsite Car and Coach Parking, the Jolly Roger Café, gift-shop and mail order service, research centre & photo sales (by prior appointment), corporate entertainment, and a free entry and optional educational service to school groups. Situated at the entrance to Portsmouth Harbour the museum is also accessible by harbour boat trips and Waterbus.

Crew of HMS Grampus cheering Submarine E11 as it leaves the Dardenelles after sinking the Turkish Battleship "Barbarousse Hairedine" 1915

In addition to expanding its collection of artefacts to build up as comprehensive a picture as possible of the Submarine Service's heritage, the Museum has considerable development plans, as well as maintaining its contribution to submarine benevolent charities.

Information & Booking:
Tel 02392 529217 x 240
Web:www.rnsubmus.co.uk

The Yorkshire Air Museum & Allied Forces Memorial
Ian Richardson - Public Relations Manager

The ancient City of York is well known for it's Roman and Viking ancestry, the awe-inspiring Minster, the famous walled City, a centre of rail heritage and much more, but there is another aspect of York that is less well known. This is the role as the Headquarters for 4 Group Bomber Command during the days of WWII. Heslington Hall, now part of the University of York, was the command centre for the airfields that were built in the surrounding area: Breighton, Burn, Driffield, Elvington, Full Sutton, Leconfield, Lissett, Melbourne, Pocklington, Rufforth and Snaith. Of these, R.A.F. Elvington was the closest to York, and one of the most interesting from a historical perspective.

RAF Elvington was established in 1942 as the home for 77 Squadron, whose ground and aircrews maintained and operated Halifax bombers, conducting numerous raids over the German heartland. From 1944, after 77 Squadron had moved to the newly built base at Full Sutton, until the end of the war, R.A.F. Elvington became the home of the only 2 heavy bomber Squadrons to be operated by the Free French Air Force from Britain. Over 2000 French personnel were based in the area, so it is small wonder that it became known as *"La Petite France"*. The French link has remained every since the two Halifax squadrons left England to become the start of the new French Air Force in 1945. After the war, the base was taken over by the U.S.A.F. who, in the early 1950's, extended the runway to become one of the longest in Europe at 1.92 miles. This was done with the view to operating the Boeing B-52 bombers, but this plan was curtailed by the advent of the Intercontinental Ballistic Missile, and these aircraft were never in fact deployed here. The runway was used as an emergency landing ground by still operational R.A.F Stations such as Church Fenton and Linton-on-Ouse until 1992. The actual wartime buildings had long

been abandoned, until, in 1983, a group of local residents and volunteers formed a Charitable Trust and began the task of clearing and preserving the site as a Museum and Allied Air Forces Memorial. The Museum opened to the public on a limited basis in 1985, following the restoration of the Control Tower. Gradually, more and more buildings were converted and built, to house the ever-increasing numbers of items donated by former veterans or their families, aviation manufacturers and Royal Air Force Stations. Today, the Museum is fully established and is the largest and most authentic of only a few original wartime bomber bases left open to the public.

Over the past few years the Yorkshire Air Museum has expanded rapidly to become one of the most fascinating and dynamic Museums of its type in the country. Recognition from the Tourism industry of the Museum's efforts resulted in us being voted the White Rose *Visitor Attraction of the Year (2001)*. A unique collection of over 40 internationally recognised aircraft and fascinating displays, all combined into this historic site, makes the Museum a very special place for aviation enthusiasts young and not so young. The aircraft collection covers aviation history from the pioneering 1849 work

preservation work in our newly refurbished aircraft restoration workshop. The presence of many former WWII veterans, air and ground crews, air gunners and the like, help to bring history alive for many visitors. Veteran Air Gunners will happily recall their tales and the black humour that existed in those dark days of WWII. For example, it was common practice for the gunners to leave some money on their beds when they left on a mission. If they did not return, their colleagues would have a 'drink on them' in the NAAFI, in tribute to a fallen comrade.

of the Yorkshire born Sir George Cayley, recognised internationally as the true "Father of Aeronautics", to WWII aircraft, including the unique Halifax bomber, the only complete example of this illustrious aircraft in the world, through to modern military jets like the Harrier GR3. By courtesy of the French Government, in view of the historic French connection, the Museum now displays the only Mirage Mk. III jet fighter in the UK.

Whilst evolving to become more professionally led, the Museum retains a strong 'volunteer' core, with around 200 'active' volunteers, working on everything from Aircraft Engineering to Gardening, and from Displays to Stewarding, and over 1000 members. The Museum is totally self-supporting, receiving no Government subsidy, apart from some Grant Aid for specific projects, and has to compete with National Museums now offering subsidised admission for a share of the visitor market. Nevertheless, the Yorkshire Air Museum is almost unique within the Museum world, as the increase in visitor numbers over the past two years alone has averaged at nearly 40% per year. The Museum is nationally registered by the Museums & Galleries Commission, which has an important bearing in terms of donations of artefacts, as these become protected and cannot be disposed of to a private collection, which is a major re-assurance to potential donors.

Our excellent displays house internationally recognised artefacts and in the many original buildings you can explore histories on a varied list of related topics. These include Barnes Wallis; Air Gunners; Airborne Forces and Home Guard, seeing how wartime life was like in the French Officers' Mess or the Airmen's Billet as well as observing aircraft

One of the most significant achievements of the Museum over the past two years has been to reach a significantly younger audience, whilst retaining the unique atmosphere of the site and the special bond that exists with veterans from those far off days. The Museum won a new army of supporters recently when we unveiled the first dedicated Memorial to the Women of the Allied Air Services on June 12th 2002. The gesture was appreciated by the hundreds of veteran servicewomen who attended on the day and the Memorial will be a permanent reminder of the role played by women in the defence of the nation, past, present and future.

Younger visitors to the Museum have enjoyed frequent opportunities to see inside the cockpits of aircraft like the newly acquired and restored Harrier GR3. The excitement of 'Jumping into a Jump Jet' often leads to a more in depth interest in aviation and the history of the Allied Air Services, so fulfilling our goal of preserving the memory of Allied Air Force personnel and educating the public in aviation history.

AIRGUNNERS' MEMORIAL ROOM

In Flanders Fields the poppies blow ....

Robert Blatchford

In Flanders fields the poppies blow
Between the crosses, row on row,
That mark our place; and in the sky
The larks, still bravely singing, fly
Scarce heard amid the guns below.

We are the Dead. Short days ago
We lived, felt dawn, saw sunset glow,
Loved, and were loved, and now we lie
In Flanders fields.

Take up our quarrel with the foe:
To you from failing hands we throw
The torch; be yours to hold it high
If ye break faith with us who die
We shall not sleep, through poppies grow
In Flanders fields.

John McCrae May 1915

John McCrae, a Canadian Army Doctor, was stationed at an advanced field dressing post near Essex Farm and alongside to the main road from Ypres to Boezinge. He was greatly affected by the hundreds of wounded soldiers treated by him, many succumbing to their wounds. The field next to the dressing station became a graveyard which grew daily. Today the Essex Farm Cemetery has 1185 graves and is adjacent to the concrete dugouts built to house the dressing station.

I have always been familiar with names such as Ypres, Kemmel, Baupaume, Menin, Messines, Vimy, Le Cateau, Peronne, Arras, Poperinge and Somme. All of them places in Belgium and France where battles had taken place during the First World War.

As a child in the nineteen fifties and sixties I knew many people who had lived through and fought in The Great War. This together with the numerous television documentaries and books such as The *Imperial War Museum's Book of The Somme* by Malcolm Brown or Lyn Macdonald's *They Called it Passchendaele* engendered a wish to visit the Western Front.

In February 2002 my wife and I visited the Northern Battlefields making our base on the Menin Road at the cosy Hotel Kasteelhof 't Hooghe a short distance from Ieper (Ypres) in Belgium.

Viewing the countryside and the town of Ypres as it is today, it is difficult to image the wasteland that was created during the various battles of the First World War. The images are black and white and in many instances it is impossible to make the connection between the landscape then and now.

The Hooge area had been subject to fierce

fighting both in and around the Hotel. Before the War had started the magnificent Chateau de Hooge had occupied the grounds. Totally destroyed in the fighting much of the grounds are now taken up with the remains of the trench network and the crater left by the huge mine which exploded there. Everywhere around there are reminders of the mass slaughter that took place between 1914 and 1918.

Ypres was reduced to rubble during the various battles over the four years of the war.

"At Reningelst there were refugees everywhere. In all these cottages there were people from Mesen, Wijtschate, Kemmel, Warneton and Hollebeke.

Everyone who knew someone, or thought they knew some-one, turned up there. We thought that it would only last two weeks. One stayed here, the other one stayed somewhere else. The tiniest corner, the smallest outhouse was full."
Georges Deconinck

"Thursday 22 April 1915.
At 3 o'clock big shells exploded over the town and surrounding area, entire streets were destroyed. Around 5 o'clock there was a big attack with poison gas. Everyone fled. The dead and wounded were lying everywhere. As if they had gone mad with panic, civilians took to the road for Veurne and Poperinge".
Diary of Gustave Delahaye, warden at the Institute of the Sacred Heart, Ieper

"Monday 3 May 1915.
At 4 o'clock, the lieutenant of the gendarmerie warned me that orders to evacuate the town had arrived, and the sector where we were living had to be evacuated by the following Thursday at the latest. We are all overtaken by deep despondency. After struggling for six months against every adversity, after having gone without comfortable every-day life for so long, with the one aim of being able to hang onto our houses, we have to resign ourselves to leaving all our things behind. What will we find when we come back?"
Diary of Aimé Van Nieuwenhove, secretary of the Comité Provisiore, Ieper

Although it was suggested that it should remain in ruins as a memorial, Ypres was rebuilt in the 1920s.

In the Grôte Markt in the centre of Ypres, stands the Cloth Hall. Originally been built in the 13th century it now houses the *In Flanders Fields Museum* and any visitor to the area should start with a visit. Described as *'an experience never to forget'* and *where you can touch the war*. To fully appreciate the experience a visitor should expect to spend several hours there.

The tableau, the exhibits and sound effects make a lasting impression of the horrors of this time. A guide book contains eye-witness accounts

used throughout the audiovisual displays. In one area the poems of the war time poets are read aloud and in some areas the eyewitness accounts are read out.

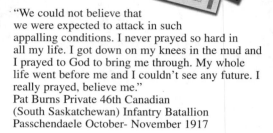

"We could not believe that we were expected to attack in such appalling conditions. I never prayed so hard in all my life. I got down on my knees in the mud and I prayed to God to bring me through. My whole life went before me and I couldn't see any future. I really prayed, believe me."
Pat Burns Private 46th Canadian (South Saskatchewan) Infantry Batallion Passchendaele October- November 1917

There was not a sign of life of any sort. Not a tree, save for a few dead stumps which looked strange in the moonlight. Not a bird, not even a rat or a blade of grass. Nature was as dead as those Canadians whose bodies remained where they had fallen the previous autumn. Death was written large everywhere. Where there had been farms there was not a stick or stone to show. You only knew them because they were marked on the map. The earth had been churned and re-churned. It was simply a soft, sloppy mess, into which you sank up to the neck if you slipped from the duckboard tracks - and the enemy had the range of those slippery ways. Shell hole cut across shell hole. Pits of earth, like simmering fat, brimful of water and slimy mud, mile after mile as far as the eye could see. It is not possible to set down the things that could be written of the Salient. They would haunt your dreams."
R. A.Colwell, Private Passchendaele January 1918

A short distance away from the Cloth Hall is the Menin Gate built as a memorial to 54,896 officers and men who have no known grave and whose names are carved on the walls. Each day at 8.00.p.m. the traffic is stopped and a group of Belgian Fire Service buglers sound the Last Post. When I visited, the names of the men who

was totally destroyed in the fighting but has now regrown within its original boundaries and appears much as it did in October and November 1914 except for the eight cemeteries nearby. The two largest of these is Hill 62, The Canadian Memorial at Mount Sorrel and the Hooge Cemetery (Commonwealth War Graves Commission). As you approach Hill 62 there is the Sanctuary Wood Museum on the right. Here there is a cafe with artefacts, photographs (many quite disturbing), and the remains of trenches. This museum is the only one to survive those that sprang up immediately after the war when relatives visiting wished to see something of the battlefield and is still owned by the same family. The trenches at the rear were part of the Vince Street and Jam Row trench system dug in 1916. It should be remembered that this is only a small

had died on that day were read out. Minutes before the traffic was stopped only a few of us were present but as the Last Post sounded the area was tightly packed with people of all ages many of them British schoolchildren. The atmosphere is by its nature very emotional.

Everywhere there are reminders of the war with small and large cemeteries dotting the countryside. As you pass or visit individual cemeteries the enormity of the loss of life during this period is a constant reminder. Small museums with various relics, most dug up from the battlefield, also dot the landscape. There is one next to our hotel, *The Hooge Crater Museum*. This is a private museum full of relics and a display about *"The Diggers"* who have spent much time undertaking archaeological exploration where battlefield areas are threatened or undergoing redevelopment. This area was where German troops used flame throwers for the first time and the huge mine constructed by the Royal Engineers was exploded. The mine crater itself is now a huge lake.

Across the Menin Road is Sanctuary Wood. This was the scene of much fierce fighting. The wood

part of a system that would have covered an extensive area.

Wherever there are museums, cafes and information centres adjacent to places such as Sanctuary Wood, there are various books and guides for sale. One such series is the *Battleground Europe* published by Leo Cooper Pen and Sword Books. These are invaluable guides to particular battle areas describing the battles in detail with maps, illustrations and useful advice. *Sanctuary Wood and Hooge* by Nigel Cave is a handy size and can be used by the reader in the 'field.'

The battles raged in all directions around Ypres and in the various battles for Passchendaele many more lives were lost. Five miles north east

It cannot be forgotten that there were casualties on both sides. Not only did the Allies suffer huge casualties but the Germans did so as well. North of Ypres is the village of Dixmunde where there is a German military cemetery. This cemetery is more melancholy than the military cemeteries of the allies. The sandstone entrance is reminiscent of a block house. Passing through it into the cemetery which is set out with oak trees you are confronted by black gravestones lying flat upon the ground with twenty names engraved upon them. I calculated that there were over 55,000 soldiers buried here. Following the ending of the war the German cemeteries were consolidated into Dixmunde, the authorities decreeing that no upright gravestones should be erected by the Germans and that all remains should be cremated. This explained the twenty names on each stone. A sad place watched over by the sculptured figures *'The Mourning Parents'* by the Munich sculptor Emil Kreiger.

Ten miles west of Ypres is the small town of Poperinge. It was here that the allied soldiers of all ranks found rest and recuperation particularly at *Talbot House.* This is where Toc H was founded by *Rev Philip 'Tubby' Clayton* in 1915 as an *'Everyman's Club'* where rank was left outside and many thousands of British soldiers took their first, and last, Holy Communion in the Chapel at the top of the house. Talbot House is still there today and is run in the same tradition as inspired by 'Tubby' Clayton.

of Ypres is The Tyne Cot cemetery which consists of the graves of 11,956 Commonwealth soldiers with a memorial wall displaying the names of 34,957 soldiers who have no known grave. This is the largest British War Cemetery in the world. The cemetery is on a slight rise below Passchendaele and looking towards Ypres from where Commonwealth troops struggled to take the slightly higher ground from the Germans. From here you can see many other much smaller cemeteries containing those who fell and were buried as the battle took place. Many who were buried were again disturbed as the battle raged backwards and forwards obliterating the landscape and the graves.

However in Poperinge approximately 70 soldiers were executed in the courtyard of The Town Hall most of them for *'desertion'*, but in all probability they were suffering from *'shell shock'* which today we call Post Traumatic Stress Disorder.

It is difficult to visualise what has taken place in the area these many years after and the vastness of it all is really too great to fully comprehend. The whole of this can be summed up by the phrase on Seigfried Sassoon's gravestone:

"I died in hell They called it Passchendaele".

Travelling into Northern France Picardy is soon reached. Here small cemeteries of both the Commonwealth and France appear to be on every field corner,at the roadside or in the centre of fields. From a distance across the fields the huge Thiépval Monument to the missing, designed by Sir Edwin Lutyens, can be seen and was an area of particularly vicious fighting during the Battle of the Somme. The battle lasted three months beginning on 1st July 1916. The Generals believed that the offensive would see the Germans driven back in a day enabling the British infantry to capture Bapaume. A stalemate·in a morass of mud developed but not before horrendous casulates had been incurred by the British. The first day saw 60,000 casualties of which 21,000 were killed and most of them fell in the first hour.

The Thiépval Memorial is carved with the names of 73,000 British and South African soldiers lost on the Somme. Around the area are other Commonwealth memorials such as the Newfoundland Memorial Park near Beaumont-Hamel. It is here that there is a green amphitheatre showing the preserved trench system. This area of about 600 metres across has been preserved in honour of 1st Newfoundlanders who lost more men than any other battalion on the first day of the battle. The small visitor centre tells the story of the battalion who were volunteers who had to buy their own uniforms and rifles before being sent to France.

The day of our visit was cold and extremely wet and it was easy to imagine the privations brought upon the troops in their life and death struggles. The heavy rain had made the ground sodden and Thiépval was particularly moving.

A short distance away is the town of Albert where the Golden Madonna at Notre Dame des Brebières shone out to the troops of both sides for miles around. Beneath the church is the Musée des Abris which recreates the life of soldiers in the trenches. The tunnel in which it is set is ten metres below ground and the gallery extends for two hundred and thirty metres beneath the church and into the public gardens.

Albert, which lay only one mile from the Front Line was fully restored, it is difficult to imagine what it was like in 1916. In the main square there are several cafes and restaurants providing time for refreshment and reflection.

Just off the Albert to Bapaume Road is La Boiselle where the Loghnagar Crater created by the largest mine exploded in the Somme can still be seen. A few kilometres north west is the village of Longueval where there was a cauldron of unimaginable suffering. It is here that The South African Brigade was ordered to take Delville Wood 'at all costs'. Over 3000 South Africans entered the woods and endured five days of savage hand to hand fighting in constant

rain when they met the Germans head on. Only 143 soldiers came out of the wood. The battle for Delville Wood lasted from 15th July 1916 into September. The broad green paths criss cross the wood as they did during the battle with only stone markers bearing the names of the 'roads'.

Beneath the canopy of the born again oaks the trench system can be traced but many areas are still too dangerous to walk because of unexploded ordnance. Apart from this it is difficult to believe that Delville Wood had once been a place of desolation with shattered tree stumps and drowned shell holes. Nearby the imposing South African Memorial comemorates this struggle.

Our visit to the Northern Battlefields ended with a visit to the field dressing station and Essex Farm Cemetery where John McCrae tended to the wounded and the dying.

It is over 88 years since the First World War began. A generation was lost in this war to end all wars. Visiting the area was incredibly moving for me. We owe these men so much and I recommend that everyone visits Northern France. There is so much to see that one visit is insufficient.

The cemeteries are maintained by The Commonwealth War Graves Commission. Their office is at 82 Elverdinge Street, Ypres. A register of those soldiers buried or comemorated is available at each cemetery and is usually found near the entrance or immediately adjacent to the memorial in a brass container. Arranged

alphabetically the register contains the name, initials, battalion and regiment of the casualty together with the reference enabling the visitor to locate the grave or inscribed comemoration. A visitors book is usually also held in the brass container. Every visitor is urged to take the time to sign the book ensuring that visitor statistics are available for the Commission. At times the register may be missing because of theft by some selfish visitors.

There are a number of operators who provide excellent tours of this area. However, the independent traveller will find the Ypres and Somme areas compact and very accessible.

Further Reading
The Imperial War Museum Book of The Western Front Malcolm Brown ISBN 0 330 48475 3 Pan Books
They Called It Passchendaele - Lyn Macdonald ISBN 0 14 016509 6 Penguin History
In Flanders Fields - Herwig Verleyen ISBN 90 5508 025 X De Klaproos Editions
The Imperial War Museum Book of The Somme - Malcolm Brown ISBN 0 330 35220 2 Pan Books
Sanctuary Wood & Hooge - Nigel Cave ISBN 0 85052 355 9 Leo Cooper Pen & Sword Books
Passchendaele - Nigel Cave ISBN 0 85052 558 6 Leo Cooper Pen & Sword Books

Military Museums

The Battlefields Trust 33 High Green, Brooke, Norwich, NR15 1HR Tel: 01508 558145 Fax: 01508 558145 Email: BattlefieldTrust@aol.com WWW: www.battlefieldstrust.com
The Museum of The Adjutant General's Corps, RHQ Adjutant General's Corps Worthy Down, Winchester, SO21 2RG Tel: 01962 887435 Fax: 01962 887690 Email: agc.regtsec@virgin.net Inc the Royal Army Pay Corps, The Royal Army educational Corps and the Army Legal Corps and part of the collections of the Royal Military Police, The Military Provost Staff Corps and the Women's Royal Army Corps
Museum of Army Flying, Middle Wallop, Stockbridge, SO20 8DY Tel: 01980 674421 Fax: 01264 781694 Email: daa@flying-museum.org.uk WWW: www.flying-museum.org.uk
Army Medical Services Museum Keogh Barracks Ash Vale, Aldershot, GU12 5RQ Tel: 01252 868612 Fax: 01252 868832 Email: museum@keogh72.freeserve.co.uk Archives on the Army Medical Services inc doctors, vetinary surgeons, dentists and some nurses CC accepted
Army Physical Training Corps Museum , ASPT, Fox Line, Queen's Avenue, Aldershot, GU11 2LB Tel: 01252 347168 Fax: 01252 340785 Email: regtsec@aptc.org.uk WWW: www.aptc.org.uk
Commonwealth War Graves Commission 2 Marlow Road Maidenhead, SL6 7DX Tel: 01628-634221 Fax: 01628-771208 WWW: www.cwgc.org
Coldstream Guards Record Office, Wellington Barracks, Birdcage Walk London, SW1E 6HQ Access is by appointment made in advance. Search fee of £25.00 per search
Fleet Air Arm Museum Records Research Centre, Box D61, RNAS Yeovilton Nr Ilchester, BA22 8HT Tel: 01935-840565 Fax: 01935-840181 Records include: WWI Ratings enlistment papers, for RN, RNAS, RNVR, RND & Royal Marines; RNAS Officers service records (copies); Fleet Air Arm Roll of Honour 1939 to date 4. RNAS + FAA papers and photographs
Firepower - The Royal Artillery Museum Royal Arsenal Woolwich, London, SE18 6ST Tel: (020) 8855 7755 Email: info@firepower.org.uk WWW: www.firepower.org.uk
Grenadier Guards Record Office, Wellington Barracks, Birdcage Walk London, SW1E 6HQ, Email: rhqgrengds@yahoo.co.uk Access is by appointment made in advance. Search fee of £25.00 per search
Guards Museum Wellington Barracks, Birdcage Walk London, SW1E 6HQ Tel: (020) 7414 3271/3428 Fax: (020) 7414 3429
Imperial War Museum Film and Video Archive Lambeth Road London, SE1 6HZ Tel: 020 7416 5291 WWW: www.iwm.org.uk/collections/film.htm
Imperial War Museum Lambeth Road London, SE1 6HZ Tel: (020) 7416-5000 Tel: (020) 7416 5348 Fax: (020) 7416 5374 (020) 7416 5246 Email: books@iwm.org.uk WWW: www.iwm.org.uk
Irish Guards Record Office, Wellington Barracks, Birdcage Walk London, SW1E 6HQ Email: bigbillaqq119@aol.com WWW: www.army.mod/ig~assoc For archives information contact Archivist in first instance. Search fee of £25.00 per search
National Army Museum Royal Hospital Road London, SW3 4HT Tel: (020) 7730-0717 Fax: (020) 7823-6573 Email: info@national-army-museum.ac.uk WWW: http://www.national-army-museum.ac.uk Incorporating Middlesex Regiment Museum & Buffs regiment Museum
Royal Air Force Museum Grahame Park Way, Hendon, London, NW9 5LL Tel: (020) 8205-2266 Fax: (020) 8200 1751 Email: groupbusiness@refmuseum.org.uk WWW: http://www.rafmuseum.org.uk
Royal Marines Museum Eastney Southsea, PO4 9PX Tel: (023) 92 819385-Exts-224 Fax: (023) 92 838420 Email: matthewlittle@royalmarinesmuseum.co.uk WWW: www.royalmarinesmuseum.co.uk No charges for research other than material costs. Donations welcome. Visits by appointment Mon to Fri 10am to 4.30pm
Royal Naval Museum H M Naval Base (PP66), Portsmouth, PO1 3NH Tel: (023) 9272 3795 Fax: (023) 9272 3942 WWW: www.royalnavalmuseum.org

Royal Navy Submarine Museum Haslar Jetty Road Gosport, PO12 2AS Tel: (023) 92510354 Fax: (023) 9251 1349 Email: admin@rnsubmus.co.uk WWW: www.rnsubsmus.co.uk Archive and photographic library by prior appointment. Unique record of service of submarine personnel
RHQ Scots Guards Archives, Wellington Barracks, Birdcage Walk London, SW1E 6HQ Email: sgarchives@dial.pipex.com Access is by appointment made in advance. Search fee of £25.00 per search
Welsh Guards Record Office, Wellington Barracks, Birdcage Walk London, SW1E 6HQEmail: rhqwelshguards@milnet.uk.net Access is by appointment made in advance. Search fee of £25.00 per search

England
Bedfordshire
Bedford Museum Bedfordshire Yeomanry, Castle Lane, Bedford, MK40 3XD Tel: 01234 353323 Fax: 01234 273401 Email: bmuseum@bedford.gov.uk WWW: www.bedfordmuseum.org
Bedfordshire and Hertfordshire Regimental Museum Luton Museum Wardown Park Luton, LU2 7HA Tel: 01582 546722 Fax: 01582 546763 WWW: www.luton.gov.uk/enjoying/museums

Berkshire
Commonwealth War Graves Commission 2 Marlow Road Maidenhead, SL6 7DX Tel: 01628-634221 Fax: 01628-771208 WWW: www.cwgc.org
R.E.M. Museum of Technology Isaac Newton Road, Arborfield, Reading, RG2 9NJ Tel: 0118 976 3375 Fax: 0118 976 3375 Email: reme-museum@gtnet.gov.uk WWW: http://www.rememuseum.org.uk
Royal Berkshire Yeomanry Cavalry Museum T A Centre, Bolton Road Windsor, SL4 3JG Tel: 01753 860600 Fax: 01753 854946
The Household Cavalry Museum Combermere Barracks, Windsor, SL4 3DN Tel: 01753 755112 Fax: 01753 755161

Buckinghamshire
Oxfordshire and Buckinghamshire Light Infantry Regimental Museum Slade Park Headington, Oxford, OX3 7JL Tel: 01865 780128

Cambridgeshire
Ely Museum The Old Goal, Market Street Ely, CB7 4LS Tel: 01353-666655 includes Cambridge Regiment displays

Cheshire
Cheshire Military Museum The Castle, Chester, CH1 2DN Tel: 01244 327617
South Lancashire Regiment Prince of Wales Volunteers Museum Peninsula Barracks, Warrington

Cornwall
Duke of Cornwall's Light Infantry Museum The Keep Bodmin, PL31 1EG Tel: 01208 72810 Fax: 01208 72810 Email: dclimis@talk21.com WWW: www.britrishlightinfantry.org.ca

County Durham
Durham Light Infantry Museum Aykley Heads Durham, DH1 5TU Tel: 0191-384-2214 Fax: 0191-386-1770 Email: dli@durham.gov.uk WWW: www.durham.gov.uk/dli

Cumbria
Border Regiment & Kings Own Royal Border Regiment Museum Queen Mary's Tower, The Castle Carlisle, CA3 8UR Tel: 01228 532774 Fax: 01228 521275 Email: rhq@kingsownborder.demon.co.uk WWW: www.armymuseums.org Museum devoted to the history of Cumbria's County Infantry Regiment 1702 to date, with information on Regular, Territorial Volunteer and Militia units associated with the Regiments incl. Soldiers; med, Museum devoted to the history of Cumbria's County Infantry Regiment 1702 to date, with information on Regular, Territorial Volunteer and Militia units associated with the Regiment. Extensive archives

Derbyshire
Regimental Museum of the 9th/12th Royal Lancers,
Derby City Museum and Art Gallery, The Strand Derby,
DE1 1BS Tel: 01332 716656 Fax: 01332 716670 Email:
diana.pealie@derby.gov.uk WWW:
www.derby.gov.uk/museums

Devon
Museum of Barnstaple & North Devon incorporating
Royal Devon Yeomanry Museum Peter A Boyd, The
Square Barnstaple, EX32 8LN Tel: 01271 346 747 Fax:
01271 346407 Email: admin@sal.org.uk
Devonshire and The Devonshire and Dorset Regiment
Archives, Wyvern Barracks, Barrack Road Exeter, EX2
6AE Tel: 01392 492436 Fax: 01392 492469

Dorset
The Keep Military Museum The Keep, Bridport Road
Dorchester, DT1 1RN Tel: 01305 264066 Fax: 01305
250373 Email: keep.museum@talk21.com WWW:
www.keepmilitarymuseum.org
Royal Signals Museum Blandford Camp Nr Blandford
Forum, DT11 8RH Tel: 01258-482248 Tel: 01258-482267
Fax: 01258-482084 WWW:
www.royalsignalsarmy.org.uk/museum/
Tank Museum Bovington, BH20 6JG Tel: 01929 405096
Fax: 01929 462410 Email: librarian@tankmuseum.co.uk
davidw@tankmuseum.co.uk WWW:
www.tankmuseum.co.uk

Essex
Essex Regiment Museum Oaklands Park, Moulsham Street
Chelmsford, CM2 9AQ Tel: 01245 615101 Fax: 01245
611250 Email: pompadour@chelsfordbc.gov.uk WWW:
http://www.chelmsfordbc.gov.uk Substantial database of Essex
service people from 1741. Family inquiries welcomed. Donations
please to The Trustee of the Essex Regiment Museum
Essex Secret Bunker, Crown Building, Shrublands Road
Mistley, CO11 1HS Tel: 01206 392271 (24 hour info line)
Kelvedon Hatch Secret Nuclear Bunker, Kelvedon Hall
Lane, Kelvedon Common, Kelvedon Hatch, Brentwood,
CM15 0LB Tel: 01277 364883 Fax: 01277 372562 Email:
bunker@japar.demon.co.uk WWW: www.japar.demon.co.uk
Visitor Access via A128

Gloucestershire
Soldiers of Gloucestershire Museum Gloucester Docks,
Commercial Road Gloucester, GL1 2EH Tel: 01452 522682
Fax: 01452 311116

Hampshire
Aldershot Military Museum Queens Avenue Aldershot,
GU11 2LG Tel: 01252-314598 Fax: 01252-342942 Email:
musim@hants.gov.uk WWW:
www.hants.gov.uk/museum/aldershot
The Museum of The Adjutant General's Corps, RHQ
Adjutant General's Corps Worthy Down, Winchester, SO21
2RG Tel: 01962 887435 Fax: 01962 887690 Email:
agc.regtsec@virgin.net Inc the Royal Army Pay Corps, The Royal
Army Educational Corps and the Army Legal Corps and part of the collections
of the Royal Military Police, The Military Provost Staff Corps and the
Women's Royal Army Corps
Army Physical Training Corps Museum , ASPT, Fox Line,
Queen's Avenue, Aldershot, GU11 2LB Tel: 01252 347168
Fax: 01252 340785 Email: regtsec@aptc.org.uk WWW:
www.aptc.org.uk
Army Medical Services Museum Keogh Barracks Ash
Vale, Aldershot, GU12 5RQ Tel: 01252 868612 Fax: 01252
868832 Email: museum@keogh72.freeserve.co.uk Archives
on the Army Medical Services inc doctors, vetinary surgeons, dentists
and some nurses CC accepted
Museum of Army Flying, Middle Wallop, Stockbridge,
SO20 8DY Tel: 01980 674421 Fax: 01264 781694 Email:
daa@flying-museum.org.uk WWW: www.flying-
museum.org.uk

The Gurkha Museum Peninsula Barracks, Romsey Road
Winchester, SO23 8TS Tel: 01962 842832, Fax: 01962
877597
The King's Royal Hussars Museum (10th Royal Hussars
PWO 11th Hussars PAO and Royal Hussars PWO),
Peninsula Barracks, Romsey Road Winchester, SO23 8TS
Tel: 01962 828540 Fax: 01962 828538 Email:
beresford@krhmuseum.freeserve.co.uk WWW:
www.hants.gov.uk/leisure/museum/royalhus/index.html
The Light Infantry Museum Peninsula Barracks, Romsey
Road Winchester, SO23 8TS Tel: 01962 868550
Queen Alexandra's Royal Army Nursing Corps Museum
Regimental Headquarters Army Medica, Keogh Barracks,
Ash Vale, Aldershot, GU12 5RQ Tel:
The Royal Green Jackets Museum (Oxford and Bucks
Light Infantry King's Royal Rifle Corps and The Rifle
Brigade), Peninsula Barracks, Romsey Road Winchester,
SO23 8TS Tel: 01962 828549 Fax: 01962 828500
Royal Hampshire Regimental Museum Serle's House,
Southgate Street Winchester, SO23 9EG Tel: 01962 863658
Fax: 01962 888302
Royal Marines Museum Eastney Southsea, PO4 9PX Tel:
(023) 92 819385-Exts-224 Fax: (023) 92 838420 Email:
matthewlittle@royalmarinesmuseum.co.uk WWW:
www.royalmarinesmuseum.co.uk No charges for research other
than material costs. Donations welcome. Visits by appointment Mon
to Fri 10am to 4.30pm
Royal Naval Museum H M Naval Base (PP66),
Portsmouth, PO1 3NH Tel: (023) 9272 3795 Fax: (023) 9272
3942 Email: WWW: www.royalnavalmuseum.org
Royal Navy Submarine Museum Haslar Jetty Road
Gosport, PO12 2AS Tel: (023) 92510354 Fax: (023) 9251
1349 Email: admin@rnsubmus.co.uk WWW:
www.rnsubmus.co.uk Archive and photographic library by prior
appointment. Unique record of service of submarine personnel

Hertfordshire
Hertford Museum (Hertfordshire Regiment) 18 Bull
Plain Hertford, SG14 1DT Tel: 01992 582686 Fax: 01992
534797 Email: enquiries@hertfordmuseum.org WWW:
www.hertfordmuseum.org

Kent
Buffs Regimental Museum The Royal Museum & Art
Gallery, 18 High Street Canterbury, CT1 2RA Tel: 01227-
452747 Fax: 01227-455047 Email:
museum@canterbury.gov.uk WWW: www.canterbury-
museums.co.uk Story of the Royal East Kent Regiment, The Buffs
and its worldwide service. Admission free.
Dover Castle, Dover, CT16 1HU Tel: 01304 211067
Princess of Wales's Royal Regt & Queen's Regt Museum
Howe Barracks, Canterbury, CT1 1JY Tel: 01227-818056
Fax: 01227-818057 Covers Infantry Regiements of Surrey, Kent,
Sussex, Hampshire and Middlesex
The Queen's Own Royal West Kent Regiment Museum
Maidstone Museum & Art Gallery, St. Faith's Street
Maidstone ME14 1LH Tel: 01622 754497 Fax: 01622 602193
Royal Engineers Library, Brompton Barracks, Chatham,
ME4 4UX Tel: 01634 822416 Fax: 01634 822419
Royal Engineers Museum of Military Engineering Prince
Arthur Road Gillingham, ME4 4UG Tel: 01634 406397
Fax: 01634 822371 Email: remuseum.rhgre@gtnet.gov.uk
WWW: http://www.army.mod.uk/armymuseums

Lancashire
The Fusiliers Museum (Lancashire), Wellington Barracks,
Bolton Road Bury, BL8 2PL Tel: 0161 764 2208
King's Own Royal Regimental Museum The City
Museum Market Square, Lancaster, LA1 1HT Tel: 01524
64637 Fax: Fax: 01524 841692 Email:
kingsownmuseum@iname.com
Museum of Lancashire (Queen's Lancashire Regiment
Duke of Lancaster's Own Yeomanry Lancashire Hussars
14th/20th King's Hussars), Stanley Street, Preston, PR1
4YP Tel: 01772 264075

Museum of the Manchester Regiment, Ashton Town Hall, Market Place Ashton-u-Lyne, OL6 6DL Tel: 0161 342 3078 museum.manchester@nxcorp1.tameside.gov.uk WWW: www.tameside.gov.uk For archives contact Tameside Local Studies Library 0161 303 7937

Museum of the Queen's Lancashire Regiment (East South and Loyal (North Lancashire) Regiments, Lancashire Regiment (PWV) and The Queen's Lancashire Regiment, Fulwood Barracks, Preston, PR2 8AA Tel: 01772 260362 Fax: 01772 260583 Email: rhqqlr@aol.com Including associated Volunteer, TA and Militia Units

South Lancashire Regiment Prince of Wales Volunteers Museum Peninsula Barracks Warrington

Leicestershire

Royal Leicestershire Regiment Museum Gallery, New Walk Museum New Walk Leicester, LE1 7FA Tel: 0116 2470403 Postal enquiries: Newarke Houses Museum The Newarke, Leicester LE2 7BY

Lincolnshire

The Queen's Royal Lancers Regimental Museum (16th/5th and 17th/21st Lancers), Belvoir Castle, nr Grantham , NG32 1PD Tel: 0115 957 3295 Fax: 0115 957 3195

London

James Clavell Library, Royal Arsenal (West), Warren Lane, Woolwich, London, SE18 6ST Tel: 020 8312 7125 Email: library@firepower.org.uk WWW: www.firepower.org.uk

Coldstream Guards Record Office, Wellington Barracks, Birdcage Walk London, SW1E 6HQ Access is by appointment made in advance. Search fee of £25.00 per search

Firepower - The Royal Artillery Museum Royal Arsenal Woolwich, London, SE18 6ST Tel: (020) 8855 7755 Fax: Email: info@firepower.org.uk WWW: www.firepower.org.uk

Guards Museum Wellington Barracks, Birdcage Walk London, SW1E 6HQ Tel: (020) 7414 3271/3428 Fax: (020) 7414 3429

Grenadier Guards Record Office, Wellington Barracks, Birdcage Walk London, SW1E 6HQ Email: rhqgrengds@yahoo.co.uk Access is by appointment made in advance. Search fee of £25.00 per search

Imperial War Museum Lambeth Road London, SE1 6HZ Tel: (020) 7416-5000 Tel: (020) 7416 5348 Fax: (020) 7416 5374 (020) 7416 5246 Email: books@iwm.org.uk WWW: www.iwm.org.uk

Irish Guards Record Office, Wellington Barracks, Birdcage Walk London, SW1E 6HQ Email: bigbillaqq119@aol.com WWW: www.army.mod For archives information contact Archivist in first instance. Search fee of £25.00 per search

National Army Museum Royal Hospital Road London, SW3 4HT Tel: (020) 7730-0717 Fax: (020) 7823-6573 Email: info@national-army-museum.ac.uk WWW: http://www.national-army-museum.ac.uk Incorporating Middlesex Regiment Museum & Buffs regiment Museum

National Maritime Museum Romney Road, Greenwich, London, SE10 9NF Tel: (020) 8858-4422 Fax: (020) 8312-6632 Email: WWW: http://www.nmm.ac.uk CC accepted

RHQ Scots Guards Archives, Wellington Barracks, Birdcage Walk London, SW1E 6HQEmail: sgarchives@dial.pipex.com, Access is by appointment made in advance. Search fee of £25.00 per search

Royal Air Force Museum Grahame Park Way, Hendon, London, NW9 5LL Tel: (020) 8205-2266 Fax: (020) 8200 1751 Email: groupbusiness@refmuseum.org.uk WWW: http://www.rafmuseum.org.uk

The Royal Regiment of Fusiliers, H M Tower of London, London, EC3N 4AB Tel: (020) 7488 5610

Welsh Guards Record Office, Wellington Barracks, Birdcage Walk London, SW1E 6HQ Email: rhqwelshguards@milnet.uk.net Access is by appointment made in advance. Search fee of £25.00 per search

Merseyside

King's Regiment Collection, Museum of Liverpool Life, Pier Head Liverpool, L3 1PZ Tel: 0151-478-4062 Fax: 0151-478-4090 Collection of 8th King's Liverpool Regiment 1685 to 1958 & the King's Regiment 1958 to date.

Norfolk

The Battlefields Trust 33 High Green, Brooke, Norwich, NR15 1HR Tel: 01508 558145 Fax: 01508 558145 Email: BattlefieldTrust@aol.com WWW: www.battlefieldstrust.com

The Mickleburgh Collection, Weybourne, Holt, NR25 7EG Tel: 01263 588210 Fax: 01263 588425 Email: jenny@mickleburgh.demon.co.uk Britains largest working military collection - tanks, model ships, suffolk & Norfolk Yeomanry collection, vehicles, guns and missiles etc

Royal Norfolk Regimental Museum Shirehall, Market Avenue Norwich, NR1 3JQ Tel: 01603 493649 Fax: 01603 765651 Email: regimental.museum@central.norfolk.gov.uk WWW: www..norfolk.gov.uk

Northamptonshire

Abington Museum and Museum of The Northamptonshire Regiment, Abington Park Museum Abington, NN1 5LW Tel: 01604 635412 Fax: 01604 238720 Email: museums@northamton.gov.uk WWW: www.northampton.gov.uk/museums

Northumberland

Fusiliers' Museum of Northumberland, The Abbot's Tower, Alnwick Castle Alnwick, NE66 1NG Tel: 01665-602151 Fax: 01665-603320 Email: fusmusnorthld@btinternet.com ,

King's Own Scottish Borderers Museum The Barracks, The Parade Berwick upon Tweed, TD15 1DG Tel: 01289 307426

A Soldier's Life 15th/19th The King's Royal Hussars Northumberland Hussars and Light Dragoons, Discovery Museum Blandford Square Newcastle-upon-Tyne, NE1 4JA Tel: 0191 232 6789 Fax: 0191 230 261 Email: ralph.thompson@tyne-wear-museums.org.uk

Nottinghamshire

Sherwood Foresters Museum and Archives, RHQ WFR, Foresters House, Chetwynd Barracks, Chilwell, Nottingham, NG9 5HA Tel: 0115 946 5415 Fax: 0115 946 9853 Email: curator@wfrmuseum.org.uk WWW: www.wfrmuseum.org.uk

Sherwood Foresters (Notts and Derby Regiment) Museum The Castle, Nottingham, NG1 6EL Tel: 0115 946 5415 Fax: 0115 946 9853 Email: rhqwfr-nottm@lineone.net WWW: www.wfrmuseum.org.uk Address for enquiries: RHQ WFR, Foresters House, Chetwynd Barracks, Chilwell, Nottingham NG9 5HA

Oxfordshire

Oxfordshire and Buckinghamshire Light Infantry Regimental Museum Slade Park Headington, Oxford, OX3 7JL Tel: 01865 780128

Shropshire

Shropshire Regimental Museum (King's Shropshire Light Infantry, Shropshire Yeomanry) Shropshire Militia, Volunteers and TA, The Castle, Shrewsbury, SY1 2AT Tel: 01743 358516 Tel: 01743 262292 Fax: 01743 270023 Email: shropshire@zoom.co.uk WWW: www.shropshireregimental.co.uk Limited information only on individuals. Does not hold service records of soldiers.

Somerset

Fleet Air Arm Museum Records Research Centre, Box D61, RNAS Yeovilton Nr Ilchester, BA22 8HT Tel: 01935-840565 Fax: 01935-840181**Somerset Military Museum (Somerset Light Infantry Yeomanry) Militia and Volunteers) County Museum** The County Museum Taunton Castle, Taunton, TA1 4AA Tel: 01823 333434 Fax: 01823 351639

Staffordshire
Museum of The Staffordshire Regiment, Whittington Barracks, Lichfield, WS14 9PY Tel: 0121 311 3240 Tel: 0121 311 3229 Fax: 0121 311 3205 Email: museum@rhqstaffords.fsnet.co.uk Museum illustrating the history of the Staffordshire Regiments and the four ancestor regiments from 1705. The museum has an extensive archive and a replica World War I trench system over 100 metres
Museum of the Staffordshire Yeomanry, The Ancient High House, Greengate Street Stafford, ST16 2HS Tel: 01785 619130 Info available on Regiment's history during Boer, WWI and WWII. There are no records of individual servicemen

Suffolk
Suffolk Regiment Museum -Museum closed to the public, Suffolk Record Office, 77 Raingate Street Bury St Edmunds, IP33 2AR Tel: 01284-352352 Fax: 01284-352355 Email: bury.ro@libher.suffolkcc.gov.uk WWW: http://www.suffolkcc.gov.uk/sro/ Museum closed to the public but archives and photographs available for inspection at the Record Office

Surrey
Regimental Museum Royal Logistic Corps, Princess Royal Barracks Deepcut, Camberley, GU16 6RW Tel: 01252 833371 Fax: 01252 833484 Email: query@rlcmuseum.freeserve.co.uk WWW: www.army-rlc.co.uk/museum The story of military logistics and the RLCs forming corps - The Royal Corps of Transport, The Royal Army Ordnance Corp, The Royal Pioneer Corps and the Army Catering Corps are told in this museum
Queen's Royal Surrey Regiment Museum (Queen's Royal, East Surrey & Queen's Royal Surrey Regiments) Clandon Park, West Clandon, Guildford, GU4 7RQ Tel: 01483 223419 Fax: 01483 224636 Email: queenssurreys@caree4free.net WWW: www.surrey-on;line.co.uk/queenssurreys
Royal Military Police Museum Roussillon Barracks, Chichester, PO19 4BN Tel: 01243 534225 Fax: 01243 534288 Email: museum@rhqrmp.freeserve.co.uk WWW: www.rhqrmp.freeserve.co.uk
Sussex Combined Services Museum (Royal Sussex Regiment and Queen's Royal Irish Hussars), Redoubt Fortress, Royal Parade Eastbourne, BN22 7AQ Tel: 01323 410300

Warwickshire
Regimental Museum of The Queen's Own Hussars (3rd King's Own and 7th Queen's Own Hussars), The Lord Leycester Hospital, High Street Warwick, CV34 4EW Tel: 01926 492035
Royal Warwickshire Regimental Museum St. John's House, Warwick , CV34 4NF Tel: 01926 491653

Wiltshire
Duke of Edinburgh's Royal Regiment (Berks & Wilts) Museum The Wardrobe, 58 The Close, Salisbury, SP1 2EX Tel: 01722-414536 Fax: 01722 421626
Royal Army Chaplains Department Museum Netheravon House, Salisbury Road Netheravon, SP4 9SY Tel: 01980-604911 Fax: 01980-604908

Worcestershire
The Worcestershire Regiment Museum Worcester City Museum & Art Gallery, Foregate Street Worcester, WR1 1DT Tel: 01905-25371 Museum Tel: 01905 354359 Office Fax: 01905-616979 Email: rhq_wfr@lineone.net Postal Address: The Curator, The Worcestershire Regimental Museum Trust, RHQ WFR, Norton Barracks, Worcester WR5 2PA
Warwickshire Yeomanry Museum The Court House, Jury Street Warwick, CV34 4EW Tel: 01926 492212 Fax: 01926 494837 Email: wtc.admin@btclick.com
Worcestershire Regiment Archives (Worcestershire and Sherwood Forester's Regiment), RHQ WFR Norton Barracks, Worcester, WR5 2PA Tel: 01905 354359 Fax: 01905 353871 Email: rhg_wfr@lineone.net, Enquires only accepted in writing by letter, email or fax
The Museum of the Worcestershire Yeomanry Cavalry, Worcester City Museum & Art Gallery, Foregate St Worcester, WR1 1DT Tel: 01905 25371 Fax: 01905 616979 Email: tbridges@cityofworcester.gov.uk

WWW: www.worcestercitymuseums.org.uk
Yorkshire - East
Museum of Army Transport Flemingate Beverley, HU17 0NG Tel: 01482 860445 Fax: 01482 872767
Yorkshire - North
Eden Camp Museum , Malton, YO17 6RT Tel: 01653 697777 Fax: 01653 698243 Email: admin@edencamp.co.uk WWW: http://www.edencamp.co.uk
Green Howards Regimental Museum Trinity Church Square Richmond, DL10 4QN Tel: 01748-822133 Fax: 01748-826561 Story of the Green Howards (Alexandra, Princess of Wales's Own Yorkshire Regiment from 1688 to date)
Royal Dragoon Guards Military Museum (4th/7th Royal Dragoon Guards & 5th Royal Inniskilling Dragoon Guards) 3A Tower Street York, YO1 9SB Tel: 01904-662790 Tel: 01904 662310 Fax: 01904 662310 Email: rdgmuseum@onetel.net.uk WWW: www.rdg.co.uk co located with Prince of Wales' Own Regiment of Yorkshire Military Museum (West & East Yorkshire Regiments)
Yorkshire Air Museum Halifax Way, Elvington, York, YO41 4AU Tel: 01904 608595 Fax: 01904 608246 Email: museum@yorkshireairmuseum.co.uk WWW: www.yorkshireairmuseum.co.uk
Yorkshire - South
King's Own Yorkshire Light Infantry Regimental Museum Doncaster Museum & Art Gallery, Chequer Road Doncaster, DN1 2AE Tel: 01302 734293 Fax: 01302 735409 Email: museum@doncaster.gov.uk WWW: www.doncaster.gov.uk
Regimental Museum 13th/18th Royal Hussars and The Light Dragoons, Cannon Hall, Cawthorne Barnsley, S75 4AT Tel: 01226 790270
York and Lancaster Regimental Museum Library and Arts Centre, Walker Place, Rotherham S65 1JH Tel: 01709 823635 Fax: 01709 823631 Email: karl.noble@rotherham.gov.uk WWW: www.rotherham.gov.uk,
Yorkshire - West
Duke of Wellington's Regimental Museum Bankfield Museum Akroyd Park, Boothtown Road, Halifax, HX3 6HG Tel: England Tel: 01422 354823 Fax: 01422 249020

Wales
Cardiff
1st The Queen's Dragoon Guards Regimental Museum Cardiff Castle, Cardiff, CF10 2RB Tel: (029) 2022 2253 Tel: (029) 2078 1271 Fax: (029) 2078 1384 Email: clivejmorris@lineone.net WWW: www.qdg.org.uk
Gwynedd
The Royal Welch Fusiliers Regimental Museum , The Queen's Tower, The Castle Caernarfon, LL55 2AY Tel: 01286 673362 Fax: 01286 677042 Email: rwfusiliers@callnetuk.com WWW: www.rwfmuseum.org.uk
Monmouth
Monmouthshire Royal Engineers (Militia), Castle and Regimental Museum The Castle Monmouth, NP25 3BS Tel: 01600-712935 Email: curator@monmouthcastlemuseum.org.uk WWW: www.monmouthcastlemuseum.org.uk Small Militia and Territorial Army Regiment. Limited and patchy collection of old ledgers.
Nelson Museum & Local History Centre Priory St Monmouth, NP5 3XA Tel: 01600 713519 Fax: 01600 775001 Email: nelsonmuseum@monmouthshire.gov.uk
Powys
South Wales Borderers & Monmouthshire Regimental Museum of the Royal Regt of Wales (24th/41st Foot), The Barracks, Brecon, LD3 7EB Tel: 01874 613310 Fax: 01874 613275 Email: swb@rrw.org.uk WWW: www.rrw.org.uk

Scotland
Ayrshire Yeomanry Museum Rozelle House, Monument Road Alloway by Ayr, KA7 4NQ Tel: 01292 445400 (Museum) Tel: 01292 264091 (Curator) The Ayrshire (ECO) Yeomanry was raised in 1798 and after 200 years existence, currently serves as one of the five squadrons in the Territorial Armoured Reconnaisance Regiment - The Queen's Own Yeomanry

Royal Scots Regimental Museum The Castle, Edinburgh, EH1 2YT Tel: 0131-310-5014 Fax: 0131-310-5019
Museum of The Royal Highland Fusiliers (Royal Scots Fusiliers and Highland Light Infantry) 518 Sauchiehall Street Glasgow, G2 3LW Tel: 0141 332 0961 Fax: 0141 353 1493
Gordon Highlanders Museum St Lukes, Viewfield Road Aberdeen, AB15 7XH Tel: 01224 311200 Fax: 01224 319323 Email: museum@gordonhighlanders.com WWW: www.gordonhighlanders.com
Queen's Own Highlanders (Seaforth & Camerons) Regimental Museum, Fort George Ardersier, Inverness, IV1 7TD Tel: 01463-224380
The Cameronians (Scottish Rifles) Museum c/o Low Parks Museum 129 Muir Street Hamilton, ML3 6BJ Tel: 01698 452163 Tel: 01698 328232 Fax: 01698 328412

Perthshire
Regimental Museum and Archives of Black Watch
Balhousie Castle, Hay Street, Perth, PH1 5HR Tel: 0131-3108530 Fax: 01738-643245 Email: bwarchivist@btclick.com

Stirlingshire
Regimental Museum Argyll and Sutherland Highlanders, Stirling Castle, Stirling, FK8 1EH Tel: 01786 475165 Fax: 01786 446038 CC accepted

Northern Ireland
Royal Ulster Rifles Regimental Museum RHQ Royal Irish Regiment, 5 Waring Street Belfast, BT1 2EW Tel: (028) 90232086 Fax: (028) 9023 2086 Email: rurmuseum@yahoo.co.uk WWW: http://www.rurmuseum.tripod.com
Royal Irish Fusilers Museum Sovereign's House, Mall East Armagh, BT61 9DL Tel: (028) 3752 2911 Fax: (028) 3752 2911 Email: rylirfusilier@aol.com
Royal Inniskilling Fusiliers Regimental Museum The Castle, Enniskillen, BT74 7BB Tel: (028) 66323142 Fax: (028) 66320359

Belgium
In Flanders Fields Museum Lakenhallen, Grote Markt 34, Ieper, B-8900 Tel: 00-32-(0)-57-22-85-84 Fax: 00-32-(0)-57-22-85-89 Email: WWW: www.inflandersfields.be

The *NEW* NATIONAL British Fair for Family and Local History

Adoption Records in England and Wales
Doreen Hopwood - a brief guide to Adoption

Just as it became the responsibility of the government to register all births, marriages and deaths in England and Wales from 1 July 1837, some ninety years later, the Adopted Children's Register was introduced to maintain a record of all adoptions after 1 January 1927. The Register of Stillbirths was established at the same time.

Prior to 1927 there was no formal adoption process, and the term "adopted" generally included fostering and guardianship. In many instances a child was simply "adopted" into the extended family or taken in by neighbours/family friends and brought up as a member of their own family. Occasionally it was arranged through a solicitor, doctor or charitable organisation but adoption was viewed as an essentially private arrangement between the parties concerned. If any documentation has survived, it is likely to be found in the relevant county record office (with the solicitors' deposited material) or with the records of the organisation. However, to access these it is necessary to know the name of the solicitor/organisation and the approximate date on which the arrangement was made.

When the Adopted Children Register came into force, it was believed that it was in the best interests of all concerned that the adopted child's break with his or her birth family should be complete and final. Parents who placed a child for adoption were told that he or she would not be able to gain access to his or her birth record. However, under legislation in the form of the 1976 Adoptions Act, it was recognised that adopted persons, whilst full members of their new families, may still wish to know about their origins. Therefore until 1975, both adopters and parents may have been given to understand that that adopted persons would never be able to discover their original names or those of their birth parents. Persons who were adopted prior to 12 November 1975 are required to receive counselling from an experienced social worker before access can be given to their original birth record. This is not compulsory for persons adopted after this date, but counselling can be taken if they wish. The main purposes of counselling is to help adopted persons to understand the information given in their adoption records and to explain some of the possible effects (both on themselves and others) if further enquiries about their birth families are pursued.

Most people who have been adopted are aware of this, and have a copy of their certificate of adoption from the Adopted Children's Register. This supersedes the original certificate of birth and is used for all legal purposes. The original birth registration is retained at the Register Office where the birth was registered and the entry in the register is endorsed "adopted". The Superintendent Registrar has no information concerning the subsequent entry in the Adopted Children's Register. The General Register Office Index of Births does NOT include adoptions, but the indexes to the Adopted Children's Registers are available for consultation at the Family Records Centre, 1 Myddleton Place, London EC1R IUX. Applications for certificates can be made in person there – the certificate will be posted on to you – or postal applications should be made to the Office of National Statistics, General Register Office (Adoptions Section), Trafalgar Road, Birkdale, Southport, Merseyside PR8 2HH. A statutory fee is payable, and telephone applications by credit/debit card can be made by telephoning 0151 471 4313. There is also a priority service for which a higher fee is charged. Leaflet ACR 99 from ONS provides full details of how to apply for a certificate from the Adopted Children's Register.
As with all birth certificates, it is possible to purchase either a full or short certificate, but the latter will not provide information to help with any family research. The full certificate shows the full names, date and place of birth and sex of the adopted person, the names addresses and occupation of the adoptive parents (at the time of the adoption), the date and name of the court making the Adoption Order and the date of entry in the Adopted Children's Register. Once the application for the certificate has been processed, the Registrar General will send most of the information from the Adoption Order to the counsellor with whom an interview has been arranged, or if counselling is not to take place, details will be posted with the certificate to the applicant. However, a copy of the original birth certificate will NOT be included. Sufficient information will be given to enable a copy to be purchased at the statutory fee. The full copy birth certificate will provide the names under which the child was originally registered, the sex, place and date of birth, the name(s) of the parent(s), occupation (where applicable) and the name and address of the person who registered the birth. The date of registration is included and the name of the registrar. If the parents were married to each other, the fathers' name and occupation is shown as well as the maiden name of the mother. If the parents were not married, it is possible that no father's details are given. These can only be included if he attended to register the birth and agreed to having his details on the certificate.

If the adoption was arranged through an adoption society or by a local authority, further records MAY be available and the counsellor can provide authorisation for the adopted person to ask the court at which the order was made for further information. If counselling has not taken place, the Registrar General will provide the authorisation. The adopted person can then pursue this with the relevant organisation or local authority. However, not all records have survived and even where they are available, they may not provide any additional information concerning the birth parents.

This process does not indicate whether or not contact between birth parents and adopted children would be welcome, but since 1 May 1991, it has been possible for adopted persons, birth parents and relatives of adopted persons to register their interest in making contact. The Adoption Contact Register provides a confidential channel by which interested parties can be put in touch with each other. Anyone who wishes to register must be over 18 years of age, and the Register is split into two sections. Part I is for adopted persons whose birth has been registered by the Registrar General, and Part II is for persons related to the adopted person. This includes birth parents, brothers and sisters or any other person related by blood, half-blood or marriage, but does not include adoptive relatives. There is also provision for the name and address of a third party/intermediary to be given if preferred. Following registration, for which a fee is payable, the adopted person will be given details of any links found, including the name and address of the relative (or intermediary). At the same time, the relative (or intermediary) will be advised that information has been passed on to the adopted person. Further information and how to register on the Adoption Contact Register can be found in Leaflet ACR 110 or on-line at www.frc.gov.uk.

Post Adoption agencies can also offer advice and their addresses and telephone numbers can be obtained from the Social Services Departments of local authorities. Another helpful guide is "Where to find Adoption Records : a guide for counsellors" by G Stafford may also be useful in locating specific records.
This article was prepared with the assistance of Nicola Fleeson, Leeds Registrars Office.

The Adopted One
Heather Rogers

It all began a long time ago during the early years of the Second World War in London. Kate was a married woman with a six month old baby boy. During the bitter cold winter of 1940 Kate had a brief affair and conceived a baby girl. She did not tell her husband. A few weeks later her husband was called up for war service in the RAF and within two years he was a Flight Sergeant. Married quarters were allocated to them and Kate and the children moved in with her husband.

Whilst living in the married quarters Kate had a deep passionate affair with another airman. He was only twenty years old and was besotted with her. Kate was twenty eight and like so many people during the war lived one day at a time. She wanted her new love no matter what and when she became pregnant again she left her husband, put her son, aged three and a half, and her daughter, Heather aged two years, into an orphanage,.and moved back to London. She took on a new identity and called herself by another name, dyed her hair and left her past behind her. At the beginning of 1943 Kate went through a bigamous marriage with her new love.

Heather was adopted from the orphanage and grew up with her adoptive parents in South Wales unaware that she had been adopted. When she was fourteen she was walking home from school when two boys from her class taunted her and said that they knew something about her. Looking at them wide eyed and amazed she pleaded with the boys to tell her. The younger one blurted out that he would kill himself if he were her. Heather looked at him strangely and demanded to know what on earth they were talking about. The other boy, who was more sure of himself shouted out and smirked. 'You are adopted' Heather looked at both boys in disbelief and ran home alone with her mind in a whirl.

Heather decided not to mention what had happened to her parents. The following Saturday pretending to have a headache Kate stayed at home instead of accompanying her parents shopping. Immediately after they had gone out Heather went into her mother's bedroom and searched through the bottom of her wardrobe finding an old biscuit tin where her mother kept insurance and other personal papers.

Heather looked through the papers making sure that she did not disturb the order they were in. In a large brown envelope at the bottom of the tin she found her adoption papers. She slumped down onto the bed and pointed to herself in the mirror crying "this is me, this is me." The tears flowed thick and fast and her stomach was in knots as she read through the papers over and over again.

Suddenly, she heard the key turn in the front door and hastily put the papers back where they belonged, wiped the tears from her eyes, closed the wardrobe door and went quietly down stairs. Heather said nothing to her parents who were busy sorting out the weekly shopping. She felt so hurt that they had never told her about her adoption and decided to keep it a secret until she was old enough to find her birth parents.

Within four years both of her adoptived parents had died and Heather was left on her own. She married at twenty, had one daughter, but the marriage did not last. In 1963 she began her search in earnest trying every avenue she could possibly think of to find her birth mother. It was not until 1981 that she discovered where her birth mother was living. When she finally made contact over the phone her birth mother told her in no uncertain terms that she did not want to have anything to do with her because she had a son in Holy Orders.

Heather was devastated and cried her heart out, but finding her birth mother did not take away the scar deep down inside that seemed to haunt her. She just wanted an hour of her mother's time to put the pieces of the jigsaw together for her but it was not to be, until many years later.

The Parting.
She stood with breath abaited and knew what she must do
How could she ever forgive herself but
    she had thought it through
No more the struggling days ahead for her two children dear
She had found them another home instead
    and one day would make it clear
That if their father had not gone away to fight the war
She would not have met another man
    whom she had fallen for
He promised her another life in a land of milk and honey
But said he could not take her children as
    he did not have the money
By now she'd fallen pregnant and could see no other way
Her husband did not want her so with
    her love she had to stay
The orphanage door opened and amongst the noise and din
A woman dressed all in white said
    'Won't you please step in?'
She had to sign some papers and left the children's things
Her mind was wracked with torment
    as she thought of what love brings
She flung her arms around them and
    whispered 'I won't be long'
They started crying for her but she knew she must be strong
She headed for the doorway and took a backward look
And saw them huddled on a bench faces
    streaming like a brook
She thought you'll thank me one day for doing you this turn
She did not think their hearts would break
    and all life long they'd yearn
To see the mother they had lost and hold her in their arms
She only thought of the man she loved as
    she was besotted by his charms.

This is my story. I am Heather and Kate is my birth mother. If you are adopted and need to find your roots I can offer confidential specialist help with my sound search package at reasonable rates. I have worked as a helpline worker with After Adoption Wales for several years and know that there is a genuine need for people to find their roots and come to terms with their past. With the knowledge that I have obtained with my own search and helping others I know of the pitfalls and feelings that surface along the way and will be only too glad to offer my services.

Heather Rogers 21, Eastmoor Road, Newport, South Wales. NP19 4NX E.mail:rogers1940@hotmail.com

(1)	(2)	(3)	(4)	(5)	(6)	(7)	(8)
No. of entry	Date and country of birth of child *(see footnotes)*	Name and surname of child	Sex of child	Name and surname, address and occupation of adopter or adopters	Date of adoption order and description of court by which made	Date of entry	Signature of officer deputed by Registrar General to attest the entry
	June 1947 England		Male		January 1951 Juvenile Court	January 1951	

CERTIFIED COPY OF AN ENTRY IN THE RECORDS OF THE GENERAL REGISTER OFFICE

Given at the GENERAL REGISTER OFFICE, TITCHFIELD, FAREHAM, HANTS

Application Number B2181-10.

CERTIFIED copy of an entry in the Adopted Children Register maintained at the General Register Office. Given at the GENERAL REGISTER OFFICE, TITCHFIELD, FAREHAM, HANTS, under the Seal of the said Office, the   day of   1990 .

GA 129636

Certificate Services - Southport

Melanie Connell - Communications Manager

The General Register Office is part of the Office for National Statistics and is the central source of certified copies of register entries (certificates) in England and Wales. Since 1837 each entry made in a register of births, marriages or deaths in England and Wales has been copied to the centrally held national record maintained by General Register Office. Certificate Services is the name given to the arm of the General Register Office (GRO) that deals with applications for copies from this record of births, marriages and deaths and is based in Southport, Merseyside.

Many customers who apply to Certificate Services for a certificate do so for legal or administrative purposes such as applying for a passport or pension but increasingly a large proportion of applications are from family historians and professional genealogists. In 2001/02 we received over 825,000 certificate applications. This is an increase of some 40% over the past five years, and interest in family history accounts for most of that increase. GRO also has separate sections that deal with adoption certificates and certain overseas records.

Family Records Centre.

Many of you will be familiar with the "public face" of Certificate Services, the Family Records Centre (FRC) at 1 Myddelton Street London EC1R 1UW. The FRC is run in partnership with the Public Record Office and aims to provide a one stop shop for family history research. The Family Record Centre provides access to:

Paper indexes of births, marriages and deaths registered in England and Wales from 1st July 1837.
Indexes of legal adoptions in England and Wales from 1927.
Indexes of births, marriages and deaths of some British citizen's abroad from the late 18th century. These include:
Consular and High Commission returns since 1849; Marine births and deaths since 1837; aircraft births, deaths and missing persons from 1947; Army returns from 1881; Regimental registers 1761-1924; Army Chaplains returns 1796-1880; deaths in World Wars I and II and the Boer War; Ionic Islands and Indian State deaths.
A CD-ROM index of births which have taken place in Northern Ireland from 1922-1999.

The FRC also has access to information on Scottish Registration. There is a computerised link to the statutory indexes of births, marriages and deaths from 1855 to the present day. A fee is charged for this service and booking may be necessary. If you wish to book to search the Scottish records please telephone 020 7533 6438.

How to go about finding a register entry

It is not possible for applicants to search through copies of the actual register entries themselves. However the indexes may be searched to identify the entry you seek. The indexes are arranged by year and then alphabetically by surname. Before 1983 the indexes are also split into the quarter of the year in which the event was registered e.g. events registered in January, February or March are indexed in the March quarter for the relevant year.

To apply for a certificate of the entry you can choose which method best suits you:

Application in person via the FRC

The Family Records Centre is open to the public at the following times:
Monday 9am-5pm; Tuesday 10am-7pm
Wednesday 9am-5pm; Thursday 9am*-7pm
Friday 9am-5pm; Saturday 9.30am-5pm
Once you have searched the indexes and identified an entry you simply complete an application form, including the GRO Reference Number listed in the index and take it to the cashiers for payment. The fee for each certificate is £6.50.

Smedley Hydro

All applications made at the FRC are transported overnight to Certificate Services at Smedley Hydro, Southport, Merseyside. Many people have asked about the unusual name of the office where their certificates are produced. Smedley Hydro was build in early Victorian times and known as the Birkdale College for the education of young gentlemen. It then became a Hydropathic Hotel whose electro-chemical baths where extremely popular "in restoring the work-weary, the enfeebled and those of a naturally delicate organisation". With the outbreak of the Second World War the building was requisitioned by His Majesty's government for the purpose of National Registration and there are now 750 people working at the Southport Office with 285 of them employed within Certificate Services.

Production Process

Once your application is received at Smedley Hydro the race then begins to have the applications sorted ready for the staff to retrieve the relevant microfilm, load the film onto a reader, find the entry, scan the image and produce the certificate ready for either posting out on the fourth working day or returning to the FRC for collection on the fourth working day. This is no mean feat when you consider that between ten and twelve thousand applications are received via the FRC every week. Last year (2001/2002) 97% of "post out" applications at the FRC were dispatched on time, with 99% of FRC "collect" cases available on time. This compares very well with our performance a couple of years ago when, due to a variety of factors, delays of many weeks were experienced. Our goal is to build on this achievement and further improve the quality of what we produce.

Application direct to GRO Southport

If it is not convenient for you to go to central London and visit the FRC, you can apply directly to GRO Southport for your certificates. It would, of course, help us to have the index reference for the entry you want, so you may wish to look this up at one of the many centres around the country which hold copies of the national GRO index on microfiche. There are over 100 such locations including libraries, County Records

Smedley Hydro, Southport
Reproduced with the permission of Martin Perry, Southport Civic Society

Offices and Family History Centres within the UK and overseas. To find out the nearest one to you telephone Certificate Services on 0870 243 7788.

Please note that it is not possible for members of the public to search the indexes at our Southport office itself. Personal callers are welcome to leave certificate applications between the hours of 9am – 5pm, Monday – Friday at GRO, Smedley Hydro, Trafalgar Rd, Birkdale, Southport.

Most applicants to GRO Southport prefer to apply by one of the following methods:

By telephone:
Our call centre may be reached by dialling 0870 243 7788. You will hear a menu selection before being transferred to an operator who can take the details of the GRO reference number(s) you want and then arrange for your certificate(s) to be posted out to you within 5 working days. The fee for this service is £8, and payment can be made by Visa, Master or Switch. Please note we do not accept Electron or American Express Cards. The Call Centre is available 6 days a week (Monday - Friday 8am-8pm Saturday 9am – 4pm) . Our Call Centre deals with a variety of enquires relating to certificate services and each week a team of 20 staff deal with nearly four and a half thousand telephone calls.

By fax or post:
You may wish to fax your certificate application to 01704 550013. Alternatively you can post in your application enclosing a cheque or postal order payable to **ONS** to : The General Register Office
PO Box 2, Southport, Merseyside, PR8 2JD

How to contact our office by email
As the e-revolution continues certificate services increasingly deal with a large number of enquiries from people who have visited our website. The address for our website is www.statistics.gov.uk, or email certificate.services@ons.gov.uk with your query.

What if you do not know the GRO reference number of the entry you want?
If you do not wish to conduct you own search of the indexes we are happy to do this for you. For a fee of £11 we will undertake a search of the indexes for the year in which you tell us the event concerned occurred, and if necessary a year either side as well if it cannot be found in that year. Due to the additional searches involved this service takes a little longer.

Once the application is received the certificate is posted out within 20 working days. Should we be unable to find the entry, we will refund your fee minus a search fee of £4.50

To assist us in the search you will need to provide as much information as possible about the person on the certificate you are trying to obtain. For a birth – full name, date of birth, place of birth and if known the parents names including the mothers maiden name. For a marriage, you will need to supply the names of both the bride and groom, date of marriage, place of marriage and if known, the fathers name for both bride and groom. For a death you will need to supply a full name, date of death, place of death and if a female their marital status. The occupation of the deceased is also helpful.

Application to a local Register Office
If you know exactly where the birth, marriage or death that you are looking for took place you may also apply to the local Register Office covering that area. The Superintendent Registrar will be able to provide you with a certificate from his or her records. Please note that the GRO reference number does not refer to these local records, and will unfortunately be of no use to them in finding the entry for you. You will be asked to provide details similar to those listed in the paragraphs above so that they can locate the entry for you.

Other services provided by GRO:
Commemorative Certificates.
Something that people may be unaware of is our Commemorative Certificate Section. For a cost of £40 they can provide a commemorative marriage certificate to mark silver, ruby, gold or diamond anniversaries. These certificates are colour printed on high quality paper and come mounted in frame within a presentation box, they do make an unusual and attractive gift. For further information call 0151 471 4256.

Overseas Section.
GRO also holds Overseas Records. They have records of the births, marriages and deaths of British Citizens overseas that have been registered with the British Registering authorities e.g. British Consuls, High Commissions, HM Forces, the Civil Aviation Authority and the Registrar General of Shipping and Seamen. Overseas certificates can be applied for in person at the FRC or alternatively, by post or by telephone at the General Register Office, Southport. They will usually be produced within 5 working days. Please telephone 0151 471 4801 or email overseas.gro@ons.gov.uk for further information.

Adoption Branch.
The Adopted Children Register (ACR) is also maintained at the General Register Office. This contains particulars of adoptions authorised by order of a court in England and Wales from 1st January 1927. An entry in the ACR replaces the original birth record and should be used for all legal purposes. An index is available at the FRC for applications for adoption certificates that are normally processed within 5 working days.

Once adopted children reach the age of eighteen they are entitled to apply for access to their original birth record. If they were adopted before 12 November 1975 they are required to attend an interview with an Adoption Counsellor before information about original birth records can be obtained. Anybody adopted after this date has the choice of either receiving this information directly or via an adoption counsellor. This facility is also available to people who have been adopted in England and Wales and are now living outside the UK. The Registrar General provides a counselling service at the FRC which supplements that provided by local authorities.

Adoptions Branch also maintains an Adoption Contact Register. This is a facility for both adopted adults and birth relatives to register an interest in contacting one another. A "link" is made when both parties register but the onus on whether contact is followed up lies with the adopted person. To date there have been

nearly 700 links. For more information on the services provided by Adoptions Branch please email adoptions@ons.gov.uk or telephone 0151 471 4313.

A new Adoption and Children Act 2002 received Royal Assent in November 2002 which proposes new methods for adopted persons and relatives to gain access to birth information. However given the breadth and complexity of the secondary legislation required, these are not expected to come into effect before 2004.

Certificate Services welcomes Feedback: We welcome feedback and customer input on the level and quality of service currently being provided. If you have any comments about our services please write to - Customer Service Unit Manager, PO Box 2, Southport, Merseyside, PR8 2JD or email certificate.services@ons.gov.uk

AIM25

~ *Archives in London and the M25 Area*
Rachel Kemsley - AIM25 Project Archivist

AIM25
Archives in London and the M25 area

Were your ancestors educated or employed in London? Over the course of the 19th and 20th centuries, hundreds of thousands of students passed through London's numerous higher education institutions. Today the University of London alone accounts for over 25 per cent of higher education activity in the UK, and the University and its colleges are one of London's largest employers. London's higher education institutions produced a large quantity of records which document their rich history, and a guide to these archives is freely available via the Internet at the AIM25 website: http://www.aim25.ac.uk

With over 5,000 records the AIM25 database covers a huge volume of sources held in nearly 50 institutions, many of them of interest to family and local historians.

The extension of higher education
From the 19th century opportunities in education were extended to larger numbers of people, increasingly across social and gender divides. Higher education in London began in the 1820s in reaction to the social and religious exclusivity of Oxford and Cambridge universities, opening education to the middle classes with the foundation of University College London (1826) - also open to nonconformists and Jews - and King's College London (1829). As the 19th century progressed, opportunities in higher education for women advanced, including the foundation of such institutions as Bedford College, Royal Holloway College, King's College for Women and its successor Queen Elizabeth College, and Westfield College.

Opportunities for other social groups advanced with the foundation of further institutions which were among the pioneers of vocational education, providing craft and technical education in subjects such as carpentry, horology, and printing, and preparation for commercial and clerical work with the

Civil Service and other metropolitan employers. This aspect of educational history is closely linked with the economic history of London. Many of these initiatives had close links with their locality, equipping men and women for employment with local industries and trades, for example the London College of Fashion (and its predecessors) and the capital's garment industry. Teacher training also developed, with the foundation of various training colleges. Within existing institutions courses were extended to cover new subjects, culminating in some cases in the foundation of new institutions, for instance the London School of Economics and Political Science (established 1895) and the School of Oriental (later Oriental and African) Studies (1916). Many new institutions were founded in this period and their history can be complex, with mergers, takeovers and changes of name: AIM25 tracks their histories and the records they produced.

Uses of higher education records
For family historians researching relatives who were students or teachers, the AIM25 website indicates where records of students and staff in higher

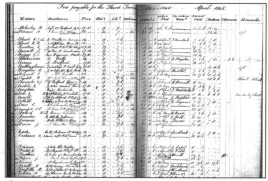

Fees book, King's College London 1845
© King's College London

Typing Class
Regent Street
Polytechnic
1890s
©King's College London

education institutions survive. Some records, in the cases of University College London and King's College London, date back to the 1820s and 1830s. Student records - for example registers and fees books listing students and, for later periods, files for individual students - may include biographical information (such as date of birth and details of schooling), attendance details, subjects studied, and examination results. An example of a fees book of 1845 from King's College London is pictured, listing students' names and addresses and detailing fees paid. In addition to official student records, more personal records sometimes survive, for instance lecture notes taken by individual students, like Edward Ballard's notes on medical lectures in the 1840s (University College London), and the notebooks of David Watson at the Royal School of Mines in the 1860s (Imperial College). Personnel records cover non-academic employees - for instance, administrative, technical, and household staff - as well as teaching staff. Users should note that more recent student and staff records may be closed. Most institutions have rich collections of photographs of their buildings, students, staff, activities and events. An example from Regent Street Polytechnic shows a typing class of the 1890s in progress.

In addition to academic and administrative records (e.g. departmental records), many institutions holds records of numerous sporting clubs and other societies, for example in debating, music and drama, in which students and staff were involved. The records document changes in leisure pursuits as participation in sports and other recreational activities increased. Particularly notable are the achievements of members of Regent Street Polytechnic, which produced Olympic champions in several sports, and was behind the evolution of sports clubs including the Polytechnic Harriers athletics club. Also a reflection of the extension of leisure activities was the increased

opportunity to travel abroad, shown by the Polytechnic Touring Association, founded in the late 19th century and pioneering cheaper travel for less affluent travellers, which eventually became part of the high street travel firm Lunn Poly.

Of interest to the local historian are records documenting the physical impact of higher education institutions on the built environment throughout London and its environs, from the fantastic Victorian architecture of Royal Holloway College, Egham (begun in 1874), to the austere grandeur of the University of London's Senate House (1936) in Malet Street, Bloomsbury. Estates records include plans and photographs. Some institutions, for instance King's College London, hold title deeds to their estates, sometimes extending back to the early modern period.

Schools and hospitals
Beyond records relating to higher education, AIM25 describes records of associated institutions, notably schools and hospitals. Schools founded in conjunction with universities included University College School (1830) and King's College School (1831). Also associated with King's College London was the Strand School, which originated as the Evening Department (1848) and provided commercial and vocational education, notably preparation for Civil Service examinations. The Polytechnic Secondary School was founded at the Polytechnic in Regent Street (1885) to provide commercial and technical education. School records may include lists of pupils, and ephemera and photographs of school events.

Hospitals covered by AIM25 include Charing Cross Hospital, Guy's Hospital, King's College Hospital, the Royal Free Hospital, the Royal London Hospital, St Bartholomew's Hospital, St George's Hospital, and St Thomas's Hospital. Their archives include admissions registers and patient records (although some records are closed, typically for 100 years, to preserve individuals' privacy). There may also be documentation on doctors, nurses and other staff; administrative records; records on their buildings; and records of other hospitals absorbed by them such as the German Hospital and the London Fever Hospital.

Records of other organisations and individuals
In addition to their own records, many higher education institutions holds extensive archives deposited by other individuals or organisations, covering a vast range of subjects including science, technology, medicine, social science, religion, language and literature, politics, law, economics, women's history, and military history. Archive collections described on AIM25 include the papers of thousands of eminent individuals in many different fields, among them politicians, soldiers, scientists, writers, and educationalists.

Of interest to the local historian are other sources relating to the history of London, including records of businesses, clubs, learned societies, and other organisations. Business records include the records of the merchants Frederick Huth and Company and the publishing firms Routledge & Kegan Paul and H K Lewis & Co (held at University College London). Philanthropic initiatives include York Place Ragged School (records of which are preserved at the University of Westminster). University College London has collections on Jewish history which include records of the Trades Advisory Council, which monitored anti-Jewish activity and advocated equal relations in trade and industry. The University of London Library holds the rules of the Agreeable United Fair Women's Friendly Society. The University of North London and the British Library of Political and
Economic Science (London School of Economics) hold rich collections on trade unionism and labour relations.

For the transport historian, collections of interest include Brunel University's substantial collection on railway history, and items at the University of London Library on railway history among its collections relating to economic history.

Outside London
Although based in London, the collections deposited in higher education institutions and covered by AIM25 are not confined to London but extend to other British localities. For instance, the University of London Library holds collections relating to land tenure in various locations, for example a report of rentals and tenants of the estates of Lord Lovat in Scotland, 1755, and accounts and rental for estates of T L Fairfax in Yorkshire and Lincolnshire, 1827-1840. The papers of the Brougham family, landowners in Westmorland and Cumberland, are held at University College London.

Further afield, there are extensive records relating to countries overseas, but even these might prove of interest to the family historian. For instance, the School of Oriental and African Studies holds records of several missionary societies, including the London Missionary Society and Methodist Missionary

Society, which over the course of the 19th and 20th centuries sent hundreds of missionaries overseas, who may be documented by letters, reports, journals and photographs in the archives.

How to use AIM25
The AIM25 website provides access to a database of records, each of which summarises the contents of an archive collection. The material may include, for instance, manuscripts, press cuttings, photographs, maps, and audio-visual recordings. Some of the collections covered have never been described previously, and most descriptions are newly available online.

Each AIM25 description is presented in a standard format and includes the biographical or administrative history of the person or organisation who created the archive, the subjects it covers, and the date it was created. Each description states whether there are more detailed lists or indexes to the archive and whether they are accessible online, or only in paper form. Other information includes quantity; language; access conditions; and location of related materials created by the same individual or organisation. From each description you can click on the website of the place which houses the archive to check its address, opening hours, and anything you might need to do before visiting, such as making an appointment or getting a letter of introduction.

Users can browse the descriptions of the archives held in each institution covered by AIM25. Alternatively you can search the descriptions in several ways. Free text searching produces hits for any term entered. You can narrow the hits by using targetted searches qualified by date or confined to a particular repository.

Indexes offer more precise hits. There are indexes for:
• *Personal names*
Over 7,000 individual names appear in the personal names index.
• *Corporate names*
The corporate names index indicates the businesses and other organisations which are covered.
• *Places*
In addition, a subject thesaurus can be searched in two ways. Firstly, you can search an alphabetical list for terms on subjects that interest you. Secondly, a subject hierarchy allows you to look at terms by navigating around subject groups. The thesaurus structure enables you to navigate using broader, narrower, related and preferred terms. For instance, if you are interested in the history of social organisations, clicking on the term 'Associations' will produce all the records relating to that subject. However, the thesaurus will also allow you to search at a higher level for all kinds of 'Organizations', or to narrow your search to look only for 'Womens organizations'. The thesaurus also suggests that you could look at related terms for 'Clubs' and 'Trade unions'. The thesaurus guides the user about which term to use, for example indicating that if you are interested in 'Business' you should search using 'Enterprises', and providing an immediate link to the preferred term.

The British Empire & Commonwealth Museum

Bristol's major new national museum

A new museum of national and international significance opened in the South West of England in September, 2002. The British Empire & Commonwealth Museum feature, in addition to its extensive archive and collections, the first permanent exhibition in the world to focus on the dramatic 500-year history of Britain's empire and its evolution into the modern Commonwealth.

The British Empire & Commonwealth Museum was established in 1986 as the Museum of Empire & Commonwealth Trust. Following a period of planning and fund-raising, the Trust in 1989 acquired a 99-year lease on a Grade I listed building in Bristol as a home for the Museum. This was the old Bristol station at Temple Meads, designed by Isambard Kingdom Brunel and last used as a working station in 1965.

Restoration work began on the building in 1993. Over £4.5 million has been spent upon the works which are nearly complete. The Trust had already started to assemble the objects, archives, photographs and other evidence such as oral history which would enable a stimulating and informative museum to be founded.

Collections
The Museum has collected material relating to the British Empire and Commonwealth since 1992. In addition to this the trust has assumed responsibility for collections made in the name of the Foreign and Commonwealth Office and the British Mercantile Marine Memorial Collection. The Museum's collections now total well over 75,000 items ranging from uniforms and other costume to domestic items and ethnographic material.

Important collections include a unique archive of over one thousand recordings covering a wide range of views, anecdotes and experiences from people who lived and worked in the British empire and the Commonwealth. Recorded are Administrators, Ayas, Foresters, Freedom Fighters, Colonial Wives, and Commonwealth Soldiers. The Museum aims to stress the ways in which the legacy of empire and the living relationship with the Commonwealth continue to influence both today's multicultural Britain and the Commonwealth countries.

The film collection is strong on footage of countries in East, West and Central Africa and the Indian sub-continent, including government-produced information and travel films (particularly the Central African Film Unit and the Northern Nigerian Information Service); newsfilm (especially political events and independence struggles in Central and East Africa); and amateur films from private collections (particulalrly good at portraying local ways of living,

Temple Meads Station, Bristol
© British Empire and Commonwealth Museum

customs and industries, together with vanished colonial lifestyles).

The Museum also holds a number of collections of television material reflecting current interest in the last years of British rule from the point of view of the governed. These include:
The Raj through Indian Eyes (2 parts); *Sex, Race and Empire;* and *The Mau Mau Emergency.*

Video and film Archive: currently nearly 300 video cassettes with plans for the creation of viewing copies. With approx. 550 reels of 16mm and 8mm film.
Sound Archive: Over 1,000 oral history.
Photograph Collection: Approx. 250,000 photographic images.
Library: Approx. 7,000 books.
Manuscripts Archive: Approx. 20,000 paper archives.Together with related material on the Museum's Accessions and Oral History Catalogues. Research collection of materials acquired in the production of *The Raj through Indian Eyes.*
Computerised Database: Moving image database currently being compiled.
Digitised Collection: Digital copies of *The Raj through Indian Eyes* are held.
Access: By arrangement only. Normally 10.00-17.00, Wed, Thu, Fri.
Viewing and listening facilities: 16mm and 35mm Steenbecks and VHS viewing facilities available on request.
Copyright: Copyright held to large part of collection. Information on request.

Pioneers in Kenya
– The story of the Grundy Family
Popular perception often has the East Africa of the early1930s peopled exclusively by hard-working government officials and gin & tonic drinking socialites. The British Empire & Commonwealth Museum, has in its collection documents and memoirs that tell a very different story of the British abroad. One such features the Grundy family.

Logging Train carrying teak , Darjeeling c 1893
© British Empire and Commonwealth Museum

the return of Hong Kong to mainland China in 1997. It will end with a look at just what living and working in Britain and the Commonwealth means today.

There will be three main sections in the Museum.

Britain builds an Empire(1480 – 1800)

How did Britain's empire begin? And who helped to build it? These galleries tells the story of the empire's early years...

- how England's merchants built private trading empires across the world
- who gained and who suffered as the empire expanded into the Americas
- and why Britain's empire became predominantly based in the east

Private traders founded Britain's early colonies. From the 1550s, merchants formed companies to import exotic goods from Asia, Africa and the Americas. They did not set out to build an empire, but they often claimed lands to keep out European rivals.

The merchants wanted to acquire what they could for Britain. The Spanish and Portuguese had already plundered the riches of Central and South America. The British settled the land in North America instead, seizing it from local people to establish new communities of emigrants. Black slaves were brought in to grow cash crops.

Closer to home in Ireland, English and Scottish Protestants forcibly took lands from Catholics. The Irish resented British domination, but many would work for the empire overseas. Were they the empire's victims, or partners in the process?

In the Seven Years War (1757–63) the British showed they were willing to fight for their empire. They captured many new colonies, including France's settlements in eastern Canada. But soon after, their own colonists in America broke free in a bloody war of independence (1775–83).

Jim and Jeanne Grundy, from the workshops of Sheffield, were among the first pioneer families in the Kenyan gold-rush, and established a gold mine in the 1920's. For a while, it looked as though the mine would never be viable. Writing to his mother in Engand, Jim says:

'Your Christmas present solved a very difficult problem for us. My insurance premium was due and Jeanne and I were wondering where on earth it would come from...The £20 just made it possible. This insurance means more than anything else to me ... if any accident happened Jeanne would get £2200, which would start her on a dairy farm.'

However, in 1933, on Jim's 40th birthday, they found a gold reef potentially worth £20,000 and fortune began to smile on them. By 1936 the mine was regularly turning a profit. Jim and Jeanne remained in mining until 1948.

The Grundy collection consists of letters, newspaper cuttings and photos and tells a very human story. As daughter Elizabeth Grundy says "...it's my family history, but it's also history *'out there.'* "

The Permanent Exhibition

The museum's permanent exhibition will be the first in the world to be dedicated to a study of Britain's dramatic 500 year colonial history. It will show how the British empire evolved into the independent nations of the Commonwealth and examine the legacy, both in Britain and worldwide, of the interchange of peoples, languages, institutions, trade and cultures.

Using authentic objects, film, photographs, sound recordings, costume and other artefacts, many never seen before in public, visitors will be offered an entertaining and engaging journey through British and world history.

The tour will feature over twenty themed galleries covering the period from explorer John Cabot's epic voyage from to Bristol to Newfoundland in 1497 to

By then Britain had already established bridgeheads in India and was reaching out to Australia and the Pacific.

The rise of Victoria's Empire (1800 – 1900)
How did Britain's empire work? And who benefited from it?

These galleries tells the story of the Victorian empire...
• how Britain expanded and controlled its empire
• who left Britain to live or work abroad
• and what it felt like to live under British rule

Britain emerged triumphant from the long wars with Napoleonic France in 1815. No country could rival its military and economic power. This proud legacy shaped the empire's progress for the next 100 years.

A new breed of confident empire-builders replaced the old company servants. Missionaries, settlers, merchants, administrators and soldiers – all felt that the empire should reflect Britain's greatness. They also shared a growing sense of imperial duty. Many believed in the idea of a 'civilizing mission'.

The empire grew rapidly. By 1900 Britain ruled most of India and Malaya, large parts of Africa and many Pacific islands. Thousands of hopeful emigrants had staked out Britain's claims to Australia, Canada and New Zealand. But, in spite of its industrial success, Britain was never big or rich enough to fully develop its colonies. It ran its empire cheaply.

In much of Africa and Asia the British ruled indirectly, using traditional leaders to collect taxes and solve disputes for them. In the white settler colonies they let the settlers govern themselves and pushed them to pay for their own defence.

Pious, dutiful and fertile, Queen Victoria was the perfect mother figure for this ever-growing imperial family. Her death in 1901 symbolized the end of an imperial era.

End of Empire (1900 – today)
How did Britain's empire come to an end? What replaced it? These galleries cover the shift from empire to Commonwealth...
• how the two world wars changed colonial attitudes
• how Britain responded to nationalists' demands for
  freedom
• the legacy of the empire in Britain today

The empire peaked after World War I. By 1921 a quarter of the world's population was ruled by Britain or owed allegiance to it. But the world was changing. Canadians, Australians and New Zealanders were establishing new nations. Asians and Africans were demanding a bigger say in running their countries. Britons too began to criticize imperial rule. A new generation of colonial officers saw it as their duty to train people for self-government.

After World War II a wave of nationalism erupted in Asia, Africa and the Caribbean. Britain freed India, Burma and Ceylon, but nationalists elsewhere were frustrated by the slow pace of change. Their polite calls for freedom turned into angry demands,

sometimes backed by violence.

Faced with a choice, Britain opted for independent friends rather than resentful colonies. One after another was freed in the 1960s and invited to join the Commonwealth. This was no longer a club for Britain and the former white colonies, but a multiracial association of free and equal nations.

A few small territories remain under British rule today. But a stronger reminder of empire exists in Britain itself. Since the 1940s, hundreds of thousands of people from the former colonies have settled here. Their presence has enriched British culture. It is a legacy to celebrate.

It is located in the historic Old Bristol station building designed by the brilliant Victorian engineer Ismabard Kingdom Brunel. Nominated as part of a world heritage site, it was the world's first purpose-built railway terminus.

A major new attraction for the South West, the Museum offers twenty themed galleries, special exhibitions, a library and archive, shop and cafe.

Open 10am - 5pm every day, except Christmas day
Adult £4.95
Senior citizen and students £4.35
Child (5 - 15 years) £2.95
Telephone: 0117 925 4980

A native King with his wife; her name is on the hat and the quantity of gold worn indicates he is a wealthy man
© British Empire and Commonwealth Museum

Worcestershire County Record Office.

Jean North Cultural Services

Worcestershire County Record Office

Over the last five years Worcestershire Office has and is still undergoing great changes. The division of the counties of Hereford and Worcester which happened on the 1st April 1998 meant that for the first time in its history the Record Office was not administered by a central administrative department of the County Council, but by a Cultural Services Division which also encompassed Archaeology, Libraries, Arts and Museums.

The main function of the Record Office is to be the corporate memory of Worcestershire County Council consequently Family and Local History interests must be seen as an offshoot of the main business of the Office

The Record Office is currently divided into three branches, including Worcestershire Library and History Centre (WLHC) and Headquarters, where all original archives are to be found. There is no charge to use either branch except for taking copies and donations are positively encouraged. By 2005 it is hoped that Worcester City Library and the Record Office will join together on one main site in the heart of the city centre, WLHC already being in place as Phase 1 of the project.

WLHC opened on the 30th April 2001 and its facilities mainly attract family historians although being in a prime site in Worcester City Centre near bus and railway stations, it has become a first call for many visitors making enquiries about the County Council. Since opening WLHC has recorded on average five hundred and forty customers per week.

There are no original documents here, records are on microfilm or microfiche, the most popular being Parish Registers, Civil Registration and of course Census Returns; these include the 1901 Census on fiche for Worcestershire and surrounding counties. There are forty four multipurpose microfilm readers, fifteen computer terminals with free use of the Internet, plus copying facilities, and also the Local Studies Library transferred from the current Worcester City Library.

Catalogues and finding aids are the same at both public branches enabling customers to consult these and gather information before starting research in either branch and to make sure that the correct office is selected as records are not transferred from branch to branch. An abundance of information leaflets in English and several other languages are also available to advise on location of records and to give advice on starting particular research e.g. House History and Adoption.

To improve it's reference service the Record Office has recently appointed an Archivist whose job is to develop the Record Office cataloguing. The aim is to

have all catalogues available via the computer database CALM (Computerisation for Archives, Libraries and Museums) which will eventually be available on-line to enable easy and remote access for information regarding Worcestershire's archives. The libraries in both branches are already catalogued on-line using OPAC (Online Public Access) Unfortunately because of limited staff numbers research for the public is not usually carried out except for looking through indexes or as training and detailed enquiries are passed to the professional researcher attached to the office.

From June1st 2002 WLHC has the distinction of being the first distribution centre for the Church of the Latter Days Saints in the UK. Customers can request films or fiche found on the Family History Library Catalogue www.familysearch.org and then place an order for them to be viewed here. Indications show that this is becoming a welcome resource for researchers who do not wish to travel or are disinclined to pay out for expensive travel arrangements to other parts of the country to view records.

Another first for the Record Office is that as an experiment the 13th July 2002 saw the first visit to the Public Record Office at Kew organised by staff for customers, 49 researchers took advantage of this and experienced a very successful trip, thus paving the way for more outreach work of this nature.

The Headquarters branch of the Office is situated just outside of the city, in the grounds of County Hall and Tony Wherry, the County Archivist is based here. This branch was reopened in September 2001 after a closure of six months whilst undergoing the successful transfer of archives from the St Helen's branch of the office which had been closed in March 2001. Headquarters did not have the capacity to house all of the combined archives and provisions had to be made for extra storage at Gloucestershire County Record Office and a courier service operates between the two County Record Offices.

The archives at Headquarters cover five miles of shelving within two strongrooms plus a high security unit. There is also an extensive library.

Worcestershire County Council's archives and Deed

Worcester Library and History Centre

Registry are held at this branch plus the archives of the Worcester Diocese, also private collections of a very varied and priceless nature. The Record Office is part of the CARN (County Archives Research Network) as a security measure and no documents can be viewed without a readers ticket which can be obtained on the production of identification showing both name and address.

The searchroom here attracts academic researchers and local historians. It has seating for twenty people plus a separate area to view maps or for use as a meeting room.

Internet Access

Reprographic services are available such as photocopying, scanning and an in-house microfilming service is located at this branch. Unfortunately at this present time there is no Conservation Unit and documents for repair are sent to outside bodies. It is hoped that with Phase 2 of the combining of the Library and Record Office in 2005 that provision will be made for an in-house unit.

Both public branches of the Record Office are involved with various projects both national and local e.g. selected inventories have been included in the Public Record Offices A2A project found at www.a2a.pro.gov.uk Worcestershire Record Office has received 801 hits during June 2002.

WLHC ran The BBC Journey into History (Census 1901) on-line project over a period of seven weeks and one hundred and five people took part. Local projects include the Oral History project on World War II, Black and Asian Studies and Memory Recall ,information about these projects can be found at www.worcestershire.gov.uk/records.

The Record Office continually looks for ways of improving the Service and attracting more and different users.This is done by staging events and an annual conference, giving talks at outside venues and running evening classes and day schools. Tours of the offices are offered and exhibitions in-house or for loan to schools or groups are varied and updated. The Friends of Worcestershire Record Office are a very active group arranging speakers for the various talks and conferences, supporting the Office financially whilst giving practical assistance with indexing and much needed help to stage events.

Worcestershire Record Office is aware of the impact made by the introduction of Information Technology and new legislation such as the Freedom of Information Act and Data Protection Act.The appointment of an Electronic Records Manager and Policy Officer into the Modern Records Unit in July 2002 ensures that the Office as a whole can keep pace with the changes whilst liasing with the Council's computer section and Legal Department.

The Modern Records Unit is the third branch of the Office and is not open to the public, it's core function is the creation, maintenance and disposal of the County Council's records whether they are paper or electronic. A computer programme CORA (Control of Registries and Archives) is already in place here and is continually updated.

To visit the two public branches appointments are not always neccessary but original documents are not issued between 12.30pm and 1.30pm

The hours of opening are the same in both public branches:- Monday 9.30am-7pm: Tuesday, Wednesday, Thursday 9.30am-5.30pm Friday 9.30am-7pm Saturday 9.30-4pm
Headquarters, County Hall, Spetchley Road, Worcester WR5 2NP
Tel : 01905 766351 Fax :01905 766363
Minicom 01905 766399
E-mail: RecordOffice@worcestershire.gov.uk

Worcestershire Library and History Centre
Trinity Street, Worcester WR1 2PW
Tel:01905 765922 Fax:01905 765925
Minicom 01905 766399
E-mail: WLHC@worcestershire gov.uk
Web Site
http://www.worcestershire.gov.uk/records

Film Readers

Notable Graves in Dorking's Historic Cemetery

Robert Blatchford describes the peaceful acres of one Cemetery

A cemetery is a source of information for the local and family historian but on closer inspection people often find them to be both peaceful and interesting places to visit.

Dorking Cemetery, nestling at the foot of Box Hill, is such a place. With the town's wealth of history it is not surprising to find such an interesting cemetery. Mole Valley District Council have produced a 42 page *'Guide to Notable Graves in Dorking's Historic Cemetery'*.

Dorking Cemetery was consecrated on 21st November 1855 and opened that month. The first burial was of Elizabeth Rose, a Non-Conformist which took place two days later. The first Church of England burial was that of Charles Wentworth on 20th December 1855 who had died at the age of fifteen months.

During the following century and a half many notables have taken their place in this historic cemetery.

George Meredith O.M. (1828 - 1909)
Novelist and Poet   Grave 4219 Plot P

The most influential period of George Meredith's youth was spent at the Moravian School at Neuwied on the Rhine where the aim was to develop the boys' faculties and inspire them with a republican spirit, a love of nature and faith in the brotherhood of man. He was for a time articled to a solicitor in London, but his interest was in writing. As this did not provide him with an adequate income, a post as reader with the publishers Chapman & Hall gave him regular employment for many years and the opportunity to encourage such writers as Thomas Hardy, R.L. Stevenson and George Gissing.

His first marriage in 1849 to a daughter of the poet Thomas Love Peacock was not successful and in 1864 he married Marie Vulliamy who had been living in The Old House in Mickleham. In 1867

they moved to Flint Cottage, Box Hill (now owned by the National Trust). Meredith had a chalet in the grounds, equipped with a hammock, and here he went to work undisturbed from early morning till late into the night. He knew the surrounding countryside well – he used to climb Box Hill every morning and walked far and wide while he was still able. With a group of friends he founded the "Sunday Tramps". They would set off with a supply of cold sausage and hock to walk the Surrey hills. One of his best-known novels Diana of the Crossways was partly inspired by Crossways Farm near Abinger Hammer, though his description of the locality does not fit the setting in several respects.

After about 1883 Meredith was gradually becoming crippled by paraplegia, but he still insisted on being taken out in his bathchair every day. He was frequently visited by friends such as James Barrie, Stevenson, Alphonse Daudet and Henry James. When he died a request from leading men of the day that he should be buried in Westminster Abbey was turned down, so his ashes were interred in Dorking Cemetery.

Although Meredith saw himself primarily as a poet, and his poetry is still quite highly regarded, he is better known as a novelist. Because of his obscure style he was never very popular with the public but his complex analyses of mood were admired by writers of his time and later.

General Sir Arthur Cotton K.C.S.I. (1803-1899)
Soldier and Irrigation Engineer.   Grave 5593 Plot 3

Arthur Cotton served with distinction in the Burma War and then spent nearly all his working life in India involved with large-scale irrigation projects, aqueducts, bridges, dams and canals. "Irrigation Cotton" became the greatest authority in India on the subject and the Government found that all his projects proved extremely profitable. His single-minded enthusiasm did however sometimes blind him to the potential of the railway. He maintained that it was on canals that future prosperity should be based. Critics exaggerated a little when they called him a One Idea Man suffering from water on the brain.

Sir Arthur came to Dorking to retire, living successively in Harrow Road East and, at the end of the 1870s, at Woodcote in Tower Hill Road, now the Garth Nursing Home. Here he involved himself in improvements in agriculture, particularly deep cultivation, but local labourers proved sceptical of his special long-tined forks. He became a well-known figure in the town on his

tricycle off to do his evangelical or temperance work. He claimed that his abstinence was the reason for his longevity.

He introduced a soup kitchen for the labourers of Dorking to encourage them not to drink beer during their working hours!

Gilliam Family
Grave 2959 PlotQ; Grave 6257 Plot 5

The Gilliam family were Stonemasons in Dorking from 1750 for over 200 years

The first member of the family to become a mason was John Gilliam of Castleford, Yorkshire. He was apprenticed in 1714 and later moved to London. Here he set up in the business which his son William took over on his death. One of the firm's most important works in London was on Somerset House when a wing was being rebuilt. Among other things they carved ox-skulls and drapery, shells above the windows of the principal floor and chimney pieces for the interior. They were also the master masons responsible for building the Fleet Prison.

In 1750 William moved to Dorking with his brother John to premises in East Street. In Dorking the firm did a considerable amount of work for Thomas Hope in The Deepdene, unpacking, mounting and setting up his collection of antique

marbles. The Gilliam family continued in the masonry trade from 1750 to the 1950s from one generation to the next, but the nature of the business gradually changed from general stonemasons to that of monumental masons. At one time nearly all the stonework in Dorking was carried out by their firm. They paved the town, worked on the Friends' meeting house and the restoration of Mickleham Church in 1823 and St Martin's churchyard in 1825. The firm was taken over in the 1950s by Messrs Sherlock & Sons who still operate as monumental masons as well as Funeral Directors.

Attlee Family Vault (9 Interments)
Graves 2704, 2709, 2714 & 2719 Plot P

The brother of Clement Attlee, Prime Minister of Great Britain, lies in the family vault here in Dorking Cemetery. There have been nine interments from 1873 to the last in 1981.

Grace Darling Edwards (1887-1963)
Grave 5290 Plot 1

Possibly a descendant of the heroine Grace Darling the famous Longstone Lighthouse Keeper's daughter, who entreated her father to row to the drowning crew and passengers of the 'Forfarshire' steamer. Her headstone bears the inscription 'A worthy descendant of a heroine'.

This article can only give a brief insight into Dorking Cemetery and its many historic graves and a visit is recommended when in the area.
For further information about Dorking Cemetery please contact Carole Brough Telephone 01306 879299

In September 2002 Dorking Cemetery was Highly Commended at the Cemetery of the Year Awards.

Kent Archive Service

Heather Forbes - Assistant County Archivist

The Kent Archives Service collects, preserves and provides access to Kent's recorded past. The collections, spanning thirteen centuries, represent an immense and priceless source of first hand information about the people, places and events that make up the county's history. There are three archive centres, located in Maidstone, Canterbury and Whitfield near Dover.

Where to carry out your research

Kent is a large county containing two ancient dioceses – Canterbury and Rochester – and a number of record offices, so it is important to know where records are held in order to pursue your research effectively. A brief summary of the collecting policies for the three Kent Archives Service offices will follow, but researchers whose interests relate to the areas of historic Kent affected by various local government reorganisations, such as Medway and the London Boroughs of Bexley and Bromley, will need to visit record offices in these areas. Please give us a call if you are uncertain which record office to visit as we will be happy to help.

Centre for Kentish Studies

Centre for Kentish Studies, Sessions House, Maidstone, Kent ME14 1XQ Tel: 01622 694363
Email: archives@kent.gov.uk Website:
http://www.kent.gov.uk/e&l/artslib/archives/home.html
Opening hours:
Monday: closed (group visits only)
Tuesday, Wednesday, Friday: 9am - 5pm
Thursday: 10am - 5pm
Saturday: 2nd and 4th every month 9am – 1pm

Collections include: Records of Kent County Council and Rochester Diocese, as well as the IGI, copies of the census and parish, borough, school and probate records, business, judicial, family and estate records for the west, mid and south Kent areas. In addition, there is an extensive collection of books on the history and topography of Kent as well as over 15,000 photographs, postcards, prints and slides, Kentish periodicals, brochures of property sales and local Acts of Parliament.

Canterbury Cathedral Archives

Canterbury Cathedral Archives, The Precincts, Canterbury, Kent, CT1 2EH
Tel: 01227 865330
Email: archives@canterbury-cathedral.org
Website:
http://www.kent.gov.uk/e&l/artslib/archives/home.html
Opening hours:
Monday – Thursday: 9am – 5pm
Friday: closed (group visits only)
Saturday: 1st & 3rd each month 9am –1pm

Collections include: Records of Canterbury Dean & Chapter, Canterbury Diocese and Canterbury City Council and its predecessors, and the parishes of Canterbury Archdeaconry (East Kent area). In addition, records of organisations, businesses and individuals from the Canterbury, Bridge, Blean, Whitstable and Herne Bay area are available as well as census and IGI material for this area. The Cathedral Archives is administered under the terms of partnership agreements between Canterbury Cathedral, Kent County Council and Canterbury City Council.

East Kent Archives Centre

East Kent Archives Centre, Enterprise Zone, Honeywood Road, Whitfield, Dover, Kent CT16 3EH
Tel: 01304 829306
Email: EastKentArchives@kent.gov.uk
Website:
http://www.kent.gov.uk/e&l/artslib/archives/home.htm

Collections include: Records from the Dover, Shepway and Thanet District Council areas. Holdings include local authority, school, hospital and estate records. For parish records relating to East Kent, please see Canterbury Cathedral Archives. Opening hours: Tuesday - Thursday: 9am – 5pm

Other Record Offices with archives relating to Kent

Medway Archives and Local Studies Centre, Civic Centre, Strood, Rochester ME2 4AU. Tel: 01634 332714. For records from within or largely relating to the Medway Council area as created in 1998, plus the parish records of Rochester Archdeaconry, and the records of the Rochester Dean & Chapter.
Bexley Local Studies and Archive Centre, Central Library, Bourne Townley Road, Bexleyheath, DA6 7HJ. Tel: 020 8301 1545.
For records within or largely relating to the London Borough of Bexley, plus parish records from the deaneries of Erith and Sidcup within the Bromley Archdeaconry.

Bromley Local Studies Library, Central Library, High Street, Bromley, BR1 1EX. Tel: 020 8460 9955. For records within or largely relating to the London Borough of Bromley, plus parish records from the Bromley Archdeaconry (except those relating to the deaneries of Erith and Sidcup – see Bexley above).

London Metropolitan Archives, 40 Northampton Road, Clerkenwell, London EC1R 0HB. Tel: 020 7332 3820.

Preparing for your visit

Good preparation before you visit can often save precious time when visiting record offices. For example, you may wish to consult the Access to Archives website which has brought together millions of catalogue entries from different archive institutions (http://www.a2a.pro.gov.uk/).
Entry to all three Kent Archives Service offices is free (including Canterbury where the usual fee to enter the Cathedral Precincts is waived for those visiting the Archives). It is advisable to reserve a document table or microfilm/fiche machine in advance to avoid disappointment. Please bring a

pencil and paper for making notes. On arrival, staff will be pleased to help you get started with your research, if required.

Kent Archives Service participates in the County Archive Research Network (CARN) scheme and you can consult original documents on production of a CARN reader's ticket. To obtain a CARN ticket please bring with you two passport sized photographs and some means of identification (such as a driving licence) showing your name, address and signature. On completion of a couple of forms on your first visit, the ticket is issued to you. If you already have a CARN ticket issued by another office, you can use that in Kent.

Research service

For those unable to visit, we offer a research service which is very popular and there is usually a turn-around time for reports of 8-10 weeks. If you wish to commission research, please contact us by post or by using the on-line form (http://www.kent.gov.uk/e&l/artslib/archives/archiverequest.html).

Tithe maps on CD-ROM

Mid-nineteenth century maps of Kentish towns and villages are now available on CD-ROM following a ground-breaking project supported by the Heritage Lottery Fund. All three offices of the Kent Archives Service now have the complete set of tithe maps on CD-ROM and it is planned to make copies available in selected libraries in due course. The aim of the project was to repair the series of maps (where necessary) and make them available in digital form in order to preserve the originals whilst improve access to researchers.

Over 75% of the maps required repair, sometimes very extensive, and this work was carried out by Cedric Chivers, a firm based in Bristol. The maps were then copied using a state-of-the-art, high resolution camera, specially constructed by ICAM, the firm responsible for the digitisation stage of the project.

The tithe maps themselves were produced following the Tithe Commutation Act of 1836 and show fields, buildings, roads, footpaths and other features of virtually every village in Kent. The accompanying awards (not included on the CD-ROMs) provide the names of owners and occupiers and brief descriptions of properties and fields. Together these documents are of great value to house and local historians, and those studying topography, agriculture, geography, place-names and genealogy. Many of these maps are the size of rolled up carpets, so it makes life a lot easier for staff and researchers alike to be able to look at the images of the maps on a computer screen. You can zoom into the area of interest, and also make printouts if you wish. Costs of copies range from under £1 for a self-service printout, to £15 for a luxury A3 colour reproduction on photographic paper (fit for display on your wall). You can also order copies of the CD-ROMs for private study at home for £35 each. We have been very pleased with the outcome of the project and look forward to sharing the results with a much wider audience.

Voyages To The Past.

Joanne Howdle - Collections And Exhibitions Officer

When I was asked to contribute this article to The Family & Local History Handbook, I had been in the post of Collection and Exhibitions Officer at The Dock Museum in Barrow-in-Furness for just two months. What am I going to write about I thought? So here goes:

In 1897, the Town Council formed its first Museum Committee, with a view to establishing a collection and finding an appropriate building for the **"Barrow Museum"**. In 1900, having made little progress, the Committee appointed a new Chairman - the local antiquarian and archaeologist, Harper Gaythorpe. Gaythorpe had a reputation for *"obtaining specimens"*, and he soon acquired the first of many donations for the collection - two Zulu spears. In 1905, the growing collection was still without a building, but nevertheless the Committee began to purchase display cases. The first display case costs £29 and 15 shillings. In 1907, the display cases were installed in the Town Hall as a temporary measure - and stayed there until 1930. In 1911, looking with an eye to the future, the Committee started to fill gaps in the collection - their first move in this direction was a scheme to collect specimens of every type of bird found locally on Walney Island.

In 1928, Alderman Bram Longstaffe took charge of the search for a permanent home for the collection and appealed to the local community for more objects because *"the things which they have in the secrets of their homes would be cherished all the more by being in the Museum"*. Whilst the search went on for a permanent home for the Museum, the collection found a new home on the first floor of Barrow Library as another temporary measure - which lasted from 1930 until 1991. The displays in the **"Museum"** over the Library become known as the **"Furness Museum"** and, for the first time, were supported by Barrow's main industry - the Shipyard. In the 1930's, Charles Craven, General Manager of Vickers, gave the Town its first collection of ship models. He commented that *"the Museum Committee apparently would not be satisfied until they got the whole Shipyard"* - the same thing has been said many times since then. During the Second World War the collection was allocated its first proper store in the Library's basement, but only on condition that it could be used as an air raid shelter. So Barrow was probably one of the earliest examples of publicly accessible Museum stores (she says tongue in cheek).

From 1942 until 1971, Fred Barnes was the Museum Curator and during that time he wrote Barrow and District (1968), the first modern account of the history of the local area. Between 1972-1974 the **"Furness Museum"** was revamped in an attempt to tell the full history of Barrow for the first time. Visitor figures peaked at 20,000 people per year.

In 1992, **Barrow Museum Service** as it is now known was relocated to The Dock Museum, the freehold of which is owned by Barrow Borough Council. In 1994, having waited over ninety years, the collection finally has a permanent home. The Dock Museum attracted over 50,000 visitors in its first year of operation and consists of two buildings side by side one of which The Dock Building, is made up of three floors of exhibition space, suspended in/straddling a Grade II, Victorian graving or dry dock.

The capital finance for the development of the site and the Museum buildings was largely provided through funding from European Regional Development Fund and Heritage Lottery Fund. And in 2001, further additions were made to the Museum including the Resource Centre, which consists of an education suite, an environmentally controlled Museum store, loading bay, Museum workrooms and offices. Along with a new café and the development of a Museum web-site. In 2001, visitor figures reached 120,000 people per year.

In 2001, BAE Systems, who currently own the Shipyard, donated their collection of ship models and photographic archive to the Museum. This material is recognised as being of national importance - a far cry from the Zulu spears donated a century earlier.

Brass Foundry, Messrs Vickers, Ltd., Barrow-in-Furness
© Robert Blatchford Collection.

Launch of Kongo
© Barrow Museum Service

found that the craftsmen, who had made **Kongo**, had been working their overtime out on bits of wood which were subsequently fitted to the model. **Kongo** is the most prestigious and most detailed model in the collection and represents one of the most famous ships built in Barrow.

The model has a solid gold walkway a centimetre wide running along part of the ship. And the little map tables in the crow's nest are decorated with detailed maps of the Japanese islands. The battle cruiser **Kongo** was built for the Japanese Navy by Vickers and was completed in 1913. Her main armament consisted of eight fourteen-inch guns, thirty-seven smaller guns and eight submerged torpedo tubes. She carried a crew of one thousand one hundred sailors.

Kongo cost £2,500,000 to build and was the last major battleship built for the Japanese Navy outside of Japan. A measure of her importance is that the Royal Navy asked for her to be leased back to Britain during World War One, although this never actually came to fruition. **Kongo** had an eventful career; she underwent two rebuilds in Japan and was sunk off Taiwan in November 1944.

The Museum Collection.
The collection held by **Barrow Museum Service** relates to the history of the Barrow area from prehistoric times to the present day. The Museum Service currently holds approximately 25,000 objects.

The Shipbuilding Collection.
In national terms this is arguably the most important part of the collection held by **Barrow Museum Service**. As it aims to represent the history and ongoing development of the Barrow Shipyard, which for much of its existence was owned by Vickers and has long been a major British shipbuilding and engineering force. The Museum Service currently holds approximately thirty-five ship, submarine, armaments and engineering models of actual or proposed Shipyard products. The ship model collection includes twelve superb ship models known as **The Vickers Ship Model Collection**, which were built by highly skilled workers at the Shipyard in Barrow from 1886 to 1935.

The Vickers Model Ship Collection has recently been restored and three of the models, the Japanese battle cruiser **"Kongo"**, the passenger liner **"Orion"** and the cargo ship **"Moveria"** are now on display at The Dock Museum. The Shipyard in Barrow built some of the most detailed models in the country. The models were originally intended for prestige and marketing purposes. In some cases the Yard would have built them before the ships were built to show the shipping lines what their ship was going look like. In other cases they would have been made at the same time as the real ship and then afterwards they'd either have been given as a gift to the shipping line or the Navy who commissioned them or the Yard would have kept them for use at trade fairs. Restoration work was carried out by Engineering Design and Models (EDM) based in Oldham. During the restoration of the **Kongo**, EDM had to remove each of the vessels 12,000 brass fittings individually in order that the model could be cleaned, repaired, repainted and then refitted. When they took the gun turrets off, there was no paint on the wooden block underneath, and EDM

The Vickers Photographic Archive.
The Vickers Photographic Archive, which was also donated to The Dock Museum by BAE Systems in 2001, provides a detailed insight into the workings of a prolific British Shipbuilding and Engineering Company. The Archive represents what Vickers thought was important to photograph at their Barrow Yard.

The Vickers Photographic Archive comprises approximately 10,000 images on glass and film negatives. The images were taken by professional photographers and span a period of almost a century of work at the Shipyard from the 1870's until the early 1960's. The Archive was built up because Vickers were interested in how they could best use their products to promote the company and photographs were a useful marketing tool. Sometimes

Launch of Orion
© Barrow Museum Service

© Barrow Museum Service

© Robert Blatchford Collection

industries that of iron mining, the Furness Railway and the Iron and Steel Works. A wide range of other local nineteenth and twentieth century industries are also represented such as the Jute Works and the shipbreaking depot.

The Social History Collection.
This collection represents the development of Barrow as a community and much of it dates to the late nineteenth and twentieth centuries. The material crosses a broad range of subjects and issues, and is especially strong in its coverage of shops and trades, household items, healthcare, entertainment, education and costume.

Visiting The Dock Museum.
Directions.
On the edge of the English Lake District, Barrow-in-Furness enjoys a coastal setting, with access from the M6 motorway, leaving at Junction 36 to follow the A590. Enter Barrow from any direction and follow the brown and white "Dock Museum" signs. By rail, finger posting takes you from Barrow station to the Museum via Abbey Road. From Hindpool Road turn left after Tesco into North Road, or from Walney Road turn right at Pizza Hut into North Road. The Museum is a few hundred yards on your right. Disabled Parking is available at the second entrance on the right.

Opening Times.
Easter to October Inclusive (Summer).
Tuesday to Friday 10am - 5pm (Last Admission 4.15pm.; Saturday and Sunday 11am - 5pm (Last Admission 4.15pm); Open Bank Holiday Mondays - High Season Only.
November to Easter (Winter).
Wednesday to Friday 10.30am - 4pm (Last Admission 3.15pm); Saturday and Sunday 11am - 4.30pm (Last Admission 3.45pm). Free Car Parking.; Free Coach Parking. Groups Welcome - Guided Tours Available.
Toilets And Baby Change Facilities.
Information In Braille And Large Print.
Accessible For Wheelchair Users (Lift Access To All Floors)., Shop., Coffee Shop.
Contact.
Administration And General Enquiries,
Telephone: 01229 894444.
Email: dockmuseum@barrowbc.gov.uk
Collections And Exhibitions Officer, Joanne Howdle,
Telephone: 01229 894445.
Email: jlhowdle@barrowbc.gov.uk

the Vickers photographers took up to two hundred images of a particular vessel if they thought it was unique. The Archive contains a detailed visual record of the construction of individual ships, from the laying of the keel to the completion of sea trials. However, you may not always find a photograph in the Archive of something you think should be there. A submarine, for example, may have become famous for a great wartime feat, but the company was often only interested in photographing it if it was the first of a class or represented a technological advance. In addition to shipbuilding images over half of the Archive relates to engineering and armaments production in the Yard, giving us a full picture of life in a Barrow Shipyard.

Funding has been secured from the Heritage Lottery Fund and the European Regional Development Fund to safeguard **The Vickers Photographic Archive** for the future. These grants have enabled the research into, and conservation and digitisation of the Archive to make it publicly accessible in three ways: on computer terminals in the Museum itself, on the Internet, and through the sales of prints.

The Archaeology Collection.
Much of this collection is local in origin and many of the objects in it are over five thousand years old. Some of the material was excavated, but much of it was found by chance in locations such as gardens, parks and school playing fields. The collection includes human and animal bones, burial urns and a large quantity of stone tools, most of which are Langdale axes. There are also a small number of bronze items and objects from the Roman and Medieval periods.

The Fine and Decorative Art Collection.
This collection is primarily comprised of paintings, prints and drawings produced by artists with local links. Most works date to the nineteenth and twentieth centuries.

The Industrial (Non-Shipbuilding) Collection.
The objects in this collection principally cover Barrow's three main nineteenth century

High Level Bridge, Barrow.

© Robert Blatchford Collection

Liverpool Record Office
David Stoker

Liverpool Record Office is located in Liverpool Central Library, which is in the city centre. It occupies one of several fine neo-classical buildings in William Brown Street in the Cultural Quarter, with Liverpool Museum and the Walker Art Gallery on either side and St George's Hall opposite. There is convenient access from all forms of public transport, including the main line railway at Lime Street Station and the coach station. The building has automatic doors, ramp and lift access.

Liverpool Record Office is run in conjunction with the Local Studies Library and Merseyside Record Office. This means that there are extensive collections all available in one place for research. There is also a major reference library in the same building with a range of printed sources useful for family history, such as London Gazette indexes, non- Liverpool street directories and parish register transcripts, and army and navy lists.

The Record Office is open for 66 hours per week, which includes evenings on every weekday, Saturday - and even Sunday opening. A large number of visitors are received - nearly 40,000 per year - and around 70% are family historians. We issue over nearly 39,000 items from our storage areas. Over 3,000 written enquiries are received each year and this total is increasing rapidly with the spread of email access.

Liverpool Record Office holds a wide range of archives which are useful for family history. The records of the City Council and its predecessors include sources such as records of freemen and burgesses and the early Town Books from the 1550s are packed with names and records of interesting incidents. There are registers of baptisms, marriages and burials from the 16th century onwards for over 100 Church of England parishes. There are similar registers from the 18th century onwards as well as registers of confirmations for over 30 Roman Catholic parishes and there are registers of many nonconformist churches. Extensive series of cemetery records are held for church, private and municipal cemeteries. A family historian once found an entry relating to the burial of just a leg in these records! There are also a number of volumes of Monumental Inscriptions. Records of many schools are held. There are also poor law records, especially the large series of admission and discharge registers for the vast Liverpool Workhouse. There are also baptism registers for the Workhouse. These include

many entries where babies and very young children have been found abandoned and named after the street in which they were found – such as James St. Vincent who was baptised in January 1850 having been left in St. Vincent Street when only four weeks old.

The Local Studies Library has much important material which can be accessed in the same reading room. As well as thousands of books on all aspects of the history of the City, there are street and trade directories from 1766 to 1970. After 1857 these also cover parts of the Wirral. There are some poll books from the 1730s to 1850s. There is a full series of electoral or voters' registers for every year from 1832 –1914, 1918-1939 and 1945 to the present. Copies of many local newspapers are held from 1756 to the present day. There is a large number of old street maps and Ordnance Survey maps.

There are extensive collections of photographs in the Record Office and in the Local Studies Library. Some of these have been digitised. There is also a fine collection of over 7,000 watercolours. Many family historians like to consult them to look at where their ancestors lived and worked.

There are also copies of the census returns for Liverpool and the surrounding area and the Wirral from 1841 to 1901, national probate indexes from 1858 to 1951, and copies of the births, marriages and deaths indexes for England and Wales from 1837 to 1996.

In addition, Merseyside Record Office holdings are accessible through the same reading room. This record office was established in 1974 to look after the records of Merseyside County Council. The office also collected and still collects archives which relate to more than one borough in Merseyside. The most frequently consulted records for family history are the

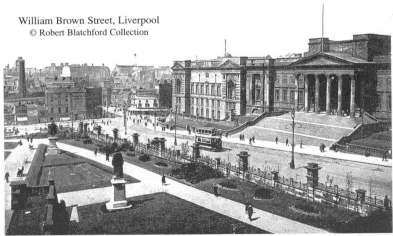

William Brown Street, Liverpool
© Robert Blatchford Collection

Pier Head, Liverpool

Coroners' inquest registers for Liverpool, Birkenhead and Wallasey.

Information is often requested on immigration and emigration but, unfortunately, no ship's passenger lists are held here. There are some at the Public Record Office, but mostly they are to be found at the country of destination. There are some copies of printed, microfilm and increasingly electronic sources held here. One collection of archives of note is the case papers of the Liverpool Catholic Children's Emigration Society from the 1880s to 1920s, which are indexed by name.

Some of the above records are on microfilm or microfiche. We have 20 machines including several self-service reader printers. However, the demand is so great that it is essential to book a machine in advance. There is a 50 pence booking fee per two-hour session. We have eight computers and it is also advisable to book these in advance. To consult original records you will need to bring formal proof of name and address so as to obtain a reader ticket on your first visit. (Please note that we are not part of the CARN scheme.) For security reasons, you will also be asked to leave any bags in lockers before entering the search room for consulting original records. There is a £1 refundable deposit for using the lockers.

Written enquiries about the contents of collections are answered. We now offer a paid research service which is currently charged at £16 per hour, or £10 for half an hour, or £3 per entry for checking and copying specific entries from sources such as directories and parish registers where full details are given. This has already proved to be very popular. A wide range of enquiries are answered from specific family history research to the naming of Liverpool (not straightforward), myths about the Liver Birds and recipes for the local delicacy of "wet nellies" (left-over cake soaked in treacle). We often can help out all branches of the media at short notice. A recent example was in searching at the request of the main local newspaper for a school photograph of the actor Ricky Tomlinson (of Royle family and Brookside fame) in the school records. Luckily we found an excellent photo and Ricky was delighted because he had no copies of photos from his school days. The local media were delighted too to reproduce the photo with his permission.

We have a range of publications. These include leaflets on many key sources for family history. These can be purchased as a pack (currently 14 leaflets for 50 pence). We also have handlists for sale on Church of England parish records, Roman Catholic parish records, and Cemetery and burial records. As well as some local history books and reproduction maps, we have for sale a CD-ROM containing 650 archive photographs with background information and ten minutes of archive film footage. We have also produced a website on schools and housing at www.pastliverpool.com. We are leading on a major project for a digitised history of the Port of Liverpool, its people and the surrounding area which will be at www.mersey-gateway.org.

A Family History Help Desk is available here almost every Tuesday afternoon. It is run by volunteers from the Liverpool Family History Society. It is open to anyone without appointment. Assistance is given to beginners and to those who have hit a particular problem or who simply do not know Liverpool. It has been very popular receiving over 700 visitors per year and we are grateful to the volunteers who have staffed it every week for several years. Some visitors have been overwhelmed by the assistance provided. A notable example is of a lady in her 60s who had come over from Australia to trace her family history and to come to terms with her harsh childhood, which included being sent as a child migrant to a farm school in Western Australia. She was struggling to find any useful information. The Help Desk volunteers gave such help and advice and persevered on her behalf until she found information on her mother, sister and brother. She wrote afterwards that: "For a long time I would not let Marie close the book. I was afraid that after all that searching I would lose it again. I cannot describe my emotion as those words appeared before my eyes. Or the emotion of, now my friends, Joyce, Harold and Marie of the Family History Help Desk, for without them I would still be looking and without them never succeeding." She eventually published her research, "Flo - child migrant from Liverpool" and has been delighted with the response and the fact that we are selling copies here.

We also have a team of volunteers indexing part of the huge collection of Liverpool registered ships' Crew Lists here. As well as building up a useful database, they have been fascinated by the colourful descriptions of some highly eventful voyages including desertions, imprisonments, and a "cook who couldn't".

We have always welcomed family historians and will continue to do so and to add to our already extensive holdings whenever possible.

Liverpool Record Office, Central Library
William Brown Street , Liverpool L3 8EW
Tel 0151 233 5817/5811
Fax (for Central Library) 0151 233 5886
Email RecOffice.central.library@liverpool.gov.uk
Opening hours : Monday to Thursday:09.00 – 20.00: Friday
09.00- 19.00 : Saturday 09.00 – 17.00: Sunday 12.00 – 16.00
Annual closure for stocktaking and special projects 3rd and 4th weeks in June.

Tom Leonard Mining Museum
A Centre for Cleveland and Yorkshire's Ironstone Mining Heritage
Jonathan Allinson - Development Manager

The Tom Leonard Mining Museum at Skinningrove is the UK's only ironstone mining museum. Situated on the beautiful Heritage coast, adjacent to the Cleveland Way, the Museum houses an impressive collection of historical artefacts and documents attributed to the region's rich mining heritage. The Museum, opened in 1983 by the friends and family of local reporter, Tom Leonard, is staffed by volunteers.

The site of the Museum originally opened as the Skinningrove Mine in August 1848. It was closed between 1856 and 1865, reopening as Loftus Mine when the Skinningrove zig-zag railway was completed. The Museum is housed in what was the Engine House of the ventilation fan and sits at the main outlet from the Loftus mine, the North Drift. At its peak, production reached approximately 1200 tons of ironstone per day, employing about 800 men and boys. Each new employee was given a numbered token, which remained theirs during their working life at the mine. Miners collected their token prior to going underground and handed it in when they returned to the surface. This enabled the Gateman to know who was underground, essential information in an emergency. The same number was chalked on the side of each tub as it was filled with ironstone so that the miner could be credited with the stone in the tub.

In 1843, just twenty years before the Loftus Mine was opened, Lord Ashley introduced an Act of Parliament excluding women, girls and boys under ten years of age from working underground. This brought to an end "the repugnant mode of conveying ironstone on the backs of ladies". The Act was not universally popular because it reduced some family incomes significantly.

Safety underground was of paramount importance. In addition to the miners' identity tokens, they were given a hard hat made of leather. It was absolutely forbidden to take cigarettes or lighters of any kind down the mine. Even to this day, gas tests are conducted daily in the North Drift before the public are allowed in and standard regulations governing the working of underground mines are still applied to ensure the safety of visitors.

A cry of "Tubs!" from the Drift mouth gave warning that a group of empty tubs had been released to run down the incline to the pit bottom. At intervals, along the sides of the drift were refuges or 'manholes', each one providing shelter to miners as the tubs rattled past. Visitors can view such refuges as well as the damage in the brick walls caused by the tubs as they rattled up and down the incline. Part of the guided tour around the Mine site and Museum includes a visit into the North Drift.

Starting at an Early Age
The doors that were used as airlocks in the Mine served ventilation purposes and were operated by young lads called 'Trappy Lads'. These young workers opened the doors to let the tubs through and closed them again afterwards. They quickly got a feel for work underground, most of their time being spent in complete darkness. Visitors can experience the chilling atmosphere and hear the 'Trappy Lad's Tale'.

At fourteen years old, a lad would be promoted to driver, to look after a horse. He would hitch the horse to two tubs at Pit Bottom and take them to the working face. Here, two full tubs would be waiting for him to take back to Pit Bottom. Twenty to thirty-five full tubs would be assembled into a 'set', attached to the rope haulage system and pulled to the surface.

Clamped to the track, near to the drift entrance is a metal bracket and a flat steel plate. This is connected by a cable to Pit Bottom. By pulling the cable, the man at Pit Bottom could signal to the engine-man at the surface when a set of tubs was ready to be hauled up by the stationary engine and haulage rope.

A set of tubs arrived every twelve to twenty-five minutes. There were at least twenty tubs in a set, each tub carried two tons. That produced approximately 600,000 tons per year (1877). The most productive year was 1881 when 654,000 tons of ironstone was drawn from the mine.

At the surface, the loaded tubs were unhooked from the rope and run out over a gantry where they were weighed and tipped into railway wagons below. From there, the stone was taken to Skinningrove Ironworks and to other iron and steel plants throughout the UK.

In 1890 the railway company tried to increase the carriage rates. Pease and Partners, the mines' owners, extended the gantry to the far side of the valley where the Loftus North Mine had just stopped production. The mine engineers dug into the existing workings and used the shaft to bring the tubs directly up to the iron-works without involving the railway company.

Working Underground
Imagine yourself a miner, starting work at 6am. Miners enter the mine at the Travelling Drift, to the north, near Skinningrove. They had up to three miles to walk underground to reach the working face before they could start digging stone and earning money. The horses were led in through the Horse Drift and also had a two to three mile walk to the face where full tubs were waiting to be taken to the Mine Bottom.

When the miner arrived at the workface, his first job was to drill a hole using a Jumper Drill. By throwing the drill repeatedly at the stone face and twisting it as it hit the stone, the miner drilled out a hole three feet deep (90cm). A photograph in the ground floor display of the Museum shows work at a high face in the Eston Mine where the seam was thirteen feet thick. At Skinningrove, the main seam was approximately nine feet thick.

An improvement, the ratchet drill, was invented by Blackett and Hutton around 1890. Such was it's popularity that it became known colloquially simply by it's maker's name. A 'Blackett and Hutton' could drill a standard three feet deep hole in fifteen minutes, a considerable improvement on the old 'throw and twist' Jumper Drill. The ratchet drill became very popular and was used until the 1950s. They were less popular at Eston Mine where the miners were initially reluctant to work with such a tool from planks high on the work surface. Pneumatic drills were introduced at Loftus Mine in 1891, powered by a steam-driven air compressor, which was installed at Skinningrove. The Museum houses tools used to create holes in the face prior to blasting.

Charging the Hole
After boring the hole to the required depth, it was cleared of rock fragments with a scraper. It was critical to clear the hole as loose fragments of stone left in the hole might cause a 'stopper'. The scraper was made of copper or brass. There were no iron or steel instruments used at this stage because of the risk of a spark igniting the gunpowder.

The miner brought his own stock of gunpowder. Each charge cost two or three pence. The charge was inserted in the hole and rammed home with a wooden tool called a 'Stemmer'. Next the 'Pricker' was hammered through the gunpowder and left lying along the bottom of the hole while clay was packed in behind the charge and hammered down hard with the stemmer. If no clay were to hand, miners would use horse dung. The pricker was carefully removed and the igniter was carefully threaded down the narrow hole. Locally, the igniter was known as a 'squib'. The fuse would allow approximately forty seconds for the miner and his filler to seek cover before it exploded the charge, releasing about two tons of stone. There is an example of a typical tin in which a miner carried his powder displayed in the Museum. At the start of each working shift, the miner went to the Magazine and drew out as much powder and as many squibs as he thought he needed for the day. He would hope never to draw too little and be left short before the end of the shift, or face a long walk back to the surface for extra stock. He would also try not to draw too much as he had to pay for it out of his wages. A miner with a good filler to load the tubs with fallen stone could mine about twenty tons of stone a day. At the end of the day, the miner would take any remaining powder home with him. Often it was left near the hearth to keep it warm and dry or even stored under his bed.

In around 1940 high explosives, as against gunpowder, came into use. Used with electrical detonators, several charges could be fired at once. Using multiple shot firing brought down a larger load of stone. The galvanometer, on display at the Museum, was used to check that the electrical circuits were complete and in working order prior to firing the shots. To have an unexploded shot left amongst the fallen stone was extremely dangerous and special safety procedures had to be followed if the shot-firer thought there was an unexploded charge.

Loading The Stone
Among the many mining photographs on display at the Museum, one particular image, taken at the beginning of the twentieth century, gives visitors an idea of miners working clothing. Cloth caps were the miners only protection. Managers might have had some form of protective helmet if they ventured underground. As a rule, protective headgear was not generally available to miners until the 1930s, and

even then it was little more than compressed cardboard.

Tubs carrying the stone ran on rails and were pulled by horses to the Mine Bottom. At the Mine Bottom, the tubs were linked into sets or trains of twenty to thirty tubs and attached to the rope haulage system, which pulled them up the North Drift. On display at the Museum is a shaft telegraph, which came from Lingdale Mine, a shaft mine as opposed to the Loftus drift mine. The telegraph indicates to the engine man who controlled the winding gear what was required by the operators at the Mine Bottom.

The Working Horses
In shaft mines, because it was difficult and time consuming to raise them up the shaft, the horses spent all their time underground. Horses in a drift mine could be walked to the surface at the end of each day. They were generally well looked after; some say they were spoilt, as the miner's wages depended upon them. If a miner got lost underground without a light, he could rely on the instincts of the horse to lead him out of the mine, even in the pitch dark.

Shire horses were used in the Loftus and Skinningrove mines. Their short, stocky, muscular bodies made them ideal for manoeuvring within the confined spaces. The Museum owns a large collection of harnesses, with many on display.

Illumination
The Museum has a representative selection of many types of lamps that were used in the Loftus Mine during its eighty active years (1865-1958). Initially, when there was no forced mine ventilation, miners would use cans to protect their candles from draughts. More sophisticated miners used a wooden box called a 'midge'. This would shelter the candle and also act to store the miner's 'bait', or mid-shift meal. Oil lamps were introduced in time. The tea-pot design was known as the 'Tommy Dim Light'. With practice and experience it was possible to lower the wick and inspect the flame for flammable gases in the mine atmosphere.

The Davy Lamp was invented in 1816, but the Upton & Roberts Lamp was the only one that did not 'pass flame' in the tests of 1835. Carbide lamps were introduced in 1920. At first they were very unpopular because the very bright light cast very dark shadows and miners found it difficult to adjust their vision. An increase in the frequency and severity of explosions in ironstone mines in the 1940s led

to the introduction of safety lamps for gas testing. By the 1950s only safety lamps were allowed in the mine.

Ventilation
At first there was no need for forced ventilation. The movement of men and tubs and horses was sufficient to refresh the air in the drifts and at the working faces. As the miners drove deeper into the hillside, natural ventilation was inadequate. The air became stagnant and carbon dioxide levels rose. The Museum tells the story of the advances made in the mining ventilation technology, with the opportunity for visitors to experience graphics and pass through the ventilation shaft and it's fan housings prior to entering the underground mining experience.

The Mining Experience
In the first part of the Mining Experience the visitor experiences the cold, dank, pitch black of the working conditions of the Trappy Lads, who waited by the ventilation doors, opening and closing them for the horse drawn tubs to pass through. The visitor has the opportunity to listen to the Trappy Lad's Tale, which gives an insight into the gloomy, unpleasant conditions experienced in the Loftus Mine.

The Tom Leonard Mining Museum provides a unique visitor experience. The visitor will walk the North Drift, descending into the hillside adjacent to rails, which would have carried tubs full of ore to the surface from Pit Bottom. In addition, mining techniques and blasting is demonstrated in the underground Mining Experience.

Visit the Tom Leonard Mining Museum and you will definitely emerge with a better understanding of the importance of this bygone industry. The opportunity to experience the underground world of an ironstone mine in the company of an enthusiastic and knowledgeable guide awaits!

Tom Leonard Mining Museum
Deepdale, Skinningrove, Saltburn By Sea, Cleveland
Tel: 01287 642877 Fax: 01287 642970
Website: www.ironstonemuseum.co.uk
E-mail: visits@ironstonemuseum.co.uk
Opening Times: Monday to Saturday: 1pm to 3:45pm (last tour 3:45pm). Tours in the company of expert guides last approximately 1.5 hours
Directions:
The Museum stands in Skinningrove valley, by the coast, just off the A174 between Saltburn & Whitby. Follow the brown signs.

Images of England
Creating an Internet home for England's listed buildings
Alexandra Saxon - Communications Officer

If you are a local or family historian there is now a new resource to aid your research. Images of England is an English Heritage and Heritage Lottery funded project, which aims to create and make accessible via the internet a 'point in time' photographic record of England's listed buildings. From palaces to pigeon lofts, medieval churches to garden sheds, Images of England is mobilising an army of volunteer photographers to capture images of every listed building in England. The project will generate new photographs of around 370,000 listed buildings and aims to record the richness of the heritage that surrounds us. The photographs are stored in a digital image library and are available to search over the internet. The project will provide the first comprehensive visual record of the nation's 370,000 listed buildings including buildings from every village and town in the land.

The practice of listing buildings began in 1947 when the importance of preservation was realised after years of wartime destruction. Since then, buildings of local and national historical importance have been listed to preserve and protect them for future generations. As well as a defining exterior image of the property, specifically taken for the Images of England project, the listed building description is also displayed on the site. This gives details of architectural features as well as, in some cases, details of architects and previous uses.

The Images of England site allows you to search under several criteria including location and building type. It can also be searched under "Associated People". For example, a search for all the buildings and structures associated with the Victorian author Charles Dickens, identified 53 listed building records that include a reference to Charles Dickens. Dickens travelled widely across England and there are a number of houses recorded on the database that the writer lived in including No. 11 Ordnance Terrace, Chatham. This was the home of the Dickens's family from 1817 – 1821. Many of the buildings found in the database were a source of influence or inspiration to Dickens in his writing. He stayed at the Royal Hotel in Great Yarmouth while writing David Copperfield and met James Sharman, Keeper of Nelson's column, on whom it is said he based the character of Ham Peggotty. The search also retrieved a photograph of a row of ten children's tombs in Kent. Known locally as "Pip's Graves", it is thought that these tombs were the inspiration for the first scene of Great Expectations.

It is not just authors who are recorded in the listed building records. Designers, architects and engineers can also be researched on the Images of England site. Searching under Isambard Kingdom Brunel results in 120 listed building records being identified. These include images of his work such as the spectacular Clifton Suspension Bridge as well as more biographical listings such as his home Cheyne Walk, Chelsea and the family tomb in Kensal Green.

Searching for "Associated People" is fine if you have a notable figure in your family or local area but if you aren't lucky enough to have such a person to research how can Images of England help you? Even if you are already familiar with the listed buildings in your locality you might never have seen the statutory listing for them. These listings might give you some surprising connections. Perhaps the stained glass in your local Parish Church is by a notable designer such as Kempe or an eminent architect might have designed a local property. All of these can be springboards for further research.

Royal Hotel,
Marine Parade,
Great Yarmouth.
Grade II listed.
©
**Mr Nigel Gallant
LRPS**
Taken as part of the
Images of England
project

Lock Keepers
Cottage, Sandiacre,
Derbyshire
Grade II listed.
©
**Mr Peter F Holt
FRPS**
Taken as part of the
Images of England
project

Peter with his sisters and his Aunt outside lock Keepers cottage in 1939
Photograph with courtesy of Peter Holt

For family history searches the Images of England database can help to put a photograph to a building with significance to your family. Perhaps a church where your grandparents were married or the house where your great-great grandparents lived. If the building was on the statutory lists at the start of the 21st Century, it is likely that you will find it on the Images of England site. The images can also be used to compare the surroundings. As each of the images is of the exterior of the building it gives a good idea of the context of the property. Comparing the recent picture on Images of England with older pictures will give you a good idea of how the area has changed.

One of the Images of England volunteer photographers, Peter Holt, had a surprise when his list of buildings to be photographed included the house he had lived in with his family between 1935 and 1946. Peter says "this was and possibly will be, the highlight of photographing listed monuments." Peter's father was a maintenance bricklayer for the Grand Union Canal company. The house, Lock Keepers Cottages in Sandiacre, Notts, went with the job. Many of the features of the house were the same as when Peter lived there including the stone slab on which he was photographed with his Aunt and two sisters before the outbreak of the Second World War. Peter has fond memories of the cottage and enjoyed being able to share them with his son as well as recording an image of it, which will be preserved for future generations to enjoy. Today the cottages are the headquarters of the Canal Preservation Society.

As well as buildings, the Images of England database also has some more unusual listings. There are over 2000 gravestones currently listed on the website. Where inscriptions are legible, they are often included in the list description. Searching using "Associated People" and "Building Type" together might get some interesting results! The database can also be used to find information and photographs on telephone and post boxes, milestones, and windmills to name but a few of the interesting but unusual listed buildings. Modern buildings also feature as listed

buildings, for example, the Trellick Tower in West London, which was designed in 1967.

Images of England is an innovative project designed to give wide access to what will be, when complete, one of the world's largest free online picture libraries. Conservationists and local groups will be able to access information needed to build detailed local records and an extraordinary educational resource will be available for everyone from school children to lifelong learners and historians. Whatever your interest in history, geography or buildings, the site is simple and quick to use allowing you to find out more about your surroundings and to appreciate the richness and variety of England's heritage wherever you are.

The Images of England website can be found at www.imagesofengland.org.uk or for further information please contact Alexandra Saxon on 01793 414779.

Tomb of Sir Marc
Isambard Brunel
and
Isambard Kingdom
Brunel,
Kensal Green
Cemetery,
Kensington, London
Grade II listed.
©
**Quiller Barrett
LRPS**
Taken as part of the
Images of England
project

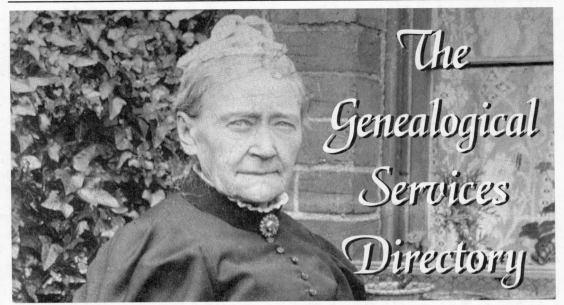

The Genealogical Services Directory

All Family History & Genealogical Societies were circulated to confirm the information is correct and up to date. Some Societies did not responded (January 2003)

British Association for Local History PO Box 1576, Salisbury, SP2 8SY Tel: 01722-332158 Fax: 01722-413242, WWW: www.balh.co.uk
East Anglian Group of Family History Societies, 42 Crowhill, Godmanchester, Huntington, Cambridgeshire, PE29 2NR Email: secretary@huntsfhs.org.uk
Federation of Family History Societies PO Box 2425, Coventry, CV5 6YX Tel: 070 41 492032 Fax: 01564 703100 Email: admin@ffhs.org.uk
Institute of Heraldic & Genealogical Studies 79 - 82 Northgate, Canterbury, CT1 1BA Fax: 01227-765617 Email: ihgs@ihgs.ac.uk WWW: www.ihgs.ac.uk
North West Group of FHS Family HistorySocieties, 4 Lawrence Avenue, Simonstone, Burnley, BB12 7HX Tel: 01282-771999 Email: ed@gull66.freeserve.co.uk
Society of Genealogists - Library 14 Charterhouse Buildings, Goswell Road, London, EC1M 7BA Tel: 020-7251-8799 Tel: 020-7250-0291 Fax: 020-7250-1800 Email: library@sog.org.uk - Sales at sales@sog.org.uk WWW: http://www.sog.org.uk
South West Group of Family History Societies 32 Marconi Close, Weston Super Mare, BS23 3HH Tel: 01934 627053,
The North East Group of Family History Societies 11 Colins Street, Great Horton, Bradford, BD7 4HF

England
Avon
Bristol & Avon Family History Society 784 Muller Road, Eastville, Bristol, BS5 6XA Tel: 0117 951 8838 Email: secretary@bafhs.org.uk WWW: www.bafhs.org.uk

Bedfordshire
Bedfordshire Family History Society, P0 Box 214, Bedford, MK42 9RX Tel: Email: bfhs@bfhs.org.uk WWW: http://www.bfhs.org.uk

Berkshire
Berkshire Family History Society, 5 Wren Close, Burghfield Common, Reading, RG7 3PF Tel: 0118-983 6523 Email: john.gurnett@btinternet.com WWW: www.berksfhs.org.uk

Birmingham
Birmingham & Midland Society for Genealogy & Heraldry 2 Castle Croft, Oldbury, B68 9BQ Tel: 0121 429 9712 Email: birmingham@terrymorter.fsnet.co.uk WWW: www.bmsgh.org

Buckinghamshire
Buckinghamshire Family History Society, PO Box 403, Aylesbury, Buckinghamshire, HP21 7GU Email: secretary@bucksfhs.org.uk WWW: http://www.bucksfhs.org.uk

Family History Societies

Buckinghamshire Genealogical Society, Varneys, Rudds Lane, Haddenham, Buckinghamshire, HP17 8JP Tel: 01844 291631 Email: eve@varneys.demon.co.uk WWW: http://met.open.ac.uk/group/kaq/bgs.htm

Cambridgeshire
Cambridgeshire Family History Society, 6 Chestnut Rise, Bar Hill, Cambridge, Cambridgeshire, CB3 8TF Email: ma.tabbitt@tesco.net WWW: www.cfhs.org.uk
Cambridge University H & G S, c/o Crossfield House, Dale Road, Stanton, Bury St Edmunds, Suffolk, IP31 2DY Tel: 01359 251050 Fax: 01359 251050 Email: president@one-name.org WWW: www.cam.ac.uk/societies/cuhags/, Membership open to members of the University but non-members may be admitted at the discretion of the Executive Committee
Fenland Family History Society, 70 Gorefield Road, Leverington, Cambridgeshire, PE13 5AT Tel: 01945 587723 Email: peter.hunter3@btinternet.com Covers Fenland areas of Cambridgeshire, Lincolnshire and Norfolk
Huntingdonshire Family History Society, 42 Crowhill, Godmanchester, Huntingdon, Cambridgeshire, PE29 2NR Tel: 01480 390476 Email: secretary@huntsfhs.org.uk WWW: www.huntsfhs.org.uk
Peterborough & District Family History Society, 33 Farleigh Fields, Orton Wistow, Peterborough, Cambridgeshire, PE2 6YB Tel: 01733 235956

Cheshire
Family History Society of Cheshire, 44 Townbridge Court, Castle Street, Northwich, Cheshire, CW8 1BG WWW: www.fhsc.org.uk
North Cheshire Family History Society 2 Denham Drive, Bramhall, Stockport, SK7 2AT Tel: 0161-439-9270 Email: roger@demercado.demon.co.uk WWW: http://www.genuki.org.uk/big/eng/CHS/NorthChesFHS
South Cheshire Family History Society incorporating S E Cheshire Local Studies Group PO Box 1990, Crewe, CW2 6FF, WWW: www.scfhs.org.uk

Cleveland
Cleveland Family History Society 1 Oxgang Close, Redcar, TS10 4ND Tel: 01642 486615

Cornwall
Cornwall Family History Society 5 Victoria Square, Truro, TR1 2RS Tel: 01872-264044 Email: secretary@cornwallfhs.com WWW: http://www.cornwallfhs.com
Cornish Forefathers Society, Credvill, Quakers Road, Perranwell, Truro, Cornwall, TR3 7PJ Tel: 0777 992 9361 (Mobile) Email: credvill@btopenworld.com WWW: www.cornish-forefathers.com

Fal Worldwide Family History Group, 57 Huntersfield, South Tehidy, Camborne, Cornwall, TR14 0HW Tel: 01209-711557 Fax: 01209-711557 Email: cfdell@clara.net WWW: http://beehive.thisiscornwall.co.uk/falwwfhg

Coventry
Coventry Family History Society, PO Box 2746, Coventry, Warwickshire, CV5 7YD Tel: (024) 7646 4256 Email: enquiries@covfhs.org WWW: www.covfhs.org

Cumbria /Cumberland
Cumbria Family History Society "Ulpha", 32 Granada Road, Denton, M34 2LJ WWW: http://www.genuki.big/eng/CUL/cumbFHS/membership.html

Cumbria
Distington Family & Local History Society 10 Mill Cottages, Distington, Workington, CA14 5SR Tel: 01946 833060, 01946 833060 Email: gillyfoster@distington.idps.co.uk WWW: www.distington.idps.co.uk
Furness Family History Society 64 Cowlarns Road, Hawcoat, Barrow-in-Furness, LA14 4HJ Tel: 01229-830942 Email: julia.fairbairn@virgin.net
WWW: www.members.aol.com/furnessfhs/fpw.htm

Derbyshire
Chesterfield & District Family History Society Skerries, 485 Newbold Road, Chesterfield, S41 8AE
Tel: 01246-471983 Email: cadfhs@chesterfield24.fsnet.co.uk
Derbyshire Ancestral Research Group 86 High Street, Loscoe, Heanor, DE75 7LF Tel: 01773-604916
Derbyshire Family History Society Bridge Chapel House, St Mary's Bridge, Sowter Road, Derby, DE1 3AT Tel: 01332 608101 WWW: www.dfhs.org.uk

Devon
Devon Family History Society PO Box 9, Exeter, EX2 6YP Tel: 01392-275917 Email: members@devonfhs.org.uk WWW: www.devonfhs.org.uk
Thorverton & District History Society Ferndale, Thorverton, Exeter, EX5 5NG Tel: 01392 860932,

Dorset
Dorset Family History Society, Unit 40 Mannings Heath Works, 18 Mannings Heath Road, Parkstone, Poole, Dorset, BH12 4NJ Tel: 01202 736261 Email: contact@dorsetfhs.freeserve.co.uk WWW: www.dfhs.freeserve.co.uk/index.htmll
Somerset & Dorset Family History Society
PO Box 4052, Sherborne, DH9 6YL Tel: 01935 389611, 01935 389611 Email: society@sdfhs.org WWW: www.sdfhs.org

Durham
Cleveland Family History Society 1 Oxgang Close, Redcar, TS10 4ND Tel: 01642 486615
Elvet Local & Family History Groups
37 Hallgarth Street, Durham, DH1 3AT Tel: 0191-386-4098 Email: Turnstone-Ventures@durham-city.freeserve.co.uk
Newton Aycliffe Family History Society, 4 Barnard Close, Woodham Village, Newton Aycliffe, County Durham, DL5 4SP Tel: 01325 315959 Email: jtb2@totalise.com
Northumberland & Durham Family History Society 2nd Floor, Bolbec Hall, Westgate Road, Newcastle-on-Tyne, NE1 1SE Tel: 0191-261-2159 WWW: http://www.geocities.com/athens/6549/

Essex
Essex Society for Family History Research Centre, Essex Record Office, Wharf Road, Chelmsford, CM2 6YT Tel: 01245 244670 Email: secretary@esfh.org.uk WWW: www.esfh.org.uk
Waltham Forest Family History Society, 49 Sky Peals Road, Woodford Green, Essex, IG8 9NE

Gloucestershire
Gloucestershire Family History Society 4 Twyver Close, Upton St Leonards, GL4 8EF Tel: 01452-52344 (RESOURCE CENTRE) Email: glosearch@hotmail.com WWW: http://www.cix.co.uk/~rd/genuki/gfhs.htm
Gloucestershire - South
Sodbury Vale Family History Group 36 Westcourt Drive, Oldland Common, Bristol, BS30 9RU
Tel: 0117 932 4133 Email: sladekf@supanet.com

Hampshire
Hampshire Genealogical Society PO Box 48, Cosham, PO6 3UN
Email: society@hgs-online.org.uk WWW: www.hgs-online.org.uk

Herefordshire
Herefordshire Family History Society 6 Birch Meadow, Gosmore Road, Clehonger, Hereford, HR2 9RH Tel: 01981-250974 Email: prosser_brian@hotmail.com WWW: www.roortsweb.com~ukhfhs

Hertfordshire
Codicote Local History Society 34 Harkness Way, Hitchin, SG4 0QL Tel: 01462 622953
Hertfordshire Family & Population History Society 2 Mayfair Close, St Albans, AL4 9TN Email: hfphs@btinternet.com WWW: http://www.btinternet.com/~hfphs/index.htm
Letchworth & District Family History Group 84 Kings Hedges, Hitchin, SG5 2QE
Royston & District Family History Society 60 Heathfield, Royston, SG8 5BN Tel: 01763 241462 Email: joyce3Atoptalise.co.uk
St. Albans & Herts Architectural & Archaeological Society 24 Rose Walk, St Albans, AL4 9AF Tel: 01727 853204
Welwyn & District Local History Society 9 York Way, Welwyn, AL6 9LB Tel: 01438 716415

Hull
Hull Central Library Family & Local History Club
Central Library, Albion Street, Kingston upon Hull, HU1 3TF Tel: 01482 616828 Fax: 01482 616827 Email: gareth2ukorigins.co.uk WWW: http://www.hullcc.gov.uk/genealogy

Isle of Wight
Isle of Wight Family History Society Spindrift, 3 Milne Way, Newport, PO30 1YF Tel: 01983 524469,
ROOTS Family & Parish History San Fernando, Burnt House Lane, Alverstone, Sandown, PO36 0HB Tel: 01983 403060 Email: peters.sanfernando@tesco.net

Kent
Folkestone & District Family History Society Brickwall Farmhouse, Dengemarsh Road, Lydd, TN29 9JH Email: levina.jones@virgin.net WWW: www.freespace.virgin.net/jennifer.killick/folkestone&districtfhs
Kent Family History Society, Bullockstone Farm, Bullockstone Road, Herne Bay, Kent, CT6 7NL WWW: www.kfhs.org.uk
Tunbridge Wells Family History Society The Old Cottage, Langton Road, Langton Green, Tunbridge Wells, TN3 0BA Tel: 01892-521495 Email: s.oxenbury@virgin.net WWW: www.tunwells-fhs.co.uk
Woolwich & District Family History Society, 54 Parkhill Road, Bexley, Kent, DA5 1HY
North West Kent Family History Society, 58 Clarendon Gardens, Dartford, Kent, DA2 6EZ Email: secretary@nwkfhs.org.uk WWW: www.nwkfhs.org.uk Membership Secretary Mr P Gosney, 28 Ingram Road, Dartford Kent DA1 1JL

Lancashire
Bolton & District Family History Society 205 Crompton Way, Bolton, BL2 2RU Tel: 01204 525472 Email: bolton@mlfhs.demon.co.uk
WWW: www.mlfhs.demon.co.uk
Cumbria Family History Society "Ulpha", 32 Granada Road, Denton, M34 2LJ WWW: http://www.genuki.big/eng/CUL/cumbFHS/membership.html
Lancashire Family History & Historical Society 15 Christ Church Street, Accrington, BB5 2LZ Tel: 01254 398579 Email: jhunt@christchurch92.freeserve.co.uk WWW: http://www.lfhhs.mcmail.com
Lancaster Family History Group 94 Croston Road, Garstang, Preston, PR3 1HR WWW: http://www.fhgroup.freeserve.co.uk
Liverpool & S W Lancashire Family History Society 11 Bushbys Lane, Formby, L37 2DX WWW: www.lswlfhs.freeserve.co.uk
Manchester & Lancashire Family History Society Clayton House, 59 Piccadilly, Manchester, M1 2AQ Tel: 0161-236-9750 Email: office@mlfhs.demon.co.uk WWW: www.mlfhs.demon.co.uk
North Meols Family History Society 9 The Paddock, Ainsdale, Southport, PR8 3PT Tel: 01704 578797 Email: nadine@xplorasia.freeserve.co.uk WWW: www.users.zetnet.co.uk/nmfhs
Oldham & District Branch of Manchester & Lancashire FHS Clayton House, 59 Piccadilly, Manchester, M1 2QA Tel: 0161 236 9750 Email: office@mlfhs.demon.co.uk WWW: www.mlfhs.demon.co.uk
Ormskirk & District Family History Society c/o Ormskirk College, Hants Lane, Ormskirk, L39 1PX Tel: 01695-578604 Email: petert@skelmersdale.ac.uk WWW: www.odfhs.freeserve.co.uk
Wigan Family History Society 464 Warrington Road, Goose Green, Wigan, WN3 6QF

Leicestershire
Leicestershire & Rutland Family History Society 11 Spring Lane, Wymondham, Leicester, LE14 2AY
Tel: 01572 787331 Email: ray.broad@ntlworld.com
WWW: www.lrfdhs.org.uk

Lincolnshire
Isle of Axholme Family History Society, Alwinton, 51 Mill Road, Crowle, Isle of Axholme, North Lincolnshire, DN17 4LW Tel: 01724 710578 Email: secretary@axholme-fhs.org.uk WWW: www.axholme-fhs.org.uk
Lincolnshire Family History Society, 10 Windsor Avenue, Holbeach, Spalding, Lincolnshire, PE12 7AN Tel: Email: chairman@lincolnshirefhs.org.uk WWW: www.lincolnshirefhs.org.uk
South Holland Family & Local History Group
6 Brendon Walk, Spalding , PE11 3AG Tel: 01775 714781,

London
East of London Family History Society 37 Medopra Road, Romford, RM7 7EP WWW: http://eolfhs.rootsweb.com
Hillingdon Family History Society 20 Moreland Drive, Gerrards Cross, SL9 8BB Tel: 01753 885602 Email: gillmay@dial.pipex.com WWW: www.hfhs.co.uk
London & North Middlesex Family History Society 7 Mount Pleasant Road, New Malden, KT3 3JZ Tel: (020) 8949-6765,
Waltham Forest Family History Society 49 Sky Peals Road, Woodford Green, IG8 9NE
Westminster & Central Middlesex Family History Society Westminster & Central Middlesex Family History Society almagamated with London & North Middlesex Family History Society, 7 Mount pleasant Road, New Malden, Surrey, KT3 3JZ Tel: 020 8949 6765
London (South East)
North West Kent Family History Society

Liverpool
Liverpool & S W Lancashire Family History Society 11 Bushbys Lane, Formby, L37 2DX WWW: www.lswlfhs.freeserve.co.uk

Manchester
Manchester & Lancashire Family History Society Clayton House, 59 Piccadilly, Manchester, M1 2AQ Tel: 0161-236-9750 Email: office@mlfhs.demon.co.uk WWW: www.mlfhs.demon.co.uk

Merseyside
Liverpool & S W Lancashire Family History Society 11 Bushbys Lane, Formby, L37 2DX WWW: www.lswlfhs.freeserve.co.uk

Middlesex
Hillingdon Family History Society
20 Moreland Drive, Gerrards Cross, SL9 8BB Tel: 01753 885602 Email: gillmay@dial.pipex.com WWW: www.hfhs.co.uk
London & North Middlesex Family History Society
7 Mount Pleasant Road, New Malden, KT3 3JZ Tel: (020) 8949-6765
West Middlesex Family History Society 10 West Way, Houslow, TW5 0JF
Westminster & Central Middlesex Family History Society almagamated with London & North Middlesex Family History Society, 7 Mount Pleasant Road, New Malden, Surrey, KT3 3JZ Tel: 020 8949 6765

Norfolk
Mid-Norfolk Family History Society Codgers Cottage, 6 Hale Road, Bradenham, Thetford, IP25 7RA, Email: melaniedonnelly@codgerscottage.fsnet.co.uk WWW: http://www.uea.ac.uk/~s300/genuki/NFK/organisations/midnfhs
Norfolk Family History Society, Headquarters, Library & Registered Office, Kirby Hall, 70 St Giles Street, Norwich, Norfolk, NR2 1LS Tel: 01603-763718 Email: nfhs@paston.co.uk WWW: www.norfolkfhs.org.uk

Northamptonshire
Northamptonshire Family History Society 2 Yewtree Court, Boothville, Peterborough, NN3 6SF Email: northamptonshire_fhs@tesco.net WWW: http://www.fugazi.demon.co.uk

Northumberland
Northumberland & Durham Family History Society, 2nd Floor, Bolbec Hall, Westgate Road, Newcastle-on-Tyne NE1 1SE Tel: 0191-261-2159 WWW: http://www.geocities.com/athens/6549/

Nottinghamshire
Mansfield & District Family History Society 15 Cranmer Grove, Mansfield, NG19 7JR, Email: flinthambe@aol.com
Nottinghamshire Family History Society 15 Holme Close, Woodborough, Nottingham, NG14 6EX WWW: http://www..nottsfhs.org.uk

Oxfordshire
Oxfordshire Family History Society 19 Mavor Close, Woodstock, Oxford, OX20 1YL Tel: 1993812258 Email: julie@kennedy91.fsnet.co.uk WWW: www.ofhs.org.uk

Rutland
Leicestershire & Rutland Family History Society 11 Spring Lane, Wymondham, Leicester, LE14 2AY Tel: 01572 787331 Email: ray.broad@ntlworld.com WWW: www.lrfdhs.org.uk

Shropshire
Cleobury Mortimer Historical Society The Old Schoolhouse, Nee Savage, Cleobury Mortimer, Kidderminster, DY14 8JU Tel: 01299 270319,
Shropshire Family History Society Redhillside, Ludlow Road, Church Stretton, SY6 6AD Email: secretary@sfhs.org.uk WWW: www.sfhs.org.uk

Somerset
Burnham & Highbridge FHS - Disbanded April 1998
Somerset & Dorset Family History Society PO Box 4052, Sherborne, DH9 6YL Tel: 01935 389611 Fax: 01935 389611 Email: society@sdfhs.org WWW: www.sdfhs.org
Weston-Super-Mare Family History Society, 32 Marconi Close, Weston Super Mare, Somerset, BS23 3HHJ Tel: 01934 627053 Email: kes.jack@virgin.co.uk
South West Group of Family History Societies, 32 Marconi Close, Weston Super Mare, Somerset, BS23 3HHJ Tel: 01934 627053 Email: kes.jack@virgin.co.uk

Staffordshire
Birmingham & Midland Society for Genealogy & Heraldry 2 Castle Croft, Oldbury, B68 9BQ Tel: 0121 429 9712 Email: birmingham@terrymorter.fsnet.co.uk WWW: www.bmsgh.org
Ancestral Rescue Club, 19 Mansfield Close, Tamworth, Staffordshire, B79 7YE Tel: 01827 65322 Email: ancestral@rescue.fsnet.co.uk WWW: www.rootsweb.com/~engarc/index.html
Audley & District Family History Society, 20 Hillside Avenue, Endon, Stoke on Trent, Staffordshire, ST9 9HH Email: famhist@audley.net
Burntwood Family History Group, 26 Coppice Close, Chase Terrace, Burntwood, Staffordshire, WS7 8BJ Email: manlaw@freeuk.co.uk WWW: www.oldminingcollege.co.uk/bfhg

Suffolk
Felixstowe Family History Society Drenagh, 7 Victoria Road, Felixstowe, IP11 7PT Tel: 01394-275631, Fax: 01394-275631 WWW: http://www.btinternet.com/~woodsbj/tths
Suffolk Family History Society, Egg Hall Cottage, 14 Birch Street, Nayland, Colchester, Essex, CO6 4JA Tel: 01206 263116 WWW: http://www.genuki.org.uk/big/eng/SFK/Sfhs/Sfhs.htm

Surrey
East Surrey Family History Society, PO Box 2506, Coulsdon, Surrey, CR5 3WF Email: secretary@eastsurreyfhs.org.uk WWW: www.eastsurreyfhs.org.uk
West Surrey Family History Society Deer Dell, Botany Hill, Sands, Farnham, GU10 1LZ Tel: 01252 783485 Email: sylviamcq@onetel.co.uk WWW: http://www.surreyweb.org.uk/wsfhs/index.html

Sussex
Sussex Family History Group 7 Tower View, Uckfield, TN22 1SB Tel: 01825 765561 Email: secretary@sfhg.org.uk WWW: http://www.sfhg.org.uk
Sussex - East
Family Roots Family History Society (Eastbourne & District) 94 Northbourne Road, Eastbourne, BN22 8QP Email: sarahslaughter@madasafish.com
Hastings & Rother Family History Society Flat 22 The Cloisters, St Johns Road, St Leonards on Sea, TN37 6JT Tel: 01424-422139, WWW: www.hrfhs.org.uk

Tyne & Wear
Northumberland & Durham Family History Society 2nd Floor, Bolbec Hall, Westgate Road, Newcastle-on-Tyne, NE1 1SE Tel: 0191-261-2159, WWW: http://www.geocities.com/athens/6549/

Waltham Forest
Waltham Forest Family History Society, 49 Sky Peals Road, Woodford Green, IG8 9NE

Warwickshire
Birmingham & Midland Society for Genealogy & Heraldry 2 Castle Croft, Oldbury, B68 9BQ Tel: 0121 429 9712 Email: birmingham@terrymorter.fsnet.co.uk WWW: www.bmsgh.org

Coventry Family History Society, PO Box 2746, Coventry, Warwickshire, CV5 7YD Tel: (024) 7646 4256 Email: enquiries@covfhs.org WWW: www.covfhs.org
Nuneaton & North Warwickshire Family History Society, 14 Amos Avenue, Nuneaton, Warwickshire, CV10 7BD WWW: www.nnwfhs.org.uk
Rugby Family History Group, Springfields, Rocherberie Way, Rugby, Warwickshire, CV22 6EG Tel: 01788 813957 Email: j.chard@ntlworld.com WWW: www.rugbyfhg.co.uk
Warwickshire Family History Society 7 Mersey Road, Bulkington, CV12 9QB Email: n.wetton.@virgin.net WWW: www.wfhs.org.uk

Westmorland
Cumbria Family History Society
"Ulpha", 32 Granada Road, Denton, M34 2LJ
WWW: http://www.genuki/big/eng/CUL/cumbFHS/membership.html

Wiltshire
Wiltshire Family History Society, 10 Castle Lane, Devizes, Wiltshire, SN10 1HJ Tel: 01380 722893 Email: wfhs@devizes39.freeserve.co.uk WWW: www.wiltshirefhs.co.uk

Worcestershire
Birmingham & Midland Society for Genealogy & Heraldry, 2 Castle Croft, Oldbury, B68 9BQ Tel: 0121 429 9712 Email: birmingham@terrymorter.fsnet.co.uk WWW: www.bmsgh.org
Malvern Family History Group, D'Haute Rive, 37 Tennyson Drive, St James' Park, Malvern, Worcestershire, WR14 2TQ Tel: 01684 561872 WWW: www.mfhg.org.uk

Yorkshire
Yorkshire Archaeological Society - Family History Section
Claremont, 23 Clarendon Road, Leeds, LS2 9NZ, WWW: http://www.users.globalnet.co.uk/~gdl/yasfhs.htm
Yorkshire Consortium of Family History Societies - London Group 121 Layhams Road, West Wickham, Kent, BR4 9HE
Yorkshire - East Yorkshire
Boothferry Family & Local History Group, 17 Airmyn Avenue, Goole, Yorkshire, DN14 6PF Email: howardrj@madasafish.com
City of York & District Family History Society, 140 Shipton Road, York, Yorkshire, YO30 5RU WWW: www.yorkfamilyhistory.org.uk
East Yorkshire Family History Society 12 Carlton Drive, Aldbrough, HU11 4SF
WWW: www.eyfhs.org.uk
Hull Central Library Family & Local History Club
Central Library, Albion Street, Kingston upon Hull, HU1 3TF Tel: 01482 616828, Fax: 01482 616827 Email: gareth2ukorigins.co.uk
WWW: http://www.hullcc.gov.uk/genealogy
Yorkshire - North
City of York & District Family History Society, 140 Shipton Road, York, Yorkshire, YO30 5RU WWW: www.yorkfamilyhistory.org.uk
Cleveland Family History Society 1 Oxgang Close, Redcar, TS10 4ND Tel: 01642 486615
Ripon Historical Society & Ripon, Harrogate & District Family History Group, 18 Aspin Drive, Knaresborough, North Yorkshire, HG5 8HH Tel: 01423 863728 Email: gdl@globalnet.co.uk WWW: www.users.globalnet.co.uk/~gdl/index.htm
Upper Dales Family History Group - affiliated to Cleveland Family History Society Croft House, Newbiggin in Bishopdale, Nr Leyburn, DL8 3TD Tel: 01969 663738 Email: glenys@bishopdale.demon.co.uk WWW: www.bishopdale.demon.co.uk
Wharfedale Family History Group 1 West View Court, Yeadon, Leeds, LS19 7HX Tel: 0113 258 5597 Email: wfhg@yorksgen.org.uk WWW: http://www.yorksgen.org.uk
Yorkshire - South
Barnsley Family History Society 58A High Street, Royston, Barnsley, S71 4RN Email: kath@barnsleyfhs.freeserve.co.uk WWW: http://www.barnsleyfhs.freeserve.co.uk
Boothferry Family & Local History Group 17 Airmyn Avenue, Goole, DN14 6PF Email: howardrj@madasafish.com
Doncaster & District Family History Society 'Marton House', 125 The Grove, Wheatley Hills, Doncaster, DN2 5SN Tel: 01302-367257 Email: tonyjunes@aol.com WWW: http://www.doncasterfhs.freeserve.co.uk
Grenoside & District Local History Group, 4 Stepping Lane, Grenoside, Sheffield, South Yorkshire, S35 8RA Tel: 0114 257 1929 Email: info@grenosidelocalhistory.co.uk WWW: www.grenosidelocalhistory.co.uk
Isle of Axholme Family History Society Alwinton, 51 Mill Road, Crowle, Isle of Axholme, DN17 4LW Tel: 01302 350849 WWW: www.linktop.demon.co.uk/axholme/
Rotherham Family History Society 12 Hall Grove, Moorgate, Rotherham, S60 2BS WWW: www.rotherhamfhs.f9.co.uk
Sheffield & District Family History Society 10 Hallam Grange Road, Sheffield, S10 4BJ, Email: secretary@sheffieldfhs.org.uk WWW: www.sheffieldfhs.org.uk

Yorkshire - West
Bradford Family History Society 2 Leaventhorpe Grove, Thornton, Bradford, BD13 3BN, Email: DFlax@aol.com WWW: http://www.genuki.org.uk/big/eng/YKS/bfhs/
Calderdale Family History Society inc Halifax & District
61 Gleanings Avenue, Norton Tower, Halifax, HX2 0NU Tel: 01422-360756, WWW: www.users.globalnet.co.uk/~cfhs/
Huddersfield & District Family History Society, 15 Huddersfield Road, Neltham, Huddersfield, West Yorkshire, HD9 4NJ Tel: 01484 859229 Email: postmaster@hdfhs.org.uk WWW: http://www.hdfhs.org.uk
Keighley & District Family History Society 2 The Hallows, Shann Park, Keighley, BD20 6HY Tel: 01535-672144
Morley & District Family History Group, 19 Hawthorne Drive, Gildersome, Leeds, West yorkshire, LS27 7YJ WWW: www.morleyfhg.co.uk
Pontefract & District Family History Society 62 Wheatfield Avenue, Oakes, Huddersfield, HD3 4FR
Tel: 01977 643358 WWW: www.genfair.com and at http://.freespace.virgin.net/richard.lockwood
Wakefield & District Family History Society 11 Waterton Close, Walton, Wakefield, WF2 6TT Tel: 01924 258163 Tel: 01924 250882 (Membership Secretary) Email: ronaldpullan@hotmail.com WWW: http://homepage.virgin.net/wakefield.fhs
Wharfedale Family History Group, 1 West View Court, Yeadon, Leeds, West Yorkshire, LS19 7HX Tel: 0113 258 5597 Email: wfhg@yorksgen.org.uk WWW: http://www.yorksgen.org.uk
Yorkshire - York
City of York & District Family History Society, 140 Shipton Road, York, Yorkshire, YO30 5RU WWW: www.yorkfamilyhistory.org.uk

Isle of Man
Isle of Man Family History Society 5 Serlborne Drive, Douglas, IM Tel: 01624-862088
WWW: www.isle-of-man.com/interests/genealogy/fhs

Channel Islands
Guernsey
Family History Section of La Société Guernesiaise, PO Box 314, Candie, St Peter Port, GY1 3TG
Jersey
Channel Islands Family History Society, PO Box 507, St Helier, JE4 5TN, Email: cifhs@localdial.com
WWW: www.user.itl.net/~glen/AbouttheChannelIslandsFHS.html

Wales
London Branch of the Welsh Family History Societies 27 Princes Avenue, Carshalton Beeches, SM5 4NZ
Email: regandpaddy@btinternet.com WWW:
Brecknockshire
Powys Family History Society Oaker's Lodge, The Vineyards, Winforton, HR3 6EA Tel: 01544 327103 Email: 114251.2276@compuserve.com WWW: http://ourworld.compuserve.com/homepages/michaelmacsorley/powys1.htm & also via Genuki
Cardiganshire
Cardiganshire Family History Society Trebrysg, Tregaron, SY25 6LH Tel: 01974-298 884 WWW: http://www.heaton.celtic.co.uk/cgnfhs
Carmarthenshire
Dyfed Family History Society 38 Brynmelyn Avenue, Llanelli, SA15 3RT Tel: 01554 774545 Email: johnhtjames@lineone.net WWW: http://www.westwales.co.uk/dfhs/dfhs.htm
Ceredigion
Dyfed Family History Society 38 Brynmelyn Avenue, Llanelli, SA15 3RT Tel: 01554 774545 Email: johnhtjames@lineone.net WWW: http://www.westwales.co.uk/dfhs/dfhs.htm
Clwyd
Clwyd Family History Society The Laurels, Dolydd Road, Cefn Mawr, Wrexham, LL14 3NH Tel: 01978-822218, WWW: www.clwydfhs.org.uk
Denbighshire
Clwyd Family History Society The Laurels, Dolydd Road, Cefn Mawr, Wrexham, LL14 3NH Tel: 01978-822218, WWW: www.clwydfhs.org.uk
Dyfed
Dyfed Family History Society 38 Brynmelyn Avenue, Llanelli, SA15 3RT Tel: 01554 774545 Email: johnhtjames@lineone.net WWW: http://www.westwales.co.uk/dfhs/dfhs.htm
Flintshire
Clwyd Family History Society The Laurels, Dolydd Road, Cefn Mawr, Wrexham, LL14 3NH Tel: 01978-822218, WWW: www.clwydfhs.org.uk
Glamorgan
Glamorgan Family History Society, 22 Parc y Bryn, Creigiau, Cardiff, Glamorgan CF15 9SE Email: secretary@glamfhs.org WWW: http://www.glamfhs.org

Gwent
Gwent Family History Society, 11 Rosser Street, Wainfelin, Pontypool, Gwent NP4 6EA Email: secretary@gwentfhs.info WWW: www.gwentfhs.info
Gwynedd
Gwynedd Family History Society 36 Y Wern, Y Felinheli, LL56 4TX Tel: 01286 871838 Email: Gwynedd.Roots@tesco.net WWW: http://www.gwynedd.fsbusiness.co.uk
Monmouthshire
Gwent Family History Society 11 Rosser Street, Wainfelin, Pontypool, NP4 6EA, Email: secretary@gwentfhs.org.uk WWW: http://welcome.to/gwent.fhs
Montgomeryshire
Montgomeryshire Genealogical Society, Cambrian House, Brimmon Lane, Newtown, Powys SY16 1BY Tel: 01686 624753 WWW: http://home.freeuk.net/montgensoc
Powys Family History Society
Oaker's Lodge, The Vineyards, Winforton, HR3 6EA Tel: 01544 327103Email: 114251.2276@compuserve.com
Pembrokeshire
Dyfed Family History Society, 38 Brynmelyn Avenue, Llanelli, SA15 3RT Tel: 01554 774545 Email: johnhtjames@lineone.net WWW: http://www.westwales.co.uk/dfhs/dfhs.htm
Powys,
Powys Family History Society, Oaker's Lodge, The Vineyards, Winforton, HR3 6EA Tel: 01544 327103
Email: 114251.2276@compuserve.com WWW: http://ourworld.compuserve.com/homepages/michaelmacsorley/powys1.htm & also via Genuki
Radnorshire
Powys Family History Society Oaker's Lodge, The Vineyards, Winforton, HR3 6EA Tel: 01544 327103Email: 114251.2276@compuserve.com WWW: http://ourworld.compuserve.com/homepages/michaelmacsorley/powys1.htm

Scotland
Scottish Genealogy Society, 15 Victoria Terrace, Edinburgh, EH1 2JL Tel: 0131-220-3677, Fax: 0131-220-3677 Email: info@scotsgenealogy.com WWW: www.scotsgenealogy.com
Aberdeen
Aberdeen & North East Scotland Family History Society 164 King Street, Aberdeen, AB24 5BD Tel: 01224-646323 Fax: 01224-639096 Email: enquiries@anefhs.org.uk WWW: http://www.anesfhs.org.uk
Angus
Tay Valley Family History Society & Research Centre Family History Research Centre, 179–181 Princes Street, Dundee, DD4 6DQ Tel: 01382-461845, Fax: 01382 455532 Email: tvfhs@tayvalleyfhs.org.uk WWW: http://www.tayvalleyfhs.org.uk
Argyll
Glasgow & West of Scotland Family History Society Unit 5, 22 Mansfield Street, Partick, Glasgow, G11 5QP Tel: 0141-339-8303, Fax: 0141-339-8303, WWW: http://www.gwsfhs.org.uk
Ayrshire
Alloway & Southern Ayrshire Family History Society c/o Alloway Public Library, Doonholm Road, Alloway, Ayr, KA7 4QQ Email: asafhs@mtcharlesayr.fsnet.co.uk
Glasgow & West of Scotland Family History Society Unit 5, 22 Mansfield Street, Partick, Glasgow, G11 5QP Tel: 0141-339-8303 Fax: 0141-339-8303 WWW: http://www.gwsfhs.org.uk
Largs & North Ayrshire Family History Society 28 Walkerston Avenue, Largs, KA30 8ER WWW: http://www.freeyellow.com/members7/lnafhs/index.html
Troon @ Ayrshire Family History Society c/o M.E.R.C., Troon Public Library, South Beach, Troon, Ayrshire, KA10 6EF, Email: info@troonayrshirefhs.org.uk WWW: www.troonayrshirefhs.org.uk
Berwickshire
Borders Family History Society 2 Fellowhills, Ladykirk, Berwickshire, TD15 1XN Tel: 01289 382060 Email: hloughAukonline.co.uk Family History Room at Old Gala House, Galashiels.
Borders
Borders Family History Society 2 Fellowhills, Ladykirk, Berwickshire, TD15 1XN Tel: 01289 382060 Email: hloughAukonline.co.uk Family History Room at Old Gala House, Galashiels.
Bute
Glasgow & West of Scotland Family History Society Unit 5, 22 Mansfield Street, Partick, Glasgow, G11 5QP Tel: 0141-339-8303 Fax: 0141-339-8303 WWW: http://www.gwsfhs.org.uk
Caithness
Caithness Family History Society Mill Cottage, Corsback, Dunnet KW1 48XQ Email: a.e.lewis@btinternet.com WWW: caithnessfhs.org.uk
Central Scotland
Central Scotland Family History Society 11 Springbank Gardens, Dunblane, FK15 9JX Tel: 01786 823937 Email:

mturner200@hotmail.com WWW: www.csfhs.org.uk
Dunbartonshire
Glasgow & West of Scotland Family History Society Unit 5, 22 Mansfield Street, Partick, Glasgow, G11 5QP Tel: 0141-339-8303 Fax: 0141-339-8303 WWW: http://www.gwsfhs.org.uk
Dundee
Tay Valley Family History Society & Research Centre 179–181 Princes Street, Dundee, DD4 6DQ Tel: 01382-461845, Fax: 01382 455532 Email: tvfhs@tayvalleyfhs.org.uk WWW: http://www.tayvalleyfhs.org.uk
Dumfries
Dumfries & Galloway Family History Society Family History Research Centre, 9 Glasgow Street, Dumfries, DG2 9AF Tel: 01387-248093 Email: shop@dgfhs.org.uk WWW: www.dgfhs.org.uk
East Lothian,
Lothian Family History Society c/o Lasswade High School Centre, Eskdale Drive, Bonnyrigg, EH19 2LA Tel: 0131-660-1933 Fax: 0131-663-6634 Email: lothiansfhs@hotmail.com WWW: www.lothiansfhs.org.uk
Edinburgh
Lothians Family History Society c/o Lasswade High School Centre, Eskdale Drive, Bonnyrigg, EH19 2LA Tel: 0131-660-1933 Fax: 0131-663-6634 Email: anne_agnew@online.rednet.co.uk
Fife
Fife Family History Society Glenmoriston, Durie Street, Leven, KY8 4HF Tel: 013333 425321 Email: fife@ffhoc.freeserve.co.uk WWW: http://www.fifefhs.pwp.bluyonder.co.uk
Tay Valley Family History Society &Research Centre 179–181 Princes Street, Dundee, DD4 6DQ Tel: 01382-461845 Tel: Fax: 01382 455532 Email: tvfhs@tayvalleyfhs.org.uk WWW: http://www.tayvalleyfhs.org.uk
Glasgow
Glasgow & West of Scotland Family History Society Unit 5, 22 Mansfield Street, Partick, Glasgow, G11 5QP Tel: 0141-339-8303 Fax: 0141-339-8303 WWW: http://www.gwsfhs.org.uk
Kinross-shire
Tay Valley Family History Society & Research Centre 179–181 Princes Street, Dundee, DD4 6DQ Tel: 01382-461845 Email: tvfhs@tayvalleyfhs.org.uk WWW: http://www.tayvalleyfhs.org.uk
Highlands and Invernesshire
Highland Family History Society c/o Reference Room, Inverness Public Library, Farraline Park, Inverness, IV1 1NH
Lanarkshire
Glasgow & West of Scotland Family History Society Unit 5, 22 Mansfield Street, Partick, Glasgow, G11 5QP Tel: 0141-339-8303 WWW: http://www.gwsfhs.org.uk
Lanarkshire Family History Society Local History Lab, Motherwell Heritage Centre, 1 High Road, Motherwell, Lanarkshire, ML1 3HU
Midlothian
Lothians Family History Society c/o Lasswade High School Centre, Eskdale Drive, Bonnyrigg, EH19 2LA Tel: 0131-660-1933 Email: lothiansfhs@hotmail.com WWW: www.lothiansfhs.org.ukk
North East Scotland,
Aberdeen & North East Scotland Family History Society 164 King Street, Aberdeen, AB24 5BD Tel: 01224-646323 Fax: 01224-639096 Email: enquiries@anefhs.org.uk WWW: http://www.anesfhs.org.uk
Orkney
Orkney Family History Society Community Room, The Strynd, Kirkwall, KW15 1HG Tel: 01856 761582 (Home) Email: olaf.mooney@virgin.net
Peebleshire
Borders Family History Society 2 Fellowhills, Ladykirk, Berwickshire, TD15 1XN Tel: 01289 382060 Email: hloughAukonLine.co.uk Family History Room at Old Gala House, Galashiels.
Perthshire
Tay Valley Family History Society & Research Centre Family History Research Centre, 179–181 Princes Street, Dundee, DD4 6DQ Tel: 01382-461845, Fax: 01382 455532 Email: tvfhs@tayvalleyfhs.org.uk WWW: http://www.tayvalleyfhs.org.uk
Renfrewshire
Glasgow & West of Scotland Family History Society Unit 5, 22 Mansfield Street, Partick, Glasgow, G11 5QP Tel: 0141-339-8303, Fax: 0141-339-8303 WWW: http://www.gwsfhs.org.uk
Renfrewshire
Renfrewshire Family History Society, c/o Museum & Art Galleries, High Street, Paisley, PA1 2BA WWW: www.renfrewshire.org.uk
Roxburghshire
Borders Family History Society 2 Fellowhills, Ladykirk, Berwickshire, TD15 1XN Tel: 01289 382060 Email: hloughAukonline.co.uk Family History Room at Old Gala House, Galashiels.

Selkirkshire
Borders Family History Society 2 Fellowhills, Ladykirk, Berwickshire, TD15 1XN Tel: 01289 382060 Email: hloughAukonline.co.uk Family History Room at Old Gala House, Galashiels.
Shetland
Shetland Family History Society 6 Hillhead, Lerwick, ZE1 0EJ Email: secretary@shetland-fhs.org.uk WWW: www.shetland-fhs.org.uk
Stirlingshire
Central Scotland Family History Society 11 Springbank Gardens, Dunblane, FK15 9JX Tel: 01786 823937 Email: mturner200@hotmail.com WWW: www.csfhs.org.uk
Stirlingshire
Glasgow & West of Scotland Family History Society Unit 5, 22 Mansfield Street, Partick, Glasgow, G11 5QP Tel: 0141-339-8303 Fax: 0141-339-8303 WWW: http://www.gwsfhs.org.uk

Northern Ireland
Irish Heritage Association A.204 Portview, 310 Newtownards Road, Belfast BT4 1HE Northern Ireland Tel: (028) 90455325
North of Ireland Family History Society c/o Graduate School of Education, 69 University Street, Belfast BT7 1HL, Northern Ireland Email: R.Sibbett@tesco.net WWW: http://www.nifhs.org
Ulster Historical Foundation Balmoral Buildings, 12 College Square East, Belfast BT1 6DD Northern Ireland Tel: (028) 9033 2288 Fax: 028 9023 9885 Email: enquiry@uhf.org.uk andrew@uhf.org.uk WWW: http://www.uhf.org.uk and www.ancestryireland.com Established in 1956 the UHF is a charitable organisation that provides a professional Irish Ancestral Research Service, publishes historical books and organises conferences

Ireland
Council of Irish Genealogical Organisations 186 Ashcroft, Raheny, Dublin 5, Ireland
Genealogical Society of Ireland 11 Desmond Avenue, Dun Laoghaire, Co Dublin, Ireland Tel: 353 1 284 2711 Email; GenSocIreland@iol.ie WWW: www.gensocireland.org
Irish Ancestry Group
Clayton House, 59 Piccadilly, Manchester, M1 2AQ Tel: 0161-236-9750 Email: mlfhs.demon.co.uk
Irish Family History Society
P0 Box 36, Naas, Email: ifhs@eircom.net WWW: http://homepage.eircom.net/~ifhs/
Ballinteer FHS 29 The View, Woodpark, Ballinteer, Dundrum, Dublin 16 Ireland Email: 01-298-8082 Email: ryanct@eircom.net
Cork Genealogical Society c/o 4 Evergreen Villas, Evergreen Road, Cork City, Co Cork, Ireland Tel: 086 8198359 Email: micaconl@eircon.ie WWW: http://homepage.eircom.net/~adcolemen
Irish Genealogical Research Society c/o 82 Eaton Square, London, SW1W 9AJ England WWW: www.igrsoc.org The Society has a library of over four thousand books and two and a half thousand manuscripts
Flannery Clan / Clann Fhlannabhra 81 Woodford Drive, Clondakin, Dublin 22 Ireland Email; oflannery@eircom.net WWW: www.flanneryclan.ie
Raheny Heritage Society 4 Thorndale Drive, Artane, Dublin 5 Tel: 01 831 9028 Lists of individuals interests supplied on request to Hon Secretary with International Reply Coupon
Wexford Family History Society 24 Parklands, Wexford, Co Wexford, Ireland Tel: 053-42273 Email: murphyh@tinet.ie
Wicklow County Genealogical Society 1 Summerhill, Wicklow Town, Co Wicklow, Ireland
Irish Family History Society P0 Box 36, Naas, Co Kildare, Ireland Email: ifhs@eircom.net WWW: http://homepage.eircom.net/~ifhs/
Irish Ancestry Group Clayton House, 59 Piccadilly, Manchester M1 2AQ England Tel: 0161-236-9750 Fax: 0161-237-3512 Email: mlfhs.demon.co.uk A specialist group of Manchester and Lancashire Family History Society

Specialist Family History Societies
Ambleside Oral History Group 1 High Busk, Ambleside, Cumbria LA22 0AW Tel: 01539 431070 Email; history@amblesideonline.co.uk WWW: www.aoghistory.f9.co.uk
Anglo-French Family History Society
31 Collingwood Walk, Andover, SP10 1PU
WWW: www.anglo-french-fhs.org
Anglo-German Family History Society 5 Oldbury Grove, Beaconsfield, Buckinghamshire HP9 2AJ England Tel: 01494 676812 Email: gwendolinedavis@aol.com WWW: www.agfhs.org.uk and www.art-science.com/agfhs A mutual self-help Society for all those with German speaking ancestry
Anglo-Scottish Family History Society
Clayton House, 59 Piccadilly, Manchester, M1 2AQ Tel: 0161-236-9750, Fax: 0161-237-3512 Email: mlfhs.demon.co.uk

Australian Society of the Lace Makers of Calais Inc
PO Box 946, Batemans Bay, 2536 Tel: 0244-718168 Tel: 0244-723421, Email: carolynb@acr.net.au
British Ancestors in India Society 2 South Farm Avenue, Harthill, Sheffield, South Yorkshire S26 7WY Tel: 44 (0) 1909 774416 Fax: +44 (0) 1909 774416 Email: editorial@indiaman.com WWW: www.indiaman.com Publishers of Indiaman Magazine, the only genealogical and history magazine in the world about the British in India and Southern asia from 1600 to 20th Century
British Assn for Cemeteries in S.Asia 76 1/2 Chartfield Avenue, London, SW15 6HQ England Tel: (020) 8788-6953 WWW: www.bacsa.org.uk Records Cemeteries. Published over 40 surveys of cemeteries in Pakistan, India, Bangladesh, Burma, Malaysia, Indonesia, Thailand and Japan South Asia (Aden to Japan)
Catholic Family History Society 45 Gates Green Road, West Wickham, Kent BR4 9DE WWW: www.catholic-history.org.uk
Cawdor Heritage Group Family & Local History Room, Nairn Museum, Viewfield Drive, Nairn, Nairnshire IV12 4EE Tel: 01667 456791 Fax: 01667 455399 Email: manager@nairnmuseum.freeserve.co.uk WWW: www.nairnmuseum.co.uk Information available on Nairnshire, census returns and Old Parish Registers
The Clans of Ireland Ltd 2 Westbourne Terrace, Quinsboro Road, Bray, County Wicklow, Ireland Tel: 01365-322353 Email: theclansofireland@ireland.com
Descendants of Convicts Group
PO Box 12224, A'Beckett Street, Melbourne 3000,
Families in British India Society 51 Taylor's Ride, Leighton Buzzard, Bedfordshire LU7 3JN Email: lawrie.butler@talk21.com
Genealogical Society of Utah (UK) 185 Penns Lane, Sutton Coldfield, West Midlands B76 1JU Tel: 0121 384 2028 Fax: 0121 384 9929
Heraldry Society PO Box 32, Maidenhead, Berkshire SL6 3FD Tel: 0118-932-0210 Fax: 0118 932 0210 Email: heraldry-society@cwcom.net
Historical Medical Equipment Society
8 Albion Mews, Apsley, HP3 9QZ, Email: hmes@antiageing.freeserve.co.uk
Hugenot & Walloon Research Association
Malmaison, Church St, Great Bedwyn, SN8 3PE
International Police Association - Genealogy Group
Thornholm, Church Lane, South Muskham, Newark, NG23 6EQ Tel: 01636 676997 Email: ipagenuk@thornholm.freeserve.co.uk
International Society for British Genealogy & Family History
P0 Box 3115, Salt Lake City, 84110-3115 Tel: 801-272-2178, WWW: http://www.homestart.com/isbgfh/
Irish Ancestry Group
Clayton House, 59 Piccadilly, Manchester, M1 2AQ Tel: 0161-236-9750, Fax: 0161-237-3512 Email: mlfhs.demon.co.uk
Irish Genealogical Research Society c/o 82 Eaton Square, London SW1W 9AJ WWW: www.igrsoc.org The Society has a library of over four thousand books and two and a half thousand manuscripts
Jewish Genealogical Society of Great Britain 48 Worcester Crescent, Woodford Green, Essex, G8 0LU Tel: 020 8504 8013 Email: pnking@onetel.net.uk WWW: www.jgsgb.org.uk
Lancashire Parish Register Society 135 Sandy Lane, Orford, Warrington WA2 9JB Email: tom_obrien@bigfoot.com WWW: http://www.genuki.org.uk/big/eng/LAN/lprs
Lighthouse Society of Great Britain Gravesend Cottage, Gravesend, Torpoint, Cornwall PL11 2LX Email: k.trethewey@btinternet.com WWW: http://www.lsgb.co.uk Holds databases of lighthouses and their keepers. SAE required for enquiries Lighthouse Encyclopaedia 2003 edition published on CD Rom only
Local Population Studies Society School of Biological Sciences (Dr SA Scott), University of Liverpool, Derby Building, Liverpool, Merseyside L69 3GS Tel: 01423-560429 Email: sscott@liverpool.ac.uk WWW: home.att.net/~jkbfa
London & North Western Railway Society - Staff History Group 34 Falmouth Close, Nuneaton, Warwickshire CV11 6GB Tel: 024 76 381090 Fax: 024 76 373577 Email: lnwrshg@aol.com WWW: www.progsol.co.uk/lnwr
North East England Family History Club
5 Tree Court, Doxford Park, Sunderland, SR3 2HR Tel: 0191-522-8344
Quaker Family History Society 1 Ormond Crescent, Hampton, Middlesex TW12 2TJ Email: info@qfhs.co.uk WWW: www.qfhs.co.uk The Society for family historians with British Quaker ancestors. Bi-annual meetings are held around the Country
Railway Ancestors Family History Society
Lundy, 31 Tennyson Road, Eastleigh, SO50 9FS Tel: (023) 8049 7465 Tel: (023) 8090 0923 Fax: (023) 8049 7465 Email: jim@railwayancestors.org.uk WWW: www.railwayancestors.org.uk
Rolls Royce Family History Society
25 Gisburn Road, Barnoldswick, Colne, BB18 5HB Tel: 01282 815778 Email: ken@ranson.org.uk
Romany & Traveller Family History Society 6 St James Walk, South Chailey, East Sussex, BN8 4BU, England WWW:

http://website.lineone.net/~rtfhs

Shap Local History Society The Hermitage, Shap, Penrith CA10 3LY Tel: 01931 716671 Email: liz@kbhshap.freeserve.co.uk

Scottish Association of Family History Societies 51/3 Mortonhall Road, Edinburgh, EH9 2HN Tel: 0131-667-0437, Fax: 0131 667 0437 Email: scots@safhs.org.uk

Society for Name Studies in Britain & Ireland 22 Peel Park Avenue, Clitheroe, BB7 1ET Tel: 01200-423771, Fax: 01200-423771,

Society of Brushmakers Descendants Family History Society 13 Ashworth Place, Church Langley, Essex CM17 9PU Tel: 01279-629392 Email; s.b.d@lineone.net WWW: http://www.brushmakers.com A society devoted to assisting research into the history and records of brush or broom maker ancestors.

Tennyson Society Central Library, Free School Lane, Lincoln LN2 1EZ Tel: 01522-552862 Fax: 01522-552858 Email: linnet@lincolnshire.gov.uk WWW: www.tennysonsociety.org.uk

The Chapels Heritage Society 2 Sandy Way, Wood Lane, Hawarden, Flintshire CH5 3JJ

Victorian Military Society PO Box 5837, Newbury, Berkshire RG14 7FJ Tel: 01635 48628 Email: beverley20@tesco.net WWW: www.vms.org.uk The leading society covering military history of all nations and races from 1837 to 1914

One Name Societies

Guild of One Name Studies 14 Charterhouse Buildings, Goswell Road, London, EC1M 7BA Tel: 01293-411136 Email: guild@one-name.org   WWW: www.one-name.org

Alabaster Society, No 1 Manor Farm Cottages, Bradenham, Thetford, Norfolk, IP25 7QE Tel: 01362-821243 Email: Laraine_Hake@compuserve.com WWW: www.alabaster.org.uk

Alderson Family History Society, 13 Spring Grove, Harrogate, North Yorkshire, HG1 2HS

Alderton Family, 16 Woodfield Drive, Gidea Park, Romford, Essex, RM2 5DH

Allsop Family Group, 86 High Street, Loscoe, Heanor, Derbyshire, DE75 7LF

Armstrong Clan Association, Thyme, 7 Riverside Park, Hollows, Canonbie, Dumfriesshire, DG14 0UY Tel: 013873 71876 Email: ted.armclan@aol.com WWW: www.armstrongclan.info

Beresford Family Society, 2 Malatia, 78 St Augustines Avenue, South Croydon, Surrey, CR2 6JH Tel: (020) 8686 3749 Fax: (020) 8681 3740, Email:, beresford@atlas.co.uk WWW: www.beresfordfamilysociety.org.uk

Blanchard Family History Society, 10 Stainers, Bishop Stortford, Hertfordshire, CM23 4GL WWW: www.blanshard.org

Bliss Family History Society, Old Well Cottage, Washdyke Lane, Fulbeck, Lincolnshire, NG32 3LB Tel: 01400 279050 Email: bliss@one-name.org WWW: http://www.members.aol.com/keithbliss/fhs/main.htm

Braund Society, 12 Ranelagh Road, Lake, Sandown, Isle of Wight, PO36 8NX, Email: braundsociety@fewiow.freeserve.co.uk

Brooking Family History Society, 48 Regent Close, Edgbaston, Birmingham, West Midlands, B5 7PL Tel: 0121 249 1226 Email: marylogan@blueyonder.co.uk WWW: www.brookingsociety.org.uk

Bunting Society, 'Firgrove', Horseshoe Lane, Ash Vale, Surrey, GU12 5LL Tel: 01252-325644 Fax: 01252-325644, Email:, firgrove@compuserve.com WWW: http://freespace.virgin.net/teebee.axmeister/BuntingSociety.htm

Caraher Family History Society, 142 Rexford Street, Sistersville, VA 26175

Cave Family History Society, 45 Wisbech Road, Thorney, Peterborough, Cambridgeshire, PE6 0SA Tel: 01733 270881 Email: hugh-cave@cave-fhs.org.uk WWW: www.cave-fhs.org.uk

Clan Davidson Association, Aisling, 67 Shore Road, Kircubbin, Newtownards, Co Down, BT22 2RP Tel: 028 427-38402 Email: clan.davidson@virgin.net

Clan Gregor Society, Administrative Office, 2 Braehead, Alloa, Clackmannanshire, FK10 2EW Tel: 01259-212076 Fax: 01259-720274, Email:, clangregor@sol.co.uk WWW: http://www.clangregor.com/macgregor

Cobbing Family History Society, 89a Petherton Road, London, N5 2QT Tel: (020) 7226-2657

Cory Society, 3 Bourne Close, Thames ditton, London, KT7 0EA WWW: www.corysociety.org.uk

Courtenay Society, Powderham Castle, Kenton, Exeter, Devon, EX6 8JQ Tel: 01626-891554 Tel: 01626-891367 Fax: 01626-890729, Email:, courtenay@courtsoc.demon.co.uk WWW: www.courtenaysociety.org

Dalton Genealogical Society, 11 Jordan Close, Leavesden, Watford, WD25 7AF Tel: 01923 661139 Email: pam-lynam@lineone.net WWW: http://members.aol.com/daltongene/index.html

East Family History Society, 45 Windsor Road, Ealing, London, W5 3UP

FHS of Martin, PO Box 9, Rosanna, Victoria, Australia 3084

FHS of Martin (UK), 63 Higher Coombe Drive, Teignmouth, Devon, TQ14 9NL

Geoghegan/McGeoghegan One Name Study, 330 Dereham Road, Norwich, Norfolk, NR2 4DL, Email: josi@geoghegan18.fsnet.co.uk WWW: www.jgeoghegan.org.uk

Hamley, Hambly & Hamlyn Family History Society (International), 59 Eylewood Road, West Norwood, London, SE27 9LZ Tel: (020) 8670-0683 Fax: (020) 8670-0683, Email:, hamley@one-name.org WWW: http://www.freespace.virgin.net/ham.famis/

Hards Family Society, Venusmead, 36 Venus Street, Congresbury, Bristol, BS49 5EZ Tel: 01934 834780 Fax: 01934 834780, Email:, rogerhards-venusmead@breathemail.net WWW: www.hards.freewire.co.uk

Holdich Family History Society, 19 Park Crescent, Elstree, Hertfordshire, WD6 3PT Tel: (020) 8953 7195 Email: apogee.dtaylor@btopenworld.com

International Haskell Family Society, 36 Hedley Davis Court, Cherry Orchard Lane, Salisbury, Wiltshire, SP2 7UE Tel: 01722 332873 Fax: 01722 410094, Email:, suzyflip@hotmail.compar

International Relf Society, Chatsworth House, Sutton Road, Somerton, Somerset, TA11 6QL Tel: 01458-274015 Email: chris.relf@bucklebury.demon.co.uk

Krans-Buckland Family Association, P0 Box 1025, North Highlands, California, 95660-1025 Tel: (916)-332-4359 Email: jkbfa@worldnet.att.net

Leather Family History Society, 134 Holbeck, Great Hollands, Bracknell, Berkshire, RG12 8XG Tel: 01344-425092 Email: s.leather@ic.ac.uk

Lin(d)field One Name Group, Southview, Maplehurst, Horsham, West Sussex, RH13 6QY Tel: 01403-864389 Email: lindfield@one-name.org WWW: http://www.lindfield.force9.co.uk/long

Mackman Family History Society, Chawton Cottage, 22a Long Ridge Lane, Nether Poppleton, York, North Yorkshire, YO26 6LX Tel: +44-(0)1904-781752 Email: mackman@one-name.org

Mayhew Ancestry Research, 28 Windmill Road, West Croydon, Surrey, CR0 2XN

Morbey Family History Group, 23 Cowper Crescent, Bengeo, Hertford, Hertfordshire, SG14 3DZ

Morgan Society of England & Wales, 11 Arden Drive, Dorridge, Solihull, West Midlands, B93 8LP Tel: 01564 774020 Fax: 01564 774020, Email:, morgansociety@tesco.net WWW: http://freepages.genealogy.rootsweb.com/~morgansociety http://homepages.tesco.net/n.morganpublications/morganpu.htm

Moxon Family Research Trust, 1 Pine Tree Close, Cowes, Isle of wight, PO31 8DX Tel: 01983 296921 Email: john.moxon@virgin.net WWW: www.moxon.org.uk

Moxon Society, 1 Pinetree Close, Cowes, Isle of Wight, PO31 8DX Tel: 01983 296921 Email: john.moxon@virgin.net

Offley Family Society, 2 The Green, Codicote, Hitchin SG4 8UR Tel: 01438-820006 Email: jrrichards@onetel.net.uk WWW: http://homepages.ntlworld.com/kevin.offley/

Orton Family History Society, 25a Longwood Avenue, Bingley, West Yorkshire, BD16 2RX, Email: derek@beckd.freeserve.co.uk WWW: www.redflag.co.uk/ortonfhs.htm

Palgrave Society, Crossfield House, Dale Road, Stanton, Bury St Edmunds, Suffolk, IP31 2DY Tel: 01359-251050 Fax: 01359-251050, Email:, DerekPalgrave@btinternet.com WWW: www.ffhs.org.uk/members/palgrave.htm

Penty Family Name Society, Kymbelin, 30 Lych Way, Horsell Village, Surrey, GU21 4QG Tel: 01483-764904 Email: PENTYTREE@AOL.COM

Percy-Piercy Family History Society, 32 Ravensdale Avenue, North Finchley, London, N12 9HT Tel: 020 8446 0592 Email: brian.piercy@which.net

Pomerology, The Keep, 3 Stokehouse Street, Poundbury, Dorchester, Dorset, DT1 3GP Tel: 01305 257570 Tel: 01305 257912 Fax: pomerology@compuserve.com

Rix Family Alliance, 4 Acklam Close, Hedon, Hull, HU12 8NA www.rix-alliance.co.uk

Rose Family Society - disbanded 1st March 2002

Serman, Surman Family History Society, 24 Monks Walk, Bridge Street, Evesham, Worcestershire, WR11 4SL Tel: 01386 49967 Fax: 01386 49967, Email:, design@johnsermon.demon.co.uk WWW: www.johnsermon.demon.co.uk

Silverthorne Family Association, 1 Cambridge Close, Swindon, Wiltshire, SN3 1JQ Tel: 01793 537103

Society of Cornishes, 1 Maple Close, Tavistock, Devon, PL19 9LL Tel: 01822 614613 Fax: 01822 614613, Email:, cornish@one-name.org WWW: www.societyofcornishes.org

Sole Society, 49 Kennel Ride, North Ascot, Berkshire, SL5 7NJ Tel: 01344 883700 Email: info@sole.org.uk WWW: www.solesociety.freeserve.co.uk

Spencer Family, 1303 Azalea Lane, Dekalb, Illinois, 60115

Stockdill Family History Society, 6 First Avenue, Garston, Watford, Hertfordshire, WD2 6PZ Tel: 01923-675292 Fax: 01923-675292, Email:, roystock@compuserve.com http://ourworld.compuserve.com/homepages/roystock

Swinnerton Society, 30 Coleridge Walk, London, NW11 6AT Tel: (020) 8458-3443 Email: roger.swynnerton@whichnet

Talbot Research Organisation, 142 Albemarle Avenue, Elson, Gosport., Hampshire, PO12 4HY Tel: 023 92589785 Email: mjh.talbot@tinyworld.cor.uk WWW: http://www.kiamara.demon.co.uk/index.html

The Goddard Association of Europe, 2 Lowergate Road, Huncoat, Accrington, Lancashire, BB5 6LN Tel: 01254-235135 Email: johnc.goddard@virgin.net WWW: www.goddard-association.co.uk

The Metcalfe Society, 57 Westbourne Avenue, Hull, East Yorkshire, HU5 3HW Tel: 01482 342516 Email: enquiries@metcalfe.org.uk WWW: http://www.metcalfe.org.uk

The Stockton Society, The Leas, 28 North Road, Builth Wells, Powys, LD2 3BU Tel: 01982 551667 Email: cestrienne@aol.com

Toseland Clan Society, 40 Moresdale Lane, Seacroft, Leeds, West Yorkshire, LS14 5SY, Fax: 0113-225-9954

Tyrrell Family History Society, 16 The Crescent, Solihull, West Midlands, B91 7PE www.tyrrellfhs.org.uk

Watkins Family History Society, PO Box 1698, Douglas, Georgia, 31534-1698 Tel: 912-383-0839 Email: watkinsfhs@alltel.net and buzzwatk@aol.com WWW: http://www.iinet.net.au/~davwat/wfhs/

Witheridge Family History Society, 2 Apsley Road, Newbridge, Bath, Somerset, BA1 3LP

AUSTRALIA

Society of Australian Genealogists Richmond Villa, 120 Kent Street, Observatory Hill, Sydney 2000 Tel: 61-02-92473953 Fax: 61-02-92414872 Email: socgenes@ozemail.com.au

NEW SOUTH WALES

1788-1820 Pioneer Association PO Box 57, Croydon, New South Wales, 2132 Tel: (02)-9797-8107

Australian Society of the Lace Makers of Calais Inc PO Box 946, Batemans Bay, New South Wales, 2536 Tel: 0244-718168, 0244-723421 Email: carolynb@acr.net.au

Bega Valley Genealogical Society Inc PO Box 19, Pambula, New South Wales, 2549

Berrima District Historical & Family History Society Inc PO Box 851, Bowral, New South Wales, 2576

Blayney Shire Local & Family History Society Group Inc c/o The Library, 48 Adelaide Street, Blayney, New South Wales, 2799 Email: blayney.library@cww.octec.org.au

New South Wales

Botany Bay Family History Society Inc PO Box 1006, Sutherland, New South Wales 1499 WWW: mypage.southernx.com.au/~bbfhs

Broken Hill Family History Group PO Box 779, 75 Pell Street, Broken Hill, New South Wales, 2880 Tel: 08-80-881321

Burwood Drummoyne & District Family History Group c/o Burwood Central Library, 4 Marmaduke Street, Burwood2134

Cape Banks Family History Society PO Box 67, Maroubra, New South Wales, NSW 2035 Email: hazelb@compassnet.com.au WWW: www.ozemail.com.au/mhazelb/capebank

Capital Territory Historical & Genealogical Society of Canberra GPO Box 585, Canberra, ACT 2601

Casino & District Family History Group Inc PO Box 586, Casino, New South Wales, 2470 Email: hughsie@nor.com

Central Coast FHG Inc PO Box 4090 East Gosford NSW 2250

Coffs Harbour District Family History Society Inc PO Box 2057, Coffs Harbour, New South Wales, 2450

Cowra FHG Inc PO Box 495, Cowra, New South Wales, 2794

Deniliquin Family History Group Inc PO Box 144, Multi Arts Hall, Cressy Street, Deniliquin, New South Wales, 2710 Tel: (03)-5881-3980 Fax: (03)-5881-1270

Dubbo & District FHS Inc PO Box 868 Dubbo NSW 2830

Family History Society - Singleton Inc PO Box 422, Singleton, New South Wales, 2330

Fellowship of First Fleeters First Fleet House, 105 Cathedral Street, Woolloomooloo, New South Wales, 2000 Tel: (02)-9360-3988

Forbes Family History Group Inc PO Box 574, Forbes, New South Wales, 2871 Tel: 0411-095311-(mobile)

Goulburn District Family History Society Inc PO Box 611, Goulburn, New South Wales, 2580

Griffith Genealogical & Historical Society Inc PO Box 270, Griffith, New South Wales, 2680

Gwydir Family History Society Inc PO Box EM61, East Moree 2400 Tel: (02)-67549235-(President)

Hastings Valley Family History Group Inc PO Box 1359, Port Macquarie, New South Wales, 2444

Hawkesbury FHG C/o Hawkesbury City Council Library, Dight Street, Windsor, 2756

Hill End Family History Group Sarnia, Hill End 2850

Hornsbury Kuring-Gai FHS Inc PO Box 680, Hornsby, 2077

Illawarra FHG PO Box 1652 South Coast Mail Centre, Wollongong 2521

Inverell District FHG Inc PO Box 367, Inverells, 2360

Leeton Family History Society PO Box 475, Centre Point, Pine Avenue, Leeton 2705 Tel: 02-6955-7199, 02-6953-2301

Little Forest Family History Research Group PO Box 87, 192 Little Forest Road, Milton , 2538 Tel: 02-4455-4780, 02-4456-4223

Email: cathyd@shoalhaven.net.au WWW: www.shoalhaven.net.au/~cathyd/groups.html

Liverpool & District Family History Society PO Box 830, Liverpool, New South Wales, 2170

Maitland FH Circle Inc PO Box 247, Maitland, New South Wales 2320WWW: www.rootsweb.com/~ausmfhc

Manning Wallamba FHS c/o Greater Taree City Library, Pulteney Street, Taree, New South Wales, 2430

Milton Ulladulla Genealogical Society Inc PO Box 619, Ulladulla, New South Wales, 2539 Tel: 02-4455-4206

Nepean Family History Society PO Box 81, Emu Plains 2750 Tel: (02)-47-353-798 Email: istack@penrithcity.nsw.gov.au WWW: www.penrithcity.nsw.gov.au/nfhs/nfhshome.htm

New South Wales Association of Family History Societies PO Box 48, Waratah, New South Wales, 2298

Newcastle Family History Society PO Box 189, Adamstown, New South Wales, 2289

Orange Family History Society PO Box 930, Orange, New South Wales, 2800

Port Stephens-Tilligerry & Districts FHS PO Box 32, Tanilba Bay, New South Wales, 2319

Richmond River Historical Society Inc PO Box 467, 165 Molesworth Street, Lismore2480 Tel: 02-6621-9993

Richmond-Tweed Family History Society PO Box 817, Ballina 2478 Email: warmer@nor.com.au

Ryde District Historical Society Inc 770 Victoria Road, Ryde 2112 Tel: (02)-9807-7137

Scone & Upper Hunter Historical Society Inc PO Box 339, Kingdon Street, Upper Hunter, Scone 2337 Tel: 02-654-51218

Shoalhaven Family History Society Inc PO Box 591, Nowra 2541 Tel: 02-44221253 Fax: 02-44212462 Email: jmoorley@shoal.net.au

Snowy Mountains Family History Group PO Box 153, Cooma, New South Wales, 2630

Wagga Wagga & District Family History Society Inc PO Box 307, Wagga Wagga, New South Wales, 2650

Wingham FHGPO Box 72, Wingham, New South Wales, 2429

Young & District FHG Inc PO Box 586, Young 2594

Blue Mountains Family History Society PO Box 97, Springwood, NSW, NSW 2777 Fax: 02-4751-2746

Dubbo & District Family History Society Inc PO Box 868, Dubbo, NSW, 2830 Tel: 068-818635

Illawarra Family History Group The Secretary, PO Box 1652, South Coast Mail Centre, Wollongong, NSW, 2521 Tel: (02)-42622212 WWW: www.magna.com.au/~vivienne/ifhg.htm

Lithgow & District Family History Society PO Box 516, Lithgow, NSW, 2790

NORTHERN TERRITORY

Genealogical Society of the Northern Territory PO Box 37212, Winnellie, Northern Territory, 0821 Tel: 08-898-17363

QUEENSLAND

Queensland Family History Society PO Box 171, Indooroonilly, Brisbane, Oueensland, 4068

Beaudesert Branch

Genealogical Soc of Queensland Inc PO Box 664, Beaudesert, Queensland, 4285

Bundaberg Genealocical association Inc PO Box 103, Bundaberg, Queensland, 4670

Burdekin Contact Group Family Hist Assn of N Qld Inc PO Box 393, Home Hill, Queensland, 4806

Caboolture FH Research Group Inc PO Box 837, Caboolture, Queensland, 4510

Cairns & District Family History Society Inc PO Box 5069, Cairns, Queensland, 4870 Tel: 07-40537113

Central Queensland Family History Asociation PO Box 8423, Woolloongabba Queensland 4102

Charters Towers & Dalrymple F H Association Inc PO Box 783, 54 Towers Street, Charters Towers, Queensland, 4820 Tel: 07-4787-2124

Cooroy Noosa Genealogical & Historical Research Group Inc PO Box 792, Cooroy, Queensland 4563 Email: info@genealogy-noosa.org.au WWW: www.genealogy-noosa.org.au

Dalby FHS incPO Box 962, Dalby, Queensland, 4405

Darling Downs Family History Society PO Box 2229, Toowoomba, Queensland, 4350

Genealogical Society of Queensland Inc PO Box 8423, Woolloongabba, Queensland, 4102

Gladstone Branch G.S.Q. PO Box 1778, Gladstone, Queensland, 4680

Gold Coast & Albert Genealogical Society PO Box 2763, Southport, Queensland, 4215

Gold Coast Family History Research Group PO Box 1126, Southport, Gold Coast, Queensland, 4215

Goondiwindi & District Family History Society PO Box 190, Goondiwindi, Queensland, 4390 Tel: 0746712156 Fax: 0746713019 Email: pez@bigpond.com

Gympie Ancestral Research Society Inc PO Box 767, Gympie, Queensland, 4570

Ipswich Genealogical Society Inc.PO Box 323, 1st Floor, Ipswich Campus Tafe, cnr. Limestone & Ellenborough Streets, Ipswich, Queensland, 4305 Tel: (07)-3201-8770
Kingaroy Family History Centre
PO Box 629, James Street, Kingaroy, Queensland, 4610
Mackay Branch Genealogical Society of Queensland Inc
PO Box 882, Mackay, Queensland, 4740 Tel: (07)-49426266
Maryborough District Family History Society
PO Box 408, Maryborough, Queensland, 4650
Mount Isa Family History Society IncPO Box 1832, Mount Isa, Queensland, 4825 Email: krp8@+opend.com.au
North Brisbane Branch - Genealogical Soc of Queensland Inc
PO Box 353, Chermside South, Queensland, 4032
Queensland FHS Inc
PO Box 171, Indooroophilly, Queensland, 4068
Rockhampton Genealogical Society of Queensland Inc
PO Box 992, Rockhampton, Queensland, 4700
Roma & District Local & Family History Society
PO Box 877, Roma, Queensland, 4455
South Burnett Genealogical & Family History Society
PO Box 598, Kingaroy, Queensland, 4610
Southern Suburbs Branch - G.S.Q. Inc
PO Box 844, Mount Gravatt, Queensland, 4122
Sunshine Coast Historical & Genealogical Resource Centre Inc
PO Box 1051, Nambour, Queensland, 4560
Toowoomba Family History Centre c/o South Town Post Office, South Street, Toowoomba, Queensland, 4350 Tel: 0746-355895
Townsville - Fam Hist Assoc of North Queensland Inc
PO Box 6120, Townsville M.C., Queensland, 4810
Whitsunday Branch - Genealogical Soc of Queensland Inc
PO Box 15, Prosperpine, Queensland, 4800
SOUTH AUSTRALIA
South Australian Genealogical & Heraldic SocietyGPO Box 592, Adelaide 5001 Tel: (08)-8272-4222 Fax: (08)-8272-4910
Email: saghs@dove.net.au WWW: dove.net.au/~saghs
South East FHG Inc PO Box 758, Millicent, South Australia, 5280
Southern Eyre Peninsula FHG
26 Cranston Street, Port Lincoln 5606
Whyalla FHG
PO Box 2190, Whyalla Norrie, South Australia, 5608
Yorke Peninsula Family History Group - 1st Branch SAGHS
PO Box 260, Kadina, South Australia, 5554
TASMANIA
Tasmanian FHS (Launceston Branch) PO Box 1290, Launceston, Tasmania 7250 Email; secretary@tasfhs.org WWW: www.tasfhs.org
Tasmanian FHS Inc PO Box 191, Launceston, Tasmania 7250 WWW: www.tasfhs.org
VICTORIA
Ararat Genealogical Society inc PO Box 361, Ararat, Victoria, 3377
Australian Institute of Genealogical Studies PO Box 339, Blackburn, Victoria, 3130 Email: aigs@alphalink.com.all WWW: www.alphalink.com.au/~aigs/index.htm
Benalla & District Family History Group Inc PO Box 268, St Andrews Church Hall, Church Street, Benalla, Victoria, 3672 Tel: (03)-57-644258
Bendigo Regional Genealogical Society Inc
PO Box 1049, Bendigo, Victoria, 3552
Cobram Genealogical Group
PO Box 75, Cobram, Victoria, 3643
East Gippsland Family History Group Inc
PO Box 1104, Bairnsdale, Victoria, 3875
Echuca/Moama Family History Group Inc
PO Box 707, Echuca, Victoria, 3564
Emerald Genealogy Group
62 Monbulk Road, Emerald, Victoria, 3782
Euroa Genealogical Group
43 Anderson Street, Euroa, Victoria, 3666
First Fleet Fellowship Victoria Inc
Cnr Phayer & Barnet Streets, South Melbourne, Victoria, 3205
Geelong Family History Group Inc PO Box 1187, Geelong, 3220
Email: flw@deakin.edu.au
WWW: www.home.vicnet.net.au/wgfamhist/index.htm
Genealogical Society of Victoria
Ancestor House, 179 Queen Street, Melbourne, Victoria, 3000
Tel: +61-3-9670-7033 Fax: +61-3-9670-4490
Email: gsv@gsv.org.au WWW: www.gsv.org.au
Hamilton Family & Local History Group PO Box 816, Hamilton, Victoria, 3300 Tel: 61-3-55-724933 Fax: 61-3-55-724933
Email: ham19.@mail.vicnet.net.au WWW: www.freenet.com.au/hamilton
Italian Historical Society 185 Faraday Street, Carlton3053
Kerang & District Family History Group
PO Box 325, Kerang, Victoria, 3579
Mid Gippsland Family History Society Inc
PO Box 767, Morwell, Victoria, 3840
Mildura & District Genealogical Society Inc
PO Box 2895, Mildura, Victoria, 3502

Narre Warren & District Family History Group
PO Box 149, Narre Warren, Victoria, 3805
WWW: www.ozemail.com.au/~narre/fam-hist.html
Nathalia Genealogical Group Inc
R.M.B. 1003, Picola, Victoria, 3639
Port Genealogical Society of Victoria Inc
PO Box 1070, Warrambool, Victoria, 3280
Email: joyceaustin@start.co.au
Sale & District Family History Group Inc
PO Box 773, Sale, Victoria, 3850
Stawell Biarri Group for Genealogy Inc
PO Box 417, Stawell, Victoria, 3380
Swam Hill Genealogical & Historical Society Inc
PO Box 1232, Swan Hill, Victoria, 3585
Toora & District Family History Group Inc
PO Box 41, Toora, Victoria, 3962
Wangaratta Genealogical Soc Inc
PO Box 683, Wangaratta, Victoria, 3676
West Gippsland Genealogical Society Inc PO Box 225, Old Shire Hall, Queen Street, Warragul, Victoria, 3820 Tel: 03-56252743
Email: watts@dcsi.net.au WWW: www.vicnet.net.au/~wggs/
Wimmera Association for Genealogy
PO Box 880, Horsham, Victoria, 3402
Wodonga FHS Inc
PO Box 289, Wodonga, Victoria, 3689
Yarram Genealogical Group Inc
PO Box 42, 161 Commercial Road, Yarram, Victoria, 3971
WESTERN AUSTRALIA
Australasian Federation of Family History Organisations (AFFHO)c/o 6/48 May Street, Bayswater, Western Australia, 6053
Geraldton FHS
PO Box 2502, Geralton 6531, Western Australia WWW: www.com.au/gol/genealogy/gfhs/gfhsmain.htm
Goldfields Branch
West Australian Genealogical Society Inc
PO Box 1462, Kalgoorlie, Western Australia, 6430
Melville Family History Centre PO Box 108 (Rear of Church of Jesus Christ Latter Day Saints, 308 Preston Point Road, Attadale, Melville, Western Australia, 6156
Western Australia Genealogical Society Inc 6/48 May Street, Bayswater, Western Australia 6053 Tel: 08-9271-4311 Fax: 08-9271-4311 Email: wags@cleo.murdoch.edu.au WWW: www.cleo.murdoch.edu.au/~wags

NEW ZEALAND
Bishopdale Branch NZ Society of Genealogists Inc.
c/o 19a Resolution Place, Christchurch, 8005 Tel: 03 351 0625
Cromwell Family History Group
3 Porcell Court, Cromwell, 9191
Fairlie Genealogy Group
c/o 38 Gray Street, Fairlie, 8771
General Research Institute of New Zealand
PO Box 12531, Thorndon, Wellington, 6038
Hawkes Bay Branch NZ Society of Genealogists Inc.
P O Box 7375, Taradale, Hawkes Bay
Kapiti Branch NZ Society of Genealogists Inc.
P O Box 6, Paraparaumu, Kapiti Coast, 6450
Mercury Bay Branch NZ Society of Genealogists Inc.
31 Catherine Crescent, Whitianga, 2856 Tel: 0 7 866 2355
Morrinsville Branch NZ Society of Genealogists Inc.
1 David St., Morrinsville, 2251
N.Z. Fencible Society
P O Box 8415, Symonds Street, Auckland, 1003
New Zealand Family History Society
P O Box13,301, Armagh, Christchurch Tel: 03 352 4506
Email: ranz@xtra.co.nz
New Zealand Family History Society Inc
PO Box 13301, Armagh, Christchurch Email: ranz@extra.co.nz
New Zealand Society of Genealogists Inc
PO Box 8795, Symonds Street, AUCKLAND, 1035
Tel: 09-525—0625 Fax: 09-525-0620
Northern Wairoa Branch NZ Society of Genealogists Inc.
60 Gordon Street, Dargaville, 300
NZ Society of Genealogists Inc. - Alexandra Branch
21 Gregg Street, Alexandra, 9181
Palmerston North Genealogy Group
P O Box 1992, Palmerston North, 5301
Panmure Branch NZ Society of Genealogists Inc.
29 Mirrabooka Ave, Howick, Auckland, 1705
Papakura Branch NZ Society of Genealogists Inc.
P O Box 993, Papakura, Auckland
Polish Genealogical Society of New Zealand
Box 88, Urenui, Taranaki Tel: 06 754 4551
Email: pgs.newzealand@clear.net.nz
Rotorua Branch NZ Society of Genealogists Inc.
17 Sophia Street, Rotorua, 3201 Tel: 0 7 347 9122
Scottish Interest Group NZ Society of Genealogists Inc.
P O Box 8164, Symonds Street, Auckland, 1003

South Canterbury Branch NZ Society of Genealogists Inc.
9 Burnett Street, Timaru, 8601
Tairua Branch NZ Society of Genealogists Inc.
c/o 10 Pepe Road, Tairua, 2853
Te Awamutu Branch NZ Society of Genealogists Inc.
Hairini, RD1, Te Awamutu, 2400
Te Puke Branch NZ Society of Genealogists Inc.
20 Valley Road, Te Puke, 3071
Waimate Branch NZ Society of Genealogists Inc.
4 Saul Shrives Place, Waimate, 8791
Wairarapa Branch NZ Society of Genealogists Inc.
34 Rugby Street, Masterton, 5901
Whakatane Branch NZ Society of Genealogists Inc.
P O Box 203, Whakatane, 3080
Whangamata Genealogy Group
116 Hetherington Road, Whangamata, 3062
Whangarei Branch NZ Society of Genealogists Inc.
P O Box 758, Whangarei, 115 Tel: 09 434 6508

SOUTH AFRICA
Genealogical Institute of South Africa 115 Banheok Road,
Stellenbosch, Western Cape, South Africa Tel: 021-887-5070
Email: GISA@RENET.SUN.AC.ZA
Genealogical Society of South Africa
Suite 143, Postnet X2600, Houghton, 2041, South Africa
Human Sciences Research Council Genealogy Information, HSRC
Library & Information Service, Private Bag X41, Pretoria 0001,
South Africa Tel: (012)-302-2636 Fax: (012)-302-2933
Email: ig@legii.hsrc.ac.za
West Rand Family History Society
The Secretary, PO Box 760, Florida 1710, South Africa

ZIMBABWE
Heraldry & Genealogy Society of Zimbabwe
Harare Branch, 8 Renfrew Road, Eastlea, Harare, Zimbabwe

NORTH AMERICA
CANADA
ALBERTA
Alberta Family Histories Society
PO Box 30270, Station B, Calgary, Alberta, T2M 4P1
Alberta Genealogical Society (Edmonton Branch)
Room 116, Prince of Wales Armouries, 10440-108 Avenue,
Edmonton, Alberta, T5H 3Z9 Tel: (403)-424-4429
Fax: (403)-423-8980 Email: agsedm@compusmart.ab.ca WWW:
www.compusmart.ab.ca/abgensoc/branches.html
Alberta Genealogical Society Drayton Valley Branch
PO Box 6358, Drayton Valley, Alberta, T7A 1R8 Tel: 403-542-2787
Email: c_or_c@telusplanet.net
Alberta Genealogical Society Fort McMurray Branch
PO Box 6253, Fort McMurray, Alberta, T9H 4W1
Alberta Gene Soc Grande Prairie & District Branch
PO Box 1257, Grande Prairie, Alberta, T8V 4Z1
Alberta Gen Society Medicine Hat & District Branch
PO Box 971, Medicine Hat, Alberta, T1A 7G8
Alberta Gen Society Red Deer & District Branch
PO Box 922, Red Deer, Alberta, T4N 5H3
Email: evwes@telusplanet.net
Brooks & District Branch Alberta Genealogical Society
PO Box 1538, Brooks, Alberta, T1R 1C4
Ukrainian Genealogical & Historical Society of Canada
R.R.2, Cochrane, Alberta, T0L 0W0 Tel: (403)-932-6811
BRITISH COLUMBIA
British Columbia Genealogical Society
PO Box 88054, Lansdowne Mall, Richmond V6X 3T6
Campbell River Genealogy Club
PO Box 884, Campbell River, British Columbia, V9W 6Y4
Email: rcase@connected.bc.ca WWW: www.connected.bc.ca/~genealogy/
Comox Valley Family History Research Group
c/o Courtenay & District Museum & Archives, 360 Cliffe Street,
Courtenay, British Columbia, V9N 2H9
Kamloops Genealogical Society
Box 1162, Kamloops, British Columbia, V2C 6H3
Kelowna & District Genealogical Society
PO Box 501, Station A, Kelowna, British Columbia, V1Y 7P1
Tel: 1-250-763-7159 Email: doug.ablett@bc.sympatico.ca
Nanaimo FHS
PO Box 1027, Nanaimo, British Columbia, V9R 5Z2
Port Alberni Genealogy Club
Site 322, Comp. 6, R.R.3, Port Alberni V9Y 7L7
Powell River Genealogy Club
PO Box 446, Powell River, British Columbia, V8A 5C2
Prince George Genealogical Society
PO Box 1056, Prince George, British Columbia, V2L 4V2
Revelstoke Genealogy Group
PO Box 2613, Revelstoke, British Columbia, V0E 2S0

Shuswap Lake Genealogical Society
R.R.1, Site 4, Com 4, Sorrento, British Columbia, V0E 2W0
South Okanagan Genealogical Society
c/o Museum, 785 Main Street, Penticton V2A 5E3
Vernon & District FHS
PO Box 1447, Vernon, British Columbia, V1T 6N7
Victoria Genealogical Society
PO Box 45031, Mayfair Place, Victoria V8Z 7G9
MANITOBA
Canadian Federation of Gen & Family History Societies
227 Parkville Bay, Winnipeg, Manitoba, R2M 2J6
WWW: www.geocities.com/athens/troy/2274/index.html
East European Genealogical Society
PO Box 2536, Winnipeg, Manitoba, R3C 4A7
La Societe Historique de Saint Boniface
220 Ave de la Cathedral, Saint Boniface, Manitoba, R2H 0H7
Manitoba Genealogical Society
Unit A, 1045 St James Street, Winnipeg, Manitoba, R3H 1BI
South West Branch of Manitoba Genealogical Society
53 Almond Crescent, Brandon, Manitoba, R7B 1A2
Tel: 204-728-2857 Email: mla@access.tkm.mb.ca
Winnipeg Branch of Manitoba Genealogical Society
PO Box 1244, Winnipeg, Manitoba, R3C 2Y4
NEW BRUNSWICK
Centre d'Etudes Acadiennes
Universite de Moncton, Moncton, New Brunswick, E1A 3E9
New Brunswick Genealogical Society
PO Box 3235, Station B, Fredericton E3A 5G9
NEWFOUNDLAND & LABRADOR
Newfoundland & Labrador Genealogical Society
Colonial Building, Military Road, St John's A1C 2C9
NOVA SCOTIA
Archelaus Smith Historical Society
PO Box 291, Clarks Harbour, Nova Scotia, B0W 1P0
Email: timkins@atcon.com
Cape Breton Genealogical Society
PO Box 53, Sydney, Nova Scotia, B1P 6G9
Genealogical Association of Nova Scotia
PO Box 641, Station Central, Halifax, Nova Scotia, B3J 2T3
Queens County Historical Society
PO Box 1078, Liverpool, Nova Scotia, B0T 1K0
Shelburne County Genealogical Society
PO Box 248 Town Hall, 168 Water St, Shelburne B0T 1W0
ONTARIO
British Isles Family History Society of Greater Ottowa
Box 38026, Ottawa, Ontario, K2C 1N0
Bruce & Grey Branch - Ontario Genealogical Society
PO Box 66, Owen Sound, Ontario, N4K 5P1
Bruce County Genealogical Society
PO Box 1083, Port Elgin, Ontario, N0H 2C0
Elgin County Branch Ontario Genealogical Society
PO Box 20060, St Thomas, Ontario, N5P 4H4
Essex County Branch Ontario Genealogical Society
PO Box 2, Station A, Windsor, Ontario, N9A 6J5
Haliburton Highlands Genealogy Group Box 834, Minden, Ontario
K0M2K0 tel; (705) 286-3154 Email; hhggroup@hotmail.com
Halton-Peel Branch Ontario Genealogical Society PO Box 70030,
2441 Lakeshore Road West, Oakville, Ontario, L6L 6M9
Email: jwatt@ica.net WWW: www.hhpl.on.c9/sigs/ogshp/ogshp.htm
Hamilton Branch Ontario Genealogical Society
PO Box 904, LCD 1, Hamilton, Ontario, L8N 3P6
Huron County Branch Ontario Genealogical Society
PO Box 469, Goderich, Ontario, N7A 4C7
Jewish Genealogical Society of Canada
PO Box 446, Station A, Willowdale, Ontario, M2N 5T1
Email: henry_wellisch@tvo.org
Kawartha Branch Ontario Genealogical Society
PO Box 861, Peterborough, Ontario, K9J 7AZ
Kent County Branch Ontario Genealogical Society
PO Box 964, Chatham, Ontario, N7M 5L3
Kingston Branch Ontario Genealogical Society
PO Box 1394, Kingston, Ontario, K7L 5C6
Lambton County Branch Ontario Genealogical Society
PO Box 2857, Sarnia, Ontario, N7T 7W1
Lanark County Genealogical Society
PO Box 512, Perth, Ontario, K7H 3K4 Email: gjbyron@magma.ca
WWW: www.globalgenealogy.com/LCGs
Marilyn Adams Genealogical Research Centre
PO Box 35, Ameliasburgh, Ontario, K0K 1A0 Tel: 613-967-6291
Niagara Peninsula Branch Ontario Genealogical Society
PO Box 2224, St Catharines, Ontario, L2R 7R8
Nipissing District Branch Ontario Genealogical Society
PO Box 93, North Bay, Ontario, P1B 8G8
Norfolk County Branch Ontario Genealogical Society
PO Box 145, Delhi, Ontario, N4B 2W9
Email: oxford.net/~mihaley/ogsnb/main.htm
Nor-West Genealogy & History Society
PO Box 35, Vermilion Bay, Ontario, P0V 2V0 Tel: 807-227-5293

Norwich & District Historical Society
c/o Archives, R.R. #3, Norwich, Ontario, N0J 1P0 Tel: (519)-863-3638
Ontario Genealogical Society
Suite 102, 40 Orchard View Boulevard, Toronto, Ontario, M4R 1B9
WWW: www.ogs.on.ca
Ontario Genealogical Society (Toronto Branch)
Box 513, Station Z, Toronto, Ontario, M4P 2GP
Ottawa Branch Ontario Genealogical Society
PO Box 8346, Ottawa, Ontario, K1G 3H8
Perth County Branch Ontario Genealogical Society
PO Box 9, Stratford, Ontario, N5A 6S8 Tel: 519-273-0399
Simcoe County Branch Ontario Genealogical Society
PO Box 892, Barrie, Ontario, L4M 4Y6
Sioux Lookout Genealogical Club
PO Box 1561, Sioux Lookout, Ontario, P8T 1C3
Societe Franco-Ontarienne DHistoire et de Genealogie
C.P.720, succursale B, Ottawa, Ontario, K1P 5P8
Stormont Dundas & Glengarry Genealogical Society
PO Box 1522, Cornwall, Ontario, K6H 5V5
Sudbury District Branch Ontario Genealogical Society
c/o Sudbury Public Library, 74 MacKenzie Street, Sudbury, Ontario,
P3C 4X8 Tel: (705)-674-9991 Email: fredie@isys.ca
Thunder Bay District Branch Ontario Genealogical Soc
PO Box 10373, Thunder Bay, Ontario, P7B 6T8
Upper Ottawa Genealogical Group
PO Box 972, Pembroke, Ontario, K8A 7M5
Waterdown East Flamborough Heritage Society
PO Box 1044, Waterdown, Ontario, L0R 2H0 Tel: 905-689-4074
Waterloo-Wellington Branch Ontario Genealogical Soc 153
Frederick Street, Ste 102, Kitchener, Ontario, N2H 2M2
Email: lestrome@library.uwaterloo.ca
WWW: www.dos.iwaterloo.ca/~marj/genealogy/ww.html
West Elgin Genealogical & Historical Society
22552 Talbot Line, R.R.#3, Rodney, Ontario, N0L 2C0
Whitby - Oshawa Branch Ontario Genealogical Society
PO Box 174, Whitby, Ontario, L1N 5S1
QUEBEC
Brome County Historical Society
PO Box 690, 130 Lakeside, Knowlton, Quebec, J0E 1V0
Tel: 450-243-6782
Federation Quebecoise des Societies de Genealogie
C.P. 9454, Sainte Foy, Quebec, G1V 4B8
Les Patriotes Inc
105 Prince, Sorel, Quebec, J3P 4J9
Missisquoi Historical Society
PO Box 186, Stanbridge East, Quebec, J0J 2H0 Tel: (450)-248-3153
Email: sochm@globetrotter.com
Quebec Family History Society
PO Box 1026, Postal Station, Pointe Claire, Quebec, H9S 4H9
Societ de Genealogie de la Maurice et des Bois Francs
C.P. 901, Trois Rivieres, Quebec, G9A 5K2
**Societe de Conservation du Patrimoine de St Fracois de la
Riviere du Sud** C P 306, 534 Boul St Francois Ouest, St Francois,
Quebec, G0R 3A0
Societe de Genealogie de Drummondville
545 des Ecoles, Drummondville, Quebec, J2B 8P3
Societe de Genealogie de Quebec
C.P. 9066, Sainte Foy, Quebec, G1V 4A8
Societe de Genealogie des Laurentides
C.P. 131, 185 Rue Du Palais, St Jerome, Quebec, J7Z 5T7
Tel: (450)-438-8158
WWW: www.societe-genalogie-laurentides.gc.ca
Societe de Genealogie et d'Histoire de Chetford Mines
671 boul. Smith Sud, Thetford Mines, Quebec, G6G 1N1
Societe d'Histoire d'Amos
222 1ere Avenue Est, Amos, Quebec, J9T 1H3
Societe d'Histoire et d'Archeologie des Monts
C.P. 1192, 675 Chemin du Roy, Sainte Anne des Monts, Quebec, G0E 2G0
Societe d'Histoire et de Genealogie de Matane
145 Soucy, Matane, Quebec, G4W 2E1
Societe d'Histoire et de Genealogie de Riviere du Loup
300 rue St Pierre, Riviere du Loup, Quebec, G5R 3V3
Tel: (418)-867-4245 Email: shgrd@icrdl.net WWW:
www.icrdl.net/shgrdl/index.html
Societe d'Histoire et de Genealogie de Verdun
198 chemin de lAnce, Vaudreuil, Quebec, J7V 8P3
Societe d'Histoire et de genealogie du Centre-du-Quebec
34-A, rue Laurier est, Victoriaville, Quebec, G6P 6P7
Tel: (819)-357-4029 Fax: (819)-357-9668
Email: geneatique@netscape.net WWW: www.geneatique.qc.ca
Societe d'Histoire et de Genealogie Maria Chapdeleine
1024 Place des Copains, C.P. 201, Dolbeau, Quebec, G8L 3N5
Societe d'Histoire et Genealogie de Salaberry de Valley Field
75 rue St Jean Baptiste, Valleyfield, Quebec, J6T 1Z6
Societe Genealogie d'Argenteuil
378 Principale, Lachute, Quebec, J8H 1Y2

Societe Genealogique Canadienne-Francaise
Case Postale 335, Place d Armes, Montreal, Quebec, H2Y 2H1
Societie de Genealogie de L'Outaouaid Inc
C.P. 2025, Succ. B , Hull, Quebec, J8X 3Z2
SASKATCHEWAN
Saskatchewan Genealogical Society 1870 Lorne Street, Regina,
Saskatchewan S4P 3E1
Battleford's Branch S askatchewan Genealogical Society
8925 Gregory Drive, North Battleford, Saskatchewan, S9A 2W6
Central Butte Branch Saskatchewan Genealogical Society
P.O. Box 224, Central Butte, Saskatchewan, S0H 0T0
Grasslands Branch Saskatchewan Genealogical Society
P.O. Box 272, Mankota, Saskatchewan, S0H 2W0 Tel: 306-264-5149
Grenfell Branch Saskatchewan Genealogical Society
P.O. Box 61, Grenfell, Saskatchewan, S0G 2B0 Tel: (306)-697-3176
Moose Jaw Branch Saskatchewan Genealogical Society
1037 Henry Street, Moose Jaw, Saskatchewan, S6H 3H3
Pangman Branch Saskatchewan Genealogical Society
P.O. Box 23, Pangman, Saskatchewan, S0C 2C0
Radville Branch Saskatchewan Genealogical Society
P.O. Box 27, Radville, Saskatchewan, S0C 2G0
Regina Branch Saskatchewan Genealogical Society
95 Hammond Road, Regina, Saskatchewan, S4R 3C8
Saskatchewan Genealogical Society
1870 Lorne Street, Regina, Saskatchewan, S4P 3E1
South East Branch Saskatchewan Genealogical Society
P.O. Box 460, Carnduff, Saskatchewan, S0C 0S0
West Central Branch Saskatchewan Genealogical Society
P.O. Box 1147, Eston, Saskatchewan, S0L 1A0
Yorkton Branch Saskatchewan Genealogical Society
28 Dalewood Crescent, Yorkton, Saskatchewan, S3N 2P7
YUKON
Dawson City Museum & Historical Society
P.O. Box 303, Dawson City, Yukon, Y0B 1G0 Tel: 867-993-5291
Fax: 867-993-5839 Email: dcmuseum@yknet.yk.ca

FAMILY HISTORY SOCIETIES - EUROPE

AUSTRIA
Heraldisch-Genealogische Gesellschaft 'Adler'
Universitatsstrasse 6, Wien, A-1096, Austria

BELGIUM
Cercle de Genealogie Juive de Belgique
74 Avenue Stalingrad, Bruxelles, B-1000, Belgium Tel: 32 0 2 512
19 63 Fax: 32 0 513 48 59 Email: mjb<d.dratwa@mjb-jmb.org>
Federation des Associations de Famille
Bruyeres Marion 10, Biez, B-1390, Belgium
Federation Genealogique et Heraldique de Belgique
Avenue Parmentier 117, Bruxelles, B-1150, Belgium
Office Genealogique et Heraldique de Belgique
Avenue C Thielemans 93, Brussels, B-1150, Belgium

CROATIA
Croatian Genealogical Society
2527 San Carlos Ave, San Carlos, CA, 94070, USA

CZECHOSLOVAKIA
Czechoslovak Genealogical Society International
PO Box 16225, St Paul, MN, 55116-0225, USA

DENMARK
Danish Soc. for Local History
Colbjornsensvej 8, Naerum, DK-2850, Denmark
Sammenslutningen af Slaegtshistoriske Foreninger
Klostermarker 13, Aalborg, DK-9000, Denmark
Email: ulla@silkeborg.bib.dk
Society for Danish Genealogy & Biography
Grysgardsvej 2, Copenhagen NV, DK-2400, Denmark WWW:
www.genealogi.dk

ESTONIA
Estonia Genealogical Society
Sopruse puiestec 214-88, Tallin, EE-0034, Estland

FINLAND
Genealogiska Samfundet i Finland
Fredsgatan 15 B, Helsingfors, SF-00170, Finland

Helsingfors Slaktforskare R.F.
Dragonvagen 10, Helsingfors, FIN-00330, Finland

FRANCE
Amicale des Familles d'alliance Canadiennne-Francaise
BP10, Les Ormes, 86220, France
Amities Genealogiques Bordelaises 2 rue Paul Bert, Bordeaux,
Aquitaine, 33000, France Tel: 05 5644 8199 Fax: 05 5644 8199

Assoc. Genealogique et Historique des Yvelines Nord
Hotel de Ville, Meulan, 78250, France
Association Catalane de Genealogie
BP 1024, Perpignan Cedex, Languedoc Rousillon, 66101,
Association de la Bourgeoisie Ancienne Francaise
74 Avenue Kleber, Paris, 75116, France
Association Genealogique de la Charente
Archives Departementales, 24 avenue Gambetta, Angouleme, Poitou
Charentes, 16000, France
Association Genealogique de l'Anjou
75 rue Bressigny, Angers, Pays de la Loire, 49100, France
Association Genealogique de l'Oise
BP 626, Compiegne Cedex, Picardie, 60206, France
Association Genealogique des Bouches-du-Rhone
BP 22, Marseilles Cedex, Provence Alpes Cote d'Azur, 1,
Association Genealogique des Hautes Alpes
Archives Departementales, route de Rambaud, Gap, Provence Alpes
Cote d'Azur, 5000, France
Association Genealogique du Pas de Calais
BP 471, Arras Cedex, Nord-Pas de Calais, 62028
Association Genealogique du Pays de Bray
BP 62, Serqueux, Normandie, 76440 Fax: 02 3509 8756
Association Genealogique du Var
BP 1022, Toulon Cedex, Provence Alpes Cote d'Azur, 83051
Association Genealogique Flandre-Hainaut
BP493, Valenciennes Cedex, Nord-Pas de Calais, 59321, **Association
Recherches Genealogiques Historique d'Auvergne** Maison des
Consuls, Place Poly, Clermont Ferrand, Auvergne, 63100, France
Bibliotheque Genealogique
3 Rue de Turbigo, Paris, 75001, France Tel: 01 4233 5821
Brive-Genealogie Maison des Associations, 11 place J M Dauaier,
Brive, Limousin, 19100, France
Centre de Recherches Genealogiques Flandre-Artois
BP 76, Bailleul, Nord-Pas de Calais, France
Centre d'Entraide Genealogique de France 3 Rue de Turbigo,
Paris, 75001, France Tel: 33 4041 9909 Fax: 33 4041 9963
Email: cegf@usa.net WWW: www.mygale.org/04cabrigol/cegf/
Centre Departemental d'Histoire des Familles
5 place Saint Leger, Guebwiller, Alsace, 68500, France
Email: cdhf@telmat-net.fr WWW: web.telemat-net-fr~cdhf
Centre Entraide Genealogique Franche Comte
35 rue du Polygone, Besancon, Franche Comte, 25000
Centre Genealogique de la Marne
BP 20, Chalons-en-Champagne, Champagne Ardennes, 51005
Centre Genealogique de Savoie
BP1727, Chambery Cedex, Rhone Alpes, 73017, France
Centre Genealogique de Touraine
BP 5951, Tours Cedex, Centre, 37059, France
Centre Genealogique des Cotes d'Armor 3bis rue Bel Orient, Saint
Brieuc, Bretagne, 22000, France Fax: 02 9662 8900
Centre Genealogique des Landes
Societe de Borda, 27 rue de Cazarde, Dax, Aquitaine, 40100, **Centre
Genealogique des Pyrenees Atlantique**
BP 1115, Pau Cedex, Aquitaine, 64011, France
Centre Genealogique du Perche 9 rue Ville Close, Bellame,
Normandie, 61130, France Tel: 02 3383 3789
Centre Genealogique du Sud Ouest Hotel des Societes Savantes, 1
Place Bardineau, Bordeaux, Aquitaine, 33000, France
Centre Genealogique et Heraldique des Ardennes
Hotel de Ville, Charleville Mezieres, Champagne Ardennes, 8000
Centre Genealogique Protestant
54 rue des Saints-Peres, Paris, 75007, France
Cercle de Genealogie du Calvados
Archives Departementales, 61 route de Lion-sur-Mer, Caen,
Normandie, 14000, France
Cercle de Genealogie et d'Heraldique de Seine et Marne
BP 113, Melun Cedex, 77002, France
Cercle de Genealogie Juive (Jewish)
14 rue St Lazare, Paris, 75009, France Tel: 01 4023 0490 Fax: 01
4023 0490 Email: cgjgeniefr@aol.com
Cercle d'Etudes Genealogiques et Heraldique d'Ile-de-France
46 Route de Croissy, Le Vesinet, 78110, France
Cercle d'Histoire et Genealogique du Perigord
2 rue Roletrou, Perigueux, Aquitaine, 24000, France
Cercle Genealogique Bull
rue Jean Jaures, BP 53, Les-Clayes-sous-Bois, 78340,
Cercle Genealogique d'Alsace
Archives du Bas-Rhin, 5 rue Fischart, Strasbourg, Alsace, 67000
Cercle Genealogique d'Aunis et Saintonge c/o Mr Provost, 10 ave
de Metz, La Rochelle, Poitou Charentes, 17000, France
Cercle Genealogique de la Manche
BP 410, Cherbourg Cedex, Normandie, 50104, France
Cercle Genealogique de la Meurthe et Moselle
4 rue Emile Gentil, Briey, Lorraine, 54150, France
Cercle Genealogique de la Region de Belfort
c/o F Werlen, 4 ave Charles de Gaulle, Valdoie, Franche Comte, 90300

Cercle Genealogique de l'Eure
Archives Departementales, 2 rue de Verdun, Evreux Cedex,
Normandie, 27025, France
Cercle Genealogique de Saintonge
8 rue Mauny, Saintes, Poitou Charentes, 17100, France
Cercle Genealogique de Vaucluse
Ecole Sixte Isnard, 31 ter Avenue de la Trillade, Avignon, Provence
Alpes Cote d'Azur, 84000, France
Cercle Genealogique des Deux-Sevres
26 rue de la Blauderie, Niort, Poitou Charentes, 79000, **Cercle
Genealogique des P.T.T.**
BP33, Paris Cedex 15, 75721, France
Cercle Genealogique d'Ille-et-Vilaine
6 rue Frederic Mistral, Rennes, Bretagne, 35200 Tel: 02 9953 6363
**Cercle Genealogique du C.E. de la Caisse d'Epargne Ile de
France-Paris**
19 rue du Louvre, Paris, 75001, France
Cercle Genealogique du Finistere Salle Municipale, rue du
Commandant Tissot, Brest, Bretagne, 29000 Fax: 02 9843 0176
Email: cgf@eurobretagne.fr WWW:
www.karolus.org/membres/cgf.htm
Cercle Genealogique du Haut-Berry place Martin Luther King,
Bourges, Centre, 18000, France Fax: 02 4821 0483
Email: cgh-b@wanadoo.fr
Cercle Genealogique du Languedoc 18 rue de la Tannerie,
Toulouse, Languedoc Rousillon, 31400, France Tel: 05 6226 1530
Cercle Genealogique du Loir-et-Cher
11 rue du Bourg Neuf, Blois, Centre, 41000 Tel: 02 5456 0711
Cercle Genealogique d'Yvetot et du Pays de Caux
Pavillion des Fetes, Yvetot, Normandie, 76190, France
Cercle Genealogique et Historique du Lot et Garonne
13 rue Etienne Marcel, Villeneuve sur Lot, Aquitaine, 47340
Cercle Genealogique Poitevin
22bis rue Arsene Orillard, Poitiiers, Poitou Charentes, 86000
Cercle Genealogique Rouen Seine-Maritime
Archives Departementales, Cours Clemenceau, Normandie, 76101
Cercle Genealogique Saone-et-Loire
115 rue des Cordiers, Macon, Bourgogne, 71000, France
Cercle Genealogique Vendeen Bat.H, 307bis, Cite de la Vigne aux
Roses, La Roche-sur-Yon, Pays de la Loire, 85000, France
Cercle Genealogique Versailles et Yvelines Archives
Departementales, 1 avenue de Paris, Versailles, 78000, France
Tel: 01 3952 7239 Fax: 01 3952 7239
Cercle Genealogique du Rouergue Archives Departementales, 25 av
Victor Hugo, Rodez, Midi-Pyrenees, 12000, France
Club Genealogique Air France CE Air France Roissy Exploitation,
BP 10201, Roissy CDG Cedex, 95703, France Fax: 01 4864 3220
Club Genealogique Group IBM France CE IBM St Jean de
Braye-Ste Marie, 50-56 ave Pierre Curie, St Jean de Braye Cedex,
45807, France
Confederation Internationale de Genealogie et d'Heraldique
Maison de la Genealogie, 3 rue Turbigo, Paris, F - 75001, **Etudes
Genealogique Drome-Ardeche**
14 rue de la Manutention, Valence, Rhone Alpes, 26000, **Federation
Francaise de Genealogie** 3 Rue de Turbigo, Paris, 75001, France
Tel: 01 4013 0088 Fax: 01 4013 0089 WWW: www.karolus.org
France-Louisuane/Franco-Americanie Commission Retrouvailles,
Centre CommercialeGatie, 80 avenue du Maine, Paris 75014 Fax: 01
4047 8321 WWW: www.noconnet.com:80/forms/cajunews.htm
Genealogie Algerie Maroc Tunisie Maison Marechal Alphonse, Juin
28 Av. de Tubingen, Aix en Provence, 13090, France
Genealogie Entraide Recherche en Cote d'Or
97 rue d'Estienne d'Orves, Clarmart, Bourgogne, 92140
Genealogie et Histoire de la Caraibe Pavillion 23, 12 avenue
Charles de Gaulle, Le Pecq, Overseas, 78230, France
Email: ghcaraibe@aol.com WWW: //members.aol.com/ghcaraibe
Groupement Genealogique de la Region dy Nord
BP 62, Wambrechies, Nord-Pas de Calais, 59118, France
Groupement Genealogique du Havre et de Seine Maritime
BP 80, Le Havre Cedex, Normandie, 76050 Tel: 02 3522 7633
Institut Francophone de Genealogie et d'Histoire
5 rue de l'Aimable Nanette, le Gabut, La Rochelle, Overseas, 17000
Tel: 05 4641 9032 Fax: 05 4641 9032
Institut Genealogique de Bourgogne
237 rue Vendome, BP 7076, Lyon, Bourgogne, 69301
Loiret Genealogique BP 9, Orleans Cedex, Centre, 45016, France
Salon Genealogique de Vichy et du Centr 48 Boulevard de Sichon,
Vichy, Auvergne, 3200, France WWW: www.genea.com
Section Genealogique de l'Assoc. Artistique-Banque de France
2 rue Chabanais, Paris, 75002, France
Societe Genealogique du Bas-Berr Maison des Associations, 30
Espace Mendez France, Chateauroux, Centre, 36000, France
Societe Genealogique du Lyonnais
7 rue Major Martin, Lyon, Rhone Alpes, 69001, France

GERMANY

Arbeirkreis fur Familienforschung e.V Muhlentorturm, Muhlentortplatz 2, Lubeck, Schleswig-Holstein, D - 23552, Germany

Bayerischer Landesverein fur Familienkunde Ludwigstrasse 14/1, Munchen, Bayern, D - 80539 Email: blf@rusch.m.shuttle.de WWW: www.genealogy.com/gene/reg/BAY/BLF-d.html

Deutsche Zentalstelle fur Genealogie Schongaver str. 1, Leipzig, D - 04329, Germany

Dusseldorfer Verein fur Familienkunde e.V Krummenweger Strasse 26, Ratingen, Nordrhein Westfalen, D - 40885, Germany

Herold - Verein fur Genealogie Heraldik und Reiwandte Wissen-Scahaften Archiv Str. 12-14, Berlin, D -14195, Germany

Niedersachsischer Gesellschaft fur Familienkunde e.V Stadtarchiv, Am Bokemahle 14 - 16, Hannover, Niedersachsen, D - 30171

Oldenburgische Gesellschaft fur Familienkunde Lerigauweg 14, Oldenurg, Niedersachsen, D - 26131, Germany

Verein fur Familien-U. Wappenkunde in Wurttemberg und Baden Postfach 105441, Stuttgart, Baden-Wuerttemberg, D - 70047, Germany

Westdeutsche Gesellschaft fur Familienkunde e.V Sitz Koln Unter Gottes Gnaden 34, Koln-Widdersdorf, Nordrhein Westfalen, D - 50859, Germany Tel: 49 221 50 48 88

Zentralstelle fur Personnen und Familiengeschichte Birkenweg 13, Friedrichsdorf, D - 61381, Germany

GREECE

Heraldic-Genealogical Society of Greece 56 3rd Septemvriou Str., Athens, GR - 10433, Greece

HOLLAND

Centraal Bureau voor Genealogie P O Box 11755, The Hague, NL - 2502 AT, Netherlands Tel: 070 315 0500 Fax: 070 347 8394 WWW: www.cbg.nl

HUNGARY

Historical Society of Hungary University of Eoetveos Lorand, Pesti Barnabas utca 1, Budapest, H - 1052, Hungary Tel: 267 0966

ICELAND

The Genealogical Society P O Box 829, Reykjavick, 121, Iceland Fax: 354 1 679840

ITALY

Ancetres Italien 3 Rue de Turbigo, Paris, 75001, France Tel: 01 4664 2722 WWW: //members.aol.com/geneaita/

NETHERLANDS

Centraal Bureau voor Genealogie P O Box 11755, The Hague, NL - 2502 AT, Netherlands Tel: 070 315 0500 Fax: 070 347 8394 WWW: www.cbg.nl

Central Bureau Voor Genealogie PO Box 11755, 2502, The Hague, Koninklijk Nederlandsch Genootschap voor Geslacht-en Wapen-Kunde P O Box 85630, Den Haag, 2508 CH, Netherlands

Koninklijk Nederlandsch Genootschap voor Geslacht-en Wapen-Kunde P O Box 85630, Den Haag, 2508 CH, Netherlands

Nederlandse Genealogische Vereniging Postbus 976, Amsterdam, NL - 1000 AZ, Netherlands Email: info@ngu.nl WWW: www.ngu.nl

Nederlandse Genealogische Vereniging Postbus 976, Amsterdam, NL - 1000 AZ, Netherlands Email: info@ngu.nl WWW: www.ngu.nl

Stichting 'Genealogisch Centrum Zeeland'

Wijnaardstraat, Goes, 4416DA Tel: 0113 232 895

Stichting 'Genealogisch Centrum Zeeland' Wijnaardstraat, Goes, 4416DA Tel: 0113 232 895

The Caledonian Society Zuiderweg 50, Noordwolde, NL 8391 KH Tel: 0561 431580

The Caledonian Society Zuiderweg 50, Noordwolde, NL 8391 KH Tel: 0561 431580

NORWAY

Norsk Slektshistorik Forening Sentrum Postboks 59, Oslo, N - 0101, Norway Tel: 2242 2204 Fax: 2242 2204

POLAND

Polish Genealogical Society of America 984 N. Milwaukee Ave, Chicago, IL, 60622, USA

Polish Genealogical Society of New Zealand Box 88, Urenui, Taranaki, New Zealand Tel: 06 754 4551 Email: pgs.newzealand@clear.net.nz

SLOVAKIA

Slovak GHS At Matica Slovenska Novomeskeho, 32, 036 52 Martin, Slovakia

SPAIN

Asociacion de Diplomados en Genealogia y Nobilaria Alcala 20, 2 Piso, Madrid, 28014 Tel: 34 522 3822 Fax: 34 532 6674

Asociacion de Hidalgos a Fuerto de Espana Aniceto Marinas 114, Madrid, 28008, Spain

Cercle Genealogic del Valles Roca 29, 5 2, Sabadell, Barcelona, 8208, Spain

Circulo de Estudios Genealogicos Familiares Prado 21, Ateneo de Madrid, Madrid, 28014, Spain

Instituto Aragones de Investigaciones Historiograficas Madre Sacremento 33, 1', Zaragoza, 50004, Spain

Instituto de Estudios Heraldicos y Genealogicos de Extremadura Lucio Cornelio Balbo 6, Caceres, 1004, Spain

Real Academia Matritense de Heraldica y Genealogia Quintana 28, Madrid, 28008, Spain

Sociedad Toledana de Estudios Heraldicos y Genealogicos Apartado de Correos No. 373, Toledo, Spain

Societat Catalona de Genealogia Heraldica Sigillografia Vexillologia P O Box 2830, Barcelona, 8080, Spain

Societat Valenciana de Genealogia Heraldica Sigillografia Vexillologia Les Tendes 22, Oliva, 46780, Spain

SWEDEN

Sveriges Slaktforskarforbund Box 30222, Stockholm, 104 25, Sweden Tel: 08 695 0890 Fax: 08 695 0824 Email: genealog@genealogi.se

SWITZERLAND

Genealogical & Heraldry Association of Zurich Dammbodenstrasse 1, Volketswil, CH-8604, Switzerland

Swiss Genealogical Society Eggstr 46, Oberengstringen, CH 8102, Switzerland WWW: www.eye.ch/swissgen/SGFF.html

Swiss Society for Jewish Genealogy P O Box 876, Zurich, CH-8021, Switzerland

Zentralstelle fur Genealogie Vogelaustrasse 34, CH-8953, Switzerland Fax: 44 1 742 20 84 Email: aicher@eyekon.ch

Family History Centres ~ *The Church of Jesus Christ of The Latter Day Saints*

Church of Jesus Christ of Latter Day Saints - North America Distribution Centre 1999 West 1700 South, Salt Lake City, Utah, 84104, United States of America

England
Bedfordshire
St Albans Family History Centre London Road/Cutenhoe Road, Luton LU1 3NQ Tel: 01582-482234

Berkshire
Reading Family History Centre 280 The Meadway, Tilehurst, Reading RG3 4PF Tel: 0118-941 0211

Bristol
Family History Centre 721 Wells Road, Whitchurch, Bristol, BS14 9HU Tel: 01275-838326

Cambridgeshire
Cambridgeshire Family History Centre 670 Cherry Hinton Road, Cambridge CB1 4DR Tel: 01223-247010,

Peterborough Family History Centre Cottesmore Close off Atherstone Av, Netherton Estate, Peterborough, PE3 9TP Tel: 01733-263374

Cheshire
Chester Family History Centre Clifton Drive, Blacon, Chester CH1 5LT Tel: 01244-390796

Church of Jesus Christ of Latter Day Saints - UK Distribution Centre 399 Garretts Green Lane, Birmingham, West Midlands, B33 0HU Tel: 0870-010-2051

Cleveland
Billingham Family History Centre The Linkway, Billingham TS23 3HG Tel: 01642-563162

Cornwall
Helston Family History Centre Clodgey Lane, Helston Tel: 01326-564503

Cumbria
Carlisle Family History Centre Langrigg Road, Morton Park, Carlisle CA2 5HT Tel: 01228-26767

Devon
Exeter Family History Centre Wonford Road, Exeter Tel: 01392-250723

Plymouth Family History Centre Mannamead Road, Plymouth PL3 5QJ Tel: 01752-668666

Dorset
Poole Family History Centre 8 Mount Road, Parkstone, Poole BH14 0QW Tel: 01202-730646

East Sussex
Crawley Family History Centre Old Horsham Road, Crawley RH11 8PD Tel: 01293-516151

East Yorkshire

Hull Family History Centre 725 Holderness Road, Kingston upon Hull HU4 7RT Tel: 01482-701439

Essex
Romford Family History Centre 64 Butts Green Road, Hornshurch RM11 2JJ Tel: 01708-620727

Gloucestershire
Cheltenham Family History Centre Thirlestaine Road, Cheltenham GL53 7AS Tel: 01242-523433

Forest of Dean Family History Centre
Wynol's Hill, Queensway, Coleford, Tel: 01594-542480

Greater Manchester
Manchester Family History Centre
Altrincham Road, Wythenshawe Road, Manchester, M22 4BJ
Tel: 0161-902-9279

Hampshire
Portsmouth Family History Centre 82 Kingston Crescent, Portsmouth PO2 8AQ Tel: (023) 92696243

Isle of Wight
Newport Family History Centre Chestnut Close, Shide Road, Newport PO30 1YE Tel: 01983-529643

Kent
Maidstone Family History Centre 76b London Road, Maidstone ME16 0DR Tel: 01622-757811

Lancashire
Ashton Family History Centre Patterdale Road, Ashton-under-Lyne OL7 Tel: 0161-330-1270

Blackpool Family History Centre Warren Drive, Cleveleys, Blackpool, FY5 3TG Tel: 01253-858218

Chorley Family History Centre Preston Temple, Chorley, PR6 7EQ Tel: 01257-226147

Lancaster Family History Centre Ovangle Road, Lancaster, LA1 5HZ Tel: 01254-33571

Rawtenstall Family History Centre Haslingden Road, Rawtenstall, Rossendale, BB4 6PU Tel: 01706-213460

Leicestershire
Leicestershire Family History Centre Wakerley Road, Leicester LE5 4WD Tel: 0116-233-5544

Lincolnshire
Lincoln Family History Centre Skellingthorpe Road, Lincoln LN6 0PB Tel: 01522-680117 Email: dann.family@diamond.co.uk

London
Hyde Park Family History Centre 64 - 68 Exhibition Road, South Kensington, London, SW7 2PA Tel: (020) 789-8561

Wandsworth Family History Centre 149 Nightingale Lane, Balham, London, SW12 Tel: (020) 8673-6741

Merseyside
Liverpool Family History Centre 4 Mill Bank, Liverpool L13 0BW Tel: 0151-228-0433

Middlesex
Staines Family History Centre 41 Kingston Road, Staines TW14 0ND Tel: 01784-462627

Norfolk
Kings Lynn Family History Centre Reffley Lane, Kings Lynn PE30 3EQ Tel: 01553-67000

Norwich Family History Centre 19 Greenways, Eaton, Norwich NR4 6PA Tel: 01603-452440

North East Lincolnshire
Grimsby Family History Centre, Linwood Avenue (NO LETTER BOX), Scartho, Grimsby DN33 2NL Tel: 01472-828876

North Yorkshire
Scarborough Family History Centre
Stepney Drive/Whitby Road, Scarborough

Northamptonshire
Northampton Family History Centre 137 Harlestone Road, Duston, Northampton NN5 6AA Tel: 01604-587630

Nottinghamshire
Mansfield Family History Centre Southridge Drive, Mansfield NG18 4RJ Tel: 01623-26729

Nottingham Family History Centre Hempshill Lane, Bulwell, Nottingham, NG6 8PA Tel: 0115-927-4194

Shropshire
Telford Family History Centre 72 Glebe Street, Wellington

Somerset
Yate Family History Centre Wellington Road, Yate BS37 5UY Tel: 01454-323004

Yeovil Family History Centre Forest Hill, Yeovil, BA20 2PH Tel: 01935-26817

South Yorkshire
Sheffield Family History Centre Wheel Lane, Grenoside, Sheffield S30 3RL Tel: 0114-245-3124

Staffordshire
Lichfield Family History Centre
Purcell Avenue, Lichfield WS14 9XA Tel: 01543-414843,

Newcastle under Lyme Family History Centre
PO Box 457, Newcastle under Lyme, ST5 0TD Tel: 01782-620653

Suffolk
Ipswich Family History Centre
42 Sidegate Lane West, Ipswich IP4 3DB Tel: 01473-723182

Lowestoft Family History Centre
165 Yarmouth Road, Lowestoft, Tel: 01502-573851

Tyne and Wear
Sunderland Family History Centre Linden Road off Queen Alexandra Road, Sunderland SR2 9BT
Tel: 0191-528-5787

West Midlands
Coventry Family History Centre Riverside Close,Whitley, Coventry Tel: (024) 76301420

Harborne Family History Centre 38 Lordswood Road, Harborne, Birmingham, B17 9QS
Tel: 0121-427-9291,

Sutton Coldfield Family History Centre 185 Penns Lane, Sutton Coldfield, Birmingham, B76 1JU Tel: 0121-386-1690,

Wednesfield Family History Centre Linthouse Lane, Wednesfield, Wolverhampton, Tel: 01902-724097

West Sussex
Worthing Family History Centre Goring Street, Worthing,West Sussex, BN12 5AR

West Yorkshire
Huddersfield Family History Centre 12 Halifax Road, Birchencliffe, Huddersfield HD3 3BS Tel: 01484-454573

Leeds Family History Centre Vesper Road, Leeds, LS5 3QT Tel: 0113-258-5297

Wirral
Birkenhead Family History Centre, Reservoir Road off Prenton Lane, Prenton CH42 8LJ Tel: 0151 608 0157

Worcestershire
Redditch Family History Centre 321 Evesham Road, Crabbs Cross, Redditch B97 5JA Tel: 01527-550657

York
Family History Centre West Bank, Acomb, York, Tel: 01904-785128

Wales
Denbighshire
Rhyl Family History Centre Rhuddlan Road, Rhyl, Denbighshire

Glamorgan
Merthyr Tydfil Family History Centre Swansea Road, Merthyr Tydfil CF 48 1NR Tel: 01685-722455

Swansea Family History Centre Cockett Road, Swansea, SA2 0FH Tel: 01792-419520

South Glamorgan
Cardiff Family History Centre Heol y Deri, Rhiwbina, Cardiff CF4 6UH Tel: (029) 20620205

Scotland
Edinburgh Family History Centre 30a Colinton Road, Edinburgh, EH4 3SN Tel: 0130-337-3049,

Glasgow Family History Centre 35 Julian Avenue, Glasgow, G12 0RB Tel: 0141-357-1024

Ayrshire
Kilmarnock Family History Centre Wahtriggs Road, Kilmarnock KA1 3QY Tel: 01563-26560

Dumfrieshire
Dumfries Family History Centre
36 Edinburgh Road, Albanybank, Dumfries DG1 1JQ Tel: 01387-254865

Fife
Kirkcaldy Family History Centre Winifred Crescent, Forth Park, Kirkcaldy KY2 5SX Tel: 01592-640041

Grampian
Aberdeen Family History Centre North Anderson Dr, Aberdeen AB2 6DD Tel: 01224-692206

Highlands
Inverness Family History Centre 13 Ness Walk, Inverness IV3 5SQ Tel: 01463-231220

Johnstone
Paisley Family History Centre Campbell street, Paisley PA5 8LD Tel: 01505-20886

Shetland
Lerwick Family History Centre Baila Croft, Lerwick, Shetland, ZE1 0EY Tel: 01595-695732 Tel: 01950-431469

Tayside
Dundee Family History Centre 22 - 26 Bingham Terrace, DundeeDD4 7HH Tel: 01382-451247

Isle of Man
Douglas Family History Centre Woodbourne Road, Douglas IM2 3AP Tel: 01624-675834

Channel Islands
Jersey
St Helier Family History Centre La Rue de la Vallee, St Mary, Jersey, JE3 3DL Tel: 01534-82171

Northern Ireland
Belfast Family History Centre 401 Holywood Road, Belfast, BT4 2GU Tel: (028) 90076250,

Londonderry Family History Centre Racecourse Road, Belmont Estate, Londonderry, Tel: Sun-only-(028) 71350179

Republic of Ireland
Co Dublin
Dublin Family History Centre The Willows, Finglas, Dublin, Co Dublin, 11 Tel: ++-353-4625609

Libraries

National

Angus Library Regent's Park College, Pusey Street, Oxford, OX1 2LB Tel: 01865 288142 Fax: 01865 288121

Birmingham University Information Services - Special Collections Main Library, University of Birmingham, Edgbaston, Birmingham, B15 2TT Tel: 0121 414 5838 Fax: 0121 471 4691 Email: special-collections@bham.ac.uk WWW: www.is.bham.ac.uk

Bristol University Library - Special Collections Tyndall Avenue, Bristol, BS8 1TJ Tel: 0117 928 8014 Fax: 0117 925 5334 Email: library@bris.ac.uk WWW: www.bris.ac.uk/depts/library

British Film Institute - Library & Film Archive, 21 Stephen Street, London, W1T 1LN Tel: 020 7957 4824 WWW: www.bfi.org.uk

British Genealogical Survey Library Kingsley Dunham Centre, Keyworth, Nottingham, NG12 5GG Tel: 0115 939 3205 Fax: 0115 936 3200 Email: info@bgs.ac.uk WWW: www.bgs.ac.uk

British Library British Library Building, 96 Euston Road, London, NW1 2DB Tel: (020) 712-7677 Email: Reader/admissions@bl.uk WWW: http://www.portico.bl.uk

British Library - Early Printed Collections 96 Euston Road, London, NW1 2DB Tel: (020) 7412-7673 Email: rare-books@bl.uk WWW: http://www.bl.uk

Caird Library - National Maritime Museum Park Row, Greenwich, London, SE10 9NF Tel: (020) 8312 6673 Fax: (020) 8312-6632 Email: ABuchanan@nmm.ac.uk WWW: http://www.nmm.ac.uk

Cambridge University Library - Department of Manuscripts & University Archives West Road, Cambridge, CB3 9DR Tel: 01223 333000 ext 33143 (Manuscripts) Tel: 01223 333000 ext 33148 (University Archives) Fax: 01223 333160 Email: mss@ula.cam.ac.uk WWW: www.lib.cam.ac.uk/MSS/

The Library & Museum of Freemasonry, Freemasons' Hall, 60 Great Queen Street, London, WC2B 5AZ Tel: (020) 7395 9257 WWW: www.grandlodge-england.org

House of Commons Library House of Commons, 1 Derby Gate, London, SW1A 2DG Tel: (020) 7219-5545 Fax: (020) 7219-3921

Institute of Heraldic and Genealogical Studies 79 - 82 Northgate, Canterbury, CT1 1BA Tel: 01227-765617 Email: ihgs@ihgs.ac.uk WWW: www.ihgs.ac.uk

Jewish Studies Library University College, Gower Street, London, WC1E 6BT Tel: (020) 7387 7050

National Gallery Library and Archive Trafalgar Square, London, WC2N 5DN Tel: 020 7747 2542 Fax: 020 7753 8179 Email: iad@ng-london.org.uk WWW: http://www.nationalgallery.org.uk

Nuffield College Library Oxford, OX1 1NF Tel: 01865 278550 Fax: 01865 278621

Rhodes House Library Bodleian Library, South Parks Road, Oxford, OX1 3RG Tel: 01865 270909 Fax: 01865 270912

Robinson Library University of Newcastle upon Tyne, Newcastle Upon Tyne, NE2 4HQ Tel: 0191 222 7671 Fax: 0191 222 6235 Email: library@ncl.ac.uk WWW: http://www.ncl.ac.uk/library/

Royal Armouries H.M Tower Of London, Tower Hill, London, EC3N 4AB Tel: (020) 7480 6358 ext 30 Fax: (020) 7481 2922 Email: Bridgett.Clifford@armouries.org.uk

Royal Commonwealth Society Library West Road, Cambridge, CB3 9DR Tel: 01223 33319 Fax: 01223 333160 Email: tab@ula.cam.ac.uk WWW: www.lib.cam.ac.uk/MSS/

Society of Antiquaries of London Burlington House, Piccadilly, London, W1J 0BE Tel: 020 7479 7084 Email: library@sal.org.uk WWW: www.sal.org.uk

Society of Genealogists - Library 14 Charterhouse Buildings, Goswell Road, London, EC1M 7BA Tel: 020-7251-8799 Tel: 020-7250-0291 Fax: 020-7250-1800 library@sog.org.uk - Sales at sales@sog.org.uk http://www.sog.org.uk

Sussex University Library Manuscript Collections, Falmer, Brighton, BN1 9QL Tel: 01273 606755 Fax: 01273 678441

The Kenneth Ritchie Wimbledon Library The All England Lawn Tennis & Croquet Club, Church Road, Wimbledon, London, SW19 5AE Tel: (020) 8946 6131 Fax: (020) 8944 6497 WWW: www.wimbledon.org Contains the world's finest collection of books and periodicals relating to lawn tennis

Trinity College Library Cambridge University, Trinity College, Cambridge, CB1 1TQ Tel: 01223 338488 Fax: 01223 338532 Email: trin-lib@lists.cam.ac.uk WWW: http://rabbit.trin.cam.ac.uk

Victoria & Albert Museum - National Art Library Cromwell Road, South Kensington, London, SW7 2RL Tel: (020) 7938 8315 Fax: (020) 7938 8461

Victoria & Albert Museum Archive of Art and Design Blythe House, 23 Blythe Road, London, W14 0QF Tel: (020) 7603 1514 Fax: (020) 7602 0980 Email: archive@vam.ac.uk WWW: www.nal.vam.ac.uk

Wellcome Contemporary Medical Archives Centre 183 Euston Road, London, NW1 2BE Tel: (020) 7611 8483 Fax: (020) 7611 8703 Email: library@wellcome.ac.uk WWW: www.wellcome.ac.uk/library Library catalogue is available through the internet: telnet://wihm.ucl.ac.uk

Wellcome Library for the History of Medicine - Department of Western Manuscripts 183 Euston Road, London, NW1 2BE Tel: (020) 7611-8582 Fax: (020) 7611 8369 Email: library@wellcome.ac.uk WWW: www.wellcome.ac.uk/library

British Library Newspaper Library Colindale Avenue, London, NW9 5HE Tel: 020-7412-7353 Fax: 020-7412-7379 Email: newspaper@bl.uk WWW: http://www.bl.uk/collections/newspaper/ The National archive collections of British and Overseas newspapers as well as major collections of popular magazines. Open Mon to Sat 10am to 4.45pm. Readers must be over 18yrs of age and provide proof

British Library of Political and Economic Science London School of Economics, 10 Portugal Street, London, WC2A 2HD Tel: 020 7955 7223 Fax: 020 7955 7454 Email: info@lse.ac.uk WWW: http://www.lse.ac.uk

British Library Oriental and India Office Collections 96 Euston Road, London, NW1 2DB Tel: (020) 7412-7873 Fax: (020) 7412-7641 Email: oioc-enquiries@bl.uk WWW: http://www.bl.uk/collections/oriental

Caird Library - National Maritime Museum Park Row, Greenwich, London, SE10 9NF Tel: (020) 8312 6673 Fax: (020) 8312-6632 Email: ABuchanan@nmm.ac.uk WWW: http://www.nmm.ac.uk

Catholic Central Library Lancing Street, London, NW1 1ND Tel: (020) 7383-4333 Fax: (020) 7388-6675 Email: librarian@catholic-library.demon.co.uk WWW: www.catholic-library.demon.co.uk

Department of Manuscripts and Special Collections Hallward Library, Nottingham University , University Park, Nottingham, NG7 2RD Tel: 0115 951 4565 Fax: 0115 951 4558 Email: mss-library@nottingham.ac.uk WWW: www.mss.library.nottingham.ac.uk

Dr Williams's Library 14 Gordon Square, London, WC1H 0AR Tel: (020) 7387-3727 Email: 101340.2541@compuserve.com , The General Registers of Protestant Dissenters (Dr William's Library Registers) were surrendered to the Registrar General and are now at The Public Record Office (RG4/4666-4673)

Huguenot Library University College, Gower Street, London, WC1E 6BT Tel: (020) 7679 7094 Email: s.massilk@ucl.ac.uk WWW: http://www.ucl.ac.uk/ucl-info/divisions/library/hugenot.htm

John Rylands University Library Special Collections Division, 150 Deansgate, Manchester, M3 3EH Tel: 0161-834-5343 Fax: 0161-834-5343 Email: spcoll72@fs1.li.man.ac.uk WWW: http://rylibweb.man.ac.uk Holdings include family muniment collections especially relating to Cheshire and major Non Conformist Archives Few genealogical records held except for family muniment collections, especially for Cheshire

Lambeth Palace Library Lambeth Palace Road, London, SE1 7JU Tel: (020) 7898 1400 WWW: www.lambethpalacelibrary.org

Library of the Religious Society of Friends (Quakers) Friends House, 173 - 177 Euston Rd, London, NW1 2BJ Tel: 0207 663 1135 Tel: 0207 663 1001, Email: library@quaker.org.uk WWW: http://www.quaker.org.uk/library Limited opening hours. Letter of introduction required. Please send SAE for details or enclose IRCs

Library of the Royal College of Surgeons of England 35-43 Lincoln's Inn Fields, London, WC2A 3PN Tel: (020) 7869 6520 Fax: (020) 7405 4438 Email: library@rseng.ac.uk

Lifelong Learning Service Theodore Road, Port Talbot, SA13 1SP Tel: 01639-898581 Fax: 01639-899914 Email: lls@neath-porttalbot.gov.uk

Liverpool University Special Collections & Archives University of Liverpool Library, PO Box 123, Liverpool, L69 3DA Tel: 0151-794-2696 Fax: 0151-794-2081 WWW: http://www.sca.lib.liv.ac.uk/collections/index.html **Methodist Archives and Research Centre** John Rylands University Library, 150 Deansgate, Manchester, M3 3EH Tel: 0161 834 5343 Fax: 0161 834 5574

Museum of the Order of St John St John's Gate, St John's Lane, Clerkenwell, London, EC1M 4DA Tel: (020) 7253-6644 Fax: (020) 7336 0587 WWW: www.sja.org.uk/history

River & Rowing Museum Rowing & River Museum, Mill Meadows, Henley on Thames, RG9 1BF Tel: 01491 415043 Fax: 01491 415601 Email: museum@rrm.co.uk WWW: www..rrm.co.uk Thames linked families especially lock keepers , boat builders

Royal Institute of British Architects' Library Manuscripts & archives Collection, 66 portland Place, London, W1N 4AD Tel: 020 7307 3615 Fax: 020 7631 1802

Royal Society of Chemistry Library & Info Centre Burlington House, Piccadilly, London, W1J 0BA Tel: (020) 7437 8656 Fax: (020) 7287 9798 Email: library@rsc.org WWW: www.rsc.org

School of Oriental and African Studies library Thornhaugh Street, Russell Square, London, WC1H 0XG Tel: 020 7323 6112 Fax: 020 7636 2834 Email: lib@soas.ac.uk WWW: http://www.soas.ac.uk/library/

South Wales Miners' Library - Swansea Hendrefoelan House, Gower Road, Swansea, SA2 7NB Tel: 01792-518603 Fax: 01792-518694 Email: miners@swansea.ac.uk WWW: http://www.swan.ac.uk/lis/swml

The Library & Museum of Freemasonry Freemasons' Hall, 60 Great Queen Street, London, WC2B 5AZ Tel: (020) 7395 9257

The Science Museum Library Imperial College Road, South Kensington, London,SW7 5NH Tel: 020 7938 8234 Tel: 020 7938 8218 Fax: 020 7938 9714

The Women's Library Old Castle Street, London, E1 7NT Tel: (020) 7320-1189 Fax: (020) 7320-1188 Email: fawcett@lgu.ac.uk WWW: http://www.lgu.ac.uk/fawcett

Thomas Plume Library Market Hill, Maldon, CM9 4PZ No Tel or Fax

Trades Union Congress Library Collections - University of North London 236 - 250 Holloway Road, London, N7 6PP Fax: 0171 753 3191 Email: tuclib@unl.ac.uk WWW: http://www.unl.ac.uk/library/tuc

United Reformed Church History Society, Westminster College, Madingley Road, Cambridge, CB3 0AA Tel: 01223-741300 (NOT Wednesdays)Information on ministers of constituent churches not members

Wellcome Library - History & Understanding of Medicine 183 Euston Road, London, NW1 2BE Tel: (020) 7611-8582 Fax: (020) 7611 8369 Email: library@wellcome.ac.uk WWW: www.wellcome.ac.uk/library Library catalogue is available through the internet: http://library.wellcome.ac.uk

England
Bedfordshire
Bedford Central Library Harpur Street, Bedford, MK40 1PG Tel: 01234-350931 Fax: 01234-342163 Email: stephensonB@bedfordshire.gov.uk

Biggleswade Library, Chestnut Avenue, Biggleswade, SG18 0LL Tel: 01767 312324 1901 census

Dunstable Library, Vernon Place, Dunstable, LU5 4HA Tel: 01582 608441 1901 census

Leighton Buzzard Library, Lake Street, Leighton Buzzard, LU7 1RX Tel: 01525 371788 1901 censusLuton Local Studies Library Luton Central Library, St George's Square, Luton, LU1 2NG Tel: 01582-547420 Tel: 01582-547421 Fax: 01582-547450

Berkshire
Ascot Heath Library Fernbank Road, North Ascot, SL5 8LA Tel: 01344 884030 Fax: 01344 884030

Berkshire Medical Heritage Centre, Royal Berkshire Hospital, London Road, Reading, RG1 5AN Tel: 0118 987 7298

Binfield Library Benetfeld Road, Binfield, RG42 4HD Tel: 01344 306663 Fax: 01344 486467

Bracknell Library (Headquarters), Town Square, Bracknell, RG12 1BH Tel: 01344 423149 Fax: 01344 411392

Bracknell Library - Local Studies, Town Square, Bracknell, RG12 1BH Tel: 01344 352515 Fax: 01344 411392

Crowthorne Library Lower Broadmoor Road, Crowthorne, RG45 7LA Tel: 01344 776431 Fax: 01344 776431

Eton College Library, College Street, , Windsor, SL4 6DB Tel: 01753 671629

Maidenhead & Windsor Local Studies Library, St Ives Road, Maidenhead, SL6 1QU Tel: 01628 796979 1901 census

Newbury Reference Library, Newbury Central Library, The Wharf, Newbury, RG14 5AU Tel: 01635 40208 1901 census

Reading Local Studies Library, Reading Central Library, Abbey Square, Reading, RG1 1QH Tel: 0118 901 5965

Reading University Library University of Reading, Whiteknights PO Box 223, Reading, RG6 6AE Tel: 0118-931-8776 Fax: 0118-931 6636 WWW: http://www.reading.ac.uk/

Sandhurst Library The Broadway, Sandhurst, GU47 9BL Tel: 01252 870161 **Slough Local Studies Library**, High Street, Slough, SL1 1EA Tel: 01753 535166

Whitegrove Library 5 County Lane, Warfield, RG42 3JP Tel: 01344 424211

Wokingham Library Local Studies, The Library, Denmark Street, Wokingham, RG40 2BB Tel: 0118 978 1368

Birmingham
Birmingham Central Library - The Genealogist, Local Studies & History Service Floor 6, Central Library, Chamberlain Square, Birmingham, B3 3HQ Tel: 0121 303 4549 Fax: 0121 464 0993 Email: local.studies.library@birmingham.gov.uk WWW: www.birmingham.gov.uk

Bolton
Central Library Civic Centre, Le Mans Crescent, Bolton, BL1 1SE Tel: 01204-333185

Bristol
Bristol Central Library Reference Section, College Green, Bristol, BS1 5TL Tel: 0117-929-9147 Tel: 0117903 7259 Fax:
Bristol University Library - Special Collections Tyndall Avenue, Bristol, BS8 1TJ Tel: 0117 928 8014 Email: library@bris.ac.uk WWW: www.bris.ac.uk/depts/library

Buckinghamshire
County Reference Library Walton Street, Aylesbury, HP20 1UU Tel: 01296-382250
High Wycombe Reference Library Queen Victoria Road, High Wycombe, HP11 1BD Tel: 01494-510241 Email: hwrlib@hotmail.com
Milton Keynes Reference Library 555 Silbury Boulevard, Milton Keynes, MK9 3HL Tel: 01908 254160 Fax: 01908 254088

Cambridgeshire
Cambridge University Library - Department of Manuscripts & University Archives West Road, Cambridge, CB3 9DR Tel: 01223 333000 ext 33143 (Manuscripts) Tel: 01223 333000 ext 33148

(University Archives) Fax: 01223 333160 Email: mss@ula.cam.ac.uk WWW: www.lib.cam.ac.uk/MSS/
Homerton College Library The New Library, Hills Road, Cambridge, CB2 2PH
Norris Library and Museum The Broadway, St Ives, PE27 5BX Tel: 01480-465101 Fax: 01480 497314 Email: norris.st-ives-tc@co-net.com
The Cambridge Library Lion Yard, Cambridge, CB2 3QD

Cheshire
Alderley Edge Library, Heys Lane, Alderley Edge, SK9 7JT Tel: 01625 584487 Fax: 01625 584487
Alsager Library, Sandbach Road North, Alsager, ST7 2QH Tel: 01270 873552 Fax: 01270 883093 Email: alsager.infopoint@cheshire.gov.uk
Barnton Library, Townfield Lane, Barnton, CW8 4LJ Tel: 01606 77343 Fax: 01606 77343
Bishops' High School Library, Vaughans Lane, Chester, CH3 5XF Tel: 01244 313806 Fax: 01244 320992, ,
Blacon Library, Western Avenue, Blacon, Chester, CH1 5XF Tel: 01244 390628 Fax: 01244 390628
Bollington Library, Palmerston Street, Bollington, SK10 5JX Tel: 01625 573058 Fax: 01625 573058
Chester Library Northgate Street, Chester, CH1 2EF Tel: 01244-312935
Congleton Library, Market Square, Congleton, CW12 1ET Tel: 01260 271141 Fax: 01260 298774 Email: congleton.infopoint@cheshire.gov.uk
Crewe Library Prince Albert Street, Crewe, CW1 2DH Tel: 01270-211123 Fax: 01270-256952 Email: ipcrewe@cheshire.gov.uk
Disley Library, Off Buxton Old Road, Disley, SK12 2BB Tel: 01663 765635 Fax: 01663 765635
Frodsham Library, Rock Chapel, Main Street, Frodsham, WA6 7AN Tel: 01928 732775 Fax: 01928 734214
Great Boughton Library, Green Lane, Vicars Cross, Chester, CH3 5LB Tel: 01244 320709 Fax: 01244 320709
Halton Lea Library Halton Lea, Runcorn, WA7 2PF Tel: 01928-715351
Handforth Library, The Green, Wilmslow Road, Handforth, SK9 3ES Tel: 01625 528062 Fax: 01625 524390
Helsby Library, Lower Robin Hood Lane, Helsby, WA5 0BW Tel: 01928 724659 Fax: 01928 726947
Holmes Chapel Library, London Road, Holmes Chapel, CW4 7AP Tel: 01477 535126 Fax: 01477 544193 Email: homeschapel.infopoint@cheshire.gov.uk
Hoole Library, 91 Hoole Road, Chester, England Tel: 01244 347401 Fax: 01244 347401
Ellesmere Port Library Civic Way, Ellesmere Port, South Wirral, L65 0BG Tel: 0151-355-8101 Fax: 0151-355-6849
Macclesfield Library Jordangate, Macclesfield, SK10 1EE Tel: 01625-422512
Stockport Local Heritage Library Central Library, Wellington Road South, Stockport, SK1 3RS Tel: 0161-474-4530 Email: localheritage.library@stockport.gov.uk
Tameside Local Studies Library Stalybridge Library, Trinity Street, Stalybridge, SK15 2BN Tel: 0161-338-2708 Tel: 0161-338-3831 and 0161 303 7937 Fax: 0161-303-8289 Email: localstudies.library@mail.tameside.gov.uk WWW: http://www.tameside.gov.uk
Warrington Library & Local Studies Centre Museum Street, Warrington, WA1 1JB Tel: 01925 442890 Fax: 01925 411395 Email: library@warrington.gov.uk WWW: www.warrington.gov.uk
Wirral Central Library Borough Road, Birkenhead, CH41 2XB Tel: 0151 652 6106 Tel: 0151 652 6107/8 Fax: 0151 653 7320 Email: birkenhead.library@merseymail.com

Cleveland
Hartlepool Central Library, 124 York Road, Hartlepool, TS26 9DE Tel: 01429 263778 1901 census
Middlesbrough Libraries & Local Studies Centre Central Library, Victoria Square, Middlesbrough, TS1 2AY Tel: 01642-263358 Fax: 01642 648077
Redcar Reference Library Coatham Road, Redcar, TS10 1RP Tel: 01642 489292 1901 census
Stockton Reference Library Church Road, Stockton on Tees, TS18 1TU Tel: 01642-393994 Email: reference.library@stockton.bc.gov.uk

Cornwall
Royal Institution of Cornwall, Courtney Library & Cornish History Research Centre, Royal Cornwall Museum, River Street, Truro, TR1 2SJ Tel: 01872 272205 Fax: 01872 240514 Email: RIC@royal-cornwall-museum.freeserve.co.uk WWW: www.cornwall-online.co.uk/ric
The Cornwall Centre Alma Place, Redruth, TR15 2AT Tel: 01209-216760 Email: cornishstudies@library.cornwall.gov.uk WWW: www.cornwall.gov.uk

County Durham
Centre For Local Studies The Library, Crown Street, Darlington, DL1 1ND Tel: 01325-349630 Email: crown.street.library@darlington.gov.uk

Durham Arts Library and Museums Department, County Hall, Durham, DH1 STY Tel: 0191-383-3595
Durham City Library Reference & Local Studies Department, South Street, Durham, DH1 4QS Tel: 0191-386-4003
Email: durhamcityref.lib@durham.gov.uk
WWW: www.durham.gov.uk
Durham University Library Archives & Special Collections
Palace Green Section, Palace Green, Durham, DH1 3RN Tel: 0191-374-3032 Email: pg.library@durham.ac.uk

Cumbria
Carlisle Library 11 Globe Lane, Carlisle, CA3 8NX Tel: 01228-607310 Fax: 01228-607333 Email: carlisle.library@cumbriacc.gov.uk WWW: http://dspace.dial.pipex.com/cumherit/index.htm
Cumbria Record Office and Local Studies Library Scotch Street, Whitehaven, CA28 7BJ Tel: 01946-852920Email: whitehaven.record.office@cumbriacc.gov.uk
WWW: , http://www.cumbria.gov.uk/archives
Cumbria Record Office & Local Studies Library 140 Duke St, Barrow in Furness, LA14 1XW Tel: 01229-894363 Email: barrow.record.office@cumbriacc.gov.uk
WWW: www.cumbria.gov.uk/archives
Kendal Library Stricklandgate, Kendal, LA9 4PY Tel: 01539-773520Email: kendal.library@cumbriacc.gov.uk
Penrith Library St Andrews Churchyard, Penrith, CA11 7YA Tel: 01768-242100Email: penrith.library@dial.pipexcom
Workington Library Vulcans Lane, Workington, CA14 2ND Tel: 01900-325170 Email: workington.library@cumbriacc.gov.uk

Derbyshire
Chesterfield Local Studies Department Chesterfield Library, New Beetwell Street, Chesterfield, S40 1QN Tel: 01246-209292 Fax: 01246-209304
Derby Local Studies Library 25b Irongate, Derby, DE1 3GL Tel: 01332 255393
Family Local Studies Library - Matlock County Hall, Smedley Street, Matlock, DE4 3AG Tel: 01629-585579 Fax: 01629-585049

Derby City Council
Derby Local Studies Library 25b Irongate, Derby, DE1 3GL Tel: 01332 255393 Fax: 01332 255381

Devon
Devon & Exeter Institution Library 7 The Close, Exeter, EX1 1EZ Tel: 01392-251017Email: m.midgley@exeter.ac.uk
WWW: http://www.ex.ac.uk/library/devonex.html
Exeter University Library Stocker Road, Exeter, EX4 4PT Tel: 01392 263870Email: library@exeter.ac.uk WWW: www.library.exeter.ac.uk
Plymouth Local Studies Library, Plymouth Central Library, Drake Circus, Plymouth, PL4 8AL Tel: 01752 305909 1901 census
Torquay Library, Lymington Road, Torquay, TQ1 3DT Tel: 01803 208305 1901 census
Westcountry Studies Library Exeter Central Library, Castle Street, Exeter, EX4 3PQ Tel: 01392-384216 Email: dlaw@devon-cc.gov.uk
WWW: http://www.devon-cc.gov.uk/library/locstudy

Dorset
Dorchester Reference Library Colliton Park, Dorchester, DT1 1XJ Tel: 01305-224448
Dorset County Museum High West Street, Dorchester, DT1 1XA Tel: 01305 262735 Email: dorsetcountymuseum@dor-mus.demon.co.uk
Poole Central Reference Library Dolphin Centre, Poole, BH15 1QE Tel: 01202 262424 Fax: 01202 262442 Email: centrallibrary@poole.gov.uk WWW: www.poole.gov.uk The local studies collection was relocated to The Waterfront Museum, Poole Some records moved to Dorset Record Office. Retains only general local history and national family history indexes.

Durham
Durham City Reference & Local Studies Library, Durham Clayport Library, Millennium Place, Durham, DH1 1WA Tel: 0191-386-4003 Fax: 0191-386-0379 Email: durhamcityref.lib@durham.gov.uk WWW: www.durham.gov.uk, 1901 census

Essex
Clacton Library, Station Road, Clacton on Sea, CO15 1SF Tel: 01255 421207 1901 census
Central Reference Library - LB of Havering Reference Library, St Edward's Way, Romford, RM1 3AR Tel: 01708 432393 Email: romfordlib2@rmplc.co.uk
Chelmsford Library
PO Box 882, Market Road, Chelmsford, CM1 1LH Tel: 01245 492758 Email: answers.direct@essexcc.gov.uk WWW: www.essexcc.gov.uk
Colchester Central Library
Trinity Square, Colchester, CO1 1JB Tel: 01206-245917 Email: jane.stanway@essexcc.gov.uk WWW: www.essexcc.gov.uk
Harlow Library, The High, Harlow, CM20 1HA Tel: 01279 413772 1901 census

Ilford Local Studies and Archives, Central Library, Clements Road, Ilford, IG1 1EA Tel: 020 8708 2417 1901 census
Loughton Library, Traps Hill, Loughton, IG10 1HD Tel: 020 8502 0181 1901 census
LB of Barking & Dagenham Local History Studies Valence House Museum, Becontree Avenue, Dagenham, RM8 3HT Tel: 020-822-75293 Fax: 020-822-75297 Email: fm019@viscount.org.uk WWW: http://www.bardaglea.org.uk/4-heritage/heritage-menu.html Heritage service includes a local history museum, and archive section. A list of resources is available upon request. Archives of the London Boroughs and Essex Parishes of Barking and Dagenham
LB of Barking & Dagenham Local History Studies Central Library, Barking, Dagenham, IG11 7NB Tel: (020) 8517-8666 Local History studies from this Library have been centralised at Valence Linbrary, Becontree Avenue, Dagenham, Essex RM8 3HT Tel & (020) 8227 5297 Email:valencelibrary@hotmail.com
Redbridge Library Central Library, Clements Road, Ilford, IG1 1EA Tel: (020) 8708-2417 Email: Local.Studies@redbridge.gov.uk WWW: www.redbridge.gov.uk
Saffron Walden Library, 2 King Street, Saffron Walden, CB10 1ES Tel: 01799 523178 1901 census
Southend Library Central Library, Victoria Avenue, Southend on Sea, SS2 6EX Tel: 01702-612621 Email: library@southend.gov.uk WWW: www.southend.gov.uk/libraries/
Thomas Plume Library Market Hill, Maldon, CM9 4PZ No facilities for incoming telephone or fax messages

Gloucestershire
Cheltenham Local Studies Centre Cheltenham Library, Clarence Street, Cheltenham, GL50 3JT Tel: 01242-532678 Fax: 01242 532673
Gloucester Library, Arts & Museums County Library, Quayside, Shire Hall, Gloucester, GL1 1HY Tel: 01452-425037 Email: clams@gloscc.gov.uk WWW: http://www.gloscc.gov.uk
Gloucestershire County Library Brunswick Road, Gloucester, GL1 1HT Tel: 01452-426979 Email: clams@gloscc.gov.uk WWW: http://www.gloscc.gov.uk
Gloucestershire Family History Society 4 Twyver Close, Upton St Leonards, GL4 8EF Tel: 01452-52344 (RESOURCE CENTRE) Tel: 01452 615143 Fax: 01452 615143 Email: glosearch@hotmail.com WWW: http://www.cix.co.uk/~rd/genuki/gfhs.htm
Gloucestershire - South
Thornbury Library St Mary Street, Thornbury, BS35 2AA Tel: 01454-865655
Yate Library 44 West Walk, Yate, BS37 4AX Tel: 01454-865661

Hammersmith
Hammersmith Central Library Shepherds Bush Road, London, W6 7AT Tel: 020 8753 3816 Fax: 020 8753 3815 WWW: www.lbhf.gov.uk

Hampshire
Aldershot Library 109 High Street, Aldershot, GU11 1DQ Tel: 01252 322456
Andover Library Chantry Centre, Andover, SP10 1LT Tel: 01264 352807 Email: clceand@hants.gov.uk
Basingstoke Library North Division Headquarters, 19 - 20 Westminster House, Potters Walk, Basingstoke, RG21 7LS Tel: 01256-473901
Eastleigh Library The Swan Centre, Eastleigh, SO50 5SF Tel: 01703 612513 Email: clweeas@hants.gov.uk
Fareham Library South Division Headquarters, Osborn Road, Fareham, PO16 7EN Tel: 01329-282715 Email: clsoref@hants.gov.uk
Farnborough Library Pinehurst, Farnborough, GU14 7JZ Tel: 01252 513838 Email: clnoref@hants.gov.uk WWW: http://www.brit-a-r.demon.co.uk
Fleet Library 236 Fleet Road, Fleet, GU13 8BX Tel: 01252 614213 Email: clnofle@hants.gov.uk
Gosport Library High Street, Gosport, PO12 1BT Tel: (023) 9252 3431 Email: clsos@hants.gov.uk
Hampshire County Library West Division Headquarters, The Old School, Cannon Street, Lymington, SO41 9BR Tel: 01590-675767 Email: clwedhq@hants.gov.uk WWW: http://www.hants.gov.uk
Hampshire Local Studies Library
Winchester library, Jewry Street, Winchester, SO23 8RX Tel: 01962 841408 Email: clceloc@hants.gov.uk WWW: www.hants.gov.uk/library
Lymington Library Cannon Street, Lymington, SO41 9BR Tel: 01590 673050 Email: clwelym@hants.gov.uk
Portsmouth City Libraries Central Library, Guildhall Square, Portsmouth, PO1 2DX Tel: (023) 9281 9311 Email: reference.library@portsmouthcc.gov.uk
Royal Marines Museum Eastney, Southsea, PO4 9PX Tel: (023) 92 819385-Exts-224 Fax: (023) 92 838420 Email: matthewlittle@royalmarinesmuseum.co.uk WWW: www.royalmarinesmuseum.co.uk No charges for research other than material costs. Donations welcome. Visits by appointment Mon to Fri 10am to 4.30pm
Southampton City Libraries - Special Collections Southampton Reference Library, Civic Centre, Southampton, SO14 7LW Tel: 023 8083 2205 Email: local.studies@southampton.gov.uk WWW: www.southampton.gov.uk

Southampton University Library Highfield, Southampton, SO17 1BJ
Tel: 023 8059 3724 Tel: 023 8059 2721 Fax: 023 8059 3007
Waterlooville Library The Precinct, Waterlooville, PO7 7DT Tel: (023)
9225 4626 Email: clsowvl@hants.gov.uk
Winchester Reference Library 81 North Walls, Winchester, SO23 8BY
Tel: 01962-846059 Fax: 01962-856615 Email: clceref@hants.gov.uk

Herefordshire
Bromyard Library 34 Church Street, Bromyard, HR7 4DP Tel: 01885
482657 No Genealogical information held
Colwall Library Humphrey Walwyn Library, Colwall, Malvern, WR13
6QT Tel: 01684 540642
Hereford Cathedral Archives & Library 5 College Cloisters, Cathedral
Close, Hereford, HR1 2NG Tel: 01432 374225 Email:
library@herefordcathedral.co.uk
Hereford Library Broad Street, Hereford, HR4 9AU Tel: 01432-272456
Ledbury Library The Homend, Ledbury, HR8 1BT Tel: 01531 632133
Leominster Library 8 Buttercross, Leominster, HR6 8BN
Tel: 01568-612384
Ross Library Cantilupe Road, Ross on Wye, HR9 7AN
Tel: 01989 567937

Hertfordshire
Bushey Museum and Art Gallery, Rudolph Road, Bushey, WD23 3HW
Tel: 020 8420 4057 1901 census
Hertfordshire Archives and Local Studies County Hall, Pegs Lane,
Hertford, SG13 8EJ Tel: 01438 737333 Email:
herts.direct@hertscc.gov.uk WWW: http://hertsdirect.org/hals
Welwyn Garden City Central Library Local Studies Section, Campus
West, Welwyn Garden City, AL8 6AJ Tel: 01438 737333
Fax: 01707 897 595

Hull
Brynmor Jones Library - University of Hull Cottingham Road, Hull,
HU6 7RX Tel: 01482 465265 Email: archives@acs.hull.ac.uk
WWW: www.hull.ac.uk/lib www.hull.ac.uk/lib/archives
**Hull Central Library Family and Local History Unit, Central
Library,** Albion Street, Kingston upon Hull, HU1 3TF Tel: 01482
616828 Fax: 01482 616827 Email: gareth@ukorigins.co.uk WWW:
http://www.hullcc.gov.uk/genealogy/famhist.php 1901 census

Isle of Wight
Isle of Wight County Library Lord Louis Library, Orchard Street,
Newport, PO30 1LL Tel: 01983-823800 Email:
reflib@llouis.demon.co.uk

Kent
Broadstairs Library The Broadway, Broadstairs, CT10 2BS Tel: 01843-
862994
Canterbury Cathedral Library The Precincts, Canterbury, CT1 2EH
Tel: 01227-865287 Email: catlib@ukc.ac.uk
WWW: www.canterbury-cathedral.org
Canterbury Library & Local Studies Collection 18 High Street,
Canterbury, CT1 2JF Tel: 01227-463608
Dartford Central Library - Reference Department Market Street,
Dartford, DA1 1EU Tel: 01322-221133
Dover Library Maison Dieu House, Biggin Street, Dover, CT16 1DW
Tel: 01304-204241
Faversham Library Newton Road, Faversham, ME13 8DY
Tel: 01759-523448 9
Folkestone Library & Local Heritage Studies
2 Grace Hill, Folkestone, CT20 1HD Tel: 01303-256710
Email: janet.adamson@kent.gov.uk
Gillingham Library High Street, Gillingham, ME7 1BG Tel: 01634-
281066 Email: Gillingham.Library@medway.gov.uk
Gravesend Library Windmill Street, Gravesend, DA12 1BE Tel: 01474-
352758
Greenhill Library Greenhill Road, Herne Bay, CT6 7PN Tel: 01227
374288
Herne Bay Library 124 High Street, Herne Bay, CT6 5JY
Tel: 01227-374896
Institute of Heraldic and Genealogical Studies 79 - 82 Northgate,
Canterbury, CT1 1BA Fax: 01227-765617 Email: ihgs@ihgs.ac.uk
WWW: www.ihgs.ac.uk
LB of Bromley Local Studies Library Central Library, High Street,
Bromley, BR1 1EX Tel: 020 8460 9955 Email:
localstudies.library@bromley.gov.uk
Ashford Library, Church Road, Asford, TN23 1QX Tel: 01233 620649
1901 census
Deal Library, Broad Street, Deal, CT14 6ER Tel: 01304 374726
1901 census
Maidstone Reference Library, St Faith's Street, Maidstone, ME14 1LH
Tel: 01622 701943 1901 census
Margate Library Local History Collection Cecil Square, Margate, CT9
1RE Tel: 01843-223626
Ramsgate Library and Museum Guildford Lawn, Ramsgate, CT11
9QY Tel: 01843-593532

**Ramsgate Library Local Strudies Collection & Thanet Branch
Archives** Ramsgate Library, Guildford Lawn, Ramsgate, CT11 9AY Tel:
01843-593532 Archives at this library moved to East Kent Archives
CentreEnterprise Zone, Honeywood Road, Whitfield, Dover, Kent CT16
3EH. A Local Studies Collection remains
Sevenoaks Library Buckhurst Lane, Sevenoaks, TN13 1LQ Tel: 01732-
453118
Sheerness Library Russell Street, Sheerness, ME12 1PL Tel: 01795-
662618 Fax: 01795-583035 WWW: www.kent.gov.uk
Sittingbourne Library Central Avenue, Sittingbourne, ME10 4AH Tel:
01795-476545 Fax: 01795-428376 WWW: www.kent.gov.uk
Sturry Library Chafy Crescent, Sturry, Canterbury, CT2 0BA
Tel: 01227 711479 Fax: 01227 710768
Tonbridge Library, Avenbury Avenue, Tonbridge, TN9 1TG Tel: 01732
352754 1901 census
Tunbridge Wells Library Mount Pleasant, Tunbridge Wells, TN1 1NS
Tel: 01892-522352 Fax: 01892-514657
University of Kent at Canterbury Library Canterbury, CT2 7NU Tel:
01227 764000
Whitstable Library 31-33 Oxford Street, Whitstable, CT5 1DB
Tel: 01227-273309 Fax: 01227-771812

Lancashire
Bacup Library, St James's Square, Bacup, OL13 9AH Tel: 01706
873324 1901 census
Barnoldswick Library, Fernlea Avenue, Barnoldswick, Colne, BB8
5DW Tel: 01282 812147 1901 census
Blackburn Central Library
Town Hall Street, Blackburn, BB2 1AG Tel: 01254 587920 Email:
reference.library@blackburn.gov.uk
WWW: www.blackburn.gov.uk/library
Bolton Central Library Civic Centre, Le Mans Crescent, Bolton, BL1
1SE Tel: 01204-333185
Burnley Central & Local Studies Library Grimshaw Street, Burnley,
BB11 2BD Tel: 01282-437115 Email:
burnley.reference@lcl.lancscc.gov.uk
Bury Central Library - References & Info Services Bury Central
Library, Manchester Road, Bury, BL9 0DG Tel: 0161-253-5871 Email:
Bury.lib@bury.gov.uk WWW: www.bury.gov.uk/culture.htm
Chethams Library Long Millgate, Manchester, M3 1SB Tel: 0161 834
7961 Fax: 0161 839 5797 Email: chetlib@dial.pipex.com
Chorley Central Library, Union Street, Chorley Lancashire, PR7 1EB
Tel: 01257 277222 1901 census
Clitheroe Library, Church Street, Clitheroe, BB7 2DG Tel: 01200
428788 1901 census
Colne Library Market Street, Colne, BB8 0AP Tel: 01282-871155
Haslingden Library, Higher Deardengate, Haslingden, Rossendale, BB4
5QL Tel: 01706 215690 1901 census
Heywood Local Studies Library Heywood Library, Church Street,
Heywood, OL10 1LL Tel: 01706 360947 Fax: 01706 368683
Hyndburn Central Library St James Street, Accrington, Lancs, BB5
1NQ Tel: 01254-872385 Email:
accrington.localstudies@lcl.lancscc.gov.uk
Lancashire Record Office Bow Lane, Preston, PR1 2RE Tel: 01772
263039 Fax: 01772 263050 Email: record.office@ed.lancscc.gov.uk
WWW: www.lancashire.gov.uk/education/lifelong/recordindex.shtm The
Lancashire Local Studies Collection is now housed here
Leigh Library Turnpike Centre, Civic Centre, Leigh, WN7 1EB Tel:
01942-404559 Email: heritage@wiganmbc.gov.uk
Leyland Library, Lancastergate, Leyland, PR5 1EX Tel: 01772 432804
1901 census
Middleton Local Studies Library
Middleton Library, Long Street, Middleton, M24 6DU
Tel: 0161-643-5228 Fax: 0161-654-0745
Morecombe Library, Central Drive, Morecombe, LA4 5DL Tel: 01524
402110 1901 census
Nelson Library, Market Square, Nelson, BB9 7PU Tel: 01282 692511
Oldham Local Studies and Archives 84 Union Street, Oldham, OL1
1DN Tel: 0161-911-4654 Email: archives@oldham.gov.uk &
localstudies@oldham.gov.uk WWW: http://www.oldham.gov.uk/archives
http://www.oldham.gov.uk/local_studies
Ormskirk Library, Burscough Street, Ormskirk, L39 2EN Tel: 01695
573448 1901 census
Prestwich Library Longfield Centre, Prestwich, M25 1AY Tel: 0161 253
7214 Tel: 0161 253 7218 Email: Prestwich.lib@bury.gov.uk
Radcliffe Library Stand Lane, Radcliffe, M26 9WR Tel: 0161 253 7160
Fax: 0161 253 7165 Email: Radcliuffe.lib@bury.gov.uk
Ramsbottom Library Carr Street, Ramsbottom, BL0 9AE Tel: 01706
822484 Fax: 01706 824638 Email: Ramsbottom.lib@bury.gov.uk
Rawtenstall Library, Haslingden Road, Rawtenstall, Rossendale, BB4
6QU Tel: 01706 227911 1901 census
Rochdale Local Studies Library The Esplanade, Rochdale, OL16 4TY
Tel: 01706 864915 Temporary address until September 2002: Floor 3
Champness Hall, Drake Street, Rochdale OL16 1PB
Salford Local History Library Peel Park, Salford, M5 4WU Tel: 0161
736 2649
Salford Museum & Art Gallery Peel Park, Salford, M5 4WU Tel: 0161
736 2649

Email: info@lifetimes.org.uk WWW: www.lifetimes.org.uk
St Anne's Library, 254 Clifton Drive, St Anne's on Sea, FY8 1NR Tel: 01253 643900 1901 census
The Harris Reference Library Market Square, Preston, PR1 2PP Tel: 01772 404010 Fax: 01772 555527 Email: harris@airtime.co.uk
Working Class Movement Library Jubilee House, 51 The Crescent, Salford, M5 4WX Tel: 0161-736-3601 Fax: 0161-737 4115

Lancashire - Wigan
Abram Library Vicarage Road, Abram, Wigan, WN2 5QX Tel: 1942866350
Ashton Library Wigan Road, Ashton in Makerfield, Wigan, WN2 9B Tel: 01942 727119
Aspull Library Oakfield Crescent, Aspull, Wigan, WN2 1XJ Tel: 01942 831303
Atherton Library York Street, Atherton, Manchester, M46 9JH Tel: 01942 404817 Tel: 01942 4044816
Beech Hill Library Buckley Street West, Beech Hill, Wigan, WN6 7PQ
Golbourne Library Tanners Lane, Golbourne, Warrington, WA3 3AW Tel: 01942 777800
Hindley Library Market Street, Hindley, Wigan, WN2 3AN Tel: 01942 255287
Ince Library Smithy Green, Ince, Wigan, WN2 2AT Tel: 01942 255287
Leigh Library Turnpike Centre, Civic Square, Leigh, WN7 1EB Tel: 01942 404557
Marsh Green Library Harrow Road, Marsh Green, Wigan Tel: 01942 760041
Orrell Library Orrell Post, Orrell, Wigan, WN5 8LY Tel: 01942 705060
Shevington Library Gathurst Lane, Shevington, Wigan, WN6 8HA Tel: 01257 252618
Standish Library Cross Street, Standish, Wigan, WN6 0HQ Tel: 01257 400496
Tyldesley Library Stanley Street, Tyldesley, Manchester, M29 8AH Tel: 01942 882504
Wigan Library College Avenue, Wigan, WN1 1NN Tel: 01942 827619
Wigan M B C - Leisure Services Department Information Unit, Station Road, Wigan, WN1 1WN

Leicestershire
Hinckley Library Local Studies Collection Hinckley Library, Lancaster Road, Hinckley, LE10 0AT Tel: 01455-635106 Fax: 01455-251385
Leicester Reference and Information Library, Bishop Street, Leicester, LE1 6AA Tel: 0116 299 5401 1901 census
Leicestershire Libraries & Information Service 929 - 931 Loughborough Road, Rothley, LE7 7NH Tel: 0116-267-8023 Fax: 0116-267-8039
Loughborough Library Local Studies Collection Granby Street, Loughborough, LE11 3DZ Tel: 01509-238466 Email: slaterjohn@hotmail.com
Market Harborough Library & Local Studies Collection Pen Lloyd Library, Adam and Eve Street, Market Harborough, LE16 7LT Tel: 01858-82127
Melton Mowbray Library Wilton Road, Melton Mowbray, LE13 0UJ Tel: 01664 560161WWW: www.leics.gov.uk
Southfields Library, Reader Development Services, Saffron Lane, Leicester, LE2 6QS

Lincolnshire
Boston Library County Hall, Boston, PE21 6LX Tel: 01205 310010
Gainsborough Library Cobden Street, Gainsborough, DN21 2NG Tel: 01427 614780
Grantham Library Issac Newton Centre, Grantham, NG1 9LD Tel: 01476 591411
Lincoln Cathedral Library Lincoln Cathedral Library, The Cathedral, Lincoln, LN2 1PZ England Tel: 01522-544544 Fax: 01522-511307
Lincolnshire County Library Local Studies Section, Lincoln Central Library, Free School Lane, Lincoln, LN1 1EZ Tel: 01522-510800 Fax: 01522-575011 Email: lincoln.library@lincolnshire.gov.uk WWW: www.lincolnshire.gov.uk/library/services/family.htm
Stamford Library High Street, Stamford, PE9 2BB Tel: 01780 763442

Lincolnshire - North East
Grimsby Central Library Reference Department Central Library, Town Hall Square, Great Grimsby, DN31 1HG Tel: 01472-323635 Fax: 01472-323634

Lincolnshire - North
Scunthorpe Central Library Carlton Street, Scunthorpe, DN15 6TX Tel: 01724-860161 Email: scunthorpe.ref@central-library.demon.co.uk WWW: www.nothlincs.gov.uk/library

Liverpool
Liverpool Record Office & Local History Department Central Library, William Brown Street, Liverpool, L3 8EW Tel: 0151 233 5817 Email: recoffice.central.library@liverpool.gov.uk WWW: http://www.liverpool.gov.uk

London
Bancroft Library, 277 Bancroft Road, London, E1 4DQ Tel: 020 8980 4366 1901 census
Bishopsgate Institute Reference Librarian, 230 Bishopsgate, London, EC2M 4QH Tel: (020) 7247-6198 Fax: (020) 7247-6318
Bracknell Library - Local Studies, Town Square, Bracknell, RG12 1BH Tel: 01344 352515 Fax: 01344 411392
Brent Community History Library & Archive 152 Olive Road, London, NW2 6UY Tel: (020) 8937 3541 Email: archive@brent.gov.uk WWW: www.brent.gov.uk
British Library British Library Building, 96 Euston Road, London, NW1 2DB Tel: (020) 712-7677 WWW: http://www.portico.bl.uk Reader/admissions@bl.uk
British Library - Early Printed Collections 96 Euston Road, London, NW1 2DB Tel: (020) 7412-7673 Fax: (020) 7412-7577 Email: rare-books@bl.uk WWW: http://www.bl.uk
British Library Newspaper Library Colindale Avenue, London, NW9 5HE Tel: 020-7412-7353 Email: newspaper@bl.uk WWW: http://www.bl.uk/collections/newspaper/ The National archive collections of British and Overseas newspapers as well as major collections of popular magazines. Open Mon to Sat 10am to 4.45pm.
British Library of Political and Economic Science London School of Economics, 10 Portugal Street, London, WC2A 2HD Tel: 020 7955 7223 Email: info@lse.ac.uk WWW: http://www.lse.ac.uk
British Library Oriental and India Office Collections 96 Euston Road, London, NW1 2DB Tel: (020) 7412-7873 Fax: (020) 7412-7641 Email: oioc-enquiries@bl.uk WWW: http://www.bl.uk/collections/oriental
Caird Library - National Maritime Museum Park Row, Greenwich, London, SE10 9NF Tel: (020) 8312 6673 Fax: (020) 8312-6632 Email: ABuchanan@nmm.ac.uk WWW: http://www.nmm.ac.uk
Catholic Central Library Lancing Street, London, NW1 1ND Tel: (020) 7383-4333 Email: librarian@catholic-library.demon.co.uk WWW: www.catholic-library.demon.co.uk
Chelsea Public Library Old Town Hall, King's Road, London, SW3 5EZ Tel: (020) 7352-6056 Tel: (020) 7361-4158 Local Studies Collection on Royal Borough of Kensington & Chelsea south of Fulham Road
Dr Williams's Library 14 Gordon Square, London, WC1H 0AR Tel: (020) 7387-3727 Email: 101340.2541@compuserve.com The General Registers of Protestant Dissenters (Dr Williams's Library Registers) were surrendered to the Registrar General and are now at The Public Record Office (RG4/4666-4673)
Ealing Local History Centre Central Library, 103 Broadway Centre, Ealing, London, W5 5JY Tel: (020) 8567-3656-ext-37 Email: localhistory@hotmail.com WWW: www.ealing.gov.uk/libraries Closed Sundays & Mondays
Fawcett Library London Guildhall University, Old Castle Street, London, E1 7NT Tel: (020) 7320-1189 Email: fawcett@lgu.ac.uk WWW: http://www.lgu.ac.uk./fawcett
Guildhall Library, Manuscripts Section Aldermanbury, London, EC2P 2EJ Tel: (020) 7332-1863 Email: manuscripts.guildhall@corpoflondon.gov.uk WWW: http://ihr.sas.ac.uk/ihr/gh/ City of London parish records, probate records, City Livery
Hammersmith Central Library Shepherds Bush Road, London, W6 7AT Tel: 020 8753 3816 Fax: 020 8753 3815 WWW: www.lbhf.gov.uk
House of Commons Library House of Commons, 1 Derby Gate, London, SW1A 2DG Tel: (020) 7219-5545 Fax: (020) 7219-3921
Huguenot Library University College, Gower Street, London, WC1E 6BT Tel: (020) 7679 7094 Email: s.massilk@ucl.ac.uk WWW: http://www.ucl.ac.uk/ucl-info/divisions/library/hugenot.htm
Imperial College Archives London University, Room 455 Sherfield Building, Imperial College, London, SW7 2AZ Tel: 020 7594 8850 Fax: 020 7584 3763 Email: archivist@ic.ac.uk WWW: http://www.lib.ic.ac.uk
Institute of Commonwealth Studies 28 Russell Square, London, WC1B 5DS Tel: (020) 7862 8844 Fax: (020) 7862 8820 Email: icommlib@sas.ac.uk WWW: http://sas.ac.uk/commonwealthstudies The Institute of Commonwealth Studies hosts and leads the CASBAH project which aims to identify and map research resources for caribbean studies and the history of Black and Asian people in Britain.
James Clavell Library, Royal Arsenal (West), Warren Lane, Woolwich, London, SE18 6ST Tel: 020 8312 7125, Email: library@firepower.org.uk WWW: www.firepower.org.uk
Jewish Museum The Sternberg Centre for Judaism, 80 East End Road, Finchley, London, N3 2SY Tel: (020) 8349 1143 Email: jml.finchley@lineone.net WWW: www.jewmusm.ort.org
Jewish Studies Library University College, Gower Street, London, WC1E 6BT Tel: (020) 7387 7050
Lambeth Palace Library Lambeth Palace Road, London, SE1 7JU Tel: (020) 7898 1400 WWW: www.lambethpalacelibrary.org
Lewisham Local Studies & Archives Lewisham Library, 199 - 201 Lewisham High Street, Lewisham, London, SE13 6LG Tel: (020) 8297-0682 Fax: (020) 8297-1169 Email: local.studies@lewisham.gov.uk WWW: http://www.lewisham.gov.uk Covering the Parishes of Lewisham, Lee & St Paul's, Deptford. Appointments advisable.

Library of the Religious Society of Friends (Quakers) Friends House, 173 - 177 Euston Rd, London, NW1 2BJ Tel: 0207 663 1135 Email; library@quaker.org.uk WWW: http://www.quaker.org/library
Library of the Royal College of Surgeons of England 35-43 Lincoln's Inn Fields, London, WC2A 3PN Tel: (020) 7869 6520 Email: library@rseng.ac.uk
Linnean Society of London Burlington House, Piccadilly, London, W1J 0BF Tel: 020 7437 4479 Email: gina@linnean.org WWW: http://www.linnean.org
Local Studies Collection for Chiswick & Brentford Chiswick Public Library, Dukes Avenue, Chiswick, London, W4 2AB Tel: (020) 8994-5295 Restricted opening hours for local history room: please telephone before visiting
LB of Camden Local Studies & Archive Centre
Holborn Library, 32 - 38 Theobalds Road, London, WC1X 8PA Tel: 020 7974 6342 Email: localstudies@camden.gov.uk WWW: www.camden.gov.uk Closed Wednesday. Open: Mon & Thurs 10 to 7pm; Tues & Fri 10 to 6pm; Sats 10 to 1pm and 2pm to 5pm
LB of Enfield Libraries Southgate Town Hall, Green Lanes, Palmers Green, London, N13 4XD Tel: (020) 8379-2724 Fax: (020) 8379 2761
LB of Greenwich Local History Library Woodlands, 90 Mycenae Road, Blackheath, London, SE3 7SE Tel: (020) 8858 4631 Email: local.history@greenwich.gov.uk WWW: www.greenwich.gov.uk The library will be moving to a new Heritage Centre autumn 2002. Please contact the library for more details
LB of Islington Central Reference Library Central Reference Library, 2 Fieldway Crescent, London, N5 1PF Tel: (020) 7619-6931 Email: local.history@islington.gov.uk WWW: http://www.islington.gov.uk Reorganisation is imminent - planned move to Finsbury Library, 245 St John Street, London EC1V 4NB (020) 7527 6931 (020) 7527 6937 Collection covers the south of the LB of Islington.
LB of Islington Finsbury Library 245 St John Street, London, EC1V 4NB Tel: (020) 7527-7994 WWW: www.islington.gov.uk/htm
LB of Lambeth Archives Department Minet Library, 52 Knatchbull Road, Lambeth, London, SE5 9QY Tel: (020) 7926 6076 Email: lambetharchives@lambeth.gov.uk
LB of Newham Archives & Local Studies Library Stratford Library, 3 The Grove, London, E5 1EL Tel: (020) 8557 8856 Fax: (020) 8503 1525
LB of Wandsworth Local studies Local Studies ServiceBattersea Library, 265 Lavender Hill, London, SW11 1JB Tel: (020) 8871 7753 Fax: (020) 7978-4376 Email: wandsworthmuseum@wandsworth.gov.uk WWW: www.wandsworth.gov.uk Open Tues & Wed 10am to 88pm, Fri 10am to 5pm, Sat 9am to 1pm - Research service offerred - £7.00 per half hour (the minimum fee) apointment advised to ensure archives, hard copy newspapers (if not microfilmed)
London University - Institute of Advanced Studies Charles Clore House, 17 Russell Square, London, WC1B 5DR Tel: (020) 7637 1731 Fax: (020) 7637 8224 Email: ials.lib@sas.ac.uk WWW: http://ials.sas.ac.uk
Manuscripts Room Library Services, University College, Gower Street, London, WC1E 6BT Tel: (020) 7387 7050 Fax: 020 7380 7727 Email: mssrb@ucl.ac.uk WWW: http://www.ucl.ac.uk/library/special-coll/
Museum in Docklands Project Library & Archives, Library & Archive, No 1 Warehouse, West India Quay, Hertsmere Road, London, E14 4AL Tel: (020) 7515-1162 Fax: (020) 7538-0209 Email: docklands@museum-london.org.uk
Museum of London Library 150 London Wall, London, EC2Y 5HN Tel: 020 7814 5588 Fax: 020 7600-1058 Email: info@museumoflondon.org.uk WWW: http://museumoflondon.org.uk
Museum of the Order of St John St John's Gate, St John's Lane, Clerkenwell, London, EC1M 4DA Tel: (020) 7253-6644 WWW: www.sja.org.uk/history
National Gallery Library and Archive Trafalgar Square, London, WC2N 5DN Tel: 020 7747 2542 Email: iad@ng-london.org.uk WWW: http://www.nationalgallery.org.uk
The Public Library 305 Queens Avenue, London, N6B 3L7 Tel: 519-661-4600
Regional Film Archive - London, British Film Institute - Library & Film Archive, 21 Stephen Street, London, W1T 1LN Tel: 020 7957 4824 WWW: www.bfi.org.uk
Royal Armouries H.M Tower Of London, Tower Hill, London, EC3N 4AB Tel: (020) 7480 6358 ext 30 Fax: (020) 7481 2922 Email: Bridgett.Clifford@armouries.org.uk
Royal B of Kensington & Chelsea Libraries & Arts Service Central Library, Phillimore Walk, Kensington, London, W8 7RX Tel: (020) 7361-3036 Email: information.services@rbkc.gov.uk WWW: www.rbkc.gov.uk
Royal Institute of British Architects' Library Manuscripts & archives Collection, 66 Portland Place, London, W1N 4AD Tel: 020 7307 3615 Fax: 020 7631 1802
Royal Soc of Chemistry Library & Information Centre Burlington House, Piccadilly, London, W1J 0BA Tel: (020) 7437 8656 Fax: (020) 7287 9798 Email: library@rsc.org WWW: www.rsc.org
School of Oriental and African Studies library Thornhaugh Street, Russell Square, London, WC1H 0XG Tel: 020 7323 6112 Fax: 020 7636 2834 Email: lib@soas.ac.uk WWW: http://www.soas.ac.uk/library/
Society of Antiquaries of London Burlington House, Piccadilly, London, W1J 0BE Tel: 020 7479 7084 6967 Email: library@sal.org.uk WWW: www.sal.org.uk

Society of Genealogists - Library 14 Charterhouse Buildings, Goswell Road, London, EC1M 7BA Tel: 020-7251-8799 Tel: 020-7250-0291 Fax: 020-7250-1800 Email: library@sog.org.uk WWW: http://www.sog.org.uk
Southwark Local Studies Library 211 Borough High Street, Southwark, London, SE1 1JA Tel: 0207-403-3507 Email: local.studies.library@southwark.gov.uk WWW: www.southwark.gov.uk
The Kenneth Ritchie Wimbledon Library The All England Lawn Tennis & Croquet Club, Church Road, Wimbledon, London, SW19 5AE Tel: (020) 8946 6131 WWW: www.wimbledon.org Contains the world's finest collection of books and periodicals relating to lawn tennis
The Library & Museum of Freemasonry Freemasons' Hall, 60 Great Queen Street, London, WC2B 5AZ Tel: (020) 7395 9257
The Science Museum Library Imperial College Road, South Kensington, London, SW7 5NH Tel: 020 7938 8234 Tel: 020 7938 8218
The Wellcome Trust 183 Euston Rd, London, NW1 2BE Tel: (020) 7611 8888 Fax: (020) 7611 8545 Email: infoserv@wellcome.ac.uk WWW: www.wellcome.ac.uk
The Women's Library Old Castle Street, London, E1 7NT Tel: (020) 7320-1189 Fax: (020) 7320-1188 Email: fawcett@lgu.ac.uk WWW: http://www.lgu.ac.uk/fawcett
Tower Hamlets Local History Library & Archives Bancroft Library, 277 Bancroft Road, London, E1 4DQ Tel: (020) 8980 4366 Ext 129 Fax: (020) 8983-4510
Trades Union Congress Library Collections 236 - 250 Holloway Road, London, N7 6PP Tel: (020) 7753 3191 Email: tuclib@unl.ac.uk WWW: http://www.unl.ac.uk/library/tuc
University of London (Library - Senate House) Palaeography Room, Senate House, Malet Street, London, WC1E 7HU Tel: (020) 7862 8475 Fax: 020 7862 8480 Email: library@ull.ac.uk WWW: http://www.ull.ac.uk
Victoria & Albert Museum - National Art Library Cromwell Road, South Kensington, London, SW7 2RL Tel: (020) 7938 8315 Fax: (020) 7938 8461
Victoria & Albert Museum - Archive of Art and Design Blythe House, 23 Blythe Road, London, W14 0QF Tel: (020) 7603 1514 Fax: (020) 7602 0980 Email: archive@vam.ac.uk WWW: www.nal.vam.ac.uk
Wellcome Library - Contemporary Medical Archives 183 Euston Road, London, NW1 2BE Tel: (020) 7611 8483 Fax: (020) 7611 8703 Email: library@wellcome.ac.uk WWW: www.wellcome.ac.uk/library Library catalogue is available through the internet: telnet://wihm.ucl.ac.uk
Wellcome Library- History & Understanding of Medicine
Wellcome Library for the History of Medicine - Department of Western Manuscripts 183 Euston Road, London, NW1 2BE Tel: (020) 7611-8582 Fax: (020) 7611 8369 Email: library@wellcome.ac.uk WWW: www.wellcome.ac.uk/library Library catalogue is available through the internet: http://library.wellcome.ac.uk
Westminster Abbey Library & Muniment Room Westminster Abbey, London, SW1P 3PA Tel: (020) 7222-5152-Ext-4830 Fax: (020) 7226-4827 Email: library@westminster-abbey.org WWW: www.westminster-abbey.org
Westminster University Archives Information Systems & Library Services, 4-12 Little Titchfield Street, London, W1W 7UW Tel: 020 7911 5000 ext 2524 Fax: 020 7911 5894 Email: archive@westminster.ac.uk WWW: www.wmin.ac.uk The archive is organisationally within the Library but is a separate entity. The University of Westminster Libraries do not have special collections relating to family and local history

Manchester
Chethams Library Long Millgate, Manchester, M3 1SB Tel: 0161 834 7961 Fax: 0161 839 5797 Email: chetlib@dial.pipex.com
Manchester Archives & Local Studies Manchester Central Library, St Peter's Square, Manchester, M2 5PD Tel: 0161-234-1979 Fax: 0161-234-1927 Email: lsu@libraries.manchester.gov.uk WWW: http://www..manchester.gov.uk/libraries/index.htm
Methodist Archives and Research Centre John Rylands University Library, 150 Deansgate, Manchester, M3 3EH Tel: 0161 834 5343
Oldham Local Studies and Archives 84 Union Street, Oldham, OL1 1DN Tel: 0161-911-4654 Email: archives@oldham.gov.uk & localstudies@oldham.gov.uk WWW: http://www.oldham.gov.uk/archives & http://www.oldham.gov.uk/local_studies

Medway
Medway Archives and Local Studies Centre Civic Centre, Strood, Rochester, ME2 4AU Tel: 01634-332714 Email: archives@medway.gov.uk & local.studies@medway.gov.uk WWW: http://cityark.medway.gov.uk

Merseyside
Crosby Library (South Sefton Local History Unit) Crosby Road North, Waterloo, Liverpool, L22 0LQ Tel: 0151 257 6401 Email: local-history.south@leisure.sefton.gov.uk The Local History Units serve Sefton Borough Council area. The South Sefton Unit covers Bootle, Crosby, Maghull and other communities south of the River Alt. The North Sefton Unit covers Southport, Formby
Wirral Central Library Borough Road, Birkenhead, CH41 2XB Tel: 0151 652 6106 Tel: 0151 652 6107/8 Fax: 0151 653 7320 Email: birkenhead.library@merseymail.com

Huyton Central Library
Huyton Library, Civic Way, Huyton, Knowsley, L36 9GD Tel: 0151-443-3738 Fax: 0151 443 3739
Email: eileen.hume.dlcs@knowsley.gov.uk
WWW: http://www.knowsley.gov.uk/leisure/libraries/huyton/index.html
Southport Library (North Sefton Local History Unit)
Lord Street, Southport, PR8 1DJ Tel: 0151 934 2119 The Local History Units serve Sefton Borough Council area. The North Sefton Unit covers Southport, Formby. The South Sefton Unit covers Bootle, Crosby, Maghull and other communities south of the River Alt
St Helen's Local History & Archives Library Central Library, Gamble Institute, Victoria Square, St Helens, WA10 1DY Tel: 01744-456952 Fax: 01744 20836 No research undertaken

Middlesex
LB of Harrow Local History Collection Civic Centre Library, PO Box 4, Station Road, Harrow, HA1 2UU Tel: 0208 424 1055 Tel: 0208 424 1056 Fax: 0181-424-1971 Email: civiccentre.library@harrow.gov.uk

Norfolk
Family History Shop & Library The Family History Shop, 24d Magdalen Street, Norwich, NR3 1HU Tel: 01603 621152, Fax: Email: jenlibrary@aol.com WWW: http://www.jenlibrary.u-net.com
Great Yarmouth Central Library Tolhouse Street, Great Yarmouth, NR30 2SH Tel: 01493-844551 Tel: 01493-842279 Fax: 01493-857628
Kings Lynn Library London Road, King's Lynn, PE30 5EZ Tel: 01553-772568 Tel: 01553 761393 Email: kings.lynn.lib@norfolk.gov.uk WWW: http://www.norfolk.gov.uk/council/departments/lis/nslynn.htm
Norfolk Library & Information Service Gildengate House, Anglia Square, Norwich, NR3 1AX Tel: 01603-215254 Email: norfolk.studies.lib@norfolk.gov.uk
Thetford Public Library Raymond Street, Thetford, IP24 2EA Tel: 01842-752048 Fax: 01842-750125 Email: thetford.lib@norfolk.gov.uk WWW: www.culture.norfolk.gov.uk

Northumberland
Alnwick Library Green Batt, Alnwick, NE66 1TU Tel: 01665-602689
Berwick upon Tweed Library Church Street, Berwick upon Tweed, TD15 1EE Tel: 01289-307320 Fax: 01289-308299
Blyth Library Bridge Street, Blyth, NE24 2DJ Tel: 01670-361352
Border History Museum and Library Moothall, Hallgate, Hexham, NE46 3NH Tel: 01434-652349 Fax: 01434-652425 Email: museum@tynedale.com
Hexham Library Queens Hall, Beaumont Street, Hexham, NE46 3LS Tel: 01434 652474 Email: cheane@northumberland.gov.uk

Nottinghamshire
Arnold Library Front Street, Arnold, NG5 7EE Tel: 0115-920-2247
Beeston Library Foster Avenue, Beeston, NG9 1AE Tel: 0115-925-5168
Eastwood Library Wellington Place, Eastwood, NG16 3GB Tel: 01773-712209
Mansfield Library Four Seasons Centre, Westgate, Mansfield, NG18 1NH Tel: 01623-627591 Email: mansfield.library@nottscc.gov.uk
Newark Library Beaumont Gardens, Newark, NG24 1UW Tel: 01636-703966 Fax: 01636-610045

Nottingham Central Library : Local Studies Centre
Angel Row, Nottingham, NG1 6HP Tel: 0115 915 2873Email: local-studies.library@nottinghamcity.gov.uk WWW: www.nottinghamcity.gov.uk/libraries
Retford Library Denman Library, Churchgate, Retford, DN22 6PE Tel: 01777-708724 Fax: 01777-710020
Southwell Minster Library
Minster Office, Trebeck Hall, Bishop's Drive, Southwell, NG25 0JP Tel: 01636-812649 Fax: 01636 815904
Email: pat@southwellminster.prestell.co.uk
Sutton in Ashfield Library
Devonshire Mall, Sutton in Ashfield, NG17 1BP
Tel: 01623-556296 Fax: 01623-551962
University of Nottingham Hallward Library, University Park, Nottingham, NG7 2RD Tel: 0115-951-4514 Fax: 0115-951-4558 WWW: http://www.nottingham.ac.uk/library/
West Bridgford Library
Bridgford Road, West Bridgford, NG2 6AT
Tel: 0115-981-6506 Fax: 0115-981-3199

Oxfordshire
Abingdon Library
The Charter, Abingdon, OX14 3LY Tel: 01235-520374
Fax: 01235 532643 Email: abingdonlibrary@hotmail.com
Angus Library Regent's Park College, Pusey Street, Oxford, OX1 2LB Tel: 01865 288142 Fax: 01865 288121
Banbury library Marlborough Road, Banbury, OX16 8DF Tel: 01295-262282 Fax: 01295-264331
The Bodelian Library Broad Street, Oxford, OX1 3BG Tel: 01865 277000 Fax: 01865 277182 WWW: www.bodley.ox.ac.uk
Henley Library Ravenscroft Road, Henley on Thames, RG9 2DH Tel: 01491-575278 Fax: 01491-576187

Centre for Oxfordshire Studies Central Library, Westgate, Oxford, OX1 1DJ Tel: 01865-815749 Email: cos@oxfordshire.gov.uk
WWW: www.oxfordshire.gov.uk
Middle East Centre St Anthony's College, Pusey Street, Oxford, OX2 6JF Tel: 01865 284706 Fax: 01865 311475
Nuffield College Library Oxford, OX1 1NF Tel: 01865 278550 Fax: 01865 278621
Pusey House Library Pusey House, 61 St Giles, Oxford, OX1 1LZ Tel: 01865 278415 Fax: 01865 278415
River & Rowing Museum
Rowing & River Museum, Mill Meadows, Henley on Thames, RG9 1BF Tel: 01491 415625 Fax: 01491 415601 Email: museum@rrm.co.uk
WWW: www.rrm.co.uk Thames linked families especially lock keepers , boat builders
Rhodes House Library Bodleian Library, South Parks Road, Oxford, OX1 3RG Tel: 01865 270909 Fax: 01865 270912
Wantage Library Stirlings Road, Wantage, OX12 7BB Tel: 01235 762291
Witney Library Welch Way, Witney, OX8 7HH Tel: 01993-703659

Peterborough
Peterborough Local Studies Collection Central Library, Broadway, Peterborough, PE1 1RX Tel: 01733 348343 Email: libraries@peterborough.gov.uk The telephone number may change in 2002

Rutland
Oakham Library, Catmos Street, Oakham, LE15 6HW Tel: 01572 722918 1901 census

Shropshire
Wrekin Local Studies Forum Madeley Library, Russell Square, Telford, TF7 5BB Tel: 01952 586575 Email: wlst@library.madeley.uk WWW: www.madeley.org.uk

Somerset
Bath Central Library 19 The Podium, Northgate Street, Bath, BA1 5AN Tel: 01225-428144 Fax: 01225-331839
Bristol University Library - Special Collections
Tyndall Avenue, Bristol, BS8 1TJ Tel: 0117 928 8014 Email: library@bris.ac.uk
WWW: www.bris.ac.uk/depts/library
Bridgewater Library Binford Place, Bridgewater, TA6 3LF Tel: 01278-450082 Fax: 01278-451027 Email: pcstoyle@somerset.gov.uk WWW: www.somerset.gov.uk
Frome Library Justice Lane, Frome, BA11 1BA Tel: 01373-462215
Nailsea Library Somerset Square, Nailsea, BS19 2EX Tel: 01275-854583
Somerset Studies Library
Paul Street, Taunton, TA1 3XZ Tel: 01823-340300
Weston Library The Boulevard, Weston Super Mare, BS23 1PL Tel: 01934-636638 Email: weston.library@n-somerset.gov.uk
Yeovil Library King George Street, Yeovil, BA20 1PY Tel: 01935-421910 Fax: 01935-431847 Email: ransell@somerset.gov.uk

Staffordshire
Barton Library Dunstall Road, Barton under Needwood, DE13 8AX Tel: 01283-713753
Biddulph Library Tunstall Road, Biddulph, Stoke on Trent, ST8 6HH Tel: 01782-512103
Brewood Library Newport Street, Brewood, ST19 9DT Tel: 01902-850087
Burton Library Burton Library, Riverside, High Street, Burton on Trent, DE14 1AH Tel: 01283-239556 Fax: 01283-239571 Email: burton.library@staffordshire.gov.uk
Cannock Library
Manor Avenue, Cannock, WS11 1AA Tel: 01543-502019 Email: cannock.library@staffordshire.gov.uk
Cheslyn Hay Library
Cheslyn Hay, Walsall, WS56 7AE Tel: 01922-413956
Codsall Library
Histons Hill, Codsall, WV8 1AA Tel: 01902-842764
Great Wyrley Library
John's Lane, Great Wyrley, Walsall, WS6 6BY
Tel: 01922-414632
Keele University Library
Keele, ST5 5BG Tel: 01782 583237 Fax: 01782 711553 Email: library@keele.ac.uk WWW: www.keele.ac.uk/library
Kinver Library
Vicarage Drive, Kinver, Stourbridge, DY7 6HJ
Tel: 01384-872348
Leek Library
Nicholson Institute, Stockwell Street, Leek, ST13 6DW Tel: 01538-483210 Email: leek.library@staffordshire.gov.uk

Lichfield Library (Local Studies Section) Lichfield Library, The Friary, Lichfield, WS13 6QG Tel: 01543-510720 Fax: 01543-411138

Newcastle Library Ironmarket, Newcastle under Lyme, ST5 1AT Tel: 01782-297310 Email: newcastle.library@staffordshire.gov.uk
Penkridge Library Bellbrock, Penkridge, ST19 9DL Tel: 01785-712916
Perton Library Severn Drive, Perton, WV6 7QU Tel: 01902-755794 Fax: 01902-756123 Email: perton.library@staffordshire.gov.uk
Rugeley Library Anson Street, Rugeley, WS16 2BB Tel: 01889-583237
Stoke on Trent City Archives Hanley Library, Bethesda Street, Hanley, Stoke on Trent, ST1 3RS Tel: 01782-238420 Fax: 01782-238499 Email: stoke.archives@stoke.gov.uk WWW: www.staffordshire.gov.uk/archives
Tamworth Library Corporation Street, Tamworth, B79 7DN Tel: 01827-475645 Email: tamworth.library@staffordshire.gov.uk WWW: www.staffordshire.gov.uk/locgov/county/cars/tamlib.htm IGI (Derby, Leics, Notts, Shrops, Staffs, Warks, Worcs). Parish registers for Tamworth. Census for Tamworth and District, 1841 - 91. Street directories for Staffs and Warks.
Uttoxeter Library High Street, Uttoxeter, ST14 7JQ Tel: 01889-256371
William Salt Library Eastgate Street, Stafford, ST16 2LZ Tel: 01785-278372 Email: william.salt.library@staffordshire.gov.uk WWW: http://www.staffordshire.gov.uk/archives/salt.htm
Wombourne Library Windmill Bank, Wombourne, WV5 9JD Tel: 01902-892032

Stockport MBC
Local Heritage Library Central Library, Wellington Road South, Stockport, SK1 3RS Tel: 0161-474-4530 Fax: 0161-474-7750 Email: localheritage.library@stockport.gov.uk

Surrey
LB of Merton Local Studies Centre Merton Civic Centre, London Road, Morden, SM4 5DX Tel: (020) 8545-3239 Fax: (020) 8545-4037 Email: mertonlibs@compuserve.com
LB of Richmond upon Thames Local Studies Library Old Town Hall, Whittaker Avenue, Richmond upon Thames, TW9 1TP Tel: (020) 8332 6820 Fax: (020) 8940 6899 Email: localstudies@richmond.gov.uk WWW: http://www.richmond.gov.uk Closed Mondays Open Tues 1-5; Wed 1-8pm; Thurs & Fri 10 to 12; Sat 10 to 12 & 1 to 5
Kingston Upon Thames Museum, North Kingston Centre, Richmond Road, New Malden, KT3 3UQ Tel: 020 8547 6738 1901 census
Surrey History Service Library Surrey History Centre, 130 Goldsworth Road, Woking, GU21 1ND Tel: 01483-594594 Fax: 01483-594595 Email: shs@surreycc.gov.uk WWW: http://.shs.surreycc.gov.uk
Sutton Central Library St Nicholas Way, Sutton, SM1 1EA Tel: (020) 8770 4745 Email: sutton.information@sutton.gov.uk WWW: www.sutton.gov.uk

Sussex
Sussex University Library Manuscript Collections, Falmer, Brighton, BN1 9QLTel: 01273 606755 Fax: 01273 678441
East Sussex -East
Brighton Local Studies Library Church Street, Brighton, BN1 1 UD Tel: 01273-296971 Fax: 01273-296962 Email: brightonlibrary@pavilion.co.uk
Hove Reference Library 182 -186 Church Road, Hove, BN3 2EG Tel: 01273-296942
Sussex - West
Worthing Reference Library Worthing Library, Richmond Road, Worthing, BN11 1HD Tel: 01903-212060 Fax: 01903-821902 Email: worthinglibrary@hotmail.com Largest library in West Sussex and specialist centre for family history sources.

Tyne and Wear
City Library & Arts Centre 28 - 30 Fawcett Street, Sunderland, BR1 1RE Tel: 0191-514235 Fax: 0191-514-8444
Local Studies Centre Central Library, Northumberland Square, North Shields, NE30 1QU Tel: (0)191-200-5424 Fax: 0191 200 6118 Email: eric.hollerton@northtyneside.gov.uk WWW: www.northtyneside.gov.uk/libraries.html
South Tyneside Central Library Prince Georg Square, South Shields, NE33 2PE Tel: 0191-427-1818-Ext-7860 Fax: 0191-455-8085 Email: reference.library@s-tyneside-mbc.gov.uk WWW: www.s-tyneside-mbc.gov.uk
Central Library Northumberland Square, North Shields, NE3O 1Q Tel: 0191-200-5424 Fax: 0191-200-611 Email: cen@ntlib.demon.co.uk
Gateshead Central Library & Local Studies Department Prince Consort Road, Gateshead, NE8 4LN Tel: 0191-477-3478 Email: a.lang@libarts.gatesheadmbc.gov.uk WWW: http://ris.niaa.org.ukw & www.gateshead.gov.uk/ls
Newcastle Local Studies Centre City Library, Princess Square, Newcastle upon Tyne, NE99 1DX Tel: 0191 277 4116 Fax: 0191 277 4118 Email: local.studies@newcastle.gov.uk WWW: www.newcastle.gov.uk
Robinson Library University of Newcastle upon Tyne, Newcastle Upon Tyne, NE2 4HQ Tel: 0191 222 7671 Fax: 0191 222 6235 Email: library@ncl.ac.uk WWW: http://www.ncl.ac.uk/library/

Warwickshire
Atherstone Library Long Street, Atherstone, CV9 1AX Tel: 01827 712395 Email: atherstonelibrary@warwickshire.gov.uk
Bedworth Library 18 High Street, Bedworth, Nuneaton, CV12 8NF Tel: 024 7631 2267 Email: bedworthlibrary@warwickshire.gov.uk
Kenilworth Library Smalley Place, Kenilworth, CV8 1QG Tel: 01926 852595 Email: kenilworthlibrary@warwickshire.gov.uk
Nuneaton Library Church Street, Nuneaton, CV11 4DR Tel: 024 7638 4027 Email: nuneatonlibrary@warwickshire.gov.uk
Rugby Library Little ElborowStreet, Rugby, CV21 3BZ Tel: 01788 533250 Email: rugbylibrary@warwickshire.gov.uk
Shakespeare Birthplace Trust - Library Shakespeare Centre Library, Henley Street, Stratford upon Avon, CV37 6QW Tel: 01789-204016 Tel: 01789-201813 Fax: 01789-296083 Email: library@shakespeare.org.uk WWW: http://www.shakespeare.org.uk
Stratford on Avon Library 12 Henley Street, Stratford on Avon, CV37 6PZ Tel: 01789 292209 Email: stratfordlibrary@warwickshire.gov.uk
Sutton Coldfield Library & Local Studies Centre 43 Lower Parade, Sutton Coldfield, B72 1XX Tel: 0121-354-2274 Tel: 0121 464 0164 Fax: 0121 464 0173 Email: sutton.coldfield.reference.lib@birmingham.gov.uk
University of Warwick Library Coventry, CV4 7AL Tel: (024) 76524219
Warwick Library - Warwickshire Local Collection (County Collection) Warwick Library, Barrack Street, Warwick, CV34 4TH Tel: 01926 412189 Tel: 01926 412488 Fax: 01926 412784 Email: warwicklibrary@warwickshire.gov.uk
Warwickshire County Library Leamington Library, Royal Pump Rooms, The Parade, Leamington Spa, CV32 4AA Tel: 01926 74272 Email: leamingtonlibrary@warwickshire.gov.uk

West Midlands
Birmingham University - Special Collections Main Library, University of Birmingham, Edgbaston, Birmingham, B15 2TT Tel: 0121 414 5838 Email: special-collections@bham.ac.uk WWW: www.is.bham.ac.uk
Dudley Archives & Local History Service Mount Pleasant Street, Coseley, Dudley, WV14 9JR Tel: 01384-812770 Fax: 01384-812770 Email: archives.pls@mbc.dudley.gov.uk WWW: www.dudley.gov.uk Family History Research
Local Studies Library Central Library, Smithford Way, Coventry, CV1 1FY Tel: 012476 832336 Fax: 02476 832440 Email: covinfo@discover.co.uk WWW: www.coventry.gov.uk/accent.htm
Sandwell Community History & Archives Service Smethwick Library, High Street, Smethwick, B66 1AB Tel: 0121 558 2561 Fax: 0121 555 6064
Sandwell Community Libraries Town Hall, High Street, West Bromwich, B70 8DX Tel: 0121-569-4909 Fax: 0121-569-4907Email: dm025@viscount.org.uk
Solihull Library Homer Road, Solihull, B91 3RG Tel: 0121-704-6977 The library is NOT an archive repository, sceondary sources only available for Solihull MBC area only
Walsall Local History Centre Essex Street, Walsall, WS2 7AS Tel: 01922-721305Email: localhistorycentre@walsall.gov.uk WWW: http://www.walsall.gov.uk/culturalservices/library/welcome.htm
Wolverhampton Archives & Local Studies 42 - 50 Snow Hill, Wolverhampton, WV2 4AG Tel: 01902 552480 Email: wolverhamptonarchives@dial.pipes.com WWW: http://www.wolverhampton.gov.uk/archives

Wiltshire
Wiltshire Buildings Record, Libraries and Heritage HQ, Bythesea Road, Trowbridge, BA14 8BS Tel: 01225 713740, Email: dorothytreasure@wiltshire.gov.uk
Salisbury Reference and Local Studies Library Market Place, Salisbury, SP1 1BL Tel: 01722 411098 Fax: 01722 413214 WWW: www.wiltshire.gov.uk
Swindon Local Studies Library Swindon Central Library, Regent Circus, Swindon, SN11QG Tel: 01793 463240 Email: swindonref@swindon.gov.uk WWW: http://www.swindon.gov.uk
Wiltshire Archaeological and Natural History Society Wiltshire Heritage Library, 41 Long Street, Devizes, SN10 1NS Tel: 01380 727369 Email: wanhs@wiltshireheritage.org.uk
Wiltshire Buildings Record Society Libraries & Heritage, Bythesea Road, Trowbridge, BA14 8BS
Wiltshire Studies Library Trowbridge Reference Library, Bythesea Road, Trowbridge, BA14 8BS Tel: 01225-713732 Email: libraryenquiries@wiltshire.gov.uk WWW: www.wiltshire.gov.uk
Swindon Borough Library, Reference Library, Regent Circus, Swindon, SN1 1QG Tel: 01793 463240 1901 census

Worcestershire
Bewdley Museum Research Library Load Street, Bewdley, DY12 2AE Tel: 01229-403573
Bromsgrove Library Stratford Road, Bromsgrove, B60 1AP Tel: 01527-575855
Evesham Library Oat Street, Evesham, WR11 4PJ Tel: 01386-442291 Email: eveshamlib@worcestershire.gov.uk WWW: www.worcestershire.gov.uk

Kidderminster Library Market Street, Kidderminster, DY10 1AD Tel: 01562-824500Email: kidderminster@worcestershire.gov.uk WWW: www.worcestershire.gov.uk

Malvern Library Graham Road, Malvern, WR14 2HU Tel: 01684-561223

Redditch Library 15 Market Place, Redditch, B98 8AR Tel: 01527-63291 Email: redditchlibrary@worcestershire.gov.uk

Worcester Library Foregate Street, Worcester, WR1 1DT Tel: 01905 765312 Email: worcesterlib@worcestershire.gov.uk WWW: www.worcestershire.gov.uk/libraries

Yorkshire

York Minster Library York Minster Library & Archives, Dean's Park, York, YO1 2JQ Tel: 01904-625308 Library Tel: 01904-611118 Archives Fax: 01904-611119 Email: library@yorkminster.org archives@yorkminster.org WWW: www.yorkminster.org

Yorkshire Archaeological Society Claremont, 23 Clarendon Rd, Leeds, LS2 9NZ Tel: 0113-245-6342 Tel: 0113 245 7910 Fax: 0113-244-1979 Email: j.heron@sheffield.ac.uk WWW: www.yas.org.uk Opening Hours: Tues,Wed 2.00 to 8.30pm; Thurs, Fri 10.00 to 5.30; Sat 9.30 to 5.00 Appointment necessary for use of archival material.

Yorkshire Family History - Biographical Database York Minster Library & Archives, Dean's Park, York, YO1 7JQ Tel: 01904-625308 Library Tel: 01904-611118 Archives Fax: 01904-611119 Email: library@yorkminster.org archives@yorkminster.org WWW: www.yorkminster.org

Yorkshire - East

Hull Central Library Family and Local History Unit, Central Library, Albion Street, Kingston upon Hull, HU1 3TF Tel: 01482 616828 Fax: 01482 616827 Email: gareth@ukorigins.co.uk WWW: http://www.hullcc.gov.uk/genealogy/famhist.php 1901 census

Beverley Local Studies Library Beverley Library, Champney Road, Beverley, HU17 9BG Tel: 01482-885358 Email: user@bevlib.karoo.co.uk

Bridlington Local Studies Library Bridlington Library, King Street, Bridlington, YO15 2DF Tel: 01262-672917 Fax: 01262-670208

East Riding Heritage Library & Museum Sewerby Hall, Church Lane, Sewerby, Bridlington, YO15 1EA Tel: 01262-677874 Tel: 01262-674265 Email: museum@pop3.poptel.org.uk WWW: www.bridlington.net/sew

Goole Local Studie Library Goole Library, Carlisle Street, Goole, DN14 5DS Tel: 01405-762187 Email: user@goolelib.karoo.co.uk

Yorkshire - North

Catterick Garrison Library Gough Road, Catterick Garrison, DL9 3EL Tel: 01748 833543 Extensive collection of some 1350 military history books available for reference or loan. Open Mon 10.am to 12, 1pm to 5.30pm; Wed 10am to 12, 1pm to 5pm; Fri 10am to 12 noon.

Harrogate Reference Library Victoria Avenue, Harrogate, HG1 1EG Tel: 01423-502744

Malton Library, St Michael's Street, Malton, YO17 7LJ Tel: 01653 692714 1901 census

North Yorkshire County Libraries 21 Grammar School Lane, Northallerton, DL6 1DF Tel: 01609-776271 Email: elizabeth.melrose@northyorks.gov.uk WWW: http://www.northyorks.gov.uk

Northallerton Reference Library 1 Thirsk Road, Northallerton, DL6 1PT Tel: 01609-776202 Email: northallerton.libraryhq@northyorks.gov.uk

Pickering Reference Library
The Ropery, Pickering, YO18 8DY Tel: 01751-472185

Richmond Library, Queen's Road, Richmond, DL10 4AE Tel: 01748 823120 1901 census

Ripon Library, The Arcade, Ripon, HG4 1AG Tel: 01765 792926 1901 census

Scarborough Reference Library Vernon Road, Scarborough, YO11 2NN Tel: 01723-364285 Email: scarborough.library@northyorks.gov.uk

Selby Reference Library 52 Micklegate, Selby, YO8 4EQ Tel: 01757-702020

Skipton Reference Library High Street, Skipton, BD23 1JX Tel: 01756-794726

Whitby Library Windsor Terrace, Whitby, YO21 1ET Tel: 01947-602554

Yorkshire - South

Archives & Local Studies Central Library, Walker Place, Rotherham, S65 1JH Tel: 01709-823616 Email: archives@rotherham.gov.uk WWW: www.rotherha.gov.uk/pages/living/learning/islib/callib.htm

Barnsley Archives and Local Studies Department Central Library, Shambles Street, Barnsley, S70 2JF Tel: 01226-773950 Tel: 01226-773938 Fax: 01226-773955 Email: Archives@Barnsley.govuk librarian@barnsley.gov.uk

Sheffield Central Library Surrey Street, Sheffield, S1 1XZ Tel: 0114 273 4711 Fax: 0114 273 5009 Email: sheffield.libraries@dial.pipex.com

Doncaster & District Family History Society Research Centre For details contact: 'Marton House', 125 The Grove, Wheatley Hills, Doncaster, DN2 5SN Tel: 01302-367257 Email: tonyjunes@aol.com WWW: http://www.doncasterfhs.freeserve.co.uk

Doncaster Libraries - Local Studies Section Central Library, Waterdale, Doncaster, DN1 3JE Tel: 01302-734307 Fax: 01302 369749 Email: reference.library@doncaster.gov.uk

Sheffield University Library Special Collections & Library Archives, Western Bank, Sheffield, S10 2TN Tel: 0114 222 7230 Fax: 0114 222 7290

West Yorkshire

The British Library Boston Spa, Wetherby, LS23 7BQ Tel: 01937-546212

Batley Library, Market Place, Batley, WF17 5DA Tel: 01924 326021 1901 census

Cleckheaton Library, Whitcliffe Road, Cleckheaton, BD19 3DX Tel: 01274 335170 1901 census

Calderdale Central Library
Northgate House, Northgate, Halifax, HX11 1UN Tel: 1422392631 WWW: www.calderdale.gov.uk

Dewsbury Library, Dewsbury Retail Park, Railway Street, Dewsbury, WF12 8EQ Tel: 01924 325080 1901 census

Huddersfield Local History Library
Huddersfield Library & Art Gallery, Princess Alexandra Walk, Huddersfield, HD1 2SU Tel: 01484-221965 Fax: 01484-221952 Email: ref-library@geo2.poptel.org.uk WWW: http://www.kirkleesmc.co.uk

Keighley Reference Library North Street, Keighley, BD21 3SX Tel: 01535-61821 Email: keighleylibrary@bradford.gov.uk WWW: www.bradford.gov.uk

Local Studies Library Leeds Central Library, Calverley Street, Leeds, LS1 3AB Tel: 0113 247 8290 Email: local.studies@leeds.gov.uk WWW: www.leeds.gov.uk/library/services/loc_reso.html

Local Studies Reference Library Central Library, Prince's Way, Bradford, BD1 1NN Tel: 01274-753661 Fax: 01274-753660

Mirfield Library, East Thorpe Lodge, , Mirfield, WF14 8AN Tel: 01924 326470 1901 census

Olicana Historical Society, 54 Kings Road, Ilkley, LS29 9AT Tel: 01943 609206

Pontefract Library & Local Studies Centre Pontefract library, Shoemarket, Pontefract, WF8 1BD Tel: 01977-727692

Wakefield Library HQ - Local Studies Department Balne Lane, Wakefield, WF2 0DQ Tel: 01924-302224 Email: wakehist@hotmail.com WWW: www.wakefield.gov.uk

Wakefield Metro District Libraries & Info Services Castleford Library & Local Studies Dept, Carlton Street, Castleford, WF10 1BB Tel: 01977-722085

Brotherton Library Department of Special Collections, Leeds University, Leeds, LS2 9JT Tel: 0113 233 55188 Email: special-collections@library.leeds.ac.uk WWW: http://leeds.ac.uk/library/spcoll/

Yorkshire - York

City of York Libraries - Local History & Ref Collection York Central Library, Library Square, Museum Street, York, YO1 7DS Tel: 01904-655631 Email: reference.library@york.gov.uk WWW: http://www.york.gov.uk

Wales

National Library of Wales Penglais, Aberystwyth, SY23 3BU Tel: 01970-632800 Email: holi@llgc.org.uk WWW: http://www.llgc.org.uk

University of Walwes Swansea library Library & Information Centre, Singleton Park, Swansea, SA2 8PP Tel: 01792 295021 Fax: 01792 295851

South Wales Miners' Library - University of Wales, Swansea Hendrefoelan House, Gower Road, Swansea, SA2 7NB Tel: 01792-518603 Fax: 01792-518694 Email: miners@swansea.ac.uk WWW: http://www.swan.ac.uk/lis/swml

Blaenau Gwent

Ebbw Vale Library Ebbw Vale Library, 21 Bethcar Street, Ebbw Vale, NP23 6HH Tel: 01495-303069 Fax: 01495-350547

Caerphilly

Bargoed Library The Square, Bargoed, CF8 8QQ Tel: 01443-875548 Fax: 01443-836057 Email: 9e465@dial.pipex.com

Caerphilly Library HQ
Unit 7 Woodfieldside Business Park, Penmaen Road, Pontllanfraith, Blackwood, NP12 2DG Tel: 01495 235584 Fax: 01495 235567 Email: cael.libs@dial.pipex.com

Cardiff

Cardiff Central Library (Local Studies Department) St Davids Link, Frederick Street, Cardiff, CF1 4DT Tel: (029) 2038 2116 Email: p.sawyer@cardlib.gov.uk WWW: www.cardiff.gov.uk

Carmarthenshire

Carmarthen Library St Peters Street, Carmarthen, SA31 1LN Tel: 01267-224822

Llanelli Public Library Vaughan Street, Lanelli, SA15 3AS Tel: 01554-773538

Ceredigion

Aberystwyth Reference Library Corporation Street, Aberystwyth, SY23 2BU Tel: 01970-617464 Fax: 01970 625059 Email: llyfrygell.library@ceredigion.gov.uk WWW: www.ceredigion.gov.uk/libraries

National Library of Wales
Penglais, Aberystwyth, SY23 3BU Tel: 01970-632800 Email:
holi@llgc.org.uk WWW: http://www.llgc.org.uk
Flintshire
Flintshire Reference Library Headquarters County Hall, Mold, CH7
6NW Tel: 01352 704411 Email: libraries@flintshire.gov.uk WWW:
www.flintshire.gov.uk
Glamorgan
Bridgend Library & Information Service Coed Parc, Park Street,
Bridgend, CF31 4BA Tel: 01656-767451 Fax: 01656-645719 Email:
blis@bridgendlib.gov.uk
Dowlais Library Church Street, Dowlais, Merthyr Tydfil, CF48 3HS Tel:
01985-723051
Merthyr Tydfil Central Library (Local Studies Dept) Merthyr Library,
High Street, Merthyr Tydfil, CF47 8AF Tel: 01685-723057 Email:
library@merthyr.gov.btinternet.com
Neath Central Library (Local Studies Department) 29 Victoria
Gardens, Neath, SA11 3BA Tel: 01639-620139
Pontypridd Library Library Road, Pontypridd, CF37 2DY Tel: 01443-
486850
Port Talbot Library 1st Floor Aberafan Shopping Centre, Port Talbot,
SA13 1PB Tel: 01639-763490
Swansea Reference Library Alexandra Road, Swansea, SA1 5DX Tel:
01792-516753 Email: swanlib@demon.co.uk Extensive holdings of trade
directories, local census returns, newspapers (partially indexed)
University of Wales Swansea library Library & Information Centre,
Singleton Park, Swansea, SA2 8PP Tel: 01792 295021 Fax: 01792
295851
Treorchy Library Station Road, Treorchy, CF42 6NN Tel: 01443-
773204 Fax: 01443-777407
Gwent
Abertillery Library
Station Hill, Abertillery, NP13 1TE Tel: 01495-212332
Chepstow Library & Information Centre Manor Way, Chepstow, NP16
5HZ Tel: 01291-635730 Tel: 01291-635731 Email:
chepstowlibrary@monmouthshire.gov.uk WWW:
www.monmouthshire.gov.uk/leisure/libraries
Newport Library & Information Service Newport Central Library, John
Frost Square, Newport, NP20 1PA Tel: 01633-211376 Email:
reference.library@newport.gov.uk WWW:
http://www.earl.org.uk/partners/newport/index.html The Local Studies
Collection contains information on all aspects of Monmouthshire and or
Gwent. A fee paying postal research service is available, which uses the
library's own resources.
Tredegar Library The Circle, Tredegar, NP2 3PS Tel: 01495-722687
Gwynedd
Canolfan Llyfrgell Dolgellau Library FforddBala, Dolgellau, LL40
2YF Tel: 01341-422771 WWW: http://www.gwynedd.gov.uk
Llyfrgell Caernarfon Lon Pafiliwn, Caernafon, LL55 1AS Tel: 01286-
679465 Fax: 01286-671137 Email: library@gwynedd.gov.uk
Merthyr Tydfil
Merthyr Tydfil Central Library (Local Studies Department) Merthyr
Library, High Street, Merthyr Tydfil, CF47 8AF Tel: 01685-723057
Email: library@merthyr.gov.btinternet.com
Treharris Library Perrott Street, Treharris, Merthyr Tydfil, CF46 5ET
Tel: 01443-410517 Fax: 01443 410517
Monmouthshire
Chepstow Library & Information Centre Manor Way, Chepstow, NP16
5HZ Tel: 01291-635730 Tel: 01291-635731 Email:
chepstowlibrary@monmouthshire.gov.uk WWW:
www.monmouthshire.gov.uk/leisure/libraries
Neath Port Talbot
Lifelong Learning Service Theodore Road, Port Talbot, SA13 1SP Tel:
01639-898581 Fax: 01639-899914 Email: lls@neath-porttalbot.gov.uk
Pembrokeshire
Pembrokeshire Libraries The County Library, Dew Street,
Haverfordwest, SA61 1SU Tel: 01437-762070 Email:
anita.thomas@pembrokeshire.gov.uk The Local Studies Library covers
people, places and events realting to The County of Pembrokeshire past
and present. The Library also houses The Francis Green Genealogical
Collection
Powys
Brecon Area Library Ship Street, Brecon, LD3 9AE Tel: 01874-623346
Fax: 01874 622818 Email: breclib@mail.powys.gov.uk
Llandrindod Wells Library Cefnllys Lane, Llandrindod Wells, LD1
5LD Tel: 01597-826870 Email: , llandod.library@powys.gov.uk
Newtown Area Library Park Lane, Newtown, SY16 1EJ Tel: 01686-
626934 Fax: 01686 624935 Email: nlibrary@powys.gov.uk
Rhondda Cynon Taff
Aberdare Library Green Street, Aberdare, CF44 7AG Tel: 01685-
885318
Vale of Glamorgan
Barry Library King Square, Holton Road, Barry, CF63 4RW
Tel: 01446-735722 Fax: 01446 734427
West Glamorgan
West Glamorgan Archive Service - Port Talbot Access Point Port
Talbot Library, Aberafan Centre, Port Talbot, SA13 1PJ Tel: 01639
763430 WWW: http://www.swansea.gov.uk/archives

Wrexham CBC
Wrexham Library and Arts Centre Rhosddu Road, Wrexham, LL11
1AU Tel: 01978-292622 Fax: 01978-292611 Email:
joy.thomas@wrexham.gov.uk WWW: www.wrexham.gov.uk

Scotland
St Andrews University Library - Special Collections Department
North Street, St Andrews, KY16 9TR Tel: 01334 462339 Fax: 01334
462282 Email: speccoll@st-and.ac.uk
WWW: http://specialcollections.st-and.ac.uk
Glasgow University Library & Special Collections Dept
Hillhead Street, Glasgow, G12 8QE Tel: 0141 330 6767 Email:
library@lib.gla.ac.uk WWW: www.gla.ac.uk/library
Edinburgh University Library, Special Collections Dept
George Square, Edinburgh, EH8 9LJ Tel: 0131 650 3412 Email:
special.collections@ed.ac.uk WWW: www.lib.ed.ac.uk
Edinburgh University New College Library Mound Place, Edinburgh,
EH1 2UL Tel: 0131 650 8957 Fax: 0131 650 6579 Email:
New.College.Library@ed.ac.uk WWW: www.lib.ed.ac.uk
Leadhills Miners's Library Main Street, Leadhills Tel: 01659-74326
National Library of Scotland George IV Bridge, Edinburgh, EH1 1EW
Tel: 0131-226-4531 Email: enquiries@nls.uk WWW: http://www.nls.uk
National Monuments Record of Scotland Royal Commission on the
Ancient & Historical Monuments of Scotland, John Sinclair House, 16
Bernard Terrace, Edinburgh, EH8 9NX Tel: 0131 662 1456 Fax: 0131
662 1477 or 0131 662 1499 Email: nmrs@rcahms.gov.uk WWW:
www.rcahms.gov.uk Website gives access to the searchable database of
NMRS Records - 'CANMORE'
National Museums of Scotland Library Royal Museum, Chambers
Street, Edinburgh, EH1 1JF Tel: 0131 247 4137 Email:
library@nms.ac.uk WWW: www.nms.ac.uk
Royal Botanic Garden The Library, 20a Inverleith Row, Edinburgh, EH3
5LR Tel: 0131 552 7171 Fax: 0131 248 2901
Scottish United Services Museum Library The Castle, Museum Square,
Edinburgh, EH1 1 2NG Tel: 0131-225-7534-Ext-2O4 Fax: 0131-225-
3848 Email: library@nms.ac.uk WWW: www.nms.ac.uk
Strathclyde University Archives McCance Building, 16 Richmond
Street, Glasgow, G1 1XQ Tel: 0141 548 2397 Fax: 0141 552 0775
Scottish Genealogy Society - Library
15 Victoria Terrace, Edinburgh, EH1 2JL Tel: 0131-220 3677 Fax: 0131
220 3677 Email: info@scotsgenealogy.com WWW:
www.scotsgenealogy.com
Aberdeen
Aberdeen Central Library - Reference & Local Studies Rosemount
Viaduct, Aberdeen, AB25 1GW Tel: 01224-652511 Tel: 01224 252512
Fax: 01224 624118 Email: refloc@arts-rec.aberdeen.net.uk
**University of Aberdeen DISS: Heritage Division Special Collections &
Archives** Kings College, Aberdeen, AB24 3SW Tel: 01224-272598
Email: speclib@abdn.ac.uk
WWW: http://www.abdn.ac.uk/diss/heritage
Aberdeenshire Library & Information Service
The Meadows Industrial Estate, Meldrum Meg Way, Oldmeldrum, AB51
0GN Tel: 01651-872707 Tel: 01651-871219/871220
Email: ALIS@aberdeenshire.gov.uk
WWW: www.aberdeenshire.gov.uk
Angus
Angus Archives Montrose Library, 214 High Street, Montrose, DD10
8PH Tel: 01674-671415 Fax: 01674-671810
Email: angus.archives@angus.govuk
 WWW: www.angus.gov.uk/history/history.htm
Archive holdings for Angus County, Arbroath, Brechin, Carnoustie,
Forfar, Montrose, Monifieth, Kirriemuir.
Angus District Montrose Library
214 High Street, Montrose, MO10 8PH Tel: 01674-673256
Tay Valley Family History Society Family History Research Centre,
179-181 Princes Street, Dundee, DD4 6DQ Tel: 01382-461845 Fax:
01382 455532 Email: tvfhs@tayvalleyfhs.org.uk
WWW: http://www.tayvalleyfhs.org.uk
Argyll
Argyll & Bute Council Archives Highland Avenue, Sandbank, Dunoon,
PA23 8PB Tel: 01369-703214
Campbeltown Library and Museum Hall St, Campbeltown, PA28 6BU
Tel: 01586 552366
Argyll & Bute Library Service Library Headquarters, Highland Avenue,
Sandbank, Dunoon, PA23 8PB Tel: 01369-703214
Email: andyewan@abc-libraries.demon.co.uk
Ayrshire
E Ayrshire Council District History Centre & Museum Baird Institute,
3 Lugar Street, Cumnock, KA18 1AD Tel: 01290-421701 Fax: 01290-
421701 Email: Baird.institute@east-ayrshire.gov.uk
WWW: www.east-ayrshire.gov.uk
East Ayrshire Libraries Dick Institute, Elmbank Avenue, Kilmarnock,
KA1 3BU Tel: 01563 554310 Tel: 01290 421701 Fax: 01563 554311
Email: baird.institute@east-ayrshire.gov.uk WWW: www.east-
ayrshire.gov.uk
East Ayrshire Libraries - Cumnock 25-27 Ayr Road, Cumnock, KA18
1EB Tel: 01290-422804

North Ayrshire Libraries Library Headquarters, 39 - 41 Princes Street, Ardrossan, KA22 8BT Tel: 01294-469137 Fax: 01924-604236 Email: reference@naclibhq.prestel.co.uk WWW: www.north-ayrshire.gov.uk

South Ayrshire Library Carnegie Library, 12 Main Street, Ayr, KA8 8ED Tel: 01292-286385 Email: carnegie@south-ayrshire.gov.uk WWW: www.south-ayrshire.gov.uk

Clackmannanshire

Clackmannanshire Archives Alloa Library, 26/28 Drysdale Street, Alloa, FK10 1JL Tel: 01259-722262 Email: libraries@clacks.gov.uk WWW: www.clacksweb.org.uk/dyna/archives

Clackmannanshire Libraries
Alloa Library, 26/28 Drysdale Street, Alloa, FK10 1JL Tel: 01259-722262 Fax: 01259-219469 Email: clack.lib@mail.easynet.co.uk

Dumfries & Galloway

Ewart Library Ewart Library, Catherine Street, Dumfries, DG1 1JB Tel: 01387 260285 Tel: 01387-252070 Email: ruth_airley@dumgal.gov.uk libsxi@dumgal.gov.uk WWW: www.dumgal.gov.uk

Dunbartonshire

Dumbarton Public library Strathleven Place, Dumbarton, G82 1BD Tel: 01389-733273 Fax: 01389-738324 Email: wdlibs@hotmail.com

Dundee

Dundee Central Library The Wellgate, Dundee, DD1 1DB Tel: 01382-434377 Fax: 01382-434036 Email: local.studies@dundeecity.gov.uk WWW: http://www.dundeecity.gov.uk/dcchtml/nrd/loc_stud.htm, Material held mainly Angus and Dundee

Tay Valley Family History Society Family History Research Centre, 179–181 Princes Street, Dundee, DD4 6DQ Tel: 01382-461845 Fax: 01382 455532 Email: tvfhs@tayvalleyfhs.org.uk WWW: http://www.tayvalleyfhs.org.uk

East Ayrshire

Auchinleck Library Community Centre, Well Road, Auchinleck, KA18 2LA Tel: 01290 422829

Bellfield Library 79 Whatriggs Road, Kilmarnock, KA1 3RB Tel: 01563 534266

Bellsbank Library Primary School, Craiglea Crescent, Bellsbank, KA6 7UA Tel: 01292 551057

Catrine Library A M Brown Institute, Catrine, KA5 6RT Tel: 01290 551717

Crosshouse Library 11-13 Gatehead Road, Crosshouse, KA2 0HN Tel: 01563 573640

Dalmellington Library Townhead, Dalmellington, KA6 7QZ Tel: 01292 550159

Dalrymple Library Barbieston Road, Dalrymple, KA6 6DZ

Darvel Library Town Hall, West Main Street, Darvel, KA17 0AQ Tel: 01560 322754

Drongan Library Mill O'Shield Road, Drongan, KA6 7AY Tel: 01292 591718

Galston Library Henrietta Street, Galston, KA4 8HQ Tel: 01563 821994

Hurlford Library Blair Road, Hurlford, KA1 5BN Tel: 01563 539899

Kilmaurs Library Irvine Road, Kilmaurs, KA3 2RJ

Mauchline Library 2 The Cross, Mauchline KA5 6AB Tel: 01290 550824

Muirkirk Library Burns Avenue, Muirkirk, KA18 3RH Tel: 01290 661505

Netherthird Library Ryderston Drive, Netherthird, KA18 3AR Tel: 01290 423806

New Cumnock Library Community Centre, The Castle, New Cumnock, KA18 4AH Tel: 01290 338710

Newmilns Library Craigview Road, Newmilns, KA16 9DQ Tel: 01560 322890

Ochiltree Library Main Street, Ochiltree, KA18 2PE Tel: 01290 700425

Patna Library Doonside Avenue, Patna, KA6 7LX Tel: 01292 531538

East Dunbartonshire

East Dunbartonshire Local Record Offices and Reference Libraries William Patrick Library, 2 West High Street, Kirkintilloch, G66 1AD Tel: 0141-776-8090 Fax: 0141-776-0408 Email: libraries@eastdunbarton.gov.uk WWW: www.eastdunbarton.gov.uk

East Renfrewshire

Giffnock Library Station Road, Giffnock, Glasgow, G46 6JF Tel: 0141-577-4976 Email: devinem@eastrenfrewshire.co.uk

Edinburgh

Edinburgh Central Library Edinburgh Room, George IV Bridge, Edinburgh, EH1 1EG Tel: 0131-242 8030 Fax: 0131-242 8009 Email: eclis@edinburgh.gov.uk WWW: www.edinburgh.gov.uk

Falkirk

Falkirk Library Hope Street, Falkirk, FK1 5AU Tel: 01324 503605 Fax: 01324 503606 Email: falkirk-library@falkirk-library.demon.co.uk WWW: www.falkirk.gov.uk Holds Local Studies Collection

Falkirk Museum History Research Centre Callendar House, Callendar Park, Falkirk, FK1 1YR Tel: 01324 503778 Fax: 01324 503771 Email: ereid@falkirkmuseums.demon.co.ukcallandarhouse@falkirkmuseums.demon.co.uk WWW: www.falkirkmuseums.demon.co.uk Records held: Local Authority, business, personal and estate records, local organmisations, trade unions, over 28,000 photographs Falkirk District

Fife

Dunfermline Library - Local History Department Abbot Street, Dunfermline, KY12 7NL Tel: 01383-312994 Fax: 01383-312608 Email: info@dunfermline.fifelib.net

Fife Council Central Area Libraries Central Library, War Memorial Grounds, Kirkcaldy, KY1 1YG Tel: 01592-412878 Email: info@kirkcaldy.fifelib.net

St Andrews Library Church Square, St Andrews, KY16 9NN Tel: 01334-412685 Fax: 01334 413029 Email: info@standres.fiflib.net

St Andrews University Library North Street, St Andrews, KY16 9TR Tel: 01334-462281 Fax: 01334-462282 WWW: http://www.library.st-and.ac.uk

St Andrews University Library - Special Collections Dept North Street, St Andrews, KY16 9TR Tel: 01334 462339 Fax: 01334 462282 Email: speccoll@st-and.ac.uk WWW: http://specialcollections.st-and.ac.uk

Tay Valley Family History Society Family History Research Centre, 179–181 Princes Street, Dundee, DD4 6DQ Tel: 01382-461845 Fax: 01382 455532 Email: tvfhs@tayvalleyfhs.org.uk WWW: http://www.tayvalleyfhs.org.uk

Glasgow

Brookwood Library 166 Drymen Road, Bearsden, Glasgow, G61 3RJ Tel: 0141-942 6811 Fax: 0141 943 1119

Glasgow City Libraries & Archives Mitchell Library, North Street, Glasgow, G3 7DN Tel: 0141 287 2937 Fax: 0141 287 2912 Email: history_and_glasgow @gcl.glasgow.gov.uk WWW: wwww.glasgow.gov.uk/html/council/cindex.htm

Glasgow University Library & Special Collections Dept Hillhead Street, Glasgow, G12 8QE Tel: 0141 330 6767 Fax: 0141 330 3793 Email: library@lib.gla.ac.uk WWW: www.gla.ac.uk/library

Social Sciences Department - History & Glasgow Room The Mitchell Library, North Street, Glasgow, G3 7DN Tel: 0141-227-2935 Tel: 0141-227-2937 & 0141-227-2938 Fax: 0141-227-2935 Email: history-and-glasgow@cls.glasgow.gov.uk WWW: www.libarch.glasgow

Isle of Barra

Castlebay Community Library Community School, Castlebay, HS95XD Tel: 01871-810471

Isle of Benbecula

Community Library Sgoil Lionacleit, Liniclate, HS7 5PJ Tel: 01870-602211

Isle of Lewis

Stornoway Library 19 Cromwell Street, Stornoway, HS1 2DA Tel: 01851-703064 Fax: 01851- 708676/708677 Email: stornoway-library1@cne-siar.gov.uk.gov.uk

Kinross-shire

Perth & Kinross Libraries A K Bell Library, 2 - 8 York Place, Perth, PH2 8EP Tel: 01738-477062 Email: jaduncan@pkc.gov.uk

Tay Valley Family History Society Family History Research Centre, 179–181 Princes Street, Dundee, DD4 6DQ Tel: 01382-461845 Fax: 01382 455532 Email: tvfhs@tayvalleyfhs.org.uk WWW: http://www.tayvalleyfhs.org.uk

Lanarkshire

Airdrie Library Wellwynd, Airdrie, ML6 0AG Tel: 01236-763221

Cumbernauld Central Library 8 Allander Walk, Cumbernauld, G67 1EE Tel: 01236-735964 Fax: 01236-458350 WWW: www.northlan.org.uk

Midlothian

Midlothian Archives and Local Studies Centre 2 Clerk Street, Loanhead, EH20 9DR Tel: 0131 271 3976 Fax: 0131 440 4635 Email: local.studies@midlothian.gov.uk WWW: www.earl.org.uk/partners/midlothian/local.html

Midlothian Libraries Local History Centre Midlothian Council Libraries Headquarters, 2 Clerk Street, Loanhead, EH20 9DR Tel: 0131-440-2210 Fax: 0131-440-4635 Email: local.studies@midlothian.gov.uk WWW: http://www.earl.org.uk.partners/midlothian/index.html

Morayshire

Forres Library Forres House, High Street, Forres, IV36 0BJ Tel: 01309-672834 Fax: 01309-675084

Moray Local Heritage Centre Grant Lodge, Cooper Park, Elgin, IV30 1HS Tel: 01343 562644 Tel: 01343 562645 Fax: 01343-549050 Email: graeme.wilson@techleis.moray.gov.uk WWW: www.morray.org/heritage/roots.html , The Moray District Record Office has now been combined with the Local studies section at Grant Lodge, Cooper Park, Elgin to form the Local Heritage Centre.

Buckie Library Clunu Place, Buckie, AB56 1HB Tel: 01542-832121 Fax: 01542-835237 Email: buckie.lib@techleis.moray.gov.uk

Keith Library Union Street, Keith, AB55 5DP Tel: 01542-882223 Fax: 01542-882177 Email: keithlibrary@techleis.moray.gov.uk

North Highland

North Highland Archive Wick Library, Sinclair Terrace, Wick, KW1 5AB Tel: 01955 606432 Fax: 01955 603000

North Lanarkshire

Kilsyth Library Burngreen, Kilsyth, G65 0HT Tel: 01236-823147

Motherwell Heritage Centre High Road, Motherwell, ML1 3HU Tel: 01698-251000 Fax: 01698-253433 Email: heritage@mhc158.freeserve.co.uk

Shotts Library Benhar Road, Shotts, ML7 5EN Tel: 01501-821556, Fax: **Orkney**

Orkney Library The Orkney Library, Laing Street, Kirkwall, KWI5 1NW Tel: 01856-873166 Email: karen.walker@orkney.gov.uk

Perthshire
Perth & Kinross Libraries A K Bell Library, 2 - 8 York Place, Perth, PH2 8EP Tel: 01738-477062 Fax: 01738-477010 Email: jaduncan@pkc.gov.uk
Tay Valley Family History Society Family History Research Centre, 179–181 Princes Street, Dundee, DD4 6DQ Tel: 01382-461845 Fax: 01382 455532 Email: tvfhs@tayvalleyfhs.org.uk
WWW: http://www.tayvalleyfhs.org.uk
Renfrewshire
Renfrewshire Council Library & Museum Services Central Library & Museum Complex, High Street, Paisley, PA1 2BB Tel: 0141-889-2350 Fax: 0141-887-6468
Email: local_studies.library@renfrewshire.gov.uk
Watt Library 9 Union Street, Greenock, PA16 8JH Tel: 01475-715628
Scottish Borders
Scottish Borders Archive & Local History Centre Library Headquarters, St Mary's Mill, Selkirk, TD7 5EW Tel: 01750 20842 Tel: 01750 724903 Fax: 01750 22875 Email: archives@scotborders.gov.uk
WWW: www.scotborders.gov.uk/libraries
Shetland
Shetland Library Lower Hillhead, Lerwick, ZE1 0EL Tel: 01595-693868 Fax: 01595-694430 Email: info@shetland-library.gov.uk WWW: www.shetland-library.gov.uk
Stirling
Bridge of Allan Library Fountain Road, Bridge of Allan, FK9 4AT Tel: 01786 833680 Fax: 01786 833680 Hold the IGI in disc form, the 1881 census on disc and have Internet access, as well as a selection of local history books relevant to their locale. Also holds microfilms of the 1851 census for Stirling
Dunblane Library High Street, Dunblane, FK15 0ER Tel: 01786 823125 Fax: 01786 823125 Email: dunblanelibrary@stirling.gov.uk
St Ninians Library Mayfield Centre, St Ninians, FK7 0DB Tel: 01786 472069 Email: stninlibrary@stirling.gov.uk
Stirling Central Library Central Library, Corn Exchange Road, Stirling, FK8 2HX Tel: 01786 432106 Fax: 01786 473094 Email: centrallibrary@stirling.gov.uk Old Parish Registers andCensus returns for all Stirling Council area
Tayside
Dundee University Archives Tower Building, University of Dundee, Dundee, DD1 4HN Tel: 01382-344095 Email: archives@dundee.ac.uk WWW: http://www.dundee.ac.uk/archives/
West Lothian
West Lothian Council Libraries Connolly House, Hopefield Road, Blackburn, EH47 7HZ Tel: 01506-776331 Email: localhistory@westlothian.org.uk
WWW: http://www.wlonline.org

Northern Ireland
Antrim
North Eastern Library Board & Local Studies Area Reference Library, Demesne Avenue, Ballymena, BT43 7BG Tel: (028) 25 6641212 Email: yvonne_hirt@hotmail.com WWW: www.neelb.org.uk
Belfast
Belfast Central Library Irish & Local Studies Dept, Royal Avenue, Belfast, BT1 1EA Tel: (028) 9024 3233 Fax: (028) 9033 2819 Email: info@libraries.belfast-elb.gov.uk WWW: www.belb.org.uk
Belfast Linen Hall Library 17 Donegall Square North, Belfast, BT1 5GD Tel: (028) 90321707
Co Antrim
Local Studies Service Area Library HQ, Demesne Avenue, Ballymena, BT43 7BG Tel: (028) 25 664121 Email: yvonne_hirst@hotmail.com WWW: www.neelb.org.uk
Co Fermanagh
Enniskillen Library Halls Lane, Enniskillen, BT1 3HP Tel: (028) 66322886 Fax: 01365-324685 Email: librarian@eknlib.demon.co.uk
Co Londonderry
Central and Reference Library 35 Foyle Street, Londonderry, BT24 6AL Tel: (028) 71272300 Email: trishaw@online.rednet.co.uk
Irish Room Coleraine County Hall, Castlerock Road, Ballymena, BT1 3HP Tel: (028) 705 1026 WWW: www.neelb.org.uk
Co Tyrone
Centre for Migration Studies, Ulster American Folk Park, Mellon Road, Castletown, Omagh, BT78 5QY Tel: 028 82 256315 Fax: 028 82 242241 Email: uafp@iol.ie WWW: www.qub.ac.uk/cms/www.folkpark.com
Omagh Library 1 Spillars Place, Omagh, BT78 1HL Tel: (028) 82244821 Fax: 01662-246772 Email: librarian@omahlib.demon.co.uk
County Down
South Eastern Library Board & Local Studies Library HQ, Windmill Hill, Ballynahinch, BT24 8DH Tel: (028) 9756 6400 Email: ref@bhinchlibhq.demon.co.uk

Ireland
National Library of Ireland Kildare Street, Dublin, 2 Tel: 661-8811 Fax: 676-6690 Email: coflaherty@nli.ie
Society of Friends (Quakers) - Historical Library Swanbrook House, Bloomfield Avenue, Dublin, 4 Tel: (01) 668-7157 Completed

computerisation of card index
Co Clare
Clare County Library The Manse, Harmony Row, Ennis Tel: 065-6821616 Email: clarelib@iol.ie WWW: www.iol.ie/~clarelib
Co Cork
Cork City Library Grand Parade, Cork Tel: 021-277110 Fax: 021-275684 Email: cork.city.library@indigo.ie
Mallow Heritage Centre 27/28 Bank Place, Mallow Tel: 022-50302
Co Dublin
Dun Laoghaire Library Lower George's Street, Dun Laoghaire Tel: 2801147 Fax: 2846141 Email: eprout@dlrcoco.ie
WWW: www.dlrcoco.ie/library/lhistory.htm
Co Kerry
Kerry County Library Genealogical Centre Cathedral Walk, Killarney Tel: 353-0-64-359946
Co Kildare
Kildare County Library Newbridge Tel: 045-431109 Fax: 045-432490
Kildare Heritage & Genealogy Kildare County Library, Newbridge Tel: 045 433602 Fax: 045-432490 Email: capinfo@iol.ie WWW: www.kildare.ie
Co Mayo
Central Library Castlebar Tel: 094-24444 Email: cbarlib@iol.ie
Co Sligo
Sligo County Library Westward Town Centre, Bridge Street, Sligo Tel: 00-353-71-47190 Fax: 00-353-71-46798 Email: sligolib@iol.ie
Co Tipperary
Tipperary County Libary Local Studies Department Castle Avenue, Thurles Tel: 0504-21555 Fax: 0504-23442 Email: studies@tipplibs.iol.ie WWW: www.iol.ie/~TIPPLIBS
Co Waterford
Waterford County Library Central Library, Davitt's Quay, Dungarvan Tel: 058 41231
Co Wexford
Enniscorthy Branch Library Lymington Road, Enniscorthy Tel: 054-36055
New Ross Branch Library Barrack Lane, New Ross Tel: 051-21877
Wexford Branch Library Teach Shionoid, Abbey Street, Wexford Tel: 053-42211 Fax: 053-21097
County Donegal
Donegal Local Studies Centre Central Library & Arts Centre, Oliver Plunkett Road, Letterkenny Tel: 00353 74 24950 Fax: 00353 74 24950 Email: dgcolib@iol.ie WWW: donegal.ie
County Dublin
Ballyfermot Public Library Ballyfermot, Dublin, 10
County Limerick
Limerick City Library The Granary, Michael Street, Limerick Tel: 061-314668 Fax: 061 411506 Email: doyledolores@hotmail.com
Dublin
Dublin Public Libraries Gilbert Library - Dublin & Irish Collections, 138 -142 Pearse Street, Dublin, 2 Tel: 353-1-677-7662 Fax: 353-1-671-4354 Email: dubcoll@iol.ie WWW: http://www.iol.ie/ dubcilib/index.html

Australia
ACT
National Library of Australia Canberra, 2600 Tel: 02 6262 1111 WWW: http://www.nla.gov.au
New South Wales
Mitchell Library Macquarie Street Sydney, 2000 Tel: 02 9230 1693 Fax: 02 9235 1687 Email: slinfo@slsw.gov.au
State Library of New South Wales Macquarie Street Sydney, 2000 Tel: 02 9230 1414 Fax: 02 9223 3369 Email: slinfo@slsw.gov.au
Queensland
State Library of Queensland PO Box 3488, Cnr Peel and Stanley Streets, South Brisbane, Brisbane, 4101 Tel: 07 3840 7775 Fax: 07 3840 7840 Email: genie@slq.qld.gov.au
WWW: http://www.slq.qld.gov.au/subgenie/htm
South Australia
South Australia State Library PO Box 419 Adelaide, 5001 Tel: (08) 8207 7235 Fax: (08) 8207 7247 Email: famhist@slsa.sa.gov.au
WWW: http://www.slsa.sa.gov.au/library/collres/famhist/
Victoria
State Library of Victoria 328 Swanston Street Walk Melbourne, 3000 Tel: 03 9669 9080 Email: granth@newvenus.slv.vic.gov.au
WWW: http://www.slv.vic.gov.au/slv/genealogy/index
Western Australia
State Library Alexander Library, Perth Cultural Centre Perth, 6000 Tel: 09 427 3111 Fax: 09 427 3256

New Zealand
Auckland Research Centre Auckland City Libraries PO Box 4138, 44 46 Lorne Street Auckland Tel: 64 9 377 0209 Fax: 64 9 307 7741 Email: heritage@auckland library.govt.nz
National Library of New Zealand PO Box 1467 Thorndon, Wellington Tel: (0064)4 474 3030 Fax: (0064)4 474 3063 WWW: http://www.natlib.govt.nz
Alexander Turnbull Library PO Box 12 349 , Wellington, 6038 Tel: 04 474 3050 Fax: 04 474 3063

Canterbury Public Library PO Box 1466 , Christchurch Tel: 03 379 6914 Fax: 03 365 1751

Dunedin Public Libraries PO Box 5542, Moray Place Dunedin Tel: 03 474 3651 Fax: 03 474 3660 Email: library@dcc.govt.nz

Fielding Public Library PO Box 264 , Fielding, 5600 Tel: 06 323 5373

Hamilton Public Library PO Box 933, Garden Place Hamilton, 2015 Tel: 07 838 6827 Fax: 07 838 6858

Hocken Library PO Box 56 , Dunedin Tel: 03 479 8873 Fax: 03 479 5078

Porirua Public Library PO Box 50218 , Porirua, 6215 Tel: 04 237 1541 Fax: 04 237 7320

Takapuna Public Library Private Bag 93508 , Takapuna, 1309 Tel: 09 486 8466 Fax: 09 486 8519

Wanganui District Library Private Bag 3005, Alexander Building, Queens Park, Wanganui, 5001 Tel: 06 345 8195 Fax: 06 345 5516 Email: wap@wdl.govt.nz

South Africa

South African Library PO Box 496 , Cape Town, 8000 Tel: 021 246320 Fax: 021 244848

Canada

Alberta

Calgary Public Library 616 MacLeod Tr SE Calgary, T2G 2M2 Tel: 260 2785

Glenbow Library & Archives 130 9th Avenue SE Calgary, T2G 0P3 Tel: 403 268 4197 Fax: 403 232 6569

British Columbia

British Columbia Archives 865 Yates Street Victoria, V8V 1X4 Tel: 604 387 1952 Fax: 604 387 2072 Email: rfrogner@maynard.bcars.gs.gov.bc.ca

Cloverdale Library 5642 176a Street Surrey, V3S 4G9 Tel: 604 576 1384 Email: GenealogyResearch@city.surrey.bc.ca WWW: http://www.city.surrey.bc.ca/spl/

New Brunswick

Harriet Irving Library PO Box 7500 Fredericton, E3B 5H5 Tel: 506 453 4748 **Loyalist Collection & Reference Library** PO Box 7500 Fredericton, E3B 5H5 Tel: 506 453 4749

Newfoundland

Newfoundland Provincial Resource Library Arts and Cultural Centre, Allandale Road St Johns, A1B 3A3 Tel: 709 737 3955 Email: genealog@publib.nf.ca WWW: http://www.publib.nf.ca

Ontario

National Library 395 Wellington Street Ottawa, K1A 0N4 Tel: 613 995 9481 Fax: 613 943 1112 Email:reference@nlc bnc.ca WWW: http://www.nlc bnc.ca

Toronto Reference Library 789 Yonge Street Toronto, M4W 2G8 Tel: 416 393 7155 **James Gibson Reference Library** 500 Glenridge Avenue St Catherines, L2S 3A1 Tel: 905 688 5550 Fax: 905 988 5490

Public Library PO Box 2700, Station LCD 1 Hamilton, L8N 4E4 Tel: 546 3408 Email: speccol@hpl.hamilton.on.ca

Public Library 85 Queen Street North Kitchener, N2H 2H1 Tel: 519 743 0271 Fax: 519 570 1360

Public Library 305 Queens Avenue London, N6B 3L7 Tel: 519 661 4600 Fax: 519 663 5396

Public Library 301 Burnhamthorpe Road West Mississauga, L5B 3Y3 Tel: 905 615 3500 Email: library.info@city.mississauga.on.ca WWW: http://www.city.mississauga.on.ca/Library

Toronto Public Library North York (Central Library) Canadiana Department, 5120 Yonge Street North York, M2N 5N9 Tel: 416 395 5623 WWW: http://www.tpl.tor.on.ca

Public Library 74 Mackenzie Street Sudbury, P3C 4X8 Tel: 01673 1155 Fax: 01673 9603

St Catharines Public Library 54 Church Street St Catharines, L2R 7K2 Tel: 905 688 6103 Fax: 905 688 2811 Email: scpublib@stcatharines.library.on.ca WWW: http://www.stcatharines.library.on.ca

Quebec

Bibliotheque De Montreal 1210, Rue Sherbrooke East Street , Montreal, H2L 1L9 Tel: 514 872 1616 Fax: 514 872 4654 Email: daniel_olivier@ville.montreal.qc.ca WWW: http://www.ville.montreal.qc.ca/biblio/pageacc.htm

Saskatchewan

Public Library PO Box 2311 Regina, S4P 3Z5 Tel: 306 777 6011 Fax: 306 352 5550 Email: kaitken@rpl.sk.ca

Public Library 311 23rd Street East Saskatoon, S7K 0J6 Tel: 306 975 7555 Fax: 306 975 7542

Areas Served by The District Land Registries for England & Wales

HM Land Registry
HM Land Registry, Lincoln's Inn Fields, London, WC2A 3PH

England
Birkenhead District Land Registry
Rosebrae Court, Woodside Ferry Approach, Birkenhead, Merseyside, L41 6DU Tel: 0151 473 1110
Tel: 0151 473 1106 Enquiries Fax: 0151 473 0366
Cheshire; London Boroughs of Kensington, Chelsea, Hammersmith, Fulham

Birkenhead District Land Registry
Old Market House, Hamilton Street, Birkenhead, Merseyside, L41 5FL Tel: 0151 473 1110
Tel: 0151 473 1106 Enquiries, Fax: 0151 473 0251
Merseyside; Staffordshire; Stoke on Trent

Coventry District Land Registry
Leigh Court, Torrington Ave, Tile Hill, Coventry, CV4 9XZ,
Tel: 01203 860860 Tel: 01203 860864
Enquiries Fax: 01203 860021
West Midlands

Croydon District Land Registry
Sunley House, Bedford Park, Croydon, CR9 3LE
Tel: 0181 781 9100 Tel: 0181 781 9103 Enquiries
Fax: 0181 781 9110
London Boroughs of Croydon, Sutton, Bromley, Bexley

Durham (Boldon House) District Land Registry
Boldon House, Wheatlands Way, Pity Me, Durham, County Durham, DH1 5GJ, Tel: 0191 301 2345 Fax: 0191 301 2300
Cumbria; Surrey

Durham (Southfield House) District Land Registry
Southfield House, Southfield Way, Durham, County Durham,
England Tel: 0191 301 3500 Tel: 0191 301 0020
Darlington; Durham; Hartlepool; Middlesbrough; Northumberland;
Redcar & Cleveland; Stockton on Tees
Tyne & Wear

Gloucester District Land Registry
Twyver House, Bruton Way, Gloucester, Gloucestershire, GL1 1DQ
Tel: 01452 511111 Fax: 01452 510050
Berkshire; Bristol; Gloucestershire; Oxfordshire; South Gloucestershire; Warwickshire

Harrow District Land Registry
Lyon House, Lyon Road, Harrow, Middlesex, HA1 2EU
Tel: (020) 8235 1181 Fax: (020) 8862 0176
London Boroughs of Barnet, Brent, Camden, Islington, City of

London; City of Westminster; Harrow, Inner & Middle Temples
Kingston Upon Hull District Land Registry
Earle House, Portland Street, Hull, HU2 8JN
Tel: 01482 223244 Fax: 01482 224278
East Riding of York; Kingston Upon Hull; Lincolnshire
Norfolk; N E Lincolnshire; North Lincolnshire; Suffolk
Leicester District Land Registry
Westbridge Place, Leicester, Leicestershire, LE3 5DR
Tel: 0116 265 4000, Tel: 0116 265 4001 Enquiries
Fax: 0116 265 4008
Buckinghamshire; Leicester; Leicestershire; Milton Keynes, Rutland
Lytham District Land Registry
Birkenhead House, East Beach, Lytham St Annes FY8 5AB
Tel: 01253 849 849 Tel: 01253 840012 Enquiries
Fax: 01253 840001 (Manchester, Salford, Stockport, Tameside & Trafford)
Fax: 01253 840002 (Bolton, Bury, Oldham, Rochdale & Wigan) Fax: 01253 840013 (Lancashire)
Greater Manchester; Lancashire
Nottingham District Land Registry
Chalfont Drive, Nottingham, Nottinghamshire, NG8 3RN
Tel: 0115 935 1166 Fax: 0115 936 0036 for Nottinghamshire, Derby; Derbyshire, Nottinghamshire; South Yorkshire West Yorkshire
Peterborough District Land Registry
Touthill Close, City Road, Peterborough, PE1 1XN
Tel: 01733 288288 Fax: 01733 280022
Bedfordshire; Cambridgeshire; Essex; Luton; Northamptonshire
Plymouth District Land Registry
Plumer House, Tailyour Road, Crownhill, Plymouth, Devon, PL6 5HY, Tel: 01752 636000, Tel: 01752 636123 Enquiries, Fax: 01752 636161
Bath; North Somerset; Cornwall; Isles of Scilly; North Somerset; Somerset
Portsmouth District Land Registry
St Andrews Court, St Michael's Road, Portsmouth, Hampshire, PO1 2JH, Tel: 01705 768888
Tel: 01705 768880 Enquiries, Fax: 01705 768768
Brighton & Hove; East Sussex; Isle of Wight; West Sussex
Stevenage District Land Registry
Brickdale House, Swingate, Stevenage, Hertfordshire, SG1 1XG, Tel: 01438 788888, Tel: 01438 788889 Enquiries
Fax: 01438 780107
Hertfordshire
London Boroughs of Barking & Dagenham, Enfield, Hackney,

Haringey, Havering, Newham, Redbridge, Tower Hamlets, Waltham Forest
Swansea District Land Registry
Ty Bryn Glas, High Street, Swansea, SA1 1PW
Tel: 01792 458877 Fax: 01792 473236
London Boroughs of Ealing, Hillingdon, Hounslow
Telford District Land Registry
Parkside Court, Hall Park Way, Telford TF3 4LR
Tel: 01952 290355 Fax: 01952 290356
Hereford; Worcester; Shropshire, Greenwich Kingston upon Thames
London Boroughs of Lambeth, Lewsiham, Merton, Richmond upon Thames, Southwark, Wandsworth
Tunbridge Wells District Land Registry
Curtis House, Forest Road, Tunbridge Wells TN2 5AQ
Tel: 01892 510015 Fax: 01892 510032 Kent
Weymouth District Land Registry

Melcombe Court, 1 Cumberland Drive, Weymouth, Dorset, DT4 9TT,
Tel: 01305 363636 Fax: 01305 363646
Hampshire Poole; Portsmouth; Southampton; Swindon
Wiltshire; Dorset
York District Land Registry
James House, James Street, York, YO1 3YZ
Tel: 01904 450000 Fax: 01904 450086
North Yorkshire; York

Wales
District Land Registry for Wales
Ty Cwm Tawe, Phoenix Way, Llansamlet, Swansea
SA7 9FQ, Tel: 01792 355000, Tel: 01792 355095 Enquiries
Fax: 01792 355055
A fuller item on The Land Registry appeared in 5th Edition of the Handbook

Cemeteries & Crematoria

This list is not exhaustive and we would be pleased to receive details of other cemeteries & crematoria to add to our future lists.

England
Avon
Bristol General Cemetery Co, East Lodge, Bath Rd, Arnos Vale, Bristol, BS4 3EW Tel: 0117 971 3294
Canford Crematorium & Cemetery, Canford Lane, Westbury On Trym, Bristol, BS9 3PQ Tel: 0117 903 8280 Fax: 0117 903 8287
Administration Office for: Canford Crematorium, Canford Cemetery, Shirehampton Cemetery, Henbury Cemetery, Avonview Cemetery, Brislington Cemetery, Ridgeway Park Cemetery
Cemetery of Holy Souls, Bath Rd, Bristol, BS4 3EW Tel: 0117 977 2386
Haycombe Crematorium & Cemetery, Whiteway Rd, Bath, BA2 2RQ Tel: 01225 423682
South Bristol Crematorium & Cemetery, Bridgwater Rd, Bristol, BS13 7AS Tel: 0117 963 4141
Westerleigh Crematorium, Westerleigh Rd, Westerleigh, Bristol, BS37 8QP Tel: 0117 937 4619
Weston Super Mare Crematorium, Ebdon Rd, Worle, Weston-Super-Mare, BS22 9NY Tel: 01934 511717
Bedfordshire
Norse Rd Crematorium 104 Norse Rd, Bedford, MK41 0RL
Tel: 01234 353701
Church Burial Ground, 26 Crawley Green Rd, Luton, LU2 0QX
Tel: 01582 722874 Fax: 01582 721867 WWW: www.stmarysluton.org
Correspondence to; St Mary's Church, Church Street, Luton LU1 3JF
Dunstable Cemetery, West St, Dunstable, LU6 1PB
Tel: 01582 662772
Kempston Cemetery, Cemetery Lodge, 2 Green End Rd, Kempston, Bedford, MK43 8RJ Tel: 01234 851823
Luton Crematorium, The Vale, Butterfield Green Road, Stopsley, Luton, LU2 8DD Tel: 01582 723700 Tel: 01582 723730, Fax: 01582 723700
Luton General Cemetery, Rothesay Rd, Luton, LU1 1QX
Tel: 01582 727480
Berkshire
Easthampstead Park Cemetry & Crematorium, Nine Mile Ride, Wokingham, RG40 3DW Tel: 01344 420314
Henley Road Cemetery & Reading Crematorium, All Hallows Road, Henley Road, Caversham, Reading, RG4 5LP
Tel: 0118 947 2433
Larges Lane Cemetery, Larges Lane, Bracknell, RG12 9AL
Tel: 01344 450665
Newbury Cemetery, Shaw Hill, Shaw Fields, Shaw, Newbury, RG14 2EQ Tel: 01635 40096
Slough Cemetery & Crematorium, Stoke Rd, Slough, SL2 5AX
Tel: 01753 523127 (Cemetery) Fax: 01753 520702 (Crematorium)
Email: sloughcrem@hotmail.com WWW: www.slough.gov.uk
Bristol
South Bristol Crematorium and Cemetery, Bridgwater Road, Bedminster Down, Bristol, BS13 7AS Tel: 0117 903 833
Fax: 0117 903 8337 Administration Office for South Bristol Crematorium, South Bristol Cemetery, Greenbank Cemetery
Buckinghamshire
Crownhill Crematorium, Dansteed Way, Crownhill, Milton Keynes, Tel: 01908 568112
Chilterns Crematorium, Whielden Lane, Winchmore Hill, Amersham, HP7 0ND Tel: 01494 724263
Cambridgeshire
American Military Cemetery, Madingley Rd, Coton, Cambridge, CB3 7PH Tel: 01954 210350 Fax: 01954 211130 Email: Cambridge.Cemetery@ambc-er.org WWW: http://www.ambc.gov
Cambridge City Crematorium, Huntingdon Rd, Girton, Cambridge, CB3 0JJ Tel: 01954 780681
City of Ely Council, Ely Cemetery, Beech Lane, Ely, CB7 4QZ Tel: 01353 669659
Marholm Crematorium, Mowbray Rd, Peterborough, PE6 7JE Tel: 01733 262639

Cheshire
Altrincham Cemetery, Hale Rd, Altrincham, WA14 2EW Tel: 0161 980 4441
Altrincham Crematorium, White House Lane, Dunham Massey, Altrincham, WA14 5RH Tel: 0161 928 7771
Chester Cemetries & Crematorium, Blacon Avenue, Blacon, Chester, CH1 5BB Tel: 01244 372428
Dukinfield Crematorium, Hall Green Rd, Dukinfield, SK16 4EP
Tel: 0161 330 1901
Macclesfield Cemetery, Cemetery Lodge, 87 Prestbury Rd, Macclesfield, SK10 3BU Tel: 01625 422330
Middlewich Cemetery, 12 Chester Rd, Middlewich, CW10 9ET Tel: 01606 737101
Overleigh Rd Cemetery, The Lodge, Overleigh Rd, Chester, CH4 7HW Tel: 01244 682529
Walton Lea Crematorium, Chester Rd, Higher Walton, Warrington, WA4 6TB Tel: 01925 267731
Widnes Cemetery & Crematorium, Birchfield Rd, Widnes, WA8 9EE Tel: 0151 471 7332
Cleveland
Teesside Crematorium, Acklam Rd, Middlesbrough, TS5 7HE Tel: 01642 817725 Fax: 01642 852424 Email: peter_gitsham@middlesbrough.gov.uk WWW: www.middlesbrough.gov.uk Also contact address for: Acklam Cemetery, Acklam Road, Middlesbrough; Linthorpe Cemetery, Burlam Road; Thorntree Cemetery, Cargo Fleet Lane; Thorntree RC Cemetery, Cargo Fleet Lane; North Ormesby Cemetery; St josephs Cemetery, Ormesby Road, Middlesbrough
Cornwall
Glynn Valley Crematorium, Turfdown Rd, Fletchers Bridge, Bodmin, PL30 4AU Tel: 01208 73858
Penmount Crematorium, Penmount, Truro, TR4 9AA Tel: 01872 272871 Fax: 01872 223634 Email: mail@penmount-crematorium.org.uk www.penmount-crematorium.org.uk
County Durham
Birtley Cemetery & Crematorium, Windsor Rd, Birtley, Chester Le Street, DH3 1PQ Tel: 0191 4102381
Chester Le Street Cemetery, Chester Le Street District Council Civic Centre, Newcastle Rd, Chester Le Street, DH3 3UT Tel: 0191 3872117
Horden Parish Council, Horden Cemetery Lodge, Thorpe Rd, Horden, Peterlee, SR8 4TP Tel: 0191 5863870
Mountsett Crematorium, Ewehurst Rd, Dipton, Stanley, DH9 0HN
Tel: 01207 570255
Murton Parish Council, Cemetery Lodge, Church Lane, Murton, Seaham, SR7 9RD Tel: 0191 5263973
Newton Aycliffe Cemetery, Stephenson Way, Newton Aycliffe, DL5 7DF Tel: 01325 312861
Princess Road Cemetery, Princess Rd, Seaham, SR7 7TD Tel: 0191 5812943
Trimdon Foundry Parish Council, Cemetary Lodge, Thornley Rd, Trimdon Station, TS29 6NX Tel: 01429 880592
Trimdon Parish Council, Cemetery Lodge, Northside, Trimdon Grange, Trimdon Station, TS29 6HN Tel: 01429 880538
Wear Valley District Council, Cemetery Lodge, South Church Rd, Bishop Auckland, DL14 7NA Tel: 01388 603396
Cumbria
Carlisle Cemetery, Richardson St, Carlisle, CA2 6AL Tel: 01228 625310 Fax: 01228 625313 Email: junec@carlisle-city.gov.uk
Penrith Cemetery, Beacon Edge, Penrith, CA11 7RZ Tel: 01768 862152
Wigton Burial Joint Committee, Cemetery House, Station Hill, Wigton, CA7 9BN Tel: 016973 42442
Derbyshire
Bretby Crematorium, Geary Lane, Bretby, Burton-On-Trent, DE15 0QE Tel: 01283 221505 Fax: 01283 224846 Email: bretby.crematorium@eaststaffsbc.gov.uk WWW: www.eaststaffsbc.gov.uk CC accepted

Castle Donington Parish Council, Cemetery House, The Barroon, Castle Donington, Derby, DE74 2PF Tel: 01332 810202

Chesterfield & District Joint Crematorium, Chesterfield Rd, Brimington, Chesterfield, S43 1AU Tel: 01246 345888 Fax: 01246 345889

Clay Cross Cemetery, Cemetery Rd, Danesmoor, Chesterfield, S45 9RL Tel: 01246 863225

Dronfield Cemetery, Cemetery Lodge, 42 Cemetery Rd, Dronfield, S18 1XY Tel: 01246 412373

Glossop Cemetery, Arundel House, Cemetery Rd, Glossop, SK13 7QG Tel: 01457 852269

Markeaton Crematorium, Markeaton Lane, Derby, DE22 4NH Tel: 01332 341012 Fax: 01332 331273

Melbourne Cemetery, Pack Horse Rd, Melbourne, Derby, DE73 1BZ Tel: 01332 863369

Shirebrook Town Council, Common Lane, Shirebrook, Mansfield, NG20 8PA Tel: 01623 742509

Devon

Drake Memorial Park Ltd The, Haye Rd, Plympton, Plymouth, PL7 1UQ Tel: 01752 337937

Exeter & Devon Crematorium, Topsham Rd, Exeter, EX2 6EU Tel: 01392 496333

Littleham Church Yard, Littleham Village, Littleham, Exmouth, EX8 2RQ Tel: 01395 225579

Mole Valley Green Burial Ground, Woodhouse Farm, Queens Nympton, South Molton, EX36 4JH Tel: 01769 574512 Fax: 01769 574512 Email: woodhouse.org.farm@farming.co.uk

North Devon Crematorium, Old Torrington Rd, Barnstaple, EX31 3NW Tel: 01271 345431

Ford Park Cemetery Trust, Ford Park Rd, Plymouth, PL4 6NT Tel: 01752 665442 Fax: 01752 601177 Email: trustees@ford-park-cemetery.org WWW: www.ford-park-cemetery.org

Tavistock Cemetery, Cemetery Office, Plymouth Rd, Tavistock, PL19 8BY Tel: 01822 612799 Fax: 01822 618300 Email: tavistocktc@aol.com WWW: www.tavistock.co.uk

Torquay Crematorium & Cemetery, Hele Rd, Torquay, TQ2 7QG Tel: 01803 327768

Dorset, Dorchester Cemetery Office, 31a Weymouth Avenue, Dorchester, DT1 2EN Tel: 01305 263900

Parkstone Cemetery, 134 Pottery Rd, Parkstone, Poole, BH14 8RD Tel: 01202 741104

Poole Cemetery, Dorchester Rd, Oakdale, Poole, BH15 3RZ Tel: 01202 741106

Poole Crematorium, Gravel Hill, Poole, BH17 9BQ Tel: 01202 602582

Sherborne Cemetery, Lenthay Rd, Sherborne, DT9 6AA Tel: 01935 812909

Weymouth Crematorium, Quibo Lane, Weymouth, DT4 0RR Tel: 01305 786984

Essex

Basildon & District Crematorium, Church Rd, Bowers Gifford, Basildon, SS13 2HG Tel: 01268 584411

Chadwell Heath Cemetery, Whalebone Lane, North Chadwell Heath, Romford, RM6 5QX Tel: 0181 590 3280

Chelmsford Crematorium, Writtle Rd, Chelmsford, CM1 3BL Tel: 01245 256946

Chigwell Cemetery, Frog Hall LaneChapman, Manor Rd, Chigwell, IG7 4JX Tel: 020 8501 4275 Tel: 020 8501 2045 Email: chigwell@tesco.net, Earliest record - April 1973**Colchester Cemetery & Crematorium,** Mersea Rd, Colchester, CO2 8RU Tel: 01206 282950

Eastbrookend Cemetery, Dagenham Rd, Dagenham, RM10 7DR Tel: 01708 447451

Federation of Synagogues Burial Society, 416 Upminster Rd North, Rainham, RM13 9SB Tel: 01708 552825

Great Burstead Cemetery, Church St, Great Burstead, Billericay, CM11 2TR Tel: 01277 654334

Parndon Wood Crematorium and Cemetery, Parndon Wood Rd, Harlow, CM19 4SF Tel: 01279 446199 Tel: 01279 423800, Email: chris.brown@harlow.gov.uk

Pitsea Cemetery, Church Rd, Pitsea, Basildon, SS13 2EZ Tel: 01268 552132

Romford Cemetery, Crow Lane, Romford, RM7 0EP Tel: 01708 740791

Sewardstone Road Cemetery, Sewardstone Rd, Waltham Abbey, EN9 1NX Tel: 01992 712525

South Essex Crematorium, Ockendon Rd, Corbets Tey, Upminster, RM14 2UY Tel: 01708 222188

Sutton Road Cemetery, The Lodge, Sutton Rd, Southend-On-Sea, SS2 5PX Tel: 01702 603907 Fax: 01702 603906 CC accepted**Weeley Crematorium,** Colchester Rd, Weeley, Clacton-On-Sea, CO16 9JP Tel: 01255 831108 Fax: 01255 831440 Also covers and is contact address for: Clacton Cemetery; Kirby Cross Cemetery; Dovercourt Cemetery; Walton on the Naze Cemetery

Wickford Cemetery, Park Drive, Wickford, SS12 9DH Tel: 01268 733335

Gloucestershire

Cheltenham Cemetery & Crematorium, Bouncers Lane, Cheltenham, GL52 5JT Tel: 01242 244245 Fax: 01242 263123 Email: cemetery@cheltenham.gov.uk WWW: www.cheltenham.gov.uk

Coney Hill Crematorium, Coney Hill Rd, Gloucester, GL4 4PA Tel: 01452 523902

Forest of Dean Crematorium, Yew Tree Brake, Speech House Rd, Cinderford, GL14 3HU Tel: 01594 826624

Mile End Cemetery, Mile End, Coleford, GL16 7DB Tel: 01594 832848

Hampshire

Aldershot Crematorium, 48 Guildford Rd, Aldershot, GU12 4BP Tel: 01252 321653

Anns Hill Rd Cemetery, Anns Hill Rd, Gosport, PO12 3JX Tel: 023 9258 0181 Fax: 023 9251 3191 WWW: www.gosport.gov.uk

Basingstoke Crematorium, Manor Farm, Stockbridge Rd, North Waltham, Basingstoke, RG25 2BA Tel: 01256 398784

Magdalen Hill Cemetery, Magdalen Hill, Arlesesford Rd, Winchester, SO21 1HE Tel: 01962 854135

Portchester Crematorium, Upper Cornaway Lane, Portchester, Fareham, PO16 8NE Tel: 01329 822533

Portsmouth Cemeteries Office, Milton Rd, Southsea, PO4 8 Tel: 023 9273 2559

Southampton City Council, 6 Bugle St, Southampton, SO14 2AJ Tel: 01703 228609

Warblington Cemetery, Church Lane, Warblington, Havant, PO9 2TU Tel:

Worting Rd Cemetery, 105 Worting Rd, Basingstoke, RG21 8YZ Tel: 01256 321737

Herefordshire

Hereford Cemetery & Crematorium, Bereavement Services office, Westfaling Street, Hereford, HR4 0JE Tel: 01432 383200 Fax: 01432 383201

Hertfordshire

Vicarage Road Cemetery, Vicarage Road, Watford, WD18 0EJ Tel: 01923 672157 Fax: 01923 672157

Almonds Lane Cemetery, Almonds Lane, Stevenage, SG1 3RR Tel: 01438 350902

Bushey Jewish Cemetery, Little Bushey Lane, Bushey, Watford, WD2 3TP Tel: 0181 950 6299 One of the burial grounds maintained by the United Synagogue

Chorleywood Road Cemetery, Chorleywood Rd, Rickmansworth, WD3 4EH Tel: 01923 772646

Dacorum Borough Council, Woodwells Cemetery, Buncefield Lane, Hemel Hempstead, HP2 7HY Tel: 01442 252856

Harwood Park Crematorium Ltd, Watton Rd, Stevenage, SG2 8XT Tel: 01438 815555

Hatfield Road Cemetery, Hatfield Rd, St. Albans, AL1 4LU Tel: 01727 819362 Fax: 01727 819362 Email: stalbans@cemeteries.freeserve.co.uk St Albans City & District Council administers three Cemeteries from Hatfield Road. The other two are situated London Road, St Albans and Westfield Road, Harpenden

North Watford Cemetery, North Western Avenue, Watford, WD25 0AW Tel: 01923 672157 Fax: 01923 672157

Tring Cemetery, Aylesbury Rd, Aylesbury, Tring, HP23 4DH Tel: 01442 822248

Vicarage Road Cemetery, Vicarage Rd, Watford, WD1 8EJ Tel: 01923 225147

Watton Rd Cemetery, Watton Rd, Ware, SG12 0AX Tel: 01920 463261

West Herts Crematorium, High Elms Lane, Watford, WD25 0JS Tel: 01923 673285 Fax: 01923 681318 Email: postmaster@weshertscrem.org WWW: www.westhertscrem.org CC accepted

Western Synagogue Cemetery, Cheshunt Cemetery, Bulls Cross Ride, Waltham Cross, EN7 5HT Tel: 01992 717820

Weston Road Cemetery, Weston Rd, Stevenage, SG1 4DE Tel: 01438 367109

Woodcock Hill Cemetery, Lodge, Woodcock Hill, Harefield Rd, Rickmansworth, WD3 1PT Tel: 01923 775188

Isle Of Wight

Shanklin Cemetery, 1 Cemetery Rd, Lake Sandown, Sandown, PO36 9NN Tel: 01983 403743

Kent

Barham Crematorium, Canterbury Rd, Barham, Canterbury, CT4 6QU Tel: 01227 831351 Fax: 01227 830258

Beckenham Crematorium & Cemetery, Elmers End Rd, Beckenham, BR3 4TD Tel: 0208650 0322

Chartham Cemetery Lodge, Ashford Rd, Chartham, Canterbury, CT4 7NY Tel: 01227 738211 Tel: 01227 738211 Minicom, Fax: 01227 738211 All burial records computerised

Gravesham Borough Council, Old Rd West, Gravesend, DA11 0LS Tel: 01474 337491

Hawkinge Cemetery & Crematorium, Aerodrome Rd, Hawkinge, Folkestone, CT18 7AG Tel: 01303 892215

Kent & Sussex Crematorium, Benhall Mill Rd., Tunbridge Wells, TN2 5JH Tel: 01892 523894
Kent County Crematorium plc, Newcourt Wood, Charing, Ashford, TN27 0EB Tel: 01233 712443 Fax: 01233 713501
The Cremation Society, 2nd Floor Brecon House, 16/16a Albion Place, Maidstone, ME14 5DZ Tel: 01622 688292/3 Fax: 01622 686698 Email: cremsoc@aol.com WWW: www.cremation.org.uk
Medway Crematorium, Robin Hood Lane, Blue Bell Hill, Chatham, ME5 9QU Tel: 01634 861639 Fax: 01634 671206 Email: paul.edwards@medway.gov.uk CC accepted
Northfleet Cemetery, Springhead Rd, Northfleet, Gravesend, DA11 8HW Tel: 01474 533260
Snodland Cemetery, Cemetery Cottage, Cemetery Rd, Snodland, ME6 5DN Tel: 01634 240764
Thanet Crematorium, Manston Rd, Margate, CT9 4LY Tel: 01843 224492 Fax: 01843 292218 Also covers: Margate Cemetery, Kent; Ramsgate and St Lawrence Cemeteries
Vinters Park Crematorium, Bearstead Rd, Weavering, Maidstone, ME14 5LG Tel: 01622 738172 Fax: 01622 630560 CC accepted
Lancashire
Accrington Cemetery & Crematorium, Burnley Rd, Accrington, BB5 6HA Tel: 01254 232933 Fax: 01254 232933
Atherton Cemetery, Leigh Road, Atherton
Audenshaw Cemetery, Cemetery Rd, Audenshaw, Manchester, M34 5AH Tel: 0161 336 2675
Blackley Cemetery & Crematorium, Victoria Avenue, Manchester, M9 8 Tel: 0161 740 5359
Burnley Cemetery, Rossendale Rd, Burnley, BB11 5DD Tel: 01282 435411 Fax: 01282 458904 WWW: www.burnley.gov.uk
Carleton Crematorium, Stocks Lane, Carleton, Poulton-Le-Fylde, FY6 7QS Tel: 01253 882541
Central & North Manchester Synagogue Jewish Cemetery, Rainsough Brow, Prestwich, Manchester, M25 9XW Tel: 0161 773 2641**Central & North Manchester Synagogue Jewish Cemetery,** Rochdale Rd, Manchester, M9 6FQ Tel: 0161 740 2317
Chadderton Cemetery, Cemetery Lodge, Middleton Rd, Chadderton, Oldham, OL9 0JZ Tel: 0161 624 2301
Gidlow Cemetery, Gidlow Lane, Standish, Wigan, WN6 8RT Tel: 01257 424127
Greenacres Cemetery, Greenacres Rd, Oldham, OL4 3HT Tel: 0161 624 2294
Hindley Cemetery, Castle Hill Road Road, Ince, Wigan, WN3 Tel:
Hollinwood Cemetery (incorporating Oldham Crematorium), Central Cemeteries Office, Roman Rd, Hollinwood, Oldham, OL8 3LU Tel: 0161 681 1312 Fax: 0161 683 5233 Email: oper.cemeteries@oldham.gov.uk WWW: www.oldham.gov.uk The Central Cemeteries Office covers seven cemeteries and one crematorium: Hollinwood, Greenacres, Crompton, Royton, Lees, Chadderton and Failsworprth Cemeteries and Oldham Crematorium
Howe Bridge Crematorium, Crematorium Management Ltd, Lovers Lane, Atherton, Manchester, M46 0PZ Tel: 01942 870811
Howebridge Cemetery, Lovers Lane, Atherton, Tel:
Ince in Makerfield Cemetery, Warrington Road, Lower Ince, Wigan
Leigh Cemetery, Manchester Rd, Leigh, WN7 2 Tel: 01942 671560 Fax: 01942 828877 WWW: www.wiganbc.gov.uk
Lower Ince Cemetery and Crematorium, Cemetery Road, Lower Ince, Wigan, WN3 4NH Tel: 01942 866455 Fax: 01942 828855 Email: t.bassett@wiganmbc.gov.uk
Lytham Park Cemetery & Cremarotium, Regent Avenue, Lytham St. Annes, FY8 4AB Tel: 01253 735429 Fax: 01253 731903
Manchester Crematorium Ltd, Barlow Moor Rd, Manchester, M21 7GZ Tel: 0161 881 5269
Middleton New Cemetery, Boarshaw Rd, Middleton, Manchester, M24 6 Tel: 0161 655 3765
New Manchester Woodland Cemetery, City Rd, Ellenbrook, Worsley, Manchester, M28 1BD Tel: 0161 790 1300
Overdale Crematorium, Overdale Drive, Chorley New Rd, Heaton, Bolton, BL1 5BU Tel: 01204 840214
Padiham Public Cemetery, St. Johns Rd, Padiham, Burnley, BB12 7BN Tel: 01282 778139
Preston Cemetery, New Hall Lane, Preston, PR1 4SY Tel: 01772 794585 Fax: 01772 703857 Email: m.birch@preston.gov.uk WWW: www.preston.gov.uk All burial records are available on microfilm at the Lancashire Record Office, Bow Lane, Preston as well as at the Cemetery Office
Preston Crematorium, Longridge Rd, Ribbleton, Preston, PR2 6RL Tel: 01772 792391 Fax: 01772 703857 Email: m.birch@preston.gov.uk WWW: www.preston.gov.uk All records relating to Preston Crematorium are held at Preston Cemetery office, New Hall Lane, Preston PR1 4SY Tel: 01772 794585
Rochdale Cemetery, Bury Rd, Rochdale, OL11 4DG Tel: 01706 645219
Southern Cemetery, Barlow Moor Rd, Manchester, M21 7GL Tel: 0161 881 2208
St. Mary's Catholic Cemetery, Manchester Rd, Wardley, Manchester, M28 2UJ Tel: 0161 794 2194   Email: cemeteries@salforddiocese.org

St Joseph's Cemetery, Moston Lane, Manchester, M40 9QL Tel: 0161 681 1582   Email: cemeteries@salforddiocese.org
Tyldesley Cemetery, Hough Lane, Tyldesley, Tel:
United Synagogue Burial Ground, Worsley Hill Farm, Phillips Park Rd, Whitefield, Manchester, M45 7ED Tel: 0161 766 2065
Wigan Council Cemeteries and Crematorium Section, 1 - 3 Worsley Terrace, Standishgate, Wigan, WN1 1XW Tel: 01942 828993 Tel: 01942 828994, Fax: 01942 828877 Email: t.boussele@wiganmbc.gov.uk
Whitworth Cemetery, Edward St, Whitworth, Rochdale, OL16 2EJ Tel: 01706 217777
Westwood Cemetery, Westwood Lane, Lower Ince, Wigan,
Leicestershire
Cemetery Lodge, Thorpe Rd, Melton Mowbray, LE13 1SH Tel: 01664 562223
Loughborough Crematorium, Leicester Rd, Loughborough, LE11 2AF Tel: 01743 353046
Saffron Hill Cemetery, Stonesby Avenue, Leicester, LE2 6TY Tel: 0116 222 1049
Lincolnshire
Boston Crematorium, Cemeteries and Crematorium Office, Marian Rd, Boston, PE21 9HA Tel: 01205 364612 Fax: 01205 364612 Email: martin.potts@boston.gov.uk www.boston.gov.uk Administers Boston Cemetery (1855), Fosdyke Cemetery (1952) and Boston Crematorium (1966)
Bourne Town Cemetery, South Rd, Bourne, PE10 9JB Tel: 01778 422796
Grantham Cemetery & Crematorium, Harrowby Rd, Grantham, NG31 9DT Tel: 01476 563083 Tel: 01476 590905 Fax: 01476 576228
Horncastle Cemetery, Boston Rd, Horncastle, LN9 6NF Tel: 01507 527118
Stamford Cemetery, Wichendom, Little Casterton Rd, Stamford, PE9 1BB Tel: 01780 762316
Tyler Landscapes, Newport Cemetery, Manor Rd, Newport, Lincoln, LN4 1RT Tel: 01522 525195
Lincolnshire - North East
Cleethorpes Cemetery, Beacon Avenue, Cleethorpes, DN35 8EQ Tel: 01472 324869 Fax: 01472 324870
North East Lincolnshire Council Crematorium & Cemeteries Department, Weelsby Avenue, Grimsby, DN32 0BA Tel: 01472 324869 Fax: 01472 324870
Lincolnshire - North
Woodlands Crematorium, Brumby Wood Lane, Scunthorpe, DN17 1SP Tel: 01724 280289 Fax: 01724 871235 Email: crematorium@northlincs.gov.uk www.northlincs.gov.uk/environmentalhealth/cemetery.htm, Central Office for holding documents for: Barton Upon Humber Cemetery, Brumby Cemetery, Crosby Cemetery, Brigg Cemetery, Scawby Cemetery, Winterton Cemetery and Woodlands Cemetery
London
Abney Park Cemetery, The South Lodgfe, Stoke Newington High St, Stoke Newington, London, N16 0LH Tel: 020 7275 7557 Fax: 020 7275 7557 Email: abney-park@ges2.poptel.org.uk WWW: www.abney-park.org.uk
Brockley Ladywell Hithergreen & Grove Park Cemeteries, Verdant Lane, Catford, London SE6 1TP Tel: 0181 697 2555
Brompton Cemetery, Fulham Rd, London, SW10 9UG Tel: 0171 352 1201
Cemetery Management Ltd, The City of Westminster Office, 38 Uxbridge Rd, London, W7 3PP Tel: 0181 567 0913
Charlton Cemetery, Cemetery Lane, London, SE7 8DZ Tel: 0181 854 0235
Chingford Mount Cemetery London Borough of Waltham Forest, Old Church Rd, London, E4 6ST Tel: 020 8524 5030
City of London Cemetery & Crematorium, Aldersbrook Rd, London, E12 5DQ Tel: 0181 530 2151
Coroners Court, 8 Ladywell Rd, Lewisham, London, SE13 7UW Tel: 0208690 5138
East London Cemetery Co.Ltd, Grange Rd, London, E13 0HB Tel: 020 7476 5109 Fax: 020 7476 8338 Email: enquiries@eastlondoncemetery.co.uk WWW: www.eastlondoncemetery.co.uk
Edmonton Cemetery, Church St, Edmonton, London, N9 9HP Tel: 0208360 2157
Eltham Cemetery & Crematorium, Crown Woods Way, Eltham, London, SE9 2RF Tel: 0181 850 2921 (Cemetery) Fax: 0181 850 7046 (Crematorium)
Gap Road Cemetery, Gap Rd, London, SW19 8JF Tel: 0208879 0701
Golders Green Crematorium, 62 Hoop Lane, London, NW11 7NL Tel: 0208455 2374
Greenwich Cemetery, Well Hall Rd, London, SE9 6TZ Tel: 0181 856 8666
London Borough of Hackney Mortuary, Lower Clapton Rd, London, E5 8EQ Tel: 0181 985 2808
Hendon Cemetery & Crematorium, Holders Hill Rd, London, NW7 1NB Tel: 0181 346 0657

Highgate Cemetery, Swains Lane, London, N6 6PJ Tel: 0181 340 1834

Honor Oak Crematorium, Brenchley Gardens, London, SE23 3RB Tel: 020 7639 3121 Fax: 020 7732 3557 Email: terry.connor@southwark.gov.uk

Islington Cemetery & Crematorium, High Rd, East Finchley, London, N2 9AG Tel: 0208883 1230

Kensal Green Cemetery, Harrow Road, London, W10 4RA Tel: 020 8969 0152 Fax: 020 8960 9744

L B S Cemeteries, Brenchley Gardens, London, SE23 3RD Tel: 020 7639 3121 Fax: 020 7732 3557 Email: terry.connor@southwark.gov.uk

Lambeth Cemetery and Crematorium, Cemetary Lodge, Blackshaw Rd, Tooting, London, SW17 0BY Tel: 0181 672 1390

Lewisham Crematorium, Verdant Lane, London, SE6 1TP Tel: 0208698 4955

Liberal Jewish Cemetery, The Lodge, Pound Lane, London, NW10 2HG Tel: 0181 459 1635

Manor Park Cemetery Co.Ltd, Sebert Rd, Forest Gate, London, E7 0NP Tel: 020 8534 1486 Fax: 020 8519 1348 Email: supt@manorpark15.fsbusiness.co.uk WWW: www.mpark.co.uk CC accepted Grave of John Cornwell VC

New Southgate Cemetery & Crematorium Ltd, 98 Brunswick Park Rd, London, N11 1JJ Tel: 0181 361 1713

Newham, London Borough of, High St South, London, E6 6ET Tel: 0181 472 9111

Plumstead Cemetery, Wickham Lane, London, SE2 0NS Tel: 0181 854 0785

Putney Vale Cemetery & Crematorium, Kingston Rd, London, SW15 3SB Tel: 0181 788 2113

South London Crematorium & Streatham Park Cemetery, Rowan Rd, London, SW16 5JG Tel: 0181 764 2255

St. Marylebone Crematorium, East End Rd, Finchley, London, N2 0RZ Tel: 0208343 2233

St. Pancras Cemetery (London Borough Of Camden), High Rd, East Finchley, London, N2 9AG Tel: 0181 883 1231

St. Patrick's Catholic Cemetery, Langthorne Rd, London, E11 4HL Tel: 0181 539 2451

St.Mary's Catholic Cemetery, Harrow Rd, London, NW10 5NU Tel: 0181 969 1145

Tottenham Park Cemetery, Montagu Rd, Edmonton, N18 2NF Tel: 0181 807 1617

United Synagogue, Beaconsfield Rd, Willesden, London, NW10 2JE Tel: 0208459 0394

West End Chesed V'Ameth Burial Society, 3 Rowan Rd, London, SW16 5JF Tel: 0181 764 1566

West Ham Cemetery, Cemetery Rd, London, E7 9DG Tel: 0208534 1566

West London Synagogue, Hoop Lane, London, NW11 7NJ Tel: 0208455 2569

West Norwood Cemetery & Crematorium, Norwood Rd, London, SE27 9AJ Tel: 0207926 7900

Woodgrange Park Cemetery, Romford Rd, London, E7 8AF Tel: 0181 472 3433

Woolwich Cemetery, Kings Highway, London, SE18 2BJ Tel: 0181 854 0740

Merseyside

Anfield Crematorium, Priory Rd, Anfield, Liverpool, L4 2SL Tel: 0151 263 3267

Southport Cemeteries & Crematoria, Southport Rd, Scarisbrick, Southport, PR8 5JQ Tel: 01704 533443

St. Helens Cemetery & Crematorium, Rainford Rd, Windle, St. Helens, WA10 6DF Tel: 01744 677406 Fax: 01744 677411

Thornton Garden Of Rest, Lydiate Lane, Thornton, Liverpool, L23 1TP Tel: 0151 924 5143

Middlesex

Adath Yisroel Synagogue & Burial Society, Carterhatch Lane, Enfield, EN1 4BG Tel: 0181 363 3384

Breakspear Crematorium, Breakspear Rd, Ruislip, HA4 7SJ Tel: 01895 632843 Fax: 01895 624209

Enfield Crematorium, Great Cambridge Rd, Enfield, EN1 4DS Tel: 0181 363 8324

Heston & Isleworth Borough Cemetry, 190 Powder Mill Lane, Twickenham, TW2 6EJ Tel: 0181 894 3830

Richmond Cemeteries, London Borough of Richmond upon Thames, Sheen Rd, Richmond, TW10 5BJ Tel: 020 8876 4511 Fax: 020 8878 8118 Email: cemeteries@richmond.gov.uk

South West Middlesex Crematorium, Hounslow Rd, Hanworth, Feltham, TW13 5JH Tel: 0208894 9001

Spelthorne Borough Council, Green Way, Sunbury-On-Thames, TW16 6NW Tel: 01932 780244

Norfolk

Colney Wood Memorial Park, Colney Hall, Watton Rd, Norwich, NR4 7TY Tel: 01603 811556

Mintlyn Crematorium, Lynn Rd, Bawsey, King's Lynn, PE32 1HB Tel: 01553 630533 Fax: 01553 630998 Email: colin.houseman@west-norfolk.gov.uk WWW: www.west-norfolk.gov.uk

Norwich & Norfolk Crematoria - St. Faiths & Earlham, 75 Manor Rd, Horsham St. Faith, Norwich, NR10 3LF Tel: 01603 898264

Sprowston Cemetery, Church Lane, Sprowston, Norwich, NR7 8AU Tel: 01603 425354

North Tyneside - North Tyneside Metropolitan Borough Council Earsdon Cemetery, Earsdon, Whitley Bay, NE25 9LR Tel: 0191 200 5861 0191 200 5860

Longbenton Cemetery, Longbenton, Newcastle Upon Tyne, NE12 8EY Tel: 0191 2661261

Whitley Bay Cemetery, Blyth Rd, Whitley Bay, NE26 4NH Tel: 0191 200 5861 Fax: 0191 200 5860

Northamptonshire

Counties Crematorium, Towcester Rd, Milton Malsor, Northampton, NN4 9RN Tel: 01604 858280

Dallington Cemetery, Harlstone Rd, Dallington, Northampton, NN5 7 Tel: 01604 751589

Northumberland

Alnwick Cemetary, Cemetary Lodge Office, South Rd, Alnwick, NE66 2PH Tel: 01665 602598 Tel: 01665 579272, Fax: 01665 579272 WWW: www.alnwicktown.com

Blyth Cemetery, Links Rd, Blyth, NE24 3PJ Tel: 01670 369623

Cowpen Cemetery, Cowpen Rd, Blyth, NE24 5SZ Tel: 01670 352107

Embleton Joint Burial Committee, Spitalford, Embleton, Alnwick, NE66 3DW Tel: 01665 576632

Haltwhistle & District Joint Burial Committee, Cemetery Lodge Haltwhistle, NE49 0LF Tel: 01434 320266 Fax: 01434 320266

Rothbury Cemetery, Cemetery Lodge, Whitton Rd Rothbury, Morpeth, NE65 7RX Tel: 01669 620451

Nottinghamshire

Bramcote Crematorium, Coventry Lane, Beeston, Nottingham, NG9 3GJ Tel: 0115 922 1837

Mansfield & District Crematorium, Derby Rd, Mansfield, NG18 5BJ Tel: 01623 621811

Northern Cemetery, Hempshill Lane, Bulwell, Nottingham, NG6 8PF Tel: 0115 915 3245 Fax: 0115 915 3246 Email: alec.thomson@nottinghamcity.gov.uk WWW: www.nottinghamcity.gov.uk/bereavement, Also covers: ~Basford Cemetery Npottingham Road, General Cemetery Waverley Street, Canning Circus and Church (Rock) Cemetery, Mansfield Road

Southern Cemetery & Crematoria, Wilford Hill, West Bridgford, Nottingham, NG2 7FE Tel: 0115 915 2340

Tithe Green Woodland Burial Ground, Salterford Lane, Calverton, Nottingham, NG14 6NZ Tel: 01623 882210

Oxfordshire

Oxford Crematorium Ltd, Bayswater Rd, Headington, Oxford, OX3 9RZ Tel: 01865 351255

Shropshire

Bridgnorth Cemetery, Mill St, Bridgnorth, WV15 5NG Tel: 01746 762386

Emstrey Crematorium, London Rd, Shrewsbury, SY2 6PS Tel: 01743 359883

Hadley Cemetery, 85 Hadley Park Rd, Hadley, Telford, TF1 4PY Tel: 01952 223418

Longden Road Cemetery, Longden Rd, Shrewsbury, SY3 7HS Tel: 01743 353046

Market Drayton Burial Committee, Cemetery Lodge, Cemetery Rd, Market Drayton, TF9 3BD Tel: 01630 652833

Oswestry Cemetery, Cemetery Lodge, Victoria Rd, Oswestry, SY11 2HU Tel: 01691 652013 Fax: 01691 652013 Email: graham.lee2@btinternet.com

Whitchurch Joint Cemetery Board, The Cemetery Lodge, Mile Bank Rd, Whitchurch, SY13 4JY Tel: 01948 665477

Somerset

Burnham Area Burial Board, The Old Courthouse, Jaycroft Rd, Burnham-On-Sea, TA8 1LE Tel: 01278 795111

Chard Town Council, Holyrood Lace Mill, Hoilyrood Street, Chard, TA20 12YA Tel: 01460 260370 Fax: 01460 260372

Minehead Cemetery, Porlock Rd, Woodcombe, Minehead, TA24 8RY Tel: 01643 705243

Sedgemoor District Council, The Cemetery, Quantock Rd, Bridgwater, TA6 7EJ Tel: 01278 423993

Taunton Deane Cemeteries & Crematorium, Wellington New Rd, Taunton, TA1 5NE Tel: 01823 284811 Fax: 01823 323152 www.tauntondeane.gov.uk/TDBCsites/crem

Wells Burial Joint Committee, 127 Portway, Wells, BA5 1LY Tel: 01749 672049

Yeovil Cemetery, Preston Rd, Yeovil, BA21 3AG Tel: 01935 423742

Yeovil Crematorium, Bunford Lane, Yeovil, BA20 2EJ Tel: 01935 476718

Staffordshire

Bretby Crematorium, Geary Lane, Bretby, Burton-On-Trent, DE15 0QE Tel: 01283 221505 Fax: 01283 224846 Email: bretby.crematorium@eaststaffsbc.gov.uk WWW: www.eaststaffsbc.gov.uk CC accepted

Cannock Cemetery, Cemetery Lodge, 160 Pye Green Rd, Cannock, WS11 2SJ Tel: 01543 503176

Carmountside Cemetery and Crematorium Leek Rd, Milton, Stoke-On-Trent, ST2 7AB Tel: 01782 235050 Fax: 01782 235050 Email: karendeaville@civic2.stoke.gov.uk

Leek Cemetery, Condlyffe Rd, Leek, ST13 5PP Tel: 01538 382616

Newcastle Cemetery, Lymewood Grove, Newcastle, ST5 2EH Tel: 01782 616379 Fax: 01782 630498 Email: jeanette.hollins@newcastle-staffs.gov.uk

Newcastle Crematorium, Chatterley Close, Bradwell, Newcastle, ST5 8LE Tel: 01782 635498 Fax: 01782 710859

Stafford Crematorium, Tixall Rd, Stafford, ST18 0XZ Tel: 01785 242594

Stapenhill Cemetery, 38 Stapenhill Rd, Burton-On-Trent, DE15 9AE Tel: 01283 508572 Fax: 01283 566586 Email: cemetery@eaststaffsbc.gov.uk WWW: www.eaststaffsbc.gov.uk

Stilecop Cematary, Stilecop Rd, Rugeley, WS15 1ND Tel: 01889 577739

Uttoxeter Town Council, Cemetery Lodge, Stafford Rd, Uttoxeter ST14 8DS Tel: 01889 563374

Suffolk

Brinkley Woodland Cemetery, 147 All Saints Rd, Newmarket, CB8 8HH Tel: 01638 600693

Bury St. Edmunds Cemetery, 91 Kings Rd, Bury St. Edmunds, IP33 3DT Tel: 01284 754447

Hadleigh Town Council, Friars Rd, Hadleigh, Ipswich, IP7 6DF Tel: 01473 822034

Haverhill Cemetery, Withersfield Rd, Haverhill, CB9 9HF Tel: 01440 703810

Ipswich Cemetery & Crematorium, Cemetery Lane, Ipswich, IP4 2TQ Tel: 01473 433580 Fax: 01473 433588 Email: carol.egerton@ipswich.gov.uk

Leiston Cemetery, Waterloo Avenue, Leiston, IP16 4EH Tel: 01728 831043

West Suffolk Crematorium, Risby, Bury St. Edmunds, IP28 6RR Tel: 01284 755118 Fax: 01284 755135

Surrey

American Cemetery, Cemetery Pales, Brookwood, Woking, GU24 0BL Tel: 01483 473237

Bandon Hill Cemetery Joint Committee, Plough Lane, Wallington, SM6 8JQ Tel: 0181 647 1024

Brookwood Cemetery, Cemetery Pales, Brookwood, Woking, GU24 0BL Tel: 01483 472222

Confederation of Burial Authorities, The Gate House, Kew Meadow Path, Richmond, TW9 4EN Tel: 0181 392 9487

Guildford Crematorium & Cemetaries, Broadwater, New Pond Rd, Godalming, Godalming, GU7 3DB Tel: 01483 444711

Kingston Cematary & Crematorium, Bonner Hill Rd, Kingston Upon Thames, KT1 3EZ Tel: 020 8546 4462 Fax: 020 8546 4463

London Road Cemetery, Figs Marsh, London Rd, Mitcham, CR4 3 Tel: 0208648 4115

Merton & Sutton Joint Cemetery, Garth Rd, Morden, SM4 4LL Tel: (020) 8337 4420 Fax: (020) 8337 4420

Mortlake Crematorium Board, Kew Meadow Path, Town Mead Rd, Richmond, TW9 4EN Tel: 0181 876 8056

Mount Cemetery, Weyside Rd, Guildford, GU1 1HZ Tel: 01483 561927

North East Surrey Crematorium Board, Lower Morden Lane, Morden, SM4 4NU Tel: 020 8337 4835 Fax: 020 8337 8745 Email: nescb.crematorium@talk21.com WWW: www.nes-crematorium.org.uk   Opened May 1958

Randalls Park Crematorium, Randalls Rd, Leatherhead, KT22 0AG Tel: 01372 373813

Redstone Cemetery, Philanthropic Rd, Redhill, RH1 4DN Tel: 01737 761592

Dorking Cemetery, Reigate Rd, Dorking, RH4 1QF Tel: 01306 879299 Fax: 01306 876821 Email: carole.brough@mole-valley.gov.uk WWW: www.mole-valley.gov.uk Victorian Cemetery concecrated in 1855 (listed Grade II in 1999)

Richmond Cemeteries, London Borough of Richmond upon Thames, Sheen Rd, Richmond, TW10 5BJ Tel: 020 8876 4511 Fax: 020 8878 8118 Email: cemeteries@richmond.gov.uk

Surbiton Cemetery, Lower Marsh Lane, Kingston Upon Thames, KT1 3BN Tel: 0208546 4463

Sutton & Cuddington Cemeteries, Alcorn Close, off Oldfields Road, Sutton, SM3 9PX Tel: 020 8644 9437 Fax: 020 8644 1373

The Godalming Joint Burial Committee, New Cemetery Lodge, Ockford Ridge, Godalming, GU7 2NP Tel: 01483 421559

Woking Crematorium, Hermitage Rd, Woking, GU21 8TJ Tel: 01483 472197 Oldest crematorium in the UK. Search fee payable

Sussex - East

Afterthoughts Grave Care, 16 Derwent Rd, Eastbourne BN20 7PH Tel: 01323 730029

Brighton Borough Mortuary, Lewes Rd, Brighton, BN2 3QB Tel: 01273 602345

Downs Crematorium, Bear Rd, Brighton, BN2 3PL Tel: 01273 601601

Eastbourne Cemeteries & Crematorium, Hide Hollow, Langney, Eastbourne, BN23 8AE Tel: 01323 766536 (Cemetery) Fax: 01323 761093 (Crematorium)

Woodvale Crematorium, Lewes Rd, Brighton, BN2 3QB Tel: 01273 604020

Sussex - West

Chichester Crematorium, Westhampnett Rd, Chichester, PO19 4UH Tel: 01243 787755

Midhurst Burial Authority, Cemetery Lodge, Carron Lane, Midhurst, GU29 9LF Tel: 01730 812758

Surrey & Sussex Crematorium, Balcombe Rd, Crawley, RH10 3NQ Tel: 01293 888930

Worthing Crematorium & Cemeteries, Horsham Rd, Findon, Worthing, BN14 0RG Tel: 01903 872678 Fax: 01903 872051 Email: crematorium@worthing.gov.uk

Tyne And Wear

Byker & Heaton Cemetery, 18 Benton Rd, Heaton, Newcastle Upon Tyne, NE7 7DS Tel: 0191 2662017

Gateshead East Cemetery, Cemetery Rd, Gateshead, NE8 4HJ Tel: 0191 4771819

Heworth Cemetery, Sunderland Rd, Felling, Gateshead, NE10 0NT Tel: 0191 4697851

Preston Cemetery & Tynemouth Crematorium, Walton Avenue, North Shields, NE29 9NJ Tel: 0191 2005861

Saltwell Crematorium, Saltwell Road South, Gateshead, NE8 4TQ Tel: 0191 4910553

St. Andrews Cemetery, Lodges 1-2, Great North Rd, Jesmond, Newcastle Upon Tyne, NE2 3BU Tel: 0191 2810953

St. Johns & Elswick Cemetery, Elswick Rd, Newcastle Upon Tyne, NE4 8DL Tel: 0191 2734127

St. Nicholas Cemetery, Wingrove Avenue Back, Newcastle Upon Tyne, NE4 9AP Tel: 0191 2735112

Union Hall Cemetery, Union Hall Rd, Newcastle Upon Tyne, NE15 7JS Tel: 0191 2674398

West Road Cemetery, West Rd, Newcastle Upon Tyne, NE5 2JL Tel: 0191 2744737

Warwickshire

Mid-Warwickshire Crematorium & Cemeteries, Oakley Wood, Bishops Tachbrook, Leamington Spa, CV33 9QP Tel: 01926 651418

Nuneaton Cemetery, Oaston Rd, Nuneaton, CV11 6JZ Tel: 024 7637 6357 Fax: 024 7637 6485

Stratford-on-Avon Cemetery, Evesham Rd, Stratford-Upon-Avon, CV37 9AA Tel: 01789 292676

West Midlands

Robin Hood Cemetery and Crematorium, Sheetsbrook Road, Shirley, Solihull, B90 3NL Tel: 0121 744 1121 Fax: 0121 733 8674

Widney Manor Cemetery, Widney Manor Road, Bentley Heath, Solihull, B93 3LX Tel:

Birmingham Crematorium 1973, 389 Walsall Rd, Perry Barr, Birmingham, B42 2LR Tel: 0121 356 9476

Birmingham Hebrew Congregation Cemetery, The Ridgeway, Erdington, Birmingham, B23 7TD Tel: 0121 356 4615

Brandwood End Cemetery, Woodthorpe Rd, Kings Heath, Birmingham, B14 6EQ Tel: 0121 444 1328

Coventry Bereavement Services, The Cemeteries & Crematorium Office, Cannon Hill Rd, Canley, Coventry, CV4 7DF Tel: 01203 418055

Handsworth Cemetery, Oxhill Rd, Birmingham, B21 8JT Tel: 0121 554 0096

Lodge Hill Cemetery & Cremetorium, Weoley Park Rd, Birmingham, B29 5AA Tel: 0121 472 1575

Quinton Cemetery, Halesowen Rd, Halesowen, B62 9AF Tel: 0121 422 2023

Stourbridge Cemetery & Crematorium, South Rd, Stourbridge, DY8 3RQ Tel: 01384 813985

Streetly Cemetery & Crematorium, Walsall Metropolitan Borough Council - Bereavement Services Division, Little Hardwick Road, Aldridge, Walsall, WS9 0SG Tel: 0121 353 7228 Fax: 0121 353 6557 Email: billingss@walsall.gov.uk Also administers: Bentley Cemetery (opened 1900), Wolverhampton Road West, Willenhall; Bloxwich Cemetery, Field Road, Bloxwich, Walsall (opened 1875), James Bridge Cemetery (opened 1857), Cemetery Road, Darlaston, Walsall; North Walsall Cemetery (opened 1996), Saddleworth Road, Bloxwixh, Ryecroft Cemetery (opened 1894), Coalpool Lane, Walsall; Steetley Cemetery & Crematorium (opened 1938/1984); Willenhall Lawn Cemetery (opened 1966); Wood Street Cemetery (opened prior to 1857), Willenhall

Sutton Coldfield Cemetery, Rectory Rd, Sutton Coldfield, B75 7RP Tel: 0121 378 0224

Sutton Coldfield Cremetorium, Tamworth Rd, Four Oaks, Sutton Coldfield, B75 6LG Tel: 0121 308 3812

West Bromwich Crematorium, Forge Lane, West Bromwich, B71 3SX Tel: 0121 588 2160

Willenhall Lawn Cemetery, Bentley Lane, Willenhall, WV12 4AE Tel: 01902 368621

Witton Cemetery, Moor Lane Witton, Birmingham, B6 7AE Tel: 0121 356 4363 Fax: 0121 331 1283 Email: wittoncem@birmingham.gov.uk

Woodlands Cemetery and Crematorium, Birmingham Rd, Coleshill, Birmingham, B46 2ET Tel: 01675 464835

Wiltshire
Box Cemetery, Bath Road, Box, Corsham, SN13 8AA Tel: 01225 742476
The Cemetery Chippenham, London Road, Chippenham, SN15 3RD Tel: 01249 652728
Devizes & Roundway Joint Burial Committee, Cemetry Lodge, Rotherstone, Devizes, SN10 2DE Tel: 01380 722821
Salisbury Crematorium, Barrington Road, Salisbury, SP1 3JB Tel: 01722 333632
Swindon Crematorium Kingsdown, Swindon, SN25 6SG Tel: 01793 822259 Holds records for Radnor Street and Whitworth Road Cemeteries, Swindon
West Wiltshire Crematorium, Devizes Road, Semington, Trowbridge, BA14 7QH Tel: 01380 871101
Wirral
Landican Cemetery, Arrowe Park Rd, Birkenhead, CH49 5LW Tel: 0151 677 2361
Worcestershire
Pershore Cemetery, Defford Rd, Pershore, WR10 3BX Tel: 01386 552043
Redith Crematorium & Abbey Cemetary, Bordesley Lane, Redditch, B97 6RR Tel: 01527 62174
Westall Park Woodland Burial, Holberrow Green, Redditch, B96 6JY Tel: 01386 792806
Worcester Crematorium, Astwood Rd, Tintern Avenue, Worcester, WR3 8HA Tel: 01905 22633
Yorkshire - East
East Riding Crematorium Ltd, Octon Cross Rd, Langtoft, Driffield, YO25 3BL Tel: 01377 267604
East Riding of Yorkshire Council, Cemetery Lodge, Sewerby Rd, Bridlington, YO16 7DS Tel: 01262 672138
Goole Cemetery, Hook Rd, Goole, DN14 5LU Tel: 01405 762725
Yorkshire - North
Fulford New Cemetery, Cemetery Lodge, Fordlands Rd, Fulford, York, YO19 4QG Tel: 01904 633151
Mowthorpe Garden of Rest, Southwood Farm, Terrington, York, YO60 6QB Tel: 01653 648459 Fax: 01653 648225 Email: robert@robertgoodwill.co.uk
Stonefall Cemetery & Cremetoria, Wetherby Rd, Harrogate, HG3 1DE Tel: 01423 883523
Waltonwrays Cemetery, The Gatehouse, Carlton Rd, Skipton, BD23 3BT Tel: 01756 793168
York Cemetery, Gate House, Cemetery Rd, York, YO10 5AF Tel: 01904 610578
Yorkshire - South
Barnsley Crematorium & Cemetery, Doncaster Rd, Ardsley, Barnsley, S71 5EH Tel: 01226 206053
City Road Cemetery, City Rd, Sheffield, S2 1GD Tel: 0114 239 6068
Ecclesfield Cemetery, Priory Lane, Ecclesfield, Sheffield, S35 9XZ Tel: 0114 239 6068 Fax: 0114 239 3757
Eckington Cemetery, Sheffield Rd, Eckington, Sheffield, S21 9FP Tel: 01246 432197
Grenoside Crematorium, 5 Skew Hill Lane, Grenoside, Sheffield, S35 8RZ Tel: 0114 245 3999
Handsworth Cemetery, 51 Orgreave Lane, Handsworth, Sheffield, S13 9NE Tel: 0114 254 0832
Hatfield Cemetery, Cemetery Rd, Hatfield, Doncaster, DN7 6LX Tel: 01302 840242
Mexborough Cemetery, Cemetery Rd, Mexborough, S64 9PN Tel: 01709 585184
Rose Hill Crematorium, Cantley Lane, Doncaster, DN4 6NE Tel: 01302 535191
Rotherham Cemeteries & Crematorium, Ridgeway East, Herringthorpe, Rotherham, S65 3NN Tel: 01709 850344
Sheffield Cemeteries, City Rd, Sheffield, S2 1GD Tel: 0114 253 0614
Stainforth Town Council, Cemetery Office, Church Rd, Stainforth, Doncaster, DN7 5AA Tel: 01302 845158
Yorkshire - West
Brighouse Cemetery, Cemetery Lodge, 132 Lightcliffe Rd, Brighouse, HD6 2HY Tel: 01484 715183
Cottingly Hall, Elland Rd, Leeds, LS11 0 Tel: 0113 271 6101
Dewsbury Moor Crematorium, Heckmondwike Rd, Dewsbury, WF13 3PL Tel: 01924 325180
Exley Lane Cemetery, Exley Lane, Elland, HX5 0SW Tel: 01422 372449
Killingbeck Cemetery, York Rd, Killingbeck, Leeds, LS14 6AB Tel: 0113 264 5247
Lawnswood Cemetery & Crematorium, Otley Rd, Adel, Leeds, LS16 6AH Tel: 0113 267 3188
Leeds Jewish Workers Co-Op Society, 717 Whitehall Rd, New Farnley, Leeds, LS12 6JL Tel: 0113 285 2521
Moorthorpe Cemetery, Barnsley Rd, Moorthorpe, Pontefract, WF9 2BP Tel: 01977 642433
Nab Wood Crematorium, Bingley Rd, Shipley, BD18 4BG Tel: 01274 584109 Fax: 01274 530419

Oakworth Crematorium, Wide Lane, Oakworth, Keighley, BD22 0RJ Tel: 01535 603162
Park Wood Crematorium, Park Rd, Elland, HX5 9HZ Tel: 01422 372293
Pontefract Crematorium, Wakefield Rd, Pontefract, WF8 4HA Tel: 01977 723455
Rawdon Crematorium, Leeds Rd, Rawdon, Leeds, LS19 6JP Tel: 0113 250 2904
Scholemoor Cemetery & Crematorium, Necropolis Rd, Bradford, BD7 2PS Tel: 01274 571313
Sowerby Bridge Cemetery, Sowerby New Rd, Sowerby Bridge, HX6 1LQ Tel: 01422 831193
United Hebrew Congregation Leeds, Jewish Cemetery, Gelderd Rd, Leeds, LS7 4BU Tel: 0113 263 8684
Wakefield Crematorium, Standbridge Lane, Crigglestone, Wakefield, WF4 3JA Tel: 01924 303380
Wetherby Cemetery, Sexton House, Hallfield Lane, Wetherby, LS22 6JQ Tel: 01937 582451

Wales
Bridgend
Coychurch Crematorium Coychurch, Bridgend, CF35 6AB Tel: 01656 656605 Fax: 01656 668108
Clwyd
Golden Memorial Care, 5 Golden Grove, Rhyl, LL18 2RR Tel: 0800 9178281
Mold Town Cemetery, Cemetery Lodge, Alexandra Rd, Mold, CH7 1HJ Tel: 01352 753820
Wrexham Cemeteries & Crematorium Pentre Bychan, Wrexham, LL14 4EP Tel: 01978 840068
Wrexham Cemetery Lodge, Ruabon Rd, Wrexham, LL13 7NY Tel: 01978 263159
Conwy County
Colwyn Bay Crematorium, Bron y Nant, Dinerth Rd, Colwyn Bay, LL28 4YN Tel: 01492 544677
Dyfed
Aberystwyth Crematorium, Clarach Rd, Aberystwyth, SY23 3DG Tel: 01970 626942
Carmarthen Cemetery, Elim Rd, Carmarthen, SA31 1TX Tel: 01267 234134
Llanelli District Cemetery, Swansea Rd, Llanelli, SA15 3EX Tel: 01554 773710
Milford Haven Cemetery, The Cemetery Milford Haven, SA73 2RP Tel: 01646 693324
Gwent
Christchurch Cemetry Christchurch, Newport, NP18 1JJ Tel: 01633 277566
Ebbw Vale Cemetery, Waun-y-Pound Rd, Ebbw Vale, NP23 6LE Tel: 01495 302187
Gwent Crematorium, Treherbert Rd, Croesyceiliog, Cwmbran, NP44 2BZ Tel: 01633 482784 Opened 1960. Records mainly on computer. No search fees payable
Gwynedd, Bangor Crematorium, Llandygai Rd, Bangor, LL57 4HP Tel: 01248 370500
Mid Glamorgan
Cemetery Section, Monks St, Aberdare, CF44 7PA Tel: 01685 885345
Ferndale Cemetery, Cemetery Lodge, Highfield, Ferndale, CF43 4TD Tel: 01443 730321
Llwydcoed Crematorium Llwydcoed, Aberdare, CF44 0DJ Tel: 01685 874115 Fax: 01685 874115 Email: enquiries@crematorium.org.uk WWW: www.crematorium.org.uk
Maesteg Cemetery, Cemetery Rd, Maesteg, CF34 0DN Tel: 01656 735485
Penrhys Cemetery, Cemetery Lodge, Penrhys Rd, Tylorstown, Ferndale, CF43 3PN Tel: 01443 730465
Trane Cemetery, Gilfach Rd, Tonyrefail, Porth, CF39 8HL Tel: 01443 670280 Tel: 01443 673991, Fax: 01443 676916
Treorchy Cemetery, The Lodge, Cemetery Rd, Treorchy, CF42 6TB Tel: 01443 772336
Ynysybwl Cemetery, Heol Y Plwyf, Ynysybwl, Pontypridd, CF37 3HU Tel: 01443 790159
South Glamorgan
Cardiff Crematorium and Thornhill Cemetery, Bereavement Services, Thornhill Road, Cardiff, CF14 9UA Tel: 029 2062 3294 Fax: 029 20692904 WWW: www.cardiff.gov.uk Opened 1953 Administered from: Bereavement Services, Thornhill Road, Llanishen, Cardiff CF14 9UA Tel 029 2062 3294 Fax 029 2069 2904 Also administers: Pantmawr Cemetery, Radyr Cemetery, Llanishen Cemetery, Llandaff Cemetery, Cathay Cemetery, Western Cemetery, Thornhill Cemetery and Cardiff (Thornhill) Crematorium
Cathays Cemetery, Fairoak Rd, Cathays, Cardiff, CF24 4PY Tel: 029 2062 3294 WWW: www.cardiff.gov.uk Opened 1859 Administered from: Bereavement Services, Thornhill Road, Llanishen, Cardiff CF14 9UA Tel 029 2062 3294 Fax 029 2069 2904
Western Cemetery, Cowbridge Road West, Ely, Cardiff, CF5 5TF Tel: 029 2059 3231 WWW: www.cardiff.gop.uk Opened 1936 - Administered from: Bereavement Services, Thornhill Road,

Llanishen, Cardiff CF14 9UA Tel 029 2062 3294 Fax 029 2069 2904
West Glamorgan, Goytre Cemetery, Neath Port Talbot CBC, Abrafan House, Port Talbot, SA13 1PJ Tel: 01639 763415
Margam Crematorium, Longland Lane, Margam, Port Talbot, SA13 2PP Tel: 01639 883570
Oystermouth Cemetery, Newton Road, Oystermouth, Swansea, SA3 4GW Tel: 07980 721 559 First internment in 1883
Wrexham
Coedpoeth Cemetery, The Lodge, Cemetery Rd, Coedpoeth, LL11 3SP Tel: 01978 755617

Scotland
Aberdeenshire
Springbank Cemetery, Countesswells Rd, Springbank, Aberdeen, AB15 7YH Tel: 01224 317323
St. Peter's Cemetery, King St, Aberdeen, AB24 3BX Tel: 01224 638490
Trinity Cemetery, Erroll St, Aberdeen, AB24 5PP Tel: 01224 633747
Aberdeen Cemeteries, St Nicholas House, Broad Street, Aberdeen, AB10 1BX Tel: 01224 523 155
Aberdeenshire (except Aberdeen City) Cemeteries (North), 1 Church Street, Macduff, AB44 1UR Tel: 01261 813387
Angus
Barnhill Cemetery, 27 Strathmore St, Broughty Ferry, Dundee, DD5 2NY Tel: 01382 477139
Dundee Crematorium Ltd, Crematorium, Macalpine Rd, Dundee, DD3 8 Tel: 01382 825601
Park Grove Crematorium, Douglasmuir, Friocheim, Arbroath, DD11 4UN Tel: 01241 828959
Dundee City Cemeteries, Tayside House Dundee, DD1 3RA Tel: 01382 434 000   Email: parks.burials@dundeecity.gov.uk
Angus (except Dundee City) Cemeteries, County Buildings, Market Street, Forfar, DD8 3WA Tel: 01307 461 460 Fax: 01307 466 220
Argyll
Argyll & Bute Council Cemeteries, Amenity Services, Kilmory, Lochgilphead, PA31 8RT Tel: 01546 604 360 Fax: 01546 604 208 Email: alison.mcilroy@argyll-bute.gov.uk WWW: www.argyll-bute.gov.uk/couninfo/dev.htm
Ayrshire
Ardrossan Cemetery, Sorbie Rd, Ardrossan, KA22 8AQ Tel: 01294 463133
Dreghorn Cemetery, Station Rd, Dreghorn, Irvine, KA11 4AJ Tel: 01294 211101
Hawkhill Cemetery, Kilwinning Rd, Saltcoats, Stevenston, KA20 3DE Tel: 01294 465241
Holmsford Bridge Crematorium, Dreghorn, Irvine, KA11 4EF Tel: 01294 214720
Kilwinning Cemetery, Bridgend, Kilwinning, KA13 7LY Tel: 01294 552102
Largs Cemetery, Greenock Rd, Largs, KA30 8NG Tel: 01475 673149
Maybole Cemetery, Crosshill Rd, Maybole, KA19 7BN Tel: 01655 884852 Fax: 01655 889621 Email: maybole.registrars@south-ayrshire.gov.uk Also contact for Crosshill, Dunure, Kirkmichael, Kirkoswald and Straiton Cemeteries
Newmilns Cemetery, Dalwhatswood Rd Newmilns, KA16 9LT Tel: 01560 320191
Prestwick Cemetery, Shaw Rd, Prestwick, KA9 2LP Tel: 01292 477759
Stewarton Cemetery, Dalry Rd, Stewarton, Kilmarnock, KA3 3DY Tel: 01560 482888
West Kilbride Cemetery, Hunterston Rd, West Kilbride, KA23 9EX Tel: 01294 822818
North Ayrshire Cemeteries, 43 Ardrossan Road, Saltcoats, KA21 5BS Tel: 01294 605 436 Fax: 01294 606 416 Email: CemeteriesOffice@north-ayrshire.gov.uk Administers: Irvine Area Dreghorn Cemetery, Station Road, Dreghorn; Knadgerhill Cemetery, Knaderhill, Irvine; Kilwinning Cemetery, Glasgow Road, Kilwinning; Shewalton Cemetery, Ayr Road, Irvine; Old P
South Ayrshire Cemeteries, Masonhill Crematorium, By Ayr, KA6 6EN Tel: 01292 266 051 Fax: 01292 610 096
Banffshire
Moray Crematorium, Clochan, Buckie, AB56 5HQ Tel: 01542 850488
Berwickshire
Scottish Borders Council Cemeteries, Council Offices, 8 Newtown Street, Duns, TD11 3DT Tel: 01361 882 600
Bute
Arran and Cumbrae Cemeteries, 43 Ardrossan Road, Saltcoats, KA21 5BS Tel: 01294 605 436 Fax: 01294 606 416 Email: CemeteriesOffice@north-ayrshire.gov.uk
Caithness
Caithness Cemeteries, Wick, Caithness, KW1 4AB Tel: 01955 607 737 Fax: 01955 606 376
Clackmannanshire
Alva Cemetery, The Glebe, Alva, FK12 5HR Tel: 01259 760354

Sunnyside Cemetery, Sunnyside Rd, Alloa, FK10 2AP Tel: 01259 723575
Tillicoultry Cemetery, Dollar Rd, Tillicoultry, FK13 6PF Tel: 01259 750216
Dumfrieshire
Dumfrieshire Cemeteries, Kirkbank, English Street, Dumfries, DG1 2HS Tel: 01387 260042 Fax: 01387 260188
Annan & Eskdale Cemeteries, Dumfries and Galloway Council, Dryfe Road, Lockerbie, DG11 2AP Tel: 01576 205 000
Dunbartonshire
Cardross Crematorium, Main Rd, Cardross, Dumbarton, G82 5HD Tel: 01389 841313
Dumbarton Cemetery, Stirling Rd, Dumbarton, G82 2PF Tel: 01389 762033
Vale Of Leven Cemetery, Overton Rd, Alexandria G83 0LJ Tel: 01389 752266
West Dumbartonshire Crematorium, North Dalnottar, Clydebank, G81 4SL Tel: 01389 874318
West Dunbartonshire Crematorium, Richmond Street, Clydebank, G81 1RF Tel: 01389 738709 Fax: 01389 738690 Email: helen.murray@westdunbarton.gov.uk
East Dunbartonshire Cemeteries, Broomhill Industrial Estate, Kilsyth Road, Kirkintilloch, G66 1TF Tel: 0141 574 5549 Fax: 0141 574 5555 Email: Alan-Copeland@EastDunbarton.gov.uk
West Dunbartonshire Cemeteries, Roseberry Place, Clydebank, G81 1TG Tel: 01389 738 709 Fax: 01389 733 493
Dunbartonshire - East, Cadder Cemetery, Kirkintilloch Road, Bishopbriggs, Glasgow, G64 2QG Tel: 0141 772 1977 Fax: 0141 775 0696
Edinburgh
Edinburgh Crematorium Ltd, 3 Walker St, Edinburgh, Midlothian, EH3 7JY Tel: 0131 225 7227
Fife
Dunfermline Cemetery, Halbeath Rd, Dunfermline, KY12 7RA Tel: 01383 724899
Dunfermline Crematorium, Masterton Rd, Dunfermline, KY11 8QR Tel: 01383 724653
Kirkcaldy Crematorium, Rosemount Avenue, Dunnikier, Kirkcaldy, KY1 3PL Tel: 01592 260277 Fax: 01592 203438
Central Fife Cemeteries, Rosemount Avenue, Dunnikier, Kirkcaldy, KY1 3PL Tel: 01592 260 277 Fax: 01592 203 438
East Fife Cemeteries, St Catherine Street, Cupar, KY15 4TA Tel: 01334 412 818 Fax: 01334 412 896
East Fife Cemeteries, Masterton Road, Dunfermline, KY11 8QR Tel: 01383 724 653 Fax: 01383 738 636
Inverness-Shire
Inverness Crematorium, Kilvean Rd, Kilvean, Inverness, IV3 8JN Tel: 01463 717849 Fax: 01463 717850
Invernessshire Cemeteries, Fulton House, Gordon Square, Fort William, PH33 6XY Tel: 01397 707 008 Fax: 01397 707 009 Service Restructuring in late 2002 transferred responsilility for all burial grounds in Lochaber area will be transferred to Highland Council, TEC Services, Carrs Corner, Fort William, PH33 6TQ Tel: 0
Badenoch & Strathspey Cemeteries, Ruthven Road, Kingussie, PH21 1EJ Tel: 01540 664 500 Fax: 01540 661 004
Inverness Cemeteries, Administration Office, Kilvean Cemetery, Kilvean Road, Inverness, IV3 8JN Tel: 01463 717849 Fax: 01463 717850 Email: derek.allan@highland.gov.uk and fiona.morrison@highland.gov.uk WWW: www.highland.gov.uk
Highland Council Cemeteries, T.E.C. Services, Broom Place, Portree, Isle of Skye, IV51 9HF Tel: 01478 612717 Fax: 01478 612255
Isle Of Cumbrae, Millport Cemetery, Golf Rd, Millport, KA28 0HB Tel: 01475 530442
Kirkcudbright
Kirkcudbright Cemeteries, Daar Road, Kirkcubright, DG6 4JG Tel: 01557 330 291
Lanarkshire
Airbles Cemetery, Airbles Rd, Motherwell, ML1 3AW Tel: 01698 263986
Bedlay Cemetery, Bedlay Walk, Moodiesburn, Glasgow, G69 0QG Tel: 01236 872446
Bothwellpark Cemetery, New Edinburgh Rd, Bellshill, ML4 3HH Tel: 01698 748146
Cambusnethan Cemetery, Kirk Road, Wishaw, ML2 8NP Tel: 01698 384481
St. Patrick's Cemetery, Kings Drive, New Stevenston, Motherwell, ML1 4HY Tel: 01698 732938
Glasgow
Campsie Cemetery, High Church of Scotland, Main Street, Lennoxtown, Glasgow, G66 7DA Tel: 01360 311127
Cardonald Cemetery, 547 Mosspark Boulevard, Glasgow, G52 1SB Tel: 0141 882 1059
Daldowie Crematorium, Daldowie Estate, Uddingston, Glasgow, G71 7RU Tel: 0141 771 1004
Glasgow Crematorium, Western Necropolis, Tresta Rd, Glasgow, G23 5AA Tel: 0141 946 2895

Glebe Cemetery, Vicars Rd, Stonehouse, Larkhall, ML9 3EB Tel: 01698 793674
Glenduffhill Cemetery, 278 Hallhill Rd, Glasgow, G33 4RU Tel: 0141 771 2446

Kilsyth Parish Cemetery, Howe Rd, Kirklands, Glasgow, G65 0LA Tel: 01236 822144
Larkhall Cemetery, The Cemetery Lodge, Duke St, Larkhall, ML9 2AL Tel: 01698 883049
Old Aisle Cemetery, Old Aisle Rd, Kirkintilloch, Glasgow, G66 3HH Tel: 0141 776 2330
St. Conval's Cemetery, Glasgow Rd, Barrhead, Glasgow, G78 1TH Tel: 0141 881 1058
St. Peters Cemetery, 1900 London Rd, Glasgow, G32 8RD Tel: 0141 778 1183
The Necropolis, 50 Cathedral Square, Glasgow, G4 0UZ Tel: 0141 552 3145
Glasgow Cemeteries, 20 Trongate, Glasgow, G1 5ES Tel: 0141 287 3961 Fax: 0141 287 3960 inc crematoria Linn and Daldowie
North Lanarkshire Cemeteries
Old Edinburgh Road, Bellshill, ML4 3JS Tel: 01698 506 301 Fax: 01698 506 309
Lanarkshire - South
South Lanarkshire Cemeteries, Atholl House East Kilbride, G74 1LU Tel: 01355 806 980 Fax: 01355 806 983
Midlothian
Dean Cemetery, Dean Path, Edinburgh, EH4 3AT Tel: 0131 332 1496
Seafield Cemetery & Crematorium, Seafield Rd, Edinburgh, EH6 7LQ Tel: 0131 554 3496
Warriston Crematorium, 36 Warriston Rd, Edinburgh, EH7 4HW Tel: 0131 552 3020
Midlothian Council Cemeteries, Dundas Buildings, 62A Polton Street, Bonnybrigg, EH22 3YD Tel: 0131 561 5280 Fax: 0131 654 2797 Email: nancy.newton@midlothian.gov.uk
City of Edinburgh Council Cemeteries, Howdenhall Road, Edinburgh, EH16 6TX Tel: 0131 664 4314 Fax: 0131 664 2031 5 private cemeteries in Edinburgh - council does not have access to their records
Lothian - West
West Lothian Cemeteries, County Buildings, High Street, Linlithgow, EH49 7EZ Tel: 01506 775 300 Fax: 01506 775 412
Moray
Morayshire Cemeteries, Cooper Park, Elgin, IV30 1HS Tel: 01343 544 475 Fax: 01343 549 050 Email: graeme.wilson@moray.gov.uk WWW: www.moray.org/heritage/roots.html
Perthshire
Perth Crematorium, Crieff Rd, Perth, PH1 2PE Tel: 01738 625068 Fax: 01738 445977 Email: dpmartin@pkc.gov.uk
Renfrewshire
Hawkhead Cemetery, 133 Hawkhead Rd, Paisley, PA2 7BE Tel: 0141 889 3472
Paisley Cemetery Co.Ltd, 46 Broomlands St, Paisley, PA1 2NP Tel: 0141 889 2260
Renfrewshire Cemeteries, Tweedie Halls, Ardlamont Square, Linwood, PA3 3DE Tel: 01505 322 135 Fax: 01505 322135
Cemeteries Division - Renfrewshire Council, Environmental Services Department, Cotton Street, South Building, Paisley, PA1 1BR Tel: 0141 840 3504 Fax: 0141 842 1179
Renfrew Cemeteries, 3 Longcroft Drive, Renfrew, PA4 8NF Tel: 0141 848 1450 Fax: 0141 886 2807
East Renfrewshire - including Neilston, Newton Mearns and Eaglesham Cemeteries, Rhuallan House, 1 Montgomery Drive, Giffnock, G46 6PY Tel: 0141 577 3913 Fax: 0141 577 3919 Email: sandra.donnelly@eastrenfrewshire.gov.uk
Roxburghshire
Roxburghshire Environmental Health - Burials, High Street, Hawick, TD9 9EF Tel: 01450 375 991
Scottish Borders
Scottish Borders Council - Burials, Paton Street, Galashiels, TD1 3AS Tel: 01896 662739 Fax: 01896 750329
Scottish Borders Council Burial Grounds Department, Council Offices, Rosetta Road, Peebles, EH45 8HG Tel: 01721 726306 Fax: 01721 726304 Email: p.allan@scot.borders.gov.uk
Shetland
Shetland Burial Ground Management Grantfield Lerwick, ZE1 0NT Tel: 01595 744 871 Fax: 01595 744869 Email: jim.grant@sic.shetland.gov.uk WWW: www.users.zetnet.co.uk/eats-operations
Stirlingshire
Larbert Cemetery, 25 Muirhead Rd, Larbert, FK5 4HZ Tel: 01324 557867
Stirlingshire Cemeteries, Viewforth, Stirling, FK8 2ET Tel: 01786 442 559 Fax: 01786 442 558 Email: mcbrier@stirling.gov.uk WWW: www.stirling.gov.uk
Falkirk Cemeteries and Crematorium, Dorrator Road, Camelon, Falkirk, FK2 7YJ Tel: 01324 503 654 Fax: 01324 503 651 Email: billbauchope@falkirk.gov.uk

Wigtown
Wigtown Cemeteries, Dunbae House, Church Street, Stranraer, DG9 7JG Tel: 01776 888 405

Northern Ireland
County Antrim
Ballymena Cemetery, Cushendall Rd, Ballymena, BT43 6QE Tel: 01266 656026
Ballymoney Cemetery, 44 Knock Rd, Ballymoney, BT53 6LX Tel: 012656 66364
Blaris New Cemetery, 25 Blaris Rd, Lisburn, BT27 5RA Tel: 01846 607143
Carnmoney Cemetery, 10 Prince Charles Way, Newtownabbey, BT36 7LG Tel: 01232 832428
City Cemetery, 511 Falls Rd, Belfast, BT12 6DE Tel: 028 90323112
Greenland Cemetery, Upper Cairncastle Rd, Larne, BT40 2EG Tel: 01574 272543
Milltown Cemetery Office, 546 Falls Rd, Belfast, BT12 6EQ Tel: 01232 613972
County Armagh, Kernan Cemetery, Kernan Hill Rd, Portadown, Craigavon, BT63 5YB Tel: 028 38339059
Lurgan Cemetery, 57 Tandragee Rd, Lurgan, Craigavon, BT66 8TL Tel: 028 38342853
County Down
City of Belfast Crematorium, 129 Ballgowan Road, Crossacreevy, Belfast, BT5 7TZ Tel: 028 9044 8342 Fax: 028 9044 8579 Email: crematorium@belfastcity.gov.uk WWW: www.belfastcrematorium.co.uk
Ballyvestry Cemetery, 6 Edgewater Millisle, Newtownards, BT23 5 Tel: 01247 882657
Banbridge Public Cemetery, Newry Rd, Banbridge, BT32 3NB Tel: 018206 62623
Bangor Cemetery, 62 Newtownards Rd, Bangor, BT20 4DN Tel: 028 91271909
Clandeboye Cemetery, 300 Old Belfast Rd, Bangor, BT19 1RH Tel: 028 91853246
Comber Cemetery, 31 Newtownards Rd, Comber, Newtownards, BT23 5AZ Tel: 01247 872529
Down District Council, Struell Cemetery, Old Course Rd, Downpatrick, BT30 8AQ Tel: 01396 613086
Down District Council - Lough Inch Cemetery, Lough Inch Cemetery, Riverside Rd, Ballynahinch, BT24 8JB Tel: 01238 562987
Kirkistown Cemetary, Main Rd, Portavogie, Newtownards, BT22 1EL Tel: 01247 771773
Movilla Cemetary, Movilla Rd, Newtownards, BT23 8EY Tel: 01247 812276
Redburn Cemetery, Old Holywood Rd, Holywood, BT18 9QH Tel: 01232 425547
Roselawn Cemetery, 127 Ballygowan Rd, Crossnacreevy, Belfast, BT5 7TZ Tel: 01232 448288
Whitechurch Cemetary, 19 Dunover Rd, Newtownards, BT22 2LE Tel: 01247 58659
County Londonderry
Altnagelvin Cemetery, Church Brae, Altnagelvin, Londonderry, BT47 3QG Tel: 01504 343351
City Cemetery, Lone Moor Rd, Londonderry, BT48 9LA Tel: 02871 362615 Fax: 02871 362085
County Tyrone
Greenhill Cemetery, Mountjoy Rd, Omagh, BT79 7BL Tel: 028 8224 4918
Westland Road Cemetery, Westland Rd, Cookstown, BT80 8BX Tel: 016487 66087

France
Russian Cemetery, Cimetiere Russe de Sainte Genevierve des Bois (Russian Cemetery), 8 Rue Léo Lagrange, 91700, Sainte Genevierve des Bois

Record Offices & Archives

National

BBC Written Archives Centre Caversham Park, Reading , RG4 8TZ Tel: 0118 948 6281 Fax: 0118 946 1145 Email: wac.enquiries@bbc.co.uk WWW: www.bbc.co.uk/thenandnowAccess by appointment only. Brief enquiries can be answered by post or telephone

Birmingham University Information Services - Special Collections Main Library, University of Birmingham, Edgbaston B15 2TT Tel: 0121 414 5838 Email: special-collections@bham.ac.uk WWW: www.is.bham.ac.uk

Black Cultural Archives 378 Coldharbour Lane, London, SW9 8LF Tel: (020) 7738 4591

Bristol University Library - Special Collections Tyndall Avenue, Bristol, BS8 1TJ Tel: 0117 928 8014 Email: library@bris.ac.uk WWW: www.bris.ac.uk/depts/library

British Coal Corporation Records & Archive Provincial House, Solly Street, Sheffield, S1 4BA Tel: 0114 279 9643

British Film Institute - Library & Film Archive, 21 Stephen Street, London W1T 1LN Tel: 020 7957 4824 WWW: www.bfi.org.uk

British Genealogical Survey Library Kingsley Dunham Centre, Keyworth, Nottingham, NG12 5GG Tel: 0115 939 3205 Fax: 0115 936 3200 Email: info@bgs.ac.uk WWW: www.bgs.ac.uk

British Medical Association Archive BMA House, Tavistock Square, London, WC1H 9JP Tel: 020 7383 6588 Fax: 020 7383 6717 WWW: www.bma.org.uk

British Universities Film and Video Council, 77 Wells Street, London W1T 3QJ Tel: 020 7393 1500 WWW: www.bufvc.ac.uk

British Waterways Archives and The Waterways Trust Llanthony Warehouse, Gloucester Docks, Gloucester, GL1 2EJ Tel: 01452 318041 Email: roy.jamieson@britishwaterways.co.uk WWW: http://www.britishwaterways.org.uk

Cambridge University Library - Department of Manuscripts & University Archives West Road, Cambridge, CB3 9DR Tel: 01223 333000 ext 33143 (Manuscripts) Tel: 01223 333000 ext 33148 (University Archives) Fax: 01223 333160 Email: mss@ula.cam.ac.uk WWW: www.lib.cam.ac.uk/MSS/

Deed Poll Records Section Room E 15 Royal Courts of Justice, Strand, London, WC2A 2LL Tel: (020) 7947 6528 Fax: (020) 7947 6807

Department of Special Collections and Western Manuscripts Bodleian Library, Oxford, OX1 3BG Tel: 01865-277152

Imperial War Museum Film and Video Archive, Lambeth Road, London SE1 6HZ Tel: 020 7416 5291 WWW:www.iwm.org.uk/collections/film.htm

Institute of Heraldic and Genealogical Studies 79 - 82 Northgate, Canterbury, CT1 1BA Fax: 01227-765617 Email: ihgs@ihgs.ac.uk WWW: www.ihgs.ac.uk

Lloyds Register of Shipping, Information Services, 71 Fenchurch Street, London EC3M 4BS Tel: (020) 7423 2531 Fax: (020) 7423 2039 WWW: www.lr.org Personal callers only. Reserarch cannot be undertaken

National Gallery Library and Archive Trafalgar Square, London, WC2N 5DN Tel: 020 7747 2542 Email: iad@ng-london.org.uk WWW: http://www.nationalgallery.org.uk

National Monuments Record Centre - English Heritage National Monuments Record Centre, Great Western Village, Kemble Drive, Swindon, SN2 2GZ Tel: 01793-414600 Email: info@rchme.gov.uk WWW: www.english-heritage.org.uk

National Monuments Record Enquiry and Research Services 55 Blandford Street, London, W1H 3AF Tel: 020 7208 8200 WWW: www.english-heritage.org.uk/knowledge/nmr

National Portrait Gallery Heinz Archive & library, 2 St. Martins Place, London, WC2H 0HE Tel: (020) 7306 0055 WWW: www.npg.org.uk

National Railway Museum Leeman Road, York, YO26 4XJ Tel: 01904 621261 Fax: 01904 611112 Email: nrm@nmsi.ac.uk WWW: www.nrm.org.uk Does not hold Railway Company staff records at PRO and NAS.

Probate Principal Registry of the Family Division, First Avenue House, 42 - 49 High Holborn, London WC1V 6NP Tel: (020) 7947 6939 Fax: (020) 7947 6946 WWW: www.courtservice.gov.uk Provision of copies to those attending in person. records of all grants of Representation (including will proved for probate) from 1858 to the present. Fee £5.00 per copy document (grant & will annexed if any)
Postal Searches: York Probate Sub Registry, Duncombe Place, York YO1 7EA

Probate Service York Probate Sub-Registry, 1st Floor, Castle Chambers, Clifford Street, York YO1 9RG UK Tel: +44 (1904) 666777 Fax: +44 (1904) 666776

Public Record Office Public Record Office, Ruskin Avenue, Kew, Richmond, TW9 4DU Tel: (020) 8876 3444 WWW: http://www.pro.gov.uk

Royal Air Force Museum - Department of Research & Information Services Grahame Park Way, Hendon, London, NW9 5LL Royal Air Force Museum, Grahame Park Way, Hendon, London NW9 5LL Tel: (020) 8205-2266 Fax: (020) 8200 1751 Email: info@rafmuseum.com WWW: http://www.rafmuseum.com

Royal Commonwealth Society Library West Road, Cambridge, CB3 9DR Tel: 01223 333319 Fax: 01223 333160 Email: tab@ula.cam.ac.uk WWW: www.lib.cam.ac.uk/MSS/

Royal Greenwich Observatory Archives West Road, Cambridge, CB3 9DR Tel: 01223 333056 Email: ajp@ula.cam.ac.uk WWW: www.lib.cam.ac.uk/MSS/

Royal Society, 6 - 9 Carlton House Terrace, London, SW1Y 5AG Tel: 020 7451 2606 Fax: 020 7930 2170 Email: library@royalsoc.ac.uk WWW: www.royalsoc.ac.uk

Shakespeare Birthplace Trust - Records Office Henley Street, Stratford Upon Avon, CV37 6QW Tel: 01789 201816 Tel: 01789 204016 Fax: 01789 296083 Email: records@sharespeare.org.uk WWW: www.shakespeare.org.uk

Society of Antiquaries of London Burlington House, Piccadilly, London, W1J 0BE Tel: 020 7479 7084 Email: library@sal.org.uk WWW: www.sal.org.uk

Society of Genealogists - Library 14 Charterhouse Buildings, Goswell Road, London, EC1M 7BA Tel: 020-7251-8799 Tel: 020-7250-0291 Fax: 020-7250-1800 Email: library@sog.org.uk - Sales at sales@sog.org.uk WWW: http://www.sog.org.uk

Traceline PO Box 106, Southport, PR8 2HH Tel: 0151 471 4811 Fax: 01704-563354 Email: traceline@ons.gov.uk To be put in touch with lost relatives and acquaintances. The ONS must be satisfied that contact would be in the best interests of the person being sought.

The Boat Museum & David Owen Waterways Archive South Pier Road, Ellesmere Port, CH65 4FW Tel: 0151-355-5017 Fax: 0151-355-4079 Email: boatmuseum@easynet.co.uk Records relating to the management, maintenance and operation of inland waterways in ngland, Scotland and Wales. Substantial Waterways library. Date range: late 17th century to 20th century.

Trinity College Library Cambridge University, Trinity College, Cambridge, CB1 1TQ Tel: 01223 338488 Fax: 01223 338532 Email: trin-lib@lists.cam.ac.uk WWW: http://rabbit.trin.cam.ac.uk

Victoria & Albert Museum - National Art Library - Archive of Art and Design Blythe House, 23 Blythe Road, London, W14 0QF Tel: (020) 7603 1514 Fax: (020) 7602 0980 Email: archive@vam.ac.uk WWW: www.nal.vam.ac.uk

Specialist Records & Indexes

Bass Museum Horninglow Street, Burton on Trent, DE14 1YQ Tel: 0845 6000598 Fax: 01283 513509 WWW: www.bass-museum.com

British Waterways Archives and The Waterways Trust Llanthony Warehouse, Gloucester Docks, Gloucester, GL1 2EJ Tel: 01452 318041 Fax: 01452 318076 Email: roy.jamieson@britishwaterways.co.uk WWW: http://www.britishwaterways.org.uk

Church of England Record Centre 15 Galleywall Road, South Bermondsey, London, SE16 3PB Tel: 020 7898 1030 Fax: 020 7898 1031 WWW: www.church-of-england.org

Department of Manuscripts and Special Collections Hallward Library, Nottingham University , University Park, Nottingham, NG7 2RD Tel: 0115 951 4565 Fax: 0115 951 4558 Email: mss-library@nottingham.ac.uk WWW: www.mss.library.nottingham.ac.uk

Guiness Archive Park Royal Brewery, London, NW10 7RR

Lambeth Palace Library Lambeth Palace Road, London, SE1 7JU Tel: (020) 7898 1400 Fax: (020) 7928-7932 WWW: www.lambethpalacelibrary.org

Library of the Religious Society of Friends (Quakers) Friends House, 173 - 177 Euston Rd, London, NW1 2BJ Tel: 0207 663 1135 Tel: 0207 663 1001 Fax: Email: library@quaker.org.uk WWW: http://www.quaker.org.uk/library

Metropolitan Police Archives Room 517, Wellington House, 67-73 Buckingham Gate, London, SW1E 6BE The Metropolitan Police do not hold any records. All records that have survived are in the PRO. Do not hold records for City of London Police or other police forces or constabularies.

National Railway Museum Leeman Road, York, YO26 4XJ Tel: 01904 621261 Fax: 01904 611112 Email: nrm@nmsi.ac.uk WWW: www.nrm.org.uk

Museum of the Royal Pharmaceutical Society, 1 Lambeth High Street, London SE1 7JN Tel: (020) 7572 2210 Fax: (020) 7572 2499 Email: museum@rpsgb.org.uk WWW: http://www.rpsgb.org.uk CC accepted. Records of pharmacists from 1841 Research fee charged £20 per person or premises researched to Non members of the Society, £10 per person or premises researched for members(Genealogical Enquiries) Enquirers may visit and undertake research themselves by appointment only at a cost of £10.00 per day

Southern Courage Archives Southern Accounting Centre, PO Box 85, Countership, Bristol, BS99 7BT

Thames Valley Police Museum Sulhamstead, Nr Reading, RG7 4DX Tel: 0118 932 5748 Fax: 0118 932 5751 Email: ken.wells@thamesvalley.police.uk Thames Valley Police formed April 1968 from Berkshire, Oxfordshire, Oxford City and Reading Borough constabularies. Only records of officers are those who served in Reading Borough and Oxfordshire.

The Museum of Berkshire Aviation Trust Mohawk Way, off Bader Way, Woodley, Reading, RG5 4UE Tel: 0118 944 8089 Fax: Email: museumofberkshireaviation@fly.to WWW: http://fly.to/museumofberkshireaviation

United Reformed Church History Society, Westminster College, Madingley Road, Cambridge CB3 0AA Tel: 01223-741300 (NOT Wednesdays), Information on ministers of constituent churches not members

Whitbread Archives - Permanently Closed The Brewery, Chiswell Street, London, EC1Y 4SD

Young's & Co's Brewery Archives Ram Brewery, High Street, Wandsworth, London, SW18 4JD

Military

Catterick Garrison Library Gough Road, Catterick Garrison, DL9 3EL Tel: 01748 833543 Extensive collection of over 1350 military history books available

Cheshire Military Museum The Castle, Chester, CH1 2DN Tel: 01244 327617

Devonshire and The Devonshire& Dorset Regiment Archives Wyvern Barracks, Barrack Road, Exeter, EX2 6AE Tel: 01392 492436 Fax: 01392 492469

Gallipoli Campaign 1915-16 Biographical Index 3966 Robin Avenue, Eugene, 97402 Email: patrickg@efn.org

Grenadier Guards Record Office Wellington Barracks, Birdcage Walk, London, SW1E 6HQ Access is by appointment made in advance. Search fee of £25.00 per search

Liddell Hart Centre for Military Archives King's College London, Strand, London, WC2R 2LS Tel: 020 7848 2015 Tel: 020 7848 2187 Fax: 020 7848 2760 Email: archives@kcl.ac.uk WWW: http://www.kcl.ac.uk/lhcma/top.htm

National Army Museum Royal Hospital Road, London, SW3 4HT Tel: (020) 7730-0717 Fax: (020) 7823-6573 Email: info@national-army-museum.ac.uk WWW: http://www.national-army-museum.ac.uk

National Army Museum Department of Archives (Photographs, Film & Sound) Royal Hospital Road, London, SW3 4HT Tel: (020) 7730-0717 Fax: (020) 7823-6573 Email: info@national-army-museum.ac.uk WWW: www.national-army-museum.ac.uk

Regimental Museum and Archives of Black Watch Balhousie Castle, Hay Street, Perth, PH1 5HS Tel: 0131-3108530 Tel: 01738 621281 ext 8530 Fax: 01738-643245 Email: bwarchivist@btclick.com WWW: www.theblackwatch.co.uk

Royal Air Force Museum Grahame Park Way, Hendon, London, NW9 5LL Tel: (020) 8205-2266 Fax: (020) 8200 1751 Email: info@refmuseum.org.uk WWW: http://www.rafmuseum.org.uk

Royal Dragoon Guards Military Museum (4th/7th Royal Dragoon Guards & 5th Royal Inniskilling Dragoons) 3A Tower Street, York, YO1 9SB Tel: 01904-662790 Tel: 01904 662310 Fax: 01904 662310 WWW: www.rdg.co.uk, co located with Prince of Wales' Own Regiment of Yorkshire Military Museum (West & East Yorkshire Regiments)

Royal Marines Museum Eastney, Southsea, PO4 9PX Tel: (023) 92 819385-Exts-224 Email:matthewlittle@royalmarinesmuseum.co.uk WWW: www.royalmarinesmuseum.co.uk No charges for research other than material costs. Donations welcome. Visits by appointment Mon to Fri 10am to 4.30pm

U.K. National Inventory of War Memorials Imperial War Museum, Lambeth Road, London, SE1 6HZ Tel: (020) 7416-5353 Tel: (020) 7416 5281 : (020) 7416 5445 Fax: (020) 7416-5379 Email: memorials@iwm.org.uk WWW: www.iwm.org.uk, Only holds records for memorials within the UK. The archive is not computerised index as yet. Aims to be online by end of 2002. The archive holds 50,000 memorials to the fallen of all conflicts

Bedfordshire

Bedfordshire & Luton Archives & Record Service County Hall, Cauldwell Street, Bedford, MK42 9AP Tel: 01234-228833 Tel: 01234-228777 Fax: 01234-228854 Email: archive@csd.bedfordshire.gov.uk WWW: http://www.bedfordshire.gov.uk

Berkshire

Berkshire Record Office 9 Coley Avenue, Reading, RG1 6AF Tel: 0118-901-5132 Fax: 0118-901-5131 Email: arch@reading.gov.uk WWW: www.reading.gov.uk/berkshirerecordoffice

Commonwealth War Graves Commission 2 Marlow Road, Maidenhead, SL6 7DX Tel: 01628-634221 Fax: 01628-771208 Email: General Enquiries: General.enq@cwgc.org Casulaty & Cemetery Enquiries: casualty.enq@cwgc.org WWW: www.cwgc.org

Eton College Library, College Library, Windsor, SL4 6DB Tel: 01753 671629

Berkshire Medical Heritage Centre, Royal Berkshire Hospital, London Road, BReading RG1 5AN Tel: 0118 987 7298

Museum of English Rural Life, Rural History Centre, University of Reading, Whiteknights PO Box 229, Reading RG6 6AG Tel: 0118-931-8664 Fax: 0118-975-1264 Email: j.s.creasey@reading.ac.uk WWW: www.ruralhistory.org/index.html, Appointments required

The Museum of Berkshire Aviation Trust Mohawk Way, off Bader Way, Woodley, Reading, RG5 4UE Tel: 0118 944 8089 Email: museumofberkshireaviation@fly.to WWW: http://fly.to/museumofberkshireaviation

West Berkshire Heritage Services, Newbury, The Wharf, Newbury RG4 5AS Tel: 01635 30511

Bristol

Bristol Record Office "B" Bond Warehouse, Smeaton Road, Bristol, BS1 6XN Tel: 0117-922-4224 Fax: 0117-922-4236 Email: bro@bristol-city.gov.uk WWW: www.bristol-city.gov.uk/recordoffice

British Empire & Commonwealth Museum Clock Tower Yard, Temple Meads, Bristol, BS1 6QH Tel: 0117 925 4980 Fax: 0117 925 4983 Email: staff@empiremuseum.co.uk WWW: www.empiremuseum.co.uk

Bristol University Library - Special Collections Tyndall Avenue, Bristol, BS8 1TJ Tel: 0117 928 8014 Fax: 0117 925 5334 Email: library@bris.ac.uk WWW: www.bris.ac.uk/depts/library

Buckinghamshire

Buckinghamshire Record Office County Offices, Walton Street, Aylesbury, HP20 1UU Tel: 01296-382587 Fax: 01296-382274 Email: archives@buckscc.gov.uk WWW: www.buckscc.gov.uk/leisure/libraries/archive

Cambridgeshire

Cambridge University Library - Department of Manuscripts & University Archives West Road, Cambridge, CB3 9DR Tel: 01223 333000 ext 33143 (Manuscripts) Tel: 01223 333000 ext 33148 (University Archives) Fax: 01223 333160 Email: mss@ula.cam.ac.uk WWW: www.lib.cam.ac.uk/MSS/

Cambridgeshire Archive Service (Huntingdon) County Record Office Huntingdon, Grammar School Walk, Huntingdon, PE29 3LF Tel: 01480-375842 Fax: 01480 375842 Email: county.records.hunts@cambridgeshire.gov.uk WWW: www.cambridgeshire.gov.uk

Cambridgeshire Archives Service County Record Office, Shire Hall, Castle Hill, Cambridge CB3 0AP Tel: 01223 717281 Fax: 01223 717201 Email: County.Records.Cambridge@cambridgeshire.gov.uk WWW: http://www.cambridgeshire.gov.uk/ and WWW: http://edweb.camcnty.gov.uk/archives 1901 census

Centre for Regional Studies Anglia Polytechnic University, East Road, Cambridge, CB1 1PT Tel: 01223-363271 ext 2030 Fax: 01223-352973 Email: t.kirby@anglia.ac.uk

Cheshire
Cheshire & Chester Archives & Local Studies
Duke Street, Chester, CH1 1RL Tel: 01244-602574 Fax: 01244-603812 Email: recordoffice@cheshire.gov.uk WWW: http://www.cheshire.gov.uk/recoff/home.htm
Cheshire Military Museum The Castle, Chester, CH1 2DN Tel: 01244 327617 Fax:
Chester Community History & Heritage St Michaels Church, Bridge Street Row, Chester, CH1 1NG Tel: 01244 317948 Tel: 01244 402110 Email: s.oswald.gov.uk
WWW:http://www.chestercc.gov.uk/chestercc/htmls/heritage.htm
All original archives transferred to Cheshire & Chester Archives & Local Studies, Duke Street, Chester. All archives must be consulted there. However, secondary sources held here
Stockport Archive Service Central Library, Wellington Road South, Stockport, SK1 3RS Tel: 0161-474-4530 Fax: 0161-474-7750 Email: localheritage.library@stockport.gov.uk
Tameside Local Studies Library Stalybridge Library, Trinity Street, Stalybridge, SK15 2BN
Tel: 0161-338-2708 Fax: 0161-303-8289
Email: localstudies.library@mail.tameside.gov.uk
WWW: http://www.tameside.gov.uk
The Boat Museum & David Owen Waterways Archive South Pier Road, Ellesmere Port, CH65 4FW Tel: 0151-355-5017 Fax: 0151-355-4079 Email: boatmuseum@easynet.co.uk
Warrington Library & Local Studies Centre Museum Street, Warrington, WA1 1JB Tel: 01925 442890 Fax: 01925 411395 Email: library@warrington.gov.uk WWW: www.warrington.gov.uk

Cleveland
Tees Archaeology - The Archaeological Service for Teeside, Sir William Gray, Clarence Road, Hartlepool TS24 8BT Tel: 01429 523455 Fax: 01429 523477 Email: tees-archaeology@hartlepool.gov.uk
Teesside Archives Exchange House, 6 Marton Road, Middlesbrough, TS1 1DB Tel: 01642-248321 Email: teeside_archives@middlesbrough.gov.uk

Cornwall
Cable & Wireless Archive & Museum of Submarine Telegraphy Eastern House,, Porthcurno, Penzance, TR19 6JX Tel: 01736 810478 Tel: 01736 810811 Fax: 01736 810640 Email: info@tunnels.demon.co.uk WWW: www.porthcurno.org.uk, Housed in one of Porthcurno's former telegraph station buildings, and adjacent to the Museum of Submarine Telegraphy, the archive is a unique resource for learning about: the history of Porthcurno
Cornwall Record Office County Hall, Truro, TRI 3AY Tel: 01872-323127 Email: cro@cornwall.gov.uk WWW: http://www.cornwall.gov.uk
Royal Institution of Cornwall, Courtney Library & Cornish History Research Centre Royal Cornwall Museum, River Street, Truro, TR1 2SJ Tel: 01872 272205 Email: RIC@royal-cornwall-museum.freeserve.co.uk WWW: www.cornwall-online.co.uk/ric
The Cornwall Centre Alma Place, Redruth, TR15 2AT Tel: 01209-216760
Email: cornishstudies@library.cornwall.gov.uk WWW: www.cornwall.gov.uk

County Durham
Centre For Local Studies The Library, Crown Street, Darlington, DL1 1ND Tel: 01325-349630 Email: crown.street.library@darlington.gov.uk
County Record Office
County Hall, Durham, DH1 5UL Tel: 0191-383-3474 Tel: 0191-383-3253 Fax: 0191-383-4500 Email: record.office@durham.gov.uk WWW: http:www.durham.gov.uk/recordoffice

Cumbria
Centre for North West Regional Studies, Fylde College, Lancaster University, Lancaster LA1 4YF Tel: 01524 593770 Fax: 01524 594725 Email: christine.wilkinson@lancaster.ac.uk WWW: www.lancs.ac.uk/users/cnwrs CC accepted Oral History Archives; Elizabeth Roberts Archive: Penny Summerfield Archive
Cumbria Archive Service
Cumbria Record Office, The Castle, Carlisle, CA3 8UR Tel: 01228-607285 Tel: 01228-607284 Fax: 01228-607270 Email: carlisle.record.office@cumbriacc.gov.uk WWW: www.cumbriacc.gov.uk/archives

Cumbria Record Office(Kendal) County Offices, Stricklandgate, Kendal, LA9 4RQ Tel: 01539 773540 Email: kendal.record.office@cumbriacc.gov.uk WWW: www.cumbria.gov.uk/archives
Cumbria Record Office & Local Studies Library (Whitehaven) Scotch Street, Whitehaven, CA28 7BJ Tel: 01946-852920Email: whitehaven.record.office@cumbriacc.gov.uk
WWW: http://www.cumbria.gov.uk/archives
Cumbria Record Office & Local Studies Library (Barrow in Furness) 140 Duke St, Barrow in Furness, LA14 1XW Tel: 01229-894363 Email: barrow.record.office@cumbriacc.gov.uk WWW: www.cumbria.gov.uk/archives
Ulverston Heritage Centre Lower Brook St, Ulverston, LA12 7EE Tel: 01229 580820
Email: heritage@tower-house.demon.co.uk WWW: http://www.rootsweb.com/~ukuhc/

Derbyshire & Derby City
Derby Local Studies Library 25b Irongate, Derby, DE1 3GL Tel: 01332 255393**Derby Museum & Art Gallery** The Strand, Derby, DE1 1BS Tel: 01332-716659 Fax: 01332-716670 WWW: www.derby.gov.uk/museums No archive material as such, but some local genealogical information available and numerous indices on local trades, etc eg clock makers, gunmakers, etc
Derbyshire Record Office County Hall, Matlock, DE4 3AG Tel: 01629-580000-ext-35207 Fax: 01629-57611 The Record Office for Derbyshire - City and County and the Diocese of Derby. The Record Office is located New Street, Matlock, Derbyshire DE4 3AG. The address at County Hall is for correspondence only
Erewash Museum The Museum, High Street, Ilkeston, DE7 5JA Tel: 0115 907 1141 Email: museum@erewash.gov.uk WWW: www.erewash.gov.uk

Devon
Beaford Photograph Archive Barnstaple, EX32 7EJ Tel: 01271-288611 Fax:
Bill Douglas Centre for the History of Cinema and Popular Culture, University of Exeter, Queen's Building, Queen's Drive, Exeter EX4 4QH Tel: 01392 264321 WWW: www.ex.ac.uk/bill.douglas
Devonshire and The Devonshire& Dorset Regiment Archives Wyvern Barracks, Barrack Road, Exeter, EX2 6AE Tel: 01392 492436
Devon Record Office Castle Street, Exeter, EX4 3PU Tel: 01392 384253 Email: devrec@devon.gov.uk
WWW: http://www.devon gov.uk/dro/homepage.html
North Devon Record Office Tuly Street, Barnstaple, EX31 1EL Tel: 01271 388607 Tel: 01271 388608 Email: ndevrec@devon.gov.uk WWW: www.devon.gov.uk/dro/homepage
Plymouth & West Devon Record Office Unit 3, Clare Place, Coxside, Plymouth, PL4 0JW Tel: 01752-305940 Email: pwdro@plymouth.gov.uk
WWW: www.plymouth.gov.uk/star/archives.htm
South West Film and Television Archive, New Cooperage, Royal William Yard, Stonehouse, Plymouth, PL1 3RP Tel: 01752 202650 WWW: www.tswfta.co.uk

Dorset
Dorset Archives Service 9 Bridport Road, Dorchester, DT1 1RP Tel: 01305-250550 Fax: 01305-257184 Email: archives@dorset-cc.gov.uk WWW: http://www.dorset-cc.gov.uk/archives Research service available. Search fee £16 per hour. £8.00 minimum charge. The service covers the areas served by Dorset County, Bournemouth Borough and the Borough of Poole.
Poole Central Reference Library
Dolphin Centre, Poole, BH15 1QE Tel: 01202 262424 Fax: 01202 262442 Email: centrallibrary@poole.gov.uk WWW: www.poole.gov.uk The local studies collection was relocated to The Waterfront Museum, Poole Some records moved to Dorset Record Office. Retains only general local history and national family history indexes.
Waterfront Musuem and Local Studies Centre
4 High St, Poole, BH15 1BW Tel: 01202 683138Email: museums@poole.gov.uk WWW: www.poole.gov.uk

Essex
Central Reference Library - L B of Havering Reference Library, St Edward's Way, Romford, RM1 3AR Tel: 01708 432393 Email: romfordlib2@rmplc.co.uk
Chelmsford Library PO Box 882, Market Road, Chelmsford, CM1 1LH Tel: 01245 492758 Email: answers.direct@essexcc.gov.uk WWW: www.essexcc.gov.uk

Essex Record Office Wharf Road, Chelmsford, CM2 6YT Tel: 01245 244644 Fax: 1245244655 Email: ero.enquiry@essexcc.gov.uk ero.search@essexcc.gov.uk (Search Service) WWW: http://www.essexcc.gov.uk/ero

Essex Record Office, Colchester & NE Essex Branch Stanwell House, Stanwell Street, Colchester, CO2 7DL Tel: 01206-572099 WWW: www.essexcc.gov.uk/ero

Essex Record Office, Southend Branch Central Library, Victoria Avenue, Southend on Sea, SS2 6EX Tel: 01702-464278 WWW: www.essexcc.gov.uk/ero

L B of Barking & Dagenham Local History Studies Valence House Museum, Becontree Avenue, Dagenham, RM8 3HT Tel: 020-822-75293 Fax: 020-822-75297 Email: fm019@viscount.org.uk WWW: http://www.bardaglea.org.uk/4-heritage/heritage-menu.html Heritage service includes a local history museum, and archive section. A list of resources is available upon request. Archives of the Essex Parishes of Barking and Dagenham and the Boroughs

L B of Barking & Dagenham Local History Studies Central Library, Barking, Dagenham, IG11 7NB Tel: (020) 8517-8666 Local History studies from this Library have been centralised at Valence Linbrary, Becontree Avenue, Dagenham, Essex RM8 3HT Tel & (020) 8227 5297

Redbridge Library Central Library, Clements Road, Ilford, IG1 1EA Tel: (020) 8708-2417 Fax: (020) 8553 3299 Email: Local.Studies@redbridge.gov.uk WWW: www.redbridge.gov.uk

Gloucestershire
British Waterways Archives and The Waterways Trust Llanthony Warehouse, Gloucester Docks, Gloucester, GL1 2EJ Tel: 01452 318041WWW: http://www.britishwaterways.org.uk,

Gloucestershire Record Office Clarence Row, Alvin Street, Gloucester, GL1 3DW Tel: 01452-425295 Fax: 01452-426378 Email: records@gloscc.gov.uk WWW: http://archives.gloscc.gov.uk Daily admission charge £2 (£1.50 for over 60's.) I/d required

Greater Manchester
Bury Archive Service 1st Floor, Derby Hall Annexe, Edwin Street off Crompton Street, Bury, BL9 0AS Tel: 0161-797-6697 Fax: 0161 797 6697 Telephone before faxing Email: archives@bury.gov.uk WWW: www.bury.gov.uk/culture.htm, May be moving to new premises in 2002 check before visiting

Greater Manchester County Record Office 56 Marshall St, New Cross, Manchester, M4 5FU Tel: 0161-832-5284 Fax: 0161-839-3808 Email: archives@gmcro.co.uk WWW: http://www.gmcro.co.uk

Wigan Heritage Service Museum History Shop, Library Street, Wigan, WN1 1NU Tel: 01942 828020 Fax: 01942 827645 Email: heritage@wiganmbc.gov.uk

Hampshire
Hampshire Local Studies Library Winchester library, Jewry Street, Winchester, SO23 8RX Tel: 01962 841408 Fax: 01962 841489 Email: clceloc@hants.gov.uk WWW: www.hants.gov.uk/library

Hampshire Record Office Sussex St, Winchester, SO23 8TH Tel: 01962-846154 Fax: 01962-878681 Email: enquiries.archives@hants.gov.uk WWW: http://www.hants.gov.uk/record-office

Portsmouth City Museum and Record Office Museum Road, Portsmouth, PO1 2LJ Tel: (023) 92827261 Fax: (023) 92875276 Email: portmus@compuserve.com

Portsmouth Roman Catholic Diocesan Archives St Edmund House, Edinburgh Road, Portsmouth, PO1 3QA Tel: 023 9282 2166 These are private archives & prior arrangements to visit have to be agreed.

Royal Marines Museum Eastney, Southsea, PO4 9PX Tel: (023) 92 819385-Exts-224 Email: matthewlittle@royalmarinesmuseum.co.uk WWW: www.royalmarinesmuseum.co.uk No charges for research other than material costs. Donations welcome Visits by appointment Mon to Fri 10 am to 4.30pm

Southampton Archive Service Civic Centre, Southampton, Hants, SO14 7LY Tel: (023) 80832251 Email: city.archives@southampton.gov.uk WWW: www.southampton.gov.uk

Southampton City Libraries - Special Collections Reference Library, Civic Centre, Southampton, SO14 7LW Tel: 023 8083 2205 Email: local.studies@southampton.gov.uk WWW: www.southampton.gov.uk Special collections include information on Southampton and Hampshire, genealogy and

maritime topics.

Wessex Film and Sound Archive, Hampshire Record Office, Sussex Street, Winchester SO23 8TH Tel: 01962 847742 WWW: www.hants.gov.uk/record-office/film.html

Herefordshire
Hereford Cathedral Archives & Library 5 College Cloisters, Cathedral Close, Hereford, HR1 2NG Tel: 01432 374225 Email: library@herefordcathedral.co.uk

Herefordshire Record Office The Old Barracks, Harold Street, Hereford, HR1 2QX Tel: 01432 260750 Email: shubbard@herefordshire.gov.uk WWW: http://www.herefordshire.gov.uk

Hertfordshire
Ashwell Education Services 59 High Street, Ashwell, Baldock, SG7 5NP Tel: 01462 742385 Email: aes@ashwell-education-services.co.uk WWW: www.ashwell-education-services.co.uk Research into the History and family histories of Ashwell and its people

Bushey Museum and Art Gallery, Rudolph Road, Bushey WD23 3HW Tel: 020 8420 4057 1901 census

Hertfordshire Archives and Local Studies County Hall, Pegs Lane, Hertford, SG13 8EJ Tel: 01438 737333 Fax: 01923 471333 Email: herts.direct@hertscc.gov.uk WWW: http://hertsdirect.org/hals Hertfordshire Archives & Local Studies is comprised of the former Herts County Record Office and Herts Local Studies Library 1901 census

Hull
Brynmor Jones Library - University of Hull Cottingham Road, Hull, HU6 7RX Tel: 01482 465265 Fax: 01482 466205 Email: archives@acs.hull.ac.uk WWW: www.hull.ac.uk/lib www.hull.ac.uk/lib/archives

Hull City Archives 79 Lowgate, Kingston upon Hull, HU1 1HN Tel: 01482-615102 Tel: 01482-615110 Fax: 01482-613051 Email: city.archives@hcc.gov.uk WWW: www.hullcc.gov.uk

Hull Central Library Family and Local History Unit, Central Library, Albion Street, Kingston upon Hull HU1 3TF Tel: 01482 616828 Fax: 01482 616827 Email: gareth@ukorigins.co.uk WWW: http://www.hullcc.gov.uk/genealogy/famhist.php 1901 census

Local History Unit Hull College, Park Street Centre, Hull, HU2 8RR Tel: 01482-598952 Fax: 01482 598989 Email: historyunit@netscape.net WWW: www.historyofhull.co.uk

Isle of Wight
Isle of Wight Record Office 26 Hillside, Newport, PO30 2EB Tel: 01983-823820/1 Fax: 01983 823820 Email: record.office@iow.gov.uk WWW: www.iwight.com/library/default.asp

Kent
Bexley Local Studies and Archive Centre Central Library, Bourne Townley Road, Bexleyheath, DA6 7HJ Tel: (020) 8301 1545 Fax: (020) 8303 7872 Email: archives@bexleycouncil.freeserve.co.uk WWW: www.bexley.gov.uk As well as being a designated local authority record office the Local Studies Centre is Diocesan Record Office for all the (C of E) Parishes within the Borough ie Rochester & Southwark Dioceses

Canterbury Cathedral Archives The Precincts, Canterbury, CT1 2EH Tel: 01227 865330 Fax: 1227865222 Email: archives@canterbury-cathedral.org WWW: www.canterbury-cathedral.org

Canterbury Library & Local Studies Collection 18 High Street, Canterbury, CT1 2JF Tel: 01227-463608

Centre for Kentish Studies / Kent County Archives Service Sessions House, County Hall, Maidstone, Kent, ME141XQ Tel: 01622-694363 Fax: 01622 694379 Email: archives@kent.gov.uk WWW: www.kent.gov.uk/e&l/artslib/ARCHIVES/archivehome.htm

East Kent Archives Centre Enterprise Zone, Honeywood Road, Whitfield, Dover, CT16 3EH Tel: 01304 829306 Fax: 01304 820783 Email: eastkentarchives@kent.gov.uk

Hythe Archives - now at East Kent Archives Centre East Kent Archives Centre, Enterprise Zone, Honeywood Road, Whitfield, Dover, CT16 3EH Tel: 01304 829306 Fax: 01304 820783 Email: eastkentarchives@kent.gov.uk WWW: www.kent.gov.uk/kcc/arts/archives/kentish.html

Institute of Heraldic and Genealogical Studies 79 - 82 Northgate, Canterbury, CT1 1BA Fax: 01227-765617 Email: ihgs@ihgs.ac.uk WWW: www.ihgs.ac.uk

L B of Bromley Local Studies Library Central Library, High Street, Bromley, BR1 1EX Tel: 020 8460 9955 Fax: 020 8313 9975 Email: localstudies.library@bromley.gov.uk
Margate Library Local History Collection Cecil Square, Margate, CT9 1RE Tel: 01843-223626 Fax: 01843-293015
Pembroke Lodge Family History Centre and Museum 2-6 Station Approach, Birchington on Sea, CT7 9RD Tel: 01843-841649 Please address all mail to 4 Station approach, Birchington on Sea
Ramsgate Library Local Strudies Collection & Thanet Branch Archives Ramsgate Library, Guildford Lawn, Ramsgate, CT11 9AY Tel: 01843-593532 Archives at this library moved to East Kent Archives CentreEnterprise Zone, Honeywood Road, Whitfield, Dover, Kent CT16 3EH. A Local Studies Collection will remain
Sevenoaks Archives Office Central Library, Buckhurst Lane, Sevenoaks, TN13 1LQ Tel: 01732-453118 Tel: 01732-452384 Fax: 01732-742682

Lancashire
Blackburn Cathedral & Archives Cathedral Close, Blackburn, BB1 5AA Tel: 01254 51491 Email: cathredal@blackburn.anglican.org WWW: www.blackburn.anglican.org
Blackburn Central Library Town Hall Street, Blackburn, BB2 1AG Tel: 01254 587920 Fax: 01254 690539 Email: reference.library@blackburn.gov.uk WWW: www.blackburn.gov.uk/library
Bolton Archive & Local Studies Service Central Library, Civic Centre, Le Mans Crescent, Bolton, BL1 1SE Tel: 01204-332185 Email: archives.library@bolton.gov.uk
Lancashire Record Office Bow Lane, Preston, PR1 2RE Tel: 01772 263039 Fax: 01772 263050 Email: record.office@ed.lancscc.gov.uk WWW: www.lancashire.gov.uk/education/lifelong/recordindex.shtm, The Lancashire Local Studies Collection is now housed here
North West Sound Archive Old Steward's Office, Clitheroe Castle, Clitheroe, BB7 1AZ Tel: 01200-427897 Fax: 01200-427897 Email: nwsa@ed.lancscc.gov.uk WWW: www.lancashire.gov.uk/education/lifelong/recordindex
Oldham Local Studies and Archives 84 Union Street, Oldham, OL1 1DN Tel: 0161-911-4654 Fax: 0161-911-4654 Email: archives@oldham.gov.uk localstudies@oldham.gov.uk WWW: http://www.oldham.gov.uk/archives http://www.oldham.gov.uk/local_studies
Rochdale Local Studies Library Arts & Heritage Centre, The Esplanade, Rochdale, OL16 4TY Tel: 01706 864915 Temporary address until September 2002: Floor 3 Champness Hall, Drake Street, Rochdale OL16 1PB
Salford City Archives Salford Archives Centre, 658/662 Liverpool Rd, Irlam, Manchester, M44 5AD Tel: 0161 775-5643
Salford Local History Library Peel Park, Salford, M5 4WU Tel: 0161 736 2649 Fax:
Tameside Local Studies Library Stalybridge Library, Trinity Street, Stalybridge, SK15 2BN Tel: 0161-338-2708 Tel: 0161-338-3831 and 0161 303 7937 Fax: 0161-303-8289 Email: localstudies.library@mail.tameside.gov.uk WWW: http://www.tameside.gov.uk
The Documentary Photography Archive - Manchester c/o 7 Towncroft Lane, Bolton, BL1 5EW Tel: 0161 832 5284 Tel: 01204-840439 (Home) Fax: 01204-840439
Traceline PO Box 106, Southport, PR8 2HH Tel: 0151 471 4811 Fax: 01704-563354 Email: traceline@ons.gov.uk To be put in touch with lost relatives and acquaintances. The ONS must be satisfied that contact would be in the best interests of the person being sought. Traceline uses the NHS Central Register. NH
Trafford Local Studies Centre Public Library, Tatton Road, Sale, M33 1YH Tel: 0161-912-3013 Fax: 0161-912-3019 Email: traffordlocalstudies@hotmail.com The collection covers the former Lancashire and Cheshire towns of Stretford, Old Trafford, Urmston, Daveyhulme, Flixton, Altincham, Bowdon, Hale, Dunham Massey, Sale, Ashton-o-Mersey, Carrington,
Wigan Heritage Service Town Hall, Leigh, Wigan, WN7 2DY Tel: 01942-404430 Fax: 01942-404425 Email: heritage@wiganmbc.gov.uk WWW: http://www.wiganmbc.gov.uk

Leicestershire
Melton Mowbray Library Wilton Road, Melton Mowbray, LE13 0UJ Tel: 01664 560161 Fax: 01664 410199 WWW: www.leics.gov.uk
Record Office for Leicestershire, Leicester and Rutland Long Street, Wigston Magna, LE18 2AH Tel: 0116-257-1080

Fax: 0116-257-1120 Email: recordoffice@leics.gov.uk
Willoughby on the Wolds Heritage Group Group Archive & Village History Enquiries, 1 Church Lane, Willoughby on the Wolds, Nr Loughborough, LE12 6SS Tel: 01509 880077

Rutland
Record Office for Leicestershire, Leicester and Rutland Long Street, Wigston Magna, LE18 2AH Tel: 0116-257-1080 Fax: 0116-257-1120 Email: recordoffice@leics.gov.uk

Lincolnshire
Lincolnshire Archives St Rumbold Street, Lincoln, LN2 5AB Tel: 01522-526204 Fax: 01522-530047 Email: archive@lincolnshire.gov.uk WWW: http://www.lincolnshire.gov.uk/archives
Lincolnshire County Library Local Studies Section, Lincoln Central Library, Free School Lane, Lincoln, LN1 1EZ Tel: 01522-510800 Fax: 01522-575011 Email: lincoln.library@lincolnshire.gov.uk WWW: www.lincolnshire.gov.uk/library/services/family.htm
North East Lincolnshire Archives Town Hall, Town Hall Square, Grimsby, DN31 1HX Tel: 01472-323585 Fax: 01472-323582 Email: john.wilson@nelincs.gov.uk

Liverpool
Liverpool Record Office & Local History Department Central Library, William Brown Street, Liverpool, L3 8EW Tel: 0151 233 5817 Fax: 0151-233 5886 Email: recoffice.central.library@liverpool.gov.uk WWW: http://www.liverpool.gov.uk

London
Alexander Fleming Laboratory Museum / St Mary's NHS Trust Archives St Mary's Hospital, Praed Street, Paddington, London, W2 1NY Tel: (020) 7886 6528 Fax: (020) 7886 6739 Email: kevin.brown@st-marys.nhs.uk
Bank of England Archive Archive Section HO-SV, The Bank of England, Threadneedle Street, London, EC2R 8AH Tel: (020) 7601-5096 Fax: (020) 7601-4356 Email: archive@bankofengland.co.uk WWW: www.bankofengland.co.uk
Bethlem Royal Hospital Archives and Museum, Monks Orchard Road, Beckenham, BR3 3BX Tel: (020) 8776 4307 Tel: (020) 8776 4053 Fax: (020) 8776 4045 Email: museum@bethlem.freeserve.co.uk The archives of the Bethlem and Maudsley NHS Trust (the Bethlem Royal Hospital and the Maudsley Hospital). Records relating to individual patients are closed for 100 years.
Bexley Local Studies and Archive Centre Central Library, Bourne Townley Road, Bexleyheath, DA6 7HJ Tel: (020) 8301 1545 Fax: (020) 8303 7872 Email: archives@bexleycouncil.freeserve.co.uk WWW: www.bexley.gov.uk, As well as being a designated local authority record office the Local Studies Centre is Diocesan Record Office for all the (C of E) Parishes within the Borough ie Rochester & Southwark Dioceses
Black Cultural Archives 378 Coldharbour Lane, London, SW9 8LF Tel: (020) 7738 4591 Fax: (020) 7738 7168
Brent Community History Library & Archive 152 Olive Road, London, NW2 6UY Tel: (020) 8937 3541 Fax: (020) 8450 5211 Email: archive@brent.gov.uk WWW: www.brent.gov.uk
British Library of Political and Economic Science London School of Economics, 10 Portugal Street, London, WC2A 2HD Tel: (020) 7955 7223 Fax: (020) 7955 7454 Email: info@lse.ac.uk WWW: http://www.lse.ac.uk
British Library Oriental and India Collections 197 Blackfriars Rd, London, SE1 8NG Tel: (020) 7412-7873 Fax: (020) 7412-7641 Email: oioc-enquiries@bl.uk WWW: http://www.bl.uk/collections/oriental
British Library Western Manuscripts Collections 96 Euston Road, London, NW1 2DB Tel: (020) 7412-7513 Fax: (020) 7412-7745 Email: mss@bl.uk WWW: http://www.bl.uk/, Note: can only respond to enquiries related to their own collections
British Red Cross Museum and Archives 9 Grosvenor Crescent, London, SW1X 7EJ Tel: (020) 7201-5153 Email: enquiry@redcross.org.uk WWW: www.redcross.org.uk, Open by appointment 10am to 4pm Monday to Friday.
British Universities Film and Video Council, 77 Wells Street, London W1T 3QJ Tel: 020 7393 1500 WWW: www.bufvc.ac.uk
Business Archives Council 3rd & 4th Floors, 101 High Street, Whitechapel , London, E1 7RE Tel: 020 7247 0024 Fax: 020 7422 0026

Centre for Metropolitan History, Institute of Historical Research, Senate House, Malet Street, LondonWC1E 7HU Tel: (020) 7862 8790 Fax: (020) 7862 8793 Email: olwen.myhill@sas.ac.uk WWW: www.history.ac.uk/cmh/cmh.main.html

Chelsea Public Library Old Town Hall, King's Road, London, SW3 5EZ Tel: (020) 7352-6056 Tel: (020) 7361-4158 Fax: (020) 7351 1294 Local Studies Collection on Royal Borough of Kensington & Chelsea south of Fulham Road

City of Westminster Archives Centre 10 St Ann's Street, London, SW1P 2DE Tel: (020) 7641-5180 Fax: (020) 7641-5179 WWW: www.westminster.gov.uk, Holds records for whole area covered by City of Westminster incl former Metropolitan Boroughs of Paddington and St Maryleborne

Corporation of London Records Office PO Box 270, Guildhall, London, EC2P 2EJ Tel: (020) 7332-1251 Fax: (020) 7710-8682 Email: clro@corpoflondon.gov.uk WWW: cityoflondon.gov.uk/archives/clro

Deed Poll Records Section Room E 15 Royal Courts of Justice, Strand, London, WC2A 2LL Tel: (020) 7947 6528 Fax: (020) 7947 6807

Documents Register Quality House, Quality Court, Chancery Lane, London, WC2A 1HP Tel: (020) 7242-1198 Fax: (020) 7831-3550 Email: nra@hmc.gov.uk

Dr Williams's Library 14 Gordon Square, London, WC1H 0AR Tel: (020) 7387-3727 Email: 101340.2541@compuserve.com The General Registers of Protestant Dissenters (Dr Williams's Library Registers) were surrendered to the Registrar General and are now at The Public Record Office (RG4/4666-4673)

Ealing Local History Centre Central Library, 103 Broadway Centre, Ealing, London, W5 5JY Tel: (020) 8567-3656-ext-37 Fax: (020) 8840-2351 Email: localhistory@hotmail.com WWW: www.ealing.gov.uk/libraries, Closed Sundays & Mondays

Family Records Centre 1 Myddleton Street, London, EC1R 1UW Tel: (020) 8392-5300 Fax: (020) 8392-5307 Email: info@familyrecords.gov.uk WWW: www.familyrecords.gov.uk

Grenadier Guards Record Office Wellington Barracks, Birdcage Walk, London, SW1E 6HQ Access is by appointment made in advance. Search fee of £25.00 per search

Guildhall Library, Manuscripts Section Aldermanbury, London, EC2P 2EJ Tel: (020) 7332-1863 Email: manuscripts.guildhall@corpoflondon.gov.uk WWW: http://ihr.sas.ac.uk/ihr/gh/ Opening hours Mon to Sat 9.30am to 4.45pm (last orders for manuscripts 4.30pm: on Sat no manuscripts produced bet 12noon and 2pm. Records: City of London parish records, probate records, City Livery

Hackney Archives Department 43 De Beauvoir Road, L B of Hackney, London, N1 5SQ Tel: (020) 7241-2886 Email: archives@hackney.gov.uk WWW: http://www.hackney.gov.uk/history/index.html, Covers Hackney, Shoreditch & Stoke Newington

Hertiage Services Consignia (formerly Post Office Heritage) Freeling House,, Phoenix Place, London, WC1X 0DL Tel: (020) 7239-2570 Fax: (020) 7239-2576 Email: heritage@consignia.com WWW: www.consignia.com/heritage, The National Postal Museum formerley in King Edward Street, London closed in December 1998. The Philatelic collection is available to view by appointment at Heritage Services Consignia

Hillingdon Local Studies & Archives Central Library, High Street, Uxbridge, London, UB8 1HD Tel: 01895-250702 Fax: 01895-811164 Email: ccotton@hillingdon.gov.uk WWW: http://www.,hillingdon.gov.uk/goto/libraries

Hounslow Library (Local Studies & archives) Centre Space, Treaty Centre, High Street, Hounslow, TW3 1ES Tel: (020) 8583 4545 Fax: 020 8583 4595

Imperial College Archives London University, Room 455 Sherfield Building, Imperial College, London, SW7 2AZ Tel: 020 7594 8850 Fax: 020 7584 3763 Email: archivist@ic.ac.uk WWW: http://www.lib.ic.ac.uk

Institute of Historical Research University of London , Senate House, Malet Street, London, WC1E 7HU Tel: (020) 7862 8740 Fax: 020 7436 2145 Email: ihr@sas.ac.uk WWW: http://ihr.sas.ac.uk

King's College London Archives Kins College, Strand, London, WC2R 2LS Tel: 020 7848 2015 Tel: 020 7848 2187 Email: archives@kcl.ac.uk WWW: http://www.kcl.ac.uk/depsta/iss/archives/top.htm Includes Student records, staff records and hospital records for King's College Hospital

L B of Hammersmith & Fulham Archives & Local History Centre The Lilla Huset, 191 Talgarth Road, London, W6 8BJ Tel: 0208-741-5159 WWW: http://www.lbhf.gov.uk

Lewisham Local Studies & Archives Lewisham Library, 199 - 201 Lewisham High Street, Lewisham, London, SE13 6LG Tel: (020) 8297-0682 Email: local.studies@lewisham.gov.uk WWW: http://www.lewisham.gov.uk Covering the Parishes of Lewisham, Lee & St Paul's, Deptford. Appointments advisable.

Library of the Royal College of Surgeons of England 35-43 Lincoln's Inn Fields, London, WC2A 3PN Tel: (020) 7869 6520 Fax: (020) 7405 4438 Email: library@rseng.ac.uk

Liddell Hart Centre for Military Archives King's College London, Strand, London, WC2R 2LS Tel: 020 7848 2015 Tel: 020 7848 2187 Fax: 020 7848 2760 Email: archives@kcl.ac.uk WWW: http://www.kcl.ac.uk/lhcma/top.htm

Linnean Society of London Burlington House, Piccadilly, London, W1J 0BF Tel: 020 7437 4479 Tel: 020 7434 4470 Fax: 020 7287 9364 Email: gina@linnean.org WWW: http://www.linnean.org

Local Studies Collection for Chiswick & Brentford Chiswick Public Library, Dukes Avenue, Chiswick, London, W4 2AB Tel: (020) 8994-5295 Restricted opening hours for local history room: please telephone before visiting

L B of Barnet, Archives & Local Studies Department Hendon Library, The Burroughs, Hendon, NW4 3BQ Tel: (020) 8359-2876 Fax: (020) 8359-2885 Email: hendon.library@barnet.gov.uk

L B of Camden Local Studies & Archive Centre Holborn Library, 32 - 38 Theobalds Road, London, WC1X 8PA Tel: 020 7974 6342 Fax: 020 7974 6284 Email: localstudies@camden.gov.uk WWW: www.camden.gov.uk, Closed Wednesday. Open: Mon & Thurs 10 to 7pm; Tues & Fri 10 to 6pm; Sats 10 to 1pm and 2pm to 5pm

L B of Croydon Library and Archives Service Central Library, Katharine Street, Croydon, CR9 1ET Tel: (020) 8760-5400-ext-1112 Fax: (020) 8253-1012 Email: localstudies@croydononline.org WWW: http://www.croydon.gov.uk/

L B of Enfield Archives & Local History Unit Southgate Town Hall, Green Lanes, Palmers Green, London, N13 4XD Tel: (020) 8379-2724 Fax: (020) 8379 2761 The collections specifically relate to Edmonton and Enfield (both formerly in Middlesex)

L B of Greenwich Local History Library Woodlands, 90 Mycenae Road, Blackheath, London, SE3 7SE Tel: (020) 8858 4631 Email: local.history@greenwich.gov.uk WWW: www.greenwich.gov.uk, The library will be moving to a new Heritage Centre autumn 2002. Please contact the library for more details

L B of Haringey Archives Service Bruce Castle Museum, Lordship Lane, Tottenham, London, N17 8NU Tel: (020) 8808-8772 Fax: (020) 8808-4118 Email: museum.services@haringey.gov.uk

L B of Islington Central Reference Library Central Reference Library, 2 Fieldway Crescent, London, N5 1PF Tel: (020) 7619-6931 Fax: (020) 7619-6939 Email: local.history@islington.gov.uk WWW: http://www.islington.gov.uk Reorganisation is imminent - planned move to Finsbury Library, 245 St John Street, London EC1V 4NB (020) 7527 6931 (020) 7527 6937 Collection covers the south of the LB of Islington.

L B of Lambeth Archives Department Minet Library, 52 Knatchbull Road, Lambeth, London, SE5 9QY Tel: (020) 7926 6076 Fax: (020) 7936 6080 Email: lambetharchives@lambeth.gov.uk

L B of Newham Archives & Local Studies Library Stratford Library, 3 The Grove, London, E5 1EL Tel: (020) 8557 8856 Fax: (020) 8503 1525

L B of Wandsworth Local studies Local Studies ServiceBattersea Library, 265 Lavender Hill, London, SW11 1JB Tel: (020) 8871 7753 Fax: (020) 7978-4376 Email: wandsworthmuseum@wandsworth.gov.uk WWW: www.wandsworth.gov.uk

London Metropolitan Archives 40 Northampton Road, London, EC1R 0HB Tel: 020 7332 3820 Email: ask.lma@ms.corpoflondon.gov.uk WWW: www.cityoflondon.gov.uk

London University - Institute of Advanced Studies Charles Clore House, 17 Russell Square, London, WC1B 5DR Tel: (020) 7637 1731 Fax: (020) 7637 8224 Email: ials.lib@sas.ac.uk WWW: http://ials.sas.ac.uk

London University - Institute of Education 20 Bedford Way, London, WC1H 0AL Tel: 020 7612 6063 Fax: 020 7612 6093 Email: lib@ioe.ac.uk WWW: http://www.ioe.ac.uk/library/

Manorial Documents Register Quality House, Quality Court, Chancery Lane, London, WC2A 1HP Tel: (020) 7242-1198 Fax: (020) 7831-3550 Email: nra@hmc.gov.uk

Manuscripts Room Library Services, University College, Gower Street, London, WC1E 6BT Tel: (020) 7387 7050 Email: mssrb@ucl.ac.uk WWW: http://www.ucl.ac.uk/library/special-coll/

Museum of London Library 150 London Wall, London, EC2Y 5HN Tel: 020 7814 5588 Email: info@museumoflondon.org.uk WWW: http://museumoflondon.org.uk

Museum of the Order of St John St John's Gate, St John's Lane, Clerkenwell, London, EC1M 4DA Tel: (020) 7253-6644 Fax: (020) 7336 0587 Email: WWW: www.sja.org.uk/history

Museum of the Royal Pharmaceutical Society Museum of the Royal Pharmaceutical Society, 1 Lambeth High Street, London, SE1 7JN Tel: (020) 7572 2210 Fax: Email: museum@rpsgb.org.uk WWW: http://www.rpsgb.org.uk, Records of pharmacists from 1841 Research fee charged £20 per person or premises researched to Non members of the Society, £10 per person or premises researched for members(Genealogical Enquiries)

National Army Museum Royal Hospital Road, London, SW3 4HT Tel: (020) 7730-0717 Fax: (020) 7823-6573 Email: info@national-army-museum.ac.uk WWW: http://www.national-army-museum.ac.uk

National Army Museum Department of Archives (Photographs, Film & Sound)
Royal Hospital Road, London, SW3 4HT Tel: (020) 7730-0717 Fax: (020) 7823-6573 Email: info@national-army-museum.ac.uk WWW: www.national-army-museum.ac.uk

National Portrait Gallery Heinz Archive & library, 2 St. Martins Place, London, WC2H 0HE Tel: (020) 7306 0055 Fax: (020) 7306 0056 WWW: www.npg.org.uk

National Register of Archives Quality House, Quality Court, Chancery Lane, London, WC2A 1HP Tel: (020) 7242 1198 Fax: (020) 7831 3550 Email: nra@hmc.gov.uk WWW: http://www.hmc.gov.uk, The National Register of Archives (NRA) is maintained by the Historical Manuscripts Commission (HMC) as a central collecting point for information concerning the location of manuscript sources for Britain

Principal Registry of the Family Division First Avenue House, 42 - 49 High Holborn, London, WC1V 6NP Tel: (020) 7947 7000 Fax: (020) 7947 6946 WWW: www.courtservice.gov.uk

Royal Air Force Museum - Department of Research & information Services Grahame Park Way, Hendon, London, NW9 5LL Tel: (020) 83584873 Fax: (020) 8200 1751 Email: info@rafmuseum.com WWW: http://www.rafmuseum.com

Royal Air Force Museum Grahame Park Way, Hendon, London, NW9 5LL Tel: (020) 8205-2266 Fax: (020) 8200 1751 Email: info@refmuseum.org.uk WWW: http://www.rafmuseum.org.uk

L B of Barking & Dagenham Local History Studies Central Library, Barking, Dagenham, IG11 7NB Tel: (020) 8517-8666 Local History studies from this Library have been centralised at Valence Linbrary, Becontree Avenue, Dagenham, Essex RM8 3HT Tel & (020) 8227 5297 Email: valencelibrary@hotmail.com

R B of Kensington & Chelsea Libraries & Arts Service Central Library, Phillimore Walk, Kensington, London, W8 7RX Tel: (020) 7361-3036 Email: information.services@rbkc.gov.uk WWW: www.rbkc.gov.uk

Royal Botanic Gardens Library & Archives, Kew, Richmond, TW9 3AE Tel: 020 8332 5414 Tel: 020 8332 5417 Fax: 020 8332 5430

Royal London Hospital Archives and Museum Royal London Hospital, Newark Whitechapel, London, E1 1BB Tel: (020) 7377-7608 Email: r.j.evans@mds.qmw.ac.uk WWW: www.bartsandthelondon.org.uk

Southwark Local Studies Library211 Borough High Street, Southwark, London, SE1 1JA Tel: 0207-403-3507 Email: local.studies.library@southwark.gov.uk WWW: www.southwark.gov.uk

St Bartholomew's Hospital Archives & Museum Archives and Museum, West Smithfield, London, EC1A 7BE Tel: (020) 7601-8152 Email: marion.rea@bartsandthelondon.nhs.uk WWW: bartsandthelondon.org.uk, Visitors to use the archive by appointment only - Mon to Fri 9.30am to 5pm

The Archives of Worshipful Company of Brewers Brewers' Hall, Aldermanbury Square, London, EC2V 7HR Tel: (020) 7606 1301

Galton Institute 19 Northfields Prospect, London, SW18 1PE

The United Grand Lodge of England Freemasons' Hall, 60 Great Queen Street, London, WC2B 5AZ Tel: (020) 7831 9811 WWW: www.grandlodge.org

Tower Hamlets Local History Library & Archives Bancroft Library, 277 Bancroft Road, London, E1 4DQ Tel: (020) 8980

4366 Ext 129 Fax: (020) 8983-4510

Twickenham Library Twickenham Library, Garfield Road, Twickenham, TW1 3JS Tel: (020) 8891-7271 Fax: (020) 8891-5934 Email: twicklib@richmond.gov.uk WWW: http://www.richmond.gov.uk, The Twickenham collection moved to Richmond Local Studies Library

University of London (Library - Senate House) Palaeography Room, Senate House, Malet Street, London, WC1E 7HU Tel: (020) 7862 8475 Fax: 020 7862 8480 Email: library@ull.ac.uk WWW: http://www.ull.ac.uk

Waltham Forest Archives Vestry House Museum, Vestry Road, Walthamstow, London, E17 9NH Tel: (020) 8509 1917 Email: vestry.house@al.lbwf.gov.uk WWW: http://.www.lbwf.gov.uk/vestry/vestry.htm Visits by prior appointment only

Westminster Abbey Library & Muniment Room Westminster Abbey, London, SW1P 3PA Tel: (020) 7222-5152-Ext-4830 Fax: (020) 7226-4827 Email: library@westminster-abbey.org WWW: www.westminster-abbey.org

Westminster Diocesan Archives16a Abingdon Road, Kensington, London, W8 6AF Tel: (020) 7938-3580 This is the private archive of the Catholic Archbishop of Westminster and is not open to the public. Pre 1837 baptismal records have been transcribed and copies are with the Society of Genealogists.

Westminster University Archives Information Systems & Library Services, 4-12 Little Titchfield Street, London, W1W 7UW Tel: 020 7911 5000 ext 2524 Fax: 020 7911 5894 Email: archive@westminster.ac.uk WWW: www.wmin.ac.uk The archive is organisationally within the Library but is a separate entity. The University of Westminster Libraries do not have special collections relating to family and local history

Public Record Office - 1901 Census Records Ruskin Avenue, Kew, TW9 4DU WWW: http://www.pro.gov.uk Records for 1901 census opened to the public in January 2002. Available on the internet, the Public Record office and main public libraries.

Manchester
Manchester Archives & Local Studies Manchester Central Library, St Peter's Square, Manchester, M2 5PD Tel: 0161-234-1979 Fax: 0161-234-1927 Email: lsu@libraries.manchester.gov.uk WWW: http://www..manchester.gov.uk/libraries/index.htm

Methodist Archives and Research Centre John Rylands University Library, 150 Deansgate, Manchester, M3 3EH Tel: 0161 834 5343 Fax: 0161 834 5574

Medway
Medway Archives and Local Studies Centre Civic Centre, Strood, Rochester, ME2 4AU Tel: 01634-332714 Fax: 01634-297060 Email: archives@medway.gov.uk local.studies@medway.gov.uk WWW: http://cityark.medway.gov.uk

Merseyside
Crosby Library (South Sefton Local History Unit) Crosby Road North, Waterloo, Liverpool, L22 0LQ Tel: 0151 257 6401 Fax: 0151 934 5770 Email: local-history.south@leisure.sefton.gov.uk The Local History Units serve Sefton Borough Council area. The South Sefton Unit covers Bootle, Crosby, Maghull and other communities south of the River Alt. The North Sefton Unit covers Southport, Formby

Huyton Central Library Huyton Library, Civic Way, Huyton, Knowsley, L36 9GD Tel: 0151-443-3738 Fax: 0151 443 3739 Email: eileen.hume.dlcs@knowsley.gov.uk WWW: http://www.knowsley.gov.uk/leisure/libraries/huyton/index.html

Merseyside Maritime Museum Maritime Archives and Library, Albert Dock, Liverpool, L3 4AQ Tel: 0151-478-4418 Fax: 0151-478-4590 Email: archives@nmgmarchives.demon.co.uk WWW: www.nmgm.org.uk

Southport Library (North Sefton Local History Unit) Lord Street, Southport, PR8 1DJ Tel: 0151 934 2119 Fax: 0151 934 2115 The Local History Units serve Sefton Borough Council area. The North Sefton Unit covers Southport, Formby. The South Sefton Unit covers Bootle, Crosby, Maghull and other communities south of the River

St Helen's Local History & Archives Library Central Library, Gamble Institute, Victoria Square, St Helens, WA10 1DY Tel: 01744-456952 No research undertaken

Wirral Archives Service Wirral Museum, Birkenhead Town Hall, Hamilton Street, Birkenhead, CH41 5BR Tel: 0151-666 3903 Fax: 0151-666 3965 Email: archives@wirral-libraries.net

Middlesex
British Deaf History Society 288 Bedfont Lane, Feltham,
TW14 9NU Fax: Email: bdhs@iconic.demon.co.uk
L B of Harrow Local History Collection Civic Centre Library,
PO Box 4, Station Road, Harrow, HA1 2UU Tel: 0208 424 1055
Email: civiccentre.library@harrow.gov.uk

Norfolk
East Anglian Film Archive, University of East Anglia,
Norwich, NR4 7TJ Tel: 01603 592664 WWW:
www.uea.ac.uk/eafa
Kings Lynn Borough Archives The Old Gaol House, Saturday
Market Place, Kings Lynn, PE30 5DQ Tel: 01553-774297 Tel:
01603 761349 Fax: 01603 761885 Email:
norfrec@norfolk.gov.uk WWW:
http://archives.norfolk.gov.uk
Norfolk Record Office Gildengate House, Anglia Square, Upper
Green Lane, Norwich, NR3 1AX Tel: 01603-761349 Fax:
01603-761885 Email: norfrec.nro@norfolk.gov.uk WWW:
http://archives.norfolk.gov.uk

Northamptonshire
Northamptonshire Central Library Abington Street,
Northampton, NN1 2BA Tel: 01604-462040 Fax: 01604-462055
Email: ns-centlib@northamptonshire.gov.uk WWW:
http://www.northamptonshire.gov.uk
Northamptonshire Studies Room collection includes census 1841
to 1891, name indexes 1851 & 1881 census, Parish Registers on
microfiche, I.G.I., trade and street directories, poll books
Northamptonshire Record Office Wootton Hall Park,
Northampton, NN4 8BQ Tel: 01604-762129 Email:
archivist@nro.northamtonshire.gov.uk
WWW: http://www.nro.northamptonshire.gov.uk
also holds Peterborough Diocesan Record Office

Northumberland
Berwick upon Tweed Record Office Council Offices, Wallace
Green, Berwick-Upon-Tweed, TD15 1ED Tel: 01289 301865
Tel: 01289-330044-Ext-265 Fax: 01289-330540 Email:
lb@berwick-upon-tweed.gov.uk WWW:
www.swinhope.demon.co.uk/genuki/NBL/Northumberland
RO/Berwick.html, GRO indexes 1837-1930
Northumberland Archive Service Morpeth Records Centre,
The Kylins, Loansdean, Morpeth, NE6l 2EQ Tel: 01670-504084
Fax: 01670-514815
WWW: http://www.swinhope.demon.co.uk/nro/

Nottinghamshire
Media Archive for Central England, Institute of Film Studies,
University of Nottingham, Nottingham NG7 2RD Tel: 0115 846
6448 WWW: www.nottingham.ac.uk/film/mace
Nottingham Central Library : Local Studies Centre Angel
Row, Nottingham, NG1 6HP Tel: 0115 915 2873 Fax: 0115 915
2850 Email: local-studies.library@nottinghamcity.gov.uk WWW:
www.nottinghamcity.gov.uk/libraries
Nottingham R.C. Diocese Nottingham Diocesan Archives
Willson House, Derby Road, Nottingham, NG1 5AW Tel: 0115
953 9803 Fax: 0115 953 9808
Nottinghamshire Archives Castle Meadow Road, Nottingham,
NG2 1AG Tel: 0115-950-4524 Admin Tel: 0115 958 1634
Enquiries Fax: 0115-941-3997 Email: archives@nottscc.gov.uk
WWW: www.nottscc.gov.uk/libraries/archives/index.htm
Southwell Minster Library Minster Office, Trebeck Hall,
Bishop's Drive, Southwell, NG25 0JP Tel: 01636-812649 Fax:
01636 815904 Email: pat@southwellminster.prestell.co.uk

Oxfordshire
Oxfordshire Archives
St Luke's Church, Temple Road, Cowley, Oxford, OX4 2EX Tel:
01865 398200 Email: archives@oxfordshire.gov.uk WWW:
http://www.oxfordshire.gov.uk

Peterborough
Peterborough Local Studies Collection Central Library,
Broadway, Peterborough, PE1 1RX Tel: 01733 348343 Email:
libraries@peterborough.gov.uk
The telephone number may change in 2002

Shropshire
Ironbridge Gorge Museum, Library & Archives The
Wharfage, Ironbridge, Telford, TF8 7AW Tel: 01952-432141
Email: library@ironbridge.org.uk WWW:

www.ironbridge.org.uk
Shropshire Records & Research Centre Castle Gates,
Shrewsbury, SY1 2AQ Tel: 01743-255350 Fax: 01743-255355
Email: research@shropshire-cc.gov.uk WWW: www.shropshire-
cc.gov.uk/research.nsf
Wrekin Local Studies Forum Madeley Library, Russell Square,
Telford, TF7 5BB Tel: 01952 586575 Fax: 01952 587105 Email:
wlst@library.madeley.uk WWW: www.madeley.org.uk

Somerset
Bath & North East Somerset Record Office Guildhall, High
St, Bath, BA1 5AW Tel: 01225-477421 Fax: 01225-477439
Email: archives@bathnes.gov.uk
Bristol University Library - Special Collections Tyndall
Avenue, Bristol, BS8 1TJ Tel: 0117 928 8014 Fax: 0117 925
5334 Email: library@bris.ac.uk WWW:
www.bris.ac.uk/depts/library
Somerset Archive & Record Service Somerset Record Office,
Obridge Road, Taunton, TA2 7PU Tel: 01823-337600
Appointments Tel: 01823 278805 Enquiries Fax: 01823-325402
Email: archives@somerset.gov.uk WWW:
http://www.somerset.gov.uk

Staffordshire
Burton Archives Burton Library, Riverside, High Street, Burton
on Trent, DE14 1AH Tel: 01283-239556 Fax: 01283-239571
Email: burton.library@staffordshire.gov.uk
Coal Miners Records Cannock Record Centre, Old Mid-
Cannock (Closed) Colliery Site, Rumer Hill Road, Cannock,
WS11 3EX Tel: 01543-570666 Employment and training
records held for ex mineworkers post 1917
Keele University Special Collections & Archives Keele, ST5
5BG Tel: 01782 583237 Fax: 01782 711553 Email:
h.burton@keele.ac.uk WWW: www.keele.ac.uk/depts/li/specarc
Lichfield Record Office Lichfield Library, The Friary, Lichfield,
WS13 6QG Tel: 01543-510720 Fax: 01543-510715 Email:
lichfield.record.office@staffordshire.gov.uk WWW:
www.staffordshire.gov.uk/archives Advance booking required.
Lichfield Records Research Service. Covers all the holdings of
the office, including Lichfield Diocesan records such as wills
including, bishop's transcripts and marriage bonds
Staffordshire Record Office Eastgate Street, Stafford, ST16
2LZ Tel: 01785-278373 (Bookings) Tel: 01785 278379
(Enquiries) Fax: 01785-278384 Email:
staffordshire.record.office@staffordshire.co.uk WWW:
www.staffordshire.gov.uk/archives For research into all
Staffordshire records including parish and nonconformist
registers, census and electoral registers contact:Staffordshire
Record Office, Eastgate Street, Stafford ST16 2LZ Lichfield
Records Research Service For research into all Lichfield
Diocesan records including will, bishop's transcripts and
marriage bonds for Staffordshire, Derbyshire, north east
Warickshire and North Shropshire 1901 census
**Staffordshire & Stoke on Trent Archive Service -Stoke on
Trent City Archives** Hanley Library, Bethesda Street, Hanley,
Stoke on Trent, ST1 3RS Tel: 01782-238420 Fax: 01782-238499
Email: stoke.archives@stoke.gov.uk WWW:
www.staffordshire.gov.uk/archives
Tamworth Library Corporation Street, Tamworth, B79 7DN
Tel: 01827-475645 Fax: 01827-475658 Email:
tamworth.library@staffordshire.gov.uk WWW:
www.staffordshire.gov.uk/locgov/county/cars/tamlib.htm, IGI
(Derby, Leics, Notts, Shrops, Staffs, Warks, Worcs). Parish
registers for Tamworth. Census for Tamworth and District, 1841
- 91. Street directories for Staffs and Warks.
William Salt Library Eastgate Street, Stafford, ST16 2LZ Tel:
01785-278372 Fax: 01785-278414 Email:
william.salt.library@staffordshire.gov.uk WWW:
http://www.staffordshire.gov.uk/archives/salt.htm

Suffolk
Suffolk Record Office - Bury St Edmunds Branch 77
Raingate Street, Bury St Edmunds, IP33 2AR Tel: 01284-352352
Fax: 01284-352355 Email: bury.ro@libher.suffolkcc.gov.uk
WWW: http://www.suffolkcc.gov.uk/sro/
Suffolk Record Office Ipswich Branch Gatacre Road, Ipswich,
IP1 2LQ Tel: 01473-584541 Fax: 01473-584533 Email:
ipswich.ro@libher.suffolkcc.gov.uk WWW:
www.suffolkcc.gov.uk/sro/ 1901 census
Suffolk Record Office Lowestoft Branch Central Library,
Clapham Road, Lowestoft, NR32 1DR Tel: 01502-405357 Fax:
01502-405350 Email: lowestoft.ro@libher.suffolkcc.gov.uk.

WWW: www.suffolkcc.gov.uk/sro/
Suffolk Regiment Archives Suffolk Record Office, 77 Raingate Street, Bury St Edmunds, IP33 2AR Tel: 01284-352352 Fax: 01284-352355 Email: bury.ro@libher.suffolkcc.gov.uk WWW: http://www.suffolkcc.gov.uk/sro/

Surrey
Domestic Buildings Research Group (Surrey) The Ridings, Lynx Hill, East Horsley, KT24 5AX Tel: 01483 283917
Kingston Museum & Heritage Service North Kingston Centre, Richmond Road, Kingston upon Thames, KT2 5PE Tel: (020) 8547-6738 Fax: (020) 8547-6747 Email: local.history@rbk.kingston.gov.uk WWW: www.kingston.gov.uk/museum/, Research service available £7.50 per half hour - max 3 hours
L B of Merton Local Studies Centre Merton Civic Centre, London Road, Morden, SM4 5DX Tel: (020) 8545-3239 Fax: (020) 8545-4037 Email: mertonlibs@compuserve.com
L B of Sutton Archives Central Library, St Nicholas Way, Sutton, SM1 1EA Tel: (020) 8770-4747 Fax: (020) 8770-4777 Email: local.studies@sutton.gov.uk WWW: www.sutton.gov.uk, The Central Library itself holds a large selection of genealogical sources. The Library is fully accessible. Please phone Archivist for opening hours and further details about holdings

Sussex
South East Film and Video Archive, University of Brighton, Grand Parade, Brighton BN2 2JY Tel: 01273 643213 WWW: www.bton.ac.uk/sefva
East Sussex Record Office The Maltings, Castle Precincts, Lewes, BN7 1YT Tel: 01273-482349 Email: archives@eastsussexcc.gov.uk
WWW: www.eastsussexcc.gov.uk/archives/main.htm
Sussex - West
West Sussex Record Office County Hall, Chichester, PO19 1RN Tel: 01243-753600
Fax: 01243-533959 Email: records.office@westsussex.gov.uk
WWW: www.westsussex.gov.uk/cs/ro/rohome.htm
Worthing Reference Library Worthing Library, Richmond Road, Worthing, BN11 1HD Tel: 01903-212060 Email: worthinglibrary@hotmail.com Largest library in West Sussex and specialist centre for family history sources.

Tyne and Wear
Local Studies Centre Central Library, Northumberland Square, North Shields, NE30 1QU Tel: 0191-200-5424 Fax: 0191 200 6118
Email: eric.hollerton@northtyneside.gov.uk
WWW: www.northtyneside.gov.uk/libraries.html
South Tyneside Central Library Prince Georg Square, South Shields, NE33 2PE Tel: 0191-427-1818-Ext-7860 Fax: 0191-455-8085 Email: reference.library@s-tyneside-mbc.gov.uk
WWW: www.s-tyneside-mbc.gov.uk
Northern Region Film and Television Archive School of Law, Arts and Humanities, Room M616 Middlesbrough Tower, University of Teeside, Middlesbrough, TS1 3BA Tel: 01642 384022 Fax: 01642 384099 Email: lenticknapp@tees.ac.uk
County Record Office Melton Park, North Gosforth, Newcastle upon Tyne, NE3 5QX Tel: 0191-236-2680 Fax: 0191-217-0905 WWW: http://www.swinnhopc.demon.co.uk/genuki/NBL/
Gateshead Central Library & Local Studies Department Prince Consort Road, Gateshead, NE8 4LN Tel: 0191-477-3478 Fax: 0191-477-7454 Email: a.lang@libarts.gatesheadmbc.gov.uk WWW: http://ris.niaa.org.ukw www.gateshead.gov.uk/ls
Newcastle Local Studies Centre City Library, Princess Square, Newcastle upon Tyne, NE99 1DX Tel: 0191 277 4116 Fax: 0191 277 4118 Email: local.studies@newcastle.gov.uk WWW: www.newcastle.gov.uk
Tyne & Wear Archives Service Blandford House, Blandford Square, Newcastle upon Tyne, NE1 4JA Tel: 0191-232-6789 Fax: 0191-230-2614 Email: twas@dial.pipex.com WWW: www.thenortheast.com/archives/

Warwickshire
Coventry City Archives Mandela House, Bayley Lane, Coventry, CV1 5RG Tel: (024) 7683 2418 Fax: (024) 7683 2421 Email: coventryarchives@discover.co.uk
Modern Records Centre University of Warwick Library, Coventry, CV4 7AL Tel: (024) 76524219 Fax: (024) 76524211 Email: archives@warwick.ac.uk WWW: http://warwick.ac.uk/services/library/mrc/mrc.html

Rugby School Archives Temple Reading Room, Rugby School, Barby Road, Rugby, CV22 5DW Tel: 01788 556227 Fax: 01788 556228 Email: dhrm@rugby-school.warwks.sch.uk WWW: www.rugby-school.warwks.sch.uk
Sutton Coldfield Library & Local Studies Centre 43 Lower Parade, Sutton Coldfield, B72 1XX Tel: 0121-354-2274 Tel: 0121 464 0164 Fax: 0121 464 0173 Email: sutton.coldfield.reference.lib@birmingham.gov.uk
Warwick County Record Office Priory Park, Cape Road, Warwick, CV34 4JS Tel: 01926-412735 Fax: 01926-412509 Email: recordoffiuce@warwickshire.gov.uk WWW: http://www.warwickshire.gov.uk Major construction work in 2002 to extend the record office. Visitors should contact by telephone in advance as public services will be closed during construction work

West Midlands
Birmingham City Archives Floor 7, Central Library, Chamberlain Square, Birmingham, B3 3HQ Tel: 0121-303-4217Email: archives@birmingham.gov.uk
WWW: http://www.birmingham.gov.uk/libraries/archives/home.htm
Birmingham Roman Catholic Archdiocesan Archives Cathedral House, St Chad's Queensway, Birmingham, B4 6EU Tel: 0121-236-2251 Fax: 0121 233 9299 Email: archives@rc-birmingham.org
Birmingham University Information Services - Special Collections
Main Library, University of Birmingham, Edgbaston, Birmingham, B15 2TT Tel: 0121 414 5838 Fax: 0121 471 4691 Email: special-collections@bham.ac.uk WWW: www.is.bham.ac.uk
Dudley Archives & Local History Service Mount Pleasant Street, Coseley, Dudley, WV14 9JR Tel: 01384-812770 Email: archives.pls@mbc.dudley.gov.uk
WWW: www.dudley.gov.uk
Sandwell Community History & Archives Service Smethwick Library, High Street, Smethwick, B66 1AB Tel: 0121 558 2561 Fax: 0121 555 6064
Solihull Library Homer Road, Solihull, B91 3RG Tel: 0121-704-6977 Fax: 0121-704-6212 NOT an archive repository, sceondary sources only available for Solihull MBC area only
Walsall Local History Centre Essex Street, Walsall, WS2 7AS Tel: 01922-721305 Email: localhistorycentre@walsall.gov.uk WWW: http://www.walsall.gov.uk/culturalservices/library/welcome.htm
Wolverhampton Archives & Local Studies 42 - 50 Snow Hill, Wolverhampton, WV2 4AG Tel: 01902-552480 Fax: 01902-552481 Email: wolverhamptonarchives@dial.pipes.com WWW: http://www.wolverhampton.gov.uk/archives

Wiltshire
Images of England Project National Monuments Records Centre, Kemble Drive, Swindon, SN2 2GZ Tel: 01793 414779 WWW: www.imagesofengland.org.uk
Salisbury Reference and Local Studies Library Market Place, Salisbury, SP1 1BL Tel: 01722 411098 Fax: 01722 413214 WWW: www.wiltshire.gov.uk
Wiltshire and Swindon Record Office Libraries HQ, Bythesea Road, Trowbridge, BA14 8BS Tel: 01225 713709 Fax: 01225-713515 Email: wrso@wiltshire.gov.uk WWW: www.wiltshire.gov.uk
Wiltshire Buildings Record, Libraries and Heritage HQ, Bythesea Road, Trowbridge BA14 8BS Tel: 01225 713740 Email: dorothytreasure@wiltshire.gov.uk
Wiltshire Studies Library Trowbridge Reference Library, Bythesea Road, Trowbridge, BA14 8BS Tel: 01225-713732 Tel: 01225 713727 Fax: 01225-713715 Email: libraryenquiries@wiltshire.gov.uk WWW: www.wiltshire.gov.uk

Worcestershire
St Helens Record Office - Worcestershire St Helens Record Office, Fish Street, Worcester, WR1 2HN Tel: 01905-765922 Email: recordoffice@worcestershire.gov.uk WWW: www.worcestershire.gov.uk/records
Worcestherire Record Office History Centre, Trinity Street, Spetchley Road, Worcester, WR1 2PW Tel: 01905 765922 Email: wlhc@worcestershire.gov.uk WWW: www.worcestershire.gov.uk/records
Worcestershire Regimental Archives RHQ The Worcestershire & Sherwood Foresters Regiment, Norton Barracks, Worcester, WR5 2PA Tel: 01905-354359

Email: rhq_wfr@lineone.net Records of the Regiment and predecessors from1694, some bibliographical details

Yorkshire
Borthwick Institute of Historical Research St Anthony's Hall, Peasholme Green, York, YO1 7PW Tel: 01904-642315 WWW:www.york.ac.uk/borthwick, Appointment necessary to use Archives. Research Service Available
Yorkshire Family History - Biographical Database York Minster Library & Archives, Dean's Park, York, YO1 7JQ Tel: 01904-625308 Library Tel: 01904-611118 Archives Fax: 01904-611119 Email: library@yorkminster.org archives@yorkminster.org WWW: www.yorkminster.org
Yorkshire - East
East Yorkshire Archives Service County Hall, Champney Road, Beverley, HU17 9BA Tel: 01482 392790 Fax: 01482 392791 Email: archives.service@eastriding.gov.uk WWW: www.eastriding.gov.uk/learning, Correspondence to County Hall, Champney Road, Beverley, HU17 9BA . Reading Room at The Chapel, Lord Roberts Road, Beverley HU17 9BQ 01482 392790 01482 392791 Appointments necessary
Hull Central Library Family and Local History Unit, Central Library, Albion Street, Kingston upon Hull HU1 3TF Tel: 01482 616828 Fax: 01482 616827 Email: gareth@ukorigins.co.uk WWW: http://www.hullcc.gov.uk/genealogy/famhist.php 1901 census
Yorkshire - North
Catterick Garrison Library Gough Road, Catterick Garrison, DL9 3EL Tel: 01748 833543 Extensive collection of over 1350 military history books available for reference or loan. Open Mon 10.am to 12, 1pm to 5.30pm; Wed 10am to 12, 1pm to 5pm; Fri 10am to 12 noon.
North Yorkshire County Record Office County Hall, Northallerton, DL7 8AF Tel: 01609-777585
Royal Dragoon Guards Military Museum (4th/7th Royal Dragoon Guards & 5th Royal Inniskilling Dragoons) 3A Tower Street, York, YO1 9SB Tel: 01904-662790 Tel: 01904 662310 Fax: 01904 662310 WWW: www.rdg.co.uk Located with Prince of Wales' Own Regiment of Yorkshire Military Museum (West & East Yorkshire Regiments)
Whitby Pictorial Archives Trust
Whitby Archives & Heritage Centre, 17/18 Grape Lane, Whitby, YO22 4BA Tel: 01947-600170 Email: info@whitbyarchives.freeserve.co.uk WWW: www.whitbyarchives.freeserve.co.uk
Yorkshire Film Archive, York St John College, Lord Mayor's Walk, York YO31 7EX Tel: 01904 716550
Yorkshire - South
Archives & Local Studies Central Library, Walker Place, Rotherham, S65 1JH Tel: 01709-823616 Fax: 01709-823650 Email: archives@rotherham.gov.uk WWW: www.rotherha.gov.uk/pages/living/learning/islib/callib.htm
Barnsley Archives and Local Studies Department Central Library, Shambles Street, Barnsley, S70 2JF Tel: 01226-773950 Tel: 01226-773938 Email: Archives@Barnsley.gov.uk & librarian@barnsley.gov.uk
Doncaster Archives King Edward Road, Balby, Doncaster, DN4 0NA Tel: 01302-859811 Email: doncasterarchives@hotmail.com WWW: doncaster.gov.uk Diocesan Record Office for the Archdeaconry of Doncaster (Diocese of Sheffield)
Sheffield Archives 52 Shoreham Street, Sheffield, S1 4SP Tel: 0114-203-9395 Fax: 0114-203-9398 Email: sheffield.archives@dial.pipex.com WWW: http://www.earl.org.uk/earl/members/sheffield/arch.htm
Sheffield Central Library Surrey Street, Sheffield, S1 1XZ Tel: 0114 273 4711 Fax: 0114 273 5009 Email: sheffield.libraries@dial.pipex.com
Yorkshire - West
Bradford Archives West Yorkshire Archive Service, 15 Canal Road, Bradford, BD1 4AT Tel: 01274-731931 Fax: 01274-734013 Email: bradford@wyjs.org.uk WWW: www.archives.wyjs.org.uk
John Goodchild Collection Local History Study Centre Central Library, Drury Lane, Wakefield, WF1 2DT Tel: 01924-298929 Primarily concerned with regional history; many tens of 000s of index cards, many tons of MSS, maps, illustrations. SAE essential for reply. No photocopying; use by prior appointment.
Local Studies Library Leeds Central Library, Calverley Street, Leeds, LS1 3AB Tel: 0113 247 8290 Email: local.studies@leeds.gov.uk WWW: www.leeds.gov.uk/library/services/loc_reso.html
Wakefield Library Headquarters - Local Studies Department Balne Lane, Wakefield, WF2 0DQ Tel: 01924-302224

Email: wakehist@hotmail.com WWW: www.wakefield.gov.uk
West Yorkshire Archive Service, Wakefield Headquarters Registry of Deeds, Newstead Road, Wakefield, WF1 2DE Tel: 01924-305980 Email: wakefield@wyjs.org.uk WWW: http://www.archives.wyjs.org.uk, This Office hold county-wide records of the West Riding and West Yorkshire and records of Wakefield Metropolitan District. Appointment always required.

West Yorks Archive Service Kirklees Central Library, Princess Alexandra Walk, Huddersfield, HD1 2SU Tel: 01484-221966 Email: kirklees@wyjs.org.uk WWW: http://www.archives.wyjs.org.uk Appointment always required
West Yorkshire Archive Service Wakefeld Registry of Deeds, Newstead Road, Wakefield, WF1 2DE Tel: 01924-305982 Email: hq@wyashq.demon.co.uk WWW: http://www.archives.wyjs.org.uk
West Yorkshire Archive Service Bradford 15 Canal Road, Bradford, BDI 4AT Tel: 01274-731931 Email: bradford@wyjs.org.uk WWW: http://www.archives.wyjs.org.uk, Appointment always required
West Yorkshire Archive Service, Calderdale Central Library, Northgate House, Northgate, Halifax, HX1 1UN Tel: 01422-392636 Email: calderdale@wyjs.org.uk WWW: http://www.archives.wyjs.org.uk, Appointment always required
West Yorkshire Archive Service Leeds Chapeltown Road, Sheepscar, Leeds, LS7 3AP Tel: 0113-214-5814 Email: leeds@wyjs.org.uk WWW: http://www.archives.wyjs.org.uk Also at Yorkshire Archaeological Society, Claremont, 23 Clarendon Road, Leeds LS2 9NZ (0113-245-6362)
Yorkshire Archaeological Society Claremont, 23 Clarendon Rd, Leeds, LS2 9NZ Tel: 0113-245-6342 Tel: 0113 245 7910 Fax: 0113-244-1979 Email: j.heron@sheffield.ac.uk WWW: www.yas.org.uk, Opening Hours: Tues,Wed 2.00 to 8.30pm; Thurs, Fri 10.00 to 5.30; Sat 9.30 to 5.00 Appointment necessary for use of archival material.
Yorkshire - York
York City Archives Exhibition Square, Bootham, York, YO1 7EW Tel: 01904-551878/9 Fax: 01904-551877 Email: archives@york.gov.uk WWW: www.york.gov.uk/heritage/museums/index
City of York Libraries - Local History & Reference Collection York Central Library, Library Square, Museum Street, York, YO1 7DS Tel: 01904-655631 Fax: 01904-611025 Email: reference.library@york.gov.uk WWW: http://www.york.gov.uk

Isle of Wight
Portsmouth Roman Catholic Diocesan Archives St Edmund House, Edinburgh Road, Portsmouth, PO1 3QA Tel: 023 9282 2166 These are private archives and arrangements to visit have to be agreed beforehand.
Isle of Wight Record Office 26 Hillside, Newport, PO30 2EB Tel: 01983-823820/1 Fax: 01983 823820 Email: record.office@iow.gov.uk WWW: www.iwight.com/library/default.asp

Isle of Man
Civil Registry Registries Building, Deemster's Walk, Bucks Road, Douglas, IM1 3AR Tel: 01624-687039 Fax: 01624-687004 Email: civil@registry.gov.im
Isle of Man Public Record Office Unit 3 Spring Valley Industrial Estate, Braddan, Douglas, IM2 2QR Tel: 01624 613383 Fax: 01624 613384
Manx National Heritage Library Douglas, IM1 3LY Tel: 01624 648000 Fax: 01624 648001 Email: enquiries@mnh.gov.im

Isles of Scilly
Islands of Scilly Museum Church Street, St Mary's, TR21 0JT Tel: 01720-422337 Fax: 01720-422337

Channel Islands
Guernsey Island Archives Service 29 Victoria Rd, St Peter Port, GYI 1HU Tel: 01481-724512
Jersey Archives Service - Jersey Heritage Trust, Clarence Road, St Helier JE2 4JY Tel: 01534 833303 Fax: 01534 833301 Do not hold genealogical sources but do have 30,000 registration cards for the population of the island 1940 - 1945 during the German occupation. 1901 census
Judicial Greffe Morier House, Halkett Place, St Helier, JE1 1DD Tel: 01534-502300 Fax: 01534-502399/502390 Email: jgreffe@super.net.uk WWW: www.jersey.gov.uk

Wales
National Library of Wales Penglais, Aberystwyth, SY23 3BU
Tel: 01970-632800 Tel: 01970 632902 Marketing Fax: 01970-
615709 Email: holi@llgc.org.uk WWW: http://www.llgc.org.uk
Department of Manuscripts
Main Library, University of Wales, College Road, Bangor, LL57
2DG Tel: 01248-382966 Fax: 01248-382979 Email:
iss177@bangor.ac.uk
National Monuments Record of Wales Royal Commission on
the Ancient & Historical Monuments of Wales, Crown Building,
Plas Crug, Aberystwyth, Wales Tel: 01970-621200 Fax: 01970-
627701 Email: nmr.wales@rcahmw.org.uk WWW:
www.rcahmw.org.uk
National Screen and Sound Archive of Wales, Unit 1, Science
Park, Aberystwyth SY23 3AH Tel: 01970 626007 Email: WWW:
http://screenandsound.llgc.org.uk
Public Record Office - 1901 Census Records Ruskin Avenue,
Kew, TW9 4DU WWW: http://www.pro.gov.uk
Anglesey
Anglesey County Archives Service
Shirehall, Glanhwfa Road, Llangefni, LL77 7TW Tel: 01248-
752080 WWW: www.anglesey.gov.uk
Carmarthenshire
Carmarthenshire Archive Service Parc Myrddin, Richmond
Terrace, Carmarthen, SA31 1DS Tel: 01267 228232 Fax: 01267
228237 Email: archives@carmarthenshire.gov.uk WWW:
www.carmarthenshire.gov.uk
Ceredigion
Archifdy Ceredigion, Ceredigion Archives Swyddfa'r Sir,
County Offices, Glan y Mor, Marine Terrace, Aberystwyth,
SY23 2DE Tel: 01970-633697 Fax: 01970 633663 Email:
archives@ceredigion.gov.uk
National Library of Wales Penglais, Aberystwyth, SY23 3BU
Tel: 01970-632800 Tel: 01970 632902 Marketing Fax: 01970-
615709 Email: holi@llgc.org.uk WWW: http://www.llgc.org.uk
Denbighshire
Denbighshire Record Office 46 Clwyd Street, Ruthin, LL15
1HP Tel: 01824-708250 Fax: 01824-708258 Email:
archives@denbighshire.go.uk WWW:
http://www.denbighshire.gov.uk Extensive refurbishment until
early Summer 2002 - telephone before visiting
Flintshire
Flintshire Record Office The Old Rectory, Rectory Lane,
Hawarden, CH5 3NR Tel: 01244-532364 Fax: 01244-538344
Email: archives@flintshire.gov.uk WWW:
http://www.flintshire.gov.uk
Glamorgan
Glamorgan Record Office Glamorgan Building, King Edward
VII Avenue, Cathays Park, Cardiff, CF10 3NE Tel: (029) 2078
0282 Fax: (029) 2078 0284 Email: GlamRO@cardiff.ac.uk
WWW: http://www.llgc.org.uk/cac/
Neath Central Library (Local Studies Department) 29
Victoria Gardens, Neath, SA11 3BA Tel: 01639-620139
West Glamorgan Archive Service County Hall, Oystermouth
Road, Swansea, SA1 3SN Tel: 01792-636589 Fax: 01792-
637130 Email: archives@swansea.gov.uk WWW:
http://www.swansea.gov.uk/archives
Swansea
Swansea Reference Library Alexandra Road, Swansea, SA1
5DX Tel: 01792-516753 Fax: 01792 516759 Email:
swanlib@demon.co.uk Extensive holdings of trade directories,
local census returns, newspapers (partially indexed)
West Glamorgan Archive Service County Hall, Oystermouth
Road, Swansea, SA1 3SN Tel: 01792-636589 Fax: 01792-
637130 Email: archives@swansea.gov.uk WWW:
http://www.swansea.gov.uk/archives
Gwent & Monmouthshire
Gwent Record Office County Hall, Croesyceiliog, Cwmbran,
NP44 2XH Tel: 01633-644886 Fax: 01633-648382 Email:
gwent.records@torfaen.gov.uk WWW: www.llgc.org.uk/cac
Gwynedd
Archifdy Meirion Archives
Swyddfeydd y Cyngor, Cae Penarlag, Dolgellau, LL40 2YB Tel:
01341-424444 Fax: 01341-424505 Email:
EinionWynThomas@gwynedd.gov.uk WWW:
www.gwynedd.gov.uk/archives/
Gwynedd Archives
Caernarfon Area Record Office, Victoria Dock, Caernarfon,
LL55 1SH Tel: 01286-679095 Fax: 01286-679637 Email:
archifau@gwynedd.gov.uk WWW:
http://www.gwynedd.gov.uk/adrannau/addysg/archifau

Conwy Record Office and Archives, Lloyd Street, Llandudno
LL30 2YG Tel: 01492 860882 Fax: 01492 860882 1901 census
Newport
Newport Library & Information Service
Newport Central Library, John Frost Square, Newport, NP20
1PA Tel: 01633-211376 Fax: 01633-222615
Email: reference.library@newport.gov.uk
WWW: http://www.earl.org.uk/partners/newport/index.html
The Local Studies Collection contains information on all aspects
of Monmouthshire and or Gwent. A fee paying postal research
service is available, which uses the library's own resources.
Pembrokeshire
Pembrokeshire Libraries The County Library, Dew Street,
Haverfordwest, SA61 1SU Tel: 01437-762070Email:
anita.thomas@pembrokeshire.gov.uk The Local Studies Library
covers peoiple, places and events relating to The County of
Pembrokeshire past and present. The Library also houses The
Francis Green Genealogical Collection
Pembrokeshire Record Office The Castle, Haverfordwest,
SA61 2EF Tel: 01437-763707 Fax: 01437 768539 Email:
record.office@pembrokeshire.gov.uk
Tenby Museum Castle Hill, Tenby, SA70 7BP Tel: 01834-842809
Fax: 01834-842809 Email: tenbymuseum@hotmail.com WWW:
tenbymuseum.free-online.co.uk
Powys
Powys County Archives Office County Hall, Llandrindod
Wells, LD1 5LG Tel: 01597 826088 Fax: 01597 826087 Email:
archives@powys.gov.uk WWW: http://archives.powys.gov.uk
West Glamorgan
**West Glamorgan Archive Service - Neath Archives Access
Point** Neath Mechanics Institute, Church Place, Neath, SA11
3BA Tel: 01639-620139 WWW: www.swansea.gov.uk/archives
West Glamorgan Archive Service - Port Talbot Access Point
Port Talbot Library, Aberafan Centre, Port Talbot, SA13 1PJ Tel:
01639 763430 WWW: http://www.swansea.gov.uk/archives
Wrexham
Wrexham Archives Service Wrexham Museum, County
Buildings,, Regent Street, Wrexham, LL11 1RB Tel: 01978-
317976 Fax: 01978-317982 Email: archives@wrexham.gov.uk

Scotland
Aberdeen Synagogue 74 Dee Street, Aberdeen, AB11 6DS Tel:
01224 582135
Dundee Synagogue St Mary Place, Dundee, DD1 5RB
Edinburgh Synagogue 4 Salisbury Road, Edinburgh, Scotland
Fax:
Grand Lodge of Scotland Freemasons' Hall, 96 George Street,
Edinburgh, EH2 3DH Tel: 0131 225 5304
General Register Office for Scotland
New Register House, Edinburgh, EH1 3YT Tel: 0131-334-0380
Tel: Certificate Order 0131 314 4411 Fax: 0131-314-4400
Email: records@gro-scotland.gov.uk WWW: http://www.gro-
scotland.gov.uk Pay per view search site: http://www.origins.net, A
fully searchable index of Scottish birth and marriage records from 1553 to
1901 and death records from 1855 to 1926 can be accessed on the
internet at http://www.origins.net
Glasgow Jewish Representative Council 222 Fenwick Road,
Giffnock, Glasgow, G46 6UE Tel: 0141 577 8200 Email:
glasgow@j-scot.org WWW: www.j-scot.org/glasgow
Glasgow University Library & Special Collections Dept
Hillhead Street, Glasgow, G12 8QE Tel: 0141 330 6767 Fax:
0141 330 3793 Email: library@lib.gla.ac.uk WWW:
www.gla.ac.uk/library
Heriot-Watt University Archives Coporate Communications,
Heriot-Watt university, Edinburgh, EH14 4AS Tel: 0131 451
3218 Tel: 0131 451 3219 & 0131 451 4140 Fax: 0131 451 3164
Email: a.e.jones@hw.ac.uk WWW: www.hw.ac.uk/archive
National Archives of Scotland HM General Register House, 2
Princes Street, Edinburgh, EH1 3YY Tel: 0131-535-1334 Fax:
0131-535-1328 Email: enquiries@nas.gov.uk WWW:
www.nas.gov.uk
National Archives of Scotland - West Search Room West
Register House, Charlotte Square, Edinburgh, EH2 4DJ Tel:
0131-535-1413 Fax: 0131-535-1411 Email: wsr@nas.gov.uk
WWW: www.nas.gov.uk All correspondence to: National
Archives of Scotland, HM General Register House, Edinburgh
EH1 3YY
National Library of Scotland - Department of Manuscripts
National Library of Scotland, George IV Bridge, Edinburgh,
EH1 1EW Tel: 0131 466 2812 Fax: 0131 466 2811 Email:
mss@nls.uk WWW: http://www.nls.uk Will answer general
enquiries but cannot undertake detailed genealogical research

National Monuments Record of Scotland Royal Commission on the Ancient & Historical Monuments of Scotland, John Sinclair House, 16 Bernard terrace, Edinburgh, EH8 9NX Tel: 0131 662 1456 Fax: 0131 662 1477 or 0131 662 1499 Email: nmrs@rcahms.gov.uk WWW: www.rcahms.gov.uk Website gives access to the searchable database of NMRS Records - 'CANMORE'

National Register of Archives (Scotland) H M General Register House, 2 Princes Street, Edinburgh, EH1 3YY Tel: 0131 535 1405/1428 Tel: 0131 535 1430 Email: nra@nas.gov.uk WWW: www.nas.gov.uk The papers mentioned on the Register are not held by the NRA(S) but are deposited elsewhere or remain in private hands. While the NRA staff are always happy to answer limited and specific POSTAL enquiries about the existence of papers relating to a particular individual or subject, theytare unable to undertake research on belalf of enquirers. Once they have advised on possible sources it is then up to enquiriers either to carry out the research themselves or to engage a record agent to do so on their behalf. Where papers remain in private hands written applications for access shoul;d be made in the first instance to the NRA(S)

Royal College of Physicians and Surgeons of Glasgow 232 - 242 St Vincent Street, Glasgow, G2 5RJ Tel: 0141 221 6072 Fax: 0141 221 1804 Email: library@rcpsglasg.ac.uk WWW: www.rcpsglasg.ac.uk

Scottish Archive Network Thomas Thomson House, 99 Bankhead Crossway North, Edinburgh, EH11 4DX Tel: 0131 242 5800 Fax: 0131 242 5801 Email: enquiries@scan.org.uk WWW: www.scan.org.uk A lottery funded project to open up access to Scotland's archives

Scottish Brewing Archive 13 Thurso Street, Glasgow, G11 6PE Tel: 0141 330 2640 Fax: 0141 330 4158 Email: sba@archives.gla.ac.uk WWW: www.archives.gla.ac.uk/sba/

Scottish Catholic Archives Columba House, 16 Drummond Place, Edinburgh, EH3 6PL Tel: 0131-5563661 These archives do not hold any genealogical material. The Catholic parish registers are still held by the parishes. There are no arrangements for personal callers.

Scottish Screen Archive, Scottish Screen, 1 Bowmont Gardens, Glasgow, G12 9LR Tel: 0141 337 7400 WWW: www.scottishscreen.com

Scottish Genealogy Society 15 Victoria Terrace, Edinburgh, EH1 2JL Tel: 0131-220 3677 Fax: 0131 220 3677 Email: info@scotsgenealogy.com WWW: www.scotsgenealogy.com

Scottish Jewish Archives Centre Garnethill Synagogue, 129 Hill Street, Garnethill, Glasgow, G3 6UB Tel: 0141 332 4911 Fax: 0141 332 4911 Email: archives@sjac.fsbusiness.co.uk WWW: www.sjac.org.uk

St Andrews University Library - Special Collections Department North Street, St Andrews, KY16 9TR Tel: 01334 462339 Email: speccoll@st-and.ac.uk WWW: http://specialcollections.st-and.ac.uk

Strathclyde University Archives McCance Building, 16 Richmond Street, Glasgow, G1 1XQ Tel: 0141 548 2397 Fax: 0141 552 0775

Aberdeen
Aberdeen City Archives Aberdeen City Council, Town House, Broad Street, Aberdeen, AB10 1AQ Tel: 01224-522513 Fax: 01224 638556
Email: archives@legal.aberdeen.net.uk
WWW: www.aberdeencity.gov.uk Also covers Aberdeenshire
Aberdeen City Archives - Old Aberdeen House Branch Old Aberdeen House, Dunbar Street, Aberdeen, AB24 1UE Tel: 01224-481775 Email: archives@legal.aberdeen.net.uk WWW: www.aberdeencity.gov.uk

Angus
Angus Archives Montrose Library, 214 High Street, Montrose, DD10 8PH Tel: 01674-671415 Fax: 01674-671810 Email: angus.archives@angus.govuk WWW: www.angus.gov.uk/history/history.htm Family history research service. Archive holdings for Angus County, Arbroath, Brechin, Carnoustie, Forfar, Montrose, Monifieth, Kittiemuir.

Argyll
Argyll & Bute District Archives Manse Brae, Lochgilphead, PA31 8QU Tel: 01546 604120 Fax:

Ayrshire
Ayrshire Archives Ayrshire Archives Centre, Craigie Estate, Ayr, KA8 0SS Tel: 01292-287584 Fax: 01292-284918 Email: archives@south-ayrshire.gov.uk WWW: http://www.south-ayrshire.gov.uk/archives/index.htm, includes North Ayrshire, East Ayrshire and South Ayrshire.

East Ayrshire Council District History Centre & Museum Baird Institute, 3 Lugar Street, Cumnock, KA18 1AD Tel: 01290-421701 Fax: 01290-421701 Email: Baird.institute@east-ayrshire.gov.uk WWW: www.east-ayrshire.gov.uk

North Ayrshire Libraries Library Headquarters, 39 - 41 Princes Street, Ardrossan, KA22 8BT Tel: 01294-469137 Fax: 01924-604236 Email: reference@naclibhq.prestel.co.uk WWW: www.north-ayrshire.gov.uk

Clackmannanshire
Clackmannanshire Archives Alloa Library, 26/28 Drysdale Street, Alloa, FK10 1JL Tel: 01259-722262 Fax: 01259-219469 Email: libraries@clacks.gov.uk WWW: www.clacksweb,org.uk/dyna/archives

Clackmannanshire Registration Office Marshill House, Marshill, Alloa, FK10 1AB Tel: 01259-723850 Fax: 01259-723850 Email: clack.lib@mail.easynet.co.uk

Dumfries & Galloway
Dumfries & Galloway Library and Archives Archive Centre, 33 Burns Street, Dumfries, DG1 1PS Tel: 01387 269254 Fax: 01387 264126 Email: libsxi@dumgal.gov.uk WWW: www.dumgal.gov.uk

Ewart Library Ewart Library, Catherine Street, Dumfries, DG1 1JB Tel: 01387 260285 Tel: 01387-252070 Fax: 01387-260294 Email: ruth_airley@dumgal.gov.uk &libsxi@dumgal.gov.uk WWW: www.dumgal.gov.ukf, Fee paid research service availble

Dundee
Dundee City Archives 21 City Square, (callers use 1 Shore Terrace), Dundee, DD1 3BY Tel: 01382-434494 Fax: 01382-434666 Email: archives@dundeecity.gov.uk WWW: www.dundeecity.gov.uk/archives.html

Dundee City Council - Genealogy Unit 89 Commercial Street, Dundee, DD1 2AF Tel: 01382-435222 Fax: 01382-435224 Email: grant.law@dundeecity.gov.uk WWW: www.dundeecity.gov.uk/dcchtml/sservices/genealogy.html

East Dunbartonshire
East Dunbartonshire Local Record Offices and Reference Libraries William Patrick Library, 2 West High Street, Kirkintilloch, G66 1AD Tel: 0141-776-8090 Fax: 0141-776-0408 Email: libraries@eastdunbarton.gov.uk WWW: www.eastdunbarton.gov.uk

East Renfrewshire
East Renfrewshire Record Offices East Renfrewshire District Council, Rouken Glen Road, Glasgow, G46 6JF Tel: 0141-577-4976

Edinburgh
Edinburgh City Archives City Chambers, High St, Edinburgh, EH1 1YJ Tel: 0131-529-4616 Fax: 0131-529-4957

Falkirk
Falkirk Library Hope Street, Falkirk, FK1 5AU Tel: 01324 503605 Fax: 01324 503606 Email: falkirk-library@falkirk-library.demon.co.uk WWW: www.falkirk.gov.uk Holds Local Studies Collection

Falkirk Museum History Research Centre Callendar House, Callendar Park, Falkirk, FK1 1YR Tel: 01324 503778 Fax: 01324 503771 Email: ereid@falkirkmuseums.demon.co.ukcallandarhouse@falkirkmuseums.demon.co.uk WWW: www.falkirkmuseums.demon.co.uk Records held: Local Authority, business, personal and estate records, local organmisations, trade unions, over 28,000 photographs Falkirk District

Fife
Fife Council Archive Centre Carleton House, Balgonie Road, Markinch, Glenrothes, KY6 7AH Tel: 01592 416504
St Andrews University Library - Special Collections Department North Street, St Andrews, KY16 9TR Tel: 01334 462339 Fax: 01334 462282 Email: speccoll@st-and.ac.uk WWW: http://specialcollections.st-and.ac.uk

Glasgow
Glasgow City Archives Mitchell Library, North Street, Glasgow, G3 7DN Tel: 0141-287-2913 Fax: 0141-226-8452 Email: archives@cls.glasgow.gov.uk WWW: http://users.colloquium.co.uk/~glw_archives/src001.htm

Glasgow University Library & Special Collections Department Hillhead Street, Glasgow, G12 8QE Tel: 0141 330 6767 Fax: 0141 330 3793 Email: library@lib.gla.ac.uk WWW: www.gla.ac.uk/library

Royal College of Physicians and Surgeons of Glasgow 232 - 242 St Vincent Street, Glasgow, G2 5RJ Tel: 0141 221 6072 Fax: 0141 221 1804 Email: library@rcpsglasg.ac.uk WWW: www.rcpsglasg.ac.uk

Glasgow University Archive Services 13 Thurso Street, Glasgow, G11 6PE Tel: 0141 330 5515 Fax: 0141 330 4158 Email: archives@archives.gla.ac.uk WWW: www.archives.gla.ac.uk

Inverness- shire
Highland Council Genealogy Centre Inverness Public Library, The Library, Farraline Park, Inverness, IV1 1NH Tel: 01463-236463 : Tel: 01463 220330 ext 9 Fax: 01463 711128
Isle of Lewis
Stornoway Record Office Town Hall, 2 CromwellStreet, Stornoway, HS1 2BD Tel: 01851-709438 Fax: 01851 709438 Email: emacdonald@cne-siar.gov.uk
Lanarkshire
South Lanarkshire Council Archives 30 Hawbank Road, College Milton, East Kilbride, G74 5EX Tel: 01355 239193 Fax: 01355 242365
Midlothian
Midlothian Archives and Local Studies Centre 2 Clerk Street, Loanhead, EH20 9DR Tel: 0131 271 3976 Fax: 0131 440 4635 Email: local.studies@midlothian.gov.uk WWW: www.earl.org.uk/partners/midlothian/local.html
Moray
Moray Local Heritage Centre Grant Lodge, Cooper Park, Elgin, IV30 1HS Tel: 01343 562644 Tel: 01343 562645 Fax: 01343-549050 Email: graeme.wilson@techleis.moray.gov.uk WWW: www.morray.org/heritage/roots.html The Moray District Record Office has now been combined with the Local studies section at Grant Lodge, Cooper Park, Elgin to form the Local Heritage Centre.
North Highland Archive Wick Library, Sinclair Terrace, Wick, KW1 5AB Tel: 01955 606432 Fax: 01955 603000
North Lanarkshire
North Lanarkshire - Lenziemill Archives 10 Kelvin Road, Cumbernauld, G67 2BA Tel: 01236 737114 Fax: 01236 781762
Orkney
Orkney Archives The Orkney Library, Laing Street, Kirkwall, KWI5 1NW Tel: 01856-873166 Email: alison.fraser@orkney.gov.uk Open Mon to Fri 9am to 1pm & 2pm to 4.45pm. Appointments preferred
Orkney Library The Orkney Library, Laing Street, Kirkwall, KWI5 1NW Tel: 01856-873166 Fax: 01856-875260 Email: karen.walker@orkney.gov.uk
Perthshire
Perth and Kinross Council Archives A K Bell Library, 2 - 8 York Place, Perth, PH2 8EP Tel: 01738-477012 Tel: 01738 477022 Fax: 01738-477010 Email: archives@pkc.gov.uk WWW: http://www.pkc.gov.uk/library/archive.htm
Regimental Museum and Archives of Black Watch Balhousie Castle, Hay Street, Perth, PH1 5HS Tel: 0131-3108530 Tel: 01738 621281 ext 8530 Fax: 01738-643245 Email: bwarchivist@btclick.com WWW: www.theblackwatch.co.uk
Scottish Horse Regimental Archives - Dunkeld Cathedral, The Cross, Dunkeld PH8 0AN Museum closed 1999 - archives now held in Dunkeld Museum. View by prior appointment
Renfrewshire
Renfrewshire Archives Central Library & Museum Complex, High Street, Paisley, PA1 2BB Tel: 0141-889-2350 Fax: 0141-887-6468 Email: local_studies.library@renfrewshire.gov.uk
Scottish Borders
Scottish Borders Archive & Local History Centre Library Headquarters, St Mary's Mill, Selkirk, TD7 5EW Tel: 01750 20842 Fax: 01750 22875 Email: archives@scotborders.gov.uk WWW: www.scotborders.gov.uk/libraries
Shetland
Shetland Archives 44 King Harald St, Lerwick, ZE1 0EQ Tel: 01595-696247 Fax: 01595-696533 Email: shetland.archives@zetnet.co.uk
Unst Heritage Centre Haroldswick, Unst, ZE2 9ED Tel: 01957 711528 Tel: 01957 711387 (Home) Fax:
Stirlingshire
Stirling Council Archives Unit 6, Burghmuir Industrial Estate, Stirling, FK7 7PY Tel: 01786-450745 Fax: 01786 473713 Email: archive@stirling.gov.uk
Strathclyde
Strathclyde Area - Genealogy Centre The Register Office, 22 Park Circus, Glasgow, G3 6BE Tel: 0141-287-8350 Fax: 0141-225-8357
Tayside
Dundee University Archives Tower Building, University of Dundee, Dundee, DD1 4HN Tel: 01382-344095 Fax: 01382 345523 Email: archives@dundee.ac.uk WWW: http://www.dundee.ac.uk/archives/
West Lothian
West Lothian Council Archives - Archives & Records Management 7 Rutherford Square, Brucefield Industrial Estate, Livingston, EH54 9BU Tel: 01506 460 020 Fax: 01506 416 167

Northern Ireland
Public Record Office of Northern Ireland 66 Balmoral Avenue, Belfast, BT9 6NY Tel: (028) 9025 5905 Fax: (028) 9025 5999 Email: proni@dcalni.gov.uk WWW: http://www.proni.nics.gov.uk
General Register Office of Northern Ireland Oxford House, 49 - 55 Chichester Street, Belfast, BT1 4HL Tel: (028) 90 252000 Fax: (028) 90 252120 Email: gro.nisra@dfpni.gov.uk WWW: www.groni.gov.uk
Northern Ireland Film Commission, 21 Ormeau Avenue, Belfast BT2 8HD WWW: www.nifc.co.uk
Presbyterian Historical Society of Ireland Church House, Fisherwick Place, Belfast, BT1 6DW Tel: (028) 9032 2284 Opening hours: Mon to Fri 10am to 12.30pm. Wed afternoons 1.30pm to 3.30pm
Belfast Central Library Irish & Local Studies Dept, Royal Avenue, Belfast, BT1 1EA Tel: (028) 9024 3233 Fax: (028) 9033 2819 Email: info@libraries.belfast-elb.gov.uk WWW: www.belb.org.uk
Belfast Family History & Cultural Heritage Centre 64 Wellington Place, Belfast, BT1 6GE Tel: (028) 9023 5392 Fax: (028) 9023 9885
Derry City Council Heritage & Museum Service Harbour Museum, Harbour Square, Derry, BT48 6AF Tel: (028) 7137 7331 Fax: (028) 7137 763 The archives of Derry City Council are an invaluable source of information for the history of both the City and the Council from the early seventeenth century to the present day.
Banbridge Genealogy Services Gateway Tourist Information Centre, 200 Newry Road, Banbridge, BT32 3NB Tel: 028 4062 6369 Fax: 028 4062 3114 Email: banbridge@nitic.net

Ireland
Church of Ireland Archives Representative Church Body Library, Braemor Park, Churchtown, Dublin 14, Tel: 01-492-3979 Fax: 01-492-4770 Email: library@ireland.anglican.org WWW: http://www.ireland.anglican.org/
Film Institute of Ireland, 6 Eustace Street, Dublin 2 Tel: 01 679 5744 WWW: www.fli.ie
Genealogical Office / Office of The Chief Herald Kildare Street, Dublin 2, Tel: +353-1-6030 200 Fax: +353-1-6621 062 Email: herald@nli.ie WWW: www.nli.ie
Grand Lodge of Ireland Freemasons' Hall, 17 Molesworth Street, Dublin 2, Tel: 00 353 01 6760 1337 :
National Archives Bishop Street, Dublin 8, Tel: 01-407-2300 Fax: 01-407-2333 Email: mail@nationalarchives.ie WWW: http://www..nationalarchives.ie
Presbyterian Historical Society of Ireland Church House, Fisherwick Place, Belfast, BT1 6DW Tel: (028) 9032 2284 Opening hours: Mon to Fri 10am to 12.30pm. Wed afternoons 1.30pm to 3.30pm
Registrar General for Ireland Joyce House, 8 - 11 Lombard Street East, Dublin 2, Tel: Dublin-711000
Dublin
Dublin City Archives City Assembly House, 58 South William Street, Dublin, 2 Tel: (01)-677-5877 Fax: (01)-677-5954
County Clare
Clare County Archives Clare County Council, New Road, Ennis, Tel: 065-28525 Tel: 065 21616 WWW: www.clare.ie
County Donegal
Donegal Ancestry Old Meeting House, Back Lane, Ramleton, Letterkenny, Tel: 00353 74 51266 Fax: 00353 74 51702 Email: donances@indigo.ie WWW: http://www.indigo.ie/~donances
Donegal County Council Archive Centre 3 Rivers Centre, Lifford, Tel: 00353 74 72490 Fax: 00353 74 41367 Email: nbrennan@donegalcoco.ie WWW: www.donegal.ie
Donegal Local Studies Centre Central Library & Arts Centre, Oliver Plunkett Road, Letterkenny, Tel: 00353 74 24950 Fax: 00353 74 24950 Email: dgcolib@iol.ie WWW: donegal.ie
County Down
Banbridge Genealogy Services Gateway Tourist Information Centre, 200 Newry Road, Banbridge, BT32 3NB Tel: 028 4062 6369 Fax: 028 4062 3114 Email: banbridge@nitic.net
County Dublin
Dublin Heritage Group Ballyfermot Library, Ballyfermot Road, Ballyfermot, Dublin, 10 Tel: 6269324 Email: dhgeneal@iol.ie
County Limerick
Limerick City Library Local History Collection The Granary, Michael Street, Limerick, Tel: +353 (0)61-314668 Fax: +353(0) 61 411506 Email: noneill@citylib.limerickcorp.ie WWW: http://www.limerickcorp.ie/librarymain.htm

Limerick Regional Archives Limerick Ancestry, The Granary, Michael Street, Limerick, Tel: 061-415125 WWW: www.mayo-ireland.ie
County Mayo
Local Record Offices The Registration Office, New Antrim Street, Castlebar, Tel: 094-23249 Fax: 094 23249

Australia

National Archives of Australia - Canberra PO Box 7425, Canberra Mail Centre, Canberra, ACT, 2610 Tel: 02-6212-3600 Email: archives@naa.gov.au WWW: www.naa.gov.au
National Archives of Australia - Hobart 4 Rosny Hill Road, Rosny Park, Tasmania, 7018 Tel: 03-62-440101 Fax: 03-62-446834 Email: reftas@naa.gov.auWWW: www.naa.gov.au
National Archives of Australia - Northern Territories Kelsey Crescent, Nightcliffe, NT, 810 Tel: 08-8948-4577
National Archives of Australia - Queensland 996 Wynnum Road, Cannon Hill, Queensland, 4170 Tel: 07-3249-4226 Fax: 07-3399-6589WWW: www.naa.gov.au
National Archives of Australia - South Australia 11 Derlanger Avenue, Collingwood, South Australia, 5081 Tel: 08-269-0100
National Archives of Australia - Sydney 120 Miller Road, Chester Hill, Sydney, New South Wales, 2162 Tel: 02-96450-100 Fax: 02-96450-108 Email: refnsw@naa.gov.auWWW: www.naa.gov.uk
National Archives of Australia - Victoria PO Box 8005, Burwood Heights, Victoria, 3151 Tel: 03-9285-7900
National Archives of Australia - Western Australia 384 Berwick Street East, Victoria Park, Western Australia, 6101 Tel: 09-470-7500 Fax: 09-470-2787,
New South Wales - State Archives Office 2 Globe Street, Sydney, New South Wales, 2000 Tel: 02-9237-0254
Queensland State Archives PO Box 1397, Sunnybanks Hills, Brisbane, Queensland, 4109 Tel: 61-7-3875-8755 Fax: 61-7-3875-8764 Email: qsa@ipd.pwh.qld.gov.auWWW: www.archives.qld.gov.au
South Australia State Archives PO Box 1056, Blair Athol West, South Australia, 5084 Tel: 08-8226-8000 Fax: 08-8226-8002,
Tasmania State Archives Archives Office of Tasmania, 77 Murray Street, Hobart, Tasmania, 7000 Tel: (03)-6233-7488 Email: archives.tasmania@central.tased.edu.au WWW: www.tased.edu.au/archives
Victoria State Archives - Ballerat State Offices, Corner of Mair & Doveton Streets, Ballarat, Victoria, 3350 Tel: 03-5333-6611 Fax: 03-5333-6609,
Victoria State Archives - Laverton North 57 Cherry Lane, Laverton North, Victoria, 3028 Tel: 03-9360-9665 Fax: 03-9360-9685,
Victoria State Archives - Melbourne Level 2 Casselden Place, 2 Lonsdale Street, Melbourne, Victoria, 3000 Tel: 03-9285-7999 Fax: 03-9285-7953,
Western Australia - State Archives & Public Records Office Alexander Library, Perth Cultural Centre, Perth, Western Australia, 6000 Tel: 09-427-3360 Fax: 09-427-3256,

New Zealand
National Archives of New Zealand PO Box 10-050, 10 Mulgrave Street, Thorndon, Wellington, New Zealand Tel: 04-499-5595 Email: national.archives@dia.govt.nz WWW: www.archives.dia.govt.nz

Africa
South Africa
Cape Town Archives Repository Private Bag X9025, Cape Town, 8000, South Africa Tel: 021-462-4050 Fax: 021-465-2960,
Dutch Reformed Church Archive PO Box 398, Bloemfontein, 9301, South Africa Tel: 051-448-9546,
Dutch Reformed Church Archive of O.F.S P O Box 398, Bloemfontein, 9301, RSA Tel: 051 448 9546,
Dutch Reformed Church Records Office PO Box 649, Pietermaritzburg, 3200 Tel: 0331-452279 Fax: 0331-452279,
Dutch Reformed Church Synod Records Office of Kwa Zulu-Natal P O Box 649, Pietermaritzburg , 3200, RSA Tel: 0331 452279 Fax: 0331 452279 Email: ngntlargrief@alpha.futurenet.co.za,
Free State Archives Private Bag X20504, Bloemfontein, Free State, 9300, South Africa Tel: 051-522-6762 Fax: 051-522-6765
Free State Archives Repository Private Bag X20504, Bloemfontein, 9300, South Africa Tel: 051 522 6762 Fax: 051 522 6765,
National Archives - Pretoria Private Bag X236, Pretoria, 1, South Africa Tel: 323 5300
South Africa National Archives Private Bag X236, Pretoria, 1
South African Library - National Reference & Preservation P O Box 496, Cape Town, 8000, South Africa Tel: 021 246320 Fax: 021 244848 Email: postmaster@salib.ac.za

Namibia
National Archives of Namibia Private Bag, Windhoek, 13250, Namibia Tel: 061 293 4386 Email: Renate@natarch.mec.gov.na WWW: www.witbooi.natarch.mec.gov.na

Zimbabwe
National Archives of Zimbabwe "Hiller Road, off Borrowdale Road", Gunhill, Harare, Zimbabwe Tel: 792741/3 Fax: 792398

EUROPE
BELGIUM
Archives de l'Etat a Liege 79 rue du Chera, Liege, B-4000, Belgium Tel: 04-252-0393 Fax: 04-229-3350 Email: archives.liege@skynet.be
De Kerk van Jezus Christus van den Heiligen Der Laaste Dagen, Kortrijkse Steenweg 1060, Sint-Deniss-Westrem, B-9051, Belgium Tel: 09-220-4316
Provinciebestuur Limburg Universititslaan 1, Afdeling 623 Archief, Hasselt, B-3500, Belgium
Rijks Archief te Brugge Academiestraat 14, Brugge, 8000, Belgium Tel: 050-33-7288 Fax: 050-33-7288 Email: rijksarchief.brugge@skynet.be
Rijksarchief Kruibekesteenweg 39/1, Beveren, B-9210, Belgium Tel: 03-775-3839
Service de Centralisation des Etudes Genealogique et Demographiques Belgique Chaussee de Haecht 147, Brussels, B-1030, Belgium Tel: 02-374-1492
Staatsarchiv in Eupen Kaperberg 2-4, Eupen, B-4700, Belgium Tel: 087-55-4377
Stadsarchief te Veurne Grote Markt 29, Veurne, B-8630, Belgium Tel: 058-31-4115 Fax: 058-31-4554

CYPRUS
Cyprus Center of Medievalism & Heraldry P O Box 80711, Piraeus, 185 10, Greece Tel: 42-26-356

DENMARK
Association of Local History Archives P O Box 235, Enghavevej 2, Vejle, DK-7100, Denmark Fax: 45-7583-1801 WWW: www.lokalarkiver.dk
Cadastral Archives Rentemestervej 8, Copenhagen NV, DK-2400, Denmark Fax: 45-3587-5064 WWW: www.kms.min.dk
Danish Data Archive Islandsgade 10, Odense C, DK-5000, Denmark Fax: 45-6611-3060, WWW: www.dda.dk
Danish Emigration Archives P O Box 1731, Arkivstraede 1, Aalborg, DK-9100, Denmark Tel: 045 9931 4221 Fax: 45 9810 2248 Email: bfl-kultur@aalbkom.dk WWW: www.cybercity.dk/users/ccc13656
Danish National Archives Rigsdagsgaarden 9, Copenhagen, DK-1218 Tel: 45-3392-3310 Fax: 45-3315-3239 WWW: www.sa.dk/ra/uk/uk.htm
Det Kongelige Bibliotek POB 2149, Copenhagen K, DK-1016 Tel: 045-3393-0111 Fax: 045-3393-2218
Frederiksberg Municipal Libraries Solbjergvej 21-25, Frederiksberg, DK-2000, Denmark Fax: 45-3833-3677, Web: www.fkb.dk
Kobenhavns Stadsarkiv Kobenhavns Radhus, Kobenhavn, DK01599, Denmark Tel: 3366-2374 Fax: 3366-7039
National Business Archives Vester Alle 12, Aarhus C, DK-8000, Denmark Tel: 45-8612-8533 Email: mailbox@ea.sa.dk WWW: www.sa.dk/ea/engelsk.htm
Provincial Archives for Funen Jernbanegade 36, Odense C, DK-5000, Denmark Tel: 6612-5885 Fax: 45-6614-7071 WWW: www.sa.dk/lao/default.htm
Provincial Archives for Nth Jutland Lille Sct. Hansgade 5, Viborg, DK-8800, Denmar Tel: 45-8662-1788 WWW: www.sa.dk/lav/default.htm
Provincial Archives for Southern Jutland Haderslevvej 45, Aabenraa, DK-6200, Denmark Tel: 45-7462-5858 WWW: www.sa.dk/laa/default.htm
Provincial Archives for Zealand etc Jagtvej 10, Copenhagen, DK-2200, Denmark Fax: 45-3539-0535 WWW: www.sa.dk/lak.htm
Royal Library Christains Brygge 8, Copenhagen K, DK-1219, Denmark Fax: 45-3393-2219 WWW: www.kb.dk
State Library Universitetsparken, Aarhus C, DK-8000, Denmark Tel: 45-8946-2022 Fax: 45-8946-2130 WWW: www.sb.aau.dk/english

FINLAND
Institute of Migration Piispankatu 3, Turku, 20500Tel: 2-231-7536 Fax: 2-233-3460 Email: jouni.kurkiasaaz@utu.fi WWW: www.utu.fi/erill/instmigr/

FRANCE

Centre d'Accueil et de Recherche des Archives Nationales 60 rue des Francs Bourgeois, Paris Cedex, 75141, France Tel: 1-40-27-6000 Fax: 1-40-27-6628

Centre des Archives d'Outre-Mer 29 Chemin du Moulin de Testas, Aix-en-Provence, 13090

Service Historique de la Marine Chateau de Vincennes, Vincennes Cedex, 94304, France

Service Historique de l'Armee de l'Air Chateau de Vincennes, Vincennes Cedex, 94304, France

Service Historique de l'Armee de Terre BP 107, Armees, 481, France Military (Army), Service Historique De L'Armee De Terre, Fort de Vincennes, Boite Postale 107 Tel: 01 4193 34 44 Fax: 01 41 93 38 90 Military (Navy), Service Historique De La Marine, Chateau de Vincennes, Boite Postale 2 Tel: 01 43 28 81 50 Fax: 01 43 28 31 60 Email: shistorique@cedocar.fr

GERMANY

German Emigration Museum Inselstrasse 6, Bremerhaven, D-2850 Tel: 0471-49096

Historic Emigration Office Steinstr. 7, Hamburg, (D) 20095, Germany Tel: 4940-30- 51-282 Fax: 4940-300-51-220 Email: ESROKAHEA@aol.com WWW: users.cybercity.dk/gccc13652/addr/ger_heo.htm

Research Centre Lower Saxons in the USA Postfach 2503, Oldenburg, D-2900, Germany Tel: 0441 798 2614 Fax: 0441-970-6180 Email: holtmann@hrzl.uni-oldenburg.de WWW: www.uni-oldenburg.de/nausa

Zentralstelle fur Personen und Familiengeschichte Birkenweg 13, Friedrichsdorf, D-61381 Tel: 06172-78263 WWW: : www.genealogy.com/gene/genealogy.html

GREECE

Cyprus Center of Medievalism & Heraldry P O Box 80711, Piraeus, 185 10, Greece Tel: 42-26-356

LIECHENSTEIN

Major Archives Record Offices & Libraries Liechtenstein WWW: www.genealogy.com/gene/reg/CH/lichts.html

NETHERLANDS

Amsterdam Municipal Archives P O 51140, Amsterdam, 1007 EC

Brabant-Collectie Tilburg University Library, P O Box 90153, Warandelaan, Tilburg, NL-5000 LE, Netherlands Tel: 0031-134-662127

Gemeentelijke Archiefdienst Amersfoort P O Box 4000, Amersfoort, 3800 EA Tel: 033-4695017 Fax: 033-4695451

Het Utrechts Archief Alexander Numankade 199/201, Utrecht, 3572 KW, Tel: 030-286-6611 Fax: 030-286-6600 Email: Utrecht@acl.archivel.nl

Rijksarchief in Drenthe P O Box 595, Assen, 9400 AN, Netherlands Tel: 0031-592-313523 Fax: 0031-592-314697 Email: RADR@noord.bart.nl WWW: obd-server.obd.nl/instel/enderarch/radz.htm

Rijksarchief in Overijssel Eikenstraat 20, Zwolle, 8021 WX, Netherlands Tel: 038-454-0722 Fax: 038-454-4506 Email: RAO@euronet.nl WWW: www.obd.nl/instel/arch/rkarch.htm

Zealand Documentation CTR P O Box 8004, Middelburg, 4330 EA, Netherlands

NORWAY

Norwegian Emigration Centre Strandkaien 31, Stavanger, 4005, Norway Tel: 47-51-53-88-63 Email: detnu@telepost.no WWW: www.emigrationcenter.com

POLAND

Head Office Polish State Archives Ul Dluga6 Skr, Poczt, Warsaw, 1005-00-950 Fax: 0-22-831-9222

Russia
Moscow
Russian State Military Historical Archive 2, Baumanskaya 3, 107864, Moscow Tel: 7 (095) 261-20-70

St Petersburg
Russian State Historical Archive (RGIA), Naberejnaya 4 (English Embankment), 190000 St Petersburg Tel: 7 (812) 315-54-35 , Tel: 7 (812) 311-09-26 Fax: 7 (812) 311-22-52

SPAIN

Archivo Historico National Serrano 115, Madrid, 28006 Tel: 261-8003- 2618004

Instituucion Fernando el Catolico Plaza de Espagna 2, Zaragoza, 50071, Espagn Tel: 09-7628-8878 Email: ifc@isendanet.es.mail

SWEDEN

Harnosand Provincial Archive Box 161, Harnosand, S-871 24, Sweden Tel: 611-835-00 Email: landsarkivet@landsarkivet-harnosand.ra.se WWW: www.ra.se/hla

Goteborg Provincial Archive Box 19035, Goteborg, S-400 12, Sweden Tel: 31-778-6800

House of Emigrants Box 201, Vaxjo, S-351 04, Sweden Tel: 470-201-20 Email: info@svenskaemigrantinstitulet.g.se

Kinship Centre Box 331, Karlstad, S-651 08, Sweden Tel: 54-107720

Lund Provincial Archive Box 2016, Lund, S-220 02 Tel: 046-197000 Fax: 046-197070 Email: landsarkivet@landsarkivet-lund.ra.se

Orebro Stadsarkiv Box 300, Orebro, S-701 35 Tel: 19-21-10-75 Fax: 19-21-10-50

Ostersund Provincial Archive Arkivvagen 1, Ostersund, S-831 31, Sweden Tel: 63-10-84-85 Email: landsarkivet@landsarkivet-ostersund.ra.se WWW: www.ra.se/ola/

Stockholm City & Provincial Archives Box 22063, Stockholm, S-104 22 Tel: 8-508-283-00 Fax: 8-508-283-01

Swedish Military Archives Banergatan 64, Stockholm, S-115 88 Tel: 8-782-41-00

Swedish National Archives Box 12541, Stockholm, S-102 29, Sweden Tel: 8-737-63-50

Uppsala Provincial Archive Box 135, Uppsala, SE-751 04, Sweden Tel: 18-65-21-00

Vadstena Provincial Archive Box 126, Vadstena, S-592 23, Sweden Tel: 143-130-30

Visby Provincial Archive Visborgsgatan 1, Visby, 621 57, Sweden Tel: 498-2129-55

SWITZERLAND

Achives de la Ville de Geneve Palais Eynard, 4 rue de la Croix-Rouge, Geneve 3, 1211 Tel: 22-418-2990 Email: didier.grange@seg.ville-ge.ch

Archives Canonales Vaudoises rue de la Mouline 32, Chavannes-pres-Renens, CH 1022, Switzerland Tel: 021-316-37-11 Fax: 021-316-37-55

Archives de l'Ancien Eveche de Bale 10 rue des Annonciades, Porrentruy, CH-2900, Suisse

Geneva
Archives d'Etat, 1 Rue de l'Hotel de Ville, Case Postale 164, Geneve 3 Tel: 41 21 319 33 95 Fax: 41 21 319 33 65

Lausanne
Archives De La Ville De Lausanne, Rue de Maupas 47, Case Postale CH-1000 Lausanne 9 Tel: 41 21 624 43 55 Fax: 41 21 624 06 01

Staatsarchiv Appenzell Ausserhoden Obstmarkt, Regierungsgebaede, Herisau, CH-9100, Tel: 071-353-6111 Email: Peter.Witschi@kk.ar.ch

Staatsarchiv des Kantons Basel-Landschaft Wiedenhubstrasse 35, Liestal, 4410 Tel: 061-921-44-40 Email: baselland@lka.bl.ch WWW: www.baselland.ch

Staatsarchiv des Kantons Solothurn Bielstrasse 41, Solothurn, CH-4509, Switzerland Tel: 032-627-08-21 Fax: 032-622-34-87

Staatsarchiv Luzern Postfach 7853, Luzern, 6000 Tel: 41-41-2285365 Email: archiv@staluzern.c WWW: www.staluzern.ch

Ukraine
Odessa, Odessa State Archive, 18 Shukovskovo Street, Odessa 270001

NORTH AMERICA - CANADA

Archives & Special Collections PO Box 7500, Fredericton, New Brunswick, E3B 5H5 Tel: 506-453-4748 Fax: 506-453-4595,

Archives Nationales PO Box 10450, Sainte Foy, Quebec, G1V 4N1 Tel: 418-643-8904 Fax: 418-646-0868

Glenbow Library & Archives 130-9th Avenue SE, Calgary, Alberta, T2G 0P3 Tel: 403-268-4197 Fax: 403-232-6569

Hudson's Bay Company Archives, 200 Vaughan Street, Winnipeg R3C 1T5 Tel: 204-945-4949 Fax: 204-948-3236 Email: hbca@chc.gov.mb.ca WWW: http://www.gov.mb.ca/chc/archives/hbca/index.html

Loyalist Collection & Reference Department PO Box 7500, Fredericton, New Brunswick, E3B 5H5 Tel: 506-453-4749 Fax: 506-453-4596,

Manitoba Provincial Archives 200 Vaughan Street, Winnepeg, Manitoba, R3C 1T5 Tel: 204-945-4949 Fax: 204-948-3236,

National Archives of Canada 395 Wellington Street, Ottawa, Ontario, K1A 0N3 Tel: 613-996-7458 WWW: http://www.archives.ca,

New Brunswick Provincial Archives PO Box 6000, Fredericton, New Brunswick, E3B 5H1 Tel: 506-453-2122 Email: provarch@gov.nb.ca WWW: www.gov.nb.ca/supply/archives

Newfoundland & Labrador Archives Colonial Building, Military Road, St Johns, Newfoundland, A1C 2C9 Tel: 709-729-0475 Fax: 709-729-0578,

Nova Scotia State Archives 6016 University Avenue, Halifax, Nova Scotia, B3H 1W4 Tel: 902-424-6060,

Ontario Archives Unit 300, 77 Grenville Street, Toronto, Ontario, M5S 1B3 Tel: 416-327-1582 Email: reference@archives.gov.on.ca WWW: www.gov.on.ca/MCZCR/archives

Public Archives & Record Office PO Box 1000, Charlottetown, Prince Edward Island, C1A 7M4 Tel: 902-368-4290 Fax: 902-368-6327 Email: archives@gov.pe.ca WWW: www.gov.pe.ca/educ/

Saskatchewan Archives Board - Regina 3303 Hillsdale Street, Regina, Saskatchewan, S4S 0A2 Tel: 306-787-4068 Email: sabreg@sk.sympatico.c WWW: www.gov.sk.ca/govt/archives

Saskatchewan Archives Board - Saskatchewa Room 91, Murray Building, University of Saskatchewan, 3 Campus Drive, Saskatoon, Saskatchewan, S7N 5A4 Tel: 306-933-5832 Email: sabsktn@sk.sympatico.ca WWW: www.gov.sk.ca/govt/archives

Yarmouth County Museums & Archives 22 Collins Street, Yarmouth, Nova Scotia, B5A 3C8 Tel: (902)-742-5539 Email: ycn0056@ycn.library.ns.ca WWW: www.ycn.library.ns.ca/museum/yarcomus.htm

UNITED STATES OF AMERICA

Alaska State Archives 141 Willoughby Avenue, Juneau, Alaska, 99801-1720, United States of America, Tel: 907-465-2270 Email: sou@bham.lib.al.usarchives@educ.state.ak.us.

Arizona Department of Library Archives & Public Records State Capitol, 1700 West Washington, Phoenix, Arizona, 85007, United States of America, Tel: 602-542-3942

Arizona Historical Foundation Library Hayden Library, Arizona State Univeristy, Tempe, Arizona, 85287, United States of America, Tel: 602-966-8331

Arkansas History Commission OneCapitol Mall, Little Rock, Arkansas, 72201 Tel: 501-682-6900,

California State Archives Office of the Secretary of State, 1020 O Street, Sacramento, 95814 Tel: (916)-653-7715 Email: archivesweb@ss.ca.gov WWW: www.ss.ca.gov/archives/archives.htm

Colorado State Archives Room 1b-20, 1313 Sherman Street, Denver, Colorado, 80203-2236, United States of America, Tel: 303-866-2390,

Connecticut State Archives 231 Capitol Ave, Hartford 6106, Tel: 0860 757 6580 Email: isref@cslib.org WWW: www. cslib.org

Daughters of the American Revolution Library 1776 D Street N W, Washington, District of Columbia, 20006-5392, United States of America, Tel: 202-879-3229,

District of Columbia Archives 1300 Naylor Court North West, Washington, District of Columbia, 20001-4225 Tel: 203-566-3690,

Family History Library of the Church of Jesus Christ of LDS 35 N West Temple Street, Salt Lake City, Utah, 84150, USA,

Georgia State Archives 330 Capital Avenue SE, Atlanta 30334-9002 Tel: 404-656-2350 WWW: http://www.state.ga.us/SOS/Archives/,

Hawaii State Library 478 South King Street, Honolulu, Hawaii, 96813

Indiana Archives Room117, 140 N Senate Avenue, Indianapolis, Indiana, 46204-2296 Tel: 317-232-3660 Fax: 317-233-1085,

Kansas State Historical Society - Archives 6425 SW Sixth Street, Topeka, Kansas, 66615-1099 Tel: 913-272-8681 Fax: 913-272-8682 Email: reference@hspo.wpo.state.ks.us WWW: www.kshs.org

Maryland State Archives Hall of Records Building, 350 Rowe Boulevard, Annapolis, Maryland, 21401 Tel: 410-974-3914,

Missouri State Archives PO Box 778, Jefferson City, Missouri, 65102 Tel: 314-751-3280,

National Archives - California 100 Commodore Drive, San Bruno, California, 94066-2350

National Archives - Colorado PO Box 25307, Denver, Colorado, 80225-0307 Tel: 303-866-2390,

National Archives - Georgia 1557 St Joseph Avenue, East Point, Georgia, 30344, Tel: 404-763-7477 Fax: 404-763-7059 Web: www.nara.gov

National Archives - Illinois 7358 South Pulaski Road, Chicago, Illinois, 60629

National Archives - Massachusetts 380 Trapelo Road, Waltham, Massachusetts, 2154,

National Archives - Massachusetts 100 Dan Fox Drive, Pittsfield, Massachusetts, 01201-8230

National Archives - Missouri 2306 East Bannister Road, Kansas City, Missouri, 64131

National Archives - New York 201 Varick Street, New York, New York, 10014 - 4811

National Archives - Northwest Pacific Region 6125 Sand Point Way NE, Seattle, Washington, 98115 Tel: 206-524-6501 Email: archives@seattle.nara.gov

National Archives - Pennsylvania Rom 1350, 900 Market Street, Philadelphia, PA 19144,

National Archives - Texas Box 6216, 4900 Hemphill Road, Fort Worth, Texas, 76115

National Archives - Washington Pennsylvania Avenue, Washington, District of Colombia, 20408,

National Archives - Pacific Alaska Region 654 West 3rd Avenue, Anchorage, Alaska, 99501 - 2145 Tel: 011-1-907-271-2443 Fax: 011-1-907-271-2442 Email: archives@alaska.nara.gov WWW: www.nara.gov/regional/anchorage.html

National Archives (Pacific Region) 1st Floor East, 24000 Avila Road, Orange County, Laguna Niguel, California, 92677 Tel: (949)-360-2641 Fax: (949)-360-2624 Email: archives@laguna.nara.gov WWW: www.nara.gov/regional/laguna.html

Nevada State Archives Division of Archives & Records, 100 Stewart Street, Carson City, Nevada, 89710 Tel: 702-687-5210,

New Jersey State Archives PO Box 307, 185 West State Street, Trenton, New Jersey, 08625-0307 Tel: 609-292-6260,

New Mexico State Archives 1205 Camino carlos Rey, Sante Fe, New Mexico, 87501 Tel: (505)-827-7332 Fax: (505)-476-7909 Email: cmartine@rain.state.nm.us WWW: www.state.nmus/cpr

Ohio State Archives 1982 Velma Avenue, Columbus, Ohio, 43211-2497 Tel: 614-297-2510,

Pennsylvania State Archives PO Box 1026, 3rd & Forster Streets, Harrisburg, Pennsylvania, 17108-1026 Tel: 717-783-3281,

South Carolina Department Archives & History 8301 Parklane Road, Columbia, South Carolina, 292223 Tel: 803-896-6100,

South Carolina State Archives PO Box 11669, 1430 Senate Street, Columbia, South Carolina, 29211-1669 Tel: 803-734-8577,

South Dakota Archives Cultural Heritage Center, 900 Governors Drive, Pierre, South Dakota, 57501-2217 Tel: 605-773-3804,

Tennessee State Library & Archives 403 7th Avenue North, Nashville, Tennessee, 37243-0312 Tel: 615-741-2764 Email: reference@mail.state.tn.us WWW: www.state.tn.us/sos/statelib

Texas State Archives PO Box 12927, Austin, Texas, 78711-2927 Tel: 512-463-5463,

Vermont Public Records Division PO Drawer 33, U S Route 2, Middlesex, Montpelier, Vermont, 05633-7601 Tel: 802-828-3700 and 802-828-3286 Fax: 802-828-3710,

Vermont State Archives Redstone Building, 26 Terrace Street, Montpelier, Vermont, 05609-1103 Tel: 802-828-2308,

Virginia State Archives 11th Street at Capitol Square, Richmond, Virginia, 23219-3491 Tel: 804-786-8929,

West Virginia State Archives The Cultural Center, 1900 Kanawha Boulevard East, Charleston, West Virginia, 25305-0300 Tel: 304-558-0230,

Wisconsin State Archives 816 State Street, Madison 53706 Tel: 608-264-6460 Fax: 608-264-6742 Email: archives.reference@ccmail.adp.wisc.edu WWW: www.wisc.edu/shs-archives

Wyoming State Archives Barrett State Office Building, 2301 Central Avenue, Cheyenne, Wyoming, 82002 Tel: 307-777-7826,

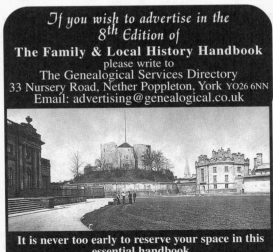

Registrars of Births, Marriages & Deaths
England, Wales and Scotland

Following is a list of Superintendent Registrars of Births, Marriages and Deaths in alphabetical order by County. We have also included details of Registration Sub Districts. **Note:** Many of the Registration Officers listed here share Office accommodation with other parties. When using the addresses given they should be prefixed "Superintendent Registrar, Register Office ...."

We offer the following advice to help readers and Superintendent Registrars

The volume and page number references which are found on the microfiche and film indexes of the General Register Office must only be used when applying for certificates from the GRO. These reference numbers are not a reference to the filing system used at local register offices and do not assist Superintendent Registrars in any way to find the entry. The General Register Office hold the records for the whole of England and Wales and therefore have their own filing system, whereas the majority of register offices are still manually searching handwritten index books which is extremely time consuming. Most offices only became computerised in the early 1990s and do not hold records before this date on computer and will never have the staff time to backlog 150 years of records. Finally, many offices are only part time, some just open a few hours per week. Unlike the larger offices they do not have receptionists or staff employed specifically to assist people researching their family history, and have to devote the majority of their time to providing certificates urgently required for passport applications, marriage bookings and pension applications.

Once the applicant has carried out their research fully using all the records and data widely available to them at no cost, they can apply to their local office with sufficient information for the Registrar to trace the entry within minutes instead of hours.

The General Register Office Trafalgar Road, Birkdale, Southport, PR8 2HH Tel: 0870 243 7788 Fax: 01704 550013

Bedfordshire
Ampthill, Court House, Woburn Street, Ampthill, MK45 2HX Tel: 01525-403430 Fax: 01525-841984 Email: denmanm@csd.bedfordshire.gov.uk
Bedford, Pilgrim House, 20 Brickhill Drive, MK41 7PZ Tel: 01234 290450 Fax: 01234 290454
Biggleswade, 142 London Road, Biggleswade, SG18 8EL Tel: 01767-312511 Fax: 01767-315033
Dunstable, Grove House, 76 High Street North, Dunstable, LU6 1NF Tel: 01582-660191 Fax: 01582-471004
Leighton Buzzard, Bossard House, West Street, Leighton Buzzard, LU7 7DA Tel: 01525-851486 Fax: 01525-381483
Luton, 6 George Street West, Luton, LU1 2BJ Tel: 01582 722603 Fax: 01582 429522
Milton Keynes, Bracknell House, Aylesbury Street, Bletchley, MK2 2BE Tel: 01908 372101 Fax: 01908 645103

Berkshire
Wokingham, The Old School, Reading Road, Wokingham, RG41 1RJ Tel: 0118 978 2514 Fax: 0118 978 2813
Bracknell Forest, Easthampstead House, Town Square, Bracknell, RG12 1AQ Tel: 01344 352027 Fax: 01344 352010
Reading and Wokingham, Yeomanry House, 131 Castle Hill, Reading, RG1 7TA Tel: 0118 901 5120, 0118 901 5194 Fax: 0118 951 0212
Slough, Slough , The Centre, Farnham Road, Slough, SL1 4UT Tel: 01753 787601 Fax: 01753 787605
West Berkshire, Peake House, 112 Newtown Road, Newbury, RG14 7EB Tel: 01635 48133 Fax: 01635 524694
Windsor & Maidenhead, Town Hall, St Ives Road, Maidenhead, SL6 1RF Tel: 01628 796422 Fax: 01628 796625

Buckinghamshire
Aylesbury Vale, County Ofices, Walton Street, Aylesbury, HP20 1XF Tel: 01296 382581 Fax: 01296 382675
Chiltern and South Bucks, Transferred to Chiltern Hills RD wef November 1998
Chiltern Hills, Wycombe Area Offices, Easton Street, High Wycombe, HP11 1NH Tel: 01494 475200, 01494 475205 Fax: 01494 475040

Cambridgeshire
Cambridge, Castle Lodge, Shire Hall, Castle Hill, Cambridge, CB3 0AP Tel: 01223 717401 Fax: 01223 717888, All churches on computer index from 1837 to date. For general searches please arrange in advance.
Ely, Old School House, 74 Market Street, Ely, CB7 4LS Tel: 01353 663824
Fenland, The Old Vicarage, Church Terrace, Wisbech, PE13 1BW Tel: 01945 467950 Fax: 01945 467950
Huntingdon, Wykeham House, Market Hill, Huntingdon, PE29 3NN Tel: 01480 375821, 01480 375822 Fax: 01480 375725
Peterborough, The Lawns, 33 Thorpe Road, Peterborough, PE3 6AB Tel: 01733 566323 Fax: 01733 566049

Cleveland
Middlesbrough, Corporation Road, Middlesbrough, TS1 2DA Tel: 01642 262078 Fax: 01642 262091
Hartlepool, Raby Road, Hartlepool, TS24 8AF Tel: 01429 236369 Fax: 01429 236373 Email: registrar@hartlepool.gov.uk
Redcar and Cleveland, Westgate, Guisborough, TS14 6AP Tel: 01287 632564 Fax: 01287 630768
Stockton-on-Tees, Nightingale House, Balaclava Street, Stockton-on-Tees, TS18 2AL Tel: 01642 393156 Fax: 01642 393159

Cheshire
Cheshire Central, Delamere House, Chester Street, CW1 2LL Tel: 01270 505106 Fax: 01270 505107
Cheshire East, Park Green, Macclesfield, SK11 6TW Tel: 01625 423463 Fax: 01625 619225
Chester West, Goldsmith House, Goss Street, Chester, CH1 2BG Tel: 01244 602668 Fax: 01244 602934
Halton, Heath Road, Runcorn, WA7 5TN Tel: 01928 576797 Fax: 01928 573616
Stockport, Town Hall - John Street Entrance, Stockport, SK1 3XE Tel: 0161 474 3399 Fax: 0161 474 3390
Tameside, Town Hall, King Street, Dukinfield, SK16 4LA Tel: 0161 330 1177 Fax: 0161 342 2625
Trafford, Town Hall, Tatton Road, Sale, M33 1ZF Tel: 0161 912 3025 Fax: 0161 912 3031
Vale Royal, Transferred to Cheshire Central wef April 1998,
Warrington, Museum Street, Warrington, WA1 1JX Tel: 01925 442762 Fax: 01925 442739
Wallasey, Town Hall, Wallasey, L44 8ED Tel: 0151-691-8505 The Wallasey is now closed, having been amalgamated with Birkenhead . All records for Birkenhead and Wallasey (ie the whole of the Wirral peninsula) are now held at Birkenhead
Wirral, Town Hall, Mortimer Street, Birkenhead, L41 5EU Tel: 0151 666 4096 Fax: 0151 666 3685, This office now holds the records formerly held at the Wallasey office, which has been closed and amalgamated with Birkenhead. Registration District now named "Wirral"

Cornwall
Bodmin, Lyndhurst, 66 St Nicholas Street, Bodmin, PL31 1AG Tel: 01208 73677 Fax: 01208 73677
Camborne-Redruth, Roskear, Camborne, TR14 8DN Tel: 01209 612924 Fax: 01209 719956
Falmouth, Berkeley House, 12-14 Berkeley Vale, Falmouth, TR11 3PH Tel: 01326 312606 Fax: 01326 312606
Kerrier, The Willows, Church Street, Helston, TR13 8NJ Tel: 01326 562848 Fax: 01326 562848
Launceston, 'Hendra', Dunheved Road, Launceston, PL15 9JG Tel: 01566 772464 Fax: 01566 772464
Liskeard, 'Graylands', Dean Street, Liskeard, PL14 4AH Tel: 01579 343442 Fax: 01872 327554
Penzance, Alphington House, Alverton Place, Penzance, TR18 4JJ Tel: 01736 330093 Fax: 01736 369666
St. Austell, 12 Carlyon Road, St. Austell, PL25 4LD Tel: 01726 68974 Fax: 01726 67048
St. Germans, Plougastel Drive, St Germans, Saltash, PL12 6DL Tel: 01752 842624 Fax: 01752 848556
Stratton, The Parkhouse Centre, Ergue Gaberic Way, Bude, EX23 8LF Tel: 01288 353209 Fax: 01288 359968
Truro, Dalvenie House, New County Hall, Truro, TR1 3AY Tel: 01872 322241 Fax: 01872 323891

Cumbria

Barrow-in-Furness, Nan Tait Centre, Abbey Road, Barrow-in-Furness, LA14 1LG Tel: 01229 894511 Fax: 01229 894513
Carlisle, 23 Portland Square, Carlisle, CA1 1PE Tel: 01228 607432 Fax: 01228 607434
Cockermouth, Fairfield, Station Road, Cockermouth, CA13 9PT Tel: 01900 325960 Fax: 01900 325962
Cockermouth (Workington Sub-district), Hill Park, Ramsay Brow, Workington, CA14 4TG Tel: 01900 325160 Fax: 01900 325161
Kendal, County Offices, Kendal, LA9 4RQ Tel: 01539 773567 Fax: 01539 773565
Kendal (Kirkby Lonsdale Sub-district), 15 Market Square, Kirkby Lonsdale, Carnforth, LA6 2AN Tel: 01524 271222
Kendal (Lakes Sub-district), Windermere Library, Ellerthwaite, Windermere, LA23 2AJ Tel: 01539 462420
Millom, The Millom Council Centre, St Georges Road, Millom, LA18 4DD Tel: 01229 772357 Fax: 01229 773412
Penrith, Friargate, Penrith, CA11 7XR Tel: 01768 242120 Fax: 01768 242122
Penrith (Alston Sub-district), Alston , Townhead, Alston, CA9 3SL Tel: 01434 381784 Fax: 01434 381784
Penrith (Appleby Sub-district), Shire Hall, The Sands, Appleby in Westmorland, CA3 8DA Tel: 01768 352976
Ulverston, Town Hall, Queen Street, Ulverston, LA12 7AR Tel: 01229 894170 Fax: 01229 894172
Whitehaven, College House, Flatt Walks, Whitehaven, CA28 7RW Tel: 01946 852690 Fax: 01946 852673
Wigton, Wigton Registry Office, Station Road, Wigton, CA7 9AH Tel: 016973 66117 Fax: 016973 66118

Derbyshire

Amber Valley, Market Place, Ripley, DE5 3BT Tel: 01773-841380 Fax: 01773-841382
Ashbourne, Town Hall, Market Place, Ashbourne, DE6 1ES Tel: 01335 300575 Fax: 01335 345252
Bakewell, Town Hall, Bakewell, DE45 1BW Tel: 01629 812261
Bakewell (Matlock Sub-district), Firs Parade, Matlock, DE4 3AS Tel: 01629-582870
Chesterfield, New Beetwell Street, Chesterfield, S40 1QJ Tel: 01246 234754 Fax: 01246 274493
Derby, 9 Traffic Street, Derby, DE1 2NL Tel: 01332 716030 Tel: 01332 716025 Fax: 01332 716021, This office holds all the South Derbyshire (formerly Swadlingcote and Gresley District) records
Erewash, 87 Lord Haddon Road, Ilkeston, DE7 8AX Tel: 0115 932 1014 Fax: 0115 932 6450
High Peak, Council Offices, Hayfield Road, Chapel-en-le-Frith, SK23 0QJ Tel: 01663 750473
High Peak (Buxton Sub-district), The Registrar's Office, Hardwick Square West, Buxton, SK17 6PX Tel: 01298 25075
High Peak (Chapel en le Frith Sub-district), The Town Hall, Chapel en le Frith, SK23 0HB Tel: 01298 813559
High Peak (Glossop Sub-district), 46-50 High Street West, Glossop, SK13 8BH Tel: 01457 852425
South Derbyshire, Traffic Street, Derby, DE1 2NL Tel: 01332 716020 Tel: 01332 716025 Fax: 01332 716021
South Derbyshire (Sub-district), The Registrars Office, Civic Way, Swadlincote, DE11 0AB Tel: 01283 213976 Fax: 01283 213976

Devon

East Devon, Dowell Street, Honiton, EX14 1LZ Tel: 01404 42531 Fax: 01404 41475
Exeter, 1 Lower Summerlands, Heavitree Road, Exeter, EX1 2LL Tel: 01392 686260 Fax: 01392 686262
Holsworthy, 8 Fore Street, Holsworthy, EX22 6ED Tel: 01409-253262
Mid Devon, The Great House, 1 St Peter Street, Tiverton, EX16 6NY Tel: 01884 255255 Fax: 01884 258852
North Devon, Civic Centre, Barnstaple, EX31 1ED Tel: 01271 388456
Okehampton, Transferred to West Devon wef July 1997,
Plymouth, Lockyer Street, Plymouth, PL1 2QD Tel: 01752 268331 Fax: 01752 256046
South Hams, Follaton House, Plymouth road, Totnes, TQ9 5NE Tel: 01803 861234 Fax: 01803 868965
Teignbridge, 15 Devon Square, Newton Abbot, TQ12 2HN Tel: 01626 206341 Tel: 01626 206340 Fax: 01626 206346
Torbay, Oldway Mansion, Paignton, TQ3 2TU Tel: 01803 207130 Fax: 01803 525388
Torridge, Council Offices, Windmill Lane, Northam, Bideford, EX39 1BY Tel: 01237 474978 Fax: 01237 473385
West Devon, Town Council Offices, Drake Road, Tavistock, PL19 0AU Tel: 01822 612137 Fax: 01822 618935

Dorset

Bournemouth, 159 Old Christchurch Road, Bournemouth, BH1 1JS Tel: 01202 551668
East Dorset, King George V Pavilion, Peter Grant Way, Ferndown, BH22 9EN Tel: 01202 892325

North Dorset, Salisbury Road, Blandford Forum, DT11 7LN Tel: 01258 484096 Fax: 01258 484090, This is a part-time office with only 2 members of staff and no receptionist. All Blandford births and deaths from 1837 to 1974 are held at Poole .
South Dorset, The Guildhall, St Edmund Street, Weymouth, DT4 8AS Tel: 01305 772611 Fax: 01305 771269
Poole, Civic Centre Annexe, Park Road, Poole, BH15 2RN Tel: 01202 633744 Fax: 01202 633725
West Dorset, Mountfield Offices, Rax Lane, Bridport, DT6 3JL Tel: 01308 456047

Durham

Darlington, Central House, Gladstone Street, DL3 6JX Tel: 01325 346600 Fax: 01325 346605
Durham Central, 40 Old Elvet, Durham, DH1 3HN Tel: 0191 386 4077 Fax: 0191 383 9961
Durham Eastern, York Road, Acre Rigg, Peterlee, SR8 2DP Tel: 0191 586 6147 Fax: 0191 518 4607
Durham Northern, 7 Thorneyholme Terrace, Stanley, DH9 0BJ Tel: 01207 235849 Fax: 01207 235334
Durham Northern (Chester le Street Sub-district), Civic Centre, Chester le Street, DH3 3UT Tel: 0191-388-3240
Durham Northern (Consett Sub-district), 39 Medomsley Road, Consett, DH8 5HE Tel: 01207-502797
Durham Northern (Stanley Sub-district), 7 Thorneyholme Terrace, Stanley, DH9 0BJ Tel: 01207-235849
Durham South Western, 30 Galgate, Barnard Castle, DL12 8BH Tel: 01833-637997 Tel: 01833-637336
Durham Western, Cockton House, 35 Cockton Hill Road, Bishop Auckland, DL14 6HS Tel: 01388 607277 Fax: 01388 664388
Durham Western (Bishop Auckland Sub-district), Cockton House, 35 Cockton Hill, Bishop Auckland, DL14 6HS Tel: 01388 603404
Durham Western (Crook Sub-district), The Community Health Clinic, Hope Street, Crook, DL15 9HU Tel: 01388-767630
Durham Western (Weardale Sub-district), The Health Centre, Dales Street, Stanhope, Bishop Auckland, DL13 2XD Tel: 01388 527074
Gateshead, Civic Centre, Regent Street, Gateshead, NE8 1HH Tel: 0191 433 3000 Tel: 0191 433 2000 Fax: 0191 477 9978
Jarrow, Suffolk Street, Jarrow, NE32 5BJ Tel: 0191-489 7595 Fax: 0191 428 0931, District abolished 2001 - records transferred to South Tyneside
South Tyneside, 18 Barrington Street, South Shields, NE33 1AH Tel: 0191 455 3915 Fax: 0191 427 7564, Records from Jarrow on abolition 2001 transferred here
Sunderland, Town Hall & Civic Centre, PO Box 108, Sunderland, SR2 7DN Tel: 0191 553 1760 Fax: 0191 553 1769

Essex

Braintree, John Ray House, Bocking End, Braintree, CM7 9RW Tel: 01376 323463 Fax: 01376 342423
Brentwood, 1 Seven Arches Road, Brentwood, CM14 4JG Tel: 01277 233565 Fax: 01277 262712
Castle Point and Rochford, Civic Centre, Victoria Avenue, Southend-on-Sea, SS2 6ER Tel: 01702 343728 Fax: 01702 612610
Castle Point and Rochford (Sub-district), District Council Offices, Hockley Road, Rayleigh, SS6 8EB Tel: 01268-776362 Fax: 01268-776362
Chelmsford, 17 Market Road, Chelmsford, CM1 1GF Tel: 01245 430700 Fax: 01245 430707
Colchester, Stanwell House, Stanwell Street, Colchester, CO2 7DL Tel: 01206 572926 Fax: 01206 540626
Epping Forest, St Johns Road, Epping, CM16 5DN Tel: 01992 572789 Fax: 01992 571236
Harlow, Watergarden Offices, College Square, The High, Harlow, CM20 1AG Tel: 01279 427674 Fax: 01279 444594
Southend-on-Sea, Civic Centre, Victoria Avenue, Southend-on-Sea, SS2 6ER Tel: 01702 343728 Fax: 01702 612610, This office now covers Southend-on-Sea, Castle Point and Rochford Registration Districts.
Thurrock, 2 Quarry Hill, Grays, RM17 5BT Tel: 01375 375245 Fax: 01375 392649
Uttlesford, Council Offices, London Road, Saffron Walden, CB11 4ER Tel: 01799 510319 Fax: 01799 510332

Gloucestershire

Cheltenham, St. Georges Road, Cheltenham, GL50 3EW Tel: 01242 532455 Fax: 01242 254600
Cirencester, Old Memorial Hospital, Sheep Street, Cirencester, GL7 1QW Tel: 01285 650455 Fax: 01285 640253
Forest of Dean, Belle Vue Centre, 6 Belle Vue Road, Cinderford, GL14 2AB Tel: 01594 822113 Fax: 01594 826352
Gloucester, Maitland House, Spa Road, Gloucester, GL1 1UY Tel: 01452 425275 Fax: 01452 385385
North Cotswold, North Cotswold , High Street, Moreton-in-Marsh, GL56 0AZ Tel: 01608 651230 Fax: 01608 651226
Stroud, Parliament Street, Stroud, GL5 1DY Tel: 01453 766049 Fax: 01453 752961

South Gloucestershire, Poole Court, Poole Court Drive, Yate, BS37 5PT Tel: 01454 863140 Fax: 01454 863145

Hampshire
Alton, 4 Queens Road, Alton, GU34 1HU Tel: 01420-85410
Andover, Wessex Chambers, South Street, Andover, SP10 2BN Tel: 01264 352943 Tel: 01264 352513 Fax: 01264 366849
Droxford, Bank House, Bank Street, Bishop's Waltham, SO32 1GP Tel: 01489 894044 Fax: 01489 892219
Hampshire North, Hampshire North , Goldings, London Road, Basingstoke, RG21 4AN Tel: 01256 322188 Fax: 01256 350745
Kingsclere & Whitchurch, Council Offices, Swan Street, Kingsclere,, Nr Newbury, RG15 8PM Tel: 01635-298714
New Forest, Public Offices, 65 Christchurch Road, Ringwood, BH24 1DH Tel: 01425 470150, Fax: 01425 471732
North-East Hampshire, 30 Grosvenor Road, Aldershot, GU11 3EB Tel: 01252 322066 Fax: 01252 338004
Petersfield, The Old College, College Street, Petersfield, GU31 4AG Tel: 01730 265372 Fax: 01730 261050
Romsey, Hayter House, Hayter Gardens, Romsey, SO51 7QU Tel: 01794 513846 Fax: 01794 830491
South-East Hampshire, 4-8 Osborn Road South, Fareham, PO16 7DG Tel: 01329 280493 Fax: 01329 823184
South East Hampshire (Fareham Sub-district), 4 - 8 Osborn Road South, Fareham, PO16 7DG Tel: 01329 280493 Fax:
South East Hampshire (Gosport Sub-district), 3 Thorngate Way, Gosport, PO12 1DX Tel: (023) 9258 0629 Fax: (023) 9258 0629
South East Hampshire (Havant Sub-district), Fernglen, Town Hall Road, Havant, PO9 1AN Tel: (023) 9248 2533 Fax: (023) 9248 2533
Portsmouth, Milldam House, Burnaby Road, PO1 3AF Tel: (023) 9282 9041 Tel: (023) 9282 9042 Fax: (023) 9283 1996
Winchester, Station Hill, Winchester, SO23 8TJ Tel: 01962 869608 Tel: 01962 869594 Fax: 01962 851912
Winchester (Eastleigh Sub-district), 101 Leigh Road, Eastleigh, SO50 9DR Tel: (023) 8061 2058 Fax: (023) 8061 2058

Herefordshire
Bromyard, Council Offices, 1 Rowberry Street, Bromyard, Hereford, HR7 4DU Tel: 01432 260258 Fax: 01432 260259
Hereford, County Offices, Bath Street, Hereford, HR1 2HQ Tel: 01432 260565 Fax: 01432 261720, Owing to the large number of sub-districts operational from 1837 to 1935 this office has a preference for genealogical enquiries by post rather than visits in person.
Kington, Old Court House, Market Hall Street, Kington, HR5 3DP Tel: 01544 230156 Fax: 01544 231385
Ledbury, Town Council Offices, Church Street, Ledbury, HR8 1DH Tel: 01531 632306
Leominster, The Old Priory, Church Street, Leominster, HR6 8EQ Tel: 01568 610131 Fax: 01568 614954
Ross, The Old Chapel, Cantilupe Road, Ross on Wye, HR9 7AN Tel: 01989 562795 Fax: 01989 564869

Hertfordshire
Bishops Stortford, 2 Hockerill Street, Bishops Stortford, CM23 2DL Tel: 01279 652273 Fax: 01279 461492
Broxbourne, Borough Offices, Churchgate, Cheshunt, EN8 9XQ Tel: 01992 623107 Fax: 01992 627605
Dacorum, The Bury, Queensway, Hemel Hemstead, HP1 1HR Tel: 01442 228600 Fax: 01442 243974
Hatfield, 19b St Albans Road East, Hatfield, AL10 0NG Tel: 01707 283920 Fax: 01707 283924
Hertford & Ware, County Hall, Pegs Lane, Hertford, SG13 8DE Tel: 01992 555590 Fax: 01992 555493
Hitchen & Stevenage, Danesgate, Stevenage, SG1 1WW Tel: 01438 316579 Fax: 01438 357197
St Albans, Hertfordshire House, Civic Close, St. Albans, AL1 3JZ Tel: 01727 816806 Fax: 01727 816804
Watford, 36 Clarendon Road, Watford, WD1 1JP Tel: 01923 231302 Fax: 01923 246852

Hull
Hull, Municipal Offices, 181-191 George Street, Kingston Upon Hull, HU1 3BY Tel: 01482 615401 Fax: 01482 615411

Isle of Wight
Isle of Wight, County Hall, High Street, Newport, PO30 1UD Tel: 01983 823230, Fax: 01983 823227

Isles of Scilly
Isles of Scilly, Town Hall, St Marys, TR21 0LW Tel: 01720 422537

Kent
Ashford with Shepway, Elwick House, Elwick Road, Ashford, TN23 1NR Tel: 01233 624666 Fax: 01233 642962
Canterbury with Swale, Wellington House, 4 St Stephen's Road, Canterbury, CT2 7RD Tel: 01227 470480 Fax: 01227 780176
Gravesend, 132 Windmill Street, Gravesend, DA12 1BE Tel: 01474

333451 Fax: 01474 564428
Maidstone, The Archbishop's Palace, Palace Gardens, Mill Street, Maidstone, ME15 6YE Tel: 01622 752891 Fax: 01622 663690
Medway, Ingleside, 114 Maidstone Road, Chatham, ME4 6DJ Tel: 01634 844073 Fax: 01634 840165
Thanet with Dover, Aberdeen House, 68 Ellington Road, Ramsgate, CT11 9ST Tel: 01843 591417 Fax: 01843 851558
Tunbridge Wells, Divisional County Offices, 39 Grove Hill Road, Tunbridge Wells, TN1 1SL Tel: 01892 527332 Fax: 01892 528518

Lancashire
Blackburn, Jubilee Street, Blackburn, BB1 1EP Tel: 01254 587524 Fax: 01254 587538
Blackburn with Darwen (Darwen & Turton Sub-district), Town Hall, Croft Street, Darwen, BB3 2RN Tel: 01254-702443 Fax:
Blackpool , South King Street, Blackpool, FY1 4AX Tel: 01253 477177 Fax: 01253 477176
Burnley and Pendle, 12 Nicholas Street, Burnley, BB11 2AQ Tel: 01282 436116 Fax: 01282 412221
Bolton, Mere Hall, Merehall Street, Bolton, BL1 2QT Tel: 01204 525165 Fax: 01204 525125
Bury, Town Hall, Manchester Road, Bury, BL9 0SW Tel: 0161 253 6027 Fax: 0161 253 6028
Chorley, 16 St George's Street, Chorley, PR7 2AA Tel: 01257 263143 Fax: 01257 263808
Fleetwood and Fylde, South King Street, Blackpool, FY1 4AX Tel: 01253 477177 Fax: 01253 477176
Fleetwood and Fylde (Fleetwood Sub-district), Fleetwood Central Library, North Albert Street, Fleetwood, FY7 6AJ Tel: 01253 874580
Fleetwood and Fylde (Fylde Sub-district), The Library, Clifton Street, Lytham, FY8 5ED Tel: 01253 737530
Hyndburn & Rossendale, The Mechanics Institute, Willow Street, Accrington, BB5 1LP Tel: 01254 871360 Fax: 01254 239391
Hyndburn and Rossendale (Rossendale Sub-district), 1 Grange Street, Rawtenstall, Rossendale, BB4 7RT Tel: 01706 215496
Lancaster, 4 Queen Street, Lancaster, LA1 1RS Tel: 01524 65673 Fax: 01524 842285
Lancaster (Garstang Sub-district), Old Posthouse, Market Place, Garstang, PR3 1ZA Tel: 01995 601651 Fax: 01995 601651
Lancaster (Preesall Sub-district), The Over Wyre Medical Centre, Pilling Lane, Preesall, FY6 0FA Tel: 01253 810722
Manchester, HeronHouse, 47 Lloyd Street, Manchester, M2 5LE Tel: 0161 234 7878 Fax: 0161 234 7888 Email: register-office@manchester.gov.uk
Oldham, Metropolitan House, Hobson Street, Oldham, OL1 1PY Tel: 0161 678 0137 Fax: 0161 911 3729
Preston and South Ribble, PO Box 24, Bow Lane, Preston, PR1 8SE Tel: 01772 263800 Tel: 01772 263808 Fax: 01772 261012
Ribble Valley, Off Pimlico Road, Clitheroe, BB7 2BW Tel: 01200 425786 Fax: 01200 425786
Rochdale, Town Hall, The Esplanade, Rochdale, OL16 1AB Tel: 01706 864779 Fax: 01706 864786
Salford, 'Kingslea', Barton Road, Swinton, M27 5WH Tel: 0161 909 6501 Fax: 0161 794 4797
West Lancashire, Greetby Buildings, Derby Street, Ormskirk, L39 2BS Tel: 01695 576009 Fax: 01695 585819
Wigan & Leigh, New Town Hall, Library Street, Wigan, WN1 1NN Tel: 01942 705000 Fax: 01942 705013

Leicestershire
Leicester, 5 Pocklington's Walk, Leicester, LE1 6BQ Tel: 0116 253 6326 Fax: 0116 253 3008
Leicestershire County Hall, Glenfield, Leicester, LE3 8RN Tel: 0116 265 6585 Fax: 0116 265 6580, Covering Coalville, Loughborough, Market Harborough, Melton Mowbray, Hinckley, South Wigston

Lincolnshire
Boston, County Hall, Boston, PE21 6LX Tel: 01205 310010 Ext 2512 Fax: 01205 356690
Bourne, Saxonhurst, 35 West Street, Bourne, PE10 9NE Tel: 01778 422269 Fax: 01778 421081
Caistor, Council Offices, Caistor, LN7 6LX Tel: 01472 851153 Fax: 01472 852678
East Elloe, 25 West Street, Long Sutton, PE12 9BN Tel: 01406 364740 Fax: 01406 365325
Gainsborough, Richmond House, Richmond Park, Gainsborough, DN21 2RJ Tel: 01427 612312 Fax: 01427 678185
Grantham, The Priory, Market Place, Grantham, NG31 6LJ Tel: 01476 561061 Fax: 01476 562235
Horncastle, Holmeleigh, Foundry Street, Horncastle, LN9 6AQ Tel: 01507 522576 Fax: 01507 524849
Lincoln, 4 Lindum Road, Lincoln, LN2 1NN Tel: 01522 552501 Fax: 01522 589524
Louth, Louth Town Hall, Eastgate, Louth, LN11 9NH Tel: 01507 603529 Fax: 01507 608346
Sleaford, PO Box 2, Council Offices, Eastgate, Sleaford, NG34 7EB Tel: 01529 414144 Ext 2520 Fax: 01529 413728
Spalding, Linden House, 1 Bath Lane, Spalding, PE11 1XP Tel:

01775 769064

Spilsby, Offord House, Church Street, Spilsby, PE23 5EF Tel: 01790 752550 Fax: 01790 752162

Spilsby (Skegness Sub-district), 30 Roman Bank, Skegness, PE25 2SG Tel: 01754 764271 Fax: 01754 612428

Stamford, 2 St Mary's Hill, Stamford, PE9 2DR Tel: 01780 756004 Fax: 01780 752659

Lincolnshire - North-East

North-East Lincolnshire, Town Hall Square, Grimsby, DN31 1HX Tel: 01472 324860 Fax: 01472 324867

Lincolnshire - North

North Lincolnshire, 92 Oswald Road, Scunthorpe, DN15 7PA Tel: 01724 843915 Fax: 01724 872668

London

Barking & Dagenham, Arden House, 198 Longbridge Road, Barking, IG11 8SY Tel: (020) 8270 4742 Fax: (020) 8270 4745

Barnet, 182 Burnt Oak, Broadway, Edgware, HA8 0AU Tel: (020) 8731-1100 Fax: (020) 8731-1111

Bexley, Manor House, The Green, Sidcup, DA14 6BW Tel: (020) 8300 4537 Fax: (020) 8308 4967

Bromley, Room S101, Bromley Civic Centre, Stockwell Close, Bromley, BR1 3UH Tel: (020) 8313 4666 Fax: (020) 8313 4699

Brent, Brent Town Hall, Forty Lane, Wembley, HA9 9EZ Tel: (020) 8937 1010 Fax: (020) 8937 1021

Camden, Camden Camden Town Hall, Judd Street, London, WC1H 9JE Tel: (020) 7974 5600 Tel: (020) 7974 1900 Fax: (020) 7974 5792

Croydon, Mint Walk, Croydon, CR10 1EA Tel: (020) 8760 5617 Fax: (020) 8760 5633

Ealing, Ealing Town Hall, New Broadway, Ealing, W5 2BY Tel: (020) 8758 8946 Fax: (020) 8758 8722

Enfield, Public Offices, Gentlemen's Row, Enfield, EN2 6PS Tel: (020) 8367 5757 Fax: (020) 8379 8562

Greenwich, Town Hall, Wellington Street, London, SE18 6PW Tel: (020) 8854 8888 Fax: (020) 8317 5754

Hackney, Town Hall, Mare Street, London, E8 1EA Tel: (020) 8356 3376 Fax: (020) 8356 3552

Hammersmith, Nigel Playfair Avenue, London, W6 9JY Tel: (020) 8748-3020 Tel: (020) 8576-5032 Fax: (020) 8748-6619

Hammersmith and Fulham, Hammersmith & Fulham Fulham Town Hall, Harwood Road, Fulham, London, SW6 1ET Tel: (020) 8576 5217 Fax: (020) 8753 2146

Haringey, Civic Centre, High Road, Wood Green, London, N22 4LE Tel: (020) 8489 2605 Tel: (020) 8489 2601 Fax: (020) 8489 2912

Harrow, The Civic Centre, Station Road, Harrow, HA1 2UX Tel: (020) 8424 1618 Fax: (020) 8424 1414

Havering, 'Langtons', Billet Lane, Hornchurch, RM11 1XL Tel: 01708 433481 Tel: 01708 433403 Fax: 01708 433413

Hendon see Barnet, 182 Burnt Oak, Broadway,, Edgware, HA8 0AU Tel: (020) 8952-0876 Tel: (020) 8952-0024 Fax: (020) 8381-2346, Transferred to Barnet wef April 1999

Hillingdon, Hillingdon Civic Centre, Uxbridge, UB8 1UW Tel: 01895 250418 Fax: 01895 250678

Hounslow, 88 Lampton Road, Hounslow, TW3 4DW Tel: (020) 8583 2090 Tel: (020) 8583 2086 Fax: (020) 8577 8798

Islington, Finsbury Town Hall, Roseberry Avenue, London, EC1R 4QT Tel: (020) 7527 6347 Fax: (020) 7527 6308

Kensington & Chelsea, The Kensington & Chelsea , Chelsea Old Town Hall, Kings Road, London, SW3 5EE Tel: (020) 7361 4100 Fax: (020) 7361 4054

Lambeth, 357-361 Brixton Road, Lambeth, London, SW9 7DA Tel: (020) 7926 9420 Fax: (020) 7926 9426

Lewisham, 368 Lewisham High Street, London, SE13 6LQ Tel: (020) 8690 2128 Fax: (020) 8314 1078

City of London, Finsbury Town Hall, Roseberry Avenue, EC1R 4QT Tel: (020) 7527 6347 Tel: (020) 7527 6357 Fax: (020) 7527 6308

Merton, Morden Park House, Morden Hall, London Road, Morden, SM4 5QU Tel: (020) 8648 0414 Fax: (020) 8648 0433

Newham, Passmore Edwards Building, 207 Plashet Grove, East Ham, London, E6 1BT Tel: (020) 8430 2000 Tel: (020) 8430 3616 Fax: (020) 8430 3127

Redbridge, Queen Victoria House, 794 Cranbrook Rd, Barkingside, Ilford, IG6 1JS Tel: (020) 8708 7160 Fax: (020) 8708 7161

Richmond upon Thames, 1 Spring Terrace, Richmond, TW9 1LW Tel: (020) 8940 2853 Fax: (020) 8940 8226

Southwark, 34 Peckham Road, Southwark, London, SE5 8QA Tel: (020) 7525 7651 Fax: (020) 7525 7652

Sutton, Russettings, 25 Worcester Road, Sutton, SM2 6PR Tel: (020) 8770 6790 Fax: (020) 8770 6772

Tower Hamlets, Bromley Public Hall, Bow Road, E3 3AA Tel: (020) 7364 7891 Tel: (020) 7364 7898 Fax: (020) 7364 7885, This office holds the records of the former RDS of Stepney, Whitechapel, Bethnal Green, Poplar, Mile End of Old Town and St George in the East Note records of the former East London RD are held by Islington Register Office.

Waltham Forest, 106 Grove Road, Walthamstow, E17 9BY Tel: (020) 8520 8617 Fax: (020) 8509 1388

Wandsworth, The Town Hall, Wandsworth High Street, SW18 2PU Tel: (020) 8871 6120 Fax: (020) 8871 8100

City of Westminster, Westminster Council House, Marylebone Road, NW1 5PT Tel: (020) 7641 1161 Fax: (020) 7641 1246

Merseyside

Knowsley, District Council Offices, High Street, Prescot, L34 3LH Tel: 0151 443 5210 Fax: 0151 443 5216

Liverpool, Liverpool , The Cotton Exchange, Old Hall Street, Liverpool, L3 9UF Tel: 0151 233 4972 Fax: 0151 233 4944

St. Helens, Central Street, St Helens, WA10 1UJ Tel: 01744 23524 Tel: 01744 732012 Fax: 01744 23524

Sefton North, Town Hall, Corporation Street, Southport, PR8 1DA Tel: 01704 533133 Fax: 0151 934 2014

Sefton South, Crosby Town Hall, Great Georges Road, Waterloo, Liverpool, L22 1RB Tel: 0151 934 3045 Fax: 0151 934 3056

Norfolk

Depwade, Council Offices, 11-12 Market Hill, Diss, IP22 3JX Tel: 01379 643915 Fax: 01379 643915

Downham, 15 Paradise Road, Downham Market, PE38 9HS Tel: 01366 388080 Fax: 01366 387105

East Dereham, 59 High Street, Dereham, NR19 1DZ Tel: 01362 698021 Fax: 01362 698021

Fakenham, Fakenham Connect, Oak Street, Fakenham, NR21 9SR Tel: 01328 850122 Fax: 01328 850150

Great Yarmouth, 'Ferryside', High Road, Southtown, Great Yarmouth, NR31 0PH Tel: 01493 662313 Fax: 01493 602107

King's Lynn, St Margaret's House, St Margaret's Place, King's Lynn, PE30 5DW Tel: 01553 669251 Fax: 01553 769942

North Walsham, 18 Kings Arms Street, North Walsham, NR28 9JX Tel: 01692 406220 Fax: 01692 406220

North Walsham (Erpingham Sub-district), Council Offices, North Lodge Park, Overstrand Road, Cromer, NR27 0AH Tel: 01263 513078

North Walsham (Smallburgh Sub-district), 18 Kings Arms Street, North Walsham, NR28 9JX Tel: 01692 403075

Norwich, Churchman House, 71 Bethel Street, Norwich, NR2 1NR Tel: 01603 767600 Fax: 01603 632677

Wayland, Kings House, Kings Street, Thetford, IP24 2AP Tel: 01842 766848 Fax: 01842 765996

Northamptonshire

Brackley, Brackley Lodge, High Street, Brackley, NN13 5BD Tel: 01280-702949

Corby, The Old Stables, Cottingham Road, Corby, NN17 1TD Tel: 01536 203141

Daventry, Council Offices, Lodge Road, Daventry, NN11 5AF Tel: 01327 302209 Fax: 01327 300011

Kettering, 75 London Road, Kettering, NN15 7PQ Tel: 01536 514792 Fax: 01536 526948

Northampton, The Guildhall, St Giles Square, Northampton, NN1 1DE Tel: 01604 745397 Fax: 01604 745399

Oundle and Thrapston, The Old Courthouse, 17 Mill Road, Oundle, Peterborough, PE8 4BW Tel: 01832 273413

Towcester & Brackley, Sunnybanks, 55 Brackley Road, Towcester, NN12 6DH Tel: 01327 350774

Wellinborough, Council Offices, Swanspool House, Wellingborough, NN8 1BP Tel: 01933 231549

Northumberland

Newcastle-upon-Tyne, Civic Centre, Barras Bridge, Newcastle-upon-Tyne, NE1 8PS Tel: 0191 232 8520 Fax: 0191 211 4970

North Tyneside, Maritime Chambers, 1 Howard Street, North Shields, NE30 1LZ Tel: 0191 200 6164

Northumberland Central , Post Office Chambers, Station Road, Ashington, NE63 8RJ Tel: 01670 812243 Fax: 01670 814255

Northumberland North First (Belford Sub-district), The Sheltered Housing Community Centre, Stone Close, Seahouses, NE68 7YL Tel: 01289 307373

Northumberland North First (Berwick Sub-district), 5 Palace Street East, Berwick on Tweed, TD15 1HT Tel: 01289 307373

Northumberland North First (Wooler Sub-district), 33 Glendale Road, Wooler, NE71 6DN Tel: 01668 281656

Northumberland North Second (Rothbury Sub-district), Court House, Front Street, Rothbury, NE66 7TZ Tel: 01669 620171

Northumberland North Second (Warkworth Sub-district), 73 Queen Street, Amble, Morpeth, NE65 0DA Tel: 01665 710744

Northumberland West (Bellingham Sub-district), Sutherland House, 3 St Cuthbert's Terrace, Bellingham, Hexham, NE48 2JR Tel: 01434 220321

Northumberland West (Haltwhistle Sub-district), Haltwhistle Library, Westgate, Haltwhistle, NE49 0AX Tel: 01434 320263

Northumberland Central, 94 Newgate Street, Morpeth, NE61 1BU Tel: 01670 513232 Fax: 01670 519260

Northumberland North First, 5 Palace Street East, Berwick upon Tweed, TD15 1HT Tel: 01289 307373 Fax:

Northumberland North Second, 6 Market Place, Alnwick, NE66

1HP Tel: 01665 602363 Fax: 01665 510079
Northumberland West, Abbey Gate House, Market Street, Hexham, NE46 3LX Tel: 01434 602355 Tel: 01434 602605 Fax: 01434 604957

Nottinghamshire
Basford (Carlton Sub-district), County Council Offices, Carlton Square, Carlton, NG4 3BP Tel: 0115-961-9663
Basford (Eastwood Sub-district), Eastwood Health Clinic, Nottingham Road, Eastwood, NG16 3GL Tel: 01773-712449
Basford (Beeston & Stapleford Sub-district), Marvin Road, off Station Road, Beeston, NG9 2AP Tel: 0115-925-5530
Newark (Southwell Sub-district), North Muskham Prebend, Church Street, Southwell, NG25 0HG Tel: 01636 814200
Basford, Highbury Road, Bulwell, NG6 9DA Tel: 0115 927 1294 Fax: 0115 977 1845
East Retford, Notts County Council Offices, Chancery Lane, Retford, DN22 6DG Tel: 01777 708631 Fax: 01777 860667
Mansfield, Registry Office, Dale Close, 100 Chesterfield Road South, Mansfield, NG19 7DN Tel: 01623 476564 Fax: 01623 636284
Newark, County Offices, Balderton Gate, Newark, NG24 1UW Tel: 01636 705455 Fax: 01636 679259
Nottingham, 50 Shakespeare Street, Nottingham, NG1 4FP Tel: 0115 947 5665 Fax: 0115 9415773
Rushcliffe, The Hall, Bridgford Road, West Bridgford, NG2 6AQ Tel: 0115 981 5307 Fax: 0115 969 6189
Worksop, Queens Buildings, Potter Street, Worksop, S80 2AH Tel: 01909 535534 Fax: 01909 501067

Oxfordshire
Oxford, Tidmarsh Lane, Oxford, OX1 1NS Tel: 01865 816246 Fax: 01865 815632

Rutland
Rutland, Catmose, Oakham, Rutland, LE15 6JU Tel: 01572 758370 Fax: 01572 758371

Shropshire
Bridgnorth, 12 West Castle Street, Bridgnorth, WV16 4AB Tel: 01746 762589 Fax: 01746 764270
Clun, The Pines, Colebatch Road, Bishop's Castle, SY9 5JY Tel: 01588 638588
Ludlow, Stone House, Corve Street,, Ludlow, SY8 1DG Tel: 01584 813208 Fax: 01584 813122
Ludlow (Craven Arms Sub-district), The Library, School Road, Craven Arms, SY7 9PE Tel: 01588 673455
North Shropshire, Edinburgh House, New Street, Wem, Shrewsbury, SY4 5DB Tel: 01939 238418
North Shropshire (Market Drayton Sub-district), Health Centre, Cheshire Street, Market Drayton, TF9 3AA Tel: 01630 657119
North Shropshire (Whitchurch Sub-district), 29 St Mary's Street, Whitchurch, SY13 1RA Tel: 01948 660902
Oswestry, Holbache Road, Oswestry, SY11 1AH Tel: 01691 652086
Shrewsbury, The Shirehall, Abbey Foregate, Shrewsbury, SY2 6LY Tel: 01743 252925 Fax: 01743 252939
Telford and Wrekin, The Beeches, 29 Vineyard Road, Wellinton, Telford, TF1 1HB Tel: 01952 248292,   Fax: 01952 240976

Somerset
Bristol, Quakers Friars, Bristol, BS1 3AR Tel: 0117 903 8888 Fax: 0117 903 8877
Mendip (Frome Sub-district), West Hill House, West End, Frome, BA11 3AD Tel: 01373 462887,
Mendip (Shepton Mallet Sub-district), 19 Commercial Road, Shepton Mallet, BA4 5BU Tel: 01749 342268
Mendip (Wells Sub-district), Town Hall, Market Place, Wells, BA5 2RB Tel: 01749 675355
Yeovil (Chard Sub-district), Holyrood Lace Mill, Holyrood Street, Chard, TA20 2YA Tel: 01460 260472 Fax: 01460 66899
Mendip, 19b Commercial Road, Shepton Mallet, BA4 5BU Tel: 01749 343928 Fax: 01749 342324
Sedgemoor, Morgan House, Mount Street, Bridgewater, TA6 3ER Tel: 01278 422527 Fax: 01278 452670
Taunton, Flook House, Belvedere Road, Taunton, TA1 1BT Tel: 01823 282251 Fax: 01823 351173
West Somerset, 2 Long Street, Williton, Taunton, TA4 4QN Tel: 01984 633116
Yeovil, Maltravers House, Petters Way, Yeovil, BA20 1SP Tel: 01935 411230 Fax: 01935 413993
Yeovil (Wincanton Sub-district), Council Offices, Churchfield, Wincanton, BA9 9AG Tel: 01963 435008 Fax: 01963 34182
North Somerset, 41 The Boulevard, Weston-super-Mare, BS23 1PG Tel: 01934 627552 Fax: 01934 412014
Bath & North East Somerset, 12 Charlotte Street, Bath, BA1 2NF Tel: 01225 312032 Fax: 01225 334812

Southampton
Southampton, 6A Bugle Street, Southampton, SO14 2LX Tel: (023) 8063 1422 Fax: (023) 8063 3431, Visa, Switch, etc are accepted. Marriage indexes are computerised from 1837 - 1900 and some others. Births and deaths computerised from 1988.

Staffordshire
Cannock Chase, 5 Victoria Street, Cannock, WS11 1AG Tel: 01543 512345 Fax: 01543 512347
Cannock Chase (Rugeley Sub-district), Council Offices, Anson Street, Rugeley, WS15 2BH Tel: 01889 585322
East Staffordshire, Rangemore House, 22 Rangemore Street, Burton-upon-Trent, DE14 2ED Tel: 01283 538701 Fax: 01283 547338
East Staffordshire (Uttoxeter Sub-district), 63 High Street, Uttoxeter, ST14 7JQ3 Tel: 01889 562168 Fax: 01889 569935
Lichfield, The Old Library Buildings, Bird Street, Lichfield, WS13 6PN Tel: 01543 510771 Fax: 01543 510773
Lichfield (Tamworth Sub-district), 26 Albert Road, Tamworth, B79 7JS Tel: 01827 62295 Fax: 01827 62295
Newcastle-under-Lyme, 20 Sidmouth Avenue, The Brampton, Newcastle-under-Lyme, ST5 0QN Tel: 01782 297581 Fax: 01782 297582, Wolstanton Registration District is split between Newcastle-under-Lyme and Stoke-on-Trent
Newcastle under Lyme (Kidsgrove Sub-district), The Town Hall, Liverpool Road, Kidsgrove, Stoke on Trent, ST7 4EH Tel: 01782 296734
South Staffordshire, Civic Centre, Gravel Hill, Wombourne, Wolverhampton, WV5 9HA Tel: 01902 895829 Fax: 01902 326779
South Staffordshire (Penkridge Sub-district), Haling Dene Centre, Cannock Road, Penkridge, ST19 5DT Tel: 01785 715260 Fax: 01785 715260
South Staffordshire (Seisdon Sub-district), Civic Centre, Gravel Hill, Wombourne, Wolverhampton, WV5 9HA Tel: 01902 895829 Fax: 01902 326779
Stafford, Eastgate House, 79 Eastgate Street, Stafford, ST16 2NG Tel: 01785 277880 Fax: 01785 277884
Stafford (Stone Sub-district), 15 Station Road, Stone, ST15 8JR Tel: 01785 812087 Fax: 01785 286123
Staffordshire Moorlands, High Street, Leek, ST13 5EA Tel: 01538 373166 Fax: 01538 386985
Staffordshire Moorlands (Biddulph Sub-district), Town Hall, High Street, Biddulph, ST8 6AR Tel: 01782 297939 Fax: 01782 297815
Staffordshire Moorlands (Cheadle & Alton Sub-district), Council Offices, Leek Road, Cheadle, Stoke on Trent, ST10 1JF Tel: 01538 752435 Fax: 01538 752435
Staffordshire Moorlands (Leek & Cheddleton Sub-district), High Street, Leek, ST13 5EA Tel: 01538 373191 Fax: 01538 386985
Stoke-on-Trent, Town Hall, Albion Street, Hanley, Stoke on Trent, ST1 1QQ Tel: 01782 235260 Fax: 01782 235258

Suffolk
Bury St. Edmunds, St. Margarets, Shire Hall, Bury St Edmunds, IP33 1RX Tel: 01284 352373 Fax: 01284 352376
Deben, Council Offices, Melton Hill, Woodbridge, IP12 1AU Tel: 01394 444331 Tel: 01394 444682 Fax: 01394 383171
Gipping & Hartismere, Milton House, 3 Milton Road South, Stowmarket, IP14 1EZ Tel: 01449 612060 Tel: 01449 612054
Ipswich, St Peter House, County Hall, 16 Grimwade Street, Ipswich, IP4 1LP Tel: 01473 583050 Fax: 01473 584331
Sudbury, 14 Cornard Road, Sudbury, CO10 2XA Tel: 01787 372904
Waveney, St Margarets House, Gordon Road, Lowestoft, NR32 1JQ Tel: 01502 405325 Fax: 01502 508170

Surrey
North Surrey, 'Rylston', 81 Oatlands Drive, Weybridge, KT13 9LN Tel: 01932 254360,   Fax: 01932 227139
West Surrey, Artington House, Portsmouth Road, Guildford, GU2 4DZ Tel: 01483 562841 Fax: 01483 573232
East Surrey, East Surrey , The Mansion, 70 Church Street, Leatherhead, KT22 8DA Tel: 01372 373668 Fax: 01372 376811, This Office now deals with all enquiries for the Reigate Office which closed in 2000
Kingston upon Thames, 35 Coombe Road, Kingston upon Thames, KT2 7BA Tel: (020) 8546 7993 Fax: (020) 8287 2888

Sussex
Brighton & Hove, Brighton Town Hall, Bartholomews, Brighton, BN1 1JA Tel: 01273 292016 Fax: 01273 292019
Hove, Transferred to Brighton & Hove RD wef November 1998, ,
Sussex - East
Crowborough, Beaconwood, Beacon Road, Crowborough, TN6 1AR Tel: 01892 653803 Fax: 01892 669884
Eastbourne, Town Hall, Grove Road, Eastbourne, BN21 4UG Tel: 01323 415051 Fax: 01323 431386
Hastings & Rother, Summerfields, Bohemia Road, Hastings, TN34 1EX Tel: 01424 721722 Fax: 01424 465296

Lewes, Southover Grange, Southover Road, Lewes, BN7 1TP Tel: 01273 475916 Fax: 01273 488073
Sussex - West
Crawley (Sub-district), County Buildings, Northgate Avenue, Crawley, RH10 1XB Tel: 01293-514545 Fax: 01293-553832
Chichester, Greyfriars, 61 North Street, Chichester, PO19 1NB Tel: 01243 782307 Fax: 01243 773671
Crawley, Town Hall, The Boulevard, Crawley, RH10 1UZ Tel: 01293 438341 Fax: 01293 526454
Haywards Heath, West Sussex County Council Offices, Oaklands Road, Haywards Heath, RH16 1SU Tel: 01444 452157 Fax: 01444 410128
Horsham, Town Hall, Market Square, Horsham, RH12 1EU Tel: 01403 265368 Fax: 01403 217078
Worthing, Centenary House, Durrington Lane, Worthing, BN13 2QB Tel: 01903 839350 Fax: 01903 839356

Warwickshire
Mid Warwickshire, Pageant House, 2 Jury Street, Warwick, CV34 4EW Tel: 01926 494269 Fax: 01926 496287
Mid Warwickshire (Leamington Spa Sub-district), 1 Euston Square, Leamington Spa, CV32 4NE Tel: 01926 428807 Fax: 01926 339923
Mid Warwickshire (Southam Sub-district), The Grange, Coventry Road, Southam, CV47 1QB Tel: 01926 812636
North Warwickshire, Warwick House, Ratcliffe Street, Atherstone, CV9 1JP Tel: 01827 713241 Fax: 01827 720467
Nuneaton and Bedworth, Riversley Park, Coton Road, Nuneaton, CV11 5HA Tel: (024) 7634 8944 Tel: (024) 7634 8948 Fax: (024) 7635 0988
Rugby, 5 Bloxam Place, Rugby, CV21 3DS Tel: 01788 571233 Fax: 01788 542024
South Warwickshire, 7 Rother Street, Stratford-on-Avon, CV37 6LU Tel: 01789 293711 Fax: 01789 261423
South Warwickshire (Alcester Sub-district), Globe House, Priory Road, Alcester, B49 5DZ Tel: 01789 765441
South Warwickshire (Shipston on Stour Sub-district), Clark House, West Street, Shipston on Stour, CV36 4HD Tel: 01608 662839
South Warwickshire (Stratford on Avon Sub-district), 7 Rother Street, Stratford on Avon, CV37 6LU Tel: 01789 293397 Fax: 01789 261423

West Midlands
Birmingham, 300 Broad Street, Birmingham, B1 2DE Tel: 0121 212 3421 Fax: 0121 303 1396
Coventry, Cheylesmore Manor House, Manor House Drive, CV1 2ND Tel: (024) 7683 3137 Fax: (024) 7683 3110
Dudley, Priory Hall, Priory Park, Dudley, DY1 4EU Tel: 01384 815373 Fax: 01384 815339
Sandwell, Highfields, High Street, Sandwell, B70 8RJ Tel: 0121 569 2480 Fax: 0121 569 2473
Solihull, Homer Road, Solihull, B91 3QZ Tel: 0121 704 6100 Fax: 0121 704 6123
Solihull North, The Library, Stephenson Drive, Chelmsley Wood, Birmingham, B37 5TA Tel: 0121-788-4376 Fax: 0121 788 4379
Stourbridge, Crown Centre, Crown Lane, Stourbridge, DY8 1YA Tel: 01384 815384 Fax: 01384 815397
Walsall, Civic Centre, Hatherton Road, Walsall, WS1 1TN Tel: 01922 652260 Fax: 01922 652262
Wolverhampton, Civic Centre, St Peters Square, Wolverhampton, WV1 1RU Tel: 01902 554989 Fax: 01902 554987

Wiltshire
Chippenham, 4 Timber Street, Chippenham, SN15 3BZ Tel: 01249 654361 Fax: 01249 658850
Devizes & Marlborough, The Beeches, Bath Road, Devizes, SN10 2AL Tel: 01380 722162 Fax: 01380 728933
Marlborough, 1 The Green, Marlborough, SN8 1AL Tel: 01672-512483, From 5/10/98 Devizes and Marlborough Districts will be merged as one district and all records will be kept at Devises.
Salisbury, The Laburnums, 50 Bedwin Street, Salisbury, SP1 3UW Tel: 01722 335340 Fax: 01722 326806
Swindon, 1st Floor, Aspen House, Temple Street, Swindon, SN1 1SQ Tel: 01793 521734 Fax: 01793 433887
Trowbridge, East Wing Block, County Hall, Trowbridge, BA14 8EZ Tel: 01225 713000 Fax: 01225 713096
Warminster, 3 The Avenue, Warminster, BA12 9AB Tel: 01985 213435 Fax: 01985 217688

Worcestershire
Bromsgrove, School Drive, Bromsgrove, B60 1AY Tel: 01527 578759 Fax: 01527 578750
Droitwich, Council Offices, Ombersley Street East, Droitwich, WR9 8QX Tel: 01905 772280 Fax: 01905 776841
Evesham, County Offices, Swan Lane, Evesham, WR11 4TZ Tel: 01386 443945, Fax: 01386 448745

Kidderminster, Council Offices, Bewdley Road, Kidderminster, DY11 6RL Tel: 01562 829100 Fax: 01562 60192
Malvern, Hatherton Lodge, Avenue Road, Malvern, WR14 3AG Tel: 01684 573000 Fax: 01684 892378
Pershore, Civic Centre, Queen Elizabeth Drive, Station Road, Pershore, WR10 1PT Tel: 01386 565610 Fax: 01386 553656
Redditch, 29 Easmore Road, Redditch, B98 8ER Tel: 01527 60647 Fax: 01527 584561
Tenbury, Council Buildings, Teme Street, Tenbury Wells, WR15 8AD Tel: 01584 810588 Fax: 01584 819733
Worcester, 29-30 Foregate Street, Worcester, WR1 1DS Tel: 01905 765350 Fax: 01905 765355

Yorkshire - East Riding
Beverley (Beverley B Sub-district), The Council Offices, Market Green, Cottingham, HU16 5QG Tel: 01482 393565 Fax: 01482 393567
Beveley (Withernsea Sub-district), 243 Queen Street, Withernsea, HU19 2HH Tel: 01482 393568 Fax: 01482 393568
Beverley (Hornsea Sub-district), The Court House, off Railway Street, Hornsea, HU18 1PS Tel: 01964 534111 Fax: 01964 534111
Bridlington, Town Hall, Quay Road, Bridlington, YO16 4LP Tel: 01482 393570 Fax: 01482 393572
Bridlington (Driffield Sub-district), 51 Manorfield Road, Driffield, YO25 5JE Tel: 01377 254051 Fax: 01377 254051
Beverley, 34 Lairgate, Beverley, HU17 8ES Tel: 01482 864205 Fax: 01482 679155
Goole, Council Offices, Church Street, Goole, DN14 5BG Tel: 01482 393580 Tel: 01482 393581 Fax: 01482 393582
Pocklington, Burnby Hall, Pocklington, YO4 2QQ Tel: 01759 303614 Fax: 01759 306722
Yorkshire - Kingston upon Hull
Hull, Municipal Offices, 181-191 George Street, Kingston Upon Hull, HU1 3BY Tel: 01482 615401 Fax: 01482 615411
Yorkshire
York, 56 Bootham, York, YO30 7DA Tel: 01904 654477 Fax: 01904 638090
Yorkshire - North
North Yorkshire Registration Service - North Yorkshire (Headquarters), Bilton House, 31 Park Parade, Harrogate, HG1 5AG Tel: 01423 506949 Fax: 01423 502105
Yorkshire - South
Barnsley, Town Hall, Church Street, Barnsley, S70 2TA Tel: 01226 773085 Tel: 01226 773080, Holds all historical records for the County of North Yorkshire (except the City of York)
Doncaster (Mexborough Sub-district), Council Offices, Main Street, Mexborough, S64 9LU Tel: 01302 735705
Doncaster, Elmfield Park, Doncaster, DN1 2EB Tel: 01302 364922 Fax: 01302 364922
Rotherham, Bailey House, Rawmarsh Road, Rotherham, S60 1TX Tel: 01709 382121 Fax: 01709 375530
Sheffield, Surrey Place, Sheffield, S1 1YA Tel: 0114 203 9423 Fax: 0114 203 9424
Yorkshire - West
Bradford, 22 Manor Row, Bradford, BD1 4QR Tel: 01274 752151 Fax: 01274 305139
Calderdale, 4 Carlton Street, Halifax, HX1 2AH Tel: 01422 353993 Fax: 01422 253370
Dewsbury, Wellington Street, Dewsbury, WF13 1LY Tel: 01924 324880 Fax: 01924 324882
Huddersfield, Civic Centre, 11 High Street, Huddersfield, HD1 2PL Tel: 01484 221030 Fax: 01484 221315
Keighley, Town Hall, Bow Street, Keighley, BD21 3PA Tel: 01535 618060 Fax: 01535 618208
Leeds, Belgrave House, Belgrave Street, Leeds, LS2 8DQ Tel: 0113 247 6707 Fax: 0113 247 6708
Pontefract, Town Hall, Pontefract, WF8 1PG Tel: 01977 722670 Fax: 01977 722676
Todmorden, Municipal Offices, Rise Lane, Todmorden, OL14 7AB Tel: 01706 814811 Ext 208 Fax: 01706 814811 Ext 208
Wakefield, 71 Northgate, Wakefield, WF1 3BS Tel: 01924 302185 Fax: 01924 302186

Wales
Anglesey
Ynys Môn, Shire Hall, Glanhwfa Road, Llangefni, Anglesey, LL77 7TW Tel: 01248 752564

Blaenau Gwent
Blaenau Gwent (Abertilley Sub-district), Council Offices, Mitre Street, Abertilley, Gwent, NP3 1AE Tel: 01495-216082
Blaenau Gwent (Ebbw Vale & Tredegar Sub-district), The Grove, Church Street, Tredegar, Gwent, NP2 3DS Tel: 01495-72269

Bridgend
Bridgend, County Borough Offices, Sunnyside, Bridgend, Glamorgan, CF31 4AR Tel: 01656 642391 Fax: 01656 667529

Caerphilly
Caerphilly (Bargoed Sub-district), Hanbury Square, Bargoed, Caerphilly, CF8 8QQ Tel: 01443-875560 Fax: 01443-822535
Caerphilly (Islwyn Sub-district), Council Offices, Pontllanfraith, Blackwood, Caerphilly, NP2 2YW Tel: 01495 235188 Fax: 01495 235298
Caerphilly, The Council Offices, Ystrad Fawr, Caerphilly Road, Ystrad Mynach, Hengoed, CF82 7SF Tel: 01443 863478 Fax: 01443 863385

Cardiff
Cardiff, The Register Office, 48 Park Place, Cardiff, CF10 3LU Tel: (029) 2087 1690 Tel: (029) 2087 1680 Fax: (029) 2087 1691

Carmarthenshire
Carmarthen, Carmarthen Register Office, Parc Myrddin, Richmond Terrace, Carmarthen, Carmarthenshire, SA31 1DS Tel: 01267 228210 Tel: 01267 228212 Fax: 01267 228215
Llanelli, County Council Offices, Swansea Road, Llanelli, Carmarthenshire, SA15 3DJ Tel: 01554 774088 Fax: 01554 749424

Ceredigion
Cardiganshire Central, The Register Office, 21 High Street, Lampeter, Ceredigion, SA48 7BG Tel: 01570 422558 Fax: 01570 422558
Cardiganshire North, Swyddfar Sir, Marine Terrace, Aberystwyth, Ceredigion, SY33 2DE Tel: 01970 633580
Cardiganshire South, Glyncoed Chambers, Priory Street, Cardigan, Ceredigion, SA43 1BX Tel: 01239 612684 Fax: 01239 612684

Conwy
Colwyn (Sub-district), Bod Alaw, Rivieres Avenue, Colwyn Bay, Conwy, LL29 7DP Tel: 01492-530430
Aberconwy, Muriau Buildings, Rose Hill Street, Conwy, Gwynedd, LL32 8LD Tel: 01492-592407
Colwyn, New Clinic and Offices, 67 Market Street, Abergele, Conwy, LL22 7BP, 01745 823976, 01745 823976
Public Protection Department - Conwy County Borough Council, Civic Offices, Colwyn Bay, Conwy, LL29 8AR Tel: 01492 575183 Fax: 01492 575204

Denbighshire
Denbighshire North, Morfa Hall, Church Street, Rhyl, Denbighshire, LL18 3AA Tel: 01824 708368 Fax: 01745 361424
Denbighshire South, The Register Office, Station Road, Ruthin, Denbighshire, LL15 1BS Tel: 01824 703782 Fax: 01824 704399

Flintshire
Flintshire East, The Old Rectory, Rectory Lane, Hawarden, Flintshire, CH5 3NN Tel: 01244 531512 Fax: 01244 534628
Flintshire West, The Register Office, Park Lane, Holywell, Flintshire, CH8 7UR Tel: 01352 711813 Fax: 01352 713292

Glamorgan
Merthyr Tydfil, The Register Office, Ground Floopr, Castle House, Glebeland Street, Merthyr Tydfil, Glamorgan, CF47 8AT Tel: 01685 723318, 01685 721849
Neath Port Talbot, The Register Office, 119 London Road, Neath, Port Talbot, SA11 1HL Tel: 01639 760020 Fax: 01639 760023

Gwent
Blaenau Gwent, The Grove, Church Street, Tredegar, Gwent, NP2 3DS, 01495 722305
Newport, The Register Office, 8 Gold Tops, Newport, Gwent, NP9 4PH, 01633 265547 Fax: , 01633 220913

Gwynedd
Ardudwy, Bryn Marian, Church Street, Blaenau Ffestiniog, Gwynedd, LL41 3HD Tel: 01766 830217
Bangor, The Register Office, Town Hall, Bangor, Gwynedd, LL57 2RE Tel: 01248 362418
Caernarfon, Swyddfa Arfon, Pennrallt, Caernarfon, Gwynedd, LL55 1BN Tel: 01286 682661
De Meirionndd, Meirionnydd Area Office Office, Cae Penarlag, Dolgellau, Gwynedd, LL40 2YB Tel: 01341 424341
Dwyfor, The Register Office, 35 High Street, Pwllheli, Gwynedd, LL53 5RT Tel: 01758 612546, 01758 701373
Penllyn, Penllyn Register Office, Fron Faire, High Street, Bala, Gwynedd, LL23 7AD Tel: 01678 521220 Tel: 01678 520893, 01678 521243
Public Protection Department - Conwy County Borough Council, Civic Offices, Colwyn Bay, Conwy, LL29 8AR Tel: 01492 575183 Fax: 01492 575204

Monmouthshire
Monmouth (Abergavenny Sub-district), Coed Glas, Firs Road, Abergavenny, Monmouthshire, NP7 5LE Tel: 01873 735435

Monmouth (Chepstow Sub-district), High Trees, Steep Street, Chepstow, Monmouthshire, NP6 6RL Tel: 01291 635725
Monmouth, Coed Glas, Firs Road, Abergavenny, Monmouthshire, NP7 5LE Tel: 01873 735435 Fax: 01837 735429

Neath Port Talbot
Neath Port Talbot, The Register Office, 119 London Road, Neath, Port Talbot, SA11 1HL Tel: 01639 760020 Fax: 01639 760023

Newport
Newport, The Register Office, 8 Gold Tops, Newport, Gwent, NP9 4PH Tel: 01633 265547 Fax: 01633 220913

Pembrokeshire
Haverfordwest, The Register Office, Tower Hill, Haverfordwest, Pembrokeshire, SA61 1SS Tel: 01437 762579 Fax: 01437 779357
Haverfordwest (Fishguard & Cemaes Sub-district), Town Hall, Fishguard, Pembrokeshire, SA65 9HE Tel: 01348 872875 Fax: 01348 872875
Haverfordwest (Haverfordwest & Milford Haven Sub-district), Tower Hill, Haverfordwest, Pembrokeshire, SA61 1SS Tel: 01437 763543 Fax: 01437 779357
South Pembroke, The Register Office, East Back, Pembroke, Pembrokeshire, SA71 4HL Tel: 01646 682432 Fax: 01646 621433

Powys
Brecknock, Neuadd Brycheiniog, Cambrian Way, Brecon, Powys, LD3 7HR Tel: 01874 624334 Fax: 01874 625781
Hay, The Borough Council Offices, Broad Street, Hay-on-Wye, Powys, HR3 5BX Tel: 01497 821371 Fax: 01497 821540
Machynlleth, The Register Office, 11 Penrallt Street, Machynlleth, Powys, SY20 8AG Tel: 01654 702335 Fax: 01654 703742
Mid Powys, Powys County Hall, Llandrindod Wells, Powys, LD1 5LG Tel: 01597 826386
Mid Powys (Builth Sub-district), The Strand hall, Strand Street, Builth Wells, Powys, LD2 3AA Tel: 01982 552134
Mid Powys (Radnorshire West Sub-district), Register Office, Powys County Hall, Llandrindod Wells, Powys, LD1 5LG Tel: 01597 826382
Newtown, Council Offices, The Park, Newtown, Powys, SY16 2NZ Tel: 01686 627862
Newtown (Llanidloes Sub-district), Town Hall, Llanidloes, Powys, SY18 6BN Tel: 01686 412353
Radnorshire East, The Register Office, 2 Station Road, Knighton, Powys, LD7 1DU Tel: 01547 520758
Welshpool & Llanfyllin (Llanfyllin Sub-district), Room 8 First Floor, Powys County Council Area Offices, Youth & Community Centre, Llanfyllin, Powys, SY22 5DB Tel: 01691 649027
Welshpool & Llanfyllllin, Neuadd Maldwyn, Severn Road, Welshpool, Powys, SY21 7AS Tel: 01938 552828 Ext 228 Fax: 01938 551233
Ystradgynlais, County Council Offices, Trawsffordd, Ystradgynlais, Powys, SA9 1BS Tel: 01639 843104

Rhonda Cynon Taff
Pontypridd, The Register Office, Court House Street, Pontypridd, CF37 1LJ Tel: 01443 486869 Fax: 01443 406587
Pontypridd (Cynon Valley Sub-district), The Annexe, Rock Grounds, Aberdare, CF44 7AE Tel: 01685 871008
Pontypridd (Rhondda No 2 Sub-district), Crown Buildings, 69 High Street, Ferndale, Rhondda, CF43 4RR Tel: 01443 730369
Pontypridd (Rhondda No1 Sub-district), De Winton Field, Tonypandy, Mid Glamorgan, CF40 2NJ Tel: 01443 433163 Fax: 01443 441677
Pontypridd (Taff Ely Sub-district), The Register Office, Courthouse Street, Pontypridd, CF37 1LJ Tel: 01443 486870 Fax: 01443 406587

Swansea
Swansea, The Swansea Register Office, County Hall, Swansea, SA1 3SN Tel: 01792 636188 Fax: 01792 636909

Torfaen
Torfaen, The Register Office, Hanbury Road, Pontypool, Torfaen, NP4 6YG Tel: 01495 762937 Fax: 01495 769049
Vale of Glamorgan, Vale of Glamorgan, The Register Office, 2-6 Holton Road, Barry, Glamorgan, CF63 4RU Tel: 01446 709490 Fax: 01446 709502

Wrexham
Wrexham, The Register Office, 2 Grosvenor Road, Wrexham, LL11 1DL Tel: 01978 265786 Fax: 01978 262061

Scotland

Aberchirder

Aberchirder, Aberchirder, AB54 5TB

Aberdeen

Aberdeen, St Nicholas House, Upperkirkgate, Aberdeen, AB10 1EY Tel: 01224-522616 Tel: 01224 522033 (search Room) Fax: 01224-522616

Aberdeenshire

Braemar, Piedmont, 9 Auchendryne Square, Braemar, AB35 5YS Tel: 01339-741501

Inverurie Oldmeldrum Skere and Echt, Gordon House, Blackhall Road, Inverurie, AB51 3WA Tel: 01467 620981 Tel: 01467 628011 (Direct) Fax: 01467-628012 Email: diane.minty@aberdeenshire.gov.uk

Maud, County Offices, Maud, Aberdeenshire, AB4 5ND Tel: 01771 613667 Fax: 0771 613204

Peterhead, Arbuthnot House, Broad Street, Peterhead, AB42 1DA Tel: 01779 483244 Fax: 01779 483246 Email: shirley.dickie@aberdeenshire.gov.uk

Strathdon, Area Office, School Road, Alford, AB33 8PY Tel: 01975 564811

Tarves, Area Office, Schoolhill Road, Ellon, Aberdeenshire, AB41 9AN Tel: 01358 720295 Fax: 01358 726410 Email: kathleen.stopani@aberdeenshire.gov.uk

Aberfeldy Dull & Weem, Municipal Buildings, Crieff Road, Aberfeldy, PH15 2BJ Tel: 01887-820773

Aberfoyle + Mentheith, Aberfoyle Local Office, Main Street, Aberfoyle, FK8 3UQ Tel: 01877 382986 Fax: 01877 382986

Aberlour

Aberlour, 46 High Street, Aberlour, AB38 9QD Tel: 01340-871635

Aboyne and Torphins

Aboyne and Torphins, District Council Offices, Bellwood Road, Aboyne, AB34 5HQ Tel: 01339-886109 Fax: 01339-86798

Airth, 100 South Green Drive, Airth, Falkirk, FK8 8JR Tel: 01324-831538

Alford, Council Office, School Road, Alford, AB33 8PY Tel: 01975-652421 Fax: 01975-563286, in corporating Sauchen (327)

Alloa

Alloa, Marshill House, Marshill, Alloa, FK10 1AD Tel: 01259-123850

Arbroath

Arbroath, 69 High Street, Arbroath, DD11 1AN Tel: 01241 873752 Fax: 01241 874805 Email: arbroath@angusregistrar.sol.co.uk

Ardgour

Ardgour, 9 Clovullin, Ardgour, by Fort William, PH33 7AB Tel: 01855-841261

Argyle and Bute

Rosneath, Registration Office, Easter Garth, Rosneath, by Helensburgh, G84 0RF Tel: 1436831679 Email: elsa.rossetter@eastergarth.co.uk WWW: www.eastergarth.co.uk

Dunoon, Council Offices, Hill Street, Dunoon, PA23 7AP Tel: 01369-704374 Fax: 01369-705948 Email: ann.sadler@argyll-bute.gov.uk

Lismore, Baleveolan, Lismore, Oban, PA34 5UG Tel: 01631 760274

Campbeltown, Council Office, Dell Road, Campbeltown, Argyll, PA28 6JG Tel: 01586 552366 Fax: 01586 552366 Email: julie.mclellan@!argyll-bute.gov.uk WWW: www.argyll-bute.gove.uk

Kilbrandon + Kilchattan, Dalanasaig, Clachan Seil, By Oban, Argyll, PA34 4TJ Tel: 01852 300380

Arrochar, Arrochar, 1 Cobbler View, Arrochar, G83 7AD Tel: 01301-702289

Assynt, Post Office House, Lochinver, Lochinver by Lairg, IV27 4JY Tel: 01571-844201

Auchlinleck, Auchlinleck, 154 Main Street, Auchlinleck, Cummock, KA18 2AS Tel: 01290-420582

Auchterderran

Auchterarder, The Aytoun Hall, 91 High Street, Auchterarder, PH3 1QD Tel: 01764 662155 Fax: 01764 662120

Auchterderran, 145 Station Road, Cardenden, KY5 0BN Tel: 01592 414800 Fax: 01592 414848

Auchtermuchty, Local Office, 15 High Street, Auchtermuchty, KY14 7AP Tel: 01337-828329 Fax: 01337-821166

Aviemore

Aviemore, Tremayne, Dalfaber Road, Aviemore, PH22 1PU Tel: 01479-810694

Ayr

Ayr, Sandgate House, 43 Sandgate, Ayr, KA7 1DA Tel: 01292-284988 Fax: 01292-885643 Email: ayr.registrars@south-ayrshire.gov.uk

Baillieston, Council Office, 89 Main Street, Baillieston, G69 6AB Tel: 0141-771-1901

Ballater, An Creagan, 5 Queens Road., Ballater, AB35 5NJ Tel: 01339 755535 Tel: 01339 755284

Banchory, Aberdeenshire Council, The Square, High Street, Banchory, AB3 1 Tel: 01330-822878

Banff

Banff, Seafield House, 37 Castle Street, Banff, AB45 1FQ Tel: 01261 812001 Tel: 01261 813439 Direct Fax: 01261 818244

Barra, Council Offices, Castlebay, Dana, HS9 5XD Tel: 01871-810431

Barrhead, Council Office, 13 Lowndes Street, Barrhead, 078 2QX Tel: 0141-8813551/2 Fax: 0141-5773553

Beauly, 7 Viewfield Avenue, Beauly, 1V4 7BW Tel: 01463-782264

Bellshill, 20/22 Motherwelt Road, Bellshill, ML4 1RB Tel: 01698-747145

Benbecula, Council Offices, Balivanich, Benbecula, South Uist, HS7 5LA Tel: 01870-602425

Biggar, 4 Ross Square, Biggar, MLI2 EAT Tel: 01899-220997

Bishopbriggs, Council Office, 1 Balmuildy Road, Bishopbriggs, G64 2RR Tel: 0141-772-1154/5

Black Isle (North), Black Isle (North), Council Offices, Ferry Road, Dingwall, IV15 Tel: 01349-863113 Fax: 01349-866164

Black Isle (South), Black Isle (South), Black Isles Centre Service Point Office, Deans Road, Fortrose, IV10 8TJ Tel: 01381-620797/8 Fax: 01381-621085

Blairgowrie, Council Buildings, 46 Leslie Street, Blairgowrie, PH10 6AW Tel: 01250-872051 Fax: 01250-876029

Bo'ness and Carriden, Registration Office, 15a Seaview Place, Bo'ness, EH51 0AJ Tel: 01506-778990

Boisdale, Post Office Hse, Daliburgh, South Uist, PA81 5SS Tel: 01878-700300

Bonar and Kincardine, Post Office, Bonar Bridge, Ardgay, IV24 3EA Tel: 01863-766219

Bonnybridge, Operating from Denny Tel: 01324-504280

Brechin, 32 Panmure Street, Brechin, DD9 6AP Tel: 01356-622107

Bressay, No 2 Roadside Bressay, Lerwick, Shetland, ZE2 9BL Tel: 01595-820356

Broadford, Fairwinds, Broadford, Skye, 1V49 9AB Tel: 01471-822270

Buckie, 1 West Church Street, Buckie, AB56 1UN Tel: 01542-832691

Bucknaven, Local Office, Municipal Buildings College Streert, Buckhaven, KY8 1AB Tel: 01592 414444 Fax: 01592 414490

Bucksburn, Nea Office, 23 Inverurie Road., Bucksburn, AB2 9LJ Tel: 01224-712866

Carnoch, Bridgend, Strathconon, Muir Of Ord, 1V6 7QQ Tel: 01997-477254

Carnoustie, Council Chambers, 26 High Street, Carnoustie, DDV 6AP Tel: 01241 853335/6 Fax: 01241 857554

Castle Douglas, District Council, 5 Street Andrew Street, Castle Douglas, D07 1DE Tel: 01557-330291

Castleton, 10 Douglas Square, Newcastleton, TD9 OQD Tel: 01387-375606

Chryston, Lindsaybeg Road, Muirhead, Glasgow, G69 9HW Tel: 0141-779-1714

Clackmannanshire, Marshill House, Marshill, Alloa, Clackmannanshire, FK10 1AB Tel: 01259-723850 Fax: 01259-723850 Email: registration@clacks.gov.uk WWW: www.clacksweb.org.uk

Clyne, Gower Lane, Brora, KW9 6NT Tel: 01408-621233

Coalburn, 'Pretoria, 200 Coalburn Road, Coolburi, ML11 0LT Tel: 01555-820664

Coigach, The Stores, Achilibuie, Ullapool, IV26 2Y0 Tel: 01854-622256

Coldstream, Operating from Duns Tel: 01361-882600

Coll, 9 Carnan Road, Isle Of Coll, PA78 6TA Tel: 01879-230329

Colonsay & Oronsay, Scalasaig Farm, Colonsay, PA6 1 7YW Tel: 01951-200357

Coupar Angus, Union Bank Buildings, Coupar Angus, PH13 9AJ Tel: 01828 628395 Fax: 01828 627147 Email: legalservices@wandlb.co.uk

Cowdenbeath, 320 High Street, Cowdenbeath, KY4 9QX Tel: 01383-313131

Crawford, 76 Carlisle Road, Crawford, Biggar, ML12 6TW Tel: 01864-502633

Crieff, 14 Comrie Street, Crieff, PH7 4AZ Tel: 01764-655151

Cumbernauld, Fleming House, Tryst Road, Cumbernauld, G67 1JW Tel: 01236-616390 Fax: 01236-616386

Cupar, County Buildings, St Catherine Street, Cupar, KYl5 4TA Tel: 01334-412200 Fax: 01334-412110

Currie, 133 Lanark Road West, Currie, EH14 5NY Tel: 0131-449-5318

Dalbeattie, Town Hall Buildings, Water Street, Dalbeattie, DG5 41X Tel: 01557-330291-Ext323

Dalmellington, Area Office, 1 New Street, Dalmellington, KA6 7QX Tel: 01292-550229 Fax: 01292-550229

Dalry, 42 Main Street, Daly, Castle Douglas, DG7 3UW Tel: 01644-430310

Delting, Soibakkan, Mossbank, Shetland, ZE2 9R13 Tel: 01806-242209

Denny, Carronbank House, Carronbank Crescent, Denny, PK4 2DE Tel: 01324-504280

Dornoch, Cathedral Square, Dornoch, 1V25 3SW Tel: 01862-810202 Fax: 01862-810166

Douglas, Post Office, Ayr Road, Douglas, ML1 I OPU Tel: 01555-851227

Dumbarton, 18 College Way, Dumbarton, G82 1LJ Tel: 01389-767515

Dumfries and Galloway

Gretna, Registration Office, Central Avenue, Gretna, DG16 5AQ Tel: 01461 337648 Fax: 01461 338459 Email: gretnaonline@dumgal.gov.uk WWW: www.gretnaonline.net, CC accepted

Thornhill, Dumfreis and Galloway Council One Stop shop, Manse Road, Thornhill, Dumfriesshire, DG3 5DR Tel: 01848 330303

Dumfries, Municipal Chambers, Buccleuch Street, Dumfries, DO 1 2AD Tel: 01387-260000 Fax: 01387-269605, incorporating New Abbey (861)

Annan, 15 Ednay Street, Annan, DG12 6EF Tel: 01461 204914 Fax: 01461 206896

Kirkcudbright, District Council Offices, Kirkcudbright, DG6 4JG Tel: 01557-330291-Ext-234 WWW: www.dumgal.gov.uk

Lockerbie, Town Hall, High Street, Lockerbie, DG11 2ES Tel: 01576-204267

Moffat, Town Hall, High Street., Moffat, DG10 9HF Tel: 01683 220536 Fax: 01683 221489 Email: alisonQ@dumgal.gov.uk

Wigtown Area, Council Sub-office, County Buildings, Wigtown, DG8 9HR Tel: 01988 402624 Fax: 01988 403201

Dunblane

Dunblane, Burgh Chambers, Dunblane, FK15 OAG Tel: 01786 823300 Fax: 01786 823300 Email: muirm@stirling.gov.uk

Dundee

Dundee City Council - Genealogy Unit, 89 Commercial Street, Dundee, DD1 2AF Tel: 01382-435222 Fax: 01382-435224 Email: grant.law@dundeecity.gov.uk WWW: www.dundeecity.gov.uk/registrars

Angus

Dundee City Council - Genealogy Unit, 89 Commercial Street, Dundee, DD1 2AF Tel: 01382-435222 Fax: 01382-435224 Email: grant.law@dundeecity.gov.uk WWW: www.dundeecity.gov.uk/registrars

Dundee, 89 Commercial Street, Dundee, DD1 2AO Tel: 01382-435222/3 Fax: 01382-435224 Email: grant.law@dundeesity.gov.uk WWW: www.dundeecity.gov.uk/registrars

Dunfermline

Dunfermline, 34 Viewfield Terrace, Dunfermline, KY12 7HZ Tel: 01383-3-12121

Dunrossness, Wiltrow, Dunrossness, Shetland, 2E2 930 Tel: 01950-460792

Duns, 8 Newtown Street, Duns, TD11 3AS Tel: 01361-882600

Durness, Mid Villa, Durine, Durness by Lairg, 1W7 4PN Tel: 01971-511340

Falkirk

Falkirk, Old Burgh Buildings, Newmarket Street, Falkirk, FK1 lIE Tel: 01324-506580 Fax: 01324-506581

East Ayrshire

Catrine, 9 Co-operative Aye, Catrine, KA5 6SG Tel: 01290-551638

Darvel Galston Newmilns, 11 Cross Street, Galston, KA4 8AA Tel: 01563 820218

Kilmarnock, Civic Centre, John Dickie Street, Kilmarnock, KA1 1HW Tel: 01563-576695/6

East Calder, East Calder Library, 200 Main Street, East Calder, EH53 0EJ Tel: 01506-884680 Fax: 01506-883944

East Kilbride, Civic Centre, Cornwall Street, East Kilbride, Glasgow, G74 1AB Tel: 01355 806472, CC accepted

East Lothian

Dunbar, Town House, 79/85 High Street, Dunbar, EH42 IER Tel: 01368 863434 Fax: 01368 865728 Email: fmcarthur@eastlothian.gov.uk

Haddington, John Muir House, Brewery Park, Haddington, EH41 3HA Tel: 01620 827308 Fax: 01620 827438 Email: sforsyth@eastlothian.gov.uk

Eastwood + Mearns, Council Offices, Easiwood Park, Roukenglen Rd, Giffnock, G46 7JS Tel: 0141-638-7588

Eday + Pharay, Eday + Pharay, Redbanks, Eday, Orkney, KW1 2AA Tel: 01857-622239

Edinburgh

Edinburgh, 2 India Buildings, Victoria Street, Edinburgh, EH1 2EX Tel: 0131 220 0349 Fax: 0131 220 0351 Email: registrars.indiabuildings@edinburgh.gov.uk, CC accepted

Ratho, Operating from 2 India Buildings Victoria Street Edinburgh, Ratho EH1 Tel: 0131 220 0349 Fax: 0131 220 0351 Email: registrars.indiabuildings@edinburgh.gov.uk, CC accepted

Edinburgh (L), 30 Ferry Road, Edinburgh, EH6 4AE Tel: 0131-554-8452

Ellon, Ellon, Area Office, Schoolhill Road, Ellon, AB41 9AN Tel: 01358 720295 Fax: 01358 726410 Email: kathleen.stopani@aberdeenshire.gov.uk

Fraserburgh, 14 Saltoun Square, Fraserburgh, AB43 5DB Tel: 01346-513281

Eyemouth, Community Centre, Albert Road, Eyemouth, TD14 5DE Tel: 01890-750690

Fife

East Neuk, Anstruther Local Office, Ladywalk, Anstruther, KYI10

3EX Tel: 01333 592110 Fax: 01333 592117

Kennoway, Sandybrae Community Centre, Kennoway, Fife, KY8 5JW Tel: 01333-351721

Lochore, Benarty Local Office, 6 Benarty Square, Ballingry, Fife, KY5 8NR Tel: 01592 414343 Fax: 01592 414363

West Fife, The Health Centre Chapel St, High Valleyfield, Dunferrnline, KY12 8SJ Tel: 01383-880682

Forfar, 9 West High Street, Forfar, DD8 1BD Tel: 01307 464973 Email: regforfar@angus.gov.uk

Forres, Forres House, High Street, Fortes, 1V36 0BU Tel: 01309-672792

Fort Augustus, Cich Collage, Fort Augustus, PH32 4DH Tel: 01320-366245

Forth, 4 Cloglands, Forth, ML11 8ED Tel: 01535-811631

Gairloch (North), Gairloch (North), 12 Bualnaluib, Aultbea, IV22 2JH Tel: 01445-731320

Gairloch (South), Gairloch (South), District Office, Poolewe, Achnasheen, Ross-shire, IV22 2JU Tel: 01445-781243 Fax: 01445-781315

Gigha, Gigha, 10 Ardminish, Gigha, PA41 7AB Tel: 01583 505249

Girthon & Anwoth, Girthon & Anwoth, 12 Digby Street, Gatehouse Of Fleet, DG7 2JW Tel: 01557 814794

Glasgow

Glasgow, 1 Martha Street, Glasgow, G1 1JJ Tel: 0141 287 7677 Fax: 0141 287 7666

Glasgow (PC), Glasgow (PC), 22 Park Circus, Glasgow, G3 6BE Tel: 0141-287-8350 Fax: 0141-225-8357

Glenrothes, Albany House, Albany Gate Kingdom Centre, Glenrothes, KY7 5NP Tel: 01592 416570 Fax: 01592 416565 Email: sophia.semple@fife.gov.uk

Golspie, Murrayfield, Main Street, Golspie, KW10 6TG Tel: 01408-633150

Grangemouth, Municipal Chambers, Bo'ness Road, Grangemouth, FK3 3AY Tel: 01324-504499

Greenock, 40 West Stewart St., Greenock, PA15 1YA Tel: 01475-714250 Fax: 01415-781647

Harris, Council Offices, Tarbert, Harris, HS3 3DJ Tel: 01859-502367 Fax: 01859-502283

Hawick, Council Offices, 12 High Street, Hawick, TD9 9EF Tel: 01450-364710 Fax: 01450-364720

Helensburgh, Council Offices, 25 West King Street, Helensburgh, G84 8UW Tel: 01436-673909

Helmsdale, 12 Dunrobin Street, Helmsdale, KW8 6LA Tel: 01431-821751

Highland

Applecross, Coire-ringeal, Applecross, Strathcarron, Ross-shire, IV54 8LU Tel: 01520-744248

Area Repository Ross and Cromarty, Council Offices, Ferry Road, Dingwall, IV15 9QR Tel: 01349 863113 Fax: 01349 866164 Email: alison.matheson@highland.gov.uk anna.gallie@highland.gov.uk, NOTE: All Statutory Registers (1855-1965) are held here for the following Districts: Alness Applecross Avoch Carnoch Coigach Contin Cromarty Dingwall Edderton Fearn Fodderty Gairloch North

Dingwall, Council Offices, Ferry Road, Dingwall, IV15 Tel: 01349 863113 Fax: 01349 866164 Email: alison.matheson@highland.gov.uk anna.gallie@highland.gov.uk, Area Repository for Ross and Cromarty

Dunvegan, Tigh-na- Bruaich, Dunvegan, Isle Of Skye, IV55 8WA Tel: 01470 521296 Fax: 01470 521519

Fort William and Ballachulish, Tweeddale Buildings, High Street, Fort William, PH33 6EU Tel: 01397 704583 Fax: 01397 702757 Email: isobel.mackellaig@highland.gov.uk WWW: www.highland.gov.uk

Glenelg, Taobh na Mara, Na Mara, Gleneig Kyle, Ross-shire, IV40 8JT Tel: 01599 522310, Only holds records from 1965

Grantown-on-Spey and Nethyridge, Council Offices, The Square, Grantown On Spey, PH26 3HF Tel: 01479-872539 Fax: 01479 872539 Email: diane.brazier@highland.gov.uk

Inverness, Registration Office, Farraline Park, Inverness, IV1 1NH Tel: 01463 239792 Fax: 01463 712412 Email: margaret.straube@highland.gov.uk WWW: www.highland.gov.uk

Kirkton and Tongue , The Service Point, NTC, Bettyhill, By Thurso, KW14 7SS Tel: 01641 521242 Fax: 01641 521242 Email: mary.cook@highland.gov.uk

Mallaig and Knoydart, Sandholm, Morar, Mallaig, Inverness-shire, PH40 4PA Tel: 01687 462592 Fax: 01687 462592

Rosskeen, Invergordon Service Point, 62 High St, Invergordon, IV18 0DH Tel: 01349 852472 Fax: 01349 853803

Tain, 24 High Street, Tain Tel: 01862 892122

Thurso Strathy and Mey, Library Buildings, Davidsons Lane, Thurso, Caithness, KW14 7AF Tel: 01847 892786 Fax: 01847894611 Email: pauline.edmunds@highland.gov.uk

Wick, Town Hall, Bridge Street, Wick, KW1 4AN Tel: 01955 605713 Fax: 01955 605713 Email: margaret.wood@highland.gov.uk

Thurso Strathy and Mey, District Office Library Buildings, Davidson's Lane, Thurso, KW14 7AF Tel: 01847 892786 Fax: 01847 894611 Email: pauline.edmunds@highland.gov.uk, Caithness Area

Repository - Genealogical Repository with on line access to GRO Scotland

Huntly, Huntly, 25 Gordon Street, Huntly, AB54 5AN Tel: 01466-794488

Insch, Marbert, George Street, Insch, AB52 6JL Tel: 01464-820964

Inveraray, Municipal Office, Inveraray, PA32 8UZ Tel: 01499-302124

Inveresk, Brunton Hall, Ladywell Way, Musselburgh, EH21 6AF Tel: 0131-665-3711

Inverkeithing, 6 Fleriot Street, Inverkeithing, KY11 1ND Tel: 01383-411742

Irvine, 106-108 Bridgegate Hse, Irvine, KA12 8BD Tel: 01294 324988 Fax: 01294324984

Islay, Council Office, Jamieson Street, Bowmore, Islay, PA43 7HL Tel: 01496-810332

Isle of Bute, Council Office, Mount Pleasant Road, Rothesay, PA20 9HH Tel: 01700-5033l/551

Isle of Lewis

Carlo Way, The Registry, Carloway, Isle Of Lewis, PA86 9AU Tel: 01851-643264

Jedburgh, Library Building, Castlegate, Jedburgh, TD8 6AS Tel: 01835 863670 Fax: 01835 863670 Email: aveitch@scotborders.gov.uk WWW: www.scotborders.gov.uk

Johnstone, 16-18 Mc Dowall Street, Johnstone, PA5 8QL Tel: 01505 320012 Tel: 01505 331771 Fax: 01505 382130 WWW: www.renfrewshire.gov.uk

Jura, Forestry Cottage, Craighouse, Jura, PA60 7AY Tel: 01496-820326

Kelso, Town House, Kelso, TD5 7HF Tel: 01573 225659, incorporates Gordon District

Kelty, Kelty Local Services, Sanjana Court, 51 Main Street, Kelty, KY4 0AA Tel: 01383-839999

Kenmore, The Old Schoolhouse, Acharn by Aberfeldy, PH15 2HS Tel: 01887-830307 Fax: Same-as-tel-no

Kilbirnie Beith & Dalry, 19 School Wynd, Kilbirnie, KA25 7AY Tel: 01505-682416 Fax: 01505-684334

Kilfinichen & Kilvickeon, The Anchorage, Fionnphori, Isle Of Mull, PA66 6BL Tel: 01681-700241

Killin, Benvue, Craignavie Road, Killin, FK21 8SH Tel: 01567-820267

Kilwinning, The Regsitrar's Office, 32 Howgate, Kilwinning, Ayrshire, KAI3 6EJ Tel: 01294-55226112 Fax: 01294 557787 Email: mmccorquindale@north-ayrshire.gov.uk

Kingussie, Council Offices, Ruthven Road, Kingussie, Inverness-shire, PH21 1EJ Tel: 01540 664529 Fax: 01540 661004, CC accepted

Kinlochbervie, 114 Inshegra, Rhiconich Lairg, IV27 4RH Tel: 01971-521388

Kinblochluichart, The Old Manse, Garve, Ross-shire, IV23 2PX Tel: 01997-414201

Kinross, 40 High Street, Kinross, KY13 7AN Tel: 01577-862405

Kirkcaldy, 7 East Fergus Place, Kirkcaldy, KY1 1XT Tel: 0I592-412121 Fax: 01592-412123

Kirkconnel, Nith Buildings, Greystone Avenue, Kelloholm, Kirkconnel, DG4 6RX Tel: 01659-67206 Fax: 01659-66052

Kirkintilloch, Council Office, 21 Southbank Road, Kirkintilloch, G66 1NH Tel: 0141-776-2109

Kirkliston, 19 Station Road, Kirkliston, EH29 9BB Tel: 0131-333-3210

Kirkmabreck, The Bogxie, Creetowm, Newton Stewart, DG8 73W Tel: 01671-820266

Kirriemuir, 5 Bank Street, Kirriemuir, DD8 8BE Tel: 01575 572845

Knoydart, Knoydart Estate Office, Inverie, Knoydart by Mallaig, PH41 4PL Tel: 01681-462331 Fax: 01687-462243

Lairg, 4 Lochside, Lairg, Sutherland, IV27 4EG Tel: 01549-402424

Langholm, Town Hall, Langholm, DG13 0JQ Tel: 01387-380255

Larbert, 318 Main Street, Lathert, FK5 3BE Tel: 01324-503580

Larkhall, Council Office, 55 Victoria Street, Larkhall, ML9 2BN Tel: 01698-882454/5

Latherton, Post Office, Latheron, KW5 6DG Tel: 01593-741201

Laurencekirk, Royal Bank Buildings, Laurencekirk, AB30 1AF Tel: 01561-377245 Fax: 01561-378020

Leadhills, Wembley, 8 Hopetoun Place, Leadhills, ML12 6YD Tel: 01659 74228

Lennoxtown, Council Office, 132 Main Street, Lennoxtown, 065 7DA Tel: 01360-311362

Lerwick, County Buildings, Lerwick, Shetland, ZE1 OHD Tel: 01595-693535-Ext-368

Lesmahagow, 40/42 Abbeygreen, Lesmahagow, ML11 0DE Tel: 01555-893314

Leven, 12 Station Road, Leven, KYS 4NH Tel: 01333-592538

Linlithgow, 29 The Vennel, Linlithgow, EH49 7EX Tel: 01506-775373 Fax: 01506-775374

Livingston, Lammermuir House, Owen Sq, Almondvale S. Livingston, EH54 6PW Tel: 01506 775833 Fax: 01506 775834

Loch Duich, Aird View, Dornie, Kyle Of Lochalsh, IV40 8EZ Tel: 01599-555201

Lochalsh, Hamilton House, Plock Road, Kyle Lochalsh, IV40 8BL Tel: 01599-534270

Lochcarron and Shieldaig, Lochcarron Service Point, Main Street, Lochcarron, IV54 8YB Tel: 01520 722241

Lochgelly, Lochgelly Local Office, Town House, Hall Street, Lochgelly, KY5 9JN Tel: 01592 418180 Fax: 01592 418190

Lochgilphead, Dairiada House, Lochnell Street, Lochgilphead, PA31 8ST Tel: 01546-604511

Lochgoilhead, Creiganvan, Lochgoilhead, PA14 8AJ Tel: 01301-703222

Lochhroom, Locality Office, 29 Market Street, Ullapool, 1V26 2XE Tel: 01854-612426 Fax: 01854-612717

Longforgan, 8 Norval Place, Longforgan, Dundee, DD2 5ER Tel: 01382-360283

Mauchline, 2 The Cross, Mauchline, Ayrshire, KA5 5DA Tel: 01290-550231 Fax: 01290-551991

Melrose, Public Library, \larket Square, Meirose, T06 9PN Tel: 01896-823114

Mid & South Yell, Schoolhouse, Ulsia, Yell, ZE2 98D Tel: 01957-722260

Midlothian

Dalkeith, 2-4 Buccleuch Street, Dalkeith, Midlothian, EH22 IHA Tel: 0131 271 3281 Tel: 0131 271 3282 Fax: 0131 663 6842 Email: dkregistrars@midlothian.gov.uk

Milnathort, Rowallan', 21 Church Street, Milnathort, KY13 7XE Tel: 01577-862536

Mochrum, Granite House, 85 Main Street, Fort William, DG8 9HR Tel: 01988-700265

Montrose, 51 John Street, Montrose, Angus, DD10 8LZ Tel: 01674-672351

Moray Council

Elgin inc Tomintoul, 240 High Street, Elgin, IV30 1BA Tel: 01343 554600 Fax: 01343 554644

Morayshire

Keith, Area Office, Mid Street, Keith, AE55 5BJ Tel: 01542 885525 Fax: 01542 885522 Email: keith.registrar@chief.moray.gov.uk

Morvern, Morvern, Dungrianach, Morvern, by Oban, PA34 5XW Tel: 01961-421662

Motherwell & Wishaw, Civic Centre, Windmillhill Street, Motherwell, ML1 1TW Tel: 01698-302222

Muckhart + Glendevon, Operating from Alloa Tel: 01259-723850

Muirkirk, 33 Main Street, Muirkirk, KA18 39R Tel: 01290-661227

Nairn

Nairn, The Court House, Nairn, IV12 4AU Tel: 01667 458510

New Cumnock, Town Hall, The Castle, New Cumnock, KA18 4AN Tel: 01290-338214 Fax: Same-as-tel.-no

New Kilpatrick, Council Office, 38 Roman Road, Bearsden, G61 2SH Tel: 0141-942-2352/3

Newburgh, Tayside Institute, High Street, Newburgh, KY4 6DA Tel: 01337-840917

Newport on Tay, Blyth Hall, Blyth Street, Newport On Tay, DD6 8BJ Tel: 01382-542839

Newton Stewarrt, The Old Town HaIl, 79 Victoria Street, Newton Stewart, DG8 6NL Tel: 01671-404187

North Ayrshire

Isle of Arran, District Council Office, Lamlash, Isle Of Arran, KA27 8JY Tel: 01770-600338 Fax: 01770-600028

Largs and Cumbrae, Moorburn, 24 Greenock Road, Largs, KA30 8NE Tel: 01475 674521 Fax: 01475 687304 Email: gmcginty@north-ayrshire.gov.uk WWW: www.north-ayrshire.gov.uk

Saltcoats, 45 Ardrossan Road, Saltcoats, KA21 5BS Tel: 01294 463312 Fax: 01294 604868 Email: j.kimmett@north-ayrshire.gov.uk WWW: www.north-ayrshire.gov.uk

West Kilbride, Kirktonhall, 1 Glen Road, West Kilbride, KA23 9BL Tel: 01294 823569 Fax: 01294 823569 Email: westkilbrideregistrar@north-ayrshire.gov.uk WWW: www.north-ayrshire.gov.uk

North Berwick

North Berwick, 2 Quality Street, North Berwick, EH39 4HW Tel: 01620-893957

North Lanarkshire

Airdrie, Area Registration Office, 37 Alexander Street, Airdrie, ML6 0BA Tel: 01236 758080 Fax: 01236 758088 Email: registrars-airdrie@northlan.gov.uk

Coatbridge, 183 Main Street, Coatbridge, ML5 3HH Tel: 01236 812647 Fax: 01236 812643 Email: registrars-coatbridge@northlan.gov.uk WWW: www.northlan.gov.uk

Kilsyth, Health Centre, Burngreen Park, Kilsyth, G65 0HU Tel: 01236 826813

Shotts, Council Ornee, 106 Station Road, Shotts, ML7 8BH Tel: 01501 824740

North Ronaldshay, Waterhouse, North Ronaldsay, Orkney, KW17 2BE Tel: 01857-633263

North Uist, Fairview' Lochmaddy, North Uist, HS6 5AW Tel: 01876-500239

Oban, Council Office, Albany Street, Oban, PA34 4AR Tel: 01631 562137 Fax: 01631 570379 Email: emma.cummins@argyll-bute.gov.uk

Old Cumnock, Council Office Millbank, 14 Lugar Street., Cummock, KA18 1AB Tel: 01290-420666 Fax: 01290-426164

Old Kilpatrick, 57 Kilbowie Road, Clydebank, G81 1BL Tel: 0141-952-1330

Orkney

Birsay, Sandveien, Dounby, Orkney, KW15 2118 Tel: 01856-771226

Orphir, The Bu, Orphir, Kirkwall, KW17 2RD Tel: 01856-811319

Sanday, Hyndhover, Sanday, Orkney, KWI7 2BA Tel: 01857 600441 Email: catharine@poona54.freeserve.co.uk

Firth & Stenness, Langbigging, Stenness, Orkney, KWI6 3LB Tel: 01856-850320

Flotta, Post Office, Flotta , Stromness, Orkney, KWI6 3NP Tel: 01856 701252

Harray, New Breckan, Harray, Orkney, KW17 2JR Tel: 01856-771233

Holm and Paplay, Netherbreck , Holm, Orkney, KWI7 2RX Tel: 01856 781231

Hoy, Laundry House, Melsetter, Longhope, Orkney, KWI6 3NZ Tel: 01856-791337

Kirkwall, Council Offices, School Place, Kirkwall, Orkney, KW15 1NY Tel: 01856 873535 Fax: 01856 873319 Email: chief.registrar@orkney.gov.uk WWW: www.orkney.gov.uk

Shapinsay, Girnigoe, Shapinsay, Orkney, KWI7 2EB Tel: 01856-711256 Email: jean@girnigoe.f9.co.uk WWW: www.visitorkney.com/accommodation/girnigoe

Stromness, Burradale, Stromness, Orkney, KW16 3JP Tel: 01856-850854

Westray, Myrtle Cottage, Pierowall Westray, Orkney, KW17 2DH Tel: 01857-677278

Paisley

Paisley, Registration Office, Cotton Street, Paisley, PA1 1BU Tel: 0141 840 3388 Fax: 0141 840 3377 WWW: www.renfrewshire.gov.uk

Papa Westray, Backaskaill, Papa Westray, Kirkwall, KW17 2BU Tel: 01857-644221

Peebles

Peebles, Chambers Institute, High Street., Peebles, EH45 8AG Tel: 01721 723817 Fax: 01721 723817 Email: showitt@scotborders.gov.uk

Penicuik and Glencorse, The Registry Office, 33 High Street, Penicuik, EH26 8HS Tel: 01968 672281 Fax: 01968 679547

Perth, Rose Terrace, Perth, PH1 5HA Tel: 01738-632486 Fax: 01738-444133, Incorporates Dunkeld (388)

Perth & Kinross

Pitlochry, District Area Office, 21 AtholI Road, Pitlochry, PH16 5BX Tel: 01796 472323 Fax: 01796 474226

Blair Athol, Operating from Pitlochry

Logierait, Operating from Pitlochry

Peterculter, Lilydale, 102 North Deeside Road, Peterculter, AB14 0QB Tel: 01224-732648 Fax: 01224 734637

Polmont + Muiravonside, Council Offices, Redding Road, Brightons, Falkirk, FK2 0HG Tel: 01324-712745

Port Glasgow, Scarlow Street., Port Glasgow, PA14 5EY Tel: 01475-742140

Portree and Raasay, Registrars Office, King's House, The Green, Portree, IV51 9BS Tel: 01478 613277 Fax: 01478 613277

Portsoy, 2 Main Street, Portsoy, Banffshire, AB45 2RT Tel: 01261 842510 Fax: 01261 842510

Prestonpans, Aldhammer House, High Street, Prestonpans, EH32 9SE Tel: 01875 810232 Fax: 01875 814921

Prestwick, 2 The Cross, Prestwick, KA9 1AJ Tel: 01292-671666

Queensferry, Council Office, 53 High Street, South Queensferry, EH30 9HN Tel: 0131-331-1590

Rannoch + Foss, Alltdruidhe Cottage, Rannoch, Pitlochry, PH17 2QJ Tel: 01882 632208

Renfrew, Town Hall, Renfrew, PA4 8PF Tel: 0141-886-3589

Rousay + Egilsay, Braehead Rousay, Kirkwall, KW17 2PT Tel: 01856-821222

Rutherglen, 1st Floor, 169 Main Street, Rutherglen, G73 2HJ Tel: 0141 613 5330 Fax: 0141 613 5335 Email: brenda.wilson@southlanarkshire.gov.uk

Sandness, 13 Melby, Sandness, Shetland, ZE2 9PL Tel: 01595-870257

Sandwick, Yeldabreck, Sandwick, Stromness, KWI6 3LP Tel: 01856-841596

Sanquhar, Council Offices, 100 High Street, Sanquhar, DG4 6DZ Tel: 01659-50347

Scottish Borders

Chirnside, White House, Chirnside Duns, TD11 3XL Tel: 01890 818339 Fax: 01890 818339 Email: davidfarmery@aladdinscave.net

Galashiels, Library Buildings, Lawyers Brac, Galashiels, TD1 3JQ Tel: 01896-752822

Lauder, The Old Jail, Mid Row, Lauder, TD2 6SZ Tel: 01578 722795

Scourie, 12 Park Terrace, Scourie by Lairg, IV27 4TD Tel: 01971-502425

Selkirk

Selkirk, Municipal Buildings, High Street, Selkirk, TD7 4JX Tel: 01750 23104

Shetland

Burra Isles, Roadside Hannavoe, Lerwick, Shetland, ZEZ 9LA Tel: 01595-859201

Fair Isle, Field, Fair Isle, Shetland, ZE2 9JU Tel: 01595-760224

Sandsting and Aigthsting, Modesty, West Burrafirth, Aithsting, Shetland, ZE2 9NT Tel: 01595 809428 Fax: 01595 809427

Fetlar, Lower Toft Funzie, Fetlar, Shetland, ZE2 9DJ Tel: 01957-733273

Foula, Magdala Foula, Shetland, 7E2 9PN Tel: 01595-753236

Lunnasting, Vidlin Farm, Vidlin Shetland, 7E2 9QB Tel: 01806-577204

Nesting, Laxfirth Brettabister, North Nesting, Shetland, ZE2 9PR Tel: 01595-694737

North Yell, Breckon, Cullivoe, Yell, ZE2 9DD Tel: 01957 744244 Fax: 01957 744352

Northmaven, Uradell, Eshaness, Shetland, ZEZ 9RS Tel: 01806 503362

Papa Stour, North House, Papa Stour, Shetland, ZE2 9PW Tel: 01595-873238

Sandwick and Cunningsbur, Pytaslee Leebitton, Sandwick, Shetland, ZE2 9HP Tel: 01950 431367 Fax: 01950 431367

Walls, Victoria Cottage, Walls, Lerwick, Shetland, ZE2 9PD Tel: 01595 809478

Whalsay, Conamore, Brough, Whalsay, ZE2 9AL Tel: 01806-566544, CC accepted

Whalsay-Skerries, Fairview, East Isle, Skerries Lerwick, ZE2 9AR Tel: 01806-515224

Slamannan, Operating from Falkirk Tel: 01324-506580 Fax: 01324-50658!

Small Isles

Slamannan, Kildonan House, Isle Of Eigg, PH42 4RL Tel: 01687-482446

South Ayrshire

Girvan Barrhill Barr Dailly Colmonell Ballantrae, Registration Office, 22 Dalrymple Street, Girvan, KA26 9AE Tel: 01465-712894 Fax: 01465-715576 Email: girvan.registrars@south-ayrshire.gov.uk, CC accepted

South Ayrshire, Maybole Crosshill Dunure Kirkmichael Kirkoswald Straiton, Council Office, 64 High Street, Maybole, KAI9 7BZ Tel: 01655 884852 Fax: 01655 889621 Email: maybole.registrars@south-ayrshire.gov.uk, CC accepted

South Cowal, South Cowal, Copeswood, Auchenlochan High Rd, Tighnabruaich, PA21 2BE Tel: 01700-811601

South Lanarkshire

Cambuslang, Council Office, 6 Glasgow Road, Cambuslang, G72 7BW Tel: 0141 641 8178 Fax: 0141 641 8542 Email: registration@southlanarkshire.gov.uk, CC accepted

Carluke, 25 High Street., Carluke, MLB 4AJ Tel: 01555 772273 Fax: 01555 773721

Hamilton, 21 Beckford Street, Hamilton, ML3 0BT Tel: 01698 454211 Fax: 01698 455746 Email: jean-lavelle@southlanarkshire.gov.uk, CC accepted

Lanark, South Vennel, Lanark, ML11 7JT Tel: 01555 673220 Tel: 01555 673221, CC accepted

South Ronaldsay, West Cara, Grimness, South Ronaldsay, KWI7 2TH Tel: 01856-831509

St Andrews, Area Office, St Man's Place, St Andrews, KY16 9UY Tel: 01334-412525 Fax: 01334-412650

Stirling

Callander, 1 South Church Street, Callander, FKI7 8BN Tel: 01877-330166

Stirling, Municipal Buildings, Corn Exchange Road, Stirling, FK8 2HU Tel: 01786-432343

Stonehaven East Kinkardine and Inverbervie, Viewmount, Arduthie Road, Stonehaven, AB39 2DQ Tel: 01569 768360 Fax: 01569-765455, Incorporates Inverbervie (343)

Stornoway and South Lochs, Town Hall, 2 Cromwell Street, Stornoway, HS1 2DB Tel: 01851-709438 Fax: 01851 709438 Email: emacdonald@cne-siar.gov.uk WWW: www.cne-siar.gov.uk/w-isles/registrars

Strathcur, Memorial Hall, Strachur, Argyll, PA27 8DG Tel: 01369-860316

Stranraer Area, Council Offices, Sun Street, Stranraer, DG9 7AB Tel: 01776 888439

Strathaven, R Bank Of Scot Blds, 36 Common Green, Strathaven, ML10 6AF Tel: 01357-520316

Strathclyde

Glasgow, 22 Park Circus, Glasgow, G3 6BE Tel: 0141 287 8350 Fax: 0141 287 8357 Email: bill.craig@pas.glasgow.gov.uk

Strathendrick, Balfron Local Office, 32 Buchanan St., Balfron, G63 0TR Tel: 01360- 40315 Fax: 01360 441254 Email: phillips@stirling.gov.uk, CC accepted

Stronsay, Strynie, Stronsay, Kirkwall, KWI7 2AR Tel: 01857-616239

Strontian, Easgadail, Longrigg Road, Strontian Acharacle, Argyll, PH36 4HY Tel: 01967-402037

Tarbat, The Bungalow, Chaplehill, Portmahomack, Portmathom Tain, IV20 1XJ Tel: 01862-871328

Tarbert, Argyll House, School Road, Tarbert, PA29 6UJ Tel: 01880-820374

Tarradale, Service Point Office, Seaforth Road, Muir Of Ord, IV6 7TA Tel: 01463-870201

Tayinloan, Bridge House, Tayinloan, Tarbert, PA29 6XG Tel: 01583-441239

Tayport, Burgh Chambers, Tayport, DD6 9JY Tel: 01382-552544

Tingwall, 20 Meadowfleld Road, Scalloway, Lerwick, Shetland, ZEI 0UT Tel: 01595-880732

Tobermory, Council Offices, Breadalbane Street, Tobernory, PA75 6PX Tel: 01688-302051

Tranent, 8 Civic Square, Tranent, EH33 1LH Tel: 01875-610278

Troon, Municipal Buildings, 8 South Beach, Troon, KA10 6EF Tel: 01292-313555 Fax: 01292-318009

Turriff, Towie House, Manse Road, Turriff, AB53 7AY Tel: 01888-562427 Fax: 01888-568559

Tyree, Crossapol, Isle Of Tyree, PA77 6UP Tel: 01879-220349

Uig(Lewis), 10 Valtos, Uig, Lewis, PA86 9HR Tel: 01851-672213

Uig(Skye) (Inverness), 3 Ellishadder, Staffin, Portree, IV51 9JE Tel: 01410-562303, records held are from 1967 to date. all previous records now held at Portree

Unst, New Noose, Ballsound Unst, ZE2 9DX Tel: 01957-711348

Uphall, 99 East Main Street, Broxburn, EH52 5JA Tel: 01506-775500 Fax: 01506-775505

Vale of Leven, Vale of Leven, 77 Bank Street, Alexandria, G83 0LE Fax: 01389-752413

Wanlochhead, Operating from Sanquhar Tel: 01659-74287

West Calder, 24 - 26 Main Street, West Calder, EH55 8DR Tel: 01506 871874

West Linton, Council Office, West Linton, EH46 7ED Tel: 01968-660267

West Lothian

Bathgate, 76 Mid Street, Bathgate, EH48 1QD Tel: 01506 776192 Fax: 01506 776194

Western Ardnamurchan, Doirlinn House, Kilchoan, Acharacle, PH36 4LL Tel: 01972-510209

Whitburn, 5 East Main Street, Whitburn, EH47 0RA Tel: 01501-678000 Fax: 01506-678026

Whiteness & Weisdale Vista, Whiteness, Shetland, ZE2 9LJ Tel: 01595-830332

Whithorn Area, 75 George Street, Whithorn, DG8 8NU Tel: 01988-500458 Email: archietaylor@supanet.com

Registration Records in The Republic of Ireland
Oifig An Ard-Chlaraitheora (General Register Office)
Joyce House, 8/11 Lombard Street East, Dublin, 2.

The General Register Office and Research Room are open Monday to Friday, (excluding public holidays) from 9.30 a.m. to 12.30 p.m. and from 2.15 p.m. to 4.30 p.m. for the purpose of searching the indexes to birth, death and marriage records and obtaining certificates. Joyce House is near the junction of Pearse Street and Westland Row Dublin

The following records are deposited in the General Register Office:-

1. Registers of all Births registered in the whole of Ireland from 1st January, 1864, to 31 December, 1921, and in Ireland (excluding the six north-eastern counties of Derry, Antrim, Down, Armagh, Fermanagh and Tyrone know as Northern Ireland) from that date.

2. Registers of all Deaths registered in the whole of Ireland from 1st January, 1864, to 31st December 1921, and in Ireland (excluding Northern Ireland) from that date.

3. Registers of all Marriages registered in the whole of Ireland from 1st April 1845, to 31st December 1863, except those celebrated by the Roman Catholic clergy.

4. Registers of all Marriages registered in the whole of Ireland from 1st January, 1864, to 31st December, 1921, and in Ireland (excluding Northern Ireland) from that date.

5. Registers of Births at Sea of children, one of whose parents was Irish, registered from 1st January, 1864, to 31st December, 1921. Register of Births at Sea of Children one of whose parents was born in the Republic of Ireland, registered after 1921.

6. Register of Deaths at Sea of Irish-born persons, registered from 1st January, 1864, to 31st December, 1921, and after 1921 of Irish born persons other than those born in Northern Ireland.

7. Registers of Births of children of Irish parents, certified by British Consuls abroad, from 1st January, 1864 to 31st December, 1921.

8. Registers of Deaths of Irish-born persons, certified by British Consuls abroad, from 1st January, 1864, to 31st December, 1921.

9. Register of Marriages celebrated in Dublin by the late Rev. J F G Schulze, Minister of the German Protestant Church, Poolbeg Street, Dublin, from 1806 to 1837, inclusive.

10. Registers under the Births, Deaths and Marriages (Army) Act, 1879.

11. Adopted Children Register – legal adoptions registered in the Republic of Ireland on or after 10th July, 1953. Note: Cost of certificates issued from the

Adopted Children Register: £5.50 for full certificate: £3.50 for short certificate: £0.70 for certificate for Social Welfare purposes.

12. Birth and Death Registers under the Defence (Amendment) (No. 2) Act, 1960.

13. Registers of certain births and deaths occurring outside the State (The Births, Deaths and Marriages Registration Act, 1972, Sec. 4).

14. Register of Certain Lourdes Marriages (Marriages Act, 1972, Sec.2).

15. Registers of Stillbirths registered in Republic of Ireland from 1st January 1995 (certified copies available to parents only).

Reading Room Searches.

There are two types of searches available to the public.

A search for a maximum of 5 years costs £1.50 whilst a general search for one day covering all years costs £12. Both are payable in advance. A photocopy of an identified entry can be purchased for £1.50.

Records for births, deaths and Catholic marriages commenced in 1864. Records for non-Catholic marriages date from 1845. Information prior to this (1864) may be available from parish records which are kept in the Genealogical Office in the National Library, Kildare Street, Dublin, 2. Records of births, deaths and marriages for Northern Ireland are only available up to 1921.

The indexes are complied on a yearly/quarterly basis in alphabetical order in the same manner as a telephone directory. Records for the years 1878 to 1903 and 1928 to 1965 are divided into four quarters ending March (which includes January, February and March), June, September and December, therefore it is necessary to check the index for each quarter in any one year. Births which were registered late are at the back of the Index for each year.

Marriages are indexed under both the maiden name of the bride and the grooms surname, therefore, if you check under each name you find a cross reference which will indicate it is the correct entry relating to the marriage.

Museums

National Collections

The Battlefields Trust 33 High Green, Brooke, Norwich, NR15 1HR Tel: 01508 558145 Email: Battlefield.trust@aol.com WWW: www.battlefieldstrust.com

The Boat Museum & David Owen Waterways Archive South Pier Road, Ellesmere Port, CH65 4FW Tel: 0151-355-5017 Fax: 0151-355-4079 Email: boatmuseum@easynet.co.uk Records relating to the management, maintenance and operation of inland waterways in England, Scotland and Wales. Substantial Waterways library. Date range: late 17th century to 20th century.

British Red Cross Museum & Archives 9 Grosvenor Crescent, London, SW1X 7EJ Tel: 020-7201-5153 Fax: 020-7235-0876 Email: enquiry@redcross.org.uk WWW: www.redcross.org.uk

Cable & Wireless Archive & Museum of Submarine Telegraphy Eastern House,, Porthcurno, Penzance, TR19 6JX Tel: 01736 810478 Tel: 01736 810811 Fax: 01736 810640 Email: info@tunnels.demon.co.uk WWW: www.porthcurno.org.uk Housed in one of Porthcurno's former telegraph station buildings, and adjacent to the Museum of Submarine Telegraphy, the archive is a unique resource for learning about: the history of Porthcurno

Commonwealth War Graves Commission Information Services, 2 Marlow Road, Maidenhead, Berkshire, SL6 7DX Tel: 01628-634221 Fax: 01628-771208

Department of Manuscripts and Special Collections Hallward Library, Nottingham University , University Park, Nottingham, NG7 2RD Tel: 0115 951 4565 Fax: 0115 951 4558 Email: mss-library@nottingham.ac.uk WWW: www.mss.library.nottingham.ac.uk

The Library & Museum of Freemasonry, Freemasons' Hall, 60 Great Queen Street, London WC2B 5AZ Tel: (020) 7395 9257, WWW: www.grandlodge-england.org.uk

Imperial War Museum Lambeth Road, London, SE1 6HZ Tel: 020-7416-5348 Fax: 020-7416-5246 Email: books@iwm.org.uk WWW: www.iwm.org.uk

Imperial War Museum Film and Video Archive, Lambeth Road, London SE1 6HZ Tel: 020 7416 5291 WWW: www.iwm.org.uk/collections/film.htm

Isles of Scilly Museum Church Street, St Mary's, Isles of Scilly, TR21 0JT Tel: 01720-422337

Labour History Archive and Study Centre 103 Princess Street, Manchester, M1 6DD Tel: 0161-228-7212 Fax: 0161-237-5965 Email: archives@nmlhweb.org lhasc@fs1.li.man.ac.uk WWW: http://rylibweb.man.ac.uk

Museums Association 42 Clerkenwell Close, London, EC1R 0PA Tel: 020-7250-1789 Fax: 020-7250-1929

The National Coal Mining Museum for England Caphouse Colliery, New Road, Overton, Wakefield, West Yorkshire, WF4 4RH Tel: 01924-848806 Fax: 01924-840694 Email: info@ncm.org.uk WWW: www.ncm.org.uk

National Dragonfly Museum Ashton Mill, Ashton, Peterborough, PE8 5LB Tel: 01832-272427 Email: ndmashton@aol.com WWW: www.natdragonflymuseum.org.uk

National Gallery St. Vincent House, 30 Orange Street, London, WC2H 7HH Tel: 020-7747-5950

National Maritime Museum Romney Road, Greenwich, London, SE1O 9NF Tel: 020-8858-4422 Fax: 020-8312-6632 WWW: www.nmm.ac.uk

National Maritime Museum, Romney Road, Greenwich, London SE10 9NF Tel: (020) 8858-4422 Fax: (020) 8312-6632, WWW: http://www.nmm.ac.uk CC accepted

National Museum of Photography, Film & Television Bradford, West Yorkshire, BD1 1NQ Tel: 01274-202030 Fax: 01274-723155 WWW: http:www.nmpft.org.uk

National Portrait Gallery 2 St. Martins Place, London, WC2H 0HE Tel: 020-7306-0055 Fax: 020-7206-0058 WWW: www.npg.org.uk

Natural History Museum Cromwell Rd, London, SW7 5BD Tel: (020) 7938 9238 Fax: 020 7938 9290 WWW: http://www.nhm.ac.uk

National Railway Museum Leeman Road, York, YO26 4XJ Tel: 01904-621261 Fax: 01904-611112 Email: nrm@nmsi.ac.uk WWW: www.nrm.org.uk

National Waterways Museum Llanthony Warehouse, Gloucester Docks, Gloucester, GL1 2EH Tel: 01452-318054 Fax: 01452-318066 Email: curatorial1@nwm.demon.co.uk WWW: www.nwm.demon.uk

North West Sound Archive Old Steward's Office, Clitheroe Castle, Clitheroe, Lancashire, BB7 1AZ Tel: 01200-427897 Fax: 01200-427897 WWW: www.nw-soundarchive.co.uk

Royal Armouries (Leeds) Armouries Drive, Leeds, West Yorkshire, LS10 1LT Tel: 0990-106666

Royal Armouries (Tower of London) HM Tower Of London, Tower Hill, London, EC3N 4AB Tel: (020) 7480 -6358 Ext 30 Fax: (020) 7481 2922

The Science Museum Exhibition Road, London, SW7 2DD Tel: 0870-870-4868 Email: sciencemuseum@nms.ac.uk

Victoria & Albert Museum Cromwell Road, South Kensington, London, SW7 2RL Tel: 020-7942-2164 Fax: 020-7942-2162

Regional Museums Organisations

The South West Museums Council Hestercombe House, Cheddon Fitzpaine, Taunton, Somerset, TA2 8LQ Tel: 01823-259696 Fax: 01823-413114 Email: robinbourne@swmuseums.co.uk

West Midlands Regional Museums Council Hanbury Road, Stoke Prior, Bromsgrove, Worcestershire, B60 4AD Tel: 01527-872258 Fax: 01527-576960 Email: wmrmc@btinternet.com

Yorkshire & Humberside Museums Council Farnley Hall Hall Lane, Leeds, West Yorkshire LS12 5HA Tel: 0113-263-8909

England

Bath & North East Somerset

Roman Baths Museum Abbey Churchyard, Bath, BA1 1LZ Tel: 01225-477773 Fax: 01225-477243

Bedfordshire

Bedford Museum Castle Lane, Bedford MK40 3XD Tel: 01234-353323

Bedford Museum Bedfordshire Yeomanry, Castle Lane, Bedford MK40 3XD Tel: 01234 353323 Fax: 01234 273401 Email: bmuseum@bedford.gov.uk WWW: www.bedfordmuseum.org

Bedfordshire and Hertfordshire Regimental Museum, Luton Museum, Wardown Park, Luton LU2 7HA Tel: 01582 546722 Fax: 01582 546763 WWW: www.luton.gov.uk/enjoying/museums

Station X - Bletchley Park, Bletchley Park Trust, The Mansion, Bletchley, Milton Keynes MK3 6EB Tel: 01908 640404, WWW: www.bletchleypark.org.uk

Cecil Higgins Art Gallery Castle Close, Castle Lane, Bedford MK40 3RP Tel: 01234-211222 Fax: 01234-327149

Elstow Moot Hall Elstow, Bedford, Bedfordshire, MK42 9XT Tel: 01234-266889 Tel: 01234-228330 Fax: 01234-228531 Email: wilemans@deed.bedfordshire.gov.uk WWW: www.bedfordshire.gov.uk

Luton Museum & Art Gallery Wardown Park, Old Bedford Road, Luton LU2 7HA Tel: 01582-546725 Email: adeye@luton.gov.uk

Shuttleworth (Flying) Collection Old Warden Aerodrome, Old Warden, Biggleswade, SG18 9ER Tel: 01767-627288 Fax: 01767-626229 Email: collection@shuttleworth.org WWW: www.shuttleworth.org

John Dony Field Centre Hancock Drive, Bushmead, Luton, Bedfordshire LU2 7SF Tel: 01582-486983

Berkshire

The Museum of Berkshire Aviation Trust Mohawk Way, off Bader Way, Woodley, Reading, RG5 4UE Tel: 0118 944 8089 Email: museumofberkshireaviation@fly.to WWW: http://fly.to/museumofberkshireaviation

Friends of Royal Borough Collection - Windsor, 14 Park Avenue, Wraysbury TW19 5ET Tel: 01784 482771

The Household Cavalry Museum, Combermere Barracks, Windsor SL4 3DN Tel: 0118 755112 Fax: 01753 755161

Blake's Lock Museum Gasworks Road, Reading RG1 3DS Tel: 0118-939-0918

Duke of Edinburgh's Royal Regiment (Berks & Wilts) Museum The Wardrobe, 58 The Close, Salisbury, SP1 2EX Tel: 01722-414536

Household Cavalry Museum Combermere Barracks, Windsor, Berkshire Tel: 01753-755112 Fax: 01753-755112

Maidenhead Heritage Centre, 41 Nicholsons Centre, Maidenhead SL6 1LL Tel: 01628 780555

Museum of English Rural Life, Rural History Centre, University of Reading, Whiteknights PO Box 229, Reading RG6 6AG Tel: 0118-931-8664 Fax: 0118-975-1264 Email: j.s.creasey@reading.ac.uk WWW: www.ruralhistory.org/index.html Appointments required

Museum of Reading Town Hall, Blagave Street, Reading, Berkshire, RG1 1OH Tel: 0118-939-9800 WWW: www.readingmuseum.org.uk

R.E.M.E. Museum of Technology, Isaac Newton Road, Arborfield, Reading, RG2 9NJ Tel: 0118 976 3375 Fax: 0118 976 3375 Email: reme-museum@gtnet.gov.uk WWW: http://www.rememuseum.org.uk

Royal Berkshire Yeomanry Cavalry Museum, T A Centre, Bolton Road, Windsor SL4 3JG Tel: 01753 860600 Fax: 01753 854946

Royal Borough Museum (Windsor & Maidenhead), Tinkers Lane, Windsor SL4 4LR Tel: 01628 796829, Email: olivia.gooden@rbwm.gov.uk

Slough Museum 278-286 High Street, Slough SL1 1NB Tel: 01753-526422

Wantage Vale & Downland Museum, Church Street, Wantage OX12 8BL Tel: 01235 771447

West Berkshire Museum The Wharf, Newbury, Berkshire, RG14 5AS Tel: 01635-30511

Bristol

Ashton Court Visitor Centre Ashton Court, Long Ashton, Bristol,

BS41 8JN Tel: 0117-963-9174

Blaise Castle House Museum Henbury, Bristol, BS10 7QS
Tel: 0117-950-6789
Bristol City Museum & Art Gallery Queens Road, Bristol, BS8
1RL Tel: 0117-922-3571 Fax: 0117-922-2047
Email: general_museums@bristol-city.gov.uk WWW:
www.bristol-city.gov.uk/museums
Bristol Industrial Museum Princes Wharf, Wapping Road, Bristol,
BS1 4RN Tel: 0117-925-1470
Bristol Maritime Heritage Centre Wapping Wharf, Gasferry Road,
Bristol, BS1 6TY Tel: 0117-926-0680
Clevedon Story Heritage Centre Waterloo House, 4 The Beach,
Clevedon, Bristol, BS21 7QU Tel: 01275-341196
Clifton Suspension Bridge Visitor Centre Bridge House, Sion
Place, Bristol, BS8 4AP Tel: 0117-974-4664 Fax: 0117-974-5255
Email: visitinfo@clifton-suspension-bridge.org.uk WWW:
www.clifton-suspension-bridge.org.uk
Exploratory Hands on Science Centre Bristol Old Station, Temple
Meads, Bristol, BS1 6QU Tel: 0117-907-9000
Georgian House, Bristol 7 Great George Street, Bristol, BS1 5RR
Tel: 0117-921-1362
Harveys Wine Museum 12 Denmark Street, Bristol, BS1 5DQ
Tel: 0117-927-5036 Fax: 0117-927-5001
Email: alun.cox@adweu.com WWW: www.j-harvey.co.uk
Red Lodge Park Row, Bristol, BS1 5LJ Tel: 0117-921-1360
WWW: www.bristol-city.gov.uk/museums

Buckinghamshire
Amersham Local History Museum 49 High Street, Amersham,
Buckinghamshire, HP7 0DP Tel: 01494-725754 Fax: 01494-725754
The Blue Max Wycombe Air Park, Booker, Marlow
SL7 3DP Tel: 01494-449810
Buckinghamshire County Museum Church Street, Aylesbury,
Buckinghamshire, HP20 2QP Tel: 01296-331441
Fax: 01296-334884
Email: museums@buckscc.gov.uk
Chesham Town Museum Project Chesham Library, Elgiva Lane,
Chesham HP5 2JD Tel: 01494-783183
Chiltern Open Air Museum Newland Park, Gorelands Lane,
Chalfont St. Giles HP8 4AB Tel: 01494-871117 Fax: 01494-872774
Milton Keynes Museum Stacey Hill Farm, Southern Way,
Wolverton, Milton Keynes, MK12 5EJ Tel: 01908-316222
Pitstone and Ivinghoe Museum Society, Vicarage Road, Pitstone,
Leighton Buzzard LU7 9EY Tel: 01296 668123 WWW:
http://website.lineone.net/~pitstonemus, Pitstone Green Museum and
Ford End Watermill
Royal Army Education Corps Museum HQ Beaconsfield Station,
Wilton Park, Beaconsfield, Buckinghamshire, HP9 2RP Tel: 01494
683232
Wycombe Museum Priory Avenue, High Wycombe HP13 6PX
Tel: 01494-421895 Fax: 01494-421897
Email: enquiries@wycombemuseum.demon.co.uk WWW:
www.wycombe.gov.uk/museum
Cambridgeshire
Museum of Classical Archaeology
Sidgwick Avenue, Cambridge, CB3 9DA Tel: 01223 335153 WWW:
www.classics.cam.ac.uk/ark.html/, Open 10.00.a.m.-5.00.p.m. Mon-
Fri Year round also 10.00.a.m.-1.00.p.m. Term Time Admission Free
Cambridge Brass Rubbing The Round Church, Bridge St,
Cambridge, Cambridgeshire, CB2 1UB Tel: 01223-871621
Cambridge Museum of Technology Old Pumping Station,
Cheddars Lane, Cambridge, Cambridgeshire, CB5 8LD
Tel: 01223-368650
Cambridgeshire Regimental Collection Ely Museum, The Old
Goal, Market Street, Ely, Cambridgeshire, CB7 4LS
Tel: 01353-666655
Cromwell Museum, The Cromwell Museum, Huntingdon Tel:
01480 375830 Email: cromwellmuseum@cambridgeshire.gov.uk
WWW: http://edweb.camcnty.gov.uk/cromwell
The Denny Farmland Museum Denny Abbey, Ely Road,
Waterbeach, Cambridge, Cambridgeshire, CB5 9PQ
Tel: 01223-860988 Fax: 01223-860988 Email: f.h.denny@tesco.net
WWW: www.dennyfarmlandmuseum.org.uk
Duxford Displays Ltd Duxford Airfield, Duxford, Cambridge,
Cambridgeshire, CB2 4QR Tel: 01223-836593
Ely Museum, The Old Goal, Market Street, Ely CB7 4LS Tel:
01353-666655 includes Cambridge Regiment displays
Fenland & West Norfolk Aviation Museum
Lynn Road, West Walton, Wisbech PE14 7 Tel: 01945-584440
Folk Museum 2 Castle Street, Cambridge CB3 0AQ
Tel: 01223-355159
Imperial War Museum - Fighter Collection
Duxford Airfield, Duxford, Cambridge, CB2 4QR
Tel: 01223-834973, 01223-835000 Fax: 01223-836956
March & District Museum March & District Museum Society,
High Street, March, Cambridgeshire, PE15 9JJ Tel: 01354-655300

Nene Valley Railway Wansford Station, Peterborough, PE8 6LR Tel:
01780 782833
Norris Library & Museum The Broadway, St Ives,
Cambridgeshire, PE27 5BX Tel: 01480-497314
Email: norris.st-ives-tc@co-net.com
Octavia Hill Birthplace Museum Trust 1 South Brink Place,
WisbechPE13 1JE Tel: 01945-476358
Peterborough Museum & Art Gallery Priestgate, Peterborough,
Cambridgeshire, PE1 1LF Tel: 01733-343329 Fax: 01733-341928
Email: museums@peterborough.gov.uk
Prickwillow Drainage Engine Museum Main Street, Prickwillow,
Ely CB7 4UN Tel: 01353-688360
Ramsey Rural Museum
The Woodyard, Wood Lane, Ramsey, Huntingdon, Cambridgeshire,
PE17 1XD Tel: 01487-815715
Sedgwick Museum University of Cambridge, Downing Street,
Cambridge, CB2 3EQ Tel: 01223-333456
Email: mgd2@esc.cam.ac.uk
Wisbech & Fenland Museum Museum Square, Wisbech PE13 1ES
Tel: 01945-583817 Fax: 01945-589050
Email: wisbechmuseum.@beeb.net
Duxford Aviation Society Duxford Airfield, Duxford CB2 4QR
Tel: 01223-835594

Cheshire
Catalyst Gossage Building, Mersey Road, Widnes, Cheshire, WA8
0DF Tel: 0151-420-1121
Cheshire Military Museum (Cheshire Regiment)
The Castle, Chester, Cheshire, CH1 2DN Tel: 01244-327617
Chester Heritage Centre - Closed August 2000
St. Michaels Church, Bridge Street, Chester CH1 1NQ
The Boat Museum & David Owen Waterways Archive
South Pier Road, Ellesmere Port, CH65 4FW Tel: 0151-355-5017
Email: boatmuseum@easynet.co.uk Records relating to the
management, maintenance and operation of inland waterways inE
ngland, Scotland and Wales. Substantial Waterways library. Date
range: late 17th century to 20th century
Grosvenor Museum 27 Grosvenor Street, Chester CH1 2DD
Tel: 01244-402008 Fax: 01244-347587
Email: s.rogers@chestercc.gov.uk WWW:
www.chestercc.gov.uk/heritage/museum
Lion Salt Works Trust
Ollershaw Lane, Marston, Northwich CW9 6ES Tel: 01606-41823
Fax: 01606-41823 Email: afielding@lionsalt.demon.co.uk
WWW: www.lionsaltworkstrust.co.uk
Macclesfield Museums Heritage Centre, Roe Street, Macclesfield,
Cheshire, SK11 6UT Tel: 01625-613210 Fax: 01625-617880
Email: postmaster@silk-macc.u-net.com
Nantwich Museum Pillory Street, Nantwich, CW5 5BQ
Tel: 01270-627104
Norton Priory Museum Trust Ltd Tudor Road, Manor Park,
Runcorn WA7 1SX Tel: 01928-569895
On The Air 42 Bridge St Row, Chester CH1 1NN
Tel: 01244-348468
Paradise Mill Park Lane, Macclesfield SK11 6TJ
Tel: 01625-618228
Warrington Museum & Art Gallery Bold Street, Warrington WA1
1JG Tel: 01925-442392
West Park Museum Prestbury Road, Macclesfield SK10 3BJ
Tel: 01625-619831
Wirral Archives Service and Museum Birkenhead Town Hall,
Hamilton Street, Birkenhead, CH41 5BR Tel: 0151-666-4010
Fax: 0151-666-3965 Email: archives@wirral-libraries.net

Cleveland
Captain Cook & Staithes Heritage Centre High Street, Staithes,
Saltburn-by-the-Sea TS13 5BQ Tel: 01947-841454
Captain Cook Birthplace Museum Stewart Park, Marton,
Middlesbrough TS7 8AT Tel: 01642-311211
Dorman Musuem Linthorpe Road, Middlesbrough TS5 6LA
Tel: 01642-813781
Green Dragon Museum Theatre Yard, High St, Stockton-on-Tees,
Cleveland, TS18 1AT Tel: 01642-393938
Margrove Heritage Centre Margrove Park, Boosbeck,
Saltburn-by-the-Sea TS12 3BZ Tel: 01287-610368
Fax: 01287-610368
North East Mills Group Research into wind and water mills in NE
England Blackfriars, Monk Street, Newcastle upon Tyne, NE1 4XN
Tel: 0191-232-9279 Fax: 0191-230-1474
WWW: www.welcome.to/North.East.Mill.Group
Preston Hall Museum Yarm Road, Stockton-On-Tees TS18 3RH
Tel: 01642-781184
Stockton on Tees Museums & Gallery Service Gloucester House,
Church Road Cleveland, TS18 1YB Tel: 01642-393983
Fax: 01642-393983
The Tom Leonard Mining Experience, Deepdale, Skinningrove,
Saltburn TS13 4AA Tel: 01287 642877

Cornwall
Automobilia The Old Mill, Terras Rd, St. Austell PL26 7RX
Tel: 01726-823092
Bodmin Museum Mount Folly, Bodmin PL31 2DB
Tel: 01208-77067
Cable & Wireless Archive & Museum of Submarine Telegraphy Eastern
House,, Porthcurno, St. Levan, Penzance, Cornwall, TR19 6
Tel: 01736-810478/810811 Fax: 01736-810640
Email: mary.godwin@plc.cwplc.com
WWW: www.porthcurno.org.uk
Charlestown Shipwreck & Heritage Centre Quay Road,
Charlestown, St. Austell, Cornwall, PL25 3NX Tel: 01726-69897
Fax: 01726-68025
Duke of Cornwall's Light Infantry Museum, The Keep, Bodmin,
PL31 1EG Tel: 01208 72810 Fax: 01208 72810 Email:
dclimis@talk21.com WWW: www.britrishlightinfantry.org.ca
Helston Folk Museum Market Place, Helston, Cornwall, TR13 8TH
Tel: 01326-564027 Email: enquiries@helstonmuseum.org.uk
WWW: www.helstonmuseum.org.uk
John Betjeman Centre Southern Way, Wadebridge PL27 7BX
Tel: 01208-812392
Lanreath Folk & Farm Museum Lanreath, Nr Looe PL13 2NX
Tel: 01503-220321
Lawrence House Museum c/o Lawrence House, 9 Castle Street,
Launceston, Cornwall, PL15 8BA Tel: 01566-773277
Maritime Museum Penzance 19 Chapel Street, Penzance TR18
4AW Tel: 01736-368890
Merlin's Cave Crystal Mineral & Fossil Museum & Shop
Molesworth Street, Tintagel PL34 0BZ Tel: 01840-770023
Mevagissey Museum Society Frazier Ho, The Quay, Mevagissey, St.
Austell, Cornwall PL26 6QU Tel: 01726-843568
National Maritime Museum (Falmouth Cornwall) 48 Arwenack
Street, Falmouth TR11 3SA Tel: 01326-313388
National Maritime Museum (Saltash Cornwall) Cotehele Quay,
Cotehele, Saltash PL12 6TA Tel: 01579-350830
Penryn Museum Town Hall, Higher Market Street, Penryn TR10
8LT Tel: 01326-372158 Fax: 01326-373004
Potter's Museum of Curiosity Jamaica Inn Courtyard, Bolventor,
Launceston, Cornwall, PL15 7TS Tel: 01566-86838
Fax: 01566-86838
Royal Cornwall Museum River Street, Truro, Cornwall, TR1 2SJ
Tel: 01872-272205

County Durham
Bowes Museum Newgate, Barnard Castle DL12 8NP
Tel: 01833-690606
Darlington Museum & Art Gallery - Closed Collection dispersed
throughout other agencies in Darlington, Tubwell Row, Darlington
DL1 1PD Tel: 01325-463795
Darlington Railway Centre & Museum North Road Station ,
Station Road, Darlington, DL3 6ST Tel: 01325-460532
Darlington Railway Preservation Society Station Road, Hopetown,
Darlington DL3 6ST Tel: 01325-483606
Discovery Centre Grosvenor House, 29 Market Place, Bishop
Auckland DL14 7NP Tel: 01388-662666 Fax: 01388-661941
Email: west.durham@groundwork.org.uk
Durham Arts Library and Museums Department, County Hall,
Durham, County Durham, DH1 STY Tel: 0191-383-3595
Durham Heritage Centre St Mary le Bow, North Bailey, Durham
DH1 5ET
Durham Light Infantry Museum, Aykley Heads, Durham DH1
5TU Tel: 0191-384-2214 Fax: 0191-386-1770 Email:
dli@durham.gov.uk WWW: www.durham.gov.uk/dli
Durham Mining Museum Easington Colliery Welfare, Memorial
Road, Easington Tel: 07931 421709 WWW: www.dmm.org.uk
Durham University Library Archives & Special Collections Palace Green
Section, Palace Green, Durham, DH1 3RN Tel: 0191-374-3032
Email: pg.library@durham.ac.uk
Fulling Mill Museum of Archaeology The Banks, Durham,
Killhope Lead Mining Centre Cowshill, Weardale, County Durham,
DL13 1AR Tel: 01388-537505 Fax: 01388-537617
Email: killhope@durham.gov.uk
WWW: www.durham.gov.uk/killhope/index.htm
North East Mills Group Blackfriars, Monk Street, Newcastle upon
Tyne, NE1 4XN Tel: 0191-232-9279 Fax: 0191-230-1474
WWW: www.welcome.to/North.East.Mill.Group
Timothy Hackworth Victorian & Railway Museum Shildon DL4
1PQ Tel: 01388-777999 Fax: 01388-777999
Weardale Museum South View, 2 Front Street, Ireshopeburn, County
Durham, DL13 1EY Tel: 01388-537417

Cumbria
Aspects of Motoring Western Lakes Motor Museum The Maltings,
The Maltings, Brewery Lane, Cockermouth, Cumbria, CA13 9ND
Tel: 01900-824448
Border Regiment & Kings Own Royal Border Regiment Museum, Queen
Mary's Tower, The Castle, Carlisle CA3 8UR Tel: 01228 532774 Fax: 01228
521275 Email: rhq@kingsownborder.demon.co.uk WWW:

www.armymuseums.org, Museum devoted to the history of Cumbria's County
Infantry Regiment 1702 to date, with information on Regular, Territorial
Volunteer and Militia units associated with the Regiment. Extensive archives
The Dock Museum North Road, Barrow-In-Furness, Cumbria, LA14
2PW Tel: 01229-894444 WWW: www.barrowbc.gov.uk
Dove Cottage & The Wordsworth Museum Town End, Grasmere,
Ambleside LA22 9SH Tel: 015394-35544
The Guildhall Museum Green Market, Carlisle CA3 8JE
Tel: 01228-819925
Haig Colliery Mining Museum Solway Road, Kells, Whitehaven
CA28 9BG Tel: 01946-599949 Fax: 01946-61896
WWW: www.haigpit.com
Friends of The Helena Thompson Museum, 24 Calva Brow,
Workington CA14 1DD Tel: 01900 603312
Lakeside & Haverthwaite Railway Haverthwaite Station, Ulverston,
LA12 8A Tel 01539 531594
Keswick Museum & Art Gallery Station Road, Keswick, Cumbria,
CA12 4NF Tel: 017687-73263 Fax: 017687-80390
Email: hazel.davison@allerdale.gov.uk
Lakeland Motor Museum Holker Hall, Cark In Cartmel,
Grange-Over-Sands LA11 7PL Tel: 015395-58509
Laurel & Hardy Museum 4c Upper Brook Street, Ulverston,
Cumbria, LA12 7BH Tel: 01229-582292
Maryport Steamship Museum Elizabeth Dock South Quay,
Maryport CA15 8AB Tel: 01900-815954
North Pennines Heritage Trust, Nenthead Mines Heritage Centre,
Nenthead, Alston CA9 3PD Tel: 01434 382037 Fax: 01434 382294
Email: administration.office@virgin.net WWW: www.npht.com
Penrith Museum Middlegate, Penrith CA11 7PT Tel: 01768-212228
Fax: 01768-867466 Email: museum@eden.gov.uk
Roman Army Museum Carvoran House, Greenhead, Carlisle CA6
7JB Tel: 016977-47485
Ruskin Museum
Coniston Institute, Yewdale Road, Coniston LA21 8DU
Tel: 015394-41164 Fax: 015394-41132
WWW: www.coniston.org.uk
Senhouse Roman Museum The Battery, Sea Brows, Maryport CA15
6JD Tel: 01900-816168
Solway Aviation Museum Carlisle Airport, Carlisle CA6 4NW
Tel: 01228-573823
Tullie House Museum & Art Gallery Castle Street, Carlisle CA3
8TP Tel: 01228-534781 Fax: 01228-810249
Ulverston Heritage Centre Lower Brook Street, Ulverston LA12
7EE Tel: 01229-580820 Fax: 01229-580820
Email: heritage@tower-house.demon.co.uk
WWW: www.rootsweb.com/~ukuhc/
William Creighton Mineral Museum & Gallery
2 Crown Street, Cockermouth CA13 0EJ Tel: 01900-828301
Fax: 01900-828001
Windermere Steamboat Museum Rayrigg Road, Windermere LA23
1BN Tel: 015394-45565 Fax: 015394-48769 WWW:
www.steamboat.co.uk

Derbyshire
Chesterfield Museum & Art Gallery No archive or library material
held., St Mary's Gate, Chesterfield S41 7TY Tel: 01246-345727
Derby Industrial Museum Silk Mill Lane, Derby DE1 3AR
Tel: 01332-255308
Derby Museum & Art Gallery The Strand, Derby DE1 1BS
Tel: 01332-716659 Fax: 01332-716670 WWW:
www.derby.gov.uk/museums
Derwent Valley Visitor Centre Belper North Mill, Bridge Foot,
Belper DE56 1YD Tel: 01773-880474
Donington Grandprix Collection Donington Park, Castle Donington
DE74 2RP Tel: 01332-811027
Donington Park Racing Ltd
Donington Park, Castle Donnington DE74 2RP Tel: 01332-814697
Elvaston Castle Estate Museum Elvaston Castle Country Park,
Borrowash Road, Elvaston, Derby DE72 3EP Tel: 01332-573799
Erewash Museum The Museum, High Street, Ilkeston, DE7 5JA
Tel: 0115-907-1141 Email: erewashmuseum@free4all.co.uk WWW:
www.erewash.gov.uk
Eyam Museum Eyam Museum Ltd, Hawkhill Road, Hope Valley,
Eyam, S32 5QP Tel: 01433-631371 Fax: 01433-630777
WWW: www.cressbrook.co.uk/eyam/museum
Glossop Heritage Centre Bank House, Henry Street, Glossop SK13
8BW Tel: 01457-869176
High Peak Junction Workshop High Peak Junction, Cronford,
Matlock DE4 5HN Tel: 01629-822831
High Peak Trail Middleton Top,, Rise End, Middleton, Matlock,
Derbyshire, DE4 4LS Tel: 01629-823204
Midland Railway Centre Butterley Station, Ripley DE5 3QZ
Tel: 01773-570140
Peak District Mining Museum Pavilion, South Parade, Matlock
DE4 3NR Tel: 01629-583834
Pickford's House Museum 41 Friar Gate, Derby DE1 1DA
Tel: 01332-255363 Fax: 01332-255277

Regimental Museum of the 9th/12th Royal Lancers, Derby City Museum and Art Gallery, The Strand, Derby DE1 1BS Tel: 01332 716656 Fax: 01332 716670 Email: diana.pealie@derby.gov.uk WWW: www.derby.gov.uk/museums
National Stone Centre Porter Lane, Wirksworth, Matlock DE4 4LS Tel: 01629-824833

Devon
Bill Douglas Centre for the History of Cinema and Popular Culture, University of Exeter, Queen's Building, Queen's Drive, Exeter EX4 4QH Tel: 01392 264321 WWW: www.ex.ac.uk/bill.douglas
Century of Playtime
30 Winner Street, Paignton TQ3 3BJ Tel: 01803-553850
The Dartmouth Museum The Butterwalk, Dartmouth TQ6 9PZ Tel: 01803-832923
Devon & Cornwall Constabulary Museum Middlemoor, Exeter, Devon, EX2 7HQ Tel: 01392-203025
Devonshire and The Devonshire and Dorset Regiment Archives, Wyvern Barracks, Barrack Road, Exeter EX2 6AE Tel: 01392 492436 Fax: 01392 492469
Dunkeswell Memorial Museum Dunkeswell Airfield, Dunkeswell Ind Est, Dunkeswell, Honiton, Devon, EX14 0RA Tel: 01404-891943
Fairlynch Art Centre & Museum
27 Fore Street, Budleigh Salterton EX9 6NP Tel: 01395-442666
Finch Foundary Museum of Rural Industry
Sticklepath, Okehampton EX20 2NW Tel: 01837-840046
Ilfracombe Museum
Wilder Road, Ilfracombe EX34 8AF Tel: 01271-863541
The Keep Military Museum
Bridport Road, Dorchester, Dorset, DT1 1RN Tel: 01305-264066
Email: keep.museum@talk21.com
WWW: www.keepmilitarymuseum.org
Museum of Barnstaple & Devon incorporating Royal Devon Yeomanry Museum The Square, Barnstaple, Devon, EX32 8LN Tel: 01271-346747 Email: admin@sal.org.uk
The Museum of Dartmoor Life, West Street, Okehampton EX20 1HQ Tel: 01837 52295 Fax: 01837 659330 Email: dartmoormuseum@eclipse.co.uk WWW: www.museumofdartmoorlife.eclipse.co.uk
Newton Abbot Town & Great Western Railway Museum
2A St. Pauls Road, Newton Abbot TQ12 2HP Tel: 01626-201121
North Devon Maritime Museum Odun House, Odun Road, Appledore, Bideford, Devon, EX39 1PT Tel: 01237-422064 Fax: 01237-422064
WWW: www.devonmuseums.net/appledore
North Devon Museum Service St.Anne's Chapel, Paternoster Row, Barnstaple, Devon, EX32 8LN Tel: 01271-378709
Otterton Mill Centre Otterton, Budleigh Salterton, Devon, EX9 7HG Tel: 01395-568521
Plymouth City Museum Drake Circus, Plymouth, Devon, PL4 8AJ Tel: 01752-304774
Royal Albert Memorial Museum Queen Street, Exeter, Devon, EX4 3RX Tel: 01392-265858
Seaton Tramway Harbour Road, Seaton EX12 7NQ Tel: 01297 20375 Email: info@tram.co.uk WWW: www.tram.co.uk
Sidmouth Museum Hope Cottage, Church St, Sidmouth EX10 8LY Tel: 01395-516139
Teignmouth Museum 29 French Street, Teignmouth, Devon, TQ14 8ST Tel: 01626-777041
Allhallows Museum of Lace & Antiquities High Street, Honiton EX14 1PG Tel: 01404-44966 Fax: 01404-46591
Email: dyateshoniton@msn.com
WWW: www.honitonlace.com
Newhall Visitor & Equestrian Centre Newhall, Budlake, Exeter EX5 3LW Tel: 01392-462453
Park Pharmacy Trust Thorn Park Lodge, Thorn Park , Mannamead, Plymouth, Devon , PL3 4TF Tel: 01752-263501

Dorset
Bournemouth Aviation Museum Hanger 600 South East Sector, Bournemouth International Airport Hurn, Christchurch, Dorset, BH23 6SE Tel: 01202-580858 Fax: 01202-580858
Bridport Harbour Museum
West Bay, Bridport, Dorset, DT6 4SA Tel: 01308-420997
Cavalcade of Costume Lime Tree House, The Plocks, Blandford Forum, Dorset, DT11 7AA Tel: 01258-453006
Christchurch Motor Museum Matchams Lane, Hurn, Christchurch BH23 6AW Tel: 01202-488100
Dinosaur Land Coombe Street, Lyme Regis DT7 3PY Tel: 01297-443541
The Dinosaur Museum Icen Way, Dorchester DT1 1EW Tel: 01305-269880 Fax: 01305-268885
Dorset County Museum and Library 66 High West Street, Dorchester DT1 1XA Tel: 01305-262735 Fax: 01305-257180 Email: dorsetcountymuseum@dor-mus.demon.co.uk
The Keep Military Museum, The Keep, Bridport Road, Dorchester

DT1 1RN Tel: 01305 264066 Fax: 01305 250373 Email: keep.museum@talk21.com WWW: www.keepmilitarymuseum.org CC accepted

Lyme Regis Philpot Museum Bridge Street, Lyme Regis DT7 3QA Tel: 01297-443370 Email: info@lymeregismuseum.co.uk
Nothe Fort Barrack Road, Weymouth DT4 8UF Tel: 01305-787243
Portland Museum Wakeham, Portland, Dorset, DT5 1HS Tel: 01305-821804
Priest's House Museum 23-27 High St. Wimborne BH21 1HR Tel: 01202-882533
Red House Museum & Gardens Quay Rd, Christchurch BH23 1BU Tel: 01202-482860
Royal Signals Museum, Blandford Camp, Nr Blandford Forum DT11 8RH Tel: 01258-482248 Tel: 01258-482267 Fax: 01258-482084 WWW: www.royalsignalsarmy.org.uk/museum/
Russell-Cotes Art Gallery & Museum
East Cliff, Bournemouth BH1 3AA Tel: 01202-451800
Shelley Rooms Museum at: Shelley Park, Beechwood Ave, Bournemouth BH5 1NE, Russell Cotes Art Gallery & Museum (Correspondence address), (Reference Shelley Rooms), East Cliff, Bournemouth, BH1 3AA Tel: 01202-451800 Fax: 01202-451851 Email: dedge@russell-cotes.demon.co.uk WWW: www.russell-cotes.bournemouth.gov.uk
Sherborne Museum Association Abbey Gate House, Church Avenue, Sherborne, Dorset, DT9 3BP Tel: 01935-812252
Tank Museum, Bovington, BH20 6JG Tel: 01929 405096 Fax: 01929 462410 Email: librarian@tankmuseum.co.uk and davidw@tankmuseum.co.uk WWW: www.tankmuseum.co.uk
Wareham Town Museum 5 East Street, Wareham BH20 4NN Tel: 01929-553448
Waterfront Museum and Local Studies Centre 4 High Street, Poole BH15 1BW Tel: 01202-683138 Fax: 01202-660896 Email: museums@poole.gov.uk WWW: www.poole.gov.uk
Weymouth & Portland Museum Service The Esplanade, Weymouth DT4 8ED Tel: 01305-765206
Shaftesbury Abbey Museum & Garden Park Walk, Shaftesbury SP7 8JR Tel: 01747-852910
Shaftesbury Town Museum Gold Hill, Shaftesbury SP7 8JW Tel: 01747-852157
Dorset – West Dorset
West Dorset Museums Service The Coach House, Grundy Lane, Bridport DT6 3RJ Tel: 01308-458703 Fax: 01308-458704 Email: j.burrell@westdorset-dc.gov.uk

Essex
Barleylands Farm Museum & Visitors Centre
Barleylands Farm, Billericay CM11 2UD Tel: 01268-282090
Battlesbridge Motorcycle Museum The
Muggeridge Farm, Maltings Road, Battlesbridge, Wickford, SS11 7RF Tel: 01268-560866
Castle Point Transport Museum Society
105 Point Road, Canvey Island SS8 7TJ Tel: 01268-684272
East England Tank Museum Oak Business Park, Wix Road, Beaumont, Clacton-On-Sea, CO16 0AT Tel: 01255-871119
Epping Forest District Museum
39-41 Sun Street, Waltham Abbey EN9 1EL Tel: 01992-716882
Essex Police Museum
Police Headquarters, PO Box 2, Springfield, Chelmsford, Essex, CM2 6DA Tel: 01245-491491 x50771 Fax: 01245-452456
Essex Regiment Museum, Oaklands Park, Moulsham Street, Chelmsford CM2 9AQ Tel: 01245 615101 Fax: 01245 611250 Email: pompadour@chelsfordbc.gov.uk WWW: http://www.chelmsfordbc.gov.uk Substantial database of Essex service people from 1741. Family inquiries welcomed. Donations please to The Trustee of the Essex Regiment Museum
Essex Secret Bunker Crown Building, Shrublands Road, Mistley, Essex, CO11 1HS Tel: 01206-392271 (24hr info)
Harlow Museum Passmores House, Third Avenue, Harlow CM18 6YL Tel: 01279-454959
Hollytrees Museum High Street, Colchester CO1 1DN Tel: 01206-282940
Kelvedon Hatch Secret Nuclear Bunker, Kelvedon Hall Lane, Kelvedon Common, Kelvedon Hatch, Brentwood CM15 0LB Tel: 01277 364883 Fax: 01277 372562 Email: bunker@japar.demon.co.uk WWW: www.japar.demon.co.uk Visitor Access via A128
Leigh Heritage Centre & Museum
c/o 13a High Street, Leigh-On-Sea, Essex, SS9 2EN Tel: 01702-470834 Email: palmtree@northdell.demon.co.uk
LB of Barking & Dagenham Local History Studies - Dagenham Valence Library & Museum, Becontree Avenue, Dagenham, Essex, RM8 3HT Tel: 020-8592-6537 Fax: 020-8227-5297 Email: fm019@viscount.org.uk WWW: www.earl.org.uk/partners/barking/index.html
Maldon District Museum 47 Mill Road, Maldon CM9 5HX Tel: 01621-842688
Mark Hall Cycle Museum Muskham Road, Harlow CM20 2LF Tel: 01279-439680

National Motorboat Museum Wattyler Country Park, Pitsea Hall Lane, Pitsea, Basildon, Essex, SS16 4UH Tel: 01268-550077 Fax: 01268-581903

Saffron Walden Museum Museum Street, Saffron Walden CB10 1JL Tel: 01799-510333 Fax: 01799-510333 Email: museum@uttlesford.gov.uk

Southend Central Museum Victoria Avenue, Southend-On-Sea, Essex, SS2 6EW Tel: 01702-434449 Fax: 01702-34980

The Cater Museum 74 High Street, Billericay, Essex, CM12 9BS Tel: 01277-622023

Valence House Museum Becontree Avenue, Dagenham RM8 3HS Tel: 020-8227-5293 Fax: 020-8227-5293 Email: valencehousemuseum@hotmail.com

Chelmsford & Essex Museum Oaklands Park, Moulsham St, Chelmsford CM2 9AQ Tel: 01245-615100 Fax: 01245-611250 Email: oaklands@chelmsford.gov.uk

Gloucestershire

Chepstow Museum
Bridge Street, Chepstow, Monmouthshire, NP16 5EZ Tel: 01291-625981 Fax: 01291-635005 Email: chepstowmuseum@monmouthshire.gov.uk

Dean Heritage Centre Soudley, Cinderford, Forest of Dean GL14 2UB Tel: 01594-822170 Fax: 01594-823711 Email: deanmus@btinternet.com

Frenchay Tuckett Society and Local History Museum, 247 Frenchay Park Road, Frenchay BS16 ILG Tel: 0117 956 9324 Email: raybulmer@compuserve.com WWW: www.frenchay.org/museum.html

Gloucester City Museum & Art Gallery
Brunswick Road, Gloucester GL1 1HP Tel: 01452-524131

Gloucester Folk Museum 99-103 Westgate Street, Gloucester GL1 2PG Tel: 01452-526467 Fax: 01452-330495 Email: ChristopherM@glos.city.gov.uk

Guild of Handicraft Trust The Silk Mill, Sheep St, Chipping Campden GL55 6DS Tel: 01386-841417

Holst Birthplace Museum
4 Clarence Road, Cheltenham GL52 2AY Tel: 01242-524846 Fax: 01242-580182

The Jenner Museum
Church Lane, Berkeley GL13 9BN Tel: 01453-810631

John Moore Countryside Museum 42 Church Street, Tewkesbury GL20 5SN Tel: 01684-297174

National Waterways Museum Llanthony Warehouse, Gloucester Docks, Gloucester, GL1 2EH Tel: 01452-318054 Email: curatorial1@nwm.demon.co.uk WWW: www.nwm.demon.uk

Nature In Art Wallsworth Hall, Tewkesbury Road, Twigworth, Gloucester, Gloucestershire, GL2 9PG Tel: 01452-731422 Email: ninart@globalnet.co.uk WWW: www.nature-in-art.org.uk

Regiments Of Gloucestershire Museum
Gloucester Docks, Gloucester GL1 2HE Tel: 01452-522682

Robert Opie Collection Albert Warehouse, The Docks, Gloucester, Gloucestershire, GL1 2EH Tel: 01452-302309

Shambles Museum 20 Church Street, Newent GL18 1PP Tel: 01531-822144

Soldiers of Gloucestershire Museum, Gloucester Docks, Commercial Road, Gloucester GL1 2EH Tel: 01452 522682 Fax: 01452 311116

The Great Western Railway Museum (Coleford) The Old Railway Station, Railway Drive, Coleford, Gloucestershire, GL16 8RH Tel: 01594-833569, 01954-832032 Fax: 01594-832032

Hampshire

The Museum of The Adjutant General's Corps, RHQ Adjutant General's Corps, Worthy Down, Winchester SO21 2RG Tel: 01962 887435 Fax: 01962 887690 Email: agc.regtsec@virgin.net, inc the Royal Army Pay Corps, The Royal Army educational corps the Army Legal Corps and part of the collections of the Royal Military Police, The Military Provost Staff Corps and the Women's Royal Army Corps

Airborne Forces Museum Browning Barracks, Aldershot, Hampshire, GU11 2BU Tel: 01252-349619 Fax: 01252-349203

Aldershot Military Historical Trust Evelyn Woods Road, Aldershot, Hampshire, GU11 2LG Tel: 01252-314598 Fax: 01252-342942

Aldershot Military Museum, Queens Avenue, Aldershot GU11 2LG Tel: 01252-314598 Fax: 01252-342942 Email: musim@hants.gov.uk WWW: www.hants.gov.uk/museum/aldershot

Andover Museum & Iron Age Museum 6 Church Close, Andover SP10 1DP Tel: 01264-366283 Fax: 01264-339152 Email: andover.museum@virgin.net or musmda@hants.gov.uk WWW: www.hants.gov.uk/andoverm

Army Medical Services Museum, Keogh Barracks, Ash Vale, Aldershot GU12 5RQ Tel: 01252 868612 Fax: 01252 868832 Email: museum@keogh72.freeserve.co.uk Archives on the Army Medical Services inc doctors, vetinary surgeons, dentists and some nurses CC accepted

Army Physical Training Corps Museum, ASPT, Fox Line, Queen's Avenue, Aldershot GU11 2LB Tel: 01252 347168 Fax: 01252 340785 Email: regtsec@aptc.org.uk WWW: www.aptc.org.uk

The Bear Museum 38 Dragon Street, Petersfield GU31 4JJ Tel: 01730-265108 Email: judy@bearmuseum.freeserve.co.uk WWW: www.bearmuseum.co.uk

Bishops Waltham Museum & Trust Brook Street, Bishops Waltham SO32 1EB Trust:- 8 Folly Field, Bishop's Waltham, Southampton, SO32 1EB Tel: 01489-894970

Eastleigh Museum 25 High Street, Eastleigh SO50 5LF Tel: 02380-643026 Email: musmst@hants.gov.uk WWW: www.hants.gov.uk/museum/eastlmus/index.html

Eling Tide Mill Trust Ltd The Tollbridge, Eling Hill, Totton, Southampton, Hampshire, SO40 9HF Tel: 023-8086-9575

Gosport Museum Walpole Road, Gosport PO12 1NS Tel: 023-9258-8035 Fax: 023-9250-1951 Email: musmie@hants.gov.uk

The Gurkha Museum, Peninsula Barracks, Romsey Road, Winchester SO23 8TS Tel: 01962 842832 Fax: 01962 877597 Email: curator@thegurkhamuseum.co.uk WWW: www.thegurkhamuseum.co.uk CC accepted The museum tells the dramatic story of service to the British Crown and people between 1815 and the present day.

Hampshire County Museums Service Chilcomb House, Chilcomb Lane, Winchester SO23 8RD Tel: 01962-846304

Havant Museum, Havant Museum, 56 East Street, Havant P09 1BS Tel: 023 9245 1155 Fax: 023 9249 8707 Email: musmop@hants.gov.uk WWW: www.hants.gov.uk/museums Also Friends of Havant Museum - Local History Section Local Studies Collection open Tuesday to Saturday 10.00.a.m. to 5.00.p.m.

HMS Warrior (1860) Victory Gate, HM Naval Base, Portsmouth PO1 3QX Tel: 02392-778600 Fax: 02392-778601 Email: info@hmswarrior.org WWW: www.hmswarrior.org

Hollycombe Steam Collection Iron Hill, Midhurst Rd, Liphook GU30 7LP Tel: 01428-724900

The King's Royal Hussars Museum (10th Royal Hussars PWO 11th Hussars PAO and Royal Hussars PWO), Peninsula Barracks, Romsey Road, Winchester SO23 8TS Tel: 01962 828540 Fax: 01962 828538 Email: beresford@krhmuseum.freeserve.co.uk WWW: www.hants.gov.uk/leisure/museum/royalhus/index.html

Light Infantry Museum Peninsula Barracks, Romsey Road, Winchester, Hampshire, SO23 8TS Tel: 01962 868550

Maritime Museum Southampton Bugle Street, Southampton SO14 2AJ Tel: 023-8022-3941

The Mary Rose Trust 1-10 College Road, HM Naval Base, Portsmouth, Hampshire, PO1 3LX Tel: 023-9275-0521

Museum of Army Flying Middle Wallop, Stockbridge SO20 8DY Tel: 01980-674421 Fax: 01264-781694 Email: daa@flyingmuseum.org.uk WWW: www.flying-museum.org.uk

New Forest Museum & Visitor Centre
High Street, Lyndhurst SO43 7NY Tel: (023)-8028-3194 Fax: (023)-8028-4236 Email: nfmuseum@lineone.net

Portsmouth City Museum & Record Office Museum Road, Portsmouth PO1 2LJ Tel: 023-9282-7261 Fax: 023-9287-5276 Email: portmus@compuserve.com WWW: ourworld.compuserve.com/homepages/portmus/

Priddy's Hard Armament Museum Priory Road, Gosport PO12 4LE Tel: 023-9250-2490

Queen Alexandra's Royal Army Nursing Corps Museum Regimental Headquarters Army Medica, Keogh Barracks, Ash Vale, Aldershot, Hampshire, GU12 5RQ

Rockbourne Roman Villa Rockbourne, Fordingbridge SP6 3PG Tel: 01725-518541

Royal Armouries Fort Nelson Down End Road, Fareham PO17 6AN Tel: 01329-233734 Fax: 01329-822092 WWW: www.armouries.org.uk

The Royal Green Jackets Museum (Oxford and Bucks Light Infantry King's Royal Rifle Corps and The Rifle Brigade), Peninsula Barracks, Romsey Road, Winchester SO23 8TS Tel: 01962 828549 Fax: 01962 828500

Royal Hampshire Regimental Museum, Serle's House, Southgate Street, Winchester, SO23 9EG Tel: 01962 863658 Fax: 01962 888302

Royal Marines Museum Archives & Library Eastney, Southsea PO4 9PX Tel: 02392-819385 Ext 224 Fax: 02392-838420 Email: mathewlittle@royalmarinesmuseum.co.uk WWW: www.royalmarinesmuseum.co.uk

Royal Naval Museum, H M Naval Base (PP66), Portsmouth PO1 3NH Tel: (023) 9272 3795 Fax: (023) 9272 3942 WWW: www.royalnavalmuseum.org

Royal Navy Submarine Museum, Haslar Jetty Road, Gosport, O12 2AS Tel: (023) 92510354 Fax: (023) 9251 1349 Email: admin@rnsubmus.co.uk WWW: www.rnsubmus.co.uk Archive and photographic library by prior appointment. Unique record of service of submarine personnel

Sammy Miller Motor Cycle Museum
Bashley Manor Farm, Bashley Cross Road, New Milton, BH25 5SZ Tel: 01425-620777

Search 50 Clarence Road, Gosport PO12 1BU Tel: 023-9250-1957
West End Local History Society, 20 Orchards Way, West End,
Southampton S030 3FB Tel: 023 8057 5244 Email:
westendlhs@aol.com WWW: www.telbin.demon.co.uk/westendlhs
Museum at Old Fire Station, High Street, West End
Westbury Manor Museum West Street, Fareham PO16 0JJ
Tel: 01329-824895 Fax: 01329-825917
Email: www.hants.co.uk/museum/westbury
Whitchurch Silk Mill 28 Winchester Street, Whitchurch RG28 7AL
Tel: 01256-892065
The Willis Museum Of Basingstoke Town & Country Life Old Town
Hall, Market Place, Basingstoke, Hampshire, RG21 7QD
Tel: 01256-465902 Fax: 01256-471455
Email: willismuseum@hotmail.com
WWW: www.hants.gov.uk/leisure/museums/willis/index.html
Winchester Museums Service 75 Hyde Street, Winchester SO23
7DW Tel: 01962-848269 Fax: 01962-848299
Email: museums@winchester.gov.uk WWW:
www.winchester.gov.uk/heritage/home.htm

Herefordshire
Churchill House Museum Venns Lane, Aylestone Hill, Hereford
HR1 1DE Tel: 01432-260693 Fax: 01432-267409
Cider Museum & King Offa Distillery 21 Ryelands Street,
Hereford, HR4 0LW Tel: 01432-354007 Fax: 01432-341641
Email: thompson@cidermuseum.co.uk WWW:
www.cidermuseum.co.uk
Leominster Museum Etnam Street, Leominster HR6 8
Tel: 01568-615186
Teddy Bears of Bromyard 12 The Square, Bromyard HR7 4BP
Tel: 01885-488329
Waterworks Museum 86 Park Street, Hereford, HR1 2RE
Tel: 01432-356653
Weobley & District Local History Society and Museum, Weobley
Museum, Back Lane, Weobley HR4 8SG Tel: 01544 340292

Hertfordshire
Bushey Museum and Art Gallery, Rudolph Road, Bushey WD23
3HW Tel: 020 8420 4057 1901 census
First Garden City Heritage Museum
296 Norton Way South, Letchworth Garden City, SG6 1SU
Tel: 01462-482710 Fax: 01462-486056
Email: egchm@letchworth.com
Hertford Museum (Hertfordshire Regiment), 18 Bull Plain,
Hertford SG14 1DT Tel: 01992 582686 Fax: 01992 534797 Email:
enquiries@hertfordmuseum.org WWW: www.hertfordmuseum.org
Hitchin British Schools 41-42 Queen Street, Hitchin SG4 9TS
Tel: 01462-452697
Hitchin Museum Paynes Park, Hitchin SG5 1EG Tel: 01462-434476
Fax: 01462-431316 Email: nhdc.gov.uk
Kingsbury Water Mill Museum
St. Michaels Street, St. Albans AL3 4SJ Tel: 01727-853502
Letchworth Museum & Art Gallery
Broadway, Letchworth SG6 3PF Tel: 01462-685647
Mill Green Museum & Mill Mill Green, Hatfield AL9 5PD
Tel: 01707-271362
Rhodes Memorial Museum & Commonwealth Centre South Road,
Bishop's Stortford CM23 3JG Tel: 01279-651746
Email: rhodesmuseum@freeuk.com
WWW: www.hertsmuseums.org.uk
Royston & District Museum 5 Lower King Street, Royston SG8
5AL Tel: 01763-242587
The De Havilland Aircraft Museum Trust P.O Box 107, Salisbury
Hall, London Colney, St. Albans, AL2 1EX Tel: 01727-822051
The Environmental Awareness Trust 23 High Street,
Wheathampstead, St. Albans AL4 8BB Tel: 01582-834580
The Forge Museum High Street, Much Hadham SG10 6BS
Tel: 01279-843301
Verulamium Museum St. Michaels Street, St. Albans AL3 4SW
Tel: 01727-751824 Fax: 01727-836282
Email: d.thorold@stalbans.gov.uk
The Walter Rothschild Zoological Museum Akeman Street, Tring
HP23 6AP Tel: 0207-942-6156 Fax: 0207-942-6150
Email: ornlib@nhm.ac.uk
WWW: www.nhm.ac.uk
Ware Museum Priory Lodge, 89 High Street, Ware SG12 9AD
Tel: 01920-487848
Watford Museum 194 High Street, Watford WD1 2DT
Tel: 01923-232297
Welwyn Hatfield Museum Service Welwyn Roman Baths,
By-Pass-Road, Welwyn, AL6 0 Tel: 01438-716096

Huntingdonshire
Peterborough Museum & Art Gallery
Priestgate, Peterborough PE1 1LF Tel: 01733-343329
Fax: 01733-341928 Email: museums@peterborough.gov.uk

Isle of Wight
Bembridge Maritime Museum & Shipwreck Centre
Providence House, Sherborne Street, Bembridge
Isle Of Wight, PO35 5SB Tel: 01983-872223
Calbourne Water Mill Calbourne Mill, Newport, PO30 4JN
Tel: 01983-531227
Carisbrooke Castle Museum Carisbrooke Castle, Newport PO30
1XY Tel: 01983-523112 Fax: 01983-532126
Email: carismus@lineone.net
East Cowes Heritage Centre 8 Clarence Road, East Cowes PO32
6EP Tel: 01983-280310
Front Line Britain at War Experience Sandown Airport, Scotchells
Brook Lane, Sandown, Isle Of Wight, PO36 0JP Tel: 01983-404448
Guildhall Museum – Newport, Isle of Wight High Street, Newport
PO30 1TY Tel: 01983-823366
The Lilliput Museum of Antique Dolls & Toy
High Street, Brading, Sandown PO36 0DJ Tel: 01983-407231
Email: lilliput.museum@btconnect.com WWW:
www.lilliputmuseum.co.uk
Natural History Centre High Street, Godshill, Ventnor PO38 3HZ
Tel: 01983-840333
The Classic Boat Museum Seaclose Wharf, Town Quay, Newport
PO30 2EF Tel: 01983-533493
Ventnor Heritage Museum 11 Spring Hill, Ventnor PO38 1PE
Tel: 01983-855407

Kent
Bethlem Royal Hospital Archives & Museum Monks Orchard
Road, Beckenham, Kent, BR3 3BX Fax: 020-8776-4045
Email: museum@bethlem.co.uk
Buffs Regimental Museum, The Royal Museum & Art Gallery, 18
High Street, Canterbury CT1 2RA Tel: 01227-452747 Fax: 01227-
455047 Email: museum@canterbury.gov.uk WWW: www.canterbury-
museums.co.uk Story of the Royal East Kent Regiment, The Buffs
and its worldwide service. Admission free.
Canterbury Roman Museum Butchery Lane, Canterbury CT1 2JR
Tel: 01227-785575
Chatham Dockyard Historical Society Museum
Likley to move 1/2/2001 to World Naval Base, Chatham, Cottage
Row, Barrack Road, Chatham Dockyard, Chatham, Kent, ME4 4TZ
Tel: 01634-844897, 01634-250647
Cobham Hall
Cobham DA12 3BL Tel: 01474-823371 Fax: 01474-822995
Dickens House Museum - Broadstairs 2 Victoria Parade,
Broadstairs CT10 1QS Tel: 01843-861232 Fax: 01843-862853
Dolphin Sailing Barge Museum Crown Quay Lane, Sittingbourne
ME10 3SN Tel: 01795-423215
Dover Castle Dover, Kent, CT16 1HU Tel: 01304-211067
Dover Museum Market Square, Dover, Kent, CT16 1PB
Tel: 01304-201066
Dover Transport Museum Old Park Barracks, Whitfield, Dover
CT16 2HQ Tel: 01304-822409
Drapers Museum of Bygones
4 High Street, Rochester ME1 1PT Tel: 01634-830647
Fleur de Lis Heritage Centre &Museum
13 Preston Street, Faversham ME13 8NS Tel: 01795-534542
Fax: 01795-533261
Email: faversham@btinternet.com
WWW: www.faversham.org
Guildhall Museum – Rochester, Kent High Street, Rochester, Kent,
ME1 1PY Tel: 01634-848717
Herne Bay Museum Centre 12 William Street, Herne Bay CT6 5EJ
Tel: 01227-367368
Hever Castle Hever, Nr Edenbridge TN8 7NG Tel: 01732-865224
Email: mail@hevercastle.co.uk WWW: www.hevercastle.co.uk
Kent Battle of Britain Museum Aerodrome Road, Hawkinge,
Folkestone CT18 7AG Tel: 01303-893140
Leeds Castle Maidstone, Kent, ME17 1PL Tel: 0870-600-8880 (Info
line) WWW: www.leeds-castle.co.uk
Maidstone Museum & Art Gallery St. Faith Street, Maidstone
ME14 1LH Tel: 01622-754497
Margate Old Town Hall Museum Old Town Hall, Market Place,
Margate CT9 1ER Tel: 01843-231213
Minster Abbey Gatehouse Museum
Union Road, Minster On Sea, Sheerness, Kent, ME12 2HW
Tel: 01795-872303
Minster Museum Craft & Animal Centre Bedlam Court Lane,
Minster, Ramsgate CT12 4HQ Tel: 01843-822312
Museum of Kent Life Cobtree, Lock Lane, Sandling, Maidstone
ME14 3AU Tel: 01622-763936 Fax: 01622-662024
Email: enquiries@museum-kentlife.co.uk
WWW: www.museum-kentlife.co.uk
Pembroke Lodge Museum & Family History Centre 2-6 Station
Approach, Birchington on Sea CT7 9RD ~Mail to: 4 Station
Approach, Birchington on Sea, Kent, CT7 9RD Tel: 01843-841649
Penshurst Place and Gardens Penshurst, Tonbridge TN11 8DG
Tel: 01892-870307 Fax: 01892-870866
Email: enquiries@penshurstplace.com WWW:

www.penshursrtplace.com

Powell-Cotton Museum Quex Park, Birchington, Kent, CT7 0 Tel: 01843-842168

Princess of Wales's Royal Regt & Queen's Regt Museum, Howe Barracks, Canterbury CT1 1JY Tel: 01227-818056 Fax: 01227-818057 Covers Infantry Regiements of Surrey, Kent, Sussex, Hampshire and Middlesex

The Queen's Own Royal West Kent Regiment Museum, Maidstone Museum and Art Gallery, St. Faith's Street, Maidstone ME14 1LH Tel: 01622 754497 Fax: 01622 602193

Romney Toy & Model Museum The Romney, Hythe & Dymchurch Railway New Romney Station, Romney TN28 8PL Tel: 01797 362353

Royal Engineers Library, Brompton Barracks, Chatham ME4 4UX Tel: 01634 822416 Fax: 01634 822419

Royal Engineers Museum Prince Arthur Road, Gillingham, Kent, ME4 4UG Tel: 01634-406397 Fax: 01634-822371 Email: remuseum.rhgre@gtnet.gov.uk WWW: www.army.mod.uk/army/museums

Royal Museum & Art Gallery 18 High Street, Canterbury, Kent, CT1 2RA Tel: 01227-452747

Sheerness Heritage Centre
10 Rose Street, Sheerness, Kent, ME12 1AJ Tel: 01795-663317

Squerryes Court Westerham, Kent, TN16 1SJ Tel: 01959-562345/563118

Tenterden Museum Station Road, Tenterden, Kent, TN30 6HN Tel: 01580-764310 Fax: 01580-766648

The C.M Booth Collection Of Historic Vehicles 63-67 High Street, Rolvenden, Cranbrook, Kent, TN17 4LP Tel: 01580-241234

The Charles Dickens Centre Eastgate House, High Street, Rochester, Kent, ME1 1EW Tel: 01634-844176

Victoriana Museum The Deal Town Hall, High Street, Deal, Kent, CT14 6BB Tel: 01304-380546

Watts Charity Poor Travellers House, 97 High Street, Rochester ME1 1LX Tel: 01634-845609

West Kent Regimental Museum Maidstone, Kent

Whitstable Museum & Gallery 5a Oxford Street, Whitstable CT5 1DB Tel: 01227-276998

Maritime Museum Ramsgate Clock House, Pier Yard, Royal Harbour, RamsgateCT11 8LS Tel: 01843-587765 Email: museum@ekmt.fsnet.co.uk WWW: www.ekmt.fsnet.co.uk

Masonic Library & Museum St. Peters Place, Canterbury CT1 2DA Tel: 01227-785625

Lancashire

Blackburn Museum & Art Gallery Museum Street, Blackburn BB1 7AJ Tel: 01254-661730

Bolton Museum & Art Gallery Le Mans Crescent, Bolton BL1 1SE Tel: 01204-332190 Fax: 01204-332241 Email: bolmg@gn.apc.org

The British in India Museum Newtown Street, Colne Tel: 01282 613129 Tel: 0976 665320 Fax: 01282 870215

Duke of Lancaster's Own Yeomanry Stanley Street, Preston PR1 4AT Tel: 01772-264074

East Lancashire Railway Bolton Street Station, Bury BL9 0EY Tel: 01772 685984

Ellenroad Trust Ltd Ellenroad Engine House, Elizabethan Way, Milnrow, Rochdale OL16 4LG Tel: 01706-881952 Email: ellenroad@aol.com WWW: http:\ellenroad.homepage.com

Fleetwood Museum Queens Terrace, Fleetwood FY7 6BT Tel: 01253-876621

The Fusiliers Museum (Lancashire) Wellington Barracks, Bolton Road, Bury, BL8 2PL Tel: 0161 764 2208

Gawthorpe Hall Habergham Drive, Padiham, Burnley BB12 8UA Tel: 01282-771004 WWW: www.lancashire.com/lcc/museums

Greater Manchester Police Museum Newton Street, Manchester, M1 1ES Tel: 0161-856-3287, 0161-856-3288 Fax: 0161-856-3286

Hall I'Th' Wood Museum Hall I Th Wood, Tonge Moor, Bolton BL1 8UA Tel: 01204-301159

Heaton Park Tramway (Transport Museum) Tram Depot, Heaton Park, Prestwich, Manchester, M25 2SW Tel: 0161-740-1919

Helmshore Textile Museums Holcombe Road, Helmshore, Rossendal BB4 4NP Tel: 01706-226459 Fax: 01706-218554

Heritage Trust for the North West Pendle Heritage Centre, Colne Road, Barrowford, Nelson, Lancashire, BB9 6JQ Tel: 01282-661704

Judge's Lodgings Museum Church Street, Lancaster LA1 1LP Tel: 01524-32808

Keighley Bus Museum Trust
47 Brantfell Drive, Burnley BB12 8AW Tel: 01282-413179 Fax: 01282-413179 WWW: www.kbmt.freeuk.com

King's Own Royal Regimental Museum, The City Museum, Market Square, Lancaster LA1 1HT Tel: 01524 64637 Fax: Fax: 01524 841692 Email: kingsownmuseum@iname.com

Kippers Cats 51 Bridge Street, Ramsbottom, Bury BL0 9AD Tel: 01706-822133

Lancashire Mining Museum - Closed wef 30/6/2000

Lancaster City Museum Market Square, Lancaster LA1 1HT Tel: 01524-64637 Fax: 01524-841692 Email: awhite@lancaster.gov.uk

Lytham Heritage Group 2 Henry St. Lytham St. Annes FY8 5LE Tel: 01253-730767

Manchester Museum University of Manchester, Oxford Road, Manchester M13 9PL Tel: 0161-275-2634

Manchester Museum Education Service University of Manchester, Oxford Rd, Manchester M13 9PL Tel: 0161-275-2630 Fax: 0161-275-2676 Email: education@man.ac.uk WWW: www.museum.man.ac.uk

Museum of Lancashire Stanley Street, Preston PR1 4YP Tel: 01772-264075 Fax: 01772-264079 Email: museum@lancs.co.uk

Museum of Lancashire (Queen's Lancashire Regiment Duke of Lancaster's Own Yeomanry Lancashire Hussar Stanley Street, Preston PR1 4YP Tel: 01772 264075

The Museum of Science and Industry In Manchester Liverpool Road, Castlefield, Manchester, M3 4JP Tel: 0161-832-2244, 0161-832-1830 24hr Info line Fax: 0161-833-2184 WWW: www.msim.org.uk

Museum of the Manchester Regiment, Ashton Town Hall, Market Place, Ashton-u-Lyne OL6 6DL Tel: 0161 342 3078 Email: museum.manchester@nxcorp1.tameside.gov.uk WWW: www.tameside.gov.uk, For archives contact Tameside Local Studies Library 0161 303 7937

Museum of the Queen's Lancashire Regiment (East South and Loyal (North Lancashire) Regiments, Lancashire Regiment (PWV) and The Queen's Lancashire Regiment, Fulwood Barracks, Preston PR2 8AA Tel: 01772 260362 Fax: 01772 260583 Email: rhqqlr@aol.com Including associated Volunteer, TA and Militia Units

North West Sound Archive, Old Steward's Office, Clitheroe Castle, Clitheroe BB7 1AZ Tel: 01200-427897 Fax: 01200-427897 Email: nwsa@ed.lancscc.gov.uk WWW: www.lancashire.gov.uk/education/lifelong/recordindex

Oldham Museum Greaves Street, Oldham OL1 1 Tel: 0161-911-4657

Ordsall Hall Museum Taylorson Street, Salford M5 3HT Tel: 0161-872-0251

Pendle Heritage Centre Park Hill, Colne Road, Barrowford, Nelson BB9 6JQ Tel: 01282-661702 Fax: 01282-611718

Portland Basin Museum Portland Place, Ashton-Under-Lyne OL7 0QA Tel: 0161-343-2878

Queen St Mill Harle Syke, Queen Street, Briercliffe, Burnley BB10 2HX Tel: 01282-459996

Rawtenstall Museum Whitaker Park, Haslingden Road, Rawtenstall Tel: 01706 226509, Email: rossendale_leisure@compuserve.com

Ribchester Roman Museum Riverside, Preston PR3 3XS Tel: 01254-878261

Rochdale Museum Service The Arts & Heritage Centre, The Esplanade, Rochdale OL16 1AQ Tel: 01706-641085

Rochdale Pioneers' Museum 31 Toad Lane, Rochdale, Lancashire Tel: 01706-524920

Saddleworth Museum & Art Gallery High Street, Uppermill, Oldham OL3 6HS Tel: 01457-874093 Fax: 01457-870336

Salford Museum & Art Gallery Peel Park, The Crescent, Salford M5 4WU Tel: 0161-736-2649 Email: info@lifetimes.org.uk WWW: www.lifetimes.org.uk

Slaidburn Heritage Centre 25 Church Street, Slaidburn, Clitheroe, BB7 3ER Tel: 01200-446161 Fax: 01200-446161 Email: slaidburn.heritage@htnw.co.uk WWW: www.htnw.co.uk and also www.slaidburn.org.uk

Smithills Hall Museum Smithills, Dean Rd, Bolton BL1 7NP Tel: 01204-841265

Weaver's Cottage Bacup Road, Rawtenstall Tel: 01706 229937 Tel: 01706 226459 Email: rossendale_leisure@compuserve.com

Whitworth Museum North Street, Whitworth Tel: 01706 343231 Email: rossendale_leisure@compuserve.com

Wigan Heritage Service - History Shop Library Street, Wigan, Greater Manchester, WN1 1NU Tel: 01942-828020 Email: heritage@wiganmbc.gov.uk

Leeds

Leeds City Art Gallery The Headrow, Leeds, LS1 3AA Tel: 0113-247-8248

Leeds Museums Resource Centre
Moorfield Road, Moorfield Industrial Estate, Yeadon, Leeds, LS19 7BN Tel: 0113-214-6526

Lotherton Hall Lotherton Lane, Aberford, Leeds, LS25 3EB Tel: 0113-281-3259 **Temple Newsham House** Temple Newsham Road, off Selby Road, Leeds, LS15 0AE Tel: 0113-264-7321

Thwaite Mills Watermill Thwaite Lane, Stourton, Leeds, LS10 1RP Tel: 0113-249-6453

Leicestershire
Abbey Pumping Station Corporation Road, Abbey Lane, Leicester LE4 5PX Tel: 0116-299-5111 Fax: 0116-299-5125 WWW: www.leicestermuseums.ac.uk
Ashby De La Zouch Museum North Street, Ashby-De-La-Zouch LE65 1HU Tel: 01530-560090
Belgrave Hall & Gardens Church Road, Belgrave, Leicester LE4 5PE Tel: 0116-2666590 Fax: 0116-2613063
Email: marte001@leicester.gov.uk
WWW: www.leicestermuseums.gov.uk
Bellfoundry Museum Freehold Street, Loughborough LE11 1AR Tel: 01509-233414
Charnwood Museum Granby Street, Loughborough, Leicestershire, LE11 3DU Tel: 01509-233754 Fax: 01509-268140
WWW: www.leics.gov.uk/museums/musinleics.htm#charnwood
Foxton Canal Museum Middle Lock, Gumley Road, Foxton, Market Harborough LE16 7RA Tel: 0116-279-2657
Harborough Museum Council Offices, Adam and Eve Street, Market Harborough LE16 7AG Tel: 01858-821085
Fax: 01509-268140 Email: museums@leics.gov.uk
WWW: www.leics.gov.uk/museums/musinleics.htm#harborough
Hinckley & District Museum Framework Knitters' Cottages, Lower Bond Street, Hinckley, Leicestershire, LE10 1QX Tel: 01455-251218
Jewry Wall Museum St. Nicholas Circle, Leicester LE1 4LB Tel: 0116-247-3021
Leicester City Museum & Art Gallery 53 New Walk, Leicester LE1 7EA Tel: 0116-255-4100
Leicester Gas Museum Closed mid 2001. No genealogical records. Archive material transferred to National Gas Archive, Aylestone Road, Leicester LE2 7LF Tel: 0116-250-3190
Leicestershire Environmental Resources Centre Holly Hayes, 216 Birstall Road, Birstall, Leicester, LE4 4DG Tel: 0116-267-1950
Email: museums@leics.gov.uk WWW: www.leics.gov.uk
The Manor House Manor Road, Donington Le Heath, Coalville LE67 2FW Tel: 01530-831259 Fax: 01530-831259
Email: museums@leics.gov.uk
WWW: www.leics.gov.uk/museums/musinleics.htm#manor
Melton Carnegie Museum Thorpe End, Melton Mowbray LE13 1RB Tel: 01664-569946 Fax: 01664-569946
Email: museums@leics.gov.uk
WWW: www.leics.gov.uk/museums/musinleics.htm#melton
Royal Leicestershire Regiment Museum Gallery, New Walk Museum, New Walk, Leicester LE1 7FA Tel: 0116 2470403 Postal enquiries: Newarke Houses Museum, The Newarke, Leicester LE2 7BY
Rutland Railway Museum Iron Ore Mine Sidings, Ashwell Road, Cottesmore, Oakham, Leicestershire, LE15 7BX Tel: 01572-813203
Snibston Discovery Park Ashby Road, Coalville LE67 3LN Tel: 01530-510851 Fax: 01530-813301
Email: museums@leics.gov.uk
WWW: www.leics.gov.uk/museums/musinleics.htm#snibston
The Guildhall Guildhall Lane, Leicester LE1 5FQ Tel: 0116-253-2569

Lincolnshire
Alford Civic Trust/Manor House Museum, Alford Manor House Museum, West Street, Alford, LN13 9DJ Tel: 01507-463073
Ayscoughfee Hall, Museum and Gardens Churchgate, Spalding, Lincolnshire, PE11 2RA Tel: 01775-725468 Fax: 01775-762715
Battle of Britain Memorial Flight Visits R.A.F Coningsby, Coningsby, Lincoln LN4 4SY Tel: 01526-344041
Boston Guildhall Museum South Street, Boston PE21 6HT Tel: 01205-365954 Email: heritage@originalboston.freeserve.co.uk
Church Farm Museum, Skegness
Church Road South, Skegness PE25 2HF Tel: 01754-766658
Fax: 01754-898243 Email: wilf@lincolnshire.gov.uk
Gainsborough Old Hall Parnell Street, Gainsborough DN21 2NB Tel: 01427-612669
Gordon Boswell Romany Museum Hawthorns Clay Lake, Spalding PE12 6BL Tel: 01775-710599
Grantham Museum St. Peters Hill, Grantham NG31 6PY Tel: 01476-568783 Fax: 01476-592457
Email: grantham_museum@lineone.net
The Incredibly Fantastic Old Toy Show
26 Westgate, Lincoln LN1 3BD Tel: 01522-520534
Lincolnshire Aviation Heritage Centre East Kirkby Airfield, East Kirkby, Spilsbury PE23 4DE Tel: 01790-763207
Lincs Vintage Vehicle Society Whisby Rd, North Hykeham, Lincoln, LN6 3QT Tel: 01522-500566
Louth Naturalists Antiquarian & Literary Society 4 Broadbank, Louth, LN11 0EQ Tel: 01507-601211
Museum of Lincolnshire Life & Museum of the Royal Lincolnshire Regiment Lincolnshire Yeomanry Old Barracks, Burton Road, Lincoln LN1 3LY Tel: 01522-528448
Fax: 01522-521264
Email: Finch@lincolnshire.gov.uk

National Fishing Heritage Centre Alexandra Dock, Great Grimsby DN31 1UZ Tel: 01472-323345 WWW: www.nelincs.gov.uk also www.nelincsevents.co.uk
Queen's Royal Lancers Regimental Museum (16th/5th & 17th/21st Lancers) Belvoir Castle, nr Grantham NG32 1PD Tel: 01159-573295 Fax: 01159-573195
Wisbech & Fenland Museum Museum Square, Wisbech PE13 1ES Tel: 01945-583817 Fax: 01945-589050
Email: wisbechmuseum@beeb.net
Lincolnshire – North Lincolnshire
North Lincolnshire Museum Oswald Road, Scunthorpe, DN15 7BD Tel: 01724-843533 Fax: 01724-270474
Email: davidwilliams@northlincs.gov.uk
WWW: www.northlincs.gov.uk/museums
Baysgarth House Museum Caistor Road, Barton-Upon-Humber DN18 6AH Tel: 01652-632318
Immingham Museum Margaret St. Immingham, DN40 1LE Tel: 01469-577066

Liverpool
King's Regiment Collection Museum of Liverpool Life, Pier Head, Liverpool, L3 1PZ Tel: 0151-478-4062 Fax: 0151-478-4090
Maritime Museum, Liverpool William Brown St. Liverpool, L3 8EN Tel: 0151-2070001

London
Alexander Fleming Laboratory Museum / St Mary's NHS Trust Archives, St Mary's Hospital, Praed Street, Paddington, London, W2 1NY Tel: 0171 7886 6528 Fax: (020) 7886 6739 Email: kevin.brown@st-marys.nhs.uk
Bank of England Archive Archive Section HO-SV, The Bank of England, Threadneedle Street, London, EC2R 8AH Tel: (020) 7601-5096 Fax: (020) 7601-4356 Email: archive@bankofengland.co.uk WWW: www.bankofengland.co.uk
Bethlem Royal Hospital Archives & Museum Archives and Museum, Monks Orchard Road, Beckenham, BR3 3BX Tel: (020) 8776 4307 Tel: (020) 8776 4053 Fax: (020) 8776 4045 Email: museum@bethlem.freeserve.co.uk The archives of the Bethlem and Maudsley NHS Trust (the Bethlem Royal Hospital and the Maudsley Hospital). Records relating to individual patients are closed for 100 years.
Bethnal Green Museum of Childhood Cambridge Heath Road, London, E2 9PA Tel: 020-8980-2415 Email: k.bones@vam.ac.uk
Black Cultural Archives 378 Coldharbour Lane, London, SW9 8LF Tel: (020) 7738 4591 Fax: (020) 7738 7168
The British Museum Great Russell Street, London, WC1B 3DG Tel: 020-7323-8768, 020-7323-8224 Fax: 020-7323-8118
Email: jwallace@thebritishmuseum.ac.uk
British Red Cross Museum and Archives 9 Grosvenor Crescent, London, SW1X 7EJ Tel: (020) 7201-5153 Fax: (020) 7235-0876
Email: enquiry@redcross.org.uk WWW: www.redcross.org.uk Open by appointment 10am to 4pm Monday to Friday.
Cabaret Mechanical Theatre Unit 33 , The Market, Covent Garden, London, WC2E 8RE Tel: 020-7379-7961
Cabinet War Rooms Clive Steps, King Charles Street, London, SW1A 2AQ Tel: 020-7930-6961 Fax: 020-7839-5897
Email: cwr@iwm.org.uk WWW: www.iwm.org.uk
Church Farmhouse Museum Greyhound Hill, Hendon, London, NW4 4JR Tel: 0208-359-2666 WWW: www.earl.org.uk/partners/barnet/churchf.htm
Clink Prison Museum 1 Clink Street, London, SE1 9DG Tel: 020-7403-6515
Crystal Palace Museum Anerley Hill, London, SE19 Tel: 020 8676 0700**Cutty Sark**
Site address: King William Walk, London SE10 9HT, Cutty Sark Offices (Enquiries address), 2 Greenwich Church Street, London, SE10 9EG Tel: 020-8858-2698 Fax: 020-8858-6976
Email: info@cuttysark.org.uk WWW: www.cuttysark.org.uk
The Design Museum Butlers Wharf 28, Shad Thames, London, SE1 2YD Tel: 020-7403-6933, 020-7940-8791 Fax: 020-7378-6540
Email: enquiries@designmuseum.org.uk
WWW: www.designmuseum.org.uk
Dickens House Museum - London 48 Doughty Street, London, WC1N 2LF Tel: 020-7405-2127 Email: Dhmuseum@rmplc.co.uk
WWW: www.dickensmuseum.com
Doctor Johnson's House 17 Gough Square, London, EC4A 3DE Tel: 020-7353-3745
Museum in Docklands Project Library & Archives, Library & Archive, No 1 Warehouse, West India Quay, Hertsmere Road, London E14 4AL Tel: (020) 7515-1162 Fax: (020) 7538-0209 Email: docklands@museum-london.org.uk and raspinal@museumoflondon.org.uk
The Fan Museum 12 Crooms Hill, London, SE10 8ER Tel: 020-8293-18889 Email: admin@fan-museum.org WWW: www.fan-museum.org
Firepower - The Royal Artillery Museum, Royal Arsenal, Woolwich, London SE18 6ST Tel: (020) 8855 7755 Email: info@firepower.org.uk WWW: www.firepower.org.uk
Florence Nightingale Museum 2 Lambeth Palace Road, London,

SE1 7EW Tel: 020-7620-0374 Email: curator@florence-nightingale.co.uk WWW: www.florence-nightingale.co.uk

Freud Museum 20 Maresfield Gardens, London, NW3 5SX Tel: 0207-435-2002, 0207-435-5167 Fax: 0207-431-5452 Email: freud@gn.apc.org WWW: www.freud.org.uk

Geffrye Museum Kingsland Road, London, E2 8EA Tel: (020) 7739 9893 WWW: www.geffrye-museum.org.uk

Geological Museum Cromwell Road, London, SW7 5BD Tel: 020-7938-8765

Golden Hinde St. Mary Overie Dock, Cathedral St, London, SE1 9DE Tel: 08700-118700

Grange Museum of Community History The Grange, Neasden Lane, Neasden, London, NW10 1QB Tel: 020-8452-8311

Guards Museum Wellington Barracks, Birdcage Walk, London, SW1E 6HQ Tel: 020-7414-3271/3428 Fax: 020-7414-3429

Gunnersbury Park Museum Gunnersbury Park, Popes Lane, London, W3 8LQ Tel: 020-8992-1612

Hackney Museum Service Parkside Library, Victoria Park Road, London, E9 7JL Tel: 020-8986-6914 Email: hmuseum@hackney.gov.uk WWW: www.hackney.gov.uk/hackneymuseum

Handel House Trust Ltd 10 Stratford Place, London, W1N 9AE Tel: 020-7495-1685

H.M.S. Belfast Morgans Lane, Tooley Street, London, SE1 2JH Tel: (020) 7940 6300 Fax: (020) 7403 0719 WWW: www.iwm.org.uk

Hogarth's House Hogarth Lane, Chiswick, London, W4 2QN Tel: 020-8994-6757

Horniman Museum 100 London Road, Forest Hill, London, SE23 3PQ Tel: 020-8699-1872 Email: enquiries@horniman.co.uk WWW: www.horniman.co.uk

Imperial War Museum Lambeth Road, London, SE1 6HZ Tel: 020-7416-5348 Email: books@iwm.org.uk WWW: www.iwm.org.uk

Island History Trust St. Matthias Old Church, Woodstock Terrace, Poplar High St, London, E14 0AE Tel: 020-7987-6041

Islington Museum Foyer Gallery, Town Hall, Upper St, London, N1 2UD Tel: 020-7354-9442

Iveagh Bequest Kenwood House, Hampstead Lane, London, NW3 7JR Tel: 020-8348-1286

James Clavell Library, Royal Arsenal (West), Warren Lane, Woolwich, London SE18 6ST Tel: 020 8312 7125 Email: library@firepower.org.uk WWW: www.firepower.org.uk

Jewish Museum 80 East End Road, Finchley, London, N3 2SY Tel: 020-8349-1143 Email: jml.finchley@lineone.net

Keats House Museum Wentworth Place, Keats Grove, London, NW3 2RR Tel: 020-7435-2062

Kensington Palace State Apartments Kensington Palace, London, W8 4PX Tel: 020-7937-9561

Kingston Museum & Heritage Service North Kingston Centre, Richmond Road, Kingston upon Thames, Surrey, KT2 5PE Tel: 020-8547-6738 Fax: 020-8547-6747 Email: local.history@rbk.kingston.gov.uk WWW: www.kingston.gov.uk/museum/

Leighton House Museum & Art Gallery 12 Holland Park Road, London, W14 8LZ Tel: 0207602-3316

Library of the Royal College of Surgeons of England 35-43 Lincoln's Inn Fields, London, WC2A 3PN Tel: 020-7869-6520 Fax: 020-7405-4438 Email: library@rseng.ac.uk

Livesey Museumfor Children 682 Old Kent Road, London, SE15 1JF Tel: 020-7639-5604 Fax: 020-7277-5384 Email: livesey.museum@southwark.gov.uk

L B of Barking & Dagenham Local History Studies - Dagenham Valence Library & Museum, Becontree Avenue, Dagenham, Essex, RM8 3HT Tel: 020-8592-6537 Fax: 020-8227-5297 Email: fm019@viscount.org.uk WWW: www.earl.org.uk/partners/barking/index.html

L B of Newham Museum Service Old Town Hall, 29 The Broadway, Stratford, London, E15 4BQ Tel: 020-8534-2274

L B of Waltham Forest - Vestry House Museum Vestry Road, Walthamstow, London, E17 9NH Tel: 020-8509-1917 Email: vestry.house@al.lbwf.gov.uk WWW: www.lbwf.gov.uk/vestry/vestry.htm

London Canal Museum 12-13 New Wharf Road, London, N1 9RT Tel: 020-7713-0836 WWW: www.canalmuseum.org.uk

London Fire Brigade Museum 94a Southwark Bridge Road, London, SE1 0EG Tel: 020-7587-2894 Email: esther.mann@london-fire.gov.uk

London Gas Museum Museum Closed - Exhibits in Storage, Twelvetrees Crescent, London, E3 3JH Tel: 020-7538-4982

London Toy & Model Museum 21-23 Craven Hill, London, W2 3EN Tel: 020-7706-8000

London Transport Museum Covent Garden Piazza, London, WC2E 7BB Tel: 020-7379-6344 Fax: 020-7565-7250 Email: contact@ltmuseum.co.uk WWW: www.ltmuseum.co.uk

Mander & Mitchenson Theatre Collection c/o Salvation Army Headquarters, PO Box 249, 101 Queen Victoria Street, London, EC4P 4EP Tel: 020-7236-0182 Fax: 020-7236-0184

Markfield Beam Engine & Museum Markfield Road, London, N15 4RB Tel: 020-8800-7061

Metropolitan Police Museum c/o Room 1317, New Scotland Yard, Broadway, London, SW1H 0BG Tel: 020-8305-2824, 020-8305-1676 Fax: 020-8293-6692

Museum of London London Wall, London, EC2Y 5HN Fax: 020-7600-1058 Email: kstarling@museumoflondon.org.uk

Museum of the Order of St John St John's Gate, St John's Lane, Clerkenwell, London, EC1M 4DA Tel: 020-7253-6644 Fax: 020-7336-0587 WWW: www.sja.org.uk/history

Museum of the Royal Pharmaceutical Society 1 Lambeth High Street, London, SE1 7JN Tel: 020-7735-9141-ext-354 Fax: 020-7793-0232 Email: museum@rpsgb.org.uk WWW: www.rpsgb.org.uk

Museum of Women's Art 3rd Floor, 11 Northburgh Street, London, EC1V 0AN Tel: 020-7251-4881

National Army Museum, Royal Hospital Road, London SW3 4HT Tel: (020) 7730-0717 Fax: (020) 7823-6573 Email: info@national-army-museum.ac.uk WWW: http://www.national-army-museum.ac.uk inc Middlesex Regiment Museum & Buffs Regiment Museum

National Gallery St. Vincent House, 30 Orange Street, London, WC2H 7HH Tel: 020-7747-5950

National Maritime Museum Romney Road, Greenwich, London, SE1O 9NF Tel: 020-8858-4422 WWW: www.nmm.ac.uk

National Maritime Museum Memorial Index National Maritime Museum, Greenwich, London, SE10 9NF Tel: 020-8858-4422 Fax: 020-8312-4422 Email: manuscripts@nmm.ac.uk WWW: www.nmm.ac.uk

National Portrait Gallery 2 St. Martins Place, London, WC2H 0HE Tel: 020-7306-0055 WWW: www.npg.org.uk

North Woolwich Old Station Musuem Pier Road, North Woolwich, London, E16 2JJ Tel: 020-7474-7244

The Old Operating Theatre Museum & Herb Garret 9a Street. Thomas's Street, London, SE1 9RY Tel: 020-7955-4791 Fax: 020-7378-8383 Email: curator@thegarret.org.uk WWW: www.thegarret.org.uk

Percival David Foundation of Chinese Art University of London, School of Oriental & African Studies, 53 Gordon Square, London, WC1H 0PD Tel: 020-7387-3909 Fax: 020-7383-5163

Petrie Museum of Egyptian Archaeology University College London, Gower Street, London, WC1E 6BT Tel: 020-7679-2884 Fax: 020-7679-2886 Email: petrie.museum@ucl.ac.uk

Pitshanger Manor & Gallery Walpole Park, Mattock Lane, Ealing, London, W5 5EQ Tel: 020-8567-1227 Email: pitshanger@ealing.gov.uk

Polish Institute & Sikorski Museum 20 Princes Gate, London, SW7 1PT Tel: 020-7589-9249

Pollock's Toy Museum 1 Scala Street, London, W1P 1LT Tel: 020-7636-3452

Pump House Educational Museum Lavender Pond & Nature Park, Lavender Road, Rotherhithe, London, SE16 1DZ Tel: 020-7231-2976

Ragged School Museum Trust 46-50 Copperfield Road, London, E3 4RR Tel: 020-8980-6405 WWW: www.ics-london.co.uk/rsm

Royal Air Force Museum, Grahame Park Way, Hendon, London NW9 5LL Tel: (020) 8205-2266 Fax: (020) 8200 1751 Email: groupbusiness@refmuseum.org.uk WWW: http://www.rafmuseum.org.uk

Royal Armouries (Tower of London) HM Tower Of London, Tower Hill, London, EC3N 4AB Tel: 020-7480-6358

Royal Artillery Regimental Museum Old Royal Military Academy, Red Lion Lane, Woolwich, London, SE18 4DN Tel: 0181 781 5628 ext 3128

Royal London Hospital Archives and Museum Royal London Hospital, Newark Whitechapel, London, E1 1BB Tel: (020) 7377-7608 Email: r.j.evans@mds.qmw.ac.uk WWW: www.bartsandthelondon.org.uk

Museum of the Royal Pharmaceutical Society Museum of the Royal Pharmaceutical Society, 1 Lambeth High Street, London, SE1 7JN Tel: (020) 7572 2210 museum@rpsgb.org.uk WWW: http://www.rpsgb.org.uk Records of pharmacists from 1841 Research fee charged £20 per person or premises researched to Non members of the Society, £10 per person or premises researched for members(Genealogical Enquiries)

Royal Regiment of Fusiliers Museum H M Tower of London, London, EC3N 4AB Tel: 0171 488 5610

Sam Uriah Morris Society 136a Lower Clapton Rd, London E5 0QJ Tel: 020-8985-6449

The Science Museum Exhibition Road, London, SW7 2DD Tel: 0870-870-4868 Email: sciencemuseum@nms.ac.uk

The Sherlock Holmes Museum 221b Baker Street, London, NW1 6XE Tel: 020-7935-8866 Email: sherlock@easynet.co.uk WWW: www.sherlock-holmes.co.uk

Sir John Soane's Museum 13 Lincolns Inn Fields, London, WC2A 3BP Tel: 020-7405-2107 WWW: www.soane.org

St Bartholomew's Hospital Archives & Museum Archives and Museum, West Smithfield, London, EC1A 7BE Tel: (020) 7601-8152 Email: marion.rea@bartsandthelondon.nhs.uk WWW:

bartsandthelondon.org.uk Archive by appointment only - Mon to Fri
Theatre Museum Russell Street, Convent Garden, London, WC2
Tel: 020 7943 4700 Email: info@theatremuseum.org
WWW: www.theatremuseum.org
Valence House Museum Becontree Avenue, Dagenham, RM8 3HT
Tel: 020-822-75293 Fax: 020-822-75297 Email:
fm019@viscount.org.uk WWW: http://www.bardaglea.org.uk/4-
heritage/heritage-menu.html
Veterinary Museum Royal Vetinerary College, Royal College Street,
London, NW1 0TU Tel: 020-7468-5165/6 Fax: 020-7468-5162
Email: fhouston@rvc.ac.uk WWW: www.rvc.ac.uk
Victoria & Albert Museum Cromwell Road, South Kensington,
London, SW7 2RL Tel: 020-7942-2164 Fax: 020-7942-2162
Wallace Collection Hertford House, Manchester Square, London,
W1M 6BN Tel: 020-7935-0687
Wellcome Trust Centre for the History of Medecine 183 Euston
Road, London, NW1 2BE Tel: 020-7611-8888 Fax: 020-7611-8545
Email: infoserv@wellcome.ac.uk WWW: www.wellcome.ac.uk
Wellington Museum Apsley House, 149 Piccadilly Hyde Park
Corner, London, W1V 9FA Tel: 020-7499-5676
Westminster Abbey Museum Westminster Abbey, Deans Yard,
London, SW1P 3PA Tel: 020-7233-0019
Wimbledon Lawn Tennis Museum Church Road, Wimbledon,
London, SW19 5AE Tel: 020-8946-6131
Wimbledon Museum of Local History 22 Ridgeway, London,
SW19 4QN Tel: 020-8296-9914

Manchester & Greater Manchester
Greater Manchester Police Museum Newton Street, Manchester,
M1 1ES Tel: 0161-856-3287, 0161-856-3288 Fax: 0161-856-3286
Manchester Jewish Museum 190 Cheetham Hill Road, Manchester,
M8 8LW Tel: 0161-834-9879, 0161-832-7353 Fax: 0161-834-9801
Email: info@manchesterjewishmuseum.com
WWW: www.manchesterjewishmuseum.com
Manchester Museum Education Service University of Manchester,
Oxford Road, Manchester, M13 9PL Tel: 0161-275-2630
Fax: 0161-275-2676
Email: education@man.ac.uk
WWW: www.museum.man.ac.uk
The Museum of Science and Industry In Manchester Liverpool
Road, Castlefield, Manchester, M3 4JP Tel: 0161-832-2244,
0161-832-1830 24hr Info line Fax: 0161-833-2184 WWW:
www.msim.org.uk
National Museum of Labour History Labour History Archive, 103
Princess Street, Manchester, M1 6DD Tel: 0161-228-7212
Fax: 0161-237-5965 Email: archives@nmlhweb.org WWW:
www.nmlhweb.org
Wigan Heritage Service - History Shop Library Street, Wigan,
Greater Manchester, WN1 1NU Tel: 01942-828020
Fax: 01942-827645 Email: heritage@wiganmbc.gov.uk

Merseyside
The Beatle Story Ltd Britannia Vaults, Albert Dock, Liverpool L3
4AA Tel: 0151-709-1963 Fax: 0151-708-0039
The Boat Museum & David Owen Waterways Archive South Pier
Road, Ellesmere Port, CH65 4FW Tel: 0151-355-5017 Email:
boatmuseum@easynet.co.uk Records relating to the management,
maintenance and operation of inland waterways in England, Scotland and
Wales. Substantial Waterways library. Date range: late 17th century to 20th
century.
King's Regiment Collection Museum of Liverpool Life, Pier Head,
Liverpool, L3 1PZ Tel: 0151-478-4062 Fax: 0151-478-4090
Merseyside Maritime Museum Maritime Archives and Library, Albert
Dock, Liverpool, L3 4AQ Tel: 0151-478-4418 Email:
archives@nmgmarchives.demon.co.uk WWW: www.nmgm.org.uk
National Museums & Galleries on Merseyside 127 Dale Street,
Liverpool L2 2JH Tel: 0151-207-0001
Port Sunlight Village Trust 95 Greendale Road, Port Sunlight,
CH62 4XE Tel: 0151-644-6466 Fax: 0151-645-8973
Prescot Museum 34 Church Street, Prescot L34 3LA
Tel: 0151-430-7787
Shore Road Pumping Station Shore Road, Birkenhead, CH41 1AG
Tel: 0151-650-1182
Western Approaches 1 Rumford Street, Liverpool L2 8SZ
Tel: 0151-227-2008 **Wirral Archives Service and Museum**
Birkenhead Town Hall, Hamilton Street, Birkenhead, CH41 5BR
Tel: 0151-666-4010 Email: archives@wirral-libraries.net
Botanic Gardens Museum Churchtown, Southport PR9 7NB
Tel: 01704-227547

Middlesex
Forty Hall Museum Forty Hill, Enfield EN2 9HA
Tel: 020-8363-8196
Hackney Museum Service Parkside Library, Victoria Park Road,
London, E9 7JL Tel: 020-8986-6914 Fax: 020-8985-7600
Email: hmuseum@hackney.gov.uk
WWW: www.hackney.gov.uk/hackneymuseum
Harrow Museum & Heritage Centre Headstone Manor, Pinner

View, Harrow HA2 6PX Tel: 020-8861-2626
Kew Bridge Steam Museum Green Dragon Lane, Brentford TW8 0EN
Tel: 020-8568-4757
Musical Museum 368 High Street, Brentford TW8 0BD
Tel: 020-8560-8108

Midlands – West Midlands
Aston Manor-Road Transport Museum Ltd 208-216 Witton Lane,
Birmingham B6 6QE Tel: 0121-322-2298
Bantock House & Park Bantock Park,, Finchfield Rd,
Wolverhampton WV3 9LQ Tel: 01902-552195 Fax: 01902-552196
Birmingham & Midland Museum Of Transport Chapel Lane,
Wythall, Birmingham, B47 6JX Tel: 01564-826471
Email: enquiries@bammot.org.uk WWW: www.bammot.org.uk
Birmingham Museum & Art Gallery Chamberlain Square,
Birmingham B3 3DH Tel: 0121-303-2834 Fax: 0121-303-1394
WWW: www.birmingham.gov.uk/bmag
Birmingham Railway Museum Ltd 670 Warwick Road, Tyseley,
Birmingham B11 2HL Tel: 0121-707-4696
Black Country Living Museum Tipton Road, Dudley DY1 4SQ
Tel: 0121-557-9643 Email: info@bcim.co.uk WWW:
www.bcim.co.uk
Blakesley Hall
Blakesley Road, Yardley, Birmingham B25 8RN Tel: 0121-783-2193
Dudley Museum & Art Gallerey
St James's Road, Dudley, West Midlands, DY1
Haden Hall Haden Hill Park, Barrs Road, Cradley Heath, West
Midlands, B64 7JX Tel: 01384-635846
Herbert Art Gallery & Museum Jordan Well, Coventry CV1 5QP
Tel: 024-76832381
Lock Museum 54 New Road, Willenhall WV13 2DA
Tel: 01902-634542
Email: http://members.tripod.co.uk/lock_museum/
Midland Air Museum Coventry Airport, Baginton Road, Baginton,
Coventry CV8 3AZ Tel: 024-7630-1033
Museum of the Jewellery Quarter 75-79 Vyse Street, Hockley,
Birmingham, B6 6JD Tel: 0121-554-3598 Fax: 0121-554-9700
Oak House Museum Oak Road, West Bromwich B70 8HJ
Tel: 0121-553-0759
Selly Manor Museum Maple Road, Birmingham, B30 2AE
Tel: 0121-472-0199
Walsall Leather Museum Littleton Street West, Walsall, West
Midlands, WS2 8EQ Tel: 01922-721153
Email: leathermuseum@walsall.gov.uk
West Midlands Police Museum Sparkhill Police Station, Stratford
Road, Sparkhill, Birmingham, West Midlands, B11 4EA
Tel: 0121-626-7181
Whitefriars Gallery London Road, Coventry CV3 4AR
Tel: 024-7683-2432
Whitlocks End Farm Bills Lane, Shirley, Solihull B90 2PL
Tel: 0121-745-4891

Norfolk
Air Defence Battle Command & Control Museum Neatishead,
Norwich, NR12 8YB Tel: 01692-633309
Bressingham Steam & Gardens Bressingham, Diss, IP22 2AB Tel:
01379 687386 Fax: 01379 688085
Bure Valley Railway Norwich Road, Aylsham, NR11 6BW Tel:
01263 733858
EcoTech Swaffham, PE37 7HT Tel: 01760 726100 01760 726109
Email: info@ecotech.rmplc.co.uk WWW: www.ecotech.org.uk
Castle Museum Castle Hill, Norwich, Norfolk, NR1 3JU
Tel: 01603-493624
City of Norwich Aviation Museum Ltd Old Norwich Road,
Horsham St Faith, Norwich, NR10 3JF Tel: 01603-893080
Diss Museum The Market Place, Diss IP22 3JT Tel: 01379-650618
Elizabethan House Museum 4 South Quay, Great Yarmouth NR30
2QH Tel: 01493-855746
Feltwell (Historical and Archaeological) Society, 16 High Street,
Feltwell, Thetford IP26 4AF Tel: 01842 828448 Email:
peterfeltwell@tinyworld.co.uk The Museum is at The Beck, Feltwell
Open Tuesday & Saturday April to September 2.00.p.m. to 4.00.p.m.
Glandford Shell Museum Church House, Glandford, Holt, NR25
7JR Tel: 01263-740081
Iceni Village & Museums Cockley Cley, Swaffham PE37 8AG
Tel: 01760-721339
Lynn Museum Old Market Street, King's Lynn, Norfolk, PE30 1NL
Tel: 01553-775001 WWW: www.norfolk.gov.uk/tourism/museums
Maritime Museum for East Anglia 25 Marine Parade, Great Yarmouth
NR30 2EN Tel: 01493-842267
The Muckleburgh Collection, Weybourne, Holt NR25 7EG Tel:
01263 588210 Fax: 01263 588425 Email:
christine@muckleburgh.demon.co.uk WWW:
www.muckleburgh.co.uk
Norfolk Motorcycle Museum Station Yard, Norwich Road, North
Walsham, Norfolk, NR28 0DS Tel: 01692-406266
Norfolk Rural Life Museum & Union Farm
Beech House, Gressenhall, East Dereham, Norfolk, NR20 4DR

Tel: 01362-860563 Fax: 01362-860385
Email: frances.collinson.mus@norfolk.gov.uk
Royal Norfolk Regimental Museum, Shirehall, Market Avenue,
Norwich NR1 3JQ Tel: 01603 493649 Fax: 01603 765651 Email:
regimental.museum@central.norfolk.gov.uk WWW:
www..norfolk.gov.uk
The North Norfolk Railway The Station, Sheringham, NR26 8RA
Tel: 01263 822045 01263 823794 WWW: www.nnrailway.co.uk
Sheringham Museum Station Road, Sheringham NR26 8RE
Tel: 01263-821871
Shirehall Museum Common Place, Walsingham, NR22 6BP
Tel: 01328-820510 Fax: 01328-820098
Email: walsingham.museum@farmline.com
Wisbech & Fenland Museum Museum Square, Wisbech PE13 1ES
Tel: 01945-583817 Fax: 01945-589050
Email: wisbechmuseum.@beeb.net
100 Bomb Group Memorial Museum, Common Road, Dickleburgh,
Diss, Norfolk , IP21 4PH Tel: 01379-740708
Inspire Hands On Science Centre Coslany Street, Norwich,
Norfolk , NR3 3DJ Tel: 01603-612612

Northamptonshire
**Abington Museum and Museum of The Northamptonshire
Regiment**, Abington Park Museum, Abington NN1 5LW Tel: 01604
635412 Fax: 01604 238720 Email: museums@northamton.gov.uk
WWW: www.northampton.gov.uk/museums
Canal Museum Stoke Bruerne, Towcester NN12 7SE
Tel: 01604-862229
Museum of The Northamptonshire Regiment Abington Park
Museum, Abington NN1 5LW Tel: 01604 635412
National Dragonfly Museum Ashton Mill, Ashton, Peterborough,
PE8 5LB Tel: 01832-272427 Email: ndmashton@aol.com
WWW: www.natdragonflymuseum.org.uk
Northampton Iron Stone Railway Trust Hunsbury Hill Country
Park, Hunsbury Hill Road, West Hunsbury, Northampton NN4 9UW
Tel: 01604-702031/757481, 01908-376821 Email: raf9687@aol.com
also bnile98131@aol.com
Northampton & Lamport Railway Preservation Society Pitsford
& Brampton Station, Pitsford Road, Chapel Brampton, Northampton,
NN6 8BA Tel: 01604 820327
Peterborough Museum & Art Gallery Priestgate, Peterborough
PE1 1LF Tel: 01733-343329 Fax: 01733-341928
Email: museums@peterborough.gov.uk
Rushden Historical Transport Society The Station, Station
Approach, Rushden, Northamptonshire, NN10 0AW
Tel: 01933-318988
Wellingborough Heritage Centre Croyland Hall, Burystead Place,
Wellingborough, Northamptonshire, NN8 1AH Tel: 01933-276838

Northumberland
**A Soldier's Life 15th/19th The King's Royal Hussars
Northumberland Hussars and Light Dragoons**, Discovery
Museum, Blandford Square, Newcastle-upon-Tyne NE1 4JA Tel:
0191 232 6789 Fax: 0191 230 2614 Email: ralph.thompson@tyne-
wear-museums.org.uk
Bellingham Heritage Centre Front Street, Bellingham, Hexham,
NE48 2DF Tel: 01434-220050
Berwick Borough Museum The Barracks, The Parade,
Berwick-Upon-Tweed, Northumberland, TD15 1DG
Tel: 01289-330933
Bewick Studios The Mickley Square, Mickley, Stocksfield NE43
7BL Tel: 01661-844055
Border History Museum & Library Moothall, Hallgate, Hexham,
Northumberland, NE46 3NH Tel: 01434-652349
Fax: 01434-652425 Email: museum@tynedale.gov.uk
Chesterholm Museum (Vindolanda Museum) The Vindolanda
Trust, Bardon Mill, Hexham, NE47 7JN Tel: 01434-344277
Fax: 01434-344060 Email: info@vindolanda.com
WWW: www.vindolanda.com
Fusiliers Museum of Northumberland The Abbot's Tower, Alnwick
Castle, Alnwick, NE66 1NG Tel: 01665-602152
Fax: 01665-603320 Email: fusmusnorthld@btinternet.com
King's Own Scottish Borderers Museum, The Barracks, The
Parade, Berwick upon Tweed TD15 1DG Tel: 01289 307426
Marine Life Centre & Fishing Museum 8 Main Street, Seahouses
NE68 7RG Tel: 01665-721257
North East Mills Group Blackfriars, Monk St. Newcastle upon
Tyne, NE1 4XN Tel: 0191-232-9279 Fax: 0191-230-1474
WWW: www.welcome.to/North.East.Mill.Group
Tynedale Council Museums Department of Leisure & Tourism,
Prospect House, Hexham, Northumberland, NE46 3NH
Tel: 01461-652351

Nottinghamshire
D.H Lawrence Heritage Durban House Heritage Centre, Mansfield
Road, Eastwood, Nottingham, NG16 3DZ Tel: 01773-717353
Flintham Museum and Flintham Society Inholms Road, Flintham,
NG23 5JF Tel: 0163.6 525111, Email: flintham.museum@lineone.net

WWW: www.flintham-museum.org.uk
Galleries of Justice Shire Hall, High Pavement, Lace Market,
Nottingham, NG1 1HN Tel: 0115-952-0555 Fax: 0115-993-9828
Email: info@galleriesofjustice.org.uk
WWW: www.galleriesofjustice.org.uk
Great Central Railway Nottingham Heritage Centre, Mere Way,
Ruddington, Nottingham, NG11 6JS Tel: 0115-940-5705
Greens Mill & Science Musuem Windmill Lane, Sneinton,
Nottingham, Nottinghamshire, NG2 4QB Tel: 0115-915-6878
Harley Gallery Welbeck, Worksop S80 3LW Tel: 01909-501700
Mansfield Museum & Art Gallery Leeming Street, Mansfield,
NG18 1NG Tel: 01623-463088 Fax: 01623-412922
Millgate Museum of Folk Life 48 Millgate, Newark NG24 4TS
Tel: 01636-655730 Email: museums@newark-sherwooddc.gov.uk
WWW: www.newark-sherwooddc.gov.uk
The Museum of Nottingham Lace 3-5 High Pavement, The Lace
Market, Nottingham NG1 1HF Tel: 0115-989-7365
Fax: 0115-989-7301 Email: info@nottinghamlace.org
WWW: www.nottinghamlace.org
Natural History and Industrial Museum The Courtyard, Wollaton
Park, Nottingham, NG8 2AE Tel: 0115-9153942
Fax: 0115-9153941
Newark (Notts & Lincs) Air Museum The Airfield, Lincoln Road,
Winthorpe, Newark, Nottinghamshire, NG24 2NY
Tel: 01636-707170 Fax: 01636-707170
Email: newarkair@lineone.net
Newark Museum Appleton Gate, Newark NG24 1JY
Tel: 01636-702358
Newstead Abbey Museum Newstead Abbey Park, Nottingham
NG15 8GE Tel: 01623-455900
Nottingham Castle Museum & Art Gallery
Castle Road, Nottingham NG1 6EL Tel: 0115-915-3700
Fax: 0115-915-3653
Nottingham Musuem Shops Canal Street, Nottingham NG1 7HG
Tel: 0115-915-6871
Ruddington Frame Work Knitter's Museum Chapel Street,
Ruddington, Nottingham NG11 6HE Tel: 0115-984-6914
Ruddington Village Museum St. Peters Rooms, Church Street,
Ruddington, Nottingham, NG11 6HD Tel: 0115-914-6645
Sherwood Foresters (Notts and Derby Regiment) Museum, The
Castle, Nottingham NG1 6EL Tel: 0115 946 5415 Fax: 0115 946
9853 Email: rhqwfr-nottm@lineone.net WWW:
www.wfrmuseum.org.uk Address for enquiries: RHQ WFR, Foresters
House, Chetwynd Barracks, Chilwell, Nottingham NG9 5HA
Sherwood Foresters Museum and Archives, RHQ WFR, Foresters
House, Chetwynd Barracks, Chilwell, Nottingham NG9 5HA Tel:
0115 946 5415 Fax: 0115 946 9853 Email:
curator@wfrmuseum.org.uk WWW: www.wfrmuseum.org.uk
Whaley Thorn Heritage & Environment Centre Portland Terrace,
Langwith, Mansfield NG20 9HA Tel: 01623-742525

Oxfordshire
Abingdon Museum County Hall, Market Place, Abingdon,
Oxfordshire, OX14 3HG Tel: 01235-523703 Fax: 01235-536814
Ashmolean Museum University of Oxford, University of Oxford,
Beaumont St, Oxford, Oxfordshire, OX1 2PH Tel: 01865-278000
Great Western Society Ltd Didcot Railway Centre, Station Road,
Didcot OX11 7NJ Tel: 01235-817200
Oxfordshire & Buckinghamshire Light Infantry Regt Museum Slade
Park, Headington, Oxford OX3 7JL Tel: 01865 780128
The Oxfordshire Museum Fletchers House, Park Street, Woodstock
OX20 1SN Tel: 01993-811456, 01993-814104 Fax: 01993-813239
Email: oxonmuseum@oxfordshire.gov.uk
Pitt Rivers Museum University Of Oxford, South Parks Road,
Oxford, OX1 3PP Tel: 01865-270927 Fax: 01865-270943
Email: prm@prm.ox.ac.uk WWW: www.prm.ox.ac.uk
River & Rowing Museum Mill Meadows, Henley on Thames RG9
1BF Tel: 01491-415625 Fax: 01491-415601
Email: museum@rrm.co.uk also alicia.gurney@rrm.co.uk WWW:
www.rrm.co.uk
The Vale & Downland Museum 19 Church Street, Wantage,
Oxfordshire, OX12 8BL Tel: 01235-771447
Email: museum@wantage.com
Wallingford Museum Flint House, High Street, Wallingford,
Oxfordshire, OX10 0DB Tel: 01491-835065
Witney & District Museum Gloucester Court Mews, High Street,
Witney, Oxfordshire, OX8 6LX Tel: 01993-775915
Email: janecavell@aol.com

Rutland
Rutland County Museum Catmose Street, Oakham, Rutland, LE15
6HW Tel: 01572-723654 WWW: www.rutnet.co.uk

Shropshire
Acton Scott Historic Working Farm Wenlock Lodge, Acton Scott,
Church Stretton, Shropshire, SY6 6QN Tel: 01694-781306
Blists Hill Open Air Museum Ironbridge Gorge Museum Trust Ltd,
Legges Way, Madeley, Telford, Shropshire, TF7 5DU

Tel: 01952-588016
Coalport China Museum Ironbridge Gorge Museum Trust Ltd, High Street, Coalport, Telford, Shropshire, TF8 7AW Tel: 01952-580650
Ironbridge Gorge Museum, Library & Archives The Wharfage, Ironbridge, Telford, TF8 7AW Tel: 01952-432141
Email: library@ironbridge.org.uk WWW: www.ironbridge.org.uk
Ironbridge Gorge Museums Ironbridge Gorge Museum Trust Ltd, Ironbridge, Telford, TF8 7AW Tel: 01952-432141
Fax: 01952-432237
Jackfield Tile Museum Ironbridge Gorge Museum Trust Ltd, Jackfield, Telford, Shropshire, TF8 7AW Tel: 01952-882030
Ludlow Museum Castle Street, Ludlow, Shropshire, SY8 1AS
Tel: 01584-875384
Midland Motor Museum Stanmore Hall, Stourbridge Road, Stanmore, Bridgnorth, Shropshire, WV15 6DT Tel: 01746-762992
Museum Of Iron Ironbridge Gorge Museum Trust Ltd, Coach Road, Coalbrookdale, Telford TF8 7EZ Tel: 01952-433418
Museum Of The River Visitor Centre Ironbridge Gorge Museum Trust Ltd, The Wharfage, Ironbridge, Telford TF8 7AW
Tel: 01952-432405
Oswestry Transport Museum Oswald Road, Oswestry SY11 1RE
Tel: 01691-671749
Rowley's House Museum Shrewsbury Museums Service, Barker Street, Shrewsbury, SY1 1QH Tel: 01743-361196
Fax: 01743-358411
Royal Air Force Museum Cosford, Shifnal, Shropshire, TF11 8UP
Tel: 01902-376200
Shropshire Regimental Museum (King's Shropshire Light Infantry, Shropshire Yeomanry) Shropshire Militia, Volunteers and TA, The Castle, Shrewsbury SY1 2AT Tel: 01743 358516 Tel: 01743 262292 Fax: 01743 270023 Email: shropshire@zoom.co.uk WWW: www.shropshireregimental.co.uk Limited information only on individuals. Do not hold service records of soldiers.

Somerset
Abbey Barn - Somerset Rural Life Museum Abbey Barn, Chilkwell Street, Glastonbury, Somerset, BA6 8DB Tel: 01458-831197 WWW: www.somerset.giv.uk/museums
Admiral Blake Museum Blake Street, Bridgwater, Somerset, TA6 3NB Tel: 01278-435399 Email: Museums@sedgemoor.gov.uk
American Museum Claverton Manor, Bath, Somerset, BA2 7BD
Tel: 01225-460503 Fax: 01225-480726
Bakelite Museum Orchard Mill, Bridge St Williton, Taunton, Somerset, TA4 4NS Tel: 01984-632133
Bath Industrial Heritage Centre Camden Works, Julian Road, Bath BA1 2RH Tel: 01225-318348 Fax: 01225-318348
Email: bathindheritage@camdenworks.swinternet.com.uk
Bath Postal Museum 8 Broad Street, Bath, Somerset, BA1 5LJ
Tel: 01225-460333 WWW: www.bathpostalmuseum.org
Bath Royal Literary & Scientific Institution 16-18 Queen Square, Bath, Somerset, BA1 2HN Tel: 01225-312084
Blazes Fire Museum Sandhill Park, Bishops Lydeard, Taunton, Somerset, TA4 3DE Tel: 01823-433964
Building of Bath Museum Countess of Huntingdon's Chapel, The Vineyards, Bath, Somerset, BA1 5NA Tel: 01225-333-895
Fax: 01225-445-473 Email: admin@bobm.freeserve.co.uk WWW: www.bath-preservations-trust.org.uk
Chard & District Museum Godworthy House, High Street, Chard, Somerset, TA20 1QB Tel: 01460-65091
Fleet Air Arm Museum R.N.A.S Yeovilton, Yeovil, Somerset, BA22 8HT Tel: 01935-840565
Fleet Air Arm Museum Records & Research Centre Box D61, RNAS Yeovilton, Nr Ilchester, Somerset, BA22 8HT
Tel: 01935-840565 Fax: 01935-840181
Glastonbury Lake Village Museum The Tribunal, 9 High Street, Glastonbury, Somerset, BA6 9DP Tel: 01458-832949
The Haynes Motor Museum Castle Cary Road, Sparkford, Yeovil, Somerset, BA22 7LH Tel: 01963-440804 Fax: 01963-441004
Email: mike@gmpwin.demon.co.uk
WWW: www.haynesmotormuseum.co.uk
Holburne Museum & Crafts Study Centre Great Pulteney Street, Bath, BA2 4DB Tel: 01225-466669
John Judkyn Memorial Garden Thorpe, Freshford, Bath, BA3 6BX
Tel: 01225-723312
Lambretta Scooter Museum 77 Alfred Street, Weston-Super-Mare, North Somerset, BS23 1PP Tel: 01934-614614 Fax: 01934-620120
Email: lambretta@wsparts.force9.net
Museum Of East Asian Art 12 Bennett Street, Bath, BA1 2QL
Tel: 01225-464640 Email: museum@east-asian-art.freeserve.co.uk
WWW: www.east-asian-art.co.uk
No.1 Royal Crescent 1 Royal Crescent, Bath, BA1 2LR
Tel: 01225-428126
Radstock, Midsomer Norton & District Museum Waterloo Road, Radstock, Bath, Somerset, BA3 3ER Tel: 01761-437722
Email: radstockmuseum@ukonline.co.uk
WWW: www.radstockmuseum.co.uk
Somerset & Dorset Railway Trust Washford Station, Washford, Watchet, Somerset, TA23 0PP Tel: 01984-640869, 01308-424630

Email: info@sdrt.org WWW: www.sdrt.org
Somerset County Museum Service Taunton Castle, Taunton, Somerset, TA1 4AA Tel: 01823-320200
Somerset Military Museum (Somerset Light Infantry Yeomanry) Militia and Volunteers) County Museum, The County Museum, Taunton Castle, Taunton TA1 4AA Tel: 01823 333434 Fax: 01823 351639
Wells Museum 8 Cathedral Green, Wells, Somerset, BA5 2UE
Tel: 01749-673477
West Somerset Museum The Old School, Allerford, Minehead, Somerset, TA24 8HN Tel: 01643-862529
William Herschel Museum 19 New King Street, Bath, BA1 2BL
Tel: 01225-311342
Somerset – North East Somerset
Roman Baths Museum Abbey Churchyard, Bath, BA1 1LZ
Tel: 01225-477773
Helicopter Museum Locking Moor Road, Weston-Super-Mare, BS22 8PL Tel: 01934-635227
North Somerset Museum Service Burlington Street, Weston-Super-Mare, BS23 1PR Tel: 01934-621028

Staffordshire
Bass Museum and Archive Horninglow Street, Burton on Trent DE14 1JZ Tel: 0845 60000598
Borough Museum & Art Gallery Brampton Park, Newcastle ST5 0QP Tel: 01782-619705
Clay Mills Pumping Engines Trust Ltd
Sewage Treatment Works, Meadow Lane, Stretton, Burton-On-Trent DE13 0DB Tel: 01283-509929
Etruria Industrial Museum Lower Bedford St, Etruria, Stoke-On-Trent, Staffordshire, ST4 7AF Tel: 01782-233144
Gladstone Pottery Museum Uttoxeter Road, Longton, Stoke-On-Trent, Staffordshire, ST3 1PQ Tel: 01782-319232
Hanley Museum & Art Gallery Bethesda Street, Hanley, Stoke-On-Trent, Staffordshire, ST1 3DW Tel: 01782-232323
Museum of The Staffordshire Regiment, Whittington Barracks, Lichfield WS14 9PY Tel: 0121 311 3240 Tel: 0121 311 3229 Fax: 0121 311 3205 Email: museum@rhqstaffords.fsnet.co.uk Museum illustrating the history of the Staffordshire Regiments and the four ancestor regiments from 1705. The museum has an extensive archive and a replica World War I trench system
Museum of the Staffordshire Yeomanry, The Ancient High House, Greengate Street, Stafford ST16 2HS Tel: 01785 619130 Email:, Info available on Regiment's history during Boer, WWI and WWII. There are no records of individual servicemen
Potteries Museum & Art Gallery Bethesda Street, Hanley, Stoke-On-Trent, ST1 3DE Tel: 01782-232323
Email: museums@stoke.gov.uk
WWW: www.stoke.gov.uk/museums
Samuel Johnson Birthplace Museum Breadmarket Street, Lichfield, Staffordshire, WS13 6LG Tel: 01543-264972 WWW: www.lichfield.gov.uk
Uttoxeter Heritage Centre 34-36 Carter Street, Uttoxeter ST14 8EU
Tel: 01889-567176

Suffolk
Christchurch Mansion & Wolsey Art Gallery Christchurch Park, Soane Street, Ipswich IP4 2BE Tel: 01473-253246
East Anglia Transport Museum Chapel Road, Carlton Colville, Lowestoft, Suffolk, NR33 8BL Tel: 01502-518459
Felixstowe Museum Landguards Fort, Felixstowe IP11 8TW
Tel: 01394-674355
Gainsborough House Society Gainsborough Street, Sudbury CO10 2EU Tel: 01787-372958 Email: mail@gainsborough.org
WWW: www.gainsborough.org
International Sailing Craft Assoc Maritime Museum
Caldecott Road, Oulton Broad, Lowestoft, Suffolk, NR32 3PH
Tel: 01502-585606 Fax: 01502-589014
Email: admin@isca-maritimemuseum.org
Ipswich Museum & Exhibition Gallery
High Street, Ipswich, Suffolk, IP1 3QH Tel: 01473-213761
Ipswich Transport Museum Ltd
Old Trolley Bus Depot, Cobham Rd, Ipswich, Suffolk, IP3 9JD
Tel: 01473-715666
Long Shop Steam Museum Main Street, Leiston, Suffolk, IP16 4ES
Tel: 01728-832189 WWW: www.suffolkcc.gov.uk/libraries_and_heritage/sro/garrett/index.html
Lowestoft Museum Broad House, Nicholas Everitt Park, Oulton Broad, Lowestoft, Suffolk, NR33 9JR Tel: 01502-511457, 01502-513795 Fax: 01502-513795
Maritime Museum Sparrows Nest The Museum, Whapload Road, Lowestoft, Suffolk, NR32 1XG Tel: 01502-561963
Mid Suffolk Light Railway Brockford Station, Wetheringsett, Stowmarket, Suffolk, IP14 5PW Tel: 01449-766899
Mildenhall & District Museum 6 King Street, Mildenhall, Bury St. Edmunds, Suffolk, IP28 7EX Tel: 01638-716970
The National Horseracing Museum & Tours 99 High Street, Newmarket CB8 8JH Tel: 01638-667333

Rougham Tower Association Rougham Estate Office, Rougham, Bury St. Edmunds, Suffolk, IP30 9LZ Tel: 01359-271471 Email: bplsto@aol.com

Suffolk Regiment Museum -Museum closed to the public, Suffolk Record Office, 77 Raingate Street, Bury St Edmund IP33 2AR Tel: 01284-352352 Fax: 01284-352355 Email: bury.ro@libher.suffolkcc.gov.uk WWW: http://www.suffolkcc.gov.uk/sro/ Museum closed to the public but archives and photographs available for inspection at the Record Office

Dunwich Museum St. James's Street, Dunwich, Saxmundham, Suffolk , IP17 3DT Tel: 01728-648796

Norfolk & Suffolk Aviation Museum Buckaroo Way, The Street, Flixton, Bungay, Suffolk , NR35 1NZ Tel: 01986-896644 WWW: www.aviationmuseum.net

West Stow Country Park & Anglo-Saxon Village The Visitor Centre, Icklingham Road, West Stow, Bury St Edmunds, IP28 6HG Tel: 01284 728718

Surrey

Bourne Hall Museum Bourne Hall, Spring Street, Ewell, Epsom, Surrey, KT17 1UF Tel: 020-8394-1734 WWW: www.epsom.townpage.co.uk

Chertsey Museum The Cedars, 33 Windsor Street, Chertsey, Surrey, KT16 8AT Tel: 01932-565764 Email: enquiries@chertseymuseum.org.uk

Dorking & District Museum The Old Foundry, 62a West St, Dorking, Surrey, RH4 1BS Tel: 01306-876591, 01306-743821

Elmbridge Museum Church Street, Weybridge, Surrey, KT13 8DE Tel: 01932-843573 Email: info@elm-mus.datanet.co.uk WWW: www.surrey-online.co.uk/elm-mus

Godalming Museum 109a High Street, Godalming, Surrey, GU7 1AQ Tel: 01483-426510 Fax: 01483-869-495 Email: museum@godalming.ndo.co.uk

Guildford Museum Castle Arch, Quarry St, Guildford, Surrey, GU1 3SX Tel: 01483-444750 Email: museum@remote.guildford.gov.uk

Haslemere Educational Museum 78 High Street, Haslemere, Surrey, GU27 2LA Tel: 01428-642112 Fax: 01428-645234 Email: haslemere_museums@compuserve.com

Kingston Upon Thames Museum, North Kingston Centre, Richmond Road, New Malden KT3 3UQ Tel: 020 8547 6738 1901 census Email: local.history@rbk.kingston.gov.uk WWW: www.kingston.gov.uk/museum/, Research service available

Merton Heritage Centre The Cannons, Madeira Road, Mitcham, Surrey, CR4 4HD Tel: 020-8640-9387

Queen's Royal Surrey Regiment Museum (Queen's Royal, East Surrey & Queen's Royal Surrey Regiments), Clandon Park, West Clandon, Guildford GU4 7RQ Tel: 01483 223419 Fax: 01483 224636 Email: queenssurreys@caree4free.net WWW: www.surrey-on;line.co.uk/queenssurreys

Regimental Museum Royal Logistical Corps Deepcut, Camberley, Surrey, GU16 6RW Tel: 01252-340871, 01252-340984

Reigate Priory Museum Reigate Priory, Bell Street, Reigate, Surrey, RH2 7RL Tel: 01737-222550

Regimental Museum Royal Logistic Corps, Princess Royal Barracks, Deepcut, Camberley GU16 6RW Tel: 01252 833371 Fax: 01252 833484 Email: query@rlcmuseum.freeserve.co.uk WWW: www.army-rlc.co.uk/museum The story of military logistics and the RLCs forming corps - The Royal Corps of Transport, The Royal Army Ordnance Corp, The Royal Pioneer Corps and the Army Catering Corps are told in this museum

Rural Life Centre Old Kiln Museum, The Reeds, Tilford, Farnham, Surrey, GU10 2DL Tel: 01252-795571 Email: rural.life@argonet.co.uk

Wandle Industrial Museum Vestry Hall Annex, London Road, Mitcham, Surrey, CR4 3UD Tel: 020-8648-0127

Woking Museum & Arts & Craft Centre The Galleries, Chobham Road, Woking , Surrey, GU21 1JF Tel: 01483-725517 Fax: 01483-725501 Email: the.galleries@dial.pipex.com

East Surrey Museum 1 Stafford Road, Caterham, Surrey , CR3 6JG Tel: 01883-340275

Sussex

Brighton Fishing Museum 201 Kings Road, Arches, Brighton BN1 1NB Tel: 01273-723064

Royal Military Police Museum Roussillon Barracks, Chichester, Sussex, PO19 4BN Tel: 01243 534225 Email: museum@rhqrmp.freeserve.co.uk WWW: www.rhqrmp.freeserve.co.uk

Sussex Combined Services Museum (Royal Sussex Regiment and Queen's Royal Irish Hussars), Redoubt Fortress, Royal Parade, Eastbourne BN22 7AQ Tel: 01323 410300

Sussex – East Sussex

Anne of Cleves House Museum 52 Southover, High St, Lewes, East Sussex, BN7 1JA Tel: 01273-474610

Battle Museum Langton Memorial Hall, High Street, Battle, East Sussex, TN33 0AQ Tel: 01424-775955

Bexhill Museum Egerton Road, Bexhill-On-Sea, East Sussex, TN39 3HL Tel: 01424-787950 Email: museum@rother.gov.uk WWW: www.1066country.com

Bexhill Museum of Costume & Social History Association Manor Gardens, Upper Sea Road, Bexhill-On-Sea, East Sussex, TN40 1RL Tel: 01424-210045

BN1 Visual Arts Project Brighton Media Centre, 9-12 Middle Street, Brighton, East Sussex, BN1 1AL Tel: 01273-384242

Booth Museum 194 Dyke Road, Brighton, East Sussex, BN1 5AA Tel: 01273-292777 Email: boothmus@pavilion.co.uk

Dave Clarke Prop Shop Long Barn, Cross In Hand, Heathfield, East Sussex, TN21 0TP Tel: 01435-863800

Eastbourne Heritage Centre 2 Carlisle Road, Eastbourne, East Sussex, BN21 4BT Tel: 01323-411189 and 01323-721825

The Engineerium The Droveway, Nevill Road, Hove, East Sussex, BN3 7QA Tel: 01273-554070 Email: info@britishengineering.com

Filching Manor Motor Museum Filching Manor, Jevington Rd, Polegate, East Sussex, BN26 5QA Tel: 01323-487838

Fishermans Museum Rock A Nore Road, Hastings, East Sussex, TN34 3DW Tel: 01424-461446

Hastings Museum & Art Gallery Johns Place, Bohemia Rd, Hastings TN34 1ET Tel: 01424-781155

Hove Musuem & Art Gallery 19 New Church Road, Hove, East Sussex, BN3 4AB Tel: 01273-290200 Fax: 01273-292827 Email: abigail.thomas@brighton-hove.gov.uk WWW: www.brighton-hove.gov.uk

How We Lived Then Museum of Shops 20 Cornfield Terrace, Eastbourne, East Sussex, BN21 4NS Tel: 01323-737143

Michelham Priory Upper Dicker, Hailsham BN27 3QS

Newhaven Local & Maritime Museum Garden Paradise, Avis Way, Newhaven, East Sussex BN9 0DH Tel: 01273-612530

Preston Manor Museum Preston Drove, Brighton, East Sussex, BN1 6SD Tel: 01273-292770 Fax: 01273-292771

Rye Castle Museum East Street, Rye, East Sussex, TN31 7JY Tel: 01797-226728

Seaford Museum of Local History Martello Tower, The Esplanade, Seaford, East Sussex, BN25 1JH Tel: 01323-898222

Wish Tower Puppet Museum Tower 73, King Edwards Parade, Eastbourne, East Sussex, BN21 4BY Tel: 01323-411620

Sussex – West Sussex

Amberley Museum Station Road, Amberley, Arundel, West Sussex, BN18 9LT Tel: 01798-831370 Email: office@amberleymuseum.co.uk

Chichester District Museum 29 Little London, Chichester, West Sussex, PO19 1PB Tel: 01243-784683 Email: chicmus@breathemail.net

Ditchling Museum Church Lane, Ditchling, Hassocks, West Sussex, BN6 8TB Tel: 01273-844744 Email: info@ditchling-museum.com

Fishbourne Roman Palace Roman Way, Salthill Road, Fishbourne, Chichester PO19 3QR Tel: 01243-785859

Horsham Museum 9 The Causeway, Horsham, West Sussex, RH12 1HE Tel: 01403-254959 Fax: 01403-217581

Marlipins Museum High Street, Shoreham-By-Sea, West Sussex, BN43 5DA Tel: 01273-462994, 01323-441279 Fax: 01323-844030 Email: smomich@sussexpast.co.uk

The Mechanical Music & Doll Collection Church Road, Portfield, Chichester PO19 4HN Tel: 01243-372646

Petworth Cottage Museum 346 High Street, Petworth GU28 0AU Tel: 01798-342100 WWW: www.sussexlive.co.uk

The Doll House Museum Station Road, Petworth GU28 0BF Tel: 01798-344044

Weald & Downland Open Air Museum Singleton, Chichester, West Sussex, PO18 0EU Tel: 01243-811363 Email: wealddown@mistral.co.uk WWW: www.wealddown.co.uk

Tyne and Wear

A Soldier's Life 15th/19thThe King's Royal Hussars Northumberland Hussars and Light Dragoons Discovery Museum, Blandford Square, Newcastle-upon-Tyne, Tyne & Wear, NE1 4JA Tel: 0191-232-6789 Fax: 0191-230-2614 Email: ralph.thompson@tyne-wear-museums.org.uk

Arbeia Roman Fort Baring Street, South Shields, Tyne And Wear, NE33 2BB Tel: 0191-4561369 Email: lizelliott@tyne-wear-museums.org.uk

Bede's World Museum Church Bank, Jarrow NE32 3DY Tel: 0191-4892106

The Bowes Railway Co Ltd Springwell Road, Springwell Village, Gateshead NE9 7QJ Tel: 0191-4161847 Email: alison_gibson77@hotmail.com WWW: www.bowesrailway.co.uk

Castle Keep Castle Garth, St. Nicholas Street, Newcastle Upon Tyne, Tyne and Wear, NE1 1RE Tel: 0191-2327938

Hancock Museum Barras Bridge, Newcastle Upon Tyne NE2 4PT Tel: 0191-2227418 Fax: 0191-2226753

Military Vehicles Museum Exhibition Park Pavilion, Newcastle

Upon Tyne NE2 4PZ Tel: 0191-281-7222
Email: miltmuseum@aol.com
Newburn Motor Museum Townfield Gardens, Newburn, Newcastle
Upon Tyne NE15 8PY Tel: 0191-2642977
North East Aircraft Museum Old Washington Road, Sunderland,
SR5 3HZ Tel: 0191-519-0662
North East Mills Group Research into wind and water mills in NE
England - promoting public access and restoration of mills., Blackfriars, Monk
Street, Newcastle upon Tyne, NE1 4XN Tel: 0191-232-9279
WWW: www.welcome.to/North.East.Mill.Group
North East Museums House of Recovery, Bath Lane, Newcastle
Upon Tyne, Tyne And Wear, NE4 5SQ Tel: 0191-2221661
Ryhope Engines Trust Pumping Station, Stockton Road, Ryhope,
Sunderland SR2 0ND Tel: 0191-5210235 WWW:
www.g3wte.demon.co.uk/
South Shields Museum & Art Gallery Ocean Road, South Shields,
Tyne and Wear, NE33 2JA Tel: 0191-456-8740 Fax: 0191-456-7850
Stephenson Railway Museum Middle Engine Lane, North Shields
NE29 8DX Tel: 0191-200-7146 Fax: 0191-200-7146
Sunderland Museum & Art Gallery Borough Road, Sunderland,
Tyne and Wear, SR1 1PP Tel: 0191-565-0723 Fax: 0191-565-0713
Email: martin.routledge@tyne-wear-museums.org.uk
Washington F Pit - Now Permanently Closed Enquiries- Sunderland
Museum & Art Gallery Tel: 0191 565 0723

Warwickshire
Leamington Spa Art Gallery & Museum Royal Pump Rooms, The
Parade, Royal Leamington Spa CV32 4AA Tel: 01926-742700
Fax: 01926-742705 Email: prooms@warwickdc.gov.uk WWW:
www.royal-pump-rooms.co.uk
Nuneaton Museum & Art Gallery Riversley Park, Nuneaton,
Warwickshire, CV11 5TU Tel: 024-7637-6473
**Regimental Museum of The Queen's Own Hussars (3rd King's
Own and 7th Queen's Own Hussars)** The Lord Leycester Hospital,
High Street, Warwick CV34 4EW Tel: Tel:01926 492035
Royal Warwickshire Regimental Museum St. John's House,
Warwick CV34 4NF Tel:01926 491653
Shakespeare Birthplace Trust - Museum Henley Street, Stratford
upon Avon CV37 6QW Tel: 01789-296083
Email: museums@shakespeare.org.uk
Warwick Castle Warwick Tel: 01926-406600WWW:
www.warwick-castle.co.uk
Warwick Doll Museum Okens House, Castle Street, Warwick,
Warwickshire, CV34 4BP Tel: 01926-495546
Warwickshire Market Hall Museum Market Place, WarwickCV34
4SA Tel: 01926-412500
Warwickshire Yeomanry Museum, The Court House, Jury Street,
Warwick CV34 4EW Tel: 01926 492212 Fax: 01926 494837 Email:
wtc.admin@btclick.com

Wiltshire
Alexander Keiller Museum High Street, Avebury, Marlborough,
Wiltshire, SN8 1RF Tel: 01672-539250
Atwell-Wilson Motor Museum Trust Stockley Lane, Calne,
Wiltshire, SN11 0 Tel: 01249-813119
Duke of Edinburgh's Royal Regiment (Berks & Wilts) Museum The
Wardrobe, 58 The Close, Salisbury, SP1 2EX
Tel: 01722-414536 Fax: 01722 421626
Lydiard House Lydiard Park, Lydiard Tregoze, Swindon, Wiltshire,
SN5 9PA Tel: 01793-770401
Royal Army Chaplains Department Museum Netheravon House,
Salisbury Road, Netheravon SP4 9SY Tel: 01980-604911
Fax: 01980-604908
Salisbury & South Wiltshire Museum The King's House, 65 The
Close, Salisbury SP1 2EN Tel: 01722-332151 Fax: 01722-325611
Email: museum@salisburymuseum.freeserve.co.uk
Sevington Victorian School Sevington, Grittleton, Chippenham,
Wiltshire , SN14 7LD Tel: 01249-783070 Fax: 01249-783070
Steam: Museum of the Great Western Railway Kemble Drive,
Swindon, Wiltshire, SN2 2TA Tel: 01793-466646
Fax: 01793-466614 Email: tbryan@swindon.gov.uk
Yelde Hall Museum Market Place, Chippenham , Wiltshire, SN15
3HL Tel: 01249-651488

Worcestershire
Almonry Museum Abbey Gate, Worcestershire, WR11 4BG
Tel: 01386-446944
Avoncroft Museum of Historic Buildings Stoke Heath, Bromsgrove
B60 4JR Tel: 01527-831363
Email: avoncroft1@compuserve.com WWW: www.avoncroft.org.uk
Bewdley Museum and Research Library Load Street, Bewdley
DY12 2AE Tel: 01229-403573
The Commandery Civil War Museum, Sidbury, WorcesterWR1
2HU Tel: 01905 361821 Fax: 01905 361822 Email:
thecommandery@cityofworcester.gov.uk WWW:
www.worcestercitymuseums.org.uk
The Elgar Birthplace Museum Crown East Lane, Lower
Broadheath, Worcester, WR2 6RH Tel: 01905-333224

Fax: 01905-333224
Kidderminster Railway Museum Station Drive, Kidderminster
DY10 1QX Tel: 01562-825316
The Mueseum of Local Life, Tudor House, Friar Street,
WorcesterWR1 2NA Tel: 01905 722349 WWW:
www.worcestercitymuseums.org.uk
Malvern Museum Abbey Gateway, Abbey Rd, Malvern,
Worcestershire, WR14 3ES Tel: 01684-567811
The Commandery Civil War Museum Sidbury, Worcester WR1
2HU Tel: 01905-361821
Worcester City Museum & Art Gallery Foregate Street, Worcester
WR1 1DT Tel: 01905-25371
Worcestershire City Museum Queen Elizabeth House, Trinity
Street, Worcester WR1 2PW
Worcestershire County Museum Hartlebury Castle, Hartlebury,
Worcestershire, DY11 7XZ Tel: 01229-250416 Fax: 01299-251890
Email: museum@worcestershire.gov.uk
WWW: www.worcestershire.gov.uk/museum
Museum of Worcester Porcelain, The Royal Porcelain Works,
Severn Street, Worcester, WR1 2NE Email: rwgeneral@royal-
worcester.co.uk
The Worcestershire Regiment Museum, Worcester City Museum &
Art Gallery, Foregate Street, WorcesterWR1 1DT Tel: 01905-25371
Museum Tel: 01905 354359 Office Fax: 01905-616979 Museum
01905 353871 Office Email: rhq_wfr@lineone.net Postal Address:
The Curator, The Worcestershire Regimental Museum Trust, RHQ
WFR, Norton Barracks, Worcester WR5 2PA
Worcestershire City Museum and Art Gallery, Foregate Street,
WorcesterWR1 1DT Tel: 01905 25371 Fax: 01905 616979 Email:
artgalleryandmuseum@cityofworcester.gov.uk WWW:
www.worcestercitymuseums.org.uk
The Museum of the Worcestershire Yeomanry Cavalry, Worcester
City Museum & Art Gallery, Foregate St, WorcesterWR1 1DT Tel:
01905 25371 Fax: 01905 616979 Email:
tbridges@cityofworcester.gov.uk WWW:
www.worcestercitymuseums.org.uk
**Worcestershire Regiment Archives (Worcestershire and Sherwood
Forester's Regiment)**, RHQ WFR Norton Barracks, WorcesterWR5
2PA Tel: 01905 354359 Fax: 01905 353871 Email:
rhg_wfr@lineone.net Enquires only accepted in writing by letter,
email or fax

Yorkshire
Yorkshire – East Yorkshire
East Riding Heritage Library & Museum Sewerby Hall,
Bridlington, East Yorkshire, YO15 1EA Tel: 01262-677874
Fax: 01262-674265 Email: museum@pop3.poptel.org.uk WWW:
www.bridlington.net/sew
The Hornsea Museum Burns Farm, 11 Newbegin, Hornsea, North
Humberside, HU18 1AB Tel: 01964-533443 WWW:
www.hornsea.com
Museum of Army Transport, Flemingate, BeverleyHU17 0NG Tel:
01482 860445 Fax: 01482 872767
Withernsea Lighthouse Museum Hull Road, Withernsea East
Yorkshire HU19 2DY Tel: 01964-614834
Yorkshire – North Yorkshire
Aysgarth Falls Carriage Museum Yore Mill , Asgarth Falls, Leyburn
DL8 3SR Tel: 01969-663399
Beck Isle Museum of Rural Life Bridge Street, Pickering YO18
8DU Tel: 01751-473653
Captain Cook Memorial Museum Grape Lane, Whitby YO22 4BA
Tel: 01947-601900 WWW: cookmuseumwhitby.co.uk/
Email: captcookmuseumwhitby@ukgateway.net
Captain Cook Schoolroom Museum Great Ayton, North Yorkshire
Tel: 01642-723358
Dales Countryside Museum Station Yard, Burtersett Road, Hawes
DL8 3NT Tel: 01969-667494 Email: dcm@yorkshiredales.org.uk
Eden Camp Museum, Malton YO17 6RT Tel: 01653 697777 Fax:
01653 698243 Email: admin@edencamp.co.uk WWW:
http://www.edencamp.co.ukA theme museum devoted to the WW2.
Video History Section of recordings of personal memories. Forces
Reunion Section. Much bibliographical information throughout the
museum
Embsay Steam Railway Embsay Railway Station, Embsay, Skipton,
North Yorkshire, BD23 6QX Tel: 01756-794727
The Forbidden Corner Tupgill Park Estate, Coverham, Middleham,
Leyburn, DL8 4TJ Tel: 01969 640638 Tel: 01969 640687
Green Howards Regimental Museum, Trinity Church Square,
RichmondDL10 4QN Tel: 01748-822133 Fax: 01748-826561 Story
of the Green Howards (Alexandra, Princess of Wales's Own Yorkshire
Regiment from 1688 to date)
Life In Miniature 8 Sandgate, Whitby YO22 4DB
Tel: 01947-601478
Malton Museum The Old Town Hall, Market Place, Malton, North
Yorkshire, YO17 7LP Tel: 01653-695136
The North Yorkshire Moors Railway PIckering Station, Pickering,
YO18 7AJ Tel: 01751 472508, Email:
info@northyorkshiremoorsrailway.com WWW:

www.northyorkshiremoorsrailway.com
Nidderdale Museum Council Offices, King Street, Pateley Bridge
HG3 5LE Tel: 01423-711225
Old Courthouse Museum Castle Yard, Knaresborough
Tel: 01423-556188
Richmondshire Museum Research enquiries must be by letter,
Ryder's Wynd, Richmond, North Yorkshire, DL10 4JA
Tel: 01748-825611
Ripon Prison & Police Museum Ripon Museum Trust, St Marygate,
Ripon, North Yorkshire, HG4 1LX Tel: 01765-690799 (24hr)
01765-690799 Email: ralph.lindley@which.net
Ripon Workhouse - Museum of Poor Law Allhallowgate, Ripon,
North Yorkshire, HG4 1LE Tel: 01765-690799
Rotunda Museum Vernon Road, Scarborough YO11 2NN
Tel: 01723-374839
**Royal Dragoon Guards Military Museum (4th/7th Royal Dragoon
Guards & 5th Royal Inniskilling Dragoon Guards),** 3A Tower
Street, York YO1 9SB Tel: 01904-662790 Tel: 01904 662310 Fax:
01904 662310 Email: rdgmuseum@onetel.net.uk WWW:
www.rdg.co.uk Co located with Prince of Wales' Own Regiment of
Yorkshire Military Museum (West & East Yorkshire Regiments)
**Royal Dragoon Guards & Prince of Wales' Own Regiment of
Yorkshire Military Museum** 3A Tower Street, York, North
Yorkshire, YO1 9SB Tel: 01904-662790 Tel: 01904-658051
Royal Pump Room Museum Crown Place, Harrogate
Tel: 01423-556188 Fax: 01423-556130
Email: lg12@harrogate.gov.uk WWW: www.harrogate.gov.uk
Ryedale Folk Museum Hutton le Hole, North Yorkshire, YO62 6UA
Tel: 01751-417367 Email: library@dbc-lib.demon.co.uk
The World of James Herriott 23 Kirkgate, Thirsk YO7 1PL
Tel: 01845-524234 Fax: 01845-525333
Email: anne.keville@hambleton.gov.uk
WWW: www.hambleton.gov.uk
Upper Wharfedale Museum Society & Folk Museum, The Square,
Grassington BD23 5AU
Whitby Lifeboat Museum Pier Road, Whitby YO21 3PU
Tel: 01947-602001
Whitby Museum Pannett Park, Whitby YO21 1RE
Tel: 01947-602908 Fax: 01947-897638
Email: graham@durain.demon.co.uk
WWW: www.durain.demon.co.uk
Yorkshire Air Museum, Halifax Way, Elvington, York YO41 4AU
Tel: 01904 608595 Fax: 01904 608246 Email:
museum@yorkshireairmuseum.co.uk WWW:
www.yorkshireairmuseum.co.uk Canadian contact: Canada Branch,
(Doug Sample CD), 470 Petit Street, St Laurent, Quebec Canada.
H4N 2H6
Yorkshire – South Yorkshire
Abbeydale Industrial Hamlet Abbeydale Road South, Sheffield,
South Yorkshire, S7 2 Tel: 0114-236-7731
Bishops House Museum Norton Lees Lane, Sheffield, S8 9BE Tel:
0114 278 2600 WWW: www.sheffieldgalleries.org.uk
Cannon Hall Museum Cannon Hall, Cawthorne, Barnsley S75 4AT
Tel: 01226-790270
Clifton Park Museum Clifton Lane, Rotherham S65 2AA
Tel: 01709-823635 Email: guy.kilminster@rotherham.gov.uk
WWW: www.rotherham.gov.uk
Fire Museum (Sheffield) Peter House, 101-109 West Bar, Sheffield
S3 8PT Tel: 0114-249-1999 Fax: 0114-249-1999
WWW: www.hedgepig.freeserve.co.uk
Kelham Island Museum
Alma Street, Kelham Island, Sheffield S3 8RY Tel: 0114-272-2106
King's Own Yorkshire Light Infantry Regimental Museum
Museum & Art Gallery, Chequer Road, Doncaster, DN1 2AE
Tel: 01302-734293 Fax: 01302-735409
Email: museum@doncaster.gov.uk WWW: www.doncaster.gov.uk
Magna Sheffield Road, Templeborough, Rotherham, S60 1DX Tel:
01709 720002 Fax: 01709 820092 Email: info@magnatrust.co.uk
WWW: www.magnatrust.org.uk
**Regimental Museum 13th/18th Royal Hussars and The Light
Dragoons** Cannon Hall, Cawthorne, Barnsley, South Yorkshire, S75
4AT Tel: 01226 790270
Sandtoft Transport Centre Ltd Belton Road, Sandtoft, Doncaster,
South Yorkshire, DN8 5SX Tel: 01724-711391
Sheffield City Museum Weston Park, Sheffield, S10 2TP
Tel: 0114-278-2600
York and Lancaster Regimental Museum, Library and Arts Centre,
Walker Place, Rotherham S65 1JH Tel: 01709 823635 Fax: 01709
823631 Email: karl.noble@rotherham.gov.uk WWW:
www.rotherham.gov.uk
Sheffield City Museum
Weston Park, Sheffield, S10 2TP Tel: 0114 278 2600 WWW:
www.sheffieldgalleries.org.uk
Sheffield Police and Fire Museum, 101-109 West Bar, Sheffield S3
8TP Tel: 0114 249 1999 WWW: www.hedgepig.freeserve.co.uk
Yorkshire – West Yorkshire
Armley Mills Canal Road, Leeds, West Yorkshire, LS12 2QF
Tel: 0113-263-7861 Fax: 0113-263-7861

Bankfield Museum
Boothtown Road, Halifax HX3 6HG Tel: 01422-354823
Bolling Hall Museum Bowling Hall Road, Bradford, West Yorkshire,
BD4 7 Tel: 01274-723057 Fax: 01274-726220
Bracken Hall Countryside Centre Glen Road, Baildon, Shipley,
BD17 5ED Tel: 01274-584140
Bradford Industrial Museum & Horses at Work Moorside Road,
Eccleshill, Bradford, West Yorkshire, BD2 3HP Tel: 01274-631756
Calderdale Museums & Arts Piece Hall, Halifax HX1 1RE
Tel: 01422-358087
Castleford Museum Room Carlton Street, Castleford WF10 1BB
Tel: 01977-722085
Cliffe Castle Museum Spring Gardens Lane, Keighley BD20 6LH
Tel: 01535-618231
The Colour Museum 1 Providence Street, Bradford, West Yorkshire,
BD1 2PW Tel: 01274-390955 Fax: 01274-392888
Email: museum@sdc.org.uk WWW: www.sdc.org.uk
Duke of Wellington's Regimental Museum Bankfield Museum,
Akroyd Park, Boothtown Road, Halifax, HX3 6HG Tel: 01422
354823 Email: Fax: 01422 249020
Eureka The Museum For Children Discovery Road, Halifax HX1
2NE Tel: 01422-330069
Keighley Bus Museum Trust 47 Brantfell Drive, Burnley, BB12
8AW Tel: 01282-413179 WWW: www.kbmt.freeuk.com
Kirkstall Abbey and Abbey House Museum Kirkstall Road, Kirkstall,
Leeds, LS5 3EH Tel: 0113 275 5821
Leeds City Art Gallery The Headrow, Leeds, LS1 3AA
Tel: 0113-247-8248
Leeds Museums Resource Centre Moorfield Road, Moorfield
Industrial Estate, Yeadon, Leeds, LS19 7BN Tel: 0113-214-6526
Lotherton Hall Lotherton Lane, Aberford, Leeds, LS25 3EB
Tel: 0113-281-3259
Manor House Art Gallery & Museum Castle Yard, Castle Hill,
Ilkley LS29 9D Tel: 01943-600066
Middleton Railway The Station, Moor Road, Hunslet, Leeds, LS10
2JQ Tel: 0113 271 0320, Email: howhill@globalnet.co.uk WWW:
wwww.personal.leeds.ac.uk/mph6mip/mrt/mrt.htm
The National Coal Mining Museum for England Caphouse
Colliery, New Road, Overton, Wakefield, West Yorkshire, WF4 4RH
Tel: 01924-848806 Fax: 01924-840694 Email: info@ncm.org.uk
WWW: www.ncm.org.uk
National Museum of Photography, Film &Television Bradford,
West Yorkshire, BD1 1NQ Tel: 01274-202030 Fax: 01274-723155
WWW: http:www.nmpft.org.uk
Royal Armouries (Leeds) Armouries Drive, Leeds LS10 1LT
Tel: 0990-106666
Saddleworth Museum & Art Gallery
High Street, Uppermill, Oldham, Lancashire, OL3 6HS
Tel: 01457-874093 Fax: 01457-870336
Shibden Hall Lister Road, Shibden, Halifax HX3 6AG Tel: 01422-352246
Skopos Motor Museum Alexandra Mills, Alexandra Road, Batley
WF17 6JA Tel: 01924-444423
Temple Newsham House Temple Newsham Road, off Selby Road,
Leeds, LS15 0AE Tel: 0113 264 7321
Thackray Medical Museum Beckett Street, Leeds LS9 7LN
Tel: 0113-244-4343 Fax: 0113-247-0219
Email: info@thackraymuseum.org WWW:
www.thackraymuseum.org
Thwaite Mills Watermill Thwaite Lane, Stourton, Leeds, LS10 1RP
Tel: 0113-249-6453
Vintage Carriages Trust Station Yard, South Street, Ingrow,
Keighley, West Yorkshire, BD21 1DB Tel: 01535-680425
Wakefield Museum Wood Street, Wakefield, West Yorkshire, WF1
2EW Tel: 01924-305351 Fax: 01924-305353
Yorkshire - York
Bar Convent Museum 17 Blossom Street, York, YO24 1AQ
Tel: 01904-643238 Fax: 01904-631792
Email: bar-convent.org.uk WWW: www.bar-convent.org.uk
Micklegate Bar Museum Micklegate, York YO1 6JX
Tel: 01904-634436
Richard III Museum Monk Bar, York YO1 2LH Tel: 01904-634191
WWW: www.richardiiimuseum.co.uk
York Archaeological Trust, 13 Ogleforth, York YO1 7FG Tel: 01904
663000 Fax: 01904 663024 Email: enquiries@yorkarchaeology.co.uk
WWW: www.yorkarchaeology.co.uk
York Castle Museum The Eye of York, York, YO1 9RW
Tel: 01904-653611 Fax: 01904-671078 WWW: www.york.gov.uk
Yorkshire Museum Museum Gardens, York, YO1 7FR
Tel: 01904-629745 Fax: 01904-651221
Email: yorkshire.museum@yorks.gov.uk
WWW: www.york.gov.uk or also www.yorkgateway.co.uk

WALES
Museum of Welsh Life St Fagans, Cardiff, CF5 6XB
Tel: 029-205-73437 Fax: 029-205-73490

Anglesey
Beaumaris Gaol Museum Bunkers Hill, Beaumaris LL58 8EP
Tel: 01248-810921, 01248-724444 Fax: 01248-750282
Email: BeaumarisCourtandGaol@anglesey.gov.uk
Maritime Museum Beach Road, Newry Beach, Holyhead, Anglesey,
LL65 1YD Tel: 01407-769745 Fax: 01407-769745
Email: cave@holyhead85.freeserve.co.uk

Caerphilly
Drenewydd Museum 26-27 Lower Row, Bute Town, Nr Rhyllney,
Caerphilly County Borough, NP22 5QH Tel: 01685-843039
Email: morgacl@caerphilly.gov.uk

Cardiff
1st The Queen's Dragoon Guards Regimental Museum, Cardiff
Castle, Cardiff CF10 2RB Tel: (029) 2022 2253 Tel: (029) 2078 1271
Fax: (029) 2078 1384 Email: clivejmorris@lineone.net WWW:
www.qdg.org.uk
Cardiff Castle Castle Street, Cardiff, CF10 3RB Tel: 029-2087-8100
Fax: 029-2023-1417 Email: cardiffcastle@cardiff.gov.uk
Techniquest Stuart Street, Cardiff, CF10 5BW Tel: 02920-475475

Carmarthenshire
Kidwelly Industrial Museum Broadford, Kidwelly,
Carmarthenshire, SA17 4UF Tel: 01554-891078
Parc Howard Museum & Art Gallery Mansion House, Parc
Howard, Llanelli, Carmarthenshire, SA15 3LJ Tel: 01554-772029

Ceredigion
Cardigan Heritage Centre Bridge Warehouse, Castle St, Ceredigion,
Dyfed, SA43 3AA Tel: 01239-614404
Ceredigion Museum Coliseum, Terrace Road, Aberystwyth,
Ceredigion, SY23 2AQ Tel: 01970-633088 Fax: 01970-633084
Email: museum@ceredigion.gov.uk
Llywernog Silver Mine (Mid-Wales Mining Museum Ltd)
Ponterwyd, Aberystwyth SY23 3AB Tel: 01970-890620
Mid-Wales Mining Museum Ltd 15 Market Street, Aberaeron,
Ceredigion, SA46 0AU Tel: 01545-570823

Conwy
Betws-y-Coed Motor Museum Museum Cottage, Betws-Y-Coed,
Conwy, LL24 0AH Tel: 01690-710760
Teapot Museum 25 Castle Street, Conwy, Gwynedd, LL32 8AY
Tel: 01492-596533

Denbigh/Denbighshire
Cae Dai Trust Cae Dai Trust/Cae Dai Lawnt, Denbigh, LL16 4SU
Tel: 01745-817004/812107
Llangollen Motor Museum Pentrefelin, Llangollen, Denbighshire,
LL20 8EE Tel: 01978-860324

Glamorgan
Glamorgan – Mid Glamorgan
Brecon Mountain Railway Pant Station, Merthyr Tydfil, CF48 2UP
Tel: 01685 722988, Email: enquiries@breconmountainrailway.co.uk
WWW: www.breconmountainrailway.co.uk
Cyfarthfa Castle Museum Cyfarthfa Park, Brecon Road, Merthyr
Tydfil, CF47 8RE Tel: 01685-723112, 01685-383704
Fax: 01685-723112
Joseph Parrys Cottage
4 Chapel Row, Merthyr Tydfil, Mid Glamorgan, CF48 1BN
Tel: 01685-383704
Pontypridd Historical & Cultural Centre
Bridge Street, Pontypridd, Mid Glamorgan, CF37 4PE
Tel: 01443-409512 Fax: 01443-485565
Ynysfach Iron Heritage Centre
Merthyr Tydfil Heritage Trust, Ynysfach Road, Merthyr Tydfil, Mid
Glamorgan, CF48 1AG Tel: 01685-721858
Glamorgan – South Glamorgan
National Museum & Galleries of Wales
Cathays Park, Cardiff CF10 3NP Tel: 029-2039-7951
Welch Regiment Museum of the Royal Regiment of Wales
The Black & Barbican Towers, Cardiff Castle, Cardiff, CF10 3RB
Tel: 029-20229367 Email: welch@rrw.org.uk
WWW: www.rrw.org.uk
Glamorgan – West Glamorgan
Cefn Coed Colliery Museum Blaenant Colliery, Crynant, Neath,
West Glamorgan, SA10 8SE Tel: 01639-750556
Glynn Vivian Art Gallery Alexandra Road, Swansea, West
Glamorgan, SA1 5DZ Tel: 01792-655006 Fax: 01792-651713
Email: glynn.vivian.gallery@business.ntl.com
WWW: www.swansea.gov.uk
Maritime & Industrial Museum Museum Square, Maritime
Quarter, Victoria Rd, Swansea, West Glamorgan, SA1 1SN

Tel: 01792-650351 Fax: 01792-652585
Email: swansea.museum@business.ntl.com
Neath Museum 4 Church Place, Neath, West Glamorgan, SA11 3LL
Tel: 01639-645741

Gwynedd
Gwynedd Museums Service Victoria Dock, Caernarvon, Gwynedd,
LL55 1SH Tel: 01286-679098 Fax: 01286-679637
Email: amgueddfeydd-museums@gwynedd.gov.uk
Bala Lake Railway Rheilffordd Llyn Tegid The Station Yr Orsaf,
Llanuwchllyn, LL23 7DD Tel: 01678 540666 WWW: www.bala-
lake-railway.co.uk
Great Orme Tramway Tramffordd Y Gogarth Goprsaf Victoria,
Church Walks, Llandudno, LL30 1AZ Tel: 01492 574003, Email:
enq@greatormetramway.com WWW: www.greatormetramway.com
Home Front Experience New Street, Llandudno, LL30 2YF Tel:
01492 871032 WWW: www.homefront-enterprises.co.uk
Llanberis Lake Railway Rheilffordd Llyn Padarn LLanberis,
LL55 4TY Tel: 01286 870549 WWW: www.lake-railway.co.uk
Llandudno & Conwy Valley Railway Society Welsh Slate Museum,
Llanberis Tel: 01492 874590
Porthmadog Maritime Museum Oakley Wharf 1, The Harbour,
Porthmadog, Gwynedd, LL49 9LU Tel: 01766-513736
The Royal Welch Fusiliers Regimental Museum, The Queen's
Tower, The Castle, Caernarfon LL55 2AY Tel: 01286 673362 Fax:
01286 677042 Email: rrwfusiliers@callnetuk.com WWW:
www.rwfmuseum.org.uk
Segontium Roman Museum Beddgelert Road, Caernarfon,
Gwynedd, LL55 2LN Tel: 01286-675625
Sir Henry Jones Museum Y Cwm, Llangernyw, Abergele, LL22
8PR Tel: 01492 575371 Tel: 01754 860661
Snowdon Mountain Railway Llanberis, LL55 4TY Tel: 0870
4580033 Fax: 01286 872518 WWW: www.snowdonrailway.co.uk
Welsh Highland Railway Tremadog Road, Porthmadog, LL49 9DY
Welsh Slate Museum Padarn Country Park, Llanberis, Gwynedd
LL55 4TY Tel: 01286-870630 Fax: 01286-871906
Email: wsmpost@btconnect.com WWW: www.nmgw.ac.uk

Merthyr Tydfil
Brecon Mountain Railway Pant Station, Merthyr Tydfil, CF48 2UP
Tel: 01685 722988, Email: enquiries@breconmountainrailway.co.uk
WWW: www.breconmountainrailway.co.uk
Cyfarthfa Castle Museum Cyfarthfa Park, Brecon Road, Merthyr
Tydfil, CF47 8RE Tel: 01685-723112, 01685-383704
Fax: 01685-723112
Joseph Parrys Cottage 4 Chapel Row, Merthyr Tydfil, Mid
Glamorgan, CF48 1BN Tel: 01685-383704
Ynysfach Iron Heritage Centre
Merthyr Tydfil Heritage Trust, Ynysfach Road, Merthyr Tydfil, Mid
Glamorgan, CF48 1AG Tel: 01685-721858

Monmouthshire
Abergavenny Museum The Castle, Castle Street, Abergavenny,
Monmouthshire, NP7 5EE Tel: 01873-854282
Castle & Regimental Museum
Monmouth Castle, Monmouth NP25 3BS Tel: 01600-772175
Chepstow Museum Bridge Street, Chepstow, Monmouthshire, NP16
5EZ Tel: 01291-625981 Fax: 01291-635005
Email: chepstowmuseum@monmouthshire.gov.uk
Monmouthshire Royal Engineers (Militia), Castle and Regimental
Museum, The Castle, Monmouth NP25 3BS Tel: 01600-712935,
Email: curator@monmouthcastlemuseum.org.uk WWW:
www.monmouthcastlemuseum.org.uk Small Militia and Territorial
Army Regiment. Limited and patchy collection of old ledgers.
Nelson Museum & Local History Centre Priory Street, Monmouth,
NP5 3XA Tel: 01600-713519 Fax: 01600-775001
Email: nelsonmuseum@monmouthshire.gov.uk
Usk Rural Life Museum The Malt Barn, New Market Street, Usk,
Monmouthshire, NP15 1AU Tel: 01291-673777

Pembrokeshire
Haverfordwest Town Museum Castle Street, Haverfordwest, SA61
2EF Tel: 01437-763087
Milford Haven Museum Old Customs House, The Docks, Milford
Haven, Pembrokeshire, SA73 3AF Tel: 01646-694496
Newport Museum & Art Gallery John Frost Square, Newport NP20
1PA Tel: 01633-840064 Fax: 01633-222615
Email: museum@newport.gov.uk
Pembrokeshire Motor Museum Keeston Hill, Haverfordwest, SA62
6EH Tel: 01437-710950
Pembrokeshire Museum Service The County Library, Dew Street,
Haverfordwest, SA61 1SU Tel: 01437-775246 Fax: 01437-769218
Pillgwenlly Heritage Community Project within Baptist Chapel,
Alexandra Road, Newport, Pembrokeshire, NP20 2JE
Tel: 01633-244893
Roman Legionary Museum High Street, Caerleon; Newport NP18
1AE Tel: 01633-423134

Tenby Museum Castle Hill, Tenby, SA70 7BP Tel: 01834-842809
Fax: 01834-842809 Email: tenbymuseum@hotmail.com WWW:
tenbymuseum.free-online.co.uk
Wilson Museum of Narberth Market Square, Narberth SA67 7AX
Tel: 01834-861719

Powys
The Judge's Lodging Broad Street, Presteigne LD8 2AD
Tel: 01544-260650 Fax: 01544-260652
WWW: www.judgeslodging.org.uk
Llanidloes Museum
Great Oak Street, Llanidloes SY18 6BN Tel: 01686-412375
Powysland Museum & Montgomery Canal Centre Canal Yard,
Welshpool, Powys, SY21 7AQ Tel: 01938-554656
Fax: 01938-554656
Radnorshire Museum Temple Street, Llandrindod Wells, Powys,
LD1 5DL Tel: 01597-824513 Fax: 01597-825781
Email: radnorshire.museum@powys.gov.uk
**South Wales Borderers & Monmouthshire Regimental Museum
of the Royal Regt of Wales (24th/41st Foot)**, The Barracks, Brecon
LD3 7EB Tel: 01874 613310 Fax: 01874 613275 Email:
swb@rrw.org.uk WWW: www.rrw.org.uk
Water Folk Canal Centre Old Store House, Llanfrynach, Brecon,
Powys, LD3 7LJ Tel: 01874-665382

Torfaen
Big Pit Mining Museum Blaenavon, Torfaen, NP4 9XP
Tel: 01495-790311
Valley Inheritance Park Buildings, Pontypool, NP4 6JH
Tel: 01495-752036 Fax: 01495-752043

Wrexham
Wrexham Museum County Buildings, Regent Street, Wrexham,
LL11 1RB Tel: 01978-317970 Fax: 01978-317982
Email: museum@wrexham.gov.uk

SCOTLAND
Scottish United Services Museum The Castle, Museum Square,
Edinburgh, EH1 2NG Tel: 0131-225-7534 Fax: 0131-225-3848
Scottish Museums Council County House, 20/22 Torphichen Street,
Edinburgh, EH3 8JB Tel: 0131-229-7465 Fax: 0131-229-2728
Email: inform@scottishmuseums.org.uk
WWW: www.scottishmuseums.org.uk

Aberdeenshire
Aberdeen Maritime Museum Shiprow, Aberdeen, AB11 5BY
Tel: 01224-337700 Email: johne@arts-recreation.net.uk WWW:
www.aagm.co.uk
Alford & Donside Heritage Association Mart Road, Alford, AB33
8AA Tel: 019755-62906
Arbuthnot Museum St. Peter Street, Peterhead, Aberdeenshire,
AB42 1LA Tel: 01779-477778 Fax: 01771-622884
Fraserburgh Heritage Society Heritage Centre, Quarry Road,
Fraserburgh, AB43 9DT Tel: 01346-512888
Gordon Highlanders Museum, St Lukes, Viewfield Road, Aberdeen
AB15 7XH Tel: 01224 311200 Fax: 01224 319323 Email:
museum@gordonhighlanders.com WWW:
www.gordonhighlanders.com
Grampian Transport Museum Alford, AB33 8AE
Tel: 019755-62292
Hamilton T.B Northfield Farm, New Pitsligo, Fraserburgh AB43
6PX Tel: 01771-653504
Museum of Scottish Lighthouses Kinnaird Head, Fraserburgh,
Aberdeenshire, AB43 9DU Tel: 01346-511022 Fax: 01346-511033
Email: enquiries@lighthousescom.co.uk
Provost Skene's House Guestrow, Aberdeen AB10 1AS
Tel: 01224-641086
Satrosphere Moved in 2000 - new address contact, 19 Justice Mill
Lane, Aberdeen, AB11 6EQ Tel: 01224-213232 Fax: 01224-211685
Email: satrosphere@ssphere.ifb.co.uk

Angus
Arbroath Museum Signal Tower, Ladyloan, Arbroath DD11 1PY
Tel: 01241-875598 Fax: 01241-439263
Email: signal.tower@angus.gov.uk
WWW: www.angus.gov.uk/history
Glenesk Folk Museum The Retreat, Glenesk, Brechin, Angus, DD9
7YT Tel: 01356-670254 Email: retreat@angusglens.co.uk WWW:
www.angusglens.co.uk
The Meffan Institute 20 High Street West, Forfar, Angus, DD8 1BB
Tel: 01307-464123 Fax: 01307-468451
Email: the.meffan@angus.gov.uk

Argyll
Campbeltown Heritage Centre Big Kiln, Witchburn Road,
Campbeltown, Argyll, PA28 6JU Tel: 01586-551400
Campbeltown Library and Museum Hall Street, Campbeltown,
Argyll, PA28 6BU Tel: 01586-552366

Castle House Museum Castle Gardens, Argyll Street, Dunoon,
Argyll, PA23 7HH Tel: 01369-701422
Kilmartin House Trust Kilmartin House, Kilmartin, Lochgilphead,
Argyll, PA31 8RQ Tel: 01546-510278 Fax: 01546-510330
Email: museum@kilmartin.org
WWW: www.kilmartin.org
Regimental Museum Argyll and Sutherland Highlanders
Stirling Castle, Stirling, Stirlingshire, FK8 1EH
Tel: 01786 475165 Fax: 01786 446038

Ayrshire
Ayrshire Yeomanry Museum, Rozelle House, Monument Road,
Alloway by Ayr KA7 4NQ Tel: 01292 445400 (Museum) Tel: 01292
264091 (Curator) The Ayrshire (ECO) Yeomanry was raised in 1798
and after 200 years existence, currently serves as one of the five
squadrons in the Territorial Armoured Reconnaisance Regiment - The
Queen's Own Yeomanry
Dalgarven Mill, Museum of Ayrshire Country Life & Costume Dalry
Road, Dalgarven, Kilwinning, Ayrshire, KA13 6PL
Tel: 01294-552448
East Ayrshire Council District History Centre & Museum Baird
Institute, 3 Lugar Street, Cumnock, Ayrshire, KA18 1AD
Tel: 01290-421701 Fax: 01290-421701
Email: Baird.institute@east-ayrshire.gov.uk
WWW: www.east-ayrshire.gov.uk
Glasgow Vennel Museum 10 Glasgow, Vennel, Irvine KA12 0BD
Tel: 01294-275059
Irvine Burns Club & Burgh Museum 28 Eglinton Street, Irvine
KA12 8AS Tel: 01294-274511
Largs Museum Kirkgate House, Manse Court, Largs, Ayrshire,
KA30 8AW Tel: 01475-687081
McKechnie Institute Dalrymple Street, Girvan, Ayrshire, KA26 9AE
Tel: 01465-713643 Email: mkigia@ukgateway.net
North Ayrshire Museum Manse Street, Saltcoats, Ayrshire, KA21
5AA Tel: 01294-464174 Email: namuseum@globalnet.co.uk
Rozelle House Rozelle Park, Ayr, Ayrshire, KA7 4NQ
Tel: 01292-445447

Banffshire
The Buckie Drifter Maritime Heritage Centre Freuchny Road,
Buckie AB56 1TT Tel: 01542-834646

Berwickshire
The Jim Clark Room 44 Newtown Street, Duns TD11 3DT
Tel: 01361-883960
Museum of Coldstream Guards Coldstream, Berwickshire

Caithness
Clangunn Heritage Centre & Museum Old Parish Kirk, Latheron,
Caithness, KW5 6DL Tel: 01593-741700
Dunbeath Preservation Trust Old School, Dunbeath KW6 6EG
Tel: 01593-731233 Email: DunTrust@aol.com
The Last House John O'Groats, Wick KW1 4YR
Tel: 01955-611250
Wick Hertiage Centre 18 Bank Row, Wick KW1 5EY
Tel: 01955-605393

Dumfries & Galloway/ Dumfriesshire
Dumfries Museum The Observatory, Dumfries, DG2 7SW
Tel: 01387-253374 Fax: 01387-265081 Email: info@dumgal.gov.uk
WWW: www.dumfriesmuseum.demon.co.uk
Ellisland Trust Ellisland Farm, Dumfries DG2 0RP
Tel: 01387-740426
Gretna Museum & Tourist Services Headless Cross, Gretna Green
DG16 5EA Tel: 01461-338441 Fax: 01461-338442
Email: info@gretnagreen.com WWW: www.gretnagreen.com
John Paul Jones Birthplace Museum Arbigland, Kirkbean,
Dumfries DG2 8BQ Tel: 01387-880613
Old Bridge House Museum Mill Road, Dumfries DG2 7BE
Tel: 01387-256904 WWW: www.dumfriesmuseum.demon.co.uk
Robert Burns Centre Mill Road, Dumfries DG2 7BE
Tel: 01387-264808
Robert Burns House Burns Street, Dumfries, DG1 2PS Tel: 01387
255297
Sanquhar Tolbooth Museum High Street, Sanquhar DG4 6BL
Tel: 01659-50186
Savings Banks Museum Ruthwell, Dumfries DG1 4NN
Tel: 01387-870640
Shambellie House Museum of Costume New Abbey, Dumfries
DG2 8HQ Tel: 01387-850375
Stranraer Museum 55 George Street, Stranraer, DG9 7JP
Tel: 01776-705088 Fax: 01776-705835
Email: JohnPic@dumgal.gov.uk

Dunbartonshire
Scottish Maritime Museum Gottries Road, Irvine, Ayrshire, KA12
8QE Tel: 01294-278283 Fax: 01294-313211
Email: jgrant5313@aol.com

Dundee

Dundee Heritage Trust Verdant Works, West Henderson's Wynd, Dundee, DD1 5BT Tel: 01382-225282 Fax: 01382-221612 Email: info@dundeeheritage.sol.co.uk WWW: www.verdant.works.co.uk

Royal Research Ship Discovery Discovery Point, Discovery Quay, Dundee, DD1 4XA Tel: 01382-201245 Fax: 01382-225891 Email: info@dundeeheritage.sol.co.uk WWW: www.rrs-discovery.co.uk

Verdant Works - A Working Jute mill West Henderson's Wynd, Dundee, DD1 5BT Tel: 01382-225282 Fax: 01382-221612 Email: dundeeheritage@sol.co.uk WWW: www.verdant-works.co.uk

Edinburgh

Heritage Projects (Edinburgh) Ltd Castlehill, Royal Mile, Edinburgh, Midlothian EH1 2NE Tel: 0131-225-7575

Huntly House Museum 142 Canongate, Edinburgh, EH8 8DD Tel: 0131-529-4143 Fax: 0131-557-3346

National Museums of Scotland - Library Royal Museum, Chambers Street, Edinburgh, EH1 1JF Tel: 0131-247-4137 Fax: 0131-247-4311 Email: library@nms.ac.uk WWW: www.nms.ac.uk

Royal Museum and Museum of Scotland Chambers Street, Edinburgh, EH1 1JF Tel: 0131-225-7534, 0131-247-4027 (Text) WWW: www.nms.ac.uk

Royal Scots Regimental Museum The Castle, Edinburgh, EH1 2YT Tel: 0131-310-5014 Fax: 0131-310-5019

Royal Yacht Britannia and Visitor Centre Ocean Drive, Leith, Edinburgh, EH6 6JJ Tel: 0131-555-5566, Group bookings 0131-555-8800 WWW: www.royalyachtbritannia.co.uk

Scottish United Services Museum The Castle, Museum Square, Edinburgh, EH1 2NG Tel: 0131-225-7534 Fax: 0131-225-3848

Scottish United Services Museum Library The Castle, Museum Square, Edinburgh, EH1 1 2NG Tel: 0131-225-7534-Ext-2O4 Fax: 0131-225-3848 Email: library@nms.ac.uk WWW: www.nms.ac.uk

Falkirk

Falkirk History Research Centre Callendar House, Callendar Park, Falkirk, FK1 1YR Tel: 01324-503778 Fax: 01324-503771 Email: ereid@falkirkmuseums.demon.co.uk WWW: www.falkirkmuseums.demon.co.uk

Fife

Andrew Carnegie Birthplace Museum Moodie Street, Dunfermline, Fife, KY12 7PL Tel: 01383-724302

Dunfermline Museum Enquiries can be made at this address for: Inverkeithing Museum, Pittencrief House Museum and St Margaret's Cave, Viewfield, Viewfield Terrace, Dunfermline, Fife, KY12 7HY Tel: 01383-313838 Fax: 01383-313837

Inverkeithing Museum Museum located at: The Friary, Queen Street, Inverkeithing, Fife. Tel: 01383-313595, Enquiries to: Dunfermline Museum, Viewfield, Viewfield Terrace, Dunfermline, Fife, KY12 7HY Tel: 01383-313838 Fax: 01383-313837

John McDouall Stuart Museum Rectory Lane, Dysart, Kirkcaldy, Fife, KY1 2TP Tel: 01592-653118

Kirkcaldy Museum & Art Gallery War Memorial Gardens, Abbotshall Road, Kirkcaldy, Fife, KY1 1YG Tel: 01592-412860 Fax: 01592-412870

Methil Heritage Centre 272 High Street, Methil, Leven, Fife, KY8 3EQ Tel: 01333-422100

Pittencrieff House Museum Museum located at: Pittencrieff Park, Dunfermline, Fife KY12 8QH Tel: 01383-722935, Enquiries to: Dunfermline Museum, Viewfield, Viewfield Terrace, Dunfermline, Fife, KY12 7HY Tel: 01383-313838 Fax: 01383-313837

Scotland's Secret Bunker Underground Nuclear Command Centre, Crown Buildings (Near St Andrews), Fife, KY16 8QH Tel: 01333-310301

Scottish Fisheries Museum Scottish Fisheries Museum Trust Ltd, St. Ayles, Harbourhead, Anstruther, Fife, KY10 3AB Tel: 01333-310628 Fax: 01333-310628 Email: andrew@scottish-fisheries-museum.org WWW: www.scottish-fisheries-museum.org

The Fife Folk Museum High Street, Ceres, Cupar, Fife, KY15 5NF Tel: 01334-828180

Glasgow

Strathclyde Police Museum, 173 Pitt Street, Glasgow G2 4JS Tel: 0141 532 2483

Glasgow Vennel Museum 10 Glasgow, Vennel, Irvine, Ayrshire, KA12 0BD Tel: 01294-275059

Heatherbank Museum Glasgow Caledonian University, Cowcaddens Road, Glasgow, G4 0BA Tel: 0141-331-8637 Email: a.ramage@gcal.ac.uk WWW: www.lib.gcal.ac.uk/heatherbank

Museum of The Royal Highland Fusilers (Royal Scots Fusilers and Highland Light Infantry), 518 Sauchiehall Street, Glasgow G2 3LW Tel: 0141 332 0961 Fax: 0141 353 1493

Scotland Street School Museum & Museum of Education 225 Scotland Street, Glasgow, Lanarkshire, G5 8QB Tel: 0141-287-0500

Inverness-Shire

Highland Folk Museum Duke Street, Kingussie, PH21 1JG Tel: 01540-661307 Email: rachel.chisholm@highland.gov.uk

Highland Folk Park Aultlarie Croft, Kingussie Road, Newtonmore, Inverness-Shire, PH20 1AY Tel: 01540-673551

Highland Railway Museum 5 Druimlon, Drumnadrochit, Inverness IV63 6TY Tel: 01456-450527

Inverness Museum & Art Gallery Castle Wynd, Inverness V2 3ED Tel: 01463-237114

Mallaig Heritage Centre Station Road, Mallaig PH41 4PY Tel: 01687-462085

Queen's Own Highlanders (Seaforth & Camerons) Regimental Museum Archives, Fort George, Ardersier, Inverness IV1 7TD Tel: 01463-224380

The Clansman Centre Canalside, Fort Augustus PH32 4AU Tel: 01320-366444

West Highland Museum Cameron Square, Fort William, Inverness-Shire, PH33 6AJ Tel: 01397-702169 Fax: 01397-701927

Isle Of Arran

Arran Heritage Museum Rosaburn House, Brodick, Isle Of Arran, KA27 8DP Tel: 01770-302636

Isle Of Islay

Finlaggan Trust The The Cottage, Ballygrant, Isle Of Islay, PA45 7QL Tel: 01496-840644

Isle Of Mull

The Columba Centre Fionnphort, Isle Of Mull, Isle Of Mull, PA66 6BN Tel: 01681-700660

Isle Of North Uist

Taigh Chearsabhagh Trust Taigh Chearsabhagh, Lochmaddy, Isle Of North Uist, HS6 5AE Tel: 01876-500293 Email: taighchearsabhagh@zetnet.co.uk WWW: www.taighchearsabhagh.org.uk

Isle Of South Uist

Kildonan Museum Kildonan, Lochboisdale, Isle Of South Uist, HS8 5RZ Tel: 01878-710343

Kinross

Perth Museum & Art Gallery George Street, Perth, Tayside, PHI 5LB Tel: 01738-632488 Fax: 01738-443505 Email: scpayne@pkc.gov.uk

Kirkcudbrightshire

The Stewartry Museum St Mary Street, Kirkcudbright, DG6 4AQ Tel: 01557 331643

Lanarkshire

Auyld Kirk Museum The Cross Kirkintilloch, Glasgow G66 1 Tel: 0141 578 0144

Barrhead Museum - Closed permanently wef 31/3/00

Biggar Museum Trust Moat Park Kirkstyle, Biggar ML12 6DT Tel: 01899-221050

The Cameronians (Scottish Rifles) Museum, c/o Low Parks Museum, 129 Muir Street, Hamilton ML3 6BJ Tel: 01698 452163 Tel: 01698 328232 Fax: 01698 328412

Discover Carmichael Visitors Centre Warrenhill Farm, Warrenhill Road, Thankerton, Biggar, Lanarkshire, ML12 6PF Tel: 01899-308169

Fossil Grove Museum Victoria Park, Glasgow G65 9AH Tel: 0141-950-1448

Greenhill Covenanters House Museum Kirkstyle, Biggar ML12 6DT Tel: 01899-221572

Heritage Engineering 22 Carmyle Avenue, Glasgow G32 8HJ Tel: 0141-763-0007

Hunter House Maxwellton Road, East Kilbride, Glasgow, Lanarkshire, G74 3LW Tel: 01355-261261

John Hastie Museum Threestanes Road, Strathaven, Lanarkshire, ML10 6EB Tel: 01357-521257

Lanark Museum 7 Westport, Lanark, Lanarkshire, ML11 9HD Tel: 01555-666680 Email: paularchibald@hotmail.com WWW: www.biggar-net.co.uk/lanarkmuseum

Low Parks Museum 129 Muir Street, Hamilton, Lanarkshire, ML3 6BJ Tel: 01698-283981, 01698-328232

New Lanark Conservation Trust Visitors Centre Mill No 3, New Lanark Mills, Lanark, Lanarkshire, ML11 9DB Tel: 01555-661345 Fax: 01555-665378 Email: visit@newlanark.org WWW: www.newlanark.org

The People's Palace Glasgow Green, Glasgow, Lanarkshire, G40 1AT Tel: 0141-554-0223

Scotland Street School Museum & Museum of Education 225
Scotland Street, Glasgow, Lanarkshire, G5 8QB Tel: 0141-287-0500
The Lighthouse 11 Mitchell Lane, Glasgow, Lanarkshire, G1 3NU
Tel: 0141-221-6362
Weavers' Cottages Museum 23-25 Wellwynd, Airdrie, Lanarkshire,
ML6 0BN Tel: 01236-747712
Auld Kirk Musuem The Cross, Kirkintilloch, Glasgow, Lanarkshire
, G66 1 Tel: 0141-578-0144

Lanarkshire - North Lanarkshire
Motherwell Heritage Centre High Road, Motherwell, North
Lanarkshire, ML1 3HU Tel: 01698-251000 Fax: 01698-253433
Email: heritage@mhc158.freeserve.co.uk

Lothian
Lothian – East Lothian
Dunbar Museum High Street, Dunbar, East Lothian, EH42 1ER
Tel: 01368-863734
John Muir House Museum 126-128 High Street, Dunbar, East
Lothian, EH42 1JJ Tel: 01368-862585
North Berwick Museum School Road, North Berwick, East
Lothian, EH39 4JU Tel: 01620-895457

Lothian – West Lothian
Almond Valley Heritage Trust Livingston Mill Farm, Millfield,
Livingston, West Lothian, EH54 7AR Tel: 01506-414957
Bennie Museum Mansefield Street, Bathgate, West Lothian, EH48
4HU Tel: 01506-634944
Kinneil Museum Kinneil Estate, Bo'Ness EH51 0AY
Tel: 01506-778530
Linlithgow's Story Annet House, 143 High Street, Linlithgow, West
Lothian, EH49 7EJ Tel: 01506-670677
Queensferry Museum 53 High Street, South Queensferry, West
Lothian, EH30 9HP Tel: 0131-331-5545

Midlothian
History of Education Centre East London Street, Edinburgh,
Midlothian, EH7 4BW Tel: 0131-556-4224
Lauriston Castle 2a Cramond Rd South, Edinburgh, Midlothian,
EH4 5QD Tel: 0131-336-2060
Nelson Monument Calton Hill, Edinburgh, Midlothian, EH7 5AA
Tel: 0131-556-2716
Newhaven Heritage Museum Pier Place, Edinburgh, Midlothian,
EH6 4LP Tel: 0131-551-4165
Scots Dragoon Guards Museum Shop The Castle, Edinburgh,
Midlothian, EH1 2YT Tel: 0131-220-4387
Scottish Mining Museum Trust Lady Victoria Colliery,
Newtongrange, Dalkeith, Midlothian, EH22 4QN
Tel: 0131-663-7519 Fax: 0131-654-1618 WWW:
www.scottishminingmuseum.com

Morayshire
Elgin Museum 1 High Street, Elgin, Morayshire, IV30 1EQ
Tel: 01343-543675 Fax: 01343-543675
Email: curator@elginmuseum.demon.co.uk
Falconer Museum Tolbooth Street, Forres, Morayshire, IV36 1PH
Tel: 01309-673701 Fax: 01309-675863
Email: alisdair.joyce@techleis.moray.gov.uk
WWW: www.moray.gov.uk
Grantown Museum & Heritage Trust Burnfield House, Burnfield
Avenue, Grantown-On-Spey, Morayshire, PH26 3HH
Tel: 01479-872478 Fax: 01479-872478
Email: molly.duckett@btinternet.com WWW:
www.grantown-on-spey.co.uk
Lossiemouth Fisheries Museum Pitgaveny Street, Lossiemouth,
Morayshire, IV31 6TW Tel: 01343-813772
Nairn Museum Viewfield House, King Street, Nairn, Morayshire,
IV12 4EE Tel: 01667-456791

Orkney
Orkney Farm & Folk Museum - Birsay Kirbister Farm, Birsay,
Orkney, KW17 2LR Tel: 01856-771268
Orkney Farm & Folk Museum - Harray Corrigall Farm Museum,
Harray, Orkney, KW17 2LQ Tel: 01856-771411
Orkney Fossil & Vintage Centre Viewforth Burray, Orkney, KW17
2SY Tel: 01856-731255
Orkney Museum Tankerness House, Broad Street, Kirkwall, Orkney,
KW15 1DH Tel: 01856-873191 Fax: 01856-871560
Orkney Wireless Museum Kiln Corner, Kirkwall, Orkney, KW15 1LB
Tel: 01856-871400
Scapa Flow Visitor Centre Lyness, Stromness, Orkney, KW16 3NT
Tel: 01856-791300
Stromness Museum 52 Alfred Street, Stromness, Orkney
Tel: 01856-850025

Perthshire
Atholl Country Collection The Old School, Blair Atholl, Perthshire,
PH18 5SP Tel: 01796-481232 Email: r.cam@virgin.net

Clan Donnachaidh (Robertson) Museum Clan Donnachaidh
Centre, Bruar, Pitlochry PH18 5TW Tel: 01796-483338
Email: clandonnachaidh@compuserve.com
WWW: donkey3@freenetname.co.uk
Clan Menzies Museum Castle Menzies, Weem, by Aberfeldy,
Perthshire, PH15 2JD Tel: 01887-820982
Dunkeld Cathedral Chapter House Museum
Dunkeld, Perthshire, PH8 0AW Tel: 01350-727601/727249
The Hamilton Toy Collection 111 Main Street, Callander,
Perthshire, FK17 8BQ Tel: 01877-330004
Meigle Museum Dundee Road, Meigle, Blairgowrie, Perthshire,
PH12 8SB Tel: 01828-640612
Perth Museum & Art Gallery George Street, Perth, Tayside, PHI
5LB Tel: 01738-632488 Fax: 01738-443505
Email: scpayne@pkc.gov.uk
Regimental Museum and Archives of Black Watch, Balhousie
Castle, Hay Street, Perth PH1 5HR Tel: 0131-3108530 Fax: 01738-
643245 Email: bwarchivist@btclick.com
Scottish Horse Regimental Museum The Cross, Dunkeld,
Perthshire, PH8 0AN

Renfrewshire
Mclean Museum & Art Gallery 15 Kelly Street, Greenock,
Renfrewshire, PA16 8JX Tel: 01475-715624
Old Paisley Society George Place, Paisley PA1 2HZ
Tel: 0141-889-1708
Paisley Museum High Street, Paisley, Renfrewshire, PA1 2BA
Tel: 0141-889-3151
Renfrewshire Council Library & Museum Central Library &
Museum Complex, High Street, Paisley, Renfrewshire, PA1 2BB
Tel: 0141-889-2350
Email: local_studies.library@renfrewshire.gov.uk

Ross-Shire
Dingwall Museum Trust Town Hall, High Street, Dingwall,
Ross-Shire, IV15 9RY Tel: 01349-865366
The Groam House Museum High Street, Rosemarkie, Fortrose,
Ross-Shire, IV10 8UF Tel: 01381-620961 Fax: 01381-621730
Highland Museum of Childhood The Old Station, Strathpeffer,
Ross-Shire, IV14 9DH Tel: 01997-421031
Email: info@hmoc.freeserve.co.uk WWW:
www.hmoc.freeserve.co.uk
Tain & District Museum Tain Through Time, Tower Street, Tain,
Ross-Shire, IV19 1DY Tel: 01862-893054
Email: info@tainmuseum.demon.co.uk
Ullapool Museum & Visitor Centre 7 & 8 West Argyle Street,
Ullapool, Ross-Shire, IV26 2TY Tel: 01854-612987
Email: ulmuseum@wavereider.co.uk
Roxburghshire
Hawick Museum & Scott Gallery Wilton Lodge Park, Hawick,
TD9 7JL Tel: 01450-373457 Fax: 01450-378506
Email: hawickmuseum@hotmail.com
Jedburgh Castle Jail Museum Castlegate, Jedburgh, TD8 6BD
Tel: 01835-863254 Fax: 01835-864750
Mary Queen of Scots House and Visitor Centre Queens Street,
Jedburgh TD8 6EN Tel: 01835-863331 Fax: 01835-863331
Email: hawickmuseum@hotmail.com

Scottish Borders
Hawick Museum & Scott Gallery Wilton Lodge Park, Hawick,
Roxburghshire, TD9 7JL Tel: 01450-373457 Fax: 01450-378506
Email: hawickmuseum@hotmail.com
Mary Queen of Scots House and Visitor Centre Queens Street,
Jedburgh, Roxburghshire, TD8 6EN Tel: 01835-863331
Fax: 01835-863331 Email: hawickmuseum@hotmail.com

Selkirkshire
Halliwells House Museum Halliwells Close, Market Place, Selkirk,
Selkirkshire, TD7 4BL Tel: 01750-20096 Fax: 01750-23282
Email: museums@scotsborders.gov.uk

Shetland
Fetlar Interpretive Centre Beach Of Houbie, Fetlar, Shetland, ZE2
9DJ Tel: 01957-733206 Email: fic@zetnet.co.uk
WWW: www.zetnet.co.uk/sigs/centre
Old Haa Museum Burravoe Yell, Shetland, Shetland Islands, ZE2
9AY Tel: 01957-722339
Shetland Museum Lower Hillhead, Lerwick ZE1 0EL
Tel: 01595-695057 Email: shetland.museum@zetnet.co.uk WWW:
www.shetland-museum.org.uk
Shetland Textile Working Museum Weisdale Mill, Weisdale,
Shetland, Shetland Islands, ZE2 9LW Tel: 01595-830419
Tangwick HAA Museum Tangwick, Eshaness, Shetland, ZE2 9RS
Tel: 01806-503389
Unst Heritage Centre Haraldswick, Unst, Shetland, ZE2 9EQ
Tel: 01957-711528 Fax: 01957-711387 (Custodian home)

Stirlingshire and Sutherland
Regimental Museum Argyll and Sutherland Highlanders, Stirling Castle, Stirling FK8 1EH Tel: 01786 475165 Fax: 01786 446038 CC accepted
Stirling
Stirling Smith Art Gallery & Museum Dumbarton Road, Stirling, FK8 2RQ Tel: 01786 471917 Fax: 01786 449523 Email: museum@smithartgallery.demon.co.uk
475165 Fax: 01786 446038
Strathnaver Museum Bettyhill, Sutherland, KW14 7SS
Tel: 01641-521418, Fax: 01641-521315

Wigtownshire
Taylor's Farm Tradition Barraer, Newton Stewart, Wigtownshire, DG8 6QQ Tel: 01671-402184 Fax: 01671-404890
Email: j.taylor@bosinternet.com

Northern Ireland
Armagh County Museum The Mall East, Armagh, County Armagh, BT61 9BE Tel: (028) 37523070
Ballymoney Museum & Heritage Centre 33 Charlotte Street, Ballymoney, County Antrim, BT53 6AY Tel: (028) 27662280
Centre for Migration Studies-Ulster American Folk Park Mellon Road, Castletown, Omagh, County Tyrone, BT78 8QY Tel: 028-8225-6315 Fax: 028-8224-2241 Email: uafp@iol.ie WWW: www.folkpark.com
also www.qub.ac.uk/cms
Down County Museum The Mall, Downpatrick, County Down, BT30 6AH Tel: (028) 446615218
Downpatrick Railway Museum Railway Station, Market St, Downpatrick, County Down, BT30 6LZ Tel: (028) 446615779
Fermanagh County Museum Enniskillen Castle Castle Barracks, Enniskillen, County Fermanagh, BT74 7HL Tel: 028-6632-5000 Fax: 028-6632-7342 Email: castle@fermanagh.gov.uk
Foyle Valley Railway Museum Foyle Road, Londonderry, County Londonderry, BT48 6SQ Tel: (028) 712265234
Friends of the Ulster Museum Botanic Gardens Botanic Gardens, Stranmillas Road, Belfast, County Antrim, BT9 5AB Tel: (028) 9068-1606
Garvagh Museum 142 Main Street, Garvagh Londonderry, BT51 5AE Tel: 028-295-58216/58188 Fax: 028-295-58993
Email: jclyde@garvaghhigh.garvagh.ni.sch.uk
Northen Ireland Museums Council 66 Donegall Pass, Belfast, BT7 1BU Tel: (028) 90550215 Fax: (028) 90550216
Email: info@nimc.co.uk WWW: www.nimc.co.uk
Odyssey Science Centre Project Office Project Office NMGNI, Botanic Gardens, Belfast BT9 5AB Tel: (028) 90682100
Roslea Heritage Centre Church Street, Roslea, Enniskillen, County Fermanagh, BT74 7DW Tel: (028) 67751750
Route 66 American Car Museum, 94 Dundrum Road, Newcastle, County Down, BT33 0LN Tel: (028) 43725223

Royal Inniskilling Fusiliers Regimental Museum, The Castle, Enniskillen BT74 7BB Tel: (028) 66323142 Fax: (028) 66320359
Royal Irish Fusilers Museum, Sovereign's House, Mall East, Armagh BT61 9DL Tel: (028) 3752 2911 Fax: (028) 3752 2911
Email: rylirfusilier@aol.com,
The Royal Irish Regiment Museum St. Patricks Barracks, Demesne Avenue, Ballymena, County Antrim, BT43 7BH
Tel: (028) 256661355
Royal Ulster Rifles Regimental Museum, RHQ Royal Irish Regiment, 5 Waring Street, Belfast BT1 2EW Tel: (028) 90232086 Fax: (028) 9023 2086 Email: rurmuseum@yahoo.co.uk WWW: http://www.rurmuseum.tripod.com
The Somme Heritage Centre 233 Bangor Road, Newtownards, County Down, BT23 7PH Tel: (028) 91823202
Fax: (028) 91823214 WWW: www.irishsoldier.org
Ulster American Folk Park Project Team Belfast 4 The Mount Albert Bridge Road, Belfast, County Antrim, BT5 4NA
Tel: (028) 9045 2250
Ulster Aviation Society Langford Lodge Airfield 97, Largy Road, Crumlin BT29 4RT Tel: (028) 94454444
Email: ernie@airni.freeserve.co.uk
WWW: www.d-n-a.net/users/dnetrazq/
Ulster Folk & Transport Museum Cultra, Holywood, Co Down, BT18 0EU
Tel: (028) 90 428428 Fax: (028) 90 428728
The Ulster History Park Cullion, Lislap, Omagh, County Tyrone, BT79 7SU Tel: (028) 8164 8188 Fax: (028) 8164 8011
Email: uhp@omagh.gov.uk
WWW: www.omagh.gov.uk/historypark.htm
Ulster Museum Botanic Gardens, Stranmillis Road, Belfast, BT9 5AB Tel: (028) 9038 1000 Fax: (028) 9038 3003
Londonderry Harbour Museum
Harbour Square, Londonderry, County Londonderry, BT48 6AF
Tel: (028) 713 377331

Ireland
Dublin Civic Museum 58 South William Street, Dublin, 2
Tel: 679-4260 Fax: 677-5954
Irish Jewish Museum 3 - 4 Walworth Road, South Circular Road, Dublin, 8 Tel: 453-1797

Belgium
In Flanders Fields Museum Lakenhallen, Grote Markt 34, Leper, B-8900 Tel: 00-32-(0)-57-22-85-84 Fax: 00-32-(0)-57-22-85-89 WWW: www.inflandersfields.be

Canada
Manitoba Museum of Man and Nature, 190 Rupert Avenue, Winnipeg, R3B 0N2 WWW: www.manitobamuseum.mb.ca HoldsThe Hudson's Bay Company's collections

---

Disclaimer

The Editor and Publishers of The Family & Local History Handbook make every effort to verify all information published. Nearly every organisation in this handbook has been contacted and asked to confirm that our information is correct. We provided reply paid envelopes and are grateful to those organisations who took the time to reply. We must express our disappointment that there were some organisations who did not reply. We cannot accept responsibilty for any errors or omissions or for any losses that may arise.

Advertisers are expected to provide a high standard of service to our readers. If there is a failure to provide such a service the Editor and Publishers reserve the right to refuse to accept advertising in future editions.

The Editor and Publishers cannot be held responsible for the errors, omissions or non performance by advertisers. Where an advertiser's performance falls below an acceptable level readers are asked to notify the Publisher in writing.

The views and opinions expressed in each of the articles are those of the author and do not necessarily reflect the opinions of the Editor.

Email and Internet or Web Addresses

Email and Web addresses shown in this book have been notified to us by the Organisation or advertiser. Unlike a normal postal address these addresses are subject to frequent change. In the case of businesses Email forwarding and Website transfer are usually provided by links to the original address. This does not always happen and the only solution is to use the various search engines available on the internet.

Many of the Browsers and Search engines will accept an address beginning with either http:// or www

Probate Records

Information from Probate records can provide vital pieces of the genealogical puzzle. Although often not as useful as records of births, marriages and deaths, which can evidence crucial links to previous generations, they can provide evidence of relatedness within generations, and often contain fascinating insights into the financial affairs of people in times past.

Probate is a process whereby some person or persons, usually the executor(s) of a Will if there was one, or one or more of the next-of-kin if there was no Will, are appointed in law to administer the estate of someone who has died. This is usually only necessary if the deceased person left fairly substantial assets, so don't expect to find any Probate record relating to the estate of a person who had little or no estate of their own. The Probate concept of 'estate' refers just to assets held in the sole name of the person who has died, and so Probate isn't necessary for the release of assets held jointly with another person. When an application for Probate is made, any Will that the deceased person left must be submitted to the Probate Registry. The Will, if judged to be valid, is thereafter kept on file, and it is normally possible for anyone to obtain a copy of it. There are exceptions, however, such as the Wills of members of the Royal family. The important point is that Wills are available from the Probate Registries only as a by-product of the Probate process: if Probate wasn't needed, then the Probate Registries have no record of the estate at all.

You should bear in mind that the Probate record, if any, will be dated some time after the date of death of the person concerned, so start searching from the year of death, or the year in which you think the person died. You should normally expect to find the Probate record within the first year or two after the date of death, and, if you have not found it within three, you can usually assume that Probate wasn't necessary. However, in a very small number of cases, Probate is granted many years after the person in question died. Take a tip from the professionals: if you don't find a probate record within the first few years, the next most likely time to search is the year in which their heir(s) died. This is because unadministered estate is most likely to come to light at that time. How far you want to go with the search will probably depend on how crucial the person in question is to your research, but there is as yet no shortcut: you will have to search the index for each year separately.

Control of Probate record-keeping passed from the Church to the state in 1858, at which point the records were unified into one Calendar index. These indexes, which summarise all Probate grants for England and Wales during a given year, act as a table of contents for the vast store of records held by the Probate Registries. If the subject of your research died before 1858, it will be more difficult to trace their Will. However, if they were very wealthy or owned a lot of land, consult the indexes of the Prerogative Court of Canterbury (PCC) first, and then those of the lesser ecclesiastical courts of the region

Reading the Will

in which they lived. PCC records are held by the Family Records Centre in London (Tel: (020) 8392 5300), but records of the lesser ecclesiastical Probate courts are highly dispersed. Try the local authority archives, such as public libraries and County Record Offices of the appropriate region, and also any local historical research institutes. Major ecclesiastical centres are also likely to have their own archives.

The table below lists the Calendar indexes held by the various Probate Registries in England and Wales. You can usually call in to consult the indexes, but check with the Registry concerned first, especially if you intend to travel any distance. Probate grants for each year are listed alphabetically by surname. The crucial parts of the Probate record are the Grant type, which is usually 'Probate', 'Administration' or 'Administration with Will', the issuing Registry, and the grant issue date. They are normally written in sequence towards the end of the index entry, but the older books give the grant date first and highlight the issuing Registry in the text of the entry. The grant type can be inferred from the text, but note that the indexes prior to 1871 listed the 'Administration' grants in a separate part of the book from the 'Probate' and 'Administration with Will' grants, so be sure to search in both places for years prior to this. In addition, there may be a handwritten number next to entries for Wills proved in the Principal Probate Registry (London) between 1858 and 1930. This is the Folio number, which is used by the Probate Registries when obtaining copies of the Will. Always make a note of this if applicable.

If the grant type is 'Administration', this tells you that the person in question did not leave a valid Will. However, the Probate Registries can still supply a copy of the grant, which is the document naming the person appointed in law as the administrator of the estate. This can provide genealogical information, especially in older grants where the relationship of the applicant to the deceased was stated. It also gives the value of the estate, although in most cases this is stated as 'not exceeding' a certain figure rather than quoting an exact amount. In fact, the Probate record contains very little information about the estate at all, and no information about its composition. Don't expect to find inventories on file for records after 1858, although they sometimes form part of the Probate record prior to this.

In many cases you can save a lot of time and money by making the search yourself, but there is a postal service by which a search is made on your behalf for a period of four years. There is a fee of £5 for this, but this includes copies of the Will and/or grant if a record is found. It also gives you the benefit of the experience of Probate staff, for instance in knowing when to search and judging under which name the record is likely to be listed. If you want the Probate Registry to conduct a search for a period longer than the standard four years, there is an additional fee of £3 for each 4-year period after the first four. Thus, an 8-year search will cost £8, a 12-year search £11, and so on.

If you want to make a postal search, contact
The Postal Searches and Copies Department,
York Probate Sub-Registry, 1st Floor, Castle Chambers, Clifford Street, York YO1 9RG UK
Tel: +44 (1904) 666777   Fax: +44 (1904) 666776

Applications for searches must be made in writing, and give the full name, last known address and date of death of the person concerned. A search can normally be made using less detail, but if the date of death is not known, you must state the year from which you want the search to be made, or give some other evidence that might indicate when the person died. If you have information about legal actions related to Probate or the disposition of assets, include that on your application. Many people find it convenient to order copies in this way even if they have already made a search of the Probate indexes and located a record relating to the subject of their research, but if this is the case, please include the grant type, issuing Registry and grant issue date on your application, as well as the Folio number if applicable (see above) as this can speed up the supply of copies considerably. The fee should be payable to "H.M.Paymaster General", and if it is paid from abroad, must be made by International Money Order or bank draft, payable through a United Kingdom bank and made out in £ sterling. If you are applying for a search as well, you can request a search of any length, and fees for this are outlined above.

The records referred to here relate only to estates in England and Wales.

The list overleaf shows what indexes the various Probate Registries hold. Most Registries will have had indexes dating back to 1858, but are not required to keep them for more than fifty years. Usually, the older indexes will have been donated to local authority archives. Contact your local public library or County/City Record Office to see what Probate records they have. If you know of any historical research institute in your area, find out if they have any Probate records. Please note that, since the York Probate Registry serves as a national centre for postal requests for searches and copies, it is not possible to inspect the Probate indexes in person there.

Probate Registries & Sub-Registries

REGISTRY	RECORDS	TELEPHONE
Bangor Probate Sub-Registry Council Offices, FFord, Bangor LL57 1DT	1946 to 1966 and 1973 to 1998	(01248) 362410
Birmingham District Probate Registry The Priory Courts, 33 Bull Street, Birmingham B4 6DU	1948 to date	(0121) 681 3400
Bodmin Probate Sub-Registry Market Street, Bodmin PL31 2JW	1858 to 1966 and 1973 to 1998	(01208) 72279
Brighton District Probate Registry William Street, Brighton BN2 2LG	1935 to date	(01273) 684071
Bristol District Probate Registry Ground Floor, The Crescent Centre, Temple Back, Bristol BS1 6EP	1901 to date	(0117) 927 3915
Carmarthen Probate Sub-Registry 14 King Street, Carmarthen SA31 1BL	1973 to 1998	(01267) 236238
Chester Probate Sub-Registry 5th Floor, Hamilton House, Hamilton Place, Chester CH1 2DA	1948 to 1966	(01244) 345082
Exeter Probate Sub-Registry Finance House, Barnfield Road, Exeter EX1 1QR	1858 to 1966 and 1973 to 1998	(01392) 274515
Gloucester Probate Sub-Registry 2nd Floor, Combined Court Building, Kimbrose Way, Gloucester GL1 2DG	1947 to 1966	(01452) 522585
Ipswich District Probate Registry Level 3, Haven House, 17 Lower Brook Street, Ipswich IP4 1DN	1936 to date	(01473) 253724
Leeds District Probate Registry 3rd Floor, Coronet House, Queen Street, Leeds LS1 2BA	1949 to date	(0113) 243 1505
Leicester Probate Sub-Registry 5th Floor, Leicester House, Lee Circle, Leicester LE1 3RE	1890 to 1966 and 1973 to date	(0116) 253 8558
Lincoln Probate Sub-Registry Mill House, Brayford Side North, Lincoln LN1 1YW	1936 to 1966 and 1973 to 1998	(01522) 523648
Liverpool District Probate Registry Queen Elizabeth II Law Courts, Derby Square, Liverpool L2 1XA	1946 to date	(0151) 236 8264
Manchester District Probate Registry 9th Floor, Astley House, 23 Quay Street, Manchester M3 4AT	1947 to date	(0161) 834 4319
Middlesbrough Probate Sub-Registry Teesside Combined Court Centre, Russell Street, Middlesbrough TS1 2AE	1973 to 1998	(01642) 340001
Newcastle-upon-Tyne District Probate Registry 2nd Floor, Plummer House, Croft Street, Newcastle-upon-Tyne NE1 6NP	1929 to date	(0191) 261 8383
Nottingham Probate Sub-Registry Butt Dyke House, Park Row, Nottingham NG1 6GR	1973 to 1998	(0115) 941 4288
Oxford District Probate Registry Combined Court Building, St.Aldates, Oxford OX1 1LY	1940 to date	(01865) 793050
Sheffield Probate Sub-Registry PO Box 832, The Law Courts, 50 West Bar Sheffield S3 8YR	1935 to 1966 and 1973 to 1998	(0114) 281 2596
Stoke-on-Trent Probate Sub-Registry Combined Court Centre, Bethesda Street, Hanley, Stoke-on-Trent ST1 3BP	1973 to 1998	(01782) 854065
Winchester District Probate Registry 4th Floor, Cromwell House, Andover Road, Winchester SO23 7EW	1944 to date	(01962) 863771
Probate Registry of Wales PO Box 474, 2 Park Street, Cardiff CF1 1ET	1951 to date	(029) 2037 6479
Principal Probate Registry First Avenue House, 42-49 High Holborn, London WC1	1858 to date	(020) 7947 6939

The Service has undergone a process of computerisation, but as yet this covers only recently-issued grants, which will be of limited interest to genealogists. However, anyone who is interested in checking up on grants since 1996 can search the Probate Service database themselves. To date, workstations for public use have been installed at the Principal Probate Registry and Manchester District Probate Registry. The Postal Searches and Copies Department at York is also completing a long period of computerisation, which should see a much-improved service to family history researchers, with clearer and more comprehensive information and quicker supply of documents.

This information is based on details supplied by the Probate Service. The details are liable to change without notice. Always telephone the Registry before visiting, to check opening times and the availability of records. While every effort is made to ensure the accuracy of these details, the Probate Service cannot be held responsible for any consequence of errors.

Please check our website at www.courtservice.gov.uk before applying for searches or copy documents by post.

English Heritage Sites

Keynon Peel Hall, Little Sutton, 1881
© Crown Copyright. National Monuments Record
From the National Monuments Record,
the public archive of English Heritage

Aldborough Roman Town
Main Street, Boroughbridge, North Yorks. YO5 9EF
Ashby De La Zouch Castle
South Street, Ashby De La Zouch, Leics. LE6 5PR
Audley End House
Saffron Walden, Essex, CB11 4JF
Aydon Castle
Northumberland, NE45 5PJ
Barnard Castle
Castle House, Barnard Castle, Durham, DL12 9AT
Battle Abbey
Battle, East Sussex, TN33 0AD
Bayham Abbey
Bayham, Lamberhurst, Kent, TN8 8DE
Beeston Castle
Beeston, Tarporley, Cheshire, CW6 9TX
Belsay Hall
Belsay, Near Ponteland, Northumberland, NE20 0DX
Berney Arms Mill
8 Manor Road, Southtown, Great Yarmouth, Norfolk, NR31 0QA
Berry Pomeroy Castle
Totnes, Devon, TQ9 6NJ
Berwick Barracks
Berwick-upon-Tweed, Northumberland, TD15 1DF
Bishop Waltham Abbey
Bishop Waltham, Hampshire, SO32 1DH
Bolsover Castle
Castle Street, Bolsover, Derbyshire, S44 6PR
Boscobel House
Brewood, Bishops Wood, Shropshire, ST19 9AR
Brinkburn Priory
Long Framlington, Morpeth, Northumberland, NE65 8AR
Brodsworth Hall
Brodsworth, Near Doncaster, South Yorks. DN5 7XJ
Brougham Castle
Brougham, Penrith, Cumbria, CA10 2AA
Buildwas Abbey
Iron Bridge, Telford, Shropshire, TF8 7BW
Busmead Priory
Colmworth, Bedfordshire, MK44 2LD
Byland Abbey
Coxwold, North Yorks, YO6 4BD
Calshot Castle
Calshot, Hants, SO4 1BR
Carisbrooke Castles
Newport, Isle Of Wight, O32 6JY
Carlisle Castle
Carlisle, Cumbria, CA3 8UR
Castle Acre Priory
Stocks Green, Castle Acre, Kings Lynn, Norfolk, E32 2XD
Castle Rising Castle
Castle Rising, Kings Lynn, Norfolk, E31 6AH
Chapter House
East Cloisters, Westminster Abbey, London, SW1P 3PE
Chester Roman Fort
Chollerford, Hexham, Northumberland, NE46 4EP
Chiswick House
Burlington Lane, Chiswick, London, W4 2RP
Chysauster Ancient Village
Newmill, Penzance, Cornwall, TR20 8XA
Cleeve Abbey
Washford, Watchet, Somerset, TA23 0PS
Clifford Tower
Clifford Street, York, North Yorkshire, YO1 1SA
Conisburgh Castle
The Ivanhoe Trust, The Priory, High St, Conisburgh, Doncaster
Corbridge Roman Site
Corbridge, Northumberland, NE45 5NT
Dartmouth Castle
Castle Road, Dartmouth, Devon, TQ6 0JN
Deal Castle
Victoria Road, Deal, Kent, CT14 7BA

Denny Abbey
Ely Road, Chittering, Cambridgeshire, CB5 9TQ
Dorchester Castle
Dorchester, Hants, O16 9QW
Dover Castle
Dover, Kent, CT16 1HU
Down House
Luxted Road, Downe, Kent, BR6 7JT
Dunstanburgh Castle
14 Queen St., Alnwick, Northumberland, NE66 1RD
Dymchurch Martello Tower
High Street, Dymchurch, Kent, CT16 1HU
Eltham Palace
Courtyard, Eltham, London, SE9 5QE
Endennis Castle
Falmouth, Cornwall, TR11 4LP
Etal Castle
Etal Village, Berwick-upon-Tweed, Northumberland, TD12 4TN
Evensey Castle
Evensey, East Sussex, BN24 5LE
Everil Castle
Market Place, Castleton, Derbyshire, S33 8WQ
Everil Castle
Castleton, Hope Valley, Sheffield, SW33 5LE
Farleigh Hungerford Castle
Farleigh Hungerford, Near Bath, Somerset, BA3 6RS
Farnham Castle
Castle Hill, Farnham, Surrey, GU6 0AG
Finchale Priory
Brasside, Newton Hall, Co Durham, DH1 5SH
Fort Brockhurst
Gunners Way, Elson, Gosport, Hants, PO12 4DS
Fort Cumberland
Fort Cumberland Rd., Eastney, Porstmouth, PO4 9LD
Framlingham Castle
Framlingham, Suffolk, IP8 9BT
Furness Abbey
Barrow In Furness, Cumbria, LH13 0TJ
Gainsborough Hall
Arnell Road, Gainsborough, Lincolnshire, DN12 2RN
Goodrich Castle
Goodrich, Ross on Wye, Worcestershire, HR9 6HY
Grimes Graves
Lynford, Thetford, Norfolk, IP26 5DE
Hailes Abbey
Near Winchcombe, Cheltenham, Glos., GL54 5PB
Halesowen Abbey
Halesowen, Huntington, West Midlands
Hardwick Old Hall
Doe Lea, Near Chesterfield, Derbyshire, S44 5QJ
Haughmond Abbey
Upton Magna, Uffington, Shrewsbury, SY4 4RW
Helmsley Castle
Helmsley, North Yorkshire, YO6 5AB

Byland Abbey, N Yorks, 1994
© Crown Copyright. National Monuments RecordFrom the
National Monuments Record, the public archive of English Heritage

Housesteads Roman Fort
Haydon Bridge, Hexham, Northumberland, NE46 6NN
Jewel Tower
Abingdon Street, London, SW1P 3JY
Kenilworth Castle
Kenilworth, Warwickshire, CV8 INE
Kenwood House
Hampstead Lane, London, NW3 7JR
Kirby Hall Deene, Corby, Northants, NN17 3EN
Kirby Muxloe Castle
South Quay, Great Yarmouth, Norfolk, NR30 2RQ
Kirkham Priory
Whitwell-on-the-Hill, North Yorks, YO6 7JS
Lanercost Priory Brampton, Cumbria, CA8 2HQ
Launceston Castle
Castle Lodge, Launceston, Cornwall, L15 7DR
Lincoln Bishops Palace
Minster Yard, Lincoln, Lincs, LN2 1PU
Lindisfarne Priory
Holy Island, Northumberland, TD15 2RX
Longthorpe Tower
Thorpe Road, Longthorpe, Peterborough, PE1 1HA
Lullingstone Roman Villa
Lullingstone Lane, Eynsford, Kent, DA4 0JA
Lyddington Bede House
Blue Coat Lane, Liecestershire, LE15 9LZ
Maison Deu
Water Lane, Ospring, Kent, ME13 0DW
Marble Hill House
Richmond Road, Twickenham, Middlesex, TW1 2NL
Medieval Merchants House
58 French Street, Southampton, Hants, SO1 0AT
Middleham Castle
Middleham, Leyburn, North Yorkshire, DL8 4QG
Milton Chantry
Gravesend, Kent
Mortimers Cross Water
Leominster, Herefordshire, HR6 9PE
Mount Grace Priory
Saddle Bridge, Northallerton, North Yorks. DL6 3JG
Muchelney Abbey
Muchelney, Langport, Somerset, TA10 0DQ
Norham Castle
Berwick-upon-Tweed, Northumberland, TD15 2JY
Okehampton Castle
Castle Lodge, Okehampton, Devon, EX20 1JB
Old Merchants House
South Quay, Great Yarmouth, Norfolk, IP13 2RQ
Old Sarum Castle
Castle Roads, Salisbury, Wilts, SP1 3SD
Old Wardour Castle
Tisbury, Salisbury, Wilts, SP3 6RR

Orford Castle Woodbridge, Suffolk, IP12 2ND
Osborne House
Royal Apartments, East Cowes, Isle of Wight, PO32 6JY
Pickering Castle Pickering, North Yorkshire, YO18 7AX
Portland Castle Castleton, Portland, Dorset, DT5 1AZ
Prudhoe Castle Prudhoe, Northumberland, NE42 6NA
Rangers House
Chesterfield Walk, Blackheath, London, SE10 8QX
Restormel Castle Lostwithiel, Cornwall, PL22 0BD
Richborough Castle
Richborough, Sandwich, Kent, CT13 9JW
Richmond Castle Richmond, North Yorkshire, DL10 4QW
Rievaulx Abbey
Rievaulx, Near Helmsley, North Yorkshire, DL10 5LB
Roche Abbey
Maltby, Rotherham, South Yorkshire, S66 8NW
Rochester Castle
The Keep, Rochester-upon-Medway, Kent, ME1 1SW
Rushton Triangular Lodge
Rushton, Kettering, Northants, NN14 1RP
Saxtead Green Post Mill
The Mill House, Saxtead Green, Suffolk, IP13 9QQ
Scarborough Castle
Castle Road, Scarborough, North Yorks. YO11 1HY
Sherborne Old Castle Castleton, Dorset, DT19 0SY
Sibsey Trader Mill
Sibsey, Boston, Lincolnshire, PE22 0SY
St. Augustines Abbey Canterbury, Kent, CT1 1TF
St. Mawes Castle St. Mawes, Cornwall, TR2 3AA
Stokesay Castle Craven Arms, Shropshire, SY7 9AH
Stonehenge Stone Circle, Wiltshire, SP4 7DE
Stott Park Bobbin Mill
Low Stott Park, Ulverston, Cumbria, LA12 8AR
Tilbury Fort Fort Road, Tilbury, Essex, RN18 7NR
Tintagel Castle
Tintagel, Cornwall, DL34 0AA
Totnes Castle Castle Street, Totnes, Devon, TQ9 5NU
Tynemouth Castle
North Shields, Tyne and Wear, NE30 4BZ
Upnor Castle
High Street, Upnor, Rochester, Kent, ME2 4XG
Wall Roman site
Watling Street, Near Litchfield, Staffs. WS14 0AW
Walmer Castle
Kingsdown Road, Deal, Kent, CT14 7LJ
Warkworth Castle
Morpeth, Northumberland, NE66 0UJ
Wenlock Priory
Much Wenlock, Shropshire, TF13 6HS
Whitby Abbey
Whitby, North Yorkshire, YO22 4JT
Wingfield Manor
South Wingfield, Alfreton, Derbyshire, DE2 7NH
Witley Court
Grest Witley, Worcestershire, WR6 6JT
Wolvesey Castle
College Street, Winchester, Hants, SO23 8NB
Wrest Park
Silsoe, Luton, Bedfordshire, MK45 4HS
Wroxeter Roman Site
Wroxeter, Shropshire, SY5 6PH
Yarmouth Castle
Quay Street, Yarmouth, Isle Of Wight, PO41 0P

Contacts:
National Monuments Record Enquiry & Research
Service, National Monuments Record Centre ,Kemble
Drive, Swindon SN2 2GZ Telephone: 01793 414600
Fax: 01793 414606
Email:
National Monuments Recordinfo@ english-heritage.org.uk
Open Tuesday to Friday, 9.30am to 5pm.

London Search Room
55 Blandford Street, London W1H 3AF
Open Tuesday to Friday 10am to 5pm.

Welsh Heritage Sites

CADW - *Welsh Heritage Sites & Locations*

Barclodiad y Gawres Burial Chamber, Anglesey
Basingwerk Abbey Flintshire
Beaumaris Castle
Beaumaris, Anglesey, LL58 8AP Tel: 01248-810361
Beaupre Castle, near Cowbridge, Vale of Glamorgan
Blaenavon Ironworks
North St, Blaenavon, Blaenau Gwent, NP4 9RN Tel: 01495-792615
Bodowyr Burial Chamber, Anglesey
Brecon Gaer Roman Fort Powys
Bronllys Castle, Bronllys, Powys
Bryn Celli Ddu Burial Chamber, Anglesey
Bryntail Lead Mine Buildings, Llanidloes, Powys
Caer Gybi Roman Fortlet, Anglesey
Caer Lêb, Anglesey
Caer y Tor Hillfort, Anglesey
Caerleon Roman Baths & Amphitheatre
High Street, Caerleon, Newport, NP18 1AE Tel: 01633-422518
Caernarfon Castle
Castle Ditch, Caernarfon LL55 2AY Tel: 01286-677617
Caerphilly Castle
Caerphilly, CF83 1JD, 029 20 883143
Caerwent Roman Town, Monmouthshire
Capel Garmon Burial Chamber
near Betws-y-Coed, Conwy
Capel Lligwy, Anglesey
Carew Cross, Carew, Pembrokeshire
Carreg Cennen Castle
Tir y Castell Farm, Trapp, near Llandeilo SA19 6TS Tel: 01558-822291
Carreg Coetan Arthur Burial Chamber
Newport, Pembrokeshire
Carswell Old House, near Tenby, Pembrokeshire
Castell Bryn Gwyn, Anglesey
Castell Coch
Tongwynlais, Cardiff, CF15 7JS Tel: 029-20-810101
Castell y Bere, near Tywyn, Gwynedd
Chepstow Bulwarks Camp, Monmouthshire
Chepstow Castle
Bridge Street, Chepstow NP16 5EZ Tel: 01291-624065
Cilgerran Castle
Castle Hse, Cilgerran, Cardigan SA43 2SF Tel: 01239-615007
Coity Castle, near Bridgend
Conwy Castle
Conwy, LL32 8AY Tel: 01492-592358
Criccieth Castle
Castle Street, Criccieth LL55 0DP Tel: 01766-522227
Cymer Abbey
c/o Vanner Farm, Llanelltyd, Dolgellau LL40 2HE Tel: 01341-422854
Denbigh Castle, Denbigh, Denbighshire
Denbigh Friary
Leicester's Church and St Hilary's Chapel, Denbighshire
Derwen Churchyard Cross, near Corwen, Denbighshire
Din Dryfol Burial Chamber, Anglesey
Din Lligwy Hut Group, Anglesey
Dinefwr Castle, Llandeilo, Carmarthenshire
Dolbadarn Castle, Llanberis, Gwynedd
Dolforwyn Castle, near Newtown, Powys
Dolwyddelan Castle
Bryn Tirion Farm, Dolwyddelan LL25 OEJ Tel: 01690 750366
Dryslwyn Castle, near Llandeilo, Carmarthenshire
Dyffryn Ardudwy Burial Chamber, Gwynedd
Dyfi Furnace, near Machynlleth, Ceredigion
Eliseg's Pillar, near Llangollen, Denbighshire
Ewenny Priory, near Bridgend
Ewloe Castle, Flintshire
Flint Castle, Flintshire
Grosmont Castle, Monmouthshire
Gwydir Uchaf Chapel, near Llanrwst, Conwy
Harlech Castle
Castle Square, Harlech LL46 2YH Tel: 01766-780552
Haverfordwest Priory, Pembrokeshire
Hen Gwrt Moated Site
Llantilio Crossenny, Monmouthshire
Holyhead Mountain Hut Group, Anglesey
Kidwelly Castle
5 Castle Road, Kidwelly SA17 5BQ Tel: 01554-890104
Lamphey Bishops Palace
Lamphey, Pembroke, SA71 5NT Tel: 01646-672224
Laugharne Castle
King Street, Laugharne SA33 4SA Tel: 01994-427906
Llanmelin Wood Hillfort, Monmouthshire
Llansteffan Castle, Carmarthenshire

Llanthony Priory, Monmouthshire
Llawhaden Castle, Pembrokeshire
Lligwy Burial Chamber, Anglesey
Loughor Castle, near Swansea
Maen Achwyfan Cross, near Whitford, Flintshire
Margam Stones Museum, Port Talbot
Monmouth Castle, Monmouthshire
Montgomery Castle, Powys
Neath Abbey, Neath Port Talbot
Newcastle Castle, Bridgend
Newport Castle, Newport city centre
Ogmore Castle and Stepping Stones, near Bridgend
Oxwich Castle
c/o Oxwich Castle Farm, Oxwich, Swansea, SA3 1NG
Tel: 01792-390359
Parc le Breos Burial Chamber, Gower Peninsula
Penarth Fawr Medieval House
near Criccieth, Ll?n Peninsula
Penmon Cross & Dovecote, Anglesey
Penmon Priory, Anglesey
Penrhos Feilw Standing Stones, Anglesey
Pentre Ifan Burial Chamber,
near Newport, Pembrokeshire
Plas Mawr Elizabethan Town House
High Street, Conwy, LL32 8DE Tel: 01492-580167
Pont Minllyn, near Dinas Mawddwy, Gwynedd
Presaddfed Burial Chamber, Anglesey
Raglan Castle
Raglan, Monmouthshire, NP15 2BT Tel: 01291-690228
Rhuddlan Castle
Castle Gate, Castle Street, Rhuddlan, Rhyl LL18 5AD
Rug Chapel/Llangar Old Church
c/o Coronation Cottage, Rug, nr Corwen, Denbighshire, LL21
9BT Tel: 01490-412025
Runston Chapel, near Chepstow, Monmouthshire
Segontium Roman Fort & Museum
Llanbeblig Rd, Caernarfon LL55 2LN Tel: 01286-675625
Skenfrith Castle, Monmouthshire
St Cybi's Well, Llangybi, Ll?n Peninsula
St Davids Bishops Palace
St Davids, Pembrokeshire, SA62 6PE Tel: 01437-720517
St Dogmaels Abbey, Ceredigion
St Lythan's Burial Chamber
near St Nicholas, Vale of Glamorgan
St Non's Chapel, St Davids, Pembrokeshire
St Quentin's Castle
Llanblethian, Cowbridge, Vale of Glamorgan
St Seiriol's Well, Penmon, Anglesey
St Winifrid's Chapel and Holy Well
Holywell, Flintshire
Strata Florida Abbey
Ystrad Meurig, Ceredigion, SY25 6BT Tel: 01974-831261
Swansea Castle, Swansea City Centre
Talley Abbey, near Llandeilo, Carmarthenshire
Tinkinswood Burial Chamber
near St Nicholas, Vale of Glamorgan
Tintern Abbey
Tintern, Monmouthshire, NP16 6SE Tel: 01291 689251
Trefignath Burial Chamber, Anglesey
Tregwehelydd Standing Stone, Anglesey
Tretower Court & Castle
Tretower, Crickhowell, Powys, NP8 1RD Tel: 01874-730279
Ty Mawr Standing Stone, Anglesey
Ty Newydd Burial Chamber, Anglesey
Valle Crucis Abbey
Llangollen, Denbighshire, LL20 8DD Tel: 01978-860326
Weobley Castle
Weobley Castle Farm, Llanrhidian, Swansea, SA3 1HB
Tel: 01792-390012
White Castle
Llantilio Crosenny, nr Abergavenny NP7 8UD
Tel: 01600-780380
Wiston Castle, Pembrokeshire

Historic Scotland

Historic Scotland is a government agency set up to care for the country's rich built heritage, which spans a period of over 5000 years. It is responsible for protecting ancient monuments, listing buildings and maintaining over 330 properties open to the public. The agency also gives grants to private owners for conservation and repair, and a team of experts carries out technical conservation and is at the forefront of research in this field. There are currently about 8000 scheduled monuments in Scotland, and each year about 380 new sites are added. Most of these lie on private land and Historic Scotland works with owners to help preserve these. Over 47,000 buildings are listed as being of special architectural or historic interest. These comprise dwelling houses (large and small), churches, city terraces, coalmines, factories, shipyards and the Forth Rail Bridge. Gardens and designed landscapes are also included. A few of the well-known properties open to the public are Edinburgh Castle, Stirling Castle, Fort George, Skara Brae and Iona Abbey. About 260 smaller sites, such as standing stones and cairns, are free to visitors. A diverse programme of events takes place at a number of properties throughout the year and free visits for schools offer an important educational opportunity.

For further information check out
www.historic-scotland.gov.uk or phone **0131 668 8600**.
You can also find out about becoming a Friend of Historic Scotland which allows you free entry to all properties as well as other benefits.

Aberdour Castle
Aberdour, Fife, KY3 0SL Tel: 01383-860519
Arbroath Abbey
Arbroath, Angus, DD11 1EG Tel: 01241-878756
Argylls Lodging
Castle Wynd, Stirling, FK8 1EJ Tel: 01786-431319
Balvenie Castle
Dufftown, Keith, Bannfshire, AB55 4GH Tel: 01340-820121
Bishop's and Earl's Palaces
Palace Road, Kirkwall, Orkney, KW15 1PD Tel: 01856-871918
Blackhouse
42 Arnol, Barvas, Isle of Lewis, HS2 9DB Tel: 01851-710395
Blackness Castle
Linlithgow, Lothian, EH8 8ED Tel: 01506 834807
Bonawe Iron Furnace
Taynuilt, Argyll, PA35 1JQ Tel: 01866-822432
Bothwell Castle
Uddingston, Glasgow, G4 0QZ Tel: 01698-816894
Broch of Gurness
Evie, Orkney, KW17 2NH Tel: 01856-751414
Caerlaverock Castle
Glencaple, Dumfries, DG1 4RU Tel: 01387-770244
Cairnpapple Hill
o6Linlithgow Palace, Linlithgow EH49 7AL Tel: 01506-634622
Calanais Vistors Centre
Callanish, Isle of Lewis, HS2 9DY, 01851-621422
Cardoness Castle
Gatehouse of Fleet, DG7 2EH Tel: 01557-814427
Castle Campbell
Dollar, Clackmannanshire, FK14 7PP Tel: 01259-742408
Corgarff Castle
White House, Strathdon AB36 8YL Tel: 01975-651460
Craigmillar Castle
Craigmillar Castle Road, Edinburgh, EH16 4SY Tel: 0131-661-4445
Craignethan Castle
Castle Cottage, Lesmahagow ML11 9PL Tel: 01555-860364
Crichton Castle
Crichton, Pathhead, Midlothian Tel: 01875-320017
Crossraguel Abbey
by Maybole, Ayrshire, KA19 8HQ Tel: 01655-883113
Dallas Dhu Distillery
Mannachie Road, Forres IV36 2RR Tel: 01309-676548
Dirleton Castle
Dirleton, East Lothian, EH39 5ER Tel: 01620-850330
Doune Castle
Castle Road, Doune, FK16 6EA Tel: 01786-841742
Dryburgh Abbey
Dryburgh, St Boswells, Melrose TD6 0RQ Tel: 01835-822381
Duff House
Banff, AB45 3SX Tel: 01261-818181
Dumbarton Castle
Castle Road, Dumbarton, Dunbartonshire, G82 1JJ Tel: 01389 732167
Dundonald Castle
Dundonald, nr Kilmarnock, Ayrshire, KA2 1AT Tel: 01563-851489

Dundrennan Abbey
Dundrennan, Kirkcudbrightshire DG6 4QH Tel: 01557-500262
Dunfermline Palace and Abbey
St Margaret Street, Dunfermline KY12 7PE Tel: 01383-739026
Dunstaffnage Castle
Dunbeg, By Oban, Argyll, PA37 1PZ Tel: 01631-562465
Edinburgh Castle
Castle Hill, Edinburgh, EH1 2NG Tel: 0131 225 9846
Edzell Castle
Edzell, By Brechin, Angus, DD9 7DA Tel: 01356-648631
Elcho Castle
Rhynd, by Perth, PH2 8QQ Tel: 01738-639998
Elgin Cathedral
Elgin, Morayshire, IV30 1HU Tel: 01343-547171
Fort George
By Ardersier, Inverness, IV1 2TD Tel: 01667-462777
Glasgow Cathedral
Cathedral Square, Glasgow, G4 0QZ Tel: 0141-552-6891
Glenluce Abbey
Glenluce, Newton Stewart DG8 0AF Tel: 01581-300541
Hermitage Castle
Newcastleton, Hawick, TD9 0LU Tel: 01387-376222
Huntingtower Castle
Huntingtower, Perth, PH1 3JR Tel: 01738 627231
Huntly Castle
Huntly, Aberdeenshire, AB54 4SH Tel: 01466 793191
Inchcolm Abbey
Incholm Island, Firth of Forth, (c/o GPO Aberdour), Fife, KY3 0UA Tel: 01383-823332
Inchmahome Priory
Port of Menteith, by Kippen, Stirlingshire, FK8 3RA Tel: 01877-385294
Jarlshof Prehistoric and Norse Settlement
Sumburgh, Shetland, ZE3 9JN Tel: 01950-460112
Jedburgh Abbey
4/5 Abbey Bridgend, Jedburgh TD8 6JQ Tel: 01835-863925
Kildrummy Castle
Kildrummy by Alford, Aberdeenshire Tel: 01975-571331
Kinnaird Head Castle Lighthouse
Stevenson Road, Fraserburgh, AB43 9DU Tel: 01346-511022
Linlithgow Palace
Linlithgow, Lothian, EH49 7AL Tel: 01506-842896
Lochleven Castle
Kinross, Tayside, KY13 7AR Tel: 07778-040483
MacLellans Castle
24 High Street, Kirkcudbright, DG6 4JD Tel: 01557-331856
Maes Howe
Stenness, near Stromness, Orkney, KW16 3HA Tel: 01856-761606
Meigle Museum
Dundee Road, Meigle, Perthshire, PH12 8SB Tel: 01828-640612
Melrose Abbey
Abbey Street, Melrose, TD6 9LG Tel: 01896-822562
New Abbey Cornmill
New Abbey, Dumfries, DG2 8BX Tel: 01387-850260
Newark Castle
Castle Road, Port Glasgow, PA14 5NH Tel: 01475-741858
Rothesay Castle
Rothesay, Isle of Bute, PA20 0DA Tel: 01700-502691
Seton Collegiate Church
Longniddry, East Lothian, EH32 0BG Tel: 01875-813334
Skara Brae
Sandwick, Orkney, KW16 3LR Tel: 01856-841815
Smailholm Tower
Smailholm, Kelso, TD5 7PQ Tel: 01573-460365
Spynie Palace
near Elgin, Morayshire, IV30 5QG Tel: 01343-546358
St Andrews Castle
The Scores, St Andrews, Fife, KY16 9AR Tel: 01334-477196
St Andrews Cathedral
The Pends, St Andrews, Fife, KY16 9QL Tel: 01334-472563
Stirling Castle
Castle Wynd, Stirling, FK8 1EJ Tel: 01786-431316
Sweetheart Abbey
New Abbey, by Dumfries, DG2 8BU Tel: 01387-850397
Tantallon Castle
North Berwick, East Lothian, EH39 5PN Tel: 01620-892727
Threave Castle
Castle Douglas, Kirkcudbrightshire, DG7 1RX Tel: 0411-223101
Tolquhon Castle
Tarves, Aberdeenshire, AB4 0LP Tel: 01650-851286
Urquhart Castle
by Drumnadrochit, Inverness-shire, IV3 2XJ Tel: 01456-450551
Whithorn Priory
6 Bruce Street, Whithorn, Wigtownshire, DG8 8PY
Tel: 01988-500508

Index to Advertisers

Index

In association with Back to Roots.co.uk Ltd

About the Editor and Publisher

Robert Blatchford LL.B (Hons)

has been involved in genealogy for several years. He is a member of The Society of Genealogists as well as Cleveland, The City of York & District, Devon, Dyfed, Glamorgan, Somerset & Dorset and Gwent Family History Societies. He is also a member of The British Association for Local History and The Poppleton History Society. A former Chairman of The City of York & District Family History Society and former Vice Chairman of the North East Group of Family History Societies. He has undertaken research in the United Kingdom & Australia.

Published by
The Genealogical Services Directory
(a trading name of GR Specialist Information Services)
33 Nursery Road, Nether Poppleton YORK, YO26 6NN England

E Mail: publishers@genealogical.co.uk
WWW: http://www.genealogical.co.uk

The Genealogical Services Directory
1st Edition Published 1997
2nd Edition Published January 1998 (Revised & Reprinted April 1998)
3rd Edition Published January 1999
4th Edition Published January 2000
© Robert Blatchford and Geoffrey Heslop

The Family & Local History Handbook
5th Edition Published January 2001   ISBN 0 9530297 4 3
6th Edition Published February 2002 ISBN 0 9530297 5 1

7th Edition Published February 2003 ISBN 0 9530297 6 X
© 2003 Robert Blatchford

ISSN 1368-9150   **ISBN 0 9530297 6 X**

Printed by
AWP
9 Advance Workshops, Wild Street, Dukinfield SK16 4DL

BACK TO ROOTS (UK) LTD

Computer Programs, Data CD's and Disks, Books and Acid Free Items

Family Historian (Postage free)	£49.95
Family Tree Maker Version 10	£29.95
Upgrade from V9	£19.95
Upgrade from any Version	£22.95

Family Treemaker Data CD's

1851 Census Extract (CD272)	£29.95
Griffiths Valuation of Ireland	£47.00
Irish Immigrants to North America	£29.00
Immigrants to the New World 1600s-1800s	£24.00
Lewis's Gazetteers of England, Ireland & Scotland	£29.00
Irish Flax Growers	£24.00
Irish Source Records 1500's-1800s	£29.00
Complete Book of Emigrants 1607-1776	£24.00
Passenger Immigration Lists 1538-1900s	£39.00
Irish to America 1846-1865	£39.00
Notable British Families 1600s- 1900s	£29.00
Value of the Pound with booklet (Postage & packing £1)	£9.95
LDS Companion (Postage & packing £1)	£18.00
Genmap Historical Mapping (Postage & packing £1)	£29.00
Brothers Keeper Family Tree (CD) Shareware (p&p 75 pence)	£5.00
TreeDraw Shareware (p&p 75 pence)	£5.00

Census

1851 Census Gloucestershire, Bristol, Somerset, Wiltshire & Worcestershire (Postage & packing 75 pence)	£15.00
1851 Census Somerset (Scanned with Surname Index) (p&p £1.50)	£29.00
1851 Census Wiltshire (Scanned with Surname Index (p&p £1.50)	£29.00
1851 Census Worcestershire (Scanned with Surname Index) (p&p £1.50)	£29.00
Marylebone 1821 & 1831 Census Index on CD	£10.50

**16 Arrowsmith Drive,
Stonehouse, Glos. GL10 2QR
Freephone 0800 2985894
E-mail: mike@backtoroots.co.uk
Web page: www.backtoroots.co.uk**

Data CDs £11.99 + postage 75p each

City of Gloucester & Districts 1920 - Residents & Street Directory
Gloucestershire Kellys 1906 - Residents & Trades
Gloucestershire Kellys 1923 - Residents & Trades
Gloucestershire Kellys 1895 - Trades & Court
Harrow 1919-20 - Residents, Trades & Street
Herefordshire Kellys 1917 - Residents & Trades
Leicestershire & Rutland Kellys 1881 - Trades
Manchester & Salford Pigots 1829 - Trades
Monmouthshire Kellys 1891 - Trades & Court
Northamptonshire Kellys 1914 - Private Residents
Nottinghamshire 1853 - Village Histories & Trades
Nottinghamshire Kellys 1881 - Trades & Court
Nottinghamshire Kellys 1916 - Residents & Trades
Nottingham Kellys 1916 - Street Directory
Nottinghamshire Kellys 1925 - Residents & Trades
Oxfordshire Kellys 1907- Residents & Trades
Preston Mannex's 1866 - Residents & Trades
Shropshire 1917 - Private Residents & Trades
South Wales Kellys 1923 - Private Residents
Somersetshire Kellys 1919 Residents & Trades
Somersetshire Pigots 1830 - Trades & Profs
Somersetshire Kellys 1914 - Residents & Trades
Somersetshire Kellys 1923 - Residents & Trades
Somersetshire Kellys 1927 - Residents & Trades
West Kensington, Hammersmith, Shepherds Bush & Fulham 1898-99 - Residents
Westmorland Pigots 1828-9 - Gentry &Trades
Wiltshire Pigots 1842 - Gentry & Trades
Wiltshire Kellys 1895 - Village Histories
Wiltshire Kellys 1895 - Trades & Court
Wiltshire Kellys 1914 - Residents & Commercial
Worcestershire Kellys 1928 - Residents & Trades

Data CDs - £15.99 + postage 75 p each

Bristol & Suburban Kellys 1923 - Street Directory
Bristol & Suburban Kellys 1923 - Residents Directory
Cardiff & Suburban Kellys 1905 - Names & Trades
South Wales Kellys 1923 - Trades Directory

Many other products in stock too numerous to list here - Send for brochure